A Multidisciplinary Science Program for High School

Level 2

BSCS SCIENCE
AN INQUIRY APPROACH

KENDALL/HUNT PUBLISHING COMPANY
4050 Westmark Drive Dubuque, Iowa 52002

BSCS Development Team

Rodger W. Bybee, PhD, *Co-Principal Investigator*
Pamela Van Scotter, *Co-Principal Investigator, Project Director*
Nicole Knapp, *Curriculum Developer, Professional Development Coordinator*
Betty Stennett, *Curriculum Developer, Professional Development Coordinator*
Steve Getty, PhD, *Curriculum Developer, Classroom-Based Research Associate*
K. David Pinkerton, PhD, *Curriculum Developer*
Cyndi Long, *Curriculum Developer, Professional Development Coordinator*
Sandy Smith, *Curriculum Developer*
C. Jane Wilson, *Curriculum Developer*
Debra Hannigan, *Curriculum Developer, Curriculum Coordinator*
David Hanych, PhD, *Curriculum Developer*
Steve Williams, PhD, *Curriculum Developer*
Hedi Baxter, *Curriculum Developer*
Molly McGarrigle, *Internal Evaluator*
Theodore Lamb, PhD, *Co-Director, Center for Research and Evaluation*
Ann Lanari, *Research Assistant*
Raphaela Conner, *Project Assistant*
Susan Hawkins, *Project Assistant*
Terry Redmond, *Project Assistant*
Pamela S. Warren, *Project Assistant*

BSCS Production Team

Barbara Perrin, *Director of Publications*
Dottie Watkins, *Production Coordinator*
Stacey Luce, *Manuscript Specialist, Permissions*
Lisa Rasmussen, *Graphic Artist*
Diane Gionfriddo, *Photo Researcher*
Angela Paoleti, *Production Assistant*

BSCS Administration

Rodger W. Bybee, PhD, *Executive Director*
Janet Carlson Powell, PhD, *Associate Director*
Pamela Van Scotter, *Director, BSCS Center for Curriculum Development*
Marcia Mitchell, *Director of Finance*
Carlo Parravano, PhD, *Merck Institute for Science Education; Chairman, BSCS Board of Directors*

Editors

Barbara Resch, Colorado Springs, CO
Francelia Sevin, *Education Editor,* Crestone, CO

External Evaluator

Doug Coulson, PhD, PS International, Arnold, MD

Artists, Designers, Photographers, Photo Research and Permissions

David Ball, Illustrator, Colorado Springs, CO
Rick Bickhart, Peaceful Solutions Design, Albuquerque, NM
Natalie Giboney, Freelance Permissions, Fort Worth, TX
Joe Hartman, Photographer, Branding Iron Media and Design, L.L.C., Colorado Springs, CO
Jane McBee, Photographer, Colorado Springs, CO
Barbara Perrin, Ibis Production Management, Colorado Springs, CO
Rick Simonson, Illustrator, Kearney, NE
Paige Thomas, Illustrator, Colorado Springs, CO
Nina Whitney, Picture Vision, Falmouth, MA

Credits can be found on page 911

ISBN 13: 978-0-7575-1734-1
ISBN 10: 0-7575-1734-X

The development of this material was funded by the National Science Foundation under Grant Numbers ESI 9911614 and ESI 0242596. Any opinions, findings, conclusions, or recommendations expressed in this publication are those of the authors and do not necessarily reflect the views of the granting agency.

Printed in the United States of America
2 3 4 5 6 7 8 9 10 12 11 10 09 08

Acknowledgments

Advisory Board Members

Marshall Berman, PhD, New Mexico State Board of Education
Kathy Comfort, PhD, Partnership for the Assessment of Standards-Based Science, WestEd, San Francisco, CA
Ginger Davis, Brevard Public Schools, FL
Melissa DeWitt, East Fairmont High School, Fairmont, WV
Christine Funk, Douglas County High School, Castle Rock, CO
Steve Getty, PhD, Colorado College, Colorado Springs, CO
Michael Hanson, Tahoma High School, Kent, WA
Jerrie Mallicoat, Titusville High School, Titusville, FL
M. Patricia Morse, PhD, University of Washington, Seattle, WA
Susan Mundry, PhD, WestEd, Stoneham, MA
Harold Pratt, PhD, Educational Consultants, Inc., Littleton, CO
Rochelle Rubin, PhD, Waterford School District, Waterford, MI
Gary Scott, San Pedro Math, Science, and Technology Center, San Pedro, CA
Ethan Smith, Tahoma High School, Kent, WA

Contributors and Reviewers

Gary Axen, PhD, New Mexico Tech, Socorro, NM
Marshall Berman, PhD, New Mexico State Board of Education
Robert Blake, PhD, Texas Tech University, Lubbock, TX
Mark Bloom, PhD, BSCS, Colorado Springs, CO
Cathy Box, Tahoka Middle School, Tahoka, TX
Heidi Carlone, PhD, University of North Carolina, Greensboro, NC
Steven Clemmens, PhD, Brown University, Providence, RI
Rocky Coleman, PhD, Colorado State University, Fort Collins, CO
George Davis, PhD, Minnesota State University, Moorehead, MN
Edward Drexler, Pius XI High School, Milwaukee, WI
Ellen Friedman, PhD, San Diego, CA
James Garrett Davis, Albuquerque, NM
Steve Getty, PhD, Colorado College, Colorado Springs, CO
Anne Haley-Mackenzie, PhD, Miami University of Ohio, Oxford, OH
David Hanych, PhD, National Science Foundation, Arlington, VA
Mary Kay Hemmenway, PhD, University of Texas, Austin, TX
William Hoyt, PhD, University of Northern Colorado, Greeley, CO
Barbara Hug, PhD, University of Michigan, Ann Arbor, MI
Jay Kauffman, PhD, University of Maryland, College Park, MD
Laura Laughran, PhD, New Directions, Tucson, AZ
Toby Merlin, MD, Centers for Disease Control and Prevention, Atlanta, GA
Samuel Milazzo, University of Colorado, Colorado Springs, CO
Gary Morgan, New Mexico Museum of Nature and Science
Jerry Phillips, PhD, BSCS, Colorado Springs, CO
Harold Pratt, PhD, Educational Consultants, Inc., Littleton, CO
Richard Reynolds, PhD, USDA Forest Service, Rocky Mountain Research Station, Fort Collins, CO
Carol Sheriff, Albuquerque, NM
Ray Tschillard, BSCS, Colorado Springs, CO
Anne Westbrook, PhD, BSCS, Colorado Springs, CO
Lawrence Woolf, PhD, General Atomics, San Diego, CA
Ted Yeshion, Cluefinders, Erie, PA

Field-Test Teachers and Leaders

Arizona

Abigail Moore, Desert View High School, Tucson, AZ

California

Dlunari Edirisinghe, Narbonne High School, Harbor City, CA
Carolyn Higuchi, Narbonne High School, Harbor City, CA
Roger Mataumoto, Narbonne High School, Harbor City, CA
Gary Scott, San Pedro Math, Science, and Technology Center, San Pedro, CA

Colorado

Kerry Adams, Alamosa High School, Alamosa, CO
Christine Funk, Douglas County High School, Castle Rock, CO
Sharon Harter, Coronado High School, Colorado Springs, CO
Dennis Lopez, District Representative, Alamosa High School, Alamosa, CO
Jim Street, Alamosa High School, Alamosa, CO
Jodi Vine Schlang, University of Denver High School, Denver, CO

Florida

Lori Braga, Melbourne High School, Melbourne, FL
Kim Bragg, District Representative, Brevard Public Schools, FL
Ginger Davis, Science Supervisor, Brevard Public Schools, FL
Elizabeth Hickey, Cocoa High School, Cocoa, FL
Catherine Hoffman, Satellite High School, Satellite Beach, FL
Edward Johnson, Cocoa High School, Cocoa, FL
Jerri Mallicoat, Titusville High School, Titusville, FL
Kip Mapstone, Eau Gallie High School, Melbourne, FL
James Meegan, Melbourne High School, Melbourne, FL
Raul Montes, Cocoa High School, Cocoa, FL
Melindy Myrick-Lupo, Eau Gallie High School, Melbourne, FL
Jon Nelson, Titusville High School, Titusville, FL
Cheryl Reve, Cocoa High School, Cocoa, FL
Lisa Scott, Satellite High School, Satellite Beach, FL
Nelson Salazar, Eau Gallie High School, Melbourne, FL
Michelle Walker, Eau Gallie High School, Melbourne, FL
Lisa Wall-Campeau, Eau Gallie High School, Melbourne, FL

Illinois

Shannon Edwards, Centennial High School, Champaign, IL
Kevin Kuppler, District Representative, Champaign, IL
Shirley Ma, Centennial High School, Champaign, IL

Indiana

Kristy Slaby, Kankakee Valley High School, Wheatfield, IN

Massachusetts

Alan Murphy, Pioneer Valley Regional High School, Northfield, MA
Lawrence Poirier, Pioneer Valley Regional High School, Northfield, MA
Jo Anne Pullen, Science Supervisor, Pioneer Valley Region School District, Northfield, MA

Michigan

John Bayerl, Fordson High School, Dearborn, MI
Herm Boatin, Science Supervisor, Dearborn Public Schools, MI
Mary Beth Henry, Dearborn High School, Dearborn, MI
Richard Klee, Science Supervisor, Dearborn Public Schools, MI
David Mayoros, Edsel Ford High School, Dearborn, MI
Robert Tyler, Dearborn High School, Dearborn, MI

Missouri

LaurAnn Robertson, Lamar High School, Lamar, MO

New Hampshire

Lise Bofinger, Concord High School, Concord, NH
Sarah Carson, Concord High School, Concord, NH
Charles Swift, Concord High School, Concord, NH

Pennsylvania

Stephen Garstka, Ridley High School, Folsom, PA
Paul McGibney, Ridley High School, Folsom, PA
Thomas Pfleger, Ridley High School, Folsom, PA

Tennessee

Laura Kile, Webb School of Knoxville, Knoxville, TN

Vermont

Merribelle Coles, Brattleboro Union High School, Brattleboro, VT
Bruce Holloway, Brattleboro Union High School, Brattleboro, VT
James Maland, District Representative, Brattleboro Union High School, Brattleboro, VT
Katherine Martin, Brattleboro Union High School, Brattleboro, VT
Scott Noren, Brattleboro Union High School, Brattleboro, VT
Julie Wheeler, Brattleboro Union High School, Brattleboro, VT

Washington

Aanika DeVries, Spring Street School, Friday Harbor, WA
Ken Loomis, Tahoma Senior High School, Covington, WA
James McLean, Science Supervisor, Kennewick School District, WA
Jim Ramsey, Kamiakin High School, Kennewick, WA
Ethan Smith, Tahoma Senior High School, Covington, WA
Walt Szklarski, Tahoma Senior High School, Covington, WA
Allison Winward, Kamiakin High School, Kennewick, WA

West Virginia

Jules Adam, Oak Glen High School, New Cumberland, WV
Melissa DeWitt, East Fairmont High School, Fairmont, WV
Joyce Duvall, Parkersburg High School, Parkersburg, WV
Diane Furman, Science Supervisor, Marion County Schools, WV
Sally Morgan, East Fairmont High School, Fairmont, WV
Joyce Pitrolo, Parkersburg High School, Parkersburg, WV
Mary Lynn Westfall, East Fairmont High School, Fairmont, WV

Wisconsin

Sue Alberti, Science Supervisor, Ashwaubenon School District, Ashwaubenon, WI
Michael Lyga, Ashwaubenon High School, Green Bay, WI
Kylie Werner, Ashwaubenon High School, Green Bay, WI
Joelle Zuengler, Ashwaubenon High School, Green Bay, WI

Contents

Unit 2

Dear Learners,

Learning—it's important. That's why the staff at BSCS developed *BSCS Science: An Inquiry Approach*. With *you* in mind, we designed a program that puts meaningful learning first.

What's meaningful learning? It's the kind of learning that's fun even though it's a lot of work. It's learning so interesting, relevant, and engaging that you find yourself understanding more than you ever have. How does that happen?

First, the program developers know you like *active* learning. You expect direct experiences with nature, not just worksheets and lectures. This is especially true in science. You want to understand through investigations, inquiry, and dialogue. That's what you'll find in these pages, along with the proper rigor so you'll be prepared for a world that needs people who can learn, think, and solve problems.

Second, learning in this program builds on *your* experiences with the natural world, which include all the disciplines of science. When you look at a rainbow, you wonder about the physics of light, the biology of your eye, the earth science of thunderstorms, and the chemistry of rain. It's the natural way to think.

Third, meaningful learning has purpose. And learners with purpose have clear goals—ones that help them focus on what's important. Your book lays out what's important with clear learning goals based on the *National Science Education Standards*. These standards help you understand the big concepts that connect all science subjects. That way, you apply one concept across many disciplines and understand more about the world around you.

Finally, the staff at BSCS knows how much learning depends on feedback. Your feedback helps us improve future editions of this program. It's the way we make science books better. So please send us your feedback. It helps us learn. Our mailing address is

BSCS Science: An Inquiry Approach
BSCS
5415 Mark Dabling Boulevard
Colorado Springs, CO 80918-3842

Sincerely,
The *BSCS Science: An Inquiry Approach* Team

Getting to Know *BSCS Science: An Inquiry Approach*

BSCS Science: An Inquiry Approach represents a new generation of textbooks for a new generation of high school science students, like you. As with all BSCS programs, *An Inquiry Approach* is an innovative science program that is centered on you, the learner. This program introduces you to the core concepts in science as inquiry, the physical sciences, the life sciences, and the earth and space sciences. In addition, the student book engages you in integration across the disciplines in ways that are relevant to your life. This program provides high school students nationwide like yourself with an important alternative to the traditional sequence of biology, chemistry, and physics.

You will notice that this program is different from other science programs you have used. This program emphasizes the big ideas in science. It also emphasizes inquiry—the way scientists do science. Throughout your learning journey, we provide you with opportunities to do science and to appreciate and better understand the nature of science. We developed this program with a team of scientists, teachers, science educators, and many students in field-test classrooms across the county.

This program supports the following goals for all students:

- To increase your understanding of fundamental concepts in the sciences
- To present science in a context that is relevant to you
- To increase your interest and achievement in science
- To strengthen your critical-thinking and problem-solving skills

Distinguishing Features of the Program

The distinguishing features of *BSCS Science: An Inquiry Approach* include the following:

- Enduring, standards-based content
- Inquiry as the overarching theme
- Activity-centered lessons
- Opportunities for structured and open investigation in areas that are meaningful to you
- Opportunities for you to design and conduct your own investigations
- Opportunities for you to consider recent research in the sciences
- A constructivist, student-centered approach
- Mathematics in the real-world setting of science
- The use of chapter organizers and science notebooks
- The BSCS 5E instructional model
- A collaborative learning environment
- An assessment package with a variety of ways you can demonstrate your learning

The Framework

The framework for *BSCS Science: An Inquiry Approach* presents a logical sequence of concepts through each year and across the years.

Each of the core units includes three chapters that present you with the fundamental concepts in each of the disciplines. The last chapter in each core unit allows you to apply what you have learned so far in integrated settings that include at least two different disciplines, such as biology and physics. In this way, we provide you with learning experiences that will help you build and deepen enduring understandings in science.

BSCS Science: An Inquiry Approach, Grades 9–11 Framework			
Units	Major Concepts Addressed at Each Grade Level		
	9	10	11
Science As Inquiry	Abilities necessary to do and understandings about scientific inquiry with a focus on:		
	• Questions and concepts that guide scientific investigations	• Design of scientific investigations • Communicating scientific results	• Evidence as the basis for explanations and models • Alternative explanations and models
Physical Science	• Structure and properties of matter • Structure of atoms • Integrating chapter	• Motions and forces • Chemical reactions • Integrating chapter	• Interactions of energy and matter • Conservation of energy and increase in disorder • Integrating chapter
Life Science	• The cell • Behavior of organisms • Integrating chapter	• Biological evolution • Molecular basis of heredity • Integrating chapter	• Matter, energy, and organization in living systems • Interdependence of organisms • Integrating chapter
Earth-Space Science	• Origin and evolution of the universe	• Geochemical cycles	• Energy in the Earth system • Integrating chapter
	• Origin and evolution of the Earth system • Integrating chapter	• Integrating chapter	
Science in a Personal and Social Perspective, Science and Technology	• Personal and community health • Natural and human-induced hazards • Abilities of technological design	• Population growth • Natural resources • Environmental quality	• Science and technology in local, national, and global challenges • Understandings about science and technology
	History and Nature of Science addressed throughout grade levels and units • Science as a human endeavor • Nature of science • History of science		

Components of the Program

BSCS Science: An Inquiry Approach is a comprehensive program that includes useful resources for you and your teacher. The major components for students include the student edition, the student edition on CD, and the *Student Resource CD*.

Student Edition

The student book is designed with students like you in mind. Each chapter and unit draws you into an engaging learning experience. In addition to being conceptually appealing, the book is visually appealing, filled with engaging art and design. Features such as the chapter organizers and openers, special reading sections, FYIs, sidebars, appealing art, the *How To* section at the back of the book, and the National Science Teachers Association SciLinks help keep your interest and allow you to take charge of your learning.

Student Edition on CD

The entire Student Edition is also on a CD, which is included in your book. This CD makes it easier to complete reading assignments. Instead of taking your textbook home, you can just take the CD with you and complete your reading assignment on the computer. This type of flexibility appeals to today's busy students.

Student Resource CD

The *Student Resource CD* (*SRCD*) provides you with concept maps for each chapter. From the concept maps, you can link to additional resources on the *SRCD*. For example, from a specific concept on a specific map, you might link to an interesting video clip, animation, or simulation related to this concept. This visually rich resource is a powerful learning tool.

Students across the Country Helped Develop This Program

We developed this program with you in mind. Students like yourself and teachers like yours across the country have used this program in their classrooms and their feedback helped us make this program even better. Now, we are able to provide you with the innovative, high-quality learning experience in the sciences that you deserve.

CHAPTER 1

Investigations by Design

Investigations by Design

Think of science as a way to explore and understand the natural world. The concepts in physical, life, and earth science connect in many ways. Making these connections helps you understand the world around you.

During this school year, you and your classmates will have opportunities to explore many ideas that span the sciences. You will explore these ideas as scientists do, through the process of scientific inquiry. Your year will be filled with activities, projects, labs, and interactive readings. Each learning experience is designed to help you better understand science content, as well as to see science as a way of knowing and understanding that content.

As you work through these activities, you will discover that your study of science is actually a study of systems. Look at the opening art for this chapter. How does each picture represent a system? You are familiar with body systems as an example of systems in life science. But, have you ever thought of a population as a system? Systems exist all around you. In physical science, there are mechanical systems and systems that include chemical reactions. The health of our planet depends on the proper functioning of systems that recycle matter. The water and the carbon cycles are examples of two such systems. As you study science and recognize these systems, you will use models, mathematics, and inquiry to study the world. You will see that the world has many aspects that are changing and many aspects that remain constant. Keep these ideas in mind as you work through the units this year and become a scientist in your own school investigating the world around you.

In chapter 1, *Investigations by Design*, you will explore the process of science. In particular, you will review some of what you already know about science. Then you will deepen your understanding of the design of scientific investigations and the characteristics that make the design a credible one. Scientists do this process every day, whether they are exploring the universe or developing new medicines. In past science classes, you learned that many questions can be answered using science. You also explored how scientists use evidence and inference to develop explanations. In this chapter, you will build on these understandings and apply rigorous criteria to scientific design.

Goals for the Chapter

By the end of chapter 1, you will be able to answer these questions:

- What characterizes a scientifically testable question?
- How do I design and conduct a scientific investigation?
- By what measures do I evaluate the design of others?
- How do I communicate the results of a scientific investigation to others?

We will introduce you to some important tools and techniques in this chapter that will continue to help you in science class every year. These tools and techniques include the following:

1. *Your science book.* This book includes many tools to help you learn science. Most important, you will find clearly drawn connections that help you understand what you are learning, how you got there, and where you are going. These connections are in the form of chapter organizers, chapter introductions, and narrative.
2. *The BSCS 5E instructional model.* You may notice that this student book is different from traditional textbooks. As you learn science this year, you will be immersed in *doing* science. You will learn through inquiry and connect science to the real world. The BSCS 5Es will guide you through your learning journey in each chapter, allowing you to build your own understanding. The 5Es are engage, explore, explain, elaborate, and evaluate. By using this model, BSCS puts into practice what we know about how students learn best.
3. *Chapter organizers.* These organizers are included in each chapter. They are a tool to help you see where you are, where you have been, and where you are headed in your learning.
4. *Learning strategies.* These strategies will help as you are developing your understanding of science. You will use these strategies as you read, organize data, reveal what you have learned, and work in groups. These learning strategies will work not only in your science class but in other classes as well. They will help you develop skills that you can also use outside of school.

5. *Toolbox activities.* These activities provide extra practice for some of the skills you will develop this year. Your teacher will share these activities with you as needed.
6. *Your science notebook.* It is critical that you keep track of your results and your growing understanding in a notebook designated for science. That way both you and your teacher will have a record of your learning.
7. *Your teammates.* When you work in a team, you will make the most of multiple minds. Learning good teamwork skills will prepare you for the work world. Many great discoveries and decisions are made as teams, not as individuals.
8. *Investigations.* When you do science, you will model the process of inquiry that scientists use. At the same time, you will learn how to ask and answer questions you have about the natural world.

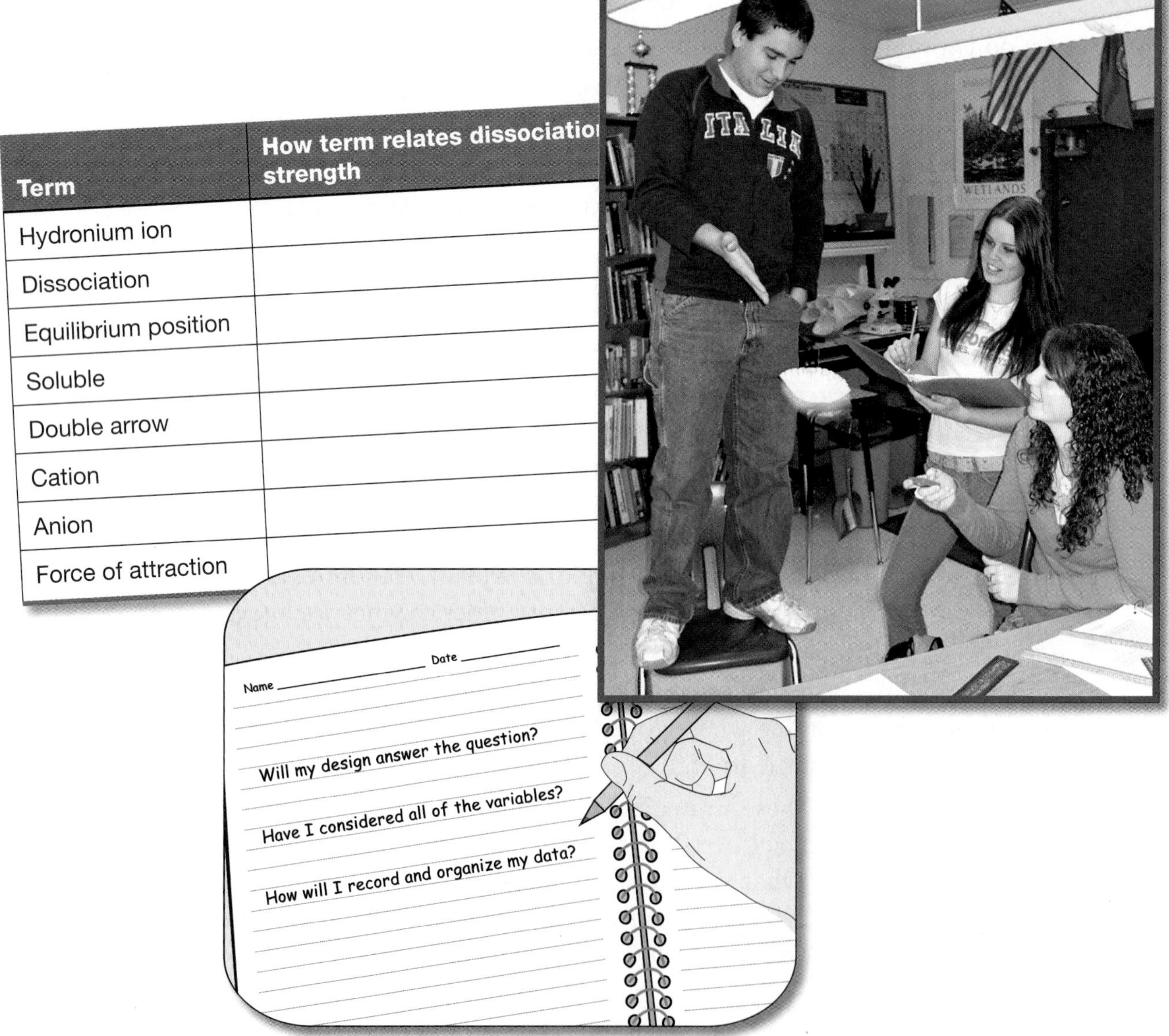

Term	How term relates dissociatio strength
Hydronium ion	
Dissociation	
Equilibrium position	
Soluble	
Double arrow	
Cation	
Anion	
Force of attraction	

WETLANDS
Name
Date
Will my design answer the question?
Have I considered all of the variables?
How will I record and organize my data?

9. *Questions.* When you ask questions of yourself and your classmates, you will contribute to your own understanding. When you answer questions posed in your book, you will demonstrate your understanding.
10. *Readings.* When you read about the work of other scientists, you will learn about their explorations of science. When you add their knowledge to the understandings about science that you are creating, your understandings will deepen.
11. *Scoring rubrics.* The scoring rubrics you will use this year outline the expectations your teacher has for the work you will do at the end of each chapter.

To learn about scientific inquiry and to use the tools and techniques of this chapter, you will participate in the following activities:

ENGAGE	A Clean Design
EXPLORE / **EXPLAIN**	Small Problem?
EXPLAIN	Why and How Do We Inquire?
ELABORATE	Valid or Deceptive?
EVALUATE	Killing Germs? Digging Deeper

ENGAGE

A Clean Design

Key Ideas:

- Careful design of scientific investigations is essential to ensure that the investigation has a good chance to provide answers.
- Scientific investigations include attention to the control of variables.

Linking Question

How can I design a scientific investigation of my own?

Investigations by Design

EXPLORE

EXPLAIN

Small Problem?

Key Ideas:

- All questions are not testable with science.
- Careful design and implementation of a scientific investigation lead to valid results.
- Communicating scientific results is important to scientific inquiry.

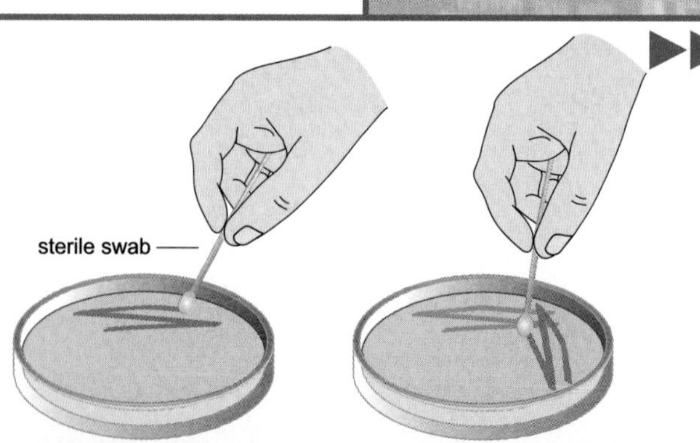

Linking Question

How does my design reflect the process of scientific inquiry?

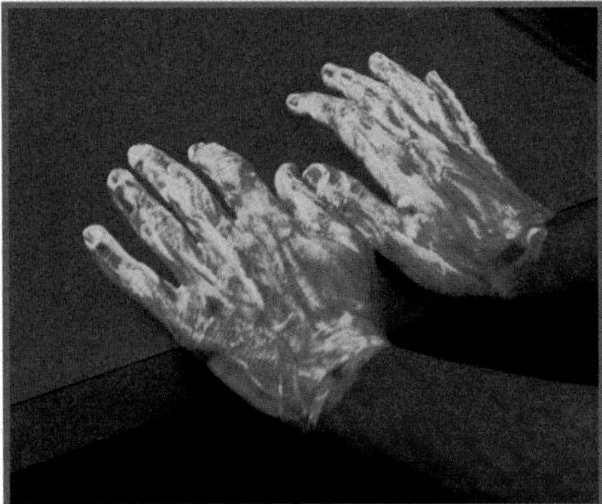

EVALUATE

Killing Germs? Digging Deeper

Key Ideas:

- Scientific investigations include
  - a testable question
  - a design that leads to valid and reliable results
  - an appropriate way of communicating and defending a scientific argument.

Linking Question

How can I demonstrate what I have learned about the process of scientific inquiry?

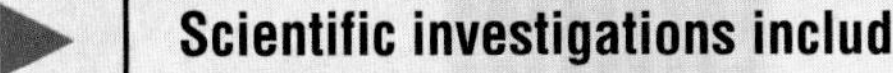

CHAPTER 1 Major Concepts

- **Scientific investigations include**
  - **A testable question**
  - **A design that leads to valid and reliable results**
  - **Observations and measurement**
  - **An appropriate way of communicating and defending a scientific argument**
- **Scientific inquiry is a systematic, nonlinear process that increases our chances of solving certain types of problems.**

ELABORATE

Valid or Deceptive?

Key Ideas:

- All "science" that is reported in the media is not valid.
- Researchers and scientists must be able to defend their arguments and reproduce their results.

EXPLAIN

Why and How Do We Inquire?

Key Idea:

Scientific Inquiry is a systematic, nonlinear process.

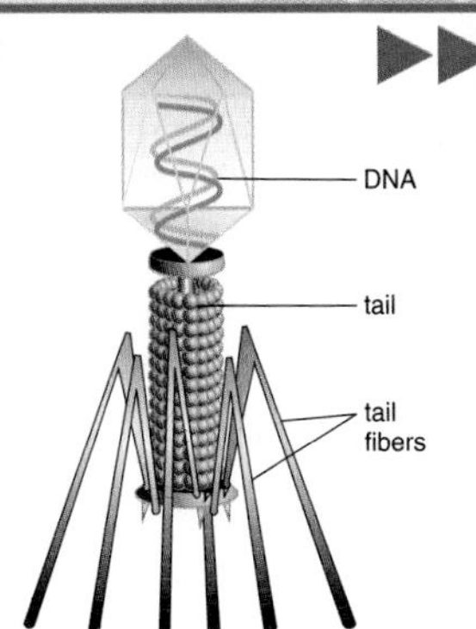

Linking Question

How can the process of scientific inquiry help me to evaluate scientific claims in the media?

ENGAGE

A Clean Design

A successful restaurant system depends on many parts working together successfully. From the production of french fries to the cleanliness of the work area and workers, everyone and every part works together to make the restaurant successful. Have you ever worked in a restaurant? If so, you know that all employees are required to wash their hands frequently (figure 1.1). If you spread disease by not washing your hands properly, then the system breaks down and the success of the restaurant suffers.

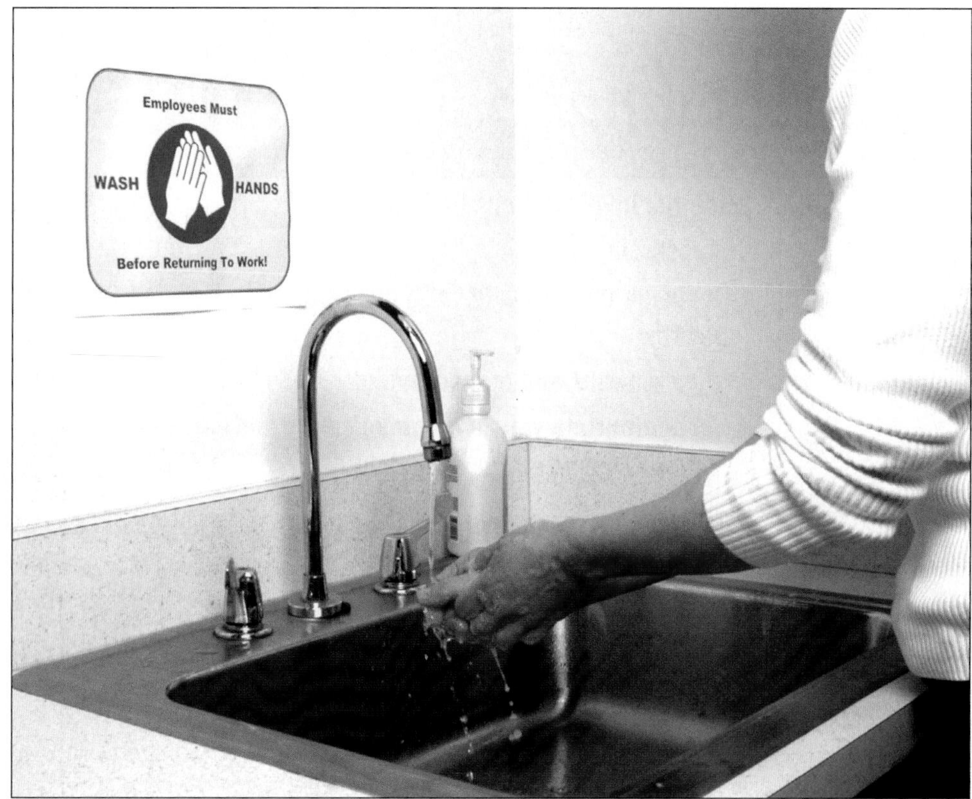

▲ **Figure 1.1 Hand washing.** Why is it so important to wash your hands regularly?

When you were younger, your parents may have reminded you to wash your hands before dinner. An important safety practice in science class and in any science laboratory is to wash your hands before leaving the lab. It should be clear to you why washing your hands in both of these situations is so important. In *A Clean Design*, you will work with a partner to investigate hand washing. You will use the simple act of hand washing as a way to think about the criteria of a good scientific investigation.

Materials

For each team of 2 students

access to germ simulator

access to an ultraviolet light source

access to hand soap and a sink

Cautions

Always use caution when using any chemical in the laboratory. Only apply the germ simulator to your hands—do not ingest it. Do not look directly into the ultraviolet light source. Looking at ultraviolet light directly can damage the corneas, lenses, and retinas of your eyes.

Process and Procedure

Germ simulator is a substance that glows when exposed to ultraviolet (UV) light (see figure 1.2). In this activity, the germ simulator represents germs (the substance is not manufactured to contain germs). This simulator is used for many applications, such as determining how well restaurant employees wash their hands.

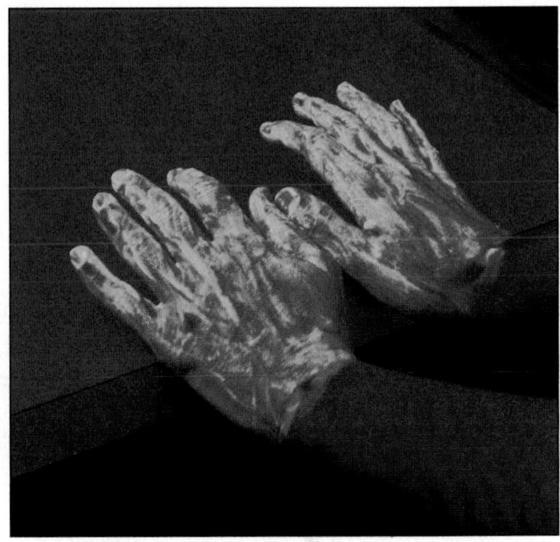

▲ **Figure 1.2**
Germ simulator. Does simple hand washing remove all the bacteria on your hands?

1. Experiment with the germ simulator and make some observations by completing Steps 1a–f.
   a. Apply a small amount of germ simulator to your hands and rub it in like lotion.
   b. When your teacher darkens the room, take turns placing your hands under the UV light. Discuss your observations with your partner.
   c. Record your observations with words and detailed drawings in your science notebook.
   d. Wash and dry your hands as you normally do.
   e. When your teacher darkens the room, place your hands under the UV light again. What do you see? Discuss your observations with your partner.
   f. Record your results in your science notebook with words and drawings.
2. Imagine that students in another high school science class observed the same phenomenon that you just witnessed. They wondered if the length of time that people spent washing their hands made a significant difference in how clean their hands got. Three lab groups, A, B, and C, designed investigations to answer the question, "Does the length of time you spend washing your hands affect the amount of germs that remain?" Use this focus question as you complete Steps 2a–c.

a. Review all the investigations and look for differences.
b. Think of a way to organize the differences in each investigation so that you can easily compare the 3 investigations. Consider using a table or a chart. Record this information in your science notebook as you read the investigations.
c. Read the investigations designed by each lab group: investigation A, investigation B, and investigation C.

Remember, germ simulator is used to *represent* germs; it is not manufactured to contain germs.

3. Discuss with your partner which investigation (A, B, or C) is most likely to give you meaningful results and answers the question, "Does the length of time you spend washing your hands affect the amount of germs that remain?"
   a. Record the investigation you chose and the reasons why you chose it in your science notebook.
   b. Record the reasons you did *not* choose the other 2 investigations.
4. Discuss the investigations and your answers as a class.

Investigation A

Procedure

1. Ask for 3 student volunteers.
2. Apply exactly 1 milliliter (mL) of germ simulator to the hands of each volunteer. Spread the germ simulator very evenly, covering both the top and bottom of their hands. Make sure that they do not touch anything.
3. Shine the ultraviolet (UV) light on the hands of each student. Identify where the germ simulator is present. Take a photograph of both the top and the bottom of their hands.
4. Label the photographs "before washing."
5. Ask all 3 students to wash their hands.
   - The first student should wash for 1 minute under warm water using exactly 2 mL of hand soap.
   - The second student should wash for 1 minute under cold water using exactly 2 mL of the same hand soap.
   - The third student should wash for 1 minute under hot water using exactly 2 mL of the same hand soap.
6. Do not let the students touch anything. Allow their hands to dry in the air completely.
7. Shine the UV light on the hands of each student. Identify where the germ simulator is present. Take a photograph of both the top and the bottom of their hands.
8. Compare the before and after photographs, looking carefully for places that glow.
9. Count the number of spots that still glow in the after photographs.
10. Compare the number of spots present on each student's hands. The hands with the fewest number of spots that glow are the cleanest.

Investigation B

Procedure

1. Ask for 1 student volunteer.
2. Set the water temperature of the sink at 30° Celsius (C).
3. Have the volunteer apply 1 mL of germ simulator to his or her hands and spread it evenly.
4. Shine the UV light on the hands of the volunteer. Take photographs of both the top and the bottom of the volunteer's hands. Label the photographs "before washing."
5. Have the volunteer wash his or her hands with water for 10 seconds using 2 mL of hand soap.
6. Let the volunteer's hands air-dry.
7. Shine the UV light on the hands of the volunteer. Identify where the germ simulator is present. Take a photograph of both the top and the bottom of the hands. Label the photographs "after washing."
8. Compare the photographs and record the results.
9. Have the student remove all the germ simulator by washing his or her hands.
10. Have the student repeat Steps 2–9, but increase the washing time to 15 seconds.
11. Repeat Steps 2–9 again, increasing the washing to 30 seconds.
12. Compare all the before and after photographs. The set of photographs that shows the least amount of germ simulator after washing indicates the amount of time you need to wash your hands in order to get rid of most germs.

Investigation C

Procedure

1. Ask for 3 student volunteers.
2. Ask all the volunteers to apply 1 mL of germ simulator to their hands and spread it evenly on both the top and the bottom of their hands.
3. Shine the UV light on the hands of each student. Identify where the germ simulator is present. Take a picture of both the top and the bottom of their hands. Label these photographs "before washing."
4. Have one of the students wash his or her hands in 27°C water for 15 seconds using 3 mL of hand soap.
5. Have a second student wash his or her hands in 27°C water for 30 seconds using 2 mL of the same hand soap.
6. Have the third student wash his or her hands in 27°C water for 45 seconds using 1 mL of the same hand soap.
7. Shine the UV light on each student's hands. Take photographs and label each "after washing."
8. Compare all the photographs. The set of photographs that shows the least amount of germ simulator after washing indicates the amount of time you need to wash your hands in order to get rid of most germs.

Reflect and Connect

Discuss the following questions with your class. Record your own answers in your science notebook.

1. What information did you and your partner use about each investigation (A, B, and C) to determine which one gave valid results? Use the terms *variable*, *control*, and *constant* in your answer.
2. Were the results from your experience with germ simulator qualitative or quantitative? Give examples to support your answer.

Results from investigations are quantitative **if the data represent measurements or specific numbers or amounts. Results are** qualitative **if the data describe features, characteristics, observations, or relative comparisons.**

3. Consider your experience with the germ simulator and the investigation procedures you examined (A, B, and C). What criteria do you think are important for designing a scientific investigation that will give valid results? Explain your criteria.

EXPLORE
EXPLAIN

Small Problem?

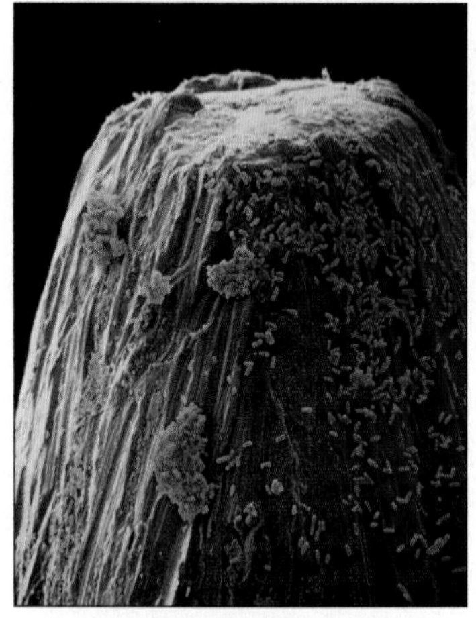

Figure 1.3 SEM image of bacteria. This image taken with a scanning electron microscope (SEM) magnifies the structures 290 times. It shows the small size and large numbers of bacteria that are present on the point of a pin.

In *A Clean Design*, the germ simulator represented common bacteria or other microorganisms that might have been on your hands. Bacteria are virtually everywhere. Figure 1.3 shows a number of bacteria on the point of a pin. These tiny organisms might or might not cause disease. If the microorganisms do cause disease, they are called **pathogenic**. If they do not cause disease, they are nonpathogenic. Many types of bacteria are even helpful. For example, a certain type of *Escherichia coli* (*E. coli*) resides in our intestines to aid the process of digestion.

Through years of study, scientists have learned a lot about bacteria. They have answered many questions by conducting scientific investigations. They carefully design the investigations so that they can collect the best possible data. Scientists then use the data as evidence to support explanations. In *Small Problem?*, you will work in a team to ask a scientifically testable question and design and conduct a scientific investigation to explore the world of bacteria through inquiry.

Part I: Developing a Question

Materials

none

Process and Procedure

When you think about what scientists do, what thoughts come to mind? If "scientists ask questions" popped into your head, then you're right. Asking questions is part of the process of scientific inquiry. But scientists are not the only people who ask questions. On a daily basis, you probably ask a few questions as well. Does that make you a scientist? Of course it does. But can you always answer your questions using science? In other words, are your questions scientifically testable? In Part I of this activity, you will work individually and with a partner to develop a scientifically testable question about bacteria.

1. Read the following fictitious story.

   Health Inspector!

   You and your friends are having lunch when there is an announcement over the intercom. The principal informs you that a health inspector will be at the school next week. The health inspector's job is to make sure the school is clean not only on the surface, but also beneath the surface in areas that we cannot see. While your principal says that everyone has done a very good job keeping the school clean, it is important to know where the health inspector might find problems. The principal asks for your help as scientists. After talking with your friends and your science teacher, you decide that there might be microorganisms like bacteria that general cleaning missed. You decide that this might be something your science class could investigate.

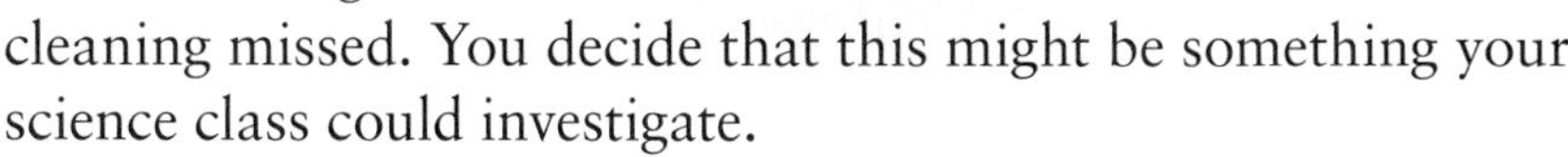

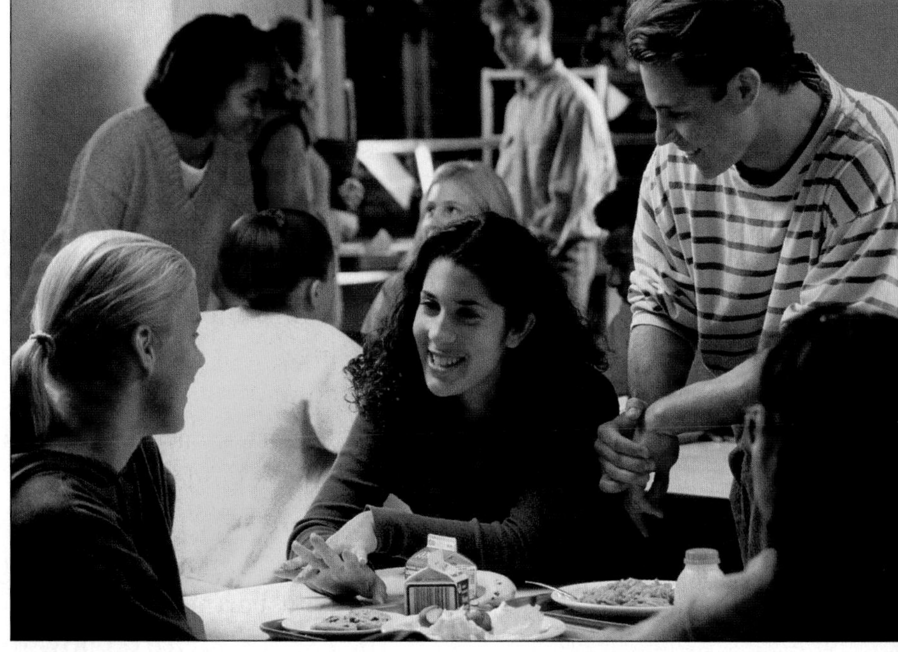

▲ **Figure 1.4** Can you and your classmates investigate the presence of microorganisms in your school?

2. Make a table similar to figure 1.5 in your science notebook. This will help you organize the information you already have.

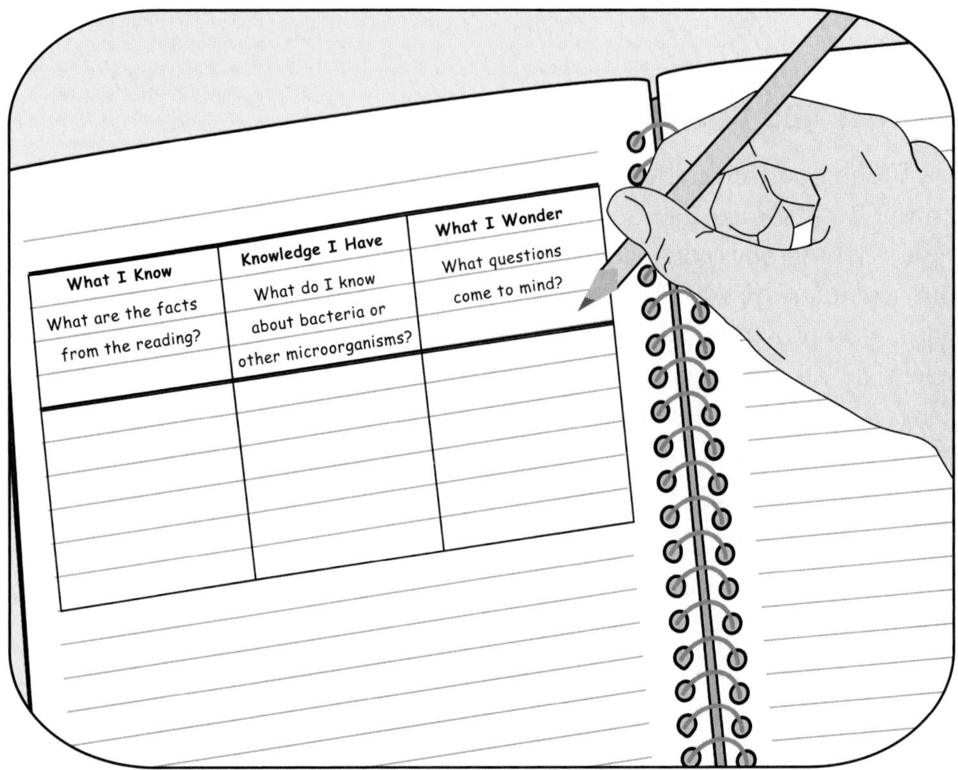

▲ **Figure 1.5 Organization table.** Make a table like this in your science notebook to organize your information.

3. Fill in your table by completing these steps.
   a. Think about what you know about the situation in *Health Inspector!* Record your ideas in the "what I know" column.
   b. Think about what you already know about bacteria. Record your ideas in the "knowledge I have" column.
   c. Think about any questions that come to mind that you could investigate. Record your questions in the "what I wonder" column.
4. Meet with a partner and share and revise your table using Steps 4a–d as a guide.
   a. *Share* your table with your partner and discuss your responses in each column. Read these responses aloud to your partner.
   b. Ask for *advice* on how to make your table more complete.
   c. *Revise* your table if you think your partner's advice is better than yours.

d. Switch roles and listen carefully to your partner.

This process of first thinking (Step 3), sharing (Step 4a), advising (Step 4b), and revising (Step 4c) is called the think-share-advise-revise (TSAR) strategy. You will use this throughout the year in every science subject area.

5. As a class, determine which questions in the "what I wonder" column are scientifically testable in your science class. Agree on which question your class will investigate.

A scientifically testable question is a question addressed and likely answered by designing and conducting a scientific investigation. Evidence gathered in the investigation supports a scientific explanation.

Stop & THINK

PART I

Answer the following questions with your class. Make notes of the class discussion of each answer in your science notebook.

1. Deciding on a scientifically testable question is the first step in designing a good investigation. Answer Questions 1a–b about these questions.
   - **a.** How did you determine which questions were scientifically testable?
   - **b.** Give an example of a question that is testable and one that is not. Explain your choices.
2. Describe how you think research scientists determine scientifically testable questions they will pursue. In your description, consider how this task by a research scientist is similar to or different from your task of choosing a testable question.

Part II: Design Time

Materials

none

Process and Procedure

In Part I of this investigation, you read about a fictional situation at your school and the possible presence of microorganisms. You developed a scientifically testable question based on the situation. In Part II, you will focus on designing a scientific investigation to answer your question. As you design your investigation, you will continue to engage in the process of scientific inquiry. What are the criteria for designing a good investigation? What evidence do you need to collect to answer the question your class is asking? Think about the three investigations you examined in *A Clean Design*. Remember that the design of the investigation leads you to either valid or invalid results (figure 1.6). You and two other students will make up one team of scientists for this activity.

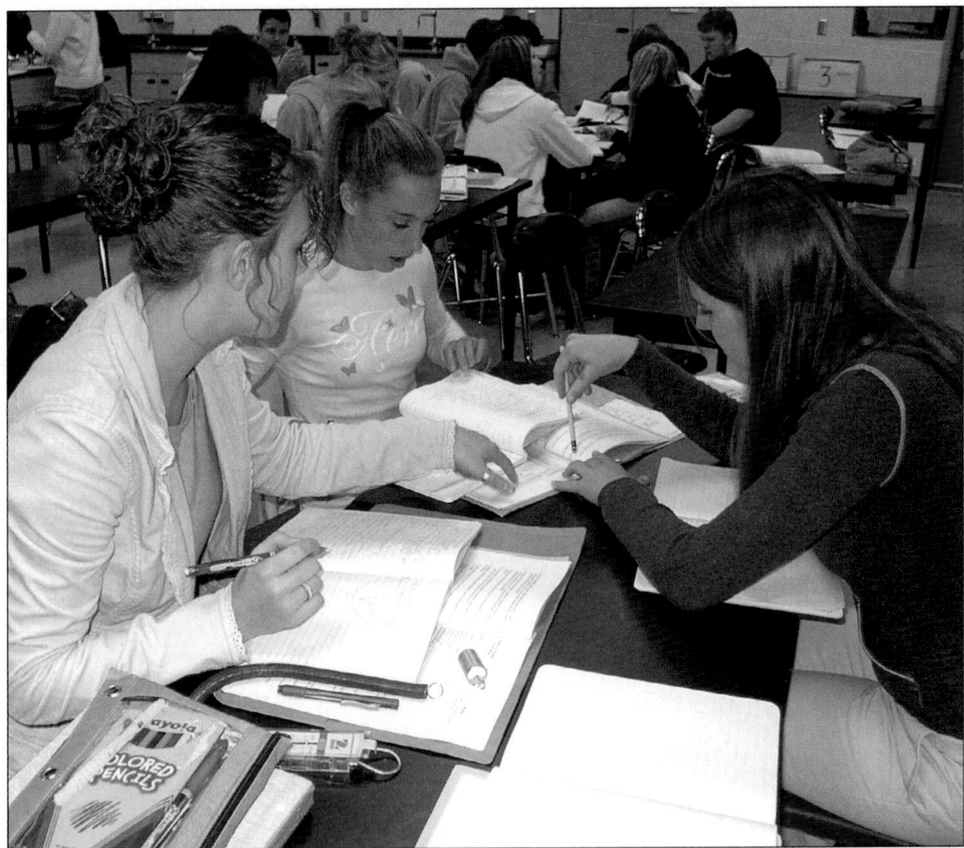

Figure 1.6 Planning an investigation. What are the criteria for a good scientific investigation? You will consider these criteria as you and your team plan a scientific investigation.

1. As a class, review what you think are the important criteria of a good scientific investigation. Take notes on your class discussion and record these ideas in your science notebook.
2. Read the protocol *Culturing Bacteria* to find out how scientists investigate bacteria. Then look at the materials that are available in your classroom.

3. With your team of scientists, design an investigation that will answer the class question from Part I. To make sure your investigation answers your question with valid results, use the following in your design.
   a. What is your rationale? How will this investigation test your question?
   b. How can you keep the investigation fair? In other words, how will you try to keep all factors or variables constant except for the one you are testing?

A well-controlled investigation only tests one factor at a time and keeps all other factors the same. Factors that are kept the same in each group are called constants. **The one factor that changes is called the** variable.

   c. How will you set up a control?

In an investigation, the control receives no treatment. All other groups are compared against the control.

   d. What type of data will you collect to answer the question?
   e. What tools will you use and what materials will you need?
   f. What safety precautions will you take?
   g. How will you organize your data? Will your data be qualitative or quantitative?
   h. How will you analyze your data? How will you develop an explanation and how will you support this explanation?
   i. How will you validate your investigation?
4. Write a step-by-step procedure for your investigation. Include labeled diagrams, charts, or tables.
5. Present your team's design and procedure to the class.
6. As a class, choose 1 procedure that all teams will follow. Record this procedure in your science notebook.

Protocol

Culturing Bacteria

Culturing bacteria or other microorganisms involves growing them on a prepared medium, such as an agar plate. Bacteria can be transferred to agar plates using different tools such as toothpicks, fingers, or pipets. The technique for these tools is described here. No matter which technique you use, bacteria are grown on plates following the same method. This method is described at the end of the protocol.

Sterile Swab or Toothpick

1. Scrape the source of the bacteria with a sterile swab or toothpick.
2. Gently (be careful not to gouge the agar) streak the bacteria from the sterile swab or toothpick in a zigzag pattern onto one side of an agar plate (see figure).
3. Draw bacteria from the first zigzag and make a new streak onto the adjacent side of the agar plate.
4. Repeat the process on a third side of the plate.

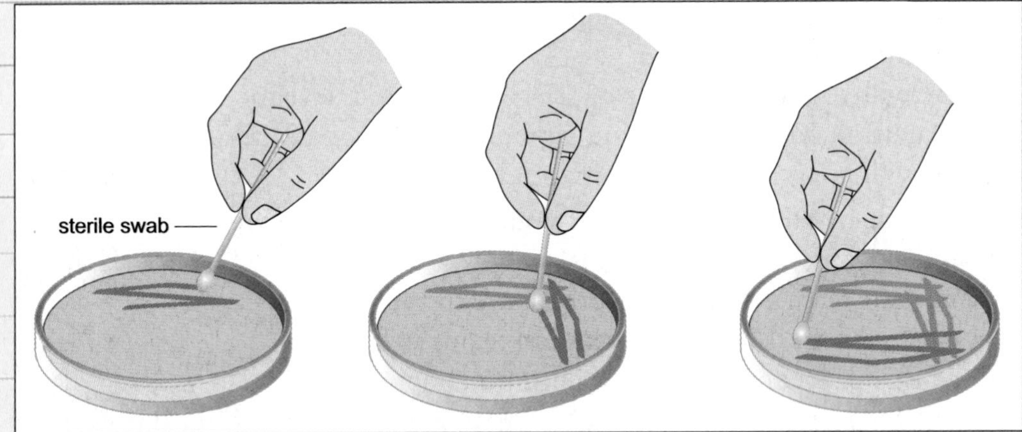

Use a cotton swab or toothpick to make zigzag patterns as shown here.

Finger

Gently (be careful not to gouge the agar) streak your finger in a zigzag pattern onto the agar plate (see figure).

Note: this method is *only* used when culturing microorganisms found on your fingers. You must *never* touch samples of microorganisms already on the agar.

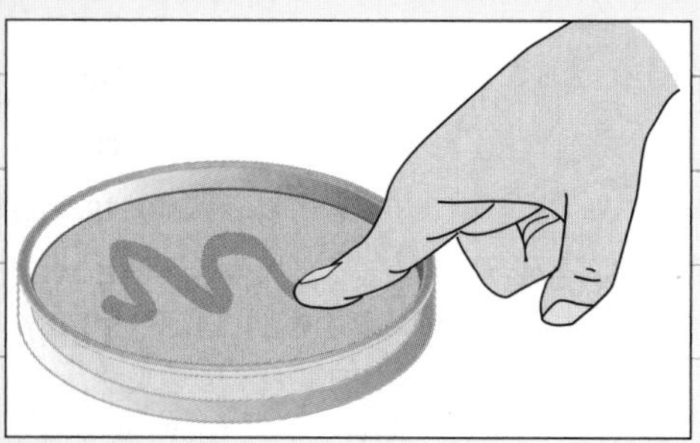

Use this method *only* if you are culturing microorganisms found on your fingers.

Pipet

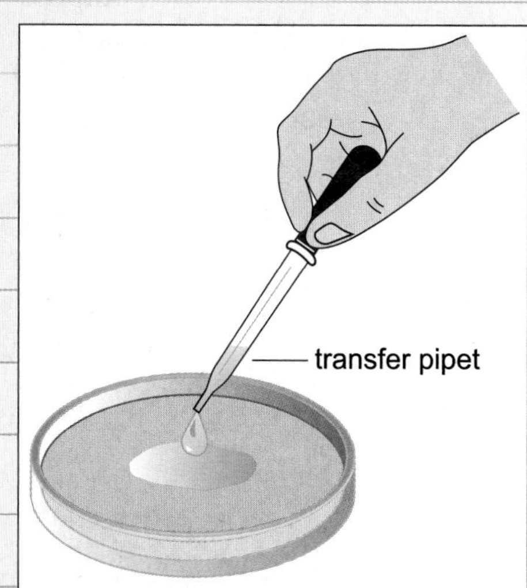

Using a transfer pipet, gently drop the source bacteria (for example, pond water or bacteria culture) onto the agar plate (see figure). Use a sterile swab to streak the sample across the agar.

Use this method if you are using pond water or a liquid source of bacteria.

Growing Bacteria

After the bacteria are transferred to the agar plate, tape the plate shut. Place the agar plate upside down in the incubator (or at room temperature) to grow.

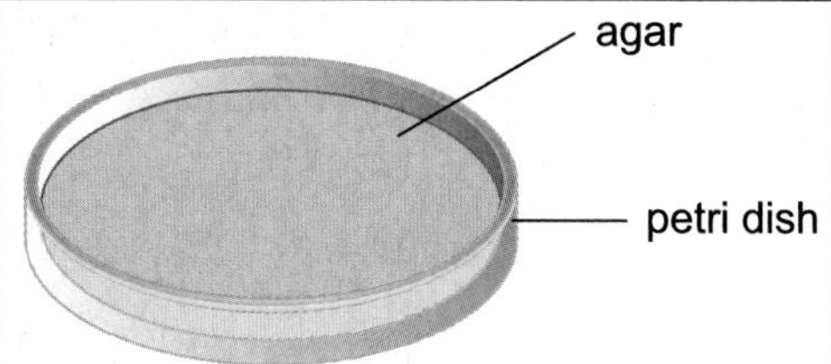

Turn your plates upside down in the incubator so condensation will not drip on the agar.

Stop & THINK

PART II

Answer the following questions with your team of scientists. Make notes of your discussion of each answer in your science notebook.

1. Consider your investigation design and the variables involved to answer Questions 1a–e.
   - **a.** What variables are held constant in your investigation?
   - **b.** What is the variable in your investigation?
   - **c.** Why is it important to test only 1 variable at a time?
   - **d.** What is your control?
   - **e.** Why do you need to have a control?
2. Think back to the 3 investigations presented in the activity *A Clean Design*. Did all of these represent sound scientific investigations? Would each investigation guide scientists to collect evidence? Would that evidence support an explanation for the question asked?
3. Describe why it is important for scientists to design scientifically sound investigations.

Part III: Conducting an Investigation

Materials

For the entire class

37°C incubator or source of warmth for growing bacteria

30% bleach solution

biohazard disposal bags

For each team of 3 students

3 pairs of safety goggles

3 pairs of gloves

2 petri dishes containing nutrient agar

2 sterile swabs

1 permanent marker

tape

other materials as needed

2 index cards

3 *Scientific Investigation Report* handouts

Cautions

Wear safety goggles and gloves while conducting the investigation. Do not open petri dishes until you are ready to use them. Tape the petri dishes shut after you collect your sample. Soak the contaminated petri dishes in a 30% bleach solution after you are finished making your observations. Properly wipe down work areas in your classroom and discard disposable items as directed by your teacher. Be sure to wash your hands before you leave your science class.

Process and Procedure

Most of the time, scientists work collaboratively to gather as much information and data as possible. Your class will now work together to conduct an investigation to answer the question you asked in Part I. The time you spent designing a scientific investigation will help you conduct a valid investigation with reliable, and interesting results. Like the student scientists in figure 1.7, it is time to put your plan to work.

▲ **Figure 1.7**
Students at work. These students have planned their investigation well and have gotten their teacher's approval. Now they are following their plan. What do you think they will find on this doorknob?

Day 1

1. Before you begin your investigation, reread the question your class is attempting to answer. Based on what you already know, what do you think the results of your investigation will show? Record your prediction as a **hypothesis** in your science notebook.

Remember, a hypothesis is a statement that suggests an explanation for an observation or an answer to a scientific problem. Your hypothesis suggests a causal relationship or an if/then relationship. You base your hypothesis on your prior knowledge.

2. Review the investigation agreed upon by your class. Verify your understanding of the procedures with your team.
3. Obtain the materials your team needs. Remember to take safety precautions.

Wear safety goggles and gloves while conducting the investigation.

4. Carry out the investigation carefully; obey all safety precautions. To complete your team's part, do Steps 4a–e.
   a. Obtain a sample from the location that your team is testing. Prepare a petri dish with the sample by following the class procedure.

Remember, the investigation needs to be as controlled as possible.

   b. Properly dispose of all materials as directed by your teacher.
   c. Tape the petri dish shut and do not open the dish again. You can make all your observations through the lid.
   d. Label your dish with the location, date, and team name.

Write on the bottom of the petri dish (the bottom contains the agar).

   e. Store your petri dish upside down in the incubator at 37°C or as your teacher directs.

Day 2

1. On an index card, write a brief description of your team's assigned test location. Retrieve your petri dish and place it next to your index card on display (figure 1.8).

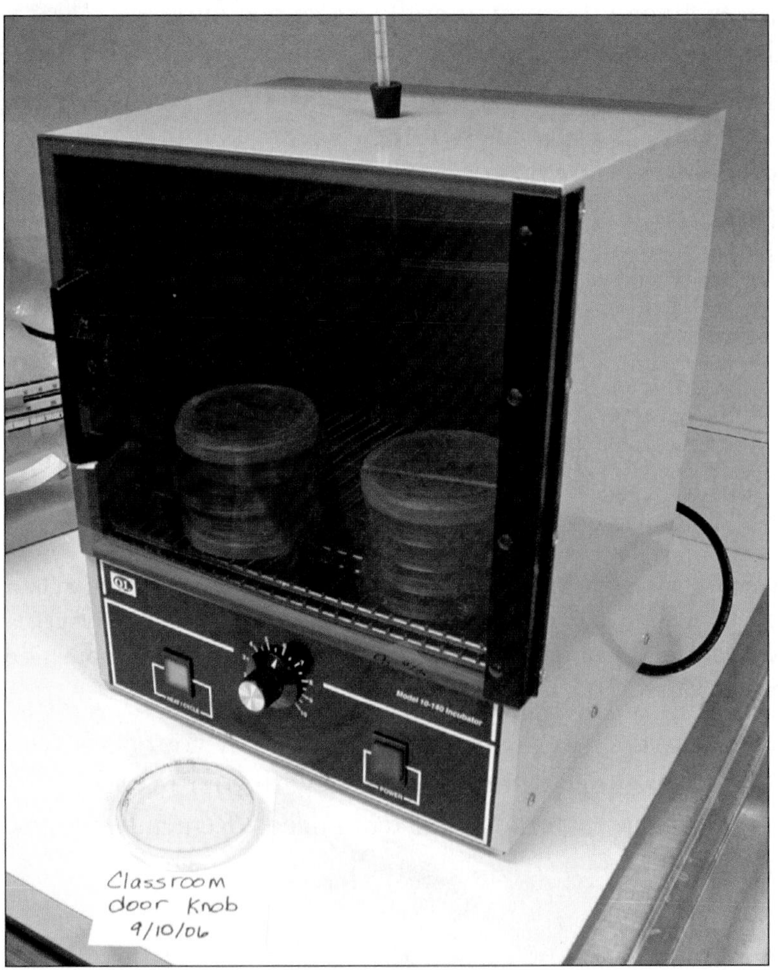

Figure 1.8 Day 2. Your bacteria have grown in the incubator. Now it's time to share your results with the rest of the class. Mark your test location on an index card.

2. Make a data table according to the class design for recording your results in the investigation. Record the table in your science notebook.
3. Examine all the petri dishes from the other teams in your class. Record your observations and results in your data table as well as those of the other teams of scientists.
4. Listen as your teacher leads a class discussion of these investigations. Make notes in your science notebook of all explanations given for the different results.

Reflect and Connect

Work first with your team and then individually to complete the following tasks.

1. Work with your team to analyze your investigation using the handout *Scientific Investigation Report*. Look at the requirements for your report and discuss with your team how you will answer each section from your investigation.
2. Write a lab report on your own of your investigation. Refer to the *Scientific Investigation Report* handout to guide you.
3. Write a cover letter to your principal that provides an overview of your investigation. This cover letter will go with your lab report. In the letter, tell your principal about your class investigation. Include the following components in the letter:
   a. An introduction about yourself and your science class
   b. Why you are doing this investigation
   c. An abstract of your investigation

An abstract is a brief summary of your investigation. It should include the problem you are trying to solve, observations, explanations, and conclusions based on evidence.

   d. Recommendations based on evidence from your results
   e. What new questions you have

Topic: common bacteria
Go to: www.scilinks.org
Code: 2Inquiry23

EXPLAIN

Why and How Do We Inquire?

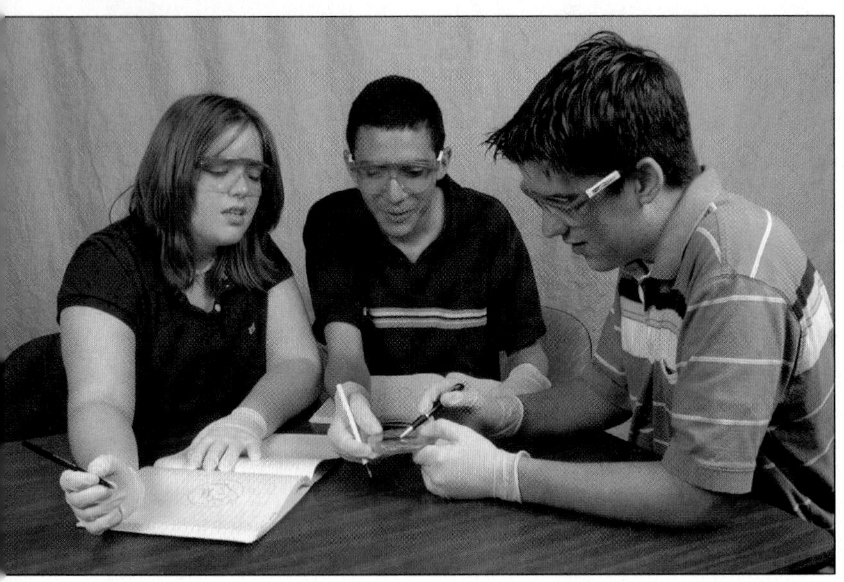

▲ **Figure 1.9 Conducting an investigation.** You have been acting as a scientist as you conducted your investigation. Now you will compare your investigation with the process of inquiry.

You have just been immersed in the process of scientific inquiry (figure 1.9). In *Small Problem?*, you developed a scientifically testable question based on a given situation. You then designed an investigation to answer that question, and you conducted that investigation. Did your investigation go smoothly? Were you able to answer your question? Do you have more questions because of the results you got from your investigation? These are all part of the process called scientific inquiry. In *Why and How Do We Inquire?*, you will identify the process you experienced as a scientist in your own school. You will work in teams for this activity.

Part I: The Process of Inquiry

Materials

For each team of 3 students

1 sheet of chart paper

1 set of markers

3 *Process of Inquiry* handouts

Process and Procedure

1. Get together with the same team of scientists you were working with in *Small Problem?* Using markers, create a flowchart or diagram on chart paper that describes the general process of scientific inquiry your team went through in Parts I, II, and III of *Small Problem?*

Do not repeat the steps in your procedure. Instead, describe in general terms what you did. For example, the first thing you might have done is make an observation or ask a question.

2. When your team has completed its flowchart or diagram, copy it into your science notebook. Then post it in your classroom.
3. Compare your chart with those of your classmates by following Steps 3a–d.
   a. Explain each step in your diagram to another team.

b. Listen as the other team explains its diagram.
c. Discuss the similarities and differences in your diagrams.
d. You all followed the same procedure. Are your charts similar? List at least 2 similarities and 2 differences.

4. With your team, study the handout *Process of Inquiry*. Compare your chart with the handout. Identify the stages on the handout that you experienced. Place an X along the paths on the handout that you experienced in your inquiry.
5. Based on information presented in the *Process of Inquiry* handout and your classmates' charts, make any additions to your chart that you feel are necessary. Make the same adjustments to the diagram in your science notebook, too.

Your diagram should depict the investigation you did in *Small Problem?* Not all scientific inquiries proceed down the same path.

6. Read *It's about Inquiry* to learn more about the process of scientific inquiry.

READING

It's about Inquiry

Asking a question and seeking answers is an obvious path to take when inquiring about the natural world. In *Small Problem*?, you developed a question and then set out to answer your question by carefully designing an investigation. You then conducted your investigation and recorded and analyzed your results. Your results might have helped you answer your question and might have presented you with new questions. You gained some knowledge and understanding of the world of bacteria and possibly identified locations in your school where bacteria were widespread. Was your scientific investigation sound? Did you collect adequate evidence? Were your results valid? Based on your experience, you can see why the design of an investigation is so important.

Scientists propose explanations based on the evidence they collect during their research. This dynamic practice of wondering and asking questions, of making detailed observations, and of developing explanations based on those observations and evidence is the process of **scientific inquiry**. It is not a linear process. Look at figure 1.10 to see the different paths scientific inquiry can take. This is how scientists study the natural world.

The Process

In your investigation of bacteria, or microorganisms, in your school, you used the fundamental process of scientific inquiry. This process is composed of the following methods:

- Make observations and ask questions that can be answered by scientific inquiry.
- Check your current knowledge and the knowledge of other scientists.
- Make a prediction or propose an answer that you can test (hypothesis).

- Test your prediction by conducting your investigation and gathering evidence through observation.
- Propose explanations based on evidence.
- Consider alternative explanations.
- Test explanations by gathering more evidence or seeing if new predictions are supported based on that explanation.
- Report (or communicate) your findings and proposed explanation.

It is important to realize that inquiry is not a prescribed, sequential process. When scientists do science, they do not just march through the steps in this order. For example, while a scientist is designing an investigation, she might come across new information that causes her to go back to her original question and change it slightly. This might lead her to make changes in the design. Or a scientist collecting data while conducting an investigation might discover a flaw in the design. This might lead him to change the design before he continues. A scientist might not only discover a flaw but might make a new discovery that also generates new questions.

In your investigation, you probably answered, or partially answered, your original question. It is likely that you also came up with new questions. If you had time, you might revise and test your explanations to be satisfied that you answered your question completely. In this way, you are "doing" science.

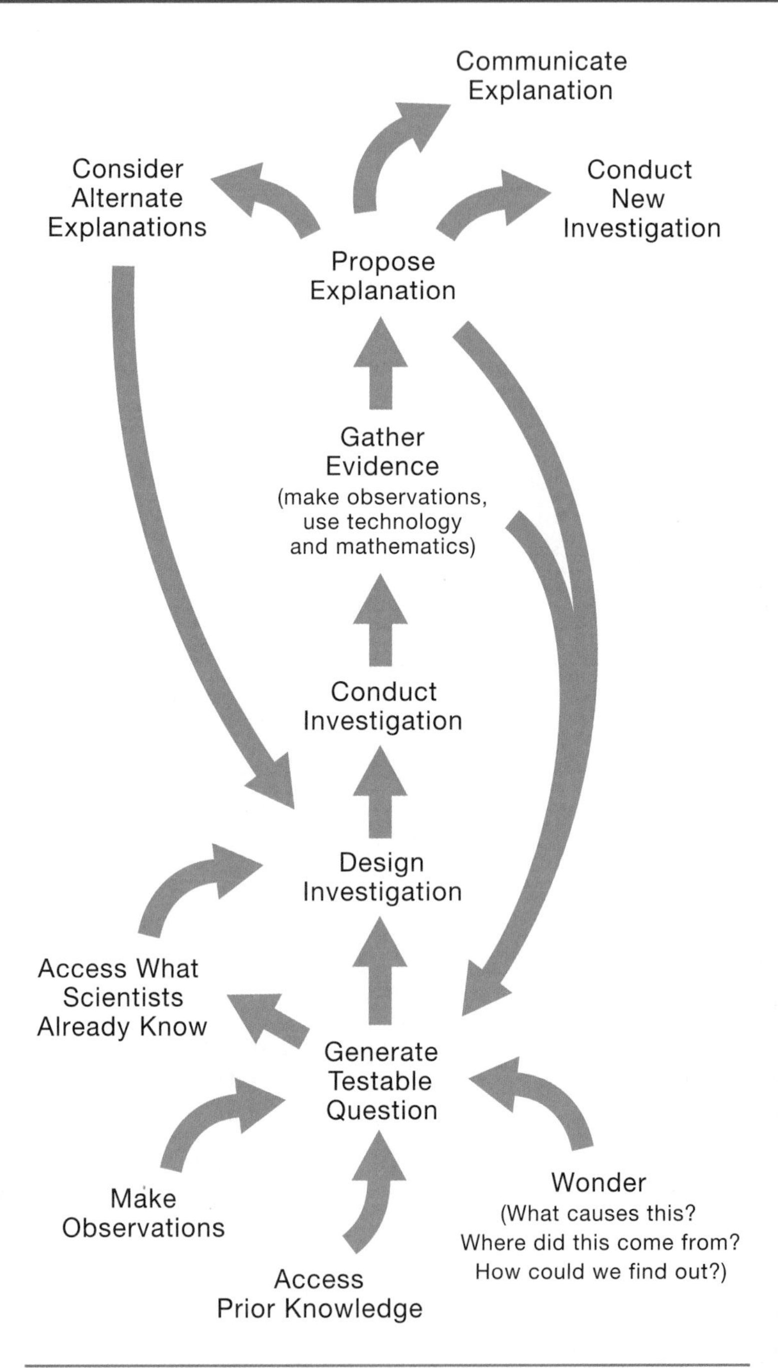

▲ **Figure 1.10 Process of inquiry.** Inquiry is a dynamic practice used to study the world around you. How did you use this process to conduct your investigation?

The Design

When scientists focus on the design of an investigation, they have to make sure that the design itself guides them to the answer to their question and controls for error (figure 1.11). If the design is poor, the results are not valid. Proper design of an investigation includes the following considerations:

- Design an investigation that answers the question in the most appropriate and direct manner.
- Control as many variables as possible. The scientist changes only the variable being tested.
- Set up a control group. Sometimes one group is not exposed to the tested variable. This group serves as a comparison group to determine that the results were due to the tested variable and not to some other factor. For example, if scientists are studying the effectiveness of a new arthritis medicine, one group does not take the medicine. Scientists compare this group with the group taking the medicine.
- Use mathematics and technology tools appropriately to collect and analyze data.
- Collect and organize data appropriately.
- Include numerous trials, samples, or subjects in each investigation.

Name
Date
Will my design answer the question?
Have I considered all of the variables?
How will I record and organize my data?

▲ **Figure 1.11 Investigation design.** What should you think about first when designing an investigation?

Stop & THINK

Answer the following questions in your science notebook.

1. What makes the design of an investigation useful and valid?
2. Now that you've learned more about the process of scientific inquiry and about designing scientific investigations, think back to your investigation in *Small Problem?* as you answer Questions 2a–b.
   - **a.** Suggest additional adjustments to the design of your investigation in *Small Problem?* Describe why you feel these adjustments are necessary.
   - **b.** How would these adjustments make the design of your investigation more valid?

Part II: Observations Leading to Discoveries

Materials

For each student

1 *Process of Inquiry* handout from Part I

Process and Procedure

1. Read *Observations Leading to Discoveries*. Use the turn-and-talk literacy strategy to help you understand the reading by following Steps 1a–h.
   a. Choose a partner to work with during this reading.
   b. Read the first paragraph of the reading silently.
   c. When both you and your partner finish the paragraph, decide which one of you will go first to complete Step 1d.
   d. Turn to your partner and summarize what you read. Relay your summary aloud as your partner listens.
   e. Listen as your partner gives you feedback on your summary. Discuss anything that is confusing to you.
   f. Each of you will read the next paragraph silently.
   g. Switch roles; this time your partner will summarize verbally and you will offer feedback.
   h. Continue this process. Read each paragraph silently and alternate roles as you summarize and offer feedback aloud.

This strategy is the turn-and-talk strategy. You will use this literacy strategy throughout the year to help you understand what you are reading.

READING

Observations Leading to Discoveries

> **"One's mind, once stretched by a new idea, never regains its original dimensions."**
> —*Oliver Wendell Holmes*

In your scientific investigation, you made discoveries about bacteria around your school by beginning with a question. Scientists learn and make discoveries by observing and asking "Why" or "What if" questions. In this reading, you will learn about a man who, when faced with a problem, helped change our way of life. He did this by making observations, asking questions, and engaging in scientific inquiry.

It was the 1840s—a time before scientists had discovered disease-causing organisms. A young Hungarian doctor, Ignaz Semmelweis (figure 1.12), worked in a hospital in Vienna, Austria. As part of his studies, he dissected cadavers (performed autopsies) in one part of the hospital. He also worked in the same hospital delivering babies in the division I ward.

▲ **Figure 1.12 Ignaz Semmelweis (1818–1865).** Semmelweis used the process of inquiry to solve a lethal problem in a Vienna hospital.

Results of Semmelweis's studies revealed that 13 percent of the women giving birth in the division I ward were dying of a disease called "childbed fever" (known scientifically as puerperal fever). Only about 2 percent of the women in the other division of the hospital were dying of childbed fever. The divisions were right next to each other, and pregnant women were cared for similarly in all ways except one: in division I, physicians and their students delivered the babies; in the other division, midwives and their students delivered the babies.

Semmelweis began to investigate. He noticed that when the hospital experienced a violent epidemic of childbed fever, no such epidemic was seen elsewhere in the city of Vienna. He observed that the death rate in home deliveries was much lower than at the hospital in which he worked. He noticed that even homeless mothers too poor to go to the hospital did not contract the fever even after delivering babies themselves in back alleys.

Semmelweis continued his inquiry. Two major correlations came to the surface. First, if the birth was especially traumatic, the mother had a greater chance of contracting childbed fever. Second, closing down division I always stopped the deaths caused by childbed fever.

Observations Leading to Discoveries, continued

Semmelweis continued to seek the cause of the high death rates from childbed fever. One day, Semmelweis's former professor of forensic pathology, a man he admired greatly, sliced his finger with a scalpel as he performed an autopsy in division I of the hospital. A few days later, the man was dead. He had become severely ill of sepsis (blood poisoning) and showed symptoms that were very similar to those seen in women with childbed fever. Devastated by his former professor's death, Semmelweis resolved to work harder to understand and prevent childbed fever.

Semmelweis hypothesized that the cause of his professor's sepsis was the same as that of childbed fever. He proposed that the source was "cadaver particles." Semmelweis thought that the attending physicians in division I transmitted these particles from cadavers to mothers during childbirth.

People could not see cadaver particles, but they could smell them. Semmelweis thought that when the invisible particles from a cadaver came in contact with an exposed surface on a patient, such as a wound, the particles were transmitted and caused the disease.

Semmelweis instituted a strict hand-washing policy (figure 1.13) for those physicians and medical students who worked in division I. Before attending patients, all medical personnel were required to wash their hands with chlorinated limewater until their skin was slippery and the smell of the cadaver was gone. Some found this practice a great inconvenience. In the first year of this policy, however, death rates dropped from about 18 percent to about 1 percent in division I. Moreover, not a single woman died from childbed fever between March and August 1848 in Semmelweis's division. Semmelweis felt he had evidence to support his idea that cadaver particles were responsible for the deaths in division I.

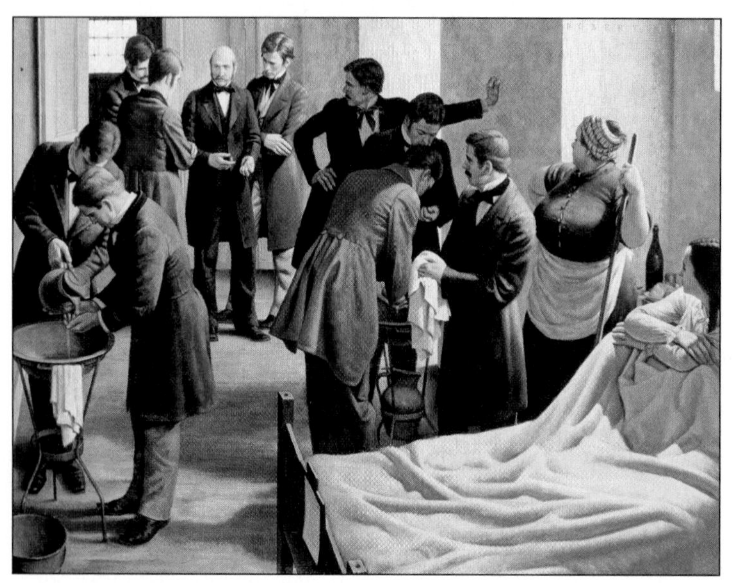

▲ **Figure 1.13 Semmelweis's hospital.** Semmelweis instituted a strict hand-washing policy to stop the spread of "cadaver particles." How did Semmelweis use the process of inquiry to solve a problem?

The connection Semmelweis made, that medical personnel were passing infection from their hands to mothers, was an incredible discovery. He made an observation, asked questions, and discovered a pattern. Observing patterns and asking questions are the guiding elements of much of science, historically and today.

Semmelweis lectured publicly in 1850 about his results and wrote a book about his discoveries in 1861. However, the medical community did not accept Semmelweis's discoveries. In fact, people criticized him both personally and professionally. It was not until 1865 that Joseph Lister (the namesake for Listerine) continued in the vein of Semmelweis's work and introduced the use of antiseptics to kill germs and reduce infection and disease. Lister said, "Without Semmelweis, my achievements would be nothing." It is now well known that hand washing is important as a way to reduce the transmission of disease. It is so important, in fact, that the Centers for Disease Control have released this statement: "Hand-washing is the single most important means of preventing the spread of infection."

Today, hand washing is part of American culture. You probably have seen signs posted in restaurant and retail restrooms stating, "Employees must wash their hands before returning to work." Schools also have programs that teach students about hand washing. There are even monitors above sinks in hospital intensive-care units to promote hand washing. The convenience of indoor plumbing, energy to heat water, special soaps, and health awareness makes hand washing part of our everyday regime. Semmelweis's work left a legacy of health and hygiene that has improved our way of life today.

SCILINKS® NSTA
Topic: antiseptics
Go to: www.scilinks.org
Code: 2Inquiry31

2. Consider what you have learned about the process of science as inquiry. Follow Steps 2a–b to explain to members of the scientific community in the 1840s what was happening in division I of the hospital.
   a. Summarize the reading as part of your explanation.
   b. Use the handout *Process of Inquiry* in your explanation. Describe the steps that Semmelweis used to solve his problem. You may use diagrams in your explanations.

Reflect and Connect

Answer the following questions on your own in your science notebook.

1. Initially, the medical community did not accept Semmelweis's discovery. Think about this as you answer Questions 1a–c.
   a. Propose an improvement to Semmelweis's process of inquiry that might have made his discoveries more readily accepted.

   Use the *Process of Inquiry* handout as your guide.

   b. Assume that Semmelweis followed the process of inquiry. Why do you think the medical profession was so reluctant to accept his ideas?
   c. Think of other examples in science where a new discovery was made and the scientific community did not immediately accept the new information. Or think of a discovery that took time to prove and demonstrate that the suggestion was correct. Record at least 1 example in your science notebook.
2. Describe why the process of scientific inquiry is not linear.

ELABORATE

Valid or Deceptive?

In the last several activities, you thought carefully about how to design investigations that will answer the scientific questions you have posed. Your understanding of the important criteria for scientific design is expanding. In *Valid or Deceptive?*, you will have an opportunity to extend your understanding by evaluating some claims made by scientists.

Have you ever read a headline that makes claims that sound too absurd to be true, like those shown in figure 1.14? You might wonder if these claims are real. Often, the writer of these articles or whoever is being interviewed makes the claim based on "scientific evidence." But how did the researcher gather evidence? Did the researcher conduct his investigation in a scientifically sound manner? Are the results of the investigation valid? You will work individually as you complete this activity, so think carefully.

Figure 1.14
Headlines in the news. Did the researcher making these claims design an investigation that gives valid results?

Materials

For each student

1 copy of *Process of Inquiry* handout

Process and Procedure

There are many decisions you'll make throughout life, as a consumer and as a part of society. Things you learn, information to which you have access, and the community that surrounds you inform your decisions. If you understand the process of scientific inquiry, you can use it to help interpret information you get from many different sources. Read the sidebar *Public Health Careers* to learn more about how a good background in science is important to reporting scientific issues.

1. Read the following headlines:
   - "Skin Patch Cuts Cravings for Sweets"
   - "Sweeteners Cause Memory Loss"
   - "Pizza Protects against Sunburn and Skin Cancer"
   - "Aspirin Cuts Risk of Ovarian Cancer"
   - "Showering Daily Increases Life Span"

2. Imagine you are a reporter assigned to interview the researcher who posted one of the claims in Step 1. It is your goal as a reporter to provide information to other citizens so that they can make informed decisions. As you think about your interview, complete Steps 2a–d.
   a. Review the *Process of Inquiry* handout and Steps 2b–d before you begin.
   b. Develop at least 10 questions that you would ask the researcher making the claim in the headline. Record these questions in your science notebook.
   c. At least 3 of your questions should focus on the "design investigation" stage of the *Process of Inquiry* handout. Address the other stages on the handout with your remaining questions.
   d. When developing your questions, consider the criteria you used when you designed the investigation in the activity *Small Problem?* Be sure that your questions help you determine the following:
      - There is evidence that supports the claim.
      - All the information is presented. Nothing seems to be ignored or deleted from the data.
      - The data are reliable and appropriate.
      - The research is reasonable and the investigation is fair.
      - The researcher or group of researchers is credible and reliable.
3. Get together with other students in your class who chose the same headline. Share your questions. Are they similar?
4. Compile a list of the 10 best questions from the discussion in Step 3 and record them in your science notebook.

Reflect and Connect

Work individually and answer the following questions in your science notebook.

1. Use what you've learned in this chapter to write answers to the 10 best questions you recorded in your science notebook. Imagine that you are the researcher. Keep in mind the characteristics of a scientific investigation and how this type of investigation resulted in the claim the researcher made.

Base your answers on your understanding about the process of scientific inquiry and designing scientific investigations. For example, the question you developed might be for the researcher who claimed that showering daily increases life span. Suppose your question was, "How many people were involved in the study?" The answer could be, "One thousand people were involved in the study over the past 20 years." This addresses a large sample size.

2. Find a science-related article in your local newspaper, a tabloid, or a magazine. Use the article and perform the tasks in Questions 2a–c.
   a. Critically review the article.
   b. Describe whether the article presents a scientific and valid argument.
   c. Do you believe the article? Why or why not?

SIDEBAR

Public Health Careers

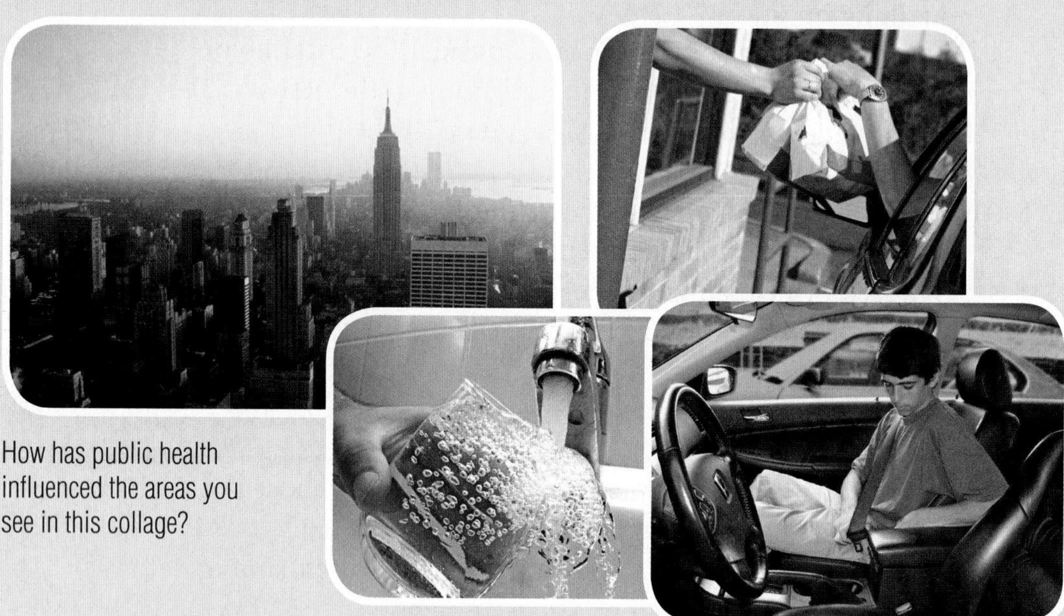

How has public health influenced the areas you see in this collage?

When you wake up in the morning, you may hear the radio announcer tell you that it is a clear day. The public health department is around to monitor air quality and the pollution level. It also develops programs to address air quality.

Next, you step into the shower. It is good to know that public health employees monitor the quality of the water you use for your shower and especially the water you drink. Did you know that one of the top 10 great achievements in public health began in 1945 when fluoride was added to drinking water in the United States? This simple act safely and inexpensively benefits both children and adults. Fluoridation prevents tooth decay in both children and adults as well as reduces tooth loss in adults. You get a fluoride treatment on your teeth every time you drink water from a tap that is monitored by public health employees.

As you get in the car to ride to school, you buckle your seat belt to keep you safe en route. Public health efforts have been successful in changing personal behavior in vehicles. These include widespread use of seat belts, child safety restraints, and motorcycle helmet use. On your ride to school, you pick up breakfast from your favorite fast-food chain. You see a sign posted that indicates the restaurant was rewarded 95 out of a possible 100 points by local public health inspectors, so you know the food is prepared safely.

Public health is important to many facets of our lives. We see the work of public health officials in regulations protecting us, from unsafe food preparation to smoke-free environments, to the safe water that we drink every day.

Because public health is involved in the safety of so many different parts of our lives, many career opportunities are available. These career choices range from research scientists to nurses to journalists. Have you ever thought of being a journalist working in the area of public health?

George Strait is a broadcast journalist with a background in science. Can you determine if the science claims from research are valid or deceptive?

Can you work under very tight deadlines? Can you write well? Do you think you would enjoy "chasing a story," which involves some basic research as well as tracking down and interviewing the experts? If so, you may want to consider a career as a health communications journalist.

George Strait (no, not the country-and-western singer!) is an award-winning health and science reporter. His undergraduate degree in science helped in his understanding of the scientific process and method and how to interpret data from scientific studies. This is exactly what you are learning in this chapter.

In 1984, George Strait was named the chief medical reporter for *World News Tonight*. At that time, there were no other specialized medical reporters on any television network. Strait appeared regularly on ABC's *World News Tonight* and *Nightline*. During that time, he received broadcast journalism's highest award, the Alfred I. duPont Award, two times. He was presented the awards for his groundbreaking series on women's health and a documentary on AIDS in minority communities.

Strait says there are three basic requirements to being a good health reporter: curiosity, the ability to write a coherent sentence, and the ability to tell a good story. He goes on to say, "Health reporting is really a question of finding information and assessing it. It requires trying to ferret out the truth and trying to fairly present what you learn."

Can you look at a scientific report and tell if the data are valid? Do you know the right questions to ask a scientist so that you can decide if her claims are believable? If so, you are on your way to being a good health and science journalist.

Topic: public health careers
Go to: www.scilinks.org
Code: 2Inquiry35

EVALUATE

Killing Germs? Digging Deeper

As you discovered in the investigation *Small Problem?*, bacteria and other microorganisms are everywhere. Some of these bacteria cause disease. Scientists have made great strides in developing products that kill bacteria (figure 1.15). The death rate due to infection has decreased as the use of antibiotics increased. People now know about good hygiene and the importance of sterilizing medical supplies. All these seem like great advances in medical science. But are they? Are there problems that could arise from using antibacterial products?

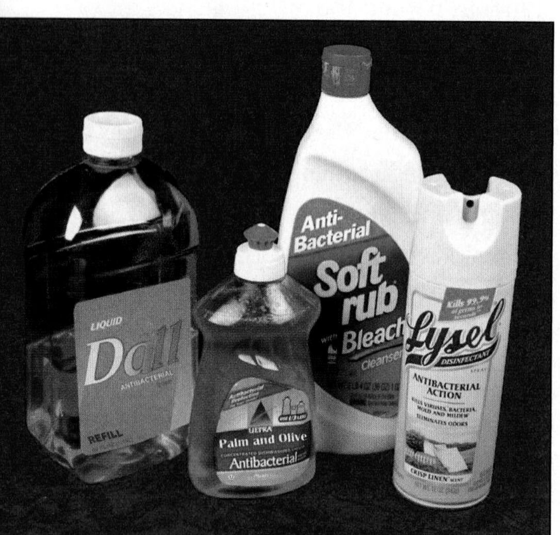

▲ **Figure 1.15**
Antibacterial products. These products are used to get rid of unwanted bacteria. Is there some danger in this?

Not all bacteria are harmful. For example, *E. coli* bacteria live in the intestinal tract of humans and other organisms. These bacteria aid digestion by helping break down foods. We use another bacteria, *Streptococcus thermophilus*, to culture yogurt. However, a specific strain of *E. coli* found in contaminated beef and other products is often lethal and group A *Streptococcus* causes strep throat and other illnesses. Antibacterial products cannot single out harmful bacteria. These products kill both the harmful and the beneficial bacteria.

Our attempts to get rid of unwanted bacteria are creating a new situation. Bacteria that are sensitive to antibiotics die. But some bacteria are no longer affected by antibiotics. They are *resistant* to antibiotics. Many scientists believe our overuse of antibiotics and antibacterial products causes antibiotic-resistant strains of bacteria to evolve. This means random changes in these bacteria's genetic material allow them to survive. Then they reproduce and pass on their resistance through their genetic material. (See figure 1.16.) Read the sidebar *Antibiotics* to learn more about how antibiotics work and how people misuse them.

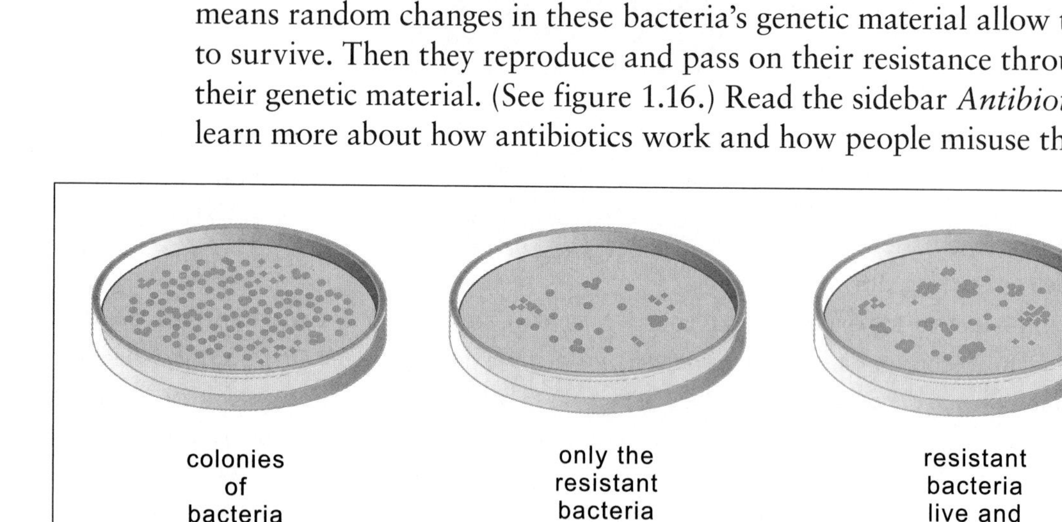

▲ **Figure 1.16 Antibiotic-resistant bacteria.** The bacteria that are sensitive to antibiotics die out. What happens to the bacteria that survive?

Is our everyday use of antibacterial products contributing to the evolution of resistant bacteria? Advertisers claim we need these products to stop the spread of disease. Do these products do what advertisers claim?

In *Killing Germs? Digging Deeper*, you will have an opportunity to demonstrate your understanding of scientific inquiry. You do this by designing and conducting a scientific investigation using antibacterial products. What you have learned throughout this chapter will help you decide what questions to ask, what tools to use, how to design a scientific investigation, how to organize your data, and how to answer your question using evidence. You will then present your findings to the rest of the class. You will work with a team for this activity.

Materials

For each team of 3 students

materials as needed to conduct an investigation focusing on antibacterial products, such as the following:

- access to an incubator or warm location
- 3 pairs of latex gloves
- 3 pairs of safety goggles
- petri dishes
- petri dishes with nutrient agar
- test tubes
- sterile swabs
- selected antibacterial or disinfectant products
- source of bacteria
- filter paper
- water
- scissors
- permanent markers

10% bleach solution

30% bleach solution

sticky notes (3 different colors)

3 *Scientific Investigation Report* handouts

3 *Killing Germs? Digging Deeper Scoring Rubric* handouts

Cautions

Wear safety goggles and gloves during your investigations. All materials that have come into contact with bacteria should be disposed of properly. Soak materials in 30% bleach solution, drain, and throw in the regular trash. Wipe down your work area with 10% bleach solution before and after the investigation. Wash your hands after the investigation.

Process and Procedure

Manufacturers have introduced many products to the market recently that they claim "kill germs," such as antibacterial and disinfectant products.

1. With your team, think of as many products as you can that have claims similar to those of the antibacterial products pictured in figure 1.15. Write your list in your science notebook.
2. Identify scientifically testable questions you might ask about the products on your list.

Think of as many questions as you can and record them in your science notebook.

3. Choose 1 question from your list in Step 2 for your team to investigate.

Your team must agree on the question to investigate. Discuss the options and justify why you would choose that particular question. Consider how you would design an investigation to answer that question, what background information you need, and if you have access to the necessary equipment and supplies.

4. Review the handout *Killing Germs? Digging Deeper Scoring Rubric* so that you understand how your teacher will grade your investigation. Discuss any questions you have with your team and your teacher.
5. In your science notebook, answer the following questions:
   a. What is the question you are investigating?
   b. What is your rationale? How will this investigation test your question?
   c. What is your hypothesis?
   d. What is the design of your investigation?

Record this as a step-by-step procedure. As a team, determine 1 design for your investigation. If you have several ideas, discuss the pros and cons of each design and make sure each member of your team agrees. Justify why you made each decision in your design. Include a list of materials you will use and safety precautions you will take.

e. What type of data will you collect?
f. How will you organize and analyze your data?
g. What is your explanation (conclusion) and what evidence supports your explanation?
h. What new questions or ideas do you have? Which might you pursue?

6. After you have designed your investigation, show your teacher your procedure for approval.
7. After you have approval from your teacher, conduct your investigation. Record your observations and data in an organized and useful way.

8. Analyze and discuss the results with your teammates. As you discuss your results, answer Questions 8a–d.
   a. How can you explain the results of your investigation?
   b. Did the results help you answer your question?
   c. What conclusion can you reach based on your investigation?
   d. How confident are you that your results answer the question you chose? Explain your answer.

Remember, to answer this question, consider how well you controlled the variables in the investigation. Discuss any sources of error.

9. Write a lab report on your own of your investigation.

Use what you learned about writing a lab report from the explore/explain activity. You may want to review the *Scientific Investigation Report* handout.

10. Prepare a visual presentation of your investigation with your team to share with the class. This could be a poster, a computer presentation, or a slide show. Look at the rubric to guide you.
11. Present your investigation to the class. Your classmates will be looking for good qualities of your investigation, ways to improve your investigation, and questions to ask you.
12. After each group presents, get together with your team for a research critique. Decide on 1 strength of the investigation, 1 way to improve it, and 1 question you have about it. Write the "strength" comment on 1 color of sticky note (designated by your teacher), the "improvement" comment on another color, and the "question" on a third color. Post your notes in the area designated by your teacher.
13. At the conclusion of each presentation, discuss the critique statements as a class. The presenters should answer questions from their classmates and address ways to improve their investigation with their own ideas.

SIDEBAR

Antibiotics

Why is it that sometimes when you feel awful, and you go to the doctor, the doctor does not give you an antibiotic? It could be that you have a virus. Antibiotics do not work on viruses.

Both bacterial and viral infections can make you sick, but bacteria and viruses are very different. Bacteria are single-celled microscopic organisms about 1/100th the size of a human cell, or 1 micrometer long. Bacteria are normally found in our bodies and in our environment, including in plants, animals, soil, and water. Most bacteria are helpful, but some harmful bacteria can cause infections. Common bacterial infections include strep throat, urinary tract infections, and diarrhea that is caused by *Escherichia coli* bacteria. Bacteria also cause diseases, such as tuberculosis and anthrax. See the figure for the three most common shapes of bacteria.

a.

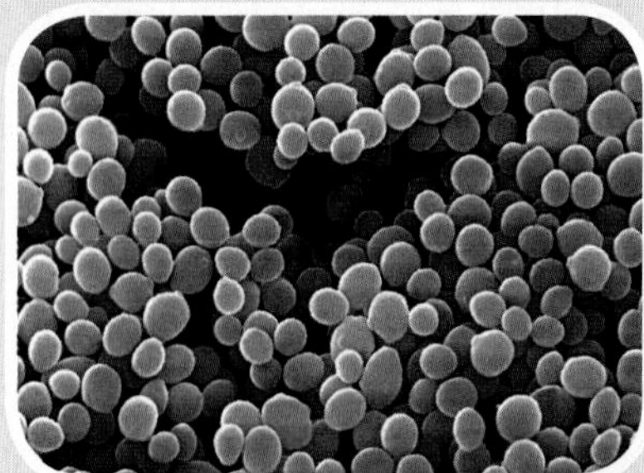

b.

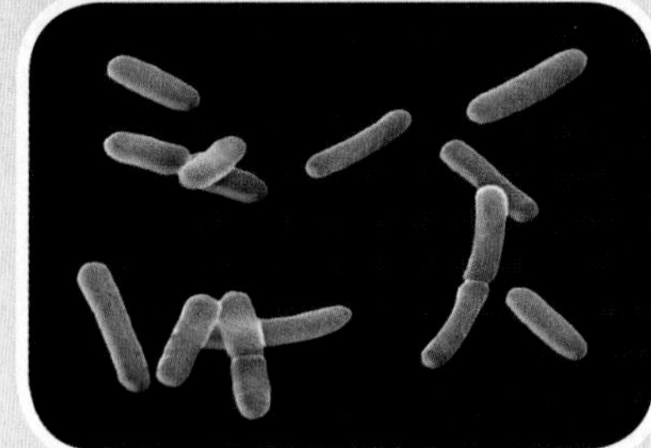

c.

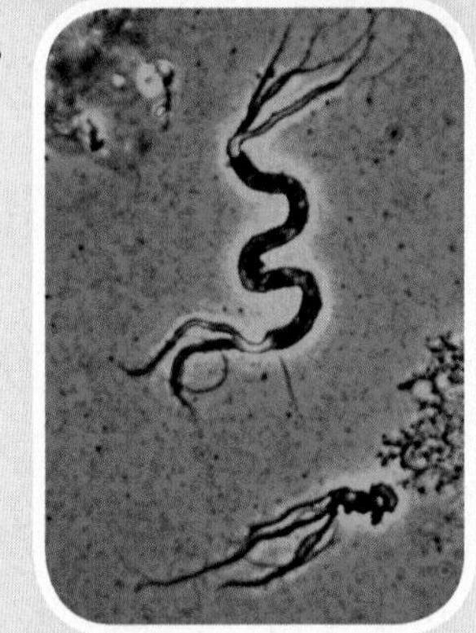

Bacterial cells. These are the three most common shapes of bacterial cells. (a) Cocci (spheres) 51,000×; (b) bacilli (rods) 24,000×; and (c) spirochetes (corkscrew) 700×.

A virus is 20–100 times smaller than a bacterium. Viruses consist only of a particle of DNA or RNA surrounded by a protective protein coat, or capsid (see figure on p. 41). Viruses survive only by infecting living cells. Most biologists classify viruses as infectious particles rather than living organisms. Common viral infections are colds, flu (influenza), and mono (mononucleosis). Other examples of viruses include chicken pox, herpes, rabies, Ebola, Asian bird flu, and AIDS.

Antibiotics kill or inhibit the growth of bacteria by interfering with the normal functions of bacteria. Antibiotics do this without harming the host organism (humans or other animals). Each antibiotic affects a unique site within a bacterial cell. Penicillin kills bacteria by attaching to their cell walls and destroying a key part of the wall. Erythromycin attacks the cell components responsible for making proteins. Other similar antibiotics include tetracycline, streptomycin, and gentamicin. Antibiotics do not work on viruses because they work on parts of bacteria that viruses do not have, such as a cell wall.

SCiLINKS® NSTA

Topic: antibiotics
Go to: www.scilinks.org
Code: 2Inquiry40

Viruses only exist within the host cell and do not carry out their own biochemical reactions.

Unfortunately, doctors and patients misuse antibiotics. Doctors sometimes prescribe antibiotics when they are not needed, such as at a patient's request or for a cold (viral infection). Patients may make the mistake of using only part of their antibiotic prescription and saving the remaining doses for later use.

a.

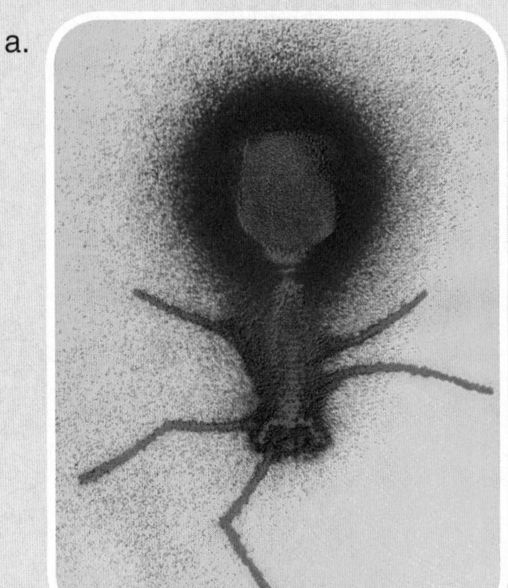

b.

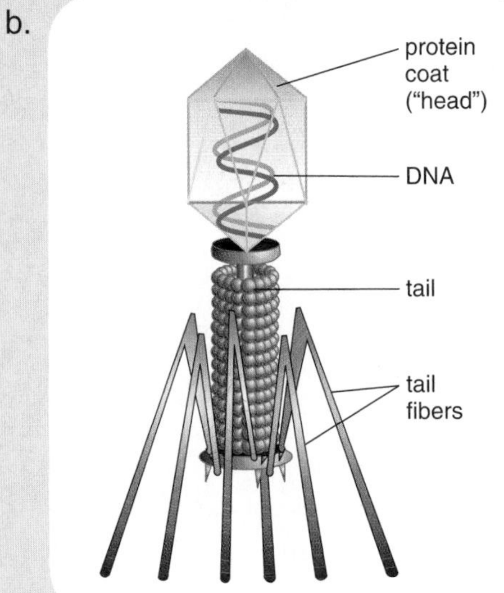

▲ **Structure of a virus.** Viruses are made of DNA or RNA and a protein coat. The electron micrograph (a) shows a virus that infects bacteria magnified 94,500 times. The diagram shown in (b) is of the same type of virus.

Misuse of antibiotics can lead to the evolution of new strains of bacteria that cannot be killed by currently used antibiotics. These bacteria are called antibiotic-resistant bacteria. Antibiotic resistance occurs when bacterial DNA spontaneously mutate. Out of the millions of bacteria living in your body, one might acquire a mutation that makes it resistant to an antibiotic. If you take an antibiotic, the susceptible bacteria will die, but the resistant bacteria might survive. A resistant bacteria cell will multiply without competition from susceptible bacteria. If the bacteria causing your illness are antibiotic resistant, an antibiotic will not cure you. Antibiotic resistance is a major health care problem.

Antibiotic resistance is inevitable because mutations allow bacteria to evolve. However, people can do things to help decrease the number of bacteria that become resistant. For example, people can reduce the spread of resistant bacteria by washing their hands. Doctors can prescribe antibiotics only when absolutely necessary, and patients can use them appropriately. People also can avoid overusing antibacterial products. By limiting the situations in which antibiotic-resistant bacteria thrive, people can use antibiotics to treat disease-causing bacterial infections successfully.

SCILINKS® NSTA

Go to: www.scilinks.org
Topic: antibiotic resistance
Code: 2Inquiry41a
Topic: super bugs
Code: 2Inquiry41b

UNIT 1

Interactions Are Interesting

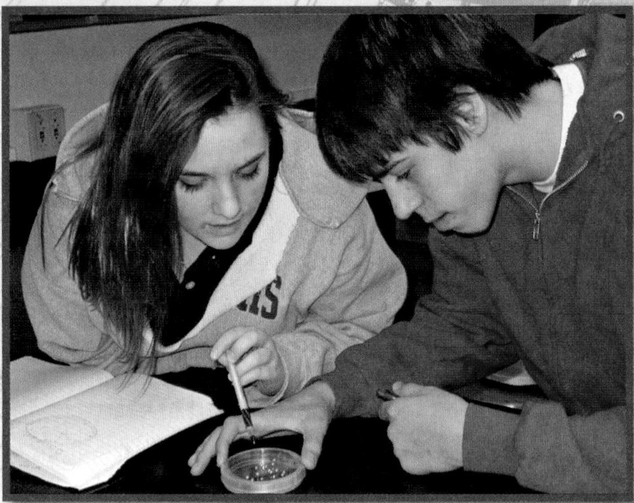

Interactions Are Interesting

Interactions make life interesting. That's why we talk to our friends, go to the amusement park, and play sports. Interactions make up our everyday experiences. They help us figure out our social and physical environment. For example, what can you tell about the interaction between the students shown in the photograph? What will the girl's reaction be? Will the interaction change the boy in any way?

Scientists study both social and physical interactions. In unit 1, *Interactions Are Interesting*, you will learn about the physical interactions common in your everyday life and try to understand them. Will the car stop in time? Does the battery have enough charge? Is the rope strong enough to hold me? These are all questions that you can answer when you study interactions.

In unit 1, you will study how forces of interaction and chemical reactions lead to changes. Then you will try to make sense of the changes, or lack of changes, you observe by looking for patterns and trends. All along, you will seek and develop explanations based on the principles that govern the physical universe. The result is a better understanding of our natural world.

▲ **Interactions are part of everyday life.** What might be the result of this interaction? Would you interact differently? What factors influence the outcome?

Goals for the Unit

By the end of unit 1, you should understand the following:

- All physical interactions between objects consist of a pair of forces, equal in size and opposite in direction. In these interactions, one force acts on one object and the other force acts on the second object.
- Changes in velocity result from net forces; no net force results in zero or constant velocity (assuming constant mass).
- Many chemical reactions involve the transfer of either electrons or protons.
- Chemical reactions involve changes in energy.
- The laws of conservation allow us to understand complex interactions.
- Investigations are guided by scientific principles and are performed to test ideas and answer questions.
- Mathematical tools and models guide and improve scientific inquiry.

▲ **Interactions can be both social and physical.** Is this rope strong enough to hold the rappeler? How can you find out? What forces are involved?

CHAPTER 2

Collision Course

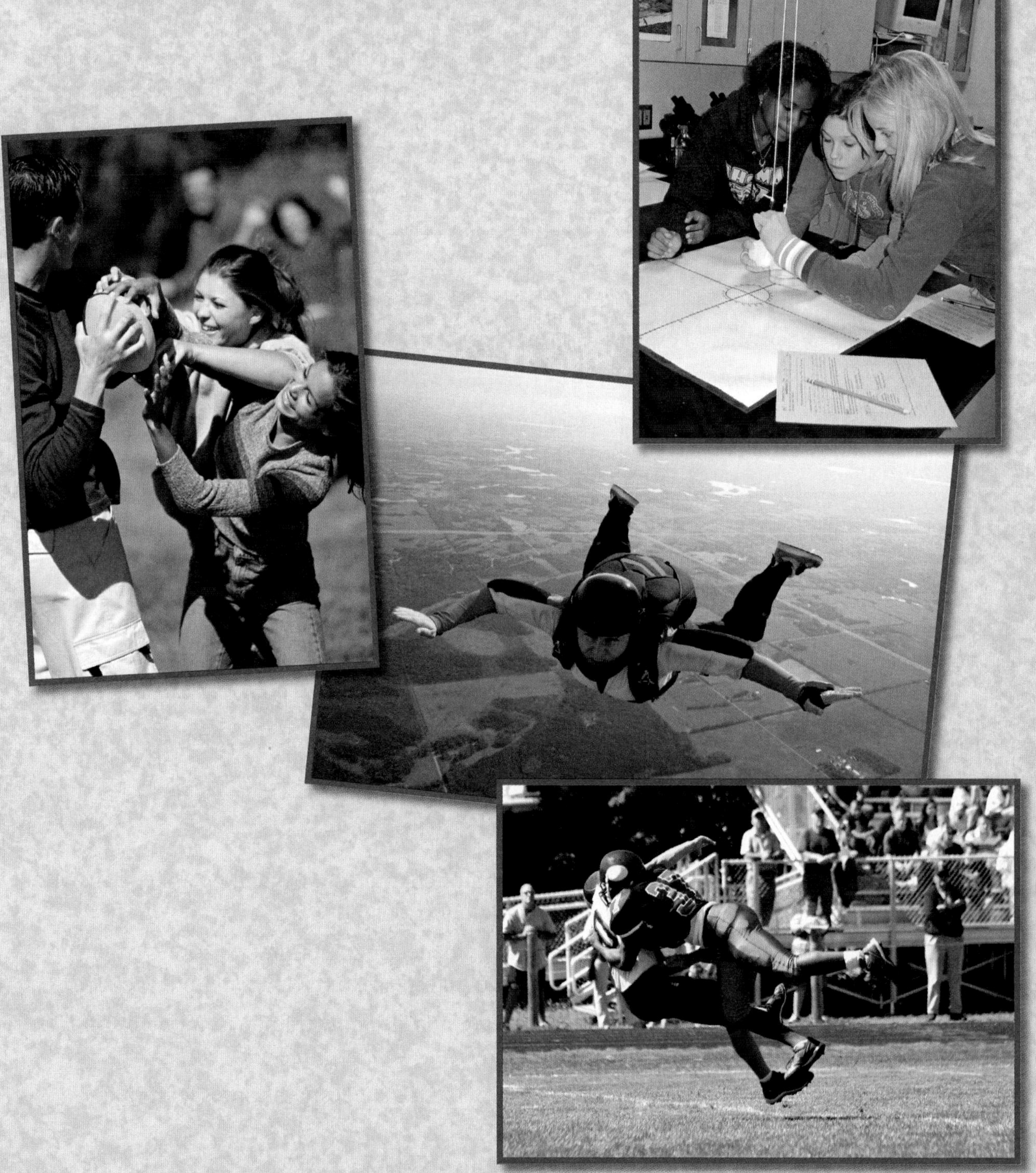

Collision Course

Collisions represent one type of interaction. One reason collisions might capture our interest is because we anticipate *changes* that they might bring about. We look at objects before and after they interact in a collision and learn from what we observe. Then we imagine what might happen if the initial conditions were different. Finally, we test those new initial conditions to see if we understand why the changes occurred.

Look at the vehicles in figure 2.1, which shows a collision about to happen. What do you anticipate? Why will it happen? What would happen if you could alter factors important to the collision? How would you determine whether your predictions were correct?

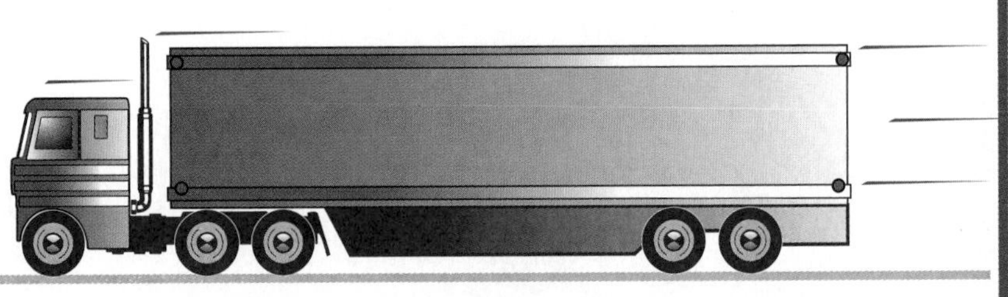

▲ **Figure 2.1**
Collisions are a type of interaction. What changes occur when two objects collide? How would those changes differ if the initial conditions were changed? How do you know?

Much of science involves answering these questions about the interactions we call collisions. Scientists observe, analyze, and evaluate the changes that the interactions between objects cause. We use this same way of thinking with *all* objects that interact, whether they are as large as cars or as small as atoms. As a result, we learn from everyday experience and can better understand the world in which we live.

Goals for the Chapter

By the end of chapter 2, you will be able to answer the following questions:

- What evidence suggests that all forces occur in pairs, equal in size and opposite in direction?
- How are impulse and change in momentum related?
- What evidence suggests that momentum is conserved?

Fortunately, you will have help answering these questions. Each activity in this chapter will give you experience with interactions. From these experiences, you will learn about the factors that affect each interaction. In the end, this knowledge will help you increase your understanding of nature.

All the activities in this chapter will help you learn about interactions.

ENGAGE	Forces Make a Lovely Pair
EXPLORE	Controlling Forces
EXPLAIN	In-Line Interactions
EXPLAIN	Getting Real: Collisions in Two Dimensions
ELABORATE	With and Without a Net
EVALUATE	Forces to Go; Forces to Stop

Chapter organizers can help you remember what you know and where you are headed. They help you organize your search to understand the material world. Look at the chapter organizer every day. Think about how the questions associated with the activity you are doing is related to one or more of the chapter's main concepts. Compare what you know now with what you knew a week ago. Think about what you will learn today. Let the chapter organizer help you map your learning and monitor your progress. That way you can look back and see what you have accomplished.

Collision Course

Linking Question

How can I determine what variables are important in finding the amount of force in an interaction?

Engage

Forces Make a Lovely Pair

Key Idea:
Interaction forces can be measured directly with a clay ball.

Explore

Controlling Forces

Key Idea:
The variables that determine the amount of force are change in velocity, mass, and/or time of interaction.

Linking Question

In a closed system, how do data from linear collisions support the law of conservation of momentum?

Explain

In-Line Interactions

Key Idea:
Both elastic and inelastic collisions exhibit conservation of momentum.

Linking Question

Is momentum conserved in two dimensions?

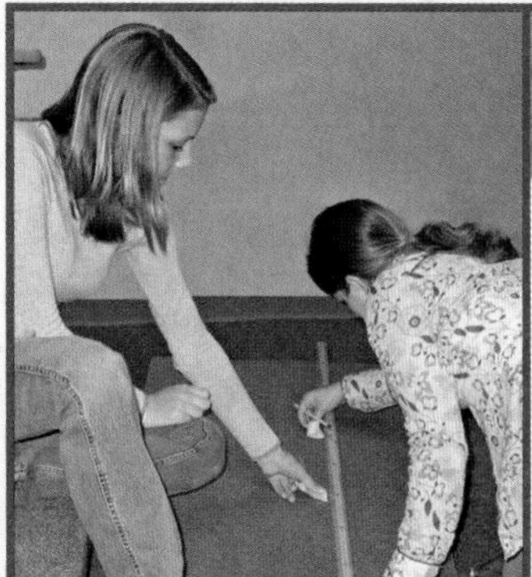

EVALUATE

Forces to Go; Forces to Stop

Key Idea:
The motion of an object changes depending on changes in the net forces acting on the object.

Linking Question

What happens to the motion of an object when net forces acting on it change?

CHAPTER 2

Major Concepts

- **All forces occur in pairs, equal in size but opposite in direction.**
- **Changing velocity indicates net forces.**
- **Momentum is conserved.**
- **Force, velocity, and momentum, as well as changes in these qualities, behave as vectors.**
- **Force is the time rate change of momentum.**

ELABORATE

With and Without a Net

Key Idea:
Objects in motion tend to stay in motion unless they experience a net force.

EXPLAIN

Getting Real: Collisions in Two Dimensions

Key Idea:
Momentum is conserved in all collisions.

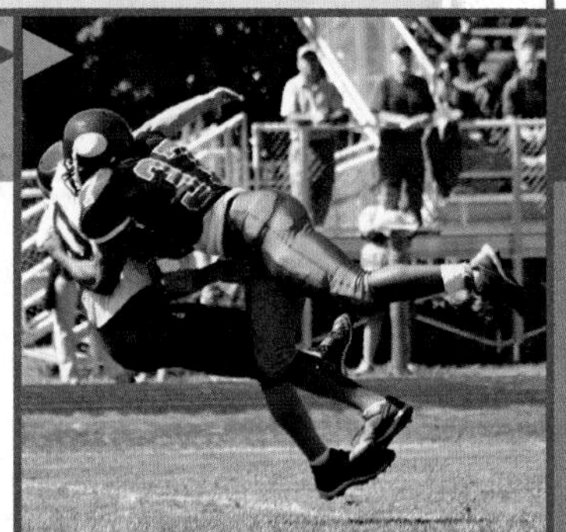

Linking Question

What kinds of changes in momentum occur with and without net forces?

ENGAGE

Forces Make a Lovely Pair

▲ **Figure 2.2**
Collisions are interactions that result in forces. Has your big toe ever collided with a soccer ball? Did your toe apply a force to the ball? Did the ball apply a force to your toe?

Collisions result in forces. Just think about the last time you stubbed your toe on a big rock or kicked a soccer ball (figure 2.2). Was the rock or soccer ball the only object to apply a force? How do you know? What's the evidence?

Interactions that produce change involve forces in some way. Scientists study change to determine how large those forces are. That way they can determine the effect of forces on objects. If a large truck and a small car collide, for example, what would the forces of the interactions be? How would those forces affect each vehicle? With the right answers, you could design a safer interior for vehicles. And a safer vehicle interior is a good application of what you learn in school.

In *Forces Make a Lovely Pair*, you and your partner will track, think about, and reach conclusions regarding two interactions, one a collision and the other a kind of tug-of-war. With a scientific mind-set, you will focus on analyzing the changes you observe and sharing what you learn so that others can understand. In this way, you will lay the groundwork for all the interactions you will study in this unit.

Part I: Moving Interactions

Materials

For each team of 2 students

1 small ball of modeling clay

Process and Procedure

Look at the two vehicles in figure 2.1. Each vehicle is about to experience a force. Will the forces be the same? Imagine what changes those forces would make.

In Part I, you and your partner will use a small ball of clay to model the forces of interaction between a large truck and a small car. But first, you will draw from previous experiences to answer a question about the forces *during* the collision. Then you will determine if your answer makes sense in light of the changes you observe.

1. Draw a sketch representing the 2 vehicles in figure 2.1 and indicate the following variables in the sketch.
   a. Relative mass of the vehicles
   b. Relative velocity of the vehicles immediately before the collision
   c. Forces acting on each vehicle during the collision

You only have to represent the *relative* sizes of these variables. In other words, simply show in some way which mass is larger or smaller. Or you may decide that some variables are equal. You do not necessarily have to use numbers.

2. Record your answer to the following question under your sketch:

   "During the collision, which force is greater, the force of the truck on the car or the force of the car on the truck?"

Draw from your previous experiences and use the words *force*, *velocity*, *time*, *momentum*, and *mass* as you state reasons for your answer. Underline these words when they appear in your sentences to help your teacher assess what you are thinking now. Remember, in science you get to change your mind based on new evidence and further thinking about a scientific question.

3. Meet with a partner and share your answer using Steps 3a–f as a guide.
   a. Review silently and *think* about the connection between what you sketched and what you wrote. Look for the most important ideas you represented.
   b. *Share* your sketch with your partner and discuss each feature of it, including labels.
   c. Read your answer aloud as you wrote it.
   d. Ask for *advice* on how to make either the sketch or the answer better.
   e. *Revise* your work if you think your partner's understanding is better than yours.
   f. Switch roles and listen carefully to your partner.

This is called the think-share-advise-revise (TSAR) strategy. You will use this throughout the year in every science subject area.

4. Participate in a class discussion and record the thoughts of other teams.
5. Model the forces of interaction between a truck and a car with a clay ball by conducting Steps 5a–d.
   a. Roll a small piece of modeling clay into a sphere about the size of a small pea (figure 2.3).
   b. Pretend your thumb is the truck and your finger is the small car shown in figure 2.1.
   c. Hold the clay ball directly between your "truck" and "car" and model the brief moment of collision by squeezing quickly, just once.
   d. Remove the clay ball carefully from your collision to preserve the changes in the shape of the sphere.

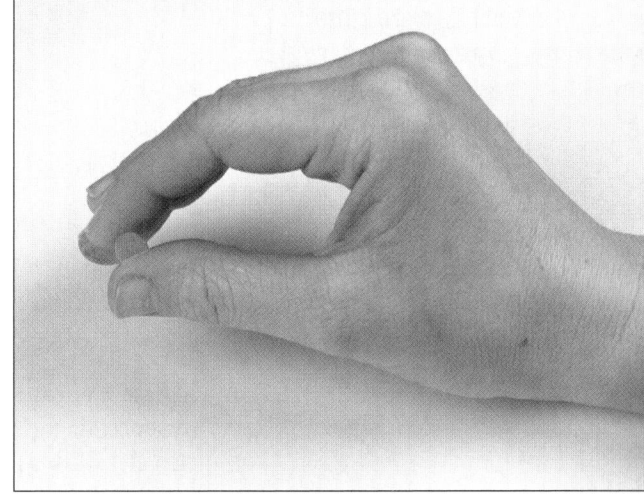

▲ **Figure 2.3**
Clay ball. The size of the clay ball is important to the success of your activity. It should only be the size of a small pea. If the clay squishes out beyond your fingers or curls on the edges, it is too big.

6. Represent your thinking about changes to the clay ball by performing Steps 6a–e.
   a. Make a before-and-after sketch of the clay ball similar to figure 2.4.

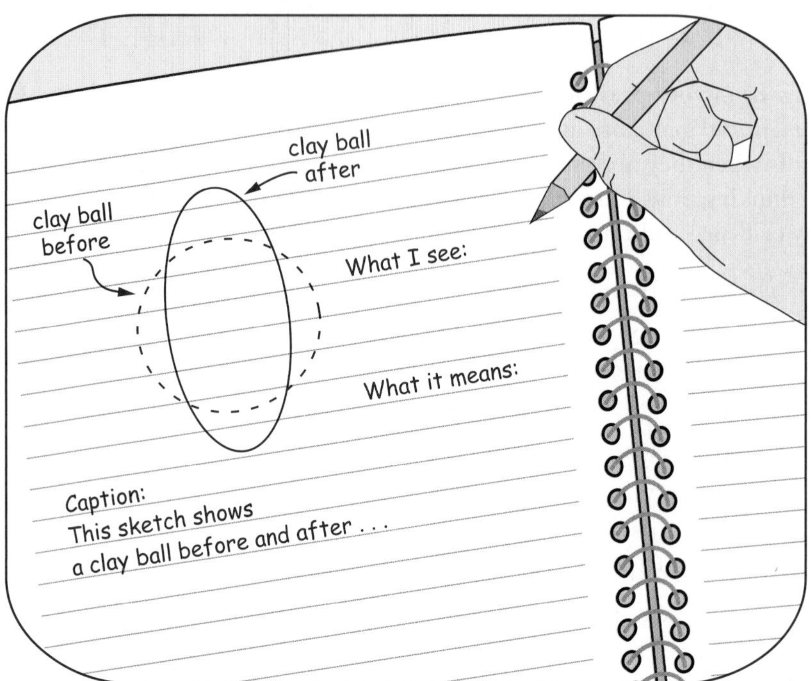

▶ **Figure 2.4 Before-and-after sketches help you make sense of change.** How you organize your observations affects your ability to make sense of the changes you record. What role do labels play in your effort to understand?

   b. Write the phrase "What I see" near the change you observe on one side of your before-and-after sketch. Then describe the squishing that the clay ball experienced.
   c. Write the phrase "What it means" just under the previous phrase. Then write what the squishing suggests about force.

These 2 phrases together are called *highlight comments* since they represent the essence, or the highlights, of your experience. You used highlight comments in Level 1 of this program to help you better understand graphs.

   d. Write additional highlight comments for the other side of your clay ball.
   e. Use the TSAR strategy with your sketches and highlight comments.
7. Write a caption under your sketch.

Captions tell the reader what is important about the sketch or figure. They convey the essential features of the figure by putting much of the highlight comments into sentence form. You will include captions on many entries in your science notebook throughout the year.

8. How do your highlight comments and caption compare with the answer you gave to the question in Step 2? Write a statement about how your thinking has changed or remained the same.

9. What questions do you have about pairs of forces that result from colliding objects? List at least 2 questions.

Stop & THINK

PART I

Read each question carefully and think about your experiences before you answer. Then record your answers in your science notebook in a way that helps your teacher find, make sense of, and give you feedback on those answers. You may want to use the TSAR strategy with classmates *before* you hand in your answers.

1. In each of the following cases, determine which (if either) of the 2 objects exerts a larger force during the interaction.
   - **a.** A very fast car hits a slow-moving truck from behind (not head on).
   - **b.** A very fast car hits a stationary (static) truck.
   - **c.** A truck pushes a car up a hill.
   - **d.** A car pushes a truck on a flat road.
   - **e.** A grasshopper hits the windshield of a fast-moving truck.
   - **f.** A baseball bat hits a baseball for a home run.
   - **g.** A north magnet gets close to another north magnet.

2. Use arrows to represent the forces at the time of collision by completing Questions 2a–b.

   Using arrows to represent forces is a common practice in science. An arrow can be any length and it points in a particular direction. The length of the arrow should represent the amount of force (longer arrow = more force). The arrowhead should point in the direction the force is acting.

   - **a.** Sketch your finger and thumb squeezing together (without the clay ball).
   - **b.** Use labeled arrows to indicate the force of your finger on your thumb and the force of your thumb on your finger.
   - **c.** Write a caption for your sketch.

3. Think of the forces involved in Question 2 as you answer 3a–b.
   - **a.** How many forces are involved in the situation described in Question 2a? Describe them in words.
   - **b.** How many objects did these forces act upon?

Part II: Static Interactions

Materials

For each team of 2 students

colored pens or pencils

Process and Procedure

Interactions result in forces. You have learned a core concept in science: *these forces* always *occur in pairs, equal in size and opposite in direction,* and *they act on two different objects*. But what if objects are not moving? Do stationary objects interact?

In Part II, you and your partner will reflect on your previous experiences with nonmoving objects and think about the forces of interaction between them. Then you will decide whether you see similarities and differences between the way moving and static objects interact.

First, you will watch an interesting interaction. Your teacher will attach two identical masses to opposite sides of a spring scale so that the masses dangle over pulleys. A sample demonstration apparatus is shown in figure 2.5.

1. Observe a 1-kilogram (kg) mass hanging freely from a spring scale. Sketch or describe this setup and record the weight (in newtons, or N) of the 1-kg mass.
2. Use your experiences from Part I to answer the question, "What will the spring scale read in figure 2.5 when the 1-kg masses are allowed to dangle freely?"

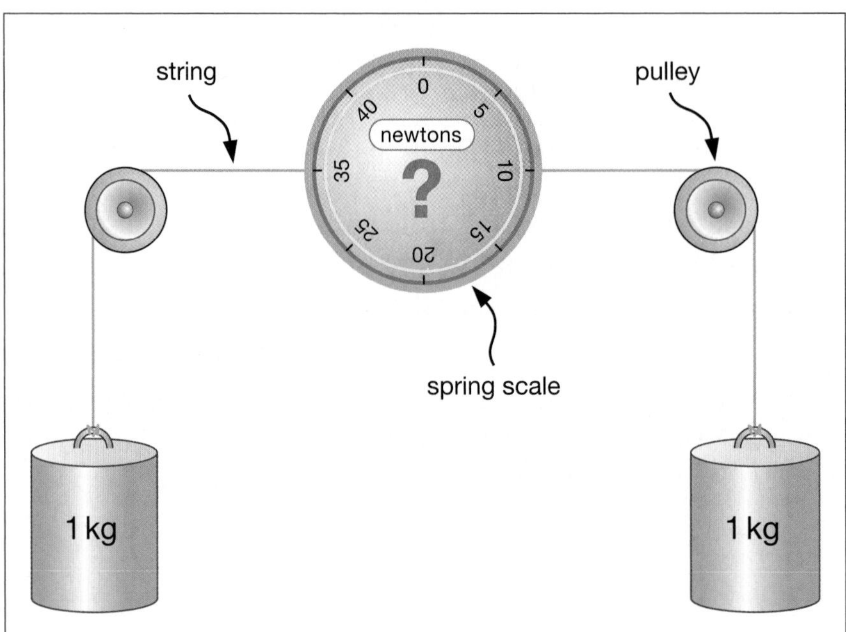

Figure 2.5 Atwood's machine. Are forces involved in this apparatus? Will the forces cause the scale dial to move? Will the masses move as well?

3. Observe the demonstration apparatus, sometimes called an Atwood's machine, as your teacher allows the masses to dangle. Record what you see.
4. Modify your answer to the question in Step 2 in light of your observations and class discussion. Use a different-colored pen or pencil to record your changes.
5. Consider other scenarios for the apparatus (different masses, uneven placement of the masses, and so on) and follow Steps 5a–d. Then perform Step 5e.
   a. With your team, make a list of these situations in the form of questions.
   b. Choose 1 scenario and add it to the class list that your teacher has started.
   c. Predict what you think will happen in each of the scenarios on the class list. Record your predictions in your science notebook.
   d. Observe as your teacher demonstrates.
   e. Modify your comments in your science notebook based on your observations and class discussion.

Reflect and Connect

Read each question carefully and think about how your experiences in this activity might lead you to an answer.

1. Copy the table in figure 2.6 into your science notebook. Then complete it to show the similarities and differences between Part I and Part II.

Concept important to interactions	Similarities between Part I and Part II	Differences between Part I and Part II
Velocity		
Mass		
Force		
Time		
Add other concepts based on your current thinking		

Figure 2.6 Similarities and differences between Part I and Part II. Use this table or a similar organizer to complete *Reflect and Connect* Question 1.

2. Imagine another demonstration apparatus similar to the one in Part II. In this apparatus, however, the weights are equal-strength north magnets and the table is a big south magnet (figure 2.7). Generate a labeled sketch of this new apparatus with highlight comments and a caption.

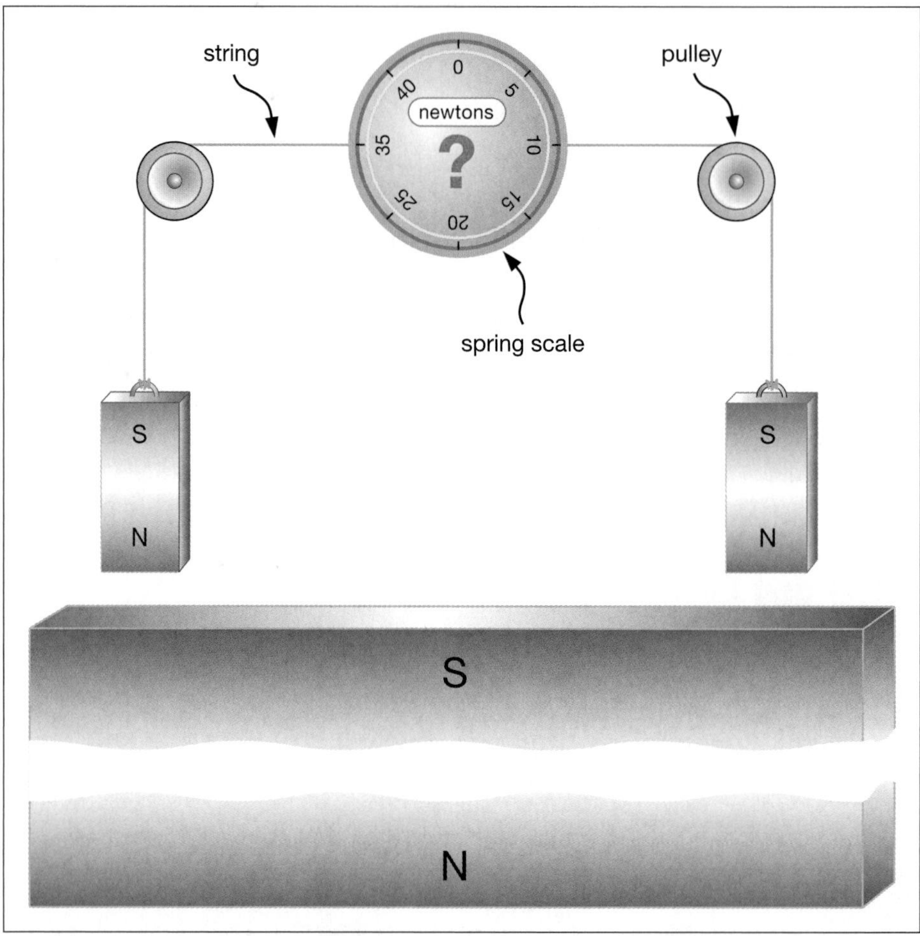

▲ **Figure 2.7 Setup with magnets.** What will the scale read with the setup pictured here?

3. Repeat Question 2, except replace the weights with electrically charged objects (both with an equal positive charge) and a negatively charged table.
4. Consider the forces you described in Questions 2 and 3 and the forces you considered in Parts I and II of this activity. How are they similar? How are they different? Use a table or a Venn diagram to organize your answers.

See *How to Use and Create Venn Diagrams* in the How To section at the back of the book.

Controlling Forces

EXPLORE

Interactions result in pairs of forces. These forces are equal in size, opposite in direction, and act on different objects. And those forces cause all kinds of changes. Is there a way to control those changes? For example, how would you change your walking speed as you move down the hallway in school? Is speeding up different from slowing down? What about sitting at your desk in class? How do forces prevent changes such as falling through your chair to the floor?

Changing your motion is an essential part of the freedom you experience in everyday life. So knowing what factors control the amount of force necessary to move about as you wish is important to you. Are those factors different for objects other than your body? For example, how much force is required to change the speed of a car moving from highway speed to a complete stop?

In *Controlling Forces*, you and your team will explore the factors that allow you to determine how much force is required to accomplish common tasks. First, you will try to understand the variables that affect force *qualitatively* (that is, mostly involving concepts). Later, you will learn about forces *quantitatively* (mostly involving measurement and some calculations). Regardless of the approach to understanding, the relationship among factors important to determining force stays the same. And as you might expect, the most complete understanding of those relationships requires both concepts *and* calculations.

Use the following question to focus your efforts in this activity: "What is the relationship among variables that affect force?" This question will help you monitor the decisions you make about collecting, analyzing, and reporting data. If something doesn't help you answer the focus question, then you should think twice about doing it.

Part I: Speed Bumps

Materials

For each team of 4 students

2 ramps

2 toy cars or trucks

various weights

1 small ball of modeling clay

tape

1 small piece of stiff cardboard

Process and Procedure

Head-on collisions can result in significant damage to automobiles and the passengers inside. So finding ways to study the forces occurring from such collisions could help scientists and engineers design better seat belts and air bags. What can you do to understand collisions better, without conducting expensive or dangerous experiments?

One approach is to use a well-designed model. A model is a representation of an actual object that exhibits most of the essential features of the object, but is easier to study. For example, you and your team can use a clay ball and toy cars to study the factors that affect forces in head-on collisions.

1. Meet with your team and develop a list in your science notebook of factors (sometimes called variables) that affect the amount of force each car experiences in a head-on collision.
2. Confer with another team to complete your list of important factors.
3. Read the following paragraph about one of the factors that you may have chosen for your list.

"How fast was I going?" This question is often asked by drivers when they are about to get a speeding ticket. Highway speed limits are in place to protect us and those around us. There is a big difference in a rear-end collision at 5 miles per hour and one at 30 miles per hour.

One of the factors that you listed may have been speed. In science, the speed of an object is often considered along with the direction the object is moving. Speed and direction make up the quantity we call velocity. Velocity is a vector. **Vectors** have both a magnitude (a size) and a direction. So the magnitude of velocity is speed. If you are stopped for speeding by a police officer, you may be concerned with the magnitude of your velocity, or your speed. If the police officer is investigating a car accident, however, she will want to know both how fast the cars were moving (their speed) and in what direction they were moving. She needs to know the velocity of the cars involved in the accident to reconstruct the accident scene.

4. Design a series of investigations to explore the qualitative relationship among velocity, mass, and force. Use the materials provided by your teacher and consider Steps 4a–f.

Design the minimum number of investigations to answer the focus question.

a. How can you use the angle of the ramp to control the velocity at collision?
b. How can you make a smooth transition (without speed bumps) between the ramp and the horizontal surface onto which the cars roll?
c. What can you do to ensure that only flat, vertical surfaces on the fronts of toy vehicles (see figure 2.8) hit the clay ball at the moment of collision?

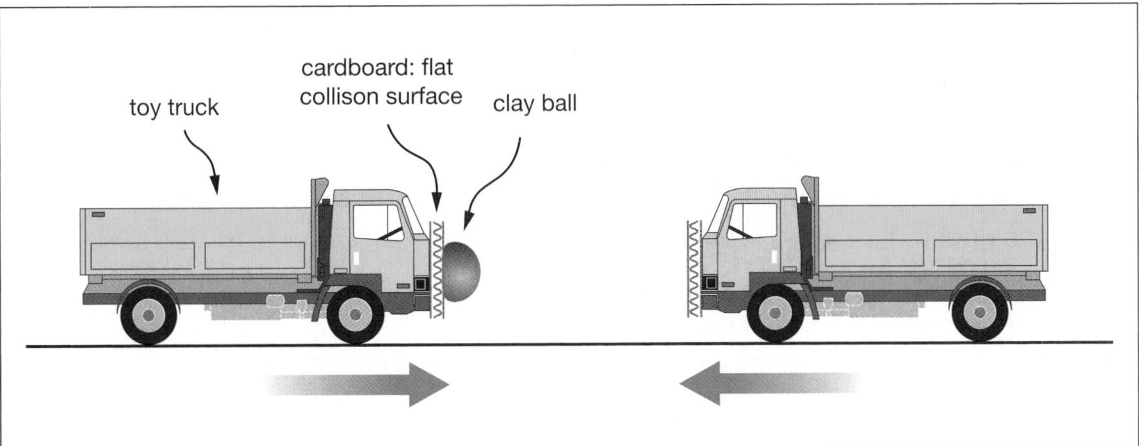

Figure 2.8 Cardboard and clay ball before collision. A flat, vertical surface helps you study the forces involved in head-on collisions.

d. How can you change the mass of the toy vehicles by amounts large enough to make a measurable difference?
e. What variables must be held constant at different times in the activity?
f. What is the best way to organize your observations in an efficient and accurate record of events?

5. Record your investigation in a step-by-step procedure that includes using data tables; obtain your teacher's approval. (Be sure to include units for all measurements.)
6. Carry out your investigation; make sure all team members record observations in their science notebooks.

Stop & THINK

PART I

Read each question carefully before writing your own answers in your science notebook. Then meet with your team and use the TSAR strategy to complete your answers. Keep careful records of what answers you changed, how, and why. This will help you and your teacher see the progress of your learning.

1. What is a general rule governing how changes in velocity affect forces on each car when the masses remain constant? Complete 1a–c to answer this question.

   Use the symbols F for force, v for velocity, and m for mass. The delta symbol, Δ, means "the change in." Mathematical symbols you can use are $=$, $<$, $>$, or $\propto$. The $\propto$ symbol means "proportional to." Use this symbol to indicate when one value is directly proportional to another.

   a. Complete the following statements:
   - As the velocity of the cars at impact increases, the force on each car at collision ________________.
   - The force of car 1 on car 2 is ________________ the force of car 2 on car 1.

   b. Using your answers to Question 1a, form the mathematical relationships in this next statement.
   F ________________ Δv as long as ________________ is held constant.

   c. What evidence did you observe to form your answer to Question 1a?

2. What is a general rule about how changes in mass affect forces on each car when the velocity at collision remains constant? State this rule in 2 ways.

   a. Apply language by writing a sentence using the words *force, mass, velocity*, and *change*.

   b. Apply mathematics by writing a relationship using the symbols F, m, v, Δ, and $\propto$.

   Use the guided format in Question 1 to help you form your answers to Question 2.

3. How might the relationships you wrote in Questions 1 and 2 change if you replaced the clay ball with a steel ball? A very "squishy" marshmallow? State what factor most affects your answer.

4 Think back to the focus question for this activity: "What is the relationship among variables that affect force?" Use the evidence from your investigation to form an answer to this question. Be sure to include *how* each variable affects force.

Part II: Safe Landing

Materials

For each team of 2 students

access to stairs

Cautions

Do not participate in this activity if you have any medical condition that prevents you from engaging in activities like jumping.

Process and Procedure

Some collisions occur horizontally, others vertically. Think about the forces when a skydiver lands on the ground (figure 2.9). How does the skydiver control these forces? Why is controlling forces important?

Safe landings depend, in part, on the ability of skydivers to control forces on their legs when they collide with Earth. How do they do that? What strategies do skydivers use to affect the way their legs respond to impacts? For example, do skydivers change their mass to produce a "softer" landing?

In Part II, you and your partner will explore ways to control forces in vertical interactions by stepping off a stair with both stiff and bent knees.

1. Predict all you can about the relative size of forces acting on you and a stair (or floor) in the following 3 situations. Do this by completing the table in figure 2.10 in your science notebook.

You will be using vectors to represent many quantities in this program. Read *FYI—Vectors in One Dimension* on page 67 to learn more about this way of representing quantities in science.

▼ **Figure 2.9 Skydiver landing.** Why is controlling forces important to this skydiver?

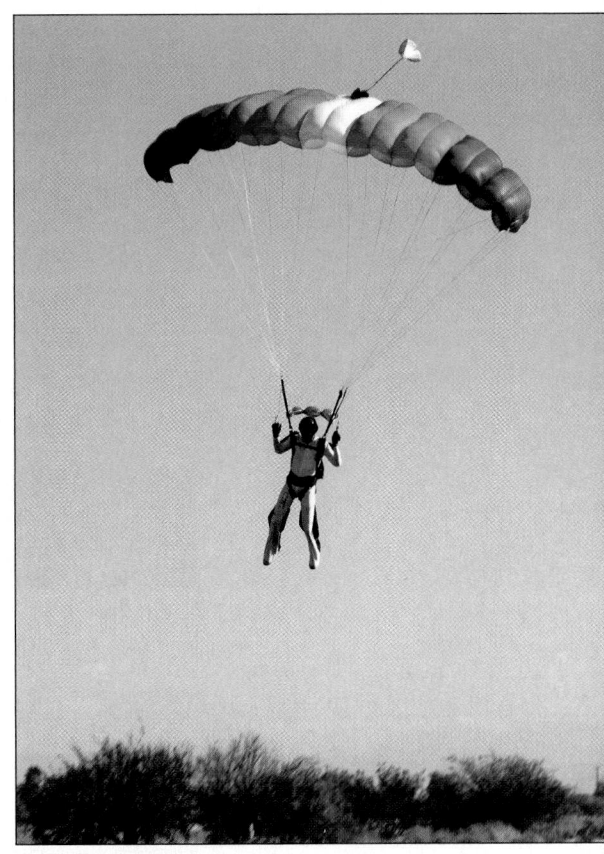

a. Situation 1: The forces on your body and the stair or floor as you are standing still

b. Situation 2: The forces on your body and the floor as you land with stiff knees

c. Situation 3: The forces on your body and the floor as you land with bent knees

Remember to label each force. The label "$F_{\text{stair on foot}}$" is one of many appropriate labels that indicate *both* the objects involved in the interaction and *on* which object the force is being applied. The first row of the table is partially completed. Fill in the first row and use it to complete the remainder of the table.

Situation	Forces involved and their magnitude	Vector sketches to represent those forces
1. Standing still	Force of me on the floor is ______ the force of the floor on me, and in the ______ direction.	$F_{\text{me on floor}}$ $F_{\text{floor on me}}$
2. Landng on next stair with stiff knees		
3. Landing on next stair with bent knees		

▲ **Figure 2.10 Predictions table.** Use this table for your predictions in Step 1.

2. Test your predictions in 2 different ways by doing Steps 2a–c. Record all your observations in a table like the one shown in figure 2.11.

   a. Copy the table in figure 2.11 into your science notebook and complete it after doing Steps 2b–c.

Situation	Forces in interaction (in words)	Forces in interaction (in vector sketches at maximum force)
Stiff knees		
Bent legs		

▲ **Figure 2.11 Forces in interaction.** Use this table to complete Steps 2b–c.

b. Stand perfectly still on a stair; then step off (with both legs stiff) to the next lower stair.

c. Stand perfectly still on a stair; then step off to the next lower stair, bending your legs as much as possible when you land.

3. What variable changed the amount of force you felt as you stepped off the stair? Complete Steps 3a–c in your science notebook to answer this question.

   a. Did a change of mass affect the forces involved in the interaction between your foot and the stair? How do you know?

   b. Did a change in the velocity *at impact* affect the forces involved in the interaction between your foot and the stair? How do you know?

Remember, the stair height was the same for both situations. So your body fell the same distance in both cases before your feet touched the next lower stair.

   c. What variable did you change (which changed the force you felt) by bending your legs during landing instead of landing with stiff legs? How do you know this variable changed?

4. If your mass (m) and your change in velocity (Δv) remain constant for a given stair, then what must be true about the product of these 2 quantities ($m\Delta v$)?

5. In your science notebook, make 2 complete sentences by joining the phrases in 5a and 5b with the proper connecting term.

Use connecting terms such as "larger than," "smaller than," "equal to," "independent of," "directly proportional to," "inversely proportional to," and "not dependent on." Your final answer in 5a and 5b should result in a complete sentence.

   a. The amount of time to stop when I land on the lower stair ________________ the force I feel when I hit the stair, for a constant mass and change in velocity.

   b. The product of mass and change in velocity ($m\Delta v$) ________________ the product of force and time to stop for a given interaction ($F\Delta t$).

Consider using unit analysis to answer Step 5b. The unit for force is the newton and can be represented by $\frac{\text{kg m}}{\text{sec}^2}$; time is in seconds, mass is in kilograms, and change in velocity is in $\frac{\text{m}}{\text{sec}}$.

   c. Check your answers with other teams. If you are still unsure of your answers, check with your teacher.

Reflect and Connect

Answer the following questions in your science notebook. Use a learning strategy that maximizes your individual understanding. Check the accuracy of your answers, using a technique that your teacher approves.

1. Explore with your classmates how scientists and engineers adjust the variable change in time (Δt) to control the forces in the following interactions. Record your ideas in your science notebook using a table like the one in figure 2.12.

Interaction	Reason it is important to control force	How force is controlled
Car hits post in parking lot with and without a 5 miles per hour (mph) bumper		
Driver hits steering wheel during crash with and without deployed air bags		
Catcher catches fastball with and without glove		
Hiking on mountain trail with and without hiking boots		

▲ **Figure 2.12 Why and how to control forces.** Use this table to organize your answer to Question 1.

2. Are there any exceptions to the statement, "Forces occur in pairs, equal in size and opposite in direction"? If yes, then give some examples. If no, then explain why there are no exceptions.
3. How do changes in Δt, m, and Δv affect force? You discovered the relationship $F\Delta t = m\Delta v$ in Step 5b. Use specific examples to answer this question.

Mathematical relationships can help you think about how a change in one variable will affect another. It may help you answer the question if you solve the relationship, $F\Delta t = m\Delta v$, for F.

4. Think about the relationships among force, change in time, mass, and change in velocity that you explored in this activity. Assume that the amount of time during which colliding cars are in contact is about the same. How might highway speed limits and vehicle size affect the force of impact in car accidents?

Vectors in One Dimension

Remember the number lines that you used in elementary school to learn negative numbers? They looked something like the following figure. Drawing vectors in one dimension is as simple as this number line. When drawing vectors, the positive and negative signs indicate the direction of the vectors. Vector quantities are those quantities that have both magnitude and direction. Force, velocity, and momentum are examples of vector quantities. The number represents the magnitude, and the algebraic sign (in one-dimensional motion) represents the direction. Deciding on the direction that will be negative is completely arbitrary. But the custom is to indicate directions to the left or west as negative and to the right or east as positive—just like a number line.

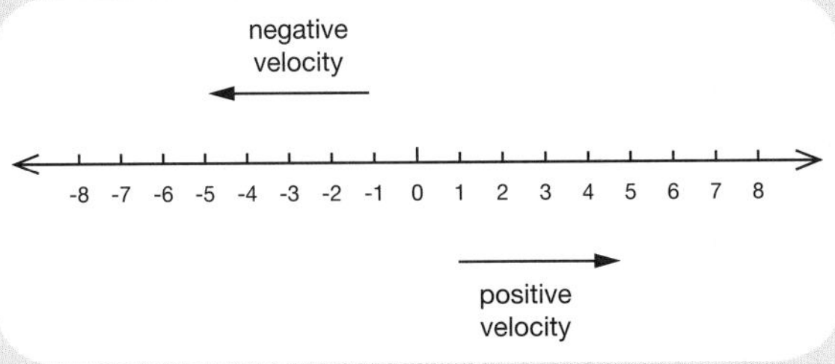

Number line. Use the idea of a number line to help you remember the sign of vectors. The sign indicates the direction of the vector.

When considering one-dimensional vectors that act vertically, positive values are usually assigned to vectors that are directed up, and negative values are usually assigned to vectors that are directed down. Similarly, if the vectors are on a flat plane, as in a map, north would be positive and south would be negative.

Some students mistake the negative values in vectors to be part of the magnitude. But a vector that is -3 is not less than a vector that is $+3$. These vectors have exactly the same magnitude; they are simply in opposite directions in one-dimensional motion. For example, a force of 3 N has the same magnitude no matter which direction it is applied. A force of -3 N applied to the left is just as much force as a force of $+3$ N to the right. The sign is only an indication of the direction.

What about adding or subtracting vectors; can it be done? Yes, you can add or subtract vectors easily using two different methods, as long as you are careful about the signs. You add or subtract vector quantities algebraically just as you would add or subtract positive or negative numbers. For example, suppose you wanted to find Δv algebraically. The initial velocity (v_i) is -16 meters per second (m/sec) and a final velocity (v_f) as 11 m/sec. Using the formula for finding Δv,

$$\begin{aligned}\Delta v &= v_f - v_i \\ &= 11\frac{\text{m}}{\text{sec}} - \left(-16\frac{\text{m}}{\text{sec}}\right) \\ &= 27\frac{\text{m}}{\text{sec}}\end{aligned}$$

You can see how important it is to keep the signs correct. This answer would indicate that the change in velocity (Δv) is 27 m/sec in the positive direction.

The second method to add or subtract vectors is to do it graphically. To do this, carefully draw vectors to scale. To keep this example simple, you will only add vectors. The formula you used before, however, subtracts vectors. How do you turn subtraction into addition? The previous formula, $\Delta v = v_f - v_i$, becomes $\Delta v = v_f + (-v_i)$. Now add the vectors graphically to find Δv. First, draw the two vectors in the appropriate direction and to scale.

V_i
- 16 m/sec
V_f
11 m/sec

Draw vectors in the appropriate direction. Begin by drawing the two vectors pointing in the direction dictated by the sign. Always draw the vectors to scale.

Vectors in One Dimension, continued

You are adding a negative v_i, so that means you will have to reverse its direction (and change the sign).

▲ **Reverse the direction.** To add a negative *vi*, you must reverse the vector's direction and change the sign.

To add vectors graphically, place them head to tail. Then draw the resultant vector from the tail of the first vector to the head of the last vector. The resultant is just the result of the vectors you are adding.

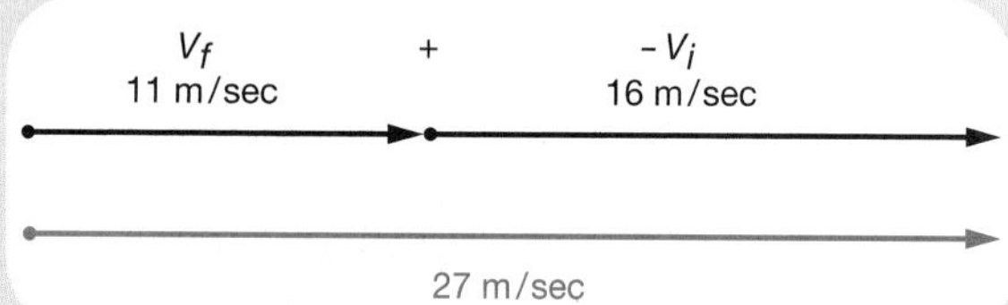

▲ **Adding vectors.** To add the vectors, place them head to tail. The resultant is drawn from the tail of the last vector to the head of the first vector. It does not matter in which order you add vectors—just like in math class.

Notice that, algebraically, the answer was positive, and it was also positive when solved graphically or by using vector math. This indicates that the answer, or the resultant, is in the positive direction, as shown by the direction of the resultant arrow in the example.

Suppose a crate had a weight of 300 N and two workers tried to lift it by the handles on the top. One worker pulled up with a force of 123 N, and the other pulled up with a force of 143 N. What would be the resultant force on the crate? Look at the following diagram, which shows three of the forces on the crate.

The resultant is the sum of these vectors. Graphically, you would solve it by placing the vectors head to tail and drawing the resultant vector from the tail of the first vector to the head of the last

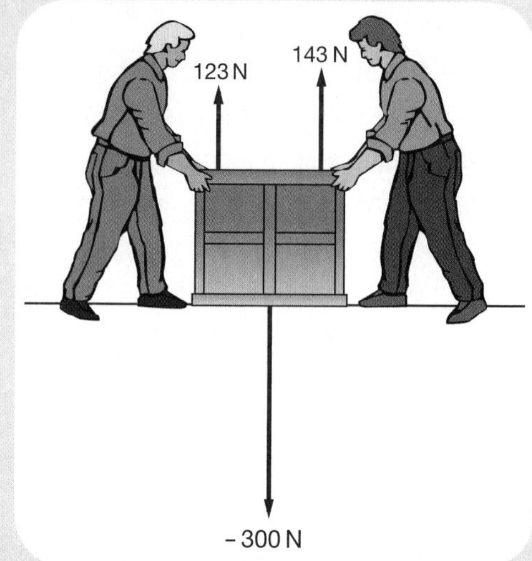

▲ **Forces on a crate.** The arrows represent three of the forces on this crate. Can the two workers lift the crate?

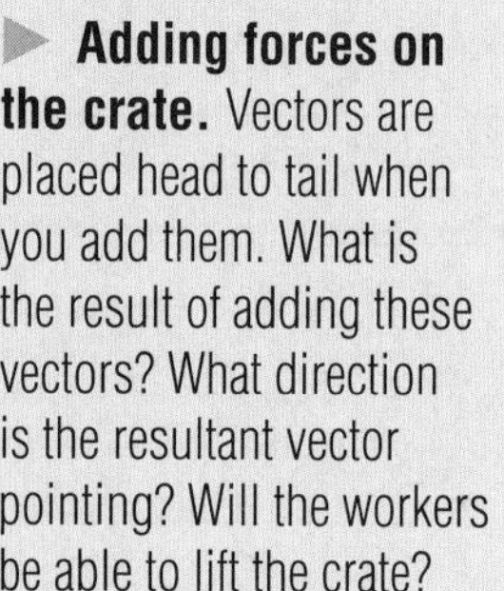

▶ **Adding forces on the crate.** Vectors are placed head to tail when you add them. What is the result of adding these vectors? What direction is the resultant vector pointing? Will the workers be able to lift the crate?

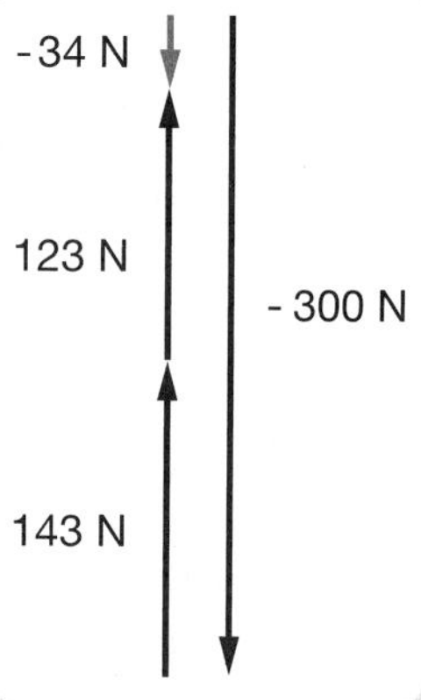

vector. All vectors must be drawn to the same scale, but the order you place them in does not matter. The vectors are placed side by side in the following figure to show overlapping vectors.

To solve for the resultant algebraically, simply add the vectors, making sure to watch the signs.

$-300 \text{ N} + 143 \text{ N} + 123 \text{ N} = -34 \text{ N}$

In both cases, the resultant is −34 N, which can be interpreted as 34 N of force in the downward direction. Will the two workers be able to lift the crate? No, the crate's weight of 300 N is too much for the two workers.

In-Line Interactions

EXPLAIN

By now you know that when objects interact in a collision, forces are involved. Those forces result in changes. Scientists want to know exactly how much change results from these forces. That is, scientists want to *quantify* what they know about force and change.

For example, think about a chunk of insulation falling from a booster rocket and colliding with the space shuttle wing. Engineers would want to know the impact force of the insulation on the wing. What changes to the wing or insulation would engineers make and what experiments would they perform? Or think about a chlorine radical (Cl·) hitting an ozone molecule (O_3) (figure 2.13). Does the force of collision cause a chemical reaction? The interaction of these atomic species is changing the concentration of the atmosphere's ozone, something you learned in Level 1 of this program. Imagine particles from a sunspot eruption interacting with Earth's magnetic field. Should satellite communications businesses be prepared for changes in the quality of transmission?

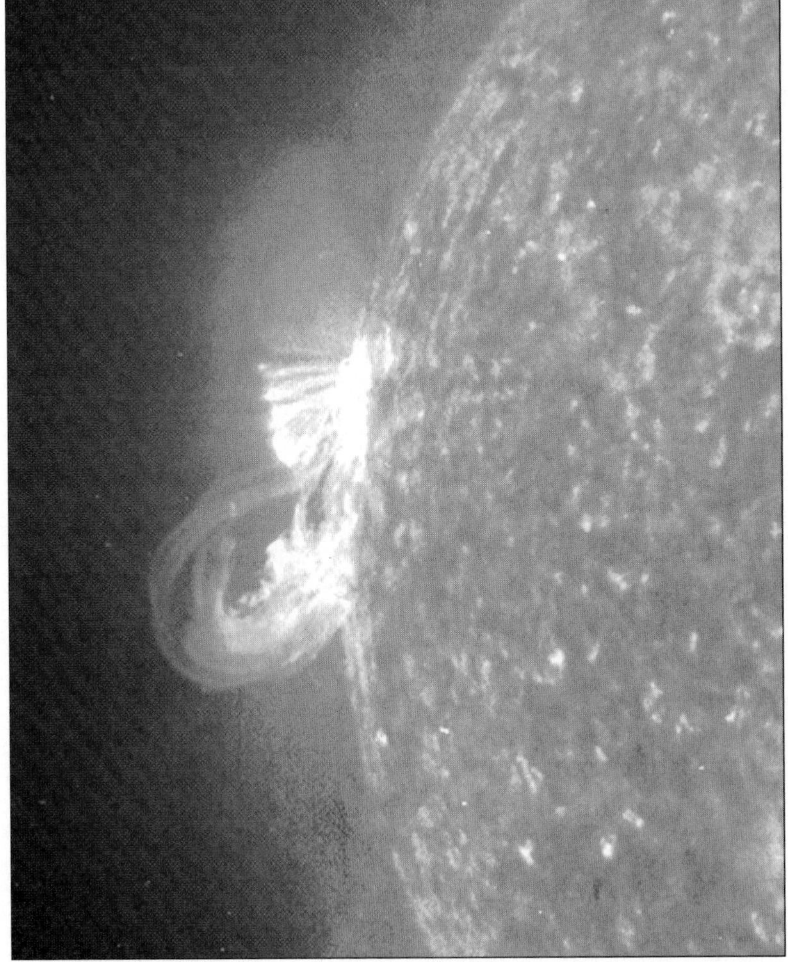

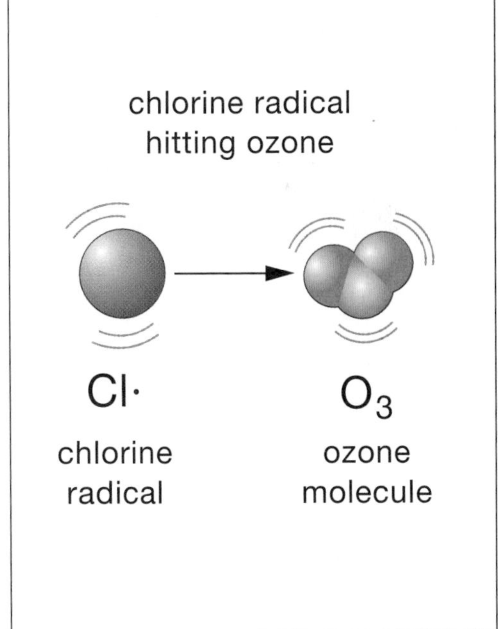

▲ **Figure 2.13 Scientists need to know the amount of force resulting from interactions.** Find the interaction in each image. Why is the amount of force important to know in each situation?

Calculating the amount of force is a crucial part of understanding nature. Being able to analyze the result of forces is key to doing well in many businesses and surviving in many sports. To see how scientists have analyzed the forces involved in many sports-related collisions, read the sidebar *Head-On Collisions*.

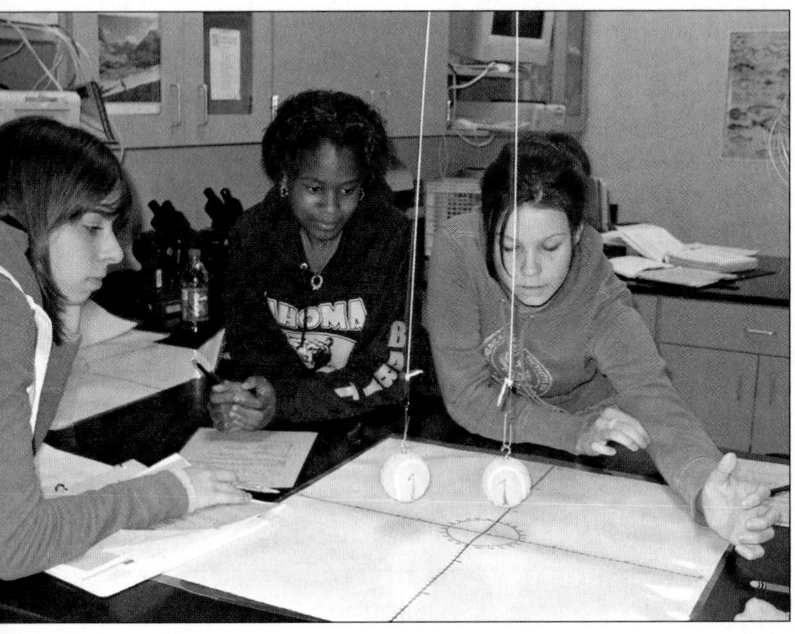

▲ **Figure 2.14 Tennis ball collisions.** How do factors before a collision of tennis balls compare with the same factors after a collision?

In *In-Line Interactions*, you will learn how to represent the amount of force and the direction of force resulting from collisions. You also will learn about an important relationship that is constant in collisions. You and your team will model these collisions, or interactions, with tennis balls (see figure 2.14).

Throughout this activity, keep in mind the following focus question: "How do factors such as velocity, mass, and others before a collision compare with the same factors after a collision?" By the end of this activity, you should be able to answer this question.

Part I: A Question of Bounces

Materials

For each team of 4 students

1 tennis ball–collision kit, which includes

- 2 tennis balls marked "1 unit of mass," with Velcro strips and cup hook
- 1 tennis ball marked "2 units of mass," with Velcro strips and a cup hook
- 2 lengths of string long enough to reach from a desk to the ceiling
- 1 collision grid with protractor markings and a center string
- paper clips
- tape

Process and Procedure

In Part I, you and your team will use colliding tennis balls as a model to quantify the amount of force resulting from collisions between any two objects.

1. Read *Tools of the Trade*, which summarizes what you have learned so far and the purpose of this activity.

SIDEBAR

Head-On Collisions

Have you ever bumped your head and "seen stars" or even blacked out? If so, you may have suffered from a mild traumatic brain injury, or MTBI. Brain injuries occur in 1.5 million people in the United States each year. Seventy-five percent of these injuries, like concussions, are classified as MTBIs. Sports-related concussions make up 300,000 of these injuries.

Head-on collision. What do you know about forces that would help you design a better helmet or soccer ball so that this player is not injured?

Research scientists are gathering data to determine what can be done to better protect athletes who play contact sports. One tool used to collect real-time data is the use of accelerometers placed in the helmets of football and hockey players. These devices measure the time rate of the change in velocity (or acceleration) experienced when a player collides with another player. The collision may also be with the wall in the case of a hockey player. These measurements are reported as *gs*, which are a comparison of the acceleration to the free fall acceleration due to gravity. For example, an acceleration of 2 *gs* would be two times the free fall acceleration due to gravity.

In recent studies, the average acceleration experienced by high school football, hockey, and soccer players ranged from 29.2 ± 1.0 *g* to 54.7 ± 4.1 *g* (see the table). The soccer measurements were made as a player, wearing an instrumented football helmet, headed a regulation soccer ball. The soccer ball was traveling at an average speed of 39.3 ± 1.8 miles per hour. You might think that soccer would be the sport that was least likely to have a high value for these impact forces. However, you must consider the head-on collisions made with a fast-moving soccer ball in this sport.

Table 1 Data collected

Parameter	Football (n = 132)	Hockey (n = 128)	Soccer (n = 23)
Peak *gs*	29.2 ± 1.0	35.0 ± 1.7	54.7[a] ± 4.1

Table of peak *gs*. This table shows the average peak acceleration during the testing of head-on collisions for football, hockey, and soccer.

Data from: Comparison of Impact Data in Hockey, Football, and Soccer from *The Journal of Trauma: Injury, Infection, and Critical Care*, Vol. 48, No. 5 (2000), p. 939 – Table 1.

Head-On Collisions, continued

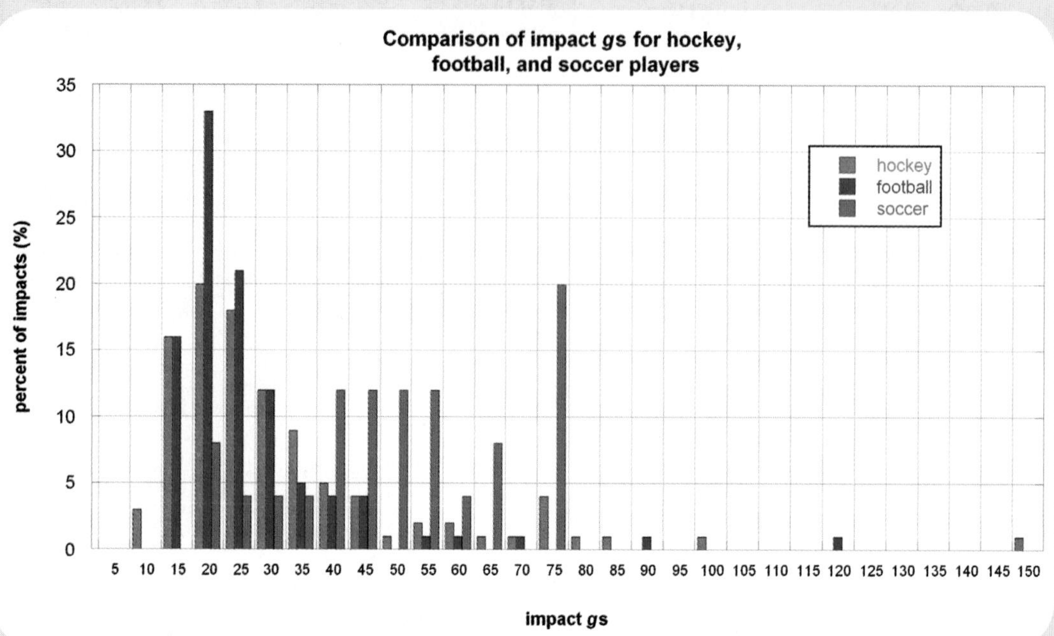

Comparing the acceleration due to impacts. This histogram compares the percentage of the impacts occurring at each *g* level for football, hockey, and soccer.

The frequency of head-on collisions in a real soccer game is less than the head-on collisions in a football or hockey game. However, a greater percentage of soccer collisions results in higher *g* values (see the figure) and therefore merits further consideration.

Science has proven that the effects of repeated mild brain injury are cumulative. Repeated low-level injuries may lead to neurological conditions because of these injuries. What can designers of football helmets, hockey helmets, or even soccer balls do to help prevent or lessen these injuries? What have you learned so far in the chapter that can be applied to this technology? Engineers of all types must understand the physics of forces and motion in order to improve our lives.

READING

Tools of the Trade

How high will a ball bounce when dropped on the floor? The rebound height depends in part on forces the ball experiences. No matter what the size or mass of an object, the forces on each object are equal in size and opposite in direction. The velocity and mass of an object can change the amount of force at impact, but the forces on each object are still equal and opposite (figure 2.15).

Newton's third law is the law of nature that states that forces come in pairs, equal in magnitude and opposite in direction. These forces always act on two *different* objects. You have seen examples of these forces in each of the activities you have completed. The force of your thumb on your finger was one force. The force of your finger on your thumb was the other force. These two forces act on two different objects, your thumb and your finger. The clay ball showed that these forces are equal and opposite as described in Newton's third law. Read more about Sir Isaac Newton and his laws in the sidebar *Newton on the Move* on page 83.

These equal and opposite forces can be represented in a simple mathematical expression: $F_{\text{thumb on finger}} = -F_{\text{finger on thumb}}$. Because force is a vector and thus has direction, forces acting in opposite directions will have opposite signs (+ and −) in algebraic representations. These vectors will point in different directions in graphic representations. Any combination of colliding objects, no matter their mass or velocity at the point of collision, can be represented similarly.

Motions along a straight line are one-dimensional motions. However, things can move in two directions along that line, to the left and to the right.

SCI LINKS NSTA
Topic: Newton's 3rd Law
Go to: www.scilinks.org
Code: 2Inquiry73

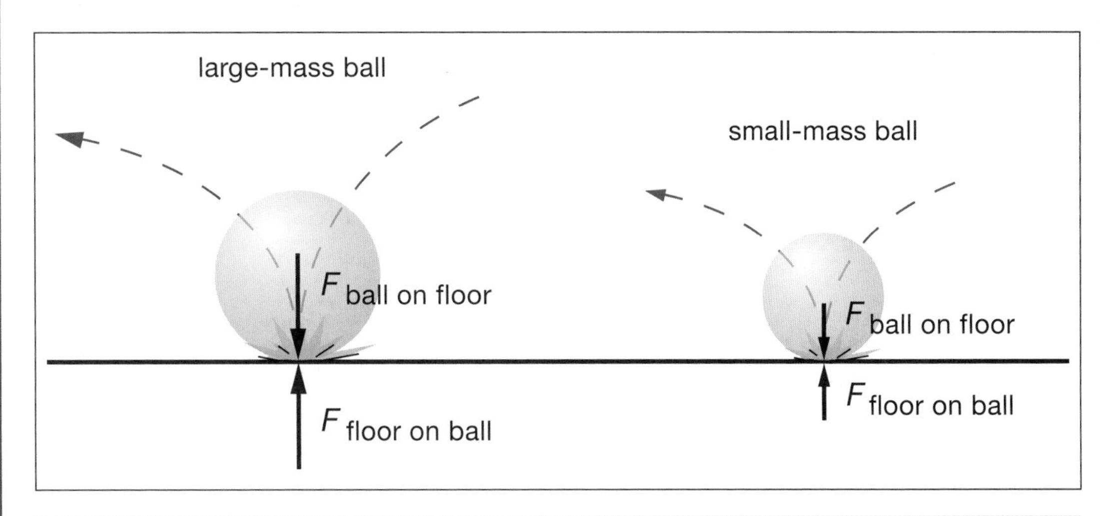

▲ **Figure 2.15 Balls of different mass.** If these balls of different mass bounce off the floor, how do the forces of interaction compare?

Tools of the Trade, continued

In this activity, you will focus on the velocity of a tennis ball. Velocity is a vector, and therefore both the magnitude of the velocity (or the speed) and the direction in which the tennis ball moves are important to consider. You read about how to add these vectors in FYI—*Vectors in One Dimension*.

It is customary to assign positive or negative directions to motions when they are moving along a straight line. Often, objects that move to the right are considered to be moving in the positive direction and objects that move to the left are considered to be moving in the negative direction. This is similar to the number lines you studied in elementary school, where numbers on the left of zero are negative and numbers on the right of zero are positive. However, it does not matter which way these motions are assigned as long as they are consistent and explained.

If you use the directions and signs described here, then velocities to the left (in the negative direction) will have a negative sign assigned to them when they are used in a mathematical equation (figure 2.16). This is the way you will tell in which direction objects are moving. These directions, represented with + and – signs, apply to other vector quantities, like force. Keeping the signs correct in your explanations, labels, and equations is important for understanding the concepts.

Often, you will use Δv, which means the change in velocity. You can calculate this by subtracting the initial velocity (v_i) from the final velocity (v_f). The formula for finding Δv is $\Delta v = v_f - v_i$.

It is very important to assign the correct sign to the velocities when using this formula. Suppose a car that is moving at a speed of 50 kilometers per hour (km/hr) speeds up to 67 km/hr. What would be the car's Δv? Since the car is going in only one direction, you can choose to have it moving in the positive direction. Solving for the car's change in velocity gives us the following:

$$\begin{aligned}\Delta v &= v_f - v_i \\ &= 67\frac{\text{km}}{\text{hr}} - 50\frac{\text{km}}{\text{hr}} \\ &= 17\frac{\text{km}}{\text{hr}}\end{aligned}$$

You will be swinging tennis balls in the next activity. If the ball moves to the right, it will have a positive velocity. If it moves to the left, it will have a negative velocity.

Remember, good experimental design requires that you repeat a measurement several times, then calculate an average value.

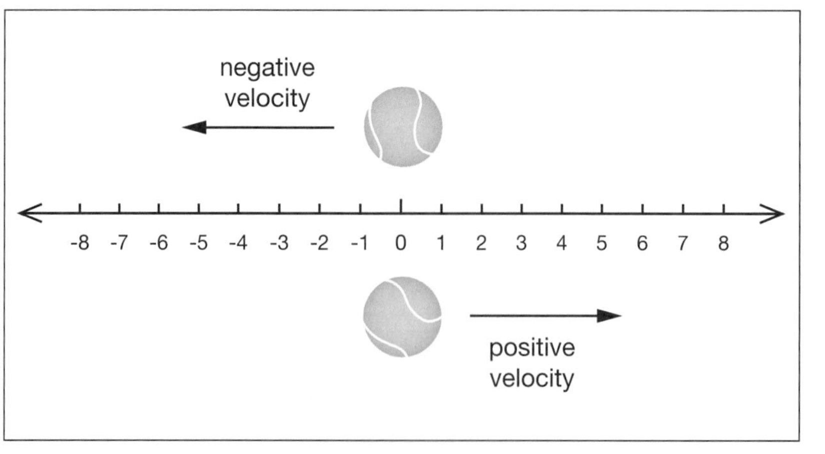

Figure 2.16 Vectors indicate both magnitude and direction. In one dimension (along a line), you can use positive and negative signs to represent the direction that vectors indicate. For example, a tennis ball moving to the left would have a negative velocity if you choose the left direction to be negative. Likewise, a tennis ball moving to the right would have a positive velocity. We will use this method in the examples in this chapter.

Experiments are not perfect, and you might observe some uncertainty in your measurements. It is unlikely that you will get the exact same measurement in each of 10 trials. You can calculate the uncertainty associated with a measurement, which will allow you to generalize about scientific laws without worrying about slight variations in measurement.

With sets of measurements, determine the average value ($\bar{x}$) from all of the trials. To estimate your uncertainty, first calculate the range, w. This is the difference between the highest and lowest values. Second, record the number of trials, n. An estimate of uncertainty (error), e, is the range divided by the square root of the number of trials, or

$$e = \frac{w}{\sqrt{n}}$$

It is typical to represent this uncertainty with a ± sign before the uncertainty value, e. This is because uncertainty represents the range of error both above and below the average. For the estimate of uncertainty above, about 60–70 percent of the trials will have values bracketed by $\bar{x} \pm e$.

For example, an average rebound velocity of 7 units to the left was averaged from five trials. The highest rebound velocity was −9 units of velocity, and the lowest rebound velocity was −5 units of velocity. The range (−9 to −5) was 4 units of velocity. So the uncertainty is calculated by dividing the range of 4 by the square root of 5 (the number of trials). This gives an uncertainty of 1.8. The average value should be reported as −7 ± 1.8 units of velocity (see figure 2.17). This tells you that most of the values lie between −8.8 and −5.2 units of velocity. The negative sign in front of the 7 represents motion in the negative direction (to the left). You can also represent uncertainty in a graph. Figure 2.18 shows how uncertainty is represented on a graph. The bars above and below the point indicate the uncertainty and are called error bars.

Scientists, engineers, and technicians all use these mathematical tools to design and test materials important to their industry. Remember the reference to bouncing balls? Are all balls equally bouncy? Would you want a golf ball to have the same bounce as a softball? What factors do scientists consider when they calculate the exact amount of force required to produce the right bounce? What are the relationships between those factors? These relationships form a law of nature that describes the motion of bouncing balls, crashing cars, and colliding galaxies, as well as any moving system in the universe.

Table of Rebound Velocities

Trial	Units of Velocity
1	−6
2	−9
3	−7
4	−6
5	−5
average	**−7**

▲ **Figure 2.17 Calculating uncertainty.** The uncertainty in your measurements can be calculated. Uncertainty values are reported as a ± value after the average, or mean, of your measurements.

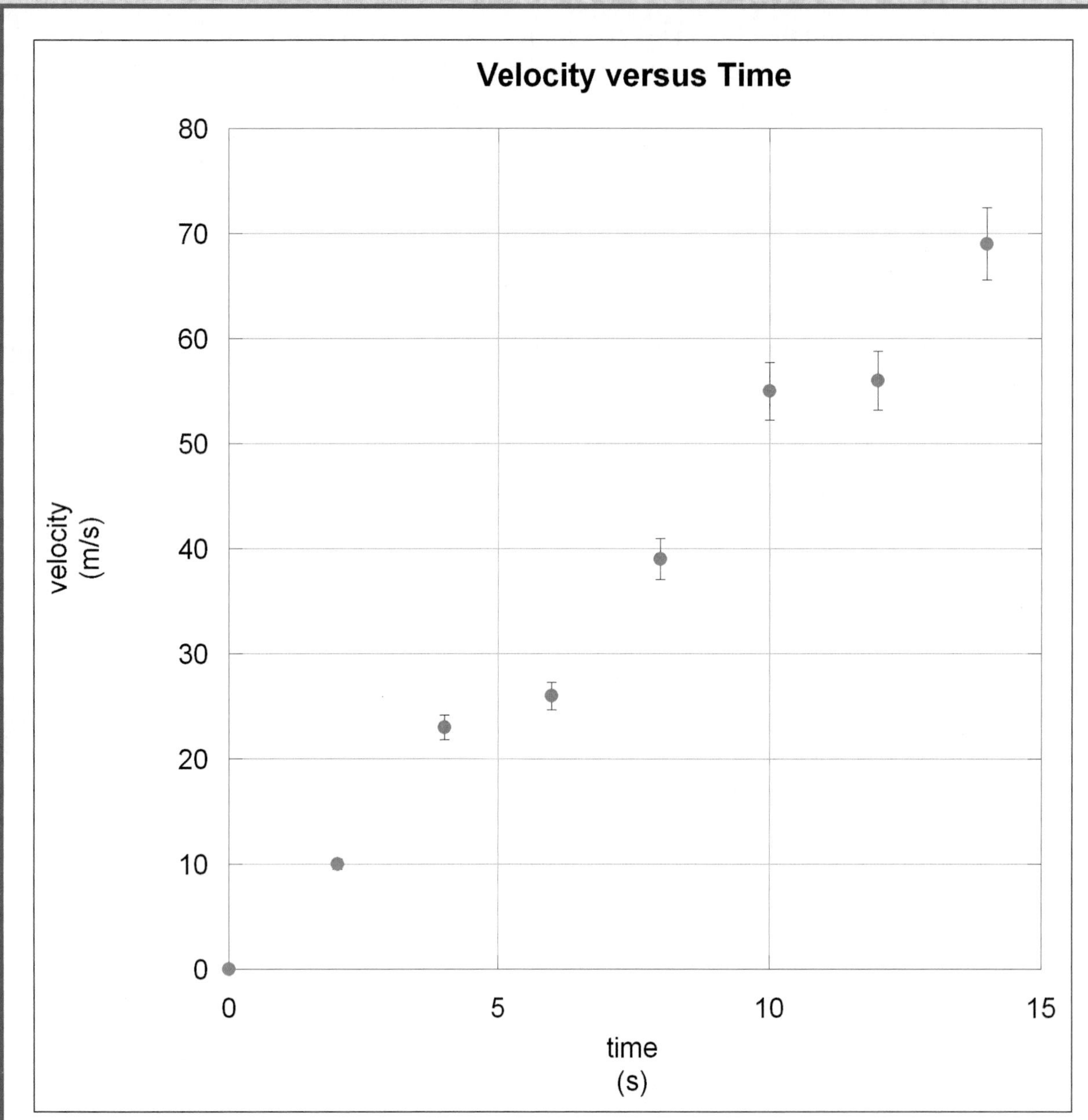

Figure 2.18 Error bars in graphs. Uncertainty can be shown in graphs by using error bars with data points. What does the uncertainty tell you about the values shown in this graph?

2. Explore how the tennis ball–collision apparatus works. In your science notebook, sketch the apparatus and label all the features you think are important.
3. Compare your thoughts from Step 2 with some of the ideas demonstrated by your teacher by answering Steps 3a–d in your science notebook.
   a. Why is it important to adjust the centers of the tennis balls to be at exactly the same level above the table?
   b. Why is it important to position the center of mass of the 2-ball system directly over the origin of your collision axes?
   c. Why is it important that the amount of time for a tennis ball to reach the origin is the same regardless of the position from which it is released (provided the string lengths are the same)?
   d. Why is it important that the speed of the tennis ball at the origin is directly proportional to the swing distance?
4. Determine how to quantify change in velocity (Δv) by doing Steps 4a–g.
   a. Suspend a 1-unit-of-mass tennis ball from each string so that the centers are the same height above the table.
   b. Separate the 2 balls, one at 20 centimeters (cm) to the left of the collision grid's origin and the other 10 cm to the right (figure 2.19).

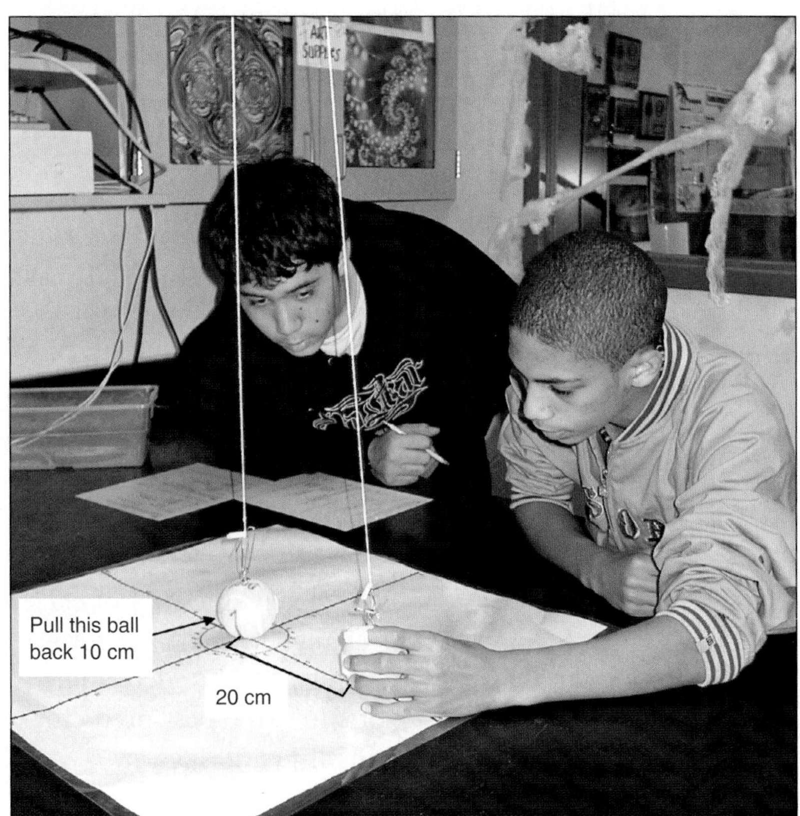

◀ **Figure 2.19 Tennis ball collisions.** Begin your testing with one tennis ball at 20 cm to the left and the other tennis ball 10 cm to the right. How would you represent the swinging with vectors once you release the tennis balls? What signs would you assign to show direction? Remember to use the direction the ball is moving at the point of collision for the initial velocity (v_i) and the direction the ball is moving after collision for the final velocity (v_f).

For convenience, refer to a ball positioned over the 20-cm mark on the left as having 20 units of velocity going to the right, *at the point of collision*. Represent this velocity with a vector arrow 20 units long, pointing to the right. Call this the initial velocity (v_i). Since this ball is moving to the right, you will assign its value a positive sign to indicate the direction. In which direction and how long should the velocity vector of the other ball be? Will the value have a positive or negative sign?

c. Release both balls simultaneously so that they *bounce* along the original axis.
d. Measure and record the maximum distance each center of mass rebounds.

Remember to record the distance that is directly below the center of mass of the tennis ball.

e. Repeat Steps 4a–d several times to determine the average value and uncertainty.
f. Determine Δv for each ball algebraically. (Use the definition for Δ, $\Delta v = v_f - v_i$, where *f* means "final" and *i* means "initial.")

Don't forget that balls moving to the right have a positive velocity and balls moving to the left have a negative velocity. This is true only because we define the right to be the positive direction.

g. Determine Δv for each ball with vector math. Use the same definition of Δ as in Step 4f, except draw vector sketches as described in *FYI—Vectors in One Dimension.*

5. Determine which velocity vectors (v_i, v_f, or Δv) are the best predictors of the forces that each ball experiences during collision by completing Steps 5a–e.
   a. Describe directions and relative magnitudes of the force on each tennis ball.

Remember the clay ball. Imagine a clay ball placed between the colliding tennis balls. What does the amount and direction of squishing tell you about the force acting on each ball?

   b. How are the directions and magnitudes of the initial velocity vectors (v_i) related (if at all) to the directions and relative magnitudes of the force each ball experiences during collisions? Provide labeled vector drawings to support your answer.
   c. Repeat Step 5a for the final velocities (v_f) of each ball.
   d. Repeat Step 5a for the change in velocity vector (Δv).
   e. Use your answers from Steps 5a–d to determine which velocity vector (v_i, v_f, or Δv) is the best predictor of the force each ball experiences. Justify your answer.

6. Develop a quantitative relationship between force (F) and change in velocity (Δv) by selecting the most appropriate math symbol or word to complete the following statements in Steps 6a–g. Be prepared to justify your choices with the class.

Possible math symbols are =, >, <, ∝; possible words are *opposite, same, directly proportional to, inversely proportional to.* You can use filler words like *and, as,* and *the.*

   a. $F_{\text{ball 2 on ball 1}}$ __________ $-F_{\text{ball 1 on ball 2}}$.

Consider the ball that starts on the left as ball 1 and the ball that starts on the right as ball 2.

   b. From previous activities, force is __________ Δt.

Think back to the activity *Safe Landing* where you stepped off a stair with both stiff and bent legs.

   c. From previous activities, force is __________ Δv.

Think back to the activity *Speed Bumps* where you changed the velocity and observed the effect on a clay ball.

   d. Force is __________ m.

Think back again to *Speed Bumps* where you changed the mass of the toy vehicle and observed the effect on a clay ball.

   e. The units for force __________ the units for $\frac{m\Delta v}{\Delta t}$.

   f. In general, for each ball, $F_{\text{on ball}}$ __________ $\frac{m\Delta v}{\Delta t}$.

   g. As a reasonable statement of cause and effect for each ball, $F\Delta t$ __________ $m\Delta v$.

7. Check your answers with another team. Discuss any differences you have and decide on the best answer. Be prepared to share your answers in a class discussion.

8. Read *Moving on Impulse* to learn more about the valuable relationship that you have just developed.

READING

Moving on Impulse

Have you ever wondered why coaches always emphasize "follow-through" in the sports of tennis, golf, baseball, and boxing? How is it that a skilled karate athlete can break a board or a stack of cement blocks with a hand or a foot (figure 2.20)? Your knowledge of the relationship of force, time, mass, and velocity can help you answer these questions. Consider the equation that you developed in previous activities:

$$F\Delta t = m\Delta v$$

The product of force and change in time ($F\Delta t$) is known as **impulse**. This is the relationship that explains the need for follow-through in many sports. It is also the scientific reasoning behind air bags and baseball or softball gloves.

Suppose you hit a fly ball into center field. The ball travels at a certain changing velocity. As it is caught by a softball player, its velocity falls to zero. The mass of the ball, however, does not change in flight. You can determine the change in velocity (Δv) as the ball goes from some initial velocity just before it is caught to zero velocity when it stops. Therefore, the $m\Delta v$ part of the equation, $F\Delta t = m\Delta v$, is constant no matter how the ball stops, in a hand or in a glove.

Now look at the other side of the equation, the $F\Delta t$. You or a ball-glove engineer can manipulate this relationship. When you catch a fly ball, do you want to feel a large force or a small force? If you don't want it to hurt very much, of course you want a small force. What could you do so that you only feel a small force? First, you could wear a padded glove. Second, you could move your hand in the direction the ball is traveling as you catch it. These two actions—using a padded glove and moving with the ball as you catch it—influence the *time* that the force acts on your hand. If you want a small force, then you want the maximum amount of time for the force to act.

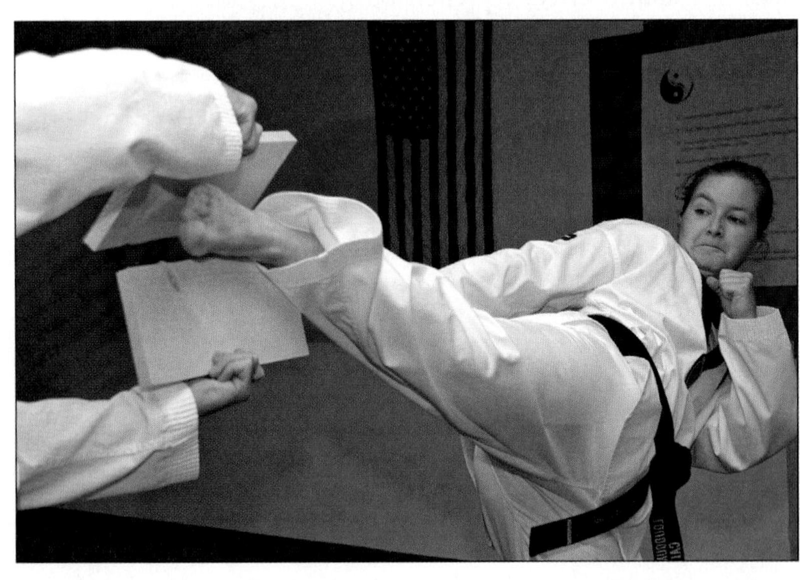

▲ **Figure 2.20 Karate kick.** Why does follow-through help this athlete break the boards?

This same idea is the explanation for follow-through. There are times when you hit a baseball or a golf ball that you want the ball to go as far as possible. In these cases, you want the ball to have the biggest change in velocity possible—the biggest Δv. Let's look at the equation again: $F\Delta t = m\Delta v$. You know that the mass of the ball doesn't change when you strike it, so the mass in the equation remains constant. How would you get the biggest change in velocity? You would want to have a large force acting over the greatest amount of time. So when you want a baseball to have a large change in velocity, you would hit it with a great amount of force. And follow-through keeps the bat in contact with the ball for the maximum amount of time.

The product of mass and velocity, mv, is known as **momentum** and is represented by the symbol p. Momentum can be thought of as mass in motion. If an object is in motion, it has momentum—if it has no motion, it has no momentum. We can see from the equation

$$p = mv$$

that an object can have a large momentum if it has a large mass or a large velocity—or both. Could a small car have the same momentum as a large truck? Yes, if the car is moving at a fast speed and the truck is moving at a slow speed, then they could have the same momentum. And, of course, if both the car and the truck were stopped, they would both have zero momentum.

SCILINKS® NSTA

Go to: www.scilinks.org
Topic: momentum
Code: 2Inquiry81a
Topic: impulse
Code: 2Inquiry81b

9. Repeat Step 4 for different tennis ball collisions, some with different mass and some with different velocities, as recommended by your teacher. Record your observations in a data table in your science notebook.

Stop & THINK

PART I

Work out answers to these questions in your science notebook individually, then meet with team members to reach consensus. Keep careful records of any changes in your answers, especially the reason for any change.

1 Consider a tennis ball hitting the floor and bouncing as you answer Questions 1a–d.

a. Draw a properly scaled and labeled before-and-after sketch representing a 0.05-kg tennis ball hitting the floor at 4.0 meters per second (m/sec), remaining in contact with the floor for 0.10 sec, then rebounding at 3.0 m/sec.

b. Draw the following 2 scaled vectors: (1) F_{max} of the floor on the ball and (2) F_{max} of the ball on the floor.

STOP & THINK, PART I, continued

Scaled vectors are those in which you use exact measurements and an explanation. For example, you may want to let 1 cm on your paper represent 1 N. You should put a key on your paper indicating 1 cm = 1 N.

c. Calculate the magnitude of force during impact. Show the equation and all your work.

d. What is the significance of the sign of the force and its relationship to Δv?

2 Think about your colliding tennis balls from the previous activity. How does the momentum before and after a collision compare for each tennis ball? Use evidence from your investigation to support your answer.

Part II: Sticky Situation

Materials

For each team of 4 students

1 tennis ball–collision kit, which includes

- 2 tennis balls marked "1 unit of mass," with Velcro strips and a cup hook
- 1 tennis ball marked "2 units of mass," with Velcro strips and a cup hook
- 2 lengths of string long enough to reach from a desk to the ceiling
- 1 collision grid with protractor markings and a center string
- paper clips
- tape

access to a computer for the animation *Elastic and Inelastic Collisions*

4 *Mathematical Relationships* handouts (or transparency)

SIDEBAR

Newton on the Move

Sir Isaac Newton (1642–1727). The English physicist and mathematician Isaac Newton was born to a poor farming family. Luckily for the scientific community, he did not like farming and turned his attention to studies at the University of Cambridge. He published the *Principia* in 1687, which became one of the most important and influential works on physics of all time.

Motion—changes in motion—forces. These are concepts that are important to everyday life. How are they connected? Is there a cause-and-effect relationship among these concepts? A famous scientist who lived over 300 years ago first made connections between these concepts. Sir Isaac Newton (1642–1727) summed up motion and the underlying causes of motion in three laws. **Newton's laws** give us the connection between cause and effect.

The law of inertia is often used to describe Newton's first law. It states that there will be no change in an object's motion unless acted upon by an outside force. In other words, if an object is in motion, it will remain in motion (along a straight line) unless some force acts upon it. A passenger in a moving car is pressed up against the seat belt as a car stops suddenly. The body continues in motion, and the force that stops it is the force supplied by the seat belt.

"Force is directly proportional to the time rate of change in velocity" is one way of stating Newton's second law. This chapter introduces this law and it is the focus of chapter 4. Newton's third law, which states, "Forces occur in pairs, equal in magnitude and opposite in direction," is the focus of this chapter. Newton's laws of motion, first published more than 300 years ago, tell us how forces affect the motion of objects. The same laws apply whether you are observing a pesky bee zigzagging through the air or a planet in orbit around the Sun. Newton's laws do not apply to the motions of very small objects like single atoms or electrons or to objects moving near the speed of light. But they apply to almost everything else.

Newton on the Move, continued

These laws have been tested throughout history. They are as valid today as when they were first written. This is significant because in the physical sciences, changes in theories and understanding are more the rule than the exception.

The laws of motion are only part of the contribution that Newton made to science. He is also known for his contributions in chemistry, light and optics, and even the discovery of calculus. However, the dispute over the person responsible for the discovery of calculus, Newton or Gottfried Wilhelm Leibniz, went on for more than 50 years. This dispute kept the citizens of Newton's country from accepting Newtonian science. Even the British mathematicians would not share the researches of the Continental colleges for over a century.

One of the best known stories about Newton is about his ideas concerning gravity. The story goes that he was sitting under an apple tree when an apple fell, hitting Newton on the head. Some stories go so far as to suggest that the apple's impact somehow made him aware of the force of gravity. Most of this story is just a legend, but there may be some truth to part of it. John Conduitt, Newton's assistant at the royal mint, described the event when he wrote about Newton's life:

"In the year 1666 he retired again from Cambridge ... to his mother in Lincolnshire and while he was musing in a garden it came into his thought that the power of gravity (which brought an apple from a tree to the ground) was not limited to a certain distance from earth, but that this power must extend much further than was usually thought. Why not as high as the Moon thought he to himself and that if so, that must influence her motion and perhaps retain her in her orbit, whereupon he fell a-calculating what would be the effect of that superposition ..." (Keesing, R. G. The History of Newton's Apple Tree, *Contemporary Physics*, 39, 377–91, 1998)

Students in physics have been constructing their understanding of these laws of nature for over 300 years. How can these laws of motion explain what we see in nature? What questions are yet to be answered about motion and gravity? Scientific discovery often comes from simple questions and the pursuit to answer those questions.

SCINKS® NSTA
Topic: Sir Isaac Newton
Go to: www.scilinks.org
Code: 2Inquiry84

Process and Procedure

In Part I, you developed a way to quantify the amount of force an object experiences during a bouncing collision: ($F = \frac{m\Delta v}{\Delta t}$). This type of collision is called an **elastic collision.** Elastic collisions occur when colliding objects rebound or bounce off each other. But not all collisions result in bouncing. Sometimes objects hit and stick together (sometimes called an **inelastic collision**).

Imagine waiting patiently in your car at an intersection. Suddenly, there is a crash from behind! The bumpers lock, and both cars skid forward. Could you determine if the other driver was speeding in addition to not paying attention?

It turns out you can, and so can the police officer investigating the accident scene (figure 2.21). To do this, you will use what you learned about force in Part I to develop a powerful tool for predicting what happens to objects in collisions. Then you and your team will design and conduct activities to test your predictive tool.

Figure 2.21 **Accident scene.** What mathematical relationships help this police officer reconstruct the accident scene? Can he determine who is at fault?

1. Participate in a class discussion by completing Question 1 on the handout or recording your thoughts in your science notebook as your teacher directs. Be sure to ask questions if you do not understand.
2. Read the following paragraphs about the important relationship that you just developed at the end of Step 1.

Recall that the product, mv, is called momentum and is given the symbol p. Momentum is a vector, like force and velocity are, since it has magnitude and direction. If an object experiences a change in velocity, it experiences a change in momentum, Δp. In what ways can you change velocity? You can change either the magnitude (the speed) or the direction of the moving object. If you do, then you change the object's momentum as well.

When a variable does not change in a before-and-after event, then that variable is conserved. Was momentum conserved when you collided two tennis balls in Part I? If you look at your data, you will see that yes, momentum was conserved within the range of uncertainty. Momentum does not change in *any* interaction between two objects even though velocities change. Momentum is conserved in both elastic and inelastic collisions. This result is called the **law of conservation of momentum.**

3. Participate in another class discussion about the *conservation* of momentum. Complete Question 2 on the handout or record your answers in your science notebook as directed by your teacher. Ask questions if you do not understand.
4. Design a step-by-step procedure using Part I as a guide for an experiment to test the design equation in Question 2d of the handout or transparency. Use a variety of masses and initial velocities. Steps 4a–f will help guide you in your design.

a. How can I model the design equation in Question 2d of the handout or transparency with the tennis ball–collision kit?
b. What masses and velocities will I use in each trial?
c. How many trials should I do, and how will I determine the uncertainty associated with my design?
d. How will I control the experiment so that I can be confident in the results?
e. What values and measurements do I need to record in my data table?
f. How can I use a summary table to display all the important relationships that have to be calculated?

5. Have your teacher approve your design and make careful notes regarding any changes you made based on feedback.
6. Carry out your step-by-step procedure; be careful to organize your data into clearly labeled tables and show all important calculations.
7. Compose a caption for your summary data table that communicates the effectiveness (or lack of effectiveness) of the data in confirming the law of conservation of momentum. Use the design equation in Question 2d of the handout or transparency.

8. Use the computer animation *Elastic and Inelastic Collisions* to model these collisions on a computer as your teacher directs.

Reflect and Connect

Work by yourself on these questions, then meet with your team and discuss any differences. Record the reasons for any changes to your original answers.

1. Think back to all the interactions you observed in Parts I and II of this activity. Momentum was conserved in each interaction. Was velocity conserved? Prove your point with labeled vector sketches, using at least 1 collision from each part (elastic collision and inelastic collision) as an example.

Use the following information for Questions 2–3.

Clouds form when water vapor condenses on tiny dust particles. Those dust particles form when smaller, electrically charged objects collide to make larger particles. In one such collision, particle A moving at 4 m/sec to the right with a mass of 0.01 grams (g) and +2 charge hits particle B moving at 3 m/sec to the left with a mass of 0.02 g and a charge of –4. They hit head on and stick together to form a larger particle onto which water vapor condenses.

2. Determine the following values for Questions 2a–c using scaled vector sketches and supporting calculations.

You must first find the final velocity of the system before finding the remaining values. Use the law of conservation of momentum in the form,

$$\Delta p_{\text{system}} = (m_A v_{f,A} + m_B v_{f,B}) - (m_A v_{i,A} + m_B v_{i,B}) = 0.$$

Since the objects hit and stick together, the equation becomes

$$m_A v_{i,A} + m_B v_{i,B} = m_{A+B} v_f.$$

a. Δv_A, Δv_B, Δv_{system}

b. Δp_A, Δp_B, Δp_{system}

c. F_A and F_B (assuming a 0.01-sec collision)

3. What is the significance of Δp_{system} that you calculated in Question 2b? What is the significance of the values of F_A and F_B from Question 2c?
4. Two volleyball players on opposite sides of the net jump into the air to hit the ball. They hit the ball at the same time, and the ball does not move but comes to rest in midair. What can you say about the original momentum of each of the player's hands? Explain your answer.
5. Answer the focus question from the beginning of this activity: "How do factors such as velocity, mass, and others before a collision compare with the same factors after a collision?"

Getting Real: Collisions in Two Dimensions

EXPLAIN

One-dimensional interactions are interesting, but not very common in everyday life. It's more common to see objects interact at various angles, not along a straight line. A small rock glances off your windshield, for example, leaving behind the results of its change in momentum. Gas molecules inside a balloon rebound off each other at all angles and hit the balloon wall, causing the inside pressure. A linebacker drives a running back out of bounds with an angled hit (figure 2.22).

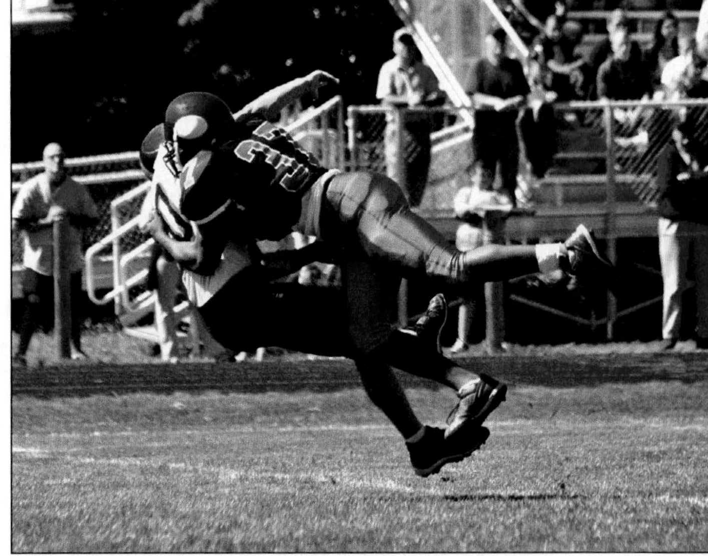

Figure 2.22 A collision in two dimensions. This linebacker knocks the running back out of bounds with an inelastic collision at an angle. What changes can you observe after a two-dimensional collision? How is a two-dimensional collision different from collisions in one dimension?

To understand these interactions, you need to think in more than one dimension. But that's easy. That's what you do every day as you negotiate the hallway during passing period or try to merge safely into traffic. In *Getting Real: Collisions in Two Dimensions*, you will use the same conceptual relationships and governing principles of nature that you learned in the previous activity, *In-Line Interactions*. Only now you will apply that knowledge to two-dimensional interactions. You and your team will reach a deeper understanding of everyday events by answering this focus question: "How does conservation of momentum help me understand and predict interactions in two dimensions?"

Materials

For each team of 4 students

1 tennis ball–collision kit, which includes

- 2 tennis balls marked "1 unit of mass," with Velcro strips and a cup hook
- 1 tennis ball marked "2 units of mass," with Velcro strips and a cup hook
- 2 lengths of string long enough to reach from a desk to the ceiling
- 1 collision grid with protractor markings and a center string
- paper clips
- tape
- 1 pen cap

Process and Procedure

In this activity, you and your team will investigate a series of events designed to test the law of conservation of momentum in two dimensions. You will model your experimental design after your experiences with one-dimensional tennis ball collisions from the previous activity. That is, you will use what you already know and understand rather than start from the beginning.

1. Review your results of Steps 2–6 from Part I of the previous activity, *In-Line Interactions*. You can use these same principles in your experimental design for this activity.
2. Assemble the tennis ball–collision kit. Then practice releasing 2 balls simultaneously at right angles along the axes provided. Your goal is to make them hit and stick together.
3. Design a step-by-step procedure to confirm the law of conservation of momentum for 2-dimensional, hit-and-stick collisions. Do this by writing answers to Steps 3a–e in your science notebook.
   a. How and by how much will you vary mass?
   b. How and by how much will you vary initial velocity (v_i) at the point of collision?

Remember, swing distance is directly proportional to the magnitude of the collision velocity.

   c. How will you predict both magnitude and direction of the final velocity (v_f) of the 2-ball system?

Your design must include a prediction each time you change either mass or velocity in your investigation. Predict the resultant vector (magnitude and direction). You must have a place to record both your prediction and the actual value of the resultant.

To check your prediction, place a pen cap at the point on your grid where you determine the 2-ball system will swing. Then observe whether the system's center of mass knocks over the pen cap.

d. How will you account for measurement uncertainty?

e. How will you organize your data efficiently and clearly? Remember to include labels, units, and a caption of explanation under the table after analyzing your results.

4. Show your design to your teacher for approval before collecting data.

5. Follow your approved, step-by-step procedure. Be sure that each team member records all observations.

6. Determine if momentum was conserved in 2-dimensional collisions, the same as you did for 1-dimensional collisions. Give evidence to support your answer.

Read *FYI—Vector Addition in Two Dimensions* to learn how to manipulate vectors in two dimensions.

Vector Addition in Two Dimensions

Using vectors to determine the result of a collision or a net force is a process that is familiar to you. You used this process in several activities in this chapter. However, the vectors you have used so far have been in a straight line—in one dimension. Now you will work with vectors that interact at angles—in two dimensions. To keep it simple, you will only work with vectors at right angles (90 degrees, or 90°) to each other. In doing this, there are several right-angle relationships that will be helpful.

First, you are familiar with the Pythagorean theorem used to calculate the length of sides in a right triangle. If you know the length of two sides, you can calculate the third by using the formula

$$a^2 + b^2 = c^2$$

In this formula, *a* and *b* refer to the two right-angle legs of the triangle and *c* is the hypotenuse (see figure).

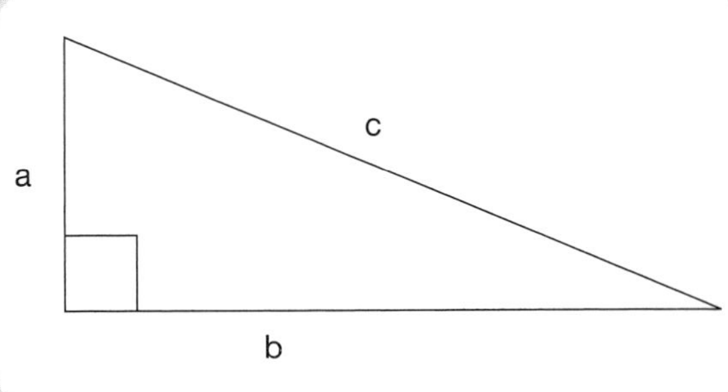

Right triangle. In this right triangle, the letters *a* and *b* refer to the two right-angle legs of the triangle. The letter *c* represents the hypotenuse.

Vector Addition in Two Dimensions, continued

In addition, there are two special-sized right triangles that, if you learn their relationships, will save you time. The first is a 45°-45°-90° triangle. In this triangle, the legs are equal lengths. The hypotenuse of this special triangle is equal to the length of a leg times the square root of 2 (see figure).

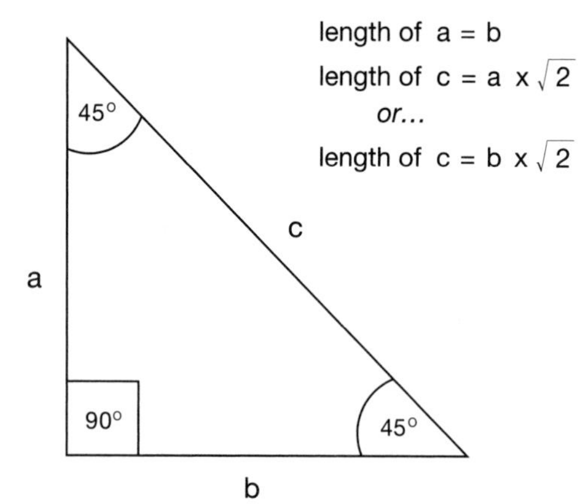

▲ **45°-45°-90° right triangle.** This special right triangle has angles of 45°, 45°, and 90°. Legs a and b are the same length. The length of the hypotenuse (c) can be calculated by finding the product of the length of one leg and the square root of 2.

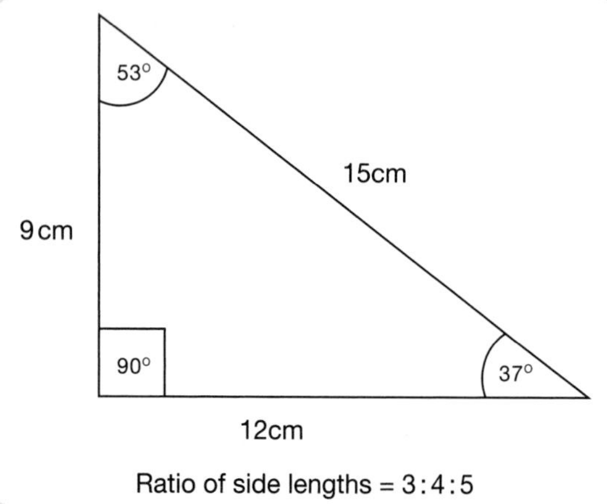

▲ **3:4:5 right triangle.** This special right triangle has leg lengths in a *ratio* of 3:4:5 with 5 representing the hypotenuse of the right triangle. For example, if the legs of the triangle were 9 cm and 12 cm, then the hypotenuse would be 15 cm long. The angles of this type of right triangle are shown in the figure.

Another special triangle is called a 3-4-5 triangle, where 5 represents the hypotenuse of a right triangle. These numbers refer to the length (or the ratio of the lengths) of each leg. The angle opposite the 4 leg is approximately equal to 53°, and the angle opposite the 3 leg is approximately equal to 37° (see figure). The sum of all the angles in any triangle is 180°. Remembering these special relationships will give you shortcuts in your calculations or vector diagrams because the length of the legs represents the magnitude or the length of the vectors.

How is vector math different in two-dimensional collisions? In one-dimensional motion, you only had to add vectors in a straight line. In two-dimensional collisions, you must consider angles, and the motion that results (the resultant) is not always obvious. But you have some feel for this type of motion because it is something you experience every day. Suppose you are playing billiards and you want the number 13 ball (orange ball) to go into the corner pocket (see figure). You know that you must hit the ball at an angle to give the orange ball the right resultant velocity (both speed and direction) to fall into the corner pocket. In doing this, you are using vector math in two dimensions and you didn't think about science or math at all!

▶ **Vector math at work.** You must hit the ball at an angle to make it go into the pocket. What are the factors you must consider to make a successful shot?

When objects collide at right angles and stick together, they will continue in a path that results from adding the two right-angle momentum vectors. This is because momentum is conserved in all types of collisions.

Suppose a car is moving east with a momentum of 15,000 kg m/sec and collides with a truck moving north with a momentum of 40,000 kg m/sec, figure (a). If the vehicles stick together at impact, what will be the final momentum of the vehicles? Take a look at how to add these vectors, which form a 90° angle. Remember, when adding vectors you place them head to tail. Start by drawing two arrows pointing in the proper direction. The vectors must be drawn to scale and be placed head to tail, figure (b).

Since momentum is conserved, you can use the initial momenta to find the final momentum of the system. The final, or resultant, momentum can be determined graphically by drawing an arrow from the tail of the first arrow to the head of the last arrow, figure (c). Now measure the length of the arrow with a ruler and determine its magnitude by using the scale.

The angle (or direction) of the vector can be found by using a protractor, figure (d).

Initial momenta of the two vehicles. Two vehicles collide as shown in (a). To add the vectors, draw the initial momenta of the two cars to scale and place the arrows head to tail as shown in (b). To find the magnitude of the final momentum of the two-vehicle system, draw the final momentum (resultant) vector from the tail of the first vector to the head of the last vector (c). Measure the length of this vector and use the scale to determine the magnitude of the vector. Finally, to find the direction of the final momentum, use a protractor to measure the angle (d).

Vector Addition in Two Dimensions, continued

For extra practice with vectors, see *Vector Addition* on the SRCD.

You can also determine its magnitude by using the Pythagorean theorem. Use it to check your answers when using vector math. Using the theorem, the answer of 42,700 kg m/sec confirms the vector math method.

$$a^2 + b^2 = c^2$$

$$\left(15{,}000\,\frac{\text{kg m}}{\text{sec}}\right)^2 + \left(40{,}000\,\frac{\text{kg m}}{\text{sec}}\right)^2 = c^2$$

$$1{,}825{,}000{,}000\,\frac{\text{kg}^2\,\text{m}^2}{\text{sec}^2} = c^2$$

$$\sqrt{1{,}825{,}000{,}000\,\frac{\text{kg}^2\,\text{m}^2}{\text{sec}^2}} = \sqrt{2}$$

$$42{,}700\,\frac{\text{kg m}}{\text{sec}} \approx c$$

Reflect and Connect

Apply your best thinking to these questions individually, and then discuss your answers as directed by your teacher.

1. A 1,300-kg car moving north at 27 m/sec collides with a 2,100-kg car moving east at 20 m/sec. They stick together. In what direction (angle) and with what speed do they move after the collision? Follow Questions 1a–c to find the answer.
   a. Solve for the final momentum using scaled vectors. Measure and label both the magnitude and the direction (angle) for the final momentum.
   b. Check your answer for the magnitude of the momentum by using the Pythagorean theorem.
   c. Use the final momentum of the system to solve for the final velocity of the 2 cars together.

Use the relationship $p_f = (m_1 + m_2)\, v_f$ to find the final velocity of the 2 cars.

2. A high school football player (100-kg mass) is running along the sidelines with a speed of 8.0 m/sec. At the same time, a cheerleader is backing up into the field of play not realizing she is straying out onto the field. She is moving at a speed of 1.0 m/sec and has a mass of 50 kg. They collide at right angles to each other. The football player wants to avoid hurting her. He paid attention in science class and knew that picking her up would be the best plan. He picks up the cheerleader at the point of collision and runs with her as he slows down rather than letting her bounce off him after the collision. How fast will they be going immediately after the collision and in what direction? Use scaled vectors and algebra to answer the question. Explain

why picking her up and running with her as he slows down will hurt the cheerleader less than letting her bounce off. Use the equation $F = \dfrac{m\Delta v}{\Delta t}$ in your answer.

3. Does adding initial velocity vectors give you the correct values for final velocity in the previous problems? Explain your answer using vectors or algebra.

With and Without a Net

ELABORATE

Now that you understand a force is required to change momentum, you can begin to see the applications of what you are learning. You understand how to calculate forces during collisions by considering change in velocity (Δv), time during the collision (Δt), and mass. The key conceptual connection is between force and the effects of force—changing momentum (Δp).

But so far in this unit, you have only looked at forces in two situations. You have seen that forces are either constant or zero. In actual everyday situations, forces change. Now you will be concerned with net forces. Think about a **net force** as the force left over after all forces are added together as vectors. There is a net force if forces on an object are not balanced—or do not all cancel. And if net forces change, so do momentum and velocity.

You can *feel* a net force or a change in velocity. Think about riding in a luxury car with your eyes closed. Or if you have flown on an airplane, think about how it feels once you have reached your cruising altitude. If you have your eyes closed, you cannot tell that you are moving even though you may be moving several hundred kilometers per hour in a plane. You are moving at constant velocity and you know that at constant velocity there is no net force. What you *can* feel is a change in momentum caused by a net force. For example, if the car or plane suddenly speeds up or slows down, you can feel it. What other motions can you feel? You can also feel the change in momentum when the car or plane changes direction. In each of the changes that you can feel, a net force caused a change in momentum.

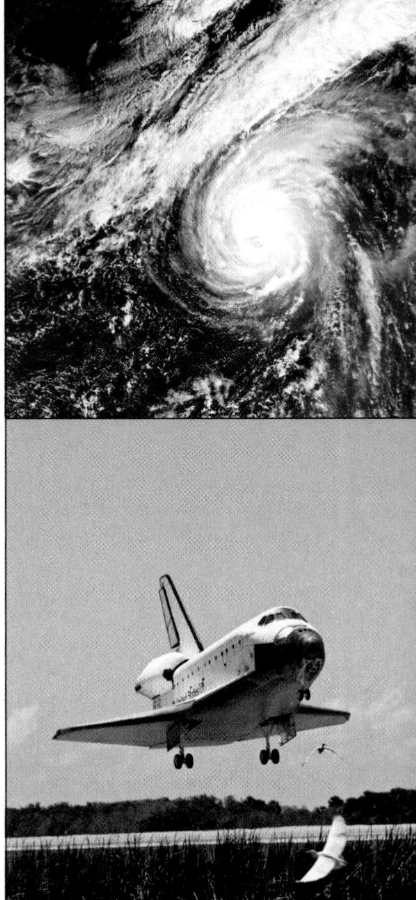

▲ **Figure 2.23 Forces change in everyday interactions.** How do you know that forces are changing in each interaction shown? What is the evidence?

Think about the changes in force when your heart beats, or the changes in momentum when a hurricane hits shore, or the changes in velocity when the space shuttle reenters Earth's atmosphere (figure 2.23). In each case, the net forces change. But as you have seen, some interactions are the result of a balance of forces (no net force). Yet whether with, or without a net force, the interactions are interesting.

In *With and Without a Net*, you and your team will apply what you know about the connection between force and changing momentum to understand everyday situations in which forces are changing. Keep your efforts focused by filtering any actions you take through the following focus question: "How do I recognize when there *is* and *is not* a net force acting on an object?"

Part I: Putting On the Brakes

Materials

For each team of 4 students

1 coffee filter (flat bottomed)

1 stopwatch

paper clips

1 chair

Process and Procedure

A common interaction exerts tremendous influence on our everyday lives. That interaction is gravity. Like all interactions, gravity is the result of a pair of forces, in this case, $F_{\text{Earth } on \text{ us}}$ and $F_{\text{us } on \text{ Earth}}$. But is that mutual force of attraction always constant? Is it the same for all objects? Does the pull of Earth's gravity result in changing or constant momentum?

In Part I, you and your team will investigate the forces acting on a person jumping out of an airplane. Then you will link what you find out to another motion, applying brakes in a car.

Cautions

Make sure the chairs you use are stable. If you have balance problems or other physical limitations, do not stand on an elevated surface.

1. Familiarize yourself with the parachutist model provided by your teacher by performing Steps 1a–b. Then record the results, using sketches with captions in your science notebook.
   a. Stand on a chair, hold a coffee filter above your head, and release it. Focus on whether the filter is speeding up, slowing down, or neither.
   b. Repeat Step 1a with 2, 4, and then 6 paper clips in the filter. Focus on the relative amount of time to hit the floor.

2. Copy the table in figure 2.24 into your science notebook. Complete this analogy table to link a parachute jump to the coffee-filter drop. Reading across each row should form a sentence. The first 2 are done for you as a guide.

Feature of a parachute jump	Feature in the coffee-filter drop	Reason
Vertical forces while riding in a plane are like	vertical forces while holding a coffee filter	because the up and down forces balance each other.
The downward velocity at the instant of jumping is like	the downward velocity at the release moment	because both start at 0 m/s.
the downward force on a parachutist is like	the downward force on ____________	because ____________ ____________.
The change in velocity after the parachute opens is like		
The distance fallen before the parachute opens is like		
Continue adding features as your team thinks of them.		

▲ **Figure 2.24 Analogy table for parachute jump and coffee-filter drop.** Use this table in Step 2 to make comparisons between a parachute jump and your coffee-filter drop. Your answers should form a logical sentence when reading across a row.

3. Read *Going Terminal* to prepare for sketching scaled vector diagrams of the forces acting on the coffee filter at several points during its fall.

A good way to get the most out of what you read is to make a T-table with the headings "fact or idea I read" and "question I have" (about the fact or idea). Then fill out the table as you read.

READING

Going Terminal

Both the parachutist and the coffee filter experience Earth's gravitational attraction (a force that pulls them toward Earth). In response, both objects pull on Earth with a force equal to Earth's pull. This is Newton's third law. The coffee filter, however, pulls on Earth with a force different from that of the parachutist. And Earth pulls on the parachutist with a force different from that of the coffee filter. Why? A person has more mass than a coffee filter, so the gravitational force between Earth and the person results in greater weight compared with a coffee filter. The vector representation of a greater force is a longer arrow. So the vector for a person's weight is longer than the vector for the weight of a coffee filter (figure 2.25). The force with which the person and the coffee filter pull back on Earth is not large enough to move Earth.

When a person jumps out of the plane or when you drop the coffee filter, the downward force results in a change in momentum ($F = \frac{m\Delta v}{\Delta t}$). You see a change in the magnitude of the velocity from 0 m/sec to some larger value. During that time, the force down remains constant. But the force of the air pushing up does not stay the same (figure 2.26). The faster the object moves, the greater the force of the air resistance pushing up. Eventually, the upward force and the downward force become equal. That is, the *net* force on the object becomes zero. The result is no more change in momentum, and thus no more change in velocity. The velocity at this point is called the **terminal velocity**, and the parachutist is moving at a constant velocity.

SCILINKS NSTA
Topic: terminal velocity
Go to: www.scilinks.org
Code: 2Inquiry96

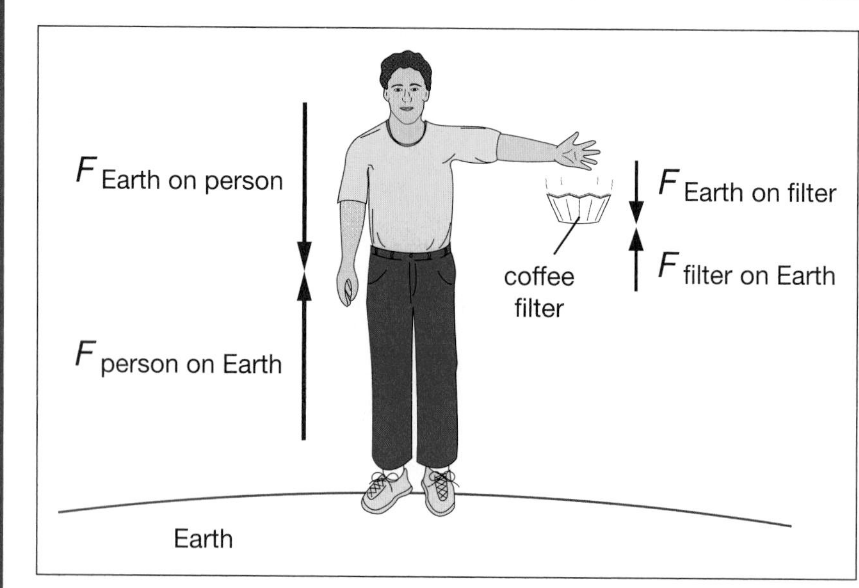

Figure 2.25
Different weight = different forces. The force that Earth pulls on the filter paper is much less than the force that Earth pulls on a person. Likewise, the force that the coffee filter pulls on Earth is less than the force that the person pulls on Earth.

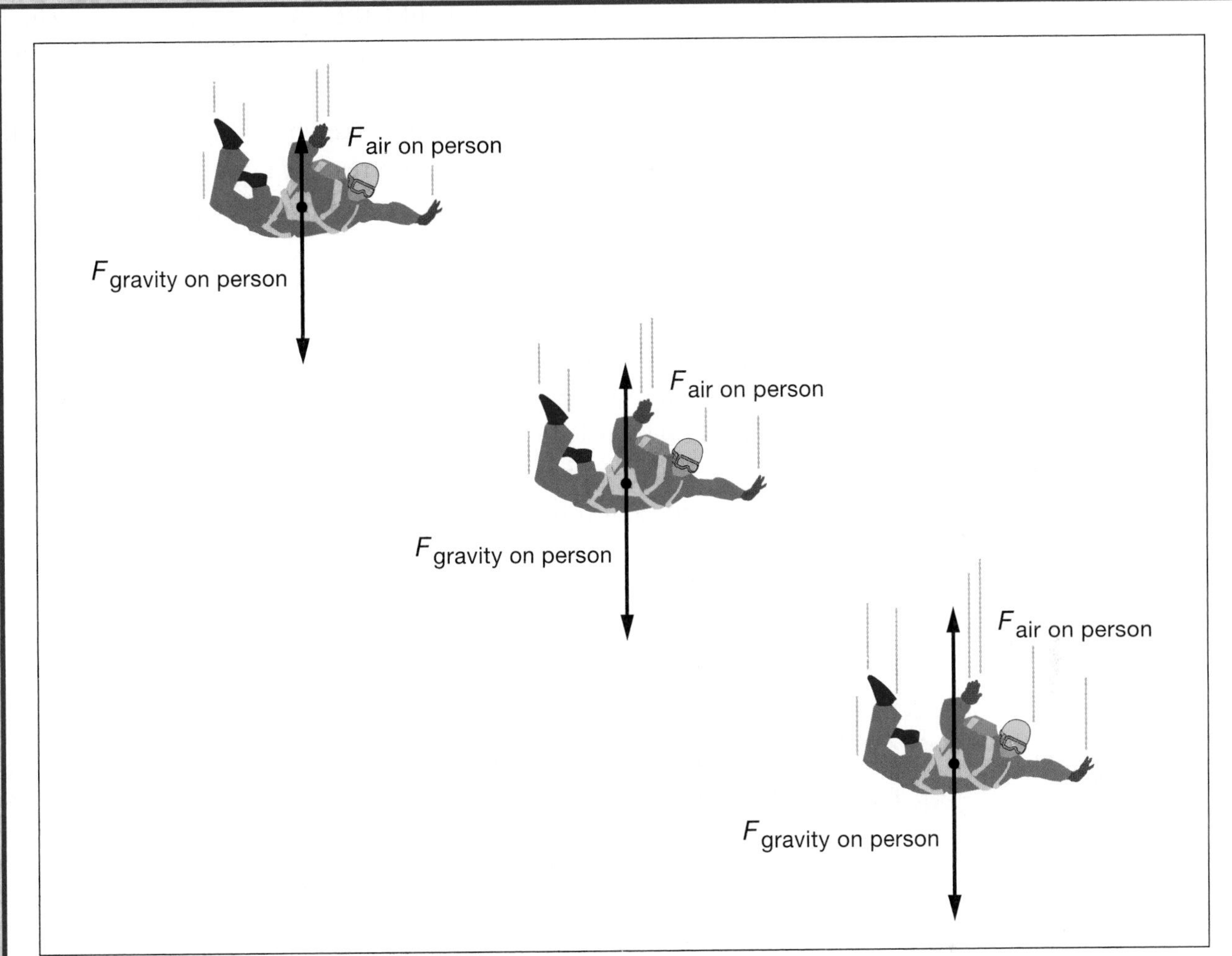

▲ **Figure 2.26 Constant and changing forces.** The force downward remains the same when a person leaves a plane because his or her weight remains the same. However, the force up due to air resistance changes as the speed of the person falling changes. At what point does the parachutist reach terminal velocity?

4. Draw 3 scaled vector sketches showing all the vertical forces acting on the coffee filter. Include sketches that show when the coffee filter is in your hand, when the filter is at some point in midair, and when the filter hits the floor. Include highlight comments and an overall caption.
5. Repeat Step 4 for the filter holding 2, 4, and 6 paper clips while it falls to the floor.
6. Compare the motion of your coffee filter to a chair as you complete Steps 6a–c.

a. Complete an analogy table like the one in Step 2 to link the filter's motions to pushing a chair across the floor, from rest to some constant velocity.
b. Draw scaled and labeled vector sketches of all the horizontal forces acting on the chair, from rest to a constant velocity.
c. Include highlight comments and an overall caption for your sketches.

7. Compare the motion of a parachute opening to applying brakes on a car by completing Steps 7a–c.
   a. Complete an analogy table like the one in Step 2 to link a parachute opening to applying brakes in a car moving at some constant velocity.
   b. Draw scaled and labeled vector sketches of all the horizontal forces acting on the car, from the initial constant velocity to a stop.
   c. Include highlight comments and an overall caption for your sketches.

Stop & THINK

PART I

Answer these questions in your science notebook individually before conferring with classmates. When your discussions cause you to change your answer, document the changes so that you and your teacher can keep track of your ongoing thinking.

1. Does the application of a constant force always result in changing momentum? Support your answer with examples that include vector sketches with labels and captions.
2. Newton's first law (or the law of inertia) states, "Objects in motion stay in motion and objects at rest stay at rest, unless acted upon by an outside net force." Explain whether Part I supports or refutes this statement by providing direct evidence from the activity.
3. A car runs out of gasoline at the top of a hill and coasts down the hill, reaching a flat region. Explain what happens by generating several force vector diagrams at several points in the car's motion downhill. Include a general caption for your sketches describing the significance of the vectors.

Part II: Fall Time

Materials

For each team of 4 students

1 coffee filter (flat bottomed)

1 stopwatch

1 meterstick or tape measure

paper clips

Process and Procedure

You learned in Part I that when the net force acting on an object is zero, two motions are possible: (1) motionless ($v = 0$ m/sec) or (2) constant velocity ($v =$ constant). But what kind of motion results when there is a *constant* net force? To find out, you and your team will use a flat-bottomed coffee filter and paper clips (figure 2.27) to model how an object falls when the only downward force is due to the pull of gravity from Earth.

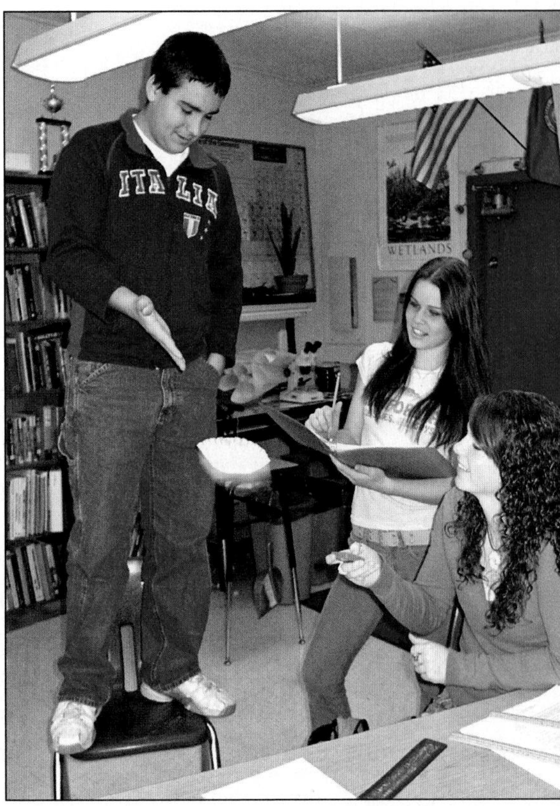

▲ **Figure 2.27**
Fall time. You and your team use a flat-bottomed coffee filter and paper clips to model how an object falls. What is the downward force on the coffee filter? Is there an upward force?

1. Predict what a time-to-floor (y-axis) versus number-of-paper-clips (x-axis) graph would look like if you continued Step 1 from Part I until there was an entire box of paper clips in the filter.
2. Design an investigation to test your prediction. Your investigation should include the following:
   - A step-by-step procedure
   - Appropriate data tables to record all measurements (including multiple trials)
   - A graph of your results including error bars and highlight comments

Don't write a caption for your graph until you have completed Step 5.

3. Carry out your investigation with your team after your teacher has approved your design and data tables.

 Cautions

Make sure the chairs you use are stable. If you have balance problems or other physical limitations, do not stand on an elevated surface.

4. Answer the true or false questions in Steps 4a–e in your science notebook regarding your xy plot of data. Include a justification for your answer (that is, "I answered false because ...")
   a. The filter reaches terminal velocity with zero paper clips. (T or F)
   b. The filter demonstrates a Δv when loaded with no paper clips. (T or F)

c. As the number of paper clips increases, the amount of time to reach the floor continues decreasing, no matter how many clips are added. (T or F)

d. Theoretically, if you placed an infinite number of paper clips in the filter, the filter would require 0 seconds to reach the floor. (T or F)

e. For objects falling near the surface of Earth, there is a limit to the amount of time they require to fall a certain distance. (T or F)

5. Read *Falling to Earth* to help you write an effective caption for the time-to-floor versus number-of-paper-clips graph from Step 2.

READING

Falling to Earth

When a parachutist first jumps out of an airplane, the only force down is the pull of gravity. Instantly, air resistance (friction) results in an upward force. The greater the magnitude of the velocity, the greater the upward force, until the force down equals the force up. The average terminal velocity of a parachutist with an unopened parachute is about 125 miles per hour or 56 m/sec. Though terminal velocity is smaller if the upward force is made greater by opening a parachute, even a falling bowling ball with no parachute reaches terminal velocity if it falls long enough. The magnitude of the terminal velocity of the bowling ball would be quite large.

However, there are times when gravitational force (gravity) is the net downward force. Can you think of some examples? What about on the Moon, where there is no atmosphere? There is no air resistance, and when an object falls or is dropped, gravity supplies a constant net force. If there is a very short distance to fall or if there is low air resistance, the fall time is not long enough to produce terminal velocity—so there is a constant net force.

Since the weight remains constant in a fall, so does the net force. And from the mathematical relationship $F = \frac{m\Delta v}{\Delta t}$, if force and mass are constant, so is the rate of change of velocity, $\frac{\Delta v}{\Delta t}$. This rate of change of velocity is the *same* for all objects close to the surface of Earth, regardless of mass, provided no upward forces exist. For the planet we live on, this constant rate of change of velocity has the average numerical value of 9.8 m/sec^2. This number, often called *g*, means that the maximum change of velocity in 1 second (sec) of free fall near the surface of Earth is 9.8 m/sec. That is, objects dropped from the same height will hit the ground at the same time, regardless of mass. So when either the falling distance is relatively short or air friction is small, the time to hit the ground will reach some constant, nonzero value. This value reflects the mutual gravitational attraction between any two objects near the surface of a particular planet. For Earth, the constant rate of change of velocity that conveys how strong Earth's gravitational field is close to the surface is 9.8 m/sec^2, on average.

6. Write a draft caption for your graph from Step 2. Then use the TSAR strategy with your team to finalize your caption.

Reflect and Connect

Think carefully about the answers to the following questions, then write answers in your science notebook. You may discuss your answers with your classmates as directed by your teacher.

1. Three students predict the relative amount of time required for a feather and a hammer, released from the same height on the Moon, to hit the ground.

   Ashley says the hammer hits in less time because the mutual gravitational attraction between the Moon and hammer produces a far greater force than between the feather and the Moon. With a greater force comes a greater change in velocity. Thus, the hammer moves more distance in less time.

   Brandon says they hit at the same time because forces occur in pairs, equal in size and opposite in direction. So the force of gravity is the same on both objects. Since the force is the same, so is the change in velocity. Thus, they hit at the same time.

   Carmella says g on the Moon is constant near the Moon's surface, though less than g on Earth because the gravitational field strength is less on the Moon than on Earth. Since g (the time rate of change of velocity) is constant near the surface, both objects experience the same change in velocity. Thus, they hit at the same time.

   Select a student position to defend and generate labeled vector sketches with highlight comments as your defense. Explain what is incorrect in the other two student explanations.

2. A team of students designed an activity to determine the mathematical relationship between drop height and time to floor for a coffee filter loaded with an entire box of paper clips. The students placed their data in the table in figure 2.28. They generated 2 xy graphs: (1) height (y-axis) versus time (x-axis) and (2) height (y-axis) versus time squared (x-axis).
   a. Generate the same 2 graphs that this team did, using the same height scale for both plots.
   b. Incorporate highlight comments onto both plots, focusing on the best-fit line that the data suggest.

▼ **Figure 2.28 Recorded data for drop height and time.** A team of students recorded the following data from an activity similar to the one you just completed. Use these data for Questions 2a–c.

Drop height (m)	Time to floor (s)
2.0	0.64
1.6	0.57
1.2	0.49
0.80	0.40
0.40	0.29
0.0	0.0

c. You know from algebra that a straight line with a constant positive slope can be represented by $y = mx + b$. Use this reminder to suggest a mathematical equation that represents the relationship between height and time for falling bodies.

Recall these relationships from the equation:

y = **the variable graphed on the** y**-axis**

m = **the slope of the line**

x = **the variable graphed on the** x**-axis**

b = **the point where the line crosses the** y**-axis (the** y**-intercept)**

3. Imagine a "clever" teenager who wanted to avoid a football workout. The conversation with a coach might go like this:

TEENAGER: "It's totally useless for me to try to push the blocking sled."

COACH: "You think so!? Why is that?"

TEENAGER: "Because of a law of nature."

COACH: "This I've got to hear."

TEENAGER: "I have been learning that forces come in pairs, equal in size and opposite in direction. When I push on the sled, the sled pushes back on me with an equal, but opposite, force. The forces cancel. Therefore, I can never get the sled moving. It's useless!"

COACH: "Now I've heard it all! I need to talk to that science teacher . . ."

Follow Questions 3a–d to analyze the motion of the blocking sled.

a. Draw a sketch of a teenager pushing a blocking sled similar to figure 2.29.

b. Use vector arrows to label the pairs of forces that occur at each of the starred areas of the sketch.

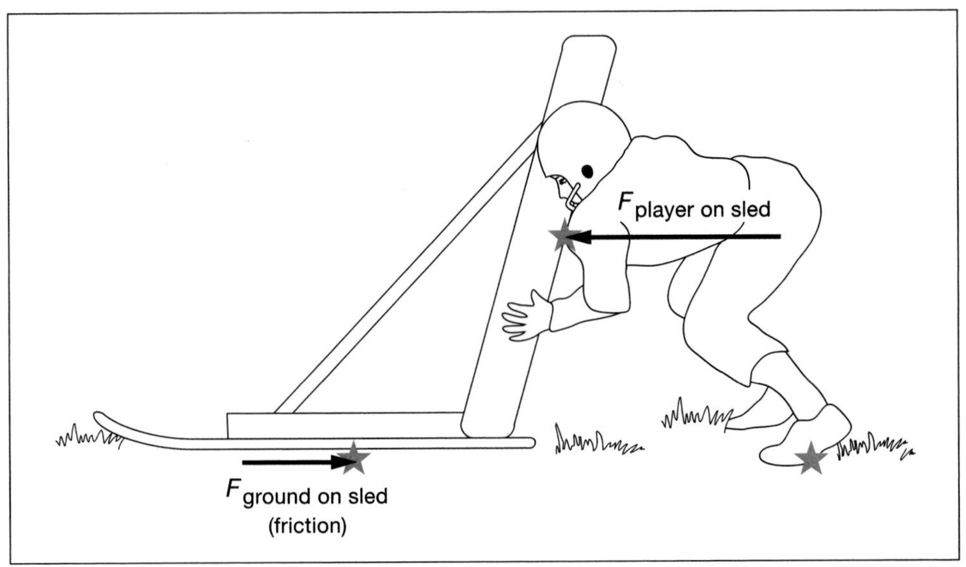

◀ **Figure 2.29 Forces involved in pushing a sled.** Draw this sketch in your science notebook. Place vectors to represent forces at each star. In some cases, one of the forces in the pair has been drawn for you.

c. Complete the table in figure 2.30 in your science notebook. Identify and comment on *all* the horizontal pairs of forces important to the question of whether the teenager can push the sled.

Objects involved in force pair	Relative size of forces in pair	Relative size of force pair compared to other two force pairs
Teenager and sled	The force of the teenager on the sled is equal and opposite to the force of the sled on the teenager.	
Teenager and ground		
Sled and ground		

▲ **Figure 2.30 Table comparing forces.** Complete this table for Question 3c.

d. Decide who is correct in his reasoning. Is it the football player trying to get out of pushing the blocking sled, or the coach who wants the player to complete the workout? Write a statement giving evidence to support your decision. To develop your statement, consider the forces that would cause a change in momentum of the sled.

4. The focus question for this activity was, "How do I recognize when there *is* and *is not* a net force acting on an object?" Use your experiences from this activity to write a short paragraph to answer this question. You may use sketches to illustrate your answer.

EVALUATE

Forces to Go; Forces to Stop

▲ **Figure 2.31**
Forces cause changes in momentum. Look at each photograph and think back to the activities in this chapter. In each activity, what evidence did you collect or observe that indicated a net force?

Forces change things. You saw this happen in each activity so far in this chapter, from colliding cars to parachuting coffee filters. That's because all net forces, *regardless of their origin*, cause changes in momentum (figure 2.31).

In Part I of *Forces to Go; Forces to Stop*, you and your team will demonstrate your understanding of the relationship between force, motion, and changing momentum. To do this, you will focus your planning and interactions on answering the following question: "How are net force and mass related for a ball rolling down a ramp, onto a carpet, and then slowing to a stop?"

Review the rubric for scoring before you start. It will help you get the best performance for the least amount of your team's limited time.

Part I: Out of Gas or Out of Momentum?

Materials

For each team of 4 students

1 balance

1 ramp

1 stopwatch

balls (same material, different mass)

tape

1 tape measure or meterstick

1 chair or box of similar height

graph paper

1 calculator (optional)

4 *Forces to Go; Forces to Stop Scoring Rubric* handouts

Process and Procedure

Imagine you are driving in a car. You glance down at your gasoline gauge and see the needle below E! But luckily, you're on top of a hill. Will you make it to the gasoline station? What factors make a difference when you have no engine force? Are there other forces to think about? What are those forces?

In this evaluate activity, you will model an out-of-gasoline scenario, using everyday objects (figure 2.32). Then you will analyze evidence and communicate your findings. Along the way, you will document how the design of your study changed due to new information and evolving understandings.

1. Meet with your team and design an experiment to answer the following question. Consider Steps 1a–e as you design your experiment.

   "What do changes in motion tell you about the relationship between force and the mass of balls rolling down a ramp, onto a carpet, and then to a stop?"

   a. Your team must generate a graph of position versus time with highlight comments and captions. You will plot time on the x-axis and position on the y-axis. This will show the core of your understanding, so be sure to consider the following as you plan your data collection for your graphs:
      - The variables you should measure and how you should control all others
      - The ramp angle you can use so that the speed and distance are easy to measure
      - A method to divide your graph so that you can record highlight comments for both the ramp and the carpet sections
      - The best way to incorporate key concepts such as mass, weight, force, momentum, impulse, vector, change, friction, and force pairs (Newton's third law) in highlight comments, captions, or both

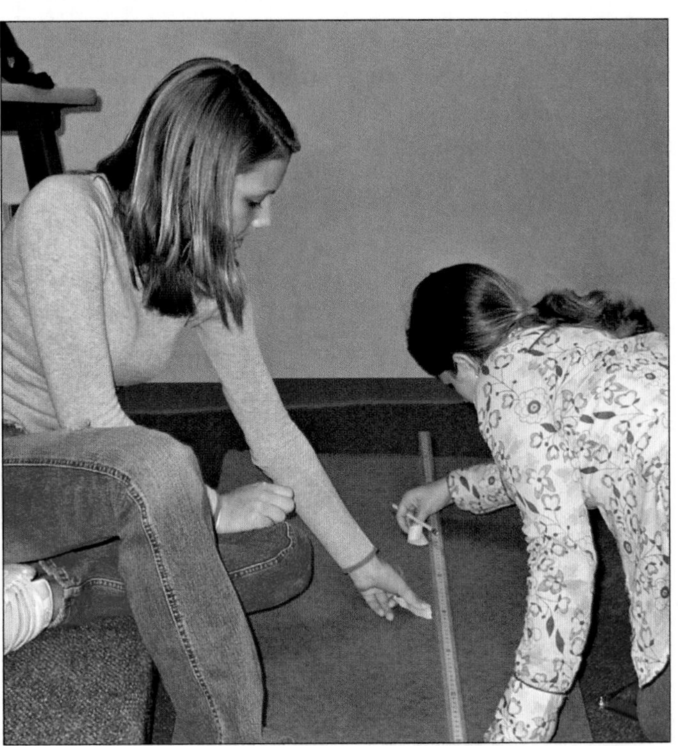

▲ **Figure 2.32 Experimental designs may change.** Answering a scientific question requires discussion and the willingness to change your approach, especially if what you started isn't working. What design will you use to answer the focus question?

Create a legend for your graph. Use a different color or different style of data point for each ball. Your graph will have 2 lines on the same graph, one for each ball.

   b. Your team must test at least 2 balls with surfaces of similar smoothness but with different mass.
   c. You must incorporate multiple trials in your analysis of any trends in data. You should include the uncertainty in your measurement and error bars on your graph.

   d. You must document each design decision and the rationale for making that decision.
   e. Your team must document the step-by-step procedure of your design.
2. Show your design to your teacher for approval and incorporate any changes before making your observations.

Be sure to indicate with underlining, highlight markers, or different-colored pens or pencils any changes you made in your design during the course of this entire activity. Record the reasons for your changes in the margin of your science notebook.

3. Before you conduct your investigation, predict what the graph will look like for each ball. Record your prediction on a separate graph. Plot the motion of both balls on the same graph with clearly labeled lines. Give your prediction to your teacher before you go on to Step 4.
4. Conduct your experiment. Then analyze your data by writing highlight comments and captions, and generate your graphs.
5. Hand in your graphs and supporting design documentation as instructed by your teacher.

Part II: Who's at Fault?

Materials

For each student

1 ruler

1 protractor

graph paper

1 calculator

1 *Who's at Fault?* handout

Process and Procedure

When there is a car accident, the drivers in the two cars often do not agree on all the facts. Consider a car accident in which the drivers approached a four-way stop from the south and from the west. The drivers do agree that they both had to stop at the intersection, controlled by stop signs in each direction, before crossing. They do agree that one of them ran through the stop sign at high speed without stopping. As often happens in car accident investigations, the most important thing they don't agree on is who ran the stop sign. The two cars' front ends are smashed; their bumpers are twisted and locked together. After the collision, the two cars came to rest on the sidewalk, where they ran over and destroyed a blue mailbox. Your job, as the investigating officer, is to determine who is telling the truth. Which car ran the stop sign? Was it the SUV or the compact car? You will work with a team to answer these questions.

1. Meet with your team and examine the following evidence and data taken from the scene of the accident:
    - Before the collision, the compact car had been heading east and the SUV had been heading north.
    - The compact car has a mass of 1,160 kg and the SUV has a mass of 3,090 kg.
    - The posted speed limit for the area is 15 mi/hr (24 km/hr).
    - The vehicles moved off together at 14.5 km/hr just after impact.
    - The mailbox that stopped the vehicles is on an angle 36° to the east of north from the center of the intersection.
    - The road conditions at the time of the accident were icy and therefore friction can be ignored.
2. Analyze the crash scene by performing Steps 2a–d. Record your thinking about each of the questions in your science notebook.
    a. What factors control the forces that the objects involved in the collisions experience?
    b. How do the vehicles' velocities change after the cars collide?
    c. What do you need to know to determine which vehicle ran the stop sign?
    d. What vectors can you use to solve the problem?
3. Write a report that provides evidence about which vehicle ran the stop sign and how you know. You should include the following in your report:
    - A description of the problem in words
    - A diagram of the problem, containing all the data from the scene
    - An explanation of the physics involved in collisions as it pertains to this situation
    - The answer to the problem (1 sentence)
    - The vector diagrams and math you used to solve the problem
    - An explanation of the steps you took to solve the problem, and why you took them

CHAPTER 3

Collisions—Atomic Style

Collisions—Atomic Style

In chapter 2, *Collision Course*, you studied the interactions of large objects such as cars and tennis balls. In chapter 3, *Collisions—Atomic Style*, you will build on your understanding of collisions as you journey into the world of chemistry. Atoms and molecules are too small to see, so you must rely on what you already know and understand and use models to help you "see" what is going on. This is why you began your learning with the physics of how tennis balls and cars collide and interact. Now it is time to think more abstractly and learn how atoms and molecules interact.

You may be asking yourself if the same laws in physics apply to chemistry. Well, you are in luck. You do not have to learn different rules for different areas in science—the same rules or laws apply. Laws in physics apply to chemistry, and—guess what—they even apply to biology and geology.

▲ **Figure 3.1**
Chemical reaction. Some chemical reactions are fast like this one, and some are slow. What conditions must be met before two substances will react?

In chemical reactions, you cannot see the individual atoms and molecules colliding. Instead, you see the results of their interactions. Look at Figure 3.1. This is definitely evidence of interaction! You may have experienced the evidence of a chemical reaction when you mixed baking soda and vinegar. What conditions must be met before two substances will interact—or *re*act? Why are some chemical reactions slow and some very fast? Can you change the speed of the reaction by manipulating conditions (often called variables) in the reaction?

Goals for the Chapter

You will have the opportunity to answer those questions as you achieve the goals for this chapter. By the end of chapter 3, you will understand

- the role of energy, concentration, catalysts, and kinetics in chemical reactions;
- changes in energy resulting from chemical reactions;
- the law of conservation of matter and the law of conservation of energy as they relate to chemical reactions;
- systems at equilibrium;
- the similarities in many relationships in the microscopic and the macroscopic worlds; and
- the abilities necessary to do scientific inquiry.

To achieve these goals, you will be involved in doing science through inquiry in the following activities:

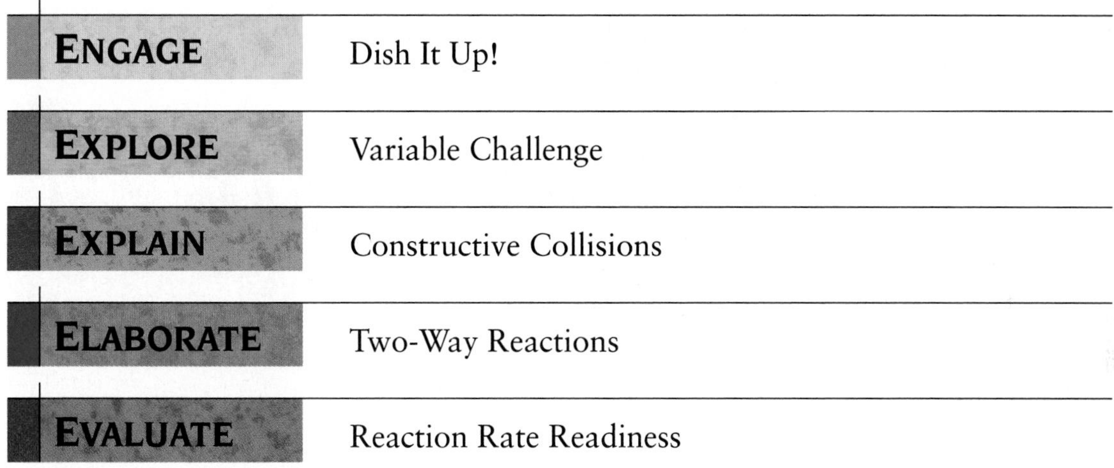

ENGAGE	Dish It Up!
EXPLORE	Variable Challenge
EXPLAIN	Constructive Collisions
ELABORATE	Two-Way Reactions
EVALUATE	Reaction Rate Readiness

Use your chapter organizer as a road map for your learning journey through this chapter. Look at it daily to review what you have studied and to see what you will study today and in the days to come.

Collisions—Atomic Style

Linking Question

How can I relate collisions between BBs to collisions on an atomic or molecular scale?

Engage

Dish It Up!

Key Idea:

Collisions between microscopic particles can be modeled using macroscopic objects.

Explore

Variable Challenge

Key Idea:

Certain factors can influence the rate of a chemical reaction.

Linking Question

What is happening on the atomic scale that can explain the changing rates of chemical reactions?

Explain

Constructive Collisions

Key Ideas:

- Energy, concentration, and the presence of catalysts or inhibitors play vital roles in the frequency of collisions between particles in a chemical reaction. This influences the rate of a chemical reaction.
- The mole is used in chemistry to represent the amount of a substance.

Evaluate

Reaction Rate Readiness

Key Idea:

You can explain chemical reactions and reaction rates by understanding collisions between particles.

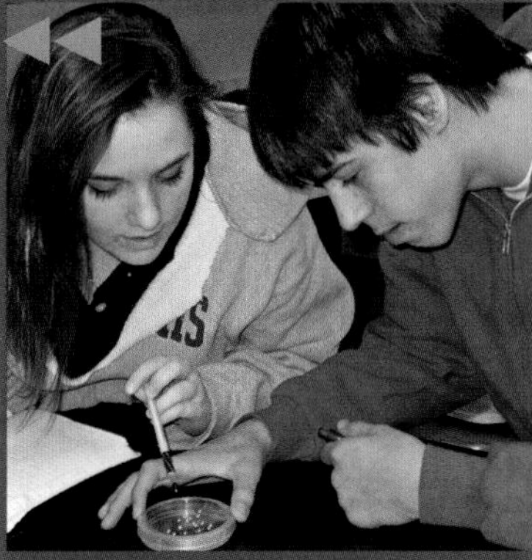

Linking Question

How can I demonstrate that I have learned about collisions between particles at the atomic scale?

CHAPTER

3 Major Concepts

- Collisions between particles can lead to reactions.
- Energy and concentration play a role in the speed of a reaction.
- The laws of conservation of matter and energy can be applied to chemical reactions.
- Chemical reactions are systems that can be in equilibrium.
- Interactions in the microscopic world are similar to interactions that occur in the macroscopic world.

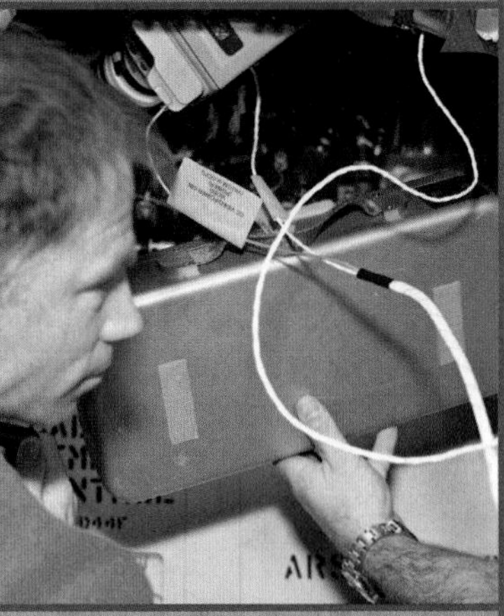

Elaborate

Two-Way Reactions

Key Ideas:

- Chemical reactions are reversible and will reach a state of equilibrium under the appropriate conditions.
- Reactions at equilibrium that are subjected to a stress will shift in a direction to relieve the stress.

Linking Question

What happens when particles in the products of a chemical reaction collide?

ENGAGE Dish It Up!

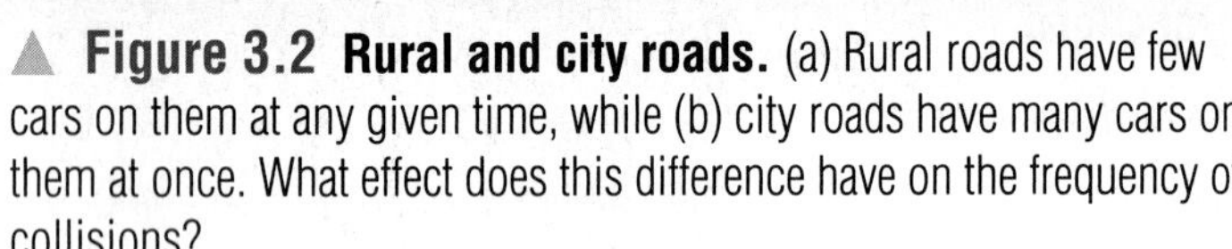

▲ **Figure 3.2 Rural and city roads.** (a) Rural roads have few cars on them at any given time, while (b) city roads have many cars on them at once. What effect does this difference have on the frequency of collisions?

Think about driving down a rural road. You probably feel like you are the only one on the road. Now think about driving on a busy highway. You might worry about your safety because of so many cars. For a particular rural road, officials determined that there were three car accidents in the last 10 years on a 16-kilometer (km, or 10-mile) segment of the road (figure 3.2). On a nearby interstate highway, however, there had been hundreds of collisions during that same time period on a 16-km segment. Can you think of reasons why this is true? Keep those ideas in mind as you work through this activity.

What do car crashes have to do with your study of chemistry? In *Dish It Up!*, you will work with a partner to discover the answer to this question. You also will develop new questions of your own. You will do this by using a petri dish with BBs to model how the atomic world behaves.

Materials

For each team of 2 students

1 petri dish containing 2 different-sized BBs

extra BBs of both sizes

Process and Procedure

1. Represent your dish and BB system in your science notebook by following Steps 1a–b.
   a. Draw a picture of the system as if you were viewing it from above.
   b. Label the BBs "large-mass BBs" and "small-mass BBs."

Your teacher has confirmed that the larger BBs have a higher mass than the smaller ones.

2. Shake the dish gently at a constant frequency of 1 complete shake (back-and-forth motion) per second. Observe the BBs and record your observations in your science notebook. As you record your observations, be sure to answer the questions in Steps 2a–c.
   a. Are the BBs colliding with one another? With the dish? What is your evidence?

Think about the evidence you observed when toy cars and tennis balls collided.

   b. Are all the BBs moving at the same speed? What is your evidence?
   c. Is the momentum of the BBs constant or changing? What is your evidence?
3. Add a few more of each type of BB to the dish. Observe what happens when you do Steps 3a–c.
   a. Repeat Steps 1 and 2. Make a new drawing of the system and answer all the questions.

Use the same "shake frequency" you used in Step 2.

   b. Label your second drawing, "after adding more BBs."
   c. Include highlight comments that help you compare the following:
      - The speed of the BBs from Step 2 with Step 3
      - The frequency of collisions occurring from Step 2 with Step 3 (Are there more, fewer, or about the same?)
4. Now shake the dish with a higher frequency than before.

Don't shake at such a high frequency that you cannot see what is happening in the dish.

5. Record your observations from Step 4 so you can effectively compare all drawings and highlight comments.
6. Write a short caption under your last drawing from Step 5. This caption should summarize what you think is going on when shake frequency and number of BBs change.
7. Exchange captions in your team and read your teammate's summary.

Reflect and Connect

Work with your partner to answer the following questions in your science notebook.

1. What conditions did you change to increase collision frequency? Record evidence that you have to support your answer.
2. Were all BBs moving at the same speed even when the shake frequency was constant? Link evidence from your observations to your explanation.
3. Compare and contrast the motions of cars on a highway, BBs in a dish, and molecules. You may organize your comparisons in a paragraph, a table, or a Venn diagram.
4. Suppose that your dish represents a laboratory beaker and the BBs represent different types of atoms or molecules in the beaker that may react. Turn and talk with your partner. Discuss the following questions. Write your best answers in your science notebook. Be prepared to discuss your reasoning with the class.
   a. What would the addition of more BBs model?
   b. What would increasing the shake frequency model?
   c. What role do collisions play in thinking about atoms and molecules in a beaker?
5. Think about what you know about chemical reactions. With your partner, come up with at least 2 questions that you still have about chemical reactions. Focus your questions on conditions you have modeled in this activity.

EXPLORE

Variable Challenge

In *Dish It Up!*, you began to think about molecules, atoms, and their interactions. BBs helped you model how microscopic objects behave. Then you related BB behavior to the world of atoms and molecules. When atoms and molecules mix together, they collide much like the BBs you saw in your model. Sometimes when molecules collide, they react.

How do you know if two chemicals are reacting? You see a change—a chemical change. A chemical reaction results in new substances. Those substances have new chemical and physical properties compared with the original substances.

You see chemical changes, or chemical reactions, every day. Some reactions are slow, like metal rusting on a car. Iron in the car's body is reacting with moisture in the air. The new substance that forms is iron oxide. This is the orange-red rust that you see on the metal. Some reactions are very fast. When gasoline burns in the engine of your car, the gasoline (mostly octane C_8H_{18}) reacts with oxygen gas (O_2). New substances form. Those substances are part of the exhaust of your car and include carbon dioxide and water. This reaction forms new substances, and you know that a chemical reaction is taking place. This reaction is much faster than the iron rusting on your car.

In *Variable Challenge*, you will work as a team to design and conduct a scientific investigation. Your teacher will demonstrate a chemical reaction. Is the reaction fast or slow? How can you determine how long it takes the reaction to occur? Use the following question to focus your activity design: "What factors speed up or slow down chemical reactions?"

Materials

For each student

- 1 pair of safety goggles
- 1 pair of disposable laboratory gloves
- 1 laboratory apron

For each team of 3 or 4 students

- 1 microwell plate
- plastic pipets
- solutions of potassium iodide (KI), sodium thiosulfate ($Na_2S_2O_3 \cdot 5H_2O$), potassium bromate ($KBrO_3$), hydrochloric acid (HCl), and starch
- baking soda ($NaHCO_3$) for acid spills
- toothpicks
- cotton swabs
- 1 sheet of blank, white paper
- additional equipment based on what variable you choose to test

Cautions

Hydrochloric acid is hazardous to skin and eyes. Wash off spills with a lot of cool water. Neutralize spills on countertops with baking soda. Wear chemical splash goggles, disposable laboratory gloves, and a chemical-resistant apron.

Process and Procedure

1. Make careful observations of the teacher demonstration by following Steps 1a–c.
   a. Draw before-and-after sketches of the reaction.
   b. Write down all the reactants under the appropriate sketches.
   c. Write a caption under each sketch to record the actions your teacher completed.
2. With your team, decide how you would determine how fast this reaction occurred.
   a. Record your best plan in your science notebook.
   b. Share your plan in a class discussion.
   c. Modify your plan based on the best information from the discussion.
3. Meet with your team and read *Reactants, Products, and Indicators.*

READING

Reactants, Products, and Indicators

Chemical reactions occur all around us. Examples include a cake baking in the oven, gasoline burning in the engines of our cars, and even digesting the foods we eat. Complex chemical reactions occur constantly in every cell of our bodies. You just witnessed a complex chemical reaction as your teacher mixed several ingredients, or **reactants**, together to produce the change. Reactants are the starting ingredients for a chemical reaction. **Products** are the new things that are produced as a result of the chemical reaction.

Scientists can determine the rate at which the reaction occurs by measuring how quickly one of the reactants disappears or how quickly one of the products appears. One of the substances used in this reaction is starch. You may have tested for the presence of starch before by dropping iodine on bread or a potato. Iodine turns dark blue to black in the presence of starch. Starch is an **indicator** in this reaction. It forms a starch-iodine substance that is dark blue. Iodine is one of the products of this reaction. When you see the dark blue color, it signals the end of the reaction.

4. With your team, formulate a scientifically testable question by following Steps 4a–f.

The question must relate to the speed of the reaction (reaction rate) your teacher just demonstrated.

   a. Think about your question carefully. Are you sure it is scientifically testable?
   b. Share your question with another team.
   c. Ask for advice on how you might improve on your question. Can you make it clearer or easier to test?
   d. Revise your work if your team thinks the advice is good.

Remember from chapter 2 that this process is called think-share-advise-revise (TSAR).

   e. Switch roles with the other team and listen carefully to what it says.
   f. Share your final question with the class as your teacher directs.

5. Work with your team to make a list of important criteria for this scientific investigation.
6. Share your ideas in a class discussion and revise your list based on the ideas proposed by other teams.
7. Read the following information about the investigation you are about to design.

   Now it is time for you to design an investigation to test your question. For this investigation, every team will follow a basic protocol, no matter what question you decide to test. Every team will

   - demonstrate the reaction in a microwell plate,
   - keep the *total* number of drops of the reactants to 20 (you might have to add drops of distilled H_2O to bring the volume to 20 drops),
   - use only 2 drops of the starch indicator and 2 drops of the $Na_2S_2O_3$,
   - add the $KBrO_3$ last, and
   - stir the reaction with a toothpick immediately after the addition of $KBrO_3$.

8. Record the detailed procedure in your science notebook.

Your design should include all the important criteria you listed in the class discussion. Also, construct a data table that outlines the number of drops of each reactant you will use in each test.

9. Choose 1 science notebook from your team to share with other teams. Place this notebook and a blank sheet of paper on your desk.

All team members should have the complete plan recorded in their notebooks.

10. With your team, visit the tables of 2 different teams and read through their designs and detailed procedures.
    a. Note anything that is unclear, that needs to be changed, or that needs to be added or omitted.
    b. Record your suggestions on the blank sheet of paper next to the notebook.
    c. Place your team's initials on the paper with your suggestions so that the team can come to you for clarification if needed.
    d. Rotate around the room until you have reviewed at least 2 plans.
    e. Your teacher will also review your plan and give you feedback.
11. Work with your team to improve the design and procedures for your investigation by completing Steps 11a–c.
    a. Carefully review the comments you received on your design and procedures.
    b. Clarify any misunderstandings with your teacher or with the other teams.
    c. Adjust your plan based on the feedback you received.

You must analyze the feedback and decide what comments to address and what comments to ignore.

    d. Rewrite your procedure if necessary and be sure to have your teacher approve your final procedure.
    e. Keep the paper that includes your peer review. Your teacher will want to look at the reviews to help evaluate your work.
12. Before you begin your investigation, reread the question you are attempting to answer. Based on what you already know, what do you think the results of your investigation will show? Record your prediction as your hypothesis in your science notebook.
13. Conduct your investigation according to your procedure.

Each member of the team is responsible for recording all the data.

14. When you finish your investigation, analyze your data and discuss them with your teammates. You may want to graph your data to see trends and patterns. What patterns do you see in your data?

15. Investigate the *Student Resource CD* (*SRCD*) animation *Kinetics2/Iodine Clock*. This activity lets you control variables to change reaction rates.

Reflect and Connect

Work as a team and use your experimental data to answer the following questions. Record any changes you make to your answers and the reasons for those changes.

1. Describe the variable you tested. Include in your answer how you controlled the other variables.
2. What can you infer from your results? How do your data support your inference?
3. How might you explain these results? Remember to base your explanation on evidence from your investigation. Use a diagram or sketch to help with your explanation. Think back to your experiences with the petri dish of BBs (figure 3.3). Use these experiences and your current understandings about collisions as you draw your sketches and write your explanation.
4. Scientists often repeat the experiments of other scientists. Are your instructions clear enough that another team could follow your procedure exactly? If someone else were going to follow your procedure and repeat your investigation, what changes would you suggest? Describe at least 2 changes you would suggest and why you would make these changes.
5. Everyone in the class needs to understand your results and explanations. Prepare to present your results, inferences, and explanations to the class.

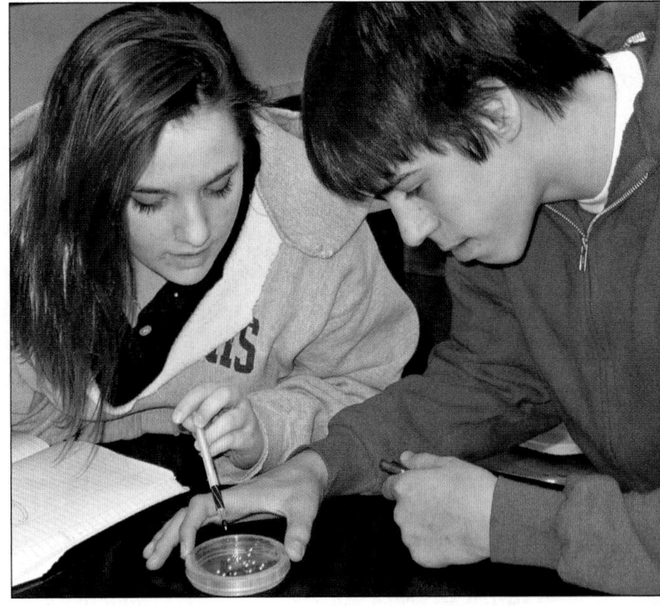

▲ **Figure 3.3 Students modeling collisions in chemical reactions.** Molecules must collide to react. How does changing the number of BBs model one of the variables you tested in this investigation? How does shaking the petri dish at a greater frequency model one of the variables you may have tested in this investigation?

Constructive Collisions

EXPLAIN

In *Variable Challenge*, you gathered evidence to determine what factors affect how fast chemical reactions occur. Why does adding drops of one reactant solution decrease the amount of time for the solution to turn blue? What happens at the atomic scale when temperature increases? Answers to these questions will help you predict how to speed up or slow down other important chemical reactions. Just imagine inventing a way to slow down rust on a highway bridge. Think of the benefit if you could speed up tumor destruction in cancer patients.

In this activity, *Constructive Collisions*, you and your team will investigate the underlying reasons why chemical reactions speed up or slow down. Those reasons involve something you already know.

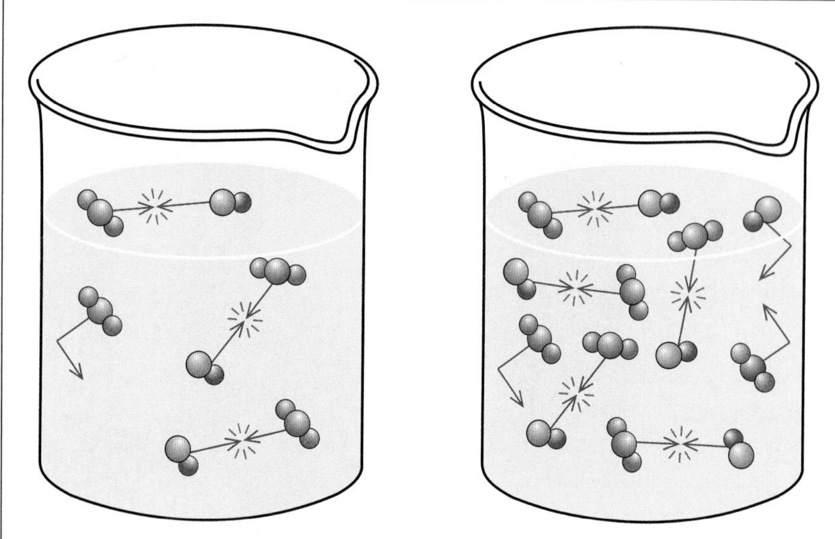

▲ **Figure 3.4 Concentrations of particles.** The beaker on the right has a higher concentration of particles in the mixture. How does an increased concentration affect the chances of collisions between particles? What does this do to reaction rate?

Particles must collide. And when they hit each other, the chances of a chemical reaction increase. You saw this when you added more BBs in *Dish It Up!* And you can see it in figure 3.4. The result: products appear in less time. But do all collisions result in the desired reaction? What are the key factors? Why do these factors speed up or slow down chemical reactions? Continue your reading in Part I of this activity to answer these questions.

Part I: Frequency Facts

To answer the questions posed in the introduction of this activity, think back to your study of macroscopic objects hitting each other. What affects a system of two tennis balls when they collide? What would happen to the chances of collision if you used three tennis balls? What would happen to a system of many BBs?

Naturally, you answer these questions by using knowledge you already have. For example, three tennis balls swinging instead of two increases the frequency of collisions. The more often collisions occur, the greater chance of a chemical reaction. Think about walking from your science class to your English class through the hallway of your school. When do you have more frequent collisions with students, during passing period or during class when the hallway is almost empty?

In Part I, you and your team will investigate how scientists change the collision frequency involved in a system of atoms or molecules. Focus your activity with this question: "How does collision frequency in macroscopic systems (tennis balls, BBs, cars in busy intersections) compare with collision frequency in microscopic systems (atoms and molecules)?"

Materials

For each team of 3 students

3 pairs of safety goggles

1 small beaker

access to a balance

small, identical items (such as paper clips, corks, pennies, sticky notes, staples) one of the following:

- aluminum foil
- sulfur
- iron filings
- copper shot
- lead shot
- water

1 wax pencil for labeling the beaker

1 pair disposable laboratory gloves

1 calculator

markers or chalk

Cautions

Wear safety goggles when working with the items. Wear disposable laboratory gloves when handling lead shot and copper BBs.

Process and Procedure

1. Read *Mole Patrol I* to learn how chemists quantify the number of particles in a solution.
2. To understand the connection between counting objects you can see and objects that are too small to see, follow Steps 2a–g.

You are making a conceptual connection between counting macroscopic objects and counting microscopic objects.

   a. Your teacher has selected several types of small, identical items. Meet with your team and decide which of these items you will use.
   b. Count out 12 of 1 item and find their total mass.
   c. Record your item name, how many you have of the item, and the total mass on the class chart that your teacher has supplied.
   d. Participate in a class discussion of the importance of this activity. As you participate and listen, take notes in your science notebook. To organize your notes, draw a line vertically down the center of the paper. Use the left side to record important relationships that you learn about in the class discussion, as well as any calculations your teacher writes on the board. You will add notes to the right side of the paper during the next activity. You can also use the left- and right-facing pages for your notes.
   e. Have 1 person from your team get the chemical substance that your teacher has assigned to your team. Place the assigned mass of that substance into a small beaker. Label your beaker with its contents and the mass.

READING

Mole Patrol I

You can increase the frequency of collisions by increasing the number of particles in a given space. Chemists call this increase an increase in **concentration**. For example, when you added more of one reactant to the reaction in *Variable Challenge*, you were increasing the concentration of that reactant. The number of particles in solution increased. But how do chemists know exactly how many particles they add to the system of particles?

Chemists know the number of particles by counting them. But counting atomic-sized particles isn't easy. So chemists count atomic-sized particles much like you count numerous small, yet visible, items.

For example, suppose you had the task of getting two dozen doughnuts from the doughnut shop; you would know that there would be 24 doughnuts. You can also count by using the mass. Consider 3,000 grams (g) of pennies. The average mass of one penny is 3 g. About how many pennies would you have? You could "count" the pennies by knowing the mass. You would know that you had about 1,000 pennies and you didn't have to count them all. The same is true for the number of particles in chemical substances.

Chemists use the **mole** (abbreviated *mol*) as a unit that refers to an amount of a substance. A mole contains 6.02×10^{23} particles. This is known as Avogadro's number and is named after Amedeo Avogadro. Chemists use the mole to count particles. If you have a mole of copper atoms, you know that you have 6.02×10^{23} atoms of copper. Chemists know that this amount of copper atoms would have a mass of 63.55 g. Where did this number come from? The average atomic mass of any element (found on the periodic table) *in grams* is known as the **molar mass** of that element. Molar mass is equal to the amount of mass in grams in 1 mol of that element.

If you increase the number of moles in a solution, you increase the concentration and the frequency of collisions. Chemists use the term **molarity** as one way to communicate the concentration of a substance. Molarity has the units of moles per liter (mol/L) and is abbreviated M.

SCILINKS NSTA
Topic: molarity
Go to: www.scilinks.org
Code: 2Inquiry124

Remember, you must consider the mass of the beaker. The mass assigned to you is only the mass of the substance that your teacher has provided.

Don't forget to think about the connection between the substance you can see and the many millions of invisible particles that constitute the substance.

f. Record the name of your substance and the mass of that substance on the class chart that your teacher has provided. Place the beaker and its contents on a desk at the front of the room.

g. Participate in another class discussion that your teacher leads. Take notes in your science notebook on the right side of the page of your notebook. Record important relationships and calculations as you did before.

3. Read *Mole Patrol II* to find out ways to convert from moles to the number of particles and to units of concentration.

READING

Mole Patrol II

Chemists use the mole concept to do some very important conversions in chemistry. Suppose you had 1.75 mol of water. How many grams of water would that be? You know from the periodic table that 1 mol of water has a mass of 18.02 g. Now start the calculation. Always start the conversion with what you are given in the problem; in this case, it is 1.75 mol of water. Then use the conversion factor: 18.02 g H_2O = 1 mol H_2O. The conversion is set up this way

$$1.75\ \cancel{\text{mol H}_2\text{O}} \times \left(\frac{18.02\ \text{g H}_2\text{O}}{1\ \cancel{\text{mol H}_2\text{O}}}\right) = 31.5\ \text{g H}_2\text{O}$$

What would the calculation look like if you measured 6.75 g of water and you wanted to know how many moles of water you had? The conversion would look like this

$$6.75\ \cancel{\text{g H}_2\text{O}} \times \left(\frac{1\ \text{mol H}_2\text{O}}{18.02\ \cancel{\text{g H}_2\text{O}}}\right) = 0.375\ \text{mol H}_2\text{O}$$

Could you find out how many molecules are in 0.375 mol of water? What information do you need? For this conversion, you need to use the number of particles in a mole, 6.02×10^{23}. The conversion would look like this

$$0.375\ \cancel{\text{mol H}_2\text{O}} \times \left(\frac{6.02 \times 10^{23}\ \text{molecules}}{1\ \cancel{\text{mol H}_2\text{O}}}\right) = 2.26 \times 10^{23}\ \text{molecules}$$

Supposed you dissolved 20 g of sodium hydroxide, NaOH, in water to make 1 liter (L) of solution. What is the molarity of the solution? (Remember, molarity has the units mol/L.) The conversion would look like this

$$20\ \cancel{\text{g NaOH}} \times \left(\frac{1\ \text{mol}}{40\ \cancel{\text{g NaOH}}}\right) \times \left(\frac{}{1\text{L}}\right) = 0.5\ \text{mol/L or } 0.5\ \text{M}$$

Stop & THINK

PART I

Practice some of these conversions on your own by working through the following questions. Be certain to check your answers and learn from any mistakes.

1. Why does a mole of lead have a higher mass than a mole of aluminum if both have the same number of atoms?
2. Work out the following conversions. Show all your work and cancellation of units.
   a. 7.36 g of aluminum = ______________ mol of aluminum.
   b. 2.55 mol of calcium contain ______________ atoms of calcium.
   c. 1.77 mol of NaCl would have the mass of ________ g.
   d. If you measured 25.6 g of sulfur, how many atoms of sulfur would you have?
   e. How many grams of sodium chloride are in 0.50 L of 1.5 M NaCl?
3. You use 2 solutions of hydrochloric acid, HCl, to dissolve zinc metal, Zn. Solution A is 1.0 M, and solution B is 2.0 M. Which solution demonstrates the greatest frequency of collisions between HCl and Zn? Explain your answer. Use molecular-level sketches in your explanation.

4. Read *Ratios in Reactions* to discover another important way chemists use moles to account for the number of particles involved in chemical reactions.

READING

Ratios in Reactions

What does the mole have to do with concentrations and chemical reactions? Scientists who construct the living space in the space shuttle certainly must understand the mole. They must remove the buildup of carbon dioxide (CO_2) in the atmosphere of the shuttle. These NASA scientists must make careful predictions about the amount of CO_2 to remove. They base their predictions on the amount each astronaut produces during the time he or she is in the shuttle. These scientists understand the mole and use that understanding to determine the amount of the absorber (lithium hydroxide, LiOH) to include on the space shuttle to absorb the CO_2 produced by the astronauts (see figure 3.5).

Look at the following chemical equation, which represents the chemical reaction just described. Remember that reactants are on the left and products are on the right of the arrow.

$$CO_{2(g)} + 2LiOH_{(s)} \rightarrow Li_2CO_{3(s)} + H_2O_{(l)}$$

reactants products

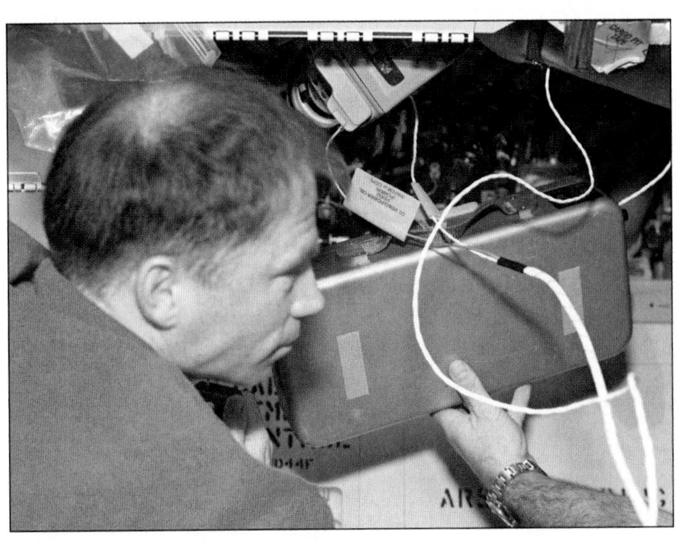

▲ **Figure 3.5 Space shuttle in-flight maintenance.** The crew aboard a 1998 mission of the space shuttle *Columbia* is installing backup lithium hydroxide canisters on the Regenerative Carbon Dioxide Removal System.

A *balanced* chemical equation gives scientists clues to the amounts of reactants that are needed for the reaction to take place. This reaction indicates that *1 mol* of carbon dioxide (CO_2) gas reacts with *2 mol* of solid lithium hydroxide (LiOH) to produce *1 mol* of solid lithium carbonate (Li_2CO_3) and *1 mol* of liquid water (H_2O). The number 2 in front of the reactant, lithium hydroxide (LiOH), is called a coefficient. It works much like coefficients in math equations—it affects everything that it is with. Is there a coefficient in front of CO_2? (One is understood but it is not written.)

The molar ratios of the particles in this reaction are $1CO_2{:}2LiOH{:}1Li_2CO_3{:}1H_2O$. As scientists prepare for a space shuttle mission, they know that for every 1 mol of carbon dioxide (6.02×10^{23} CO_2 particles) produced by the astronauts, they must provide 2 mol of lithium hydroxide (12.04×10^{23} LiOH units). Knowing these mole ratios is essential to the safety of the astronauts aboard spacecrafts.

This equation is balanced with coefficients. Coefficients show that the same number and kinds of atoms are present at the beginning of the reaction (in the reactants) as at the end of the reaction (in the products). This supports the **law of conservation of matter**, which states that matter is conserved in ordinary chemical and physical changes. Count the atoms in this reaction to verify that it supports this law. Set up a T-table as shown in figure 3.6 to check if this equation is balanced.

$$CO_{2(g)} + 2LiOH_{(s)} \rightarrow Li_2CO_{3(s)} + H_2O_{(l)}$$

If you must balance an equation, only add coefficients to balance it. Never change the subscripts to balance a chemical equation. Look at the reaction of hydrogen (H_2) and oxygen (O_2) to produce water:

$$H_{2(g)} + O_{2(g)} \rightarrow 2H_2O_{(l)}$$

Count the atoms to decide whether the equation is balanced. You should see that it is not balanced. Write down the equation in your science notebook and try to balance it on your own before you continue.

It would be easy to balance the equation by just adding a subscript of 2 at the end of H_2O. Did you try that? If you did, you just turned water (H_2O) into hydrogen peroxide (H_2O_2)! You cannot balance a chemical equation by changing subscripts because that changes the substance. Only use coefficients to balance chemical equations. The balanced chemical equation should look like this:

$$2H_{2(g)} + O_{2(g)} \rightarrow 2H_2O_{(l)}$$

The ratio of the reactants and products in this reaction is 2 mol of H_2 to 1 mol of O_2 to 2 mol of H_2O.

The balanced chemical reaction does not tell you anything about the rate at which the reaction will occur. It does, however, give you information about the relative amounts of reactants needed and the amounts of products formed in the reaction.

SCiLINKS® NSTA
Topic: conservation of matter
Go to: www.scilinks.org
Code: 2Inquiry128

Atoms in reactants	Atoms in products
1C	1C
2Li	2Li
2H	2H
4O	4O
2 O in CO_2 + 2 O in the 2LiOH (remember, the coefficient affects all elements in the compound, LiOH)	3 O in Li_2CO_3 + 1 O in H_2O

▲ **Figure 3.6 Balancing chemical equations.** Use this process as you balance chemical equations to keep track of atoms in the reaction.

Stop & THINK

PART I continued

4. Explain why increasing the concentration of the reactants speeds up a chemical reaction. Use the concept of collisions of particles in your answer.
5. Relate a balanced chemical reaction to the law of conservation of matter. Balance this equation, which shows the combustion of methane (CH_4), and use it in your answer

$$CH_4 + O_2 \rightarrow CO_2 + H_2O$$

6 Use your knowledge of the mole to answer Questions 6a–b.

a. What is the molar mass of sodium?

b. If you have 2.3 mol of sodium, how many grams of sodium do you have?

7 Molar ratios can be used to determine quantities in chemical reactions. Use these ratios to answer Questions 7a–d.

a. What is the molar ratio of carbon dioxide to water in the reaction in Question 5?

b. If you began the reaction with 3 mol of CH_4, how many moles of O_2 would you need for it to react completely with the CH_4?

c. How many moles of CO_2 and H_2O would be produced?

d. If 25.7 g of water were produced, how many moles of methane were used?

Part II: Energize Those Reactions

Materials

For each student

1 pair of safety goggles

1 resealable plastic bag of substance A, provided by your teacher

1 container of substance B, provided by your teacher

1 resealable plastic bag of substance C, provided by your teacher

1 container of substance D, provided by your teacher

Cautions

You must wear safety goggles during this activity. Do not at any time touch the chemicals.

In Part I, you found out how chemists keep track of the number of particles available for a chemical reaction. You discovered that more moles of reactant particles mean a greater frequency of collision and an increased chance for chemical reaction. But is increased collision frequency the only factor affecting reaction rate? What about how hard particles hit—the energy of collision? After all, a slight bump by a fellow student in the hallway produces a very different reaction than a running crash.

In Part II, you will investigate the role of energy in chemical reactions. From this core understanding, you will learn in the next activity how energy-producing and energy-consuming reactions affect the rate of chemical reactions.

Process and Procedure

1. Read about the combustion of gasoline in *It Only Takes a Spark* to explore the aspects of energy important to chemical reactions.

READING

It Only Takes a Spark

Gasoline, primarily the hydrocarbon octane (C_8H_{18}), reacts with oxygen gas to produce carbon dioxide and water according to the balanced chemical equation

$$2C_8H_{18} + 25O_2 \rightarrow 16CO_2 + 18H_2O + \text{heat}$$

This reaction occurs in the engine of your car. However, you know that you can have a can of gasoline sitting outside in the air (which contains oxygen gas) and the reaction does not take place, at least not fast enough for you to see the effects. The gasoline does not explode even though there is a high concentration of gasoline and sufficient oxygen present in the air. It does not burn even though octane and oxygen particles are colliding all the time.

What would make this gasoline react quickly? Of course, you must add energy in the form of a spark or fire from a match for it to react. But why? What are the underlying reasons why the relatively small amount of energy in a spark can produce huge amounts of energy in a gasoline explosion?

2. Develop and discuss your ideas about the questions posed at the end of the reading *It Only Takes a Spark*. Be ready to contribute your answers to a class discussion.

Keep a record of your discussion in your science notebook.

3. Compare and contrast your class discussion notes from Step 2 with the following reading, *Boulder Analogy*.

READING

Boulder Analogy

Energy in chemical reactions, such as burning gasoline, is a lot like pushing a boulder up a hill (see figure 3.7). Once you get the boulder up the hill, the boulder will roll down the hill spontaneously. This is similar to the way chemical reactions take place. Once a molecular collision results in particles with enough energy, the reaction continues on its own.

When the energy into a system is less than the energy out of a system ($E_{in} < E_{out}$), the reaction releases energy to the environment ($E_{in} - E_{out} =$ energy released). Chemists call the net energy associated with a chemical reaction **enthalpy**. Its symbol is ΔH. For a reaction that releases energy to the outside environment, enthalpy is negative ($-\Delta H$). The result you measure directly from $-\Delta H$ is a temperature increase of the surroundings. Reactions with $-\Delta H$ are called **exothermic** reactions. Chemists represent the energy relationships in a heat-producing reaction in an enthalpy diagram such as figure 3.8.

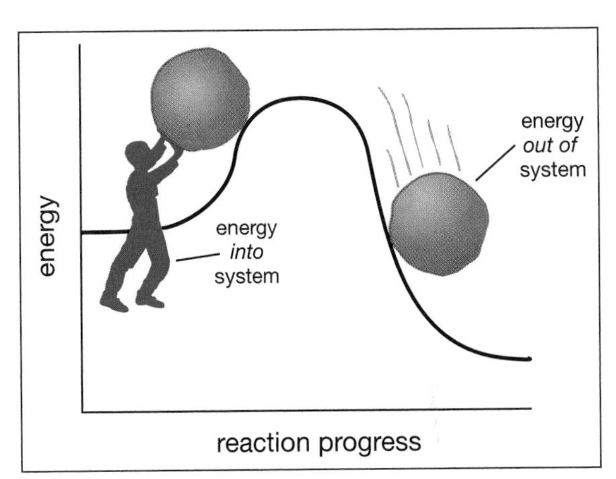

▲ **Figure 3.7 Energy input uphill, energy output downhill.** Why does it take energy input to push a boulder uphill? How would you measure the energy out of the system?

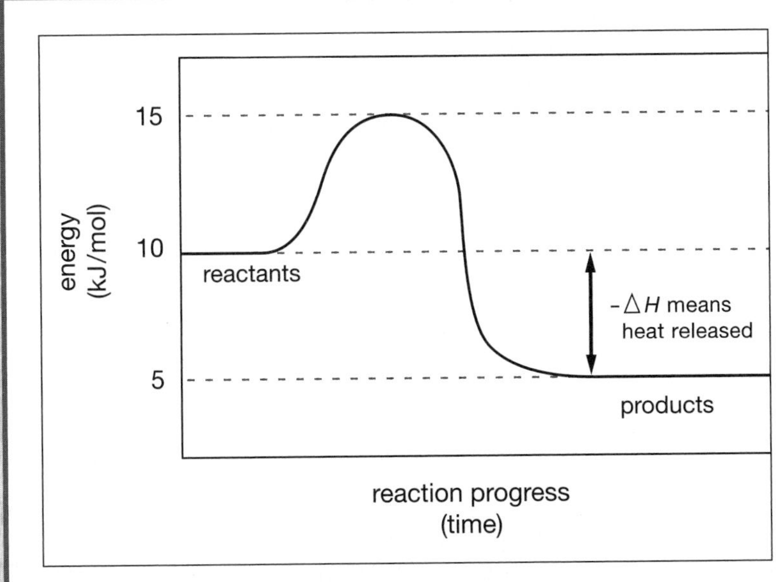

◀ **Figure 3.8 Enthalpy diagram for an exothermic reaction.** Enthalpy diagrams show energy differences between reactants and products. Always subtract the energy of the products from the energy of the reactants. What is always the algebraic sign of ΔH for exothermic reactions?

4. To feel the energy of a chemical reaction safely, do Steps 4a–g.
   a. Draw a sketch of the substances you are using in this activity. Record the color and state of the substances. Touch their containers to see if the substances feel hot, cold, or about room temperature. Label your sketches with these observations.
   b. Continue to make observations by following Steps i–v.
      i. Carefully open the plastic bag containing substance A.
      ii. Pour substance B into the bag.
      iii. Immediately close the bag and mix the contents by kneading the bag.
      iv. If necessary, open the bag to release the gas produced.
      v. Record all your observations of the bag and its contents in your science notebook.
   c. Repeat the instructions in Step 4b, only this time use substances C and D.
   d. Meet with a classmate and share your observations. Listen as your classmate shares his or her observations.
   e. If you and your classmate disagree on any observations, or you discover that you missed an important observation, be prepared to share this with the class in a discussion.
   f. Listen as your teacher leads a class discussion of these reactions. Share your ideas about the reactions and your observations with the class.
   g. Work with your team to develop an enthalpy diagram for reactions that feel cool. Reactions that cool the outside environment are called **endothermic** reactions.

Label your enthalpy diagram with the following key words: *reactants*, *products*, and $+\Delta H$. Remember that the positive sign means the heat content of the products is greater than the heat content of the reactants.

5. Read *The Ins and Outs of Heat* to understand the reasons at the atomic level for the heat involved in chemical reactions.

READING

The Ins and Outs of Heat

Burning gasoline produces great amounts of heat. At the atomic level, where does that heat come from? It comes from the chemical reaction. Specifically, the energy comes from the energy associated with breaking and forming chemical bonds.

Remember from Level 1 of this program that chemical bonds can be modeled as tiny springs, holding atoms in molecules together. At different temperatures, the springs make atoms in the molecule vibrate back and forth with different frequencies. Different kinds of atoms are bonded together with springs of different strength.

What must happen to the bonds of reactant molecules to result in product molecules? Indeed, reactant molecule bonds must break before product molecule bonds can form. For bonds to break, the springs must be stretched apart. As with any spring, this requires energy input. This is similar to the energy input required to push a boulder up a hill.

What happens when product molecules form new bonds? This would be like a spring contracting. Energy is released to the environment. The exact amount of energy depends on the spring strength and number of bonds involved. When more energy is released by bonds forming than is required to break bonds, the reaction produces heat and warms the outside environment. You feel the heat and measure a temperature increase.

All chemical reactions involve breaking reactant particle bonds and forming product molecule bonds. The net energy result can be either positive or negative. This results in the outside environment either cooling or heating. Chemists often represent the relationship between bond energy and net energy by

$$\Delta H = \Sigma(\text{bonds broken}) - \Sigma(\text{bonds formed}).$$

In sentence form, this expression reads: "The change in enthalpy (ΔH) equals the sum of all the energy of bonds broken minus the sum of all the energy of the bonds formed."

The Σ symbol (capital of the Greek symbol sigma) means "to find the sum of." For example, $\Sigma(3 + 6)$ equals 9.

Topic: enthalpy
Go to: www.scilinks.org
Code: 2Inquiry133

Stop & THINK

PART II

Read each question carefully before you answer it in your science notebook. Then check your answer and make corrections.

1. Consider the reaction

$$H_{2(g)} + Cl_{2(g)} \rightarrow 2HCl_{(g)}.$$

a. This reaction requires 671 kJ of energy to break all the reactant bonds, and 854 kJ of energy are released when all the product molecules form. Use this information to determine if the reaction warms or cools the outside environment. Show all your work.

Remember, kJ stands for kilojoules, or 1,000 joules of energy.

b. Sketch an enthalpy diagram for this reaction. Clearly indicate the relative energy content of reactants, products, and the ΔH.

STOP & THINK, PART II, continued

2 Many chemical reactions cool the outside environment. Remember, these reactions are called endothermic reactions. Consider the generic endothermic reaction, heat + A + B = C + D and answer Questions 2a–b.

a. What does the enthalpy diagram look like for this reaction? Sketch it in your science notebook.

b. Label your enthalpy diagram with ΔH along with its correct algebraic sign and the relative energy of reactants and products.

3 Label the following processes as endothermic or exothermic.

a. Chemical bonds are broken.
b. New chemical bonds are made.
c. Heat is absorbed.
d. The reaction container feels cold.
e. Heat is released.
f. ΔH is negative.
g. Energy of the products is greater than the energy of the reactants.

4 There are many practical uses for endothermic and exothermic reactions. Name 1 practical application for each of these types of chemical reactions.

Part III: Economize and Catalyze

Materials

none

Process and Procedure

1. Select an effective literacy strategy and then read *Catalysts Change Reaction Rates.*
2. Apply what you understand from the reading by answering Questions 2a–e in your science notebook.
   a. What is the approximate activation energy in kilojoules per mole of the uncatalyzed reaction in figure 3.9?
   b. From reading the scale in figure 3.9, what is the activation energy of the catalyzed reaction?
   c. Look at the plot in figure 3.9. What effect does adding a catalyst have on the enthalpy of reaction?
   d. How would adding a catalyst speed up a chemical reaction? Use your knowledge of collision frequency to form your answer.

READING

Catalysts Change Reaction Rates

You know that for a chemical reaction to take place, bonds must be broken and new bonds must form. The energy needed to break the bonds in the reactant is the **activation energy**, E_a, of the reaction. Look at the energy plot in figure 3.8. The hill formed by the solid line is the activation energy in the enthalpy diagram.

There are ways to decrease the height of the energy hill, E_a, without changing the chemical reaction. One way involves adding a substance called a **catalyst**. The dashed line in figure 3.9 represents a reaction with a catalyst. What does adding a catalyst do to the reaction rate?

You see that a catalyst will speed up a chemical reaction by lowering the activation energy. That's because the energy of activation is about 3 kilojoules per mole (kJ/mol) or 2 kJ/mol less than the uncatalyzed reaction. You might think of it this way:

> Suppose you are participating in track at your school. Your event is the high jump. You may be able to clear the bar set to over 1.75 meters (m, or 5 feet, 9 inches), but only with a great deal of energy. However, if they lower the bar to 1 m (about 3 ft), you will be able to jump over the bar with much less energy.

Catalysts that occur in living systems are called **enzymes**. You have witnessed the effects of the enzyme catalase in your body if you have ever poured hydrogen peroxide in a cut. As the hydrogen peroxide interacts with the enzyme in your body, the decomposition of H_2O_2 occurs very rapidly. How do you know that the hydrogen peroxide is decomposing rapidly? You see the formation of oxygen gas bubbles.

Finally, one reason catalysts are so valuable in industry and life is that they are not used up in a chemical reaction. That is, you can add a catalyst and have the reaction speed up without having to add more and more catalyst.

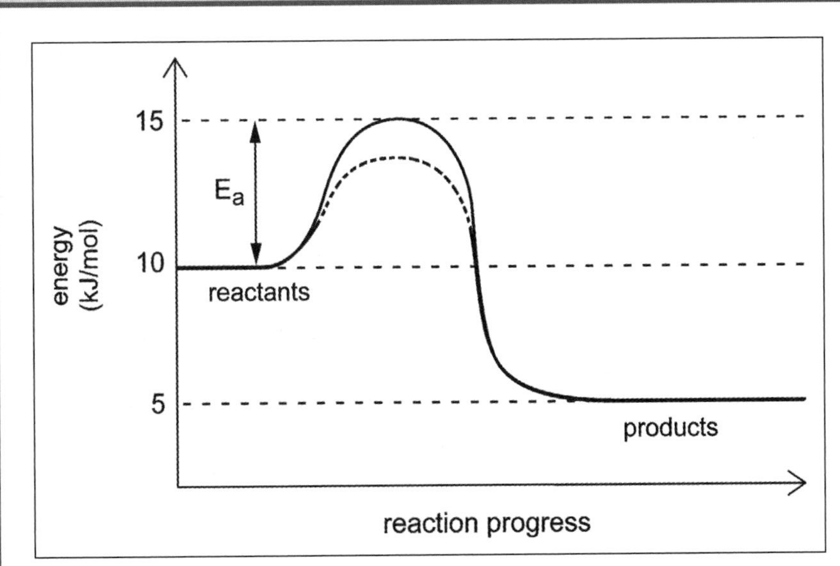

▲ **Figure 3.9 Catalyzed and uncatalyzed reactions.** In which reaction is the energy of activation lower? What effect does this have on the rate of reaction? What evidence would you collect to support your answer?

Topic: catalyst
Go to: www.scilinks.org
Code: 2Inquiry135

e. Collision frequency and energy are not the only factors affecting the rate of a chemical reaction. Read *FYI—Molecular Orientation* to find out more.

Reflect and Connect

Answer the following questions on your own in your science notebook. Then check your answers with several classmates.

1. Copy the table in figure 3.10 into your science notebook. Complete the table by drawing a labeled sketch in the middle column for each of the ways listed that can change the rate of a chemical reaction. You may want to draw a before-and-after sketch to make your point. Your sketch can be a picture or a graph, but it must represent your best understanding. Next, complete the last column with a caption for your sketch or graph and your understanding of the reasons why each of these ways changes the rate of a chemical reaction. Be sure to include *how* the rate changes.
2. There is always an expiration date on a bottle of hydrogen peroxide (H_2O_2). Suppose you just got a paper cut on your finger and you are looking through your medicine cabinet and find an old bottle of H_2O_2. The H_2O_2 expired at least 2 years ago, but you decide to use it on the paper cut anyway. Are you in danger since the hydrogen peroxide has gone "bad"? What would you expect to see as you poured the expired H_2O_2 on your cut? Explain your ideas. Include a balanced equation in your explanation.
3. Catalytic converters on cars use the metals rhodium and platinum as catalysts to convert potentially dangerous exhaust gases to carbon dioxide, nitrogen, and water. Why don't cars need to have the rhodium and platinum replaced after they are used?

Ways to change the rate of a chemical reaction	Sketch or graph	Caption
Increase concentration		
Decrease concentration		
Add a catalyst		

▲ **Figure 3.10 Answer table.** Set up this table in your science notebook. Leave plenty of room for pictures and sketches. To make sure that you will have enough room, you may want to complete one row before you add the next row to your table.

Molecular Orientation

You have studied chemical reactions and their dependency on collisions. Not all collisions are effective in producing chemical reactions. That is because a minimum energy is required for the reaction to occur. However, experiments show that the observed reaction rate is much smaller than expected. What does this mean? Many collisions, even though they have the required energy, still do not produce a reaction. Why not?

Consider the following chemical reaction that shows the reaction of carbon monoxide (CO) with nitrogen dioxide (NO_2) to produce carbon dioxide (CO_2) and nitrogen monoxide (NO).

$$CO + NO_2 \rightarrow CO_2 + NO$$

We can represent the molecular chemical reaction as shown in the following:

$$CO + NO_2 \rightarrow CO_2 + NO$$

The atoms can be represented as shown in the following figure.

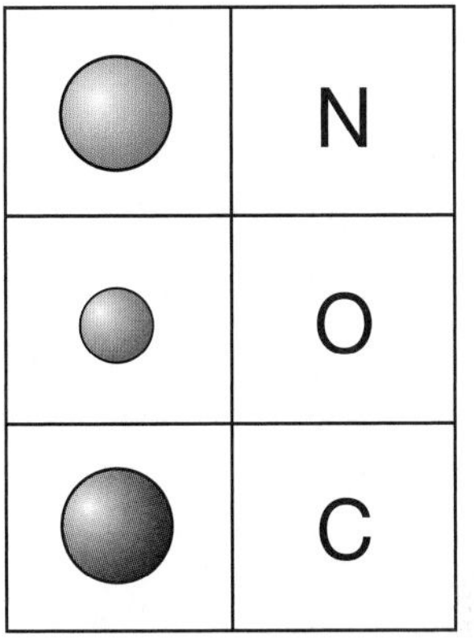

Atom representations. We will represent the atoms in this reaction with these shades.

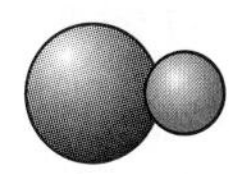

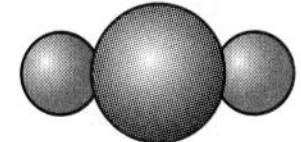
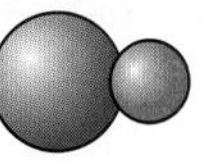

Molecular chemical reaction. Look at the molecular models of the reactants in this chemical reaction. What must happen for the reaction to occur?

If you examine the reaction closely, you can see that one oxygen atom must break apart from the NO_2 molecule and bond with the CO molecule. In the process of the reaction, an intermediate particle called the activated complex forms. Let's look at different possible collisions of the two reactant particles in detail. A successful chemical reaction would look like the following figure.

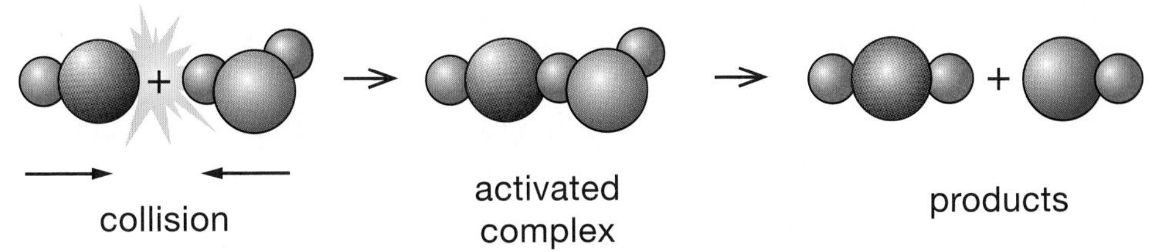

Successful chemical reaction. What makes this collision one that leads to a chemical reaction?

Molecular Orientation, continued

Other collisions do not result in a chemical reaction. Why not? One possibility that you have studied is that the collision occurs but the reaction does not take place. This may be because the collision does not occur with enough energy. Remember, the particles must collide with at least the activation energy for a reaction to occur. If the particles do not have enough energy, they simply rebound from each other, resulting in no chemical reaction, as seen in the illustration to the right.

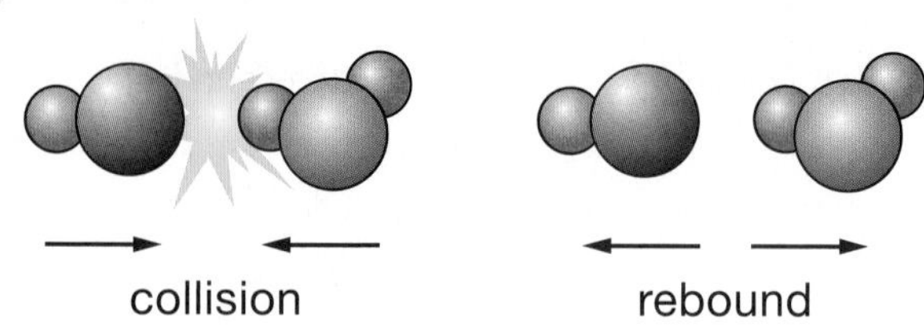

Unsuccessful collision. Everything is in place for this reaction to occur. Why doesn't the collision produce a chemical reaction?

Look at the collisions illustrated in the figure below. Neither of these collisions results in a reaction even though the particles collide with more than enough energy in both instances. Compare all the figures and see if you can see why these do not result in a chemical reaction. Can you tell?

Careful study of these examples indicates that in order for a successful collision to occur, the carbon atom in a CO molecule must collide with an oxygen atom in an NO_2 molecule at the moment of impact. Only in that way can a temporary bond between the carbon atom and an oxygen atom form. The collisions shown in the illustration above do not lead to a reaction because the molecules collide with the incorrect orientation. In other words, the carbon atom does not contact an oxygen atom at the moment of impact, and the molecules simply rebound.

Chemical reactions depend on collisions. However, you have seen that all collisions do not result in a successful collision—one that leads to a chemical reaction. These collisions must occur with the appropriate amount of energy and the reacting particles must collide in the proper orientation.

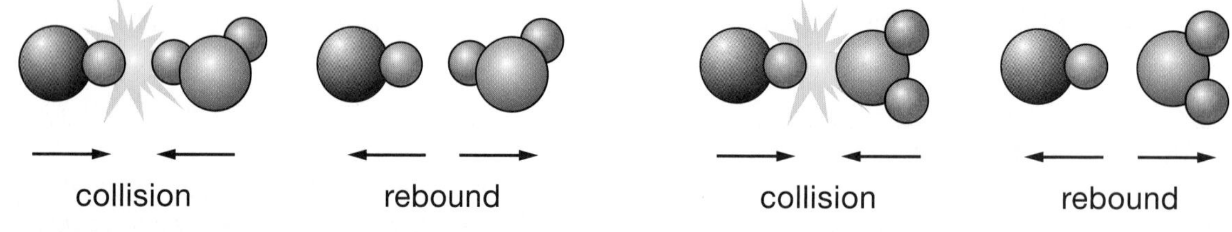

Two examples of unsuccessful collisions. Examine these illustrations carefully and compare them with the figure of a successful collision. Why don't these two collisions produce a chemical reaction even though the particles collide with enough energy?

4. Explain why it is best to store chemicals in dark, tightly sealed bottles and in an environment that has cool or moderate temperatures.
5. How many items are in a mole? List at least 3 words other than "mole" and "dozen" that represent a fixed number of items and use them in a sentence.

Careers in Catalysis Research

SIDEBAR

What would you do if you were a chemist? Mostly, you would try to understand and apply chemical reactions. You would think of better ways to make the chemicals we need for everyday life. And many times, you would apply your knowledge to destroying chemicals. Why would you want to get rid of some chemical substances?

One important reason involves producing safer, cleaner chemical processes. This area of research, sometimes called "green chemistry," seeks environmentally friendly methods of producing the chemical substances we need for everyday living. That's important because many useful products, such as pesticides, detergents, and diesel fuel, produce harmful effects in humans and in the environment.

Researchers from Carnegie Mellon University have developed a catalyst that speeds up several chemical reactions. The name of this catalyst is iron-tetraamido macrocyclic ligand (Fe-TAML). The type of chemical reaction Fe-TAML speeds up is called oxidation. Rusting of metals and burning of fuels are examples of oxidation reactions. In all oxidation reactions, oxidant molecules take electrons from neighboring compounds. Hydrogen peroxide (H_2O_2) and oxygen (O_2) are example oxidants. Oxidation can result in molecules tearing apart.

Why would chemists want to tear apart certain molecules? Some molecules, such as pesticides, do important jobs. But inevitably, they become part of what we eat or of important ecosystems such as estuaries. These molecules oxidize to harmless substances very slowly. Catalysts can speed up their destruction by speeding up the oxidation process. This is how Fe-TAML works.

▲ **Many chemists study how to make better catalysts.** What do chemists need to know about enthalpy, activation energy, and reaction rate in order to know when their product is better?

In the next figure, you can see an iron atom at the core of the Fe-TAML molecule in the representation of this catalyst. The iron atom is surrounded by proteinlike molecules. In concentrations as low as 10 parts per million, Fe-TAML speeds up the oxidation of environmentally harmful compounds. When mixed with an oxidant like hydrogen peroxide, Fe-TAML reduces chlorinated pesticides to relatively harmless molecules.

Fe-TAML increases the decomposition rate of other chemical reactions. It catalyzes the cleanup of paper-mill wastewater. The cleaner and clearer water is safer for fish and allows more light to reach underwater plants. Fe-TAML takes the sulfur out of diesel fuel in a two-step process. This saves time and money compared with the current multistep method. Sulfur in fuels fouls

Careers in Catalysis Research, continued

emission-control equipment and produces compounds that contribute to acid rain. Finally, research suggests that Fe-TAML will catalyze the destruction of anthrax spores. Anthrax is a deadly disease used in biological weapons. The spores are very resistant to oxidation in natural environments. But Fe-TAML breaks apart the spores and destroys the disease. Spraying a dilute solution of hydrogen peroxide and a catalyst on military troops could save many lives.

You can see how important knowledge of catalysts is to professional chemists. In high school, these researchers studied math and science each year. After an undergraduate science major, many practicing chemists attain graduate degrees. But learning does not end with formal schooling. These researchers read and study for the rest of their careers. The results speak for themselves. We have access to the chemical substances that make our modern lives possible.

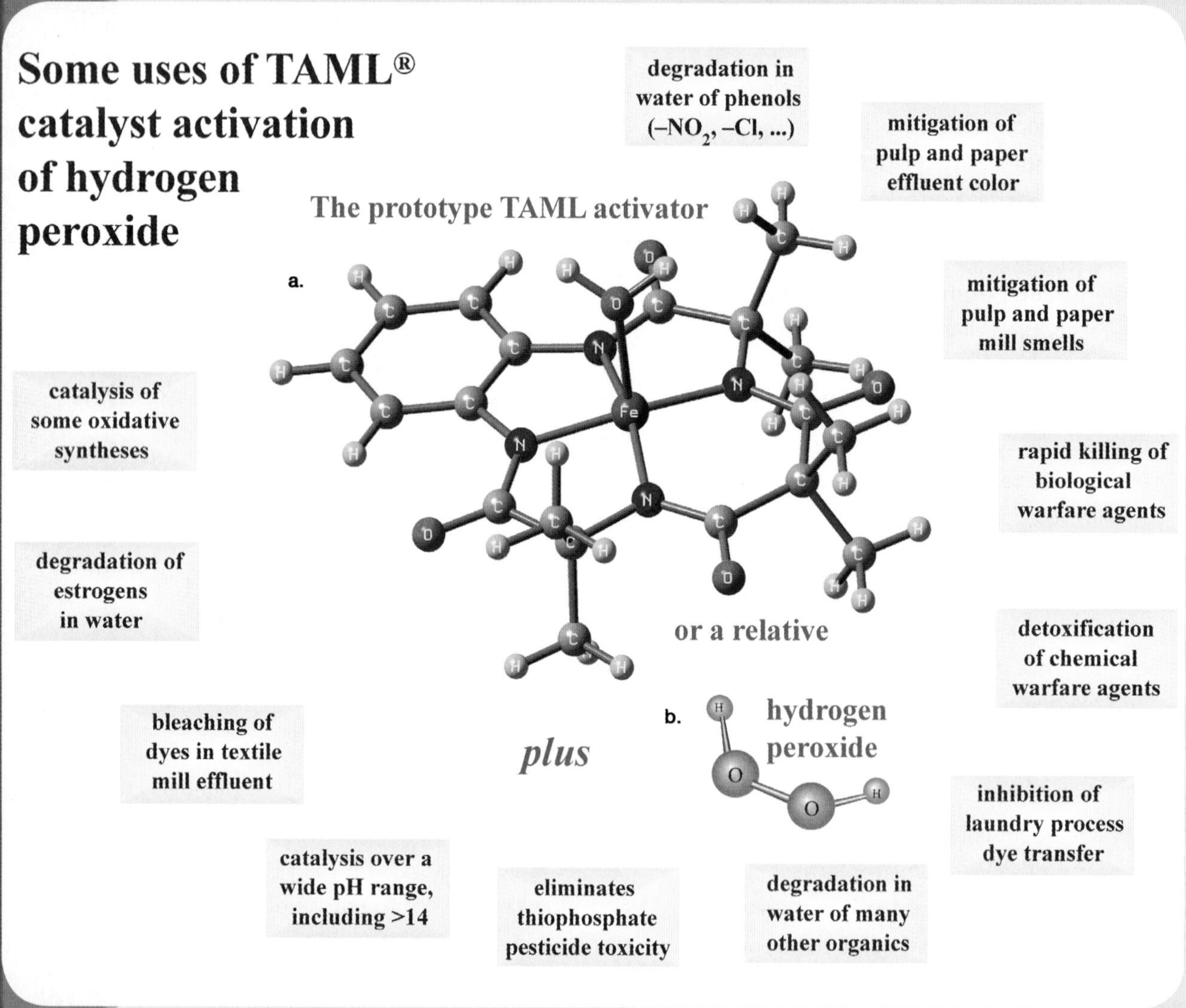

Some uses of TAML® catalyst activation of hydrogen peroxide

degradation in water of phenols (–NO_2, –Cl, ...)

mitigation of pulp and paper effluent color

The prototype TAML activator

a.

mitigation of pulp and paper mill smells

catalysis of some oxidative syntheses

rapid killing of biological warfare agents

degradation of estrogens in water

or a relative

detoxification of chemical warfare agents

b. hydrogen peroxide

bleaching of dyes in textile mill effluent

plus

inhibition of laundry process dye transfer

catalysis over a wide pH range, including >14

eliminates thiophosphate pesticide toxicity

degradation in water of many other organics

▲ **Fe-TAML and hydrogen peroxide molecule.** (a) Notice the iron (Fe) atom in the center of the Fe-TAML molecule. (b) The hydrogen peroxide molecule is actually much smaller than the Fe-TAML molecule.

Two-Way Reactions

ELABORATE

Chemical changes occur when particles collide with the proper amount of energy. You have looked at how different factors can change collision frequency and in turn change the rate of the chemical reaction. You are changing something in the chemical system to produce the results you want. But have you ever thought about the collisions that occur in the system *after* the products have been produced? Do collisions stop at this point? If the particles in the product are also colliding in the system, what might you predict would happen?

Two-Way Reactions helps you answer these questions. You and your team will apply what you already know about concentration and energy to an important class of chemical reactions—equilibrium reactions.

Part I: Reversible Reactions

Materials

For each team of 4 students

- 4 pairs of safety goggles
- 4 pairs of safety gloves
- 4 laboratory aprons
- 1 dropper pipet
- 1 small test tube or microwell plate
- 1 mL of 1.0 M chromate solution (K_2CrO_4)
- 3.0 M sulfuric acid (H_2SO_4)
- 6.0 M sodium hydroxide (NaOH)
- colored pencils or markers

Cautions

Wear safety goggles, gloves, and an apron at all times. Do not allow any solution to touch your skin. If any solution touches your skin, wash the affected area with large amounts of cool water and tell your teacher.

In Part I, you and your team will gather visible evidence, such as color change, for reversible reactions. Then you will think about what might be happening at the invisible level. That is, you will collect macroscopic evidence and infer what occurs at the microscopic level.

Process and Procedure

1. Test for color changes in a chromate ion (CrO_4^{2-}) solution by doing Steps 1a–f.
   a. Put on all safety gear and gather your materials.
   b. Place about 1 mL (15–20 drops) of 1.0 M chromate ion solution in a small test tube.

c. Sketch what you see in your science notebook, including color.

Label this sketch "beginning" and save room for a caption. Also list the chemicals you think are inside the test tube.

d. Add at least 2 but not more than 10 drops of 3.0 M H_2SO_4 slowly until you see an obvious color change.

Label this sketch "middle" and save room for a caption. Also list the chemicals you think are inside the test tube.

e. Compare the solution from Step 1d with the dichromate solution your teacher shows you. Add comments to your middle sketch based on what you see.

f. Add drops of 6.0 M NaOH until another color change occurs.

Label this sketch "end" and save room for a caption. Also list the chemicals you think are inside the test tube.

2. Read *Switch-A-Roo I* and look for ways to apply your knowledge about collisions to the color changes you saw in Step 1.
3. Use the reading *Switch-A-Roo I* to write captions under each sketch from Step 1. The captions tell the story of what is happening at the atomic level.
4. Use the TSAR strategy with a team member to make your captions the best they can be.
5. Represent the changes you observed in Step 1 in a sketch graph by following Steps 5a–d.

   a. Copy the sketch graph in figure 3.12 into your science notebook.

Make the graph large and leave plenty of room for highlight comments and a caption.

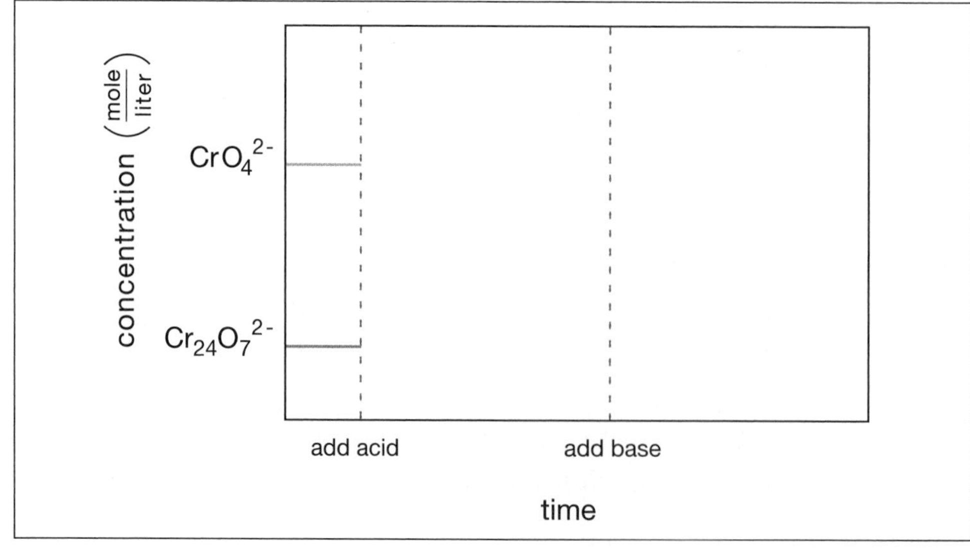

Figure 3.12 Concentration changes. Use these axes as a guide to chart changes in concentration of the chromate and dichromate ions over time. What do the flat regions mean? What happens to the lines when the equilibrium position shifts?

READING

Switch-A-Roo I

Changes are constantly occurring. Scientists try to determine whether these changes are permanent. Can you think of a change that is not permanent? Consider water freezing; is this physical change permanent? Liquid water can freeze and ice can melt. Liquid water can evaporate and then condense back into a liquid state. These processes are examples of reversible reactions as shown in figure 3.11. You should be glad these changes are not permanent; the fact that they are reversible is the focus of the water cycle on Earth. You will learn more about the water cycle in chapter 10, *The Water System*.

▲ **Figure 3.11 A reversible process.** How would you reverse this process? Are chemical reactions reversible?

What about chemical reactions? Can they be reversed? You saw evidence that this was possible in Step 1 of this activity. When particles collide with enough energy, products are formed. The particles of the products also collide and can reverse the original process to form more reactants. Theoretically, all chemical reactions are reversible given certain conditions.

Here is the reversible reaction from Step 1:

$$2CrO_4{}^{2-}{}_{(aq)} + 2H_3O^+{}_{(aq)} \rightleftarrows Cr_2O_7{}^{2-}{}_{(aq)} + 3H_2O_{(aq)}$$

yellow chromate	hydronium ion	orange dichromate	water
reactants		products	

You begin with a yellow solution that is not changing color. That's evidence for no change in concentration—no macroscopic change. Then you add some sulfuric acid (H_2SO_4), which is a source of the hydronium ion, H_3O^+. Hydronium ions are responsible for the acid characteristics of sulfuric acid. The concentration of H_3O^+ increases. What does this do to the collision frequency between the chromate and hydronium ions? What does this do to the rate of the forward reaction?

When reactant concentrations increase, the rate of the forward reaction increases for a moment, resulting in more product. You see the evidence. The chromate solution turns orange. This indicates the formation of dichromate ion ($Cr_2O_7{}^{2-}$), which is orange. The reaction remains the same color, indicating no change in concentration. Next, you add the base, sodium hydroxide (NaOH). The base neutralizes the acid, decreasing the hydronium ion concentration. There is a relative increase in product concentration. Product molecules collide more frequently and form reactant molecules. The rate of the reverse reaction increases. Within moments, the color stabilizes again, but to a different color.

b. Use colored pencils to chart the changes in concentration of the chromate and dichromate ions you observed in Steps 1a–f.

You do not need exact concentrations. Remember, flat lines mean no change in concentration. Curving or sloping lines mean the concentration is changing at that moment.

c. Write highlight comments for each section (beginning, middle, and end), and then write an overall caption.

d. Participate in a class discussion about this graph and make changes to your graph as needed.

Interact with the animation titled *Equilibrium* on your *SRCD* to see how reversible reactions affect concentrations of reactants and products.

Stop & THINK

PART I

Answer these questions in your science notebook. Compare your answers with those of a classmate before continuing.

1. What do the flat portions of the graph indicate about what is going on macroscopically? What is going on microscopically?
2. What do the curved or sloped portions of the graph indicate about what is going on macroscopically? What is going on microscopically?

6. Read *Switch-A-Roo II* to find out what your graph tells you about reversible reactions.

READING

Switch-A-Roo II

There is a high concentration of reactants and almost no products at the beginning of a chemical reaction. The forward reaction rate is high, and the reverse reaction rate is low. The concentration of both the reactants and the products changes; thus, the rates change. Eventually, the rate of the forward reaction equals the rate of the reverse reaction. The system is said to be at **equilibrium**. A reversible chemical reaction is in chemical equilibrium when the rate of its forward reaction equals the rate of its reverse reaction. A graph showing the rates of forward and reverse reactions at equilibrium would have two horizontal lines. These flat lines would not have to be at the same rate. They would have to indicate nonchanging reaction rates for the forward and reverse reactions.

It may appear that a chemical reaction has stopped when it reaches equilibrium. That's because the concentrations of the reactants and products are not changing. However, this is not the case. On the molecular level, particles are still moving, colliding, and interacting. The equilibrium of chemical reactions is a *dynamic* system. What does that mean? Consider two island cities connected by a bridge. Cars move continuously from one city to the other. At equilibrium, the rate of the cars going in one direction equals the rate of the cars going in the opposite direction. Cars are not stopped (static) but are constantly in motion (dynamic). The cars are also moving both ways at the same time. The number of cars in each city is not changing because the cars leaving each city are equal to the cars entering each city.

Does chemical equilibrium imply anything about the concentrations of the reactants and the products? The answer is yes ... and no. By definition, a chemical reaction reaches equilibrium when the rates of the forward and the reverse reactions are equal. At this point, the concentrations of the reactants and the products are constant. But this does not mean that the concentrations of the reactants and the products are equal, just that there is no *net* change in the concentrations. Think about the analogy of the two cities. The number of cars in each city is not changing, but that does not necessarily mean the number of cars in each city is the same.

Let's summarize conditions of chemical equilibrium:

- The reaction is reversible.
- The forward reaction moves at the same rate as the reverse reaction.
- The forward and reverse reactions happen at the same time.

Here's a specific example in the form of a gas phase chemical reaction

$$H_2O_{(g)} + CO_{(g)} \rightleftarrows H_{2(g)} + CO_{2(g)}$$

What happens when the same concentrations of $H_2O_{(g)}$ and $CO_{(g)}$ are mixed? Notice that the concentrations of the reactants and products change over time and eventually become constant, as shown in figure 3.13.

Since the mole ratio of the reactants is 1:1, the concentrations of both reactants change the same way. The same reasoning is true for the products. Rarely do chemical reactions reach equilibrium and the concentrations of the reactants and products become equal. It is more likely that the forward or the reverse reaction is favored. In a reaction in which the

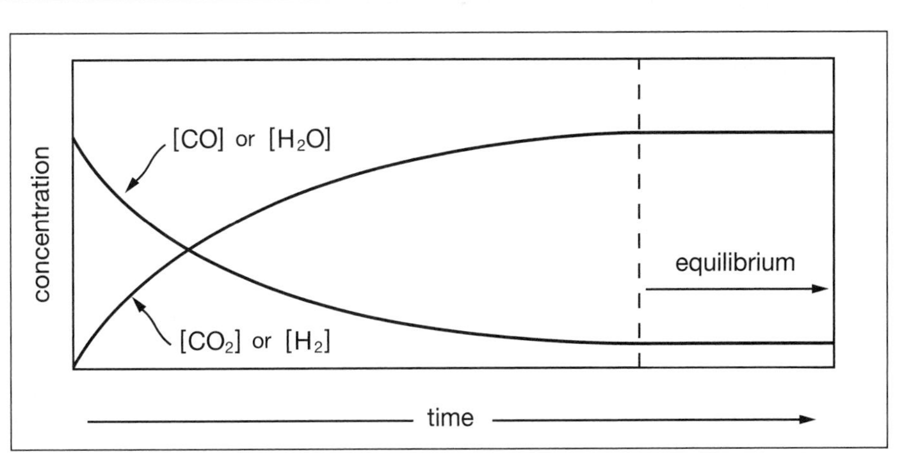

Figure 3.13 Concentration graph. The concentrations of both the reactants and the products in this reaction eventually become constant. But are the concentrations equal? What does this say about the equilibrium position of this reaction?

forward reaction is favored, the concentration of the products is higher at equilibrium than the concentration of the reactants.

Consider when the reverse reaction is favored. At equilibrium, there will be a higher concentration of reactants than products. Chemists identify these reactions with an **equilibrium position**. If the equilibrium position lies far to the right, it means the forward reaction is favored. What would it mean if the equilibrium position were to the left? The reverse reaction is favored and the reactants (on the left) would be in higher concentration than the products at equilibrium.

SCILINKS NSTA
Topic: chemical equilibrium
Go to: www.scilinks.org
Code: 2Inquiry146

Stop & THINK

PART I continued

3. Sometimes you may see a chemical equation written this way:

$$A + B \underset{\longleftarrow}{\rightharpoonup} C + D$$

Use your understanding of equilibrium position to explain why the equation is written this way.

4. Describe and explain how the concentrations of each of the reactants and products will change as the system *approaches* equilibrium for this reaction.

5. Describe and explain the concentrations of each reactant and product *at* equilibrium using the equation in Question 3.

7. Develop a general rule for predicting which side of an equilibrium expression is favored when you change concentrations.

Look at the animation *Le Châtelier's Principle* on the *SRCD* to help you understand the general principle.

8. Read *Stressed Out I* and compare your prediction rule with the one from the reading. Do systems at equilibrium stay at equilibrium? Use this as a focus question as you read *Stressed Out I*.

READING

Stressed Out I

You know how to recognize a chemical reaction at equilibrium. Now consider whether all reactions remain at equilibrium. Reactions will stay at equilibrium as long as conditions are constant. Changes to the system may disrupt the equilibrium. Look at an example of a system at equilibrium.

$$N_{2(g)} + 3H_{2(g)} \rightleftarrows 2NH_{3(g)}$$

This is a very important chemical reaction in the agricultural industry. It represents the production of ammonia (NH_3), which is used in large quantities as fertilizer. If you could observe a closed container at room temperature of sufficient concentrations of N_2 and H_2, you would observe no changes. If you could take a sample of gas in the system, you would see that there is no apparent change in the concentrations over time. Why? The reaction is either at equilibrium or the reaction rates are so slow that no changes can be detected. If this system is at equilibrium, then chemists must change the system to drive the reaction to the right. This change produces more NH_3. When we change conditions for a system at equilibrium, it places a stress on the system and upsets the equilibrium. The reaction will shift right to produce more products or shift left to produce more reactants, depending on the stress. The direction that the reaction will shift depends on the stress.

Look at a generic equation for a system at equilibrium

$$A + B \rightleftarrows C + D$$

One condition that can be changed easily is adding or removing either a reactant or a product. If the reaction is at equilibrium, and you increase the concentration of A, this is considered a stress on the system. The system will shift in one direction or the other to relieve the stress. This is known as **Le Châtelier's principle**. If more A is added to the reaction, which way, left or right, will use up this extra A? The forward reaction (shifting to the right) will consume A, so the reaction shifts to the right. Eventually, the system will reach equilibrium again. What if you added some of the product D? Which way would the reaction shift to relieve the stress? The reverse direction or to the left uses D, so the reaction will shift to the left.

What if C were *removed* from the system? You will use the chart in figure 3.14 to look at this situation more closely. The stress was the removal of C as indicated by the down arrow. Since it is the stress, you will put it in parentheses.

Stress	A	+ B	$\rightleftarrows$	C	+ D
Removal of C				(↓)	

▲ **Figure 3.14 Stress chart.** Use this chart to organize your thinking. The stress is indicated in parentheses.

Now decide which direction the reaction will shift to relieve the stress. According to Le Châtelier's principle, the system will shift in a direction to relieve the stress. The stress is too little C since it was removed. To relieve the stress, the system will shift in a direction to make more C. Which direction will it shift? The reaction will shift to the right to relieve the stress and reestablish equilibrium. Place a right arrow in the table to indicate the direction of the shift (figure 3.15).

What happens to the concentrations of all the other reactants and products when a shift occurs? The concentrations change. Shifting to the right causes the reactants, A and B, to be consumed and produce the products, C and D. Therefore, the concentrations of the reactants will decrease and the concentrations of the products will increase. Now add arrows to the chart to indicate the change in concentrations of all the other reactants and products (figure 3.16).

The stress on the system was the removal of C, and even though the system shifts in a direction to make more C, equilibrium will be reestablished before the original concentration of C is reached. Therefore, the concentration of C is still lower at the new equilibrium.

SCILINKS NSTA
Topic: Le Châtelier's Principle
Go to: www.scilinks.org
Code: 2Inquiry148

Stress	A + B		⇄	C + D	
Removal of C			→	(↓)	

▲ **Figure 3.15 Stress chart showing shift.** Add an arrow to indicate the direction that the reaction will shift according to Le Châtelier's principle.

Stress	A + B		⇄	C + D	
Removal of C	↓	↓	→	(↓)	↑

▲ **Figure 3.16 Completed stress chart.** Now add up or down arrows to indicate if the reactant or product will increase or decrease in concentration.

Stop & THINK

PART I continued

6 Consider this reaction and answer Questions 6a–b.

$$AB + CD \rightleftharpoons AD + CB$$

a. Set up a chart similar to figure 3.16 using the equation above.

b. Complete the table by using arrows to represent the stress, the direction of the shift, and the changes of concentrations of all reactants and products. Use the following stresses:

- Adding more CD
- Removing AB
- Increasing the concentration of AD

7 Using the last stress described in Question 6b (increasing the concentration of AD), describe in words what happens to the system. Include in your description all the changes in direction and concentration. Use Le Châtelier's principle to support your answer.

Part II: Temperature Shifts

Materials

For each team of 4 students

- 4 pairs of safety goggles
- 4 pairs laboratory gloves
- 4 laboratory aprons
- 1 sealed plastic pipet with cobalt chloride solution
- 1 ice bath
- hot water
- colored pencils or markers

Cautions

Wear safety goggles and an apron at all times. Pipets are sealed but should one leak, do not allow any solution to touch your skin. If any solution touches your skin, wash the affected area with large amounts of cool water and tell your teacher. Do not use hot water.

In Part I, you applied what you know about particles colliding and concentration to understand chemical systems at equilibrium. You know how to make equilibrium reactions shift in predictable ways. In Part II, you will apply what you know about Le Châtelier's principle and heat to predict shifts in an equilibrium system due to changes in temperature.

Process and Procedure

1. Study the following cobalt chloride equilibrium reaction and predict what will happen when you place the sealed pipet in very hot water and in ice water.

Use the stress chart technique you learned in Part I and your knowledge of enthalpy diagrams.

$$50kJ + Co(H_2O)_6{}^{2+}{}_{(aq)} + 4Cl^-{}_{(aq)} \rightleftharpoons CoCl_4{}^{2-}{}_{(aq)} + 6H_2O_{(l)}$$

pink (under $Co(H_2O)_6{}^{2+}$) — blue (under $CoCl_4{}^{2-}$)

2. As a team, design an investigation to test your prediction by writing a step-by-step procedure in your science notebook.
3. Gain your teacher's approval of your design, then conduct your investigation.
4. Make a sketch graph like the one from Part I, Step 5 of all the changes you observed by conducting your investigation.
5. Apply what you know about Le Châtelier's principle to write a general rule about equilibrium shifts due to changes in temperature. Write your rule in your science notebook.
6. Compare your rule with what you learn from reading *Stressed Out II* and modify your rule as appropriate.

READING

Stressed Out II

Chemists use Le Châtelier's principle regularly to get the products they want from a chemical reaction. If the desired product is on the right of the chemical reaction, chemists will introduce stresses to shift the reaction to the right to produce more of this product. Is changing the concentration the only way to stress a system? No, changing the temperature will stress the system as well.

Recall that an exothermic reaction releases heat from the reaction. Remember that these reactions feel hot because of the release of heat. This release of heat can be thought of as a product of the chemical reaction. On which side of the reaction should you include the heat if the reaction is an exothermic reaction? It will be included on the right side of the chemical equation with the products.

Since you have been using generic chemical equations, you will continue and just add the word "heat" to the appropriate side of the reaction. In a true chemical reaction, the number of kilojoules would be written in the equation.

$$\text{A} + \text{B} \rightleftharpoons \text{C} + \text{D} + \text{heat}$$

exothermic reaction

If the reaction is endothermic, then heat is absorbed in the reaction and the heat is written on the left as part of the reactants

$$\text{A} + \text{B} + \text{heat} \rightleftharpoons \text{C} + \text{D}$$

endothermic reaction

Consider the reaction

$$\text{A} + \text{B} + \text{heat} \rightleftharpoons \text{C} + \text{D},$$

an endothermic reaction. How could chemists increase or decrease the temperature of the system to shift the reaction to the right? When you try to answer this question, consider heat as a reactant just as it is written. Then solving the problem is no different than you have learned before. Put this reaction in a table as you did before to organize your thoughts (figure 3.17).

Think about what happens when the temperature decreases. In what direction would the reaction shift? (Remember to think of heat as a reactant.) The reaction would shift in a direction to relieve the stress and attempt to raise the temperature (increase heat). This would shift the reaction to the left. That is not what you want in this case. Instead, if you want to shift the reaction to the right, then you must increase the temperature. The reaction will shift in a direction to get rid of this extra heat. That direction is to the right. The completed chart would look like figure 3.18.

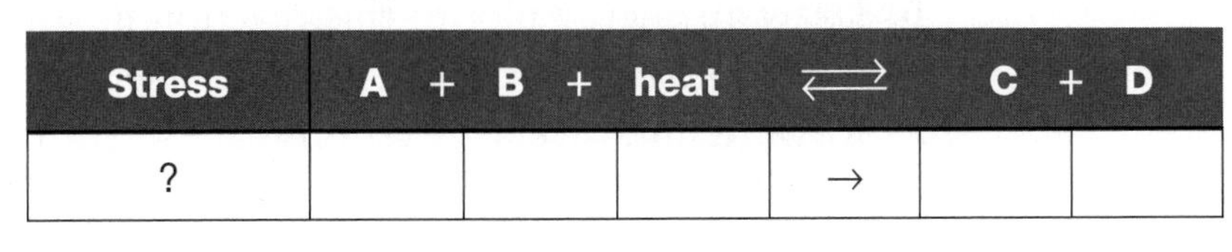

Stress	A +	B +	heat	$\rightleftharpoons$	C +	D
?				→		

▲ **Figure 3.17 Stress chart that includes heat.** This chart includes heat in the equation. Is this simulated reaction an exothermic or an endothermic chemical reaction?

Stress	A +	B +	heat	$\rightleftharpoons$	C +	D
Increased temperature	↓	↓	(↑)	→	↑	↑

▲ **Figure 3.18 Completed stress chart with heat.** When heat is added to this simulated chemical reaction at equilibrium, the reaction shifts to the right. This decreases the concentration of the reactants and increases the concentration of the products.

Reflect and Connect

Answer each question in your science notebook. Revise your answers after you check them.

1. List all the conditions of a chemical system at equilibrium.
2. Explain Le Châtelier's principle and give an example of a stress and its effect on a chemical system.
3. Consider the following situations. Do they represent a system at equilibrium? Write a sentence for each situation and indicate if it is at equilibrium and how you know.
   a. A coach substituting players in a basketball game
   b. Your school during the beginning of the day when everyone is arriving
   c. A person rowing a boat upstream at the same rate as the current
   d. Irrigation water pumped from the Ogallala Aquifer (an underground water supply)

4. Consider the enthalpy plot of an exothermic reaction.
   a. Does the forward or the reverse reaction have a higher activation energy?
   b. Draw an energy plot of this reaction in your science notebook and label the activation energies for both the forward and reverse reactions ($E_{a(forward)}$ and $E_{a(reverse)}$).
   c. Which reaction, forward or reverse, would you expect to have a faster reaction rate if concentration and temperature of the reactants were the same? Explain your answer.
5. What if chemical reactions did not behave as we know they do? What if they were not reversible? What if they never reached equilibrium? Consider this scenario and write a paragraph that describes how the world would be if chemical processes were not reversible.

EVALUATE

Reaction Rate Readiness

Thus far in unit 1, *Interactions Are Interesting*, you have learned a lot about the interactions that occur when collisions take place. In chapter 2, you studied these interactions on a macroscopic scale, and in this chapter you journeyed into the molecular world of chemistry. You saw that there is no fundamental difference in the behavior of large objects such as tennis balls and very small particles in chemical reactions.

In *Reaction Rate Readiness*, you will have the opportunity to demonstrate your understanding of the ideas of moving particles and what factors influence the way that these particles interact. In Part I, you and a partner will begin by organizing your knowledge in a way that will help you review what you have learned. Then in Part II, you will express your understanding individually on a constructed-response test. Your teacher will give you feedback on this part of the activity. In science, it is important that we learn from our mistakes and be able to correct them. You have the opportunity to do this in Part III when you will revise your answers based on your teacher's feedback.

Part I: Map It!

Materials

For each team of 3 or 4 students

note cards

markers

butcher paper

1 *Reaction Rate Readiness Scoring Rubric* handout

Process and Procedure

1. Organize your learning from this chapter.

Meet with your team and carefully review the rubric for this activity with your partners. Use it to guide your work.

2. Develop a list of words or short phrases that describe the main ideas of the chapter. For example, you should definitely list "chemical reactions" as one of your ideas.
3. Share your team's list with another team. Add any new ideas you hear to your list and omit any ideas you discover that might be included within another concept.
4. List each of these words or phrases on separate note cards. Everyone on your team should have a set.
5. Work with your team to develop summary notes about each topic. These notes can be in the form of a bulleted list of things you think are important to each topic, sentences describing each topic, or diagrams or sketches with labels. Use your book and your science notebook to develop your notes. Put these summary notes on the back of the note cards to make study cards.
6. Use your study cards (topic side up) to construct a concept map on a large piece of butcher paper. Use markers to draw lines between concepts that are connected in some way. Take turns with your teammates and explain the connections and the importance of each word you have on your study cards. Write the connections on your map. Question each other to make sure you understand the material. Be prepared to discuss your concept map with your teacher and with other classmates.
7. As a team, talk through your concept map with your teacher. Listen for anything that you may have forgotten or misunderstood. Make additions or deletions to your map or your study cards based on feedback from your teacher.
8. Take your study cards home and use them to prepare for Part II.

Part II: Test It!

Materials

For each student

1 *Chemical Reaction Rates and Equilibrium* handout

Process and Procedure

1. Obtain a copy of the test and work individually to compose your best answer to the questions. Be sure to answer each question completely and to your best ability.
2. You have 1 class period to answer the questions, so plan your time accordingly.

Part III: Revise It!

Materials

For each student

1 *Reaction Rate Readiness Scoring Rubric* handout

the scored copy of your test

1 sheet of paper

access to stapler

Process and Procedure

1. Look over your scored test. Circle the number of each question for which you did not receive full credit. Working with these questions is the objective for this part of the evaluate activity.
2. Your teacher will provide feedback as a discussion of the concepts that are important to each question. Participate in a class discussion of how to demonstrate that you have learned from your mistakes.

3. Follow the procedures outlined in the *Learn from Mistakes Protocol*. Put all your work on a separate sheet of paper. If you have questions or do not understand how to use the protocol, ask your teacher.
4. When you are finished using the protocol for each question, staple your work to your original test and hand it in to your teacher.

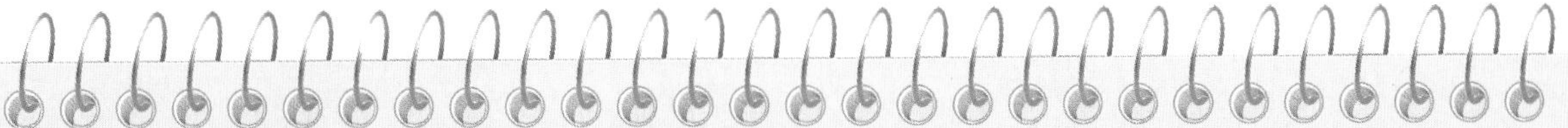

Protocol

Learn from Mistakes (LFM) Protocol

School is not just a place to deposit right answers. Sometimes you make mistakes. In fact, most people make mistakes when they try to learn something, especially when the subject is difficult or new. When you learn to identify and explain what is incorrect about a wrong answer, you have a better chance of avoiding that mistake again.

For each of the questions that you missed or did not receive full credit, perform the following steps. By doing so, you can earn up to 50 percent of the difference between your raw percent score and 100 percent. Before you begin, write your raw percent score at the top of the page along with a list of the numbers of the questions you missed.

1. Represent the original question in a different way than it was represented on the test. For example, if the question was mostly words, represent it as a sketch. If it was mostly a sketch, represent it in words. When you use words, paraphrase the question in your own words. Do not copy the question word for word. Label a sketch with all variables, especially the unknown. If the problem mentions any change in condition, show before-and-after sketches.
2. Identify and explain the mistake you made in the answer you selected. Focus on explaining any conceptual misunderstandings. When you explain what is incorrect, show how the misconception would lead to a contradiction with what you see in nature. Explanations such as "I read the problem wrong" and "I pushed the wrong button on the calculator" will receive no credit.
3. Show the correct solution or answer. When necessary, show all governing equations—first in symbol form, then with number and unit values. Place proper units and labels on your answers. Include an explanation of why the answer is reasonable.

CHAPTER 4

Physics Is Moving

Physics Is Moving

In chapter 2, *Collision Course*, you learned how to identify forces and the relationships between force and momentum, mass, velocity, and time. Then in chapter 3, *Collisions—Atomic Style*, you applied what you learned to molecules colliding. But knowing that forces exist or how much and in which direction they are applied is just the beginning. What kinds of changes do forces cause or prevent that are important to your everyday existence? In short, what do forces do?

Think about the astronauts in weightlessness, as in figure 4.1. How can they appear to be free from the force of gravity? Are they? How does a spacecraft keep moving around Earth in orbit? The cheerleader in figure 4.1 seems to defy gravity, but forces play a role in her motion. What are those forces?

▲ **Figure 4.1 What role do forces play?** Are these astronauts free from the force of gravity? What forces are involved to propel this cheerleader in the air?

One thing net forces do is cause changes in motion. Just think how important certain kinds of motions are to your everyday life. You already know about linear changes in velocity getting you from street to highway speeds. But there's also circular motion in a clothes dryer, pendulum motion in a grandfather clock, spring motion in the shock absorbers of a car, and projectile motion in a basketball free throw. In fact, each of these motions can be entertaining, as in amusement park rides like the ones shown in the opening art for this chapter.

In chapter 4, *Physics Is Moving*, you will learn about the physics of motion, especially those motions that make everyday interactions easier, more enjoyable, or more efficient. In this way, you will use what you learn in school to understand the motions of daily life. And you will use that same understanding in future courses and in the world of work.

Goals for the Chapter

By the end of chapter 4, you will be able to answer the following questions:

- How does the mathematical relationship between force, mass, and acceleration explain changes in motion or lack of changes in motion?
- Why are vertical and horizontal motions independent of each other?
- What are the similarities and differences among spring motion, uniform circular motion, projectile motion, and pendulum motion?

Fortunately, you will have help answering these questions. Each activity in this chapter gives you experience that allows you to learn directly from different types of motion. From these experiences, you gain knowledge of the factors affecting each motion and the relationships among those factors. In the end, you will increase your understanding of everyday interactions and of nature.

All the activities in this chapter will help you learn about interactions.

ENGAGE	Going through the Motions
EXPLORE	Acceleration Indication
EXPLAIN	Constantly Accelerating
EXPLAIN	Back and Forth, Up and Down
ELABORATE	Sky High Motion
EVALUATE	Moving toward Understanding

Chapter organizers can help you remember what you know and where you are headed. They help you organize your quest to understand the world around you. Look at the chapter organizer every day. Think about where you are in its organization. Compare what you know now with what you knew a week ago. Think about what you will learn today. Let the chapter organizer help you map your learning and monitor your progress. That way you can look back and see what you have accomplished.

Physics Is Moving

Engage

Going through the Motions

Key Ideas:

- Motion can be represented on graphs.
- All objects fall with the same acceleration near Earth's surface.

Linking Question

What instrument can I use to measure acceleration?

Explore

Acceleration Indication

Key Idea:

Accelerometers show the direction and relative magnitude of acceleration for many common motions.

Linking Question

What motions display constant acceleration?

Explain

Constantly Accelerating

Key Idea:

The motions of free fall and circular show a constant acceleration.

Linking Question

What kind of motion results from changing acceleration?

EVALUATE

Moving toward Understanding

Key Idea:

The relationship, $F_{net} = ma$, helps explain free fall, spring, pendulum, circular, and projectile motion.

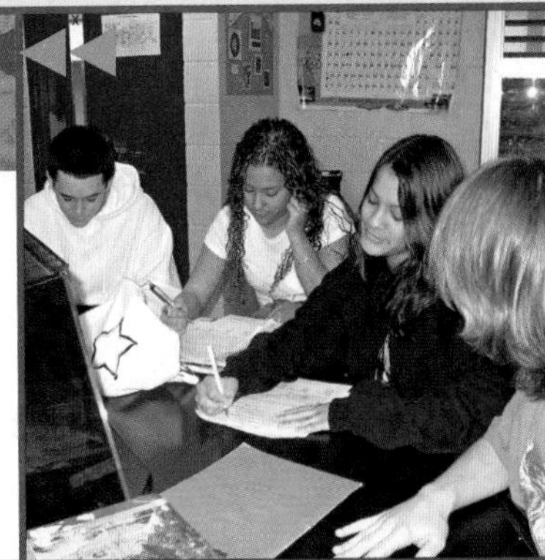

Linking Question

How can I find out what I know about force and motion?

CHAPTER 4 Major Concepts

- **All motion graphs for an object describe the same motion, but from different perspectives.**
- **F_{net} and acceleration are constant in some motions and change for others.**
- **F_{net} and acceleration are not always in the same direction as the velocity or displacement.**
- $F_{net} = ma$

ELABORATE

Sky High Motion

Key Idea:

Many satellites mimic circular motion.

EXPLAIN

Back and Forth, Up and Down

Key Idea:

Spring and pendulum motion result from varying acceleration.

Linking Question

How are these common motions applied to satellites in orbit?

ENGAGE

Going through the Motions

Maps are important to our lives. You may have used a map of your school to find your science classroom on the first day of school. Your parents use maps to find the best route for your family vacation or a business trip. Maps such as the one in figure 4.2 tell us locations, distances, and the direction to places around the world. But they do not tell us anything about our velocity as we travel from place to place. In *Going through the Motions*, you will work with graphs that will tell you many things about your motion. Many graphs can tell you locations, distances, and direction, just as a map can. However, with the graphs you will use in this activity, you can find out other information as well—quantities such as velocity and changes in velocity.

In Part I, you will work with a team to go through the motions depicted on two different types of graphs. In Part II, you and your team will examine the motion of falling objects. As you experience the different ways to represent motion graphically, you will learn about important features of motion graphs.

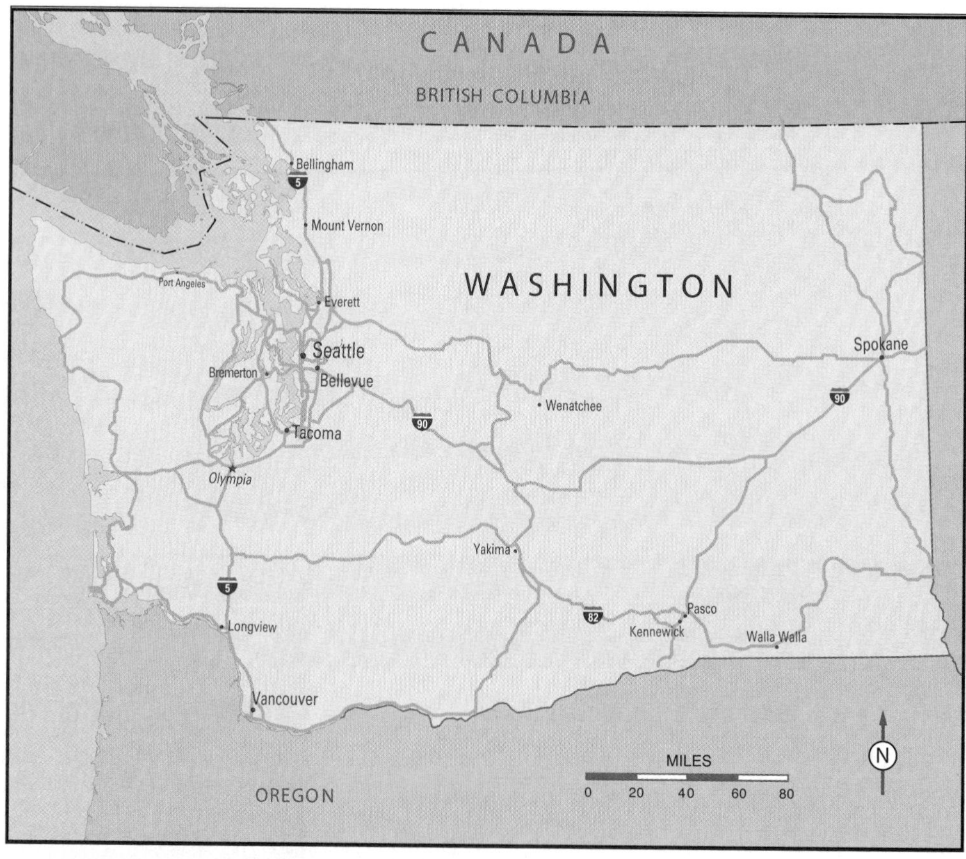

▲ **Figure 4.2 Map of Washington state.** What can you learn from a map? How are maps similar to or different from motion graphs?

Part I: Walk the Line

Materials

none

Process and Procedure

1. Meet with your team and study the motions depicted in figure 4.3. Steps 1a–h list characteristics of a motion graph that are significant. Locate these characteristics on the graph and discuss with your team what motion each represents. Record your ideas in your science notebook.
   a. Straight, flat line
   b. Positive sloping line
   c. Negative sloping line
   d. Positive y value
   e. Negative y value
   f. $y = 0$
   g. Steepness or slope of the line
   h. Straight line versus a curved line
2. Model the horizontal motion shown on the graph in figure 4.3. Decide how to model it by walking in a straight line. Prepare to demonstrate your motion to the class.
3. Model your motion for the class as your teacher directs. Watch other teams as they model the motion and explain their ideas.

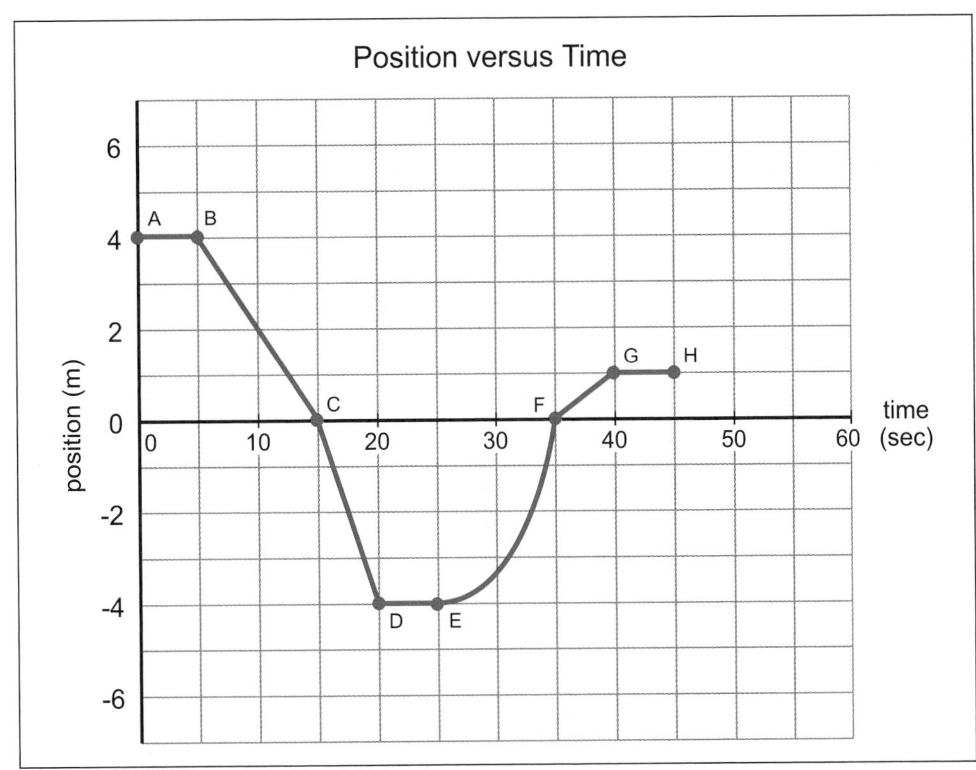

Figure 4.3 Position versus time graph. Use this graph for Part I. What motion does each characteristic of the graph represent?

4. Copy the graph into your science notebook and write a description of the motion based on the best ideas from the class.
5. Repeat Steps 1–4 for the graph pictured in figure 4.4. Note that this is a velocity versus time graph.

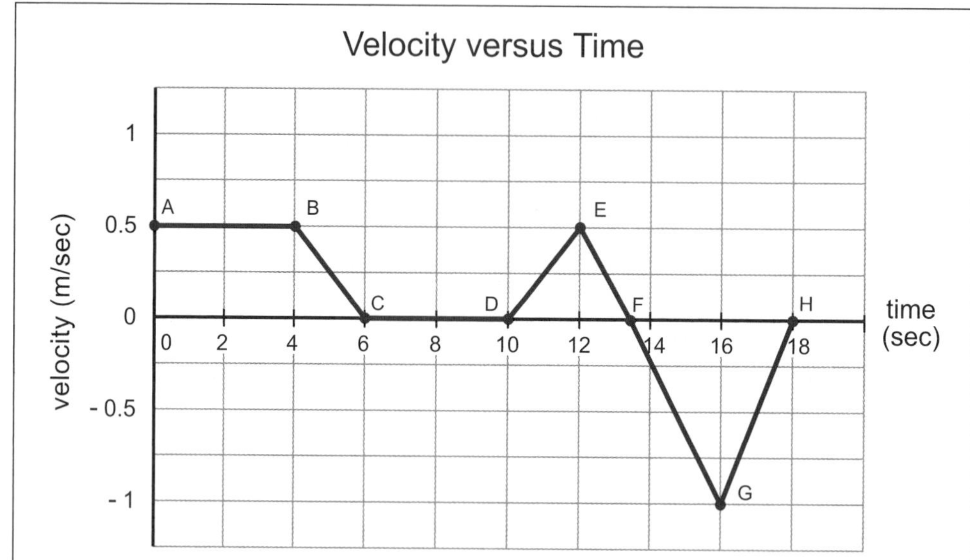

▶ **Figure 4.4 Velocity versus time graph.** Refer to this graph for Step 5. What motion does each feature of the graph represent? How is this graph different from a position versus time graph?

Stop & THINK

PART I

Work individually and record your answers in your science notebook. Check your answers with a classmate or with your teacher.

1. Examine the graph pictured in figure 4.5. Use the information in the labeled sections to write a description of the motion shown in the graph. Be sure to describe both lines and what happens at the time at position I.
2. Examine the section B–C on the graph shown in figure 4.5 and answer Questions 2a–c.
   - **a.** What feature of this part of the graph is constant?
   - **b.** What is the general formula used to calculate the slope of a line?
   - **c.** Calculate the slope using the values from the graph in figure 4.5.

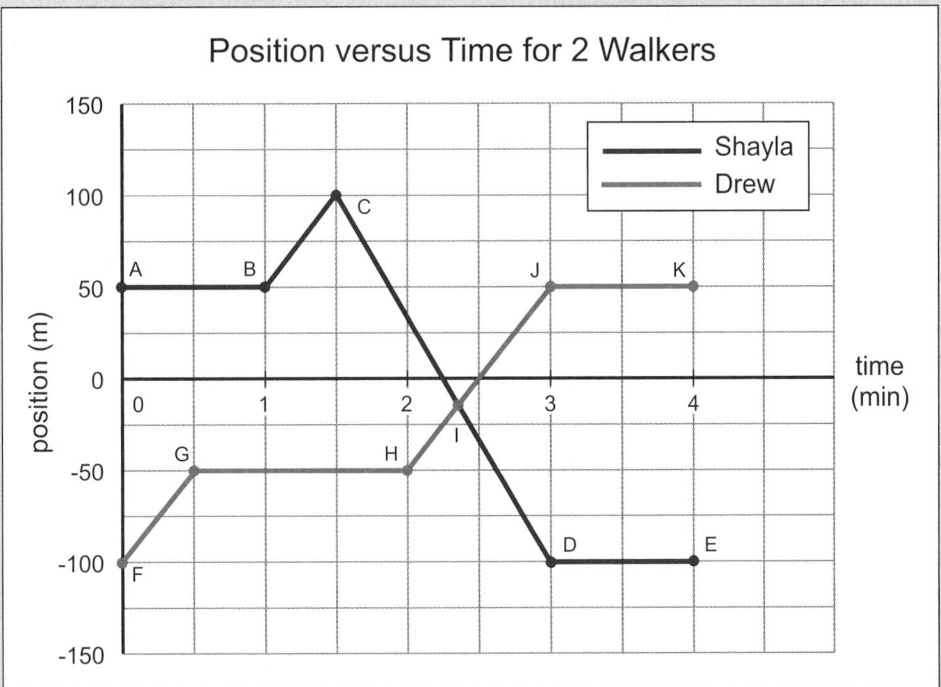

▲ **Figure 4.5 Position versus time graph.** Use this graph for *Stop and Think* Questions 1 and 2. Describe the motion shown by each of these lines.

Part II: All Fall Down

Materials

For each team of 3 students

1 spring scale

2–4 different-sized hanging masses, 200 gram (g) and greater

1 hardbound book

1 sheet of paper

1 pair of scissors

Process and Procedure

Not all motions are horizontal, like those in Part I. Many are vertical. In Part II, you and a team of two other students will use a model to represent two falling objects of different mass (figure 4.6). Then you will design a step-by-step procedure to enact your design and determine what story this tells about forces and motion.

Finally, you will propose a qualitative graph of this motion that illustrates the story graphically. A qualitative graph is one type of motion graph that you will be working with throughout this chapter.

1. Complete Steps 1a–c as you determine the motion of 2 falling objects.
   a. Trim a sheet of paper so that it has the same area as the cover of your student book.
   b. Prepare a table in your science notebook to record your observations of the 2 falling objects. You will drop these objects as described in the following list:
      - Book and paper falling from identical heights as independent objects
      - Book and paper released at the same time, but with the paper under the book
      - Book and paper released at the same time, but with the paper on top of the book
      - Book and paper released at the same time, but with the paper crumpled into a tight ball that is released at the side of the book
   c. Use the *Observation Guidelines* described at the end of this activity to guide your final, step-by-step procedure.
2. Obtain your teacher's approval and follow your approved design.
3. Draw qualitative graphs of the motion of these falling objects on both a position versus time graph and a velocity versus time graph.

Qualitative graphs are motion graphs that have labeled axes but do not necessarily have numbers on the axes. This type of graph shows only the basic shape of the line without having to plot *xy* ordered pairs.

4. Share your graphs with the class in a class discussion. Modify your graphs based on the best ideas of the class.
5. Work with your team to fill in the missing words for the following sequence of relationships.

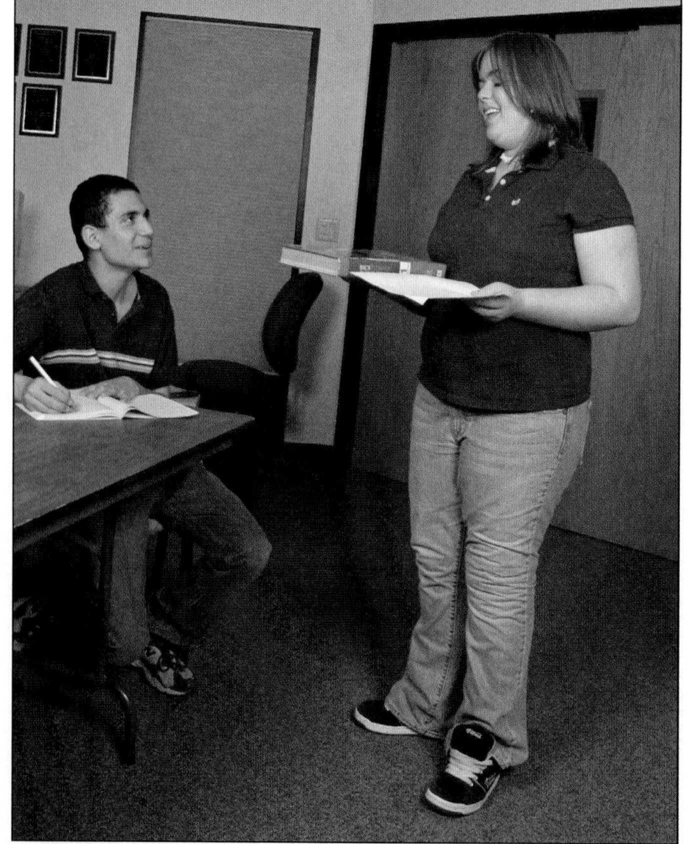

◀ **Figure 4.6 Fall time.** What important observations should you make as you conduct your investigation?

a. The heavier an object is, __________ the force between Earth and the object.
b. The force of gravity (weight) on an object is __________ __________ the object's mass.
c. As an object's weight increases, the ratio $\frac{Force_{gravity}}{mass}$ __________ __________.

6. Test your answer to Step 5c by using different masses (to represent the book and the paper) and a spring scale. You may test more than 2 different masses. Organize your data in an appropriate way in your science notebook. Include a column in your data table for the value of the ratio $\frac{Force_{gravity}}{mass}$.
7. What is the significance of the value you found from the ratio of $\frac{Force_{gravity}}{mass}$?

Reflect and Connect

Work alone or with a team as your teacher directs to answer the following questions.

1. Why does the shape of objects that are falling in the air affect the time it takes them to hit the ground? Include force vector sketches with labels and captions in your answer.
2. Draw a position versus time graph and a velocity versus time graph to compare each of the scenarios in Questions 2a–b. Use highlight comments and captions to formulate your answer.
   a. Two objects with different mass falling on Earth
   b. A book falling on Earth and a book falling on the Moon
3. State the relationship between 2 ratios of force to mass, ($\frac{Force_{gravity}}{mass}$ or $\frac{F_g}{m}$), one for a heavy object and one for a lightweight object. Then use what you have learned to write an equation that shows the relationship between this ratio for the heavy object, the light object, and *g* (the acceleration due to gravity). State this relationship in both a mathematical form and a word sentence.

Observation Guidelines

You were not born knowing how to make good-quality scientific observations. But you can learn. Effective scientists have made good-quality observations for centuries. The following questions related to making observations are not a step-by-step procedure. Rather, they are guidelines (in the form of questions) to help you *think* your way through observations. When done well, observations help you link what you see to what it means. This is the very heart of science.

- How is each procedural step related to the focus question or problem you are investigating?
- What is the best way to represent the initial conditions (with tables, sketches, graphs, equations, or sentences)?
- What is the best way to record the final conditions?
- What is the best way to record what happens *during* the investigation?

You need to focus on what is happening during the investigation, but sometimes changes occur very quickly. In these cases, you must plan carefully so that you are not distracted by writing down your data.

- How do you know that the changes you see are the result of the variable that you are manipulating and not other variables?
- Will multiple trials increase your confidence in what you see?
- What is the best way to keep a record of your initial ideas and how those ideas change during the course of the investigation?

Explore — Acceleration Indication

Graphs tell us many things about the motion they represent. You have seen that you can know the position, direction, and even the velocity of an object by analyzing a simple position versus time graph. When motion is graphed on a velocity versus time graph, there is much more you can learn about the motion. What does a straight line tell you on this type of graph? Slope is calculated the same in all types of graphs as $slope = \frac{\Delta y}{\Delta x}$. Since the y-axis represents velocity and the x-axis represents time in a velocity versus time graph, this formula becomes $slope = \frac{\Delta v}{\Delta t}$. This is the time rate of change in velocity. Sound familiar?

It should, because you learned about this in chapter 2. This ratio is commonly called **acceleration** and is represented by the symbol *a*. You learned in chapter 2 that any time there is a net force, there is a change in momentum. You also learned that if velocity is changing, then there is a net force. Net forces cause accelerations—and an object is accelerating if its velocity is changing. This means speeding up, slowing down, or changing directions are forms of acceleration. Read *FYI—Newton's Third Law Meets Newton's Second Law* for a better understanding of how the forces you have been studying compare.

In *Acceleration Indication*, you and a partner will learn a different means of indicating the direction and size of acceleration. This new approach involves building an instrument called an accelerometer. You will use the accelerometer (figure 4.7) as you design a series of investigations to study the kinds of motions important to everyday life.

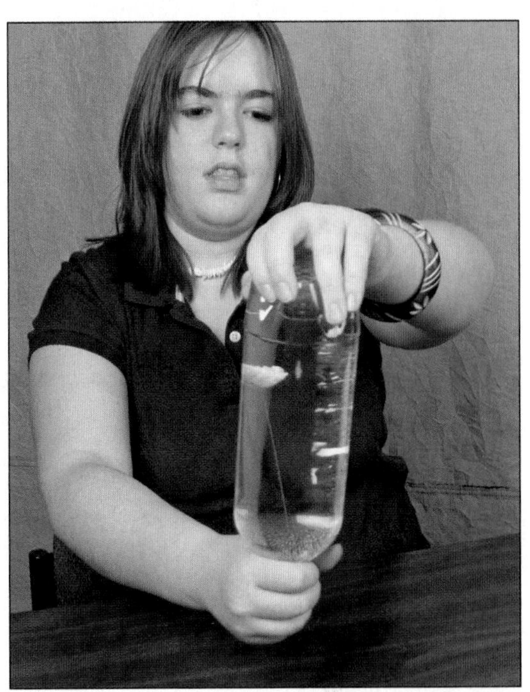

▲ **Figure 4.7 Using your accelerometer.** In this activity, you will learn how to use a homemade accelerometer to observe the direction and relative size of acceleration.

During this entire investigation, continue to ask yourself this question: "What is the accelerometer telling me about the relationship between acceleration and force?"

Materials

For each team of 2 students

1 plastic soda bottle with cap (20 oz or larger)

thread

1 packing peanut (nonwater soluble) or cork

water

Process and Procedure

Scientific instruments can help you gain terrific insights into natural events. But their effectiveness is limited in part by the person observing the instrument. So matching accurate and precise observations with quality instruments produces the highest-quality data. From that, scientists have the best opportunity of determining what the data mean.

As you follow the procedure, keep in mind the importance of matching good investigation design, proper instrument use, and careful observations. This match will help you understand more about motions common to your daily life.

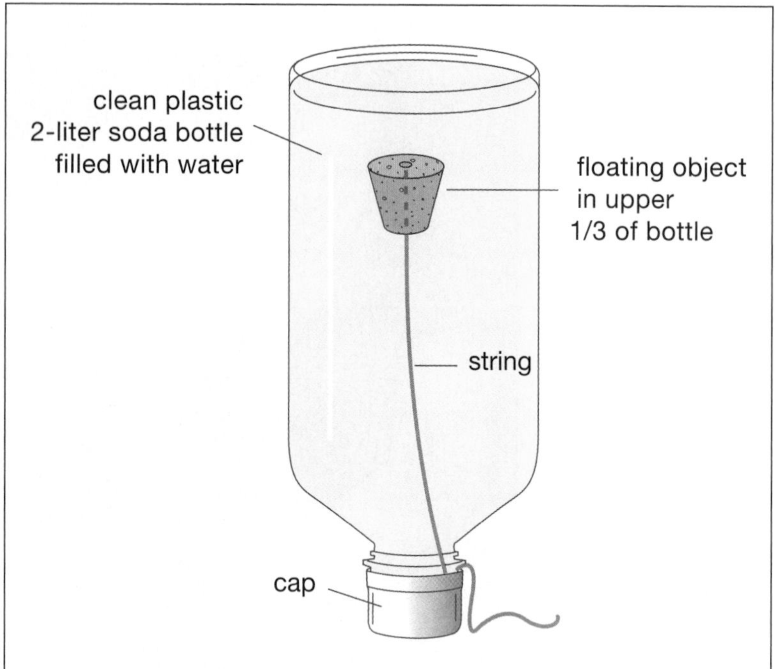

▲ **Figure 4.8 Soda bottle accelerometer.** Make sure that the peanut or cork floats in the upper one-third of the inverted bottle.

1. Obtain the materials used to construct an accelerometer. Then complete Steps 1a–c to assemble it to look like the one in figure 4.8.
   a. Find a piece of packing peanut or a cork that fits into the mouth of a plastic soda bottle. Tie it securely to one end of a piece of strong thread.
   b. Fill the bottle completely with water and place the peanut or cork inside. Be sure to include enough string inside the bottle for the peanut or cork to float in the upper one-third of the bottle when the bottle is inverted.
   c. Cap the bottle securely, invert it, and check for leaks.
2. Practice using your accelerometer before you study certain motions by doing Steps 2a–c.
   a. Stand at arm's length away from your partner, holding the inverted accelerometer at eye level between you.
   b. Holding the bottle far to the left, imagine that the soda bottle is a race car getting ready to start a race. Then accelerate the bottle sharply to the right.
   c. Repeat Steps 2a–b until you and your partner can both reproduce the *direction* and the *magnitude* of the peanut or cork's lean during the speeding up and slowing down process.
3. Use the *Observation Guidelines* from the engage activity, *Going through the Motions*, to devise a set of investigations to characterize acceleration for the motions in Steps 3a–f.

You can also find the *Observation Guidelines* in the *How To* section at the back of your book.

In all tests, keep the accelerometer inverted and perpendicular to the floor.

   a. Positive acceleration starting from rest, then moving along a straight line
   b. Negative acceleration from some constant speed to a stop
   c. Acceleration because of Earth's gravitational field (g)

You may have to exaggerate the downward motion of the soda bottle with a sharp downward pull in order to notice any movement of the peanut or cork.

   d. Movement in a circle (with the radius parallel to the floor) at a constant rate
   e. Motion of a pendulum
   f. A walk across the room at a constant velocity

4. Show your plan to your teacher for approval, then carry out your investigations.
5. Meet with another team. Use an appropriate discussion strategy to reach consensus about the direction and magnitude of acceleration in each motion listed in Step 3.
6. Report your consensus from Step 5 in the form of a sketch of each motion. Include 2 vectors on each sketch: force and acceleration.

Reflect and Connect

Write answers to the following questions in your science notebook. Then meet with 1 or 2 other classmates to check your thinking. If the team cannot reach a consensus, explain to your teacher the key features of any disagreement.

1. What can you say about the net force and the acceleration in each of the motions from Step 3?
2. Sketch what your accelerometer would look like during a bungee jump by completing Steps 2a–d.
   a. Sketch your accelerometer somewhere from the start to the middle of your fall.
   b. Sketch your accelerometer exactly at the middle of your fall.
   c. Sketch your accelerometer somewhere from the middle of your fall to the bottom.
   d. Repeat Steps 2a–c and sketch your return trip to the start of your fall.

For this thought investigation, you'll also have to imagine a stretchy string tied to the peanut or cork.

3. Suppose a particularly athletic cheetah accelerates from rest toward a gazelle at a constant acceleration of 3.0 meters per second squared (m/sec^2).
   a. What is the cheetah's velocity in 2 seconds (sec)? In 6 sec?
   b. How long does it take for the cheetah to obtain a speed of 32 meters per second (m/sec)?
   c. Suppose the cheetah is loping at a constant speed of 1.0 m/sec before accelerating. Answer Questions 3a and b with this new initial condition.

Newton's Third Law Meets Newton's Second Law

Forces cause change—sometimes. If all the forces on an object are balanced, then the object's motion will not change. The object could either remain stationary or move along at a constant velocity. The *change* in motion and the forces involved in the changes are the focus of this chapter. This focus is also Newton's second law: a net force causes a mass to accelerate. Net forces cause a change in motion. Newton's third law of motion was the focus of chapter 2: forces occur in pairs—equal in size, opposite in direction—and act on two separate objects. How are these two laws of motion related?

Consider a cart that is not moving (see figure a). This cart is equipped with a digital force meter that will indicate the force produced by the cart. The students in the picture also have digital force meters. Their meters indicate the forces they exert on the cart. Only some of the horizontal forces are shown in order to simplify the diagram.

The force pairs according to Newton's third law are labeled in each figure. All force pairs show forces that are equal in magnitude and opposite in direction. You should also notice that in each force pair, the two forces act on two separate objects. Can you name them?

Will the cart move? To determine if the cart will move, you must consider the forces acting *on the cart* and then use Newton's second law. These forces are a subset of all the force pairs described in Newton's third law. The forces that determine the motion of the cart are only the forces acting *on the cart.* Figure (b) shows those forces in red.

You can tell from the illustration that the forces on the cart are balanced—they are equal in size and opposite in direction. If you added scaled vectors of these two forces, you would get a net force of zero. Newton's second law tells you that if there is no net force on an object, then there is no change in the object's motion—no acceleration according to the formula $F_{net} = ma$. Sometimes the situation of balanced forces is called Newton's first law of motion: objects will remain in their current motion unless outside forces act on that object. Since the forces on the cart are balanced, there will be no acceleration. Can you think of a circumstance where there would be acceleration? Consider figure (c).

If the girl is pushing to the left with 40 newtons (N) and the boy is pushing to the right with 30 N, the forces *on the cart* are unbalanced. There is a net force of 10 N to the left on the cart. According to Newton's second law, the cart will accelerate in the direction of the net force—to the left. You can also find the value of the acceleration by using the formula $F_{net} = ma$. For a cart with a mass of 500 kilograms (kg),

$$\begin{aligned} F_{net} &= ma \\ a &= \frac{F_{net}}{m} \\ &= \frac{10\text{N}}{500\text{ kg}} \\ &= 0.02\,\frac{\text{N}}{\text{kg}} \text{ or } 0.02\,\frac{\text{m}}{\text{s}^2}. \end{aligned}$$

This means that the cart will move to the left and speed up 0.02 m/sec every second as long as the net force on the cart remains 10 N.

You can see that Newton's third law and Newton's second law are not two unrelated laws of motion. They are very much connected and are used to explain motion. So how is it that you can lift your backpack from the floor to your back? Aren't the forces involved always in pairs—equal and opposite? This is true, but the force pairs, equal in size and opposite in direction, act on the backpack and on other things. A subset of these force pairs, only the forces on the backpack, determine the motion of the backpack and whether you can lift it from the floor.

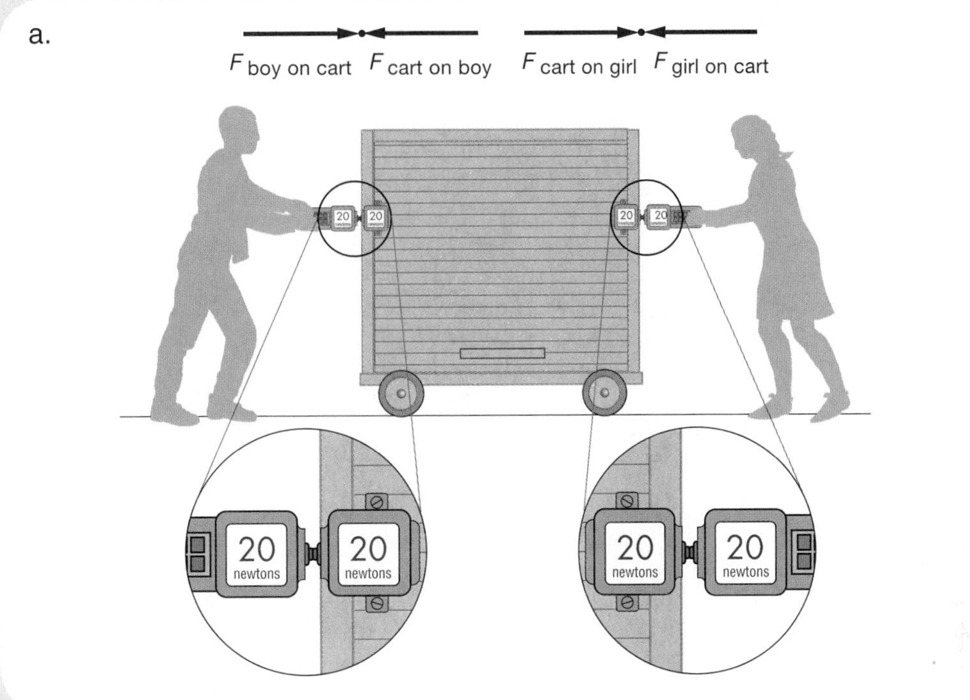

Newton's third law forces. Newton's third law forces always act on two separate objects. These force pairs are balanced. How do you know if the cart will move?

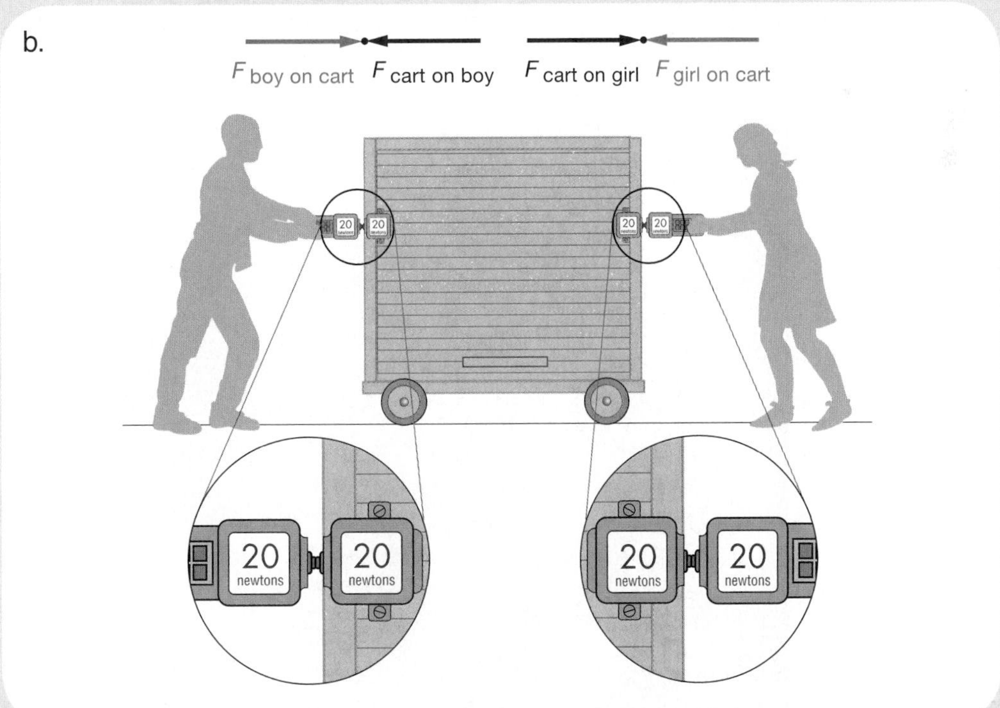

Cart that does not accelerate. When the two forces on the cart (indicated in red) are balanced, the cart will not accelerate.

Newton's Third Law Meets Newton's Second Law, continued

c.

$F_{\text{boy on cart}}$ $F_{\text{cart on boy}}$ $F_{\text{cart on girl}}$ $F_{\text{girl on cart}}$

30 newtons 30 newtons

40 newtons 40 newtons

Newton's second law forces. To decide if the cart's motion will change, you only need to examine the forces on the cart. The motion will change according to Newton's second law.

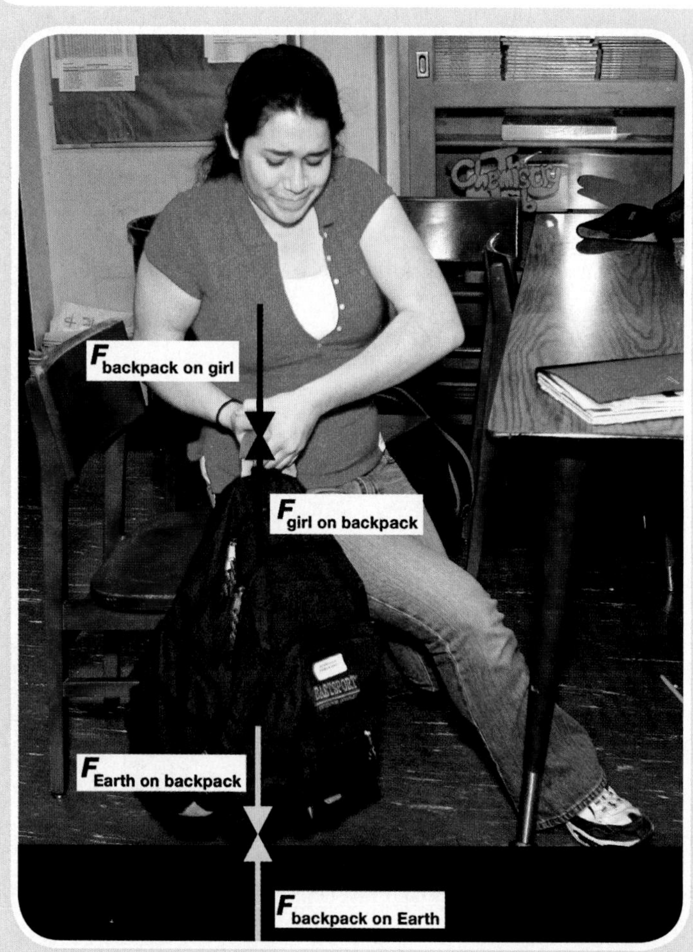

Lifting a backpack. What forces determine the motion of the backpack?

Constantly Accelerating

In the explore activity, *Acceleration Indication*, you learned an instrumental means of determining net forces by measuring acceleration. You found out how an accelerometer helps you characterize changes in velocity (acceleration), and thus changes in momentum. The result was a better understanding of the forces required to produce certain types of common motion.

As you were using your accelerometer, you noticed that some motions produced accelerations that were constant. This was evident during the motion when the cork or peanut leaned in one direction with a constant magnitude, or "lean." This happened when you modeled free fall and circular motion. Would the acceleration of the teenagers on this amusement park ride (figure 4.9) be constant or changing? In *Constantly Accelerating*, you will look at these two motions in detail. In the process, you will learn more about net forces and accelerations that are constant.

▲ **Figure 4.9**
Physics can be fun. Do these teenagers experience a constant or a changing acceleration on this amusement park ride?

Part I: Leftovers

Materials

For each team of 2 students

1 ball

2 rulers for drawing graphs

Process and Procedure

In Part I, you will work individually and in a team to analyze and understand the motion of a ball tossed in the air. (You will not use an accelerometer.) Throughout this activity, use the following focus question to help you stay on track: "What are the relationships among force, position, velocity, time, and acceleration for a ball tossed in the air?"

1. Work with your team as you examine the motion of a ball tossed in the air. Steps 1a–c will help you.
   a. Prepare to make a motion graph by drawing and labeling 2 graph axes in your science notebook. Arrange them like figure 4.10.
   b. Toss a ball straight up into the air and catch it at the same level that you released it.
   c. Assume that it takes 2 sec for the ball to complete the round-trip. Plot the motion of the ball on the position versus time graph.

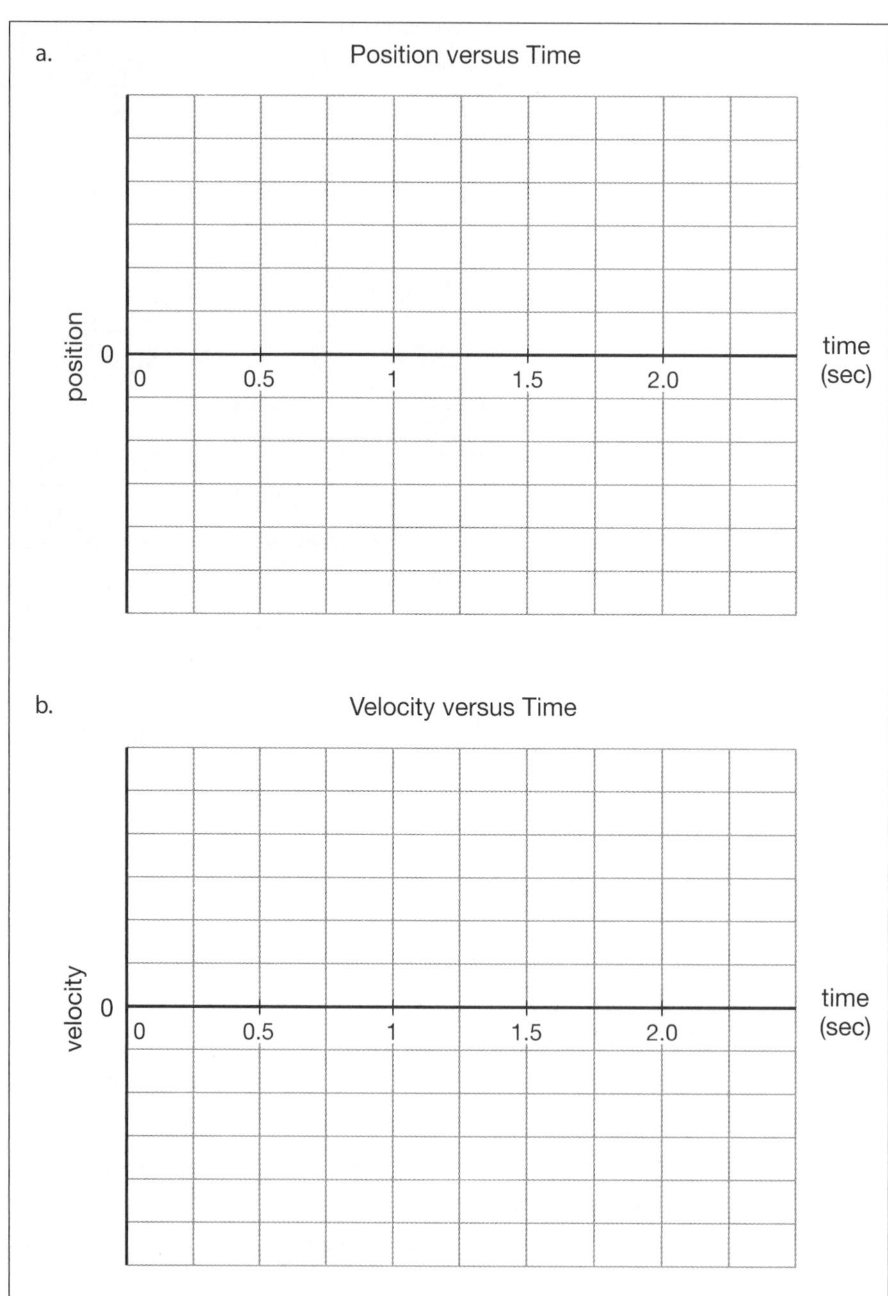

▶ **Figure 4.10 Graph axes for Step 1a.** Copy these axes into your science notebook. Notice that graph (a) plots position versus time and graph (b) plots velocity versus time. Make sure that your time axes (*x*-axes) align vertically.

Only plot the ball's motion when the ball is *not* touching your hand. Consider the point immediately after the ball leaves your hand to be at time = 0 sec and position at 0 meters (m).

2. Identify the following important features of your graph. Steps 2a–f will help you label them.
   a. Location or locations of maximum height
   b. Location or locations where the ball is moving with the fastest speed
   c. Location or locations where the ball is moving with the slowest speed
   d. Section of the path in which the ball's speed is decreasing
   e. Section of the path in which the ball's speed is increasing
   f. Location or locations where the ball changes direction
3. Mark points on your graph at the following locations.
   a. Beginning of the motion
   b. Middle of the motion
   c. End of the motion
4. Think about the velocity at each of the 3 points you marked in Step 3. Graph these 3 points on the velocity versus time graph and connect your points. Include highlight comments with your graph.

Consider whether you should connect your points with a straight line or a curved line. To make your decision, think about how the velocity is changing.

5. Use a strategy such as think-share-advise-revise (TSAR) to check your answers with another team.

You can find instructions for the TSAR strategy in the *How To* section at the back of your book.

6. Sketch several scaled force vectors to represent the forces acting on the ball at several points in the ball's path. Completing Questions 6a–c will help you.
   a. Resketch the path of the ball so that you have a clean diagram.
   b. Simplify your task by assuming zero air resistance and by only considering ball locations away from the hand, such as the positions from Steps 2a–f.
   c. Write highlight comments for each force vector and a caption under your sketch.
7. Help your teacher plan how to conduct a quick survey of classroom thinking. Record the number of students whose vector sketches showed the following.
   a. The force of gravity (the weight of the ball) always points down.

b. The force of gravity (the weight of the ball) always is the same length.
c. The force of the hand is left over from the toss.
d. There is zero force at the highest point.
e. The force decreases as the ball approaches the highest point.
f. The force increases as the ball returns to the hand.

8. Modify your force vectors after a classroom discussion of the survey results. Be especially careful to record what and why you changed anything. Revise your caption and highlight comments based on the best ideas of the class.

9. Read the following paragraphs as you prepare to examine figure 4.11 and complete Steps 9a–f.

   Scientists are continuously looking for relationships between variables that they test. You, too, are acting as a scientist when you analyze a motion graph and determine what each part of the graph represents. Many relationships can be discovered while observing motion and representing that motion on different types of graphs. So far in this activity, you have looked at both position versus time graphs and velocity versus time graphs. You also analyzed the forces responsible for the motion of a ball tossed in the air. How are all of these variables related?

   The motion of an object has many characteristics. Think about a car's motion. You can describe the car's velocity, position, or acceleration. The distance the car traveled in a given amount of time is another characteristic to consider. Think about these relationships and characteristics of motion as you complete the next steps in this activity.

   a. Examine the graph in figure 4.11.
   b. Describe the motion the graph represents.
   c. Calculate the slope of the line using the general formula for the slope. Be sure to include units in your calculation.
   d. State the value related to motion that you are calculating when you find the slope of the line on a position versus time graph.
   e. Describe the meaning of the sign (+ or −) assigned to this value.
   f. Write a summary statement that describes what you have learned in Step 9. Include the words *slope*, *position*, *velocity*, *direction*, *time*, *positive*, and *negative* in your description.

10. Find another valuable relationship between position versus time graphs and velocity versus time graphs by completing Steps 10a–e.

a. Draw a velocity versus time graph for the motion shown in figure 4.11. Base your graph on the value you calculated in Step 9c.
b. Shade in the rectangle bounded by –5 m/sec and 10 sec.
c. Find the area of this rectangle; pay close attention to the units.
d. What characteristic of motion does this value represent? Write a sentence describing this characteristic and how you determined its value.

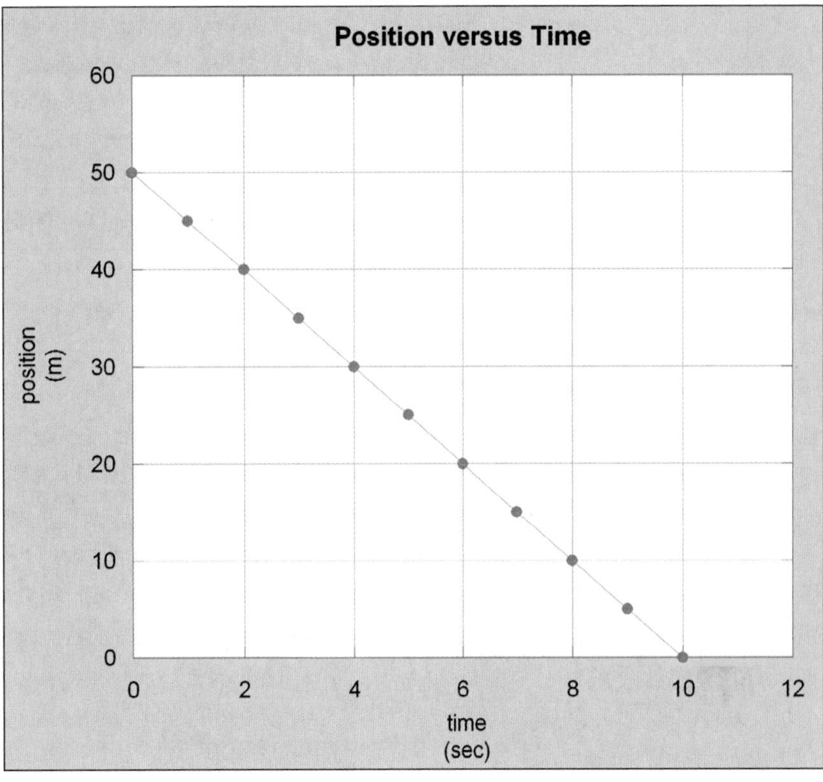

▲ **Figure 4.11 Graph for Step 9.** Use this motion graph to answer Steps 9a–f.

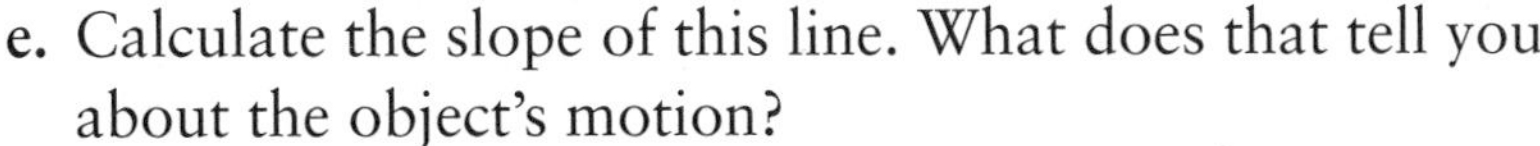

e. Calculate the slope of this line. What does that tell you about the object's motion?

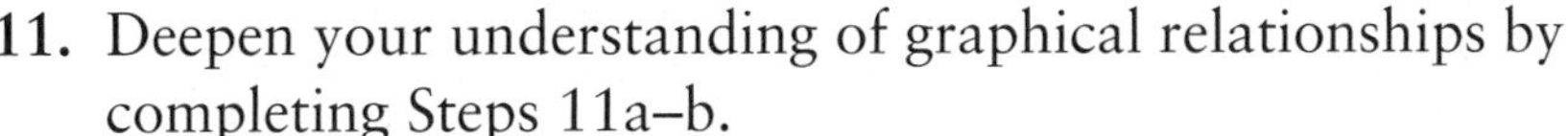

11. Deepen your understanding of graphical relationships by completing Steps 11a–b.
    a. Study the graph in figure 4.12 of a car's motion that starts from rest. Describe the motion of the car using the words *velocity*, *acceleration*, *constant*, *direction*, and *positive* or *negative*.

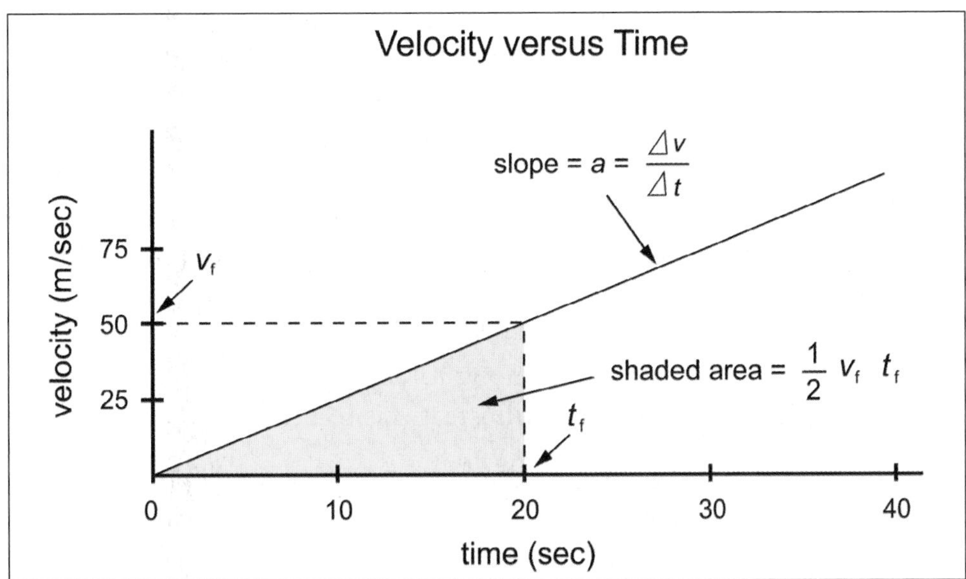

◀ **Figure 4.12 Velocity versus time graph for Step 11.** Refer to this graph as you complete Step 11.

Mathematical equation	Justification for the equation
$\Delta x = \Delta t$	*This is the general statement or relationship to calculate distance when velocity is constant and time is given.*
x = shaded area	(Think back to Step 10.)
$A = \frac{1}{2}$ *(base)(height)*	
$x = \frac{1}{2}(t)(v)$	
$v = at$	*This is a way to calculate velocity when the acceleration is constant and the motion begins at zero velocity at $t_x = 0$.*
$\Delta x = \frac{1}{2}(t)(a)(t)$	
$\Delta x = \frac{1}{2}at^2$	

▲ **Figure 4.13 Answer table for Step 11b.** Copy this table to help you organize your answers for Step 11b. Some justifications have been filled in for you. Use the graph in figure 4.12 to help you with some of the answers.

b. Copy the table in figure 4.13 into your science notebook. Write detailed explanations or justifications in the table for each of the following mathematical steps. These steps progress in a logical sequence. Some of the justifications have been completed for you.

Each motion begins from rest (or $t_i = 0$) from a position that is defined as the origin (or $x = 0$), and the object moves in the positive direction. For the sake of convenience, let x represent position, v represent velocity, t represent time, and a represent acceleration.

12. Calculate the slope of the line in figure 4.12. Then describe the characteristic of motion that this value represents.
13. Calculate the distance the car in figure 4.12 traveled in 20 sec, starting from rest. Use the relationship you derived in Step 11b and the value you calculated in Step 12 in your calculation.
14. Write a short paragraph summarizing what you have learned about the relationships among force, acceleration, velocity, and position. Use graphs and illustrations to clarify your summary.

Stop & THINK

PART I

Work individually to answer these questions in your science notebook. Then compare your answers with those of a classmate. If the answers differ, involve a third student or your teacher.

1. A classmate says, "At the highest point, the ball slows to 0 m/sec. Since Newton's second law suggests that objects at rest have no net force acting on them, then the ball has no net force acting on it at the top of the toss. That's why I drew no force vector at the top."

   Respond to your classmate in writing. Carefully detail what you agree and disagree with in this classmate's comments. Be sure to explain why.

   In the elaborate activity from chapter 2, *With and Without a Net*, you learned that there were 2 examples of motion where there was no change in velocity: zero velocity ($v = 0$ m/sec) and constant velocity ($\frac{\Delta v}{\Delta t} = 0$).

2. A different classmate talks about the forces acting on the ball on the way to the top by saying, "There are 2 forces acting on the ball while it moves to the top—the force of gravity down and the force of my hand up. Since the ball is not moving at a constant speed, there are unbalanced forces. This happens because the hand force is greater than the gravity force at the beginning of the toss and, gradually, the hand force becomes smaller until it becomes zero at the top. Then gravity takes over, making the ball accelerate down."

   Respond to these comments by writing in your science notebook. Use the key concept words *force, velocity, change, constant, acceleration,* and *momentum* in your response.

3. Suppose you stand behind a chair and give it a shove. After a short distance, the chair leaves your hands and coasts to a stop. For the chair's motion *after leaving your hands*, explain the similarities and differences between the ball toss and the coasting chair. Copy and fill out the table in figure 4.14 to list your comparisons.

STOP & THINK, PART I, continued

Feature of motion	Similarity	Difference
Orientation of motion (vertical or horizontal)		
Force from person		
Force of gravity		
Force of friction		
Velocity		
Acceleration		
Momentum		

▲ **Figure 4.14 Comparison table.** Think about the similarities and differences between the motion of a ball tossed in the air and a chair shoved across the floor. Use this table to organize your comparisons.

4. Write justifications or explanations in your science notebook for each of the following mathematical relationships.

   Consider using a table like the one in Step 11b.

   a. $F_{net} = \frac{m\Delta v}{\Delta t}$

   b. $a = \frac{\Delta v}{\Delta t}$

   c. $F_{net} = ma$

5. Suppose you measure a constant acceleration of −2.0 m/sec for a 0.035-kg ball rolling up and down a ramp. What is the net force on the ball (both for direction and magnitude)? How would you determine whether or not the net force is constant?

6. How long does it take a diver to reach the water below a 10-m diving platform?

7. A dragster covers a quarter mile in 6.0 sec, accelerating constantly all the way. What is its acceleration in m/sec^2?

8 Consider the motion of a ball rolling down a ramp, onto the carpet, and finally coming to a stop. The motion is shown on the graph in figure 4.15. Complete Questions 8a–d for this situation.

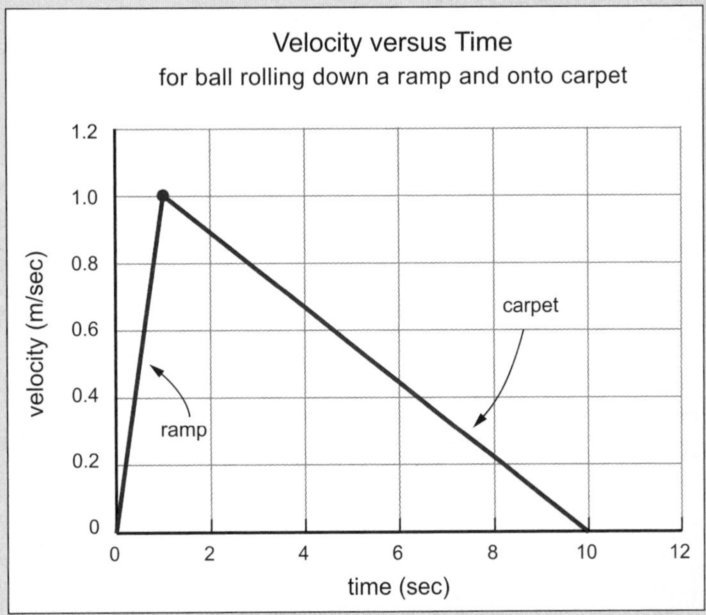

Figure 4.15 Velocity versus time graph for a ball rolling down a ramp and onto carpet. What quantities can you determine from this graph? How does the acceleration of the ball compare to *g*?

Think back to the evaluate activity, *Forces to Go; Forces to Stop*, from chapter 2 for a reminder.

a. Write a short paragraph describing the physical conditions necessary to produce this graph of a rolling ball. Pay particular attention to the forces involved.

b. Calculate the acceleration associated with both sections of the graph. Be sure to show the connection between slope and the algebraic definition for acceleration: $a = \frac{\Delta v}{\Delta t}$.

c. Determine which section of the graph, if any, depicts positive velocity, negative acceleration, and a backward force. Explain how 1 ball can have this set of motions at the same time.

d. Compare and contrast your calculated values of acceleration from Question 8b to the constant *g*. Be especially careful to use *g* as a way to determine if your calculated accelerations are reasonable.

Part II: Projectile Motion

▲ **Figure 4.16 Hitting the bull's-eye.** At what angle and speed would you have to throw the dart to hit the bull's-eye?

One nice thing about analyzing motion is that the same set of principles applies to most motions in our everyday environment. So once you understand those principles, you can describe the motion of everything from mountains to molecules. Now that's a good use of what you learn in school!

What kind of motion would result if you threw a ball horizontally, as fast as you could? Once the ball left your hand, what path would the ball follow? Where would it land? How long would it take to hit the ground? What angle and speed would you have to throw a dart to hit a bull's-eye (figure 4.16)?

As in each of the preceding activities, force is the key. Once you determine what forces act on the ball during flight, you can understand acceleration, velocity, and position. And as before, you can communicate your understanding of motion using a variety of methods.

In Part II, you and your team will apply what you already know about forces and motion to understanding the motion of a ball tossed horizontally. This motion is often called projectile motion.

Materials

For each team of 4 students

- 1 ring stand assembly
- 1 plastic ruler
- 2 coins (same denomination)
- 2 marbles
- 1 stopwatch
- 1 meterstick
- tape
- flat, rigid surface, approximately 40 × 100 cm

Process and Procedure

Projectile motion involves motion in the horizontal plane (often parallel to the ground) and in the vertical plane (perpendicular to the ground). That is, there is motion in two dimensions. But are there forces in two dimensions?

To answer this question, you and your team will investigate the motion of two objects, both beginning their motion at exactly the same time from the same height. The only difference is that one object drops straight down and the other receives a hit in the horizontal direction.

1. Suppose the 2 objects discussed in the preceding paragraph are identical marbles. Predict how many "clicks" you would hear if the horizontally and vertically moving marbles begin motion at the same time (figure 4.17). (A click is the sound of a marble hitting the floor for the first time.) Explain your reasoning.
2. Test your prediction with a plastic ruler and 2 coins, as instructed by your teacher.
3. Sketch the position of each coin at several regular time intervals *after* the motion begins. Include the following in your sketches.
   a. Scaled and labeled force vectors for each position
   b. Highlight comments that focus on the force vectors
4. Explain in your science notebook how you know whether or not there was a leftover plastic ruler force acting on the coin that projected sideways.

Use sketches and words in your answer.

5. Explain how you know whether or not there was a constant net force acting on both coins.

Sometimes motion is difficult to analyze because it happens too fast. If you can slow the motion, yet maintain the relationship among all the key concepts, then you can have time to make better observations. In Step 6, you will slow down the motion so that you can make better observations. You will use rolling marbles to simulate the motion of the pennies.

6. Use the materials recommended by your teacher to assemble a tilted, flat surface and a ball ramp. Your apparatus needs to have the following features.
   a. The tilted surface is very stable and its angle of tilt is less than 10 degrees (°).

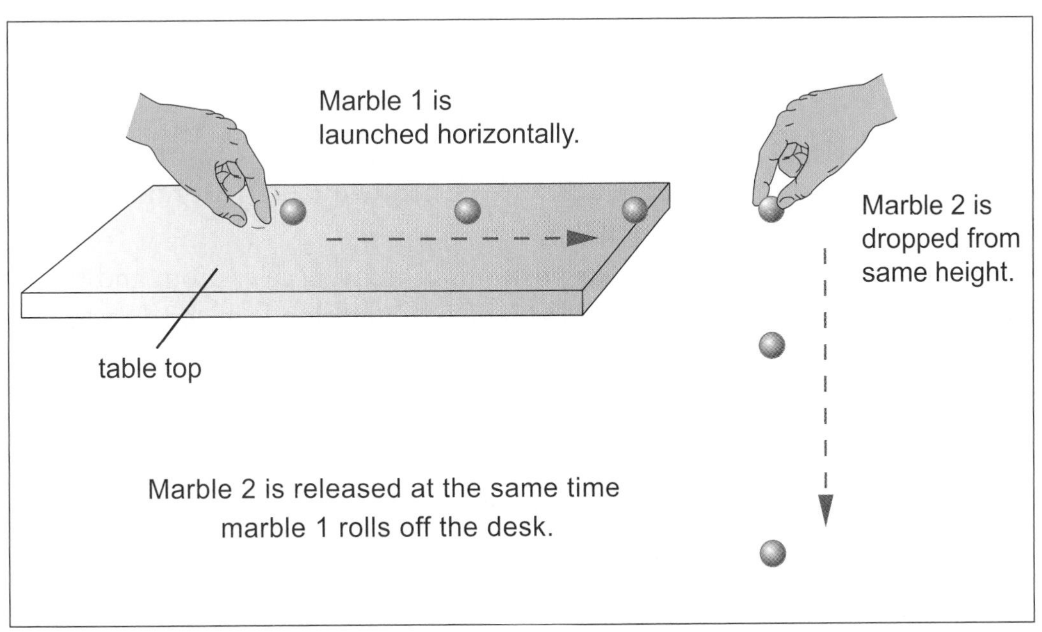
Marble 1 is
launched horizontally.
Marble 2 is
dropped from
same height.
table top
Marble 2 is released at the same time
marble 1 rolls off the desk.

Figure 4.17 Marble launch and drop. If one marble is dropped and another is launched horizontally at the same time, which one will hit the ground first? Or will they hit at the same time?

b. The ball ramp attaches to the top right corner of the tilted surface. It projects the ball horizontally, without bouncing, as the ball moves from the ball ramp to the tilted surface.
c. The ball ramp is very stable and its angle of tilt does not change during a set of trials.

7. Investigate whether the results of your penny experiment transfer to this apparatus. Consider the following during your investigation.
   a. The *Observation Guidelines*

You used the *Observation Guidelines* in the engage activity. You can find the guidelines in that activity or in the *How To* section in the back of your student book.

   b A variety of angles for the ball ramp
   c. A variety of angles for the tilted surface

8. Summarize your findings from Step 7; use at least 2 forms of scientific communication. Then compare your summary with the summaries of at least 2 classmates. Check with your teacher if you have any questions.

Examples of scientific communication that you may want to use are paragraphs, charts or tables, graphs, or mathematical equations or relationships.

9. Relate what you have learned to the information in the reading *Motion in Two Dimensions, Force in One Dimension*. Read the passage with a partner, using a strategy that works best to help you understand the reading.
10. Use what you have learned in this activity to explain the title of the reading, *Motion in Two Dimensions, Force in One Dimension*. Use 2 different types of scientific communication to form your explanation.

Challenge Opportunity

11. Select 1 set of angles for the ball ramp and tilted surface from your investigation in Step 7. Generate qualitative graphs for the criteria in Steps 11a–b.
    a. Motion graphs for position, velocity, acceleration, and force (aligned by time axes): The ball's motion is in the direction parallel to the top edge of the tilted surface (that is, only in the plane of the board).
    b. Motion graphs for position, velocity, acceleration, and force (aligned by time axes): The ball's motion is perpendicular to the top edge of the tilted board (that is, only in the plane of the board).

READING

Motion in Two Dimensions, Force in One Dimension

You have learned that when an object is launched horizontally, the motion in the horizontal direction is *independent* of the motion in the vertical direction. (This is also true for objects launched at an angle.) You saw evidence of this when two pennies landed at the same time, although one penny was launched horizontal to the ground. Even though that penny had an initial horizontal velocity, the velocity and acceleration in the vertical direction were unaffected. Because of this, the penny landed at the same time as the one dropped from the same height.

The curved path of a projectile may seem complicated. But we can simplify it by looking at the horizontal and vertical motions separately. We can do this since they act independently of each other. The horizontal component of the motion of a ball thrown off a balcony is the same as the horizontal motion of the ball rolling along a flat surface. (That is, if we can ignore the slowing effect of friction). The ball rolls along the surface at a constant velocity. The ball moves equal distances in the same intervals of time. The ball has no horizontal acceleration. Similarly, a ball thrown as a projectile off a balcony has this same horizontal motion. The horizontal position of the ball at any time can be calculated by using the formula $\Delta x = v_x \Delta t$, where v_x represents the velocity (v) in the x, or horizontal, direction.

The vertical motion of a ball thrown off a balcony is equivalent to the vertical motion of a ball dropped from the same height. The ball accelerates downward in the direction of the force of gravity. You can use the relationship you discovered in Part I, Step 11 to calculate either the vertical position or the time of the fall. This relationship, for vertical motion starting from rest, is represented by $\Delta y = \frac{1}{2}at^2$ when $t_i = 0$. Since the ball is in free fall, the acceleration it experiences is the acceleration due to gravity (g). Thus, the equation becomes $\Delta y = \frac{1}{2}gt^2$ when downward is defined as in the positive direction.

Topic: projectile motion
Go to: www.scilinks.org
Code: 2Inquiry187

12. Use what you know about the independence of horizontal and vertical motions to plot the actual position of the ball at 0.1-sec time intervals. Follow Steps 12a–d to accomplish this.

Do this for only 1 tilted surface angle and 1 ball ramp angle.

a. Determine the ball's exit speed from the ball ramp.

b. Determine the vertical acceleration of the ball on the tilted surface.
c. Use the calculated values from Steps 12a–b to determine the horizontal and vertical positions of the ball at 0.1-sec intervals.
d. Check the accuracy of your measurements and calculations by placing a small piece of tape on each position you determined in Step 12c. Then watch how close the ball rolls to those tape marks.

Don't forget to reproduce exactly both the ball ramp and the tilted surface angles from Steps 12a–b.

Stop & THINK

PART II

Read through each question completely before answering it in your science notebook. Check your answers with classmates before proceeding to the next activity.

1. Suppose an airplane carrying a heavy crate of food for flood victims flies parallel to the ground at an altitude of 1,500 m and a speed of 200 m/sec. It then releases the crate of food. Disregard the effect of air resistance when answering Questions 1a–e.
   - **a.** What do the relative positions of the plane and crate look like for equal time intervals? The time intervals start at the moment of release and end when the crate hits the ground.
   - **b.** How many seconds does it take the crate to hit the ground?
   - **c.** How many horizontal meters away from the release point will the crate hit the ground?
   - **d.** How many meters will the plane travel horizontally from the release point until the time the crate hits the ground?
   - **e.** Describe what the crate would look like to you from the airplane.
2. Suppose you rode along on the top part of a ship's mast carrying a heavy ball. (The mast is the tall beam perpendicular to the ship's deck). The ship travels at a constant velocity of 4 m/sec, and you hold the ball 12 m above the deck.
   - **a.** Relative to the mast, where would the ball hit when you dropped it?
   - **b.** Use what you understand about force, acceleration, vertical, and horizontal motion to explain your answer in Question 2a.

3. Repeat Questions 2a–b, except answer them for a ship that is accelerating.
4. Repeat Questions 2a–b, except answer them for the ball's landing point relative to a dock directly between the ship and the shore.

Part III: Uniform Circular Motion

Materials

For each team of 4 students

accelerometer from the explore activity

Process and Procedure

In Part II, the force of gravity always points perpendicular to Earth's surface. The force of gravity constantly pulls the object straight down. Then why does a projectile's path curve? It curves because of Newton's second law. When there is a net force, there will be a change in motion. Since there is a net vertical force, the object accelerates toward Earth's surface. The combination of horizontal constant velocity and vertical *changing* velocity results in curved motion.

For a projectile that is thrown horizontally, the horizontal velocity and gravity are perpendicular only at the instant the motion begins. After that, the projectile's velocity vector begins to point increasingly downward. It is no longer perpendicular to the force of gravity (figure 4.18).

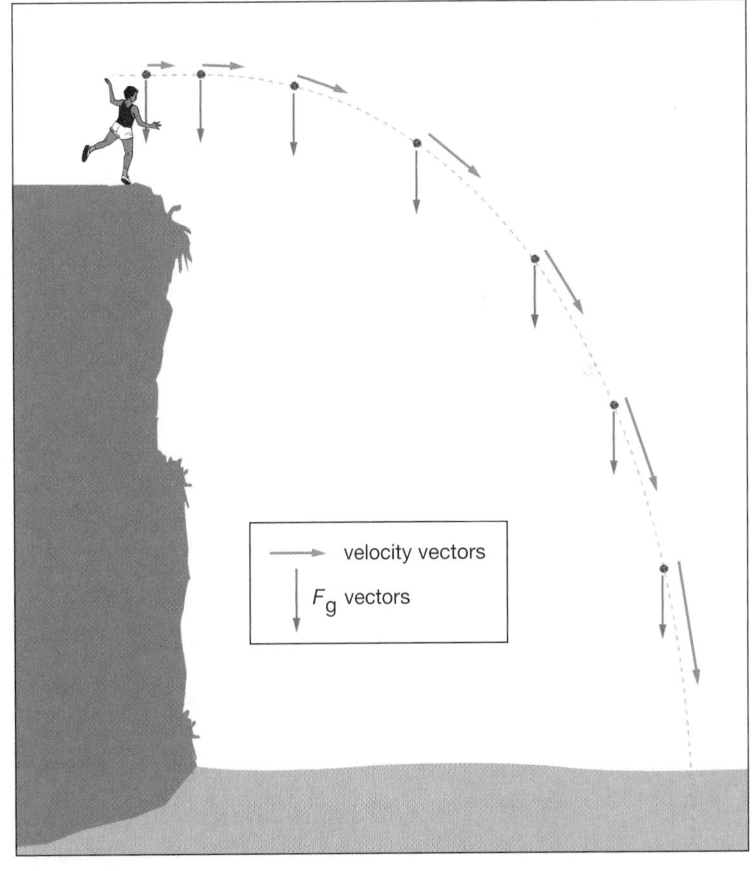

▲ **Figure 4.18 Velocity vectors on a projectile.** At the instant the projectile motion begins, the horizontal velocity vector is perpendicular to the force due to gravity. How does the geometric relationship of these two vectors change as the motion of the projectile continues?

There is another type of common motion in which the net force is *always* perpendicular to the velocity. And that's the motion you will investigate with your team in Part III.

1. Place your accelerometer on the table in front of you, and then complete Steps 1a–c.

Focus on the water in your accelerometer for these steps. Don't focus on the floating cork or peanut until you are asked specifically about it.

   a. Draw a scaled force vector diagram of all the forces acting on the water.
   b. Label each vector with the source of the force.
   c. Include a caption explaining why the water isn't moving relative to the bottom of the bottle.

2. Use the *Observation Guidelines* in this chapter to focus on your accelerometer. As you stand, hold the bottle by its top, with the long axis of the bottle *parallel* to the ground, and begin to spin it like helicopter blades.

The spinning bottle will form a circle. Be sure each team member observes both the center of the circle and the outside of the circle. Try to keep the spin rate as constant as possible. You may have to pour some water out so it is only half full.

3. Analyze the water's motion by doing Steps 3a–e.
   a. List all the quantities that are constant when the water is not moving relative to the bottom of the bottle during spinning. Include evidence for each item in your list.
   b. Draw scaled and labeled force vector diagrams (viewed from above) of the forces acting on the water when it is not moving relative to the bottom of the bottle during spinning.

Since the water is not falling down during spinning, omit the gravity force vector. Focus only on the force or forces involved with circular motion. Draw diagrams for at least 2 different positions around the circle.

   c. Add a labeled velocity vector of the water to your diagrams from Step 3b.
   d. Add a labeled acceleration vector of the water to your diagrams from Step 3b.

Use your accelerometer to confirm the direction of the acceleration and force vectors you are drawing for uniform circular motion. You will have to spin in a circle while holding the long axis of the accelerometer *perpendicular* to the floor during this step. Observe the lean of the cork or peanut to determine the direction of the acceleration and force. Fill the accelerometer with water if necessary.

   e. Repeat Steps 3b–d for at least 2 other positions of the water as the bottle moves in a circle.

4. Meet with your team and discuss the following questions and tasks. Then write responses in your science notebook.
   a. What is the geometric relationship (perpendicular, parallel, or always at, say, 20°) between force and velocity vectors for uniform circular motion? State the evidence for your answer.
   b. Describe the magnitude of the velocity (the speed) of the water for uniform circular motion.
   c. If the speed is not changing during uniform circular motion and there is a net force, then how can the water accelerate?

Use vector sketches in your answer.

   d. Generate a sketch, as viewed from above, of what would happen to the bottle if you suddenly released it as you were spinning it.

Reflect and Connect

Answer each question in your science notebook, then confer with your teammates to check your thinking. If you change any answer, record what you changed and why.

1. Why is the path of projectile motion curved? Use vectors, words, equations, or all of these in your answer.
2. Compare and contrast uniform circular motion, projectile motion, and the motion of a ball tossed in the air. Choose a method that helps you organize this information. Examples include tables, Venn diagrams, and paragraphs.
3. Some amusement parks have a ride that spins people around in what looks like a huge salad spinner. At a certain spin rate, the floor drops away, yet everyone "sticks" against the wall. Develop a labeled vector sketch with a caption to explain how this happens.

Read the sidebar *Amusement Park Designer* to learn more about careers that involve the physics of amusement park rides.

4. Calculate the speed you are moving due to Earth's rotation. (The radius of Earth = 6.36×10^6 m.)
5. Pretend that you are a NASA scientist and propose a plan to simulate gravity in a space station located in outer space. Use your understanding of circular motion to describe your plan.

SIDEBAR

Amusement Park Designer

Going for a Ride

Do you love the thrill of climbing to great heights and then, seconds later, dropping so fast that your stomach flies up into your throat? Next come the loops, twists and corkscrews, all of which make for an exciting minute or two. Such is the experience of a roller coaster ride—a favorite among vacationers of all ages. These machines of motion are a demonstration of engineering know-how. And designing them can be even better than riding them.

"Everyone has opinions about what makes for a good roller coaster ride, but they don't stop to think that someone actually has to design them," says Scott Andersen, P.E., a structural engineer with Arrow Dynamics in Clearfield, Utah. "It's an uncommon thing that I do for a living."

Roller coasters have been around for more than a century, enticing people's adventurous nature by defying gravity. Andersen carries on that tradition by building coasters that boast multiple loops or sheer, almost 90-degree drops. Thrill seekers today are given the rides of their lives.

Like designing any new product, it all begins with putting an idea on paper.

"We begin with the layout of the ride, whether it will be looping or not and how many loops. Most parks have something in mind when they come to us," he explains. "Then we figure out how long to make the track and how high the lift has to be to get you around the coaster. We also check the G-Forces and velocity."

After the coaster's design is completed, Andersen refines the track specifications, including its support structure. The track consists of the rails for the cars to ride on and the ties between them. "The ties are similar to railroad ties and we design them and calculate the spaces between them. Then we figure out the support, which is called the strongback," he says. "Finally, we connect the strongback to the saddle or the support structure, which are the columns that support everything."

When all that is configured and tested, the coaster is shipped to the amusement park for final assembly. There, Andersen adds his final structural touches before handing the coaster off to electrical engineers to finish the testing before opening the ride to the public.

Certainly, roller coaster design is unlike most engineering jobs, but there are several reasons Andersen found himself drawn to it, and it's not because he loved them as a kid. "My dad and sister were nuts about coasters," he says. "They would ride them three or four times each. But once was enough for me."

SCiLINKS® NSTA
Topic: amusement park physics
Go to: www.scilinks.org
Code: 2Inquiry193

Excerpted with permission from the article "Jobs Off the Beaten Track" by Anne Baye Ericksen appearing on Graduating Engineer and Computer Career Online, www.graduatingengineer.com. Copyright Career Recruitment Media/AlloyEducation.

Back and Forth, Up and Down

EXPLAIN

In *Constantly Accelerating*, you applied your ability to observe and analyze motion. You discovered that a ball tossed in the air or thrown horizontally exhibits constant acceleration. Acceleration is also constant in circular motion, although its direction is different. What is the cause of the constant acceleration? A constant net force. The mutual gravitational attraction between the ball and Earth causes constant acceleration in vertical motions. But what kind of motion results when forces change?

At the very least, you would say that changing forces result in changing acceleration. That's because you know the relationship $F_{net} = ma$. This relationship links what you can see (acceleration) to what it means (the object experienced a net force). Can you think of some common motions in which the acceleration is changing?

▲ **Figure 4.19 The pendulum motion of a grandfather clock.** Is the acceleration of this pendulum constant or changing?

Perhaps you thought of the motion of car tires as they bounce up and down over a bumpy road. Or you thought of the back and forth motion of a pendulum in a grandfather clock (figure 4.19). In fact, any motion that varies in a repeating way over time (periodic motion) exhibits changing acceleration. So the swaying motion of skyscrapers after an earthquake is due to changing acceleration. Even a vibrating guitar string moves back and forth due to varying acceleration. Oxygen molecules oscillate at a greater frequency when temperature increases. This microscopic motion also represents changing acceleration.

All these motions are worth understanding. But in *Back and Forth, Up and Down*, you and your team will only study two motions: motions caused by springs and by pendulums. You will analyze the relationships among force, mass, velocity, acceleration, and time for these two motions. Once you understand the relationships in spring and pendulum motions, you will be able to understand complex periodic motion, such as earthquakes, guitar strings, and molecules.

Part I: Changing Forces

Materials

For each team of 3 students

1 spring scale (scaled in newtons)

1 spring

1 string

2 weights (approximately the same mass)

1 pair of scissors

access to a computer

animations *Simple Pendulum* and *Spring Pendulum* on the *Student Resource CD (SRCD)*

Process and Procedure

The key to understanding periodic motion is force. If you know what the net force on an object is at any point in time, you can determine the acceleration. Once you know the acceleration, you can predict the velocity and, ultimately, the object's position. With accurate knowledge of position and time, you can understand that object's motion.

In Part I, you and your team will think about the forces acting on similar objects that exhibit periodic motion. You will use force vectors to determine the net force at key locations in the motions of a spring and a pendulum. Then in Parts II and III, you will determine how forces relate to aspects of motion, such as time, position, velocity, and acceleration.

1. Conduct a qualitative investigation of the force a spring applies to a scale that you hold in your hand.
   a. Lay the spring on a table. Have a team member hold one end firmly. Attach the other end to the scale as shown in figure 4.20.

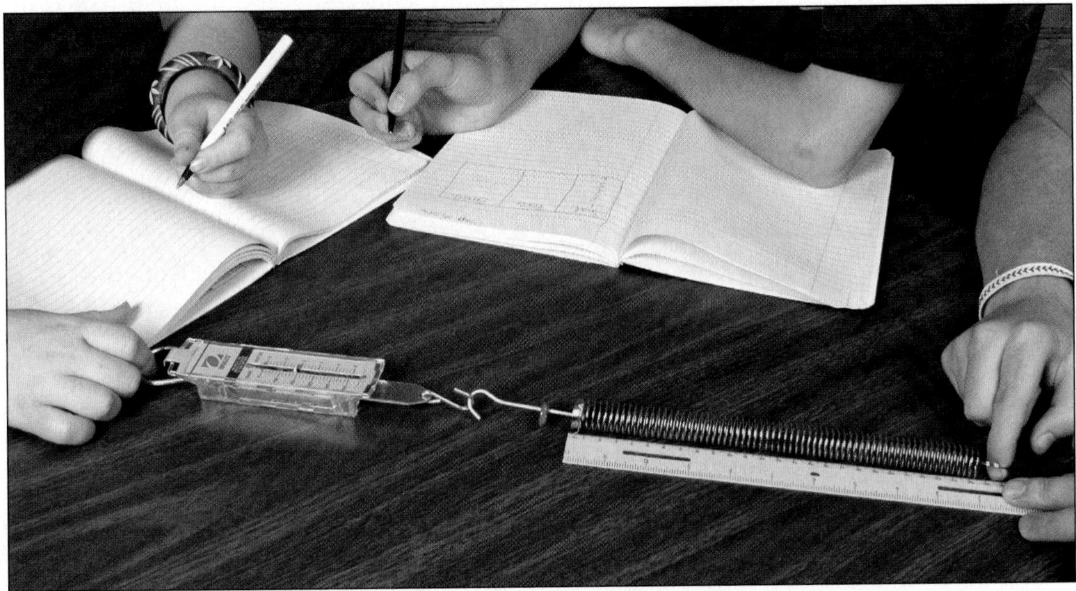

▲ **Figure 4.20 Students with a spring scale and a spring.** Use the scale to stretch and relax the spring. What is the relationship between the amount of force and the amount of stretch of your spring?

   b. Use the scale to stretch and relax the spring.
   c. Sketch the spring, scale, and hand in 2 different "stretch" positions. Include scaled force vector diagrams with labels for those 2 positions.
   d. Generate a qualitative *xy* plot of the force of the spring (vertical axis) versus the position (horizontal axis). Include highlight comments and a caption.
   e. Select an effective technique to compare your sketches, graphs, and comments with team members.
   f. Write a summary statement for what you have learned in Step 1.
2. Connect the results from your qualitative investigation in Step 1 to a quantitative relationship by reading *Changing Forces*.

READING

Changing Forces

When you pull on a spring, the spring pulls back on you. What do you remember about the "pull-back" force of the spring as you pull in the opposite direction? Because force always occurs in pairs, equal in size and opposite in direction, the pull-back force is equal to your pulling force. If you pull with a scale, the reading on the scale indicates the numerical value of the mutual forces, but not the direction. You determine direction from observations.

As you pull with a greater force, the scale reading increases. Why? The scale reading increases because the spring force increases, but maintains its opposite direction from your pulling direction. The more you pull on the spring, the more the spring pulls back on you. That is, the spring force changes depending on the amount of stretch. *The force is not constant.*

How can you predict the amount of spring force for a given stretch without using a scale every time you need to know the force? You have already learned how graphs and equations can help you answer this question. Study each feature of figure 4.22 to make the connection between your qualitative investigation and mathematics. The graph in figure 4.22 shows the force of the spring on your hand as you stretch the spring different amounts (figure 4.21).

In your math classes, you may have used the equation for a straight line in a graph: $y = mx + b$. In the equation, x and y are simply the quantities on the x- and y-axes; b is the y-intercept, or where the graphed line crosses the y-axis; and m is the slope of the line. Since the line in figure 4.22 is a straight line, you can apply this equation and discover the mathematical relationship of the stretch of a spring and the force. Because the graphed line appears to cross the y-axis at the origin (0,0), you can omit b from the equation. The equation is now $y = mx$. Can you see how this equation is equivalent to $F = -\text{k}\Delta x$?

The symbol Δx represents the stretch of the spring where $\Delta x = x_{\text{stretched}} - x_{\text{unstretched}}$. The symbol –k represents the slope. This mathematical relationship is the equation for a line. The symbol, k, is called the spring constant. The spring constant is different for

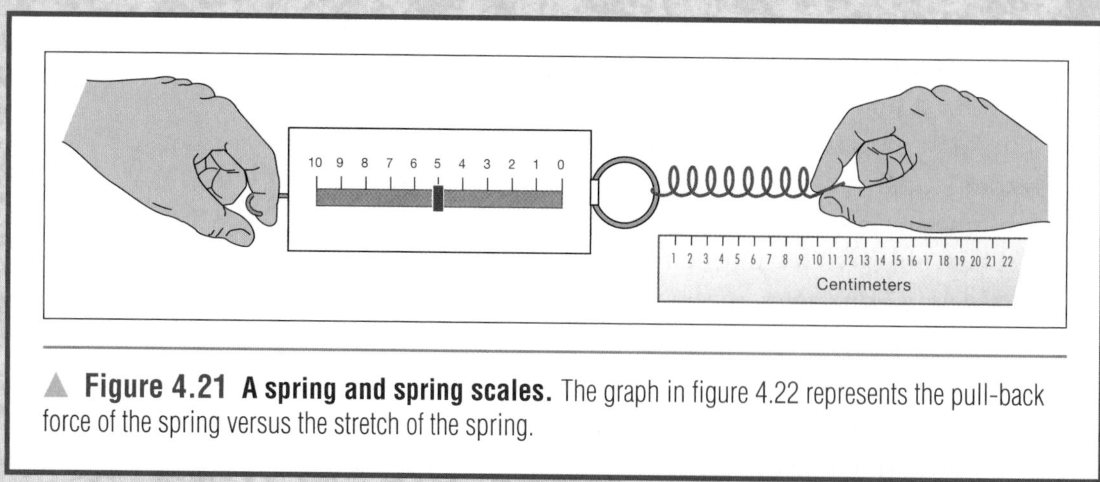

▲ **Figure 4.21 A spring and spring scales.** The graph in figure 4.22 represents the pull-back force of the spring versus the stretch of the spring.

every spring. Stiff springs, like the ones for automobile suspensions, have large spring constants. Soft springs, like the ones in some ballpoint pens, are small. In all cases, k helps characterize the way springs perform and the kind of motion springs might produce.

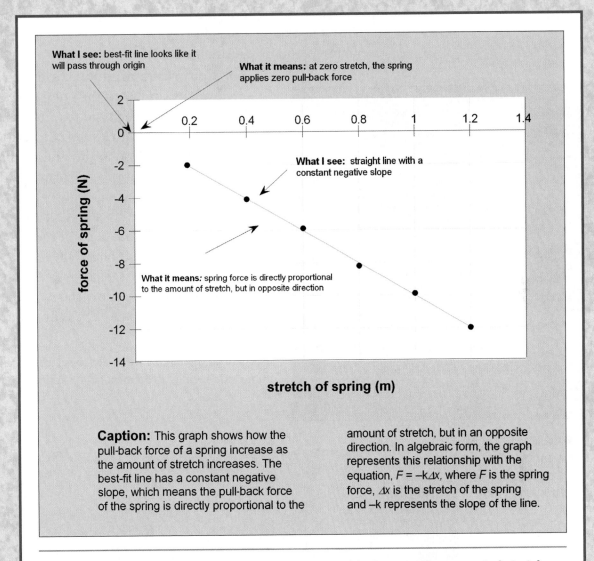

What I see: best-fit line looks like it will pass through origin

Caption: This graph shows how the pull-back force of a spring increase as the amount of stretch increases. The best-fit line has a constant negative slope, which means the pull-back force of the spring is directly proportional to the amount of stretch, but in an opposite direction. In algebraic form, the graph represents this relationship with the equation, $F = -k\Delta x$, where F is the spring force, Δx is the stretch of the spring and $-k$ represents the slope of the line.

▲ **Figure 4.22 Pull-back force of the spring on an object versus the amount of stretch.** Inspect both scales and the best-fit line shown to see if they are reasonable compared with your qualitative investigation. Read each highlight comment and caption to compare your thoughts with the ideas presented here. How similar are they?

Topic: periodic motion
Go to: www.scilinks.org
Code: 2Inquiry197

3. Connect the relationship between the force and the stretch of a spring, $F = -k\Delta x$, to both spring and pendulum motion by completing Steps 3a–d.
   a. Attach your spring to a fixed object as instructed by your teacher. Then hang a weight from your spring and let it oscillate up and down (figure 4.23).
   b. Construct a pendulum, using a weight similar to the one used in Step 3a. The time required to complete 1 entire swing (1 period) should be close to the time required for the weight on the spring to make 1 oscillation (figure 4.24).
   c. Generate side-by-side sketches similar to figure 4.25 of these 2 motions. Use a blank sheet of paper in your science notebook and be sure to show the weights at 5 positions (A–E) as shown in figure 4.25.

Plan ahead by making these sketches large enough to include highlight comments and captions later.

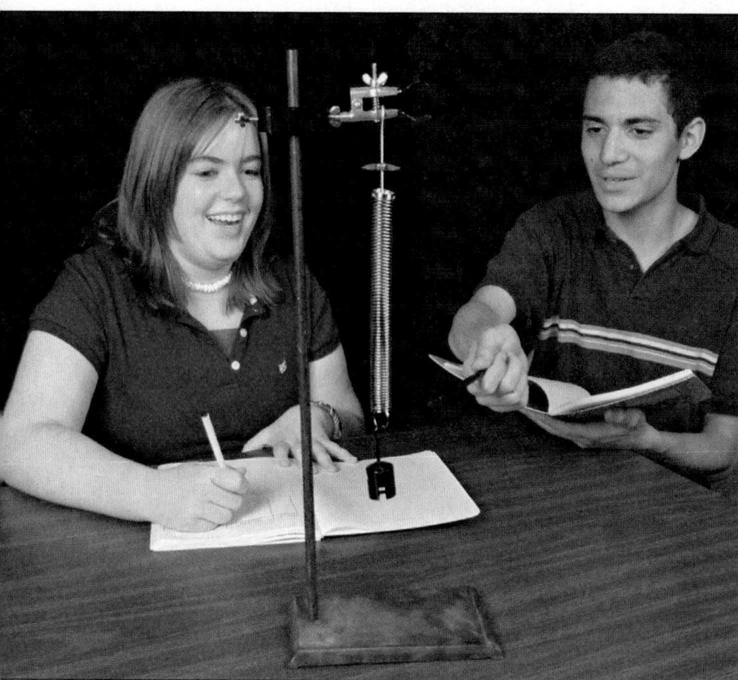

▲ **Figure 4.23**
Weight on a spring. Your weight should oscillate from your spring, as shown in this photograph.

► **Figure 4.24 Weight on a pendulum.** The weight should swing back and forth like a pendulum. Try to manipulate your pendulum so that the time required to complete 1 swing (1 period) is the same as the time required for the weight on the spring to make 1 oscillation.

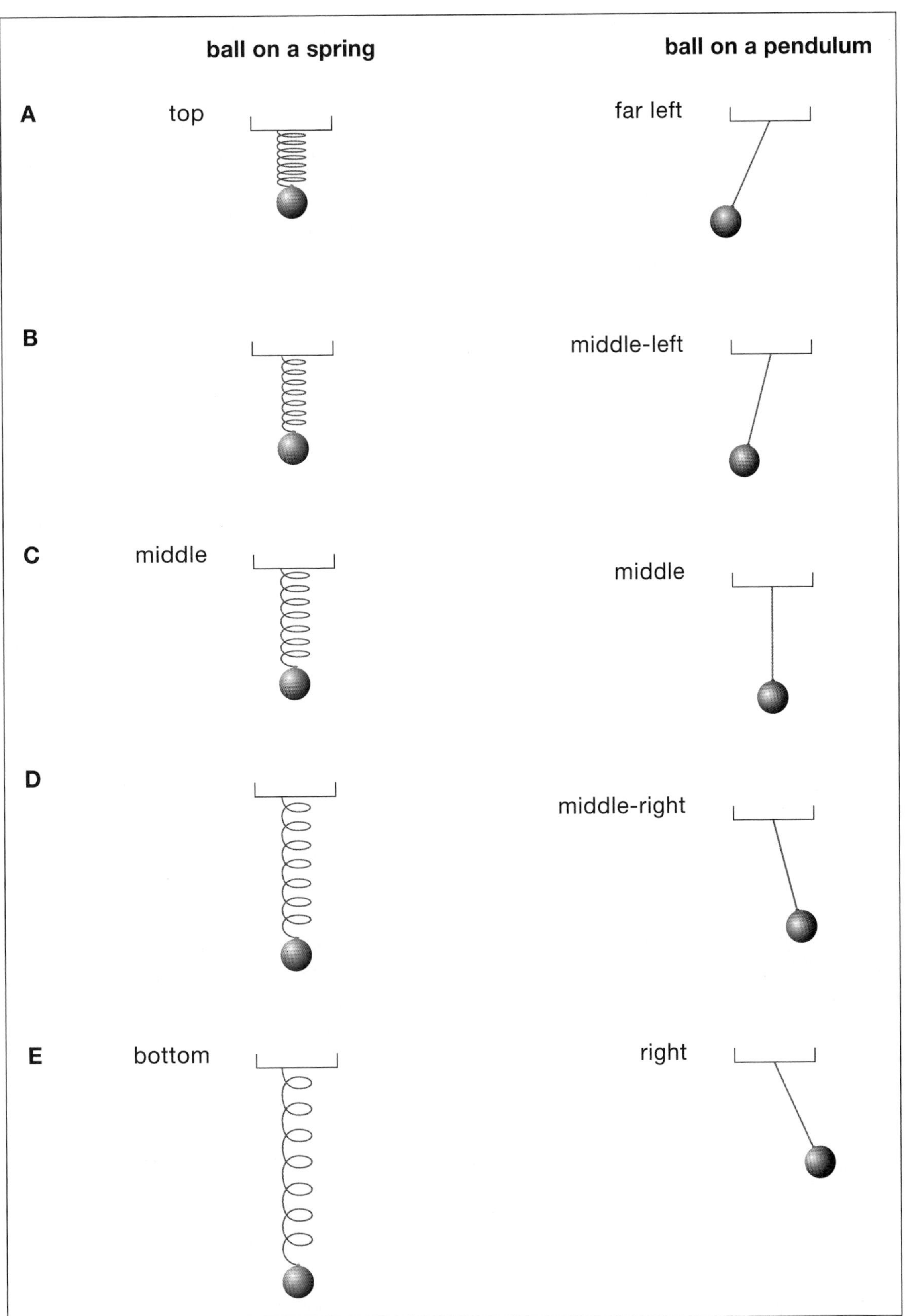

▲ **Figure 4.25 Positions for sketches.** Generate sketches for the 5 positions labeled A to E.

d. Label each position with qualitative descriptions of the motion. Use words like *fastest, slowest, stationary, increasing speed*, and *decreasing speed*.

4. Incorporate scaled force vector diagrams for at least positions A, C, and E of the *spring*. Include the following in your diagrams.

   a. Labeled arrows to represent the direction and relative magnitude of the pull-back force of the spring

Remember that $F = -k\Delta x$ tells you about the amount of pull-back force for each relative stretch position.

   b. Labeled arrows to represent the direction and magnitude of the gravitational force acting on the weight

   c. Labeled arrows to represent the direction and magnitude of the *net* force acting on the oscillating weight

Remember to use vector addition to determine the net force.

5. Meet with your team and decide how to repeat Step 4 for the *pendulum*.
6. Write an overall caption under your sketches. Explain how the sketches, along with vectors, demonstrate changing forces as the weights move back and forth or up and down.

Include the words *momentum, net force, acceleration, velocity, position*, and *time* in your caption.

7. Copy the table in figure 4.26 into your science notebook. Complete the table in order to find similarities in 2 examples of periodic motion.

You may choose another form of showing similarities, such as Venn diagrams or a paragraph explanation.

Position (or motion) of the spring	Position (or motion) of the pendulum	Reason
Top	Far left (or far right)	The speed is zero and the weight is reversing direction.
Bottom		
Middle		
Between top and middle, going down		
Between middle and bottom, going down		
Between bottom and middle, going up		
Between middle and top, going up		

▲ **Figure 4.26 Analogy table linking pendulum and spring motions.** This table will help you make connections between pendulum and spring motions.

8. Complete Steps 8a–d as you view the animation *Simple Pendulum* on the *Student Resource CD* (*SRCD*).

   a. Select the button for velocity on the bottom right and start the animation.
   b. Note direction of the velocity vector compared with the direction of the motion of the pendulum. Record this comparison in your science notebook.
   c. Repeat Steps 8a–b 2 more times, first choosing the acceleration button and then the force button.
   d. Summarize your findings about the direction of these vectors in relation to the direction of the pendulum motion. Write your summary in a sentence and illustrate it with diagrams.

9. Repeat Steps 8a–d for the animation *Spring Pendulum,* also on the *SRCD*.

Stop & THINK

PART I

Read each question carefully before answering it in your science notebook. Then use an effective learning technique to check and revise your answers.

1. Consider 2 different springs as you answer Questions 1a–e. Spring A has a spring constant of $k = 25$ N/m (newtons per meter), and spring B has a spring constant of $k = 50$ N/m.
   a. Make a qualitative graph in your science notebook of spring force versus stretch for each spring.
   b. Suppose you placed identical weights on the ends of each spring and let them hang. Which weight would hang lower and why? (Assume each spring was originally the same length.)
   c. Suppose you allowed identical masses to oscillate from each spring. Which period would be greatest?
   d. Which spring pulls back with a force of 25 N when stretched 50 centimeters (cm)? Show your justification.
   e. Suppose you were making a bed mattress out of a group of identical springs. Would you use spring A or spring B? Explain the advantages and disadvantages of each. Remember, an average student might weigh 700 N.

2. Include a new set of vectors on your sketches from Steps 4 and 5 to depict the relative acceleration at each position.

STOP & THINK, PART I, continued

3 Summarize what you have learned about changing forces and their affect on velocity and acceleration in periodic motion. Use sentences and sketches to form your summary.

Part II: Time Matters

Materials

For each team of 3 students

1 spring scale (scaled in newtons)

1 spring

1 string

2 weights (approximately the same mass)

1 pair of scissors

1 stopwatch

Process and Procedure

In Part I, you began your in-depth analysis of periodic motion by examining the forces involved in spring and pendulum motions. You learned that a changing net force produces a changing acceleration, which in turn changes velocity and position in a repeating pattern.

The repeating pattern of motion depends on the period of oscillation. This is the time required for one complete cycle of motion. For spring motion, the period is the time from release to the time when the weight returns to the release point. For a pendulum, it is the time from "tick" to "tock" and back to tick. The period of Earth revolving around the Sun is one year, or about 365 days.

So time matters. For example, it would be a big deal if the periodic motion called "one day" changed due to some cosmic force. Because time matters, you and your team will study the factors (sometimes called variables) that affect the time associated with periodic motion (figure 4.27). Focus your efforts in Part II with this question: "What factors affect the period of spring and pendulum motions?"

1. Meet with your team and develop an overall investigation strategy to determine what factors affect the period of oscillation for spring and pendulum motions. Steps 1a–c will help you develop your strategy.

   a. Use appropriate features of the *Observation Guidelines*.

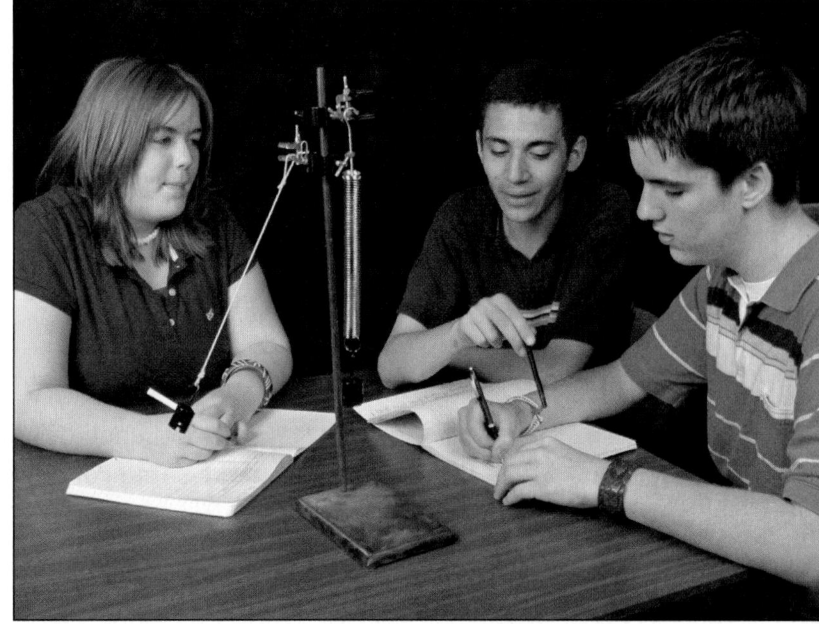

▲ **Figure 4.27**
Planning your investigation. What factors will you investigate to answer the focus question?

   b. Use multiple forms of representing and communicating your understanding, including words (in complete sentences), sketches, graphs, and equations.
   c. Use a step-by-step procedure that students your age could follow without difficulty.
2. Check with another team and compare your overall strategies. Obtain your teacher's approval before you conduct your investigation.
3. Conduct your overall investigation. Be careful to reflect on the results of each step along the way.
4. Using the data from your investigation, formulate a complete answer to the focus question for Part II.

Stop & THINK

PART II

Review your observations and results from Part II before writing answers in your science notebook to the following questions.

1. You have become an astronaut for NASA and you are trying out one of your high school experiments on the new colony on the Moon. If you repeated your investigation from this activity using both the pendulum and the spring, how would your results compare?
2. A friend of yours has a grandfather clock that keeps time poorly. It runs slow. Your friend says, "I know how to make it keep proper time. I will decrease the mass of the object at the end of the pendulum. That will speed up the swing rate because the equation $F_{net} = ma$ says lighter objects accelerate faster. Thus, the lighter pendulum mass has less mass and will move faster." Choose a convincing mix of explanation techniques to either confirm or refute your friend's comments.

Part III: Graph-o-holic

Materials

For each team of 2 students

colored pencils

graph paper

access to a computer

animations *Simple Pendulum* and *Spring Pendulum* on the *Student Resource CD* (*SRCD*)

Process and Procedure

Part III is a challenge opportunity. You will use what you have learned to make some connections. You will continue to create and compare graphs because that is a good method to find relationships. You and a partner will construct these graphs by aligning them by their x-axes. That way, it will be easier to compare the motions.

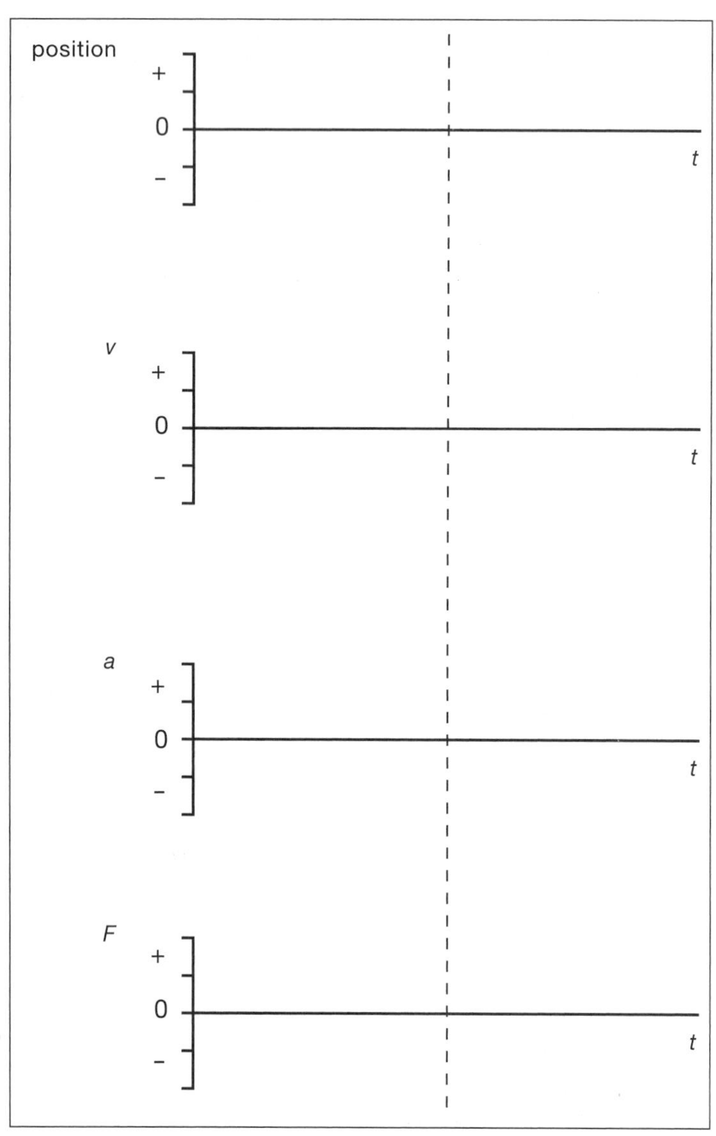

▲ **Figure 4.28 Aligned graph axes.** Draw your graphs on a clean page in your science notebook. Vertically align the time axes for all of the graphs.

1. Draw qualitative graphs of *either* 1 full period of oscillation for spring motion *or* 1 full period of oscillation for pendulum motion. Steps 1a–f will help you organize your graphs.
   a. Use figure 4.28 as a guide to organize your graphs. Note that the time axes are aligned.
   b. Assume that the motion starts to the left for the pendulum and at the top of the oscillation for spring motion. (This is position A on figure 4.25.)
   c. Plot high-confidence points of the motion.

High-confidence points are points for position and velocity that you are sure of. Think about times where position, velocity, acceleration, or force is equal to zero.

d. Connect the high-confidence points with a line.

Should you use a straight or a curved line?

e. Label each graph with points of maximum and minimum values of position, velocity, acceleration, and force.

f. Write a caption for your set of graphs that communicates the relationships of each graph.

2. Find at least 1 team that analyzed a different motion from your team's and choose an effective strategy to compare and contrast each set of graphs.

Possible strategies include but are not limited to T-tables, paragraphs, Venn diagrams, and annotated sketches.

3. View the animation *Simple Pendulum* on the *SRCD* again. Complete Steps 3a–d as you watch.
   a. Select the button on the bottom right for velocity and start the animation.
   b. What is the direction of the velocity vector compared with the direction of the pendulum's motion?
   c. Repeat Steps 3a–b 2 more times, first choosing the acceleration button and then the force button.
   d. Check your graphs from Step 1 and revise them if necessary. Remember to mark your revisions in a different color.
4. Repeat Steps 3a–d for the animation *Spring Pendulum*, also on the *SRCD*.

Reflect and Connect

Answer these questions in your science notebook. Then use a strategy such as TSAR to finish your answers.

1. Imagine holding a soda bottle accelerometer while you swing back and forth on a playground swing. Make a series of 3 sketches similar to figure 4.29. Add the string and cork to show what the side view of your accelerometer would look like at both extremes and at the middle of the swing. Provide highlight comments for each sketch.
2. Answer Questions 2a–e about the meaning of the words "negative" and "positive" when referring to motion and graphs.
   a. What is the physical meaning of negative position?

When thinking about the physical meaning, consider how, where, or in what direction an object is moving.

   b. What is the physical meaning of negative velocity?
   c. What is the physical meaning of negative acceleration?

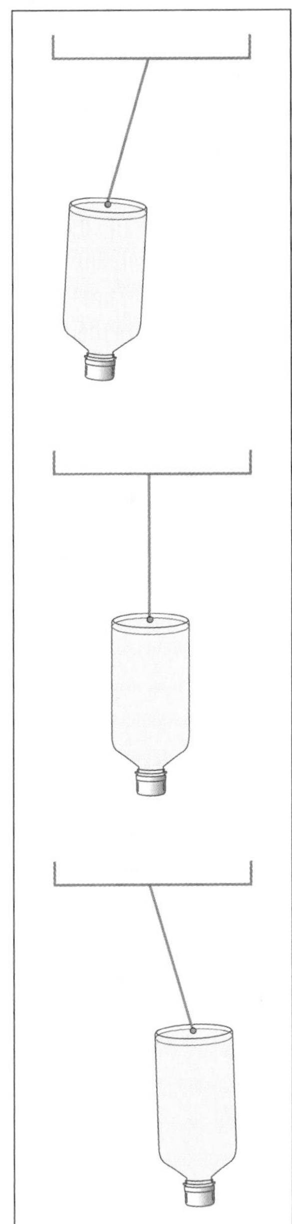

▲ Figure 4.29
Swinging accelerometer. Imagine holding a soda bottle accelerometer while you swing back and forth on a playground swing. What would the string and cork look like as you moved like a pendulum?

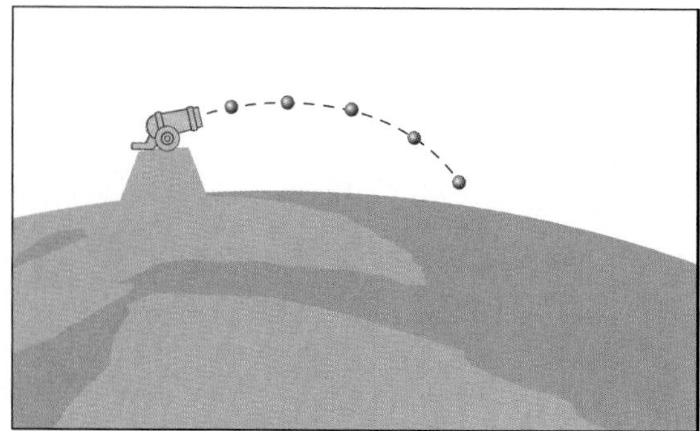

▲ **Figure 4.30 Cannon firing.** What would the path of the cannonball look like if the cannon could fire the ball with higher and higher initial velocity?

d. What is the physical meaning of negative force?

e. How do you convey the meaning of negative relative to positive on graphs? In algebraic equations? In vectors? With words?

3. Chemists often think of chemical bonds as invisible springs connecting atoms. Suppose you were investigating the motion between parts of 2 acid molecules.

a. Acetic acid: $CH_3COO \xleftrightarrow[\text{bond}]{\text{chemical}} H$

b. Propanoic acid: $CH_3CH_2COO \xleftrightarrow[\text{bond}]{\text{chemical}} H$

If both acids were at the same temperature, which one would oscillate with the smallest period and why?

4. Think of other periodic motions, like the Moon orbiting Earth or your favorite CD spinning. Choose a method to compare and contrast circular motions like these with pendulum and spring motions. Consider changing or nonchanging force, acceleration, velocity, and position. Find at least 1 classmate who used a comparison technique different from yours. Ask your classmate to explain his or her comparison.

5. Suppose you shot off a cannon from a tall mountain. The path of the cannonball would curve as shown in figure 4.30. Imagine firing the cannon with higher and higher initial velocity. What would the path of the cannonball look like? Describe at least 2 very different scenarios; use both sentences and sketches in your descriptions.

ELABORATE

Sky High Motion

The motions that you have studied in this chapter are all the result of forces. Some of those forces are the result of the force of gravity. Can you think of which motions result from gravity? Is a paintball shot from a paintball gun affected by gravity? The path of the paintball curves as it falls due to its original horizontal velocity after leaving the gun and the force of gravity. Imagine having a super powerful paintball gun that could shoot the ball at extremely high velocities. At some velocity, the paintball would fall in a curved path that matched the curvature of Earth. You have put the paintball in orbit!

The motion of the paintball in an imaginary orbit around Earth is an example of the circular motion that you learned about in a previous activity. However, the circular motion you studied did not result from gravity. Remember twirling around, holding a plastic bottle of water?

The force that kept the bottle moving in a circular motion was the force of your hand on the bottle. And that force pointed toward you.

Think about the motion of the Moon around Earth. The Moon moves in an almost circular path, but what force keeps it in motion around Earth? There is nothing physical holding the Moon in orbit around Earth, but rather, the force of gravity supplies this force. The Moon is a satellite of Earth. A **satellite** is any object that orbits another object. Figure 4.31 shows an example of a satellite that orbits Earth.

In *Sky High Motion*, you will work with a team to investigate different types of satellites and different types of orbits. You will apply your understanding of forces, acceleration, velocity, motion, and direction as you explain your satellite's motion to the class. Your task is to prepare a presentation with a visual display that conveys one application of the understanding you have developed so far in this chapter.

Materials

For each team of 3–4 students

access to the Web

access to reference materials in the library

computers or poster materials for visual display

▲ **Figure 4.31 Satellite in orbit.** What type of satellite will you investigate in this activity? What type of orbit will be appropriate for your satellite? Apply what you have learned about forces to understand how your satellite stays in orbit.

Process and Procedure

Work with your team to complete the following tasks. As you work, focus on this question: "How can I apply what I have learned about forces and motion to satellite motion?"

1. Research different types of artificial satellites and choose one that interests your team.

Use a combination of library and Web resources. Make sure to keep a record of all of your references. See *How to Cite References and Avoid Plagiarism* and *How to Conduct an Effective Web Search* in the *How To* section at the back of your book.

Topic: satellites
Go to: www.scilinks.org
Code: 2Inquiry208

2. Research the different types of orbits that satellites make and determine the type of orbit that is best for the satellite your team chose.
3. Individually, draw a carefully labeled illustration of Earth and your satellite in orbit. Use labeled vectors to represent the relative sizes and direction for force, acceleration, and velocity for your satellite. Show at least 4 different positions along the path of the orbit.
4. Decide with your team the best way to communicate your understanding of forces and motion for your satellite. Use the following criteria to prepare your report and presentation for the class. Your final product must include the following.
   a. Verbal presentation by the team
   b. Visual display
   c. Diagram of your satellite in orbit, complete with qualitative scaled vectors for force, acceleration, and velocity

   Revise one of your team's diagrams from Step 3 to reflect the best ideas of the team.

   d. Description of your satellite and its use
   e. Description of advances in science that have resulted from your satellite technology
   f. Description of the type of orbit that your satellite follows and why this type is the best one for your satellite
   g. Comparison of the force of gravity on your satellite and the force of gravity on you

   Read *FYI—Universal Gravitation* to understand how you will make these comparisons. Each member of your team will need to do a separate calculation.

   h. Distance from Earth, the velocity of your satellite, and the period of revolution of your satellite

   Compare satellites that are close to Earth and farther from Earth. Which ones must move faster and why? How do their periods compare?

   i. List of your references with at least 2 references from resources other than the Web.

5. Divide up the tasks of the project. Make sure everyone on the team has a role gathering information, applying knowledge, preparing the visual display, and presenting the material.
6. Develop at least 3 questions that you will ask other teams during the presentations. These questions should be consistent with the requirements of the activity and should not be meant to "stump" the other teams.

Reflect and Connect

Answer the following questions either individually or with a partner as your teacher directs. Record your answers in your science notebook.

1. If you could somehow stop a satellite from moving, it would simply crash into Earth. Why, then, don't satellites that appear in the same spot above Earth simply crash into Earth?
2. Some satellites follow an elliptical orbit, as shown in figure 4.32. In fact, the orbit of Earth around the Sun is very slightly elliptical. In perfectly circular orbits, the magnitude of the velocity (the speed) of the satellite is constant. Would the speed of the satellite in figure 4.32 be constant or changing? Justify your answer with your understanding of forces.
3. Use figure 4.32 to indicate positions in the orbit where the satellite experiences the following.
   a. Maximum force of gravity
   b. Minimum force of gravity
   c. Maximum speed
   d. Minimum speed
   e. Greatest momentum
   f. Least momentum
   g. Increasing speed
   h. Decreasing speed

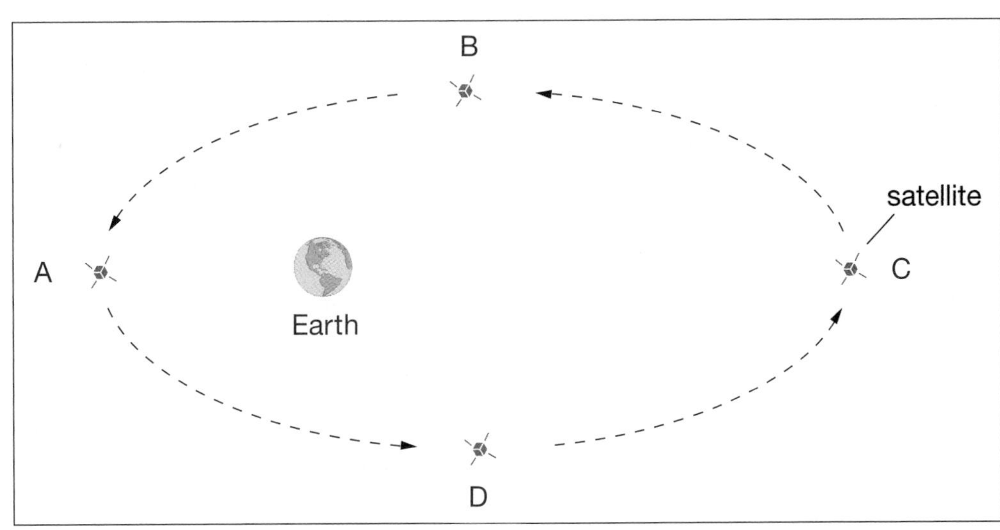

Figure 4.32 Elliptical satellite path. Would a satellite in an elliptical orbit have a constant or a changing velocity? Note: Distances are not to scale.

4. List any new problems or ethical issues that have resulted from satellite technology.
5. Describe at least one new area of research that satellite technology has provided to scientists.

Universal Gravitation

The force of gravity is something all too familiar to you. As an infant, you "studied" gravity as you adjusted to its effects when you dropped your bowl of cereal off the high chair or when you fell while learning to walk. As you grew older, you naturally learned to compensate for the force and accelerations produced by gravity as you learned to kick a soccer ball, catch a baseball, or shoot a basketball. How would you have to adjust if you were playing these sports on a planet other than Earth? Gravity has influenced the way we do everything on Earth. It has even influenced the course of evolution.

Level 1 of this program introduced the universal law that describes the mutual gravitational force of attraction between any two objects. Every object exerts a force on every other object due to mutual gravitational attraction. This force is directly proportional to the masses of the objects and inversely proportional to the square of the distance between their centers. You can use this relationship to calculate the force of gravity between Earth and a satellite. The equation for this relationship, known as the universal law of gravitation, is

$$F_{gravity} \text{ or } F_g = \frac{Gm_1m_2}{d^2}, \text{ where}$$

G = universal gravitation constant $(6.67 \times 10^{-11} \frac{m^3}{kg\ sec^2})$,

m_1 and m_2 = masses of two objects in kilograms,

d = the distance (in meters) between the centers of mass of the two objects.

In Level 1, this relationship was used to find the force of gravity between galaxies, students, and a student and Earth. In fact, you can use it to calculate the force between any two objects if you know their masses and the distance between their centers of mass. For objects near Earth's surface, the distance between the objects is simply the radius of Earth (6.38×10^6 m). The mass of Earth is 5.98×10^{24} kg.

This universal law of gravitation is related to Newton's second law in the following way. The equation you have learned for Newton's second law is,

$$F_{net} = ma.$$

For an object in free fall, the only force acting on the body is that due to the gravitational force. Then from the universal law of gravitation, the equation becomes,

$$\frac{GmM}{r^2} = ma.$$

In this equation, m represents the mass of the object, and M represents the mass of Earth. So for objects near Earth and canceling the mass on both sides of the equation, the equation becomes,

$$\frac{GM}{r^2} = a.$$

An object that is attracted to Earth by gravity accelerates with constant acceleration of

$$\frac{GM}{r^2}.$$

For ease of writing, we rename the term, $\frac{GM}{r^2}$, g. Thus, the acceleration due to gravity is g.

All of the values in $\frac{GM}{r^2}$ are constants, so putting in the values for these constants in the expression gives us the following:

$$\frac{GM}{r^2} = a$$

$$\frac{\left(6.67 \times 10^{-11} \frac{m^3}{kg\ s^2}\right)\left(5.98 \times 10^{24}\ kg\right)}{(6.38 \times 10^6\ m)^2} = a$$

$$\frac{\left(6.67 \times 10^{-11} \frac{\cancel{m^2} \times m^1}{\cancel{kg}\ s^2}\right)\left(5.98 \times 10^{24}\ \cancel{kg}\right)}{4.07 \times 10^{13}\ \cancel{m^2}} = a$$

$$9.80\ \frac{m}{s^2} = a$$

This is our familiar acceleration due to gravity near Earth's surface.

Unit 1, *Interactions Are Interesting*, has introduced you to the laws of motion described by Sir Isaac Newton. In fact, he is also responsible for finding the relationships described in the universal law of gravitation. It took Newton 20 years to prove that this law is valid for large objects like the planets as well as very small particles.

Moving toward Understanding

EVALUATE

In this chapter, you have linked net force to many types of motion in a match between cause and effect. The result is your increased ability to explain, understand, and apply motions common to your everyday environment. These are motions such as free fall, spring motion, pendulum motion, projectile motion, and uniform circular motion. That's a lot of understanding.

Now it is time to demonstrate what you know and understand. Of course, learning is ongoing. So the test you will take in this activity is vital feedback that helps you and your teacher make the best plans for your long-term benefit.

First, you will work with team members to review the relationships among concepts important to motion. Then you will take a test on your own to demonstrate your understanding of force and motion. After the test, you will learn how to use feedback to improve your understanding.

Part I: Structured Review

Materials

For each team of 4 students

4 *Concept Map* handouts

4 *Moving toward Understanding Scoring Rubric* handouts

colored markers

1 large piece of paper

Process and Procedure

There are many effective ways to review for a test. One technique is to reexamine what you know about the key concepts of the chapter (figure 4.33). Focusing on the *relationships* among those concepts and how those relationships help you solve problems is particularly effective.

Concept maps are one way to represent and communicate the relationships among concepts important to force and motion. You generated a concept map in chapter 3, *Collisions—Atomic Style.* The map communicated which concept you thought was most important and which concepts are most closely related. Your map showed the concepts you are most likely to use when you solve problems and the ones you tend not to use. Concept maps give you feedback about the way you approach thinking and solving problems in science.

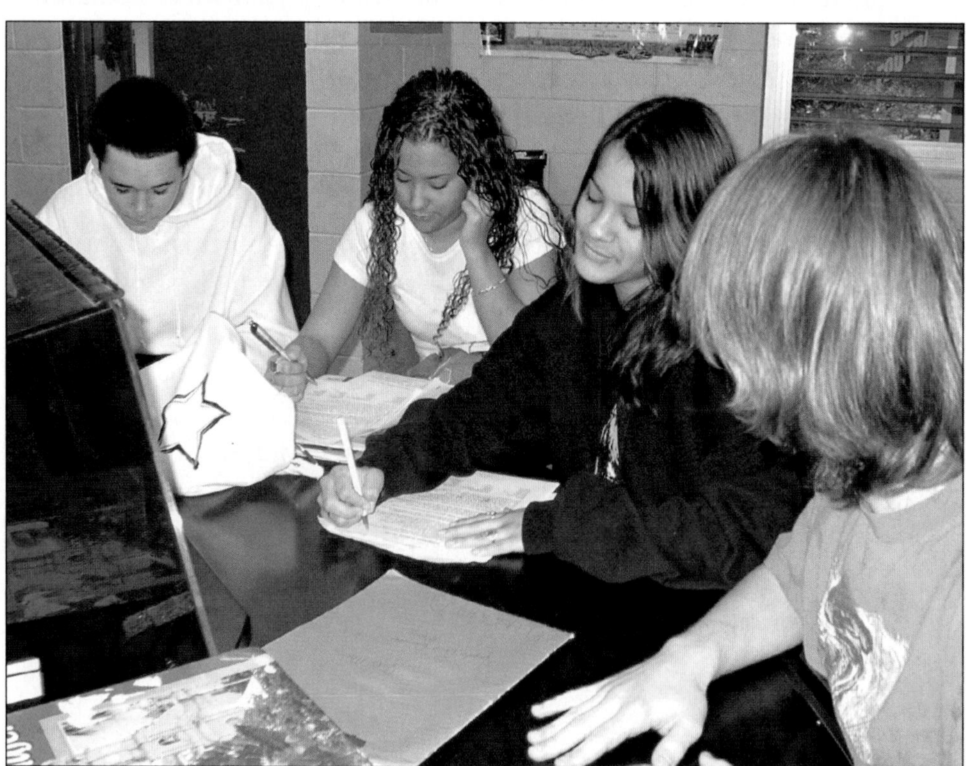

Figure 4.33
Structured review. These students are working together to focus on the relationships among the concepts covered in this chapter. In this way, they will be prepared for the upcoming chapter assessment.

In Part I, you and your team will use completed concept maps to consider different ways of thinking. In doing so, you will review and strengthen your own understanding about force and motion.

1. Review the *Moving toward Understanding Scoring Rubric* handout to understand what is expected of you for this activity. Ask your teacher for clarification if you do not understand any part of the rubric.
2. Examine the *Concept Map* handout, which shows 2 concept maps created from concepts in this chapter. Use this handout to complete Steps 2a–e.
   a. Develop a list of criteria with your class of the important features of a concept map. List those features that will convey the best understanding of the concepts.
   b. Decide which concept map shows a better understanding of the concepts in this chapter based on the criteria from your class discussion.
   c. Write a justification for your selection of the best concept map.
   d. Redraw the concept map you chose onto a large piece of paper using colored markers.
   e. Add connecting language to your concept map that communicates the relationship of the connected words.
   f. Add other details to your concept map that will help you review the material in this chapter.
   g. Take turns explaining the concepts in your map to your teammates. Use language that explains the relationship between concepts. Be prepared to share your ideas with other teams, the class, or your teacher.

Part II: Multiple-Choice Test

Materials

For each student

1 multiple-choice test booklet

Process and Procedure

1. Obtain a copy of the multiple-choice test from your teacher.
2. Follow your teacher's instructions and work individually to complete the test.
3. Hand in your test when you are finished.

Part III: Learn from Mistakes

Materials

For each student

the scored copy of your test

Process and Procedure

Now it's time to get feedback on what you know and understand. The feedback is called learning from mistakes. Be prepared to analyze your individual test results for patterns in what you understood and what is still challenging for you. Then use the process of scientific inquiry to learn from mistakes you may have made.

Your teacher will score your test from Part II and give you immediate feedback. Part of that feedback will be a discussion of the concepts important to each question.

1. Participate in a class discussion of how to demonstrate that you have learned from mistakes.
2. Read the *Learn from Mistakes* (*LFM*) *Protocol* carefully before you begin to make corrections.
3. Follow the *LFM Protocol* for each question you missed and turn in your paper as instructed by your teacher.

Protocol

Learn from Mistakes Protocol

School isn't just a place to deposit right answers. Sometimes we make mistakes. In fact, most humans make mistakes when they try to learn something, especially when the subject is difficult or new. When you learn to identify and explain what is incorrect about a wrong answer, you have a better chance of not making that mistake again.

For each of the questions you missed on the test, perform the following steps. If you do, you can earn up to 50 percent of the difference between your raw percent score and 100 percent. Be sure to write your raw percent score at the top of the page along with a list of the numbers you missed.

1. Represent the original question in a different way than it was represented on the test. For example, if the question was mostly words, represent it as a sketch. If it was mostly a sketch, represent it in words. When you use words, paraphrase the question in your own words. Do not copy the question word for word. Label any sketch with all the variables, especially the unknown. If the problem mentions any change in condition, show a before-and-after sketch.
2. Identify and explain the mistake you made in the answer you selected. Focus on explaining any conceptual misunderstandings. When you explain what is incorrect, show how the misconception would lead to a contradiction with what you see in nature. Explanations like, "I read the problem wrong" and "I pushed the wrong button on the calculator" will receive no credit.
3. Show the correct solution or answer. When necessary, show all governing equations, first in symbol form, then with number and unit values. Always place proper units and labels on answers. Include why the answer is reasonable.

CHAPTER 5

Forces of Attraction

Forces of Attraction

You have been studying how horizontal and vertical forces act on objects that are falling, spinning, swinging, or simply moving along a tabletop. You can see the effects of these forces. These forces cause a change. But what do these forces have to do with chemical reactions? Do forces in chemical reactions cause a change? If so, then how do the changes that molecules undergo compare to the changes large objects experience?

Recall that electrons are negatively charged, and the nucleus of an atom is positively charged. The nucleus contains positively charged protons and neutral neutrons. The force of attraction between the positively charged nucleus and the negatively charged electrons is the force that holds the atom together. The strength of that force and the mutual attraction of charged particles are the keys to understanding the chemical reactions that you will study in chapter 5, *Forces of Attraction*. Look at the opening art to see the similarities between macroscopic and microscopic forces.

There are many ways to classify or group chemical reactions. From chapter 3, *Collisions—Atomic Style*, you may think of grouping chemical reactions according to their rate. Relatively slow reactions such as an iron nail rusting would fall into one group, and the very rapid reaction of vinegar and baking soda would fall into a different group. In this chapter, you will look at two very important categories of chemical reactions. They are oxidation-reduction reactions and acid-base reactions. These reactions are some of the most familiar and important reactions in nature.

You may wonder why some nails rust and others do not. What metal is used to make the nails that do not rust? Or are the nonrusting nails ordinary nails that are simply treated in some way? These questions can be answered by understanding the chemistry behind oxidation-reduction reactions. You will be pleased to know that you already have the knowledge foundation to make this learning easier. What you learned about forces in the previous chapter will help you better understand these interactions on an atomic scale.

The strength of forces will also help you understand why some acids and bases are weak and some are strong. We eat pickles that are stored in vinegar (a weak acid), but you know that battery acid (a very strong acid) will harm us if it gets on our skin or in our eyes. So you see that some acids are weak enough to even be edible, but others will damage our bodies. What makes one acid strong and another weak? Is it the concentration of the acid or is it something fundamentally different about the molecular makeup of the acid? Or is it both?

Goals for the Chapter

As you work through the activities in this chapter, you will have the opportunity to conduct investigations, work with your classmates, and answer questions individually about chemical reactions. By the end of this chapter, you should be able to answer these questions:

- What does it mean for an acid or base to be "strong"?
- What does pH mean, and how does the pH scale work?
- Why does iron rust but gold does not?
- Can we predict how metals will react?
- How are forces of attraction for ions such as the hydrogen ion (H^+) and negatively charged electrons (e^-) involved in chemical reactions?
- What are the applications of these types of chemical reactions?

To help you answer these questions and others, you will participate in the following activities:

ENGAGE	Ranking Tasks
EXPLORE	Gathering Evidence
EXPLAIN	Acids and Bases
EXPLAIN	Redox Reactions
ELABORATE	Electrochemistry
EVALUATE	Nail It Down

Use your chapter organizer as a road map for your learning journey through this chapter. Look at it daily to review what you have studied and to see what you will study today and in the days to come.

Forces of Attraction

Linking Question

How can I verify my classifications and rankings with evidence?

ENGAGE

Ranking Tasks

Key Ideas:

- Students can use their experiences to identify acids and bases and rank them according to degrees of acidity and basicity.
- Students can use their experience to rank metals by their degree of reactivity.

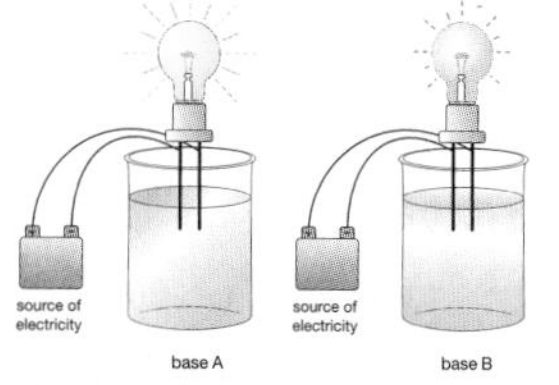

EXPLORE

Gathering Evidence

Key Ideas:

- Acids and bases have specific ranges of pH values.
- Metal reactivity can be determined based on observable evidence.

Linking Question

How can I use my knowledge of forces to explain acid-base behavior?

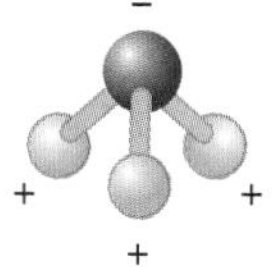

EXPLAIN

Acids and Bases

Key Ideas:

- Acids and bases vary in strength due to the forces of attraction of ions.
- Both strength and concentration play a role in determining the pH of substances.

Linking Question

Can I use my knowledge of forces of attraction to also explain oxidation-reduction reactions?

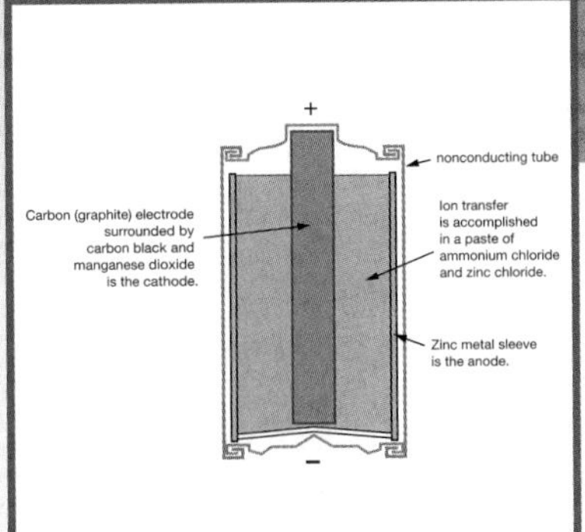

EVALUATE

Nail It Down

Key Idea:
Corrosion is a process that can be controlled by understanding acid-base and redox chemistry.

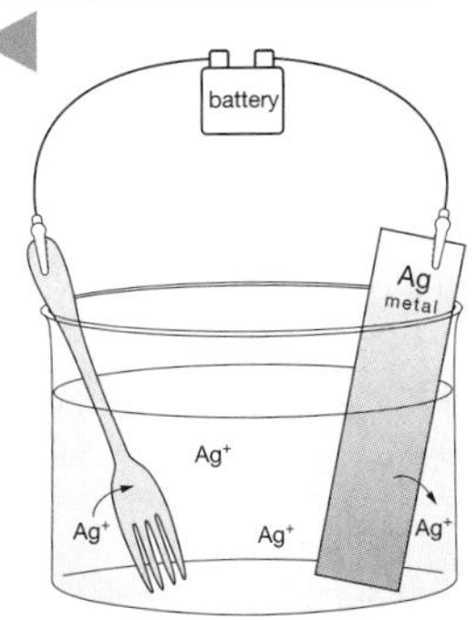

Linking Question

How can I demonstrate what I have learned about acid-base and oxidation-reduction reactions?

CHAPTER 5

Major Concepts

- **Acids and bases vary in strength and concentration and affect pH.**
- **Acid-base processes can be explained by the relative attractions for hydrogen ions.**
- **The activity of elements depends on the relative attractions for electrons.**
- **Oxidation-reduction reactions can be designed to give the desired results.**

ELABORATE

Electrochemistry

Key Idea:
By understanding the strength of reducing and oxidizing agents, redox reactions can be designed to produce useful processes and products.

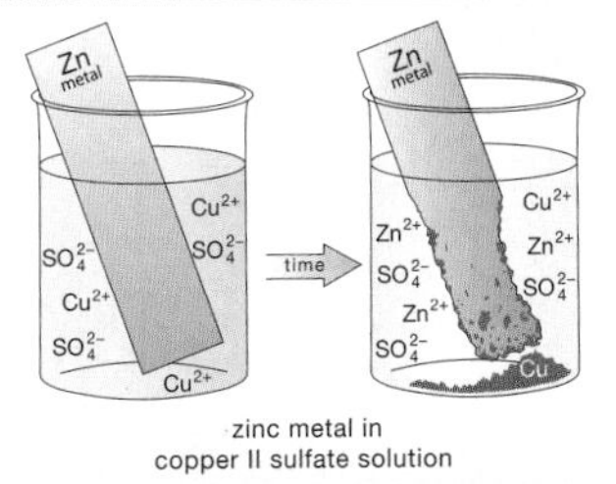

zinc metal in copper II sulfate solution

EXPLAIN

Redox Reactions

Key Idea:
Reactivity is predictable based on the competition for electrons in redox reactions.

Linking Question

Can I design redox reactions to produce useful processes and products?

ENGAGE

Ranking Tasks

Life is packed with competitions. There is competition for class rank, to be first in line at the movie theater, or to be first chair in your section of the band. Often, competition results in ranking things from best to worse or strongest to weakest. Sometimes ranking tells you something about the properties of objects. For example, the venom from a brown recluse spider is ranked as one of the most poisonous. A ranking system for how poisonous different spiders are helps you learn what spiders can be potentially deadly and what spiders are virtually harmless. In this activity, you and your team will be ranking items and substances. Understanding how these items rank will help you understand something about their properties.

Does battery acid harm you if it gets on your skin? What about lemon juice? Have you ever accidentally spilled drain cleaner on your hand? What were the results? In Part I of *Ranking Tasks*, you will use your everyday experiences with some common substances to first sort and then rank the substances according to what you currently know about them. Later, you will connect your ranking to the force of attraction between electrically charged objects.

Part II is similar to Part I. You will think about the reactivity of some metals. What might you notice about some nails that are left outside for a long period? Do all nails behave this way? You will think about these things as you work with a partner to rank metals according to how reactive they are with other substances.

Use the following question to focus your thinking and actions in this and the next four activities: "How do forces of attraction and repulsion help me understand chemical reactions?"

Part I: Acid, Base, or Neutral?

As you work through Part I of *Ranking Tasks*, think about your experiences with the substances that are listed on the cards that you will receive. Talk with your teammates and use your current understanding to complete the task.

Materials

For each team of 2–4 students

Card Pack 1

Property Card Pack

Process and Procedure

1. Meet with your team and obtain *Card Pack 1* from your teacher. Spread the cards face up on your desk or table.
2. Discuss each of the substances on the cards. Talk about your experiences with each of them.

If there is a substance listed on a card that no one on your team recognizes, ask another team for help.

3. Use your everyday experiences and general knowledge about each substance to complete Steps 3a–b.
   a. Make a chart with 3 columns in your science notebook on a blank, left-hand page. Place the substances on each card into 1 of 3 categories: acid, base, or neutral.

Each team member should make a chart in his or her notebook.

   b. Make a chart with the same 3 categories on the right-hand page and record your justifications for placing each substance in one of those categories.

What experiences do you have that led you to classify a substance as acid, base, or neutral? What evidence do you have for your reasoning? Use this evidence for your justifications.

4. Use the *Property Card Pack* to complete Steps 4a–d.
   a. With your team, read through the 2 cards in the *Property Card Pack*.
   b. Summarize these properties in a new chart in your science notebook.

Be sure to use headings that make sense in your chart.

   c. Make any changes to your categories based on new information.

Scientists classify or group things in many different ways, but they are always looking for similarities between things in the same group. If new evidence surfaces, they may change their groups or move items from one group to another.

   d. Record any changes *and* reasons for those changes in your charts.

Consider using a different-colored pen for any change you make. This helps you find and remember what you learned. It also helps you track your thinking.

5. Rank your acid and base items according to which substances you think are more or less acidic and more or less basic.
6. Participate in a class discussion of your rankings.

As you participate, share your rankings and your reasoning. Listen as others share their ideas about this ranking task.

7. Record any new ideas you hear or questions that you have in your science notebook.

Stop & THINK

PART I

Work individually as you answer these questions about Part I. Then consult with your team and record any changes you make, including the reasons for those changes.

1. What were the main criteria that you used in first grouping the substances?
2. How did your ideas change as you learned new information?
3. Antacids are used to neutralize excess stomach acid. How do you think this works?
4. You may have heard of pH and know that it relates to acids and bases. The scale that measures pH goes from 0 to 14 and is illustrated in figure 5.1. Copy this scale into your science notebook and indicate where you would put each of the substances you just worked with on the scale. Use your current understanding to place these substances on the scale. Don't worry about being exactly correct; you will learn more about the pH scale in the next activity.

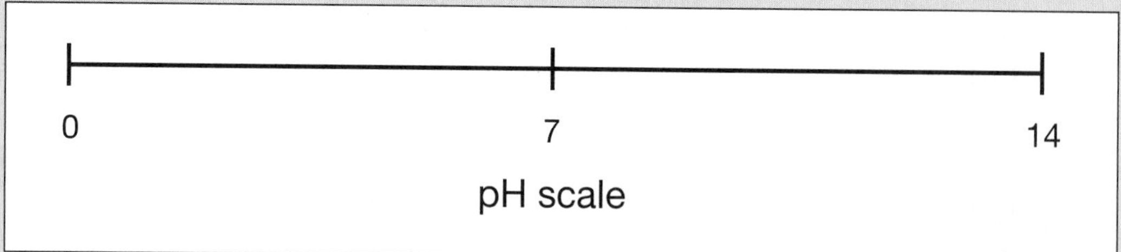

Figure 5.1 pH scale. Copy this scale into your science notebook. Where would the substances you worked with in Part I fall on this scale?

Part II: Active or Not?

Materials

For each team of 2–4 students

Card Pack 2

Process and Procedure

Many things in our world are made of metals, from our jewelry to huge skyscrapers. Do all metals behave in the same way? What chemical properties are important to consider when choosing which metal to use for a particular application? Some metals react by simply being exposed to the atmosphere. Other metals are very nonreactive. Knowing how metals rank in reactivity is important information to use when deciding the best metal to use for certain purposes. Use your experiences with metals of different kinds as you work with your team to complete another ranking task.

1. Meet with your team and obtain *Card Pack 2*. Spread the cards face up on your desk or table.
2. Design a step-by-step procedure to rank the metals in *Card Pack 2* from "most reactive" to "least reactive."

   Use your experiences with charts from Part I of this investigation to guide your design. Each team member should have a design in his or her science notebook.

3. Agree as a team on your design, then obtain your teacher's approval before conducting your design.
4. Follow your design to obtain a ranking of metal reactivity.
5. Participate in a class discussion of your rankings.

   As you participate, share your rankings and your reasoning. Listen as others share their ideas about this ranking task. Record any new ideas you hear or questions that you have in your science notebook.

Reflect and Connect

Answer these questions in your science notebook based on what you know and understand. Then work with your team members to check your thinking. Make revisions to your answers as needed.

1. How do you know that a metal is reacting with another substance? (That is, what is the evidence?)
2. Iron rusts but gold does not rust. Why don't we use gold to manufacture nails? Give at least 2 reasons why.
3. Electrolytes are substances that, when placed in water, conduct an electric current. For an electric current to flow, some type of charged particle (either ions or electrons) must be free to move.

Look at the 2 pictures in figure 5.2. What do the results of these 2 experiments tell you about the 2 bases in the figure?

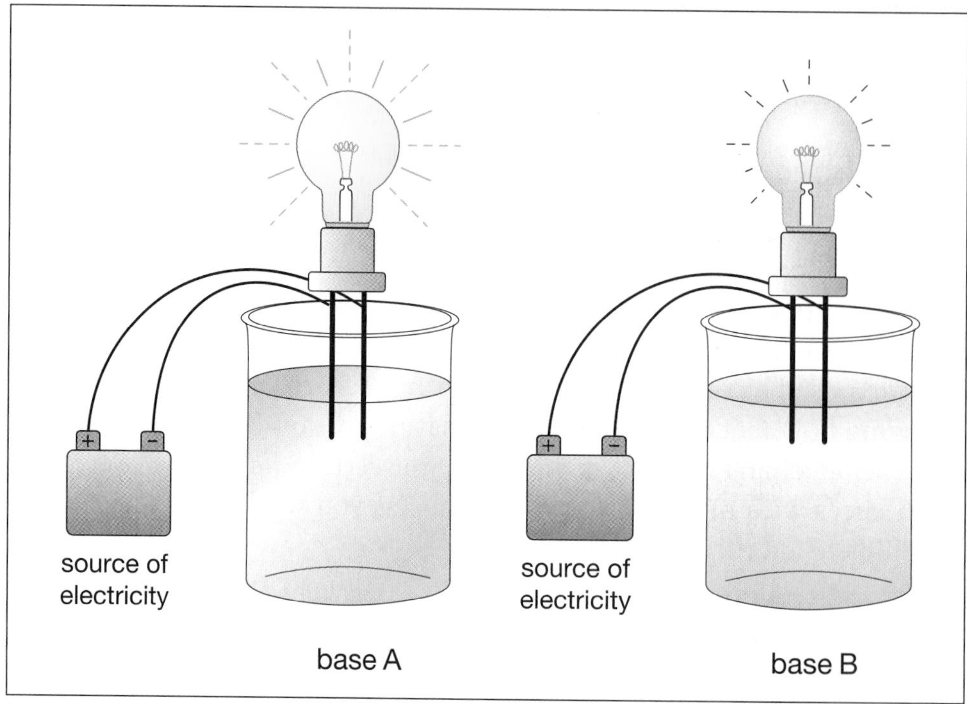

Figure 5.2 **Electrolytes in solution.** What do the results of these two experiments tell you about the different bases in solution? The concentration of the base in water is the same for both bases.

4. Consider this list of acids and their chemical formulas: hydrochloric acid (HCl), sulfuric acid (H_2SO_4), nitrous acid (HNO_2), and acetic acid (CH_3COOH, also written as $HC_2H_3O_2$). What do all these acids have in common?

EXPLORE

Gathering Evidence

There were certainly different rankings and groupings within your class for the previous activity. Did it frustrate you when your teacher did not give you the accepted answers for the tasks? Scientists often go long periods before they know if their ideas are supported by other evidence. They must wait for more evidence to verify their ideas. You have seen that knowing what spider is most poisonous is important to your safety. When you are ranking things such as poisonous spiders, it is important to have your rankings correct. Otherwise, you may mistake a potentially harmful spider for a harmless one.

But you are lucky. You do not have to wait long to find out if your rankings from the last activity are correct. You will gather your own evidence to develop explanations as you work with a team to verify your rankings.

Part I: pH Evidence

Materials

For each team of 2–4 students

2–4 pairs of safety goggles

2-4 pairs of safety gloves

2–4 laboratory aprons

microwell plates or small beakers

disposable plastic pipets

samples of common substances such as

- drain cleaner
- lemon juice
- baking soda solution
- ammonia
- vinegar
- rainwater
- soap solution
- antacid solution
- simulated stomach acid

pH meter, universal indicator solution, or pH paper

Cautions

Wear safety goggles, safety gloves, and lab aprons and take care not to touch any of the substances used in this activity. Even though you are working with household solutions, substances such as drain cleaner can be extremely harmful.

Process and Procedure

You began thinking about pH at the conclusion of the last activity. How is it used to rank acids and bases? Work with your team to test your rankings using pH.

1. Determine which end of the scale represents acids and which end represents bases by following the procedures in Steps 1a–f.

You saw in the last activity how pH is used when ranking acids and bases.

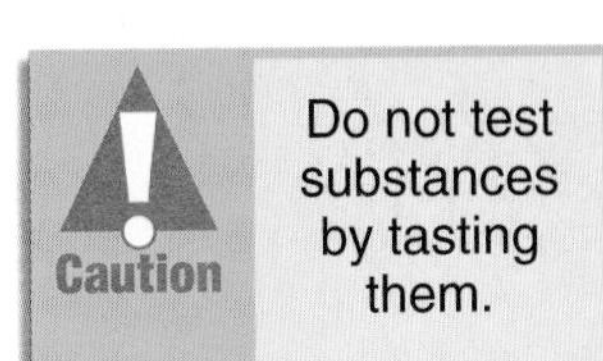

Caution
Do not test substances by tasting them.

a. Choose one of the substances that you know tastes sour.

Remember, one of the properties of acids is that it tastes sour.

b. Determine the pH of your substance. Use either a pH probe or an indicator as your teacher directs.

c. Draw another pH scale in your science notebook. Mark the divisions 0–14 from left to right along the scale. Label only 0, 7, and 14 on the scale.

Your scale should look similar to figure 5.1.

d. Record the pH and the name of your substance in your notebook.

e. Is this substance an acid or a base? Record your answer and justification in your notebook.

f. Does the pH value for this substance lie on the left or the right side of your scale? Record your answer in your notebook.

2. Use the drain cleaner to complete Steps 2a–d.

One property of bases is that they react to break down fats and oils. This makes bases good candidates for drain cleaners.

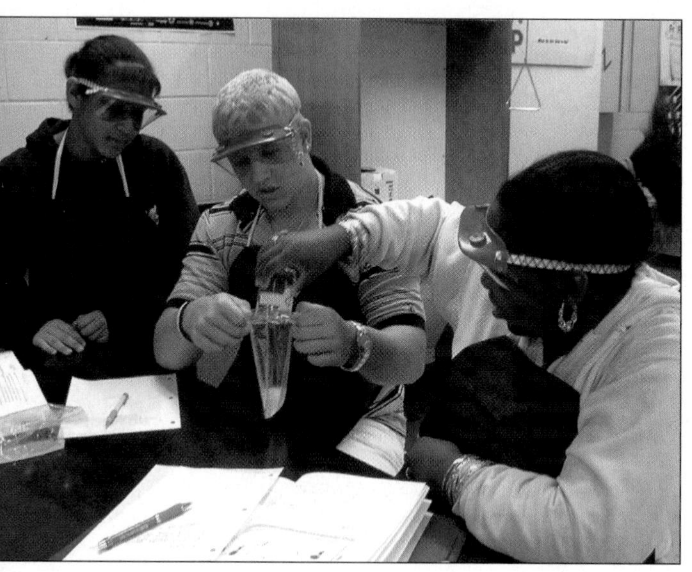

a. Determine the pH of your drain cleaner. Use either a pH probe or an indicator as your teacher directs.

b. Record the pH and the name of the drain cleaner in your science notebook.

c. Is this substance an acid or a base? Record your response in your notebook.

d. Does the pH value for this drain cleaner lie on the left or the right side of your scale? Keep records of your answer.

3. Label your pH scale with "acid" and "base" on the appropriate sides of the scale.

4. What do you think a pH of 7 means about the amount of acid and base present?

5. Design a step-by-step procedure to determine the pH of all your substances. Use your answers to the questions in Steps 5a–f to guide your design.

a. How will you determine the pH of each substance?

b. How will you make sure that there is no contamination of the samples?

c. What is the most efficient and organized way to keep track of all your data?

d. How will you rank these substances on the pH scale?

e. What safety precautions do you need to consider?

f. How will you clean up when you are finished?

6. After you have answered these questions and designed your tests, compare your design with the design of another team. Finally, have your teacher approve your design.
7. Conduct the tests that you have designed.

Stop & THINK

PART I

1. Suppose you needed a mild base to use as a gentle cleaner. You would not want to use a base that was extremely strong because it might be harmful to certain surfaces or to your skin. Knowing the degree of acidity or basicity (sometimes called alkalinity) is important in this case, and ranking is a way to confirm this. Using your experiences with these substances and the results of your pH tests, rank your acids from most acidic to least acidic. Rank your bases in a similar way.

   Be sure to label your rankings properly so that your teacher can interpret your answers.

2. Use arrows to label the pH scale that you drew in Step 1c to indicate increasing acidity and increasing basicity.

   You will have to use 2 separate arrows, one for acids and one for bases.

3. The cells of your skin contain lipids (or fats). Use what you know about the properties of acids and bases to explain why bases can be harmful to your skin.
4. You predicted the relative degrees of acidity and basicity in the engage activity, *Ranking Tasks*. Compare your results in this activity with your original predictions by answering the following questions.
   a. What substances changed in your rankings based on your tests?
   b. How did their grouping (acid or base) or ranking (more or less acidic or basic) change based on your tests?

Part II: Reactivity Evidence

Materials

For each team of 2–4 students

2–4 pairs of safety goggles

2–4 laboratory aprons

2–4 pairs of safety gloves

Test tube racks, test tubes

samples of the following metals:

- iron (Fe)
- copper (Cu)
- zinc (Zn)
- tin (Sn)
- aluminum (Al)
- magnesium (Mg)

3 M hydrochloric acid (HCl)

Cautions

Wear safety goggles, safety gloves, and lab aprons for each part of this experiment. Hydrochloric acid is corrosive; use care when working with acids. Wash your hands at the conclusion of the lab.

Process and Procedure

One of the properties of metals is their reactivity with other substances. Knowing their reactivities is important in making decisions for those who select building materials. Imagine if the supporting materials in your home or school were constructed with a metal that is highly reactive. The metal would disintegrate and the building would no longer be safe.

In the engage activity, you learned that acids react with some metals to produce a gas. You can use this property of acids and metals to determine their relative reactivities. That is, you can rank the chemical reactivity of metals. Work with a team to design and conduct chemical tests to verify your rankings from the previous activity.

Use the following question to focus your thinking and actions in this part of the activity: "How does chemical reactivity help me rank metals?"

1. Design an investigation to test the relative reactivities of the metals provided by your teacher. In planning your design, answer the questions in Steps 1a–f.
   a. Some metals react with air and form a coating on their outer surface. How will you ensure that the reaction is with the metal and not with the coating?
   b. What are some outside variables and how will you control them?
   c. How will you determine the reactivity of each metal?
   d. What is the best, and most organized, way to record your data?
   e. What safety precautions should you consider?
   f. How will you clean up when the investigation is finished?

2. Compare your design with the design of another team.

Make adjustments in your design based on advice from your classmates. Always have your teacher approve your design before proceeding.

3. Following all safety procedures, conduct your investigation. Wear safety goggles, safety gloves, and lab aprons and don't forget to wash your hands at the conclusion of the lab.
4. Rank your metals from most reactive to least reactive and record your ranking in your science notebook.
5. Read the following 2 paragraphs to learn how you can identify the gas produced in these chemical reactions.

The four typical gases produced in a chemical reaction are carbon dioxide (CO_2), oxygen (O_2), chlorine (Cl_2), and hydrogen (H_2). You can identify chlorine gas by its odor. You will recognize the smell of chlorine gas if you have ever been at a swimming pool. Chlorine kills bacteria in pools. Chlorine gas results when bleach reacts with water and other substances in the pool. Chlorine gas is toxic and should never be smelled directly.

Carbon dioxide, oxygen, and hydrogen are odorless gases. Scientists verify whether these gases are produced in chemical reactions by using a lighted wooden splint. If the gas is carbon dioxide, the flame will extinguish when the splint is placed in the presence of the gas. If the gas is oxygen, a glowing splint will relight when placed near where the gas is produced. If the gas produced is hydrogen, you can identify the gas by the "pop" you hear when you place a lighted splint near the gas that is produced.

6. Record your observations as your teacher demonstrates the procedure to test the type of gas produced.
7. What gas do you think is produced in the tests you conducted with your metals?

Use your knowledge of chemical reactions and the reactants involved to justify your answer.

8. Test the gas produced in the reactions with your metals and hydrochloric acid. Record the results in your science notebook.

You may have to add another small piece of metal if the bubbling has ceased.

9. Choose 1 metal and write the reactants of the chemical reaction that you investigated. Write the reactants in the form of a chemical equation.
10. Does the type of gas produced make sense based on the law of conservation of matter? Explain your answer.

11. To complete the chemical reaction you started in Step 8, do Steps 11a–c.
    a. Add the gas that is produced as a product of the chemical reaction.
    b. Is this the only product? Why or why not? Explain your answer based on the law of conservation of matter.
    c. Complete the chemical reaction with all the reactants and products.

Reflect and Connect

Develop answers to these questions on your own. After you have written your best ideas in your science notebook, check your thinking with classmates or your teacher.

1. How did your rankings of metals in the last activity differ from your predictions in the engage activity? What evidence did you use to modify your rankings?
2. You learned how to balance equations in chapter 3. Work through Questions 2a–d, which are related to chemical reactions with metals.
    a. Balance the following equation, which represents the chemical reaction of sodium and an acid.

    $$Na + HI \rightarrow H_2 + NaI$$

    b. What is the gas produced in this reaction and where did it come from?
    c. What is the symbol for the acid in this equation?
    d. A certain concentration of this acid has a pH of 1.3. Would you consider this to be very acidic? Why?
3. You used a strong acid to produce the chemical reactions in Part II of this activity. Would you expect the same results with a weak acid? Explain your reasoning.

EXPLAIN

Acids and Bases

Have you ever been stung by an ant or a bee? If you have, you have personally experienced the effects of formic acid (HCOOH). The sting you feel is the result of an injection of formic acid into your skin. Is formic acid a strong or a weak acid? Judging by what you feel, you may think it is a strong acid, but how do you know? What is it about acids and bases that makes one strong and another weak?

You have learned that you can rank acids and bases according to their pH. This helps identify them as more or less acidic or basic. What is the difference, on the atomic level, between acids and bases? You may have thought about this as you were working through the previous activities. In *Acids and Bases*, you will have the chance to answer this question. You will determine what it is about the atomic makeup of these substances that makes the difference.

This activity will help you develop your own explanations about the strength of acids and bases.

Materials

For each team of 2 students

marshmallows

toothpicks

markers

Process and Procedure

Acids and bases are an integral part of life and life processes. You have seen that many products that you use every day have properties of acids or bases. But did you know that your body functions best in a very narrow pH range? The acidity or alkalinity of your blood can give clues to doctors about your health. If this balance is disrupted, you can become very ill.

Topic: blood pH
Go to: www.scilinks.org
Code: 2Inquiry233

Understanding acids and bases involves understanding protons, charges, and forces. This actually makes your work a lot easier since you have already learned about these three concepts. All you have to do now is understand them in the context of acid-base chemistry.

As with many concepts in science, there are multiple ways to define or think about acids and bases. For the purposes of this chapter, we will use a general description of acids recognized by the Swedish chemist Svante Arrhenius (1859–1927). This model of acids and bases, known as the Arrhenius model, describes an **acid** as a chemical compound that increases the concentration of hydrogen ions (H^+) in solution. A **base** is described as a chemical compound that increases the concentration of hydroxide ions (OH^-) in solution. How do acids and bases increase the number of these ions? Are there differences in the extent to which some acids or bases form these ions? You will work with a partner to understand the chemistry behind acids and bases and what causes one to be strong or weak.

1. Read *Dissociation* to find out where OH^- (hydroxide) and H^+ (hydrogen) ions come from.

READING

Dissociation

You have seen examples of many acids and have examined their chemical formulas. Some examples include hydrochloric acid (HCl), sulfuric acid (H_2SO_4), nitrous acid (HNO_2), and acetic acid (CH_3COOH). Most acids, including these, have hydrogen in them, and often hydrogen is written first in the chemical formula. You may recall studying dissociation in previous science classes. Dissociation occurs when compounds break apart to form charged particles. When these acids are placed in water, the acid molecule dissociates to varying degrees according to the following general acid dissociation equation:

$$HA_{(aq)} \rightleftharpoons H^{+}_{(aq)} + A^{-}_{(aq)}$$

HA is the general chemical formula to represent an acid.

According to Arrhenius, bases are substances that increase the number of OH^- in solution; thus, many bases contain an OH^- (hydroxide) group. Some chemical equations representing dissociation of bases can be represented generally, like the following:

$$MOH_{(aq)} \rightleftharpoons M^{+}_{(aq)} + OH^{-}_{(aq)}$$

MOH is the general chemical formula for metal hydroxides such as sodium hydroxide (NaOH) or potassium hydroxide (KOH). Metal hydroxides are bases.

2. Complete Steps 2a–c to develop a model of acids at the atomic level.
   a. Build a model of a general acid (HA) molecule using 2 marshmallows and a toothpick.
   b. With a marker, label one marshmallow "H^+" and the other marshmallow "A^-."
   c. Draw a picture of this molecule on a blank page in your science notebook so that you will have a permanent record. Leave room to add other pictures and labels to the right of this diagram. Label this picture "acid dissociation."
3. Write the dissociation reaction for the following substances. Use the general examples from the reading as your guide.
   a. Hydrochloric acid (HCl)
   b. Acetic acid (CH_3COOH)
   c. Sodium hydroxide (NaOH)
   d. Lithium hydroxide (LiOH)

4. Complete Steps 4a–c to generate a model of a base.
   a. Build a model of a general hydroxide, represented by MOH.

Use 3 marshmallows instead of 2, along with the correct number of toothpicks.

   b. With a marker, label each atom and charge.

The hydroxide will stay together, and the OH pair has a negative charge. The M (which represents the metal) will always have a positive charge. Put the O and the H very close together in your model—these atoms stay together in the reaction.

   c. Draw a picture of this molecule on a blank page in your science notebook so that you will have a permanent record. Leave room to add other pictures and labels to the right of this diagram. Label this picture "base dissociation."
5. Using your models as props, explain the dissociation of an acid and a base to your partner. Switch roles when you are finished.
6. Read *Water Works* to see what happens to the water molecule in the presence of acids and some bases.

READING

Water Works

When an acid dissociates in water, the acid breaks apart into positive hydrogen ions (H^+, really just protons) and negative ions. These ions form a solution with water, which is a polar molecule. Recall that water molecules, while being neutral overall, are very polar and have an unequal distribution of charge around the molecule (figure 5.3). When the hydrogen ion is in the presence of a polar water molecule, the ion will be attracted to the water molecule's negative end. This plus-minus attraction results in the formation of the more stable hydronium ion.

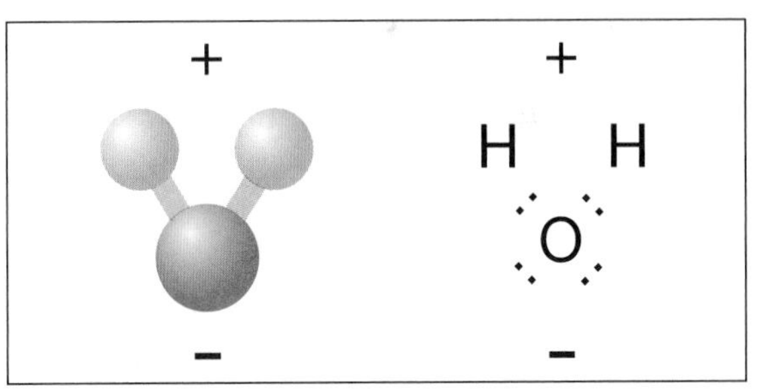

▲ **Figure 5.3 A polar water molecule.** The unequal distribution of the electrons around this neutral water molecule cause one end of the molecule to have a partial negative charge and one end to have a partial positive charge.

Water plays an important role in some base processes as well. According to Arrhenius, a base is a substance that increases the number of hydroxide or OH^- ions in solution. Consider the gas ammonia (NH_3). When ammonia dissolves in water, initially it retains its molecular formula, NH_3. Then it reacts with water to form hydroxide ions. It does not dissociate into ions to any significant amount. So there must be something different occurring besides simple dissociation.

Water Works, continued

Ammonia (figure 5.4) is a polar molecule, like water. The ammonia molecule exhibits a force of attraction to hydrogen atoms in water. When ammonia comes close to water, the ammonia molecule "rips off" one of the hydrogens from the water molecule. This happens because the force of attraction between hydrogen and ammonia is stronger than the force of attraction between the hydrogen atom and water. Note that the ammonia molecule takes the hydrogen nucleus only, not the hydrogen's electron.

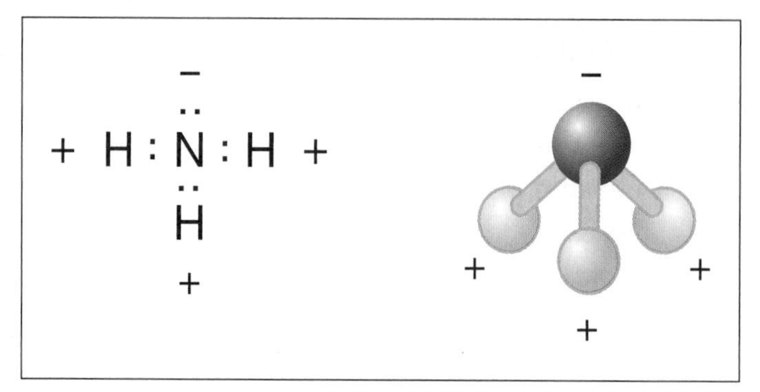

▲ **Figure 5.4 Ammonia molecule.** This molecule produces hydroxide ions in water. What role does water play in this reaction?

7. Follow Steps 7a–e to build 2 water molecule models. You will use these models to learn about acid and base processes.
   a. Assemble 3 marshmallows together in the shape shown in figure 5.3.
   b. Use your marker to label the hydrogen atoms and the oxygen atom.
   c. Place 2 pairs of dots on the top sides of the oxygen atom to represent the 2 pairs of unshared electrons.

Recall that unshared electrons are electrons that are not shared between 2 atoms.

   d. Use figure 5.3 as your guide and mark the appropriate end of the water molecule with the correct charge.

The water molecule, as a whole, is neutral, but the distribution of charge is not even. Part of the molecule has a slight positive charge and the opposite end of the molecule has a slight negative charge. This permanent separation of charge makes the molecule polar.

   e. Draw a picture of this molecule beside the acid molecule you drew in Step 2c. Add a plus sign between them to represent the reactants in a chemical equation. Leave room to add the products later.
8. Work with your model and complete Steps 8a–g.

Working with a model will help you understand the processes in acid-base chemistry that are too small to observe, especially the formation of hydronium ions.

a. Remove the H^+, or proton, from the acid molecule and attach it to the negative portion of the water molecule. Attach it where you have marked 1 of the pairs of unshared electrons.

b. You have just made hydronium. What is the chemical formula for hydronium? Record your answer in your science notebook.

c. Water is a neutral molecule, and you have added a proton, or H^+. What is the charge of hydronium (H_3O^+)? Add it to your formula from Step 8b.

d. Draw your hydronium ion as one of the products of the chemical reaction you started in Step 2c.

e. What is the other product of this reaction? Draw it as part of the chemical reaction. Record your answer in your science notebook.

f. Write the chemical formulas underneath your drawings to complete the chemical reaction.

Don't forget to add charges where appropriate.

g. What is water's role in this reaction? Record your answer in your science notebook.

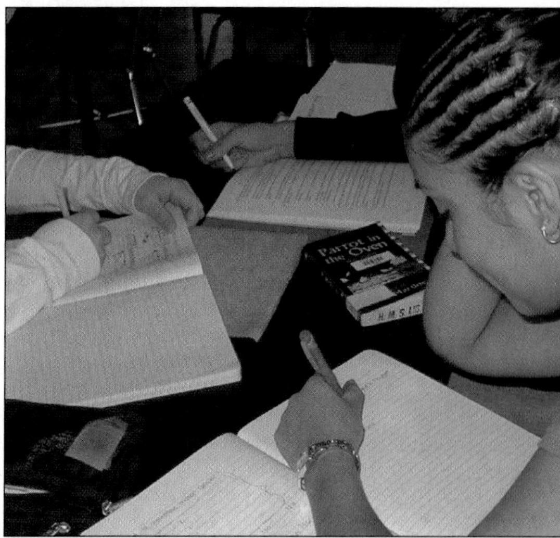

9. Compete the dissociation reaction for the general base that you started in Step 4c by following Steps 9a–d. This reaction is similar to the one you just completed for acids.

   a. Model dissociation by separating the molecule into its 2 ions according to the general equation.

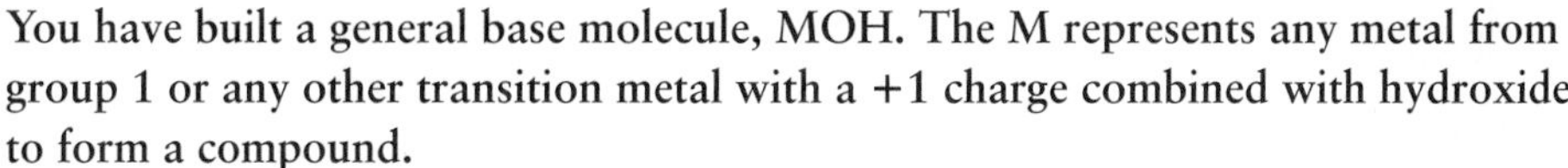

You have built a general base molecule, MOH. The M represents any metal from group 1 or any other transition metal with a +1 charge combined with hydroxide to form a compound.

   b. Draw the 2 resulting ions as the product of the dissociation reaction you started in your science notebook in Step 4c.

   c. Be sure to include the charges of each ion and write the names of each particle underneath the drawing.

   d. What role does water play in this dissociation reaction? Record your answer in your science notebook.

10. Follow Steps 10a–d to model the dissociation of bases like ammonia.

   a. Build a molecule to represent the polar ammonia molecule. It should look similar to figure 5.4.

   b. Draw the ammonia molecule and the water molecule as reactants. Use your second water molecule for this reaction.

c. Use your models as props to discuss how water and ammonia react.

Be sure to include what happens to produce hydroxide ions, a description of the charges, and the forces that are involved.

d. Draw the 2 resulting ions as the product of this reaction. Be sure to include the charges and write the names of each particle underneath the drawing.

11. Complete the T-table in figure 5.5 in your science notebook as you read *Acid-Base Strength*.

Term	How term relates dissociation and acid-base strength
Hydronium ion	
Dissociation	
Equilibrium position	
Soluble	
Double arrow	
Cation	
Anion	
Force of attraction	

Figure 5.5 T-table for the reading *Acid-Base Strength*. Find the terms in the reading. Then explain in the right-hand column how each term helps relate dissociation and acid-base strength.

READING

Acid-Base Strength

Have you ever worked on a car and accidentally gotten battery acid on your clothing or skin? This acid can be very dangerous. Car battery acid is typically the strong acid, sulfuric acid (H_2SO_4). Bases like drain cleaner and oven cleaner can be harmful to your skin as well. They typically contain a strong base such as sodium hydroxide (NaOH). These acids and bases are strong and can be potentially dangerous if not handled properly. However, you shampoo your hair or wash your hands with bases every day. Are those bases strong or weak? Just because an acid is defined as weak, does that mean it is harmless? What are the fundamental differences at the molecular level between strong and weak acids and bases?

In the reading *Dissociation*, you saw the general acid equation represented with a double arrow. What does that mean? You studied reversible reactions and reactions at equilibrium in chapter 3. The same general equation with the water molecule included in the reaction would look like this:

$$HA_{(aq)} + H_2O_{(l)} \rightleftarrows H_3O^+_{(aq)} + A^-_{(aq)}$$

Some acids dissociate very readily, and some hardly dissociate at all. We call acids that dissociate completely **strong acids**, and those acids that do not dissociate readily **weak acids**. Acids that are strong, such as hydrochloric acid (HCl), could be written like this:

$$(a)\ HCl_{(aq)} + H_2O_{(l)} \longrightarrow H_3O^+_{(aq)} + Cl^-_{(aq)}$$

or

$$(b)\ HCl_{(aq)} + H_2O_{(l)} \rightleftharpoons H_3O^+_{(aq)} + Cl^-_{(aq)}$$

Since the HCl molecule dissociates almost completely, there essentially would be no HCl molecules remaining. Equation (a) is usually used to represent this. In this acidic solution, there would only be hydronium ions, chloride ions, and few HCl molecules. The equilibrium position for this reaction lies far to the right, as shown by the arrows. Equation (b) shows a very slight reverse reaction, thus the shorter arrow to the left.

A weak acid such as acetic acid (CH_3COOH), since it dissociates much less, would reach equilibrium and is written as

$$CH_3COOH_{(aq)} + H_2O_{(l)} \rightleftharpoons H_3O^+_{(aq)} + CH_3COO^-_{(aq)}$$

In this weak acidic solution, there would still be molecules of CH_3COOH and water as well as some hydronium ion (H_3O^+) and acetate ion (CH_3COO^-). Only about 0.4 percent of the CH_3COOH molecules are dissociated at any one time in a solution containing 1 mole (mol) of CH_3COOH molecules per liter (L) of solution. The equilibrium position for this process lies far to the left, as shown by the arrows in the equation.

Some basic solutions behave similarly. For the metal hydroxides, it is as simple as knowing if the hydroxide is soluble. If it is soluble, then the hydroxide will dissociate completely in water and, essentially, the dissociation reaction goes to completion. Sodium hydroxide (common household lye) is very soluble in water and would be represented like this:

$$NaOH_{(aq)} \longrightarrow Na^+_{(aq)} + OH^-_{(aq)}$$

Sodium hydroxide is considered a strong base. So are all the other group 1 hydroxides. However, the reaction you modeled in the previous steps represents a reaction of a weak base. Ammonia is a weak base because, even though it produces hydroxide ions in water by removing a hydrogen ion from the water molecule, most of the NH_3 molecules do not react in solution. The reaction of NH_3 and H_2O should be represented using a double arrow.

What is the difference in these two types of acids and bases? What is it about their molecular makeup that makes one strong and dissociate completely and the other weak and only dissociate slightly? You can answer this by considering the competitive forces involved in the chemical reaction.

For the acid to dissociate, the hydrogen ion must be lost from the acid molecule and attach to the water molecule. The force of attraction between the water molecule and the hydrogen ion must be sufficient to remove the hydrogen ion from the anion (A^-). Positive ions are called **cations**, and negative ions are called **anions**. For a strong acid, the H^+ ion is pulled from the anion in the acid molecule by the stronger force of attraction by the water molecule. For weak acids, the acid anion has a stronger attraction for the H^+ than water, so the acid molecule stays intact. For bases, water either acts as the dissolving agent or donates one of its hydrogen ions to produce OH^- ions.

12. Discuss Questions 12a–d with your partner and record your best answers in your science notebook.
    a. What causes the force between the hydrogen ion and the anion (A^-) in the acid molecule?

Think about the force between the H^+ and the A^- in the HA molecule.

    b. What causes the force between the water molecule and the proton (H^+) once the proton is removed from the acid molecule?

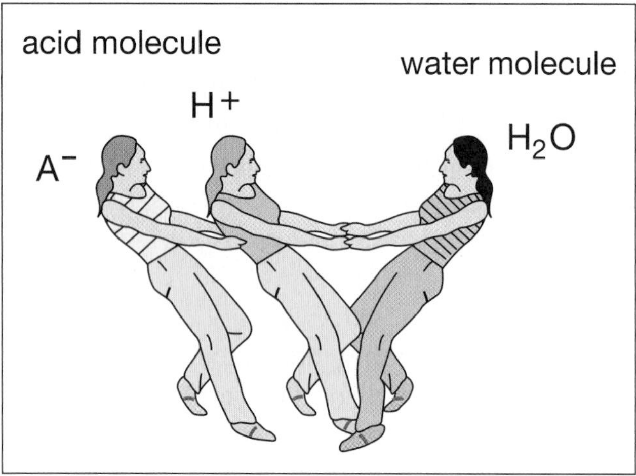

Figure 5.6 Strong and weak acids differ because of the amount of dissociation of the acid molecule. For the molecule to dissociate, which force is stronger?

    c. Strong acids readily lose a hydrogen ion (hydrogen nucleus) to water. To which particle is the hydrogen most strongly attracted, water or the anion of the strong acid? Write your answer in terms of relative strengths of attraction. See figure 5.6.
    d. Weak acids *do not* easily lose a hydrogen ion (hydrogen nucleus) to water. To which particle is the hydrogen most strongly attracted, water or the anion of the weak acid? Write your answer in terms of relative strengths of attraction. See figure 5.6.

13. Write the dissociation reaction for the following acids in your science notebook.

Consider if the acid is strong or weak and use your knowledge to represent the equation with the appropriate arrows. Make water part of the chemical reaction.

    a. Nitrous acid (HNO_2) (weak)
    b. Hydrogen cyanide (HCN) (weak)
    c. Hydroiodic acid (HI) (strong)

14. For each of the acids in Step 13, indicate if water or the anion in the acid molecule (A^- in the HA molecule) has the greatest attraction for the hydrogen ion. Justify your answer.
15. Look back to your experiment in Part I of the explore activity, *Gathering Evidence*. Find the pH of vinegar to answer the questions in Steps 15a–b.

Dilute acetic acid is what we commonly call vinegar. Acetic acid is considered a weak acid.

a. Is this value closer to the left side of the pH scale or to the neutral position on the pH scale?

b. Does this surprise you? Why or why not?

16. Read *A Matter of Concentration* to find out what concentration has to do with pH values and acid-base strength.

READING

A Matter of Concentration

You may have noticed that the pH values of some *weak* acids are low, indicating increased acidity. This may seem counterintuitive to you since you might think that weak acids will have pH values near 7, or neutral. What is the reason for this? It all has to do with the strength of the acid *and* the concentration of the acid. We use "strong" and "weak" to indicate the extent to which an acid (or base, for that matter) dissociates when placed in water. The concentration refers to how much of the substance is dissolved in water.

A strong acid or base can be either concentrated or dilute. We can say the same for a weak acid or base. Just keep in mind that "concentrated" and "dilute" refer to the number of particles in the solution and "strong" and "weak" refer to the extent to which these acid or base particles dissociate.

One way that chemists express concentration is in *molarity* (M), or moles of solute per liters of solution. What does it mean to have a 1 M solution of hydrochloric acid? It means that there is 1 mol of HCl dissolved in enough water to make 1 L of solution. The formula for calculating molarity is

$$M = \frac{\text{moles of solute}}{\text{liters of solution}}$$

In this example, HCl is the solute. If you had 0.10 mol HCl in a liter of solution, what would be the concentration of the solution? This solution would have a concentration of 0.10 M and would be expressed as 0.10 M HCl.

The pH scale is based on concentrations such as these. pH stands for "power of hydrogen," and the scale reflects the concentration of the hydrogen ions in solutions. You know that the more hydrogen or hydronium ions in solution, the more acidic the solution. This relationship is extended to basic solutions as well.

SCILINKS® NSTA
Topic: molarity
Go to: www.scilinks.org
Code: 2Inquiry241

Stop & THINK

You have looked at the differences in the pH values on the pH scale and how concentrations determine the pH values. Take a closer look and compare how strong and weak acids are different from concentrated and dilute acids.

1 Acid molecules can be represented generally by using HA. Use this designation as you complete Questions 1a–g.

a. Draw 4 beakers that will represent different acidic solutions. Use a blank page in your science notebook and allow room for highlight comments outside the beakers and drawings inside the beakers. Label your 4 beakers from "1" to "4."

b. Title beaker 1 "strong acid" and beaker 2 "weak acid."

c. Using 5 molecules of acid and 5 molecules of water, illustrate the differences in these 2 acids once they are dissolved in water.

You can use just general chemical symbols or you can draw atomic representations of each particle. In either case, be sure to label everything clearly.

d. Title beaker 3 "concentrated strong acid" and beaker 4 "concentrated weak acid."

e. Using the same method of illustration as you did in Question 1c, represent solutions of concentrated strong and weak acids.

For easier comparison, change the number of acid particles for each acid by the same amount.

f. Write highlight comments on your drawings for "What I see" and "What it means."

g. Share your drawings with another team.

Consider using the think-share-advise-revise (TSAR) strategy.

2 You learned to use molarity to represent concentrations of solutions. Consider 1 M solutions of a strong acid and a weak acid. Use the relationships =, >, >>, <, and << to answer Questions 2a–b.

a. For a 1 M strong acid solution,

- a concentration of H_3O^+ __________ 1 M.
- a concentration of HA __________ 1 M.
- a concentration of A^- __________ 1 M.

b. For a 1 M weak acid solution,

- a concentration of H_3O^+ __________ 1 M.
- a concentration of HA __________ 1 M.
- a concentration of A^- __________ 1 M.

17. Look at the simulation *Determination of the Molarity of an Acid or Base Solution* on the *Student Resource CD* (*SRCD*). In it, you will find out how to use acid-base neutralization chemistry to determine the concentration of unknown solutions. This process is called **titration**.

Reflect and Connect

Show your best thinking and write answers to the following questions in your science notebook. After you are done, revise your answers based on discussions with your teammates.

1. You have learned a lot about ions in solution in this activity. You also learned in earlier classes that electrolytes are substances that, when dissolved in water, will produce an electric current. Electric currents will flow through a solution in which ions are present. The more ions present, the more current flows. Choose the example from each pair that would be a stronger electrolyte. (If you think they are equal, then say so.) Consider all amounts to be equal. Justify each selection.
   a. A 1 M solution of HCl or a 1 M solution of CH_3COOH
   b. A 1 M solution of HNO_3 or a 0.5 M solution of HNO_3
   c. A solution of 0.5 M LiOH and a solution of 0.5 M NH_3
2. Use the general form for an acid (HA) and the general form for a base (MOH) to answer Questions 2a–b.
   a. Write a chemical reaction that represents a reaction between a strong acid such as hydrochloric acid and a strong base such as sodium hydroxide.
   b. Write highlight comments for the reactants and products.
3. Water contains both H^+ and OH^- because of its self-ionization. Explain why water is neutral even though it contains these ions.
4. Describe how you could have a solution of a strong base with the same pH as a solution of a weak base. Use the words *strong*, *weak*, *concentrated*, and *dilute* in your answer.
5. Consider the following particles listed in order of decreasing attraction to H^+ ions: $F^- > H_2O > Br^-$. Which is the stronger acid, HF or HBr? Explain your answer. Use chemical equations in your answer.
6. Think about the reaction you observed in Part II of the explore activity. You used a dilute solution of hydrochloric acid (HCl). You put different metals in the acid, and a gas was produced that you identified as hydrogen gas (H_2). Write a chemical equation for this reaction using magnesium as the metal.

7. The gastric juice in your stomach has a H^+ concentration between 0.01 and 0.1 M. When a person suffers from acid indigestion, the pH of the gastric juice (a strong acid) drops below the normal range. Often, a dose of antacids (made from a weak base) will alleviate the symptoms of indigestion.
   a. In what pH range is gastric juice, acid or base?
   b. Describe how taking an antacid will help a person suffering from indigestion. Include in your answer what kind of reaction this is, the expected products, and their pH range.
   c. Why would it be inadvisable to use a strong base as an antacid?

EXPLAIN

Redox Reactions

Magnesium burns in air to produce the bright white light in many fireworks. Iron in the body of a car starts to rust where the paint is scratched off. Metabolic processes in our bodies process sugars, fats, and proteins to provide the energy necessary for life. Gold ions react to form a layer of gold atoms on a necklace to give us less expensive gold-plated jewelry. The combustion of the fuel in a rocket propels the rocket into outer space. What do all these chemical processes have in common? These reactions may seem unrelated. But in fact, they are all the same type of chemical process. These reactions represent a category of reactions called oxidation-reduction reactions, or redox reactions.

Historically, oxidation reactions were defined as reactions in which an element combines with oxygen to form an oxide. The rusting of an iron nail to form iron oxide is an example. Reduction was represented as the reverse reaction. Here a chemical process removes the oxygen from the oxide to yield the pure metal. It was called reduction because the pure metal weighs less than the oxide. This reaction is still very important in industry. The removal of oxygen from iron ore in steelmaking is still the first step in the process today.

Topic: oxidation-reduction reactions
Go to: www.scilinks.org
Code: 2Inquiry244

However, now we define these reactions in a more general way. **Oxidation-reduction reactions** or **redox reactions** involve the transfer of electrons. This is similar to the way acids transfer protons. It's similar because both the electron and proton are charged particles. And just like your study of acids and bases, your prior knowledge of forces will help you understand redox reactions. Can you see this transfer take place? No, electrons are much too small to see. But you can see the results of a redox reaction. From the evidence you can see, you infer what happens at the atomic level.

What would it look like if metal ions such as silver (Ag^+) in a solution were to gain electrons? You will work with a partner and individually to answer this and other questions as you conduct investigations and read about these very important chemical reactions.

Materials

For each team of 2 students

2 pairs of safety goggles

2 laboratory aprons

2 pairs of safety gloves

1 petri dish

1 dissecting scope or 2 hand lenses

silver nitrate solution ($AgCl_{(aq)}$)

1 dropping pipet

thin copper wire

tape

white paper

colored pencils

Cautions

Wear safety goggles, safety gloves, and a lab apron during the experiment and do not touch any chemicals or solutions. Silver nitrate is toxic by ingestion and inhalation. It may cause irritation to skin, eyes, and mucous membranes. Use care in handling this chemical. Avoid contact with skin and clothing. Silver nitrate will permanently stain skin, nails, and clothing.

Process and Procedure

What changes can you observe when a redox reaction occurs? Work with your partner as you observe a redox reaction and discover how and where electrons are being transferred.

1. Tape a piece of thin copper wire to the inside of a petri dish. Make sure the wire is flat against the bottom of the dish.
2. Sketch your setup following Steps 2a–f.

Make your sketch large enough to record important detail. Leave room around the sides for comments.

   a. Sketch a top view of your setup. Focus on a small area of the center of your wire.
   b. You will add a few drops of silver nitrate ($AgNO_3$) solution to the center of your wire. But *before* you add it to your wire, draw this "puddle" of $AgNO_3$ solution. Do not add the $AgNO_3$ at this time.
   c. Label your copper wire.
   d. Label the ions in solution on your drawing.

The silver nitrate dissolved to form a solution. Therefore, there are silver ions (Ag^+) and nitrate ions (NO_3^-) in the solution.

e. Use your colored pencils to make your sketch more realistic.

f. Title your drawing "before reaction."

> **Caution**
> Don't let silver nitrate touch your skin.

3. Place 2–3 drops of the silver nitrate solution in the center of your petri dish. Make sure that the drops cover the copper wire.
4. Place the dish under a dissecting scope immediately or examine the reaction with the hand lenses. Watch the reaction for several minutes.
5. After the reaction has proceeded for several minutes, compare the results with the color of the "before reaction" solution. Describe any changes you see in your science notebook.

To help you see color changes, carefully lay the dish on a sheet of white paper. You may have to wait a few minutes to notice any change from the colorless solution.

6. Sketch the results of this reaction by following Steps 6a–c.
   a. Draw a picture of your petri dish and the results of this chemical reaction. Use the same view and scale as you did in Step 2. Include the wire, the solution, and the new substance that was formed. Do not label anything yet.
   b. Add color to your drawing with your colored pencils to represent the colors in the reaction.
   c. Title this sketch "after reaction."
7. Discover what these crystals are by working with your partner and following Steps 7a–c.

Remember the law of conservation of matter: atoms are neither created nor destroyed. So the atoms making up the crystals in your petri dish must have been present at the beginning, but in another form.

a. Write the particles present at the beginning as reactants in a chemical equation.

These were labeled in your "before" sketch. Write them down as reactants in a chemical equation. Don't forget to include charges. Since copper is in its elemental state, it has no charge.

b. Write your ideas for products to complete your chemical reaction.

Think about the possibilities for the new substances formed as the products of your chemical reaction. Remember, atoms in their elemental state have no ionic charge.

c. Share your ideas with another team and follow the TSAR strategy to formulate and record your best ideas.

8. Share your ideas in a class discussion led by your teacher. Write down any changes or new ideas that you hear in the discussion.
9. In your science notebook, fill in any missing atoms and charges in Steps 9a–b.

Notice that some of the atoms involved in this chemical reaction changed charges.

a. $Cu_{(s)} \longrightarrow \_\_\_\_\_\__{(aq)}$

b. $Ag^{+}_{(aq)} \longrightarrow \_\_\_\_\_\__{(s)}$

10. Determine whether the electric charge is balanced in the equations from Steps 9a–b by following Steps 10a–c.
    a. Determine the total charge on the reactant side of each equation and see if it is the same as the total charge on the product side. Treat each reaction separately.
    b. Write the total charge under each side of each reaction.
    c. Check your answer with another team and modify your science notebook if necessary.
11. What is the charged particle responsible for changes to the metals in these chemical reactions? What charge does the particle have?

Remember, atoms contain electrons (−), protons (+), and neutrons (0).

12. Add the charged particle you identified in Step 11 to balance the total charge for each chemical reaction by following Steps 12a–d.
    a. Remember that mass *and* charge are conserved in chemical reactions. This means the total amount of charge on both sides of a chemical reaction must be the same.
    b. Decide to which side of each equation you must add some of the charged particles selected in Step 11.
    c. Determine the appropriate number of these particles you must add to ensure conservation of charge.
    d. Incorporate these charged particles into each reaction from Step 9 by using coefficients.
13. Apply a reading strategy to *The Redox Exchange* to increase your understanding of the terms half reaction, lose electrons, gain electrons, oxidized, reduced, oxidation, reduction, spectator ion, and oxidation number.

READING

The Redox Exchange

The reactions you have been working with are called **half reactions**. They represent only half of the chemical reaction taking place. Did you notice that the nitrate ion did not appear in these half reactions? That is because the NO_3^- ion does not change in any way during the chemical reaction. It is a spectator ion. Think back to adding iron to hydrochloric acid in the explore activity. At the beginning of the reaction, these atoms and ions were present:

$$Fe_{(s)} \qquad H^+_{(aq)} \qquad Cl^-_{(aq)}$$

At the end of the reaction, the following atoms, ions, and molecules were present:

$$Fe^{2+}_{(aq)} \qquad H_{2(g)} \qquad Cl^-_{(aq)}$$

Note the ion that is unchanged in the chemical reaction. The chloride ion (Cl^-) is the spectator ion in this reaction. The two half reactions for this redox reaction would be

(a) $Fe_{(s)} \longrightarrow Fe^{2+}_{(aq)} + 2e^-$ and
(b) $2H^+ + 2e^- \longrightarrow H_{2(g)}$.

Always check to see that the reactions are balanced according to mass and charge. Notice in reaction (a) how Fe changes from having a charge of zero to a charge of plus 2 (written Fe^{2+}). You can see from the two electrons on the product side that Fe lost two electrons in the process. Atoms or ions that lose electrons are said to be **oxidized**. When something is oxidized, its oxidation number or charge increases. An **oxidation** reaction is a half reaction in which electrons show up on the product side of the arrow. That is, electrons are lost.

Ions have charges. These charges are the same as the ion's oxidation number. All elements have oxidation numbers even if they do not form ionic compounds. These oxidation numbers can be helpful in determining what is oxidized and what is reduced in a redox reaction. Oxidation numbers are given to atoms according to the charge they would have if the electrons are all assigned to the atom with the highest attraction for electrons—the most electronegative atom.

In reaction (b), hydrogen changes from having a charge of 1^+ to zero charge since H_2 is the elemental state of hydrogen. Electrons are gained to make this change. Atoms or ions that gain electrons are said to be **reduced**. The charge is reduced or the charge moves to a more negative direction. A **reduction** reaction is a half reaction in which electrons are gained. One way to remember this is to think of the mnemonic device OIL RIG, which stands for "Oxidized Is Loss and Reduced Is Gain."

There are two equations—two half reactions—for one process. These reactions can be "added" together. First, you must make sure that both reactions are balanced according to mass (the same number and kinds of atoms on both sides). Second, the reaction must be balanced according to charge, adding electrons to either side to balance the reaction. The third step is to see if the same number of electrons is in both reactions. If one substance loses two electrons, then another substance must gain two electrons. If the number of electrons is not the same, use a coefficient to balance the electrons. Remember, if you change the coefficient of one substance in the half reaction, you must change the coefficients of all substances in the half cell by the same factor. It is like multiplying everything by the same number—it will still be balanced. The last step is to double-check your combined equation to make sure it is balanced according to mass and charge.

Check the equations to see how to add them together and produce one overall redox equation for the reaction. Start by collecting all the reactants on the left and all the products on the right.

Did you notice that the same number of electrons appear on opposite sides of the equation in the half reactions? That is because if one substance loses electrons, then another must gain those electrons. Oxidation and reduction must come as a pair of reactions; if something is oxidized, then something else must be reduced. The transfer of electrons makes redox reactions occur.

$$Fe_{(s)} \longrightarrow Fe^{2+}_{(aq)} + 2e^-$$

$$2H^+ + 2e^- \longrightarrow H_{2(g)}$$

$$2H^+ + \cancel{2e^-} + Fe_{(s)} \longrightarrow Fe^{2+}_{(aq)} + \cancel{2e^-} + H_{2(g)}$$

(You can cancel anything that appears on both sides.)

$$2H^+ + Fe_{(s)} \longrightarrow Fe^{2+}_{(aq)} + H_{2(g)}$$

14. Reads Steps 14a–e and determine which steps you have already accomplished for the half reactions from Step 10.
    a. Balance each half reaction according to mass.
    b. Balance each half reaction according to charge.
    c. Make the number of electrons gained and lost the same by using coefficients.
    d. Add half reactions together, canceling out electrons.
    e. Double-check the final reaction for balance (both mass and charge).
15. Check your reaction with the reaction of another team or with your teacher for accuracy.
16. Add labels to your equations by following Steps 16a–e.
    a. Label the half reaction that is oxidation.
    b. Label the half reaction that is reduction.
    c. On the combined equation, label the particle that is oxidized.
    d. On the combined equation, label the particle that is reduced.
    e. Go back to the "after" sketch that you did in Step 6. Identify the solution that is now the puddle and the crystals forming on the wire. Label these on your sketch.

17. Read the following paragraph and answer the questions in Steps 17a–f in your science notebook.

When a particle loses electrons (is oxidized), another particle is the agent that caused the oxidation. **Oxidizing agent** is the term given to this particle. The same is true for particles that gain electrons (are reduced). There is another particle that is the agent that gives up an electron or electrons in the process. This particle is called a **reducing agent**.

a. What particle *caused* the oxidation in your reaction?

It will be the one that has stolen the electron!

b. On the combined equation from Step 14, label the particle "oxidizing agent."

c. What particle *caused* the reduction in your reaction?

It will be the one that donated the electron!

d. On the combined equation from Step 14, label the particle "reducing agent."

e. What is the relationship between the particle that is oxidized and the reducing agent?

f. What is the relationship between the particle that is reduced and the oxidizing agent?

18. When you studied acid and base reactions, you learned about the role that forces play in determining if an acid or a base is strong or weak. Forces play an essential role in redox reactions as well. Read *Fundamental Forces* to discover the role of forces in redox reactions.

READING

Fundamental Forces

Understanding forces helps you understand the strengths of acids and bases. For example, the competitive forces on an H^+ determine relative acid strength. Understanding forces helps you understand redox reactions as well. That's because redox reactions involve competitive forces on electrons. Electrons move from one atom or ion to another in redox reactions. Because of the electron's charged nature, at least two particles will be competing for the electron. Who will win? The answer lies with how easily the atom gives up electrons.

Look back to your results from Part II of the explore activity where you placed different metals in hydrochloric acid solution (HCl). You have already looked at one of the redox reactions from this activity. This reaction happened when you placed iron in the acid.

Iron readily gave up two electrons to the hydrogen ions to produce hydrogen gas and the iron II ion (Fe^{2+}). How did that reaction compare with the reaction of magnesium and the acid? You noticed that the "fizzing" was much more vigorous with the magnesium metal than with the iron metal. What did that tell you? You said that magnesium was more reactive than the iron. This must mean that magnesium gives up its electrons more readily to hydrogen than iron. The force of attraction of the hydrogen ion for the electron must be greater than the magnesium's force of attraction. Hydrogen wins. The electron is transferred to the hydrogen ion (H^+), and the result is hydrogen gas (H_2).

What happened when you put copper in the HCl? You should have observed no fizzing. What does that mean? There were still H^+ ions that have a force of attraction for electrons, but the copper does not give them up. Did copper or hydrogen win the struggle for the electron? Did copper or hydrogen have the strongest force of attraction for the electron? The copper ion's force of attraction for its electrons is greater than the attractive force that the H^+ has for an electron. So copper keeps its electrons and no reaction occurs.

The table in figure 5.7 shows the relative strengths of reducing and oxidizing agents. The strongest reducing agents (most easily oxidized) are on the top left. Lithium (Li) is the strongest reducing agent. These agents lose electrons very easily and therefore are very reactive. These metals are close to the same order that you found in the explore activity.

The strongest oxidizing agents (most easily reduced) appear on the bottom right of the table. You see that fluorine (F_2) is the strongest oxidizing agent. Strong oxidizing agents have a strong force of attraction for electrons. Recall that fluorine has the highest electronegativity of all elements. This supports the fact that F_2 is the strongest oxidizing agent. The general trend for these agents is shown in figure 5.8.

You can use the information in the table shown in figure 5.7 to predict if a redox reaction will occur. Think back to the reaction you observed at the beginning of this activity. You placed solid copper in a solution that contained silver ions. Look at the placement of copper and the silver ion (Ag^+) in the table in figure 5.7. For a reaction to occur, copper must lose electrons to the silver ions in solution. From the table, you can see that copper is a stronger reducing agent than silver. In other words, copper loses electrons more easily than silver and is more reactive. Elements shown on this table lose electrons to the positively charged ions of any element below them in the series. The more

Reducing agents	Oxidizing agents
Li	Li^+
K	K^+
Ca	Ca^{2+}
Na	Na^+
Mg	Mg^{2+}
Al	Al^{3+}
Zn	Zn^{2+}
Cr	Cr^{3+}
Fe	Fe^{2+}
Ni	Ni^{2+}
Sn	Sn^{2+}
Pb	Pb^{2+}
H_2	H_3O^+
Cu	Cu^{2+}
I^-	I_2
Hg	Hg_2^{2+}
Ag	Ag^+
Br^-	Br_2
Cl^-	Cl_2
F^-	F_2

increasing strength (reducing agents: upward) — increasing strength (oxidizing agents: downward)

Figure 5.7 Relative strengths of oxidizing and reducing agents. You can use this table to predict redox reactions.

active an element from this table is, the greater its tendency to lose electrons. This makes it the strongest reducing agent.

What if you switched the reaction around and placed solid silver in a solution that contained copper ions? Would a reaction occur? Since silver appears below copper in the table and is a weaker reducing agent, no reaction would occur. Consider the following equation:

$$Cu + 2Ag^{+} \longrightarrow Cu^{2+} + 2Ag$$

This pair is reactive. This pair is stable (nonreactive).

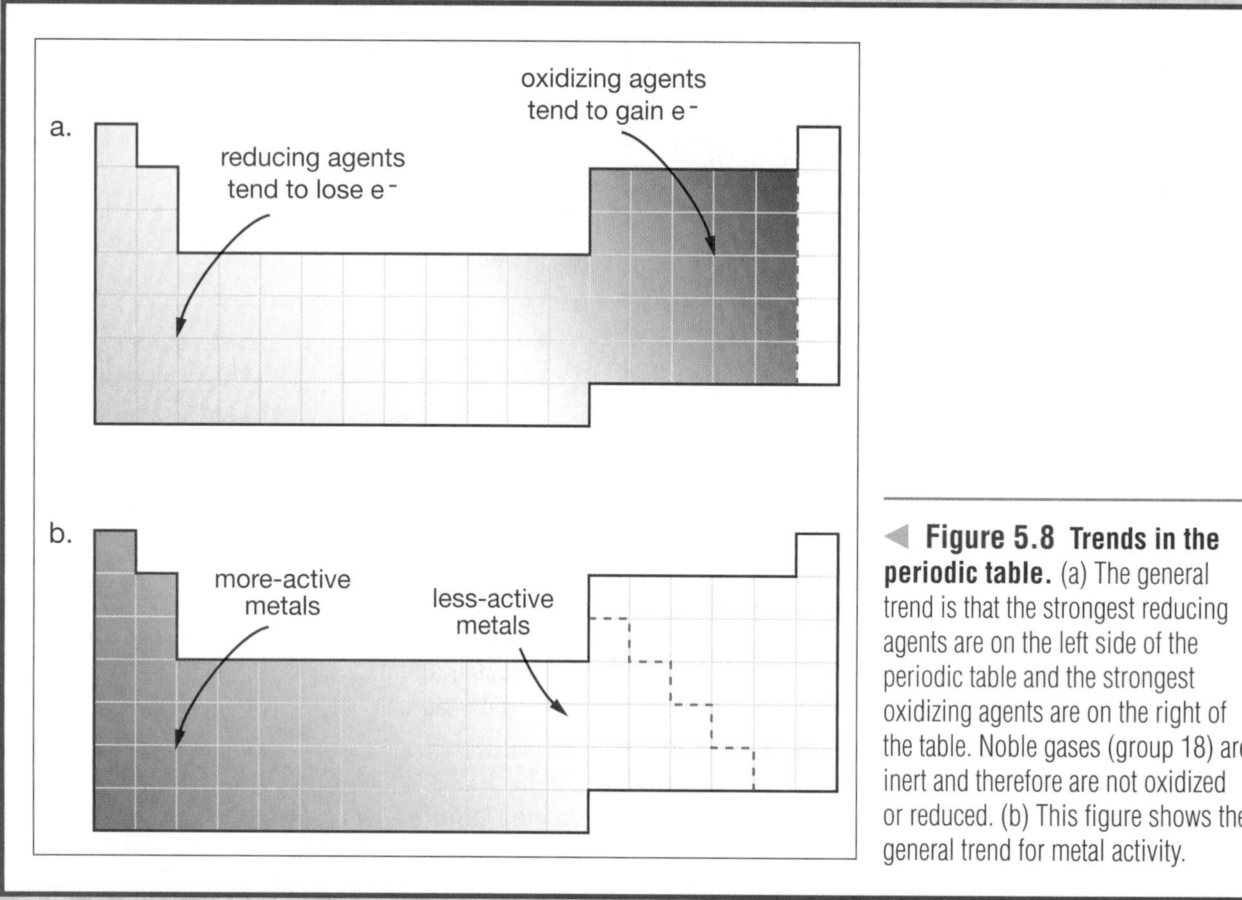

Figure 5.8 Trends in the periodic table. (a) The general trend is that the strongest reducing agents are on the left side of the periodic table and the strongest oxidizing agents are on the right of the table. Noble gases (group 18) are inert and therefore are not oxidized or reduced. (b) This figure shows the general trend for metal activity.

Reflect and Connect

Answer the following questions in your science notebook.

1. Redox reactions are important reactions to your everyday life. A redox reaction involving a biochemical process occurs when cut fruit turns brown on the surface. Colorless compounds are oxidized by the oxygen gas (O_2) in the air to produce a

brown pigment on the surface of cut fruit. The skin of the fruit keeps this from happening much the same way paint on a car keeps its body from rusting. Is there any way to keep a fruit salad from turning brown before you eat it? Yes, add lemon juice. The citric acid in lemon juice acts as an antioxidant in this chemical reaction. When the lemon juice (or a commercial additive) is added to your fruit salad, the oxygen in the air reacts to oxidize the citric acid. The citric acid loses electrons to the oxygen more readily than the fruit-browning compounds and, in so doing, it spares the fruit from oxidation and turning brown. The citric acid is a stronger reducing agent than the compounds in the fruit.

Knowing the strength of oxidizing and reducing agents is important in trying to protect substances from unwanted reactions. Which is the stronger oxidizing agent in each of the following pairs? Explain how you arrived at your answer.

a. Cu^{2+} or Fe^{2+}

b. H_2 or Cl^-

c. Pb or Cu

2. Describe the reactions or nonreactions set up for you in Questions 2a–c. If a reaction occurs, describe what you would see. If no reaction occurs, explain why.

   a. A piece of lead (Pb) is placed in a solution of zinc chloride ($ZnCl_2$)

   b. A piece of chromium (Cr) is placed in a solution of copper II nitrate ($Cu(NO_3)_2$)

   c. A piece of nickel (Ni) is placed in a solution of hydrochloric acid (HCl)

3. A Breathalyzer test for roadside alcohol investigations is a redox reaction. The reaction occurs as Cr^{6+} ions are reduced to Cr^{3+} ions. What does that mean? Use the terms *loses*, *gains*, *electrons* (include the number involved), *oxidation*, and *reduction* in your explanation.

4. Magnesium is a reactive metal and can lose electrons readily. It reacts slowly with water. The 2 half reactions depicting the oxidation of magnesium as it reacts with water follow. Complete Questions 4a–c using these reactions.

$$Mg \longrightarrow Mg^{2+}$$
$$H_2O \longrightarrow H_2 + OH^-$$

   a. Which reaction represents oxidation and which represents reduction?

Remember that these 2 processes occur in pairs.

b. Using the process you learned earlier, balance these 2 half reactions and combine them into 1 overall redox reaction.
c. Would the resulting solution be acidic or basic? Explain your answer.

ELABORATE

Electrochemistry

What do an MP3 player, a laptop computer, a cell phone, and your school calculator have in common? They all use the chemistry of redox reactions as a source for the electric current. That current makes these devices work. Often, the source for the electric current is a battery. How do batteries work? Redox reactions within the battery supply electric current. But are these redox reactions occurring even if the battery is still in its package? In *Electrochemistry*, you will apply your understandings of redox reactions and use some of your knowledge about acid-base chemistry to the practical application of these reactions.

Electrons move from reducing agent to oxidizing agent, from metal atoms to metal ions. When you place a metal into a solution of HCl, the electrons move from atom to ion. Energy is lost as heat. What would happen if you separated these oxidation and reduction agents and made the electrons flow through a wire? Could you harness these moving electrons to produce useful work?

You will investigate this possibility in Part I. Then in Part II, you will look at instances where you can force a reaction to take place that would not normally do so. You can do this by adding energy. This will be the focus of Part II.

Part I: Electricity by Chemistry

Materials

For each student

1 pair of safety goggles

Process and Procedure

What would happen if you bit down on aluminum foil and it touched one of your fillings? If you have done this, you may have felt a tiny shock and felt the pain go through your tooth to the nerve hiding beneath your filling. You had just created a battery in your mouth and a tiny amount of electricity was generated when the foil, the silver amalgam filling, and the electrolyte solution provided by your saliva all came into contact with one another. In Part I, you will work individually and with a team to investigate what it takes to make a battery and what redox and acid-base chemistry are involved in the process.

In the introduction for this activity, you read about getting something useful out of electric current. This current comes from redox reactions. But when a redox reaction takes place in a beaker, the reaction and the transfer of electrons are instantaneous. You get no useful work from the system. But if you separate the oxidation and reduction parts of the reaction, you can cause the electrons to flow through a wire. Then you can get something useful out of the process. The flow of charge in a particular direction is called an **electric current**. What causes this charge to flow?

1. Make a T-table in your science notebook with the headings "term" and "how term relates to voltaic cells."
2. Complete the T-table as you read *A Battery of Cells*. Use the following terms in the left-hand column: *spontaneous reaction*, *electric current*, *competition for electrons*, *reducing agent*, *oxidizing agent*, *active metal*, *salt bridge*, *anode*, *cathode*, and *useful work*.

READING

A Battery of Cells

The type of electrochemical cell that produces electricity is called a voltaic cell. Another name for this type of electrochemical cell is a galvanic cell. In a **voltaic cell**, a spontaneous chemical reaction generates an electric current. Metals are often used as electrodes. Electrodes are the part of an electrochemical cell where oxidation or reduction often takes place. If you used zinc and copper for electrodes, then an oxidation reaction takes place at the zinc electrode. That happens because zinc is a more active metal than copper.

Reduction takes place at the copper electrode. This happens because the electrons lost by the zinc are diverted to the copper electrode. By conducting this reaction in a beaker, you can see what is going on. If you place a piece of zinc into a solution of copper II sulfate ($CuSO_4$), will a reaction occur? Check the table in figure 5.7 for the answer. Notice that zinc is a more active metal than copper; zinc is a stronger reducing agent, and the reaction will occur. When this reaction occurs, as pictured in figure 5.9, the electrons are transferred instantaneously. Zinc atoms lose electrons and become zinc ions in solution, and copper ions in solution attract these electrons and form copper atoms. These copper atoms form, or plate out, on the zinc strip.

Let's separate these two reactions by using two beakers and two solutions. Put the zinc metal into a solution that contains zinc ions and put the copper metal into a separate beaker that contains copper ions. Figure 5.10 shows this setup.

Will the electrons lost by the zinc atoms in figure 5.10 be transferred to the copper ions in the other beaker? The electrons have no mechanism in which to get from one beaker to another. What if you connect the two pieces of metal with a piece of conducting wire as in figure 5.11?

Now there is a mechanism in which the electrons can flow from the zinc metal to the copper ions. But will the current flow? It will, but only for an instant. When the current begins to flow, charge builds up in each beaker, causing the flow to stop. Consider the beaker with the zinc metal and the zinc ions in solution. Zinc loses electrons to form zinc ions (Zn^{2+}), and the electrons move through the wire to the other beaker. Here they go into the solution and are quickly taken up by the copper ions to form copper metal. The zinc side develops a buildup of positive charge, and therefore it is harder and harder to lose more electrons. The copper side develops a buildup of negative charge and, because like charges repel, it becomes harder and harder to take on more negative electrons, and the reaction stops. To remedy this, something must be in place to keep the charge balanced or the reaction will not proceed. Look at figure 5.12 to see how a salt bridge is used to balance the charge.

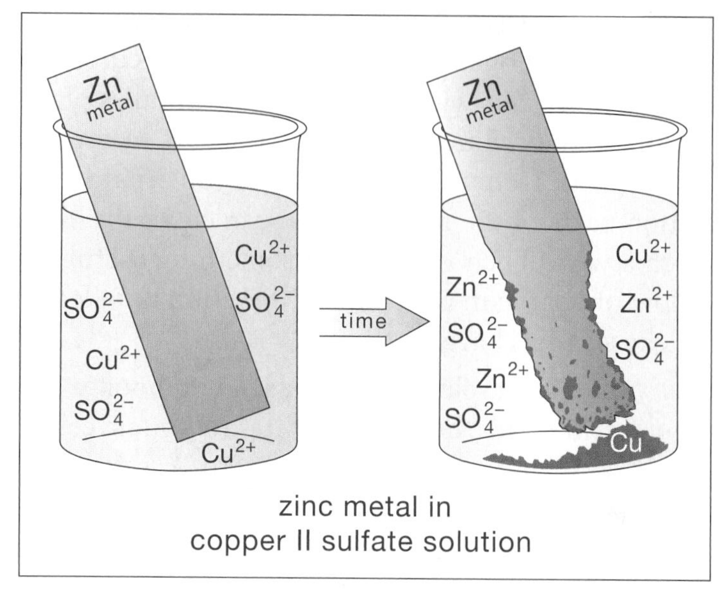

▲ **Figure 5.9 Redox reaction of zinc and copper II sulfate.** In this reaction, the electrons are transferred very quickly. Notice that the zinc strip is "eaten away" as zinc atoms lose electrons and become zinc ions in solution. The blue color of the solution fades in time because the copper II ions that give the solution its color are gaining electrons and becoming copper atoms. These atoms either attach to the zinc metal or fall off into the beaker. Sulfate ions (SO_4^{2-}) are spectator ions.

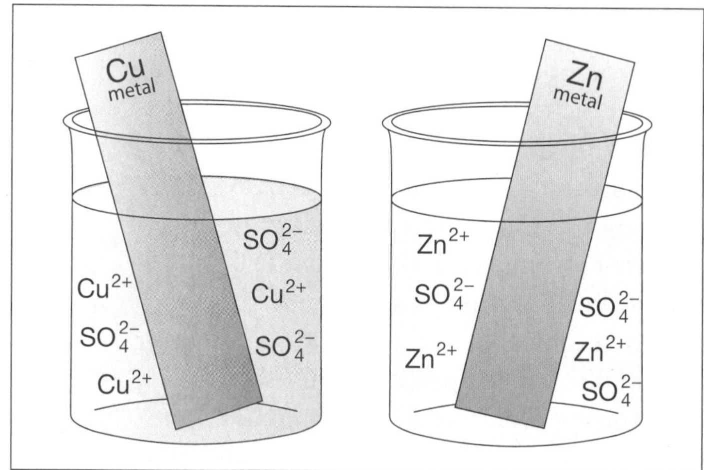

▲ **Figure 5.10 Separate beakers for each half redox reaction.** The reactions are separated in this setup, but will the reaction occur? How will the electrons lost by the zinc be transferred to the copper ions?

The salt bridge can be made from any soluble salt because there will be both positive and negative ions in solution. The salt solution is usually held in place by some type of gel or porous plugs. Notice that the electrodes are labeled "**anode**" and "**cathode**." Oxidation always occurs at the anode, and reduction always occurs at the cathode. You can remember this by remembering that oxidation and anode both start with vowels and reduction and cathode start with consonants. Another important thing to note is that the electrons flow from anode to cathode (from A to C).

In voltaic cells, chemical reactions are used to produce electricity. These chemical reactions occur because of the careful selection of reducing and oxidizing agents that will react. This type of reaction is essential to our way of life, as so many of the devices we use today are powered by batteries. A battery is an application of this type of chemistry. The proper setup of reducing agents and oxidizing agents can convert chemical energy into electrical energy to do useful work.

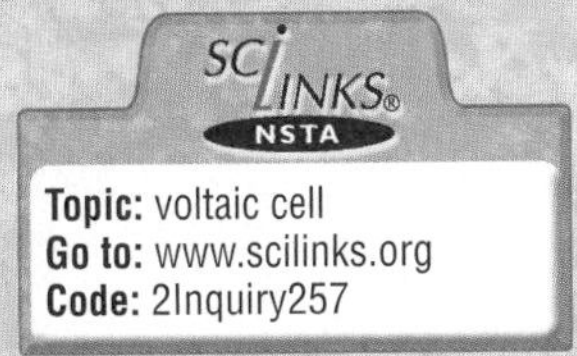

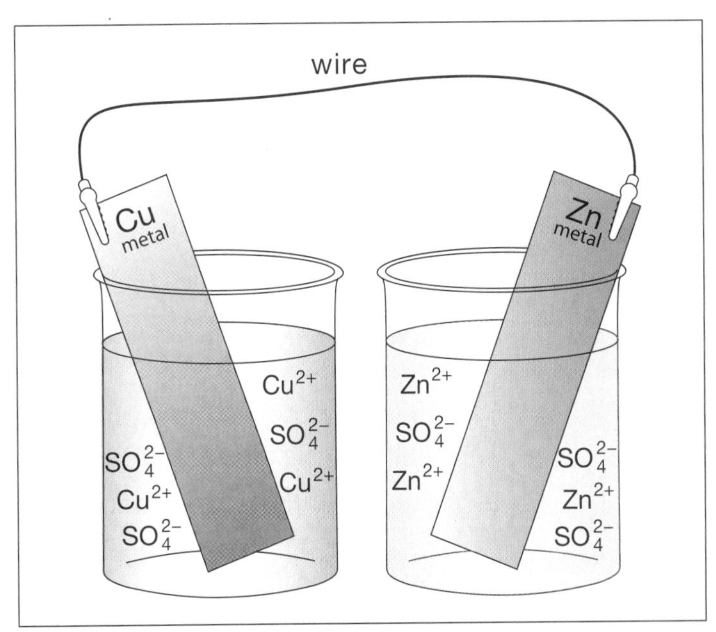

▲ **Figure 5.11 Metal strips connected with a wire.** The reactions are separated in this setup and connected with a wire. Will the reaction occur now that there is a pathway for the electrons to move?

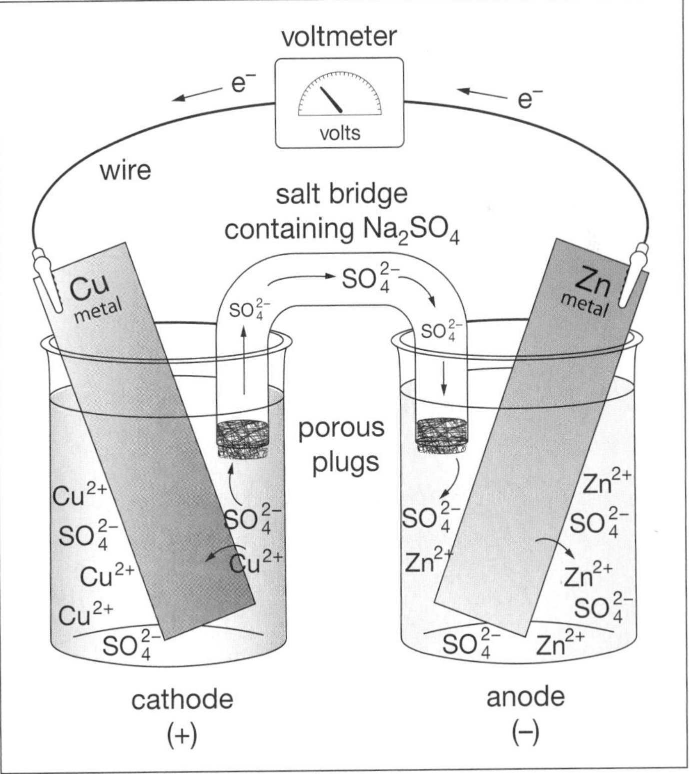

▲ **Figure 5.12 Voltaic cell.** The reaction will occur in this setup because there is a salt bridge to keep the charge balanced in each beaker.

3. Compare and contrast your T-table with the T-table of 1 or more classmates. Record any changes you made to your table and the reasons for those changes.

Stop & THINK

PART I

1 Sketch the illustration in figure 5.12 in your science notebook. Complete 1a–c using this drawing.

a. Write the half reaction that occurs at each half cell.

b. Label the cell in which oxidation occurs and the cell in which reduction occurs.

c. Balance both half reactions and add them together to form 1 equation.

2 Sometimes a salt bridge will be replaced by a porous boundary (one that allows particles to move through it) between the 2 solutions (see figure 5.13).

a. Explain why either a salt bridge or a porous boundary is needed.

b. Why would a porous boundary work as well as a salt bridge?

3 Would the reaction in the cell depicted in figure 5.13 continue indefinitely? Why or why not?

4 Suppose you took the mass of each of the electrodes before you made this voltaic cell. How would the mass before the reaction compare with the mass after the reaction for each metal? Explain any changes.

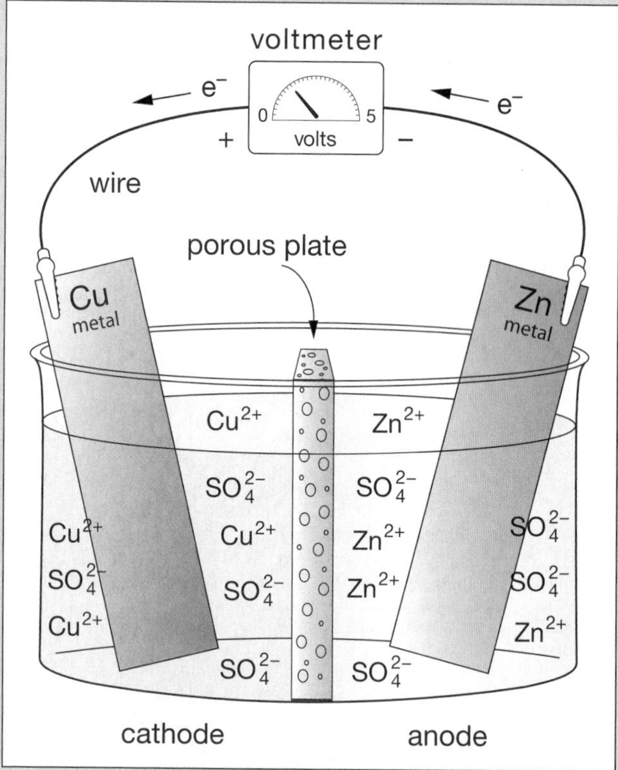

Figure 5.13 Voltaic cell with porous plate. Why will the reaction occur in this setup?

Look at the animation *Voltaic Cells* on the *SRCD* to see voltaic cells in action.

5 Consider life without batteries. Write a short essay depicting life without batteries. Include how you would feel and how you would have to adapt to this way of life.

Part II: Batteries Included

Materials

For each team of 2–3 students

2–3 pairs of safety goggles

1 plastic pipet

1 100-mL beaker or small cup

clear aquarium tubing

1 9-volt battery with battery clip

2 small alligator clips

2 pencil leads (minimum diameter of 7 mm)

copper II chloride solution ($CuCl_2$)

The reactions that occur in voltaic cells convert chemical energy to electrical energy. These reactions are spontaneous. However, many reactions are not spontaneous. You have seen the reaction that occurs when a piece of copper is placed in a solution of silver nitrate. Silver crystals form as the electrons are transferred from the copper metal to the silver ions in the solution. What would you expect to happen if you placed a piece of silver in a solution of copper nitrate? If you look at figure 5.7, you see that silver is a weaker reducing agent than copper, so no reaction will occur. This reaction is not spontaneous. Other reactions are nonspontaneous as well. Consider the decomposition of water:

$$2H_2O \longrightarrow 2H_2 + O_2$$

This does not occur spontaneously, but you can make the reaction happen by applying an electric current to water. See figure 5.14. Note the two half reactions that occur at the electrodes. Water is reduced at the cathode and hydrogen gas is produced. Notice that OH^- ions are also produced. This would make the solution at the cathode basic.

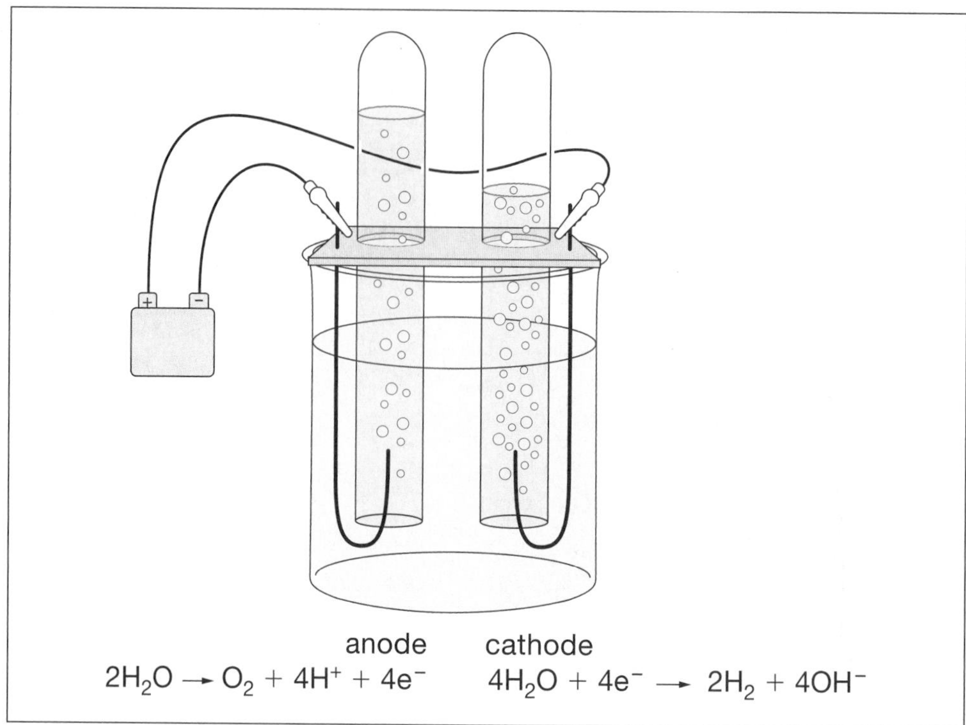

▲ **Figure 5.14 Electrolysis of water.** The electrolysis of water produces hydrogen gas and OH^- ions at the cathode and oxygen gas and H^+ ions at the anode. What do you notice about the volumes of gas produced at each electrode? What is the significance of this ratio?

Water is oxidized at the anode and oxygen gas is produced. Since H^+ ions are produced at the anode, what does this tell you about the pH of the solution near the anode?

Applying an electric potential causes current to flow and can force nonspontaneous reactions to occur. These types of reactions use electrical energy to produce a chemical change. Instead of the reaction proceeding in the same way as in voltaic cells, these reactions *require* a battery (source of electric potential).

Electrolytic cells are cells that include a battery as an energy source. Look at figure 5.15 to see a comparison of these cells.

In Part II, you will work with a team to make an electrolytic cell. As you observe the changes that occur, you will use your understanding of redox reactions to explain the chemistry involved.

Process and Procedure

The nature of metals is characterized by their ability to donate electrons to form ions. Because metals are typically such good reducing agents, most metals are not found in nature in their pure form. They occur as metal ores, and some chemical means must be used to separate

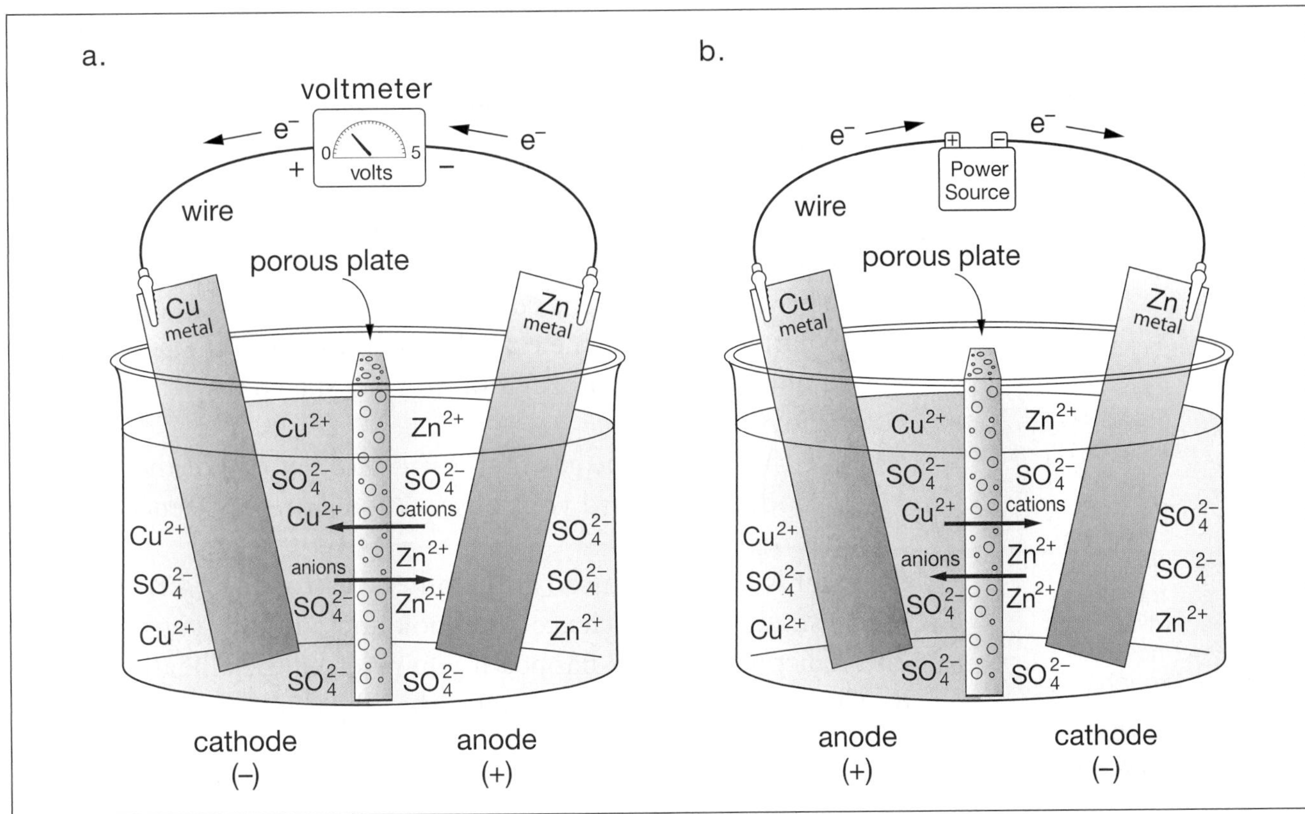

▲ **Figure 5.15 (a) Voltaic cell and (b) electrolytic cell.** Both of these cells involve chemical energy and electrical energy. Notice that the flow of electrons is in the opposite direction (but still from anode to cathode) for an electrolytic cell compared with a voltaic cell.

the metal from other substances in the ore. Suppose you wanted to extract copper metal from a solution of copper II chloride ($CuCl_2$). To do this, the copper ions in the solution (Cu^{2+}) must gain two electrons to become copper metal (Cu). This reaction is not spontaneous, and therefore you must set up an electrolytic cell.

1. Set up your investigation apparatus by following Steps 1a–f.
   a. Place your length of tubing in a U shape in your beaker.
   b. Use your pipet to fill the tube with the copper II chloride ($CuCl_2$) solution to about 5 mm from the top of each end of the tube.
   c. Attach the alligator clips to the wires on the battery clip. The clip should not be on the 9-volt (V) battery at this time.
   d. Carefully attach the alligator clips to 2 pencil leads, 1 on each clip.
   e. Immerse 1 pencil lead into each end of the filled tube.

Be careful with the pencil leads; they break easily.

f. Attach the battery clip to the 9-V battery. Your setup should look like figure 5.16.

2. As the reaction proceeds, sketch the setup in your science notebook. Make the drawing large enough to add labels, highlight comments, and captions later.
3. After a few minutes, note any changes to the system or observations you make. Add these to your sketch.
4. Note which electrode is connected to the negative terminal of the battery and which electrode is connected to the positive terminal. Add this information to your sketch if you have not already done so.
5. Note the odor of the gas that is produced at one of the electrodes and record your observations in your science notebook.
6. What is being produced at the other electrode? Describe the substance in your science notebook and add it to your sketch.
7. Predict what would happen if you reversed the alligator clips.
8. Check your prediction. Reverse the alligator clips by disconnecting the battery clip from the battery and flipping the connection. You will have to hold the connection in place because it will not snap onto the battery.

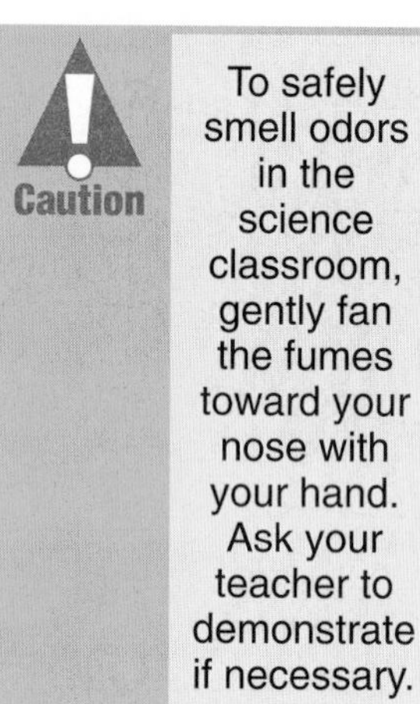

Caution
To safely smell odors in the science classroom, gently fan the fumes toward your nose with your hand. Ask your teacher to demonstrate if necessary.

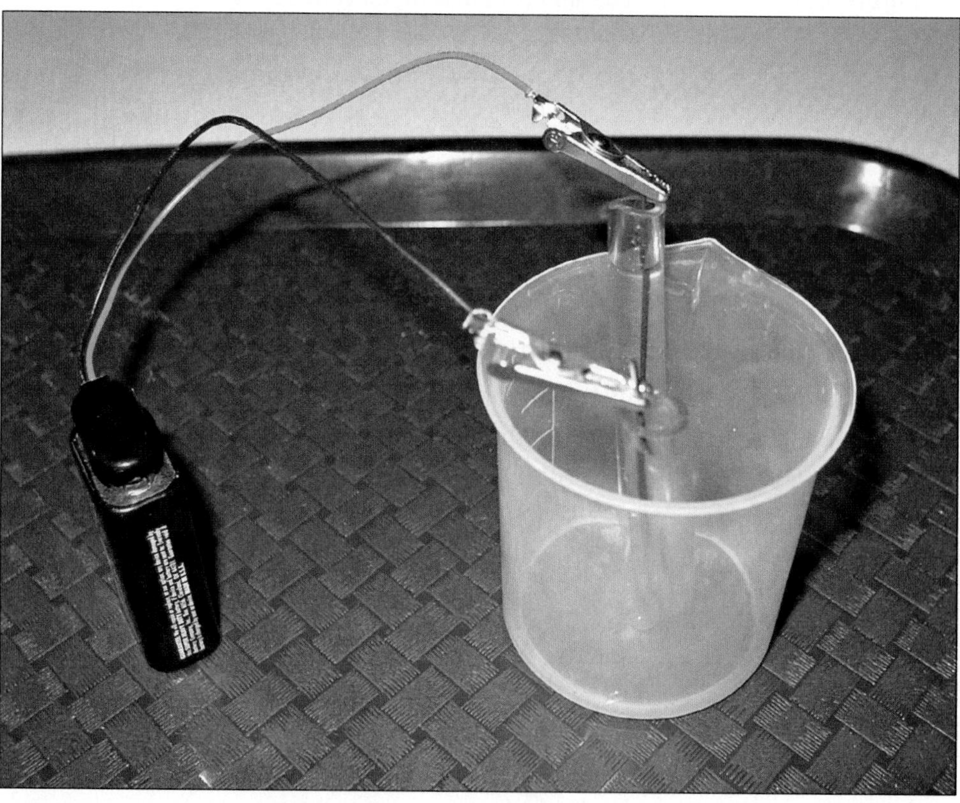

Figure 5.16 Electrolytic cell setup. Your lab setup should look like this.

9. Disconnect the battery from the clip and clean up the lab as you teacher directs.
10. Add highlight comments to your sketches by responding to "What I see" and "What it means."
11. Label all parts of the sketch including the balanced half reactions that are taking place at each electrode.
12. Write a balanced overall chemical reaction for the redox reaction that is occurring. Place this on your sketch. Remember that the gas that is produced is diatomic (occurs as X_2).
13. For a short history of the chemistry of the kinds of batteries we use every day, read the sidebar, *Current History*.

Reflect and Connect

1. Electroplating is sometimes used to coat a less expensive metal with a more expensive metal. Sterling silver flatware, or silverware, is made of solid silver and is very expensive. Less expensive silverware can be made by plating silver onto items that are made from less expensive metals. This can be arranged by making an electrolytic cell where a piece of pure silver and an item such as a fork are used as electrodes. These electrodes are placed in a solution containing silver salts and a battery is connected, as shown in figure 5.17.

   Why is it necessary to supply energy to reactions in an electrolytic cell such as the one pictured in figure 5.17?
2. What is the purpose of the solid silver metal as one of the electrodes in figure 5.17?
3. Sketch figure 5.17 in your science notebook and label the cathode and the anode. Include the half reaction that is occurring at each electrode.
4. If copper is placed in a solution of silver ions, then no battery is necessary for silver to plate out on the copper as you saw in a previous activity. Why is a battery not necessary for this process?
5. Use a Venn diagram to compare and contrast voltaic cells and electrolytic cells.

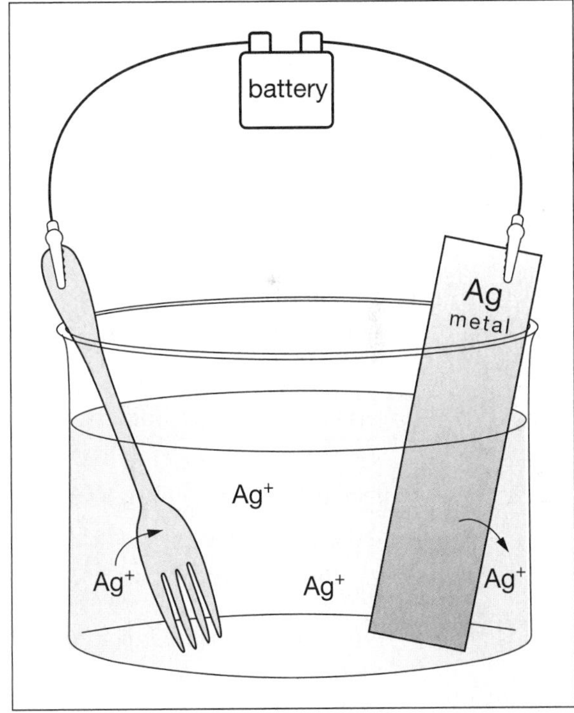

▲ **Figure 5.17 Electroplating cell.** Electroplating silver onto a less expensive metal can make beautiful silverware and is much less expensive than solid silver utensils.

SIDEBAR

Current History

What do batteries supply that powers electric motors in CD players, the electromagnetic signal in a cell phone, and the screen display of a laptop computer? Batteries provide much of the flow of electrons required to accomplish this and other work important in our daily lives.

But how did batteries come about? How do they produce electric current? Certainly people couldn't always go to a store and buy them. It turns out that the first modern battery can be traced to the work of Alessandro Volta, an Italian scientist. Volta reinterpreted the work that his countryman, Luigi Galvani, had accomplished with electricity. Galvani studied how dissected frog legs twitched when hooked up to metal connectors and lightning occurred. He thought "animal electricity" caused the twitching. But Volta thought the muscle twitches were induced by electric current flowing between two dissimilar metals connected by the moist flesh of the frog's leg. This led Volta to develop the first device that demonstrated the chemical production of electric current. In 1799, Volta arranged a vertical pile of metal disks (zinc with copper or silver). He then separated those disks from each other with paperboard disks that had been soaked in a salt solution. This stack was the first electric battery.

In 1802, William Cruickshank designed the first electric battery capable of being mass produced. He arranged sheets of dissimilar metals (copper and zinc) of equal size in a box. The box was then filled with an electrolyte of dilute acid. This flooded design resisted drying out and provided more energy than Volta's disk arrangement.

In 1836, John Daniell invented the first battery that produced a constant and reliable source of electric current over a long period of time. And in 1866, Georges Leclanché patented a new battery. He assembled his original cell in a porous pot. The positive electrode consisted of crushed

HIP/Ann Ronan Picture Library/Art Resource, NY

▲ **Volta explaining his first battery.** What role did dissimilar metals play in Volta's thinking about batteries? Why was moisture important?

manganese dioxide (MnO_2) with a little carbon mixed in. The negative pole was a zinc rod. The zinc rod and the pot were immersed in an ammonium chloride ($AlCl_3$) solution, which served as the electrolyte. Leclanché's battery became the forerunner to the world's first widely used battery, the carbon-zinc cell (see the modern carbon-zinc battery in the figure).

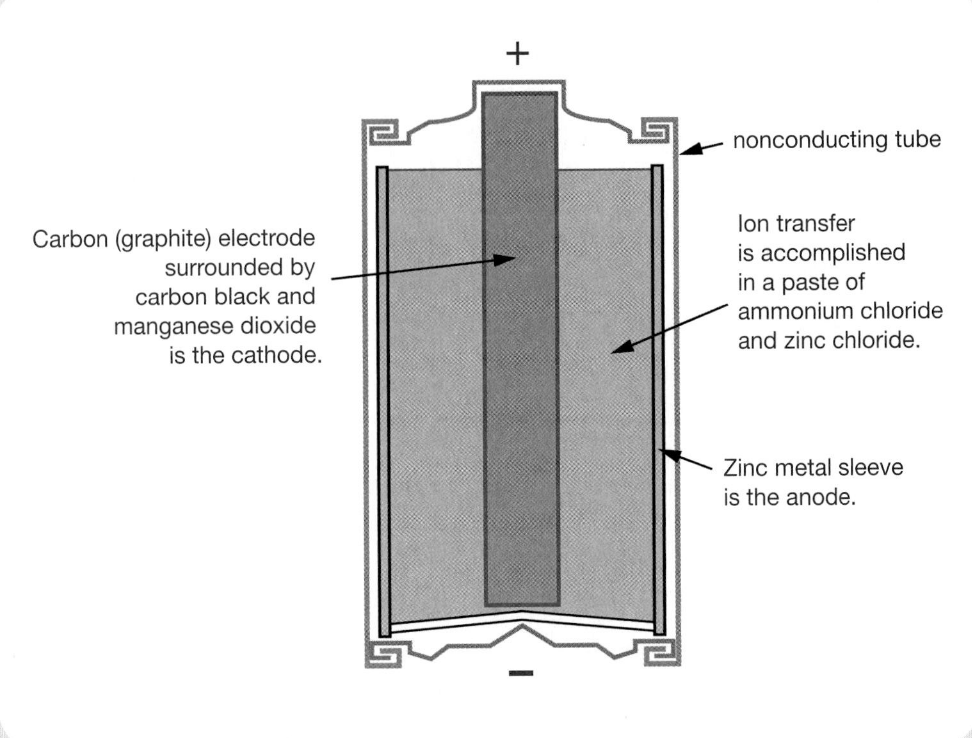
+
nonconducting tube
Carbon (graphite) electrode surrounded by carbon black and manganese dioxide is the cathode.
Ion transfer is accomplished in a paste of ammonium chloride and zinc chloride.
Zinc metal sleeve is the anode.
–

Cross section of a carbon-zinc battery. Where does oxidation take place? Where does reduction take place? How does a battery produce a reliable source of electric current?

The chemical reactions that produce electric current in this cell are approximated by

$$Zn_{(s)} \longrightarrow Zn^{2+}_{(aq)} + 2e^- \quad \text{anode}$$

$$2NH^+_{4(aq)} + 2MnO_{2(s)} + 2e^- \rightarrow Mn_2O_{3(s)} + H_2O_{(l)} + 2NH_{3(aq)} \quad \text{cathode}$$

The voltage of this cell is initially about 1.5 V, but decreases as energy leaves the cell. It also has a short shelf life and deteriorates rapidly in cold weather. While these batteries have a long history of usefulness, they are declining in application since some of their problems are overcome in alkaline batteries.

Alkaline batteries overcome some of the problems with carbon-zinc batteries by using potassium hydroxide in place of ammonium chloride in the electrolyte. Potassium hydroxide is a base, or alkaline, material, hence the name "alkaline" batteries. The half reactions are

$$Zn_{(s)} + 2OH^-_{(aq)} \rightarrow Zn(OH)_{2(s)} + 2e^- \quad \text{anode}$$

$$2MnO_{2(s)} + H_2O_{(l)} + 2e^- \rightarrow Mn_2O_{3(s)} + 2OH^-_{(aq)} \quad \text{cathode}$$

These cells have a much longer shelf life and perform better in cold weather. They avoid the use of the zinc-corroding ammonium ions and do not produce any gaseous products.

EVALUATE

Nail It Down

Many very important chemical reactions involve the transfer of charged particles such as protons in acid-base chemistry and electrons in redox chemistry. You have studied many of these reactions in this chapter. You are now prepared to demonstrate your knowledge in this evaluate activity. You will work both individually and with a partner to complete this activity.

Materials

For each team of 3 students

3 pairs of safety goggles

3 petri dishes

gelatin solution containing indicators

3 iron nails

6-cm magnesium ribbon

6-cm copper wire

3 *Corrosion Engineering Scoring Rubric* handouts

Cautions

Be careful with metals; sharp edges can cut you. Handle the gelatin mixture with care. Do not touch the mixture. Wear safety goggles during the laboratory portion of this activity.

Process and Procedure

1. Study the scoring rubric for *Corrosion Engineering* and determine how you will be evaluated on your work.
2. Read the following article and the description of the job for which you have just been hired.

Cost of Corrosion Study Unveiled

The U.S. Federal Highway Administration (FHWA) released a breakthrough two-year study on the corrosion of metals. The study addressed the direct costs of metallic corrosion in U.S. industry. Example industries include infrastructure, transportation, and manufacturing. Initiated by government and private organizations, the study provides current cost estimates and identifies national strategies to minimize the impact of corrosion.

Results of the study show significant costs. For example, the total annual estimated direct cost of corrosion in the United States is a staggering $276 billion—approximately 3.1 percent of the nation's gross domestic product. The study reveals that although corrosion management has improved, the United States must find more and better ways to encourage, support, and implement improved corrosion control practices.

Corrosion—a Natural but Controllable Process

Corrosion is a naturally occurring phenomenon. It is commonly defined as the deterioration of a substance (usually a metal) or its properties because of a reaction with its environment. Like other natural hazards, corrosion can be dangerous and expensive. Corrosion can damage everything from automobiles, home appliances, and drinking water systems to pipelines, bridges, and public buildings. Over the past 22 years, the United States has suffered 52 major weather-related disasters—including hurricanes, tornadoes, tropical storms, floods, fires, droughts, and freezes. These natural disasters have shown total losses of more than $380 billion (averaging $17 billion annually). According to the current U.S. corrosion study, the direct cost of metallic corrosion is $276 billion *on an annual basis.* Unlike weather-related disasters, corrosion can be controlled, but at a cost.

Corrosion Control Methods

Various time-proven methods for preventing and controlling corrosion depend on several factors. These factors include the specific metal to be protected; environmental concerns such as humidity, exposure to salt water or industrial environments; and the type of product to be processed or transported. The most commonly used methods include protective coatings, corrosion-resistant alloys, plastics, and cathodic protection. Cathodic protection is a technique used on pipelines, underground storage tanks, and offshore structures that creates an electrochemical cell in which the surface to be protected is the cathode and corrosion reactions are lessened.

The U.S. Federal Highway Administration (FHWA) has just hired you as a corrosion prevention specialist to help with a project to control corrosion in the reinforcing metal rods embedded in the concrete of bridges and overpasses. Your knowledge of redox and acid-base chemistry will be important in helping to solve a major corrosion problem. These reinforcement rods are made of iron, and corrosion is a continuing problem. Because of this recent report, the FHWA is aware of the problem and the costs involved in repairing and maintaining structures affected by corrosion. They want you to advise them on the proper use of cathodic protection for these rods.

3. Read the following information to learn more about your new job.

   To help you give the FHWA the best advice, you will conduct a set of experiments, record observations, and gather data. You will use the evidence from your experiments to write a report that will advise the FHWA of the benefits and problems of using cathodic corrosion control. The financial executives who will be reading your report have a limited background in chemistry, so you will have to include the chemistry background for them to understand your arguments.

   You learned about cathodes earlier in this chapter. Cathodic protection is the prevention of corrosion of a metallic structure by causing it to act as the cathode rather than as the anode of an electrochemical cell. This is done successfully by carefully selecting metals based on their relative reactivities.

   Financial advisers have given you important information. You have money to buy the metals that you need for this type of protection. But they have asked you to consider using copper since they have a source for copper that is inexpensive. You must argue either for or against using copper as part of the protection process for the iron rods. For your argument, you must have evidence. You can use your chemistry knowledge, but you also need experimental proof that this method will or will not work. And, if it doesn't work, you must be ready to supply the advisers with an alternative solution.

4. To help with this assignment, prepare 3 petri dishes with a gelatin solution. The gelatin will set into a semisolid material that will allow the reaction to occur undisturbed.

Your teacher has mixed 2 chemicals in the gelatin solution that will act as indicators for some of the reactions that take place. The first is an indicator that turns blue when the following process occurs: $Fe \longrightarrow Fe^{2+}$. The other indicator is phenolphthalein and turns pink when a solution reaches pH 8. Your teacher also added salt to the gelatin solution to speed up the corrosion process.

a. Prepare two of the iron nails by wrapping the middle of one nail with a piece of copper and the middle of the other nail with a piece of magnesium. Leave one nail unwrapped.
b. Place one nail in each of your three petri dishes.
c. Pour the liquid gelatin solution over the three nails. Pour enough gelatin solution to almost but not completely cover each nail.
d. Do not disturb the dishes. Allow the gelatin to congeal.

5. As you wait for the gelatin to congeal, make careful observations.

You will want to draw diagrams and add color and detailed labels and captions to your drawings. If you have access to a digital camera, take pictures of the reactions. You will need this evidence when you write your report.

6. Consider the indicators in the gelatin solution as you answer the questions in Steps 6a–e.

You will use your answers when you create your report to your advisers. Remember, they want you to use copper. Is this a good idea? You must support your case *for* or *against* using copper. A table of relative strengths of oxidizing and reducing agents is shown in figure 5.18.

a. What is the pH range of the original gelatin mixture? How do you know?
b. What does this pH indicate?
c. What color indicates that the iron nail is corroding?
d. What is the balanced redox half reaction for this process?
e. Is it an example of oxidation or reduction? How do you know?

7. Answer the questions in Steps 7a–d about how the pH of the solution changed.

a. What is the evidence of a pH change?
b. What is the pH range of this area around the nails?

Reducing agents	Oxidizing agents
Li	Li^+
K	K^+
Ca	Ca^{2+}
Na	Na^+
Mg	Mg^{2+}
Al	Al^{3+}
Zn	Zn^{2+}
Cr	Cr^{3+}
Fe	Fe^{2+}
Ni	Ni^{2+}
Sn	Sn^{2+}
Pb	Pb^{2+}
H_2	H_3O^+
Cu	Cu^{2+}
I^-	I_2
Hg	Hg_2^{2+}
Ag	Ag^+
Br^-	Br_2
Cl^-	Cl_2
F^-	F_2

increasing strength (reducing agents, upward) — increasing strength (oxidizing agents, downward)

Figure 5.18 Table of relative strengths of oxidizing and reducing agents. Use this table to determine the relative strengths of reducing agents.

c. What does this pH range tell you about the type and concentration of ions present in this part of the solution?
d. What is the difference between a concentrated acid or base and a strong acid or base?

8. Read the information below and answer the questions in Steps 8a–c.

In some parts of the gelatin solution near the nails, the dissolved oxygen in the solution (O_2) and the water (H_2O) together are the reactants of the redox half reaction:

$$O_2 + H_2O \longrightarrow ?$$

Either H^+ ions are produced or OH^- are produced.

a. Describe 2 lines of evidence for the ion that is produced.
b. Balance this redox half reaction according to mass and charge.
c. Is this oxidation or reduction? How do you know?

9. Combine the 2 balanced half reactions from the questions in Steps 6 and 8 to form an overall balanced redox reaction. Label the oxidizing agent and the reducing agent.

10. Read the following information and use it to answer the questions in Steps 10a–b.

In 1 dish, it appears that only 1 process of oxidation-reduction chemistry is occurring because only 1 color is appearing.

a. Is it possible to have only oxidation or reduction? Why or why not?
b. Why can't you see evidence of the other process?

11. Describe what would happen if you used a battery and connected one terminal to the copper wire and the other terminal to the iron nail in the petri dish. What would you see happening? Describe the process.

12. Label your sketches or photographs completely and write captions for each. Your labels should include the following:

a. The anode and the cathode
b. The point where oxidation occurs and the point where reduction occurs
c. Half reactions that are occurring at each anode and cathode

Look back at your diagrams. You will need to redraw them in your report.

13. Make a decision. Is copper the best choice for this process? Is magnesium the best choice for this process? Do you have another metal that you think would be better than either of these? Whichever way you answer, you must justify your decision, provide evidence that it is the best decision, and convey your reasoning in a way that your advisers will understand.
14. Prepare a report. It must contain illustrations, explanations, and justifications for your decision on the best metal to use to prevent the corrosion of the iron support rods.

Read over the scoring rubric again to make sure you understand your teacher's expectations for the report.

UNIT 2

Inside Life

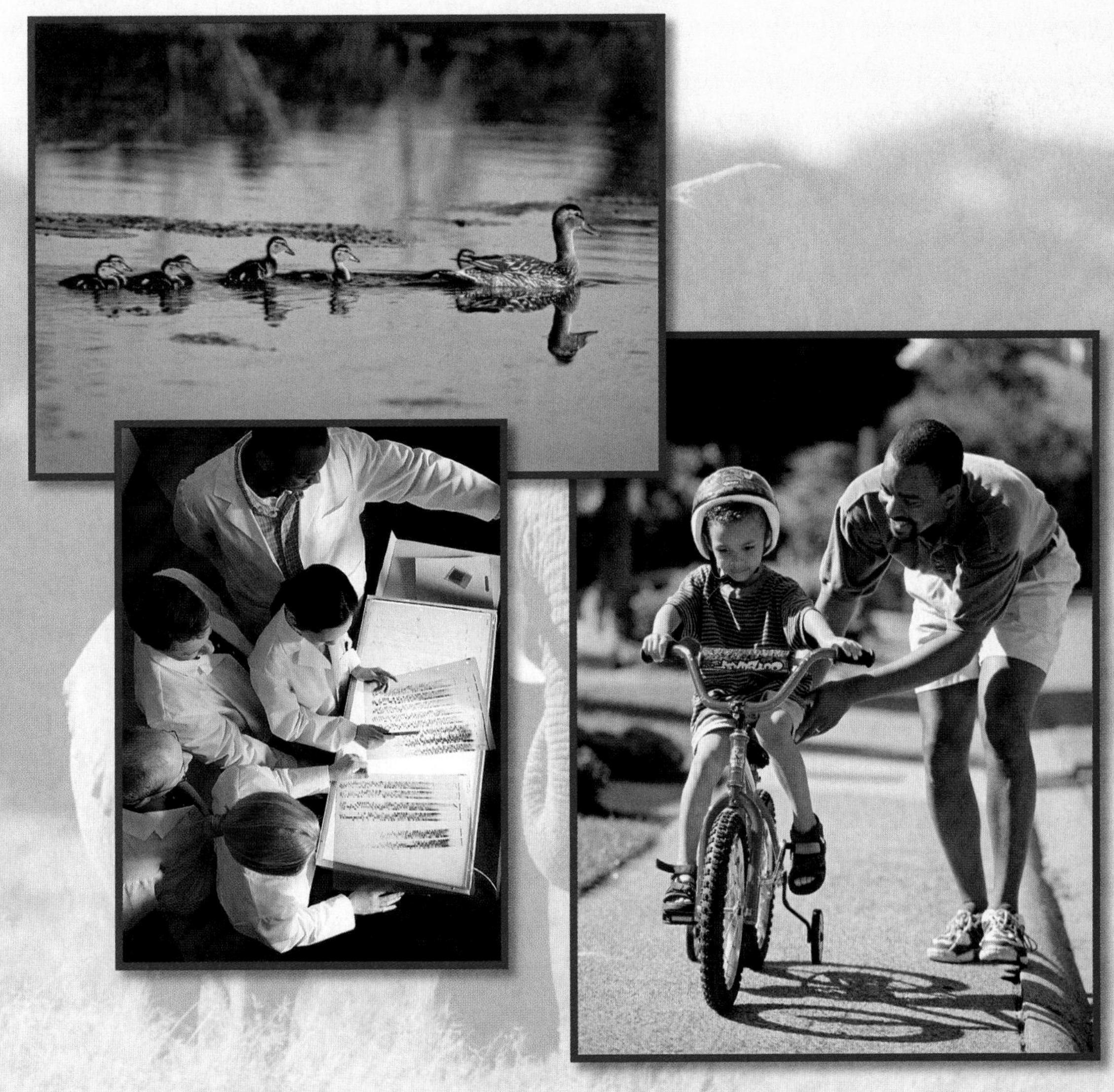

Inside Life

Millions of different species of bacteria, plants, animals, and other organisms live on Earth today. Fossil evidence indicates that many more species have become extinct. In fact, scientists estimate that about 95 percent of the species that have lived on Earth are extinct. Some fossils closely resemble living organisms of today. Look at the illustration of the Thrinaxodon, a mammal-like reptile that lived about 240 to 220 million years ago. How do you think that it might be similar to the marten pictured beside it? Martens live in forests, are excellent climbers, and prey on red squirrels and chipmunks.

Other organisms that lived in the past and present have unique physical features, such as Dimetrodon with a sail on its back or the platypus with a bill and webbed feet. Dimetrodons lived about 280 to 260 million years ago and were more closely related to mammals than reptiles. Its sail was probably used to regulate body temperature. Platypuses are mammals with some reptilelike characteristics such as egg laying.

In unit 1, *Interactions Are Interesting*, you learned that interactions in both physical and chemical systems lead to changes. In unit 2, *Inside Life*, you will learn that interactions both within and between living systems lead to changes.

Goals for the Unit

In unit 2, you will learn about change in living systems. By the time you finish the unit, you should understand the following:

- Evolution of species occurs through the process of natural selection acting on genetic variation.
- Parents transmit genetic information to offspring through gametes.
- Genetic variation results from cells containing two copies of each gene and from mutation.
- DNA carries the code for the characteristics of all living things.
- DNA serves as the template for proteins, which are substances essential to life.
- Genetic engineering makes it possible to transfer DNA sequences from one organism to another.
- Genetic engineering brings up ethical issues that are influenced by multiple factors.

As you learn about change in living systems, you also will refine your ability to do science and develop a better understanding of scientific inquiry. You will

- use math and models to gather data,
- develop and revise explanations using evidence, and
- communicate information using a variety of methods.

CHAPTER 6

Exploring Change

Exploring Change

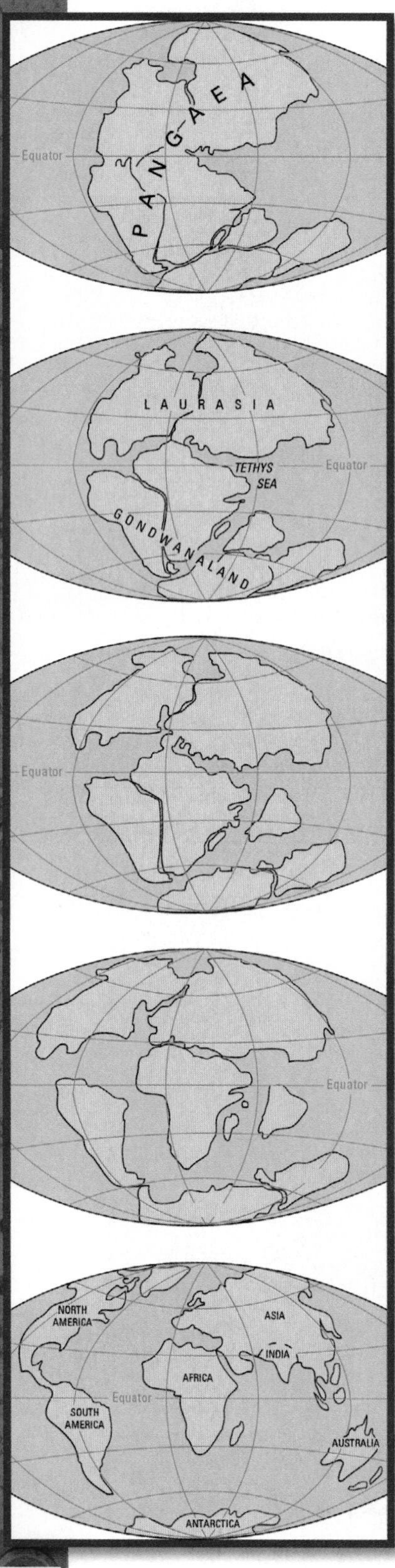

Have you ever thought about how much things around you change? What evidence do you have that change has occurred? For example, what changes do you see happening in figure 6.1? In chapter 6, *Exploring Change*, you will explore the concept of change in living systems. But don't be surprised if change doesn't always occur. In living systems, change is happening all the time, from small scales to large scales. Some changes happen very rapidly. Think of the change that takes place in you each morning as your alarm goes off, calling your body from sleep to wakefulness. Other changes in living systems take place more slowly. Think of the changes in you from the time you were an infant until now—a high school student. Other changes happen even more slowly, across millions of years. Think of the changes that occurred to produce the differences you see in the opening photographs.

Goals for the Chapter

In chapter 6, you will have an opportunity to use your critical-thinking skills to investigate evidence for change across time on Earth. By looking at the evidence, you will develop an understanding of the following concepts:

- Living systems on Earth change across time and have changed across time since the beginning of life on Earth. Many of these changes may have come about through changes in the environment.
- Species evolve across time through the mechanism of natural selection and genetic variation.
- Evolution helps account for the similarities and differences in species that existed in the past and that are alive today.

◀ **Figure 6.1 Geologic and biological change.** Change occurs across time and on both large and small scales. What evidence do you look for that change has occurred?

You will be better able to understand these concepts by participating in the following activities:

ENGAGE	Unity and Diversity
EXPLORE	Gifts from the Past
EXPLAIN	Clocks in Rocks
EXPLORE	Who Will Survive?
EXPLAIN	Learning about Life: A Great Discovery
ELABORATE	Twine Time
EVALUATE	Ancient Elephants

Use the chapter organizer to determine how each activity connects to the other.

Exploring Change

Linking Question

How do we know the relative age of rock layers?

ENGAGE

Unity and Diversity

Key Idea:
Observing organisms allows us to see unity and diversity.

EXPLORE

Gifts from the Past

Key Idea:
The arrangement of rock layers can tell us the relative age of the layers and any fossils.

Linking Question

How are rock layers dated on an absolute scale?

EXPLAIN

Clocks in Rocks

Key Idea:
Radioactive isotopes help date rocks on an absolute scale.

Linking Question

How does competition among organisms affect populations?

EXPLORE

Who Will Survive?

Key Idea:
Strategies for survival affect the population of all organisms.

EVALUATE

Ancient Elephants

Key Idea:
Evidence for elephant evolution can be pieced together to explain modern day elephants.

Linking Question

Did modern day elephants evolve from ancient ancestors?

ELABORATE

Twine Time

Key Idea:
The events of evolution have occurred over vast time periods, mostly before the present.

Linking Question

On what scale did the changes associated with evolution take place?

EXPLAIN

Learning about Life: A Great Discovery

Key Idea:
Darwin described the mechanism of evolution—natural selection.

Linking Question

What is the historical background of evolution?

CHAPTER 6 Major Concepts

Evolution explains the diversity of life on Earth

- **Organisms change across time**
- **Natural selection explains how species change across time**
- **Multiple lines of evidence that confirm evolution**
- **Physical properties change**

ENGAGE

Unity and Diversity

Earth is inhabited by a variety of living things. How much do you know about life on Earth? Have you ever thought about all the types of organisms that live on Earth? Scientists observe and compare different types of organisms to learn more about them. As scientists gather information about each type of organism, they begin to organize their observations and identify patterns. Many scientists have discovered that life on Earth reveals a pattern of unity and diversity. In the activity *Unity and Diversity*, you will work individually and with your class to discover if you see a pattern of unity and diversity in the life on Earth. Begin by looking for a pattern in the organisms pictured in figure 6.2.

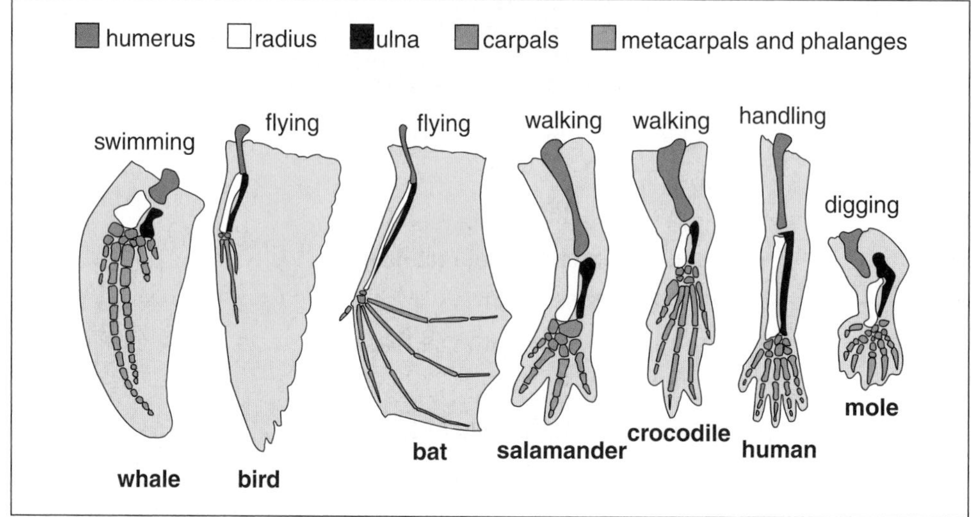

Figure 6.2
Variation in arms.
Do you notice any similarities or differences in the arms of different organisms? How do these similarities and differences affect the way an organism survives in its environment?

Materials

For each student

1 *Unity and Diversity* handout

Process and Procedure

1. Work in a team of 3 to complete the *Unity and Diversity* handout provided by your teacher.
2. Compare the 3 organisms you described on the handout with the organisms described by other teams in the class. Are they the same? What do you notice about them?
3. What other kinds of organisms can you think of? Contribute to a class list of organisms, which your teacher will compile on the board.
4. How are the organisms listed on the board similar to one another? How are the organisms different from one another?

5. Participate in a class discussion of the similarities and differences among the organisms. Record the results of your class discussion in your science notebook.

Reflect and Connect

Work on your own to answer the following questions. Record your best thinking in your science notebook.

1. Describe what you think scientists mean when they talk about the unity and diversity of life on Earth.
2. Why do you think organisms are similar? Why are they different? Explain your reasoning.
3. Consider the similarities and differences in organisms.
   a. You grouped organisms according to their similarities and separated them according to their differences. How did these tasks help you understand the unity and diversity of life on Earth?
   b. When else do you organize things according to their similarities and differences?

Gifts from the Past

EXPLORE

In the activity *Unity and Diversity*, you learned that life on Earth is diverse, yet many organisms share similar characteristics. How do scientists know about organisms that lived on Earth in the past? How do they piece together life on Earth? Scientists continuously discover evidence of how Earth and the life on it have changed across time. Figure 6.3 provides one example of a discovery of past life on Earth.

In *Gifts from the Past*, you will have an opportunity to work individually, with a partner, and with your class. You will use your critical-thinking skills and observational skills to piece together some important ideas about change. Focus your investigation with this question: "What do rock layers tell us about the relative age of organisms?"

▲ **Figure 6.3 Mammoth discovery.** A volunteer from a Denver museum carefully removes dirt from a mammoth tusk uncovered by a construction crew. The tusk was discovered in July 2002 while workers were digging up an area in Denver for a housing development. How often do you think evidence of past life is discovered?

Materials

Fossil Deposition animation on the *Student Resource CD* (*SRCD*)

Process and Procedure

1. You might have already studied the rock cycle and how rocks are formed, but you might not know as much about rock layers. Do you know a little or a lot about rock layers? Look at the sediment column your teacher has created. Then participate in a class discussion about stratigraphy, which is the study of rock layers (called strata).
2. With a partner, study the layers of rock in figure 6.4. Then do Steps 2a–c to show what you have learned about rock layers.

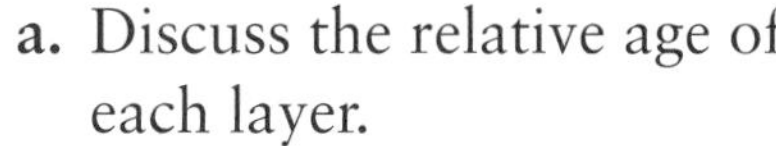

   a. Discuss the relative age of each layer.
   b. Sketch the major rock layers in your science notebook and label them from oldest to youngest.
   c. Write a few sentences under your drawing to explain why you labeled the rock layers the way you did.

▲ **Figure 6.4**
Rock layers. Erosion often exposes rock layers such as these along Highway 68 in Maryland. Layers of rock, called strata, hold fascinating records of time. Geologists use stratigraphy to help determine the relative age of rock layers by looking at the position of the strata.

3. There are probably many times in your life that you have been on a road that ran along a wall of exposed rock layers. But you might not have thought about what you could learn from the rocks. To think more about what you might learn, discuss Questions 3a–b with your partner. Record your answers in your science notebook.
   a. Describe how you think rock layers help geologists determine a sequence of events in Earth's history.
   b. What other kinds of information could you learn from a study of rock layers?
4. Remains of organisms are often found in layers of rock and provide scientists with information about life on Earth. To learn more about this kind of evidence, read the following paragraphs. Then discuss your understanding with your partner.

Evidence from geologists' studies of rock layers reveals some interesting information about organisms. Many types of organisms from the past no longer exist today. In fact, many of the types of organisms that have lived on Earth are now extinct; they no longer exist on Earth. The next time you walk outside, look around you. What types of plants and animals do you see? These organisms are only a small fraction of the life on Earth today and an even smaller fraction of the life that has existed across time. Figures 6.5 and 6.6 provide examples of organisms that lived in the past on Earth.

Take a look at the *Fossil Deposition* animation on the *Student Resource CD* (*SRCD*) to get an idea of how fossils are dated by the layers of rock they are found in.

What evidence do we have in rock layers that extinct organisms once existed? **Fossils** are one example of a type of evidence that scientists discover and study. When the hard parts of organisms (such as bones and teeth) are buried under silt, mud, and sand, a fossil forms across time. Look at figure 6.7 to see an example of how a fossil is formed. Entire organisms can become fossilized when they get trapped in ice (woolly mammoths), tar pits (saber-toothed cats), and tree sap, which becomes amber when hardened (insects). Fossils also can be imprints, such as a footprint or an imprint of a leaf. These remains or traces of organisms provide a geologic record of ancient life. Using fossil evidence as one piece of the puzzle, and the sequence of rock layers as another, scientists can construct a historical account of life.

▲ **Figure 6.5 Extinct dinosaur (*Ornitholestes*).** Many organisms such as the *Ornitholestes* pictured here are extinct. Fossils of *Ornitholestes* aren't found in rock layers younger than 65 million years old. How do you think pictures and exhibits of ancient animals are made? How do we know what the outside of a dinosaur or a prehistoric mammal looked like?

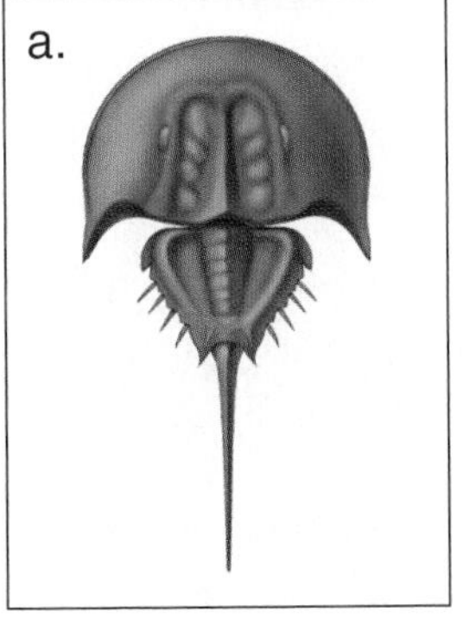

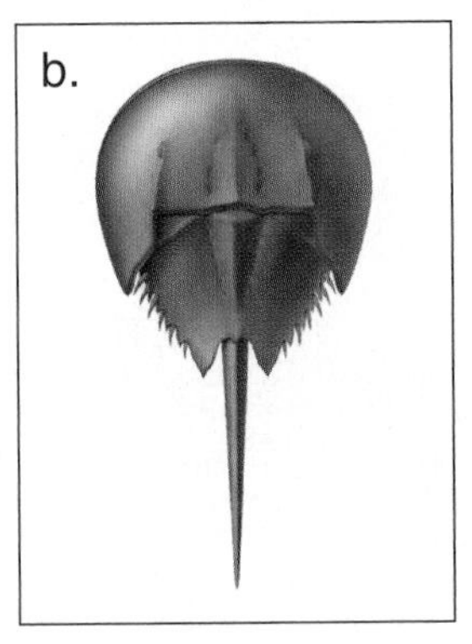

◄ **Figure 6.6 Living fossil.** Many species of horseshoe crab have existed during Earth's history. (a) This species of horseshoe crab (*Paleolimulus avitus*) lived about 250 million years ago. (b) This species of horseshoe crab (*Limulus polyphemus*) is found along the East Coast of the United States. Another three species of horseshoe crabs are found in other parts of the world. What is your evidence that horseshoe crabs have changed a little or a lot across time?

Figure 6.7
Fossil formation.
(a) Dead organisms or their skeletons may remain intact in underwater sediments through long periods of time. Eventually, minerals circulating in underground water replace the bone of the skeletons, forming fossils. (b) Buried fossils may be brought to the surface by any of the forces that uplift segments of Earth's crust. Once near the surface, the fossil-containing rock layers are exposed to erosion, which can free the fossils from the rock.

5. Fossils provide additional evidence of Earth's history. Choose a fossil from those shown in figure 6.8 and study it closely.
6. Use your observation skills to make some inferences about the fossils in figure 6.8. Identify some distinctive characteristics of the fossils and use this knowledge to answer the following questions in your science notebook.

Figure 6.8 Fossil organisms: (a) crinoid, (b) fern, (c) trilobite, and (d) polychaete. Do any of these fossils look similar to organisms you have seen before?

a. Describe what you think the organism is. What kind of organism is it? Where might it have lived?

b. Do you think there are similar organisms alive today, or did the organism only exist in the distant past? Explain your reasoning.

c. What other evidence would you want to collect to understand more about this organism?

How could you find out about its environment? How could you know when it lived?

7. Think about what you have learned so far about the rock layers. Fossils often are uncovered during excavation for the construction of new buildings and roads. With your partner, study the rock layers and fossils pictured in figure 6.9.

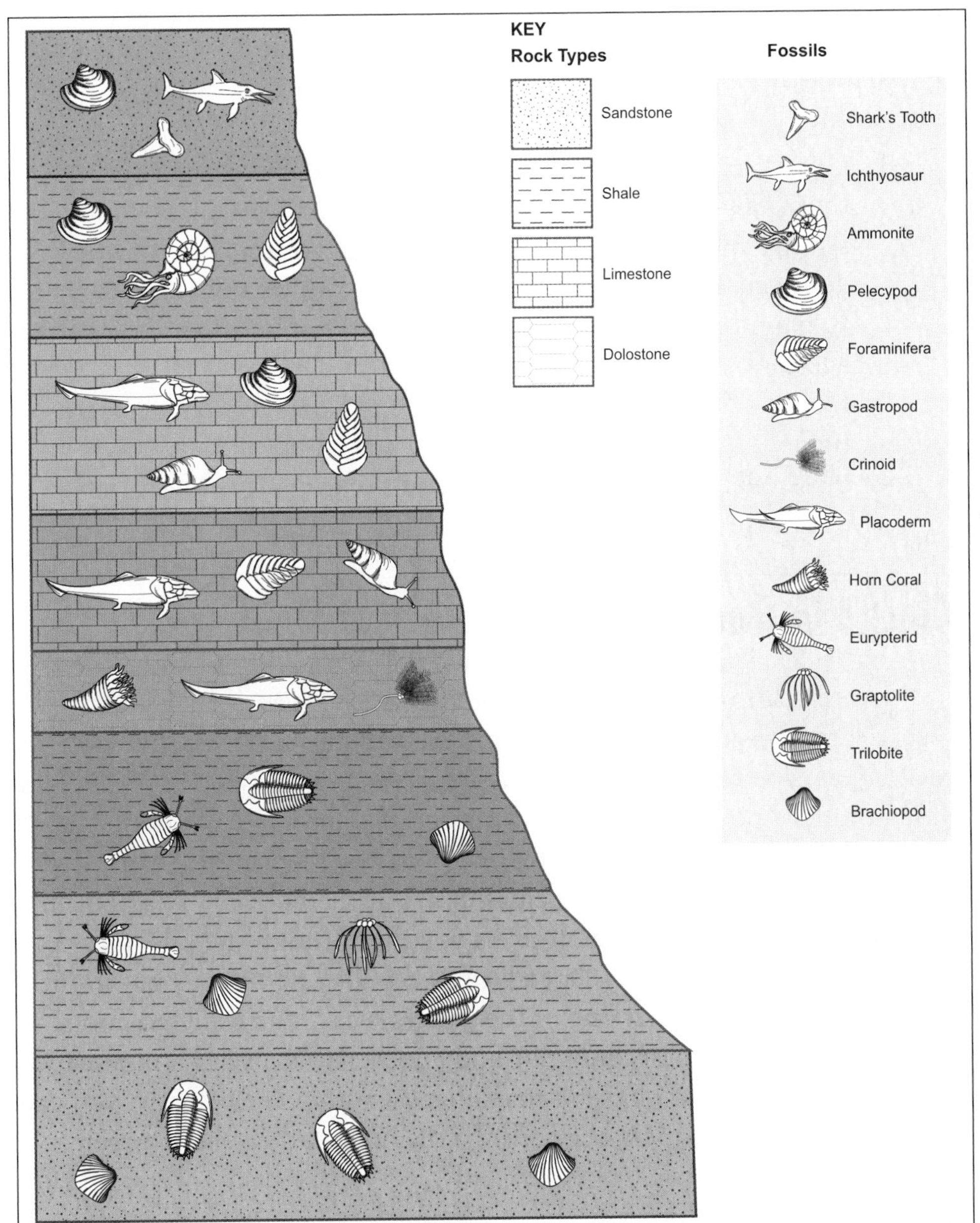

Figure 6.9
Fossils and rock layers correlate. Several fossils have been found in the newly exposed rock. What kind of information can you gather from the fossils and rock layers?

8. Use figure 6.9 to answer Questions 8a–c in your science notebook.
   a. Which fossil is older, the dinosaur bone or the coral? Explain your reasoning.
   b. Choose 2 fossils and describe the environment that you think they might have lived in.
   c. How have the environment and the organisms that live in it changed at this location?
9. You have been building on your previous understanding of rock layers. To learn how your understanding of rock layers has changed, look at the sediment column from Step 1 again and participate in a class discussion.

Reflect and Connect

Answer the following questions individually in your science notebook.

1. Go explore your environment. Find an object or structure that is a good model of rock layers to help you understand stratigraphy. Describe your model or draw a picture of it in your science notebook. Then explain your analogy.
2. Explain how rock layers are used to help determine the relative age of fossils.
3. How does the fossil record provide evidence for change across time?
4. How exact is relative age? Do you think you could find the exact age for a fossil? How?

EXPLAIN

Clocks in Rocks

Now you know how to determine the relative age of rock layers by their relative positions. You also know that by using the relative age of rock layers, you can infer which fossils are older and which are younger based on their position. You might recognize that you can apply your knowledge to other situations. Think about your locker at school. The papers you threw in there last semester are at the bottom. The book you just put in today is at the top. As you dig through the pile, all your work is correlated to (depends on) how long ago it was put in the locker. Now imagine that one of the papers was a dated memo about class changes from your counselor and another was a school newspaper (see figure 6.10). If you haven't rearranged your locker recently, you can infer the age of the papers between the memo and the school paper.

Rocks aren't stamped with a date, but geologists can determine the age of rocks. What tools do they use? In *Clocks in Rocks*, you will see that geologists use the properties of atoms and nuclei, something you have already studied.

Figure 6.10 Papers stacked in a locker. How old are the papers below the memo? Above the memo?

Materials

For each student

1 penny

1 cup

graph paper

Cautions

Hold your hand firmly over the opening of the cup so that pennies don't fly out and hit anyone.

Process and Procedure

1. Draw a T-table in your notebook with the headings "Key Word" and "Meaning of Key Word." Then read *Radiometric Dating* and complete your T-table as you read.

READING

Radiometric Dating

In the late 19th century, scientists discovered that some minerals in rocks contain radioactive elements. Radioactive elements have different forms. These forms are called **isotopes**. You might remember from Level 1 of BSCS *Science: An Inquiry Approach* that isotopes are atoms of the same element. But they have different numbers of neutrons. For example, all potassium atoms have 19 protons, but different isotopes of potassium have 20, 21, or 22 neutrons. These give atomic masses of 39, 40, and 41. Some isotopes are radioactive. The potassium isotope with 21 neutrons (potassium-40) is radioactive and is commonly used in geologic dating.

The nuclei of radioactive isotopes such as potassium-40 are unstable. They break down spontaneously. When they break down, they form stable isotopes across time. In this process, called **radioactive decay**, an isotope loses particles from its nucleus. The result is an isotope of a new element. The original element, called the **parent element**, decays into the new element, called the **daughter element**. The rate of decay from parent to daughter is reflected in a number called the **half-life**. The half-life of a radioactive isotope is the length of time it takes for exactly one-half of the parent atoms to decay to daughter atoms. Figure 6.11 illustrates the process of radioactive decay.

Each radioactive isotope has a unique half-life. Many radioactive isotopes have rapid rates of decay. They lose their radioactivity within a few days or years. Other isotopes decay slowly. A few of these isotopes are useful as geologic "clocks." That's because they tell the amount of time since the rock was formed.

For example, radioactive isotopes of uranium decay into lead. The half-life for one of these isotopes is 704 million years. If uranium-235 was a mineral in a rock, half of it would decay into lead-207 in 704 million years. Therefore, after 704 million years, equal amounts of uranium-235 and its daughter product lead-207 would be present in the mineral. After another 704 million years (a total of 1.4 billion years), only one-quarter of the original uranium isotope would be left. Scientists measure the amount of parent and daughter element in a rock. They use these amounts to calculate how many half-lives have passed.

Geologists must purify and concentrate minerals in rocks that contain radioactive isotopes. When they study the youngest rocks, they see that very little of the parent element may have decayed. When they study the oldest rocks, they find that a substantial amount of the parent element has decayed into a stable element. Geologists can measure the presence of several different isotopes to help them determine the age of rocks. Figure 6.12 shows the half-lives of some elements commonly used in radiometric dating.

Scientists have spent the last 100 years establishing the techniques and developing the technology used in radiometric dating. After the discovery of radioactivity in the late 1800s, physicists began experimenting with how to measure decay rates. By the 1950s, physicists were using mass spectrometers to measure the amount of

SCILINKS® NSTA
Topic: radioactive decay
Go to: www.scilinks.org
Code: 2Inquiry290

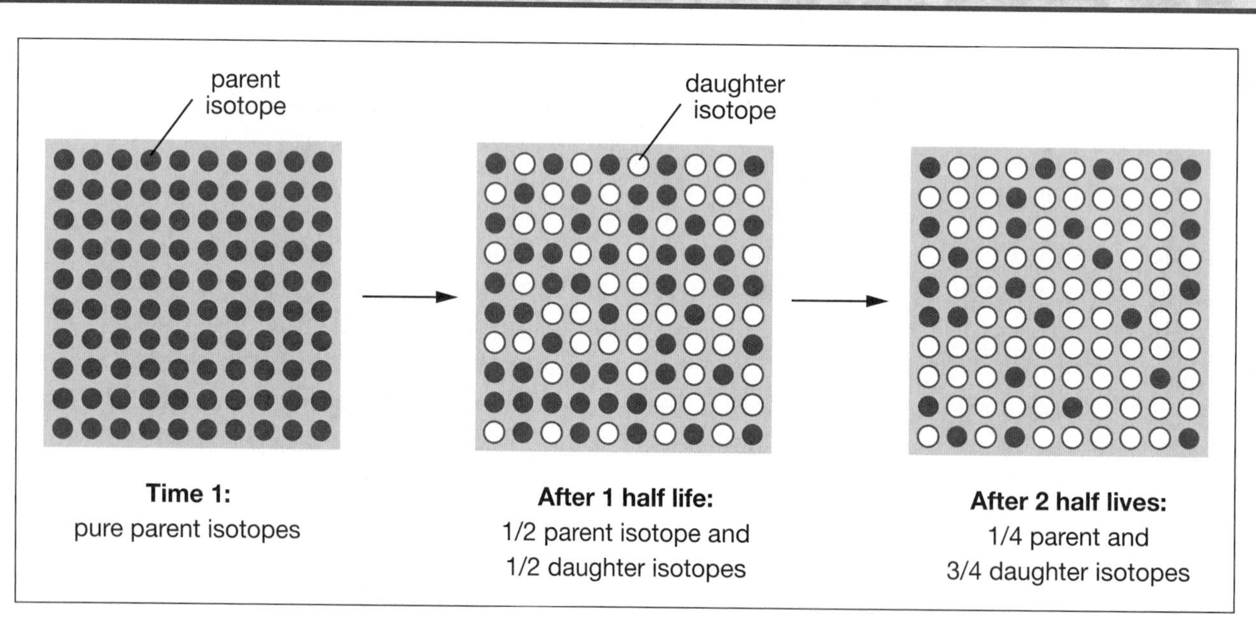

▲ **Figure 6.11 Radioactive decay.** When an igneous rock forms, some minerals in the igneous rock contain only parent isotopes. After one half-life of the radioactive element has passed, the rock contains one-half parent and one-half daughter isotopes. After two half-lives have passed, the rock contains one-quarter parent isotopes and three-quarters daughter isotopes. How many daughter isotopes will the rock contain after three half-lives have passed?

various isotopes found in rock samples. Now more than 50 years later, geologists use the radiometric dating techniques developed by physicists to determine the absolute ages of rocks. Radiometric dating has helped scientists establish that Earth formed about 4.6 billion years ago (see figure 6.13).

Isotope		Half-life of parent (years)	Useful range (years)
Parent	**Daughter**		
Carbon-14	Nitrogen-14	5,730	100–50,000
Potassium4-0	Argon-40	1.3 billion	100–0.5 billion
Rubidium-87	Strontium-87	47 billion	10 million–4.6 billion
Uranium-238	Lead-206	4.6 billion	10 million–4.6 billion
Uranium-235	Lead-207	710 million	10 million–4.6 billion

▲ **Figure 6.12 Radioactive elements.** This table shows some of the radioactive elements used in radiometric dating. Some elements such as uranium have more than one radioactive isotope. Notice that the half-life for carbon is much smaller than the half-life for the other elements. Isotopes with long half-lives decay very slowly.

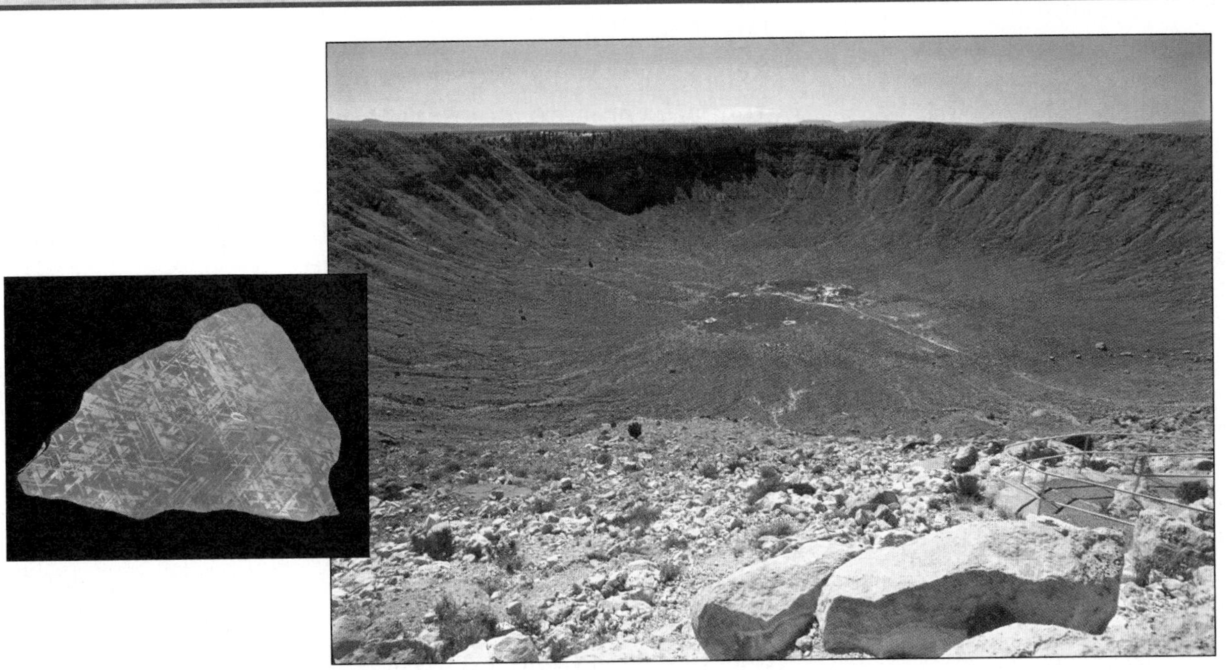

▲ **Figure 6.13 Meteorites tell the age of Earth.** This famous crater located in northern Arizona was formed by the Canyon Diablo meteorite. Meteorites are material left over from the creation of the solar system. Therefore, scientists expect Earth to be the same age as the meteorites. Scientists use radiometric dating techniques on meteorites such as Canyon Diablo to determine the age of the solar system. All data from these techniques suggest that the solar system is about 4.6 billion years old. Therefore, Earth is about 4.6 billion years old.

2. Radioactive isotopes have properties that make them useful to scientists. Work on the following task to show what you have learned about radioactive isotopes so far. Record your response in your science notebook.

   Explain how scientists use the isotopes of some elements to determine the age of rocks. Include the following words in your description: *isotope*, *radioactive decay*, *parent*, *daughter*, *half-life*.
3. Sometimes it is easier to understand a complicated process such as radiometric dating after you model it in an activity. Obtain a penny and a cup to model radioactive decay.
4. Begin the activity with the class standing. Each of you represents a radioactive atom.
5. To determine if your atom decays, do Steps 5a–c.

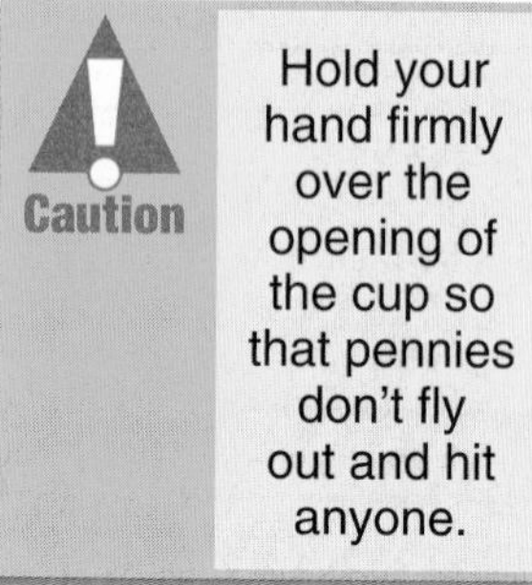

Caution
Hold your hand firmly over the opening of the cup so that pennies don't fly out and hit anyone.

   a. Place the penny in your cup. Hold the cup in one hand while covering it with the other hand.
   b. When your teacher tells you to start, begin shaking the cup. Shake for 10 seconds or until your teacher tells you to stop.
   c. Turn the cup over and look to see if you have heads or tails. If you have heads, sit down. Your atom has decayed.
   d. Your teacher will record the results of the first round on the board.
   e. Repeat these steps until the entire class is sitting (decayed).
   f. To represent more atoms and collect more data, repeat Steps 4 and 5 two more times.
6. Using the numbers in the table recorded by your teacher, plot the data on a graph. Place your graph in your science notebook. Then compare your graph to the graphs showing exponential and linear change in *FYI—Changing Rates of Change*.

Always include highlight comments and a caption for *xy* plots you place in your notebook.

7. Answer the following questions in your science notebook.
   a. Explain how the penny activity modeled radioactive decay.
   b. What was the half-life for your class isotope? Show your calculations.
   c. Describe the curve in the graph you plotted in Step 6. Did the number of decay events stay the same, increase, or decrease with the passage of time (each trial)?
8. Where would you find rocks that contain radioactive isotopes? Learn more about the rocks used in radiometric dating by reading the following paragraph. Discuss your understanding with your partner.

Radioactive isotopes can be found in rocks from volcanoes, such as ash layers and lava flows. A variety of radioactive elements tend to become concentrated in these types of rocks. Radiometric clocks "start" when a rock is formed. Once the rock has solidified, the products of decay can begin to accumulate in the minerals. Radiometric dating measures the amount of time that has passed since the rock was formed. Because volcanic rocks often contain many radioactive elements, scientists can use many radiometric dating techniques and compare the results. Volcanic ash layers can be valuable to scientists because they are deposited worldwide. Scientists can find the same deposit at many locations on Earth.

Reflect and Connect

Discuss the following questions with your partner and record your own answers in your science notebook.

1. Explain how radiometric dating works.

What are scientists measuring in rocks? How do they use the measurements to determine the age of rocks?

2. Study figure 6.14 and determine the age range of the limestone and sandstone layers. Record your response in your science notebook. Be sure to explain your reasoning.

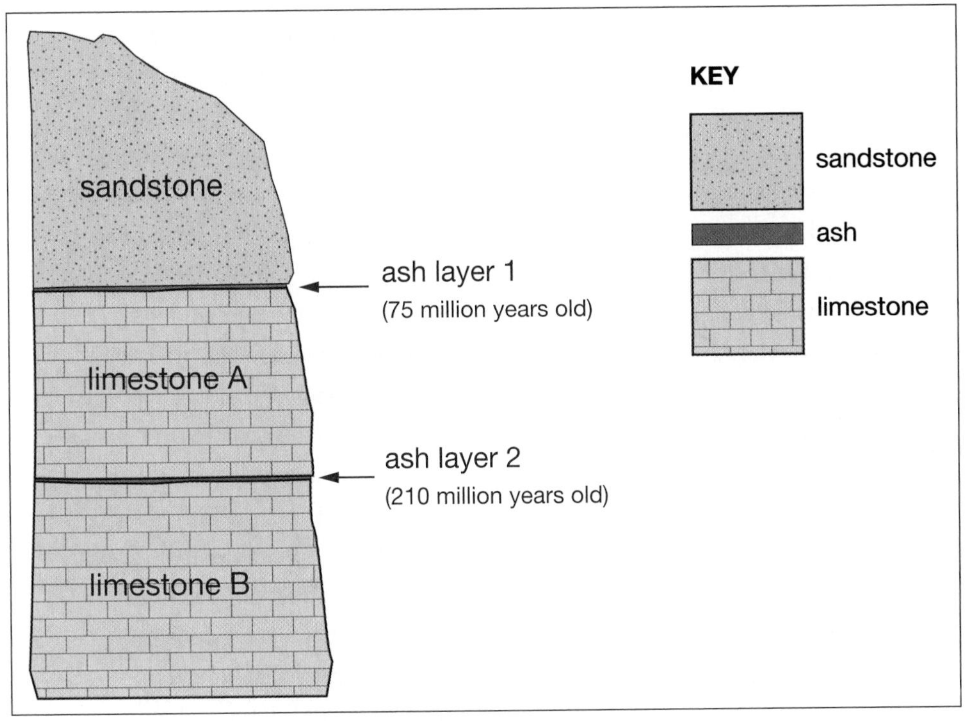

Figure 6.14 Limestone and sandstone layers. This rock column contains three types of rock (limestone, sandstone, and 2 ash deposits). Ash deposit 1 is approximately 75 million years old according to radiometric dating techniques; ash layer 2 is 210 million years old. Use what you know about rock layers and radiometric dating to estimate the age range of both limestone layers and the sandstone layer.

Changing Rates of Change

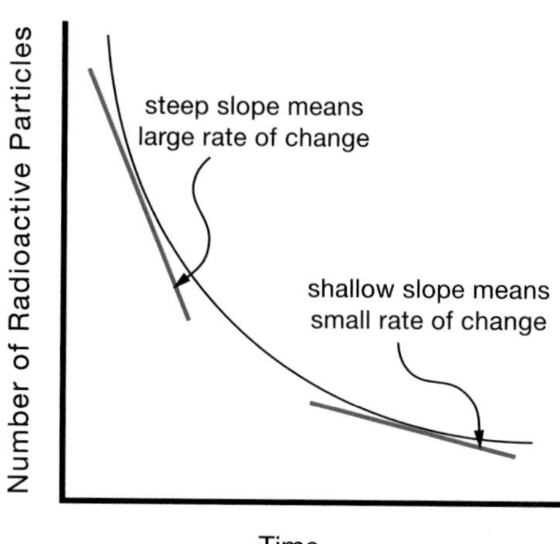

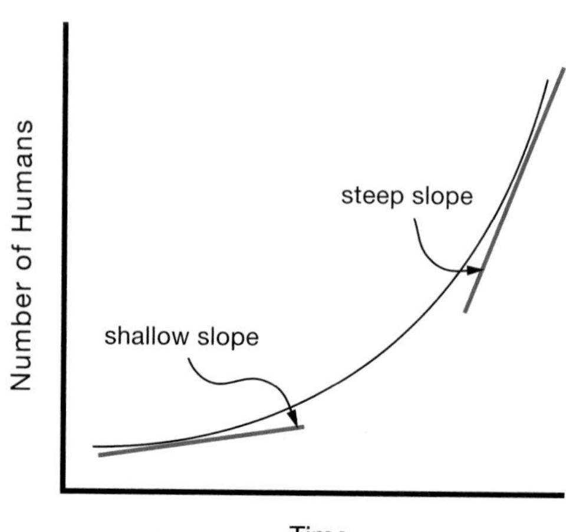

Rates of change can change. (a) Radioactive decay begins quickly and then slows down. How do the slopes show this? (b) Human population increases slowly at the beginning and then increases even more. How do the slopes show this?

Radioactive decay results in changes to the original amount of radioactive isotope. In fact, many phenomena result in changes to the original amount of "stuff." For example, populations of organisms, concentrations of chemical reactants, the position of an accelerating car, and even the value of investments change over time. How these things change has much in common. Scientists seek to understand the common features of change that these phenomena share. Using that knowledge, they can predict what will happen at some future point in time.

Look at the graphs of radioactive decay and human population increase. Note how they are both curved. This suggests they are related mathematically. Though one graph shows decreases and the other shows increases, they both show slow and fast rates of change. You can see the differences in rates of change by looking at the slopes at specific times. A steep slope means a large rate of change, and a shallow slope means a small rate of change.

Now contrast changing rates to nonchanging rates, as shown in the following graphs. Observe the amount of change for equal time periods. Note how curved lines show different amounts of change when compared with lines with no curve. Scientists associate curved lines with **exponential** mathematical relationships. This simply means the equation used to describe the line has an exponent in it. You will see the same curved line anytime something changes by the same percentage in each time period. For example, an inflation rate of 4 percent results in exponential increases in costs.

You have already seen many examples of exponential relationships in this program. Study the following table to refresh your memory. As you continue learning about science, remember to look for curved lines. When you see them, think about the amount of change. It's not always constant. When it's not constant, exponential growth or decay occurs. And exponential changes affect your predictions dramatically.

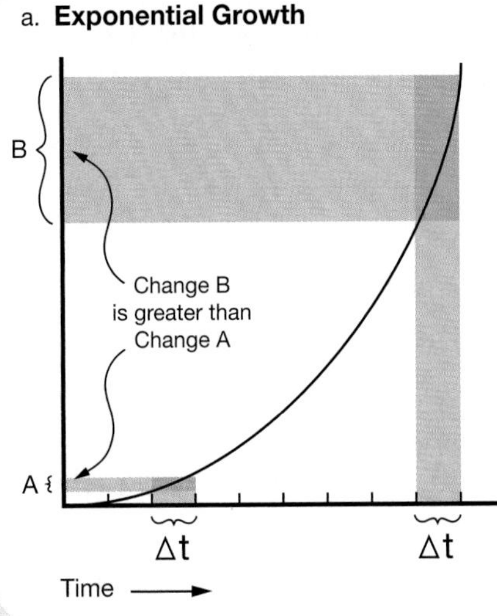

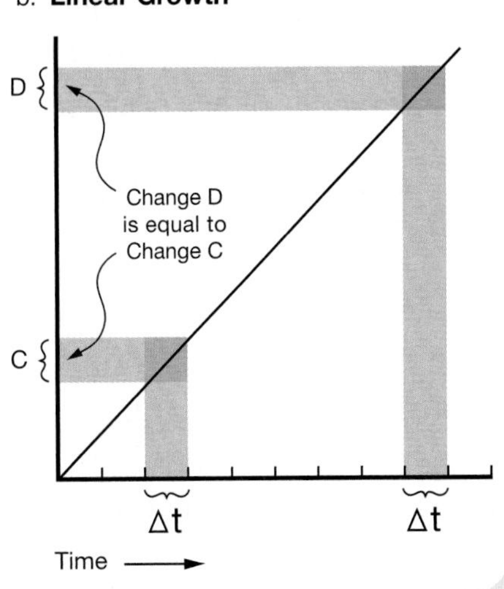

Topic: exponential growth
Go to: www.scilinks.org
Code: 2Inquiry295

Exponential and linear change. (a) Exponential growth results in an increase in the amount of change over time. (b) Linear growth results in the same amount of change for each time unit.

Subject	Equation	Graph	Phenomena
Earth Science/ Space Science	$C = C_o e^{-kt}$ C = amount of radioactive isotope C_o = original amount	C_o, C, Time	Radioactive Decay
Biology	$L = L_o e^{-kt}$ L = amount of medicine L_o = original dose	L_o, L, Time	Medicine half-life in human body
Chemistry	$A = A_o e^{-kt}$	A_o, A, Time	Decrease in amount of reactants in chemical reaction
Physics	$x = \frac{1}{2} at^2$	x, Time	Acceleration of an object from rest
Economics	$P = P_o e^{rt}$ P = amount of money P_o = original amt. of money r = annual interest rate	P, P_o, Time	Exponential growth of money due to constant interest rate

e = 2.178, t = time, k = constant

Examples of exponential change. Look for examples of exponential change that you recognize. Find the exponent in each equation. The *e* is a constant equal to 2.72. Similarly, *k* is a constant associated with the material in question and *t* represents time.

3. How do fossils, rock layers, and radiometric dating techniques work together to provide evidence for change across time?
4. Do organisms ever change? What evidence would you look for to support the idea that an organism has different characteristics now than in the past?

EXPLORE

Who Will Survive?

You have been learning about the evidence that supports the idea that things change across time. The fossil record provides one piece of evidence. The type of organisms at a particular location can change across time, for example, from ocean organisms to terrestrial (land) organisms. Because the type of organisms changed, we know that the environment in that location changed. You will consider this idea again in chapter 13, *Time for Change*, for the history of life in Colorado. But the same species of organism also can change across time. What do you think happens across time to cause a species to look different?

▲ **Figure 6.15**
Predator and prey. Will the rabbit survive? What factors influence the answer? What physical changes would result in more successful coyotes?

In *Who Will Survive?*, you will simulate how this change might occur. In each simulation, you will act as the predator. In Part I, you will explore what happens across time to a population of prey that has variations in its characteristics. In Part II, you will explore what happens across time to populations of predators and prey when they both have variations in their characteristics. In both parts, focus your thinking with this question: "What variables affect who will survive?"

Part I: Predator and Prey

In Part I, you and your classmates will represent predators in an environment. Beans will represent the species of organisms that are your prey. The different colors and shapes of the beans will represent variation within the species of prey. After the simulation, you will analyze the selective effects of predation in this simulation. That analysis will help you gain a better understanding of how the average characteristics of a population can change across many generations.

A species is a group of organisms that reproduces most successfully with individuals of the same type. A population is a group of organisms of the same species that lives in a particular area.

Materials

For each team of 4 students

3 plastic cups or other containers

3 forceps (optional)

25 lentils, 25 split peas, 25 navy beans, and 25 red beans in a bag labeled "starting population"

50 lentils* in a bag

50 split peas* in a bag

50 navy beans* in a bag

50 red beans* in a bag

1 empty bag

1 meterstick

4 colored pencils similar to the color of the dried beans

2 sheets of graph paper

1 large sheet of wrapping paper

2 *Three Generations* handouts

4 *Predictions across Time* handouts

*Vary the type of bean according to the environment you use.

Cautions

Use utensils properly.

Process and Procedure

1. Spread out your wrapping paper in one of the locations provided by your teacher. The wrapping paper will represent a habitat. Crumple the paper to make the habitat more 3-dimensional.
2. Decide on your roles for the activity.

Three members of your team will be predators of beans (the prey). As predators, each of you will hunt the prey in your environment. The fourth member will be the game warden, who will keep track of the hunting.

3. Draw a data table in your science notebook similar to the one in figure 6.16.

Population	Number of individuals			
	Lentils	Split peas	Navy beans	Red beans
First Generation Starting				
First Generation Surviving				
Second Generation Starting				
Second Generation Surviving				
Third Generation Starting				

▲ **Figure 6.16 Data table for Part I.** Adjust the bean types in your data table according to the bean types you will use in your simulation.

4. Examine the beans in the bag labeled "starting population." Record the number of individuals of each color in your table as the first-generation starting population.

The beans (prey population) represent a variation in the color of individuals within a species. The individuals of this species can be 1 of 4 color variations (lentils, split peas, navy beans, or red beans). There should be 25 "individuals" of each color.

5. Set up the simulation as follows.
   a. Predators: Obtain a cup to put your captured prey in. Face away from the selected environment.
   b. Game warden: Spread the beans from the bag labeled "starting population" throughout the selected habitat. Keep the boundaries to about 1 meter (m) by 1 m.

Spread the beans as uniformly as possible so that no beans are sticking together or covering others.

6. Begin the simulation as follows.
   a. Game warden: Direct the predators to face the environment and begin picking up prey.

Tell predators to use a pinching motion with one hand (or forceps) to pick up beans 1 at a time. They must pick up only 1 bean at a time and place it in their cup before taking another bean. Predators should locate the prey using their eyes. Make sure they locate their prey before picking it up.

Direct the predators to stop when only 25 percent of the prey remains. For a starting population of 100, 75 will be removed so that 25 remain.

b. Predators: For a team of 3 predators, each predator should pick up 25 prey.

7. Finish round 1 of predation in your simulation as follows.

a. Predators: Place the "eaten" prey from your cup into the empty bag. You might need to reuse these later to represent offspring.

b. Game warden: Collect the remaining (surviving) prey from the environment and sort them by type. Count the number of each color of prey that "survived."

To make them easier to count, arrange the beans in rows.

c. Game warden and predators: Record in your data table the number of each color of prey that survived as the first-generation surviving population.

8. Prepare for round 2 of predation in your simulation as follows.

a. Game warden: Simulate reproduction among the surviving prey by adding 3 new beans of the same color for each surviving prey. The number of each type of surviving prey is recorded in your data table (Step 7c).

These beans represent offspring. Obtain them from the bags containing the single colors of beans. If necessary, use the beans that have already been eaten.

Thoroughly mix the prey that survived with their offspring. You should end up with a total of 100 prey.

b. Game warden and predators: Record the number of each color of prey in your data table as the second-generation starting population.

9. Repeat Steps 5 through 7 for round 2 of predation. Use the second-generation starting population as your prey. When your simulation is complete and you have recorded your results, sort the colored beans into their respective plastic bags. Then return the bags to the materials area.

10. Suppose each surviving prey after round 2 produced 3 offspring. How many prey of each color would there be? Record this information as the third-generation starting population in your data table.

11. Prepare 2 graphs to show how many of each color prey were in the starting population at the beginning of each generation.

Sometimes it is helpful to describe the results of your investigation in a different way. Graphing your data can represent the information visually from your data table.

To make your graphs, follow these directions.

a. Choose 2 team members to prepare graphs. Each team member can make a different kind of graph.

One team member can make a bar graph. The other can make a line graph. Then you can compare them.

b. Both graphs should show the number and color of prey for all 3 generations.

c. Use different-colored pencils that correspond to the 4 colors of the prey.

d. Somewhere on your graph paper indicate what the habitat looked like.

You could paste a sample of the wrapping paper or write a description of the habitat.

12. While 2 team members are making graphs, the remaining team members should do the following.

a. Get a *Three Generations* handout. On the handout, each generation is represented by 50 circles and each circle represents 2 individuals.

b. Color each circle to represent members of the starting population of each generation. Use colored pencils that correspond to the colors of prey. For example, if there were 30 split peas in the second-generation starting population, you would color 15 of the circles with a green pencil. You can color only half of a circle if your numbers are not divisible by 2.

c. Somewhere on your handout indicate what the habitat looked like.

You could paste a sample of the wrapping paper or write a description of the habitat.

13. Compare the completed graphs and handout. Answer Questions 13a–c with your class. Record your own answers in your science notebook.

a. Which colors of prey survived better than others in the second- and third-generation starting populations?

b. Predators did not select the surviving prey as much as they did prey of other colors. Why?

c. What effect did capturing a particular color of prey have on the number of that color in the generations that followed?

14. You have been thinking about how different factors affected the survival of prey. Now work in your team to predict what might have happened to the prey population across time. Record your ideas in your science notebook.
    a. Predict the starting populations (of all 4 colors) for the next 4 generations. You do not have to predict actual numbers, but describe a trend.
    b. Compare your prediction with the data supplied on the *Predictions across Time* handout. Describe similarities and differences. Explain why you see these patterns. Does your prediction match the predictions on the handout? Explain how you arrived at your prediction.

Stop & THINK

PART I

As a team, study your graphs and the circle diagrams. Consider the following questions and record your team's responses in your science notebook.

1. Describe the simulation as a sequence of events. What was happening to the population of prey at each step in the sequence?
2. Which of the 3 methods of presenting data—the data table, the graphs, or the circle diagrams on the handout—helped you most easily interpret the data? Why?
3. What conclusions can you draw from your data?

Part II: Bird Beaks

In Part I of this investigation, you discovered how predators affect the variation that exists within a population of prey across time. In Part II, you and your team will investigate how **variation** in characteristics of predators affects their survival and their population across time. You will simulate how birds collect their food. The variation within the population of predators is their beaks—they vary in size, shape, and function. Figure 6.17 shows examples of birds with different beaks. What happens to birds with a variety of beaks when the food source changes?

a.

b.

c.

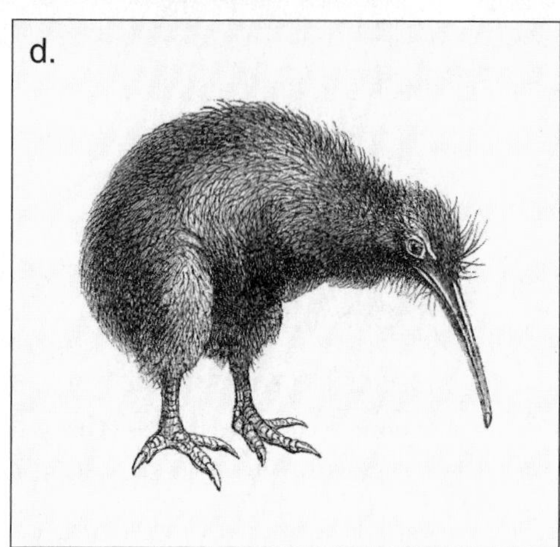
d.

Figure 6.17 Birds have different beaks. Different bird species have different types of beaks. Look at each bird beak: (a) eagle, (b) duck, (c) finch, and (d) kiwi. What influences might have led to the diversity of beak function you see?

Materials

For each team of 4 students

- 1 forceps
- 4 cups
- 1 container (plastic tub or dishpan) filled with water
- 1 spoon
- small marbles in a container (approximately 60)
- raisins (approximately 60)
- uncooked elbow macaroni (approximately 60)
- Styrofoam peanuts (packing material, approximately 60)
- 1 or 2 toothpicks
- 1 clothespin (spring type)
- 1 box top (used to contain prey, especially marbles)
- 4 plastic sandwich bags

Cautions

Use utensils properly.

Process and Procedure

1. Get in your team of 4. Select a utensil (toothpick, clothespin, spoon, or forceps) and a cup from the materials your teacher distributes. Each member of your team must have a different utensil.

The utensils represent types of bird beaks for different species of birds. The cups represent a bird's stomach.

2. You will use the utensil as a bird beak to collect food. Read the following descriptions about how you will collect food with the different bird beaks.
   - Clothespin: Hold the clothespin at the very end so that it opens as wide as possible. Pinch and release with 1 hand.
   - Toothpick: Hold the toothpick in 1 hand and use it to carefully spear the food. Use 1 finger of the opposite hand to push the food off the toothpick into the cup.
   - Forceps: Hold the forceps with 1 hand and squeeze to collect the food.
   - Spoon: Hold the end of the spoon and scoop the food. Use only 1 hand.
3. Obtain bird food from your teacher. You should see that you have marble "seeds," raisin "slugs," macaroni "worms," and Styrofoam "water bugs."
4. Design an investigation to answer this question: "Suppose only 1 food source is available at a time in an environment. Which of the 4 birds living in the environment would be most likely to obtain food and survive?"

   To design the investigation, think about the following things.

   a. How could your experience with the investigation in Part I help you design this investigation?

   b. How many different trials do you need to run?

How many different food sources are you testing?

   c. In a real environment, the 4 birds would be competing for the food source. What does that mean about what the 4 team members will be doing in the investigation?

   d. What would a data table look like for your investigation? Draw one in your science notebook.

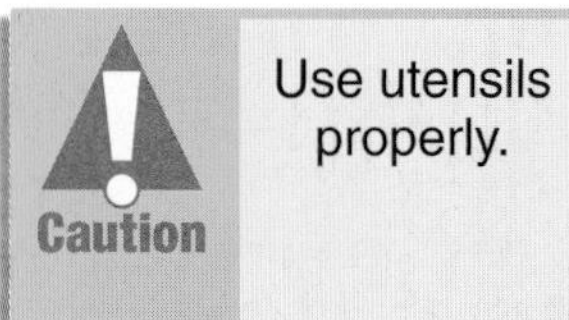
Caution
Use utensils properly.

5. When you have an designed your investigation, check it with your teacher.
6. Conduct your investigation. Record your results in your data table.
7. When you have completed your investigation, return your materials to the storage area.
8. Share your data with the rest of the class as your teacher directs.
9. Compare the results from your team's investigation with other teams' results by discussing the following questions as a class.
   a. Which beak captured the greatest variety of foods?
   b. Which beak was best at capturing an individual food?

Was there a beak that successfully captured only 1 or 2 types of food?

10. In Part I, you simulated 3 generations of a prey population. Now make some predictions about what would happen to the predator population in this simulation after several generations. Answer Questions 10a–c in your science notebook.

    Which bird would have the greatest chance to survive if

    a. there were flooding and only water bugs were left? Why?
    b. there were a drought and only seeds were left? Why?
    c. changes occur so that there is some food but a limited supply of each kind? Why?
11. Read the following paragraph. Then use the TSAR procedure to answer the following questions:
    - How does variation in the predator population affect the foods the organism can eat?
    - How might the variation be an advantage or a disadvantage to the predator?

    Characteristics of a species, such as beak shape, influence what abilities to eat an organism will have. These abilities influence how likely an individual is to survive. A characteristic can change to an advantage or a disadvantage when an organism's environment or its prey changes. Individuals that are better at coping in an environment are more likely to survive and reproduce. When they reproduce, these individuals pass their advantageous characteristics on to their offspring. The result is that, across time, more individuals will have characteristics that help them survive in a particular environment.

Reflect and Connect

Answer the following questions in your science notebook.

1. Think about the concepts of variation and survival as you answer Questions 1a–b in your notebook.
   a. How does variation affect the survival of an individual in a population?
   b. How does the survival of a particular individual affect the makeup of future generations of a population?
2. What might cause a population of organisms within a species to change across time? List at least 3 causes.

Think about variations within a species and between species.

3. The fossil record contains evidence for descent with modification in organisms. What would the fossil record of birds look like in the following scenario?

   Hundreds of thousands of years ago, the 4 birds and 4 food types you investigated in Part II lived in a particular location. Across time, the macaroni worms became the primary food source. This affected the 4 populations of birds.

   Draw a series of rock layers and label the fossils you would find in each.

Think about how the fossils in the rock layers for the years with more macaroni worms would differ from fossils in other layers.

4. Think about simulations and models as you answer Questions 4a–b in your notebook.
   a. In what specific ways do the simulations in Parts I and II model how populations change across time?

For Part I, how is the environment simulated? Through variation? Reproduction? For Part II, how were characteristics modeled?

   b. In what ways do these simulations simplify what actually happens to populations across time? Provide specific examples.

EXPLAIN

Learning about Life: A Great Discovery

In the previous activities, you have been looking at evidence for change across time. Along the way, you have been developing an understanding of biologic **evolution**—a theory that explains how species change across time. So how did the theory of evolution come about? How long has the theory been around? And who first thought of it? Although many scientists and philosophers contributed ideas, we generally attribute the theory of evolution to Charles Darwin (see figure 6.18). In *Learning about Life*, you will work with a partner to learn about Darwin and the evidence that supports his theory of evolution.

Materials

Natural Selection handout (optional)

Process and Procedure

1. In your notebook, predict which animals should be most alike, ones from the same continent or ones from different continents. Share your prediction with your partner.
2. Read *The Voyage* to learn how Darwin's travels answered the question about similarity among animals.
3. Compare your prediction from Step 1 to what you learned from reading, *The Voyage*.
4. Read *Fossils* to understand the role of buried evidence in Darwin's theory.

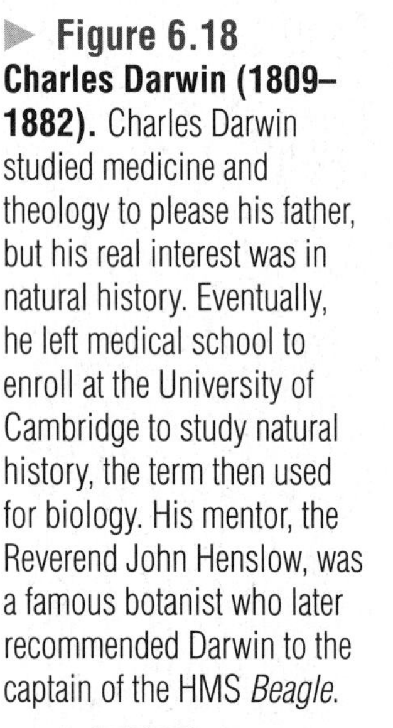

Figure 6.18 Charles Darwin (1809–1882). Charles Darwin studied medicine and theology to please his father, but his real interest was in natural history. Eventually, he left medical school to enroll at the University of Cambridge to study natural history, the term then used for biology. His mentor, the Reverend John Henslow, was a famous botanist who later recommended Darwin to the captain of the HMS *Beagle*.

READING

The Voyage

Darwin changed his focus from medicine to theology in college. He was presented with an opportunity of a lifetime at the age of 22. In 1831, he was invited to go on an incredible journey aboard a ship. He was to explore, observe, and map the voyage. Figure 6.19 shows the path of the voyage. It turned out that on this journey Darwin began his study to explain the great diversity of life. Darwin's observations of nature led him to reject many cherished ideas about the natural world. As a result, he developed a different understanding. His study eventually led to new ideas about geologic and biological change across time and to the theory of evolution.

Darwin's 5-year journey began aboard the ship the *Beagle*. The primary mission of the *Beagle* was to chart sections of the coast of South America. While the ship's crew completed that work, Darwin made remarkable observations. Darwin also collected thousands of specimens and took detailed notes on all that he saw.

Darwin noticed that many plants and animals have **adaptations**. Adaptations are characteristics that help an organism survive and reproduce within a particular environment. Specialized body structures such as protective shells or wings are examples of adaptations. Many organisms use the same type of body structure for different functions. Darwin found

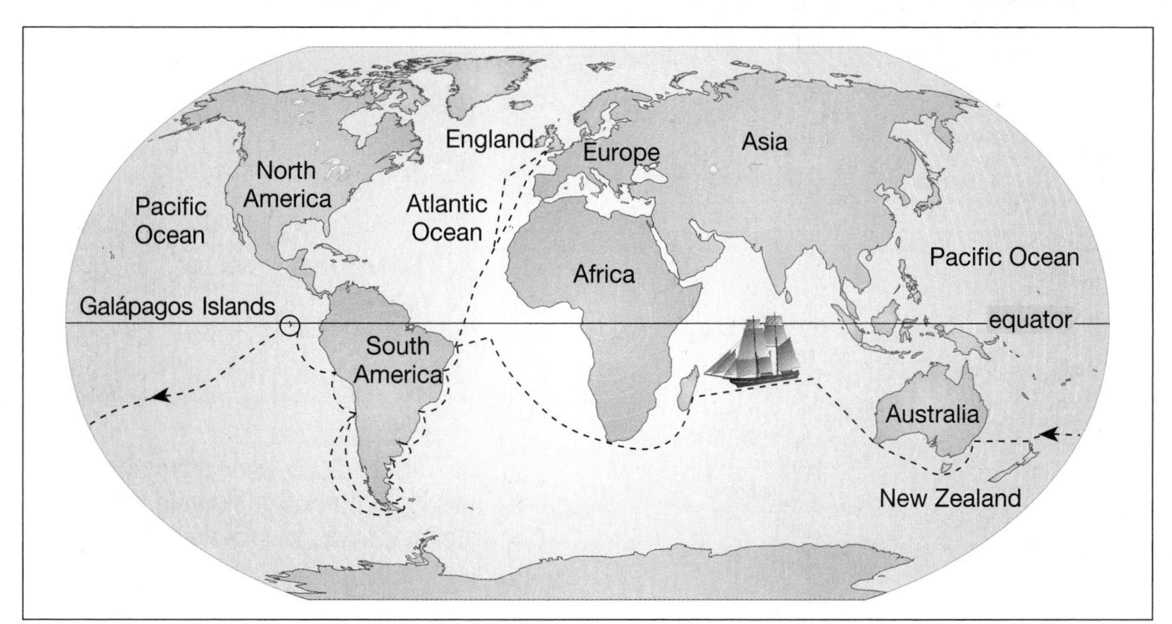

Source: Darwin Museum Down House. Courtesy of the Royal College of Surgeons of England

▲ **Figure 6.19 Voyage of the HMS *Beagle*.** Darwin sailed around the world on the *Beagle*. The route included stops in South America and a stay in the Galápagos Islands. During the trip, Darwin collected evidence that he later used to support the theory of evolution.

three birds in South America that used their wings for purposes other than flight (penguin, steamer duck, and rhea). Each bird wing showed a different adaptation. Study figure 6.20 and think about what adaptation each bird has.

Darwin had many questions about his observations. One of the most important questions had to do with the geographical distribution of the organisms. Although similar to organisms in Europe, the plants and animals that lived in South America and the southeastern Pacific were distinct. That was not surprising. But what perplexed Darwin was the fact that organisms living in temperate (mild) areas of South America were more similar to organisms living in tropical areas of South America than to organisms living in temperate regions of Europe. Orchids, army ants, marine iguanas, and penguins are species well suited to their environment. Yet each seemed to be related to species living in other parts of that huge continent. How could one account for both the similarities and the differences among species? How could one account for their specific patterns of geographical distribution?

Topic: adaptations
Go to: www.scilinks.org
Code: 2Inquiry308

▲ **Figure 6.20 Wing adaptations: (a) South American penguin, (b) steamer duck, and (c) rhea.** For what purpose do you think each bird's wings are adapted?

Stop & THINK

QUESTIONS 1–2

Read each question before writing an answer in your notebook. Then compare your answers to a teammate's. Revise your answers based on what you learn.

1. List 3 adaptations from the human body and explain why they are important.
2. What surprised Darwin about the adaptations of animals on the same continent compared to those on different continents?

READING

Fossils

Darwin did not just make observations of living organisms. He also paid careful attention to the fossils he found. He noticed that younger rock layers contained fossils that looked very similar to species that still existed. He also noticed that older rock layers had fewer fossils but they looked like existing species. Two examples of fossils discovered by Darwin are shown in figure 6.21. Remember that younger rock layers are found closer to the surface. Older rock layers are found in the lower layers farther beneath the surface.

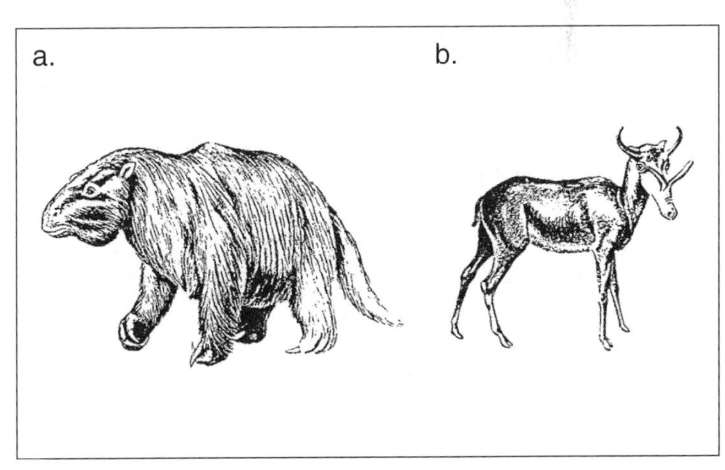

▲ **Figure 6.21 Similar species in the past and present: (a) extinct *Megatherium*, (b) extinct *Syndyoceras*.** Darwin found abundant fossil remains. Many of the remains were similar but not identical to similar existing species. What do these species remind you of? Similar species of both animals live in South America today.

The fossils found in rocks of different ages differ because life on Earth has changed. For example, if we begin at the present layer of rock

Fossils, continued

and examine older and older layers of rock, we eventually will come to a layer where no fossils of humans are present. Farther down through the layers, we will come to layers where no fossils of mammals are present, and so on.

Fossils are not the only piece of evidence for change across time. Scientists have identified six other lines of evidence that support evolution. They are (1) the structural similarities among organisms, (2) the geographical distribution of organisms, (3) the embryological similarities among organisms, (4) the pattern of organism groupings, (5) the molecular similarities among organisms, and (6) the direct observation of evolutionary changes in the laboratory and in the wild.

Stop & THINK

QUESTION 3

3 Use what you have learned so far about Darwin and work with your partner to complete the following tasks. Record your own responses in your science notebook.

a. Give examples of types of evidence that Darwin gathered to develop the theory of evolution. Record at least 3.

b. Compare the types of evidence Darwin gathered with the types of evidence you have learned about in this chapter. Think about these things when you respond:

- Did anything Darwin observed remind you of something you learned about earlier in this chapter?
- Were any of Darwin's observations new information for you?

5. Make a T-table in your notebook with the headings "Fact or Idea from Reading" and "Question I Have."
6. Complete the T-table you drew in Step 5 as you read *Natural Selection*.
7. Exchange T-tables with your partner and attempt to answer each other's questions. You may want to talk to other students or your teacher as well.
8. Read *Evolution* to discover the role of "descent with modification" in evolution.

READING

Natural Selection

On the Galápagos Islands, Darwin took particular notice of the incredible variety of plants and animals. He also noticed how these same plants and animals varied from island to island and from habitat to habitat on the same island. When he arrived back in England, he studied the specimens he had collected much more carefully. He began to think about the variety of species and how this variety came to be. He also thought about how these many organisms could coexist and how they were geographically distributed.

Darwin knew that the characteristics of organisms varied, but he did not know what caused those variations or how these characteristics were passed on to the next generation. It turns out that near the same time, two other scientists were working on these very ideas. You will learn about these two scientists in the next two chapters.

Although he could not explain what caused variation in organisms, Darwin observed that the individuals of any species have a lot of variation in their characteristics. Darwin reasoned that variations in a population might result in some individuals being slightly better adapted to a certain environment than others. Because well-adapted organisms tend to survive, they are more likely to produce more offspring. The adaptations that improved their ability to survive then would be passed to their offspring.

Across time, as this pattern continued, future generations would look more and more like the well-adapted organism. The other organisms that were not as well adapted would die out. We now generally refer to this process as **natural selection**. Natural selection is a mechanism for biological evolution. Evolution only occurs when there is variation within a population and when there are mechanisms that affect variation.

You experienced the process of natural selection in the activities you did in this chapter. In a population of one species, well-camouflaged prey (beans) had a better survival rate and produced more offspring than prey that stood out against the background. Let's think about this. The characteristic of blending in with the environment is an advantage to that individual. This helps to be hidden from a predator. In other words, this characteristic was adaptive. It was "selected for" in nature. Predators were the **selective pressure**. They acted as a selective pressure that influenced which prey survived. Across time, organisms that lacked this adaptive characteristic tended to die out. Organisms that were more easily spotted were more often eaten! In this example, natural selection acted on a color variation within a species.

"Selection" can be a confusing term. Selection occurs in a population when an individual possesses a characteristic that increases its chances of survival.

The finches found on the Galápagos Islands are good examples of similar bird species with different beaks. A few million years ago, one species of finch migrated to the Galápagos Islands from Central or South America. The ancestral finch species was a ground dweller and ate seeds. Evidence collected by scientists supports the idea that 13 species of finch have evolved from this single common ancestor. Across time, each species of finch developed

Natural Selection, continued

distinctive beak sizes and shapes as well as distinctive behaviors that were adaptive to particular environments. The bill of each species of finch is adapted for different purposes such as cracking the shells of seeds, pecking wood, and probing flowers for nectar (figure 6.22).

We saw natural selection acting on variation within a species. Natural selection can also act on variations that exist across species. Variation in beak shape occurs randomly. A variation in beak shape may cause some species of birds to be better adapted to some environments than other species are. Species of birds that are best adapted to an environment survive and produce more offspring than other bird species. Successful individuals within a species will pass along their adaptation to the next generation. In this scenario, natural selection is acting among several species. Competition among species for limited food resources acts as a selective pressure between species.

The fossil record indicates that there has been a consistent change in the plant and animal species in a region from one period in Earth's history to another. New species appear, and other species disappear as they become extinct. Species face changes in their environments across

SCILINKS® NSTA
Topic: natural selection
Go to: www.scilinks.org
Code: 2Inquiry312

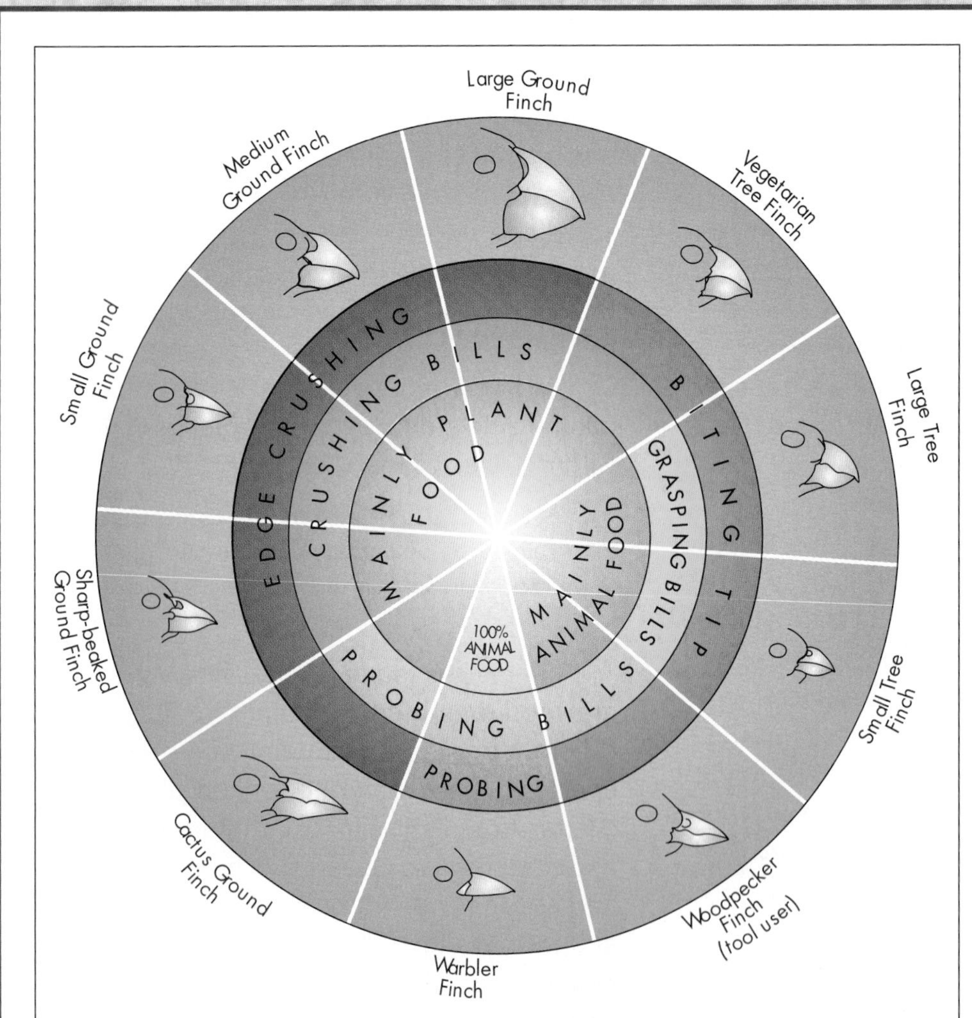

Figure 6.22 Galápagos finches. The Galápagos finches were able to use many different food sources because few species competed with them. The variations in the sizes and shapes of the beaks show how the beak structure of each finch species has adapted to gathering its primary food source.

time. Some species might have adaptations that increase the chances to survive in an environment that has changed. Species that lack those helpful adaptations might become extinct. To learn about some extinct organisms, study figure 6.23.

What determines an organism's ability to survive and reproduce despite various selective pressures? Generally, a mix of characteristics is the answer. It is not only one or two characteristics that help organisms adapt in a particular environment. Organisms, however, do not *acquire* these characteristics to help them survive. These characteristics occur naturally among individuals in a population. This is a result of natural, inherited variation. Selective pressures in the environment act on differences in individuals. These pressures influence which organisms survive to contribute their characteristics to the next generation.

▲ **Figure 6.23 Adaptations.** Not all adaptations help organisms survive if the environment changes. Look at each extinct organism: (a) *Ornitholestes*, (b) dodo bird, (c) Stellar's sea cow, and (d) Tasmanian wolf. Try to decide what adaptation did not help the organism survive.

READING

Evolution

Individual organisms do not evolve. Instead, populations of species evolve. Darwin's theory of evolution by natural selection proposes this idea. Characteristics of a population can sometimes change dramatically because of natural selection. Eventually, scientists recognize the population as a distinct species. This new species is different from the ancestor. Here we return to Darwin's basic idea: descent with modification.

Descent with modification provides a powerful explanation for the similarities we see among closely related forms of life. Descent with modification also explains the similarities we see in all forms of life. Modification, variation, and natural selection provide an explanation for the differences we see among organisms.

Across time, all types of organisms changed and inherited new characteristics from their parents. All species must have descended from a common ancestor. As billions of years passed on Earth, new characteristics appeared in organisms. These characteristics help the organisms survive. Beneficial characteristics pass from generation to generation. Eventually, the differences in this new population are so great that the new population branches off from the ancestral population. Figure 6.24 shows how scientists illustrate the results of evolution as a branching tree or bush.

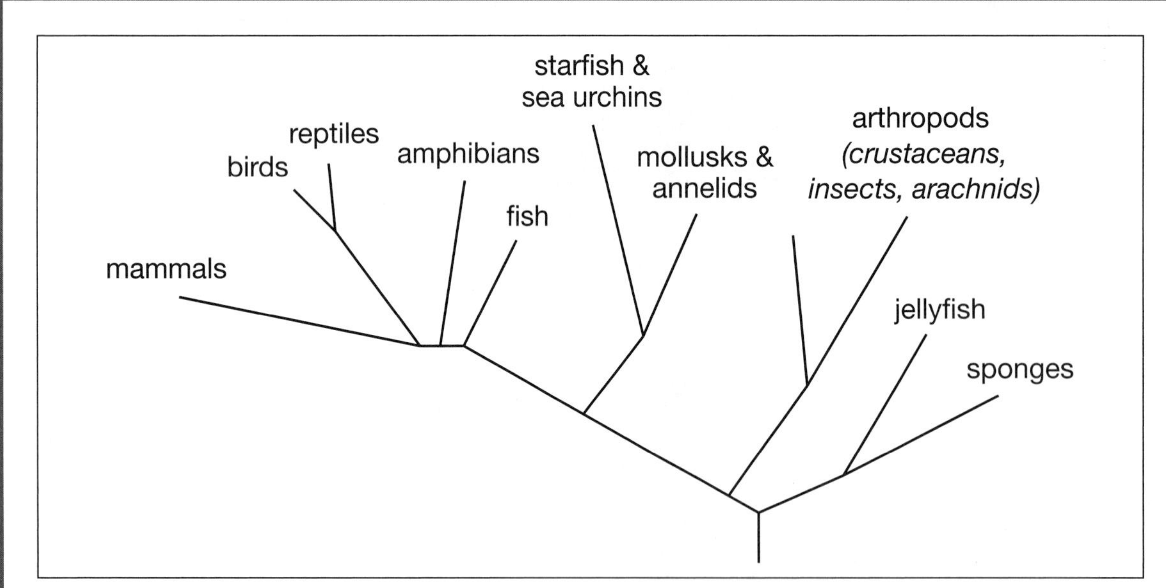

Figure 6.24 Tree of life. Different species diverge from a common lineage much like branches of a tree diverge from the trunk.

Stop & THINK

QUESTION 4

Read each question and task carefully. Record your own responses in your science notebook and then compare your answers to a classmate's.

4 Work with your partner to complete the following tasks.

a. Explain how Parts I and II in the explore activity *Who Will Survive?* simulated the process of natural selection differently. Think about the following:
   - Was the variation within 1 species or across different species?
   - Were the selective pressures different?

b. Explain how an antibiotic acts as a selective pressure on a population of bacteria.

One characteristic of bacteria is their resistance or lack of resistance to an antibiotic.

c. Explain how you think evolution helps to explain the diversity of life on Earth.

You will learn how evolution helps to explain the unity of life on Earth in the next 2 chapters.

9. Read *Summary* before working with your partner to answer each question in *Reflect and Connect*.

READING

Summary

It took Darwin more than 20 years to come up with his theory. Only then was he confident enough to publish it in 1859. In his book *On the Origin of Species*, Darwin presented his theory of biological evolution and descent with modification. Darwin did not use the word "evolution" in the first edition. Instead, he proposed the concept of descent with modification (figure 6.25). This phrase expressed his view that all organisms on Earth are related through descent from some unknown ancestor that lived long ago. This idea helped

Darwin explain the diversity of organisms that he encountered on his travels. The phrase also explained the patterns in geographical distribution that he observed.

Darwin theorized that the process of evolution might have been going on for millions of years. His theory predicted that similar species existing today are related and that they descended from a common ancestor. Darwin's ideas provide an explanation for changes in the number and diversity of organisms that we see in the fossil record. The fossil record provides evidence of the extinction of species as well as evidence of the new species that survived changes in the environment. The fossil record also provides evidence of long periods of time with little change. One fossil record is shown in figure 6.26.

Darwin was not the only naturalist to think about the ideas of evolution through natural selection. A biologist named Alfred Russel Wallace developed the same explanation. In his letter to Darwin, Wallace enclosed a draft of a scientific paper that described a theory of evolution. His theory was less detailed than Darwin's theory, but almost identical in its basic outline.

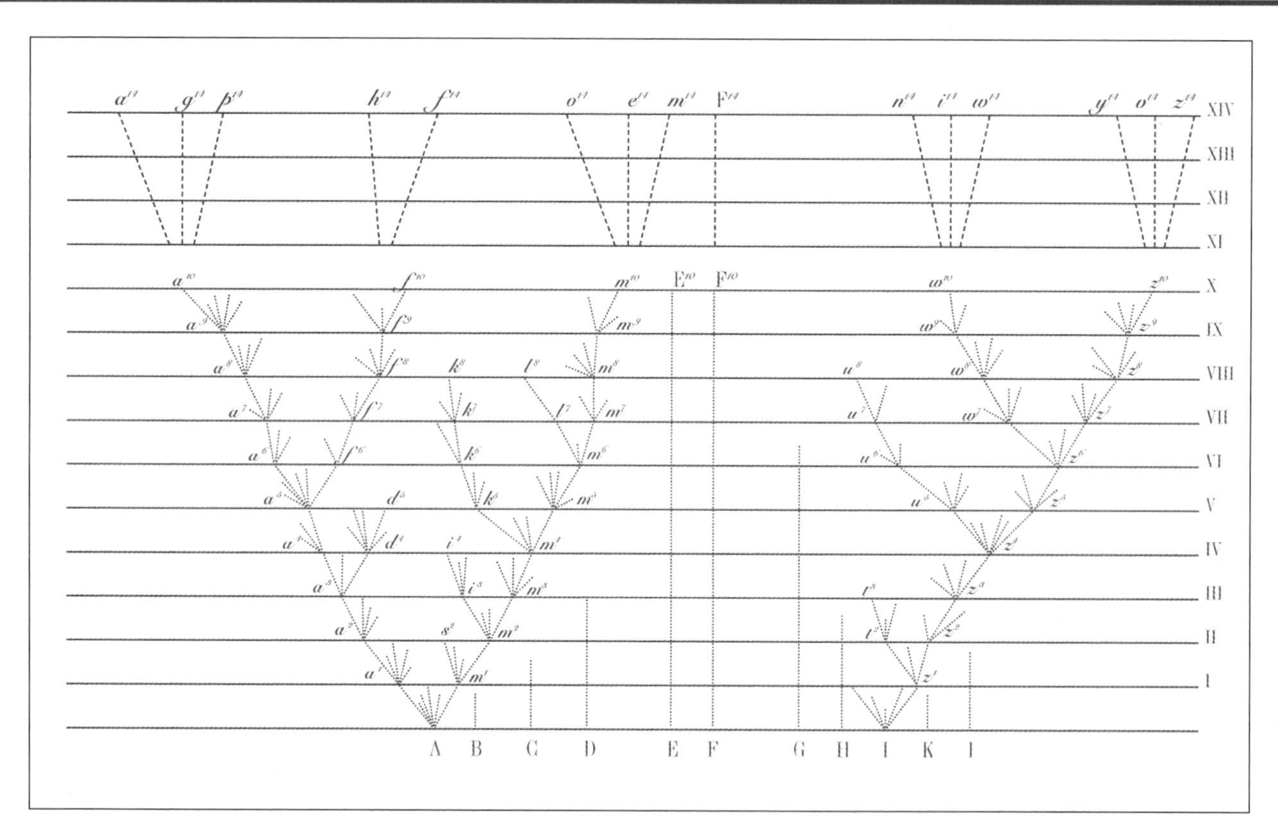

▲ **Figure 6.25 Descent with modification.** Depiction of Darwin's drawing of descent with modification.

Occurrence (in millions of years ago)	Appearance*	Name	Year of Discovery	Description*
55		*Mesonychid*	prior to 1989	• Hyena-like land mammal • 4 long legs • Slender tail
50		*Ambulocetus*	1989	• Land and sea mammal • 4 short legs with feet • No tail fluke but probably swam like an otter
46		*Rodhocetus*	1994	• Whale-like sea mammal • Legs shorter than *Ambulocetus* • May have been able to move awkwardly on land • Strong tail for swimming
40		*Prozeuglodon*	1994	• 15-foot long aquatic mammal • Tiny 6-inch hind legs that could not support weight on land • Tail fluke for swimming

*Based on fossils of skeleton

Source: From C. Zimmer, Back to the Sea, January 1995, *Discover* magazine, pp. 82-84.

SIDEBAR

Unpopular Ideas

Throughout history, people have had many ideas about the natural world. Before the 17th century, people believed that Earth was the center of the universe. This belief was called geocentricism. As more and more evidence supported the idea that the Sun was the center of the solar system (heliocentrism) and Earth was one of many planets that revolved around it, the old idea was rejected. However, the rejection of this idea took time and much scientific evidence.

Each time an idea is expressed, that idea is open to review by the scientific community. Before Darwin published his ideas about natural selection in *On the Origin of Species*, he spent 20 years thinking carefully about his ideas and testing them with new observations and evidence.

Charles Darwin was not the first person to propose a natural explanation for life. More than two dozen naturalists before him developed natural explanations. These explanations had an evolutionary theme. In fact, natural explanations for diversity, unity, and adaptation date back at least 2,600 years. Most of these explanations were based on philosophical reasoning. There was little evidence to support these explanations. In contrast, Darwin had evidence to back up his theory of evolution by natural selection.

Darwin tried to anticipate every possible objection others would have. He used evidence to answer each new objection. This process strengthened his argument. As a result, his ideas withstood scrutiny from the scientific community and the public. This process of skeptical review is an essential part of science.

Skeptical review involves the careful examination of ideas. The examination depends on evidence. It does not depend on emotional judgments or opinions. Skeptical review works to eliminate individual bias and subjectivity. Other people must be able to determine whether an idea is consistent with the evidence. In this way, public scrutiny leads to new observations and the advancement of science.

Many ideas proposed by skillful scientists must be set aside because additional observations and evidence do not support the ideas. Some withstand the test of time and accumulated evidence, increasing our knowledge about the natural world.

Science is a process—growing in some directions, changing in others. Many ideas we consider fundamental to science today were once very unpopular. For example, consider Darwin's idea that all life has a common ancestry. In parlors and tearooms across England in the 1800s, people mocked Darwin for his theory. Biological evolution still disturbs some people today, more than 150 years later.

Darwin was cautious and used the methods of science to slowly and carefully build a body of evidence to support his ideas. The theory of evolution has withstood the test of time and is the foundation upon which modern biology is structured. Today, scientists continue to refine and add to our knowledge about evolution and how it works. Scientists also continue to contribute ideas and support them with evidence.

Darwin was not alone in his time in proposing a new explanation in science.

New ideas that went against the popular view of Earth's history were emerging. Many people believed that Earth had existed unchanged since its relatively recent formation. Darwin was influenced by the work of geologists James Hutton and Sir Charles Lyell. They began to gather evidence to indicate that Earth was changing all the time. These changes occurred over millions of years. They saw that Earth's crust had made vertical movements in England. New sediments had formed in freshwater lakes. They found fossils of sea animals in land formations and in rocks thrusting high above the ocean. They found volcanoes erupting to form mountains, such as Mount Etna in Italy. They believed that these geologic processes, on both small and large scales, had been operating throughout the history of Earth, continuously modifying its form.

To justify their observations, geologists found it necessary to create a vast timescale of Earth's history. By doing this, however, they questioned the social and religious views of the day. For this, they were sometimes accused of heresy.

Today, we accept these views and the scale for Earth's history, a doctrine known as uniformitarianism. The idea is, "the present is the key to the past." Processes we see today have taken place on Earth since its formation. Example processes are the carving of canyons by rivers, the deposition of layers of silt in still water, the eruptions of volcanoes, and the blowing of sand into dunes.

Radiometric dating of rocks has shown the age of Earth to be approximately 4.6 billion years old. This dating validates Hutton and Lyell's idea that Earth is much older than people of their time believed. Like Darwin's work, the work of these scientists laid the foundation for our understanding of an important science. That science is geology, or the study of Earth.

Scientists with new models and new theories do not always agree with one another. Darwin's *On the Origin of Species* drew upon Sir Charles Lyell's book *Principles of Geology*. Lyell did not, however, up to that time, share Darwin's belief in evolution, even though both of these scientists' ideas depended on the view that Earth's history was long and ever changing.

After reading Darwin's book, Lyell began a series of studies. He wrote *The Geological Evidences of the Antiquity of Man*. In this book, and in his *Principles of Geology*, Lyell added powerful arguments of his own from the science of geology. These ideas supported Darwin's theory of evolution by natural selection. Darwin clearly understood the pressure Lyell underwent for refuting the popular views of the day. Darwin said, "Considering his age, his former views, and position in society, I think his action [to support the theory of evolution] has been heroic."

It's not easy to propose new ideas, even when there is a chance that you're right. So what do scientists do when faced with criticism about their ideas? They continue to gather evidence to support their ideas until the sheer amount of evidence convinces even those who are skeptical.

Reflect and Connect

Answer the following questions with your partner. Record your final answers in your notebook.

1. Explain what evolution means. Include the following words in your description: *adaptation*, *population*, *natural selection*, *selective pressure*, *variation*, and *species*.
2. Explain why some species become extinct.
3. Describe how you think the theory of evolution helps explain Earth's history.
4. You may have been surprised that Darwin wasn't the only scientist to come up with the theory of evolution. Describe why you think scientists make similar discoveries or develop similar explanations around the same time.

ELABORATE

Twine Time

Now that you have had an opportunity to share some of your ideas about change on Earth, let's put that change in a context. Let's see when in the history of our Earth these changes might have taken place. Some of the events in Earth's history are shown in figure 6.27. We have reliable evidence from radiometric dating that dates Earth back billions of years. During *Twine Time*, you will learn more about that evidence. To get a better sense of Earth's history, you will develop a timeline dating from Earth's formation, approximately 4.6 billion years ago, to the present day. You will work in teams of four for this activity.

Materials

For each team of 4 students

20 m of twine, marked every meter

1 tape measure

tape (multiple colors)

markers

colored pencil

1 set of biological and abiotic event cards

4 *Events in Evolution* handouts

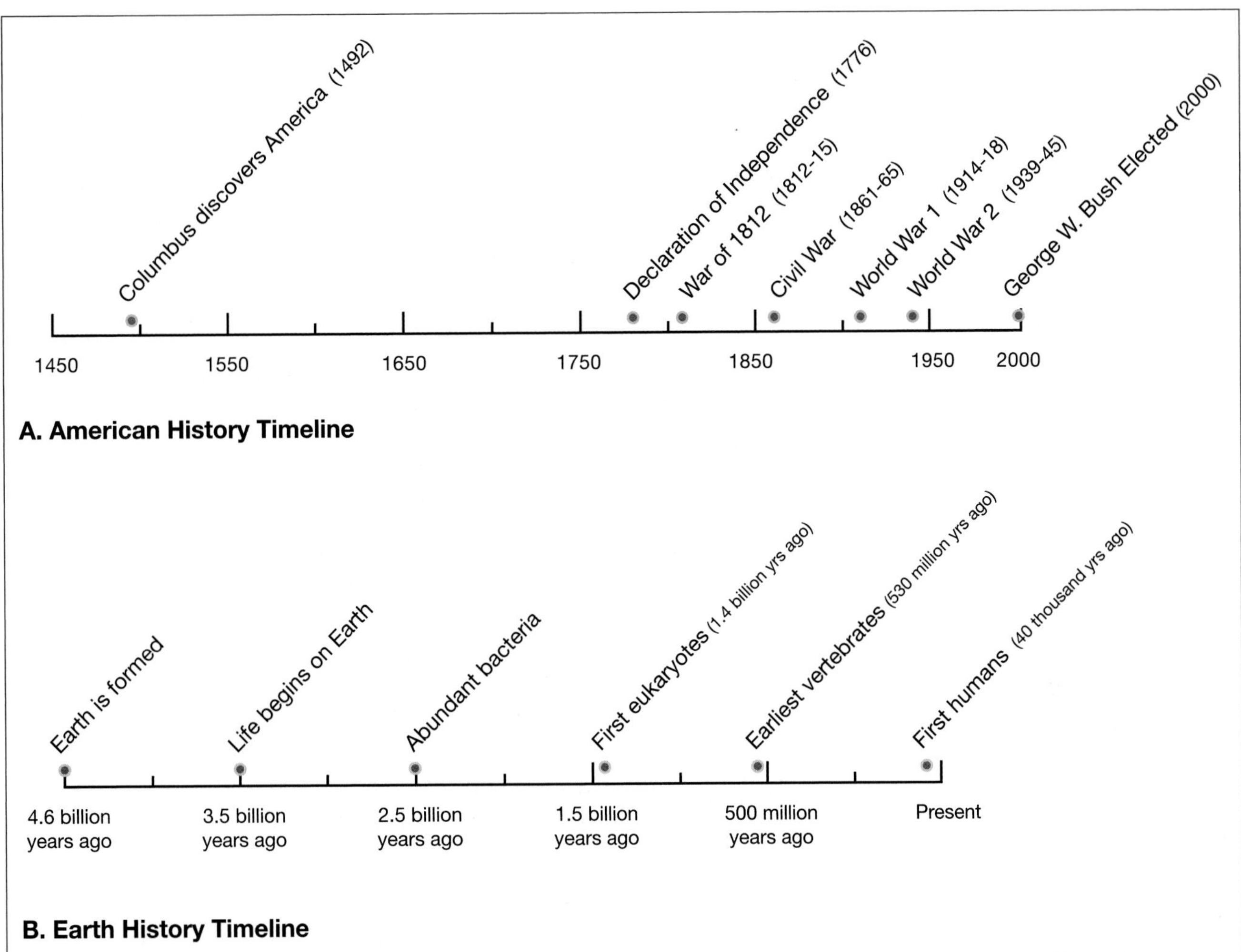

Figure 6.27 Record of events. We have clear records about recent history and present-day events. As we look farther into the past, records are less clear or nonexistent.

Process and Procedure

1. Obtain the biological and abiotic event cards.
2. Sort the event cards into 2 piles: biological events and abiotic events. Use a colored pencil to lightly shade the abiotic event cards.

The term abiotic **describes the physical and chemical (nonliving) aspects of an environment. Here we are talking about Earth's environment.**

3. Place the biological event cards on your desk in the order in which you think they occurred. Think about why you placed each card where you did. Be prepared to contribute your ideas in a class discussion.
4. Repeat Step 3, this time using the abiotic event cards.
5. Compare your order of events with the order proposed by other teams.

a. Listen as each team explains why it placed the cards the way it did.
b. As a class, decide the order of the events for each group, biological and abiotic.
c. Record the order of biological and abiotic events in your science notebook. If you disagree with the placement of an event, make a note of where you would put it and why.

6. Decide which biological event and abiotic event you think occurred closest to the middle point of Earth's history (about 2.3 billion years ago). Record your 2 predictions in your science notebook by circling the events you chose in the lists of biological and abiotic events.

Remember that the events must occur between now and 4.6 billion years ago.

7. As a team, spread out the twine for your timeline and secure it on the floor, the wall, between 2 posts, or on the athletic field. Then do the following tasks.
   a. Label the twine to indicate which end represents the present day and which end represents when Earth formed.
   b. Your twine is 20 m long and represents 5 billion years. Calculate how many years are represented in 1 m. Record your answer in your science notebook.
   c. Calculate how many years are represented in 1 centimeter. Record your answer in your science notebook.
   d. Determine where 1 billion years ago would be found on your timeline. Use colored tape to mark this spot and use a marker to write "1 billion years ago" on the tape.
   e. Repeat Step 7d for 2 billion, 3 billion, and 4 billion years ago.

Your teacher has marked the twine every meter.

8. Study the handout *Events in Evolution* that your teacher gives you. The table shows what scientists have discovered about events in Earth's history. How does the actual order of events compare with the order you recorded in your science notebook?
9. Place the event cards in the correct spot on your timeline. To do this, you will need to do the following.
   a. Divide the event cards among your team members. You will need to do a few calculations to determine where to place them.
   b. Use the values you calculated in Step 7 to help you place each card on the timeline.
   c. Fold your event cards over the twine at the appropriate spot.

10. Examine your timeline and those from other teams to answer Questions 10a–d. Record your answers in your science notebook.
    a. What patterns do you see in the placement of events? Find at least 4 patterns.
    b. What surprised you about the timelines?
    c. How close were your predictions of the halfway point in Earth's history that you made in Step 6? What does this tell you?

Give a specific reason why your prediction was accurate or inaccurate. Then explain what the prediction and the real timeline helped you learn.

    d. How does the amount of time you've been alive compare mathematically with the amount of time Earth has been around? Where would your life fall on the timeline? What do you think about this?

11. Look at the timelines and the geologic clock displayed by your teacher. Discuss as a class what you've discovered about the past 4.6 billion years.

Reflect and Connect

Answer the following questions in your science notebook.

1. Compare your timeline and the clock diagram displayed by your teacher in Step 11. Which did you find more helpful as a representation of Earth's history? Why?
2. Look at the events that represented changes in Earth's surface or atmosphere. Compare the location of these events on the timeline with the events showing the appearance of different plant and animal life. How do you think these events are related?
3. Explain how you think the process of natural selection and evolution might lead to the appearance of new species.

Think about the Galápagos finches discovered by Darwin.

SIDEBAR

Ongoing Research, Ongoing Evolution

Imagine working on one question for more than 30 years. That's exactly what Peter and Rosemary Grant have been doing on several of the Galápagos Islands. What kind of question would require that much work to answer?

Simply put, the Grants' question was, "Does evolution take place in short time frames?" The Grants (and several graduate students) first needed to identify a natural setting that gave them a reasonable chance of collecting data to answer their question. They chose to study a species of finch (small, seed-eating birds) that lives on a small island named Daphne Major, located a few hundred miles west of Ecuador. The finch population remained isolated from outside influence and was small enough for the Grants to identify *every* bird by sight.

The researchers knew they would have to document changes in the finch population over a few years' time. A key measurement was beak depth (depicted above the graph). The Grants determined that shallow-beaked birds cannot open hard seeds, but deep-beaked birds can. During droughts, more hard seeds exist than soft seeds. Thus, deep-beaked birds tend to survive and produce more offspring than do shallow-beaked birds. The result in the next generation of birds is a change in the finch population from shallow-beaked birds to deep-beaked birds.

But the Grants knew one such occurrence of this change was not sufficient to show ongoing evolution. As all researchers do, they needed to reproduce their results. To do so, they continued measuring beak-depth changes in medium ground finches over several cycles of wet and dry years. The results are shown in the graph.

You can see the same thing the Grants saw. During dry years, the population of the medium ground finch changed. More deep-beaked birds survived and reproduced because they could use the hard seeds better than the shallow-beaked birds. This difference in survival rate influenced the distribution of finches, favoring deep-beaked

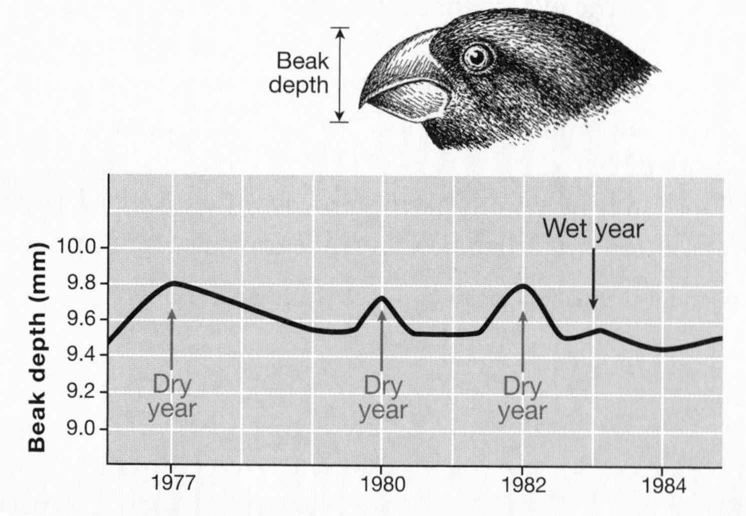

Changes in beak depth over time. The graph shows evolutionary changes in beak depth in medium ground finches on the Galápagos island of Daphne Major under different environmental conditions. How much did average beak depth change between dry years and wet years in the 1970s and 1980s?

birds. Thus, the population of deep-beaked birds spiked during dry years.

What would happen to the medium ground finch if dry years continued for thousands of generations? What would happen if many wet years occurred in a row? With no other influences, the population of medium ground finches would show deeper beaks as a result of many dry years. Similarly, many wet years in succession would produce more shallow-beaked birds. In short, the species would evolve in response to changes in the environment.

The Grants' work has shown evidence for ongoing evolution. In conjunction with the fossil record and other lines of evidence, evolution explains the changes we see in species across millions of years *and* in our lifetime.

EVALUATE

Ancient Elephants

Throughout this chapter, you have been learning about change across time. You began by learning about how rock layers, fossils, and radiometric dating are evidence of change across time. Then you learned that Charles Darwin developed an explanation for change across time in life-forms on Earth. You also learned about natural selection, which is the mechanism of evolution or a means through which evolution occurs. In *Ancient Elephants*, you will work individually to demonstrate your understanding of evolution by using your growing knowledge of rock layers, fossils, and change across time to piece together a story about the evolution of elephants.

Materials

For each student

1 *Proboscidean and Rock Layers* handout

1 *Proboscidean Pictures* handout

1 *Ancient Elephants Scoring Rubric* handout

Process and Procedure

1. Imagine that you are part of a research team studying the evolution of elephants. Read the following paragraph to learn about your work.

   Elephants and their closest relatives are called proboscideans. Scientists named them this because of their long trunk, which is also called a proboscis. In your search to learn more about proboscideans, you have obtained a picture of a column of rock layers. Some of the rocks consist of an ash layer that scientists have been able to date. Some of the rock layers also contain fossils of proboscideans. Based on the fossilized skeletons, artists have illustrated what the proboscideans and their environment might have looked liked. Your research team must use what you know to piece together what might have happened to proboscideans across time.

2. Look carefully at the rock column and the proboscideans pictured in the handout *Proboscidean and Rock Layers* and in the *Proboscidean Pictures* handout.
3. You learned a lot about the study of rock layers and change across time in this chapter. Using what you have learned, you can make some inferences about the proboscideans from the rock column and the pictures of the environments. To demonstrate your understanding of the concepts in this chapter, answer Questions 3a–c. When you respond to each question, explain how you arrived at your answer.
   a. When did the different proboscidean species live relative to one another? Which species lived most recently and which species lived farther in the past?
   b. Determine the time period in which each of the proboscideans might have lived.

Look at the rock layers where their fossils first appear and last appear.

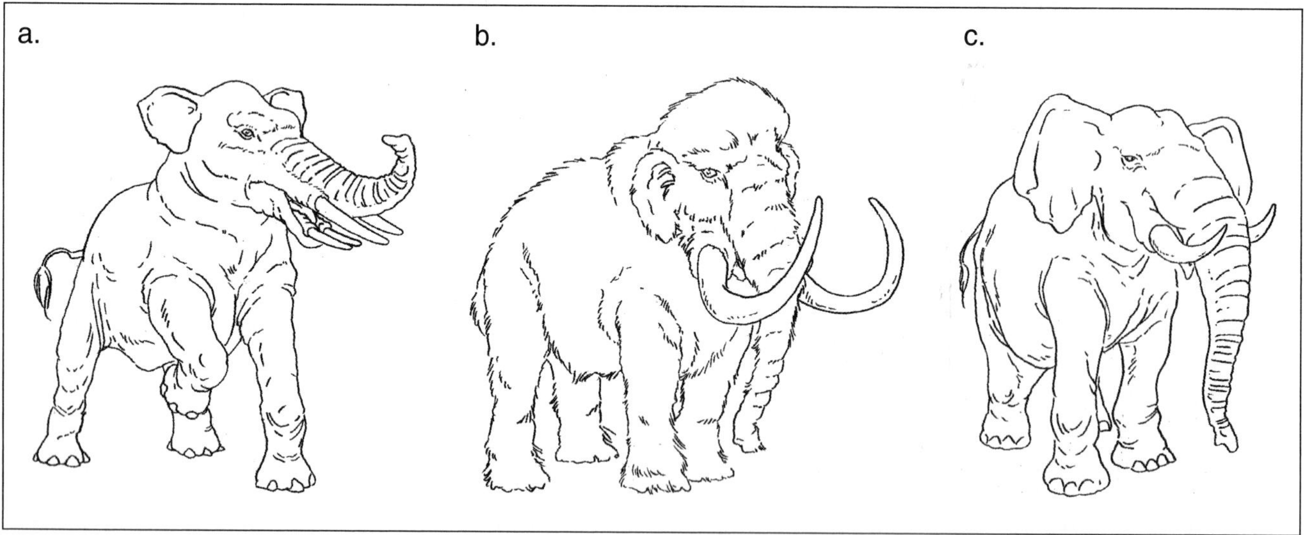

Figure 6.28 Three types of proboscideans (a) Gomphothere, (b) wooly Mammoth, (c) African elephant

c. Consider a proboscidean that is descended from gomphotheres and is a common ancestor of African elephants and mammoths. In which rock layers would you look for a fossil of this proboscidean? Respond using a clearly labeled drawing or a written description. Briefly explain your answer.

4. Scientists piece together evidence from locations around the world to learn more about proboscideans. In this way, they know more than they can learn from only 1 set of rock layers. To learn what else scientists know about proboscideans, read the following paragraph about mammoths. Then answer Questions 4a–c.

Mammoths migrated out of Africa about 2 million years ago. Several species of mammoth evolved from the ancestral African mammoth. One of these species was the woolly mammoth, which lived from about 350,000 to 10,000 years ago. Scientists have collected the oldest woolly mammoth fossils from Siberia and western Europe. More recent fossils of woolly mammoths have been collected in North America as well as in Asia and Europe. Younger fossils are more abundant near the Arctic Circle. Because scientists have found frozen carcasses of woolly mammoths in Siberia and Alaska, they know the mammoths were covered with a thick coat of hair. Mammoths are extinct in all parts of the world today.

a. Describe a selective pressure that might have caused the woolly mammoth to evolve from the ancestral mammoth. Explain how this selective pressure could lead to the evolution of a woolly mammoth.

b. Explain what has caused some species of proboscideans to become extinct. You might not know the exact reasons, but you can use what you have learned in this chapter to develop a general explanation.

c. Describe how the process of natural selection leads to a diversity of species. Use the evolution of gomphotheres into the African elephant and the ancestral mammoth as an example. Include the following words in your explanation: *adaptation*, *population*, *natural selection*, *selective pressure*, *variation*, and *species*.

5. The rock column pictured on the *Proboscidean and Rock Layers* handout is particularly useful because scientists could date some of the rock layers. How do scientists determine the age of rocks? Think about the following when constructing your answer:
   - Why are some rocks used more often than others?
   - What do scientists measure during this process?
   - Why is knowing the half-life important?
6. It is difficult to watch evolution happen across millions of years, yet scientists are certain of the theory of evolution. That is because they have a lot of evidence of change across time and descent from common ancestors. Give at least 2 examples of evidence for change across time and explain why each supports the theory of evolution.
7. Read the following statement. Use what you have learned about natural selection and evolution to explain why you think the statement is an accurate or inaccurate description of how species change across time.

   "Giraffes developed their long necks and legs because of generation after generation of giraffes stretching to eat leaves high in the trees."

CHAPTER 7

Tracking Traits

Tracking Traits

Throughout the last chapter, *Exploring Change*, you learned that living systems have changed across time. Organisms share many characteristics, but some species have different characteristics from their ancestors. For example, extinct organisms, such as the elephant-like *Gomphotherium*, share characteristics such as large size and tusks with African elephants that exist today. However, *Gomphotherium* had tusks in the upper and lower jaw, but modern African elephants only have tusks in the upper jaw.

In the activity *Ancient Elephants*, you thought about how natural selection could lead to the appearance of new species of elephants, such as woolly mammoths. But how are characteristics such as large size and tusks passed from one generation to another? What characteristics do you think have been passed down to the elephant's offspring pictured in the opening art? In chapter 7, *Tracking Traits*, you will learn about this process, which is called **inheritance**. Inherited characteristics are called **traits**. Some examples of visible traits include eye color, hair color, and the presence or absence of dimples. Other traits are not visible, such as blood type. What is inheritance and what are the mechanisms that are responsible for it?

Goals for the Chapter

You will explore the concept of inheritance and see how this concept contributes to your understanding of change in living systems. By the end of this chapter, you will be able to answer the following questions:

- How are traits passed from one generation to another generation?
- Why do members of the same family have different traits?
- Why are some traits hidden in one generation and expressed in the next generation?
- What can we learn from our understanding of inheritance patterns?

You will be better able to answer these questions by participating in the following activities:

ENGAGE	It Runs in the Family
EXPLORE	What Shows Up?
EXPLAIN	How Do We Get Our Traits?
EXPLAIN	All about Alleles
ELABORATE	Inheritance Patterns
EVALUATE	Passing Genes—Who Gets What?

The chapter organizer is your guide for learning about inheritance. Use it to review what you have learned and to see what new things you will be learning.

Tracking Traits

Engage

It Runs in the Family

Key Idea:
Family members tend to share some of the same traits.

Linking Question

How can I investigate if traits are inherited?

Explore

What Shows Up?

Key Idea:
Some offspring have the same traits as the parents, but other offspring have different traits from the parents.

Linking Question

How are traits inherited, and how is meiosis part of the process of inheritance?

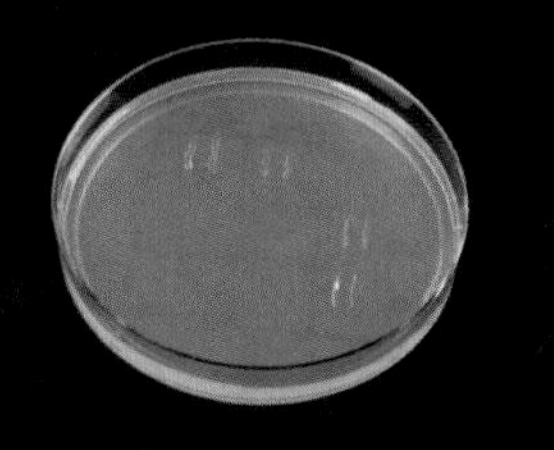

Explain

How Do We Get Our Traits?

Key Ideas:
- Genes determine the traits exhibited by an organism.
- Genes for the same trait can exist in different forms called alleles.
- The transfer of genetic information occurs through gametes.
- Meiosis produces gametes that have half the genetic material of other body cells.

Linking Question

How can we make predictions about what traits offspring will inherit?

Evaluate

Passing Genes—Who Gets What?

Key Ideas:

- Each parent contributes one-half of the genetic makeup of the offspring.
- Meiosis facilitates the transfer of genetic information from one generation to the next through gametes.
- Differences in the traits between generations result from individuals having different alleles of the same gene.
- Traits are inherited through different inheritance patterns.

Linking Question

How can I use what I have learned to demonstrate my understanding of how traits are inherited and the process of meiosis?

CHAPTER 7 Major Concepts

- **Traits are transmitted from parent to offspring through gametes.**
- **Meiosis results in the formation of gametes that contain half the genetic information of other cells.**
- **Cells contain two copies of each chromosome and therefore two copies of each gene.**
- **Variations in the traits of different generations are explained by the fact that each individual gets two copies of each gene.**

Elaborate

Inheritance Patterns

Key Ideas:

- Tools such as pedigrees help make predictions about the traits of offspring.
- Traits can be autosomal dominant, autosomal recessive, or sex linked.

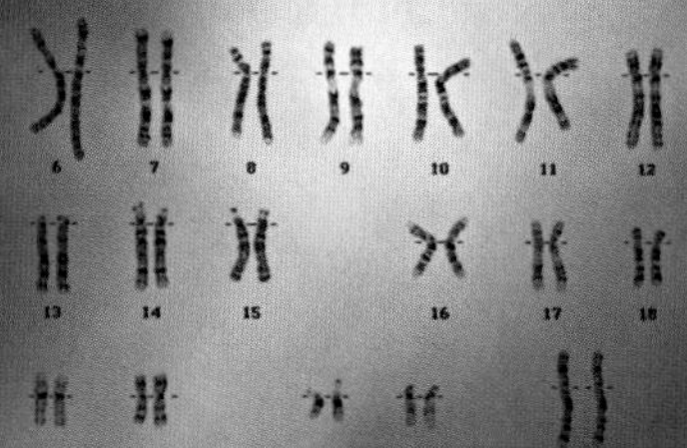

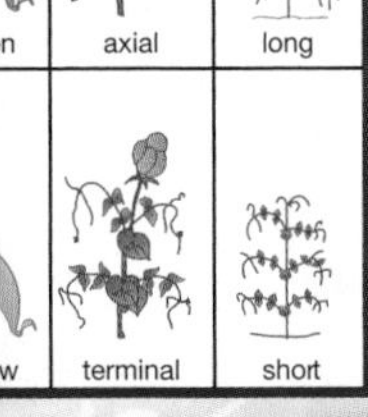

Explain

All about Alleles

Key Ideas:

- Tools such as Punnett squares help make predictions about the traits of offspring.
- Gametes have one representative from each chromosome pair, allowing offspring to receive different combinations of alleles from their parents.

Linking Question

Are there patterns in how traits are inherited?

ENGAGE

It Runs in the Family

Members of the same family share many traits. Children with tall parents often grow to be tall adults. Grandchildren sometimes look astonishingly like the photographs of their grandparents at a similar age. A mother beams proudly when people mistakenly think she and her daughter are sisters.

Some traits that run in families affect more than how you look (figure 7.1). The biological process that makes offspring look like their parents can also transfer genetic disorders from one generation to the next. How does this all happen? In *It Runs in the Family*, you will begin to think about how traits are inherited. You will explore how our knowledge of inheritance has led to the understanding of genetic disorders.

Materials

none

Process and Procedure

1. Read the "Dear Counselor" letter in figure 7.2 with your class. You will learn some of the questions a teenager has for a genetic counselor when he learns his father has a disorder.
2. Consider the questions and thoughts "Afraid and Wanting to Know More" has about how inheritance works. What are your ideas about inheritance?
   a. Generate 2 statements about inheritance.
   b. Share your statements with the class. Your teacher will record your statements.
   c. Record the class list of statements in your science notebook.
   d. Make a note of whether you think each statement is true or false.
   e. Participate in a class discussion about inheritance.

You might think your statements are true, but you might disagree with some of the other statements. You will have an opportunity to look back at the list later in the chapter when you have learned more about inheritance.

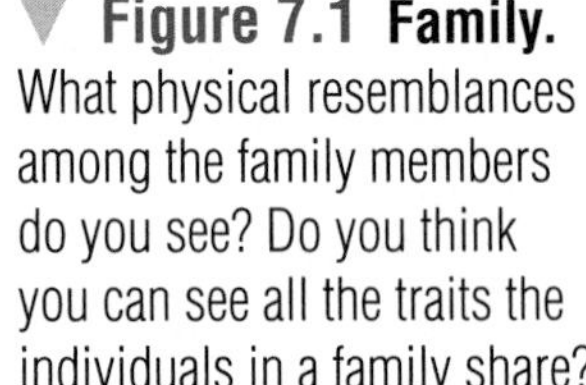

Figure 7.1 Family. What physical resemblances among the family members do you see? Do you think you can see all the traits the individuals in a family share?

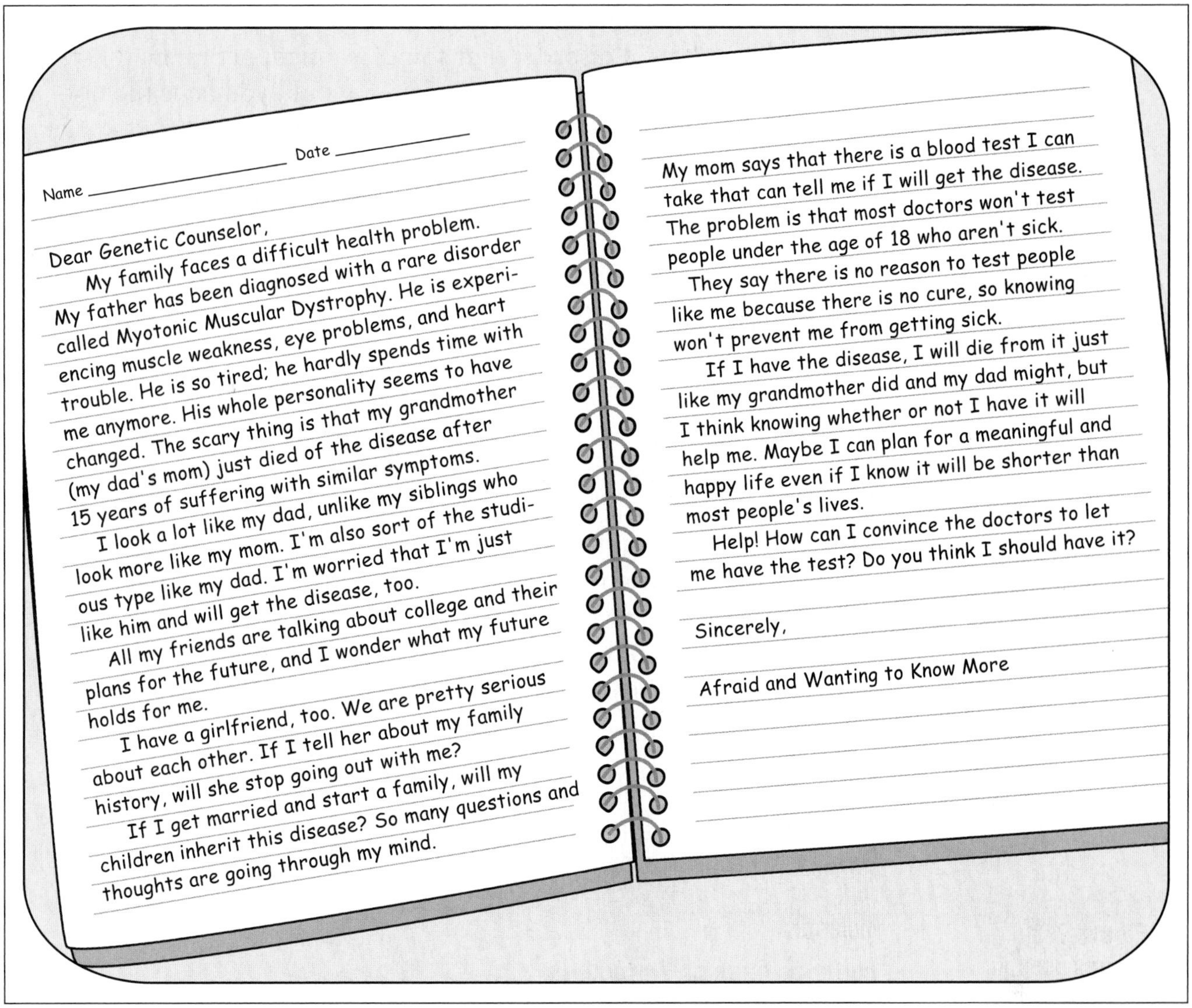

Name

Date

Dear Genetic Counselor,

My family faces a difficult health problem. My father has been diagnosed with a rare disorder called Myotonic Muscular Dystrophy. He is experiencing muscle weakness, eye problems, and heart trouble. He is so tired; he hardly spends time with me anymore. His whole personality seems to have changed. The scary thing is that my grandmother (my dad's mom) just died of the disease after 15 years of suffering with similar symptoms.

I look a lot like my dad, unlike my siblings who look more like my mom. I'm also sort of the studious type like my dad. I'm worried that I'm just like him and will get the disease, too.

All my friends are talking about college and their plans for the future, and I wonder what my future holds for me.

I have a girlfriend, too. We are pretty serious about each other. If I tell her about my family history, will she stop going out with me?

If I get married and start a family, will my children inherit this disease? So many questions and thoughts are going through my mind.

My mom says that there is a blood test I can take that can tell me if I will get the disease. The problem is that most doctors won't test people under the age of 18 who aren't sick.

They say there is no reason to test people like me because there is no cure, so knowing won't prevent me from getting sick.

If I have the disease, I will die from it just like my grandmother did and my dad might, but I think knowing whether or not I have it will help me. Maybe I can plan for a meaningful and happy life even if I know it will be shorter than most people's lives.

Help! How can I convince the doctors to let me have the test? Do you think I should have it?

Sincerely,

Afraid and Wanting to Know More

▲ **Figure 7.2 "Dear Counselor" letter.** What questions would you have for a genetic counselor if someone in your family had a genetic disorder?

Reflect and Connect

Answer the following questions individually and then discuss your answers as a class. This is an opportunity to share your ideas and current understanding with your classmates. It is likely that you will also generate more questions.

1. Why does "Afraid and Wanting to Know More" think he could have myotonic muscular dystrophy (MMD)?
2. Suggest some characteristics that people acquire during their lifetimes. What is the difference between acquired characteristics and traits that are inherited? Make a list of acquired characteristics and a list of inherited traits.

3. What do you think doctors can observe in the blood that tells them about a disorder that someone might get in the future?
4. If you were the writer of the letter, would you have the test performed? Why or why not?
5. In your opinion, should people under the age of 18 be allowed to be tested for a genetic disorder? Give reasons for your thoughts.

EXPLORE

What Shows Up?

In *It Runs in the Family*, you discussed some of your ideas about inheritance. How do we know that traits are inherited? Scientists have conducted experiments on a wide variety of organisms to learn more about heredity. They choose organisms that are easy to handle, have short life cycles, produce large numbers of offspring, and, most important, have variation among the individuals in the population. Figure 7.3 shows some examples of organisms that have contributed to our understanding of heredity.

In *What Shows Up?*, you will work with a partner to conduct an investigation of your own on one of these organisms: yeast. By making observations of yeast, you will begin thinking about how traits are passed on.

Part I: The First Generation

Materials

For each team of 2 students

2 pairs of safety goggles

access to biohazard bags or buckets with 10% bleach solution

Figure 7.3 Organisms used in genetics experiments. Scientists have used (a) yeast, (b) fruit flies, (c) rats, and (d) corn in genetics experiments for many years.

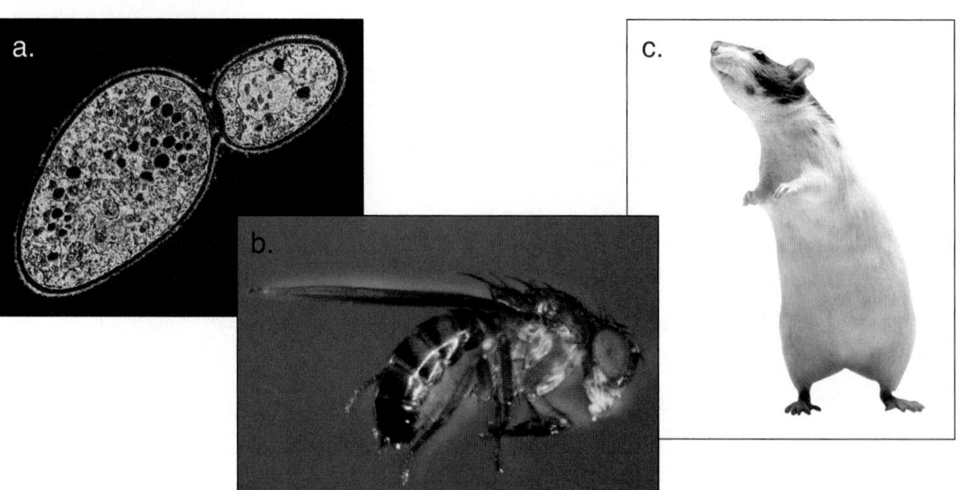

1 microscope slide

1 coverslip

1 dropper

1 pair of forceps

1 yeast nutrient agar plate (YED)

microscope

10% bleach solution

access to incubator set at 30°C

access to 2 subcultures of strain 2 (red-colored) yeast colonies (a2 and alpha2)

access to 2 subcultures of strain 3 (cream-colored) yeast colonies (a3 and alpha3)

access to sterile toothpicks or sterile inoculating loops

1 small cup of water

1 glass marking pencil or marker

Cautions

The yeast used in this investigation are nonpathogenic laboratory strains. "Nonpathogenic" means the yeast cannot cause disease. However, it is always good practice to disinfect all materials that come in contact with live organisms. Make sure your lab area is clean. Wipe the top surface of your lab area with a 10% bleach solution before and after the investigation. Wear goggles while working with the agar plates and yeast. Pull your hair or loose clothing back if necessary. Wash your hands thoroughly before leaving the laboratory. Dispose of all materials as directed by your teacher.

Process and Procedure

1. Observe the yeast subcultures provided by your teacher. What do you think yeast cells will look like through a microscope? Record your ideas in your science notebook.
2. Get a closer look at yeast cells using a microscope by completing Steps 2a–g.
   a. Obtain a clean microscope slide.
   b. Add a drop of water to the slide.
   c. Put on your safety goggles. Touch a sterile toothpick to a colony of yeast from one of the subcultures provided by your teacher.

Safety Goggles

d. Touch the end of the toothpick containing yeast to the water on the slide. Stir gently. Dispose of the toothpick according to your teacher's instructions.
e. Place a coverslip over the drop of water.
f. Observe the slide using the high-power objective of the microscope. Look for small, circular yeast cells.
g. (optional) Make a second slide from a yeast colony of the other color using a fresh toothpick and compare the 2 slides.

3. Make a detailed sketch of a few yeast cells in your science notebook.
4. Work with a partner to discuss how you can investigate inheritance using yeast by completing Steps 4a–d. You may not know exactly what inheritance is, but be patient. This activity will help you begin to understand how inheritance occurs. Record your ideas in your science notebook.
   a. Read *Yeast* to learn about the organism and how it reproduces.
   b. Describe how yeast reproduce using a labeled drawing.
   c. What visible trait do baker's yeast exhibit?
   d. Discuss with your partner how you might investigate what traits yeast pass to the next generation through reproduction.

READING

Yeast

Yeast are a type of fungus. Other common fungi include mushrooms, truffles, and molds. Yeast are single-celled microorganisms that are known for their ability to ferment (break down) carbohydrates (see figure 7.4). Yeast are found in a wide variety of natural habitats such as plant leaves, soil, and on the skin surface and in the intestinal tracts of warm-blooded animals. Yeast are also cultivated for commercial use. They are used in the baking industry to expand and raise dough and are used to ferment the sugars of grains to produce alcoholic beverages. In this activity, you will work with the yeast *Saccharomyces cerevisiae*, commonly called baker's or brewer's yeast.

Figure 7.4 Baker's yeast. When yeast ferment the sugars in flour, they are converting the sugar into carbon dioxide and ethanol. Yeast are not the only microorganisms found in food products. The next time you are in the store, look at the ingredient list on a container of yogurt. The active cultures are bacteria.

After your experience in chapter 1, *Investigations by Design*, you might be more familiar with a different kind of single-celled organism, bacteria. Bacteria are very different from yeast; they are prokaryotes (organisms without a cell nucleus). Yeast are eukaryotes (organisms with a cell nucleus). Plants, animals, and fungi are all eukaryotes. Many eukaryotic microorganisms, such as yeast, do not have two "sexes" (male and female). Instead, certain types of yeast occur in two mating types: mating type *a* and mating type *alpha*. The mating types are morphologically the same. That is, the mating types look identical. But mating only occurs between yeast cells of the opposite mating type. When cells of opposite mating types (a and alpha) come in contact, they secrete hormonelike substances called **pheromones**. These pheromones cause cells of the opposite mating type to develop into new yeast cells. You can **cross**, or mate, yeast strains of opposite mating types and let them grow to see what the resulting generation looks like. A cross is a deliberate mating to study how traits are passed from parents to offspring.

Yeast can also reproduce asexually by budding and may grow into a visible colony that contains up to 100 million cells. Budding is the development of a new cell from the outgrowth of a parent cell. Buds look like bubbles growing on the side of the yeast cell. The buds separate from the parent yeast cell, forming new yeast cells.

There are many strains of baker's yeast. **Strains** of yeast are the same species but are physiologically distinct, meaning they function differently from one another. The strain of yeast used for baking bread is different from the strains of yeast used in scientific experiments. You will be using two strains of yeast in this activity. They will be identified as strain 2 and strain 3. Strain 2 exhibits a red color trait. Strain 3 exhibits a cream color trait. Now that you know more about yeast, remember to complete the tasks in Step 4.

5. Work with your partner and use the protocol to investigate what color traits are passed on from different strains of yeast. Steps 5a–d will serve as a guide.
   a. Read *Yeast Monohybrid Cross Protocol* to learn a technique for studying the traits passed from one generation of yeast to the next.

A monohybrid cross **is a mating of individuals to study 1 trait.**

   b. Discuss what yeast strains you should cross to study the color trait in baker's yeast.
   c. Draw a mating grid in your science notebook showing which strains and mating types you will cross.

The mating grid should look like the mating grid you would draw on a petri dish to cross yeast.

   d. Have your teacher approve your mating grid.
6. Follow Part I of *Yeast Monohybrid Cross Protocol* to grow parent colonies. Use your mating grid to guide your work.

Protocol

Yeast Monohybrid Cross Protocol

Part I: Growing Parent Colonies

Wipe the top surface of your lab area with a 10% bleach solution.

1. Obtain a yeast nutrient agar plate.
2. Label the *bottom* of an agar plate along the edge (so that you can observe growth later) with the date, your name, and your partner's name.
3. Draw a grid on the *bottom* of the agar plate and label it with the strains and mating type you will use. (See the mating grid figure.) The "boxes" in your grid should be large enough to allow space to streak the agar with yeast, as shown in the mating grid figure.

This grid will help you keep track of the yeast strains you will cross in Part II.

4. Make streaks of 4 strains of yeast in the appropriate part of the grid by completing Steps 4a–d.
   a. Put on your safety goggles.
   b. Find a single yeast colony on a subculture of yeast strain.

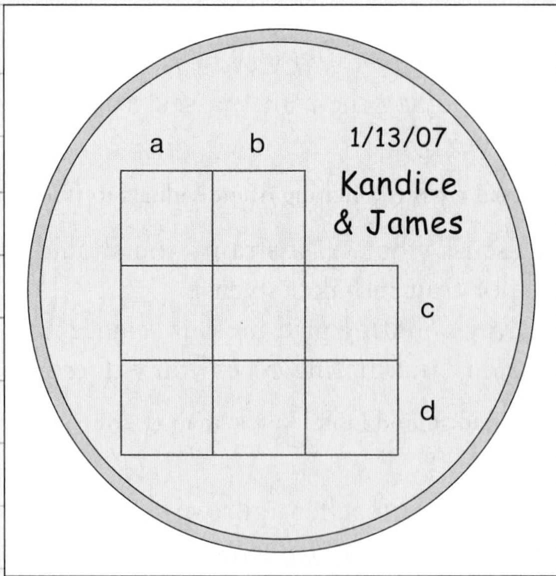

Mating grid. Each side of the grid should be labeled with the mating type and the strains being used. For example, one side might be labeled "alpha2" and "alpha3" and the other side "a2" and "a3."

Look for areas of growth that are isolated and have a circular shape. When you compare the growth of the red-colored strains with the cream-colored strains, you might notice that the red-colored strains have less growth (the colonies are smaller). Don't worry about the size of the colony you pick. You will pick up hundreds of yeast cells by touching even the smallest colony.

c. Touch a sterile toothpick to the single yeast colony you have chosen. Using the end of the toothpick with yeast, make a short streak on the agar in the part of the grid that matches the yeast strain and mating type you have. Be careful not to tear the agar.

d. Discard the toothpick in the disposal area provided by your teacher.

Try to keep everything as sterile as possible. Do not touch the end of the toothpick that you are going to use to streak the yeast. Use a different toothpick for each strain of yeast.

e. Select another single yeast colony from the same subculture.

f. Repeat Steps 4c–d, placing a second streak next to the first. This will give you 2 parent colonies of the same strain of yeast from which to choose in Part II.

5. Repeat Steps 4b–f with the 3 remaining yeast strains. Make sure you streak each strain in the correct part of the mating grid. Your plate should look like the one in the figure.

6. Place the lid back on the plate. Seal the plate with parafilm or tape according to your teacher's instructions. Place your plate upside down in an incubator set at 30° Celsius (C). Allow the parent colonies of yeast to grow at least 1 day. You need enough growth so that you can cross the parent colonies in Part II.

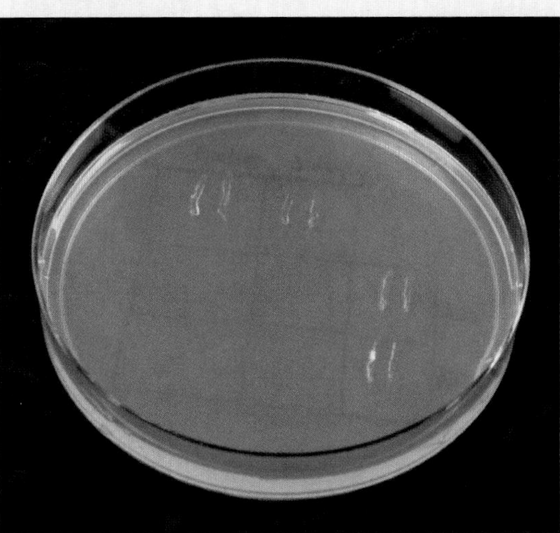

Streaked plate. Your plate should have two streaks for each yeast strain and mating type.

Agar plates should be stored upside down with the lid on the bottom. This prevents condensation from forming on the agar. If you don't have an incubator, store your agar plate in the area provided by your teacher.

7. Wipe the top surface of your lab area with 10% bleach solution after storing your agar plate.
8. Wash your hands after storing your agar plate.

Part II: Crossing Parent Colonies

1. Wipe the top surface of your lab area with 10% bleach solution.
2. Put on your safety goggles.
3. Use the yeast crosses diagram as a guide to cross yeast in Steps 3a–d.

Safety Goggles

   a. Touch a sterile toothpick to one of the (a) streaks, as shown in the diagram of yeast crosses. Then touch the toothpick to the agar in the box directly below it.

Remember to be careful not to tear the agar.

   b. Discard the toothpick in the disposal area provided by your teacher.
   c. Touch a sterile toothpick to one of the (c) streaks. Then touch it to the agar close to the spot you just made in Step 2a. Discard the toothpick.
   d. Obtain a sterile toothpick and mix the 2 spots of yeast together as shown in the mating yeast figure. Discard the toothpick.

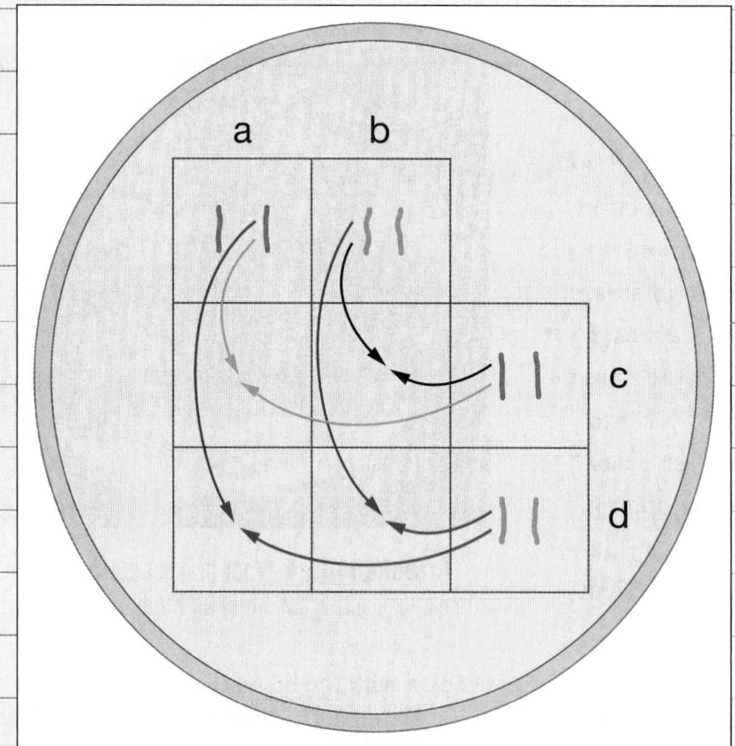

Yeast crosses. Your plate should have four possible crosses: streak (a) with (c), (a) with (d), (b) with (c), and (b) with (d).

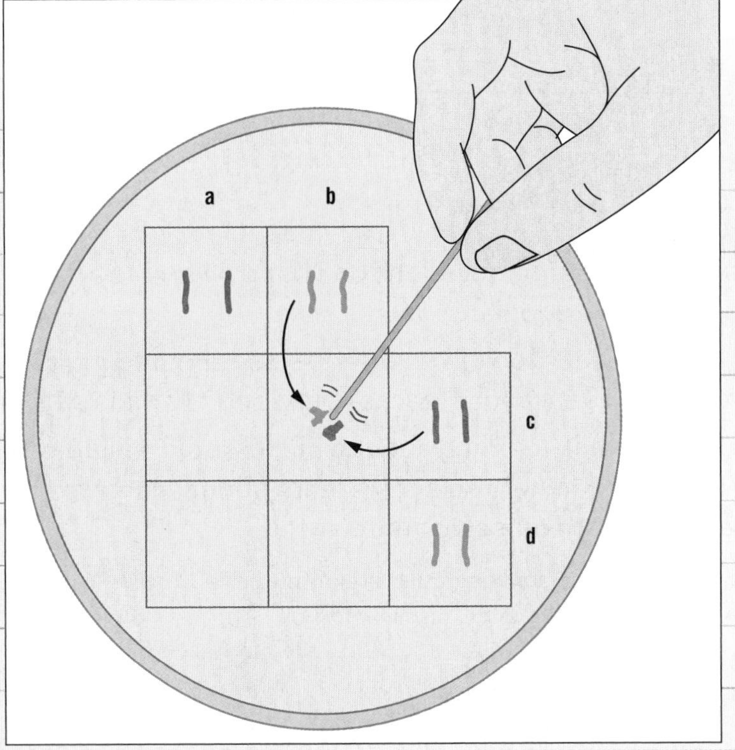

▲ **Mating yeast.** Mate yeast by using a fresh toothpick to mix two spots of yeast together. Make sure you mix yeast of opposite mating types. In this figure, streaks (a) and (b) are the opposite mating type of streaks (c) and (d).

3. Repeat Steps 2a–d, crossing streak (a) with (d), (b) with (c), and (b) with (d). The yeast cross diagram illustrates how to make the crosses.
4. Place the lid back on the plate after you have completed all the crosses.
5. Seal the plate with parafilm or tape according to your teacher's instructions.
6. Place your plate upside down in an incubator set at 30°C. You should see the results of your crosses after 24 hours.
7. Wipe the top surface of your lab area with 10% bleach solution.
8. After making observations of the results of your crosses, dispose of the plate according to your teacher's instructions.
9. Wash your hands after handling your agar plate.

Stop & THINK

PART I

Answer the following questions on your own and record your answers in your science notebook.

1. Did the yeast cells look like you expected them to look after seeing the subcultures of yeast your teacher provided? Explain why or why not.
2. How do you think learning about a microscopic, single-celled organism, such as yeast, can help scientists learn about a large multicellular organism, such as ourselves (humans)?

For example, how can studying other organisms help scientists learn about disorders such as MMD, discussed in the last activity?

Part II: Mating Game

Now that you have grown parent colonies, you will mate the yeast. After the yeast reproduce, you will see how the offspring colonies compare with the parents.

Materials

For each team of 2 students

- 2 pairs of safety goggles
- biohazard bag or bucket with 10% bleach solution
- 1 agar plate with yeast growth from Part I
- access to incubator set at 30°C
- 1 pair of forceps
- parafilm or tape
- access to sterile toothpicks
- colored pencils

Cautions

The yeast used in this investigation are nonpathogenic laboratory strains. However, it is always good practice to disinfect all materials that come in contact with live organisms. Make sure your lab area is clean. Wipe the top surface of your lab area with a 10% bleach solution before and after the investigation. Wear goggles while working with the agar plates and yeast. Pull your hair or loose clothing back if necessary. Wash your hands thoroughly before leaving the laboratory. Dispose of all materials as directed by your teacher.

Process and Procedure

1. Get your agar plate from your teacher.
2. Follow Part II of *Yeast Monohybrid Cross Protocol* to cross your yeast strains.
3. Draw a sketch of your agar plate showing the grid and the location of the yeast. Label the yeast strains and the color of the yeast using colored pencils.
4. Work with your partner to discuss your ideas about the investigation by completing Steps 4a–b. Record your ideas in your science notebook.
   a. Why did you cross specific strains of yeast?
   b. Predict the results of your cross. Record your prediction and justify your prediction for each cross.
5. Discuss the following questions as a class and record your answers in your science notebook.
   a. Why were you able to make a prediction about the results of your cross?

What previous experiences have you had that helped you make your prediction?

   b. When someone tells you he has a Dalmatian, you can predict that this Dalmatian will look like all other Dalmatians even before seeing it. But what if someone tells you she has a mixed-breed dog and she thinks the parents are a beagle and Pomeranian, like those pictured in figure 7.5. What do you think her mixed-breed dog looks like? Why?

All organisms have traits that make them distinct. The yeast you worked with were either red or cream. Dogs are different colors, different sizes, and have different lengths and textures of hair.

   c. Why do you think offspring look something like their parents?
6. Observe the colonies produced when you crossed the parent yeast colonies. The new colonies are called the first generation. Discuss with your partner how the actual results compare with your predictions.
7. Add your results and highlight comments to your drawing from Step 3.

▲ **Figure 7.5 Two dog breeds.** Both (a) beagles and (b) Pomeranians are dogs, but they look very different.

Reflect and Connect

Answer the following questions individually in your science notebook. Then compare your answers with a partner's and adjust your answers if you learn something new.

1. Were you surprised at the results of the cross? What was unexpected in your results and why?
2. Why do you think you obtained the results that you did?
3. How did this yeast experiment help you learn more about heredity?
4. What new questions do you have about the yeast strains? What future experiments could you try with your yeast to answer these questions?

EXPLAIN

How Do We Get Our Traits?

▲ **Figure 7.6 Gregor Johann Mendel (1822–1884).** Experimenting in his monastery garden, Mendel developed the fundamental principles of heredity that became the foundation of modern genetics.

You have been thinking about traits that are passed from one generation to the next. You might be surprised to learn that until the 1860s, people did not even realize that organisms inherited their traits from a previous generation. In the 1860s, a man by the name of Gregor Mendel began to change people's thinking about how organisms acquire their traits. Mendel discovered some of the fundamental principles of **genetics**. Genetics is the science of heredity.

In Part I, you will read about Mendel and his work (figure 7.6). Then you will take a look at the process of meiosis, which determines what traits are inherited. In Part II, you will develop your understanding of meiosis by modeling the process with clay.

Part I: Mendel's Discoveries

Materials

none

Process and Procedure

1. Complete an analogy map while you read *Mendel: The Founder of Genetics*. The headings for your analogy map should be "Part of Yeast Investigation," "Part of Mendel's Pea Plant Experiment," "How the Yeast Investigation Is Similar to Mendel's Pea Plant Experiment."

READING

Mendel: The Founder of Genetics

Gregor Mendel grew up as Johann Mendel in a German-speaking region of Austria (now the eastern part of the Czech Republic). Mendel grew up in a peasant farming family. Because his family had very little money, his only way of getting an advanced education was to become a monk. He joined the St. Thomas monastery (figure 7.7) in 1843 and was assigned the name Gregor. This particular order of monks encouraged teaching and research and was a wonderful place for Mendel to further his studies.

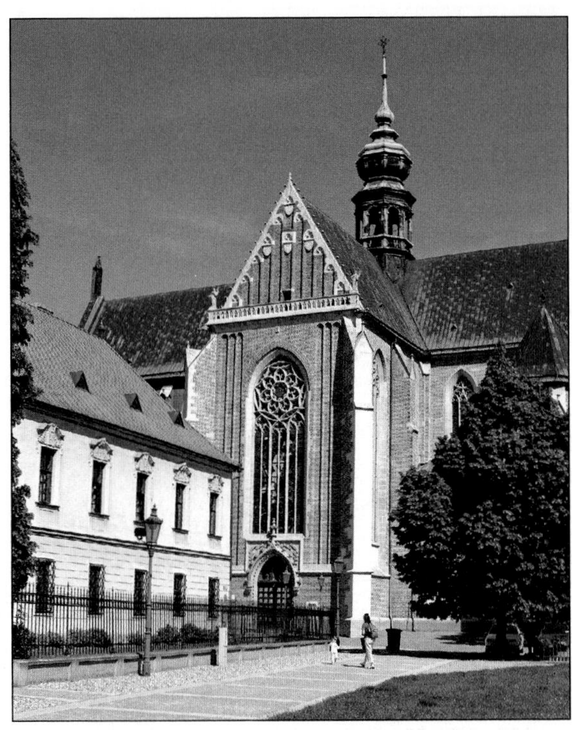

Figure 7.7 St. Thomas monastery. The monastery is located in Brünn, which was a large city of 70,000 even in the 1800s. Brünn, now called Brno, had many fine schools and scientific societies.

Mendel was exposed to the ideas of scientists and mathematicians during his first 10 years at the monastery. At one point during his studies, he learned about plant breeding methods. He also learned about a particular plant, the common garden pea (*Pisum sativum*), which was well suited for crossbreeding because of its easily identifiable characteristics. Mendel was particularly interested in the inheritance of animal and plant features—or traits. As a result, he began investigating inheritance patterns in the pea plants he had learned about.

Garden pea flowers contain both male and female reproductive parts, as shown in figure 7.8. Under natural conditions, a pea plant usually self-pollinates. However, plant breeders can collect pollen grains from flowers of one pea plant and transfer them to the flowers of another pea plant. This technique, called cross-pollination, results in seeds (from pea pods) that are the offspring of two pea plants, not just one.

To begin his work, Mendel spent 2 years collecting various strains of garden peas and tested each strain to make sure it was genetically true, or true breeding. True-breeding plants produce offspring, through self-pollination, that are identical to themselves generation after generation. Mendel worked with strains that were true breeding except for one trait. These plants would show one of two different forms of this trait, while all other traits were exactly the same. For example, plants were either tall or short, or produced either green or yellow seeds. By having distinct and contrasting forms of only one trait, Mendel could follow the differences in that trait in the offspring. Figure 7.9 shows the seven traits of pea plants that Mendel investigated in his experiments.

Mendel: The Founder of Genetics, continued

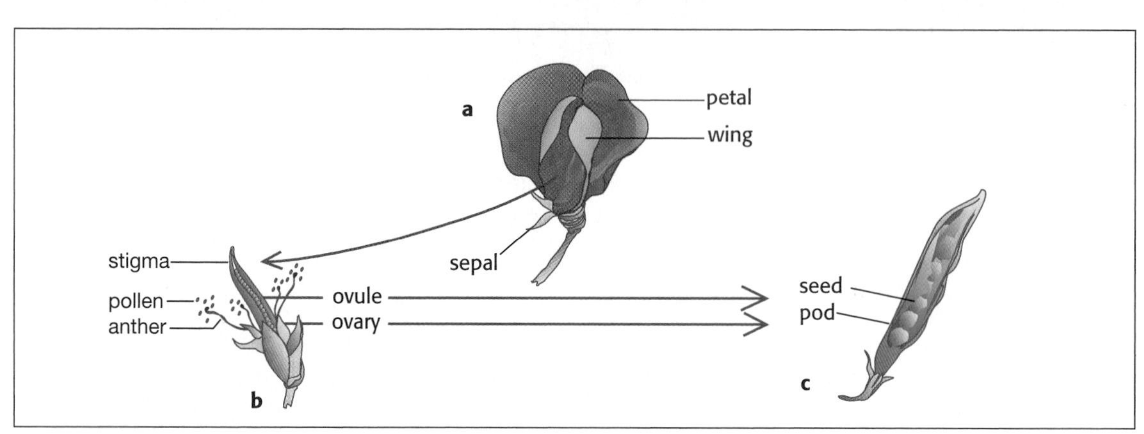

▲ **Figure 7.8 Pea flower reproductive parts.** The petals of the pea flower (a) completely enclose the reproductive organs. As a result, self-pollination occurs when the pollen from the anthers falls on the stigma of the same flower (b). Pollen tubes then grow down through the female reproductive organ to the ovules (immature seeds) in the ovary. The ovules develop into seeds, and the ovary wall develops into the pea pod (c).

seed shape	seed color	seed-coat color	pod shape	pod color	flower position	stem length
round	yellow	colored	inflated	green	axial	long
wrinkled	green	white	constricted	yellow	terminal	short

▲ **Figure 7.9 Traits of garden peas.** Are you surprised at the variation in the traits of garden pea plants?

Mendel worked with many generations of pea plants over many years. In one of his breeding experiments, Mendel crossed pea plants that produced yellow seeds with pea plants that produced green seeds. Mendel then looked at the traits in the resulting generation. All the members of the resulting first generation produced yellow seeds.

You probably wondered what happened to the red color trait in your yeast experiment. Mendel, too, wondered what happened to the trait of green seeds in his experiment. Mendel felt that the green pea trait was not lost for good, so he took his experiment one step further. Mendel crossed members of the first generation (called F_1) with themselves (self-pollination) and looked at the resulting generation (called F_2). He found that in the F_2 generation, about 75 percent (3 out of every 4) of the offspring produced yellow seeds and about 25 percent (1 out of every 4) produced green seeds. Figure 7.10 illustrates the crosses and the results.

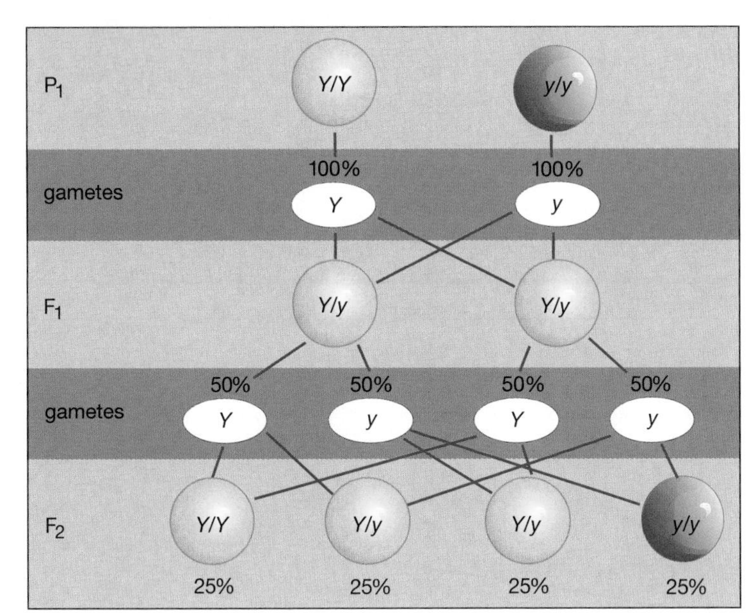

▲ **Figure 7.10 Yellow seed and green seed cross.** Two generations of one of Mendel's crosses using yellow and green seeds. Note that the alleles of a gene segregate, or separate, during gamete formation.

Mendel determined that whether seeds were yellow or green was determined by factors. We now call these factors **genes**. Genes determine the traits expressed by an organism—the traits that an organism has. They are the basic unit of information passed along from generation to generation through inheritance. Between 1854 and 1863, Mendel patiently grew thousands of pea plants, conducting different crosses. He repeated the same two-generation cross, shown in figure 7.10, with the six other traits.

After many years of study, and many plant breeding experiments, Mendel concluded that some expressions of traits were masked by other expressions of the trait. If the trait was the one that showed up in the first generation, he called it the **dominant** trait. If the trait did not appear again until the second generation, he called it the **recessive** trait.

Mendel realized that each trait existed in different forms. For example, the color trait could be yellow or green. The height trait could be tall or short. We now call different forms of the same gene **alleles**. For the gene that controls the height of a pea plant, there are two alleles. One allele results in the production of a tall plant. The other allele results in a short plant. The allele for the dominant form (tall plant) is commonly represented by a capital letter (in this cross, *T* for tall plants). The allele for the recessive form is represented by the same letter in lowercase (*t* for short plants).

Alleles form the genetic plan, or **genotype**, of an organism. The genotype of an individual is responsible for its **phenotype**. Phenotype describes the appearance or observable traits of an individual, such as seed color or petal shape. For instance, garden peas can have the tall plant or the short plant phenotype. Mendel found that both the *TT* and *Tt* genotypes produce the same phenotype exhibiting the dominant trait: tall plants. The *tt* genotype only produces the phenotype exhibiting the recessive trait: short plants.

If the alleles are the same (*TT* or *tt*), they are **homozygous**. An individual can be homozygous dominant or homozygous recessive for a trait.

Mendel: The Founder of Genetics, continued

The true-breeding plants that Mendel used to start his experiments were either homozygous dominant (*TT*) or homozygous recessive (*tt*). If the alleles are different (*Tt*), they are **heterozygous**. Heterozygous offspring are called **hybrids**.

Phenotype is not determined solely by the genotype, however. Environmental factors play a critical role as well. For example, the average height of Japan's human population increased by several inches during the early and middle 20th century (see figure 7.11). Did the genetic plan for the entire population change? No, the environment for the population changed. Japanese children had more nutritious diets in the early and middle 1900s than did children of earlier generations. Poor diet is an environmental factor. This environmental limitation prevented earlier generations from getting as tall as permitted by their genetic plan. Complex phenotypes involve many genetic and environmental factors.

Mendel's work is the basis for the modern study of heredity and variation. Geneticists now call his work Mendelian genetics. His experiments were unique in four important ways. First, he concentrated on one trait at a time. Second, he used large numbers of organisms to minimize the influence of chance on his data. Third, he combined the results of many identical experiments. Fourth, he used the rules of probability to analyze his results. By using these methods, Mendel was able to recognize distinctive patterns of inheritance.

Mendel's experiments defined the basic unit of inheritance, genes, but he could provide no information about its physical or chemical nature. Unable to see genes in his studies, he inferred their existence from his experiments. The answer to the riddle of what genes are and how they work could not be known until nearly 100 years later. This was when techniques for studying biological molecules were developed.

Topic: genetic traits
Go to: www.scilinks.org
Code: 2Inquiry350

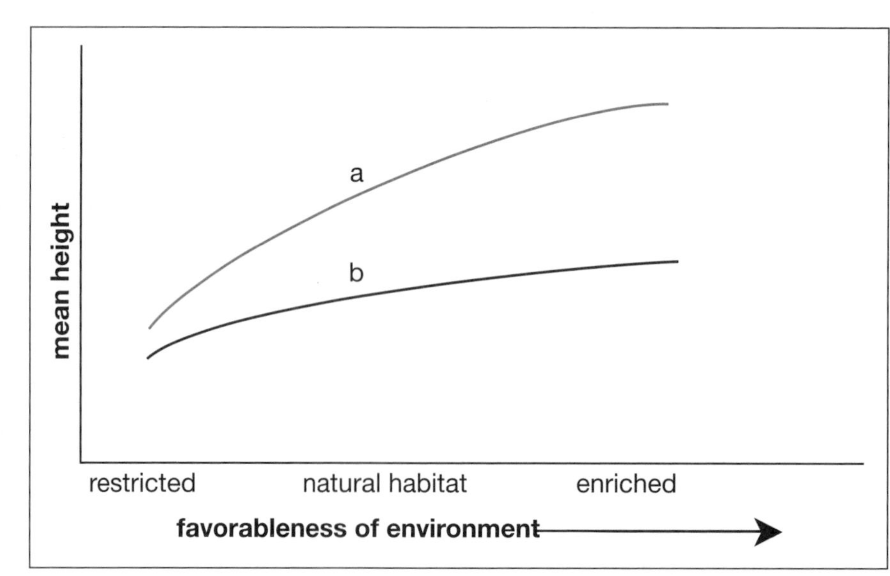

Source: Based on data from I. I. Gottesman and L. L. Heston. (1972). *Genetics, Environment, and Behavior*. Academic Press.

▲ **Figure 7.11 Height in Japanese boys and girls in relation to environmental conditions.** Improved environmental conditions in Japan led to a phenotype for increased height during the early and middle 20th century. Curve A represents 13-year-old girls and curve B represents 15-year-old boys. The units for both mean height and environmental conditions are not to scale.

2. Explain which of the following pairs of traits from Mendel's experiments is dominant and which is recessive and why.

Write out the possible genotypes for each trait if you are unsure which is dominant and which is recessive.

   a. The yellow or green seeds in Mendel's experiment
   b. The red- or cream-colored yeast in the investigation from the last activity

3. Answer the following questions to show what you learned about Mendel's discoveries.
   a. Describe the difference between genotype and phenotype. Include in your description what determines the traits exhibited by an organism.
   b. Why do you think Mendel is often referred to as the "Founder of Genetics"?
   c. Do you think most of what we know about an area of science is the result of research across many years or the result of a few experiments? Why?

4. Select a technique you have found that helps you understand as you read. Apply your technique to the reading titled *Chromosomes and the Genes They Contain.*

Some example techniques include T-tables, importance pyramids, and the TSAR process.

READING

Chromosomes and the Genes They Contain

In *Mendel: The Founder of Genetics*, you read about Mendel's experiments with peas and learned that the traits of an organism are determined by its genes. Specifically, the genetic information for an organism is stored in **DNA** (deoxyribonucleic acid) molecules. Genes are small sections of DNA molecules. In humans and other eukaryotes, the DNA molecules are organized into distinct structures called **chromosomes**. Each chromosome contains just a small part of an organism's total genetic information. The DNA in each chromosome, however, contains enough information for many phenotypic traits. For example, the very tip of just one human chromosome contains the piece of genetic information that causes blood to clot.

Humans have 46 chromosomes (23 pairs) in the nucleus of just about every cell of their bodies. The number of chromosomes varies from species to species and does not necessarily have to do with the complexity of the organism. Ants have two chromosomes, dogs have 78, cats have 38, and some species of ferns have 1,000.

Chromosomes and the Genes They Contain, continued

In humans, the first 22 pairs of chromosomes are called **autosomes**. The 23rd pair is referred to as the **sex chromosomes** because the chromosomes in that pair determine whether a person is male or female. If an individual has two X chromosomes in the 23rd pair, she is female. If an individual has one X and one Y chromosome in the 23rd pair, he is male.

Each of the 46 human chromosomes contains many genes. The largest chromosome contains about 3,000 genes. The smallest one, the Y chromosome, contains only about 230 genes. Figure 7.12 illustrates some of the many genes present on two human chromosomes. Each gene occupies a specific location on the chromosome.

Populations of organisms have more than one form of most genes. You learned about these forms of genes, or alleles, when you read about Mendel's experiments. For example, some individuals in the human population have a blood type gene that specifies type A blood. Others have a version of the same gene that specifies type B blood. Remember that the particular combination of alleles determines the organism's phenotype. To learn what your alleles might be if you have type A blood, see figure 7.13.

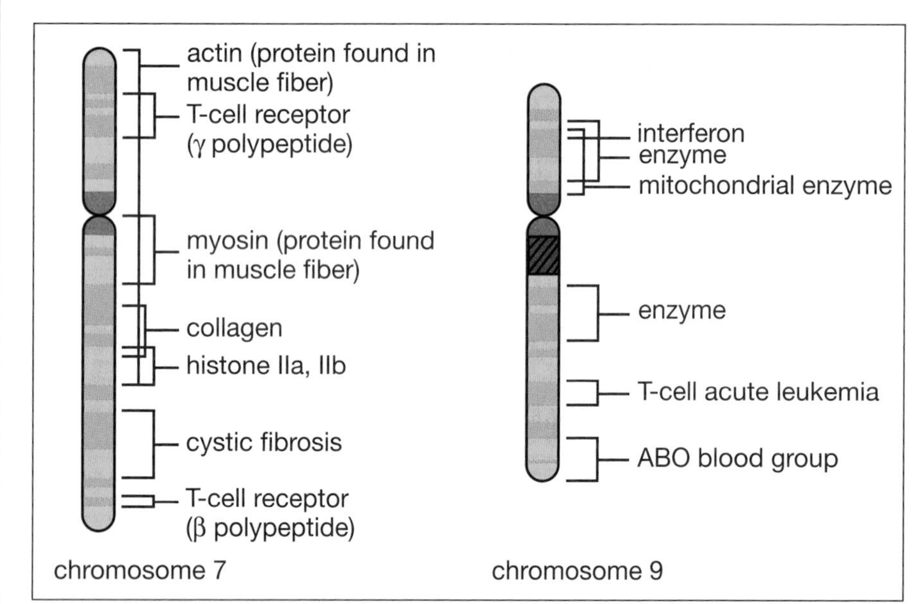

▲ **Figure 7.12 Genes on a chromosome.** Each chromosome carries many genes. This illustration shows a few of the genes that have been mapped to two human chromosomes, chromosome 7 and chromosome 9. Humans have two copies of each of 23 different human chromosomes, which carry an average of 1,000 genes each.

Phenotype	Genotype(s)
O	OO
A	AA, AO
B	BB, BO
AB	AB

▲ **Figure 7.13 Blood types.** Humans can be one of four blood types (O, A, B, or AB). In this table, the alleles are represented by A, B, and O. You have two blood type alleles because you receive one blood type allele from each parent.

Topic: chromosomes
Go to: www.scilinks.org
Code: 2Inquiry352

Organisms that are the result of sexual reproduction generally receive two alleles for every gene. One allele comes from one parent. Another allele comes from the other parent. For a trait like seed color of peas, an offspring that results from a cross receives one allele from each parent, either *Y* or *y*. Despite the notion that offspring might look more like one parent than the other, an offspring receives exactly one-half of its genetic information from each parent. How does this happen? Think about this as you read in the next section about how sex cells are produced. Read FYI—*Asexual Reproduction* to learn how some organisms reproduce asexually.

5. Answer the following questions to keep track of what you have learned about chromosomes in humans.
   a. How many chromosomes are present in human cells?
   b. How many pairs of autosomes and sex chromosomes do humans have? Describe the difference between autosomes and sex chromosomes.
   c. If 2 human body cells joined, how many chromosomes would be in the newly formed offspring cell? What problems do you think could arise if this happened?
6. Use a visual representation to show the relationship between the following terms: *chromosomes*, *genes*, *alleles*, and *traits*. Label your representation to show how the terms are related. An example is provided in figure 7.14.

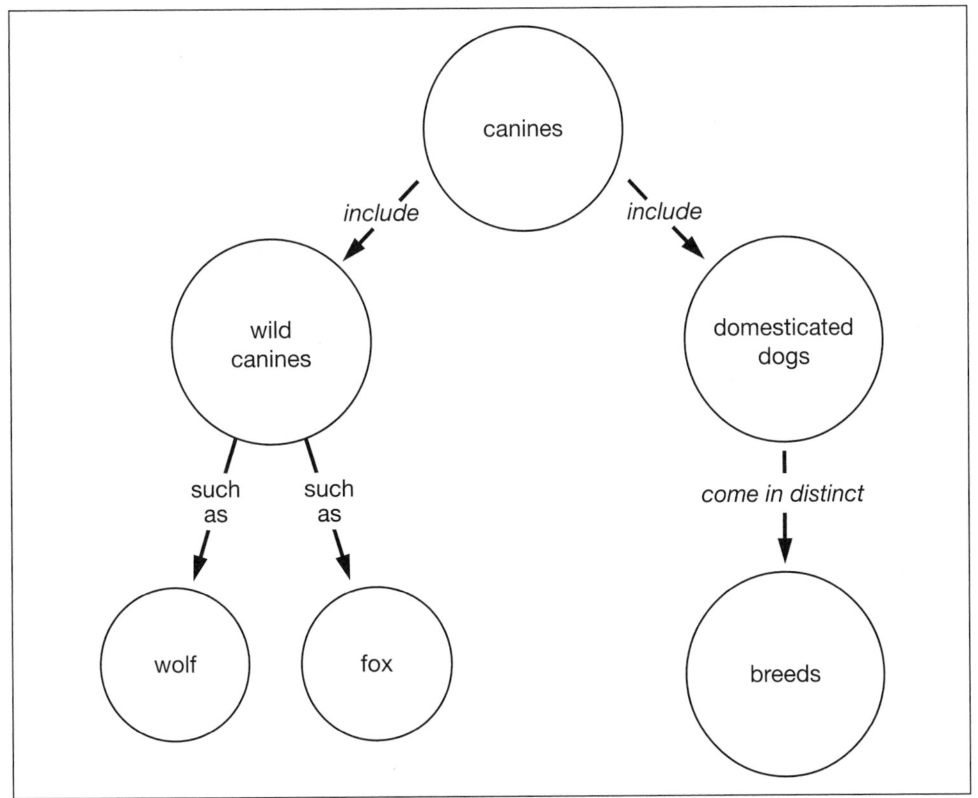

Figure 7.14 Canid graphic organizer. Canids are carnivorous members of the dog family. Examples of canids include foxes, wolves, coyotes, jackals, dingoes, and domestic dogs. Notice how phrases are used to connect the major words ("canid," "domesticated dogs," and "breeds").

Asexual Reproduction

During sexual reproduction, both parents pass genetic information to their offspring. Sexual reproduction increases the amount of genetic variation in a population because sexual reproduction combines genetic information from two different individuals.

Not all organisms reproduce sexually. Many organisms reproduce through **asexual reproduction**. In asexual reproduction, individuals originate from a single parent. Either the parent divides into two (or more) individuals, or new individuals arise as buds from the parent's body. Because new individuals arise from only one parent, asexual reproduction does not increase genetic variation in a population. Instead, new individuals are genetically identical to the parent organism.

Some animals and plants can reproduce both sexually and asexually. For example, the potato is a flowering plant that can use sexual reproduction to produce seed, but it also can reproduce asexually. In plants, this is called vegetative reproduction. The little "eyes" on potatoes are actually buds—groups of cells that can undergo rapid mitosis and develop into new plants. The buds can sprout and begin to grow, as shown in the figure.

The yeast you investigated in *What Shows Up?* reproduced both sexually and asexually. When you crossed the yeast, they reproduced sexually. How do you think yeast reproduced asexually? Yeast reproduce asexually through budding, a type of vegetative cell division, which is similar to potatoes budding. The division of yeast cells begins with an unbudded cell. Then yeast cells bud, and the bud grows to nearly the size of the "parent" cell. The nucleus of the parent cell divides, and the two cells separate. You might have noticed that your yeast colonies grew larger across time. Yeast cells divide rapidly, causing colonies to grow quickly under the right conditions.

Budding potatoes. After a dormant period, some of the eyes or buds on a potato begin to sprout and form shoots. The shoots like you see in this photo can develop into new potato plants.

7. Continue using the technique you selected in Step 4 or switch to a new technique to read *Meiosis: The Mechanism behind Patterns of Inheritance.*

READING

Meiosis: The Mechanism behind Patterns of Inheritance

In sexual reproduction, genetic information is passed from generation to generation by cells called **gametes**. Gametes have only *half* the genetic information of other body cells. They have half the chromosomes and thus half the alleles.

How and when does this reduction occur? Most of the solution to this question was discovered just before the beginning of the 20th century. The key is a process called **meiosis**. Meiosis is the special type of cell division that produces gametes (egg and sperm cells) in male and female organisms that reproduce sexually. Meiosis accomplishes three major tasks: (1) It reduces the number of chromosomes in gametes to half of all the chromosomes found in body cells. (2) It forms cells that will allow each parent to contribute equal amounts of genetic information to the offspring. In humans, the gametes have 23 chromosomes in each cell. (3) It creates gene combinations in the offspring that are distinct from the parents.

Following the chromosomes during meiosis provides a way to understand certain patterns of inheritance. In all cells other than gametes, chromosomes occur in matching pairs. This is called the **diploid** condition. For each pair, one chromosome came from the mother's egg cell and one chromosome came from the father's sperm cell. The maternal and paternal chromosomes of each pair contain genes that affect the same traits. As you learned earlier, however, the alleles for each gene may be different.

In contrast, gametes (egg, or ovum, and sperm) contain only *one* chromosome from each matching pair. Gametes are **haploid**: they contain half the number of chromosomes that other body cells such as skin and nerve cells have. In sexual reproduction, a sperm fertilizes the ovum and the nuclei of both cells fuse to form a new cell with the correct number of chromosomes. The single cell that results from the joining of the egg and the sperm is called a **zygote**. The zygote will have matching pairs of chromosomes. Each pair is composed of one chromosome from the egg and one chromosome from the sperm. Thus, fertilization restores the diploid number of chromosomes in the zygote. What would happen if chromosome numbers were not halved during meiosis? The number of chromosomes would double with each generation! Such a condition in humans and other animals would lead to the death of the zygote.

The zygote begins a series of cell divisions, through the process of **mitosis**, to produce an **embryo**. Mitosis forms many new cells, each with 46 chromosomes (23 pairs) if the organism is a human. Those cells eventually specialize into tissues and organs, giving rise to the human body. Each new cell formed has the genetic makeup of the zygote.

Sometimes two sperm fertilize two eggs. When this happens, fraternal twins are produced. Fraternal twins really are no more genetically similar to each other than other siblings are. At other times, one sperm fertilizes one egg and, for reasons that scientists do not completely understand yet, the cell doubles in chromosome number and then splits into separate zygotes. Identical twins are the result of one sperm fertilizing one egg. Identical twins have identical genetic information.

Meiosis: The Mechanism behind Patterns of Inheritance, continued

Meiosis is similar to the process of mitosis. In meiosis, as in mitosis, the number of chromosomes doubles at the beginning of the process. In mitosis, one cell division follows, restoring the usual diploid number of chromosomes. In meiosis, however, cell division occurs *twice*. The process results in four cells, each with the haploid number of chromosomes. The four cells produced by meiosis each have just one set of chromosomes. In humans, meiosis results in one large egg cell for females and four sperm cells for males (see figure 7.15).

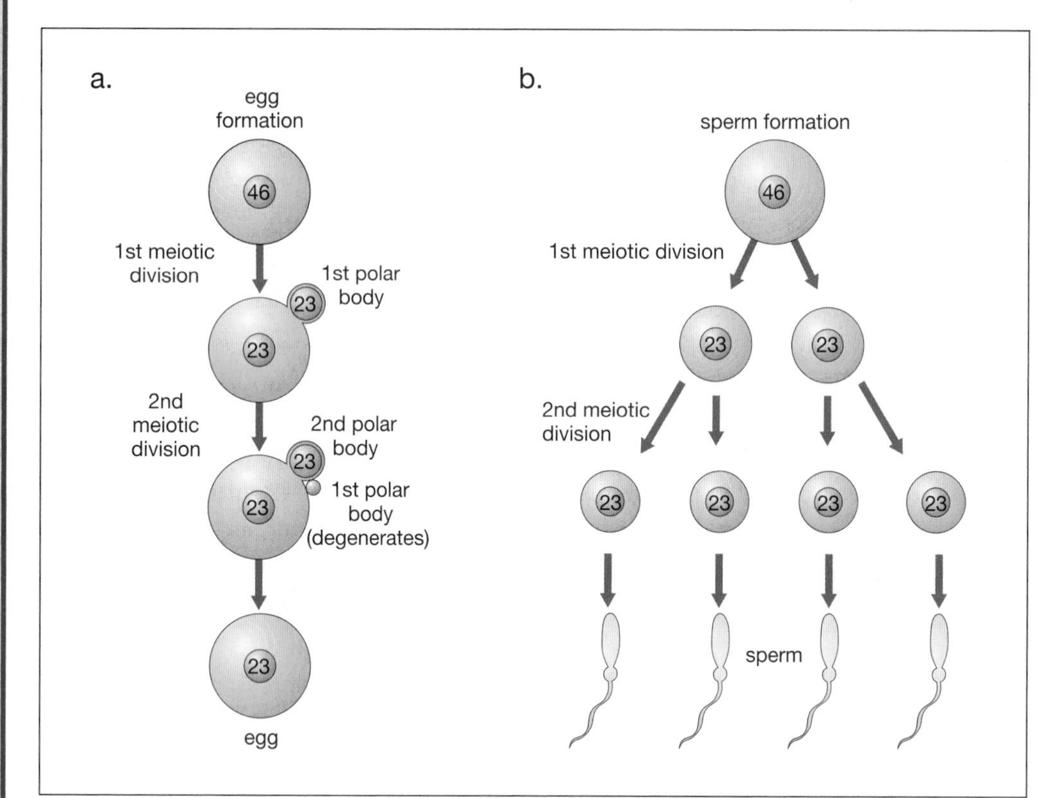

Figure 7.15 Human gamete formation. In human males, meiotic division usually results in four equal-sized sperm, each with 23 chromosomes. The formation of an egg is somewhat different. Two unequally sized cells are formed in the first meiotic division. The larger cell of the two again produces a smaller cell in the second meiotic division. The result is one large ovum that can be involved in reproduction and three polar bodies that will not be involved in reproduction. The polar bodies are by-products of meiosis in female animals and will eventually disintegrate. What do you think is the advantage of producing a large egg? Think about what the yolk provides for a developing chick.

Figure 7.16 illustrates what happens to one pair of chromosomes during meiosis. Let's examine the process in more detail. Just before meiosis begins, each chromosome pair doubles. During the first meiotic cell division, the two doubled chromosomes separate into two cells. Each of these cells contains one doubled chromosome. During the second meiotic cell division, the doubled chromosome in each cell separates into two more cells. This second cell division results in a total of four cells. Each cell contains one chromosome from the original pair.

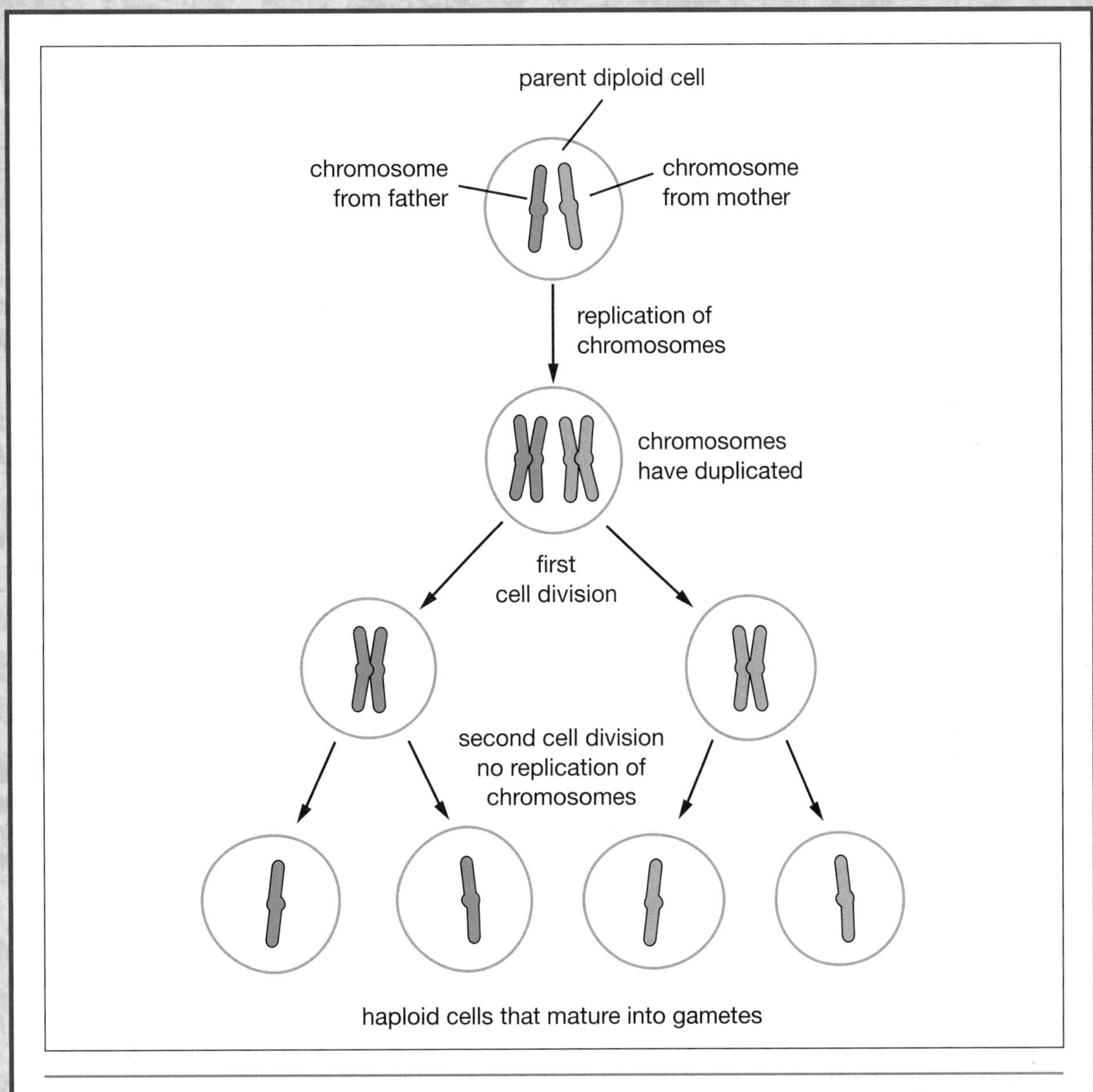

▲ **Figure 7.16 Meiosis.** Meiosis consists of one replication of chromosomes followed by two cell divisions.

SCILINKS® NSTA
Topic: meiosis
Go to: www.scilinks.org
Code: 2Inquiry357

Meiosis: The Mechanism behind Patterns of Inheritance, continued

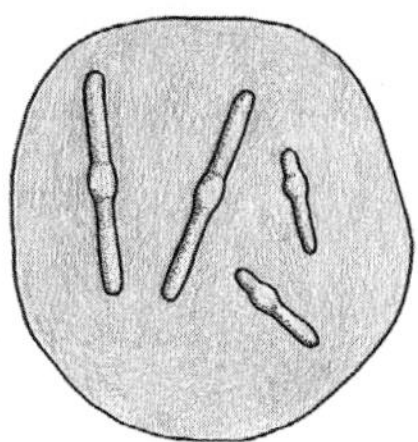

diploid parent cell

a This cell has 2 pairs of chromosomes.

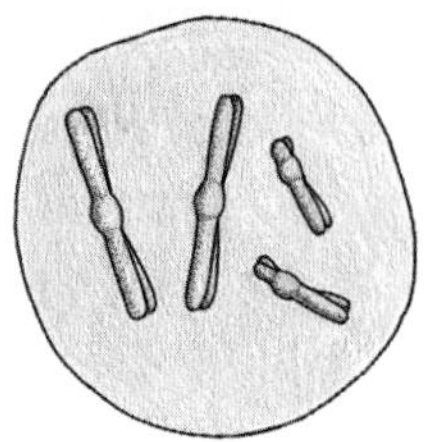

beginning of meiosis prophase 1

b Just before this diploid cell begins meiosis each chromosome is replicated.

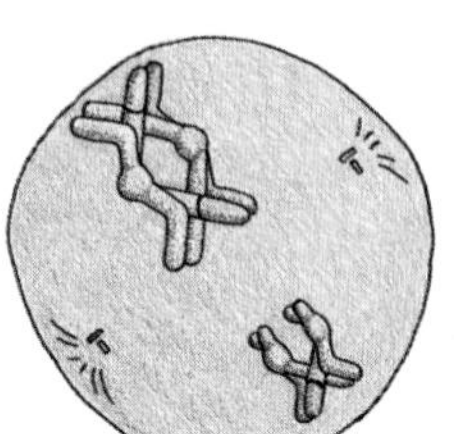

crossing-over

c The pairs of replicated chromosomes become closely aligned and join in several places. At these junctions, equivalent pieces of the chromosome pair might exchange places. This exchange process, called crossing over, results in the switching of alleles. Because the chromosomes involved in the exchange originally came from different parents, a new combination of information now exists.

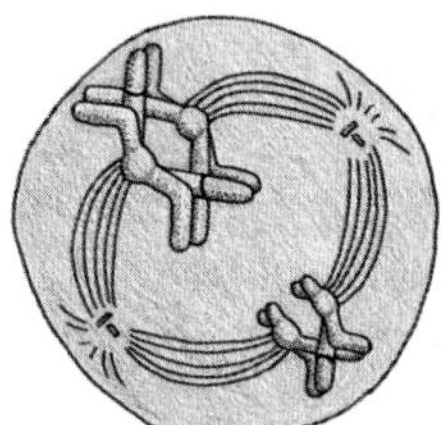

metaphase 1

d The joined chromosomes line up along the middle of the cell. Cytoplasmic fibers attach to each replicated chromosome.

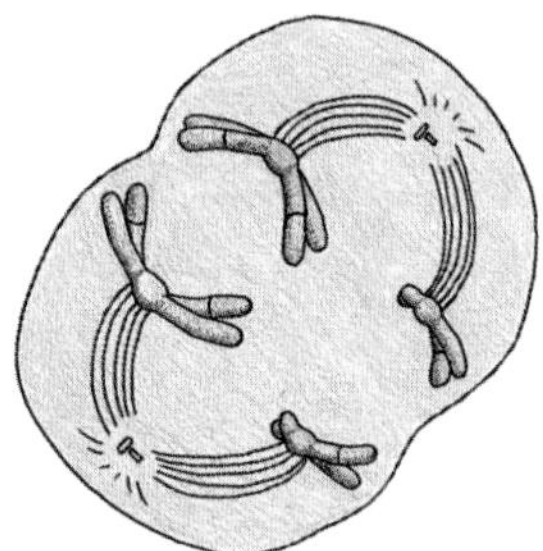

anaphase 1

e The cytoplasmic fibers pull apart each pair of duplicated chromosomes during the first cell division.

▲ **Figure 7.17 The stages of meiosis.** This figure illustrates the events of meiosis for a cell that has two pairs of chromosomes.

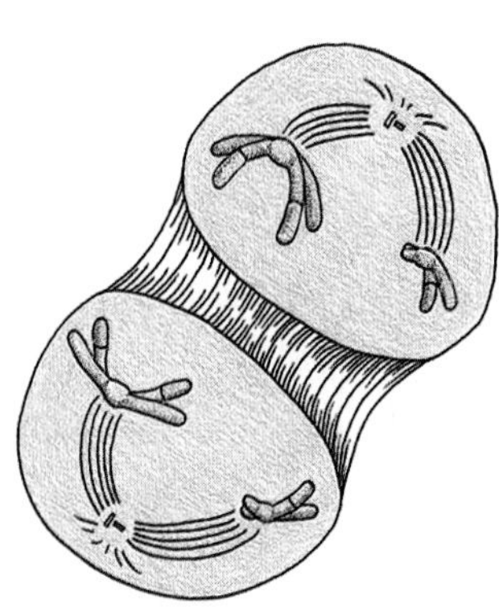

telophase 1

f Each new cell resulting from this division contains two doubled chromosomes, one from each pair.

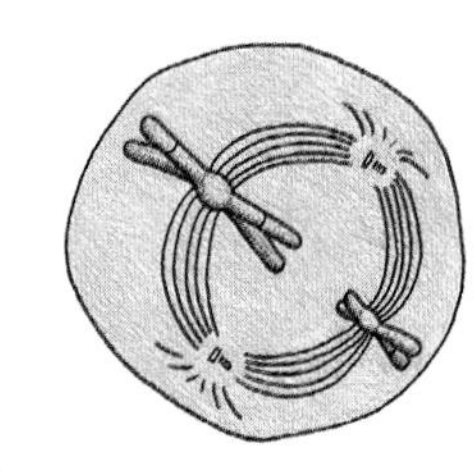

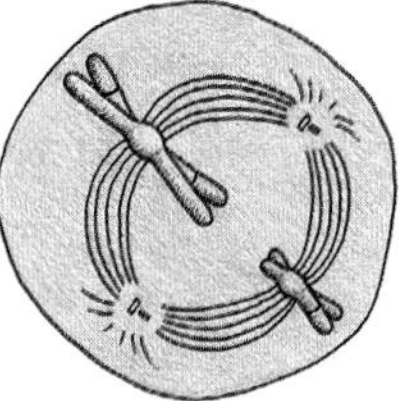

metaphase 2

g A second cell division now takes place with no further replication of chromosomes. During this cell division, there are no matching chromosome pairs. Instead, the doubled chromosomes line up in single file.

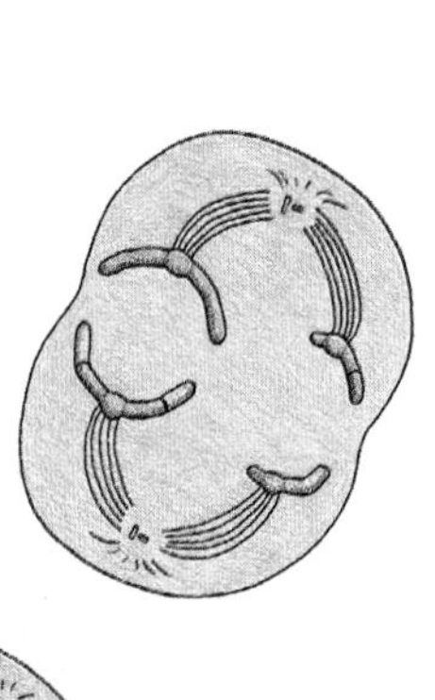

anaphase 2

h Fibers pull apart each doubled chromosome.

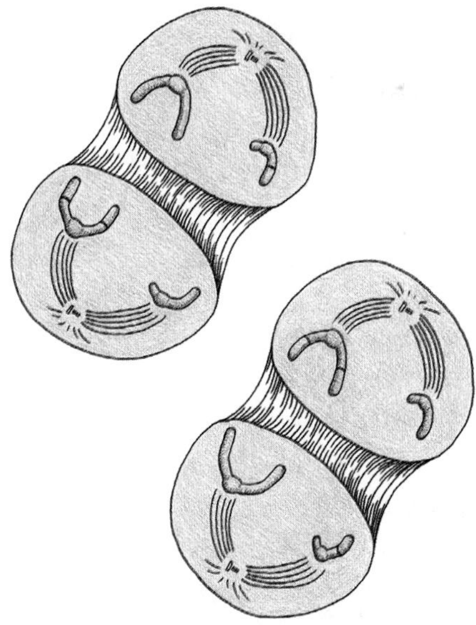

telophase 2

i Each of the resulting four offspring cells has a single set of chromosomes and is haploid. Mature human gametes form from the products of meiosis.

8. Study figure 7.17, which shows the events of meiosis in a cell with two pairs of chromosomes. Then record your answers to Questions 8a–d in your science notebook.
   a. How many chromosomes do human cells have before meiosis?
   b. How many *pairs* of chromosomes do human cells have?
   c. How many chromosomes do they have after meiosis? Explain why this is so.
   d. Describe the difference between haploid and diploid cells.
9. Read *Sorting Genes* and complete the following tasks to show your understanding of how offspring can have different combinations of alleles from the same parents.
   a. Describe how the principle of independent assortment and the principle of segregation might help explain the variation in a species, such as humans or pea plants.
   b. Copy and complete the table from figure 7.18 in your science notebook. Use the information in the figure to help you fill in the blank spaces.
   c. Determine the number of ways to get each genotype (*gg*, *Gg*, or *GG*) using the information from figure 7.18.
   d. Calculate the probability of each genotype (*gg*, *Gg*, or *GG*). Show your work.

READING

Sorting Genes

Gregor Mendel worked out the principles of simple inheritance decades before the scientists understood how cells carry out meiosis. He accomplished this astounding intellectual achievement by designing creative experiments, making observations, keeping detailed records, and applying mathematical reasoning to his results.

Meiosis explains Mendel's key discoveries. One of Mendel's discoveries was the **principle of independent assortment**. In meiosis, the chromosome pairs separate independently. When Mendel looked at multiple traits of pea plants, such as seed color and seed shape, he found that specific seed colors are not inherited with specific seed shapes. Genes governing those two traits undergo **independent assortment**. Independent assortment occurs because the genes for seed color and seed shape are located on different chromosomes. The movement of one chromosome does not depend on the movement of another chromosome.

Mendel also understood that offspring received alleles from each parent. Mendel called this separation the **principle of segregation**. Remember that (1) genes are located on chromosomes and (2) alleles are versions of a gene. Alleles on the two chromosomes in a pair segregate (separate) when the two chromosomes separate during meiosis. Each gamete, therefore, receives only one allele for a given gene. You will model how meiosis explains the principle of segregation in Part II.

Understanding meiosis also allows us to make predictions about the genotypes and phenotypes of offspring. We can predict the frequency of offspring genotypes when parents of a known genotype mate and produce large numbers of offspring. Figure 7.18 presents an example using guinea pigs. Short hair is a dominant trait in guinea pigs. *G* represents the allele for short hair, *g* the allele for long hair. Both parents are heterozygous for short hair (*Gg*). Each parent produces equal numbers of *G* and *g* gametes through meiosis. When fertilizations occur, the gametes join in random combinations. In this case, ½ of the egg and ½ of the sperm contain the *G* allele. We can, therefore, expect that ¼ (½ × ½ = ¼) of the offspring will have the homozygous genotype *GG* of short hair.

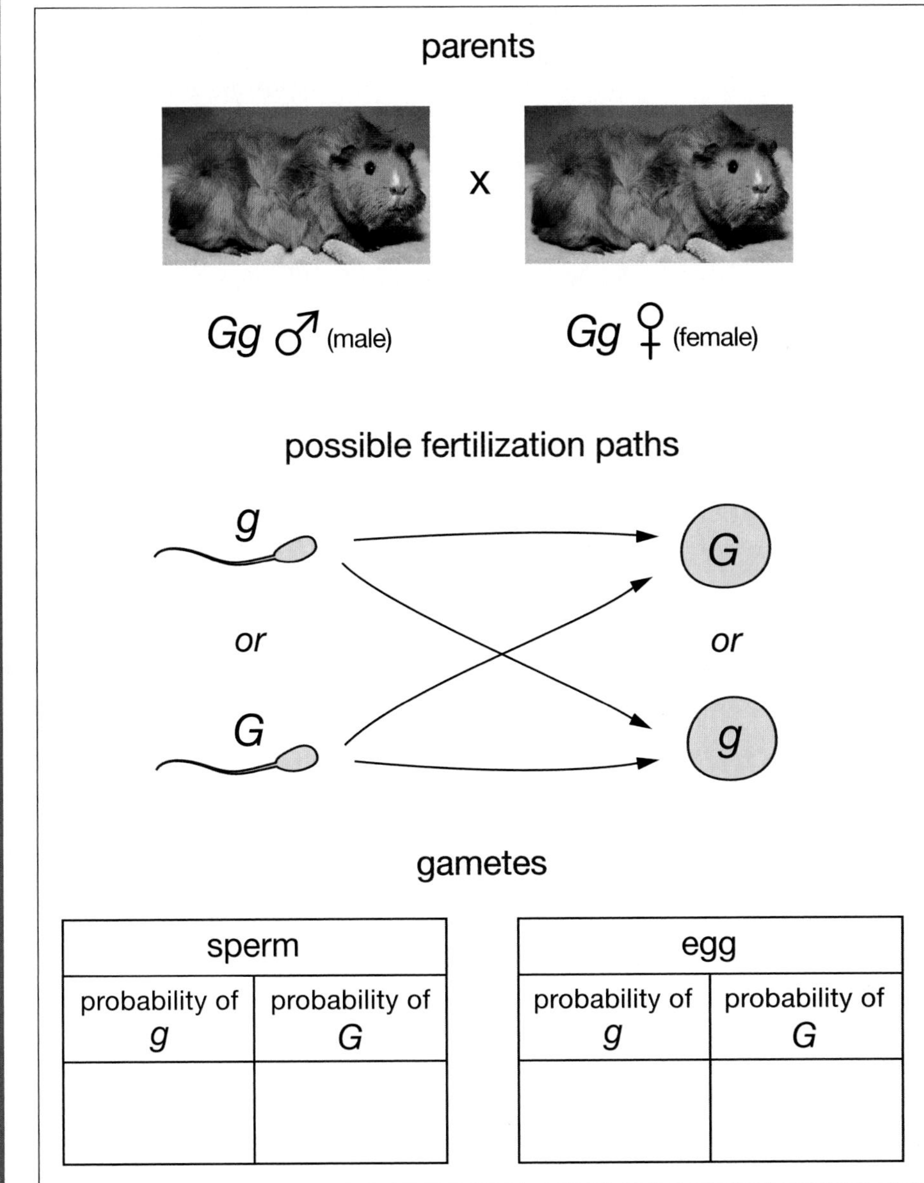

Figure 7.18 Predicting genotype. Allele segregation occurs in a regular pattern that makes it possible to predict offspring. If the genotypes of the parents are known, then the gametes that result can be known as well. If one parent was homozygous for short hair (*GG*), how many offspring would you expect to be genotype *GG*?

Sorting Genes, continued

What about the other half of the ova (plural of ovum) and sperm—those that carry the *g* allele? Fertilization of these gametes will probably result in about ¼ of the offspring having the homozygous genotype *gg* of short hair. The rest of the offspring will be heterozygotes. Half of the heterozygotes will come from unions of *G* egg with *g* sperm. The other half will come from unions of *g* egg and *G* sperm. (Both are written *Gg* because biologists record the dominant trait first, regardless of which parent passes it on.) Of the resulting offspring at one mating, ¾ will have short hair (½ *Gg* plus ¼ *GG*) and 1/4 will have long hair (*gg*). Biologists refer to this pattern as a 3:1 phenotypic ratio (¾:¼, reduced to lowest terms).

The laws of inheritance do not allow us to make exact predictions for a specific mating, however. Each fertilization involves the union of a single egg and a single sperm out of *many* possible egg and sperm. We cannot predict with absolute certainty that a particular mating will result in a zygote that is *Gg*, for example. Flipping a coin illustrates this phenomenon. Is it possible to toss four heads in a row with a coin? What about tossing 100 heads in a row? The predicted result of getting heads in a coin toss is 50:50, a prediction that can be verified by observing a large number of tosses. You might not be surprised at tossing four heads in a row, but you would be surprised at tossing 100 heads in a row.

Imagine that the parent guinea pigs in figure 7.18 have a litter of four. Recall that both parents are heterozygous (*Gg*) for the short hair allele. If we examine *many* such litters, we probably would find that ½ of the offspring had the *Gg* genotype, ¼ the *GG* genotype, and ¼ the *gg* genotype. However, it is quite possible that in any given litter, all may have the *GG* genotype or all may have the *gg* genotype. Isn't it possible to toss four heads in a row with a coin? You may have to flip a coin many times to get the same number of heads and tails. Similarly, many matings would have to occur to get the frequencies of genotypes predicted by the parents' alleles.

SCI LINKS® NSTA

Topic: independent assortment
Go to: www.scilinks.org
Code: 2Inquiry362

Stop & THINK

PART I

Complete the following tasks and questions with a partner and record your answers in your science notebook.

1 Using what you just learned about meiosis, work with your partner to complete the following tasks.

a. Write a description in your science notebook of how the major events in meiosis lead to a reduced amount of genetic information in gametes. Include in your answer how many gametes are produced by a single parent and explain why the process of meiosis results in this number of gametes. You may want to use sketches as you complete this task.

b. Create a flowchart to record the steps for how an individual chromosome behaves during the process of meiosis. Provide labels if necessary on your flowchart.

c. Check your answers with your classmates and then your teacher. You will use this information in Part II.

2 Answer the following questions about the yeast investigation.

a. Which yeast colonies contained half the number of chromosomes: the parent colonies or the first generation? Explain your answer.

b. What would have to happen before you could cross the first generation of yeast with itself as Mendel did with his pea plant experiments?

Do you think scientists such as Mendel learn everything there is to know about an area of study?

Part II: Modeling Meiosis

The fruit fly (*Drosophila melanogaster*) is commonly used in genetic experiments. Studies of fruit flies have demonstrated the direct relationship between genes and chromosomes. In this part of the activity, you will follow the chromosomes and genes of a male fruit fly gamete through the process of meiosis.

Materials

For each team of 2 students

red and blue play dough

1 large sheet of paper

1 small sheet of scratch paper

1 pair of scissors

paper

Process and Procedure

1. Develop a plan for simulating meiosis. Your simulation plan should include the following elements. They will help you develop an effective plan on your own. Record your plan in your science notebook.

The simulation will be your own visual representation of the various stages of meiosis. Refer to the reading *Meiosis: The Mechanism behind Patterns of Inheritance* in Part I for details about meiosis. Use your answers from Question 1 of *Stop and Think—Part I* as a guide.

   a. A male fruit fly (a diploid animal) that has 2 pairs of chromosomes
   b. Circles on a large sheet of paper to represent cells at different stages of meiosis
   c. A way to represent *replication* of chromosomes before meiosis begins

You will learn about the details of replication in chapter 8, *Instructions for Life*.

   d. Play dough to represent 2 different pairs of chromosomes
   e. Different colors of play dough to represent the chromosome of each pair that came from the female parent and the male parent
   f. Labels to represent genes for each chromosome (see figure 7.19)
2. Have your teacher approve your plan.
3. Carry out your plan to simulate meiosis by completing Steps 3a–b.
   a. Using your cell-diagram circles, move your chromosome models through the process of meiosis and into the sperm.

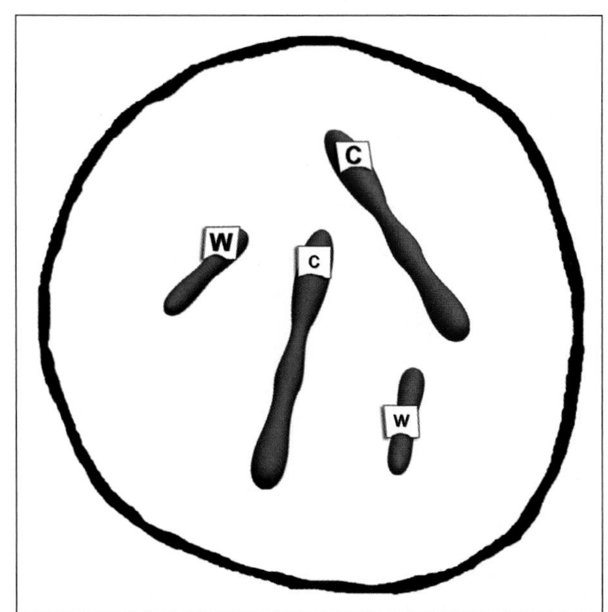

▲ **Figure 7.19 Simulating meiosis.** Clay models and paper labels can represent chromosomes and genes in a diploid animal cell.

b. Sketch in your science notebook how you line up the chromosome models during each meiotic division.

4. Think about how you just modeled meiosis and answer the following questions with a partner.

   a. In your model, what is the genotype of each sperm for eye color and wing color?

   b. What other genotypes are possible?

Check the results of other teams.

   c. At what points would you change how you positioned your chromosome models to obtain the other possible genotypes?

Reflect and Connect

Work on your own to answer the following questions. Record your answers in your science notebook.

1. What can you say for sure about the alleles for a particular trait in an organism that exhibits a recessive phenotype? A dominant phenotype?
2. Explain how your cell diagrams and the answers to Questions 8a–d from Part I of this activity illustrate how meiosis accomplishes segregation of alleles.
3. If an organism has the genotype *AA*, what can you say about the alleles present in the gametes that gave rise to that organism?
4. Consider how tall you are, how tall you will likely be when you are fully grown, and how tall you might have been if you were raised in a very different situation. How do your genes and the environment interact to determine how tall you will be?

Modify the diagram in figure 7.20 to illustrate your answer. Explain why you modified the diagram.

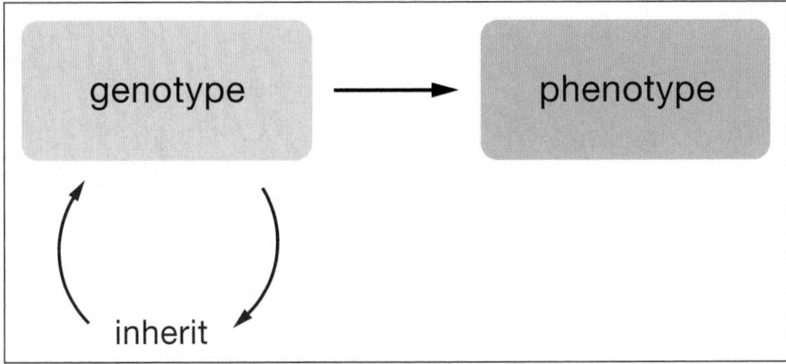

▲ **Figure 7.20 Relationship between genotype and phenotype.** How do genes and the environment interact to determine your phenotype (your traits)?

SIDEBAR

When Meiosis Has a Glitch

It is amazing that processes like meiosis and mitosis occur continuously without any significant problems. Cells divide to produce new body cells, and certain cells form gametes. These processes occur like a well-orchestrated symphony. However, sometimes there are mistakes that occur during the processes of meiosis and mitosis.

If a mistake during meiosis is major, a gamete will not form. Many gametes containing an error are not involved in fertilization. Those errors are "lost." We are not aware of their existence. In other instances, the gamete containing the error forms and is involved in the production of a zygote. The effects of the error can be

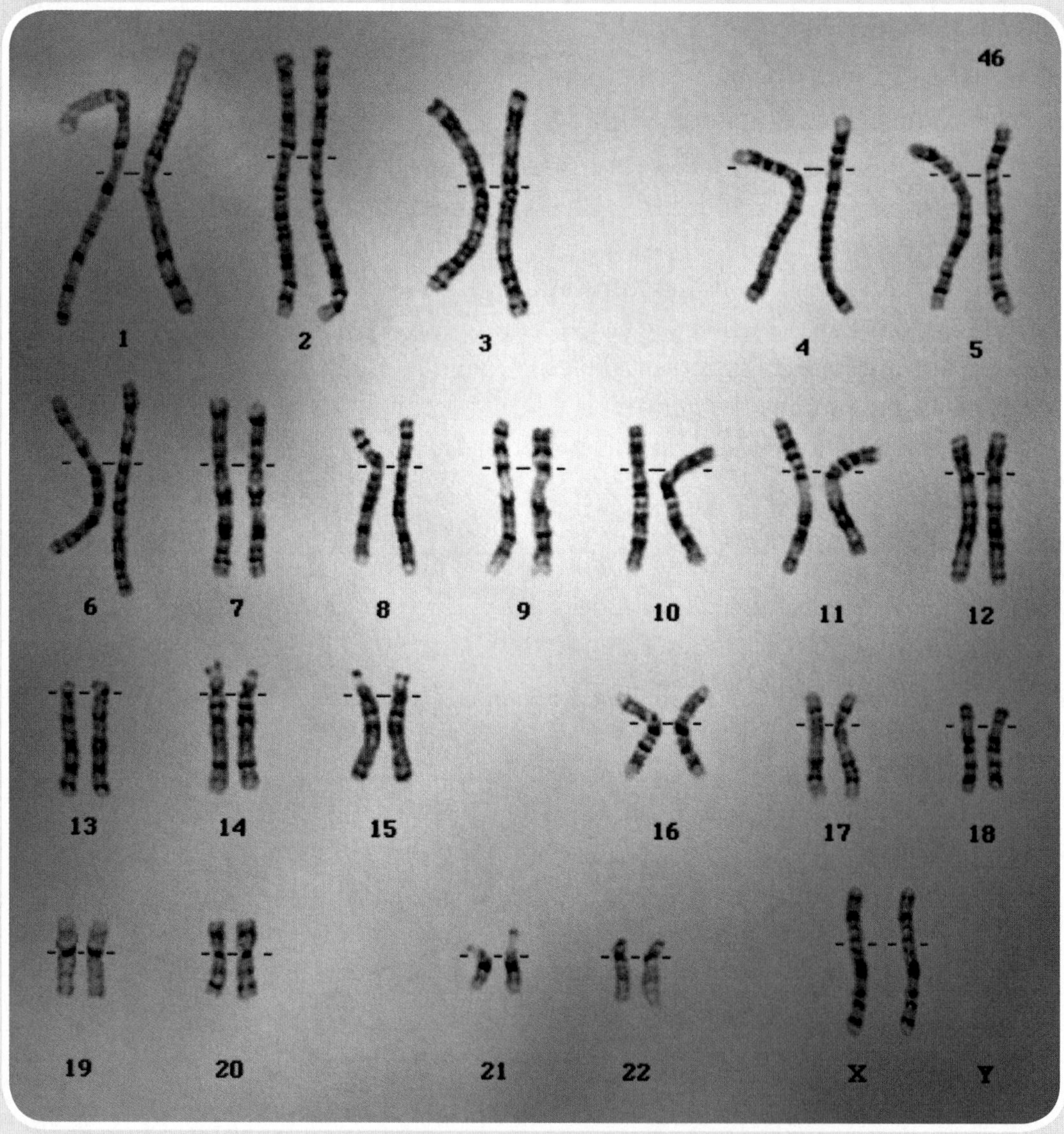

▲ **Karyotype of a human.** A karyotype is the appearance and characteristics of chromosomes in a cell. The karyotype on the right is prepared by cutting out individual chromosomes from a photograph and matching them, pair by pair. Is this the karyotype of a male or a female?

detrimental and the effects are different depending on which chromosome has the error.

Scientists can actually take cells, stain them, and take a picture of the chromosomes. The appearance and characteristics of chromosomes in a cell is called a **karyotype**. Look at the figure showing a karyotype from a cell of a normal human (image on the left). You will notice that the chromosomes are scattered. This is the way they occur in the nucleus of the cell. The chromosomes have been arranged into pairs in the image on the right. Looking at chromosomes in pairs helps us understand how genetic information is inherited.

Down syndrome, often referred to as trisomy 21, occurs when there is an extra chromosome in the 21st pair (see figure). Down syndrome affects about 1 in every

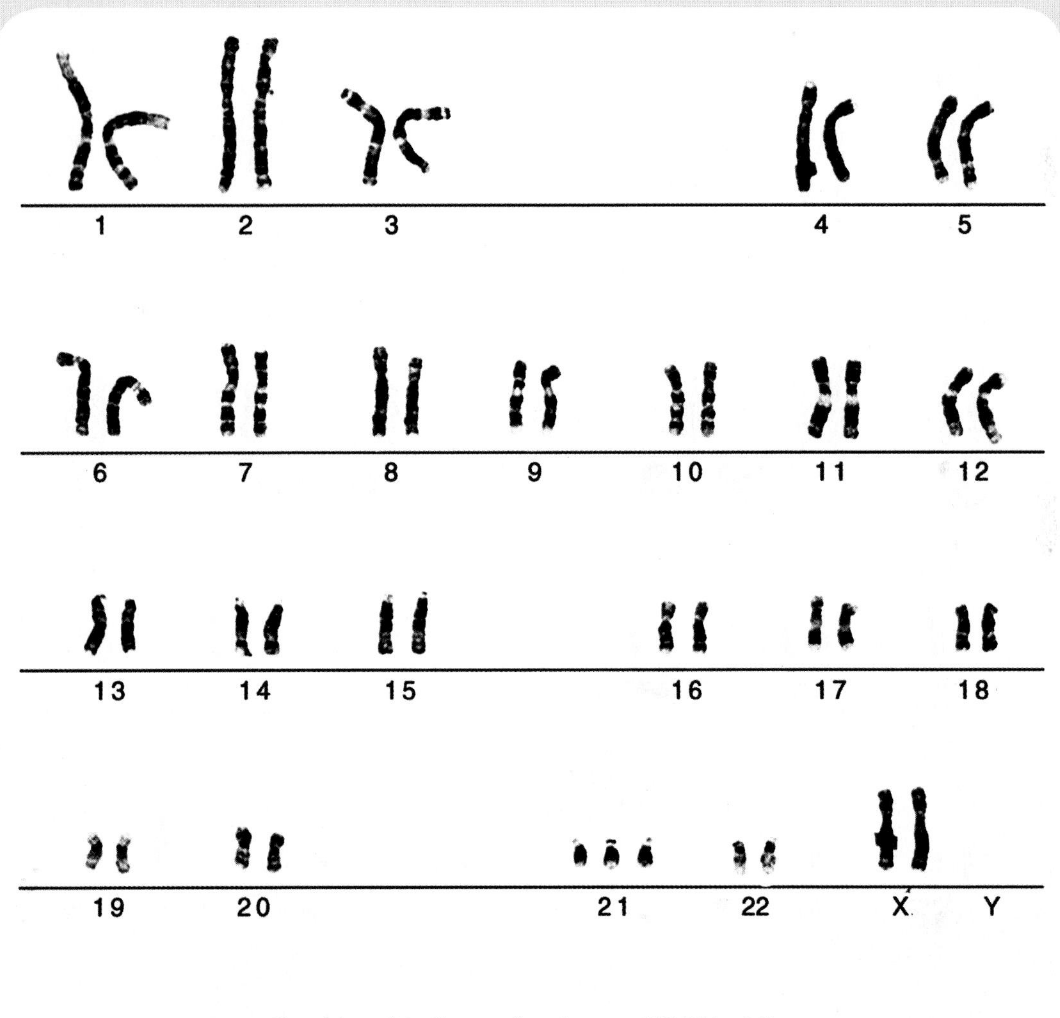

▲ **Karyotype of Down syndrome.** How many chromosomes were present in the gametes that resulted in a cell with 47 chromosomes?

1,000 births worldwide. Extra genetic material is responsible for the characteristics of Down syndrome. The severity varies from individual to individual. People with Down syndrome have some degree of mental retardation, slow physical development, and organ abnormalities. The most common physical features of those with Down syndrome include short stature, low muscle tone, and altered facial features. Often, males with Down syndrome are sterile but females may be fertile.

Turner's syndrome occurs when chromosomes fail to separate during meiosis. Normally, chromosome pairs separate before cell division. Occasionally, the two X chromosomes do not separate and eggs are produced with either two X chromosomes or no X chromosomes,

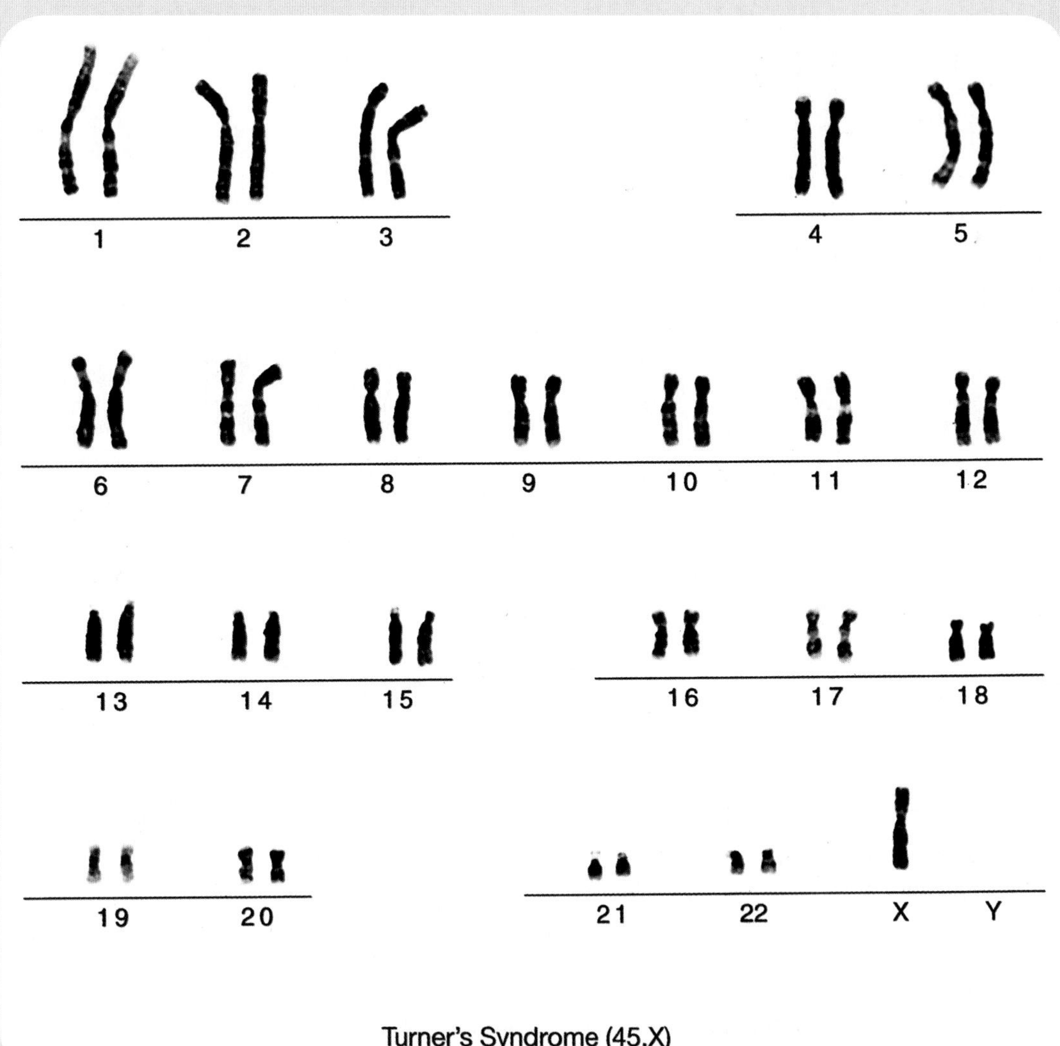

Karyotype of Turner's syndrome. How many chromosomes would be present in a gamete that results in Turner's syndrome?

instead of the normal one X chromosome in an egg. Individuals with Turner's syndrome are born with only one X chromosome, but no second X or Y chromosome.

Turner's syndrome affects approximately 1 out of every 2,500 female live births worldwide. As with Down syndrome, some individuals with Turner's syndrome may have only a few characteristics of the syndrome. Others may have many. Almost all people with Turner's syndrome have short stature and loss of ovarian function, making them sterile, but the severity of these problems varies considerably among individuals. In general, individuals with Turner's syndrome have normal intelligence. This characteristic is different from many other chromosomal syndromes, such as Down syndrome.

You will notice that the chromosomes affected in these instances involve chromosomes that are small. Individuals with too many or too few chromosomes (**aneuploidy**) of the larger pairs likely will not survive. That is because there is a great deal of genetic information in the larger pairs. Many individuals with aneuploidy of the sex chromosomes do not suffer from significant detrimental effects because there is less genetic information on the sex chromosomes than on the others. However, people with aneuploidy of the sex chromosomes are often sterile. If their condition is not severe, people with aneuploidy often lead full and productive lives.

All about Alleles

EXPLAIN

You have learned that an organism's traits are determined by the genes it carries on its chromosomes. You also know how organisms are able to pass their genes from one generation to the next. Even though you have an understanding of how traits are inherited, you still might wonder why some people in a family have a trait while others do not. Much of what we know about human genetics is used to predict what traits we will inherit.

In *All about Alleles*, you will work alone to learn how the traits of offspring can be predicted. Then you will work with a partner to piece together the complicated process of heredity by simulating the inheritance of traits through two generations.

Part I: Punnett Squares

Mendel knew what traits his true-breeding pea plants carried. Do you think he might have been able to predict what traits the offspring from a cross would carry? In this part of the activity, you will learn how predictions can be made.

Materials

none

Process and Procedure

1. Read the following paragraph to learn about one of the tools scientists use to make predictions about the traits of offspring.

   Punnett squares are a mathematical tool that provides a way to predict all the possible outcomes for combining alleles from parents in a cross. When you predict something, you make a statement that something will or will not happen with a certain amount of confidence. In the study of heredity, this type of prediction is expressed in terms of **probability**. Probability is an area in mathematics that predicts the chances that a certain event will occur. Geneticists use probability to predict the outcomes of matings.

2. Set up a Punnett square that you can use to predict the results of a cross between a tall heterozygous (hybrid) garden pea plant and a short homozygous recessive garden pea plant. The tall allele is dominant over the short allele. To do this, do the following.

   a. Sketch a Punnett square like the one shown in figure 7.21 in your science notebook.

   b. Determine the alleles of each parent (a tall and a short pea plant) using the information provided about the parent plants.

   c. Write the alleles of one parent across the top of your Punnett square and the alleles of the other parent along the left side of your Punnett square. Make sure you write only 1 allele next to each box.

   Only 1 letter goes above or to the left of each box. It does not matter which parent is on the side or the top of the Punnett square.

▲ **Figure 7.21 Punnett square.** A Punnett square looks similar to a windowpane.

3. Determine the alleles of the offspring by taking each allele from the parent column and combining it with an allele from the parent row in the corresponding square, as shown in figure 7.22. Remember that each parent contributes 1 allele for each trait to the offspring.

The predicted alleles of the offspring are the likely outcome of a cross of a tall and a short pea plant, not the actual outcome.

4. Answer the following questions about your Punnett square for each phenotype.

   What fraction of the offspring would you predict to have each of the following phenotypes? Record your response in your science notebook as a percentage or as a ratio, such as 1:2.

   a. The dominant phenotype for height

   b. The recessive phenotype for height

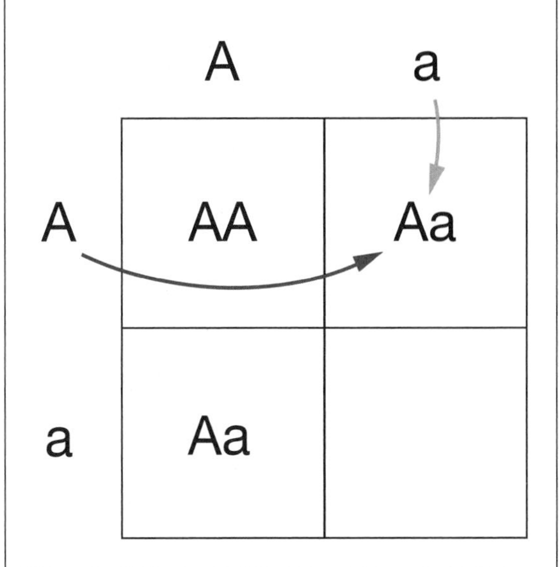

Figure 7.22 Filling in a Punnett square. In this example, both parents are heterozygous. They both carry a dominant and a recessive allele (Aa) for a trait. Complete the Punnett square by taking an allele from the top and combining it with an allele from the left. What alleles will the offspring represented by the lower left box have?

Stop & THINK

PART I

Work on the following tasks on your own and record your answers in your science notebook.

1. Think back to the yeast experiment you conducted. How could you have used a Punnett square to predict the outcome of your experiment? Explain your answer and draw a Punnett square to show the predicted outcomes.

   The yeast experiment was similar to a cross between heterozygous parents. Imagine that strain 2 (red color) and strain 3 (cream color) were different alleles of the color trait.

2. Why do you think a Punnett square is a useful predictive tool? Describe in what way you think the usefulness of a Punnett square might be limited.

Part II: Making a Human

Most traits are the result of the interactions of many genes. Geneticists are still working to understand all the interactions. However, there are a few traits or disorders that are better understood because they are the result of different alleles on a single gene, such as the traits of pea plants that Mendel studied. Traits or disorders that are the result of single genes are sometimes called *Mendelian*. Some human traits, such as dimples, also appear to be the result of a single gene and follow dominant or recessive inheritance patterns. To simplify the study of inheritance patterns, you will work with a partner to investigate some human traits that follow these patterns. If the study of genetics interests you, read the sidebar *Careers in Genetics* to learn about the diverse jobs available in the field of genetics.

Materials

For each student

access to sodium benzoate tasting paper

index cards

1 marker

access to 9 bags of chromosomes (each for a different trait)

Cautions

This activity uses sodium benzoate tasting paper. Although food and drink items should not be allowed in the lab, sodium benzoate is designed for use in the lab to test a genetic trait. Use the paper according to your teacher's instructions and then discard it immediately in a trash can.

Process and Procedure

1. Study figure 7.23, which lists 9 common human traits that seem to follow dominant and recessive inheritance patterns.

Human genetics is very complex and often involves more than 2 alleles for a trait. This activity is simplified, but it will give you an idea of how dominant and recessive patterns of inheritance work.

Trait	Dominant	Recessive
Dimples	Having dimples (DD or Dd)	No dimples (dd)
Ear lobes	Free (EE or Ee)	Attached (ee)
Mid-digit hair	Having mid-digit hair (MM or Mm)	No mid-digit hair (mm)
Freckles	Freckles (FF or Ff)	No freckles (ff)
Number of fingers	6 on each hand (HH or Hh)	5 on each hand (hh)
Chin	Dimple in center cleft (CC or Cc)	No dimple in center (cc)
Taster of Sodium Benzoate	Can taste (TT or Tt)	Cannot taste (tt)
Albinism	Has pigmentation (PP or Pp)	Lacks pigments (pp)
MMD (also called Steinhart's disease)	Having MMD (SS or Ss)	Not having MMD (ss)

▲ **Figure 7.23 Common human traits.** These traits seem to follow dominant and recessive inheritance patterns. What do you notice about the genotypes for dominant traits compared with recessive traits?

2. Answer the following questions about the traits in figure 7.23. Record your answers in your science notebook.
   a. Which of the traits listed in the chart do you have? According to the chart, what are your alleles for each of these traits?

If you have not already done so, obtain sodium benzoate tasting paper from your teacher. Use the paper according to your teacher's instructions to determine whether you have the dominant or recessive trait for tasting sodium benzoate.

   b. Did any of these traits or dominant and recessive patterns surprise you? Why?
3. Simulate with a partner how alleles might separate during meiosis and randomly recombine during fertilization. Steps 3a–c will help guide your work.
   a. Assume the roles of lab technicians who are making a human by uniting a donated sperm and an egg cell in the lab. When this is done to help infertile couples conceive a child, it is known as in vitro fertilization.
   b. Make a data table that looks like figure 7.24 in your science notebook. Title it "First Generation."
   c. Decide which one of you will work with the sperm cell and which one will work with the egg cell.

This is a simulation involving cards that represent alleles. You will not be working with real cells.

Trait	Father's alleles	Father's allele contributed to child	Mother's alleles	Mother's allele contributed to child	Child's alleles	Trait expressed in child
Sex						
Dimples						
Ear lobes						
Mid-digit hair						
Freckles						
Number of fingers						
Chin						
Taster of Sodium Benzoate						
Albinism						
MMD						

▲ **Figure 7.24 First-generation traits.** Use a table similar to this one to record the alleles of the parents and a child.

4. Determine the gender of the new offspring by completing Steps 4a–g.
   a. Use index cards to represent chromosome pairs. Each index card (chromosome pair) carries 2 alleles, 1 for each chromosome.
   b. Obtain an index card to represent each parent.
   c. Label the cards as follows. The technician on your team who works with the female gamete (egg) labels that card with two *X*s for sex chromosomes. The technician on your team who works with the male gamete (sperm) labels one-half of that card with *X* and the other half with *Y*.
   d. Cut the mother's and father's sex chromosomes in half. What does this step represent in the process of meiosis?
   e. Place the sex chromosome cards face down, so that the blank side of the cards faces up.
   f. Shuffle your 2 cards by yourself and randomly choose 1 chromosome without looking. Place it on the table in front of you face down.

Recall from your reading that chromosomes separate randomly during meiosis and might combine during fertilization. In this step, you are simulating how this might happen.

   g. Turn your card and your partner's card over. What sex is the new child? Fill in the information in your data table.

5. Determine the other traits of the child by completing Steps 5a–c. Determining the other traits of the child is a little more difficult because you need to know the alleles of the parent gametes.
   a. Draw a chromosome pair from the teacher's bag of cards to learn what alleles each parent carries for dimples. Each chromosome carries 1 allele.

The technician working with the sperm cell draws the chromosome pair for the father. The technician working with the egg cell draws the chromosome pair for the mother. Each technician keeps his or her own chromosome pair.

   b. Fill in this information for the mother's and father's alleles in your data table.
   c. Repeat Steps 5a–b for the remaining traits.
6. How will you know which alleles are passed on to the child? Recall that humans have pairs of chromosomes and they receive 1 chromosome of each pair from their mother and the other from their father. Complete the following tasks to find out.
   a. Cut the father's and mother's chromosome pairs for dimples in half. What does this step represent in the process of meiosis?
   b. Turn upside down your pair of chromosomes that carries the alleles for dimples, so that you cannot see the alleles. Shuffle them as you did for the sex chromosomes. Randomly choose an allele and place it face down on the table in front of you.
   c. Turn over the cards after both technicians have contributed an allele for dimples. Record the allele for dimples that is contributed from each parent in your data table.
   d. Combine the 2 contributed alleles in the column labeled "Child's Alleles." This step simulates the chromosomes coming together during fertilization.
   e. Begin a stack of cards that represents the child's chromosomes. Place the "unused" alleles in another stack and put them aside.
   f. Repeat Steps 6a–e for the remaining traits. When you are finished, you should have 1 pile of chromosome cards on the desk that represents all the alleles of the offspring.
7. Use the information in figure 7.24 to determine the traits the child expresses based on his or her allele pairs. Record the traits, such as dimples or no dimples, in your data table.

Congratulations! You have made a new human being.

8. Place the chromosomes not used in a stack and put them aside. Keep the chromosomes of the child in a stack. You will follow them into the next generation.

9. Determine the traits for a second-generation child by doing the following.
   a. Gather the first-generation child's chromosomes and separate them into their chromosome pairs.
   b. Find another team that has a child with the opposite sex of your team's child. Ask your teacher for help if you cannot find a child of the opposite sex.
   c. Pretend the in vitro child has grown up and is married to the other team's child. The two are now going to have a child.
   d. Make another data table in your notebook like figure 7.24. Title it "Second Generation."
   e. You already know the alleles that each parent has for each trait. Record this information in your second-generation data chart.
   f. Starting with the sex chromosomes, and using the chromosomes from each team's children, repeat the procedure you followed for the first in vitro child. With the cards face down, shuffle the chromosome pairs and randomly choose 1 chromosome from each pair. Look at the resulting pair of chromosomes and record them on your data table.
   g. Complete the remainder of your data table to determine the traits of the second-generation child.

Reflect and Connect

Work on your own to answer the following questions in your science notebook. Be prepared to share your understanding with your classmates.

1. Draw a picture of the second-generation child from Part II that shows off his or her traits. Label the traits he or she carries, including those that are not apparent.

2. Outline the steps of the simulation and describe how they simulated the processes of meiosis and fertilization.
3. Compare the simulation with what actually happens during meiosis in humans.

Think about the number of chromosomes (autosomes and sex chromosomes) in the simulation compared with the number of chromosomes in the human body.

4. If the mother of "Afraid and Wanting to Know More" from the engage activity earlier in this chapter does not have MMD, what are the chances that "Afraid and Wanting to Know More" has the disorder? Draw a Punnett square from this investigation that shows how you arrived at your answer.

Refer back to figure 7.23 if you do not remember what the alleles are for a person who has or does not have MMD.

SIDEBAR

Careers in Genetics

Do you find genetics interesting? If you do, many career options exist in a variety of areas such as medicine, pharmaceuticals, law, agriculture, and business. Depending on what career you are interested in you need different kinds of training.

Medical technicians are sometimes involved in the field of genetics. For example, technicians called phlebotomists collect blood samples from patients, which can be used for genetic testing. Technicians generally have an associate's degree from a community college or a certificate from a hospital or technical school. Medical technicians need to have good eyesight, steady hands, and the ability to follow procedures accurately.

Forensic science technicians examine biological evidence from crime scenes to identify individuals. They also provide testimony on laboratory findings for criminal cases. Forensic science technicians generally have either an associate's degree or a bachelor's degree.

Genetics technologists study the morphology or structure of chromosomes and their relationship to disease. A technologist prepares cell samples for analysis. Genetics technologists analyze the samples using microscopes and computer image analysis. An important part of their job is generating reports that outline the results from their analysis. Technologists usually have a bachelor's degree with a major in medical technology or one of the life sciences.

Remember "Afraid and Wanting to Know More" from the first activity? He wrote to a genetic counselor about his concerns regarding a genetic disorder he might have inherited from his father. Genetic counselors try to help people make sense of what scientists know about genetic disorders. They look at an individual's family history, interpret information about a disorder, explain the inheritance patterns (see photo), and review the options for genetic testing. They also help individuals and families cope with changes to their life that may occur after learning test results. Genetic counseling is a good career if you are interested in genetics but would also like to interact with people. In the future, jobs in genetic counseling may become more common as the use of genetic testing increases. Genetic counselors must have a master's degree in genetic counseling.

The business world requires people with an understanding of genetics as well. With a bachelor's degree in a biological science, you can work in a variety of areas such as management, marketing, writing, sales, and public relations. Many agricultural, biotechnology, and pharmaceutical companies need individuals with an understanding of genetics to help them better market and sell their products. For example, agricultural companies might want to sell seeds for a new corn plant that is drought resistant. Some lawyers also need to be familiar with genetics. Ethical and legal issues associated with genetics arise and require the expertise of lawyers. Patent lawyers also are important for determining intellectual property such as new processes or products developed by genetics researchers.

If you would like to conduct research to understand genetic disorders and improve human health, you might be interested in becoming a medical scientist. They work in government, private company, or university laboratories exploring new areas of research. For example, a new field in the drug industry is pharmacogentics. Pharmacogentics is the study of how genes influence an individual's response to drugs. Individuals respond to the same drugs and dosages in different ways because of genetic variations among the human population. Scientists working in this field research how medications can be adjusted based on genetic factors. Medical scientists require a doctor's degree (PhD) in a life science to gain the skills necessary to direct research programs. Often medical scientists have a medical degree as well. A medical degree is necessary if the scientist will interact directly with patients. For example, a medical scientist might need to dispense gene therapy or perform procedures to remove tissue.

Many jobs are available in the field of genetics. The education required to enter this field varies depending on the job. Some require a doctor's degree, but many jobs are available for individuals with an associates or bachelor's degree. No matter what career route you choose, a good background in math and science during high school is important for working in the field of genetics.

SCILINKS® NSTA
Topic: genetic counseling
Go to: www.scilinks.org
Code: 2Inquiry378

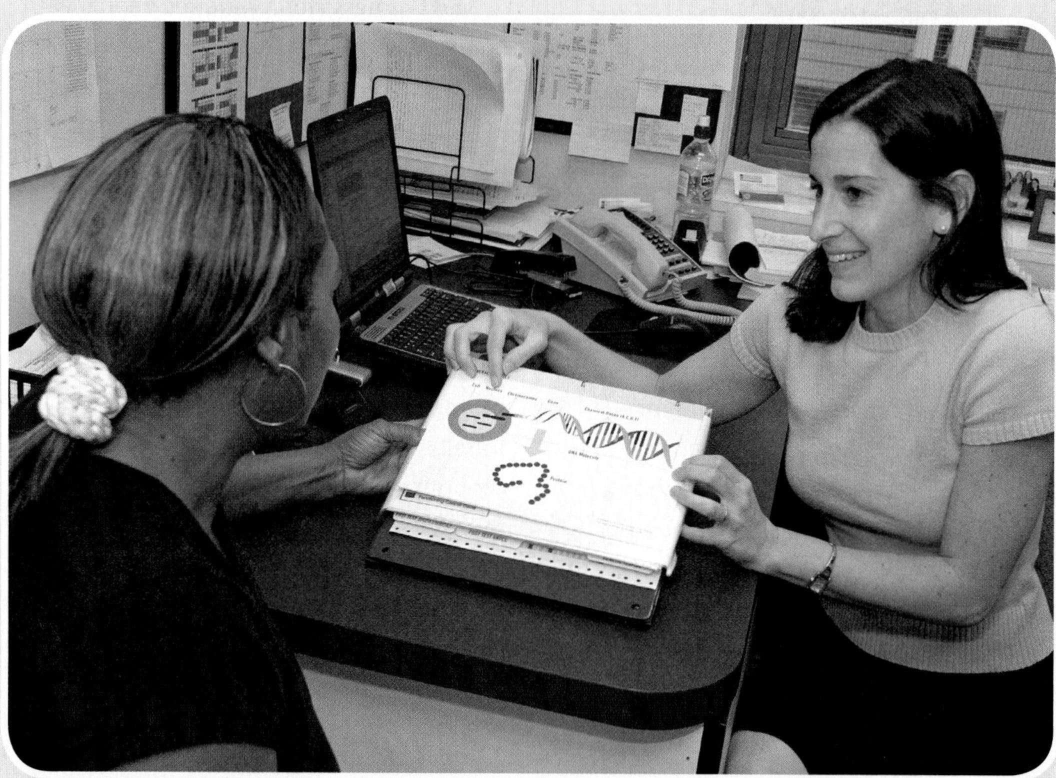

▲ **Genetic counselor.** Genetic counselors describe the genetic disorder and how it is inherited and help an individual decide if he or she wants to be tested for the disorder.

Inheritance Patterns

ELABORATE

Observing patterns is an important part of science. By making many observations, scientists have noticed patterns among family members and their ancestors. By continuing to look at these patterns, scientists now have a better understanding of inheritance. In the previous activities, you observed how traits are passed from one generation to the next. You also learned that tools such as Punnett squares are used to make predictions about the traits that will be inherited. Another tool used by geneticists is a pedigree. In this activity, you will work with a partner to use pedigrees to help you identify patterns of inheritance and make predictions based on these patterns.

Part I: Interpreting a Pedigree

In Part I, you will look at a new tool, called a pedigree, and begin to understand how certain traits follow patterns. You will then be able to apply this knowledge to create a pedigree in Part II.

Materials

For each student

1 *Pedigree* handout

Process and Procedure

1. Read the following 2 paragraphs and check your understanding of inheritance and pedigrees with your partner.

   Inheritance is the process through which characteristics of an organism are passed from one generation to the next. "Afraid and Wanting to Know More" from the engage activity was concerned that he had inherited MMD. A disorder is genetically linked, which means that it can be inherited, when the trait can be passed from one generation to the next by a specific gene or set of genes. If a pattern of inheritance is determined for a disorder, this information can be used to predict the risk of future generations inheriting the disorder.

   One way to determine the pattern of inheritance for a disorder is to look at its occurrence within a family across multiple generations. The information is drawn up using a tool called a pedigree. Geneticists use pedigrees to study the inheritance of genes in humans. A **pedigree** is very similar to a family tree, except that a pedigree is a tool that is used to follow a trait through multiple generations of a family. You also might be familiar with the use of pedigrees by dog or horse breeders. Figure 7.25 shows an example of a dog pedigree and a family tree.

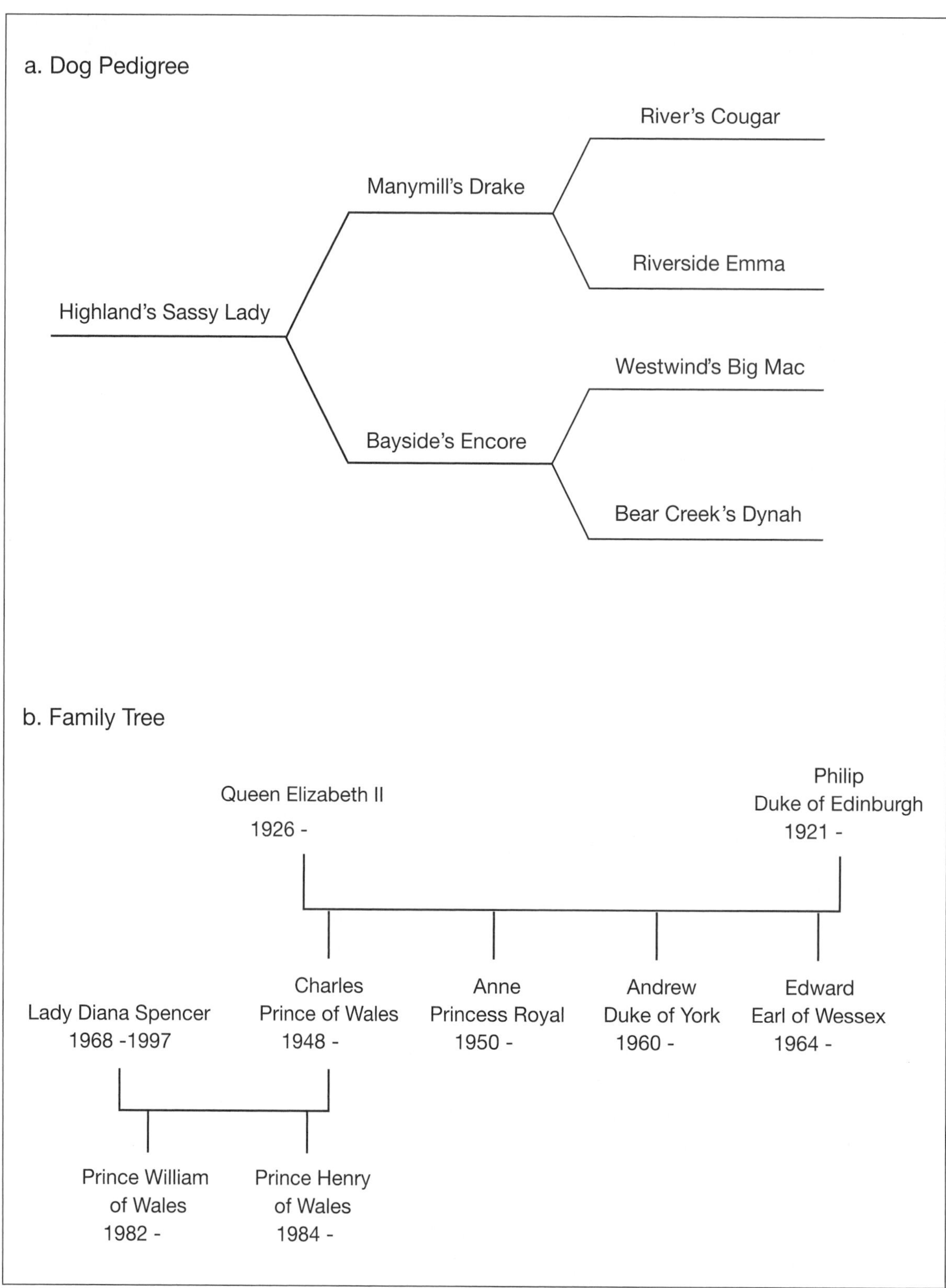

▲ **Figure 7.25 Dog pedigree and family tree.** (a) Dog pedigrees show the male's name on the top part of the branches. Females are shown on the bottom part of the branches. You might notice that dogs are often given unusual names that include the name of the kennel that owns the dog. (b) Family trees, such as this one shown of the British royal family, often show the birth and death dates for each of the individuals on the tree. Notice that the pedigree and the family tree do not have information about genetics.

	Male	Female		
Unaffected	□	○	□—○	Mating
Affected	■	●		1st generation
Carrier	◧	◐		2nd generation

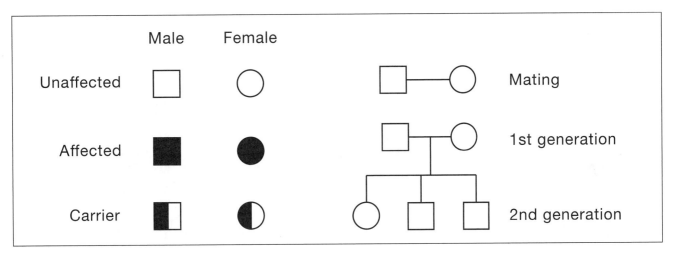

▲ **Figure 7.26 Symbols used in pedigrees.** Pedigrees make it easier to look at the occurrence of a trait within a family. The trait might be a physical characteristic such as eye color, or the trait might be a disease. Unaffected individuals do not express the trait. Affected individuals express the trait. Carriers carry the trait, but do not express the trait. A horizontal line between a circle and a square indicates mating; vertical lines indicate the children from the mating.

2. Study figure 7.26 to learn what each of the symbols used in a pedigree represents. You will use this information to interpret pedigrees in the steps that follow.
3. Study the pedigrees shown in figure 7.27. Do you notice any patterns? Describe patterns that you observe in the way the trait is passed to each generation. Record your ideas in your science notebook.
4. Read the following descriptions and decide which of the pedigrees from figure 7.27 shows the inheritance pattern for the following.
   a. A sex-linked trait
   b. An autosomal dominant trait
   c. An autosomal recessive trait

Use what you know about dominant and recessive traits. Which of the traits in Mendel's experiments skipped a generation: the dominant trait or the recessive trait?

Some traits are **sex linked**. A sex-linked trait is carried on one of the sex chromosomes. A common sex-linked (in this case, X-linked) trait is color blindness. The gene for color blindness is carried on the X chromosome, but not the Y chromosome. Most sex-linked traits are located on the X chromosome. The X chromosome is longer and holds more genes than the Y chromosome. Recall from reading about meiosis that 22 of the 23 pairs of human chromosomes are called autosomes. Autosomal traits are carried on any chromosome other than a sex chromosome. Traits can be **autosomal dominant** or **autosomal recessive**.

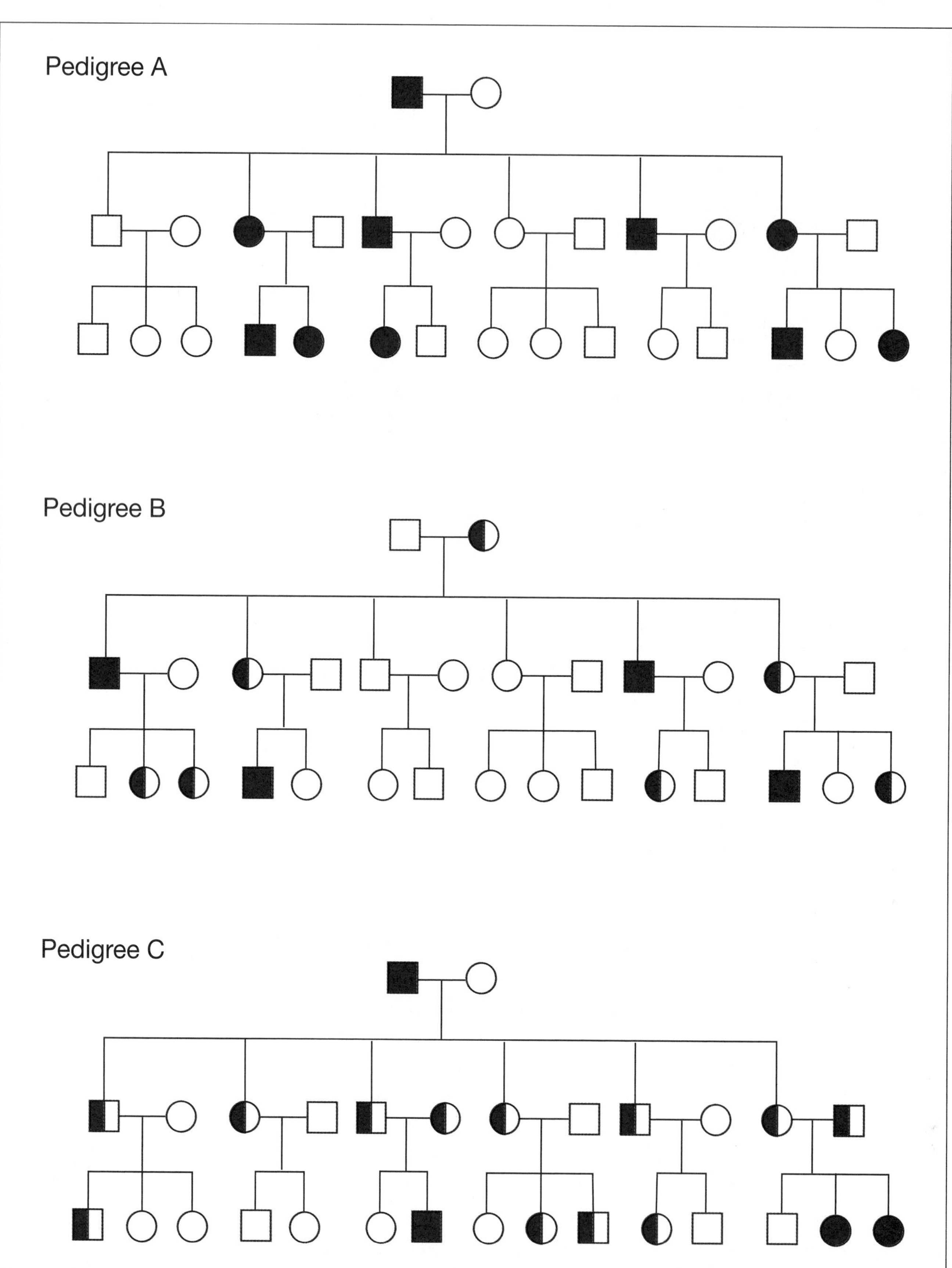

▲ **Figure 7.27 Pedigrees A, B, and C.** This figure illustrates three different inheritance patterns. Can you find the pattern?

5. Read the following paragraph to learn how to represent the allele for a sex-linked recessive trait.

   You just learned that some traits are carried on one of the sex chromosomes. Most of these traits are **X-linked recessive,** like color blindness discussed in the previous step. One example of a sex-linked trait is fruit fly eye color. The eye color gene for fruit flies is carried on the X chromosome, making it an X-linked trait. The X chromosome carrying a dominant red eye allele is symbolized by X^R. If the X chromosome carries the recessive white eye allele, it is symbolized by X^r. Study figure 7.28 to learn which genotypes have the red eye trait and which genotypes have the white eye trait.

6. Answer the following questions about sex-linked recessive traits.
   a. Why do you think the male fruit fly with the genotype X^rY has white eyes?
   b. What genotype do you think a female fruit fly would have if she had white eyes?
   c. Why do you think eye color in fruit flies is called an X-linked recessive trait?

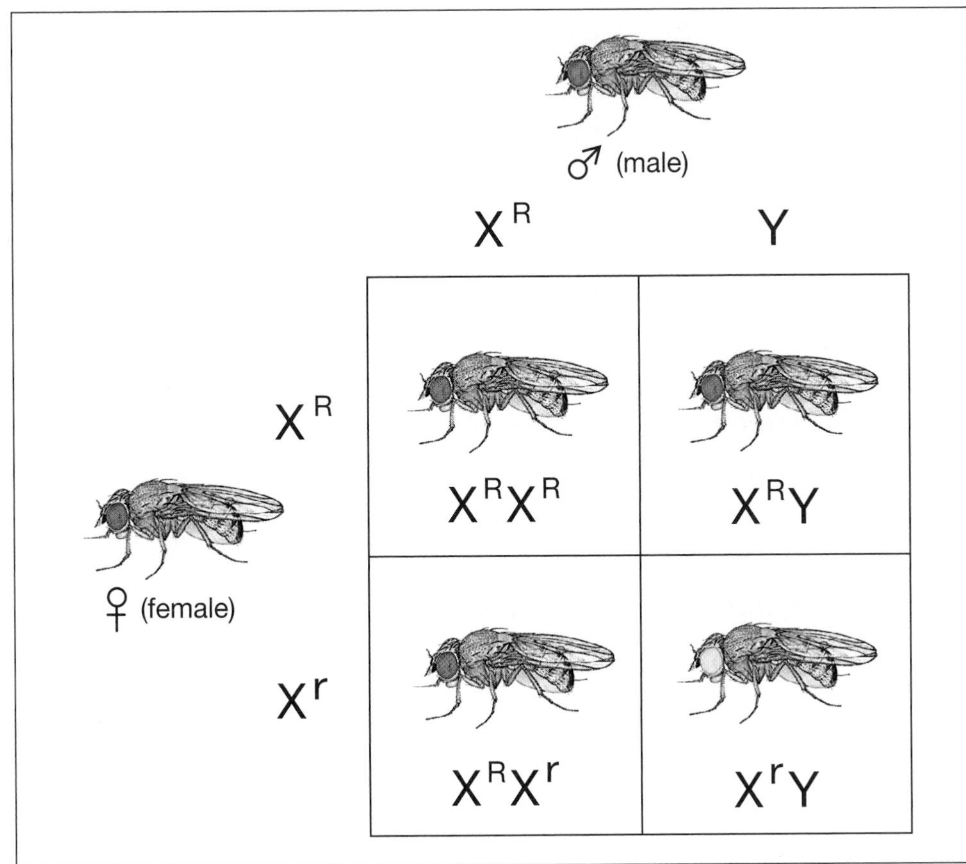

Figure 7.28 Fruit fly Punnett square. Eye color in fruit flies is an X-linked trait. The X chromosome carries the allele for eye color.

7. Study the inheritance patterns in the *Pedigree* handout. Use the information provided to do Steps 7a–c.
   a. Find the characteristics described for each inheritance pattern.
   b. Make notes on the handout indicating each characteristic.
   c. Label the alleles of each individual on the pedigree. For simplicity, use *A* and *a* as the alleles.
8. With a partner, use the handout and what you already know about inheritance to decide if each statement describes an autosomal dominant, autosomal recessive, or sex-linked recessive pattern. Some might describe more than 1 pattern. Record your answers in your science notebook.
   a. Brothers and sisters are equally likely to have the trait.
   b. Family members from all generations have the trait.
   c. The trait can be inherited from either parent.
   d. Men in the family are more likely to have the trait.
   e. The trait might appear in offspring without appearing in their parents.

Stop & THINK

PART I

1. What are some differences between the patterns of sex-linked traits and those of autosomal traits?
2. What are some differences between dominant and recessive trait patterns?
3. Create a Punnett square for fruit flies where the parents' genotypes are X^RY and $X^r X^r$ and answer the following questions.
   a. What are the possible genotypes?
   b. What is the phenotype for each genotype?
   c. What is the probability of each genotype occurring?
4. Explain why a person with two dominant alleles cannot be a carrier.

Part II: Making a Pedigree

In Part II of this investigation, you will apply your understanding of alleles and pedigrees to make your own pedigree.

Materials

none

Process and Procedure

SCiLINKS
NSTA
Topic: dominant and recessive traits
Go to: www.scilinks.org
Code: 2Inquiry385

1. Read the following story about Ben, a high school student who finds out that he has inherited a genetic disorder.

   During his senior year of high school, Ben started weighing his options for life after graduation. First Ben thought about finding a job. Then he decided to check the possibility of attending college. Ben applied to a variety of colleges throughout the United States. As Ben began receiving acceptance letters in the mail, he was not satisfied with any of his choices.

   Eventually, he decided to take advantage of his excellent grades and pursue a passion for flying. Ben visited and applied to the U.S. Air Force Academy.

   Ben was accepted into the academy but he still needed to pass one more test: a full physical exam. He passed the physical without any problems except for the eye exam. It turned out that Ben's eyesight was fabulous. The problem was his ability to distinguish between colors. What appears red and green to many of us does not appear the same to Ben.

   Ben already had a private flying license and had been flying for 2 years. Ben can still fly airplanes privately, but he cannot enter the Air Force Academy. Ben's mother remembered that Ben's cousin Chris had experienced the same type of disappointment as a young adult. Ben contacted Chris and found that he, too, was accepted to the academy but could not pass the eye exam. Instead, he attended college and became a successful software designer.

   In the end, Ben decided to attend Michigan Tech. Even though it was not his first choice, Ben was excited to move to the dorms and study aeronautical engineering.

   The genetic disorder that both Ben and Chris exhibit is red-green color blindness. The phenotype, or observable trait, of color blindness is the inability to distinguish the colors red and green. People with red-green color blindness also do not see as well at night as those individuals without red-green color blindness.

2. Draw Ben's pedigree showing 3 generations. Ben and his cousin Chris will be the third generation and their grandparents will be the first generation. Use the following information (and information from the story) in your diagram.
   - A first-generation male is color blind.
   - There are 3 daughters and 1 son in the second generation; all are married.
   - Two of the second-generation daughters have 2 children (1 girl and 1 boy) and 1 daughter has 3 children (2 boys and 1 girl).
   - The second-generation son has 4 children (2 boys and 2 girls).
   - Ben and Chris, the third generation, are both descendants of daughters in the second generation.
   - Label Ben and Chris on your diagram.
   - Label each person on the pedigree with the alleles that he or she is likely to carry for color blindness.
3. Determine the probably that Ben was going to inherit the color-blindness trait. Assume that his father was not color blind. Draw a Punnett square with Ben's parents and explain how likely his parents were to have a boy with color blindness.

Using a Punnett square when creating a pedigree can help determine all the possible traits offspring might have or carry.

Reflect and Connect

Discuss the following questions with your teammate. Record your answers in your science notebook.

1. Why are pedigrees useful tools to illustrate inheritance patterns?
2. What pattern of inheritance did you draw for Ben and Chris's family? Explain why you say this.
3. From Part II of the explain activity *All about Alleles*, construct a pedigree for your team's in vitro child, following the patterns of inheritance for dimples. Start from the original parents and label the alleles for dimples next to each individual. On that same pedigree, follow the pattern for color blindness. Label the alleles for color blindness next to each individual.

Passing Genes—Who Gets What?

EVALUATE

Throughout this chapter, you have been exploring the inheritance of traits. You observed the traits of two generations of yeast. Then you learned that traits are inherited through the process of meiosis. You modeled meiosis using play dough and the inheritance of alleles for a hypothetical child. You have also used Punnett squares and pedigrees to illustrate how alleles are inherited by family members. All these experiences have contributed to your understanding of inheritance and meiosis. In *Passing Genes—Who Gets What?*, you will work individually and with a partner to demonstrate your understanding of inheritance and meiosis. You will do this by interpreting the inheritance pattern of a genetic disorder and creating a pedigree that shows the inheritance of the disorder.

Materials

For each team of 2 students

current resources

plain paper

access to the "gene pool"

ruler

markers

2 *Passing on Genes—Who Gets What? Scoring Rubric* handouts

Process and Procedure

What if there was a genetic disorder in your family? What inheritance patterns could you figure out if you understood the disorder? In this evaluate activity, you will have the opportunity to demonstrate what you know about inheritance by tracing a specific disorder through several generations.

1. Review the *Passing on Genes Scoring Rubric* handout so that you learn the expectations for this activity.
2. Imagine that you and your partner are siblings. You have just learned that a third sibling has been diagnosed with a genetic disorder.
   a. Select a genetic disorder from the container provided by your teacher to find out which disorder your sibling has.
   b. Do you already know something about the disorder you selected? What are some questions you have about the disorder? Record your ideas in your science notebook.

3. Obtain information about the genetic disorder your sibling has from your teacher.
    a. Look for the following information:
        - The cause of the disorder
        - The symptoms, effects, and possible cures
        - The inheritance pattern
    b. Record your findings in your science notebook. Make sure you take notes on your own because you will be using them to complete the next steps.
4. Work with your partner to decide the sex of your sibling. Justify your decision with the information you learned about the genetic disorder in Step 3.

Use what you know about the inheritance pattern of the disorder. For some disorders, the alleles of individuals with the disorder are different depending on gender.

5. Determine the alleles for you and your sibling's mates by doing these things.
    a. Go to your teacher's "gene pool" and draw a pair of alleles. This will be your mate's alleles for the trait. You and your partner will draw for your mates. If necessary, draw a pair of alleles for your sibling's mate.

Your teacher will provide the gene pool. Before drawing a pair of alleles for your sibling, think about the symptoms of your sibling's disorder. Is your sibling expected to survive to a reproductive age? Is drawing for his or her mate appropriate?

    b. Record the alleles of your mate, your partner's mate, and your sibling's mate, if appropriate, in your science notebook. Then return the alleles to the gene pool.
    c. Work with your partner and decide what you and your partner's alleles are. Use what you have learned in the chapter and the information provided about your sibling's disorder to help you decide.

Make sure you have recorded the alleles for you, your siblings, and their mates. You will use this information in the next step.

    d. Record the alleles of you and your partner in your science notebook.
6. Work individually to create a pedigree of your hypothetical family.
    a. Use what you know about your sibling's disorder and the alleles of the rest of the family members to determine how the disorder could be inherited through 3 generations.

b. Include your parents (first generation); you, your mate, your partner and mate, and your affected sibling and mate (second generation); and a third generation based on the couples' alleles.

c. Generate as many offspring from each couple as you choose to.

7. Label the alleles for *all* the individuals on the pedigree after you have all 3 generations drawn for your pedigree. For the sake of consistency, use the letters *A* and *a* to represent the alleles.

8. Write a paragraph that describes how one of the offspring in the third generation got his or her alleles. Include in your description what determines the sex of the offspring and the number of chromosomes (autosomes and sex chromosomes) found in the cells of most humans. Include the following words in your description:
   - *Meiosis*
   - *Gametes*
   - *Chromosomes*
   - *Genes*
   - *Alleles*

9. Briefly describe the importance of meiosis. Include information about the amount of genetic information passed from each parent to the offspring.

CHAPTER 8

Instructions for Life

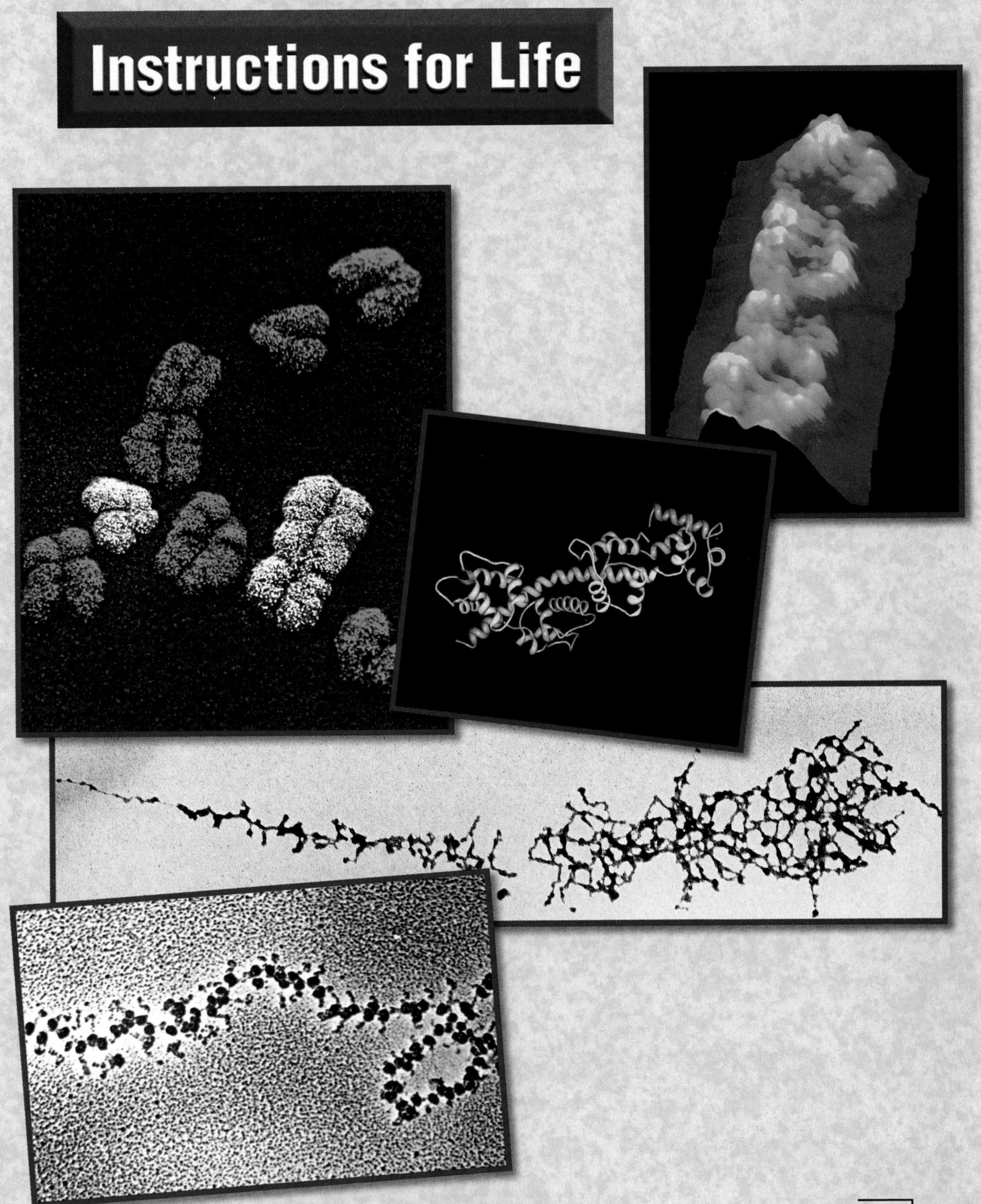

Instructions for Life

In chapter 7, *Tracking Traits*, you learned that chromosomes carry traits from one generation to the next. What is so special about chromosomes, and how do they carry all this information with them? How can chromosomes instruct an organism to have certain characteristics? How do organisms that do not have chromosomes, such as bacteria, pass genetic information to their offspring?

In chapter 8, *Instructions for Life*, you will learn about the molecule in the chromosomes that gives organisms their traits. This molecule is capable of storing and carrying genetic information whether it is packaged in chromosomes or not. You will learn what information is stored in this molecule and how it is stored. You will begin your investigation of this molecule by extracting it from living cells. Then you will explore the structure of this molecule. You will learn the significance of the code in this molecule and how this code contains the instructions for life. The structure of this molecule is the same for all organisms, yet the code can change, giving rise to changes in organisms. Scientists use this code as evidence to support the theory of evolution. When you finish this chapter, you will have extensive knowledge about this molecule. You will share your knowledge in the evaluate activity by educating someone else about this important molecule.

Goals for the Chapter

In chapter 8, you will learn about the genetic code that carries the instructions for life. You will learn how this code is passed from one generation to another, and you also will learn how the instructions code for proteins. By the end of this chapter, you will be able to answer the following questions:

- What is the code found in all living things and what is it composed of?
- How are genes and chromosomes related to the code?
- How does the code pass its information to newly formed cells?

- How does the code synthesize proteins?
- Why are proteins essential for life?
- How do mutations in the code affect individuals and populations?
- How can the code serve as evidence for evolution?

You will be better able to answer these questions by participating in the following activities:

ENGAGE	Just the Fax
EXPLORE	What Is This Stuff?
EXPLAIN	Clips of DNA
EXPLAIN	Words to Live By
EXPLAIN	Transcription and Translation—the Road to Making Proteins
ELABORATE	Nobody's Perfect
ELABORATE	DNA and Evolution
EVALUATE	Sharing Your Knowledge

Use the chapter organizer to think about what you will learn today and where you are headed. It will help you map your learning about the genetic code.

Instructions for Life

Engage

Just the Fax

Key Idea:
Codes can carry a lot of information.

Linking Question

How can you extract the substance that makes up the chromosomes and carries the code of life?

Explore

What Is This Stuff?

Key Idea:
The same substance can be extracted from three different organisms.

Linking Question

What is DNA made of and how is it inherited?

Explain

Clips of DNA

Key Ideas:
- DNA is a long chain of repeating subunits called nucleotides.
- Copies of DNA are made through DNA replication.
- DNA replication is important in mitosis and meiosis.

Linking Question

What is significant about the words from the *Just the Fax* activity and how are they related to DNA?

Explain

Words to Live By

Key Idea:
Proteins are essential for life.

Linking Question

How does DNA store the information that directs protein production?

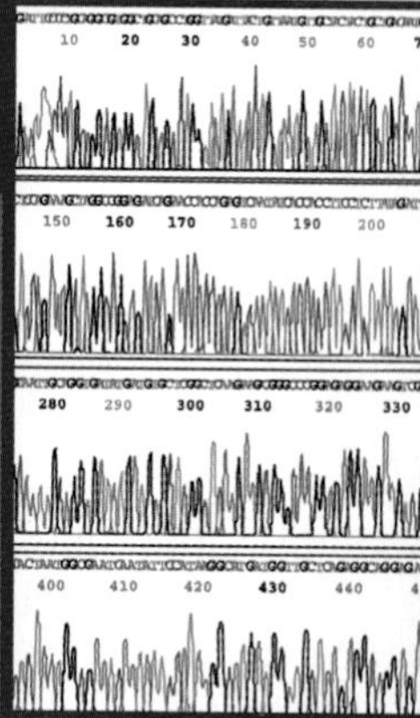

EVALUATE

Sharing Your Knowledge

Key Ideas:
- DNA is the genetic code for all living things.
- DNA replicates to transmit genetic information to newly formed cells.
- DNA serves as a template for making proteins.
- Mutations in DNA result in changes in proteins.

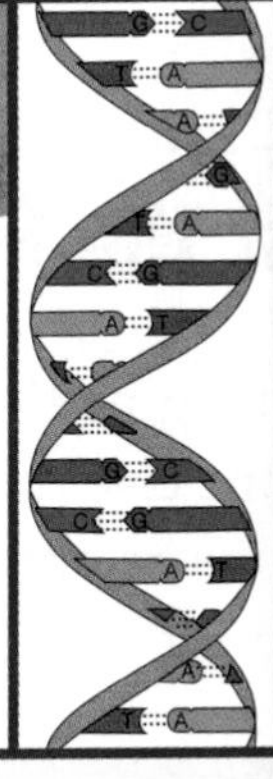

Linking Question

How can I use what I have learned to demonstrate my understanding of DNA?

ELABORATE

DNA and Evolution

Key Ideas:
- DNA can be used to determine the relatedness of organisms.
- DNA can be used as evidence to support theories of evolution.

Linking Question

How do scientists know how similar the genetic code is among different organisms?

ELABORATE

Nobody's Perfect

Key Ideas:
- Mutations can be beneficial, detrimental, or neutral to organisms
- Mutations lead to variability in populations.

CHAPTER 8

Major Concepts

- **DNA is found in all living things and carries the genetic code for their characteristics.**
- **DNA can replicate to pass its genetic information to newly formed cells.**
- **DNA serves as a template for making proteins.**
- **Proteins are substances essential to life.**
- **Mutations in DNA result in changes in proteins that can be advantageous, detrimental, or neutral (have no effect) to individual organisms and their species.**
- **Similarities in DNA show relatedness of organisms.**

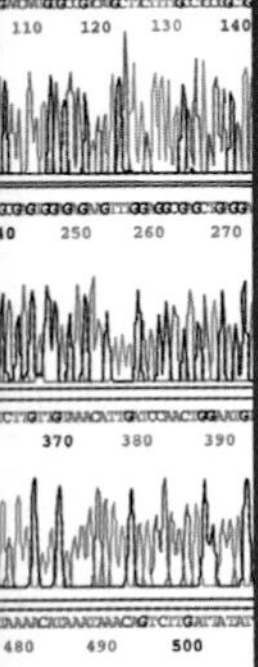

EXPLAIN

Transcription and Translation—the Road to Making Proteins

Key Ideas:
- Protein synthesis occurs through a two part process that involves transcription and translation.
- During transcription, part of a DNA sequence is copied into a complementary sequence of mRNA.
- During translation, the information on mRNA is converted to form a long protein chain.

Linking Question

What happens if a mistake occurs during DNA replication, transcription, or translation?

ENGAGE

Just the Fax

Imagine that you want to send a note to a friend but you don't want anyone else to know what it says. What could you do? One of your options might be to write the note using a code. People use codes quite often for many different reasons. You might be surprised at where we find codes. Figure 8.1 shows some common examples of how people use codes.

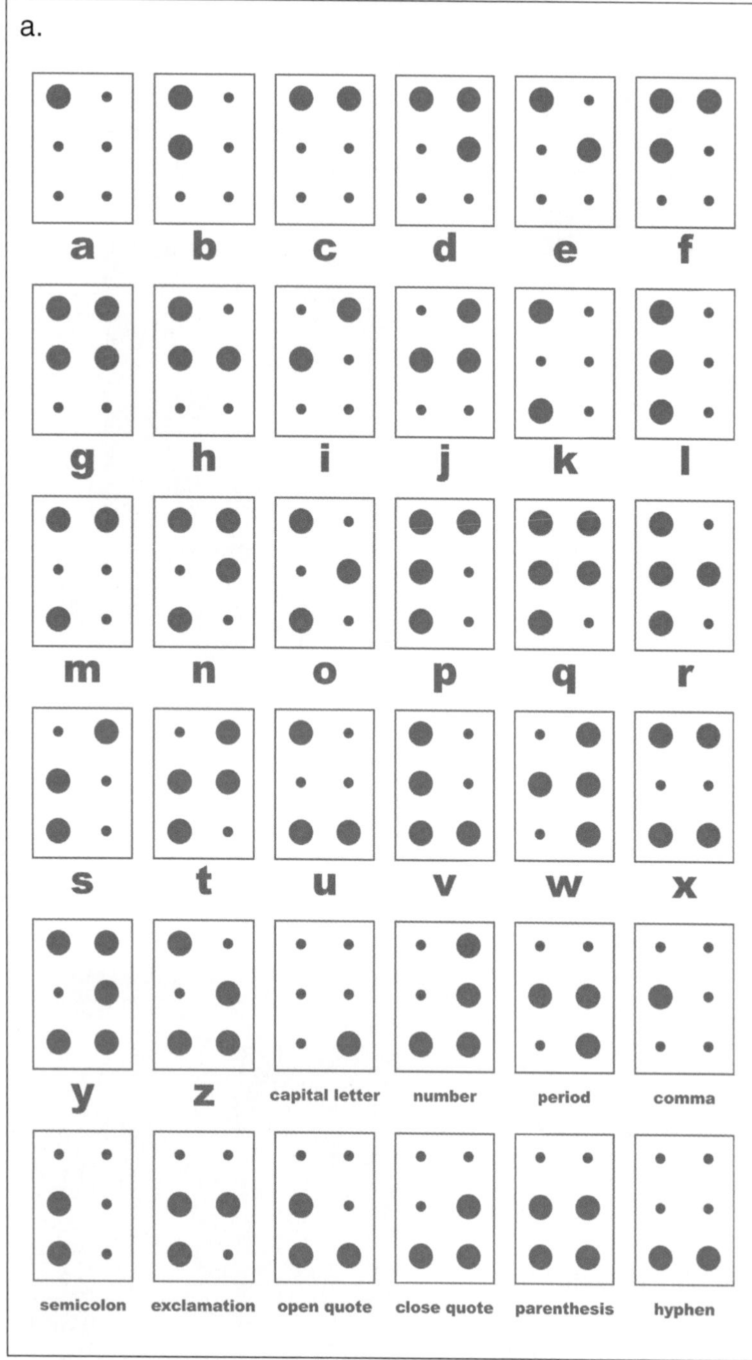

Figure 8.1 Different types of codes. (a) Braille alphabet, (b) bar code, (c) alarm keypad. How do people use these codes?

In *Just the Fax*, you will experience one code that people use to communicate with one another. Later in the chapter, you will relate your understanding of this code to how a code can direct life's processes.

Materials

For each student

coded message

graph paper

1 large sheet of paper

sticky notes

access to reference material

Process and Procedure

1. Obtain a message from your teacher.
2. Try to determine what your message says. Can you figure it out?
3. Compare your message with a partner's message and discuss the following questions with your partner. Record your ideas in your science notebook.
   a. What is similar and what is different about your message compared to your partner's message? How do you know?
   b. What information do you need before you can read your message?
4. Read the following paragraphs to help you decipher your message.

   Your message was written using digital coding. Digital coding allows us to program computers for many different applications such as games, word processing, and mathematics. Digitally encoded information allows us to take pictures or video and put them on the computer. Television is based on interpreting a digital code. Communication networks also are digitally encoded.

   To get a sense of how a digital code can provide information, think about how the first fax machines worked. Fax machines provide us with the technology to send an exact copy of a document across telephone lines. The information is transmitted using a digital code. Simple fax machines use the numbers 0 and 1 as a code. In fax machines, an optical device looks for bright light. White on a document has high reflectivity (bright light), and the code is 0. Black on a document has low reflectivity, and the code is 1. An image in a document consists of many densely packed dots. So a fax machine codes the document as a series of 0s and 1s. It transmits the code and prints black dots or leaves blank spots. When all the code is printed, the document is reproduced exactly like the original. Look at figure 8.2 to see how some fax machines interpret a code.

Document	Optical reading (reflectivity)	Code	Means	Action
White	High	0	Off	Blank
Black	Low	1	On	Dot

▲ **Figure 8.2 Interpreting fax machine code.** Some fax machines use 0s and 1s to transmit a message.

5. Obtain a sheet of graph paper from your teacher. Use it to help you decipher the code following these guidelines.
   a. Starting at the top left corner of your graph paper, match each square on the graph paper to the corresponding number (0 or 1) in the code. Proceed from left to right across one row then start on the next row.
   b. If the code says "1," fill in the box. (This is your "dot.")
   c. If the code shows a "0," leave the box blank. If you run out of room on your graph paper, staple another sheet to it.

You might find it easier to work with a partner to decipher your message. If so, help each other with each of your codes.

6. When you have revealed your message, record your word on the class list as directed by your teacher.
7. Copy the class list into your science notebook.

Reflect and Connect

Work individually to answer these questions. Record your answers in your science notebook.

1. Would you have been able to read the message if guidelines were not provided for you? Explain your answer.
2. Digital coding only uses 2 symbols (0s and 1s). How many different words are on the class list? Could the same code be used to make more words? Explain your answer.
3. The letter "e" is part of many words.
   a. Give 3 examples of how the addition of an "e" at the end of a word alters its meaning.

b. Explain how the addition of an "e" is like the code for a fax machine or a bar code.

4. What do you think the words in the class list have in common? Show what they have in common by placing all the words in a concept map as directed in 4a–d.
   a. Write each word on a separate sticky note.
   b. Arrange the sticky notes on a large sheet of paper.
   c. Add linking words between the class words to show what they have in common.
   d. Copy the concept map into your science notebook. You will revisit this concept map in the activity *Words to Live By*.

Review the end of chapter 3, *Collisions—Atomic Style*, to remind yourself how to create a concept map with linking words.

5. Gather information about what your word means. Later in the chapter, you will discuss the words from the class list in more detail. Answer Questions 5a–e as you gather information about your term.
   a. What is it?
   b. What is its function?
   c. Where is it found?
   d. What is it made of?
   e. Why is it important?

You will likely have to look in a few sources, such as on-line encyclopedias. Looking at Web sites and textbooks that focus on biology will also help you. A dictionary alone will not give you enough information to complete the assignment.

What Is This Stuff?

EXPLORE

In chapter 7, you learned that chromosomes carry genetic information. In *Just the Fax*, you saw how codes are used for storing information. Could a code on the chromosomes be responsible for giving organisms their unique characteristics? After all, there are millions of species of organisms, all with their own unique characteristics. That is quite a bit of information! A code would be one way to store this information.

If there is such a code, where is it found? What does it look like? Is this code found in all organisms? Does it look the same for all organisms? In *What Is this Stuff?*, you will work with a partner to go inside the cells of some common living things to search for the substance that makes up the chromosomes and carries the code of life.

Part I: Extracting Information

Materials

For each team of 2 students

2 pairs of safety goggles

2 safety aprons

1 5-mL graduated cylinder

1 10-mL graduated cylinder

1 large test tube

1 test-tube rack

1 50-mL beaker containing 20 mL of filtered material (from your teacher)

1 wooden splint or metal spatula

Woolite liquid detergent

meat tenderizer

cold ethanol

1 clock or timer

Cautions

During this investigation, wear safety goggles at all times. Ethanol is very flammable. Make sure there are no open flames or burners turned on nearby. Keep the lids on all of the solutions when not in use. Do not inhale any fumes. Be sure to wash your hands thoroughly after this investigation. Wash your hands thoroughly after handling the filtrate. Wipe counters with a dilute bleach solution if you spill any filtrate.

Process and Procedure

1. Look at the names of the organisms your teacher has written on the board.
   a. Think back to the activity *Unity and Diversity* in chapter 6. What are some things these organisms have in common?
   b. Write down your ideas in your science notebook.

2. Read the protocol *Extracting the Substance of Life* to learn how you can search for the special substance that organisms have in common. You will need to get into the cells of organisms to find it.
3. Gather the materials you need and follow the protocol.

Protocol

Extracting the Substance of Life Protocol

Be sure to wear your safety goggles and safety apron.

1. Obtain a 20-mL sample of filtered material from your teacher. Record what organism this material came from in your science notebook.

Your teacher made this material by putting the substance in a blender with salt and water and blending it for 15 seconds.

2. Add 3 mL of Woolite detergent to your sample and swirl the mixture *very gently*.
3. Allow the mixture to sit for 10 minutes. *Very gently* swirl the mixture every few minutes.
4. After 10 minutes, *very carefully* and *slowly* pour all the mixture into a large test tube.
5. Using the tip of a wooden splint, add a small amount of meat tenderizer to the mixture. Stir the mixture *very gently* with the wooden splint just enough to mix in the meat tenderizer.
6. Obtain cold ethanol from your teacher.
7. Carefully tilt the test tube at a 45-degree angle.
8. *Very slowly* pour the ethanol down the inside of the test tube as shown in the illustration. Try not to let the ethanol get mixed into the mixture. Pour until you have about the same amount of ethanol in the tube as you have of the mixture.

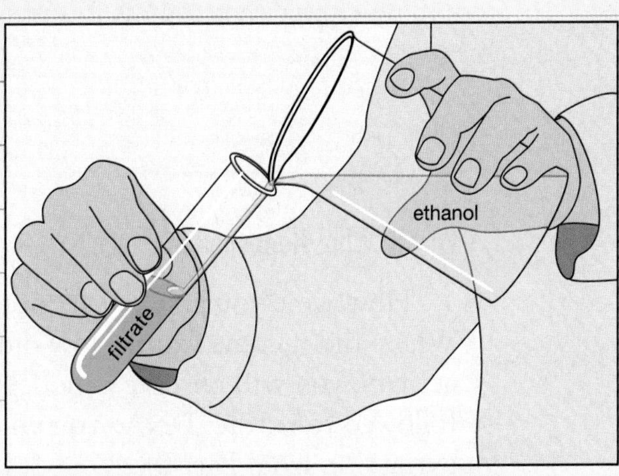

Adding ethanol to the mixture. Slowly pour ethanol into the test tube. Be careful to pour it down the side so that it forms a layer on top of the mixture. Pour until you have about the same amount of ethanol and mixture in the test tube.

4. Answer the following questions in your science notebook as you follow the protocol.
   a. What do you see happening in the ethanol layer? Record your observations.

Recall what you know about solubility.

   b. What does the material in the ethanol layer look like?
   c. The substance that you just extracted from an organism is **deoxyribonucleic acid (DNA)**. DNA carries the code for all of life. You extracted the very material that directs all the major processes of life! You have probably at least heard of DNA. List 3 things you already know about DNA.
5. Observe other teams' results.
6. Discuss the similarities and differences between their results and yours. Does DNA look similar among the organisms your class used? Record your thoughts in your science notebook.
7. Consult with your teacher if you want to perform any further investigations with the DNA. Only perform investigations that your teacher approves.

Stop & THINK

PART I

Work individually to answer these questions. Record your answers in your science notebook.

1. Does DNA appear to be the same for all organisms? What is your evidence? What could you do to be more certain of your answer?
2. How could you show that DNA is found only in living or once-living things?

Part II: What Happened in the Cells?

How were you able to get enough DNA to see it in the test tube? Where did it come from? How did you reach it? In this part of the activity, you will observe a model that explores the protocol you followed to extract DNA. You will relate this model to your DNA extraction from Part I.

Materials

none

Process and Procedure

1. Think about the purpose of each step in the protocol. What happened to the filtered material during each step? Discuss your thoughts with your partner. To help prompt your thinking, do the following.
   a. Look at figure 8.3 to refresh your memory of cell parts.
   b. Locate the chromosomes in figure 8.3.
   c. Read through the protocol again including how your teacher made the material to give to you.

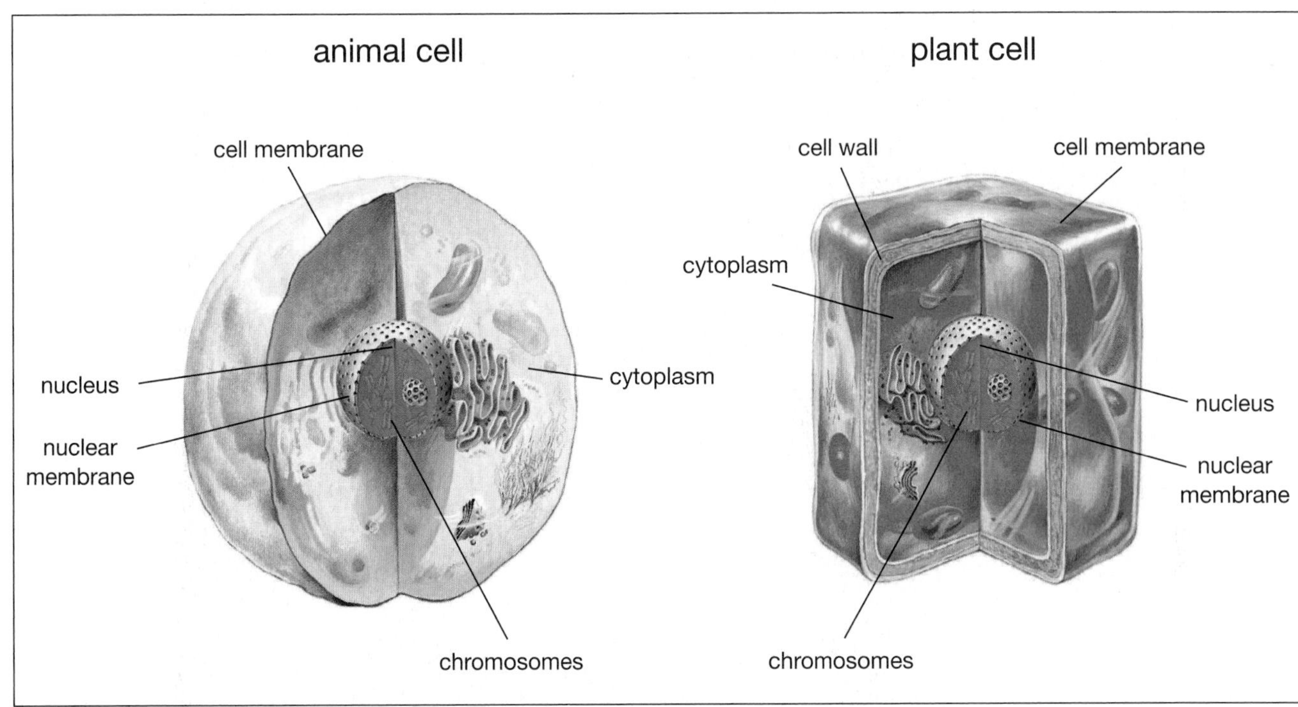

▲ **Figure 8.3 Plant and animal cells.** How did you extract DNA from cells?

2. Look at the model that your teacher has prepared. This model represents 1 cell. Watch as your teacher conducts a demonstration with the model and think about how this demonstration relates to your investigation.

3. In your science notebook, make a copy of the table shown in figure 8.4. Fill in the table, which relates the DNA extraction process to your teacher's demonstration.

Part in the model	What part of the cell is represented in the model?	What happens to the part in the demonstration?	How did you achieve this step in your DNA extraction?

▲ **Figure 8.4 Comparing DNA extraction with the teacher demonstration.** How did you reach the DNA?

Reflect and Connect

Answer these questions individually. Write your answers in your science notebook.

Describe in your own words what you did at the cellular level to extract DNA from your organism.

1. You probably did not have much success in finding a code in the DNA that you extracted. In fact, scientists didn't find the code in DNA until the 1950s. Why do you think it was so difficult to find the code in DNA?
2. How did observing the teacher demonstration help you understand your DNA extraction process?

EXPLAIN

Clips of DNA

In *What Is This Stuff?*, it might have seemed that you magically made a substance appear out of a blended mess! In reality, however, you have just taken a journey inside the many cells of an organism. At the end of that journey, you isolated DNA—deoxyribonucleic acid. You learned that all organisms have DNA. If all organisms have DNA, then it must be pretty important to life. What is so special about DNA and how does it code for the many traits of so many organisms? In *Clips of DNA*, you will begin to answer these questions as you look closer at DNA to learn about its structure.

Part I: The Structure of DNA

DNA makes up part of the chromosomes in cells. The DNA that you extracted in the explore investigation of this chapter sure did not look like pictures you have seen of chromosomes. This is because you extracted such an enormous quantity of DNA from many cells. In order to look at chromosomes, you would have to isolate just one cell and look at it in a way that would not disrupt the chromosomes.

Imagine that DNA is represented by the fiber that your teacher pulled from the yarn at the end of the explore activity. If you have looked at DNA with a microscope, it probably looked stringy or like a blob. If you had the technology and capabilities to look at DNA closer than you can with a microscope, what would you see? What makes up DNA? In Part I, you will work with a partner to begin to learn how DNA relates to chromosomes and what DNA, itself, is made of.

Materials

For each team of 2 students

25 red paper clips

25 yellow paper clips

25 green paper clips

25 blue paper clips

tape

cups to hold the paper clips

Process and Procedure

1. Read *The Code in DNA* to learn about DNA's structure and use Steps 1a–b as a guide. As you are reading, pay close attention to the components of DNA. You will apply your understanding of this reading by making a model of DNA.
   a. Create an analogy map comparing a train with DNA. The headings for your analogy map should be "Part of a Train," "Part of DNA," and "How the Part of the Train Is Similar to a Part of DNA."
   b. Compare your analogy map with another student's map. Revise or add information to your analogy map based on what you learn from your classmate.

READING

The Code in DNA

DNA is the genetic material required for the building, maintenance, and regulation of the cells of all living organisms. Recall from chapter 7 that in humans and other eukaryotes DNA molecules are organized into structures called chromosomes. That is, each chromosome consists of one, unbroken DNA molecule and many protein molecules. As figure 8.5 shows, the DNA coils tightly into beadlike clusters.

In *What Is This Stuff?*, you extracted the molecule containing the genetic code, DNA, from three organisms. This code is inherited and carries with it the instructions for all of life. You probably did not see a code in your DNA sample. Even scientists had a difficult time finding the code in DNA. A biologist by the name of Johann Friedrich Miescher first isolated DNA in 1869, but the code was not discovered until the 1950s. This is because DNA is very small. In order to find the code that DNA carries, scientists had to look very deeply into the DNA and examine it at the molecular level. When scientists looked closely at the molecular structure of DNA, they could see DNA's code. Instead of numbers like a digital code,

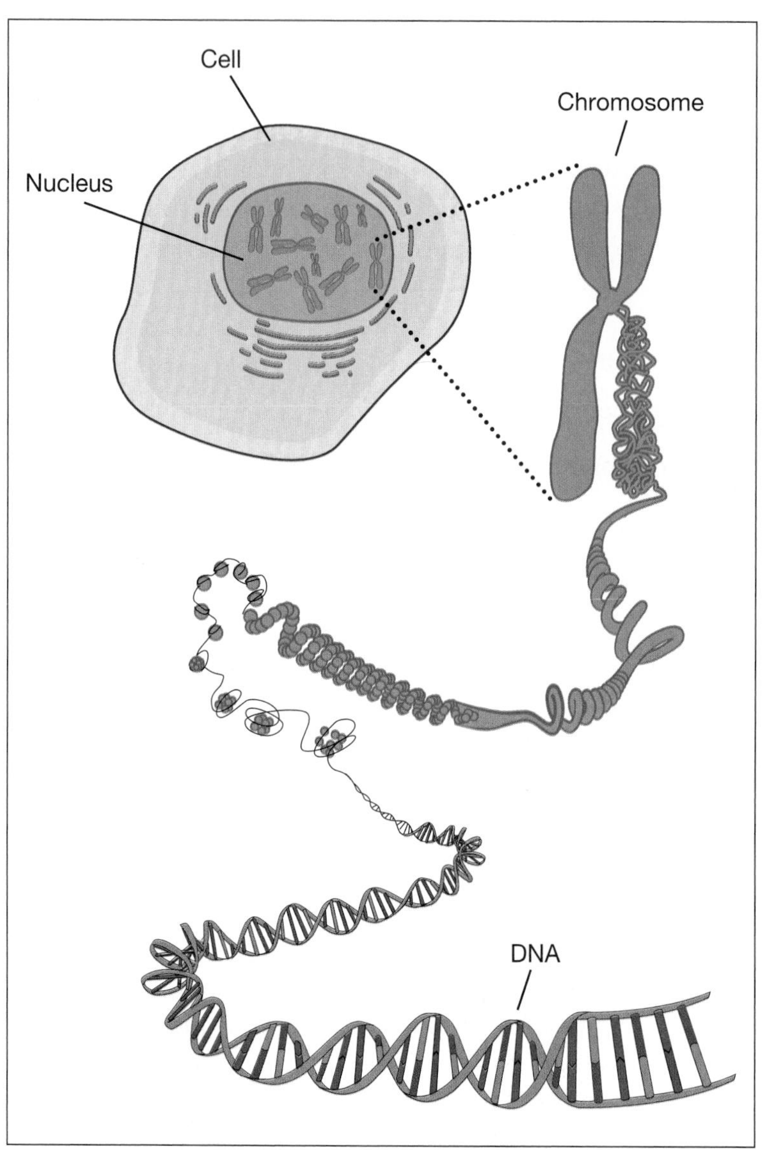

▲ **Figure 8.5 Eukaryotic chromosome structure.** In eukaryotes, chromosomes are found within the nucleus. Each chromosome consists of one molecule of DNA. The molecule is wrapped tightly into beadlike structures. Fully extended, the DNA in one human chromosome would be about 5 centimeters long. What advantage might efficient packing of DNA offer a cell?

DNA's code is made up of a string of molecules. These special molecules are called **nucleotides**. Each nucleotide, in turn, is made up of three components: a sugar molecule, a phosphate group, and a molecule with nitrogen in it, which is called a nitrogen base. To learn more about the discoveries that have contributed to our understanding of DNA, read the sidebar *In Search of DNA* and look at *FYI—A DNA Timeline*.

In DNA, there are four types of nucleotides. Each nucleotide is different because of its nitrogen base. Figure 8.6 shows one type of nucleotide with the nitrogen base: cytosine.

To simplify how DNA is written, scientists label the entire nucleotide with a letter to represent its base. For example, scientists refer to a nucleotide with the cytosine base as "C." The other nitrogen bases in DNA are adenine (A), guanine (G), and thymine (T).

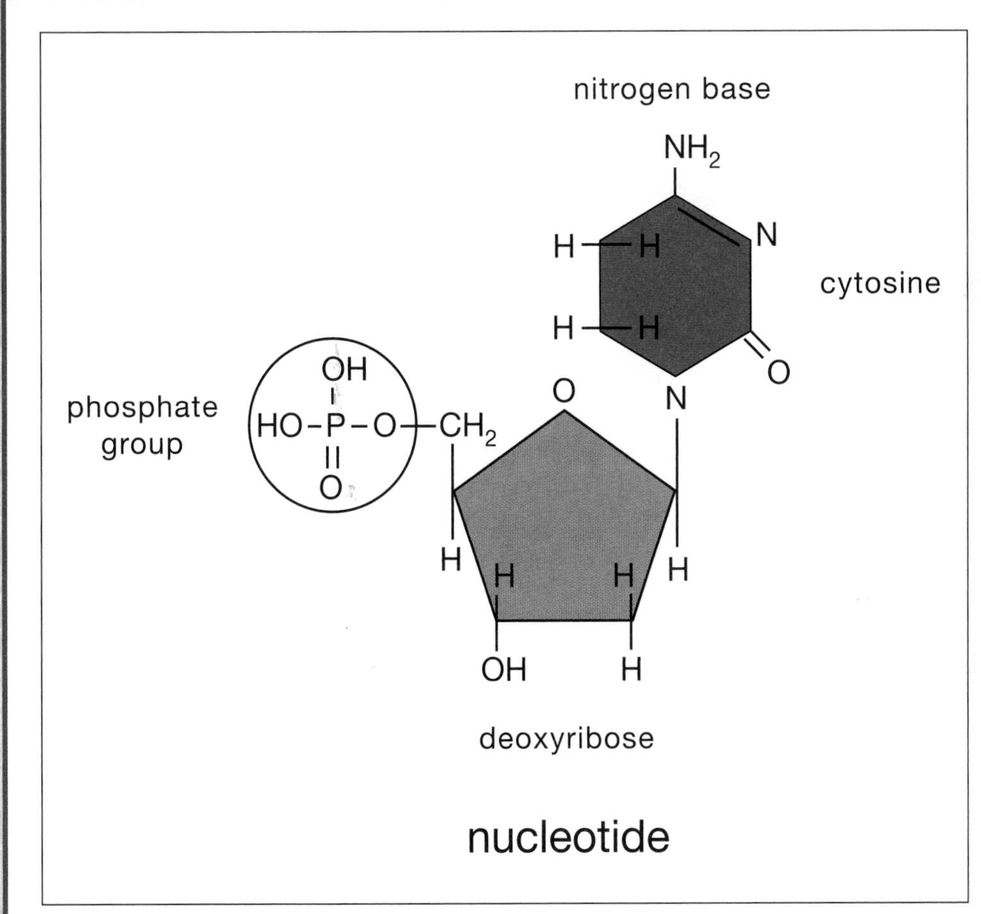

▲ **Figure 8.6 Nucleotide with cytosine as the nitrogen base.** A DNA nucleotide is made up of a phosphate group, a sugar (deoxyribose), and a nitrogen base.

The Code in DNA, continued

A DNA strand is a very long strand of nucleotides. These nucleotides are held together by covalent bonds. Figure 8.7 shows a DNA strand of nucleotides.

There are billions of nucleotides in the cells of every organism. You can think of a DNA strand as a very long train with four different designs of railcars. The designs of the cars represent the different types of nucleotides (A, C, T, and G). The arrangement of nucleotides (the order of the railcars) is called the DNA sequence. Figure 8.8 illustrates a segment of DNA using the train analogy. Each of the four types of cars corresponds with one of the four types of nucleotides.

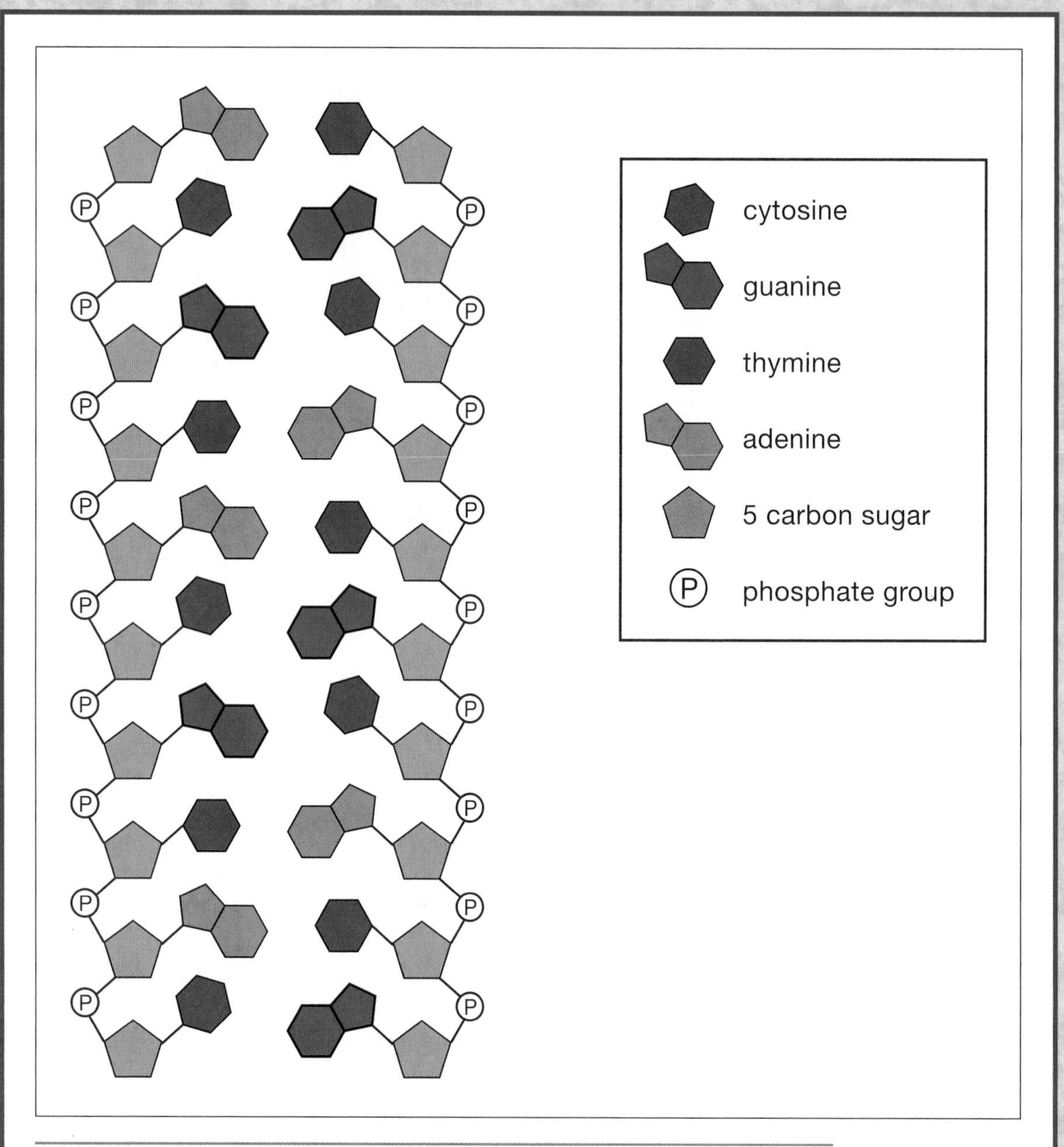

▲ **Figure 8.7 DNA strand.** DNA is in long strands consisting of many nucleotides.

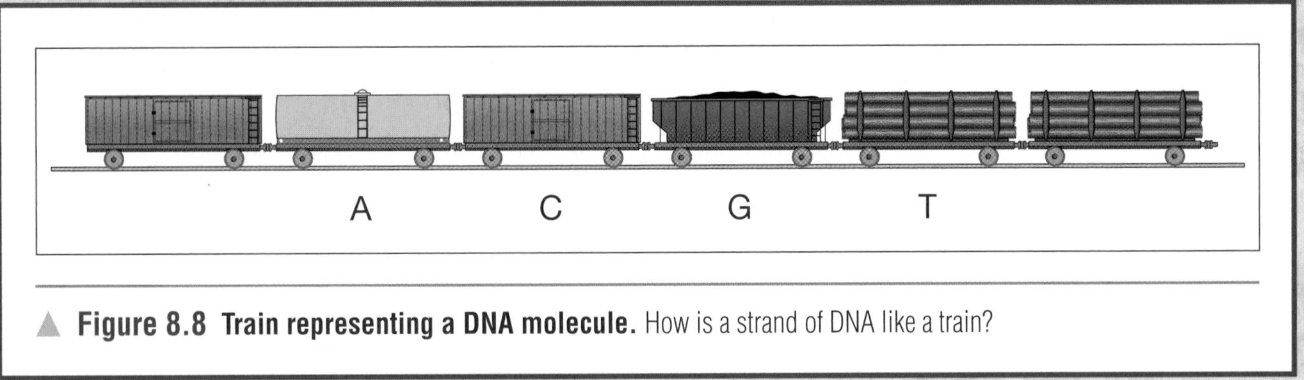

▲ **Figure 8.8 Train representing a DNA molecule.** How is a strand of DNA like a train?

2. Work with a partner and make a model of DNA by completing Steps 2a–c. Often, making a model helps people understand how things work.
   a. Collect 15 paper clips of 4 different colors (red, blue, yellow, and green).
   b. Build a chain of paper clips using different colors. Make the chain 15 paper clips long, in any order. This chain represents a very small section of DNA.

Attach the paper clips end to end to form a long chain.

   c. Label this chain by attaching tape to your starting end.
3. Determine the DNA sequence of your chain by following Steps 3a–c.
   a. Look at the table in figure 8.9 to learn what each colored paper clip represents in your DNA model.
   b. Record the DNA sequence of your chain in your science notebook.
   c. Verify the sequence by comparing the sequence you recorded with that of your partner.

Nucleotide	Color of paper clip
A (adenine)	Green
T (thymine)	Red
G (guanine)	Yellow
C (cytosine)	Blue

▲ **Figure 8.9 Nucleotide key.** In your model, each color of paper clip represents each different nucleotide.

4. Spread your paper clip chain out on your desk and discuss the answers to the following questions with your partner. Record your answers in your science notebook.
   a. What subunit of DNA does each paper clip represent?
   b. Describe what makes this paper clip chain a good model of DNA. What could you do to improve this model? Give reasons for your answer.
   c. Compare your strand of DNA with another team's strand. What are the similarities and differences between the 2 strands?

Recall from the *Just the Fax* activity that all the messages consisted of 0s and 1s. Each message was unique, however, because of how the 0s and 1s were arranged.

5. Read *Double the Code* to learn more about DNA's molecular arrangement. You know about the parts that make up DNA and a little bit about how those parts are arranged in a sequence. However, the parts alone are only one piece of what makes DNA special.

READING

Double the Code

A complete DNA molecule is double stranded. This means that there are two long strands of DNA bonded to each other to form a double helix. The nucleotides play a key role in how the double-stranded molecule is connected. Adenine on one strand always bonds with thymine on the other strand. Similarly, guanine always bonds with the cytosine. Because the nucleotides bond this way, they are said to form complementary base pairs (the base refers to A, T, G, or C). Each nitrogen base only bonds with one other nitrogen base. The two DNA strands are held together by hydrogen bonds between the complementary base pairs. Figure 8.10 shows the **complementary base pairing** between two DNA strands.

So, if two parallel trains moving in opposite directions represent double-stranded DNA, each railcar would represent a nucleotide. The cars would line up so that all of one type of car would pair with a specific type of car from the other train pointed in the opposite direction. This models the complementary base pairing of DNA. A person leaning out of one of the cars and grabbing the hand of a person leaning out of the paired car would represent the hydrogen bonds.

The structure of a DNA molecule is called a double helix. A helix is a spiral form. DNA is a double helix because it has two connecting strands and is twisted in a helical way. Figure 8.11 shows the double helix structure of DNA.

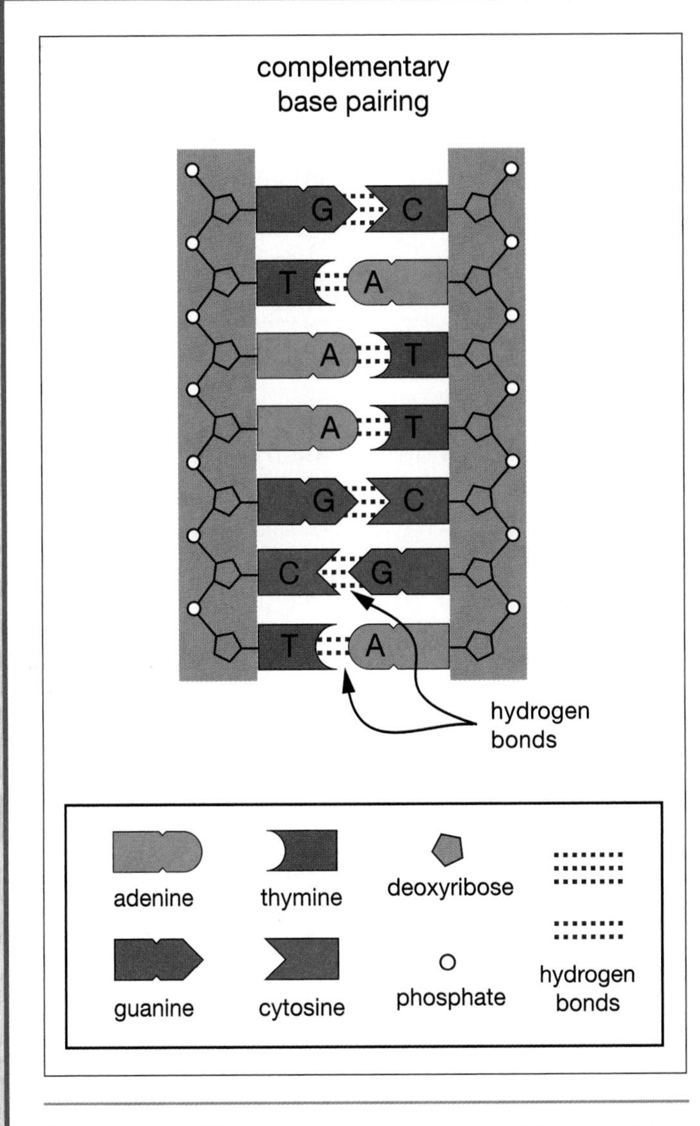

▲ **Figure 8.10 Complementary base pairing in DNA.** What are the rules of complementary base pairing?

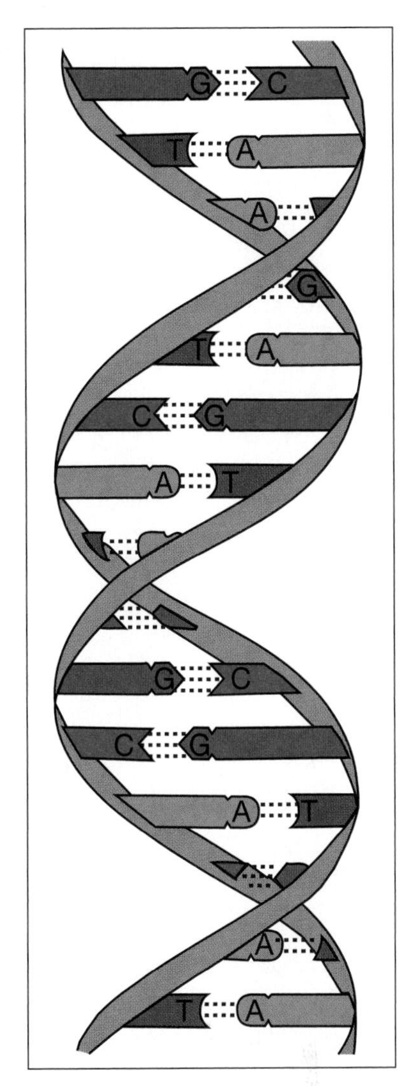

▲ **Figure 8.11** The DNA molecule forms a double helix.

6. Make a model of a DNA double helix and show what you have learned about the structure of DNA by following Steps 6a–g. Record your answers in your science notebook.
   a. Build a new paper clip chain that represents the complementary strand of your original chain. Record the sequence in your science notebook as shown in the following:

      original sequence ______________________________

      complementary sequence ______________________________
   b. Line up your 2 paper clip chains so that the complementary nucleotides are next to each other (side by side).
   c. Pick up the 2 chains and hold them by one end so that the chains dangle vertically.
   d. Put your pencil tip through the bottom paper clip from each strand.
   e. Turn your pencil so that the 2 chains begin to twist slightly.
   f. Record your observations and sketch the appearance of the chains in your science notebook.
   g. Repeat the twisting process. Continue to turn your pencil until it will not turn anymore. What do you notice the DNA strand doing? Are you surprised at your results? Record your observations in your science notebook.

Stop & THINK

PART I

Discuss these questions with your partner. Record your thoughts in your science notebook.

1. Describe the code that DNA carries. How many parts to the code are there?
2. How does the sequence of nucleotides on one strand provide a template or guide for the sequence of subunits on the other strand?
3. Sketch a representation of a DNA double helix using the train analogy. Include a key with your sketch.

Part II: DNA Replication

So far, you have studied the structure of DNA. But the structure alone does not tell you how DNA is inherited or what information it carries. In Part II, you will see how DNA's form enables it to perform its functions. You will answer the question, "How does the structure of DNA allow it to pass on the genetic information that it carries in its nucleotides?" Later in the chapter, you will experience how this information gives organisms their traits.

Materials

For each team of 2 students

- 25 red paper clips
- 25 yellow paper clips
- 25 green paper clips
- 25 blue paper clips
- cups to hold the paper clips

Process and Procedure

1. Read *Copying DNA* to learn how DNA makes copies of itself. As you read, use the focus question, "How are DNA replication and meiosis related?" to guide your thinking.

READING

Copying DNA

DNA carries the code that gives organisms their traits. In order for DNA to get its code into every cell, DNA must make a copy of itself. This process is called replication and is very important for forming gametes and for making other new cells. Remember from chapter 7 that gametes have half the genetic information of other cells.

The first step in the process of **DNA replication** is the separation of the DNA strands. Special chemicals called **enzymes** cause the DNA molecule to separate. Enzymes are a type of protein that helps reactions occur. **DNA polymerase** is the enzyme involved in DNA replication. The hydrogen bonds between the nitrogen bases of the two strands are weaker than the covalent bonds between nucleotides in a DNA strand. In the train analogy, the hands clasping between trains are weaker than the links between the railcars on each train. Because the bonds between the trains are weaker, the two trains separate just as the DNA polymerase causes the two DNA strands to separate along the hydrogen bonds.

Once the DNA is separated into two strands, each strand can serve as a template to be copied. A template is a pattern or guide. DNA polymerase adds nucleotides one at a time to a new strand that is complementary to the original template. The nucleotides are added according to complementary base pairing (see figure 8.12). Do you remember the rules of complementary base pairing? If the template DNA strand has an A, then a T will be added to the new strand. If a G comes next in the template DNA strand, then a C will be added to the T in the new strand. New strands form along each of the separated strands.

DNA replicates for two reasons: to go into gametes that can result in offspring, and to go into new cells for growth and maintenance. Once DNA has replicated, a copy of the original DNA can go into new cells. Each new cell formed will contain a copy of the original DNA sequence. In chapter 7, you learned how the process of meiosis forms gamete cells. Prior to meiosis, the chromosomes doubled through the process of DNA replication. Recall that eukaryotic chromosomes consist of one DNA molecule. Thus, when DNA replicates, the chromosome doubles. During later stages of meiosis, cell division ensures that the resulting gametes (sperm and egg) have half the number of chromosomes as the original parent cell.

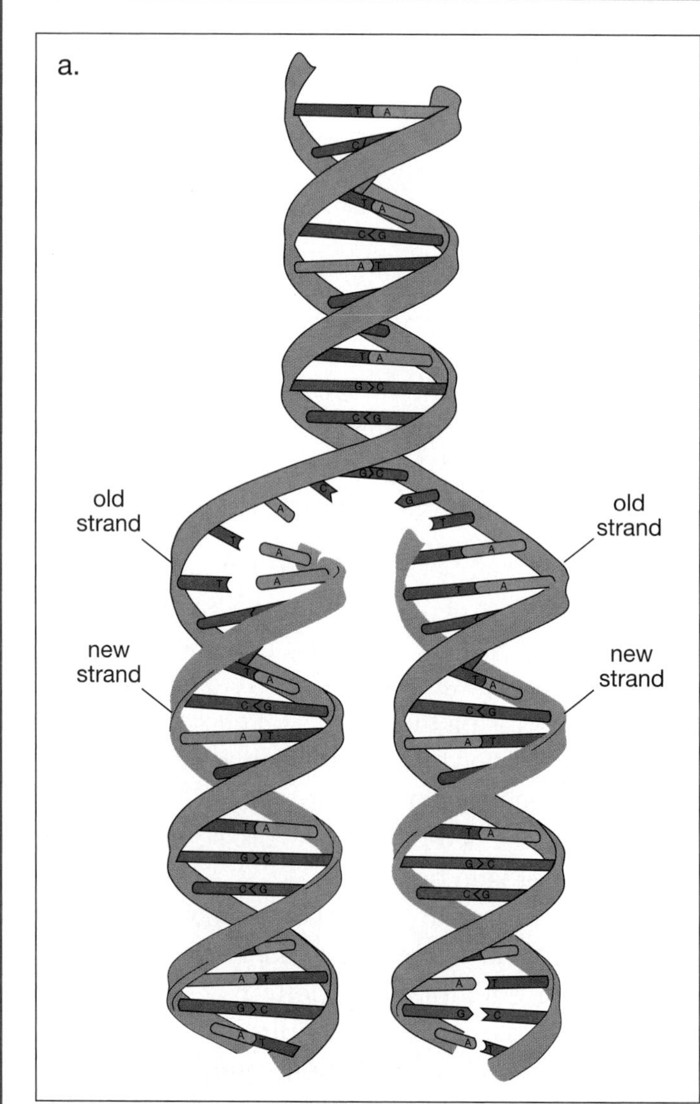

Figure 8.12 DNA replication. (a) During DNA replication, the strands come apart at the bonds between the nucleotides. DNA replicates by adding nucleotides. Eventually, two DNA molecules are produced. Each molecule is exactly alike, and each has one old and one new strand. (b) New nucleotides are added one by one with the original strands serving as templates for the production of new strands. What base would be added next?

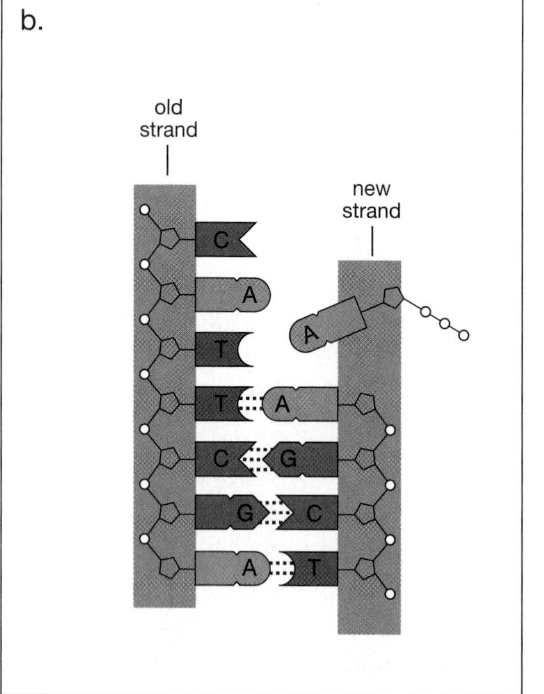

After an egg is fertilized, the zygote (fertilized egg) has one complete set of chromosomes. The zygote cell continues to divide to make more cells. The major process involved in producing these new cells is called mitosis. In mitosis, the DNA replicates and then the cell goes through a series of stages that results in new cells that each contains the same genetic information as the original zygote. The stages that the chromosomes go through during mitosis are similar to those in meiosis except that the cell only divides to the point where each new cell has a complete set of chromosomes. Any cells that divide by mitosis will contain genetic information identical to the original cell. Look at figure 8.13, which shows how cells divide through mitosis.

Topic: mitosis
Go to: www.scilinks.org
Code: 2Inquiry415

parent cell

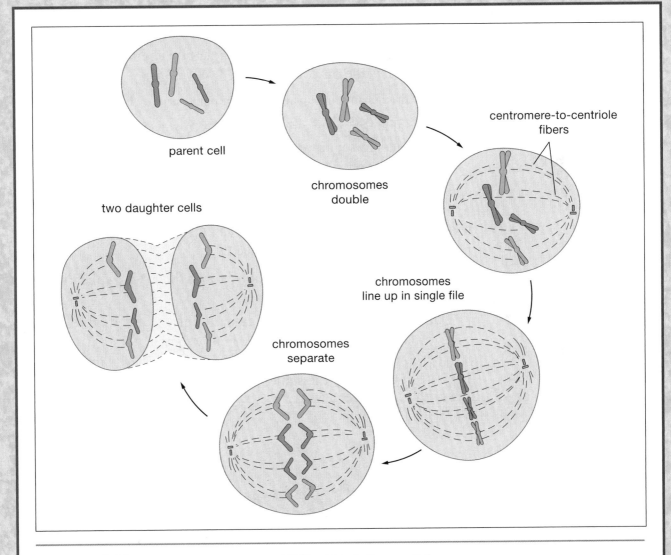

chromosomes double

centromere-to-centriole fibers

chromosomes line up in single file

chromosomes separate

two daughter cells

▲ **Figure 8.13 Mitosis.** How does a copy of DNA get into both new cells?

2. Answer Questions 2a–e to show what you have learned about DNA replication. Record your ideas in your science notebook.
   a. How does being double stranded help DNA replicate?
   b. How did the chromosomes double during meiosis?
   c. Why does each new cell contain copies of the original DNA?
   d. Why is DNA replication necessary to organisms?
   e. Compare your answers with a classmate's. Then add to or revise your answers based on what you learn from his or her responses. Record your changes in your science notebook including what you changed and why.
3. Model DNA replication using your paper clips by following Steps 3a–c.
   a. Reassemble your original 2 paper clip chains so that they lie side by side on your desk.

Make sure the 2 chains line up according to complementary base pairing.

   b. Imagine that your fingers are DNA polymerase. Use your fingers to separate the chains as shown in figure 8.14.
   c. Replicate your DNA by pairing up free paper clips with each chain. Use the extra paper clips you have as your free nucleotides.

Refer to the table in figure 8.9 and to figures 8.14 and 8.15 to guide the replication process in your paper clip model.

4. Answer the following questions about the DNA replication model.
   a. After replicating your original double-stranded DNA, how many strands of DNA do you now have?
   b. Compare your paper clip DNA with another team's strands. How are they the same? How are they different?

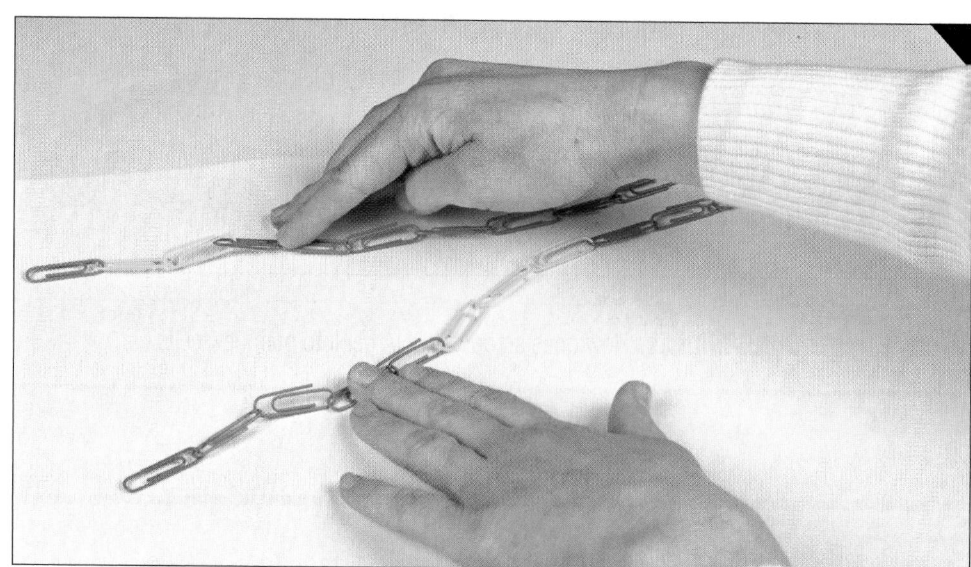

Figure 8.14
Separating strands. How do your fingers represent DNA polymerase?

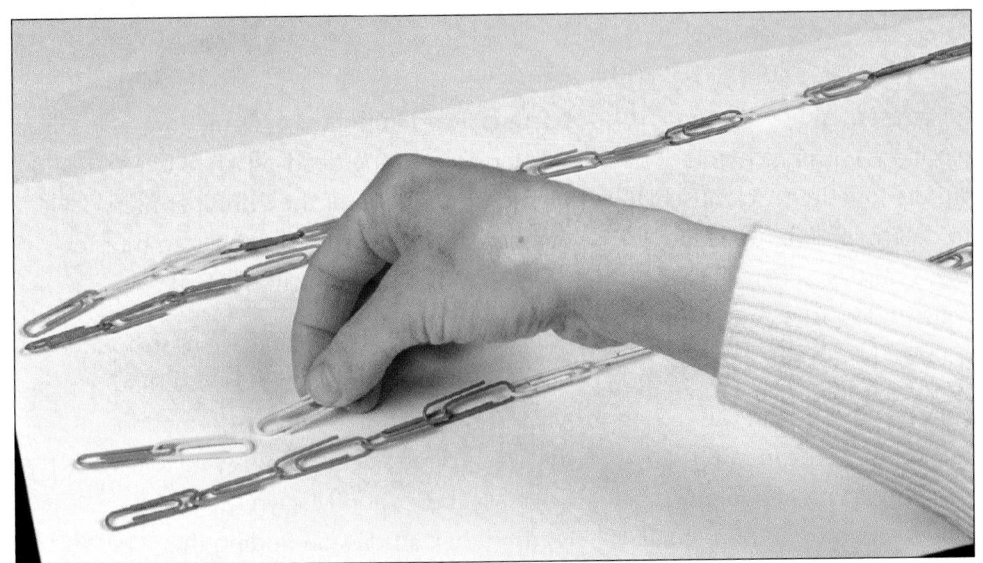

◀ **Figure 8.15**
Adding paper clips. How does adding paper clips to your model show DNA replication?

Reflect and Connect

Discuss the following questions with your partner. Record your best thinking in your science notebook.

1. How is the fax code with 0s and 1s similar to the code in DNA?
2. Study figure 8.13 in *Copying DNA*, which shows the stages of mitosis. Then compare that figure with figure 7.17 in chapter 7, which shows the stages of meiosis. Answer the following questions.
   a. How does the genetic information from a parent get into the gametes?
   b. Why is DNA replication important during mitosis?
   c. If DNA did not replicate accurately, what do you think would happen to new cells?
   d. Generate a Venn diagram comparing the processes of meiosis and mitosis.
3. Why did your DNA model differ from the models of other teams? Do you think this happens with cellular DNA? Explain your reasoning.
4. What is the benefit of the double-stranded characteristic of DNA?
5. How do models like your paper clip model help you understand science concepts?

SIDEBAR

In Search of DNA

In chapter 7, you learned how Gregor Mendel's investigations with pea plants proved that traits are inherited. Scientists' next task was to determine *how* traits are inherited. Scientists quickly began their search for the inherited substance that gives organisms their traits.

The first major breakthrough in the search for this substance came in 1869. A Swiss biologist and medic named Johann Friedrich Miescher wanted to find out what chemicals were in the nuclei of cells. For his search, Miescher collected pus cells from discarded surgical bandages and broke down these cells with chemicals from a pig's stomach. In the cells, Miescher found a white, phosphorous-containing substance that he named nuclein. Miescher conducted similar studies on the heads of salmon sperm cells and found the same substance. What Miescher discovered was DNA. And he believed that DNA was the substance responsible for inheritance. Unfortunately, Miescher did not have enough evidence to support his ideas about DNA. Most scientists of the time ignored Miescher's discovery. They thought the key to inheritance was in the proteins of organisms.

The first hint that DNA was responsible for carrying genetic information came in the 1920s from an experiment conducted by Fred Griffith, an English medical officer. Griffith worked with a type of bacteria that had two forms. One form of the bacteria was deadly and the other form was harmless. Griffith injected mice with living cells of the harmless bacteria together with dead cells from the disease-causing bacteria. The mice died. When Griffith examined the dead mice, he found both types of bacteria living in the mice. Somehow, some substance from the dead cells had been picked up by some of the living harmless bacteria. Griffith called this ability to transfer genetic information transformation.

It was not until 1943 that scientists found direct evidence to support the idea that DNA was responsible for transformation. In that year, three scientists—Oswald Avery, Colin MacLeod, and Maclyn McCarty—focused their studies on finding the substance responsible for transformation. They knew that extracts from transformed cells contained protein, RNA, and DNA. But they did not know which substance carried the information for transformation. The three scientists worked meticulously using the process of elimination. They destroyed each substance one at a time to see what the effect on transformation was. When they destroyed the RNA and the protein, transformation took place as usual. When they destroyed the DNA, transformation did not take place. Their experiment provided evidence that DNA was the substance responsible for transformation and therefore the carrier of genetic information.

Some scientists were still not convinced that DNA was the carrier of genetic information. In 1952, two scientists, Alfred Hershey and Martha Chase, provided visual evidence that DNA was the molecule that carried genetic information. They used a radioactive isotope to follow the DNA for a virus as it infected a host. By following the viral cycle, they saw that the virus injected its host with DNA to provide the information for viral replication. Hershey and Chase proved once and for all that the genetic information was in the DNA, not in the protein coat of the virus.

Once scientists were convinced that DNA was the carrier of genetic information, the race was on to understand its structure and how it carried the code for all the variations of life. In the late 1940s and early 1950s, many scientists focused their efforts on understanding the structure of DNA and cracking its code. In 1950, Edwin Chargaff found that certain bases of DNA always occurred at a 1:1 ratio. He discovered that in DNA molecules, there was always as much adenine as there was thymine and as much cytosine as there was guanine. This discovery would later contribute greatly to identifying the molecular structure of DNA.

In 1953, a scientist named Rosalind Franklin took thin strands of DNA, exposed them to an extremely fine beam of X-rays, and examined the resulting patterns. She painstakingly took several photographs from many angles and under many conditions. When she looked at the photographs, she found a specific, now famous, pattern starting to emerge (see figure). Franklin showed her findings to her colleague, Maurice Wilkins. Wilkins then shared Franklin's data with two other scientists, James Watson and Francis Crick. Watson and Crick had also been working on understanding the structure of DNA. When they saw Franklin's photographs, they suggested that DNA was a molecule made up of two chains of nucleotides arranged in a helix. When they learned of Chargaff's findings, they added to their model by pairing adenine with thymine and cytosine with guanine.

Watson and Crick's model explained how DNA could serve as a template for passing genetic information. The model fit the experimental data of the time so well that the scientific community accepted it almost immediately. In 1962, Watson, Crick, and Wilkins won the Nobel Prize in Physiology. Rosalind Franklin died at age 37 in 1958. At that time, the Nobel Prize was awarded only to living recipients. Had she been alive, Rosalind Franklin might have also been awarded the Nobel Prize.

It took almost 90 years from the time DNA was discovered until scientists completely understood its structure and function. Now that scientists have this knowledge, they can help us understand how DNA codes for all of life.

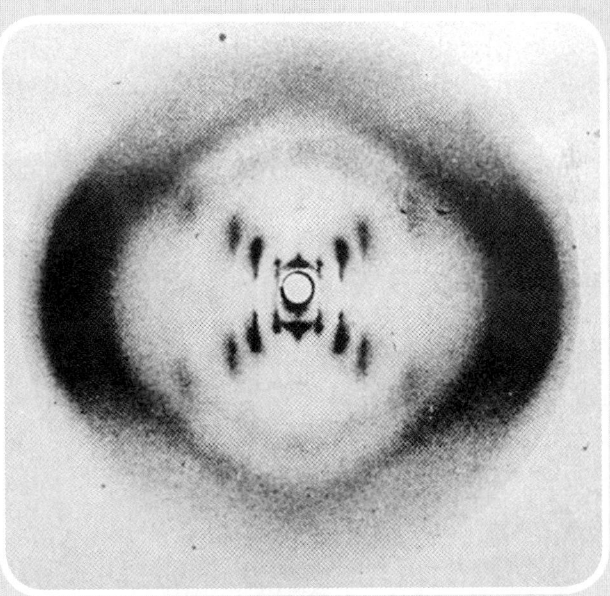

▲ **Rosalind Franklin's X-ray diffraction photograph of DNA taken in 1953.** This photo showed, for the first time, the double helix shape of DNA.

DNA Timeline

This timeline depicts when discoveries became generally known to the scientific community, not when the Nobel Prize was awarded. Often, the prizes were awarded much later.

1869
DNA was first isolated by Johann Friedrich Miescher. He discovered the substance in the pus on soiled bandages.

1953
Wilkins and Franklin produce X-ray diffraction patterns of DNA.

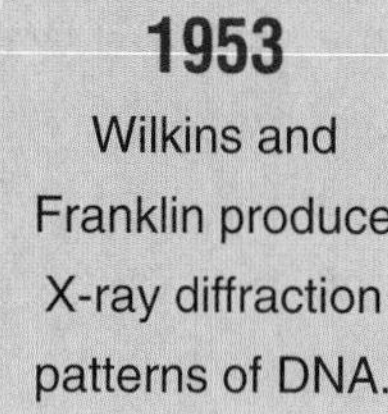

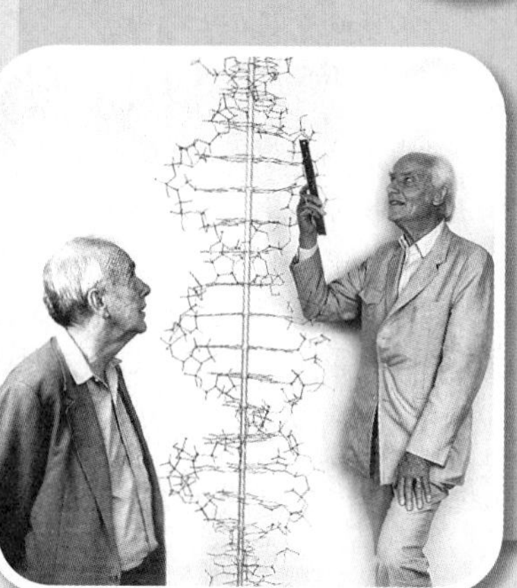

Watson and Crick discover the structure of DNA.

AUG = methionine

1966
Holly, Khorana, and Nirenberg crack the genetic code.

1944
Avery, MacLeod, and McCarty show that the hereditary material in bacteria is DNA.

1951
McClintock discovers that genes are transposable. They can change position on chromosomes.

1958
Messelson and Stahl demonstrate semi-conservative replication of DNA.

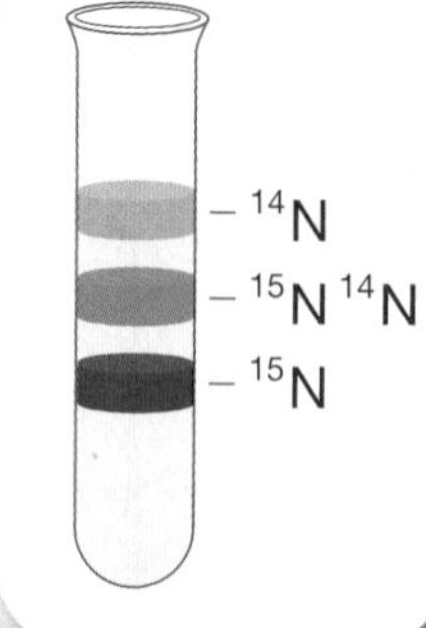

1970
Arber, Nathans, and Smith discover restriction enzymes.

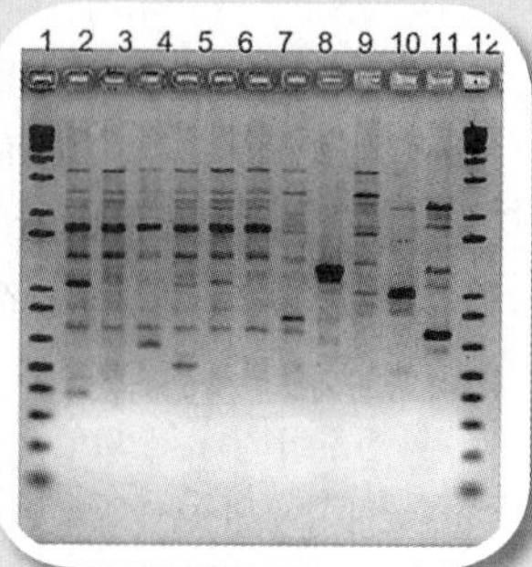

Denotes research that received a Nobel Prize.

1977
Maxam, Gilbert, and Sanger develop rapid DNA sequencing methods. These methods made it practical to study DNA sequences.

1981
1982
Foreign genes expressed in mice and fruit flies result in the creation of the first transgenic animals.

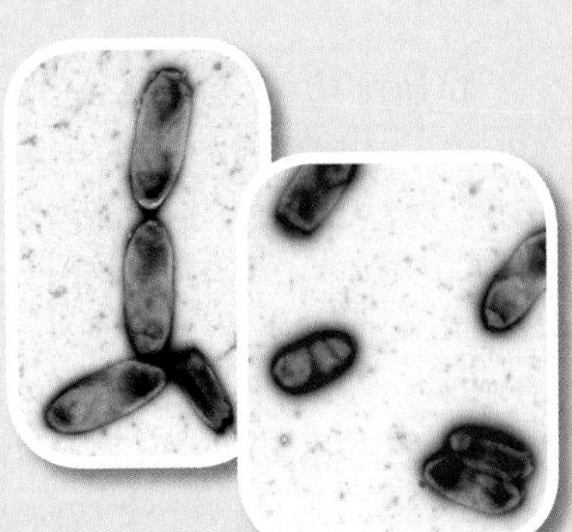

1995
Venter, Frazier, and Smith sequence the first genomes of two free living organisms, the bacterium *Haemophilis influenzae* and the bacterium *Mycoplasma genitalium.*

2005
Chimpanzee and dog genomes sequenced.

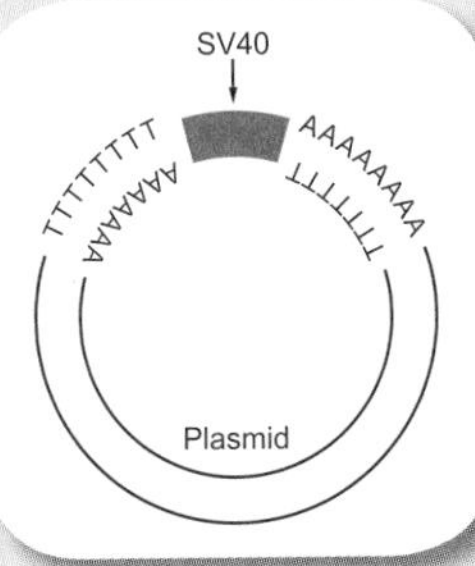

1972
Berg creates first recombinant DNA molecule.

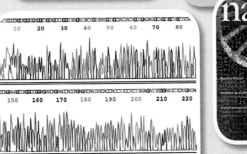

1990
National Institutes of Health and Department of Energy begin the Human Genome Project.

2001
Rough draft of the human genome published. The results were released simultaneously by the federal government and a private company.

2003
Completion of the Human Genome Project announced.

EXPLAIN

Words to Live By

In *Just the Fax*, each member of your class was given the task of finding information about the word you deciphered in your binary code. Now that you have completed the task, it is time to compile the information you gathered. You might be wondering what this assignment has to do with your study of DNA. Surprisingly, these words have a great deal to do with DNA's significance. To connect these words to DNA, however, you first need to understand what is important about these terms. In *Words to Live By*, you will experience the connection between these words and DNA's role in life.

One way to help understand new information is to organize it in a way that makes sense to you. Once you organize information, you can begin to make connections and determine relationships. In this activity, you will work with a partner to organize the words you decoded in the first activity, *Just the Fax*.

Materials

For each student

completed assignment from the *Just the Fax* activity

1 5×7 in index card

1 large piece of construction or butcher paper

markers

1 *Term Chart Completed* handout (optional)

Process and Procedure

1. Pair up with someone who researched the same word that you researched. If no one else investigated your word, pair up with any available person.
2. Compare what you learned about the word with your partner by completing Steps 2a–c.
   a. Read the information that your partner gathered about the word.

Remember the 5 questions you were to answer about your word. If you need help remembering, look back at *Reflect and Connect*, Question 5 from the *Just the Fax* activity.

   b. Combine your information to get a thorough description of your word (if you researched the same word as your partner). If you had different words, help each other decide on a thorough description of your terms.
   c. Label an index card with headings that describe the research you conducted on your word.

Fill out your index card neatly with the information you gathered about your word. If you did not research the same term as your partner, help each other complete the cards.

3. Present your word aloud to the class when your teacher calls on you.

Read your information using a clear, strong voice. Present the information slowly enough so that your classmates can take notes about important points. Then post your word on the board.

4. Listen carefully as other teams describe their words. Take notes in your science notebook by writing down the important information about each term.
5. Review each of the words posted on the board and decide what they have in common by completing Steps 5a–c. Record your ideas in your science notebook.
   a. In what ways are these words different?
   b. Decide what these words have in common. Justify your answer.

One of the words describes what is common among all the terms.

   c. When you have an idea, check with your teacher. Are you surprised at the commonality of the words? Explain why or why not.

If you are having difficulties making sense of these words, ask your teacher for a copy of the *Protein Summary* handout.

6. Organize the words into a concept map to show the relationship among them using Steps 6a–c as a guide.
   a. Decide on a way to sort these words into categories that make sense to you. Then divide each category further into subcategories. Record your categories and the criteria for your categories in your science notebook.
   b. Revise your concept map from the *Just the Fax* activity to show your organization scheme. Start by rearranging the sticky notes on the large piece of paper.

Remember to add linking words and use verbs to show how these terms relate to one another.

   c. Copy your concept map into your science notebook to create a permanent record of it.
7. Post your concept map as instructed by your teacher. Think about the following questions as you look at other concept maps.
   a. Did other teams organize the terms the same way you did?
   b. Do the other concept maps make sense to you?

Reflect and Connect

Answer the following questions individually. Record your answers in your science notebook.

1. Describe why proteins are essential for life. Use specific examples from this activity in your discussion.
2. Why are very different substances such as hormones and the components of spider silk both classified as proteins?
3. How does a graphic organizer help you understand concepts?

EXPLAIN

Transcription and Translation—the Road to Making Proteins

You learned in the activity *Words to Live By* that proteins are very important to life. Life could not happen without proteins. Proteins are what give organisms their traits. How do organisms make the specific proteins they need for all the processes of life? Most genes contain the information required to build proteins. Genes are segments of DNA that code for an organism's traits. Therefore, the path to protein production begins with DNA. In *Transcription and Translation*, you and a partner will crack the code carried in DNA to see how DNA stores the genetic information that directs specific protein production. To learn what scientists know about our genes, read the sidebar *Mapping the Human Genome.*

Part I: Transcription

To understand how DNA relates to protein production, you need to understand a few processes that occur in the cell on the way to protein production. The first step on the road to protein production is the construction of another nucleic acid, **ribonucleic acid** (**RNA**). RNA is constructed through a process called **transcription.** Transcription is similar to DNA replication except that transcription copies only part of the nucleotide sequence in DNA. In Part I of this activity, you will learn how transcription occurs.

Materials

For each team of 2 students

25 red paper clips

25 yellow paper clips

25 green paper clips

25 blue paper clips

25 silver paper clips

cups to hold the paper clips

Process and Procedure

1. Assemble a DNA sequence in preparation for modeling transcription by following Steps 1a–b.
   a. Look in your science notebook to see what your DNA sequence was from the activity *Clips of DNA*.
   b. Reassemble both strands and place them next to each other to represent the double-stranded structure of DNA.

Remember, this strand represents only a very short section of an entire DNA molecule.

2. Read *Making RNA* to learn about RNA and how to model transcription. Refer back to other readings or illustrations if it helps you organize your understanding.

READING

Making RNA

Throughout this chapter, you have been thinking about how DNA carries a code. DNA actually stores information in the form of a code. The code that DNA carries leads to protein production or protein synthesis. Using just four nucleotides, DNA codes for the production of hundreds of thousands of proteins in all organisms. A DNA sequence that codes for a protein is a gene.

Though DNA carries the code, it cannot produce proteins without another molecule called RNA, which is ribonucleic acid. RNA is similar to DNA in that it also is made of nucleotides. Each nucleotide in RNA has a sugar, a phosphate group, and a nitrogen base. But, as you can tell from the name, RNA is a little different from DNA. The sugar molecule in RNA is ribose instead of deoxyribose. There are also two important structural differences between RNA and DNA. In RNA, the nitrogen base thymine (T) is replaced by uracil (U), and RNA is usually single stranded instead of double stranded.

You might remember from your study of cells in earlier science classes that proteins are made in the ribosome of the cell. For proteins to be produced, the code carried in DNA needs to be read. But DNA cannot leave the nucleus of the cell in eukaryotic organisms. If DNA cannot leave the nucleus, how does the information carried on DNA get to the ribosome? There exists a special molecule called **messenger RNA** or mRNA. As the name *messenger* suggests, mRNA carries the message from the DNA sequence. Its only role is to carry a *message* of the DNA sequence to the place in the cell where the sequence can be translated.

The mRNA molecule reads the code on the DNA sequence using a process called transcription. Transcription is the process in which part of a DNA sequence is copied into a complementary sequence of ribonucleic acid (RNA). During transcription, the two strands of DNA separate and a strand of RNA is copied along one strand of the DNA molecule. Figure 8.16 shows you how RNA is formed. Transcription happens in the nucleus of cells in eukaryotic organisms.

Making RNA, continued

Cells make three major types of RNA. The first type, mRNA, is necessary for carrying information for the DNA in the cell's nucleus to the cell's cytoplasm where the proteins will be made. Transfer RNA (tRNA) and ribosomal RNA (rRNA) function in the process of assembling amino acids to make proteins.

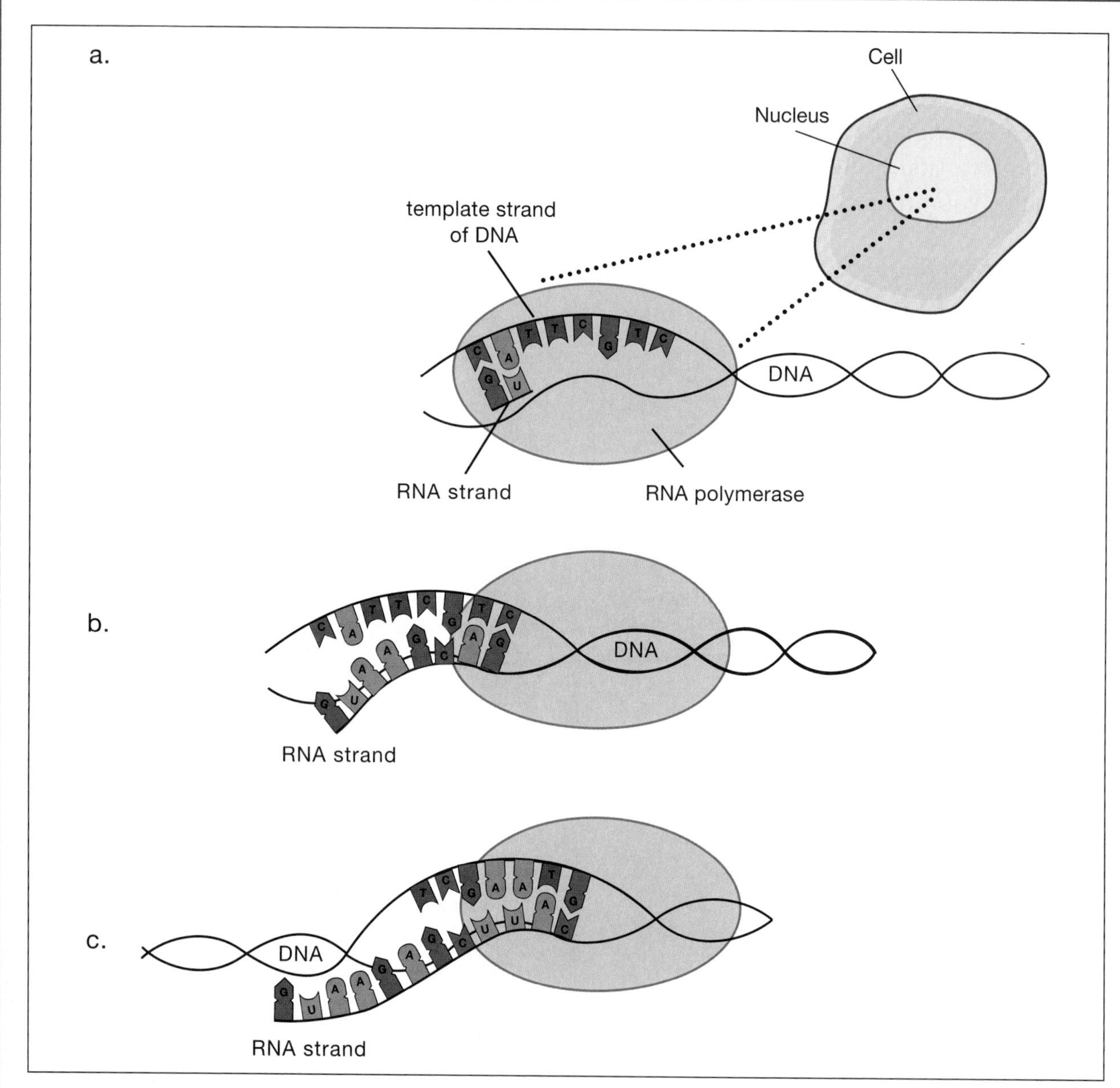

Figure 8.16 Transcription. (a) An enzyme synthesizes RNA from a template strand of DNA. (b) Note that as the RNA polymerase moves along the DNA, the double helix is unwound and the DNA and RNA nucleotides interact. (c) The DNA behind the enzyme re-forms a double helix. Eventually, when the enzyme that is building the RNA reaches the end of the gene, the DNA and RNA are released. Recall that genes code for proteins. What do you notice about the nucleotides on the DNA strand and the RNA strand?

3. To model what happens in transcription, work with a partner to carry out Steps 3a–f.

   a. Use your fingers to separate the double-stranded paper clip chain as you did for DNA replication. When DNA separates, it can either replicate or serve as a template for making proteins. Choose one of the strands for transcription.

   b. Use paper clips to transcribe your DNA sequence by making a strand of mRNA that is complementary to your DNA strand.

Remember, RNA has the nucleotide uracil instead of thymine. Use silver paper clips to represent uracil.

   c. Record your original DNA sequence and your mRNA sequence in your science notebook.

   original DNA sequence ______________________________

   mRNA sequence ______________________________

   d. Trade your original DNA strand with another team's original DNA strand from the previous activity.

   e. Practice transcription by transcribing the other team's strand. Record the original DNA sequence and the mRNA sequence in your science notebook.

   original DNA sequence ______________________________

   mRNA sequence ______________________________

   f. When you are finished with transcription, double-check your sequences with the other team.

Topic: transcription
Go to: www.scilinks.org
Code: 2Inquiry427

Stop & THINK

PART I

Participate in a class discussion of these questions. Record agreed-upon answers in your science notebook.

1. How is DNA transcription like DNA replication? How are the 2 processes different?

2. In this activity, you transcribed 2 different DNA strands. Each one was only 15 nucleotides long. That seems pretty short.

   a. How many different arrangements of nucleotides are possible in a strand of DNA that is 15 nucleotides long?

STOP & THINK, PART I, continued

b. How would the number in Question 2a compare with the number of different arrangements of nucleotides possible in a real strand of DNA?

3 How did transcribing 2 different strands of DNA help you understand the process of transcription?

Part II: Translation

Once the cell has formed a strand of mRNA from the DNA template, that mRNA strand can leave the nucleus and travel through the cytoplasm to the ribosomes. DNA is too large to leave the nucleus, but mRNA is small enough to fit through tiny pores. Proteins are made in the ribosomes. The next process on the road to making proteins is called **translation**. After transcription, the mRNA has information, but still needs to pass on the information for making proteins. Translation is the process of reading the information on mRNA and using that information to make proteins. Up until now, you have modeled the processes of DNA replication and transcription using paper clips. In Part II, you will switch gears a little to simulate both transcription and translation in a role-playing exercise. This simulation will help you get an overview of how proteins are made from start to finish.

Materials

none

Process and Procedure

1. Work in teams of 3 and arrange your desks to form a small circle. Label the area "ribosome." This circle will represent a ribosome in the cytoplasm of a cell. Each person in the team will play a role in protein synthesis.
2. Before you begin the role-playing activity, study the following guidelines:
   - DNA is located only in the nucleus of the cell in eukaryotic organisms. In natural settings, DNA cannot leave the nucleus! (For this activity, your teacher has marked an area that represents the nucleus.)
   - In RNA, uracil replaces thymine.
   - RNA is a single-stranded instead of double-stranded molecule.

- Proteins are made from long chains of amino acids.
- Proteins begin forming at a specific RNA sequence called a "start" codon. A **codon** is a sequence of 3 adjacent nucleotides on mRNA. For example, the codon that corresponds to the amino acid tryptophan consists of this sequence of nucleotides: UGG.

3. Decide who in your team will play each of these 3 major roles for the simulation. You will switch roles for the next rounds.

mRNA: This stands for messenger RNA. Messenger RNA transcribes the DNA template and delivers the message from the nucleus to the cytoplasm of a cell.

rRNA: This stands for ribosomal RNA. **Ribosomal RNA interprets the transcribed code as sections of 3 nucleotides. These sections are called codons.**

tRNA: **tRNA stands for** transfer RNA. **tRNA has a section of 3 nucleotides that is complementary to specific codons on the mRNA. This section on the tRNA is called an anticodon. The tRNA picks up amino acids using the information from its anticodon. It then assembles the amino acids into chains to make proteins at the ribosome. In this simulation, you will facilitate translation by moving the cards that represent tRNA.**

4. Role-play transcription in your team of 3 following Steps 4a–d as a guide.
   a. **mRNA:** Go to the nucleus (the teacher's desk) to get the DNA message.
   b. **mRNA:** Take a pen and your science notebook to "transcribe" the DNA sequence that your teacher assigns you. You cannot simply write down the DNA sequence. You are mRNA and you must transcribe the sequence in the nucleus.

The mRNA strand is produced by forming a strand of RNA that is complementary to the DNA strand. Remember, uracil replaces thymine.

   c. **mRNA:** Return to the ribosome with the transcribed message.

This is the last step in transcription. Translation begins when mRNA interacts with the ribosome.

   d. **rRNA:** Divide the mRNA strand into sections of 3 nucleotides each. Do this by drawing a vertical line between every third nucleotide. These sections of 3 nucleotides represent codons.

5. Role-play translation by following Steps 5a–h.

During translation, the mRNA code is deciphered and the language of RNA is translated into amino acids. Translation is like translating from one language to another language. You are going to take the language from RNA and translate it to make proteins.

a. tRNA: Use the codons to find amino acids. Do this by taking the sequence of codons and looking for anticodons listed on the cards placed around the room. The cards actually represent tRNA but you are facilitating the process.

An anticodon is a sequence of 3 nucleotides on a tRNA molecule that are complementary to an mRNA codon.

b. tRNA: Find a card with the correct anticodon. Bring it back to the ribosome and flip it over to reveal the word on the back of the card.

c. **mRNA, rRNA,** and tRNA: Record the word located by the tRNA in your science notebook.

d. tRNA: Return the card immediately to its original location so that other teams can find it. In the cell, the tRNA would actually take amino acids to assemble the proteins, but you need to return the card back to where you got it from.

e. tRNA: Continue matching the codons from your mRNA to the anticodons on the cards until all of the codons from your mRNA are translated.

f. tRNA: Record the words from the anticodon cards in sequential order. You should end up with a sentence.

g. tRNA: Check with your teacher to see if your sentence is correct. Record the sentence in your science notebook.

h. tRNA: Using the numbers on the sentences, read the sentences aloud in numerical order. Notice that you have now formed a paragraph. Record the paragraph in your science notebook.

6. Switch roles and repeat Steps 3–5.
7. Switch roles one last time and complete Steps 3–5 again.
8. To help you relate this role-playing simulation to what happens during protein synthesis in cells, complete Steps 8a–c.
   a. Read the following paragraph about protein synthesis and study figure 8.17.
   b. Create an analogy map comparing the simulation with protein synthesis. Use the headings "Part of Simulation" and "How It Is Similar to Protein Synthesis."
   c. What do the following analogies from this simulation represent in a real cell?
      - A word
      - A sentence
      - The paragraph

This activity used role playing to simulate the complex processes involved in protein synthesis. In real cells, amino acids are the basic building blocks of proteins and therefore the building blocks of life. The ribosome is like a protein factory: all the components needed for translation gather here to produce a product. Each set of three nucleotides on the tRNA code for amino acids. The tRNA pulls amino acids from the cell one at a time, forming a chain. The amino acid chains make up the specific needed proteins. Figure 8.17 shows how proteins are synthesized in the cell in the process of translation.

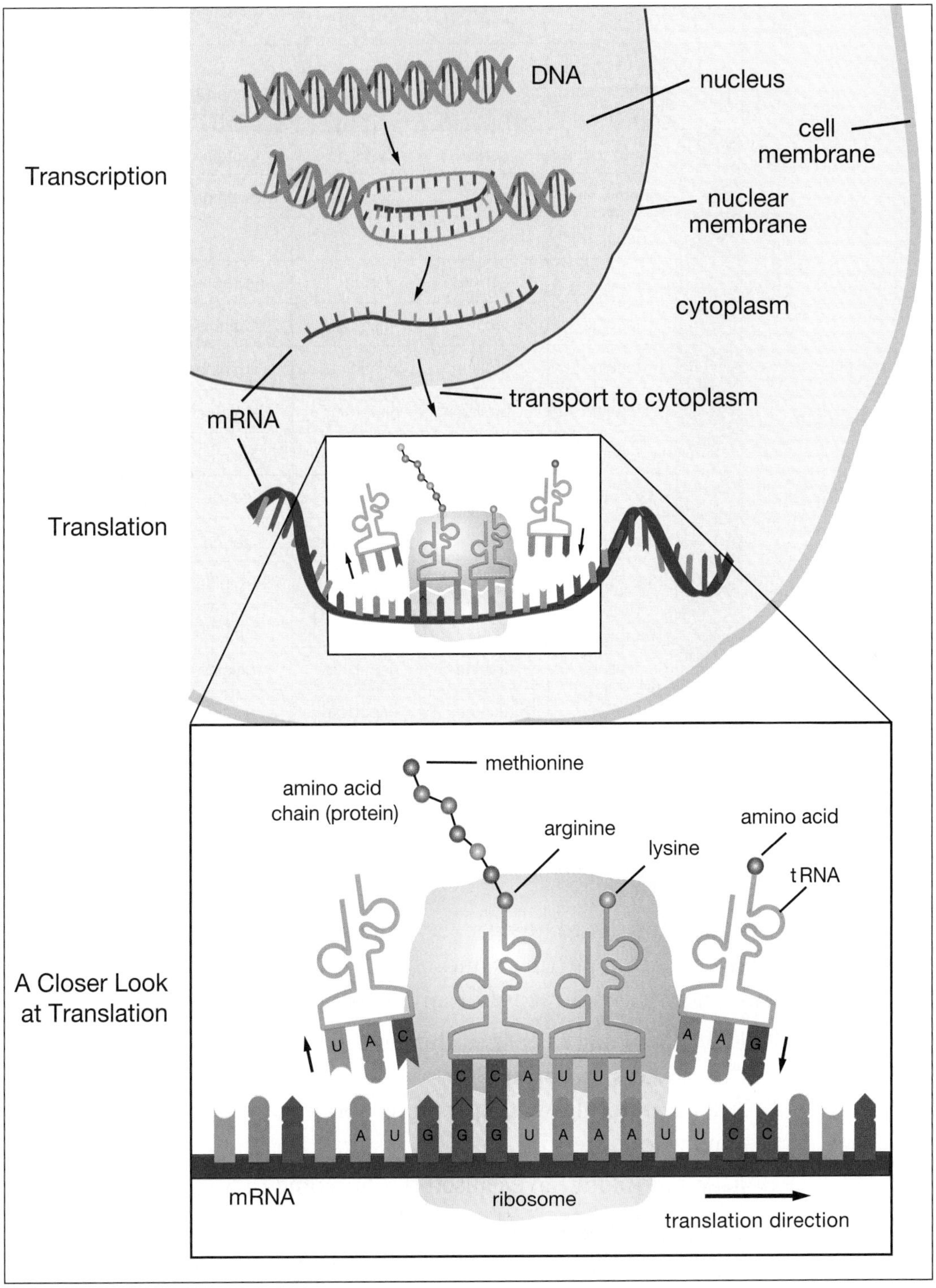

Figure 8.17 Protein synthesis. During protein synthesis, information stored in DNA is copied into mRNA through transcription. Then the mRNA enters the cytoplasm and attaches to a ribosome. To transfer the genetic code into a protein, tRNA with a specific amino acid attached reads each codon of mRNA. How was your role-playing activity like protein synthesis?

9. Answer the following questions about nucleotide sequences.
   a. How many arrangements of nucleotides are possible if you take 4 nucleotides, 3 at a time?
   b. Look at figure 8.18. This figure shows the codons for the amino acids in nature. How does your answer from Question 9a compare with the number of amino acids in nature?
   c. What is the corresponding nucleotide sequence for the amino acid valine?

First Base	Second Base: U	Second Base: C	Second Base: A	Second Base: G	Third Base
U	phenylanine	serine	tyrosine	cysteine	U
U	phenylanine	serine	tyrosine	cysteine	C
U	leucine	serine	stop	stop	A
U	leucine	serine	stop	tryptophan	G
C	leucine	proline	histidine	arginine	U
C	leucine	proline	histidine	arginine	C
C	leucine	proline	glutamine	arginine	A
C	leucine	proline	glutamine	arginine	G
A	isoleucine	threonine	asparagine	serine	U
A	isoleucine	threonine	asparagine	serine	C
A	isoleucine	threonine	lysine	arginine	A
A	(start) methionine	threonine	lysine	arginine	G
G	valine	alanine	aspartate	glycine	U
G	valine	alanine	aspartate	glycine	C
G	valine	alanine	glutamate	glycine	A
G	valine	alanine	glutamate	glycine	G

▶ **Figure 8.18 Codons.** The genetic code is written in nucleotide triplets, or codons, in a strand of mRNA. Each codon specifies an amino acid, as shown in the boxes. To use the table, follow a codon's three nucleotides to arrive at the corresponding amino acid. What amino acid does the codon GGA code for?

Reflect and Connect

Work individually to answer these questions. Then compare your answers with a partner's and revise your answers as you learn something new. Keep a record of any revision in your science notebook.

1. Describe what happened during the translation process. Why is this process important?
2. Answer the following questions about round 3 of the simulation (Step 7).
   a. What might have caused the outcome in Step 7 of the activity?
   b. Do you think this happens in nature? Explain your answer.

3. In your own words, or in a diagram, briefly describe the relationships among nucleotides, DNA, genes, chromosomes, cells, and traits in an organism.
4. Did the word and sentence analogy help you understand the complex process of protein synthesis? Why or why not?

SCILINKS
NSTA
Topic: protein synthesis
Go to: www.scilinks.org
Code: 2Inquiry433

SIDEBAR

Mapping the Human Genome

As technology advances, and our understanding of the mechanism of inheritance increases, we continue to discover more about the human genome. In 2003, scientists finished mapping the entire human genome. The biggest surprise at the completion of the project was that there were fewer genes than scientists had expected.

A **genome** is all of the information coded in the DNA of an organism. It contains the complete set of genetic instructions for making an organism. Human cells that have nuclei (with the exception of egg and sperm cells) normally contain 22 pairs of autosomes (nonsex chromosomes), plus two sex chromosomes (XX or XY). Remember, these chromosomes contain DNA. When the Human Genome Project (HGP) was completed, scientists learned the entire sequence of human DNA and the location of each gene in our chromosomes.

Two major groups worked independently to sequence the human genome. The HGP was the public group, which was funded in the United States primarily by the Department of Energy and the National Institutes of Health. Several other countries were also involved. The other group was a

▲ **Automated DNA sequencing.** Scientists use machines to help them sequence multiple samples of DNA. Each of the colors on the screen represents one of the four nitrogen bases.

Mapping the Human Genome, continued

private company called Celera Genomics Corporation.

Human DNA contains approximately 3.2 billion base pairs of DNA. So determining the sequence, and finding and mapping the genes was a tremendous task. If the DNA sequence of the human genome was compiled in books, we would need about 200 volumes at 1,000 pages each to hold all this information. Scientists learned that there are approximately 25,000 genes in human DNA.

The major findings of mapping the human genome include the following:

- Scientists were surprised at the small number of genes. It appears that humans have only a few thousand more genes than the roundworm *C. elegans*.
- Humans are 99.99 percent similar to one another in our DNA. It does not appear that there is much variation in the human population.
- Genes appear to be concentrated in random areas along the genome, with vast expanses of noncoding DNA in between.
- Chromosome 1 has the most genes (about 3,000); the Y chromosome has the fewest (about 230).
- Sperm carry twice as many mutations as eggs. This is interesting because mutations are a major source of genetic errors and also lead to variations in a population.
- We do not know the functions for more than half of the genes that were discovered.
- Some genes appear to have come from bacteria that infected our ancestors millions of years ago. This discovery provides additional evidence of evolution.
- Less than 2 percent of the genome codes for proteins.

The human genome map will help in diagnosing, treating, and preventing disease in the future. As genes are isolated, scientists will be able to find small differences in DNA sequences. These variations might be the cause of some genetic disorders in people. Once scientists identify these variations, they may be able to develop treatments and cures for some of the diseases. Eventually, treatments may even be customized to individual genetic profiles. Customizing treatments likely would increase their effectiveness and reduce adverse drug reactions. Some diseases might be cured either by altering the proteins produced or, eventually, by gene therapy (fixing the gene).

As more genes are identified, scientists are finding genetic basis for psychiatric disorders. Identifying such genes will help our understanding of the causes of depression, schizophrenia, and other mental disorders. Once the contributions from those genes are understood, it will be possible to develop better medications.

The process of mapping the human genome has also given rise to new fields of study, such as bioinformatics, proteomics, and pharmacogenics. Bioinformatics uses sophisticated data management systems and computers to identify genes in the DNA sequence data and establish their functions. Proteomics is the study of protein structure, function, and interactions. Pharmacogenics is the study of how genetic variation affects the body's response to drugs. Research in these areas might someday lead to the development of drugs specifically tailored to an individual's genetic makeup.

Mapping the human genome has generated some important ethical concerns that as individuals and society as a whole, we will have to address. Scientists are developing new technologies that can sequence an individual's genome for less than $1,000. This technology has already set in motion questions about personal privacy. For example, "Who will have the right to see individuals' genetic information?" "Could this information be used against people in the workplace?" "Would insurance companies have access to individual genetic information?" and "Should families have the right to see profiles of other family members?" Federal and state governments are struggling with legislation to protect genetic privacy.

Far-reaching questions also arise when we think about the entire human population. Should our genes be "fixed"? At what point do we decide what is a detrimental condition? As we develop new treatments and cures, what will happen to the dynamics of the human population? Will humans live longer? Will diseases such as cancer be eradicated? How will tinkering with genetics affect the human population as a whole?

These ethical concerns that surround the human genome will affect you in your lifetime. What questions should you ask and what information will you need to understand the important decisions that will be made as a result of mapping the human genome?

SCILINKS® NSTA
Topic: Human Genome Project
Go to: www.scilinks.org
Code: 2Inquiry435

Nobody's Perfect

ELABORATE

The processes of DNA replication, transcription, and translation are amazing. These processes are occurring in the cells of all living things, every second of every day. If you take all the DNA from your body cells and place it end to end, your body alone contains more than 3 million miles of DNA! Much of that DNA is either replicating or being used as a template for transcription.

Most of the time, the processes of DNA replication, transcription, and translation occur without any problems. The processes remain constant. However, eventually mistakes do occur. These mistakes are called **mutations**. Mutations lead to changes in DNA sequences. You experienced some consequences of mutations in the activity *Transcription and Translation—the Road to Making Proteins*. In that activity, a mutation affected your sentences. In *Nobody's Perfect*, you will work by yourself and with a partner to apply what you learned in the sentence activity to understand how real mutations affect life.

Part I: A Natural Mistake

When you hear the word "mutation" or "mutant," many thoughts and ideas likely come to mind. You might have seen horror movies with a wild mutant running around or alien mutants landing on Earth. Mutations do cause changes in organisms, and the movies are a great way to sensationalize these changes. But what happens when real DNA mutates? In Part I of this activity, you will identify some of your current thoughts about mutations and check those thoughts as you learn about mutations in nature.

Materials

none

Process and Procedure

1. Share what you know about mutations with a classmate and the class by following Steps 1a–d.
   a. Share some ideas you have about mutations with a classmate. Based on your discussion, develop 3 statements about mutations and record them in your science notebook.
   b. Read your statements aloud to contribute to a class list.
   c. Record the statements from the class list in your science notebook.
   d. Decide whether you think each statement is true or false. Explain your reasoning in your science notebook.

2. Read *We All Make Mistakes* to learn about mutations. Use this question to focus your reading: "In what ways do mutations affect organisms?"

READING

We All Make Mistakes

What happens when a mutation in DNA occurs? The consequences of a mutation might or might not have an effect on the message the DNA is sending. Imagine a blueprint for a building. The length of a wall might be written on the blueprint as 30 meters (m). What if the architect accidentally spills something on the blueprint? The carpenter begins to measure the boards according to the lengths on the blueprint, but reads 33 m instead of 30 m. The carpenter might notice this mistake and repair it (as some DNA-repairing enzymes do in the cell). If the carpenter does not fix the error, however, it might affect the structural properties of the building.

Some mutations in DNA happen spontaneously during the normal process of DNA replication. Some mutations happen as a result of natural factors such as radiation. Certain types of radiation such as ultraviolet radiation from the Sun can cause mutations in DNA. Mutations can also be caused by environmental or chemical toxins. Chemicals found in tobacco smoke, charcoal-grilled foods, and toxic waste contain substances that can cause mutations.

The third time you went through the protein synthesis activity, there was a mutation in all of the DNA sequences. You might have noticed, however, that some sentences still made sense. Mutations in DNA do not always have negative effects. Sometimes they have no observable effect on organisms. In other cases, mutations can benefit organisms. In every population, there are many genes coding for traits that exist because of mutations in DNA and new combinations of genes formed during meiosis. How do those mutations stay in a population and how do they help populations? The traits that result from mutations are not always detrimental to the organism. Therefore, the organism thrives and reproduces, passing the trait to its offspring. The traits that result from mutations and recombination lead to variability within populations. You might remember from chapter 6, *Exploring Change*, that variability within a population enables the population to survive through natural selection.

While some mutations might not make a difference to an organism, others might have a great impact on an individual organism. Fortunately, many harmful mutations are fixed before they cause any harm. The cell has repair enzymes that patrol DNA for defects. If a mutation is detected, the damaged nucleotides are cut out and replaced with correct nucleotides. However, the mistakes are not always caught. Just as the carpenter might not detect the mistake in the blueprint, the repair mechanisms in a cell might not always catch or be able to repair mutations. Some inherited mutations are passed to future generations and affect entire populations of organisms. To learn about some examples of how mutations have affected populations, read the sidebar *Mutations and Society*.

When a mutation occurs in any cell other than a gamete (sperm or egg cell), each new cell produced from that cell will carry the mutation. When mutations occur in nongamete (somatic) cells, they only affect the individual. They are not passed to offspring. As the cells carrying the mutation continue to divide, they produce a group of mutated cells within an organism. Cancer is one example of mutated cells growing out of control.

When a mutation is in the DNA of a gamete, it is known as a genetically linked mutation and it can be inherited by the offspring. For example, Huntington's disease and cystic fibrosis are genetically linked conditions that you learned about in chapter 7. In these conditions, and many others like them, certain needed proteins malfunction. If a person does not have these needed proteins, he or she often suffers ill effects and might have a shortened life span. These mutations are passed on through the gametes, sperm and egg, from the parents.

SCILINKS® NSTA
Topic: mutations
Go to: www.scilinks.org
Code: 2Inquiry437

3. Participate in a class discussion of the reading and show your understanding of mutations by answering Questions 3a–c.
   a. Answer the focus question: In what ways do mutations affect organisms?
   b. How can mutations occur?

c. Why can mutations in gametes have a different effect than mutations in nongamete cells?

4. Look back at your responses to the 3 statements you developed in Step 1. Would you change any of your answers? Record your corrected responses in your science notebook.

Stop & THINK

PART I

Work with your partner to answer the following questions. Record your answers in your science notebook.

1. Why does each new cell carry a mutation from the original cell?
2. How are genetically linked mutations passed from generation to generation? Show your understanding by drawing a diagram. Write a caption for your diagram that explains your answer in words.

   Review figure 7.17 in chapter 7 to help you answer this question. Start with a cell containing only 1 pair of chromosomes.
3. Can organisms avoid mutations? Explain your reasoning.

Part II: Mutations Lead to Variation

In *We All Make Mistakes*, you learned that mutations lead to variability in populations and you know that variability helps species survive. Variations are present in all populations of organisms. Some of these variations are not easily observed while others are quite noticeable. We often overlook variability within populations, yet it is an important feature of successful populations.

How does variation in a population help it survive? In Part II, you will work with a partner to observe variability within a population and think about how variability is important to species survival.

Materials

For each team of 2 students

1 ruler

1 container of 25 seeds (all of the same type)

graph paper

access to measuring tools

Process and Procedure

1. Obtain a container of 1 type of seeds. These seeds are representatives from their population.
2. Look at the seeds with your partner. Is there much variation among them? Record all the ways in which the seeds might vary from one another in your science notebook.
3. Decide on 1 variation to investigate within this seed population. To help you decide, think about what you could measure as evidence of this variation. Record your decision in your science notebook.
4. Make a data table to record your data in your science notebook.
5. Investigate your chosen variation in your population of seeds. Record your data in your science notebook.
6. Make a graph of your data. Include highlight comments and a caption with the graph.
7. Analyze your graph by completing the following tasks.
   a. Describe the amount of variation you observed in your population of seeds.
   b. Describe the shape of your graph. Where in the graph are most of the seeds found?
   c. What might have caused the variation in your seed population? Describe 2 possible factors.
8. Read the following paragraph, which describes how seeds are adapted for survival. Seeds themselves are specialized in ways to help them survive. Focus your thinking with the question, "How do you think variation might be related to seed survival?"

   Many people do not realize that seeds contain living things. Seeds contain baby plants and seeds are necessary for plant species to survive. Plants produce seeds when their ovules (eggs) are fertilized by pollen. This process is much like the sperm and egg uniting in animals to form a zygote. A seed actually contains a living baby plant (embryo) surrounded by stored food. Look at figure 8.19 to see a diagram of the inside of a seed.

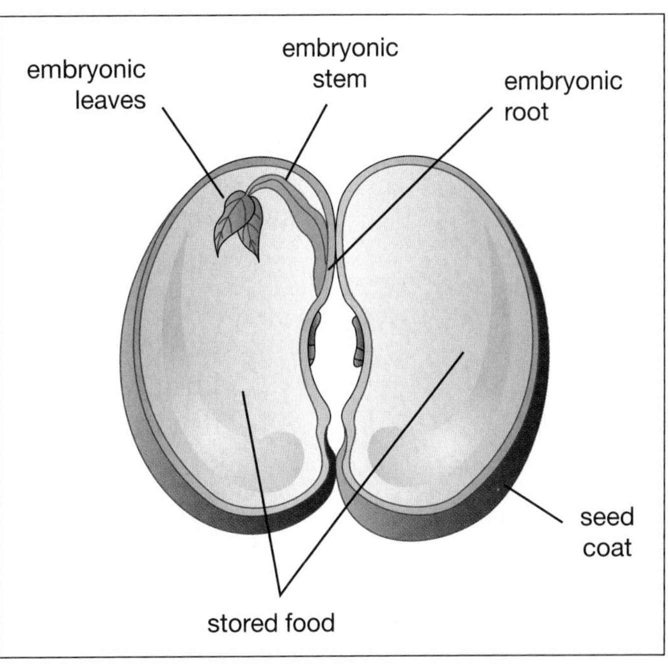

▲ **Figure 8.19 Longitudinal section of a bean seed.** In seeds, the embryo uses the stored food until conditions are right for it to germinate (sprout) and begin growing toward the surface. Seeds depend on the stored food until they can reach the light and begin making their own food through photosynthesis. Sometimes seeds have to wait quite awhile before conditions become favorable for growth. Many animals such as birds, squirrels, and chipmunks eat seeds before they germinate.

9. Answer the following questions using your graph from this activity and the reading in Step 8.
   a. Which group within your population of seeds would most likely not be eaten by birds? Explain your reasoning.
   b. Predict what your bar graph would look like several years from now if the environment slowly changed and became darker. Show your predictions using a dotted line on your graph labeled "d." Explain your reasoning.
   c. What would your bar graph look like several years in the future if the environment slowly changed and the winters became longer? Show your predictions using a dotted line on your graph labeled "w." Explain your reasoning.

Reflect and Connect

Work individually to answer the following questions. Record your answers in your science notebook.

1. How might variability within a population help that population survive?
2. How might mutations help your population of seeds survive?
3. Imagine there is a mutation in the DNA of a few of the seeds that caused the production of a protein that made the seeds slightly larger. How would that affect your population of seeds? Explain your reasoning.
4. How do mutations relate to the evolution of a species? Give examples using your experiences in this unit.

Think back to chapter 6 when you completed the activity *Who Will Survive?* In that activity, you captured seeds that represented different variations within the same species. You determined that influences, such as predators, can make survival of some individuals more likely than others. Differential survival can cause a species to change over time—to evolve.

5. Look back at your initial responses to the statements in Step 1 of Part I. Would you change any of your responses? Why or why not? Write your corrected responses in your science notebook.

SIDEBAR

Mutations and Society

Variability is important for species survival. Humans depend on other organisms. Therefore, the variation in the populations of other organisms can affect our way of life. One example of how variation within a population has affected our society is the Irish potato famine of 1845. The Irish grew potatoes for more than 200 years without any major problems. Most of the potato crops in Ireland were composed of two varieties of potatoes, the *Lumper* and the *Cup*. When a fungus was brought over from North America, it destroyed the entire *Lumper* and *Cup* potato crops. Had there been more varieties of potatoes planted, some might have been resistant to the species of fungus and survived. Because of the lack of variety, nearly the entire food source for the people in Ireland was wiped out.

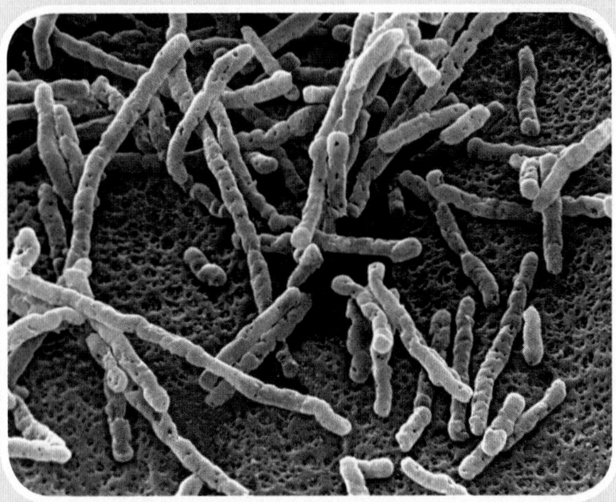

▲ ***Clostridium difficile.*** *Clostridium difficile* is a bacterium that causes diarrhea and occasionally more serious intestinal conditions. Outbreaks of *C. difficile* infections have become more prevalent in hospitals since 2004. Scientists think that a new strain has developed that is more resistant to some types of antibiotics.

Unfortunately, some variations help unwanted organisms to survive. One example is bacteria. Bacteria reproduce quickly. This rapid rate of reproduction increases the chance that mutations will appear in the DNA sequences of a bacteria population. Some species of bacteria have mutated enough to be resistant to antibiotics, and as a result can survive antibiotic treatments. The offspring of these mutated bacteria also are resistant. Eventually, many strains of bacteria will be resistant because these few bacteria had the mutation. It is hard for doctors to treat diseases caused by antibiotic-resistant bacteria.

Sometimes one mutation can affect a population in both positive and negative ways. Sickle-cell disease in humans causes red blood cells to become sickle shaped, which leads to blocked blood vessels. This causes pain and damage to areas that are not receiving an adequate blood supply. People who are carriers for the sickle-cell trait, however, are less likely to suffer from malaria than those without the sickle-cell trait. Malaria kills more than 1 million people each year around the world. Resistance to malaria is a major survival advantage for people who live in areas where malaria is a problem.

Mutations in DNA can be unwelcome, but they are also what enable species to survive. They might cause disease or even death. However, without mutations, we would not have the variation within populations or the diversity of life we have on the planet today.

ELABORATE

DNA and Evolution

In *Nobody's Perfect*, you learned that mutation and new combinations of genes formed during meiosis can lead to variation in a population of organisms. But how do scientists know how similar the genetic code is among different organisms? New advances in technology allow scientists to understand more about DNA. Scientists can isolate genes, study their sequence, and determine what proteins they code for. This knowledge can help scientists learn more about how closely organisms are related to one another. Scientists predict how closely related organisms are by looking for similarities in their DNA sequences. Using this information, scientists can determine the common ancestors for organisms and predict how the organisms evolved.

In *DNA and Evolution*, you will work individually to see how scientists use DNA to determine how closely related species are. You will learn how scientists use this evidence to support the theory of evolution.

Materials

none

Process and Procedure

1. Predict which pair of organisms (a, b, or c) you think are the most closely related to each other. Explain your reasoning.
   a. Gorillas and chimpanzees
   b. Humans and gorillas
   c. Humans and chimpanzees
2. Study the 3 DNA sequences in figure 8.20. Scientists use DNA sequences to determine how closely related species are.
3. Compare the DNA sequences. Which 2 organisms appear to be the most closely related? What is your evidence?

Human DNA :	T	C	C	G	T	A	T	T	T	G	G	T	T	G	G	C	T	A	A	T
Gorilla DNA :	T	C	C	G	G	G	G	A	A	G	G	T	T	C	A	T	C	C	G	G
Chimpanzee DNA :	T	C	C	G	G	G	G	A	A	G	G	T	T	G	G	C	T	A	A	T

▲ **Figure 8.20 Sections of DNA sequences from three primates.** Each DNA sequence represents a small section of a gene that codes for the protein hemoglobin and is labeled with the name of the organism it was taken from.

4. Read the following paragraphs that describe 2 hypotheses of how primates evolved. As you are reading, think about how the 2 theories are similar and how they are different.

   Most scientists agree that humans, gorillas, and chimpanzees shared a common ancestor at one time in evolutionary history. However, one group thinks the fossil record shows that gorillas, chimpanzees, and humans split from one common ancestor at the same time. Their model for this split is shown in figure 8.21a.

   A second group thinks the fossil record shows there were two splits. In the first split, gorillas split from the common ancestor. Humans and chimpanzees then shared another common ancestor for perhaps 2 million years. They then split again and evolved into their present species. The model for this pattern of splitting is shown in figure 8.21b.
5. Use the DNA sequences from Step 2 to investigate this debate. Which model in the evolutionary debate is more accurate based on the DNA evidence? Justify your answer.

Reflect and Connect

Work alone to answer the following questions. Record your answers in your science notebook.

1. How is DNA used to determine relatedness among organisms?
2. How can DNA be used as evidence for common ancestry? Use a diagram like the one in figure 8.21 to support your answer. Include a caption with your diagram to indicate which organisms are more closely related.

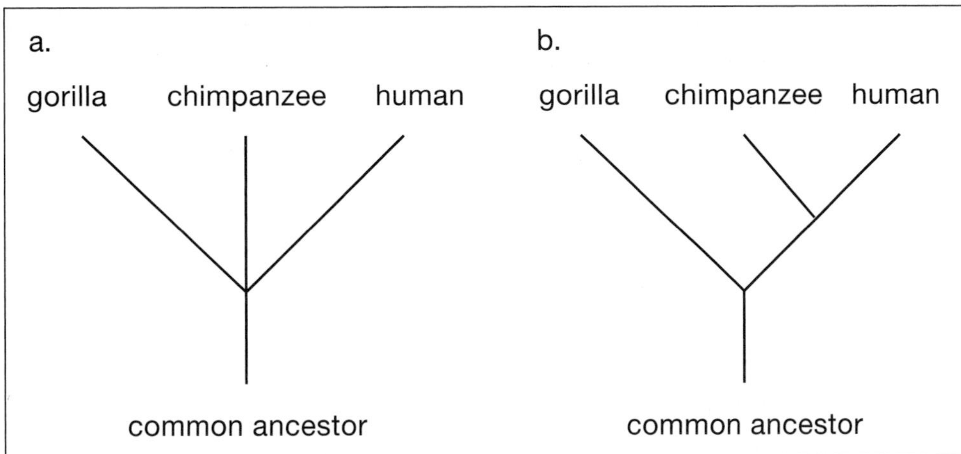

▲ **Figure 8.21 Models of primate evolution.** Diagram (a) shows that gorillas, chimpanzees, and humans share one common ancestor. Diagram (b) shows that chimpanzees and humans have a different common ancestor than gorillas. This also suggests that chimpanzees and humans are more closely related than chimpanzees and gorillas or humans and gorillas.

3. Imagine you could obtain DNA from common ancestors that lived millions of years ago. How would their DNA sequences compare with the species that now exist? Think about how the DNA sequence changes over time to explain your reasoning.
4. How can DNA evidence be used to support the theory of evolution?

EVALUATE

Sharing Your Knowledge

Many people know that DNA is the code of life but most do not understand how it works. In this chapter, you have learned a great deal about DNA. You have learned about its structure and function and why it is so significant to life. In *Sharing Your Knowledge*, you will summarize what you know about DNA to help someone else understand how it functions as the code of life.

Imagine that a new student just transferred to your school. Your teacher has asked you to help bring him up to date on what you have been learning about DNA. But how can you go about condensing the major ideas about DNA for this new student? You decide that the most efficient way to teach him about DNA is to prepare a summary. In this summary, you will address the main concepts you learned in this chapter and show how these concepts are related.

One method you might use to prepare your summary is to create a graphic organizer. Graphic organizers are visual representations of information such as concept maps or story boards. Other ways to prepare a summary include flash cards, game boards, a skit, a summary essay, or a PowerPoint presentation. For this activity, you get to decide which technique you want to use. If you are more comfortable with graphic organizers, then that may be the way you want to go. If you are a good writer and find that writing is a good way to summarize major ideas, then you would probably want to write an essay. The choice is up to you. No matter what summary method you choose, however, you will make a model of DNA to include with your summary.

Materials

For each student

note cards

materials for creating a summary

1 *Example Concept Map* handout (optional)

1 *Sharing Your Knowledge Scoring Rubric* handout

Process and Procedure

1. Review the *Sharing Your Knowledge Scoring Rubric* to see what your teacher expects of you for this activity.
2. Hold a brainstorming session with your class. Make a list of the terms, processes, and concepts that you learned about in this chapter. Your teacher will record your ideas on the board.

Brainstorming is a process of generating ideas about a specific subject without judging their quality. (You will review the ideas later.) You may want to go back through the chapter and your science notebook to help you identify all the topics, concepts, and terms that relate to DNA.

3. Write the terms and concepts from the class list on the board in your science notebook; include any topics your teacher adds to the list. Place a star next to the terms identified by a star on the class list.
4. List each of these terms on a separate note card.
5. Work with your partner to develop notes that summarize each term. Use the information from your science notebooks and student books. Record your notes in a bulleted list, as sentences that describe each topic, or with labeled diagrams or sketches. Put these notes on the back of the cards.
6. With your partner, decide how the terms are connected and rank the importance of each by following Steps 6a–d.
   a. Arrange your cards in a hierarchy to show the relative importance of each idea about DNA.

A hierarchy is a way of organizing or ranking things.

   b. Arrange the cards on a table according to the hierarchy you assigned in Step 6a.
   c. Rearrange the cards so that those ideas that are connected in some way are placed next to each other.
   d. Sketch the arrangement of the cards in your science notebook. Describe briefly why you arranged the cards as you did.
7. Summarize what you know about DNA by completing Steps 7a–b.
   a. Make a model of DNA. You can use a model similar to the one in this chapter or develop a new model of your own.
   b. Choose your summary method. You can use concept maps, story boards, flash cards, game boards, a skit, a summary essay, or a PowerPoint presentation.

If you choose to design a concept map, you might want to use the hierarchy from Step 6 as a starting point. To complete the assignment successfully, however, you must create a new concept map and follow the guidelines in Step 8.

Whatever method you choose, be sure to show your understanding of the terms and concepts and how they relate to one another. In addition, you must use all of the starred terms (see Step 3).

8. Prepare your summary individually. Your finished product should include the following parts:
   - Title: Describe what your summary is about.
   - Terms and concepts: Use all the terms and concepts generated from the class brainstorming session as well as those your teacher added. Circle all the terms in your summary.
   - Additional terms: You might find that there are some terms that are associated with DNA that did not come up in the brainstorming session. Add these terms and circle them in another color.
   - Relationships and connections: Your summary must show clear connections and relationships between and among the terms and concepts. How are the terms related? What do they have to do with one another? Make the connections clear.
   - Organization: Make sure your summary is neat and easy to follow.
   - DNA model critique: Describe how the model accurately represents DNA; point out at least 1 weakness of the model.
9. Evaluate your summary using the scoring rubric and the requirements listed in Step 8.
10. Describe at least 2 ways you could improve your summary.

CHAPTER 9

Genetic Engineering

Genetic Engineering

In the last 40 years, science has greatly increased our understanding of the structure and function of DNA. Scientists have also improved their ability to work with it in the laboratory. In fact, our increasing ability to study and manipulate DNA has led to a revolution in the ways that scientists conduct research. That, in turn, has changed how many industries conduct their day-to-day business.

Although the technologies are new, our basic interest in studying and manipulating genetic information is not new. For centuries, humans have selectively bred plants and animals to produce organisms with desirable traits. Traditional methods of agricultural breeding were the earliest forms of genetic engineering. In selective breeding, humans cross plants or animals that have desirable traits to produce new generations.

▲ **Figure 9.1**
Electrophoresis. Scientists have developed many powerful techniques for examining DNA.

In recent years, scientists have developed more powerful techniques for examining DNA at the molecular level (figure 9.1). These techniques make it possible to change the genotypes of organisms. Many other new techniques allow scientists to alter the DNA of a species in much more detailed ways than the older methods of selective breeding. It is now possible to introduce genes into an organism that neither parent possessed. It is even possible for scientists to remove genes from one organism and introduce them into an unrelated organism.

In chapter 9, *Genetic Engineering*, you will apply your understanding about DNA, heredity, and evolution from *Exploring Change*, *Tracking Traits*, and *Instructions for Life* (chapters 6, 7, and 8) to the field of genetic engineering. **Genetic engineering** introduces new traits into organisms. One of the best known applications of genetic engineering is the creation of genetically modified organisms (GMOs). In this chapter, you will simulate advanced methods in genetic engineering and consider various decisions about the ethics of using these methods. You will also learn how these methods include the fields of chemistry and earth science, as well as biology. In the process, your understanding of changes in genetic material will deepen. You will learn that these changes cause living organisms to develop in new ways.

Goals for the Chapter

In chapter 9, you will learn about genetic engineering. By the end of this chapter, you will be able to answer the following questions:

- What components of a cell are involved in genetic engineering?
- What laboratory processes are involved in genetic engineering?
- How do scientists apply the processes of genetic engineering to solve everyday problems?
- What is a systematic way of addressing bioethical questions?

You will have the opportunity to answer these questions by participating in the following activities:

ENGAGE	Company Policy
EXPLORE	Moving Genes—Recombinant DNA Technology
EXPLAIN	How Can It Be Done?
ELABORATE	Biotechnology and Society
EVALUATE	Can It Be Done? Should It Be Done?

Chapter organizers help you monitor your progress through a chapter. This organizer will help you see what you will learn about genetic engineering. Review it as you complete an activity to see what you have accomplished.

Genetic Engineering

Engage

Linking Question

What is one of the key processes of genetic engineering?

Company Policy

Key Idea:

Genetically altered food poses many ethical considerations.

Explore

Moving Genes—Recombinant DNA Technology

Key Idea:

Cutting, recombining, and transferring DNA fragments follows a specific sequence of procedural steps.

Linking Question

Are all techniques similar and what are some specific applications of the general recombinant DNA process?

Explain

How Can It be Done?

Key Idea:

Gene therapy, drug therapy, tissue engineering, and gene "bullets" are examples of recombinant DNA processes.

EVALUATE

Can It Be Done, Should It Be Done?

Key Idea:

Both scientific knowledge about genetic engineering processes and a systematic approach to solving ethical dilemmas are required to solve modern problems.

Linking Question

Will a model ethics problem-solving process help me address current bioethics issues?

CHAPTER 9

Major Concepts

- **Genetic material can be transferred from one organism to another by human intervention.**
- **Only small parts of DNA are required to be transferred from one organism to another in order to affect large changes.**
- **Genetic engineering processes create some organisms with beneficial characteristics and some with damaging characteristics.**
- **Ethical considerations about genetic engineering can be approached systematically, like inquiry.**

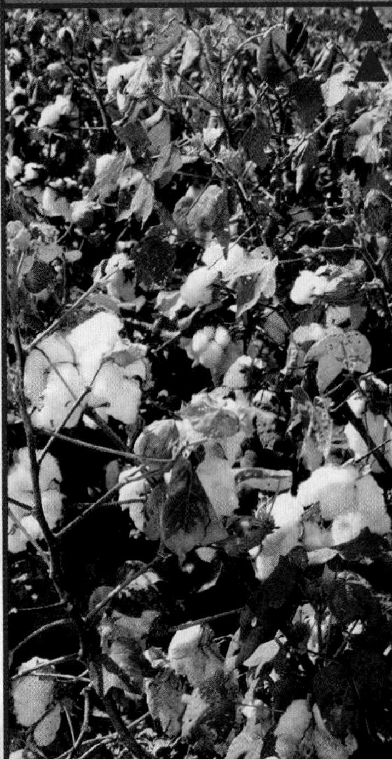

Linking Question

What are some technologies dependent on genetic engineering and what ethical issues do these technologies introduce?

ELABORATE

Biotechnology and Society

Key Ideas:

- Many areas of science utilize genetic engineering processes to address important applications.
- Ethical questions can be approached systematically, much like inquiry.

ENGAGE

Company Policy

▲ **Figure 9.2 Genetically modified food.** Are these foods safe to eat? What would you need to know to find out?

Genetically engineered food—what is it? Does it affect you? Where does it come from? How is it processed? Is it safe? These are all questions careful consumers ask (figure 9.2). Scientists and engineers also ask these questions as they develop new technologies. With these new technologies come new issues that societies need to address. You will begin thinking about these issues in a systematic way as you work individually and in a team in *Company Policy*.

Materials

For each team of 4 students

2 markers, each a different color

butcher paper or poster paper

Process and Procedure

1. Read the magazine advertisement shown in figure 9.3 carefully. As you read the policy, use this focus question to guide your thinking: "What do I need to know about genetically engineered food to form an educated opinion?"
2. Write 5 questions that come to mind after reading the ad. Word your questions as if you were a consumer and title your questions, "Consumer Questions."

EDEN FOODS

Eden – GEO-Free Assurance Since 1993

Foreseeing the commercialization of genetically engineered food, Eden established our policy against genetically engineered organisms (GEOs) and their derivatives in food in February 1993. Eden's Purchasing Department, working with our suppliers, has protected our patrons and does everything possible to make sure our food is free of GEOs.

In 1998 the *New York Times* hired a laboratory to test for GEOs in eleven soy and corn based foods, and the only one that tested negative was EDENSOY soymilk.

Eden Foods is doing everything possible to protect our customers from the genetically engineered food experiment.

The EDEN brand is your best assurance of freedom from GEOs. We take every available step to ensure our avoidance of GEOs, including:

- In-house GEO testing of each batch of corn and soybeans.
- Our traditional methods of processing and fermentation, rather than pharmaceutical enzymes.
- Knowing our growers, suppliers, and their families.
- Supporting consumer and environmental organizations working for the mandatory labeling of GE food and ingredients.

13 February 1993

Dear EDEN Patron,

The trend to commercialize genetically engineered food compels Eden Foods to assure you that we will not support or participate in this movement away from natural foods as they are manifest by Nature.

Please let this letter serve as our affidavit and your assurance that Eden Foods will not purchase or sell any food or food ingredient known to be genetically engineered and, that we will act to best ensure our avoidance of such.

You can depend upon Eden Foods to be diligent in avoiding any aspect of the commercialization of genetically engineered food. We object to the introduction of these foods for human consumption in any manner, for any reason. We are fundamentally opposed to these foods for moral, ethical, and practical reasons.

With more than twenty-four years in the natural foods industry, I remain unaware of any other food company that spends a greater percentage of its time or money to be certain of the growing, ingredients, and processing used for foods carrying its brand name.

Very truly yours,
Michael J. Potter
Chairman and President

◀ **Figure 9.3 Company policy.** This company advertises its policy regarding genetically engineered food.

Always record your thinking in your science notebook. That way, you can go back and track how new information changed your views and helped you learn.

3. Read your questions in a team of 4 students and listen to your team members as they read their questions.

For each question, be sure to ask the questioner why it is important to him or her as a consumer.

4. With your team, write 5 questions that you would ask as the president of this company before you would agree to establish this policy for your company. Title these questions, "Company Executive Questions."
5. Decide as a team how to organize both the consumer and company executive questions on a large sheet of butcher paper so that the entire class can read and understand your questions.
6. Copy your team's list of consumer and company executive questions in your science notebook. Then post your team's list on butcher paper in the classroom.

Reflect and Connect

Answer the following questions in your science notebook;w use complete sentences. Read your answers to your team members and listen to them read their answers. Record any new thoughts that result from hearing your teammates' answers.

1. As a consumer who likes this company's products, how might this policy be a hassle for you?
2. As a consumer, what would you appreciate about this company's policy?
3. As the company's executive, what are some of the advantages and disadvantages to establishing this company policy? How might establishing this policy hurt the company? How might this policy help the company?
4. Speaking for yourself now, would you eat genetically altered food? What information or evidence about genetically altered food do you want to have in order to make your decision?

EXPLORE

Moving Genes—Recombinant DNA Technology

In *Company Policy*, you might have asked questions like, "What is genetic engineering?" and "How is it done?" In *Moving Genes*, you will begin to understand what is involved in genetic engineering as you explore one technique used in genetic engineering.

In this activity, you will be a genetic engineer! You will use a paper model to simulate recombinant DNA technology. You will work with a partner to simulate standard techniques used in genetic engineering.

Materials

For each team of 2 students

1 pair of scissors

transparent tape

1 highlighter or light-colored marker

1 *Plasmid* handout

1 *Insulin Gene* handout

1 *Restriction Enzymes* handout

Process and Procedure

1. Watch as your teacher demonstrates the first steps in 1 type of recombinant DNA technology.

2. Use an analogy map to record what you learn in a class discussion. Use the headings "Cell Model," "*E. coli* Cell," and "Human Blood Cell."

For help in creating an analogy map, see *How to Use and Create Organizing Tables* in the back of the book.

3. Study figure 9.4 and read the following paragraph about the small, circular piece of material that was in the *Escherichia coli* cell model. Add new information to your analogy map as you read.

   Scientists use **plasmids** to transfer fragments of DNA, such as the gene that codes for a particular protein. Plasmids are circular, double-stranded pieces of DNA that occur naturally in some bacteria. Review the picture of a typical bacterial cell (figure 9.4).

4. Collect the materials you need for this activity and the 3 handouts provided by your teacher.

5. As a team of 2, you will create the starting material for recombinant DNA technology. To begin, create your own *E. coli* plasmid by following these steps.

Most plasmids that are used in research have been manipulated by scientists to perform a certain function.

   a. Cut out the double-stranded DNA sequence from the *Plasmid* handout (figure 9.5). Be sure to cut along the dotted lines.
   b. Tape the 5 sections together end to end.

You may tape the plasmid strips together in any order.

   c. Tape the ends of the entire strip together so that the plasmid is circular. Make sure to tape the circle where you can see the base pairs on the outside.

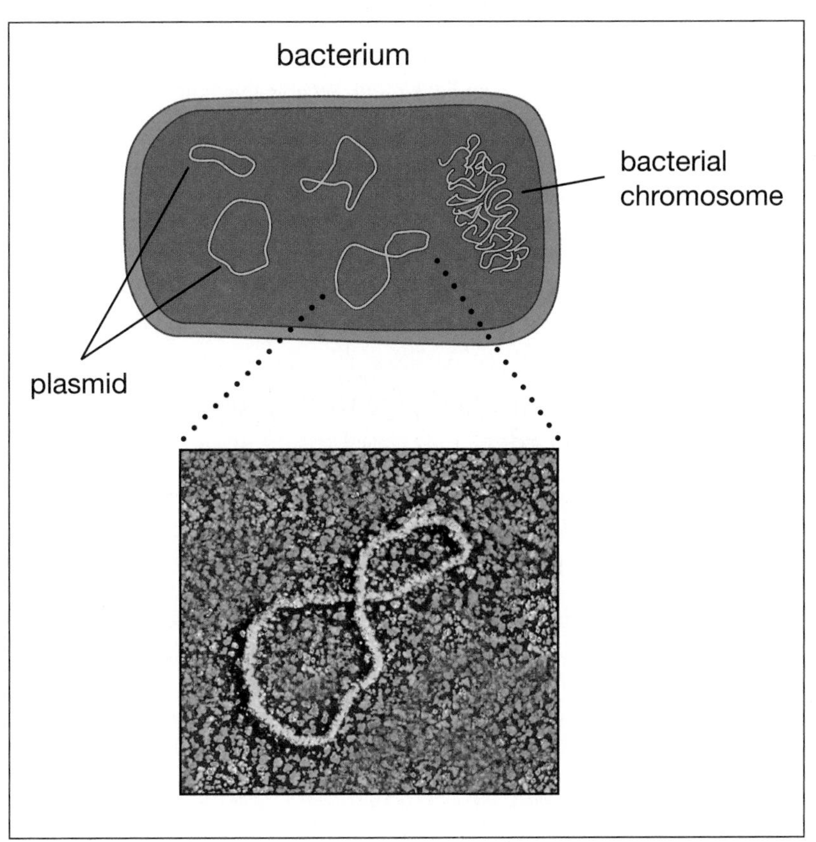

Figure 9.4 Typical bacteria cell. This figure shows a typical bacteria cell with DNA and plasmids. A plasmid is a small circular piece of DNA found in some bacteria and other prokaryotic cells. What features of the bacteria cell would have to be changed in order for genetic engineering to occur? Note the figure is not to scale.

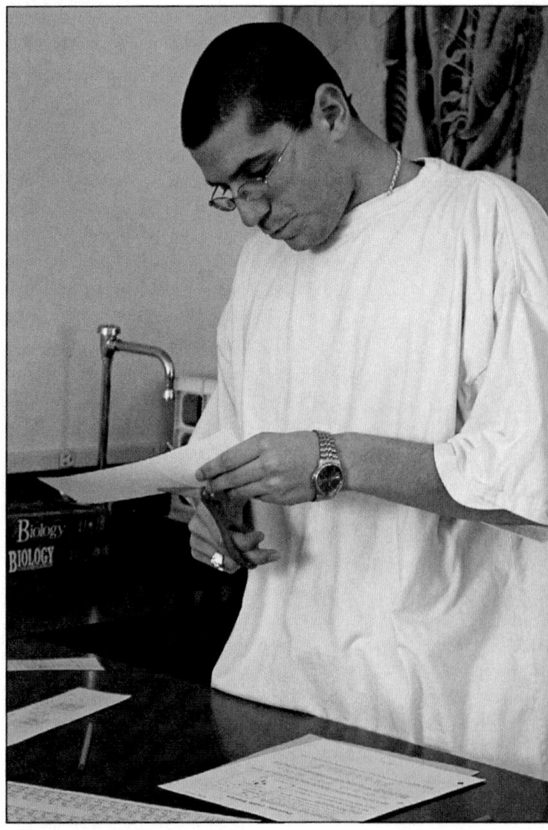

Figure 9.5 Cutting paper plasmids. Cut out the double-stranded DNA sequence from the *Plasmid* handout.

6. You have a model of a paper plasmid similar to the one that was in the cell model at the beginning of this activity (figure 9.6). This particular plasmid has a gene that codes for a certain trait. Examine your plasmid and record that trait.

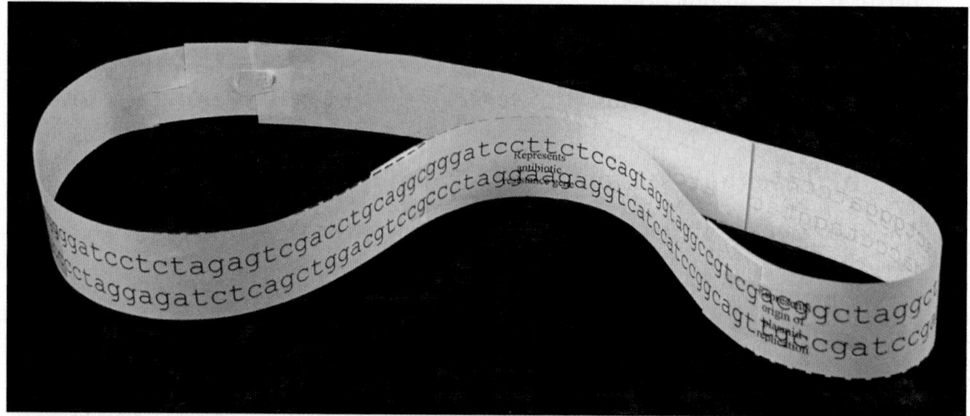

▲ **Figure 9.6 Paper plasmid.** Your model of a paper plasmid should be similar to this one. The model includes a gene that codes for a particular trait. What is this trait?

7. Now create your second piece of starting material for recombinant DNA technology, a piece of human DNA.
   a. Create a piece of human DNA by cutting out the double-stranded DNA sequence from the *Insulin Gene* handout. This piece of DNA contains the insulin gene that you will manipulate.
   b. Cut along the dotted line and tape the sections together end to end in numerical order.

Be sure to tape the strips representing the human DNA in order as it is in the normal human DNA sequence. In reality, scientists can't specify the order of DNA, so they discover and study it as it naturally exists.

8. To learn what molecular biologists do with these pieces of DNA in genetic engineering, read *Manipulating DNA*.

READING

Manipulating DNA

Through genetic engineering, foreign DNA is introduced into an organism. To do this, scientists need to isolate fragments of DNA. How do scientists isolate and manipulate the genes they are interested in? One method scientists commonly use is called recombinant DNA technology. **Recombinant DNA technology** is the process of cutting DNA at specific locations and putting the pieces back together. The fragments of DNA usually contain part of a gene. This technology allows scientists to isolate specific genes and learn what the genes code for. This technology opens many doors in genetic engineering.

Scientists can put the genes into another organism. For example, if a gene from a cow is put into a bacterium, the bacterium can express the cow protein coded by the added gene.

One of the first genes inserted into another organism was the gene that codes for insulin. Insulin is a protein hormone. A healthy pancreas produces insulin whose function is to signal cells, like muscle, liver, and fat cells, to take up glucose (sugar). One type of diabetes is caused by a lack of insulin. People with diabetes rely on recombinant DNA technology to produce cloned human insulin as a treatment for diabetes (see figure 9.7).

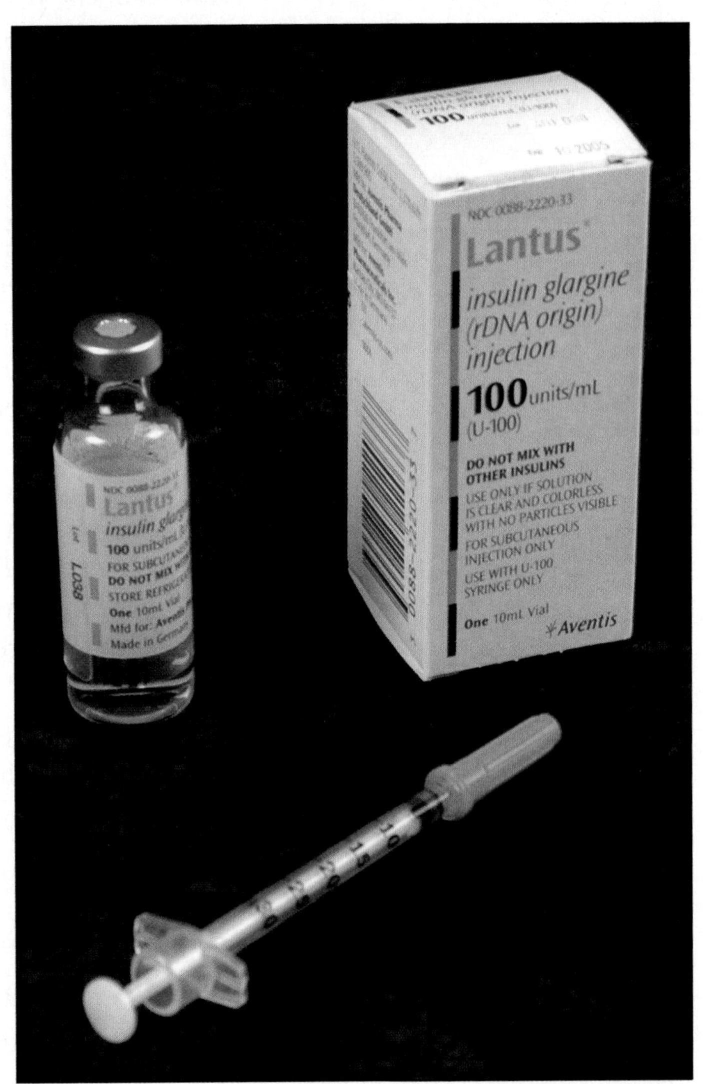

▲ **Figure 9.7 Recombinant human insulin.** At one time, insulin could only be obtained from cattle and hog pancreases. It was in short supply, expensive, and was not effective for some individuals because it was slightly different from human insulin. In 1982, the U.S. Food and Drug Administration approved the recombinant human insulin. Since then, human insulin has been produced inexpensively.

9. Answer Questions 9a–b about the plasmid and human DNA model in your science notebook. Compare and contrast your answers to your teammate's answers. Adjust your answers based on what you learn from others.
   a. What are the differences between a plasmid and a section of human DNA? What are the similarities?
   b. What would a scientist need to do before he or she could remove a gene from a section of DNA?
10. Read the following paragraph to learn how scientists put a plasmid into a strand of DNA. This process is how scientists use recombinant DNA technology to move genes. As you read, use this question to focus your reading: "How do restriction enzymes work?"

    Restriction enzymes are an important tool that scientists use. Essentially, restriction enzymes work like scissors that cut at specific locations along a DNA strand. There are thousands of restriction enzymes that occur naturally in bacteria. Because restriction enzymes cut DNA at specific locations, scientists can use them as a tool to isolate a specific segment of DNA. Each enzyme cuts at a unique DNA sequence called a **restriction site.**

    Your scissors will be used as restriction enzymes in this activity. On the *Restriction Enzymes* handout, several restriction enzymes are listed next to the DNA sequence at which they cut. But remember that the gene you are interested in must stay intact.
11. Study the DNA sequences where the restriction enzymes cut (restriction site) on the *Restriction Enzymes* handout. Write 1 question you have about how restriction enzymes work in your science notebook.

Read your question to your teammate, and then listen to his or her question. Help each other with the answers.

12. Prepare the *human* DNA strand by following Steps 12a–d.
   a. Locate the restriction sites described on the *Restriction Enzymes* handout.
   b. Label all of the places along the human DNA segment where a specific restriction enzyme would cut.
   c. Mark each site with the name of the restriction enzyme.
   d. Draw a line indicating where the enzyme would cut.

Not every enzyme will cut along this section of DNA.

13. Read the following paragraph, which describes the different ways restriction enzymes work.

When studying the restriction sites in Step 12, did you notice differences in how the enzymes cut DNA? For example, *Eco* RI cuts between the G and the A in a six-nucleotide sequence. This leaves what is called a "sticky end" on both ends of the DNA. Sometimes the cut leaves a "blunt end," like the *Hpa* I restriction enzyme. Figure 9.8 shows double-stranded DNA cut with restriction enzymes. The top row of letters represent one strand, and the bottom row of letters represent the complementary strand. You can see where the enzymes have cut. Figure 9.8a shows DNA cut with an enzyme, leaving sticky ends, and figure 9.8b shows DNA cut with an enzyme, leaving blunt ends.

14. Think about which restriction enzymes you can use to cut out the insulin gene. Highlight the sites where you can cut out the gene, and record the restriction enzymes you would use. Do not cut out the gene yet.
15. Answer the following questions about restriction enzymes in your science notebook.
    a. Which restriction enzymes would you use to cut out the insulin gene? Why?
    b. What other information might you need before making your final choice?

▲ **Figure 9.8 Restriction enzyme.** The DNA in (a) is cut with a restriction enzyme that leaves sticky ends. The DNA in (b) is cut with an enzyme that leaves blunt ends.

Your goal is to put the insulin gene into the plasmid.

16. Prepare a plasmid by locating restriction sites on the *plasmid* DNA. Use the *Restriction Enzymes* handout as a guide and complete Steps 16a–d.
    a. Locate the restriction sites described on the *Restriction Enzymes* handout.
    b. Label all the places along the plasmid where a restriction enzyme would cut.
    c. Mark each site with the name of the restriction enzyme.
    d. Draw a line indicating where the enzyme would cut.
17. Compare the restriction sites you found on both the human DNA and the plasmid. Identify which restriction enzyme(s) you should use to cut out the insulin gene and to cut the plasmid DNA.

Remember that the insulin gene needs to be placed into the plasmid.

When you cut out the insulin gene, you will need a place to put it for processing. We can use plasmid DNA for this purpose. In fact, plasmids can serve as vectors. Vectors are used to carry a gene to an organism. The gene within the plasmid can then be replicated, transcribed, and translated, all within a host organism, such as the bacteria *E. coli*. Plasmids use the machinery of the host bacteria to do this.

You learned that vectors in physical science are quantities with size and direction.

18. Using the *Restriction Enzymes* handout as a guide, follow these steps.
    a. Decide where to cut the DNA sequence on your human DNA strand.
    b. Compare your decision with another team's. Then have your teacher approve your decision.
    c. Use your scissors as a restriction enzyme to cut the DNA sequence at the sites you have identified.
19. Remove the insulin gene from the human DNA segment. Isolate the gene by removing the rest of the DNA (throw it away).
20. Cut the DNA sequence on your plasmid at the sites you have identified.

You only need to open up the plasmid to insert the insulin gene. You accomplish this by using enzymes.

21. Answer Questions 21a–b about the simulation in your science notebook.
    a. What happens to the plasmid when you cut it?
    b. Compare the ends of the plasmid DNA with the ends of the isolated insulin gene. What do you notice?

22. It is now time to put the insulin in the plasmid. Another enzyme, called **ligase**, assists in the formation of bonds between adjacent, complementary DNA ends. Your tape will play the role of the ligase.
    a. Insert the insulin gene in the plasmid DNA in the appropriate place.
    b. Tape the ends together.
    c. Does it fit?
23. Read the following paragraph about the next steps in recombinant DNA technology.

    How do you get protein from a plasmid? Your goal in this activity was to take the gene for insulin from human DNA and insert it into the plasmid. But the engineering does not stop there. After you have the plasmid with the insulin gene inserted, what comes next? You know that this gene codes for insulin and you want to "manufacture" a lot of insulin. So the plasmid must be put back into the *E. coli* cells. The *E. coli* reproduce rapidly and the new gene is expressed, giving *E. coli* a new trait. Remember from chapter 8 that gene expression results in the production of a particular protein. Many drugs are now made this way. Scientists insert a gene coding for the desired protein into a bacterium, and the desired trait is expressed.

Reflect and Connect

Answer the following questions in your science notebook and then discuss your answers with your partner. Record what you learn from your discussion in your science notebook.

1. What is the role of the plasmid in recombinant DNA technology?
2. What is the role of the gene in recombinant DNA technology?
3. Next to each task in Question 3a–c, explain how you simulated the task in this activity.
    a. Identify a specific gene and remove it from a chromosome.
    b. Find a DNA carrier, or vector, to place into living host cells.
    c. Join the gene to the vector.
4. Why is the location of the restriction site important? Which sites would work and which would not? Why?
5. The technique you modeled in this activity will produce abundant *E. coli* cells that contain the gene that codes for the production of insulin. What would be the next steps to have insulin available for diabetic patients?

SIDEBAR

Agarose Gel Electrophoresis

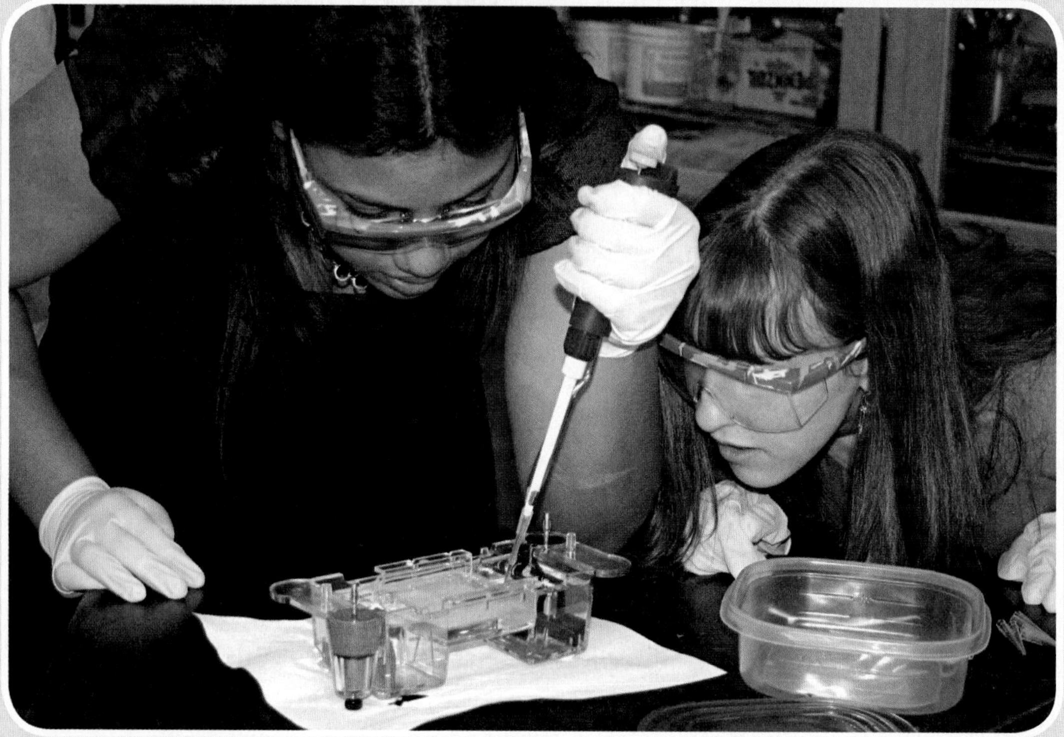

Electrophoresis. These students are conducting an investigation using agarose gel electrophoresis. This process separates DNA fragments by size using an electric field. Once separated, the fragments can be identified or compared with a known sample.

In this chapter, you have been learning about how scientists recombine DNA in useful ways. An insulin gene can be put in plasmid DNA so that insulin may be produced in great quantities for use in medicine. A luciferase gene that glows when expressed can transform bacteria to make them glow. (Luciferase comes from fireflies.) These are just two examples of the many ways to use recombinant DNA technology.

How do scientists know when the DNA fragments are recombined correctly? How can they identify and isolate genes? Scientists apply their understanding of physical science by taking advantage of the way DNA molecules behave in an electric field. In a process called **agarose gel electrophoresis**, scientists separate DNA fragments by size and then identify the fragments.

A substance called *agarose* helps separate the DNA fragments. Agarose is extracted from seaweed. Agarose gel has the consistency of gelatin that has very small holes or pores in it and works like a fishnet. A fishnet set in the ocean allows small fish to travel through the net, but slows down or catches the big fish. Agarose gel allows small DNA molecules to pass through quickly, medium-sized DNA molecules to pass through more slowly, and large DNA molecules to pass through slowly, if at all. Agarose gel electrophoresis is a filtering process.

But how does a DNA molecule begin its travels? An agarose gel is set into a container called a "gel box." The gel box contains a solution with positively and negatively charged ions. On one end of the gel box there is a positive electrode, and on the other end there is a negative electrode. When an electric current is applied to this system, it creates an electric field.

It is here that scientists use their understanding of physical science as a tool in biology. They know that opposite charges attract and that like charges repel. DNA is a negatively charged molecule. As an organic acid, negatively charged oxygen atoms branch out from phosphates on the outside of the DNA molecule. Because of this negative charge, DNA travels to the positively charged electrode and is repelled by the negatively charged electrode. The DNA travels horizontally through an agarose gel from the negative electrode to the positive electrode. In fact, the term electrophoresis means "to carry with electricity."

As the DNA travels through the agarose gel, it separates according to size. Scientists have developed DNA molecular-weight markers with DNA fragments of known sizes. These markers are used to "size" the DNA fragments on the agarose gel. Then the DNA is stained with a chemical called ethidium bromide. Ethidium bromide penetrates the DNA, allowing the DNA to be seen under an ultraviolet light.

The fragments, or genes, are filtered using agarose gel electrophoresis. Genes can be identified and isolated using this process. The figure below shows how DNA is separated out using gel electrophoresis.

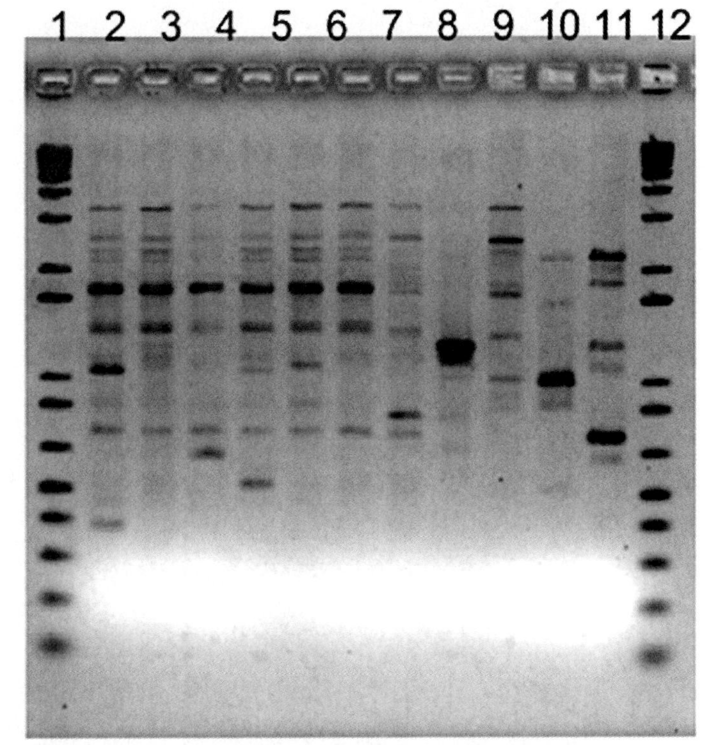

Electrophoresis result. What do the positions of the dark spots mean?

SCILINKS® NSTA
Topic: electrophoresis
Go to: www.scilinks.org
Code: 2Inquiry463

EXPLAIN

How Can It Be Done?

In *Moving Genes—Recombinant DNA Technology*, you explored how genes can be manipulated and recombined so that, when the gene is introduced into bacteria, it produces a desired characteristic. With recombinant DNA technology, we have the ability to change DNA in organisms by adding genes, transferring genes, and stopping the functioning of certain genes. Genetic engineering is the process of changing the genes of an organism. As advancements in this field continue, our understanding of gene function also advances. When new genes, usually from another source, are added to an organism, the organism being changed is called a **transgenic organism**. Transgenic organisms (figure 9.9) are becoming increasingly common.

▲ **Figure 9.9 Genetically engineered organisms.** Can you tell if these organisms are transgenic? How did scientists alter their DNA and why?

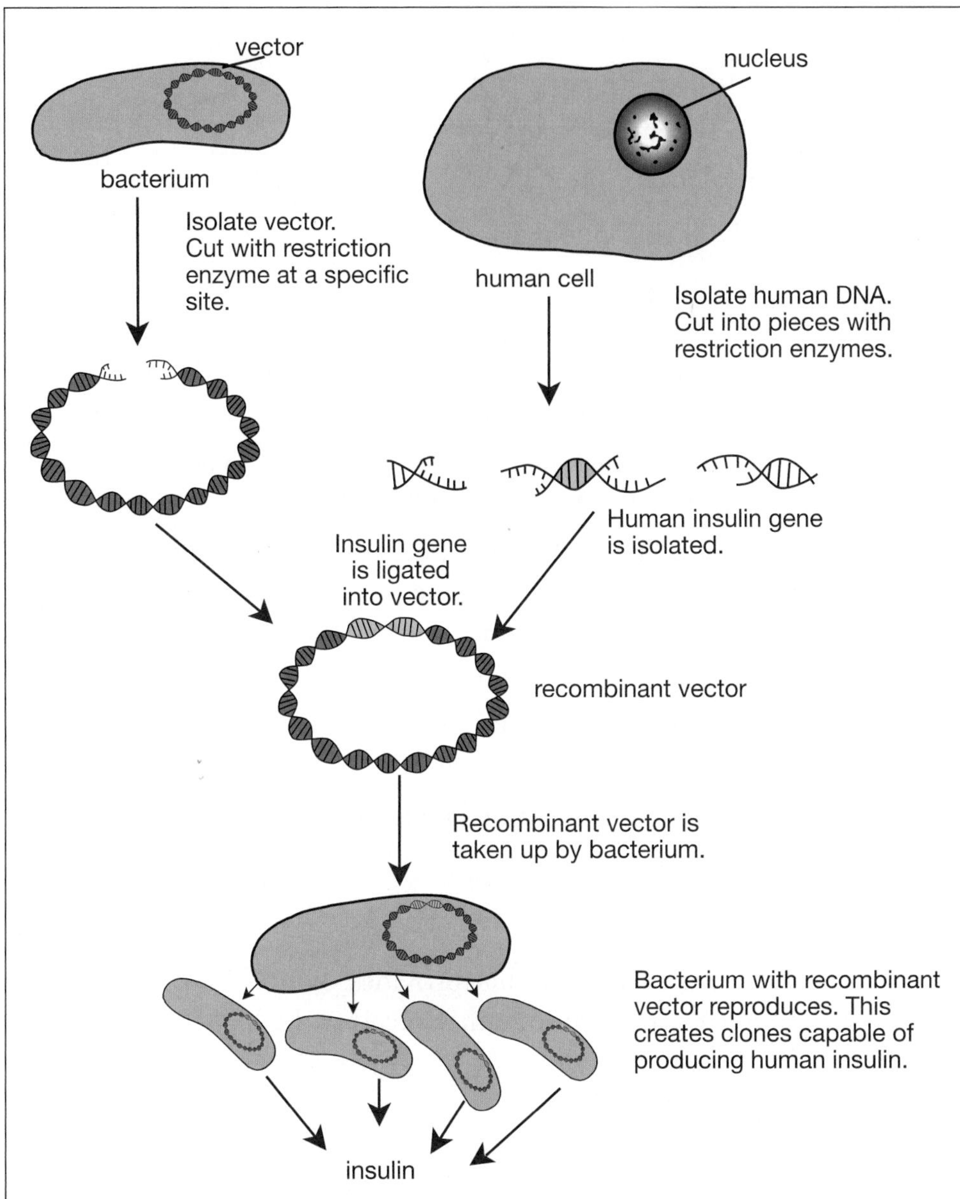

▲ **Figure 9.10 Sequence of recombinant DNA.** How do vectors and fragments combine to make a changed organism?

Review figure 9.10, which summarizes the sequence you followed in the *Moving Genes* activity.

Scientists use many techniques in genetic engineering to obtain a desired result, such as constructing an organism that expresses a new gene. In *How Can It Be Done?*, you will work with a teammate to gain a better understanding of some commonly practiced techniques in genetic engineering and how they might be applied. You will then compare and contrast the techniques. If you would like to learn about careers in the field of genetic engineering and other related fields, read the sidebar *Biomedical Engineering: Making a Good Living.*

Materials

For each team of 2 students

2 copies of the handout assigned to your team

2 5×7 in index cards

colored pencils or thin-line markers

Process and Procedure

1. With your teammate, read the sequence of steps described on the handout distributed by your teacher.

Your teacher also will distribute index cards. The color on top of the index card should match the color written at the top of the handout.

2. On your own, draw a labeled diagram on your index card. Your diagram should show the sequence of steps used in the genetic engineering technique you are describing. You may help each other, but you will each make a card.

You will use this card to teach someone else about this technique, so make your diagram clear and label it carefully. You will not be present to describe the process.

   The following items must be labeled on your diagram:
   a. Desired gene
   b. Plasmid
   c. Bacteria
   d. Donor organism (one that provides the DNA)
   e. Recipient organism (one that receives the DNA)
   f. Chromosome
   g. Vector

Use red to draw the desired gene each time.

3. Copy your diagram into your science notebook.
4. On the back of the card, write the type of applications the technique is used for.
5. When all of the teams have finished their diagrams, trade cards with 2 other teams so that your team has 2 new cards (2 different colors).

If your team drew red cards originally, your team should trade to get 2 new colors. For example, your team could end up with a yellow card and a blue card.

6. Look at the new cards and answer Steps 6a–b in your science notebook.
   a. Compare these 2 new techniques with the one you diagrammed. In what ways are they similar to the technique you drew?
   b. Why do you think the applications vary so much?

7. Post the diagram cards in your classroom; group cards of the same color together.

Reflect and Connect

Answer the following questions in your science notebook. Use an effective technique to check your answers.

1. Summarize the major steps common to all the techniques used in genetic engineering. Why are they common steps?
2. Were the same genetic engineering techniques repeated in different types of applications? Explain why this would occur.
3. Do you think genes in gamete cells (sex cells) can be altered? Describe how this could happen.

SIDEBAR

Biomedical Engineering: Making a Good Living

What do you need to know to make a good living? Of course, it depends on what you want to do. And that depends on the things you like to do, your talents, and your determination. One career field that combines interesting work, helping others, and great pay is biomedical engineering.

Biomedical engineering is a broad family of career fields. Each branch combines science with technology to enhance the lives of those in need of health care. Look at the graphic organizer with biomedical engineering in the center bubble. Notice how many fascinating career possibilities link to biomedical engineering. No wonder biomedical engineering jobs are projected to grow by more than 31 percent by 2010.

Just imagine being part of the bioinstrumentation team that developed the personal blood-sugar tester, which diabetes patients need to monitor their blood sugar. What would it be like to be the biomedical engineer who made it possible to transplant a pig's heart into a human? Think how it would change lives if you invented the first artificial shoulder? This is the kind of work biomedical engineers do.

Naturally, rewarding careers demand careful preparation. You have to know a lot about living systems, science, and mathematics. In addition, working professionals need to speak and write effectively, especially about science and mathematics concepts. These demands translate to taking as many core classes in high school as possible. Plus, you need to do well in them. It's hard work, but it's also interesting and rewarding. In the end, you not only make a good living, you make living good.

Biomedical Engineering: Making a Good Living, continued

Biomedical Engineering Careers

BIOINSTRUMENTATION
Computers to help diagnose/treat disease

GENETIC ENGINEERING
Moving genetic material from one genome to another

ORTHOPAEDIC ENGINEERING
Understanding and improvement of bones, joints, and connective tissues

MEDICAL IMAGING
Uses sound and electromagnetic radiation to develop diagnostic images

CLINICAL ENGINEERING
Management of technology as interface between health care professionals and patients

BIOMATERIALS
Living/nonliving materials to replace/improve the human body

BIOMECHANICS
How statis, dynamics, fluids, solids, and thermodynamics apply to biological systems

REHABILITATION ENGINEERING
Help improve physical and cognitive functioning of people with injury or disease

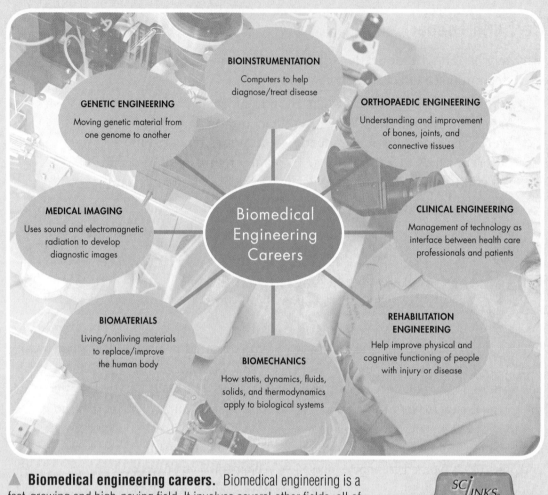

▲ **Biomedical engineering careers.** Biomedical engineering is a fast-growing and high-paying field. It involves several other fields, all of which require core knowledge about science, mathematics, and human communication.

Go to: www.scilinks.org
Topic: biomedical engineer
Code: 2Inquiry468a
Topic: genetic engineering
Code: 2Inquiry468b

ELABORATE

Biotechnology and Society

When certain needs arise, sometimes we can address those needs through advances in science and technology. Indeed, the need to solve problems is a major incentive for advances in science—and especially in technology. Through technology, humans adapt the natural world to suit themselves and their needs. This is true for both individuals and for societies. Across time, technology leads to changes in our culture.

When a solution involves technology *and* living organisms, we call it **biotechnology**. Recombinant DNA technology has created many new forms of biotechnology. Read the sidebar *Biotechnology in the Fields* to learn about one biotechnology that is helping cotton farmers. Because we have the ability to manipulate genes, and genes produce proteins, we can solve many problems.

As you know from your work in chapter 8, proteins are complex molecules found in all living things. As important as DNA and genes are, proteins (figure 9.11) are where the action is. They have many amazing functions, such as breaking down what we eat, moving muscle, and transporting molecules. Proteins keep certain bacteria alive at the depths of the oceans and at the far reaches of the Arctic. Proteins cause some insects to secrete unusual chemicals, give animals their color, and cause fireflies to glow. Enzymes are a type of protein that speeds up chemical reactions in organisms.

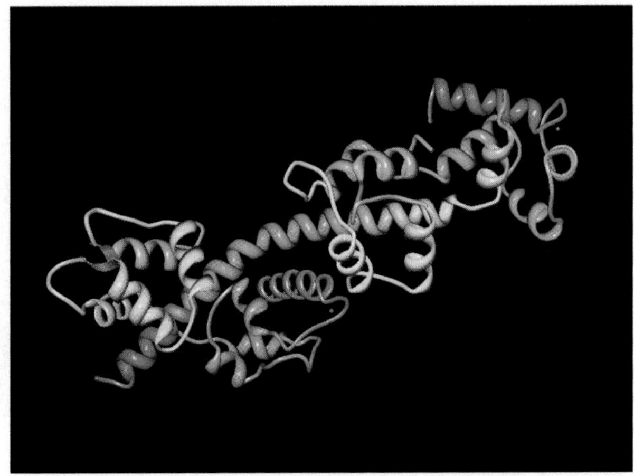

▲ **Figure 9.11 Model of a protein molecule.** Proteins such as this one control many functions of life.

In *Part I—Meeting a Need*, you will learn about some examples of biotechnology. Then, in *Part II—Bioethics*, you will learn about the ethical dilemmas that biotechnology raises.

Part I: Meeting a Need

Earlier in this chapter, you learned that, through recombinant DNA technology, a scientist can incorporate a gene directly into an organism. That gene is expressed so that an organism produces a desired protein. As scientists learned more about how genetic engineering could help us in medicine and agriculture, they began to wonder if genetic engineering could help humans in other ways as well. Could we genetically engineer a bacterium that breaks down oil and withstands salt water? Could we then release this new kind of bacterium to "eat" oil spills? If we could accomplish this, could we go further? Could we genetically engineer organisms to produce detergents? The applications of recombinant DNA technology in genetic engineering are only limited by our current understanding of science and technology and our imagination. What does the future hold?

Materials

For each class

access to the Web

other resources as needed

Process and Procedure

1. As a class, conduct a brainstorming session on some challenges or problems that we face in our lives, in our society, and in our world. Choose one classmate to write down the ideas. Circle the ones you think could be addressed using genetic engineering techniques.
2. Copy the table from figure 9.12 into your science notebook and fill it out as you read about 4 applications of genetic engineering. As you read each example, focus on this question, "How has genetic engineering solved this problem?"

Name of organism(s) involved	Description of problem	How genetic engineering solved problem

▲ **Figure 9.12 Genetic engineering table.** Use this table to organize the information about 4 applications of genetic engineering.

No More Toxic Dump Sites

Every living organism ingests nutrients and produces a waste by-product as a result. Certain bacteria thrive on the chemical components of waste products ("one person's trash is another's treasure"). Their metabolic process converts these hazardous or unwanted materials into less harmful products. The use of microorganisms to degrade waste is called **bioremediation**.

Some examples of bioremediation include organisms that feed on hydrocarbons (oil), methylene chloride (a toxic waste product), detergents, and sulfur. Many of these organisms exist naturally, but new advances in the use of transgenic organisms (those that have been genetically modified) are allowing science to genetically engineer custom-made microbes to perform the duties of digesting unwanted waste. Oil spills may be cleaned up using these microbes.

Transgenic microorganisms have been developed that contain genes for bioluminescence (glowing), coupled with a gene for waste degradation. These microorganisms glow when they are working, and stop glowing when they are done. This indicates when the waste is completely removed. Scientists can monitor the amount of light emitted and determine how much biodegradation is occurring.

Bacteria have been discovered that can live in an environment of very high radiation. *Deinococcus radiodurans* (figure 9.13) has the ability to repair damage within its DNA that is caused by radiation. Scientists are working toward genetically engineering other microorganisms to clean up radioactive waste sites using what they have learned about *Deinococcus radiodurans*.

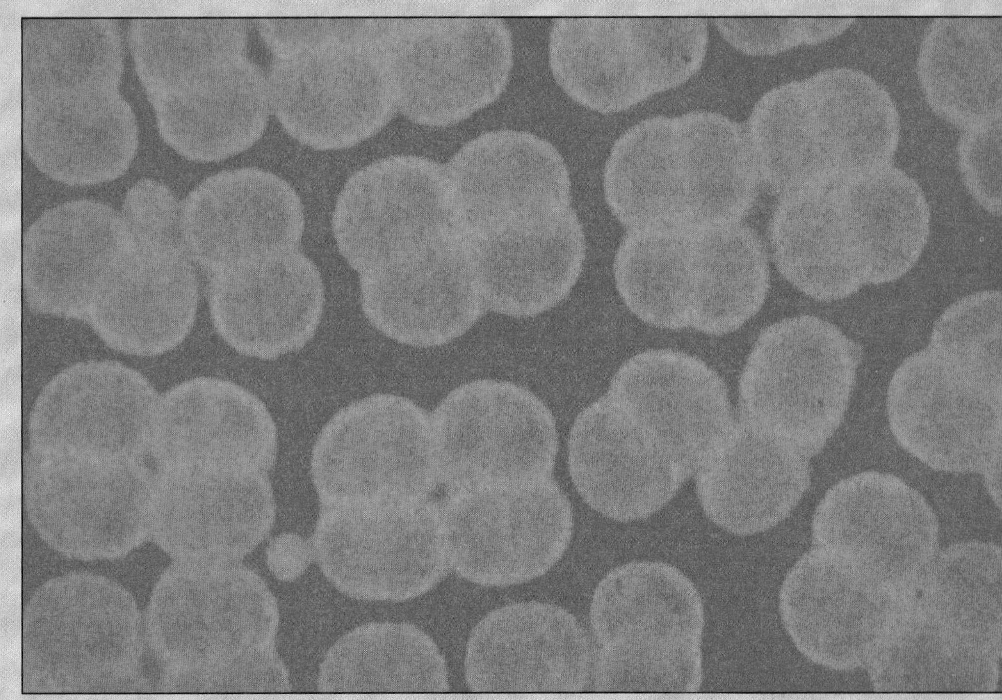

Figure 9.13 ***Deinococcus radiodurans.*** This bacterium can live in an environment of very high radiation. *D. radiodurans* has the ability to repair damage within its own DNA caused by radiation. Could this trait be genetically engineered to clean up the environment damaged by nuclear wastes?

Genetically Engineered Blue Jeans

A scientist named David Gibson was working with a strain of *E. coli* that could eat hydrocarbons. One day he noticed that the bacterial spots in his petri dishes had turned a brilliant blue. Looking back over his notes, he realized that those were the particular microbes to which he had just added a new gene. The gene he added coded for an enzyme called toluene dioxygenase. He analyzed the blue pigment and reasoned that the color had been produced when the enzyme converted a simple nutrient called indole into indigo. Indigo is the world's largest selling dye and the one that makes blue jeans blue. Presently, indigo is produced chemically, and the process generates toxic by-products. If bacteria could be genetically engineered to produce indigo, the result could be a more environmentally friendly pair of pants (see figure 9.14).

Figure 9.14 Blue jeans. Could cotton plants be genetically engineered to contain the gene to produce the blue pigment indigo?

Gold Rush

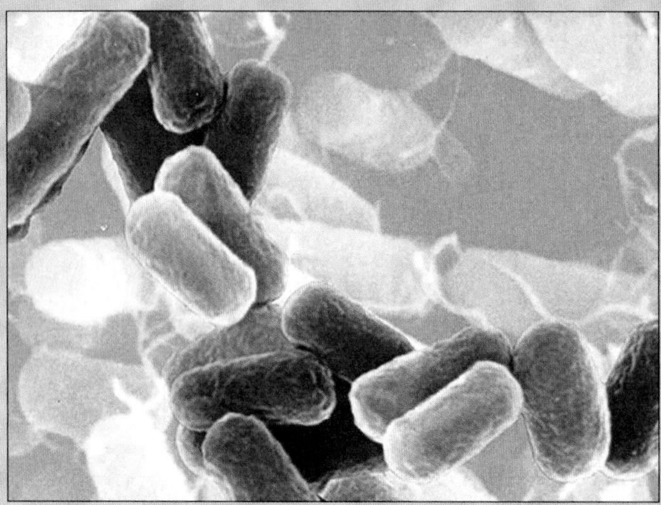

Figure 9.15 Thiobacillus ferooxidans. This bacterium can "chew up" copper ore, releasing pure copper that is collected in solution.

Mining is a process that is expensive and time consuming, and it causes a lot of pollution. Efforts are underway to genetically engineer microbes to mine needed minerals. The bacterial strains must be able to withstand heavy metals (such as mercury, cadmium, and arsenic). These microbes must also be able to extract needed minerals from earth. Some naturally occurring bacteria, such as *Thiobacillus ferooxidans* (figure 9.15), "chew up" ore, and copper is released and collected in solution. Scientists are studying how microorganisms can be genetically engineered to withstand heavy metals while leaching out desired minerals.

A Cleaner Way

Most laundry detergents and stain removers contain enzymes (figure 9.16). Enzymes are proteins that help to facilitate processes that occur in organisms. Why are enzymes in laundry detergents? One of the things that enzymes can do is break down proteins. Your digestive system produces many enzymes to break down the food you eat. The enzymes break down the food into basic building blocks that your body uses to build tissue.

Many of the stains that end up on your clothing contain proteins. Some examples of stains that contain proteins are blood, food, grass, and perspiration. The manufacturers of laundry detergents have been using enzymes in their products for many years. These enzymes have traditionally been chemically (synthetically) produced. With recombinant DNA technology, researchers can now find organisms that have genes that naturally produce a desired enzyme. Each gene produces a specific enzyme. One enzyme might break down blood, while another enzyme (possibly from a different organism) breaks down grass stains. These genes can then be spliced into microbes, causing them to produce enzymes that break down a variety of stains. The enzymes can then be added to detergents. Genetic engineering techniques used for producing laundry detergents may be more efficient and environmentally friendly than synthetic detergents.

Figure 9.16 Stain removers in detergents. Why are enzymes in laundry detergents?

3. Look back at your original list from Step 1 of some challenges and problems that humans face. Which items on the list did you think genetic engineering could address? Now that you have read about these unique applications, is there anything new you would like to add to the list? Discuss your ideas and add them to your list. Then draw a rectangle around needs that you *now* think could be addressed by the use of genetic engineering.
4. The genetic engineering applications in these readings are just a few of the ones scientists are working on. The field of biotechnology is growing rapidly. Using the Web, research other applications of biotechnology. In your science notebook, describe 2 uses of biotechnology that take advantage of genetic engineering techniques.

Stop & THINK

PART I

Answer the following questions in your science notebook. Remember to incorporate other classmates' viewpoints into your learning.

1. Why would we want to use biotechnology to make a product instead of making it in a laboratory?
2. What would be some advantages and disadvantages to having microorganisms mine minerals for us?
3. How might these applications of biotechnology, which are being used to solve problems, create new problems? Explain your answer.
4. View the video, *Genetic Engineering in California Agriculture* on the SRCD. Record at least 2 new things you learned about genetic engineering.

SIDEBAR

Biotechnology in the Fields

You have learned that it is possible for scientists to remove genes from one organism and introduce them into an unrelated organism. The new DNA formed through that process is called recombinant DNA. One example of how scientists are using recombinant DNA technology to address a practical problem involves the cotton plant. A pest called a bollworm attacks cotton plants often (see photo). This pest damages cotton crops and costs millions of dollars each year to control. Researchers, however, have known for a long time that a bollworm will die if it eats the common bacterium *Bacillus thuringiensis* (*B.t.* for short). A protein that the bacterium produces is partially digested in the worm's gut and poisons the worm. Because that protein is so effective, for years farmers have sprayed *B.t.* bacteria on their cotton crops to discourage the bollworms from eating them. That protective measure has its drawbacks, though. Sunlight breaks down *B.t.*, and rainfall easily washes it off the plants.

Through genetic engineering, however, researchers have overcome those drawbacks. The figure on the next page shows how scientists can manipulate the DNA of a cotton plant. The new genetically engineered cotton plants (GE cotton) contain recombinant DNA. The GE cotton plants produce a bacterial protein, *B.t.* toxin, in their leaves. In other words, they are engineered to protect themselves from bollworms. When a bollworm begins nibbling on the leaves, it eats the *B.t.* protein and dies. In addition to cotton, food crop plants can be engineered to produce the *B.t.* protein because it is not toxic to humans.

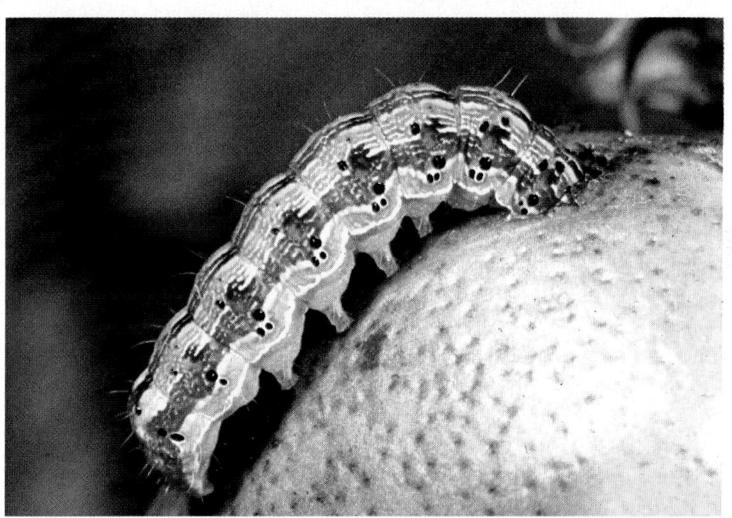

▲ **Bollworm attacking cotton boll.** This pest of cotton plants can be controlled with pesticides or with genetically engineered cotton. What are the advantages and disadvantages to each method?

A benefit of such technology is that farmers can use less insecticide, decreasing the amount of toxic chemicals that enter the water supply and food web. The new technology, however, has not been completely effective. Farmers using the engineered cotton in 1996 reported that many bollworms survived in the new crop. Additional pesticides had to be applied, though the total amount was reduced. The surviving bollworms raise concerns about what prolonged exposure to *B.t.* may do to the bollworm's resistance to the bacterium's toxicity. There also are concerns for the

Biotechnology in the Fields, continued

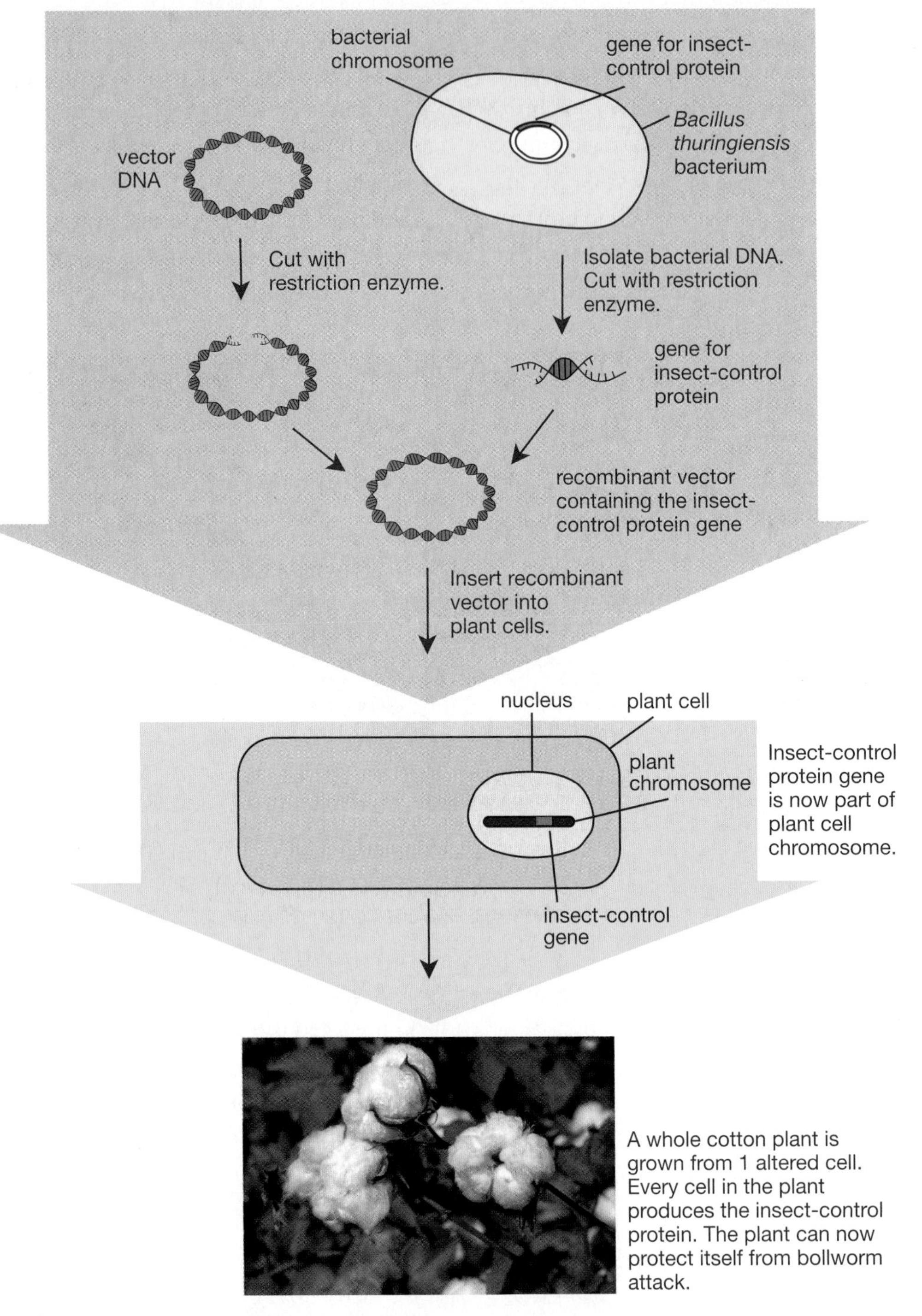

bacterial chromosome
gene for insect-control protein
Bacillus thuringiensis bacterium
vector DNA
Cut with restriction enzyme.
Isolate bacterial DNA. Cut with restriction enzyme.
gene for insect-control protein
recombinant vector containing the insect-control protein gene
Insert recombinant vector into plant cells.
nucleus
plant cell
plant chromosome
Insect-control protein gene is now part of plant cell chromosome.
insect-control gene
A whole cotton plant is grown from 1 altered cell. Every cell in the plant produces the insect-control protein. The plant can now protect itself from bollworm attack.

▲ **Genetic engineering of cotton.** The toxic insect-controlling protein gene from *Bacillus thuringiensis (B.t.)* is isolated. This is done with the same DNA-cutting restriction enzyme that is used to cut the DNA vector. Scientists combine these two pieces of DNA. They then insert the recombinant DNA into a plant cell. An entire plant grows from that one cell. The plant can now protect itself from the bollworm.

other organisms that encounter *B.t.* through this technique. Though current tests show that the *B.t.* toxin is nontoxic for most animals, including many beneficial insects, it has the potential to harm endangered and threatened species of moths and butterflies.

GE cotton represents 21 percent of the total cotton planted globally. Since its introduction in 1996, cotton has been one of the lead crops to be genetically engineered, and GE cotton has been one of the most rapidly adopted technologies ever. Varieties of GE cotton with multiple traits are now available. The current varieties that have commercial importance address crop management or agronomic traits that assist with pest management (Bt) or herbicide tolerance (HT). Although insect resistance and herbicide tolerance are the only traits currently available in biotech cottons, a broad range of other traits is under development using modern biotechnology. These may directly affect agronomic performance, stress tolerance, fiber quality, and yield potential.

SCILINKS NSTA
Topic: genetically engineered crops
Go to: www.scilinks.org
Code: 2Inquiry477

Part II: Bioethics

By now, you can see that biotechnology possibly could address many of the world's problems. But, with any new technology comes responsibility. Is there a danger that biotechnology can be used irresponsibly? What about ethics? Should we use biotechnology for every problem possible? **Ethics** refers to the morals of individuals and society. Morals are values and beliefs about what is acceptable behavior. An ethical question asks what "should" or "ought" to be done in a particular situation so that the values of society or the individuals involved are upheld while society and individual needs are met. **Bioethics** is the term we use when the ethical issue is raised by developments in life science technologies, such as new medical technologies.

In *Part II—Bioethics,* you will face an ethical dilemma. You will use a decision-making model to decide on the best solution, while taking into account all viewpoints.

Materials

For each team of 2 students

ruler

Process and Procedure

Work with a partner for this activity.

1. Study the following description of a decision-making model and discuss it with your class.

Bioethics Decision-Making Model

1. Define the ethical question being posed.

   Usually an ethical question contains a subjective opinion based on a particular cultural frame of reference. An example of an ethical question might be, "Should there be a law that requires motorcycle riders to wear helmets?" (see figure 9.17).

2. Identify the relevant facts of the case.

   Look at the case from all angles and generate a list of facts.

In the motorcycle helmet example, the facts would center on the numbers of deaths and injuries associated with motorcycle accidents, individual rights, and societal values.

▲ **Figure 9.17 Motorcycle riders and helmets.** Should there be a law that requires motorcycle riders to wear helmets?

3. Identify the stakeholders.

   Stakeholders are individuals, organizations, or other entities that are directly affected by the outcome or decision. Stakeholders sometimes can be difficult to identify because individuals whose opinions cannot be heard (such as infants, animals, and those with minority opinions) may be stakeholders.

In our example, some of the stakeholders are motorcycle riders, insurance companies, and police officers.

4. Address the moral values of society that apply to the case.

   These can include a wide variety of qualities, such as fairness to the various shareholders, privacy, freedom of choice, respect for life or property, religious beliefs, political orientation, and cultural values.

In the motorcycle helmet example, our society's value of human life is weighed against the individual right to choose whether or not to wear a helmet.

5. Consider all of the possible solutions to the dilemma.

   Reflect on possible solutions from multiple perspectives. Consider different points of view—ones contrary to your own.

6. Choose the best possible solution.

   In this final step, a decision is made based on the previous steps. The decision takes into account the facts, the stakeholders, and the moral values of those represented as stakeholders.

2. Draw a table in your notebook that looks like figure 9.18. Make the blank boxes large and leave plenty of room to write under each heading.

	Define the ethical question.	List the relevant facts of the case.	Identify the stakeholders in the case.	Identify the values that play a role in this case.	List several possible solutions to resolve the conflict.	Choose an acceptable solution(s) and justify.
Issue #1						
Issue #2						

▲ **Figure 9.18 Decision-making table for ethical questions.** How can you use this table to organize difficult decisions involving ethics?

3. Read *Bioethical Issue 1.*
4. With your teammate, fill in the table you drew in your notebook for *Bioethical Issue 1* by following the 6 steps of the decision-making model.
5. Participate in a class discussion of ideas for each step of the model and fill in a table for the class as a whole.
6. Following the class discussion, fill in the last column of your table.
7. Read *Bioethical Issue 2.*
8. Fill out the second row of your table individually.

Bioethical Issue 1

Some people do not produce enough growth-hormone (figure 9.19). The deficiency causes them to be significantly shorter than the average person. Doctors used to treat the deficiency with a growth hormone extracted from cadavers shortly after death. This technique worked, but there was a short supply of the growth hormone. Today recombinant DNA techniques enable us to propagate bacteria that produce enough of the growth hormone to supply doctors with the hormone for the individuals who need it. Eventually, we may be able to insert the gene for growth hormone into individuals who have the deficiency, allowing them to produce the growth hormone in their cells. Such a procedure would be a type of **gene therapy**. Gene therapy is the insertion of normal or genetically altered genes into cells as part of the treatment of disorders that have a genetic component. What if other people (without the deficiency), such as athletes who want to be taller, want to use the growth hormone? Should they be allowed to use the hormone therapy?

▲ **Figure 9.19 Growth-hormone deficiency.** Growth-hormone deficiency causes individuals to be shorter than the average person. Recombinant DNA techniques may be able to provide gene therapy for sufferers of this disorder. Should everyone be allowed to use this hormone therapy?

Bioethical Issue 2

Genetic engineering is used quite extensively in agriculture. Crops can be genetically engineered to be resistant to drought or frost. Plants can even be engineered to produce their own pesticide (figure 9.20). People have a variety of opinions about genetically engineered foods. One concern is that some people might have an allergy to a new protein. If people eat food that has the new protein, they may have an allergic reaction. Some people think that if a crop is only used for livestock consumption, it is acceptable to genetically engineer it. Others feel that allergies happen no matter what and that genetic engineering is no different from what happens in nature. Some people say that all genetically modified foods should be labeled. Still others believe that genetic engineering should not be conducted at all. Some farmers say genetic engineering saves crops and money and that using genetic engineering technology is better than spraying crops with toxic substances. Others feel that, because we can't control genetically engineered crops from crossing with crops that aren't engineered, we shouldn't plant them at all. What do you say?

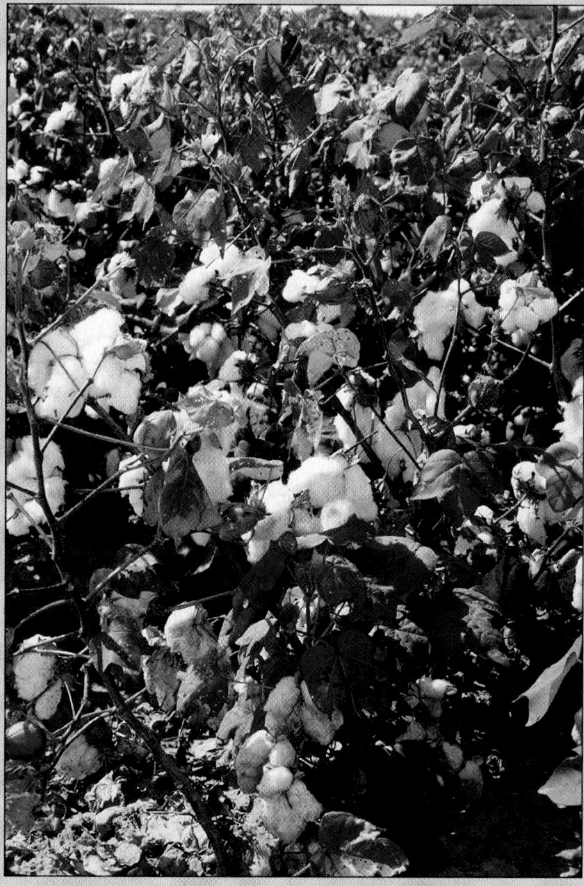

Figure 9.20 Cotton field. Genetically engineered cotton is developed to produce higher yields and reduce the use of pesticides and herbicides.

Reflect and Connect

Answer the following questions in your science notebook. Don't forget how valuable it is to check with your teacher or classmates regarding your answers.

Go to: www.scilinks.org
Topic: bioethics
Code: 2Inquiry482a
Topic: gene therapy
Code: 2Inquiry482b

1. Why might different people come up with different biotechnology solutions to the same problem?
2. Give an example of a conflict between an individual's desire and the morals of society.
3. Is there a way to distinguish between which biotechnology solutions are needed and which are not?
4. How is the process of ethical analysis related to scientific analysis? How is it different?

EVALUATE

Can It Be Done? Should It Be Done?

Throughout this chapter, you have explored many aspects of biotechnology. We now have the technology to treat genetic disorders, increase agricultural yields, clean up environmental pollution, and even change the way we obtain valued resources. Because of existing biotechnology, our society also faces many individual, social, ethical, and legal questions.

Imagine a societal problem that biotechnology could solve. Or imagine a unique biotechnology application that you would like to see implemented. The genetic engineering application that you propose could solve a problem or change a current situation.

In *Can It Be Done? Should It Be Done?*, you will work as a team to propose a new biotechnology application. You will have an opportunity to present your idea to the Genetic Engineering Advisory Board (GEAB) for review (figure 9.21). In doing so, you will demonstrate your understanding of the concepts in this chapter. The class will represent the GEAB and hear your presentation, review your proposal, and determine whether or not it should be implemented. The GEAB will vote on whether it can be done and whether it should be done.

Materials

For each team of 4 students

resource materials or access to the Web

poster paper

markers

4 *Can It Be Done? Should It Be Done? Scoring Rubric* handouts

other materials as needed for presentation

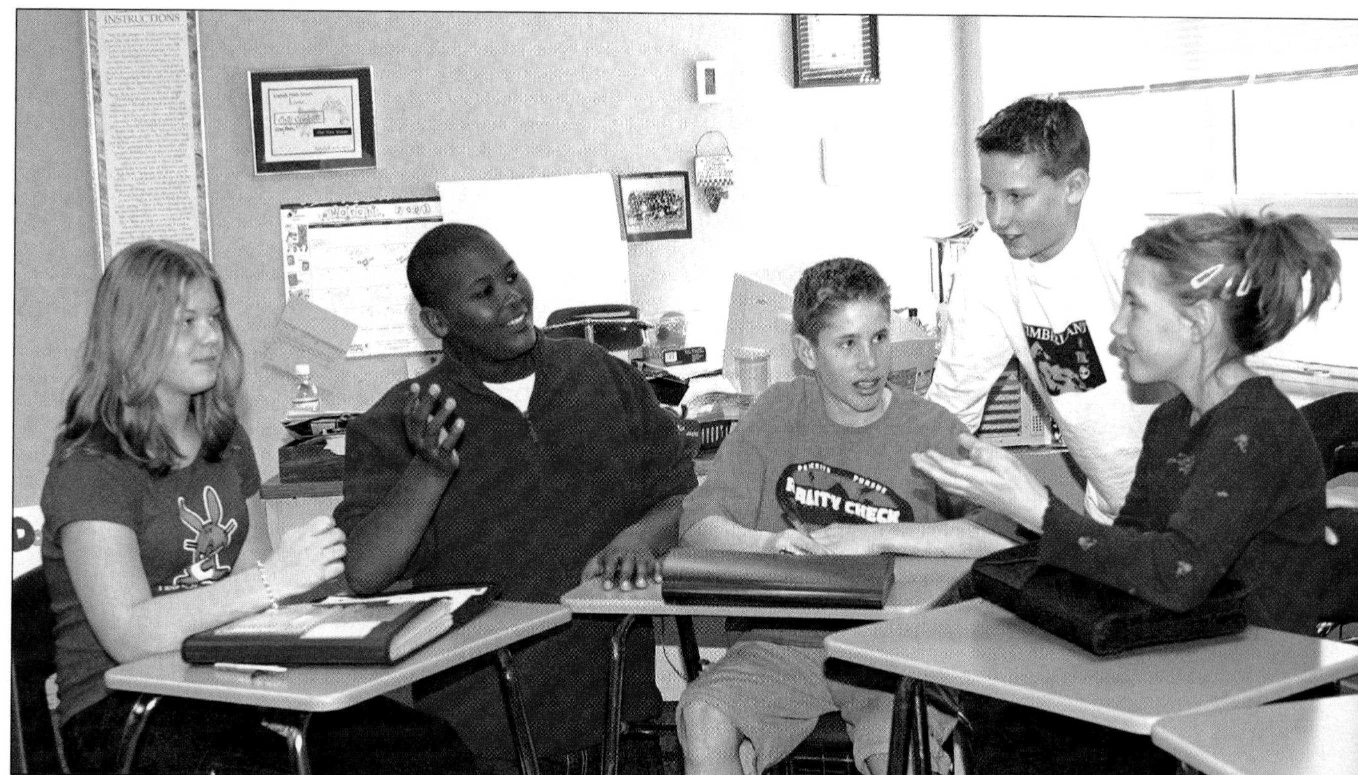

▲ **Figure 9.21 GEAB meeting.** You will have the opportunity to present your ideas for biotechnology to the Genetic Engineering Advisory Board. What do you need to do to prepare for your presentation?

Process and Procedure

1. Read through the entire activity before you begin, and study the scoring rubric your teacher distributes.
2. Form a team of 4 and work through Steps 2a–d.
   a. Discuss some current issues with your team that could someday be addressed using biotechnology. Think about issues that may help individuals or society as a whole or that are just something unique to do.
   b. Imagine you could change anything genetically. What would it be? Could it be done? Should it be done?
   c. Decide on 1 genetic engineering application that addresses a need and that you would like to exist.
   d. Be sure that the application you choose does not already exist. Conduct some research in the library or on the Web to find out.

3. As a team, discuss Questions 3a–f, and record your best answers in your science notebook.
   a. Is this biotechnology a necessity or only for those with lots of money?
   b. Why would you want this to happen? What is the need that you are addressing?
   c. How could you implement your plan? Include in your plan, what organisms it involves, what techniques it involves, and at what level it takes place (for example, body cell, gamete cell, plasmid, or chromosome).
   d. Who are the stakeholders? Why are they the stakeholders?
   e. Summarize why and how you would implement this technology.
   f. Could this technology have other applications? Describe some of them.
4. Assign each person on your team a role in preparing the presentation to the GEAB. Discuss the following roles and establish who will take which role.
   - *Genetic engineer.* Genetic engineers are the technicians that manipulate the DNA of an organism with tools such as recombinant DNA technology. In this case, the genetic engineer proposes how the technology could be implemented.
   - *Evolutionary biologist.* The evolutionary biologist concentrates efforts on the evolutionary consequences of using this technology.
   - *Marketing or public educator.* The public educator communicates with the GEAB about the risks and benefits to both society and individuals that are associated with the use of the technology.
   - *Ethicist.* The ethicist focuses on the moral and ethical considerations of implementing the technology.
5. Each team member works on his or her own part of the presentation, following Steps 5a–d. Be ready to contribute to the team's presentation.
   a. Genetic engineer
      - Describe the technique that you will use to implement your plan. In your description, include the vectors involved.

- Describe current technology that is similar to your technique. Discuss problems that you would need to overcome in order to get the technology to work. What roadblocks may prevent you from implementing this technology?
- Describe possible side effects to organisms and any problems associated with using the technology. Consider the recipient organism, provider organism, and any other organisms involved in transmission.
- Write a step-by-step sequence of what you will do to implement your plan.
- Draw and label a graphic showing how your team would implement your plan.

b. Evolutionary biologist
- List all organisms that would specifically be involved. Include their genus and species.
- Explain how this technology could help an organism adapt to its environment.
- Predict how overuse of this technology could affect an entire population of organisms. Consider life span, variations, and survival rates.
- Explain how using this technology could have an effect on natural selection. Provide a scenario by drawing a diagram.
- Describe how implementing this technology could affect the population of organisms that you are working with. Also, describe how your plan could affect the populations of two other organisms.
- Describe how using this technology could affect the gene frequency distribution in either the recipient populations of organisms or the vector.

c. Marketing or public educator
- Describe how this technology will help both the individual and society. Discuss the major benefits of using this technology.
- Describe the current model of genetic engineering that the technique is most like.
- Provide other examples of how society is currently using this same type of technology.
- Describe the successes, drawbacks, and milestones that this type of biotechnology has had in real life.

- Describe how using this technology may affect economics or politics.
- Discuss who would favor the use of this technology and why.
- Draw a logo that represents your team's proposed technology.

d. Ethicist

- Would using this technology change life as we know it?
- Describe possible negative consequences of using the technology. Consider the recipient species, transport (vector) species, other species, and the environment.
- Who might object (morally, ethically, religiously) to implementing this technology and why? Consider religions, cultures, human rights groups, animal rights groups, others.
- Discuss some reasonable alternatives to using this technology that may provide a compromise to some people who may object.
- Discuss how money would play a role in the use of this technology. Who would pay for it?
- Prepare a chart that shows both sides of this issue.

6. After team members have completed their assigned parts, get together to prepare your final presentation. Assemble the graphics into an organized format, such as a poster, and prepare your discussion. You are going to present your proposal to the GEAB for their approval.

7. Prepare to give your classmates high-quality feedback on their presentations by following Steps 7a–c.

a. Read the scoring rubric that your teacher gives you.

b. Write in your notebook any questions you have about how to use the rubric while your classmates make their presentations.

c. Ask your questions as part of a class discussion and write your answers in your notebook and hand it in to your teacher.

Reflect and Connect

Answer the following questions in your science notebook. Use an effective strategy to check your answers.

1. What criteria did you consider when evaluating a new biotechnology? For each proposal presented, decide whether you would want to see the technology implemented. Support your decision with at least 3 statements.
2. In your opinion, what was the most unique technology presented? Do you think this technology is possible? Explain your answer.
3. Describe how the topic of genetic engineering spans across science disciplines, such as physical science, earth science, and life science.

UNIT 3

Moving Matter

Moving Matter

Look around. You probably see a lot of objects in your classroom. Some objects, like doors, outlets, or jewelry, might be made of metals. Other objects may consist of wood, such as desks, pencils, or buildings. How many things can you see made of plastic? You know well by now that all these objects are made of different kinds of atoms.

Take, for example, a carbon atom in your clothes. Where do you think a carbon atom might have been just before becoming part of your clothes? Was it in a ball of cotton? Was the carbon atom in a fossil fuel that was used to make synthetic fibers? Where might the atom have been one stage just before that? How might the stages link to form a history for that atom?

In unit 3, *Moving Matter*, you will explore how atoms that make up matter cycle and move among Earth's systems. Sometimes it's easy to see matter moving, such as with water flowing in a river or falling from the sky. At other times, the moving matter is very large, but difficult to visualize. Examples include currents in the oceans or even moving **tectonic plates**.

Systems, scale, and cycles—those are the big ideas in this unit. For example, how many kinds of cycles do you think might be represented in the unit's opening photograph? Write down some ideas in your science notebook. You'll return to this question later.

Goals for the Unit

By the end of unit 3, you should understand the following:

- Matter moves around Earth between reservoirs in geochemical cycles.
- Many kinds of technology help scientists measure moving matter in Earth's cycles.
- Geochemical cycles such as water, carbon, ice ages, and plate tectonics operate over timescales from days to millions of years.
- Geochemical cycles often involve reactions that change the chemical form and properties of the matter.
- Systems on Earth have reservoirs of matter, inputs and outputs, and fluxes of matter between those reservoirs.
- Carbon sinks in the geologic past are now valuable sources of fossil fuels and energy.
- Plate tectonics, mountain building, and erosion have slowly shaped the surface of Earth; many patterns of life on continents and in the oceans are linked to plate tectonics.

CHAPTER 10

The Water System

The Water System

As seen from space, water covers more than 70 percent of Earth's surface. This feature sets Earth apart from other planets in our solar system. Water is also vital for life. Humans cannot survive more than a few days without water. Even the hardiest desert plants and animals need some water to survive. On a personal level, humans need water for drinking, sanitation, bathing, and food preparation. In addition, humans use water for recreation, growing crops, sustaining livestock, mining, and producing goods. Water certainly matters to people and to all life on Earth.

In chapter 10, *The Water System*, you will look at water from a new point of view: a systems perspective. To do this, you will review what you already know about systems and expand your understanding of them. The world consists of many types of systems. You will describe some of these systems. You will analyze their size and boundaries, their parts, and their interactions. You will also look at how matter moves in systems.

Goals for the Chapter

You will apply your growing understanding of systems to water systems, ranging from your local water system up to the global water system. As you explore these systems, you will focus on both the location and the flow of water through one of Earth's systems, the hydrosphere. By the end of this chapter, you will be able to answer questions like these:

- Where does water exist on Earth?
- How much water do you use?
- What is the global water system?
- How does water move through the global water system?
- What is the earth system and how is the water system part of it?

At the end of this chapter, you will demonstrate your understanding of the water system by analyzing the Great Salt Lake as a system. You will work as a team to create a feature article on the Great Salt Lake (figure 10.1). This natural water system is unique in the United States. Do you know some reasons why? At the same time, the Great Salt Lake system faces issues similar to

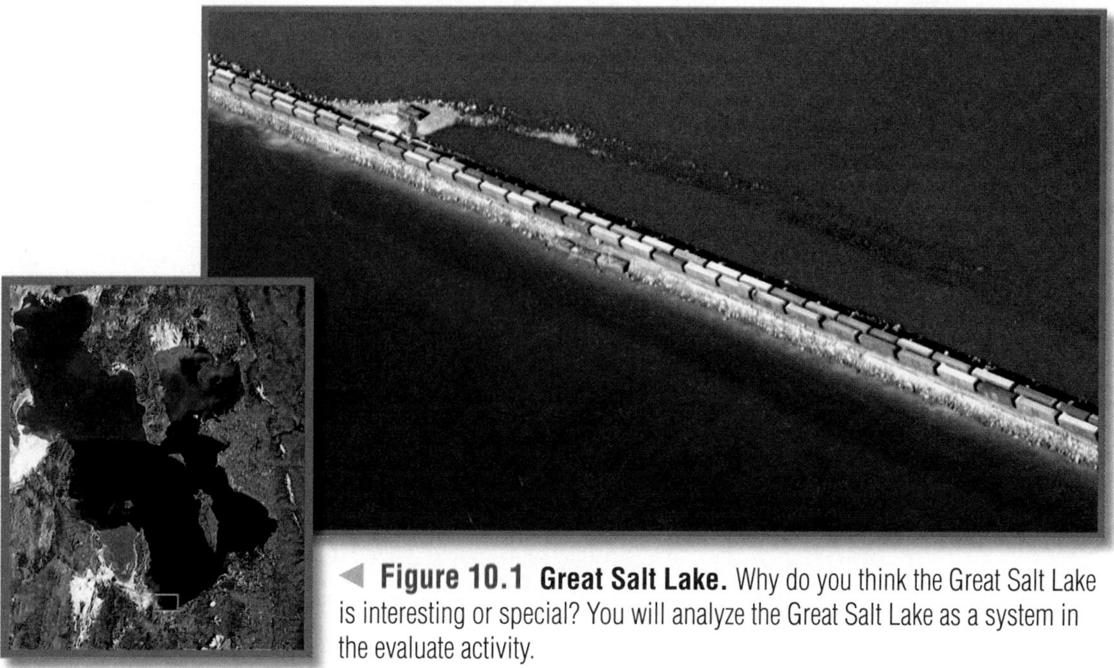

◀ **Figure 10.1 Great Salt Lake.** Why do you think the Great Salt Lake is interesting or special? You will analyze the Great Salt Lake as a system in the evaluate activity.

other lake systems on Earth. Can you think of other bodies of water that might be like the Great Salt Lake?

You will be better able to answer these questions by participating in the following activities:

ENGAGE	Entertaining Systems
EXPLORE / **EXPLAIN**	System Structures
EXPLORE	Beyond the Drinking Fountain
EXPLAIN	Expanding Boundaries
ELABORATE	The Global Water System
EVALUATE	A Salty Situation

This chapter also uses a chapter organizer. You should use it every day to think about where you are in its organization. Review each day the major concepts shown in the organizer. What is your understanding of these concepts? You can use the organizer to help monitor your progress. The organizer also will show your progress toward the evaluate activity, *A Salty Situation*.

Linking Question

How would you describe the parts of a system?

ENGAGE

Entertaining Systems

Key Idea:
Systems are part of our world.

The Water System

EXPLORE

EXPLAIN

System Structures Part I—A Bathtub System

Key Idea:
Bathtubs have some simple features that help you understand systems.

System Structures Part II—Systems Syntax

Key Idea:
Several words help you describe systems.

System Structures Part III—Fast-food Flowchart

Key Idea:
A restaurant is a system with inputs and outputs.

Linking Question

Where does your drinking water come from?

EXPLORE

Beyond the Drinking Fountain

Key Idea:
Water is vital in your community from initial treatment to waste treatment.

Linking Question

How is water distributed on continental North America?

EVALUATE

A Salty Situation

Key Idea:
Science, technology, dialogue, and clear writing are essential in understanding and solving community challenges, such as those with water resources.

Linking Question

How do ecosystems and communities interact in a natural system of water?

ELABORATE

The Global Water System Part I—Global Reservoirs

Key Idea:
A model can be used to show the sizes of water reservoirs on Earth.

The Global Water System Part II—Global Water Movement

Key Idea:
Balancing water fluxes shows how fast water moves in the water cycle.

The Global Water System Part III—Residence Time

Key Idea:
You can estimate the time that water or other matter spends in a reservoir.

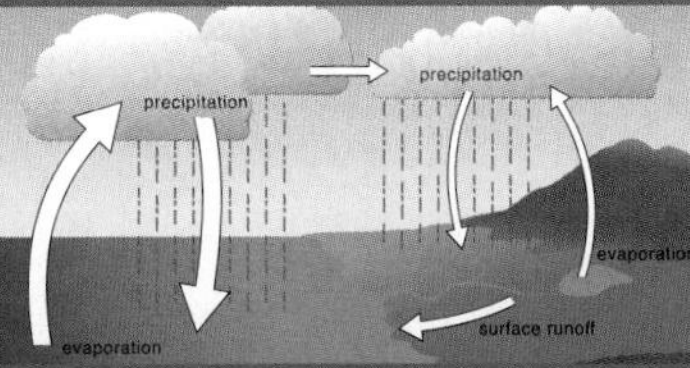

CHAPTER 10 Major Concepts

- Water on Earth cycles between several main reservoirs in the hydrosphere, geosphere, atmosphere, and biosphere.
- Knowing inputs and outputs lets you determine changes in reservoirs in the water system.
- Water helps define the Earth system, and a vital resource for humans.
- Many technologies let scientists monitor different parts of the water system.

EXPLAIN

Expanding Boundaries Part I—Where Is the Water?

Key Idea:
Water is transported in North America by evaporation, transpiration, precipitation, and river flow.

Expanding Boundaries Part II—The Water We Use

Key Idea:
The U.S. uses many millions of gallons of water per day.

Linking Question

How does water in your community link to a global water cycle?

ENGAGE

Entertaining Systems

Systems make up our world. You are probably already familiar with systems such as the digestive and reproductive systems in your body. Or you probably have used a computer system in your school or at home.

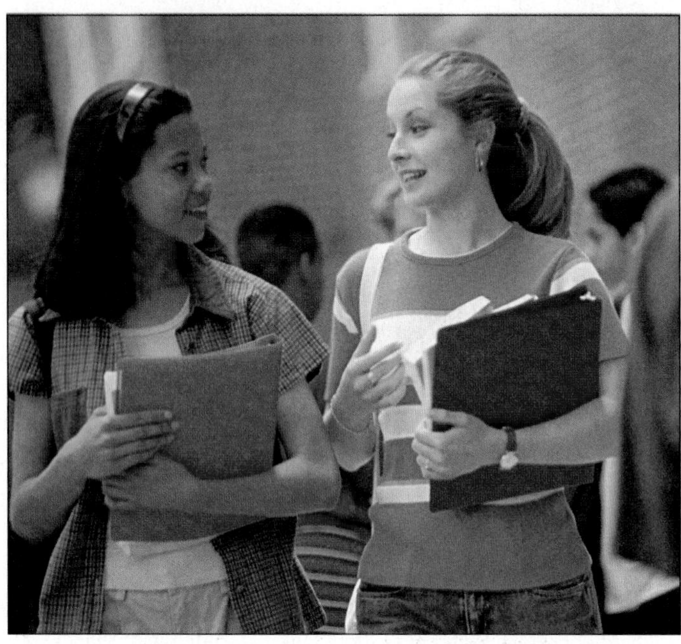

▲ **Figure 10.2**
Systems. Look at the natural and human systems in this photograph. What is similar about these systems? What is different?

But what first comes to mind when you see the word "system"? What exactly is a system? How big, or how small, is a system? What kinds of systems are shown in figure 10.2? In *Entertaining Systems*, you will work individually and then in a team to explore and share what you already know about systems that you interact with every day—entertainment systems.

Materials

For each team of 3 students

1 sheet of oversized paper

2 large markers

Process and Procedure

1. Work alone to make a list of systems that are related to entertainment. Write down at least 5 systems in your science notebook. Be prepared to share your list with your class.

Think of entertainment as a broad category. What are your favorite forms of entertainment? What sorts of things do you need so that the entertainment system works properly?

2. When you have completed your list, form a team with 2 other students. Answer the following questions in your science notebook.
   a. Do your team members think about an entertainment system as you do?
   b. What are the similarities and differences among the entertainment systems on your 3 lists?
   c. Which systems are you a part of? Carefully explain why you think so.
3. As a team, determine 3 or 4 general characteristics that are shared by all the entertainment systems on the 3 lists. Write these general characteristics on an oversized sheet of paper and post them in the classroom according to your teacher's instructions.

4. In your team, select 1 entertainment system that includes each of you. Complete Steps 4a–c for that system.
   a. Develop a diagram or sketch that represents that system. Label the parts of the system.
   b. Show how you fit into that system.
   c. Develop a figure caption that describes the main parts of the diagram or sketch.
5. Follow your teacher's instructions to share with the class ideas from your team list and your sketch or diagram. A recorder will list the ideas for everyone to review and compare.

Reflect and Connect

Work on your own to answer the following questions. Record your best thinking in your science notebook.

1. Use a table (or chart) in your science notebook to record your ideas for each of these categories.
   a. What I know about systems
   b. What I think I know about systems
   c. What I wonder about systems
2. Look at the list of entertainment systems you developed as a class. Have you ever thought about these things as systems before? Why do you think it is helpful to think about entertainment as a system?
3. Write the names of 2 other systems (not entertainment) in your science notebook. Describe how these 2 systems have the characteristics of a system that your team determined in Step 3.

Decide whether it might be helpful for you to use a sketch, diagram, or highlight comment.

System Structures

EXPLORE

EXPLAIN

In *Entertaining Systems*, you developed a list of characteristics common to systems. Does material or energy flow through those systems? How do the parts of a system interact? You already started thinking about the kinds of interactions in systems in the unit *Interactions Are Interesting*.

In *System Structures*, Part I, you will work in a team to explore the movement of matter by modeling a bathtub system. Then in Part II, you will work with a partner to learn the terminology used to describe systems. In Part III, you will work with a team and use your understanding of systems to analyze a fast-food restaurant system.

Part I: Bathtub System

Materials

For each team of 3 students

1 1-L plastic bottle or container

1 100-mL graduated cylinder

1 stopwatch

Process and Procedure

You will work in a team to model a bathtub system using a small container with a hole and a faucet to provide water. Your team's challenge is to fill your container up to a mark and keep the water level exactly at this mark. Then you will quantify (measure) what is happening in your bathtub system.

1. Get into teams of 3 and go to the area designated by your teacher. Review figure 10.3, which shows a bathtub setup and how you might represent it in your science notebook.

Water is an important resource that shouldn't be wasted. Read all the steps before beginning this activity. Then complete the steps that require water as quickly as possible so that you minimize the water used.

2. Fill your container with water until the water reaches the mark on the container. Then make the necessary adjustments to the flow rate of water to keep the water level exactly at the mark. Record answers to the following in your science notebook.
   a. What adjustments did you make to your system? What did you change?
   b. What could you not change?

Recall that a rate of flow is sort of like a velocity, or rate of motion. It tells the change that occurs in a given amount of time.

3. Several variables indicate the size of the system and how long it takes for the system to change. Measure these and record the results with proper units in your science notebook.
   a. Use a graduated cylinder to measure the flow rate at the faucet. How much water enters the cylinder in a given time period, such as 10 seconds (sec)?

Check that your units for flow rate here make sense. Also confirm that the water is still coming out of the faucet at the same speed that it was in Step 2.

   b. Write in your notebook the flow rate in terms of the mass of water (grams, abbreviated as g). What property of water do you use to determine flow rate as mass?

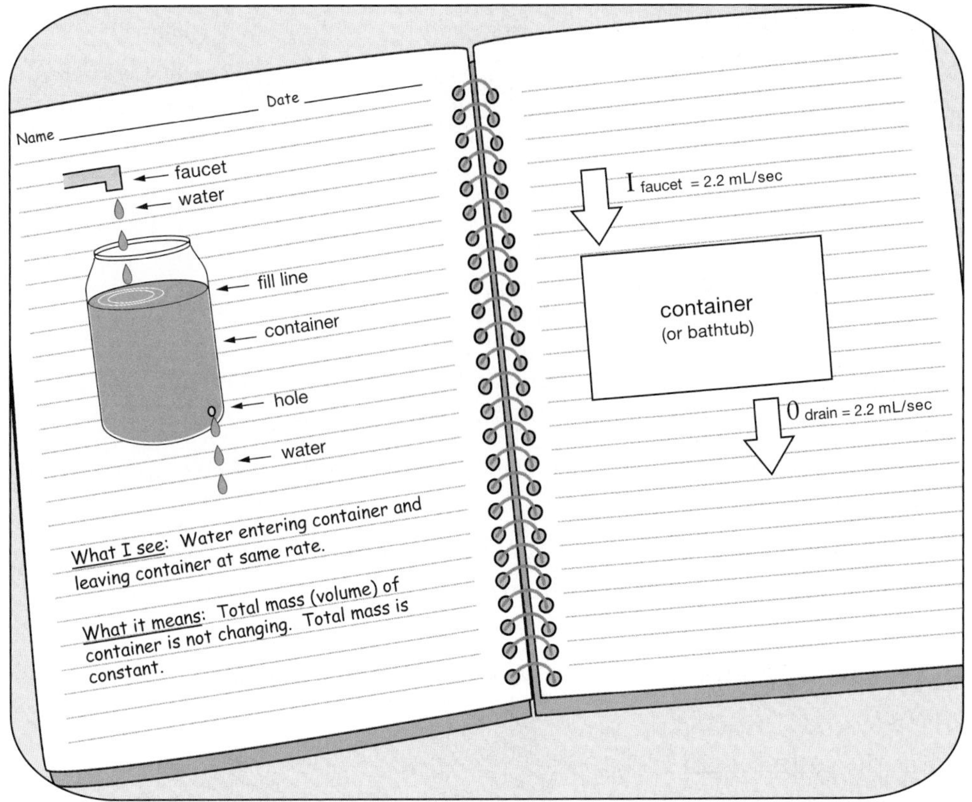

Figure 10.3 Sketch and box diagram in science notebook. This diagram shows some elements of science notebooks, such as name, date, labels, and measurement (2.2 mL/sec). The sketch to the left includes simple phrases for "what I see/what it means." The sketch to the right represents the water container as a box with water flowing in and out.

c. Repeat Steps 3a–b for the water flowing out of the container and for the volume of the container.

d. What is the mass of the water in the container at the mark?

4. Develop a simple diagram or sketch for your setup of a bathtub system. Model your diagram like figure 10.3. You should include labels for things like the following in your diagram.

   a. Flow rate into the container (show rates and units for volume change)

   b. Flow rate out of the container (show rates and units for volume change)

   c. Volume of the container (show rates for mass)

   d. Highlight comments or figure caption

Stop & THINK

PART I

Work with your team to complete the following tasks. Record your answers in your science notebook.

1. Your bathtub system was balanced when you kept the water at the same level. You also considered chemical reactions that were balanced in chapter 5, *Forces of Attraction*. How are these 2 balanced systems similar?
2. In a balanced system, what is the relationship between the flow rate into and the flow rate out of the system? Use numbers to explain your answer.
3. Describe what would happen to your bathtub system if the following had happened.
   - **a.** You made the hole bigger.
   - **b.** You changed the position of the hole (not the size).
   - **c.** You moved the mark higher in your container.
   - **d.** You increased the flow rate from the faucet.

Part II: Systems Syntax

Materials

none

Process and Procedure

1. Follow your teacher's directions for completing the following reading on systems.

READING

Systems Are Everywhere

By modeling the bathtub system in Part I, you began to define a system. But how do scientists define a system? A **system** is any collection of things that interact with one another. Many systems accomplish a very specific set of functions, while other systems appear chaotic. You were investigating a simple system when you modeled a bathtub system. In science, everything in the physical world is part of a system.

Systems are open or closed depending on how they relate to their surroundings and how the boundaries are defined. **Open systems** exchange both energy and matter with the surrounding environment. **Closed systems** exchange only energy with the surrounding environment. A potted plant is an open system. The plant exchanges oxygen and carbon dioxide with the atmosphere. However, a plant in a sealed, glass terrarium is a closed system. Energy enters the terrarium system daily, but matter is not exchanged. Water circulates only within the terrarium.

Earth is essentially a closed system. Solar energy enters the system, and infrared radiation given off by Earth escapes to space. Matter does not enter or leave Earth. Or does it? Meteors and interstellar dust constantly bombard Earth's atmosphere. Much of this dust vaporizes after entering the atmosphere. Occasionally, a meteorite will reach Earth's surface. But the mass of matter added to Earth is small compared with the mass of Earth.

Every system has **boundaries**, or physical limits. The boundary for a terrarium is the glass container. A container also provided the boundary for the bathtub system you modeled. Expanding the boundaries can increase the number of components and interactions involved in the system.

Within the boundaries, the system contains a particular amount of material. The amount of material entering the system is **input**, and the amount of material leaving the system is **output**. Systems can change with time because the inputs and outputs may be different. If the inputs and the outputs are equal, a system might not appear to change at all. It is in a state of balance. You considered balanced chemical equations earlier in this program.

Even simple systems can have more than one input and one output. For example, trees take in water through their roots, carbon dioxide from the air, and energy through their leaves. Trees expel oxygen and water vapor through their leaves and give off heat as a result of burning stored energy during respiration. The rate that material, such as water, moves into or out of a system, such as a tree, often varies. For example, trees in many parts of North America take in more water in summer when they are growing than in winter when they may be dormant.

How does changing one part of a system affect the whole system? A common saying is "Change is the only constant." An important feature of natural systems is that they are dynamic—they are always changing. Changes in systems are identified by comparing the inputs (I) and the outputs (O). If the inputs are greater than the outputs, the change in the system is positive. If the outputs are greater than the inputs, the change in the system is negative.

Systems Are Everywhere, continued

An outdoor pool is a good example (figure 10.4). The pool receives water from precipitation, and additional water can be added from a faucet. The pool loses water through evaporation. The inputs are water from the faucet and precipitation. The output is evaporation.

When inputs equal output, the volume of water in the pool remains the same. However, if the pool receives more water from precipitation and the output remains the same, the water level in the pool will increase. The change in volume is positive. If more water evaporates and the inputs remain the same, the water level in the pool will decrease. This change in volume is negative. Water circulation in the filtration system does not change the total amount of water. You can show this as

$$\pm \text{ change in pool volume} = \text{inputs} - \text{outputs} = (I_{faucet} + I_{rain}) - (O_{evaporation}).$$

Systems can also be characterized by how fast they change mass or volume. You studied rates of change earlier in the year when you saw that velocity was the change in distance over an amount of time, or $v = \frac{\Delta x}{\Delta t}$. With systems, the **flux** tells how fast, or the rate, that matter enters or leaves a system. And just like with inputs and outputs, systems can have fluxes in and fluxes out.

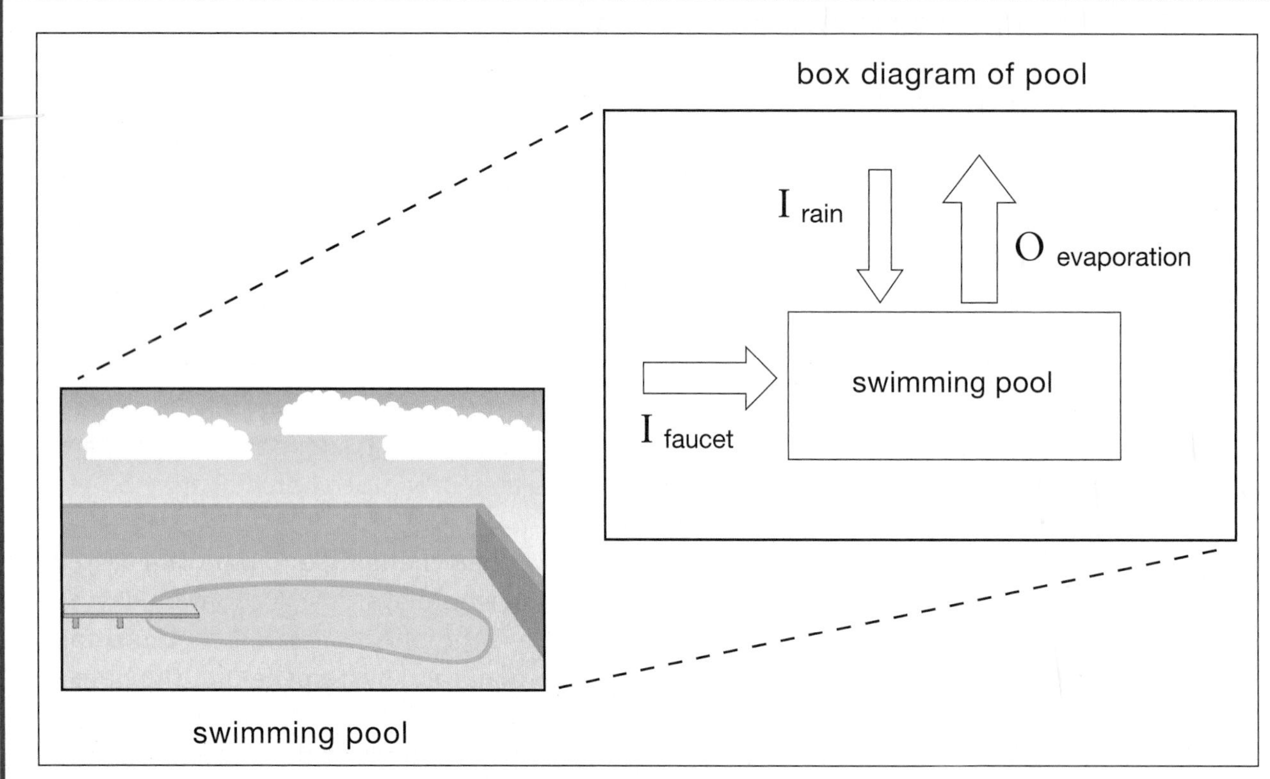

Figure 10.4 Box diagram of a pool system. Box diagrams are a way to visually represent systems. The arrows show inputs (I) and outputs (O) of mass to the box. The subscripts show how to label independent inputs and outputs. Arrow sizes represent the amounts of mass (water) entering and leaving the box.

With the pool example, during July the pool might receive water input that changes the level at a rate of 5 centimeters (cm) per month (about 2 inches [in] of summer rain). At the same time, evaporation might equal a net loss at a rate of 15 cm per month. You can see that there is a net decrease in water level of 10 cm per month. This is expressed in an equation as volume (V):

$$\pm \text{ rate of change in pool volume} = \frac{\Delta \text{Volume}}{\Delta \text{time}} = \frac{\Delta \text{V}}{\Delta \text{t}} \text{ or}$$

$$\frac{\Delta V}{\Delta t} = (\text{flux in} - \text{flux out}).$$

One point is very important. Simple equations like this can be used for any kind of system. But you do need to check that the units match on each side of the equation. Rather than volume per time, each side of the equation could also have units such as mass of carbon per time.

Pool systems tend to change, but a balance can be maintained between the inputs and outputs. You already investigated such balances in chemical systems in *Interactions Are Interesting*. With a pool system, changes in the precipitation or evaporation rates might change the water level of the pool. The manager of a pool would try to maintain the same water level in the pool by adding water from a faucet. In this case, the rate of change is zero and—you guessed it—the flux in has to equal the flux out. This is easy to show.

$$\pm \text{ rate of change in pool volume} = 0 = (\text{flux in} - \text{flux out}) \text{ or}$$

$$\text{flux in} = \text{flux out}$$

The inputs and outputs into natural systems change, but overall they need to maintain a balance. For example, water plays an important role in your body. On average, 55–65 percent of your body consists of water. A healthy body has just the right amount of water inside and outside each cell. When you sweat from hot weather or exercise, your body loses water (figure 10.5). Your body tries to regain balance by sending a message to make you feel thirsty. In response, you drink more water. Your increased water input balances your increased water output.

Your body systems can get out of balance if you don't have access to water. Without water, your body systems will have difficulty functioning properly and their malfunction could lead to death. Inputs and outputs, such as water in our body systems, are an important part of systems. These inputs and outputs change to maintain a balanced system.

▲ **Figure 10.5 Athletes competing.** You can sweat up to 1 liter of water per hour while exercising or competing in sports. You must balance this output with an input—drinking water or a sports drink.

Topic: systems
Go to: www.scilinks.org
Code: 2Inquiry505

Stop & THINK

PART II

Work individually or with one partner to complete the following tasks. Record your answers in your science notebook.

1. Answer the following questions about the bathtub system from Part I.
   a. Was the bathtub system open or closed? Explain your reasoning.
   b. Identify the inputs and outputs.

2. Return to the box diagram in figure 10.3 in Part I. Redraw this diagram in your science notebook using vocabulary and ideas from the reading *Systems Are Everywhere*. Use as a model the diagram in figure 10.4. Assume the system is balanced and use the flow rate you calculated in Step 2 of Part I.

   Include the input and output fluxes on your diagram. You will need to adjust the number and size of the input and output arrows to fit the bathtub subsystem.

3. Look back at the drawing of the bathtub system you created in Part I. Explain how the box diagram you just created in Question 2 is different from the drawing in figure 10.3.

4. Imagine that a full-time worker earning $10 per hour is paid $1,600 per month. The worker has monthly expenses for housing ($700); food ($350); utilities (water, electricity, heat; $150); transportation (car insurance, repairs, gas; $100); car loan payment ($75); and medical insurance ($80).
   a. Make a T-table showing inputs and outputs per month to the worker's bank account.
   b. Does the worker have money left each month for other needs, such as clothing, vacations, going out to eat, or buying furniture or recreational items? Explain the net change in the system per month.
   c. How much extra does the worker gain per year? Is it enough to buy a new car?

5. Figure 10.6 shows a farm pond with inputs and outputs. They are from streams (str), rain, evaporation (evap), and a spring. Which expression best shows the net change in water volume in the farm pond? Explain in your science notebook which answer you selected.

a. Change in volume = $(I_{str} + I_{spring} + I_{rain}) + (O_{evap} + O_{str})$
b. Change in volume = $(I_{str} + I_{rain}) - (O_{evap} + O_{str} + I_{spring})$
c. Change in volume = $(I_{str} - O_{str}) - O_{evap} + (I_{spring} + I_{rain})$
d. Change in volume = $(O_{evap} + O_{str}) - (I_{str} - I_{spring} + I_{rain})$
e. Change in volume = $(I_{str} + I_{spring} + I_{rain}) - (O_{evap} + O_{str})$

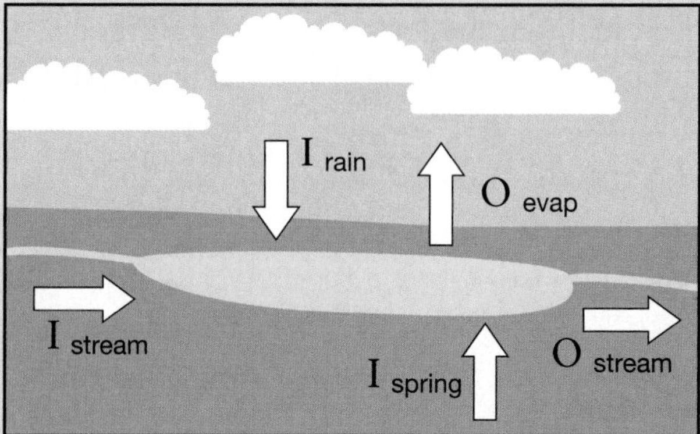

Figure 10.6 Farm pond box diagram. This box diagram for a farm pond has three inputs (stream, rain, spring) and two outputs (evaporation, stream).What balance of these inputs and outputs shows the net change in water level for the farm pond?

6 Recall the container from Part I. It had a hole that let water flow out and a volume of 1.2 liters (L). Imagine that water flows in at a rate of 400 milliliters per minute (400 mL/min), and flows out at 300 mL/min.

a. How many milliliters (mL) does the container hold?
b. How long does it take for the container to fill?
c. If the container is full and water coming in is turned off, how long would you predict for the container to drain to empty?
d. Imagine that the container is empty and it still has a flow rate out the drain of 300 mL/min. What flow rate into the container (input) will give 1.0 L of water in 5 minutes?

Part III: Fast-food Flowchart

Materials

none

Process and Procedure

The bathtub you modeled is a simple system. Other systems you will encounter could be more complicated. They may have multiple inputs and outputs. You will see that natural water systems may be like this. But for now, let's use another example to represent how mass moves through a system. You are probably familiar with this system—a fast-food restaurant.

When did you last have french fries? A lot of people enjoy eating french fries, yet they take for granted that they can buy them ready to eat. What does it take to get an order of french fries into your hands? Where do they come from and how many steps are required before you purchase them? You can answer these questions with a systems approach. In Part III of the activity, you will work in a team to investigate how french fries move through a fast-food restaurant.

1. Large systems often include smaller systems within them. Before diagramming a fast-food restaurant system, read *Systems within Systems*.

READING

Systems within Systems

Large systems may have other systems contained within them. These are called **subsystems**. Subsystems can have their own parts and interactions. For example, a pasture where cattle graze is a system that also includes interactions between grasses and cattle. Each plant also constitutes a subsystem that interacts with the air and soil. An amusement park is another example of a system. Each ride and concession stand is a subsystem within the larger amusement park. The aquarium in figure 10.7 shows another example of subsystems within a larger system.

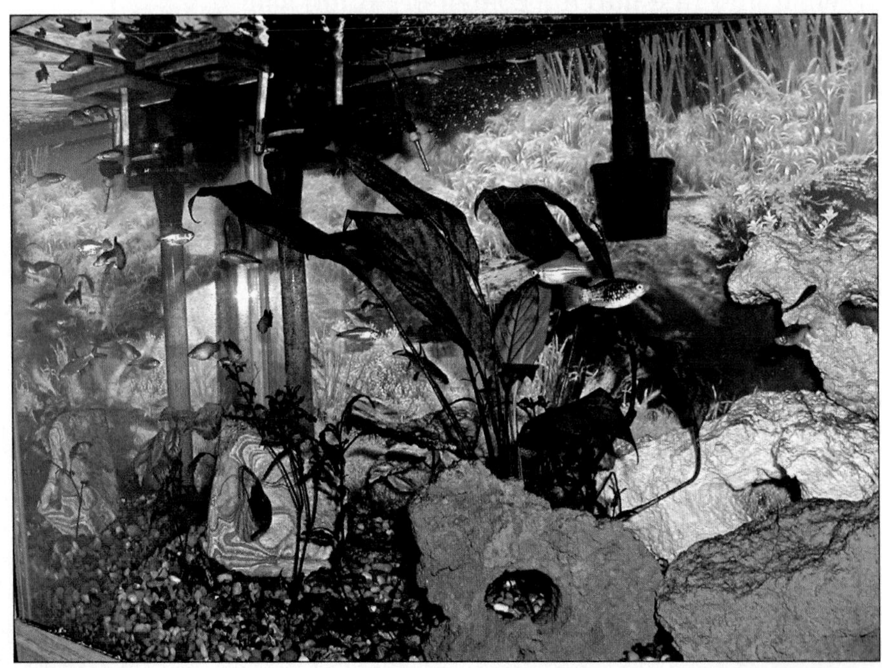

◀ **Figure 10.7**
Systems and subsystems. Examine the things in this aquarium. How many subsystems can you find in the photograph?

The function of a whole system is different from the function of each of its parts. As a whole, a car is a mode of transportation. The parts of a car are subsystems with functions including gasoline combustion, steering, braking, and lighting. A car would not function properly without each of these smaller subsystems.

Life on Earth is also a web of natural and human-made systems. Your body and life are part of a network of subsystems and larger systems. For example, your body consists of subsystems such as the circulatory, respiratory, reproductive, and muscular systems. These subsystems interact with one another. When you exercise and use your muscles, your heart beats faster and your respiration increases. Oxygen from the air moves into your lungs and is absorbed into the blood. Then the circulatory system increases the flow of oxygen-rich blood to the muscles. You also are a part of larger systems such as a family system, a community, a school system, an ecosystem, and even the solar system.

Here's another example of subsystems—using the World Wide Web. From your Web browser, your computer connects to an Internet service provider (ISP). When connected to the ISP, you become part of its network. The ISP can in turn connect you to a larger network and so on. Each network is its own system. Your personal computer also consists of hardware and software systems including the processor, power supply, keyboard, operating system, and programs.

We are surrounded by systems. We are parts of systems. You are able to investigate and determine the size and properties of these systems.

2. Using what you know about systems, subsystems, and fast-food restaurants, answer the following questions.
   a. What are the major parts of a fast-food restaurant system?
   b. What are some inputs and outputs of a fast-food restaurant system?
   c. What are the boundaries of a fast-food system?
   d. How do you think a fast-food restaurant is a subsystem of a larger system?

For example, money flows into and out of a fast-food restaurant. The flow of money is part of a larger economic system. We can think about a fast-food restaurant as a subsystem of the economic system.

   e. Think of a fast-food restaurant as the larger system. What are 3 or more subsystems of the fast-food restaurant system?
3. Develop a diagram of a series of subsystems showing where the french fries come from and how they get into your hands. Where were the fries before they got into your hands? Where were they before that? And before that?

You may have developed a diagram like figure 10.8 in the activity *Entertaining Systems*.

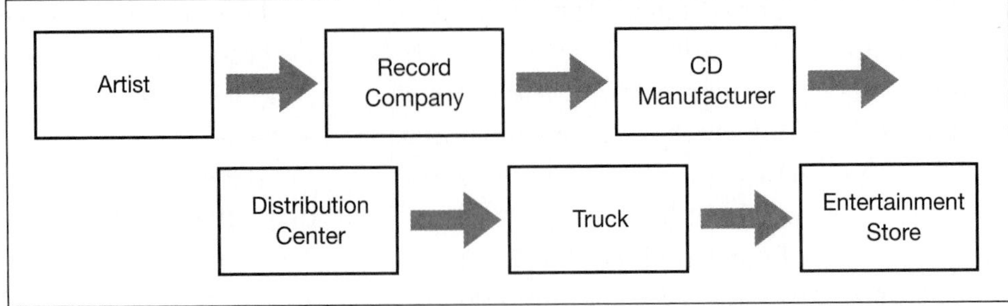

▲ **Figure 10.8 Entertainment system flow diagram.** This flow diagram shows steps to get a CD to a store. Each box is a subsystem. The arrows indicate matter moving through the systems. For example, a CD manufacturer needs music from the record company before it can produce a CD.

4. Pick 1 subsystem (box) in your diagram. Describe and draw any interactions it has with other systems. Consider the movement of both matter and energy in this side chain. Where was the matter and energy before arriving at that system? Where was the matter and energy before that? Share your ideas with your team and use the diagram in figure 10.9 as a model.

For example, you might have labeled the first box before the fries were in hand, "heat lamp." A side chain off of a heat lamp might include the electricity that makes the lamp work. The electricity is supplied by a power plant that may get its power from fossil fuels.

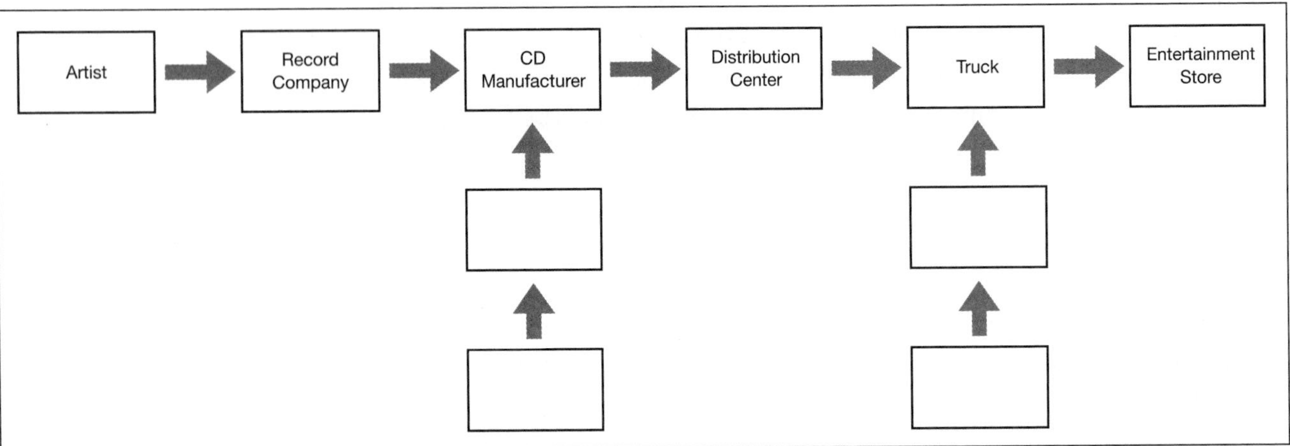

▲ **Figure 10.9 Interactions between subsystems.** Add one or more chains of boxes to your previous diagram. The new chain of boxes (subsystems) represents the flow of matter and energy into one of the subsystems in your diagram. For example, what does the truck need to function?

5. Draw circles around the subsystems that are part of the fast-food restaurant system. Circle "fast-food restaurant system." Identify another subsystem in your diagram and draw the boundaries for that subsystem. Label the system you have identified.
6. Use the following data about french fries to calculate the input and output fluxes. Label the inputs and outputs and record the fluxes as kilograms per week (kg/wk) in the diagram.
   - Fry Daze fast-food restaurant receives a delivery of 50 cases of french fries every week.
   - Each case weighs 20 kilograms (kg).
   - Every week, 5 percent of the french fries spoil before they can be sold, with the rest purchased by hungry customers.
7. To check your understanding of fluxes, draw a box diagram of the fast-food restaurant system similar to the one in figure 10.4. Show the fluxes of french fries for the restaurant that you calculated in Step 6. Adjust the size of the input and output arrows to fit the french fry subsystem.

Reflect and Connect

Answer the following questions on your own in your science notebook.

1. What are some of the characteristics of systems? Look at the list of characteristics you developed in *Entertaining Systems*. How do your previous ideas about systems compare with what you learned in this activity? Describe any similarities and differences.

Decide if a strategy such as a T-table or a Venn diagram is useful here.

2. Describe how the following changes would affect the fast-food restaurant system from Part III. The fast-food restaurant sells fewer french fries each day.
   a. Will the number of fries in the restaurant increase or decrease?
   b. How can the owner of the fast-food restaurant adjust the system to maintain the same amount of fries stored in the freezer? Explain your answer.
   c. Imagine that potato crops in Idaho are damaged and the cost of potatoes increases by 5 percent. Estimate how the costs associated with the fluxes in your box diagram from Step 6 in Part III might change.
3. Does a systems approach help you view fast-food restaurants differently? Explain your ideas in your science notebook.

EXPLORE

Beyond the Drinking Fountain

When did you last have a drink of water? You know how important water is. You cannot live without it, yet many people take water for granted. They turn on the faucet, and there it is. They use it to drink, to cook, and to clean. But where does the water in the faucet come from? And where does it go?

In *Beyond the Drinking Fountain*, you will work in a team to explore your local water system in order to answer these and other questions. As you do this activity, be sure to use what you learned from previous work with bathtubs, pools, and restaurants and recall how you diagrammed inputs and outputs. This will help you develop a better understanding of your local water system, both before and after faucets or drinking fountains.

Materials

For each team of 3 students

access to resource materials

Process and Procedure

Every community has important local issues related to water. Perhaps county officials have discovered that a local fishing hole is contaminated. Maybe the city council is trying to decide whether or not to add fluoride to the water. Is there a water shortage? Imagine that because of recent events around a local water issue, your teacher has asked your class to prepare a display for the school hallway that will both interest and inform fellow students about the local water system. You will work in teams to prepare a proposal for the layout of the display. Your proposal will include a diagram and related information about the water system.

You will not actually build the display, so you can propose any type of display you want, even if the materials to make it are hard to find or expensive. The goal is to obtain information and decide on an effective way to present the information.

1. What does your team know about the local water system? Write in your science notebook answers to the following questions.
   a. Where do you think that the water in your school comes from?
   b. Where do you think that the water in your school goes?

Answer Questions 1a–b with written phrases as well with as diagrams to show your thinking.

2. Research your local water system with your team to answer more specifically Questions 1a–b. Write answers in your science notebook, using both sentences and diagrams with labels. Consider getting information on the following:
   - The boundaries of your local water system
   - The parts or subsystems in the local water system (for example, its use in houses, business, and agriculture)
   - The interactions between parts of the local water system
   - Whether the system is dynamic and changing or the source of water is constant
3. Gather data about the flow of water, or fluxes, in your local water system. Do these amounts change over time? Record your data as a box diagram, with values for inputs and outputs, in the proposal for your display.

As you find information, you might encounter a variety of units used to report water data. Read more about these units in *FYI—Units for Water Volumes and Flow Rates.*

4. As your team does research, note interesting information to display about your local water system. Consider information about local water issues, interesting facts or figures, or creative ways of displaying data.
5. Prepare a design for the layout of your display. The display needs to inform and interest other students in your school about the local water system. The layout should include the following.
   a. A sketch of the hallway display
   b. A description of any visuals you are proposing to use in the display, including the box diagram
   c. Examples of data you have found
   d. A list of all references and sources of information
6. Share your team's display layout with the class.

Units for Water Volumes and Flow Rates

Containers. What units of volume are used for the beverages you drink? What units would you use to describe the volume of water in this reservoir?

When you open the refrigerator for a drink, you might reach for a can of soda or a glass of milk. Containers for these drinks have volume as ounces or gallons (or liters). It is much tougher to visualize the volume of water in lakes or river systems, or the water used in towns or cities, each day or each year. How would you do this? You will see different units for volume when researching water systems.

In water systems, scientists often describe volumes with units of **acre-feet** (**af**). This is the volume of water that covers 1 ac of land with water that is 1 ft deep. A football field is a good analogy. Without the end zones, football fields are 300 ft long and 160 ft wide, for a total area of 48,000 square feet (ft^2). One acre of land is 43,560 ft^2, so a football field is within 10 percent of the area of 1 ac of land. Thus, 1 af of water will cover a football field with 1 ft of water, for about 273 of the 300 feet in length. This is to about the 91 yard line. This may sound like a lot of water. But compared with the volumes of water in natural systems, this is a drop in the bucket.

Public utilities often report water use either in acre-feet or in **millions of gallons** (**Mgal**). How much is 1 million gallons of water? A good way to think about this is to compare 1 Mgal of water with 1 af of water. As indicated earlier, 1 af is 43,560 ft^3. Similarly, 1 cubic foot of water equals 7.48 gallons (1 ft^3 = 7.48 gal). Combining these, making sure that units cancel, shows that 1 Mgal is the same as about 3.07 af. Or 1 Mgal is just 1 ac covered with about 3 ft of water.

$$\left(1\ \cancel{\text{Mgal}}\right) \times \left(\frac{10^6\ \cancel{\text{gal}}}{1\ \cancel{\text{Mgal}}}\right) \times \left(\frac{1\ \cancel{\text{ft}^3}}{7.48\ \cancel{\text{gal}}}\right) \times \left(\frac{1\ \text{af}}{43{,}560\ \cancel{\text{ft}^3}}\right) = 3.07\ \text{af}$$

For towns or cities, rates of water use are often recorded as **millions of gallons per day**, (**Mgal/d**). In Colorado Springs, Colorado, for example, water

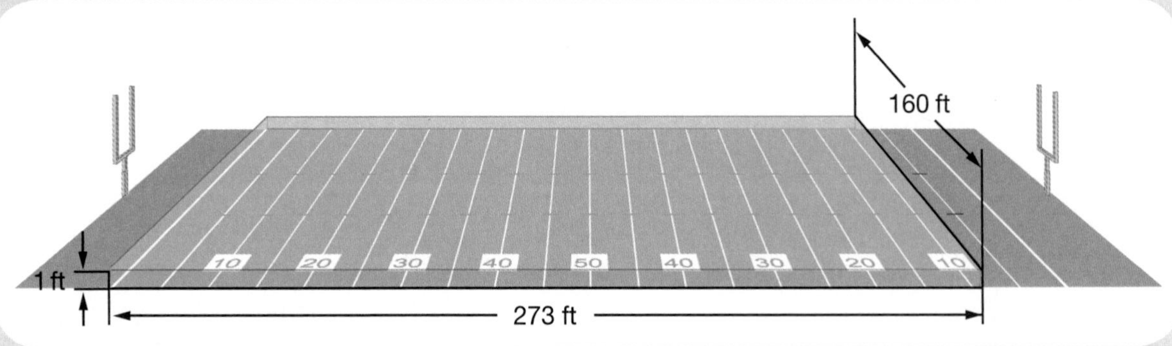

Acre-feet of water. How much water is 1 acre-foot (1 af) of water?

use in 1999 for nearly 400,000 customers was at a rate of about 74.3 Mgal/d. How many acre-feet per year (af/yr) is this? It is about 83,000 af/yr. By converting depths of feet to miles, you can show that this would cover a football field in water nearly 16 miles (mi) deep. That's a lot of water!

$$\left(\frac{74.3 \text{ Mgal}}{1 \text{ day}}\right) \times \left(\frac{3.07 \text{ af}}{1 \text{ Mgal}}\right) \times \left(\frac{365.25 \text{ day}}{1 \text{ yr}}\right) = 83{,}314 \frac{\text{af}}{\text{yr}}$$

$$\left(83{,}314 \frac{\text{acre}\cdot\text{ft}}{\text{yr}}\right) \times \left(\frac{1 \text{ mile}}{5{,}280 \text{ ft}}\right) = 15.8 \frac{\text{acre}\cdot\text{mile}}{\text{yr}}$$

Scientists also need to record the rate of water flow in rivers and streams. They do this in units of **cubic feet per second (cfs)**. First, imagine filling a 1-ft cube with water, for a total volume of 1 ft^3. If 1 ft^3 of water passes a point each second, the rate of flow is said to be 1 ft^3 per second, or 1 cfs. While this might not seem like a lot, it is! A flow rate of 1 cfs for one day delivers nearly 2 af of water (1 cfs = 1.983 af/day). Or a flow rate of 1 cfs fills a football field to a depth of 1 ft in just half a day. But this is only for 1 ft^3. A river is many times wider than this.

Water flow rates in cubic feet per second are measured at stream gauges all over North America. Many of these data are available in real time on the World Wide Web from organizations such as the U.S. Geological Survey. When you see rates at thousands of cubic feet per second, this leads to accumulations of millions of acre-feet of water per year—all of which are flowing to the ocean!

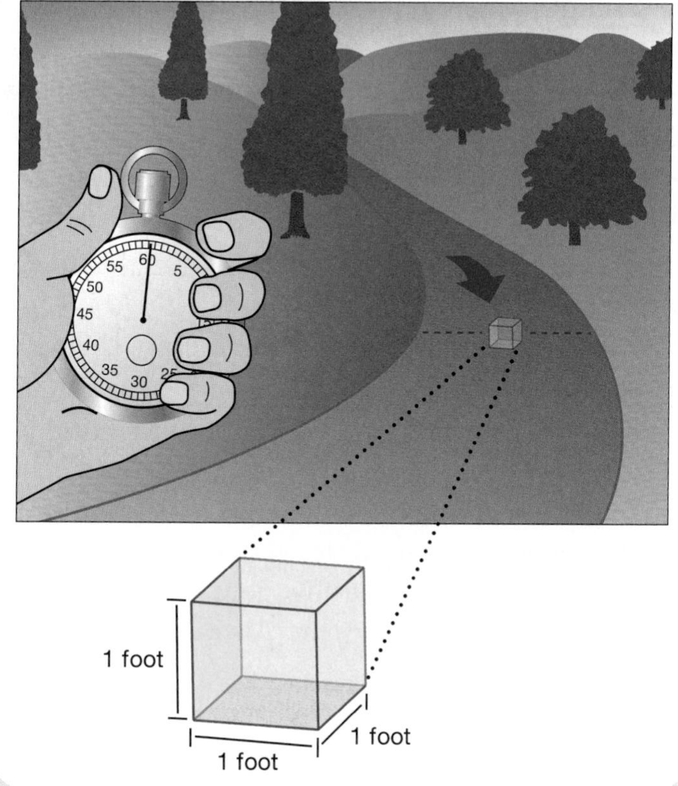

Cubic feet per second of water. How fast does water flow at 1 cubic foot per second (1 cfs)? Is this a large or small amount of water?

Reflect and Connect

Work individually to answer the following questions. Write your responses in your science notebook.

1. Show the path of a water molecule (H_2O) through your local water system by linking a series of subsystems. Each of the subsystems should be a part of your local water system. The first box should show the first subsystem where the water molecule enters your local system at a boundary. The last box should show the subsystem where the water molecule leaves your local water system at the other side of the boundary. Add boxes and arrows as needed. Use figure 10.10 as a model.

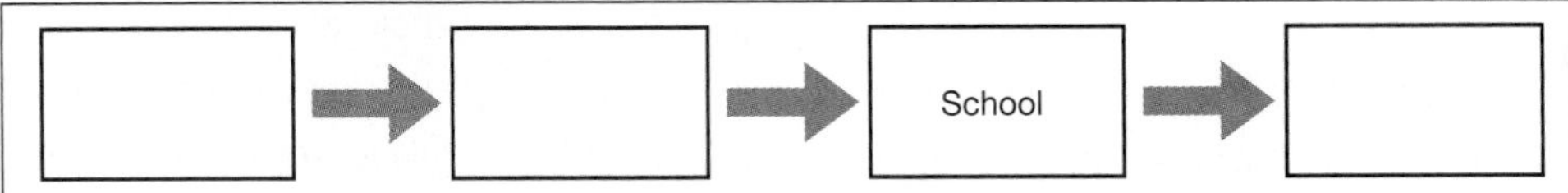

▲ **Figure 10.10 Water through subsystems.** Examine the boxes and arrows in the diagram. Fill in the boxes to show the path of a water molecule through the subsystems of your local water system.

2. Sources of drinking water are typically either surface water or groundwater.
   a. What is the source of water in your community, and how much water does your community use?

Again, make sure that you use proper units by checking the *FYI—Units for Water Volumes and Flow Rates.*

   b. What factors affect the amount of water available to your community?
   c. Under what circumstances might a community change its primary source of water?
3. Write 2 sentences telling how you are a part of the local water system.
4. Write 2 sentences describing possible impacts of your local water system on a neighboring water system.
5. Write in a short paragraph about how your local water system is like the fast-food restaurant system. Also describe how these 2 systems are different.
6. Imagine that 3 acres (ac) of land are covered with water that is 2 feet (ft) deep.
   a. About how many millions of gallons (Mgal) of water is that?
   b. If people use this much water each day, how many million gallons is this per year?
   c. Use a ratio to compare your answer in Question 6b with the rate of water use in your community.

Expanding Boundaries

EXPLAIN

The water that flows out of the drinking fountain is part of the school's water system. In turn, the school's water system is part of your local water system. In the previous investigation, *Beyond the Drinking Fountain*, you explored your local water system. You identified the boundaries of this system. What happens when those boundaries are extended even further? In *Expanding Boundaries*, you will work in teams to expand the boundaries of your local water system and to explore the larger water system of the United States.

Part I: Where Is the Water?

Materials

For each team of 3 students

1 marker or yellow highlighter

3 *North America, Rivers and Streams* handouts

Process and Procedure

Just as french fries are a part of a fast-food restaurant, which is part of the larger fast-food system, your local water system is part of a larger system. Some of this system is shown in figure 10.11. In Part I of this investigation, you will work in teams of three to examine the larger water system of the United States. Your focus will be on the natural flow of water within and around the United States.

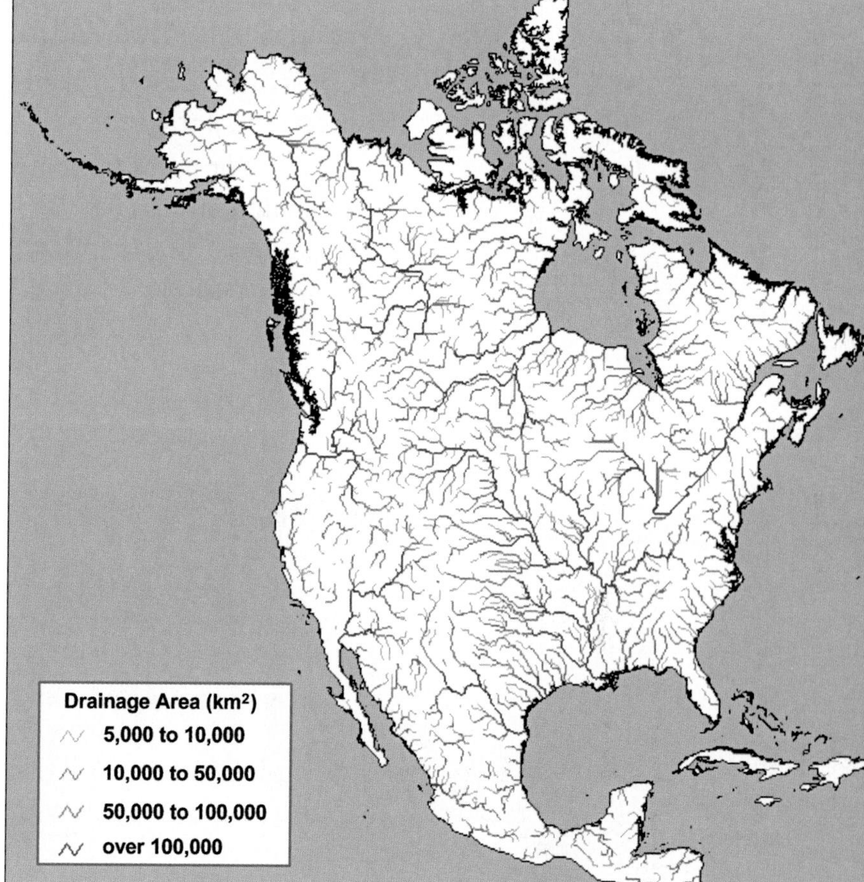

▲ **Figure 10.11 Rivers of North America.** This map shows the network of rivers and streams crossing North America. Where is your community on this map?

1. Answer Questions 1a–c in your team. Show your answers by labeling the map on the handout *North America, Rivers and Streams.*
   a. Mark the boundaries of the water system on the handout. What are the boundaries of the water system?
   b. Where is water stored? Identify and label the major storage areas for water.
   c. Draw and label arrows to reflect processes that move water into and out of the system.

2. Read the information in the following paragraph. Check your understanding with your team.

   Each year, the United States receives enough precipitation to cover the entire country to a depth of 30 in. That is approximately 4,200,000 Mgal/d. Scientists call these 30 in of precipitation the U.S. water budget. Of the 30 in of rainfall, 21.5 in (3,010,000 Mgal/d) returns to the atmosphere through **evapotranspiration.** This general process includes both evaporation and transpiration. **Evaporation** occurs when water in the liquid phase passes into the gas phase. **Transpiration** is water loss by plants. (One tree can lose as much as 50 gal of water a day!) Most of the remaining 8.5 in of precipitation (1,190,000 Mgal/d) flows over the land in rivers and returns to the ocean. A small percentage seeps into the ground.

3. Construct a box diagram to summarize the information in the preceding paragraph.
   a. Use 1 or more boxes to represent the storage of water in the United States.
   b. Use arrows to represent the flow of water into and out of the water storage areas.

This is a flux if it is a volume per time.

   c. Label the arrows with symbols that represent the name of the process that is moving water.

Stop & THINK

PART I

Refer to the paragraph in Step 2 and the box diagram you made in Step 3 to discuss the following questions with your team. Write your answers in your science notebook.

1. Why do you suppose the 30 in of precipitation that falls in the United States is called the water budget?
2. The 30 in of precipitation is not evenly distributed. Figure 10.12 shows yearly rainfall in the Lower 48 states. Write answers to the following questions.
   a. What regions have the highest rainfall?
   b. What regions have the lowest rainfall?
   c. What impact does the distribution of rainfall have on the inputs and outputs of the system?

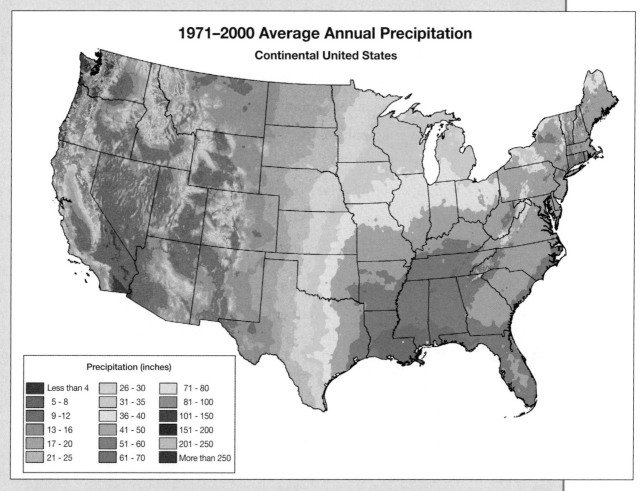

1971–2000 Average Annual Precipitation

Continental United States

Precipitation (inches)

Less than 4	26 - 30	71 - 80
5 - 8	31 - 35	81 - 100
9 -12	36 - 40	101 - 150
13 - 16	41 - 50	151 - 200
17 - 20	51 - 60	201 - 250
21 - 25	61 - 70	More than 250

▲ **Figure 10.12 Annual U.S. precipitation.** This map shows the distribution of annual precipitation in the United States. How much rain falls where you live?

3 Figure 10.13 shows an observer on the bank of a river and 1-ft cubes extending across and into the river. Imagine that the wall of cubes represents the movement of water down the river. If 1 wall passes the observer each second, what is the flow rate of the river?

► **Figure 10.13 Water cubes down a river.** Examine the boxes and arrows in the diagram. Fill in the boxes to show the path of a water molecule through the subsystems of your local water system.

Part II: The Water We Use

Materials

For each team of 3 students

graduated cylinders (100 mL, 50 mL, 25 mL, 10 mL)

2 water containers (minimum 300 mL each)

8 water containers (minimum 150 mL each)

water

food coloring (blue, yellow)

1 calculator

tape for labeling containers

Process and Procedure

Up to now, you have focused on the characteristics of water systems. This includes boundaries, components, interactions, and flow rates. This has helped you understand the source of the water in the drinking fountain at your school. But how else do humans use water? In Part II of this investigation, you will work in teams of three to explore the major ways that water is used in the United States.

In Part I, you diagrammed the U.S. water system. Which part of the system does the water we use come from? In the activity *Beyond the Drinking Fountain*, you learned that the two general sources of drinking water for schools are surface water and groundwater. Next, you will investigate water use in the U.S. water system.

1. Complete the following tasks to explore water sources in the United States.
   a. In 2000, the rate of water withdrawal from the ground was 83,400 Mgal/d. Surface water was used at a rate of 262,000 Mgal/d. Estimate the total water use.
   b. Construct the table with the headings "Source of Water," "Rate of Withdrawal (Mgal/d)," and "Total (%)."
   c. Show in a diagram how you could represent these data graphically. In other words, explain and sketch the types of graphs that you could use to show these data.
   d. On average, estimate how many gallons of water a single person uses per day. In 2000, there were about 281 million people in the United States.
   e. Does this number seem high or low to you? What uncertainties or factors in your estimate from Step 1d might make the estimate inaccurate?

2. The large volumes of water used in the United States are difficult to imagine. Sometimes it helps to see what you are investigating. Obviously, you cannot measure 262,000 Mgal. Instead, you will create a smaller model of water use. Follow these steps.
   a. Use a scale of 1 mL of water for each 1,000 Mgal/d to measure volumes of water to represent groundwater and surface water.
   b. Place the measured volumes in separate, labeled containers.
   c. Place a few drops of blue food coloring in the container representing surface water.
   d. Place the same number of drops of yellow food coloring in the large container representing groundwater.

Keep your model accessible. You will be modeling the amounts of water used in Steps 5 and 6.

3. Review with your team the 4 main categories of water use for the United States. Which of these categories are used in your town or city? Which category do you think is the biggest water user? Write a reason why in your science notebook.
   a. Domestic—public supply
      - Water for drinking, food preparation, bathing, washing clothes and dishes, flushing toilets, and watering lawns and gardens
      - Water for motels, hotels, restaurants, office buildings, and other commercial facilities and military, educational, and other governmental institutions
   b. Industrial—mining
      - Water for industrial processing, washing, and cooling in facilities that manufacture products
      - Water for the extraction of naturally occurring minerals
   c. Thermoelectric
      - Water for the generation of electric power with fossil fuel, nuclear, or geothermal energy
   d. Irrigation—livestock
      - All water artificially applied to farm and horticultural crops and golf courses
      - Water for livestock, feedlots, dairies, fish farms, and other on-farm needs
4. Now you know the 4 main categories of water use in the United States. But how much of the water used comes from surface water or groundwater? Which category would you guess uses the most water? To answer those questions, follow these steps.

Source	Surface Water (262,000 Mgal/day)			Groundwater (83,400 Mgal/day)			Totals	
Water Use Category	**Percent of Surface Water**	**Rate of Water Use (Mgal/d)**	**Scaled Volume of Water (mL)**	**Percent of Ground-water**	**Rate of Water Use (Mgal/d)**	**Scaled Volume of Water (mL)**	**Volume of Water (Mgal/d)**	**Scaled Volume of Water (mL)**
A	52%	136,000	136	0.5%	417	0.417	136,417	136.4
B	32%			71%				
C	10%			23.5%				
D	6%			5%				
Totals								

Source: Hutson, et. al., 2004, *Estimated use of water in the United States in 2000*: Reston, Va., U.S. Geological Survey Circular 1268.

Figure 10.14 Water source and use in the United States in 2000. Percentage values are rounded. For the scale model, 1 mL of water represents 1,000 Mgal/d. Which of the four water use categories do you think uses the most surface water? Groundwater?

a. Review with your team figure 10.14, which shows the percentage of water use per category. The use categories are shown in the left-hand column. Each letter (*A*, *B*, *C*, and *D*) represents 1 category of water use in figure 10.14, but you don't know which one! Write ideas in your science notebook for how you could figure this out.

b. Calculate the missing amounts of water by converting the percentages into actual volumes of surface water or groundwater for the indicated use. Figure 10.14 provides values to do this. Show your work and record your answers in your science notebook.

For example, 52 percent of the withdrawn surface water is used for category A. Since total surface water is 262,000 Mgal/d, 52 percent of this amount is approximately 136,000 Mgal/d.

c. Calculate the scaled, missing amounts of water. Using the scaling in Step 2a, 136,000 Mgal would be represented by 136 mL of water.

5. To help you visualize the water, use the water from the scale model you started in Step 2 to make a model showing water use. The categories in figure 10.14 correspond with the use categories shown in Step 3. Measure the appropriate amounts of surface water (blue) and pour each into a container labeled with "A," "B," "C," or "D." Follow the same procedure to distribute the groundwater (yellow) into the appropriate water use containers.

6. Fill in the right side of figure 10.14. Do this by summing the water per use category (A, B, C, or D) from the surface water and the groundwater. Your volumes should also be shown in the completed figure 10.14. Check that the measured amount is equal to the calculated amounts.
7. Record observations about the contents of the 4 different water use containers. What do the colors of the waters tell you?
8. Determine which water use categories (A, B, C, and D) correspond to which of the 4 categories described in Step 3. Record your predictions next to the table in your science notebook. Check your answers with your teacher.

Also think about how you would use a pie chart or a bar graph to represent data in these categories.

9. What happens to water after it is used? Discuss this question with your team and represent your ideas in a sketch. Check your thinking with information from a transparency provided by your teacher.
10. Consider interactions between parts of the water system. For the following changes, discuss the likely impact the change would have on the water use system. Record your best thinking in your science notebook and refer to prior diagrams as evidence.
    a. The United States experiences several consecutive years of above-average rainfall.
    b. The U.S. population grows significantly.
    c. Several major groundwater sources (aquifers) are severely depleted by overuse.
    d. Significant advances in solar and wind energy reduce the use of thermoelectric power.

Reflect and Connect

Work with your team to answer the following questions in your science notebook. Always show all work for any calculations.

1. The water use system you explored in Part II is a subsystem of the water budget you worked with in Part I. Answer Questions 1a–d to compare the amount of water in the U.S. water budget with the amount of water used in the United States.
    a. Determine the ratio of the U.S. water budget (in Mgal/d) to the rate of U.S. water use (in Mgal/d). Explain your answer.
    b. Determine how much water it would take to represent the U.S. water budget using the scale 1 mL = 1,000 Mgal/d.

c. Compare U.S. water use with the amount of water that flows out of a large river system. Calculate the ratio of the flow rate of the Mississippi River to the daily water use of the United States. Repeat the calculation for another one of the river systems shown in figure 10.15.

d. Write in your science notebook a statement comparing water use with the water budget.

2. Flow rates of water (fluxes) are often shown as mass of water per time. Analyze the following calculation for the flux of water in the Mississippi River. If the comparison is not correct, write the correct calculation in your science notebook.

$$420{,}000\,\frac{\cancel{\text{Mgal}}}{\text{day}} \times \frac{10^6\,\cancel{\text{gal}}}{1\,\cancel{\text{Mgal}}} \times \frac{0.1\,\cancel{\text{L}}}{1\,\cancel{\text{gal}}} \times \frac{1\,\cancel{\text{g water}}}{1\,\cancel{\text{mL}}} \times \frac{1\text{ kg water}}{10^3\,\cancel{\text{g water}}} = 8.4 \times 10^8\,\frac{\text{kg water}}{\text{day}}$$

Remember that canceling units in the denominator and the numerator is vital. If units do not cancel, that is the first clue that a calculation might not be correct.

3. Obtain information about water use within your local water system. You may have located this information in the activity *Beyond the Drinking Fountain*. Compare water use at your local level with water use in the United States.

a. How does water use in your local water system compare with water use in the United States?

b. What local factors might account for any differences?

4. Describe how the following systems are related to one another, using sentences or a diagram. Where possible, identify these systems by name (for example, include the name of your high school and your specific watershed).

a. U.S. water system

b. School's drinking water system

c. Local water use system

d. Local watershed

e. Regional water drainage basin

f. U.S. water use

River System	Flow Rate (Mgal/day)
Mississippi	420,000
St. Lawrence	244,000
Mackenzie	220,000
Columbia	181,000
Yukon	141,000
Nelson	80,000
Frazer	72,000
Colorado (1960s)	14,500
Rio Grande (Laredo, TX)	1,740

Figure 10.15 Flow rates for rivers in North America. This table shows the flow rates for the nine largest rivers in North America where they enter the ocean. What factors do you think control the flow rates?

Source: Berner, E. K., & Berner R. A. (1987). *The global water cycle: Geochemistry and environment*. Englewood Cliffs, NJ: Prentice Hall.

The Global Water System

ELABORATE

In the activity *Beyond the Drinking Fountain*, you looked at water on a local scale. Then you expanded your view to the United States in the investigation *Expanding Boundaries*. In *The Global Water System*, you will expand your view to the water system at a global scale. You will work with a team of 2 students to think of the water cycle as one big system. This accounts for all the water on Earth.

Part I: Global Reservoirs

Materials

For each team of 2 students

1 1-L bottle of water

6 containers

Process and Procedure

More than 70 percent of Earth's surface is covered with water. In Part I of this investigation, you will learn how water is distributed across Earth. Have you ever thought about where all the water on Earth is stored? Discuss the following questions with a partner and record your answers individually in your science notebook.

1. What does the term *reservoir* mean to you? Talk about this term with your partner and prepare to share your ideas with the class.
2. Listen as your teacher describes how scientists study the global water system and use the term reservoir.
   a. Identify global water reservoirs on Earth. Share your ideas with your partner.
   b. Compare your ideas with the actual reservoirs listed on the transparency shown by your teacher. Did you and your partner think of all the reservoirs? Why or why not?
   c. Is all the water from the global reservoirs available for human use? Why or why not?
3. Write ideas in your science notebook about the size of global reservoirs of water.
   a. Which reservoirs do you think hold the most mass of water?
   b. Which reservoirs do you think hold the least mass of water?

4. Obtain materials to make a scale model of global water reservoirs using 1 L of water and the containers (or beakers) provided by your teacher. Have each container represent a global reservoir. Label your reservoirs and be prepared to share your model with the class.
5. Observe the data your teacher will show you.
   a. Use the volumes given in the table shown on the transparency *Global Water Reservoirs* to calculate the percentage of the global water found in each reservoir. Record your answers in a table in your notebook.
   b. Could you represent these data in a pie chart or a bar graph? Use a sketch to explain how in your science notebook.
   c. Calculate the volume of water (in mL) for each reservoir in a scale model that uses 1 L of water to represent all global water. For example, if lakes and rivers were 10 percent of the total global water, 100 mL (10 percent of 1,000 mL) would represent this reservoir. Record your answers in a table in your science notebook.

Stop & THINK

PART I

Work individually to answer the following questions. Record your answers in your science notebook.

1. A **reservoir** is any environment in which matter is stored. Can you think of systems other than water systems that have reservoirs? For example, a reservoir in a banking system would be a vault. Describe at least 1 reservoir other than a banking system and the system to which it belongs.
2. Describe how you think all the water reservoirs on Earth could be considered part of a system.

Part II: Global Water Movement

Materials

For each team of 2 students

2 sheets of blank paper

colored pencils (optional)

Process and Procedure

The flow of water around Earth is the largest scale for water systems. This movement of water is commonly referred to as the water cycle. The water cycle is one of several geochemical systems you will learn about in this unit. A **geochemical cycle** describes the storage and movement of a particular chemical, water in this case, through the earth system. A geochemical cycle could include another element or nutrient, such as carbon phosphorus, calcium, or iron. Geochemical cycles explain how matter moves between reservoirs on Earth.

Topic: geochemical cycle
Go to: www.scilinks.org
Code: 2Inquiry527

You have diagrammed the inputs and outputs moving through several systems involving humans. Examples are a fast-food restaurant, a swimming pool, and water use in the United States. Now you will learn about and diagram the inputs and outputs for a natural system, the global water system. The inputs and outputs move matter, water in this case, between different reservoirs. Complete the following tasks with a partner and sketch your ideas on a blank sheet of paper.

1. Use the data in figure 10.16 and from Part I to create a simple box diagram of the global water system. Follow these steps.

Box diagrams of systems help you visualize the parts of a system and how those parts interact.

   a. Identify which reservoirs listed in figure 10.16 contain water. List how many of them are there.
   b. Sketch on the blank sheet of paper the boxes for each reservoir in Step 1a.
   c. Use arrows to show fluxes between and to connect the reservoirs (boxes) given in figure 10.16. Write flux values next to the arrows on your diagram when you know them.

You may not wish to use the symbols I and O in this diagram. This is because the input for one part of a system might also be the output for another part of the system. For example, rain over the ocean is an input of water for the ocean, but an output relative to the atmosphere.

   d. Consider land to be 1 large reservoir for water. Identify several subsystems within the land that would contain water.

Recall your findings from Part I.

Water transport process	Flux (rate of water movement)	
	km^3/year	$\times 10^3$ km^3/year
Evaporation from land to atmosphere	71,000	71
Evaporation from ocean to atmosphere	434,000	434
Precipitation from atmosphere to land	107,000	107
Precipitation from atmosphere to oceans	398,000	398
Runoff from land to oceans	?	?
Water vapor flux from atmosphere over oceans to atmosphere over land	?	?

Source: Berner, E. K., & Berner R. A. (1987). *The global water cycle: Geochemistry and environment.* Englewood Cliffs, NJ: Prentice Hall.

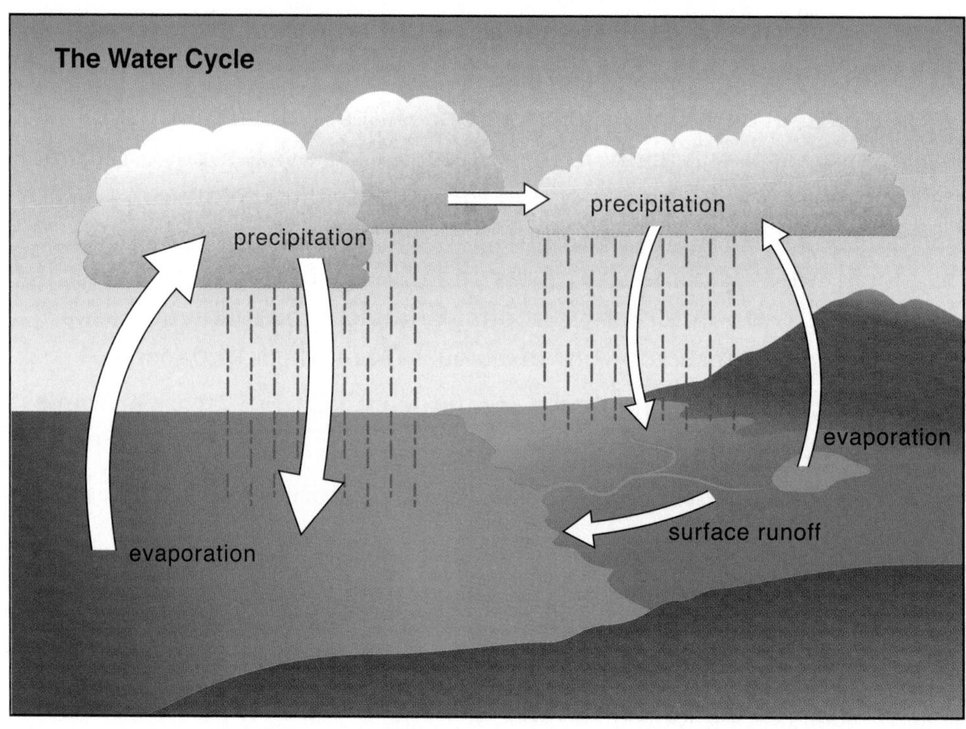

▶ **Figure 10.16**
Water cycle fluxes. The fluxes of water between reservoirs differ for the land and the ocean (10^3 km^3/year = thousands of cubic kilometers per year). These are fluxes because they tell the volume (or mass) per year. How can you determine the flux rate for runoff and water vapor moving between the atmosphere above the ocean and the atmosphere above land?

2. Use what you know about systems to determine the values of the fluxes missing in figure 10.16. First, consider the ocean as a subsystem of the global water system.
   a. Identify the inputs and outputs for the ocean due to precipitation and evaporation.
   b. Assume that the mass of water in the ocean is constant. What then must be true about the total inputs and outputs of water for the ocean? Explain this both as a sentence and as a mathematical expression.

Recall your system inputs and outputs from Part II of the activity *System Structures*.

SCILINKS NSTA
Topic: water cycle
Go to: www.scilinks.org
Code: 2Inquiry528

c. Use the flux of water from land into the ocean (river runoff) to balance the total inputs and outputs for the ocean. This is easiest to do with a simple equation.

d. Determine the value of water flux for continental runoff in rivers, and thus, a missing value in figure 10.16.

3. Second, consider the atmosphere above land as a subsystem of the global water system.

   a. Identify the inputs and outputs for the atmosphere above land.

Divide the atmosphere into 2 boxes if you have not already. One box is the atmosphere over the ocean, and the other is the atmosphere over land.

   b. Assume that the mass of water vapor in the atmosphere above land is constant. What must be true about the total inputs and outputs of water for the atmosphere above the land?

   c. Use the flux of water vapor from above the ocean to the atmosphere above the land to balance the total inputs and outputs for the atmosphere above land.

   d. Determine the value of water flux from the atmosphere above the ocean to the atmosphere above the land, and thus, the other missing value in figure 10.16.

4. The numbers you have been working with are an average across time. Consider what would happen if the system changed. Imagine that during an extreme year, the evaporation rate of the ocean increased because of warmer temperatures near the equator.

   a. How would the increase in evaporation rate over the ocean affect the other fluxes?

   b. Describe an effect this change would have on a reservoir other than the ocean.

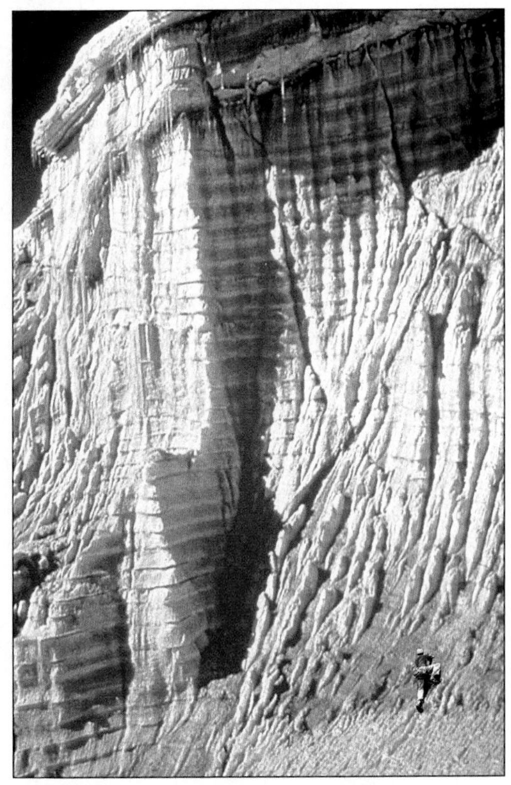

▲ **Figure 10.17**
Annual snow layers. This photograph shows a cliff of ice where part of a glacier has broken away. The layers show a record of the cycle of yearly snowfall when these layers were on top of the glacier. White layers are winter snowfall. Brown stripes represent dust falling on the snow in summer. What does this tell you about the water cycle?

5. Consider a different change in the global water system. What if the global climate becomes colder, and precipitation on the continents falls as snow. If the snow cannot melt away during the summer, then some snowfall is retained from each year on land. This accumulating snow grows into glaciers with yearly layers (figure 10.17).

   a. What changes would you predict for the global water cycle?

   b. Is the system still in balance for the ocean? In other words, do the inputs equal the outputs?

6. As you finish, listen to directions from your teacher regarding collecting your diagram.

Stop & THINK

PART II

Complete the following questions in your science notebook.

1. Why do you think it is important to think about water on Earth? What can you learn by looking at the global water system?

2. You probably were familiar with the water cycle. Think about how a systems approach has helped you look at the water cycle differently.

   a. Recall a water cycle diagram that you have seen in the past. As best you can, sketch it in your science notebook. How does that diagram compare with the global water system you worked with in this activity?

   Consider using a strategy such as a Venn diagram or a T-table to list similarities and differences.

   b. Describe how you think a systems approach to the global water cycle might help you better understand the water cycle.

   A systems approach focuses on the whole system and how all the parts of the system interact. How would this approach help you make predictions about what might happen if the system changed?

Part III: Residence Time

Materials

none

Process and Procedure

Have you ever thought about the average length of time a library book is on a shelf before it is checked out? Or how long a music CD sits on the store shelf before being sold? On a bigger scale, how long do you think $1 remains in a bank before heading back out into the economy?

In Part III of this investigation, you will learn how to estimate the time that matter, such as water, stays in a reservoir before moving to another reservoir. Discuss the following questions with a partner and record your answers individually in your science notebook.

1. Do you think that a water molecule spends more time in the ocean or in the atmosphere before moving to the next reservoir? Explain your reasoning.
2. How much time do you think a water molecule spends in the ocean? The atmosphere? Would you guess times of seconds, hours, days, or years? Discuss your best guess with your partner. Be ready to share your ideas and explain your reasoning with the class.
3. Read the following to learn how scientists estimate these values and then study figure 10.18.

   Residence time is the average length of time that matter in a system remains in a given reservoir. This value is estimated when there is no long-term change in the system. Residence time is calculated from the mass of material in the reservoir, divided by either the total flux in, or the total flux out, for the reservoir. Remember that flux has units of mass per time. You can also use volume if you remember that mass is related to volume by density.

$$\text{residence time} = \frac{\text{mass of matter (or volume) in reservoir}}{\text{total flux in (or flux out) for reservoir}}$$

   A reservoir can have multiple inputs or outputs. In these cases, residence time is estimated from the sum of the inputs or outputs. If you use only one of several inputs, for example, you will underestimate the rate of mass coming into the reservoir and leaving the reservoir. The inputs and outputs can be used interchangeably because the system is balanced. That is, the inputs and outputs are equal.

   Here's an example. Assume a bathtub is filled with 24 gal of water and the input of water from the faucet is 3 gallons per minute (gal/min). The residence time for bathwater before it leaves the bathtub through the drain is calculated as 24 gal divided by 3 gal/min. The residence time for bathwater in this system is 8 minutes. So a water molecule entering this bathtub would remain in the bathwater for an average of 8 minutes before leaving through the drain. If the bathtub held 18 gal of water, the residence time would decrease to 6 minutes.

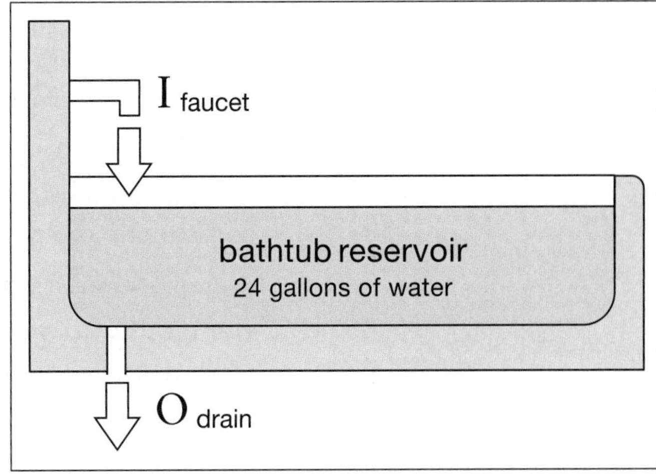

Figure 10.18 Residing in a bathtub. If inputs and outputs are equal, they can be used to estimate residence time for a molecule of water in bathwater before it leaves the tub down the drain.

4. Imagine a water molecule entering the ocean from precipitation or continental runoff. Estimate the residence time for a water molecule in the ocean.
   a. Identify the volume of water in the ocean.
   b. Determine the total flux of water into (or out of) the ocean.
   c. Calculate the residence time. Use a sentence to compare this answer with Step 2.
5. Imagine a water molecule entering the atmosphere. Follow the procedure in Step 3 to estimate the residence time for that water molecule in the atmosphere.

Your answer may make more sense after converting to days. Use a volume of water in the atmosphere of 15,000 km^3.

Reflect and Connect—Part III

Work with your partner to complete these questions.

1. How close was your prediction of how long a water molecule is in the ocean (residence time) to the number you calculated in Step 4c? Were you surprised by the residence time for water in the ocean?
2. Residence time applies to more than just water systems. For example, the residence time for a CD in a department store might be 1 week and the residence time for a calcium atom in the ocean is 850,000 years. How do you think residence time helps you better understand a system? How do you think residence time might help you make predictions about a system?

Calcium enters the ocean from rocks that weather and dissolve on Earth's surface. Calcium is highly soluble in seawater, so it tends to have a long residence time. Calcium can leave seawater when marine organisms use calcium to build their shells. You'll learn more about this in the next chapter.

3. Recall your experiment in Part I of *System Structures* where you maintained the water level at a mark on your container. Estimate the residence time for a water molecule in that system.

Use the procedure in Step 4 to help organize values for this calculation.

4. One group of researchers has estimated that the residence time for a water molecule stored as ice in a glacier and polar ice reservoir is 27,500 years. Assume the system is balanced (the inputs and outputs are equal). Would the residence time increase or decrease if Earth entered an ice age and more water were stored in the polar ice reservoir? Explain your reasoning using the equation for residence time.

5. In 1993, what was the residence time for a water molecule in the Great Salt Lake? That year, the rate of water entering the Great Salt Lake was nearly equal to the rate of water lost to evaporation. The input and output rates were about 3.5 million af/yr. That year, the volume of water in the Great Salt Lake was about 16 million af.

A Salty Situation

EVALUATE

In *The Global Water System*, you investigated some characteristics of systems, in particular water systems. You have learned that water systems can be described by their boundaries, their components, and the rate that water moves into or out of parts of a system. You also learned about your local water system. This system can be thought of as a subsystem of continental water systems. You might even think of continental water systems as a part of the largest water reservoir on Earth—the hydrosphere.

In *A Salty Situation*, you will first work as a class, then as a team, to investigate a dilemma for a large water system. It is the Great Salt Lake in Utah. Decisions and choices need to be made regarding the uses and management of water in the Great Salt Lake system. What will you recommend?

Part I: The Lake

Materials

For each team of 3 students

3 sets of handouts, consisting of the following:

- *Map of the Great Salt Lake*
- *Water Numbers for the Great Salt Lake*
- *Humans at the Great Salt Lake*

3 *Salty Situation Scoring Rubric* handouts

1 set of 3 handouts, consisting of the following:

- *Shrimp Survival*
- *Minerals: Resources from the Great Salt Lake*
- *A Unique and Evolving Ecosystem*

Process and Procedure

It is early in the 21st century, and communities around the Great Salt Lake, Utah, have a dilemma (figure 10.19). Changes in the salinity of the lake have caused a salt imbalance between the northern and southern portions. The salt imbalance is affecting the local ecosystem, the mineral industry, and the brine shrimp industry (figure 10.20). Something needs to be done. Or does it?

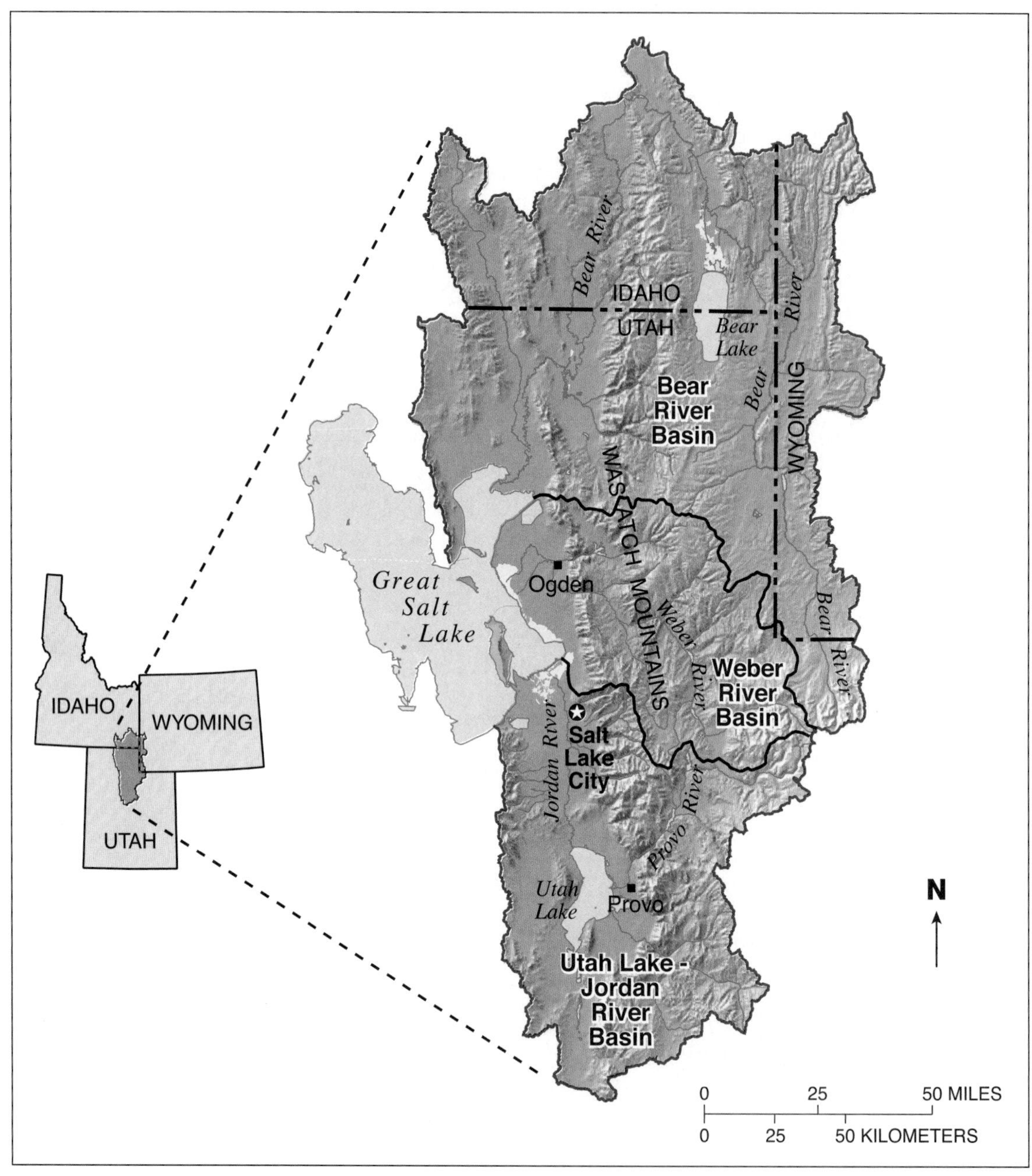

▲ **Figure 10.19 Great Salt Lake map.** This map shows the Great Salt Lake, Utah, and the three major watersheds for rivers draining into the lake. Salt Lake City and the Wasatch Mountains are to the east.

In an effort to help the community decision makers understand the issue, your team has been asked to write a feature article for the local newspaper. Your class has been selected because of its ability to analyze the issue from a systems perspective. Here is a chance to apply your understanding of systems to a new situation. Your feature article will include a description of the Great Salt Lake as a system and will provide a recommendation of how to manage the Great Salt Lake system.

▲ **Figure 10.20**
Brine shrimp. This brine shrimp is about 1 cm long. Brine shrimp are an important part of the ecology of the Great Salt Lake.

Before you begin your work, become familiar with the evaluate *Salty Situation Scoring Rubric* provided by your teacher. Use the rubric to guide your work.

1. As a class, make a list of questions about the Great Salt Lake and the salt imbalance dilemma being faced. If you were in the position of making a decision about what to do—or what not to do—what facts and data would you need?
2. Get in your team of 3 and gather information about the Great Salt Lake. Each team member will become an expert in 1 of 3 categories (water, human impacts, or salinity) for the Great Salt Lake system. Information about salinity is in the sidebar *Why Is the Great Salt Lake So Salty?* Carefully complete the reading for your expert group. You might want to conduct further research on your own. Prepare to contribute to a class discussion.

You will have copies of all the handouts. In this step, you are only responsible for reading the handout for your expert group. Keep all the handouts to use as reference in this activity. All team members need to understand the sidebar *Why Is the Great Lake So Salty?*

3. What did you learn about the Great Salt Lake? Participate in a class discussion of the Great Salt Lake as a system. Your teacher will ask you to share what you learned from your handout.

Take notes as you listen to other experts share what they learned. You will need to understand all parts of the Great Salt Lake system to complete this activity.

4. Record in your science notebook who and what depend on the Great Salt Lake. Changes in the Great Salt Lake system affect the local economy and the local ecosystem. In your team of 3, become an expert on 1 of the following special interest groups: the brine shrimp industry, the mineral industry, or the GSL Friends group. You can do further research on your own. Prepare to contribute to a class discussion.

GSL Friends is a community group whose mission is to preserve and protect the Great Salt Lake ecosystem. You may come across information from this group on the World Wide Web.

5. How do other systems (such as industries or ecosystems) interact with the Great Salt Lake system? Participate in a class discussion of how the brine shrimp industry, mineral industry, and the ecosystem are affected by the Great Salt Lake system. Share what you know about your special interest group. Provide information that will help answer the following questions.
   a. How would you describe your group? What connection does the group have to the Great Salt Lake?
   b. What does your group bring to the Great Salt Lake region? What value does it have?
   c. How does your group depend on the Great Salt Lake?
   d. How have changes in the Great Salt Lake, such as the salt imbalance, affected your group?

SIDEBAR

Why Is the Great Salt Lake So Salty?

If you live near a river or lake, the water might not be clear. With a magnifying glass, you might see fine particles of silt, organic matter, or microorganisms. This is the **suspended load** in natural waters. The suspended load is all the particles, either floating or suspended, carried by the water.

All natural waters also have a **dissolved load**. These are elements and molecules in an ionic form that are dissolved in the water. This is easy to show by dissolving sugar or table salt (NaCl) in water. In natural waters, the dissolved load often includes cations (Ca^{+2}, Na^{+1}, Mg^{+2}, or K^{+1}), anions (Cl^{-1} or HCO_3^{-1}), and the dissolved gases CO_2 and O_2. **Salinity** refers to the amount of dissolved ions in the water. Dissolved ions are always present in natural waters, even though they cannot be seen. The ions come from rocks and minerals that weather and degrade in rain and snow. This process helps explain why the Great Salt Lake is so salty.

The Great Salt Lake is the largest remaining part of the ancient Lake Bonneville. Lake Bonneville was a huge lake formed by meltwater from glaciers during the last major ice age approximately 30,000 to 20,000 years ago. Over the last 10,000 years, the climate in the region has become drier and warmer. Over this time period, more water evaporated from Lake Bonneville than flowed into it. As water evaporates, it concentrates the ions in the shrinking lake, making it more and more salty. The salts of various types accumulate on the shores of the lake.

Currently, three main rivers drain from the mountains to the Great Salt Lake: the

▲ **Great Salt Lake.** The shores of the Great Salt Lake, Utah, are very salty. This is due to the evaporation of water and the precipitation of salt compounds at the shoreline.

Bear, Weber, and Jordan rivers (see *Water Numbers for the Great Salt Lake* handout). The region that these rivers cover makes up most of the **watershed** for the Great Salt Lake. A watershed is the area of land that drains into a particular body of water. Within that entire watershed, the streams and rivers slowly weather and dissolve rocks and minerals. While this process is quite slow, the Great Salt Lake watershed is large, about 21,500 square miles. Thus, there is a lot of rock to erode and weather.

These rivers have flowed into the Great Salt Lake for hundreds of thousands of years. Today, they deliver nearly 2 million acre feet of water per year, and perhaps 2 million tons of dissolved salts. Yet the average level of the Great Salt Lake does not change much. This is because the rate of evaporation equals the total flow rates into the lake.

During evaporation, the dissolved ions do not enter the atmosphere as gaseous molecules, so they remain dissolved in the lake. With time, the dissolved ions increase in concentration in the lake water as more ions are added to the lake, and water continues to evaporate. We detect the dissolved ions as a salty taste to the water. This same process of large rivers transporting dissolved ions from the continents to the ocean is what makes the ocean salty as well. The scale of the ocean system is much larger though.

SCILINKS® NSTA

Topic: salinity
Go to: www.scilinks.org
Code: 2Inquiry537

Part II: The Article

Materials

none

Process and Procedure

A newspaper in Salt Lake City, Utah, is doing a feature article on Great Salt Lake. In the past, the paper has printed pro and con articles about issues facing the Great Salt Lake. These articles address one specific issue. For the feature article, the paper wants to address a much more complex issue. Changes in the Great Salt Lake since the railroad levee was built have affected the lake and the interests of several special interest groups. Because of your experience with this issue, the paper will hire your team to write the feature article. Your team's work with systems will give the most complete evaluation of the Great Salt Lake and will take into account the special interest groups.

In addition to describing the Great Salt Lake as a system, the paper wants you to include a recommendation in the article. The recommendation will propose how local agencies should manage the lake to meet the needs of all three groups. The Great Salt Lake is managed by three Utah state agencies: the Utah Geological Survey, the Division of Water Resources, and the Division of Wildlife Resources. They monitor salinity levels in the lake and the species inhabiting the lake. These agencies work together to make decisions about how to maintain a balance between using the Great Salt Lake's natural resources and maintaining a healthy lake ecosystem. Your team will have to take into account all parts of the Great Salt Lake system and all special interest groups when writing your recommendation.

1. Work as a team to use what you have learned about the lake and the issue to write a feature article on the Great Salt Lake. Remember, your article must use a systems perspective. It should include the following in the explanation section:
   - A paragraph explanation of the Great Salt Lake system
   - A box diagram with labels showing the boundary of the system, parts of the system, and fluxes (inputs and outputs) of the system
   - Accurate and appropriate systems language
   - Interactions that occur with parts of the Great Salt Lake system (You can develop a diagram for this.)

2. The article should also include the following regarding a recommendation by your team for how the Great Salt Lake system should be managed. Use specific evidence from your research to
   - write 2–3 paragraphs that use accurate information of the management of the Great Salt Lake and its salt imbalance,
   - use evidence and data to argue how your proposed solution would change or stabilize salt balance in the Great Salt Lake system, and
   - describe how the management plan either does or does not address the needs of the different interest groups.

In your recommendation, you must consider how changing the system will affect everyone and everything dependent on the Great Salt Lake system. You might think about what costs are involved and who or what will benefit. Use the evidence you have gathered about the Great Salt Lake to decide what you think is most important.

3. Review the overall quality of your article. Is the article
   - neat and easy to read,
   - composed as a feature article that you might find in a newspaper,
   - written in a clear manner with summarizing data and information, and
   - complemented by neat diagrams or maps of the Great Salt Lake?
4. Turn in your article to your teacher.

CHAPTER 11

Carbon on the Move

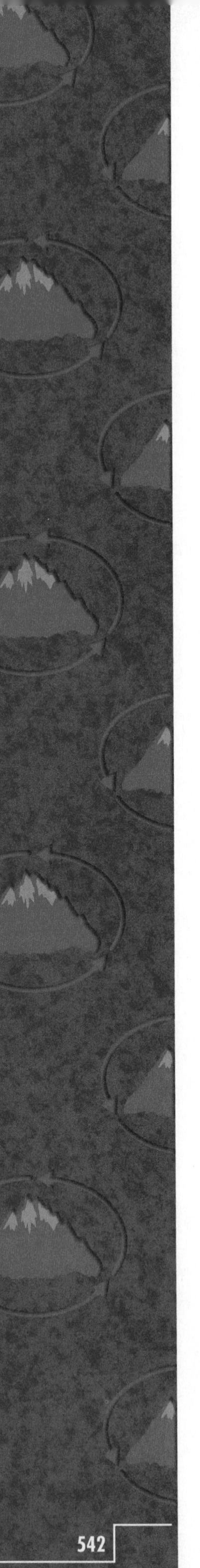

Carbon on the Move

Carbon. It is a diverse element, and it is vital for life. In your body, for example, carbon makes up about 50 percent of your tissues and about 28 percent of your bones. That is a lot. Carbon also makes up roughly half of the various tissues in plants. And you've probably learned about photosynthesis. Remember, this is the process that transfers carbon from the atmosphere to plants or other photosynthesizing organisms. Carbon links to life in many ways.

But carbon's reach does not stop with life. Carbon is also found in nonliving (abiotic) objects such as minerals, like diamond. Carbon is also a part of many types of rocks, such as limestone or rocks with fossil fuels (petroleum, coal, and natural gas). Yet even before arriving on Earth and becoming part of an organism, such as you, carbon is manufactured in stars in our Milky Way Galaxy. In other parts of the galaxy, carbon is found as hydrocarbons in massive molecular clouds. Carbon is part of many kinds of systems at many scales.

Goals for the Chapter

How might you characterize carbon to a friend who was not in your science class? How is carbon part of your clothes, foods, or medicines? How many forms of carbon are there? How does carbon relate to the energy that society needs? Chapter 11, *Carbon on the Move*, will help you answer questions like those. By the end of this chapter, you will learn the following:

- Earth has a fixed amount of carbon.
- Some substances with carbon can be analyzed with simple tests.
- Carbon moves among several main reservoirs on Earth.
- Carbon transport involves reactions that change the properties of the carbon substances.
- Simple reactions simulate the carbon cycle.
- Some carbon sinks in the geologic past are now valuable sources of fossil fuels.

In the last chapter, you learned that the water cycle describes water (H_2O) in systems of various sizes and forms. For example, words such as "evaporation" and "transpiration" describe how water moves between plants and air. You saw that moving the water or changing its form involved changes in energy.

But what are some of the ways that carbon moves around Earth? You will investigate the ways in this chapter. To understand this, you will simulate in your classroom a number of simple chemical reactions that involve carbon. A **simulation** is a small-scale model or test of a much larger process. Your simulations will help you transfer what you learn about carbon to larger systems on Earth—much larger, global systems. As you can see in the opening photos to the chapter, these systems include the ocean and the atmosphere.

In this chapter, you will complete the following activities:

ENGAGE	Characterizing Carbon
EXPLORE	Carbon Changing Costumes
EXPLAIN	The Carbonated Geosphere
EXPLORE	Fossil Carbon
ELABORATE	The Flux Is the Crux
EVALUATE	Carbon Quest

Chapter organizers help you see what you have learned and where you are headed. They help you organize your understanding of the physical world. As you have been learning in this program, when you are organized, it is easier to learn.

Look at the chapter organizer every day. Think about where you are in its flow. Compare what you know now with what you knew a week ago. Think about what you will learn today. Let the chapter organizer help you map your learning and monitor your progress. That way, you can look back and see what you have accomplished.

Carbon on the Move

Linking Question

What kinds of reactions move carbon around Earth?

ENGAGE

Characterizing Carbon

Key Idea:

Indicator solutions let you monitor carbon movement in simple systems.

EXPLORE

Carbon Changing Costumes

Key Idea:

Simple reactions with carbon-bearing substances at 8 stations represent carbon transport between different settings on Earth.

Linking Question

Where do reactions with carbon occur on Earth?

EXPLAIN

The Carbonated Geosphere

Key Idea:

Carbon is a key part of terrestrial (land), atmospheric, and oceanic settings. Carbon is stored in these settings as organic and inorganic carbon.

Linking Question

Are humans part of the carbon cycle?

EVALUATE

Carbon Quest

Key Idea:

You can answer questions, and revise your answers, about your understanding of the carbon cycle. You learn things better by critically evaluating your own work.

Linking Question

How much do you understand about carbon cycles?

ELABORATE

The Flux Is the Crux

Key Idea:

Carbon cycles at different rates among carbon reservoirs. The carbon flux and reservoir size tells how long an average carbon atom resides in a reservoir.

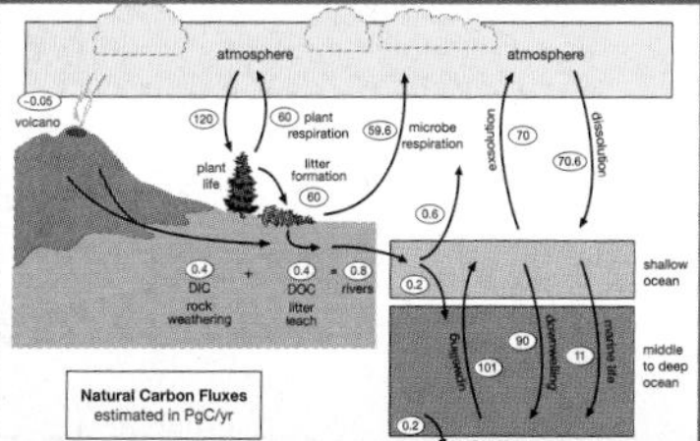

Linking Question

How fast does a carbon atom move around Earth?

CHAPTER 11

Major Concepts

- Some substances with carbon can be analyzed with simple tests.
- Earth has a fixed amount of carbon; that carbon moves among several main reservoirs.
- Carbon transfer involves chemical reactions with changes in atomic structures of carbon, and in properties of the carbon-bearing material.
- Simple reactions simulate carbon cycling in the natural world.
- Some carbon sinks in the geologic past are now valuable sources of fossil fuels and energy for society.

EXPLORE

Fossil Carbon
Part I: Carboniferous Combustion

Key Idea:

Energy production and fossil fuel combustion make carbon dioxide. Geologic data shows the pattern of humans adding CO_2 to the atmosphere.

Fossil Carbon
Part II: Showing the Carbon Cycle

Key Idea:

A series of reactions with carbon can be linked to represent key parts of the carbon cycle.

ENGAGE

Characterizing Carbon

What color is carbon? You might say that carbon is black like charcoal, coal, or graphite, or clear and sparkly like a diamond. But what about other objects with carbon, such as leaves, gasoline, seashells, plastics, white marble sculptures, or you? What about gases in the atmosphere that contain carbon? How would you characterize carbon in these objects?

After a few minutes, you may realize that this is not a simple question. A description might even be tricky for a system where carbon changes from one substance to another. For example, what about a burning log in a fireplace—where does carbon in the wood go? The more you think about it, the more complex the answer seems.

A good way to start learning about carbon is to consider carbon in small parts. Leave carbon complexity aside for the moment and try to think about carbon in simple ways. In fact, that is a good way to break down and simplify any system. In *Characterizing Carbon*, you will work with a team to explore two interesting processes with carbon. Keep in mind how these investigations might relate to carbon moving around Earth. Color gives a clue here, but the colors you see are not the color of carbon.

Investigation 1

Materials

For each team of 3 students

2 plastic bottles or jars with tightly sealing caps

universal indicator solution

seltzer water

1 ruler

1 sheet of plain white paper

Process and Procedure

In this activity, you will do two investigations with carbon and a water system in a team of three students. Listen carefully to your teacher for instructions about materials for the two investigations. For each investigation, keep this focus question in mind: "In what form is the carbon?"

1. Put 1 sample of seltzer water about 2–3 centimeters (cm) deep in each of 2 plastic containers. Quickly add 6 drops of universal indicator to each and close the containers immediately.

Keep both containers closed very tightly to preserve as much fizz as possible.

2. Complete Steps 2a–c and record your observations in your science notebook.
   a. Select 1 of the water containers as the control. After the universal indicator is added, do not open the control. Place this container on the sheet of white paper and do not move it.
   b. Shake the other container vigorously for 15 seconds (sec). Open the seal on the lid briefly to release the fizz. Close the container.

You can also tilt the container for about 5 sec so that the water comes near the opening. But do not pour out any water!

   c. Repeat Step 2b about 10 times until no more fizz is escaping.
3. During each step, compare the color of the shaken sample with your control. Record in your science notebook all the changes occurring between your sample and the control.
4. Describe in your science notebook the relationship between the amount of fizz and the color.
5. Copy figure 11.1 into your science notebook. Make a qualitative graph showing the amount of fizz relative to the color that you observe.
6. Record in your science notebook your team's ideas about the following questions.
   a. What do you know about seltzer water?
   b. What was happening as you released the fizz?
   c. What process on Earth might this investigation model?
   d. How do you think this investigation involved carbon?

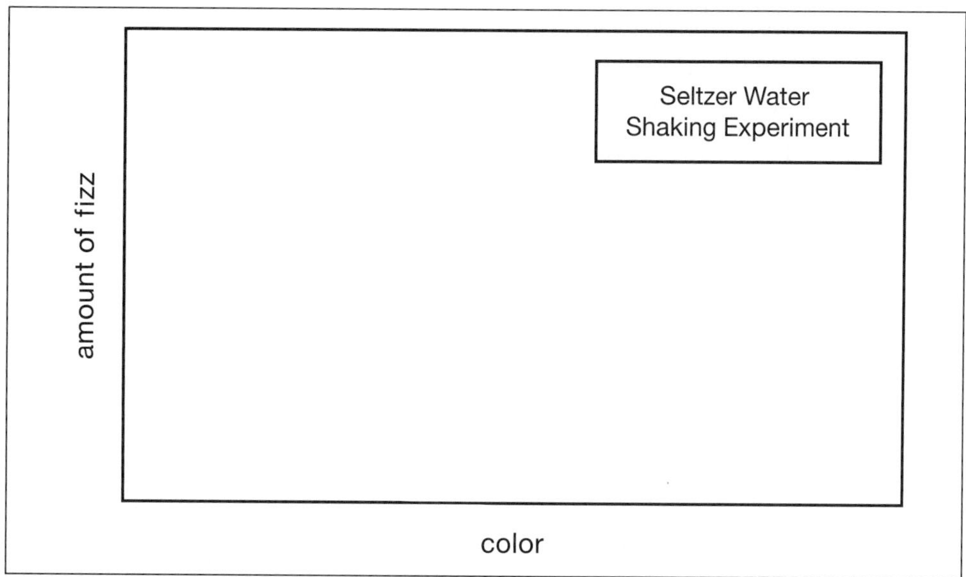

Figure 11.1 Experiment to shake seltzer water. Use these axes to plot the amount of fizz versus the color of shaken seltzer water. Copy this diagram into your science notebook and label the axes according to your observations.

Investigation 2

Materials

For each team of 3 students

3 pairs of safety goggles

1 pair of gloves or cloth

2 beakers (at least 350 mL) or tall glass jars

water solution with bromthymol blue (BTB)

1 10×10 cm square of aluminum foil

1 sheet of white paper

1 ruler

1 small piece of tape

1–2 pieces of dry ice (about 2 cm per side)

Caution
Wear safety goggles. Only handle dry ice with a cloth or gloves.

Process and Procedure

1. Get 2 glass containers. Add the mixture of water and bromthymol blue (BTB) indicator to a depth of 1.5 cm in each container.
2. Place 1 of the containers on a sheet of white paper at least 10 cm from the experiment beaker. Use this container as the control.
3. Squeeze aluminum foil around your thumb to make a holder for 1–2 pieces of dry ice. Use a small piece of tape to attach the foil holder above the water inside one of the jars (figure 11.2).
4. Obtain from your teacher a small piece of dry ice (roughly 2 cm per side). What do you think the dry ice is?
5. Quickly place the dry ice in the foil holder in the open container. Make observations for the next 3–4 minutes (min).
   a. What happens to the dry ice?
   b. What happens to the water?
   c. What happens to the control?

You can place a cover on your container if you have air currents in your classroom.

6. Discuss with your team the sequence of events or changes that must occur for the dry ice to interact with the water. Record this sequence of events as boxes connected by arrows in your science notebook.
7. Discuss with your team where the dry ice goes and how you think it interacts with the water.

8. Use a strategy such as think-share-advise-revise (TSAR) to explore the character of carbon in this investigation.

If you have time, your team can repeat this experiment by dropping a small piece of dry ice into the water/BTB mixture. Does that test confirm or refute your ideas?

Reflect and Connect

Discuss the following questions with your team and write answers in your science notebook.

1. What gases, liquids, or solids were the parts of each investigation? What is your evidence?
2. For each investigation, revisit the focus question, "In what form is the carbon?"
3. Discuss and record some settings on Earth where you think carbon dioxide (CO_2) goes into liquids.
4. Discuss and record some other settings in the natural world where you think CO_2 leaves or exits fluids.
5. Discuss the following reactions and answer Questions 5a–f.

$$CO_{2(aq)} + H_2O_{(aq)} \rightleftharpoons H_2CO_{3(aq)} \rightleftharpoons HCO_3{}^{1-}{}_{(aq)} + H^{1+}{}_{(aq)}$$

   a. What 2 common molecules combine to make carbonic acid (H_2CO_3)?
   b. When H_2CO_3 dissociates, what are the acid and base components?
   c. Did the water in investigation 1 gain or lose CO_2? What is your evidence?
   d. Did the water in investigation 2 gain or lose CO_2? What is your evidence?
   e. Which direction would the reaction above shift for a system that lost CO_2 by fizzing? Would the system be more or less acidic?
   f. Which direction would the reaction above shift for a system that gained CO_2? Would the system be more or less acidic?

▼ Figure 11.2 Beaker with dry ice holder. Gently tape the aluminum foil holder inside the beaker to suspend the dry ice above the water. Place a cover on the beaker if you have strong air currents in your area of the classroom. How does the dry ice interact with the water? What happens to the water?

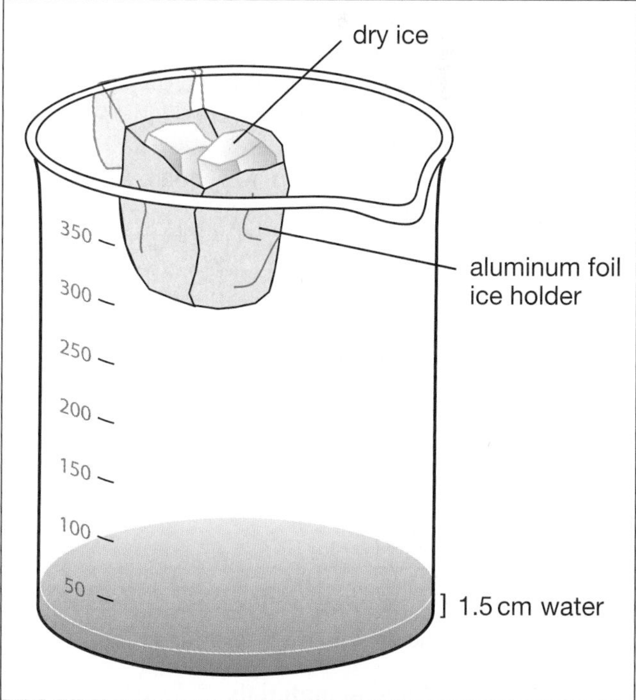

EXPLORE

Carbon Changing Costumes

In the engage activity, *Characterizing Carbon*, you experienced carbon on the move. You saw a form of carbon move into and out of water. The color changes in the solution indicated that a chemical reaction was taking place.

On a bigger scale, carbon can participate in many chemical reactions as it moves through natural systems. Photosynthesis is an example of this that you have already studied in Level 1 of this program. Here the carbon changes from a simple molecule to a complex one. During photosynthesis, carbon in CO_2 is converted to organic compounds. Examples of these compounds are starch and cellulose.

In *Carbon Changing Costumes*, you will explore eight simple reactions with carbon. These reactions simulate a series of real carbon pathways. As you carry out the reactions, think about how they relate to the world around you. Also think with your team about how some of the reactions might relate or link together. This helps you understand the pathways of carbon movement around Earth.

Materials

For each team of 3 students

See figure 11.3 for materials for the stations.

Cautions

Wear safety goggles for investigations with chemical reactions and open flames.

Station	Materials per team of 3
2	2 500-mL beakers or jars 1 stirring spoon or rod 1 funnel 1-cup measuring cup 1 filter paper or coffee filter soil, or bag of potting soil or rotting vegetation tap water
3	2 test tubes 2 antacid tablets with calcium carbonate ($CaCO_3$) 2 test tubes vinegar (5% acetic acid, CH_3COOH) tap water 1 calculator
4	3 pairs of safety goggles 2 test tubes 1 test-tube holder Bunsen burner or other heat source 1 scale or weighing station sodium bicarbonate ($NaHCO_3$) 1 dropper bottle of universal indicator solution tap water 1 3×3 cm aluminum foil square matches or flame source
5	2 beakers, at least 300 mL 2 spoons for stirring sodium bicarbonate ($NaHCO_3$) calcium chloride ($CaCl_2$) 1 dropper bottle of universal indicator solution tap water
8	1 test tube or small beaker 1 dropper bottle of distilled water with BTB indicator tap water 1–2 straws

Note: Materials for stations 1, 6, and 7 are at those stations.

▲ **Figure 11.3 Table of materials.** Refer to this table for a summary of materials needed at each station by each team.

Process and Procedure

In the next two class periods, you will explore reactions with carbon at eight stations. At each station, record your answers in your science notebook. Pay particular attention to the chemical reaction that moves carbon from reactants to products. The class will complete station 8 together.

1. Copy the large diagram in figure 11.4 onto a full page in your science notebook. Title it "Carbon Environs." At the end of the activity, your diagram should show the locations of all stations. Feel free to be creative. Add color, shading, or other enhancements to improve your diagram. At each station, you will
   - identify with your team in which natural environment you think the reaction occurs and
   - write the station number on the diagram in the appropriate environment.
2. Listen to your teacher for suggestions or instructions about the stations. Complete all the stations, but not necessarily in numeric order.

Station 1

What does it mean for a gas to dissolve, or be "soluble," in a liquid? How does this relate to gas escaping or leaving a liquid? You will think about these questions in this investigation.

1. Look at the 4 bottles of seltzer water labeled from 1 to 4. Sketch the setup in your science notebook and add the appropriate labels.
2. What variable could be different between the bottles?

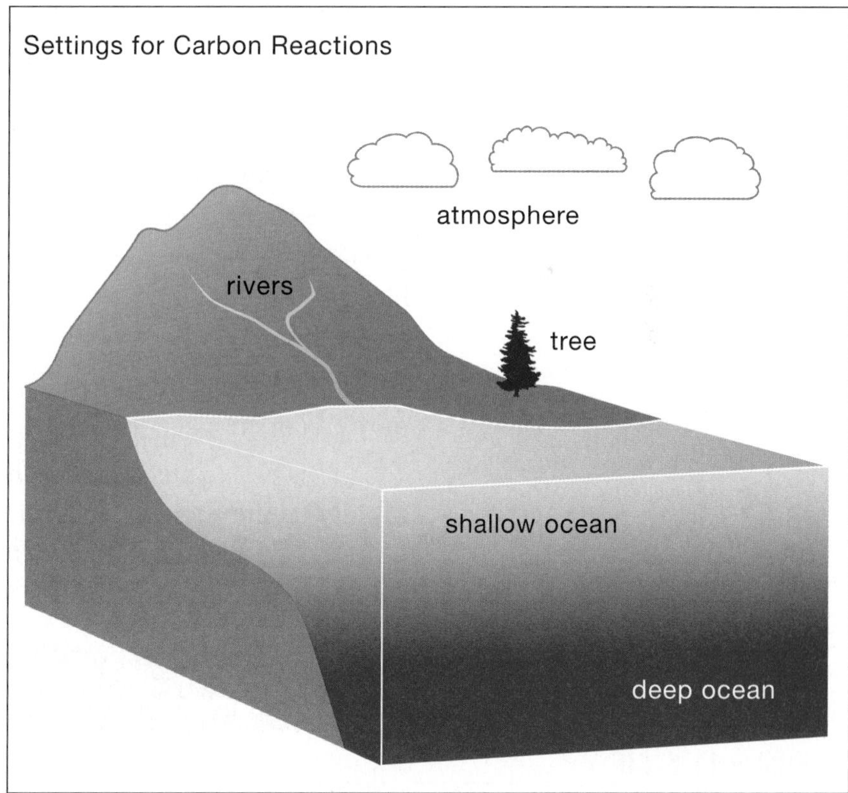

Figure 11.4 Carbon environs. This diagram shows natural settings for carbon reactions on land and in the ocean and the atmosphere. Where on the diagram do you think carbon reactions for the eight stations occur? Copy this diagram onto a full page in your science notebook. You will add the number of each station to show where you expect its reaction to occur.

3. Copy the table in figure 11.5 into your science notebook. Record your observations for the experiment in this data table.
4. On the count of 3, your teacher will quickly open all 4 bottles. What do you observe? Discuss as a class whether the bottles behave similarly or differently.
5. You have been learning that gases like CO_2 either escape from fluids or dissolve into fluids. Use figure 11.5 to record your ideas and observations for Questions 5a–c.
   a. Discuss as a class which of the bottles lost CO_2 the fastest.
   b. You have learned that the **solubility** of a substance indicates how much will dissolve in a liquid. If CO_2 has a high solubility in a liquid, does the CO_2 tend to leave the liquid or remain in the liquid?
   c. Write a chemical equation showing the escape of CO_2 gas from water. Write another equation showing that CO_2 dissolves in water.
   d. If CO_2 escapes quickly from a liquid, does this mean that CO_2 has a low solubility or a high solubility in that liquid?
   e. In which of the bottles (1–4) is CO_2 solubility the highest? That is, which bottle has the least fizzing?
6. Discuss as a class what variable differs between the bottles. Write how CO_2 solubility relates to that variable.
7. Draw in your science notebook axes for a simple graph showing how CO_2 solubility (on the *y*-axis) changes with the variable in Step 6 (on the *x*-axis).
   a. Use your observations to draw a line on that graph.
   b. Does the line in the plot show a direct or an indirect relationship?
8. Write the following sentence in your science notebook and fill in the blanks:

   "This experiment shows that carbon in CO_2 moves more rapidly to the atmosphere from ________ water than from ________ water. This means that carbon dioxide is more soluble in ________ water than in ________ water."

Bottle number	Observations when opened	Rate of CO_2 escape (fast/slow)	CO_2 solubility (high/low)
1			
2			
3			
4			

Figure 11.5 CO_2 solubility table. Make a data table like this in your science notebook to record observations of the 4 bottles of seltzer.

9. Add the station number to your carbon environs diagram in your science notebook.

Station 2

What happens as rainwater percolates through organic **soils**? Do this investigation to explore how natural waters interact with soil.

1. Add 2 cups (c) of water to a beaker.
2. Add ½ c of soil or rotten vegetation to the beaker. Stir thoroughly with a stirring rod or spoon for 1–2 min. Write about the mixture and draw a diagram of it in your science notebook.
3. Prepare a filter assembly with a clean beaker beneath it. Transfer the mixture into the funnel and collect the fluid that drains.
4. What does the filtered solution look like? Explain.
5. Write your ideas for what forms you think carbon takes in the soil. What forms do you think carbon takes in the filtered solution?
6. Write the following sentence in your science notebook and fill in the blanks:

   "Compared with processes in nature, this experiment represents movement of carbon from __________ to __________."
7. Add the station number to your carbon environs diagram in your science notebook.

Station 3

Here is a different type of investigation with carbon. Some antacid tablets are mostly calcium carbonate ($CaCO_3$), and thus contain carbon.

1. Imagine that the antacid tablets represent a carbonate rock. For the 0.5 grams (g) of $CaCO_3$ in a tablet, what percentage of it is carbon?

Use the gram atomic weights for the 3 elements in $CaCO_3$ to estimate. Sum the weights and determine the proportion of carbon.

2. Obtain 2 test tubes. Place 3 inches (in) of acetic acid (CH_3COOH) in one test tube, and 3 in of water in another test tube.
3. Add 1 antacid tablet to each test tube. What happens in each tube?
4. Balance the following reaction with your team. Check that it is charge and mass balanced.

$$CaCO_3 + 2CH_3COOH \longrightarrow Ca^{2+}{}_{(aq)} + \underline{?}CH_3COO^{1-}{}_{(aq)} + \underline{?}H_2O + \_\_\_\_\_$$

5. Did you see evidence for the reaction product in the far right side of the equation in Step 4? What was the evidence?
6. In nature, a better model of rock weathering is the reaction between calcium carbonate and carbonic acid, H_2CO_3. Weak carbonic acid forms in rainwater as CO_2 dissolves in raindrops.
   a. Write the reaction to make carbonic acid (H_2CO_3) from rainwater and CO_2.
   b. Complete the following reaction in your science notebook. Be sure to check with your team for charge and mass balance.

$$CaCO_3 + H_2CO_3 \longrightarrow \underline{?}Ca^{2+}{}_{(aq)} + \underline{?}HCO_3{}^{1-}{}_{(aq)}$$

   c. In the reaction in Step 6b, does the chemical reaction remove CO_2 from the atmosphere or add CO_2 to the atmosphere? Agree on an answer with your team and write your evidence in your science notebook.
   d. How does the reaction in Step 4 with acetic acid compare with the reaction between carbonic acid and $CaCO_3$? In particular, did the reaction of calcium carbonate with acetic acid consume or produce CO_2?
7. Write the following sentence in your science notebook and fill in the blanks:

   "Compared with processes in nature, this experiment represents movement of carbon from the __________ to __________."
8. Add the station number to your carbon environs diagram in your science notebook.

Station 4

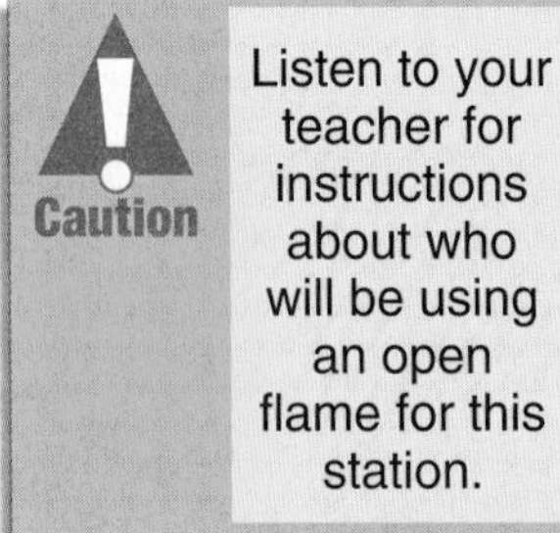

Listen to your teacher for instructions about who will be using an open flame for this station.

Limestone is a rock that contains a lot of carbon. The carbon is in calcium carbonate, $CaCO_3$ (figure 11.6). Often, rocks like limestone get pushed deep into the earth, where it is very hot. What do you think happens to the rock? You can simulate a heated carbonate rock with a similar material, sodium bicarbonate, $NaHCO_3$. This is just baking soda.

1. What do you think will happen if you heat sodium bicarbonate ($NaHCO_3$)? Complete the following chemical reaction. Use the reaction to write a prediction in your science notebook. The reaction shows 1 reaction product.

$$NaHCO_3 + \text{heat} \longrightarrow NaOH_{(s)} + \underline{\qquad}$$

It is OK to be wrong about a prediction. Scientists use predictions to see how well they understand systems. The key is thinking carefully about why you didn't get the correct answer. This will help you make a better prediction the next time.

2. Complete Steps 2a–f to heat and weigh sodium bicarbonate ($NaHCO_3$).
   a. Measure the mass of a small test tube.
   b. Weigh 1.5–2 g $NaHCO_3$ onto foil or weighing paper. Carefully transfer the powder to the bottom of the test tube.
   c. Heat the test tube for about 3 min. Obtain a dull red glow for the glass and powder. Record all changes that you observe for the $NaHCO_3$.
   d. After heating, gently cover the test tube with a small piece of foil. This keeps the sample from absorbing water vapor.
   e. Let the test tube cool for at least 1 min. If needed, cool the test tube further by immersing it in several inches of water.

Do not get water inside the test tube or around the foil on the top of the test tube.

   f. When the test tube is at room temperature, completely dry the exterior, remove the foil cover, and weigh the test tube plus the powdery substance.
3. Summarize the masses of the reactants and the products.
   a. Write the masses of sodium bicarbonate and product 1 (NaOH):

      mass of reactant $NaHCO_3$ = ________

      mass of product 1 NaOH = ________

   b. How would you determine the mass of product 2? Explain this in your science notebook and write the mass in the form shown.

      mass of product 2 ________ = ________

   c. What percentage of the initial reactant mass is product 2?
4. Chemical reactions are important predictive tools. For example, the completed reaction for Step 1 shows that 48 percent by mass of reaction products should be $NaOH_{(s)}$. Use this data about the reaction to answer Questions 4a–d.
   a. For your initial mass of $NaHCO_3$, predict the mass of NaOH from your experiment.
   b. Explain how similar or different your answers are for measured and predicted masses in Steps 3 and 4. If your answers are different, list sources of error that you think might account for this.
   c. What percentage of the initial mass of reactant do you infer for product 2? Show in your science notebook 2 different ways to calculate this.

Figure 11.6
Fossiliferous limestone.
This limestone has fossils of shells. The shells consist of calcium carbonate, $CaCO_3$. How much carbon is this?

   d. What is product 2? Explain your evidence in your science notebook.
5. Show that the reaction product NaOH differs from reactant $NaHCO_3$.
   a. Dissolve the remaining NaOH in the test tube with 20–30 milliliters (mL) of water.
   b. Dissolve a similar amount of $NaHCO_3$ in 20–30 mL of water in a test tube.
   c. Add 5 drops of universal indicator to each.
   d. Which test tube has a stronger base? Does this correlate with NaOH or with $NaHCO_3$? Explain your evidence.
6. Return to the limestone ($CaCO_3$) analogy, rather than the sodium bicarbonate ($NaHCO_3$) analogy. Complete the following reaction and use it to predict what happens when the $CaCO_3$ in limestone is heated in the earth.

$$CaCO_3 + \text{energy} \longrightarrow CaO_{(s)} + \_\_\_\_$$

7. Write the following sentence into your science notebook and fill in the blanks:

   "Compared with processes in nature, this experiment represents movement of carbon from ____________ to the ____________."
8. Add the station number to your carbon environs diagram in your science notebook.

Station 5

What do you think the seafloor looks like at a depth of 1–2 kilometers (km)? Yes, it is dark with many unfamiliar forms of life. Complete this investigation to simulate carbon changing forms in the ocean.

1. Think of different ways for carbon to move from the shallow ocean to greater depths. Explain these ideas as best you can in your science notebook.
2. Obtain 2 glass beakers, at least 300 mL in volume. In the first, add 150 mL of water. Add a spoonful of baking soda ($NaHCO_3$) and stir until the solution is clear.
3. In the other beaker, add 150 mL of water. Add 1 large spoonful of calcium chloride ($CaCl_2$) and stir until the solution is completely clear.

Have different team members prepare the 2 solutions. If you cannot entirely dissolve either of the powders, add another 50 mL of water and stir.

4. Dissolving $NaHCO_3$ and $CaCl_2$ in water are 2 disassociation reactions. Complete the following reactions and write them in your science notebook.

$$2NaHCO_{3(s)} \longrightarrow 2Na^{1+}_{(aq)} + \underline{\qquad}_{(aq)}$$

$$CaCl_{2(s)} \longrightarrow \underline{?}Ca^{2+}_{(aq)} + \underline{?}Cl^{1-}_{(aq)}$$

5. What do you think will happen if you mix these 2 solutions? Make a prediction with a chemical reaction by completing Steps 5a–c.
   a. Take the reaction products in Step 4 and rearrange them as reactants. You will mix the 2 solutions in Step 7.
   b. Predict the reaction products from mixing the solutions. Write this prediction in your science notebook.

Note that sodium (Na^{1+}) and chlorine (Cl^{1-}) are very soluble and remain dissolved in a solution.

   c. Show your prediction to your teacher before you begin Step 6.
6. Add 8 drops of universal indicator solution to each beaker. Record the color.
7. Pour the contents of the beakers together. Describe carefully what you see.
   a. What color is the mixture? What does that tell you about the pH of the mixture?
   b. How many reaction products form in the mixture? Describe these very carefully. What happens to the mixture after 20–30 sec?
   c. Make a sketch of the beaker with the mixture; add appropriate labels that show your main observations.

This is a good place to use the labeling strategies "What I see" and "What it means."

8. Evaluate your prediction strategy from Step 5. Consider what you saw and the reactants in this experiment. What is your evidence for the solid? Write a complete chemical reaction.
9. Write the following sentence in your science notebook and fill in the blanks:

   "Compared with processes in nature, this experiment represents movement of carbon from ____________ to the ____________."

10. Add the station number to your carbon environs diagram in your science notebook.

Station 6

You've studied photosynthesis in this program in several contexts. You know that plants use this process to make the food and tissues that they need. Review the chemical reaction for photosynthesis at this station.

1. Observe and sketch the plant at this station. The plant is growing and needs carbon to grow leaves, branches, roots, and a thicker trunk. Draw a sketch of the plant that shows labels and a scale.
2. Balance the following photosynthesis reaction. Recall that reaction products are glucose ($C_6H_{12}O_6$) and 6 molecules of oxygen gas (O_2). Glucose is one of many thousands of kinds of carbon molecules (figure 11.7).

   $$\_\_\_\_ + \_\_\_\_ + \text{energy} \longrightarrow C_6H_{12}O_6 + 6O_2$$

   The reaction product is represented here as glucose. A prior step (not shown) builds a 3-carbon sugar that plants convert to glucose.
3. What forms does carbon appear in for the reactants and the products?
4. Write the following sentence in your science notebook and fill in the blanks:

   "Compared with processes in nature, this experiment represents movement of carbon from the __________ to __________."
5. Add the station number to your carbon environs diagram in your science notebook.

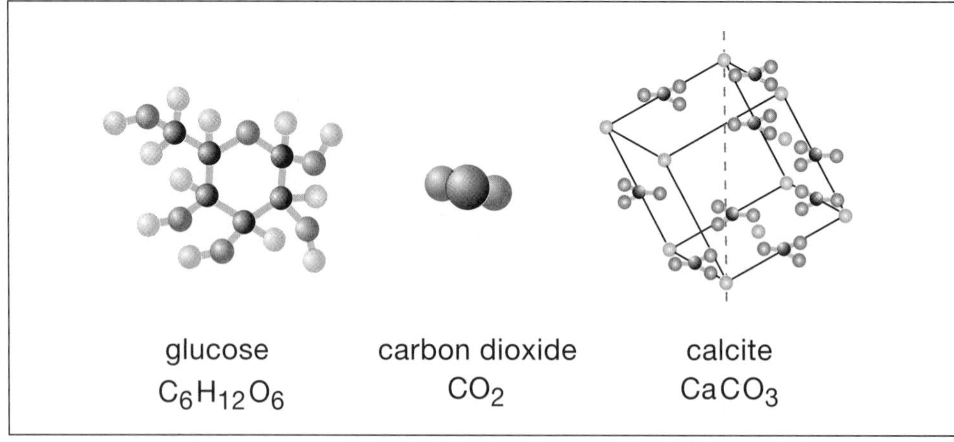

▲ **Figure 11.7 Molecular diagrams with carbon.** The carbon atom is highly versatile and forms hundreds of thousands of kinds of molecules. These 3 diagrams show the atomic structure of carbon in glucose, carbon dioxide, and the mineral calcite ($CaCO_3$).

Station 7

What might you see if you dug into soils on a forest floor? Mostly, you would see a lot of leaves and branches in a state of decay. But where does the carbon go that is in that vegetation? You explored one such carbon pathway in soils in station 2. See another pathway at this station.

1. View, touch, and smell the decaying vegetation at this station. Have a member of your team read the following paragraph about decaying vegetation.

   In Level 1 of this program, you learned about cellular respiration. During cellular respiration, the cells in your tissues use oxygen and sugars to produce energy for your body. Because this kind of respiration uses or consumes oxygen, it is called **aerobic respiration.** In soils, small organisms called **microbes** "eat" and use fallen vegetation as a source of energy. Some of these are single-celled organisms. Thus, microbial respiration leads to the decay that you see.

2. Use glucose ($C_6H_{12}O_6$) as a product of photosynthesis. Glucose is not quite cellulose, or the parts of plants with leaves, wood, roots, or bark. Still, it is a good molecule to model the decay of vegetation in soils.

   a. Complete the following reaction for microbial respiration with oxygen. Assume that microbes consume glucose. Make sure that the reaction is charge and mass balanced.

   $$C_6H_{12}O_6 + \underline{?}O_2 \longrightarrow \underline{\qquad} + \underline{?}H_2O + \text{energy}$$

   b. What must be the reaction product on the blank line in Step 2a?

3. Follow Steps 3a–c to learn about another kind of cellular respiration.

   a. Use a reading strategy with your team to read the following paragraph.

   Many microbes live deep in soils, the ocean, or even the intestines of animals. In those settings, the microbes do not have oxygen for respiration. Yet they still consume glucoselike molecules to produce energy and stay alive. This energy-generating process is still called respiration. But without oxygen, it is called **anaerobic respiration.** These microbes are sometimes called **anaerobes.** You have already studied anaerobic fungi—yeast. They consume sugar and produce ethanol (C_2H_5OH). Yeast do this without oxygen.

b. Complete the following reaction for anaerobic respiration by microbes.

$$C_6H_{12}O_6 \longrightarrow 2C_2H_5OH + \underline{\quad\quad} + \text{energy}$$

Is your reaction charge and mass balanced? You might recall that this process is called fermentation.

c. How many moles (mol) of reaction products are made from 1 mol of $C_6H_{12}O_6$?

4. Balance the reaction for the anaerobic production of methane (CH_4). Other anaerobes produce methane from glucose in swamps and from the intestines of animals.

$$C_6H_{12}O_6 \longrightarrow \underline{?}CH_4 + \underline{?}CO_2 + \text{energy}$$

5. Write the following sentence in your science notebook and fill in the blanks:

   "Compared with processes in nature, this experiment represents movement of carbon from __________ to the __________."

6. Add the station number to your carbon environs diagram in your science notebook.

Station 8

Complete the following steps to investigate cellular respiration further. Recall that you have already studied cellular respiration in Level 1 of this program.

1. For a molecule of glucose ($C_6H_{12}O_6$), complete and balance the following chemical reaction. This represents cellular respiration for a plant or an animal.

$$C_6H_{12}O_6 + \underline{?}O_2 \longrightarrow \underline{\quad\quad} + \underline{?}H_2O + \text{energy}$$

2. Fill a test tube with 10 mL of water. Add 5 drops of BTB solution from a dropper bottle. Swirl gently until the solution is a uniform color.
3. Obtain a straw and blow gently into the blue solution. What color does the solution turn? What does the change in color tell you about the acidity of the solution?

It may help you to refer to the reaction in Question 5 of the *Reflect and Connect* from the engage activity. Yellow means more acidic, blue more basic.

Cautions

Do not draw water up the straw. Only blow out through the straw.

4. What are the reaction products of cellular respiration? How did the color change serve as evidence for the reaction products?
5. Rinse the solution out of the test tube when you are finished.
6. Write the following sentence in your science notebook and fill in the blanks:

   "The process of cellular respiration moves carbon from __________ to the __________."
7. Add the station number to your carbon environs diagram in your science notebook.

Reflect and Connect

Discuss the following questions with your team and write answers in your science notebook. For all chemical equations, confirm that they are charge and mass balanced.

1. At station 5, you used baking soda ($NaHCO_3$) to make a solution with a high concentration of bicarbonate $(HCO_3)^{1-}$. If $CO_{2(g)}$ dissolves in the ocean or a lake, write a reaction with water (H_2O) to show one way to make a bicarbonate ion $(HCO_3)^{1-}$.

It will help you to recall the acid-base reactions in the engage activity.

2. Geologists test whether a rock is limestone by looking for a "fizz" when they put a drop of hydrochloric acid (HCl) on it. Assuming that the fizz is a release of CO_2, balance the following reaction to represent this handy field test for limestone.

$$CaCO_3 + 2HCl \longrightarrow \underline{?}^{2+} + \underline{?}^{1-} + \underline{\qquad} + \underline{?}CO_{2(g)}$$

3. A solution in a beaker is nearly saturated in $NaHCO_3$. Another beaker contains limewater, a solution nearly saturated in calcium hydroxide $Ca(OH)_2$. Predict what happens when the 2 solutions are mixed.
   a. Write a dissociation reaction for 2 mol of $NaHCO_3$.
   b. Write another dissociation reaction for 1 mol of $Ca(OH)_2$.
   c. List the reaction products from the steps above. Imagine that these are reactants when one of the beakers is poured into the other to make a mixture.
   d. Use your results at station 5 to predict the reaction products for Question 3c. Check your equation for charge and mass balance.

Recall that sodium (Na^{1+}) and the hydroxide ion (OH^{1-}) are very soluble and stay in solution.

4. Review station 7 with the 3 respiration reactions from glucose ($C_6H_{12}O_6$).
   a. Write each of these reactions together in your science notebook and label them.
   b. Starting with 1 mol of glucose, which of the 3 respiration reactions generates the most CO_2?
   c. Which of the 3 reactions generates the least CO_2?
   d. What are the molar ratios of CO_2 produced in each of the 3 respiration reactions?
5. CO_2 dissolves into the ocean in both polar and equatorial areas. Would CO_2 dissolve more readily into cold polar oceans or warm equatorial oceans? Use your data from station 1 to explain your answer.
6. Which station or stations represent a reaction that is the basis for food chains in ecosystems? Use 2 examples to explain your answer.

EXPLAIN

The Carbonated Geosphere

In the explore activity, *Carbon Changing Costumes*, you saw carbon change costume through chemical reactions. Carbon can move between substances in the liquid, solid, or gas state. You probably even noted that some stations had reactions that were the reverse of other stations.

Indeed, carbon takes many forms. This is because its bond structure is so versatile, as you have been learning in science. But to change settings on Earth and participate in different reactions, carbon has to move around. You have probably traced the flow of water (H_2O) between different reservoirs. The movement of water between reservoirs is the water cycle.

What about carbon? How does carbon move around between different geologic and biologic settings? In *The Carbonated Geosphere*, you and your team will analyze carbon transport on Earth.

Materials

For each team of 3 students

3 *Carbon Chemical Reaction Table* handouts

3 *Carbon Transport Table* handouts

Process and Procedure

Begin by observing as a class 2 containers with water and substances with carbon.

1. Look at the containers of water your teacher has set up. Are they similar or different? Can you tell which one has dissolved $NaHCO_3$? Discuss these containers as a class and answer Questions 1a–c in your science notebook.
   a. Discuss what forms of carbon you think might be in the 2 containers of water. What is your evidence, and how might you test your ideas?
   b. What do you think will happen if the 2 are mixed? Write a prediction.
   c. What ideas do you have about the geologic or biologic setting that the mixture might represent?
2. Obtain the *Carbon Chemical Reaction Table* and the *Carbon Transport Table* handouts. Refer to these tables with your team as you complete the following reading. The tables are an important tool to help you map pathways of carbon on Earth.
3. Use a reading strategy with your team to complete the following reading, *Carbon Transport across the Globe*. This will help you learn more about how carbon moves around Earth.

READING

Carbon Transport across the Globe

Terrestrial Carbon and Fall Colors

What is it like in the woods, the mountains, or a city park on a brisk fall day? What indicates the changing seasons to you? Maybe you note that the Sun is at a lower angle in the sky, or that not only are leaves changing colors, but many are fluttering to the ground. The leaves fall amidst limbs or trees that have fallen, as well as the remains of other leaves that fell to the forest floor last fall.

Each year, this process repeats itself in forests. Vegetation that grew in the spring and summer is transferred to forest floors in the fall. The buildup of leaves and limbs on the forest floors is called **litter** (figure 11.8). This process moves carbon from trees to the forest floor. As litter, the carbon in that organic material can enter a new series of decay pathways.

When litter starts to decay, it is sometimes called **humus**. In the explore activity, you saw several possible fates for carbon in the humus of the forest floor. Do you remember what these were? One was microbes that consume humus. For the microbes, this is a stage of cellular respiration. Much of the carbon is converted to CO_2.

Another fate for carbon in the humus occurs from the rinsing or leaching of the humus by rainwater. As the rainwater then drains to rivers, the carbon may remain in particles of organic

Carbon Transport across the Globe, continued

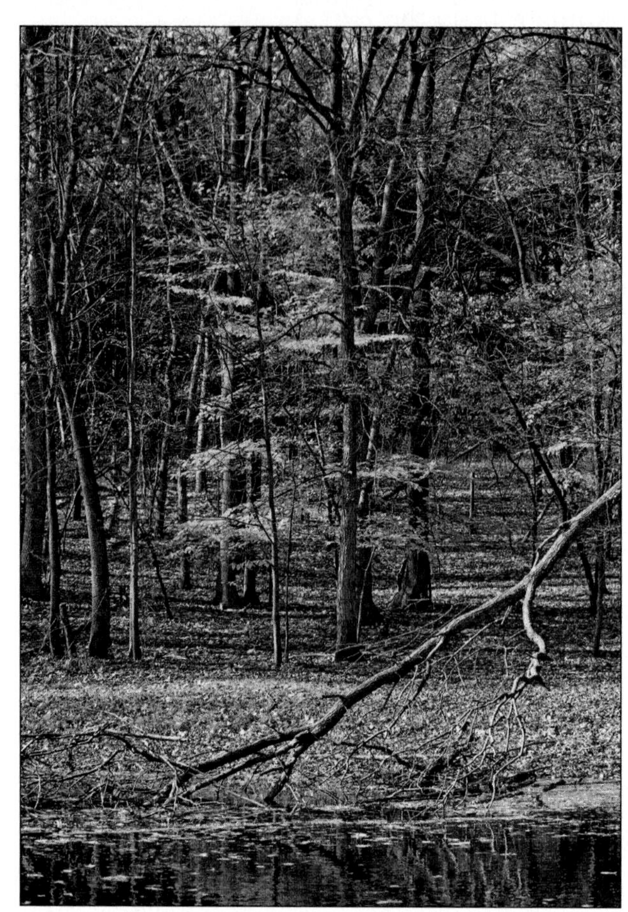

▲ **Figure 11.8 Fall leaves.** These trees are losing their leaves in the fall. Carbon in leaves, limbs, and trunks fall to the forest floor to become litter.

matter. This is often called **dissolved organic carbon**, or **DOC** for short. Rivers carry DOC to the ocean—that's where rivers go (figure 11.9).

But carbon also takes another form in rivers. This is the carbon from rock weathering, such as the weathering of limestone ($CaCO_3$). Do you recall the reaction that makes the bicarbonate ion HCO_3^{1-} from rock weathering? Rivers also carry a lot of this carbon. Since $CaCO_3$ is not organic carbon ($CaCO_3$ doesn't "grow on trees," so to speak), it is called **dissolved inorganic carbon**, or **DIC** for short.

Maybe you have heard the word **terrestrial**. This refers to something found on land. The processes above describe terrestrial carbon—that is, the carbon in forests, rocks, rivers, and lakes. There are two other key parts of Earth with a lot of carbon. You can probably guess what those are.

Atmospheric Carbon

Think back to one of your first activities with seltzer water. Your team noted a very common reaction product that carried carbon straight into the atmosphere. What was it? That's right—it was carbon dioxide, CO_2. The atmosphere doesn't have a huge concentration of carbon as CO_2, but it is enough to support processes like photosynthesis. **Atmospheric mixing** is a key process to help transport and move that carbon around. Rivers are one way to move carbon from the land to the ocean. But atmospheric mixing is a faster way to move carbon around Earth.

With atmospheric mixing, for example, the movement of carbon from the land to the ocean occurs in two steps. Wind moves the atmosphere from the land over the ocean. Then CO_2 dissolves from the atmosphere into the ocean. You have seen in several activities how CO_2 dissolves into water. This also happens with the ocean.

How else does carbon get to the atmosphere? Look at your tables. Another key transport process is **volcanic degassing**. This moves carbon in CO_2 from inside Earth to the atmosphere. But how did the carbon get into the earth? If you study more geology, you will learn how rocks like limestone get pushed deep into the earth. Recall station 4, where $CaCO_3$ decomposes under heat and pressure, releasing CO_2 gas. This is what happens to limestone when it is pushed into the earth.

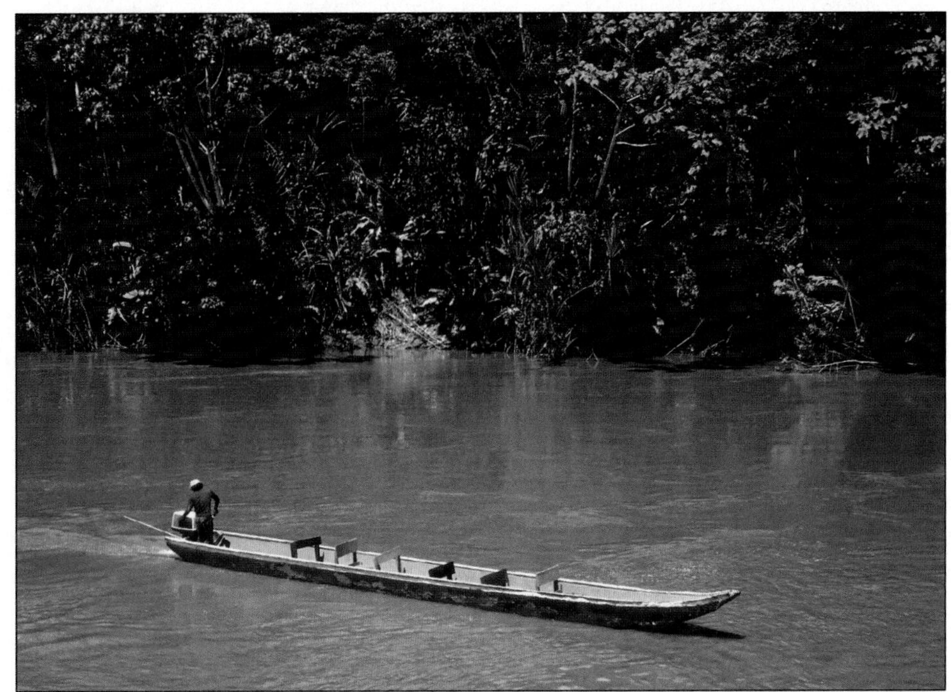

◀ **Figure 11.9**
River transport. This lowland river has dark water, in part due to the high content of dissolved organic carbon. Even though you cannot see it, the river also carries a lot of dissolved inorganic carbon.

Stop & THINK

Gather around the 1–2 new containers of water at the front of the class. Listen to directions from your teacher for what to do to the containers.

1. Record the following in your science notebook.
   a. What are the components of the setup? You should be answering questions such as, "What do you see?" "How big are the containers?"
   b. Make a sketch with labels of one of the containers. Review what the BTB indicator detects and what it is evidence of.
   c. Watch carefully what happens as your teacher starts the experiment. Write your observations in your notebook.
2. Answer Questions 2a–b about the role of carbon in the experiment.
   a. What compounds of carbon would you predict in the experiment?
   b. What does the experiment tell you about the movement of carbon? In what types of settings on Earth might such movement of carbon occur?
3. Use a reading strategy for your team to continue the reading.

Carbon Transport across the Globe, continued

Oceanic Carbon

Envision carbon moving in terrestrial settings. These settings have a lot of vegetation, and we are familiar with these environments. The transport occurs by processes such as respiration, making forest litter, and carrying DIC and DOC in rivers. Blowing trees, flags, or kites are evidence of CO_2 in the atmosphere being mixed up. But what about the ocean? Is there much carbon that moves around the ocean? What forms would this carbon take?

Indeed, the ocean transports massive amounts of carbon around the globe. In fact, the ocean is the largest reservoir of "active," or mobile carbon on Earth. When ocean waters mix, a massive flux of carbon results. You have used the word "flux" for the mass of matter that is moved in a given amount of time.

You learned that the ocean covers about 70 percent of Earth, making it the largest reservoir of water. The ocean ranges from vast, shallow banks teeming with life, to deep, cold, dark trenches over 11 km deep. These waters are deeper than Mount Everest, the tallest mountain on Earth. How could you visualize the transport and mixing of carbon from shallow ocean waters to deep ocean waters? Actually, you've already done a simulation of this process.

Think back to the tall bottle in the *Stop and Think* demonstration. Your teacher forced CO_2 into water. The BTB indicator recorded changes in acidity, which were a response to adding CO_2 to the water. Depending on the setup, you might have even seen yellow volumes, or patches, of relatively carbon-rich water moving to the bottom of the container. Did you also see blue cells of water moving to the surface? This also happens in the ocean. Upwelling and downwelling transport vast amounts of carbon.

But what chemical forms does carbon take in the ocean? You know this as well. In the ocean, it is just DIC and DOC from rivers, or CO_2 that dissolves in the ocean from the atmosphere.

DOC enters the ocean from rivers. (Recall that DOC comes from the leaching of soils and vegetation.) In the ocean, DOC is eaten by microorganisms and converted to CO_2. This CO_2 can either escape to the atmosphere, be used for photosynthesis, or be converted to HCO_3^{1-}. The latter, the bicarbonate ion, is inorganic carbon (DIC). Another source of DIC into the ocean comes from rivers due to rock weathering. Inorganic carbon is then available to marine animals to make their shells.

So several processes add carbon to the ocean—DIC and DOC from rivers, and CO_2 from the atmosphere. You saw that CO_2 solubility was higher in cold water than in warm water. Cold waters in polar regions (the Arctic and the Antarctic) are much better at absorbing CO_2 from the atmosphere than are warm waters at the equator. Remember the simple experiment you did with several bottles of seltzer water? The CO_2 was more soluble in cold water than in warm water.

How else is carbon transported in the ocean? Another way is by marine animals. These animals consist largely of carbon, and they range in mass from phytoplankton to whales (figure 11.10). **Phytoplankton** are microorganisms at the ocean's surface that use dissolved CO_2 in photosynthesis. Phytoplankton are primary **producers**. They are the foundation of the marine food web, just as plants are the primary producers on land.

Many marine organisms also build houses or shells out of calcium carbonate, $CaCO_3$. At some point, these organisms are either eaten, which moves their carbon up the food chains, or they die. When they die, their carbon sinks to the bottom of the ocean.

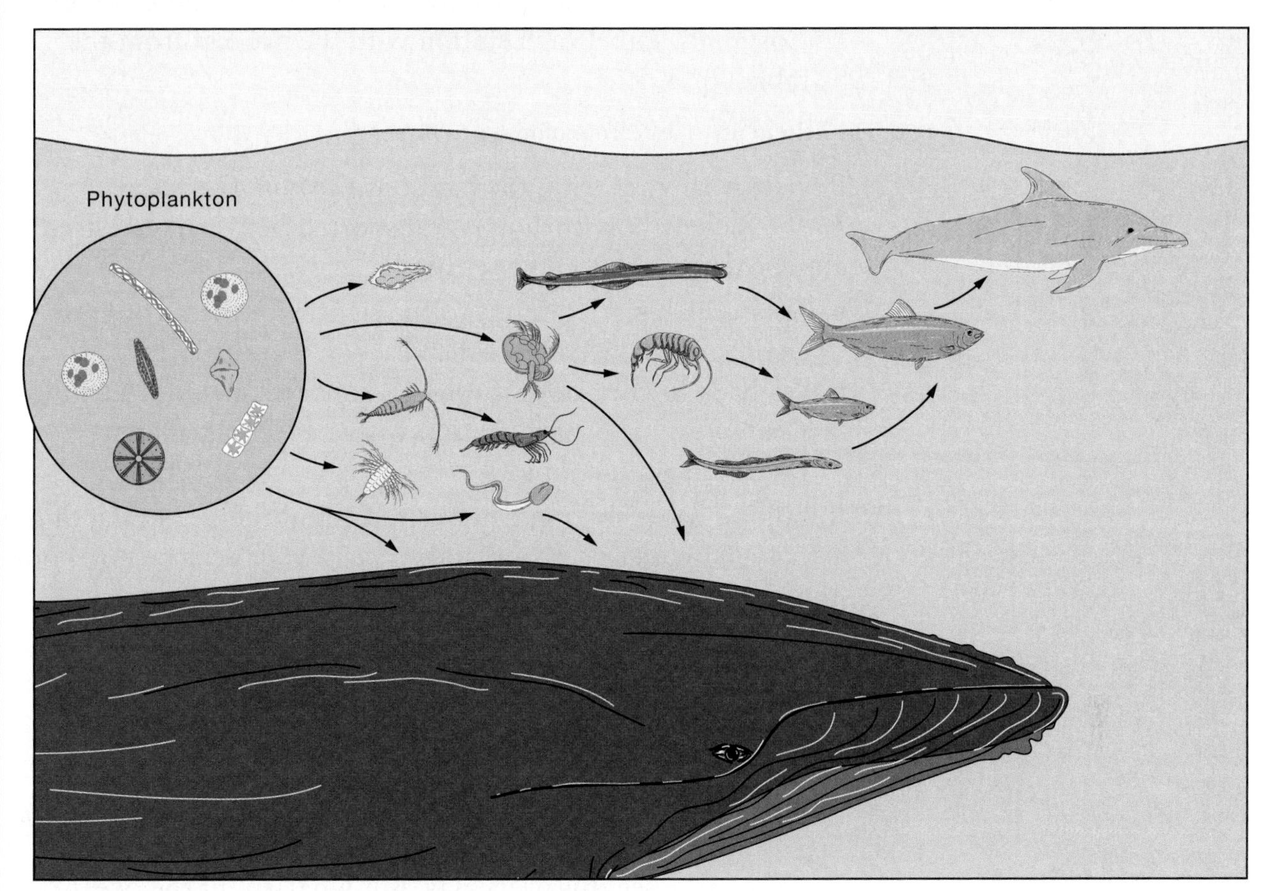

▲ **Figure 11.10 Life in shallow oceans.** Several types of life exist at different water depths in the ocean. Ultimately, all of these organisms rely on photosynthesis for their food.

Reflect and Connect

After completing the reading with your team, discuss and answer the following questions. Your team should prepare to share its ideas with the class.

1. Review the handout *Carbon Chemical Reaction Table*. Review the reactions with carbon.
   a. Fill in the blank columns to the right with examples of carbon-bearing reactants and products.

Review your carbon environs diagram to see whether the reactions occur in the ocean, the atmosphere, or terrestrial settings.

b. Go back in your notes to the stations in *Carbon Changing Costumes*. Label each station with the process from the table.

It may help to use a different-colored pen or pencil.

2. Review with your team the handout *Carbon Transport Table*. Review how carbon is transported between terrestrial, atmospheric, and oceanic settings.
   a. Fill in the blank columns to the right with the settings or environments between which carbon is transported.
   b. Go back in your notes to the stations in *Carbon Changing Costumes*. Label each station with a carbon transport process from the table.
3. Recall the water mixing demonstrations at the beginning of this activity. Discuss as a group and write in your science notebook how the mixing experiments can help you remember the chemical forms of DIC and DOC in carbon cycling.
   a. Which experiment models the transport and mixing of carbon in the ocean? Explain why.
   b. Which experiment models carbon in rivers? What is the evidence?
4. Trees and vegetation store carbon in terrestrial environments. You probably see this every day. But what about the ocean? What organisms do you think store carbon in the ocean? For example, what organisms can carry out photosynthesis beneath the ocean's surface? Figure 11.10 provides a clue. Does much carbon reside there?
5. What does the title of the activity *Carbon Changing Costumes* mean to you?

EXPLORE

Fossil Carbon

You have explored carbon transport around the globe that is independent of human actions. But how do we fit into the picture? Humans rely on carbon in many ways. It is a key part of our bodies, our environment, and our economy. In this manner, we are also a part of carbon pathways around Earth.

Do humans affect carbon movement around Earth? The answer is pretty simple. We do. Every time we turn on a light, use the grill, or drive our cars, we are converting carbon from one form to another. In Part I of *Fossil Carbon*, you and your team will investigate how human needs for energy have become part of carbon cycling. Then in Part II, you will use your learning to construct a model of the carbon cycle.

Part I: Carboniferous Combustion

Materials

For each team of 3 students

1 metal spoon

paper towels

1 ice cube

1 ruler

1 candle

matches

1 *Atmospheric CO_2 Records* handout

▲ **Figure 11.11**
Burning candle. What are the reaction products of a burning candle?

Go to: www.scilinks.org
Topic: fossil fuels
Code: 2Inquiry569a
Topic: hydrocarbons
Code: 2Inquiry569b

Process and Procedure

Gather with your team to complete the following steps. Keep in mind how the investigation relates to fossil fuels as a source of energy.

1. Place a metal spoon on a paper towel, and put a cube of ice on the metal spoon. Over 5–10 min, the ice should conform to the shape of the spoon. The spoon will get very cold.
2. Use a reading strategy with your team for the following paragraph on fossil fuels and hydrocarbons.

   Fossil fuels include many carbon-bearing substances. Humans rely on these substances every day for transportation, electricity, and warmth in our homes. We call them **fossil fuels**, or **hydrocarbons**, for a simple reason. Fossil fuels consist of hydrogen and carbon compounds from geologic deposits of organic carbon. Of course, these hydrocarbons began as organic molecules that were cellulose, wood, bark, or starches in plants, or were even animal remains. Fossil fuels formed many millions of years ago. You have probably heard of fossil fuels such as coal, petroleum, or natural gas. Combusting these fuels provides valuable energy for society. As such, this combustion is an exothermic reaction.
3. Complete these steps to investigate a burning candle. A burning candle is a simple example of combusting hydrocarbons.
   a. Candles may consist of several kinds of wax, or paraffin. A general formula for wax is $C_nH_{(2n+2)}$, where n can vary from about 20 to 30. Write the formula for paraffin with a value of $n = 20$.
   b. Make a T-table showing values of n from 20 to 25 and the corresponding formula for paraffin.
   c. Is a burning candle a source of energy? Explain why.
4. How would you write a chemical reaction for the combustion of fossil fuels? Start with the chemical reaction for burning a candle (figure 11.11). Use these steps to determine the 2 reactants.

a. Use paraffin with a value of $n = 20$ as 1 reactant.
b. What gas needs to be present for a combustion reaction? This is your second reactant.

5. Determine 1 of the reaction products using the cold spoon and a lit candle.
   a. Check that your metal spoon is very cold. The ice should be melted into the shape of the spoon.
   b. Draw away all the water around the ice with a paper towel. Completely dry the bottom of the spoon with a dry paper towel. The spoon should be very cold and completely dry on the bottom.

Your teacher may have dry ice to use on the spoon. This will make the spoon much colder than ice, and it will not melt.

   c. Hold the cold, dry spoon about 1 cm above the tip of the candle flame. What do you see happening on the bottom of the spoon?
   d. What is the substance on the bottom of the spoon? How could you test what the substance is? Describe a test in your science notebook for that substance. Show it to your teacher—if it's a good test, you may be allowed to try it.
6. Candle combustion has a second reaction product. Follow these steps and your teacher's directions to determine this product.
   a. Get from your teacher water with BTB indicator that is sky blue. Add this to a depth of 0.5 cm in each of 2 flat glass dishes. Place each on a white sheet of paper.
   b. Place 3 or 4 very short (or cut) candles in the water. Light them.
   c. Place a glass lid on top of 1 of the containers, but do not let the candles extinguish. As the candle flames dim, slide the lid sideways to let in more oxygen.
   d. What do you observe happening to the color of the water in the 2 containers?
   e. What molecule could be causing this effect? Explain several lines of evidence.

Don't put your finger too close to the flame, or you will discover this reaction product firsthand.

7. Write a third reaction product of combusting fossil fuel. This is the whole reason that we use fossil fuels.
8. Write the complete chemical reaction for candle combustion in these steps. Use a candle formula of $C_{20}H_{42}$.
   a. Make a T-table with reactants in the left column and products in the right. Label the columns.
   b. Reconfigure reactants and products around an arrow, as in a chemical reaction.
   c. Work with your team to balance the equation.

To balance the equation, start by equating the number of carbons on the left with the number on the right. Then balance the hydrogen. Balance the oxygen last.

d. Return to the *Carbon Chemical Reaction Table* from the explain activity, *The Carbonated Geosphere*. Add the reaction from Step 8c to line 10 on the handout. Write in the process "fossil fuel combustion."

9. Complete the following 2 sentences in your science notebook.

a. "Two settings or locations where hydrocarbons are combusted to make energy are __________ and __________."

b. "This experiment simulates the movement of carbon from __________ to the __________ to the __________."

Stop & THINK

PART I

After completing the reading in Step 2 with your team, discuss and answer the following questions.

1 Fossil shells have carbon in calcium carbonate, $CaCO_3$. Could you combust shells, a source of fossil carbon, to use as fuel? Use evidence from this chapter in your answer.

It may help you to use the terms endothermic and exothermic.

2 Propane (C_3H_8) is a hydrocarbon used for energy. Balance the following reaction for combusting propane.

$$C_3H_8 + \underline{?}O_2 \longrightarrow \underline{?}CO_2 + \underline{?}H_2O + \text{energy}$$

3 Natural gas is an important source of energy. It is close to a mixture of about 50 percent methane (CH_4) and 50 percent ethane (C_2H_6). Balance the following reaction for combusting natural gas.

$$CH_4 + C_2H_6 + \underline{?}O_2 \longrightarrow \underline{?}CO_2 + \underline{?}H_2O + \text{energy}$$

4 Figure 11.12 shows concentrations of CO_2 in the atmosphere measured each month in Hawaii from 1958 to 2002. Tick marks on the year axis represent January 1.

a. Draw a best-fit line through the center of the squiggle pattern. What is the slope of the line you drew? Be sure to include units on the slope.

Recall that slope is change in y (Δy) divided by change in x (Δx). You may also know this as "rise over run."

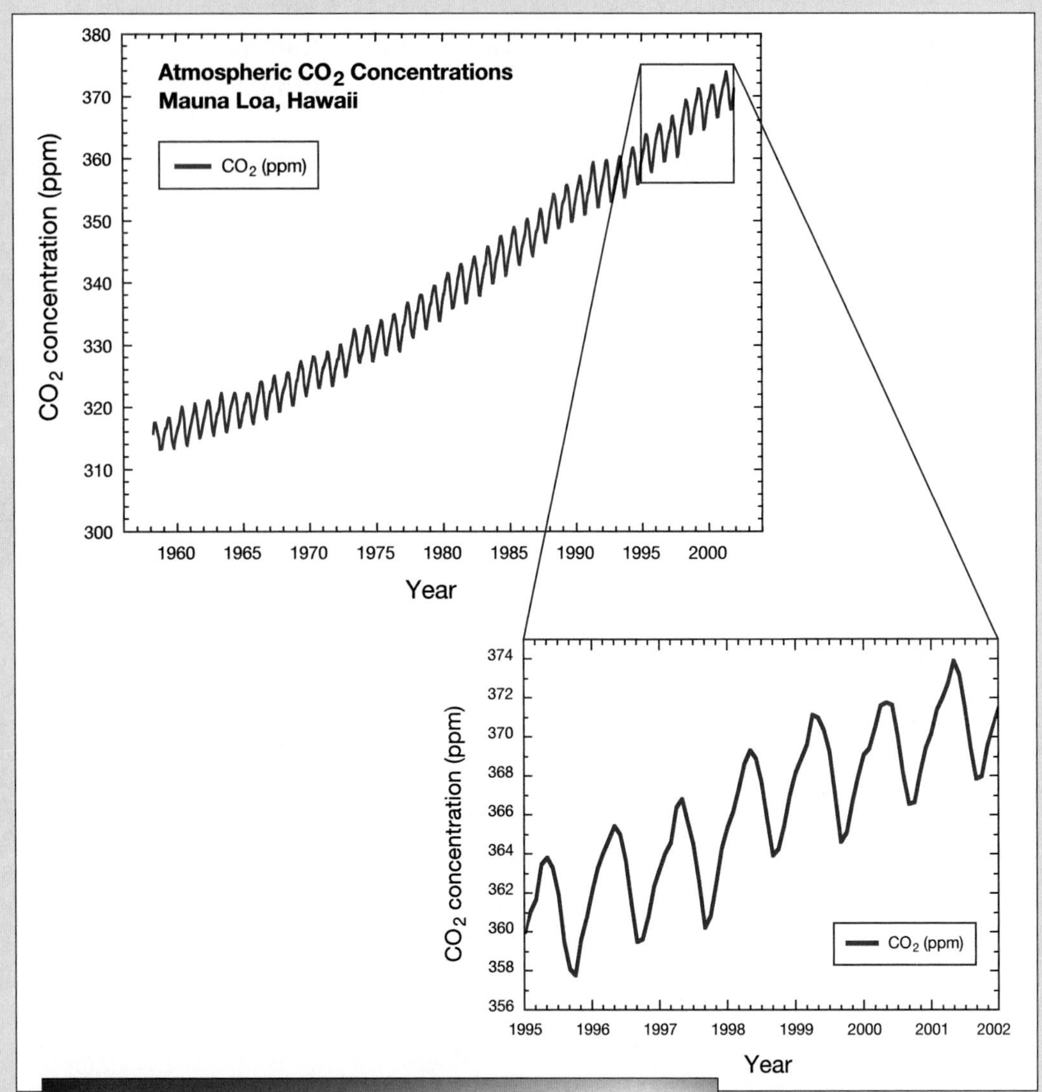

STOP & THINK, PART I, continued

Atmospheric CO_2 Concentrations
Mauna Loa, Hawaii

CO_2 (ppm)

CO_2 concentration (ppm)

380 370 360 350 340 330 320 310 300

1960 1965 1970 1975 1980 1985 1990 1995 2000

Year

CO_2 concentration (ppm)

374 372 370 368 366 364 362 360 358 356

CO_2 (ppm)

1995 1996 1997 1998 1999 2000 2001 2002

Year

Figure 11.12 Atmospheric CO_2 concentration, 1958–2002. In this plot of atmospheric CO_2 concentration from 1958 to 2002, measurements were taken each month from the top of Mauna Loa, Hawaii. The detail shows the CO_2 curve from 1995 to 2002. How many kinds of patterns do you see in these data?

Source: Keeling, C.D. and T.P. Whorf, 2005. Atmospheric CO2 records from sites in the SIO air sampling network. In *Trends: A compendium of Data on Global Change*. Carbon Dioxide Information Analysis Center, Oak Ridge National Laboratory, U.S. Department of Energy, Oak Ridge, TN, U.S.A.

b. What months of the year does CO_2 increase in concentration? How much does CO_2 concentration typically increase?

c. What months of the year does CO_2 decrease in concentration? How much does CO_2 concentration typically decrease?

d. What month in each year is CO_2 the highest?

e. Think about the month you identified in Step 4d. What happens each year during that month that would affect the concentration of CO_2 in the atmosphere?

Not counting equatorial forests, the Northern Hemisphere has much more vegetation than the Southern Hemisphere.

f. What process in plants can explain the annual pattern in figure 11.12?

5 Figure 11.13 shows a record of CO_2 concentrations in the atmosphere over the past 1,000 years. The CO_2 is recovered from air bubbles in ice cores from Antarctica (see figure 11.14). The ice cores were recovered at a location called Law Dome.

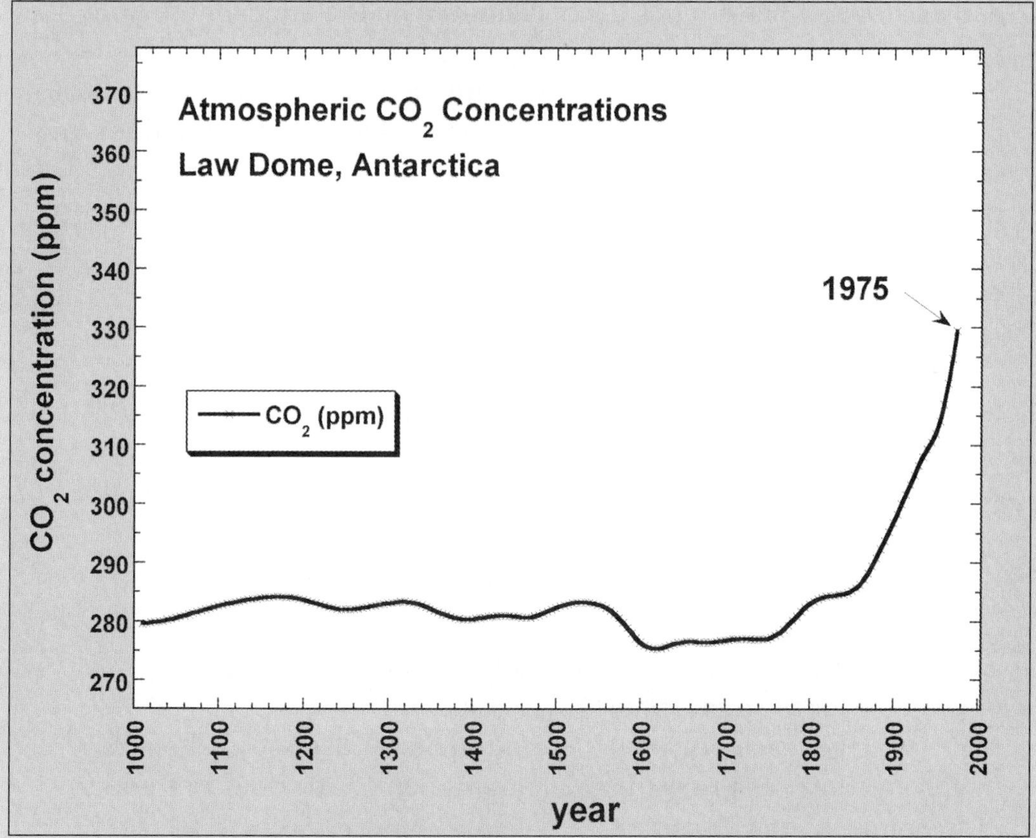

Source: Etheridge, et.al., 1998. Historical CO2 records from the Law Dome DE08, DE08-2, and DSS ice cores. In *Trends: A compendium of Data on Global Change*. Carbon Dioxide Information Analysis Center, Oak Ridge National Laboratory, U.S. Department of Energy, Oak Ridge, TN, U.S.A.

▲ **Figure 11.13 Atmospheric CO_2 concentrations, 1000–1975.** These data were measured from air bubbles preserved in a glacier at Law Dome, Antarctica. What overall pattern do you note here?

STOP & THINK, PART I, continued

Figure 11.14 Working with an ice core sample. Small bubbles in this ice core preserve a record of past CO_2 contents in the atmosphere.

a. Describe the pattern of CO_2 concentration in the atmosphere from 1000 to 1750.

b. Compare the pattern from Step 5a with the pattern from 1750 to 2000.

c. Estimate the slope of the line from about 1900 to 1975. How does this compare with the slope you estimated from Step 4a?

d. Discuss with your team some possible explanations for this change. Write those reasons in your science notebook.

e. Refer back to the data from Mauna Loa in figure 11.12. On your handout, neatly draw a box showing the limits of figure 11.12 from 1958 to 2002.

f. Write an X on the graph for Law Dome to show CO_2 concentrations in 2002.

g. What does this tell you about changes in CO_2 concentrations in the atmosphere?

6. Use FYI—*Fill 'er Up!—What's in Your Tank?* to answer the following questions about CO_2. Assume complete combustion of octane (C_8H_{18}).

a. A typical gas tank is 15 gallons (gal). How much CO_2 does that produce for the atmosphere?

b. On average, each person in the United States uses 461 gallons of gasoline per year. How many kilograms (kg) of CO_2 does this add to the atmosphere?

c. The United States has a population of about 290 million people. Estimate how many kilograms of CO_2 the United States adds to the atmosphere each year.

Fill 'er Up!—What's in Your Tank?

When were you last in a car or bus? Did you ride in one of those to school today? Did you use a car or bus to go shopping last weekend? You know that a transportation system won't work without a source of energy. That energy usually comes from a fossil fuel, particularly gasoline. Scientists are concerned that the amount of gasoline humans use might be affecting Earth's climate.

Gasoline is made by distilling and refining crude oil that is extracted from the ground. The final chemistry depends on the kind of crude oil, the refining process, and the additives. Still, most of gasoline is a hydrocarbon that can represented with $C_nH_{(2n+2)}$. While *n* for gasoline may vary from 7 to 11, a good example is octane, with $n = 8$. The formula for octane is C_8H_{18}.

What happens to gasoline after it is combusted in a car's engine? What are the reaction products, and how much of each is produced? Let's take a look by starting with 1 gal of octane that is fully combusted in a car's engine.

Step 1 is to write a balanced reaction of octane plus oxygen to produce water, carbon dioxide, and energy. The following reaction shows that 1 mol of octane needs 12.5 mol of O_2 ($^{25}/_2$) to produce 8 mol of CO_2 and 9 mol of H_2O and energy:

$$C_8H_{18} + \left(\frac{25}{2}\right)O_2 \longrightarrow 8CO_2 + 9H_2O + \text{energy}$$

Step 2 is to determine how many moles of octane are in 1 gallon. We will use the following conversion factors:

- 3.786 liters (L) = 1 gal
- density of octane = 702.5 grams per liter (g/L)
- gram atomic weight of octane = 114 grams per mole (g/mol)

$$\left(1\ \cancel{\text{gal octane}}\right) \times \left(\frac{3.786\ \cancel{\text{L oct}}}{1\ \cancel{\text{gal oct}}}\right) \times \left(\frac{702.5\ \cancel{\text{g oct}}}{1\ \cancel{\text{L oct}}}\right) = 2{,}659.7\ \text{g octane}$$

$$\left(2{,}659.7\ \cancel{\text{g octane}}\right) \times \left(\frac{1\ \cancel{\text{mol oct}}}{114\ \cancel{\text{g oct}}}\right) = 23.3\ \text{mol octane}$$

Step 3 is to calculate the moles of the reaction products and convert them to mass. We'll start with CO_2:

$$\left(23.3\ \cancel{\text{mol octane}}\right) \times \left(\frac{8\ \cancel{\text{mol CO}_2}}{1\ \cancel{\text{mol octane}}}\right) = 186.4\ \text{mol CO}_2$$

$$\left(186.4\ \cancel{\text{mol CO}_2}\right) \times \left(\frac{44\ \cancel{\text{g CO}_2}}{1\ \cancel{\text{mol CO}_2}}\right) \times \left(\frac{1\ \cancel{\text{kg CO}_2}}{10^3\ \cancel{\text{g CO}_2}}\right) = 8.2\ \text{kg CO}_2$$

So, 1 gal of octane gasoline produces about 8.2 kg of CO_2, or about 18 pounds (lb) of CO_2. Because about 27 percent of a CO_2 molecule is carbon, this is the same as adding about 5 lb of carbon to the atmosphere (18×0.27).

Fill 'er Up!—What's in Your Tank?, continued

The same approach shows how much water is produced. Start with the octane:

$$\left(23.3\ \cancel{\text{mol octane}}\right) \times \left(\frac{9\ \cancel{\text{mol}\ H_2O}}{1\ \cancel{\text{mol octane}}}\right) \times \left(\frac{18\ \cancel{g\ H_2O}}{1\ \cancel{\text{mol}\ H_2O}}\right) \times \left(\frac{1\ \cancel{kg\ H_2O}}{10^3\ \cancel{g\ H_2O}}\right) = 3.78\ \text{kg}\ H_2O$$

The sum of the reaction products, water and carbon dioxide, is 11.99 kg (3.78 kg H_2O + 8.21 kg CO_2). But how do you get about 12 kg of reaction products from only 2.66 kg of octane? Does that make sense? Don't forget the other reactant—oxygen. Here's the mass of oxygen used in the combustion:

$$\left(23.3\ \cancel{\text{mol octane}}\right) \times \left(\frac{12.5\ \cancel{\text{mol}\ O_2}}{1\ \cancel{\text{mol octane}}}\right) \times \left(\frac{32\ \cancel{g\ O_2}}{1\ \cancel{\text{mol}\ O_2}}\right) \times \left(\frac{1\ \cancel{kg\ O_2}}{10^3\ \cancel{g\ O_2}}\right) = 9.33\ \text{kg}\ O_2$$

Now you see that the total mass of the reactants is also 11.99 kg (9.33 kg O_2 + 2.66 kg octane).

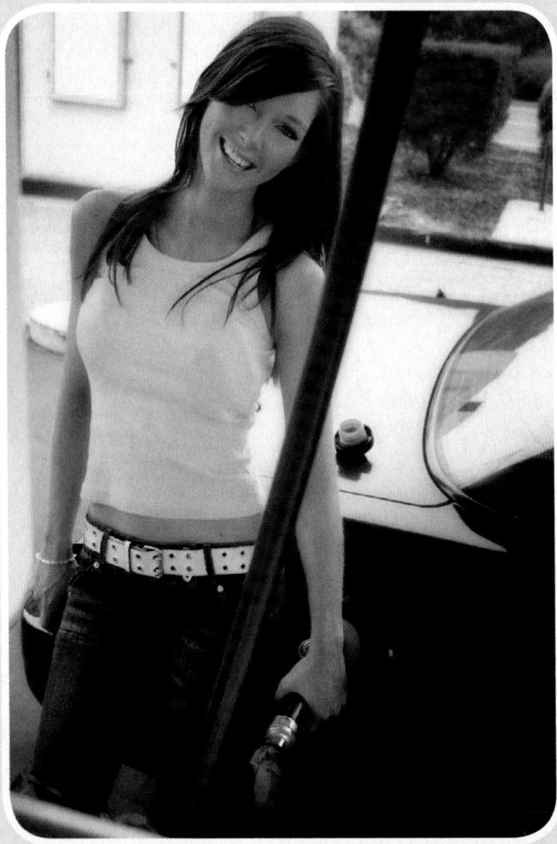

▲ **Pumping gas.** Humans rely on petroleum products like gasoline as an inexpensive source of energy, especially for transportation. How many gallons of gas does a car tank hold?

This equals the mass of the products. Does this relationship between reactants and products sound familiar? It should—the law is the **conservation of mass**.

But real cars don't completely combust gasoline made of pure octane. Rather, their incomplete combustion makes smog, particularly in cities. That smog contains nitrogen oxides, the poisonous gas carbon monoxide (CO), and unburned hydrocarbons (soot).

Why should humans be concerned about adding CO_2 to the atmosphere? First, CO_2 in the atmosphere is a greenhouse gas. This means that it traps and retains heat from the Sun inside Earth's atmosphere. Many scientists are concerned that increasing global temperatures could affect the balance of animals in food webs in ecosystems. Climate change also is linked to sea level change, and perhaps to patterns of food production for humans.

Second, besides photosynthesis, CO_2 is also removed from the atmosphere by dissolving into the ocean. You have seen that adding CO_2 to water makes water more acidic. Many scientists are seeing evidence for the impact of increased acidity (decreasing pH) on the ability of marine organisms such as corals and clams to form shells and protective structures of calcium carbonate.

Part II: Showing the Carbon Cycle

Materials

For each team of 3 students

15 sticky notes

1 pair of scissors

1 pencil and eraser

3 pieces of clear tape

1 sheet of 11×17 in paper (optional)

colored pencils (optional)

1 *Terrestrial, Atmospheric, and Oceanic Carbon Cycling* handout

You have explored a lot of carbon reactions so far. You have also been thinking about how carbon moves around. Now it's time for your team to map out a way that these processes join together in the carbon cycle. You'll focus on Earth of course, even though the carbon cycle would be very different on other planets or moons (see sidebar, *Titanic Carbon*).

Process and Procedure

Gather in a team of three for the following steps. Be prepared to share, describe, and answer questions about your carbon cycle in a class discussion.

1. Obtain a copy of the handout *Terrestrial, Atmospheric, and Oceanic Carbon Cycling*. Tape the backs together to make a single sheet about 11×17 in.

Your teacher may also provide large sheets of paper to use as a background. Model the background environmental setting from the handout.

2. Use your completed *Carbon Chemical Reaction Table* and *Carbon Transport Table* to write each of the 10 carbon reactions on a different sticky note. Then write each of the 5 transport processes on a separate sticky note.

Use the main reaction path for microbial respiration.

3. Attach each sticky note to the background in a position where the reaction or transport process might occur. Discuss your reasons for the placement of each sticky note.

During your discussion, you may adjust or move any sticky note.

4. Use your pencil to draw lines and link the different carbon reactions and transport processes.

5. Decide on any other visual props or diagrams that you can add to your map of the carbon cycle. For example, what might you add to help visually represent reaction 10?

Reflect and Connect

Discuss and answer the following questions based on your diagram of the carbon cycle. These questions make sure that your team is seeing the links and connections in the carbon system.

1. Complete this check on possible carbon paths. You should be able to follow a carbon atom in a continuous path from arrow to arrow from a power plant, to the atmosphere, into phytoplankton in the shallow ocean, to the deep ocean, and then to sediments. Does your diagram represent this path of carbon?
2. Complete this check on possible carbon paths. You should be able to follow carbon with arrows from the atmosphere, to forests, to litter, to rivers, to the ocean, and into organisms like corals. Does your diagram represent this path of carbon?

SIDEBAR

Titanic Carbon

From all signs, the mission was going well. The capsule plummeted into the thick, orange haze surrounding Titan—Saturn's largest moon. Still, other missions like this had ended in disaster. In the past decade, several spacecraft to Mars had "gone silent" during descent. They had probably crashed directly onto the planet's surface. But those were the risks. Such missions were the only way to study the chemistry of other parts of the solar system.

The descending capsule was the Huygens probe, launched only 3 weeks before (December 2004) from the *Cassini* spacecraft. The *Cassini* spacecraft had spent the past 7 years traveling to Saturn and its 31 moons. *Cassini* had been able to image the outer parts of Titan's atmosphere (see figure). Now it would be up to the Huygens probe to penetrate the upper layers of Titan's atmosphere and to explore the dense, lower atmosphere and Titan's surface.

All evidence was that Titan would have carbon in several forms. But what would they be? Was there evidence for a carbon cycle or even life on Titan? What might that carbon cycle look like?

The carbon cycle on Earth involves gases in the atmosphere, liquids in the hydrosphere, and solids in the geosphere and biosphere. Interactions among these four parts of Earth make up the carbon cycle as the carbon changes forms by chemical reactions. A cycle on Titan would also need to include evidence for transport of

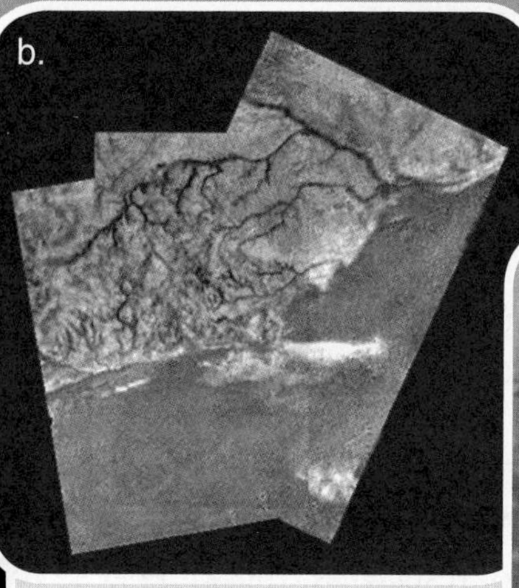

▲ Three views of hydrocarbons on Titan. (a) The first image, taken by the *Cassini* spacecraft, shows layering of gases, mostly N_2 and CH_4, in Titan's atmosphere. (b) This image was taken by the Huygens probe in January 2005 during its descent to the surface. It shows river channels that join and drain a liquid, probably liquid CH_4, from left to right. (c) The last image shows blocks of "dirty ice" and CH_4 on the surface of Titan.

carbon-bearing substances and chemical reactions. The evidence wasn't hard to see.

The mission controllers waited anxiously as the Huygens probe plummeted into the orange haze and toward Titan's surface. Soon, features became clear, showing shapes that resembled river channels and a coastline (see figure). Given temperatures of nearly −300° Fahrenheit at Titan's surface, the liquid could not be H_2O. The liquid likely came from "rains" of liquid methane (CH_4) or ethane (C_2H_6).

Amazingly, after a safe landing, the probe operated for about 2 hours. It sent back a close-up view of Titan's surface (see figure) and detected hydrocarbon gases in the lower atmosphere. Scientists believe that these images show pieces of solid ice (H_2O) or methane (CH_4) blocks. Then the Huygens probe went silent.

Since January 2005, scientists have learned much more about Titan's atmosphere. Like Earth, Titan's atmosphere is about 80–90 percent nitrogen (N_2). Titan's atmosphere also has carbon compounds, particularly CH_4. Dissociation of N_2 and CH_4 by ultraviolet radiation from the Sun results in other hydrocarbons and nitrogen compounds. These include C_2H_6 (ethane), C_3H_8 (propane), C_2H_2 (acetylene), C_2H_4 (ethylene), C_3H_4 (methylacetylene), HCN (hydrogen cyanide), HC_3N (cyanoacetylene), C_2N_2 (cyanogen), and H_2 (hydrogen). There is also evidence for CO_2 (carbon dioxide) and CO (carbon monoxide), just like on Earth, but no free oxygen (O_2).

So, it would appear that Titan has a carbon cycle, of sorts. Combined with the absence of O_2, Titan may be similar to Earth before life formed, but perhaps somewhat colder. Studying carbon pathways on Titan helps us understand our planet and the prospects for life elsewhere in the universe.

ELABORATE

The Flux Is the Crux

Have you seen photographs of the Amazon River basin in South America? It is a vast area of massive trees and dense jungles (figure 11.9). The Amazon basin is almost as big as the United States. Surely the Amazon basin stores massive amounts of carbon. Could anything on Earth have *more* carbon than dense tropical jungles?

You have learned that reservoirs store matter, be it water or carbon. You could even think of a bank as a reservoir—banks store dollars. You also learned that fluxes tell the rate that matter moves into and out of reservoirs. In *The Flux Is the Crux*, you and your team will apply these concepts to carbon in the geosphere. You will be able to figure out the main reservoirs of carbon on Earth. This is a key part of our being able to live on Earth.

Materials

1 calculator

Process and Procedure

Gather with your team and record all information and ideas in your science notebook. This activity will help you to be successful in the evaluate activity, *Carbon Quest.*

1. Discuss with your team whether you think there is more carbon in Earth's atmosphere or in all the vegetation on Earth. Write your reasons or evidence in your science notebook.

Scientists often refer to the biosphere as the living part of the planet. This can include all plants, animals, and soils, plus analogous parts of the ocean.

2. Use a reading strategy with your team for the following paragraphs about rates of carbon transport in the carbon cycle.

   Dissolved carbon flows down a river to the ocean. Maybe the carbon is in a bicarbonate ion used by a clam to build its shell. Or imagine carbon entering a plant by photosynthesis and then leaving the plant by respiration after a week. Or what about carbon in the atmosphere, dissolving into the ocean, and then quickly entering phytoplankton by photosynthesis?

   In each of these cases, carbon is mobile. That carbon moves quickly between carbon reservoirs on Earth. In some cases, the carbon might even cycle back and forth, such as in the photosynthesis-respiration path. Such interactions occur over days, weeks, or perhaps a few years. For this reason, this carbon might be called **active** or **mobile carbon**. Sometimes this quickly moving carbon is referred to as the **biologic carbon cycle**.

In contrast, other parts of Earth have large amounts of carbon that interact much more slowly in the ocean, land surface, or atmosphere. This carbon is mostly beneath Earth's surface. It is stored in geologic deposits of limestone or hydrocarbons such as coal, petroleum, or natural gas. These geologic reservoirs of carbon are viewed as **inactive carbon** because they were not part of rapid carbon cycling at Earth's surface. Some geologists call this the **geologic carbon cycle.** This is because such carbon reservoirs require millions of years to develop, mature, and cycle.

Go to: www.scilinks.org
Topic: biologic carbon cycle
Code: 2Inquiry581a
Topic: geologic carbon cycle
Code: 2Inquiry581b

3. Recall your carbon reactions and transport processes from earlier in this chapter. Answer the following 2 questions.
   a. Discuss with your team 2 paths or processes where carbon in the geologic carbon cycle is transferred to become active, biologic carbon.
   b. Discuss with your team 2 paths or processes where carbon in the biologic carbon cycle is transferred to become inactive, geologic carbon.

It may be helpful to use a sketch with labels to illustrate your answers.

4. Copy figure 11.15 into your science notebook (including the blank columns) and complete the following steps. The table shows the main active reservoirs of carbon on Earth and their masses.
   a. Rewrite the mass of carbon (g C) from column 2 as the mass of carbon with the exponent of 10^{15} in column 3. Remember how to move decimals and change the exponent.

If you were changing 1,000 g to kilograms, you would use these steps:

$$1{,}000 \text{ g} = 1.0 \times 10^{3} \text{ g} = 1 \text{ kg}$$

   After you have done this, do a visual check with your team to make sure that the values make sense.
   b. In column 4, show the mass of carbon as petagrams of carbon (Pg C). Use the conversion where 1 petagram of carbon equals 10^{15} grams of carbon (1 Pg C = 10^{15} g C).
   c. At the bottom of column 4, sum the carbon in Pg C for all the reservoirs.
   d. In column 5, calculate the percentage of active carbon in each reservoir.
   e. Make a T-table in your science notebook. List the reservoirs from largest to smallest in the left column and include their percentages in the right column.
   f. Sketch in your science notebook how you would represent the result from Step 4d as a bar graph and a pie chart.

Carbon reservoir	Mass of carbon (g C)	Mass of carbon (g C with × 10^{15} notation)	Mass of carbon (Pg C)	Percentage of active carbon (% total carbon)
Soils	1.66×10^{18}			
Marine life	3.0×10^{15}			
Shallow ocean	9.0×10^{17}			
Middle, deep ocean	3.71×10^{19}			
Atmosphere	5.9×10^{17}			
Vegetation	6.4×10^{17}			
		Total Pg C		

Source: Sarmiento, J.L. & Gruber, N. 2002. Sinks for anthropogenic carbon. *Physics Today*, 55(8) 30-36, and Intergovernmental Panel on Climate Exchange, 2001. Climate change 2001: The scientific basis. Chapter 3: The carbon cycle and atmospheric carbon dioxide.

▲ **Figure 11.15**
Carbon reservoir table. Use a table like this one to help you organize the data from the 6 main reservoirs of mobile carbon. Fill in the columns for petagrams of carbon (Pg C), total carbon, and the percentage of active carbon.

5. Answer the following questions based on your completed table from figure 11.15. Use petagrams of carbon to compare reservoir sizes (for example, 50 is 2 times larger than 25).
   a. What are the first- and second-largest reservoirs of active carbon on Earth? Are these the reservoirs that you expected?
   b. Reevaluate your team's response to Step 1. (Is there more carbon in Earth's atmosphere or in all the vegetation on Earth?)
   c. Soils are a key player in the active carbon cycle. How many times larger is the amount of carbon in soils than in the atmosphere? In vegetation?
   d. Notice that land animals are not included in figure 11.15. Why do you think they are not included?
6. Estimate how much carbon is in the inactive, or geologic, carbon cycle by following Steps 6a–d.
   a. Geologists think that sediments and muds beneath the ocean have about 1.5×10^{22} g C. Show how you move decimals to express this number in Pg C.
   b. Geologists estimate that sediments on continents hold about 7.6×10^{22} g C. Express this as Pg C.
   c. How many Pg C from Steps 6a–b?
   d. How many times larger are estimates for carbon in all geologic sediments (Step 6c) compared with carbon in the active (biologic) carbon cycle?

Many of the estimates that you have made in the last 2 questions are sometimes called "back of the envelope" calculations. You can do them on a small piece of paper to make a quick approximation or comparison. But do these in your science notebook.

7. Use a reading strategy with your team for the following reading, *Carbon Taking Up Residence*. Do you remember from chapter 10 how flux was used for french fries and water? This is the same, but with carbon.

READING

Carbon Taking Up Residence

The word **flux** indicates the amount of matter that moves into, or out of, a reservoir in a given time. Reservoirs that interact and exchange matter are a **system**. In this chapter, the matter has been carbon. When there are several inputs (or outputs), all the inputs (or outputs) need to be added together for the reservoir.

For example, figure 11.16 shows fluxes of carbon (Pg C) per year between reservoirs of carbon on Earth. Four arrows point to the

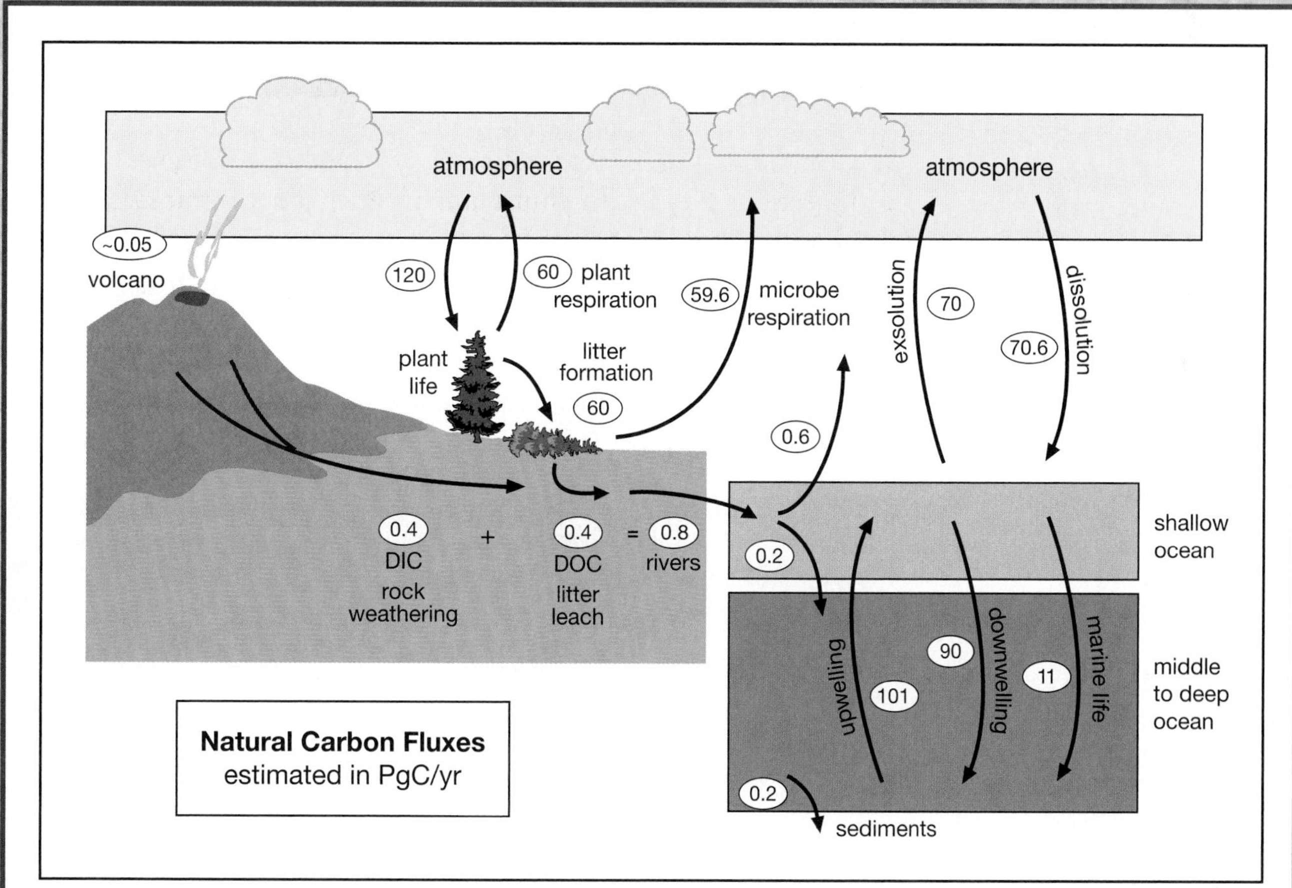

▲ **Figure 11.16 Natural carbon flux.** This diagram shows fluxes of natural carbon between major reservoirs of carbon in the geosphere. Units are petagrams of carbon (10^{15} g C) per year. Where are the largest fluxes of carbon?

Carbon Taking Up Residence, continued

atmosphere. Thus, the atmosphere receives carbon from respiration by vegetation (60.0), microbes in the soils (59.6), river carbon moving to the atmosphere (0.6), and CO_2 leaving the shallow ocean (70.0). The total flux to the atmosphere is about 190.2 Pg C per year (60 + 59.6 + 0.6 + 70 = 190.2 Pg C/yr). With humans, emissions of carbon from fossil fuels increase the flux to the atmosphere by about 5–6 Pg C/yr. This is about 2–3 percent of the total.

If a reservoir is accumulating carbon over time, it is a carbon **sink**. The reservoir has inputs of carbon greater than outputs. An example is seafloor sediments. Carbon accumulates there, making geologic sediments. On the other hand, if a reservoir of carbon is losing carbon over time to other reservoirs, it is a carbon **source**. The reservoir has outputs of carbon greater than inputs. Examples of carbon sources are volcanic eruptions and rock weathering. These provide new carbon for the active carbon cycle.

Residence time tells, on average, the amount of time that matter is in a reservoir. For carbon, short residence times mean that carbon cycles quickly to a neighboring reservoir. Long residence times indicate that carbon stays in the reservoir for much longer times. Only then does the carbon move to the next reservoir in a cycle. Here is a key point: residence time comes from dividing the mass in a reservoir by the total flux into (or total flux out of) the reservoir.

8. Copy figure 11.17 into your science notebook. Discuss Questions 8a–d with your team and explain your answers in your notebook.
   a. Consider using fossil fuels to make energy. Are fossil fuels a source or a sink of carbon to the ocean? Explain your evidence and reasons.
   b. Enter estimates for mass of carbon per reservoir in column 2 of figure 11.17. Refer to your work in Step 4 (figure 11.15).

Carbon reservoir	Mass of carbon (Pg C)	Individual carbon flux per year (Pg C/yr)	Total carbon flux per year (Pg C/yr)	Average residence time (yr)
Soils				
Marine life				
Shallow ocean				
Middle, deep ocean				
Atmosphere				
Vegetation				

Figure 11.17 Carbon mass, flux, and residence time. Copy this table into your science notebook. Use it to record fluxes for the 6 major carbon reservoirs on Earth. Estimate residence times of carbon in those systems.

c. Examine figure 11.17 with your team. Enter the total flux from inputs or outputs per reservoir into column 3 of your table.

Remember, if a reservoir has several inputs or outputs, they must be summed together for the total flux for that reservoir. Tally the individual fluxes listed in column 3 for the total in column 4.

d. Calculate residence time in years and enter the number in column 5.

9. Complete Questions 9a–c about residence times of carbon in different reservoirs on Earth.
   a. Where does carbon reside for the longest period of time? Explain whether this makes sense to your team, and why or why not.
   b. Where does carbon reside for the shortest period of time? Explain whether this makes sense to your team, and why or why not.
   c. How much longer or shorter are the residence times for carbon in soils compared with vegetation (forests)? Explain whether this makes sense to you.

Reflect and Connect

After creating a carbon cycle with your team, discuss and answer the following questions.

1. What is the residence time for a given dollar in a bank? Use the fictional Bank of the Lower 48, with total holdings of $10 billion. Transfer rates per business day average $7.5 million. How long on average does a dollar stay in the bank before moving out again into the economy?
2. See figure 11.16, which shows estimates for fluxes of natural carbon into and out of the atmosphere. Note that the units are petagrams of carbon per year (Pg C/yr).
   a. In your science notebook, make a T-table with values for inputs and outputs of carbon for the atmosphere.
   b. Show total fluxes for the atmosphere at the bottom of each column. How similar or different are these?
   c. Given these estimates, is the atmosphere gaining or losing carbon?
   d. Fossil fuels are adding carbon to the atmosphere at a rate of 5–6 Pg C/yr. What percentage of the total flux into or out of the atmosphere is this?
   e. Scientists estimate that the ocean and vegetation absorb about 1.5–2.0 Pg C/yr. What percentage of the 5–6 Pg C from humans is this?

◀ **Figure 11.18 Mount Everest.** This photograph shows Mount Everest and the buff-colored limestone band near the peak. Limestone consists of organisms such as clams. Clams remove carbon from the ocean to build shells of calcium carbonate ($CaCO_3$).

3. Imagine that you are an atom of carbon, Carl Carbon, in the elbow of 1 of your teammates. At a time in the past, you were in a clam in a limestone that was slowly dissolving and weathering near the top of Mount Everest (figure 11.18). The clam in the limestone formed 480 million years ago in a shallow ocean on the southern part of continental Asia.

   Develop with your team a sequence showing a possible history for Carl Carbon. Begin before the atom became part of the limestone and ended up in your teammate. For a carbon atom weathered from Mount Everest, what series of reactions and transport could move the atom to a human in the United States? Be prepared to share your ideas with the class. Use the x-axis to represent time; add labels to show the location or setting of the carbon above.

   You can check a map to see river basins and drainage patterns from Mount Everest.

EVALUATE

Carbon Quest

Indeed, carbon is on the move. You see this all around through processes like photosynthesis, the decay of vegetation in soils, or the use of fossil fuels. You have even worked with some other types of carbon reactions that in nature move carbon from one reservoir to another.

You have also seen how carbon is stored in reservoirs in limestone or coal layers. These range from carbon stored in the deepest, coldest oceans, to carbon stored atop Mount Everest, the highest mountain on Earth.

In *Carbon Quest*, you will complete a short assessment on key features of the carbon cycle. Then you will use the *Learn from Mistakes (LFM) Protocol* from Chapter 4, to analyze, discuss, and explain your answers. This gives you the chance to revise incorrect answers and improve your grade.

Materials

For each student

1 *Carbon Quest* handout

1 pencil

1 calculator

Process and Procedure

1. Review as a class the *LFM Protocol* (on page 155). To summarize, you will
   - take a short test on the carbon cycle,
   - participate in a discussion about questions that you or your classmates might have missed, and
   - write an explanation for why one of your wrong answers was not correct and what the correct answer would be.
2. Get from your teacher the handout *Carbon Quest*. Take about 15 min to complete the multiple-choice questions on the handout. All answers must be given on the attached answer sheet.
3. Turn in the answer sheet to your teacher.
4. Participate in a class discussion about questions where you or your classmates had incorrect answers. Note that your teacher will not necessarily give you the correct answer. By analyzing the wrong answers, however, you should be able to explain the reason why another answer is the correct one.

It is OK to ask questions during this session. You should also keep notes on questions you missed.

5. For each of the questions you missed on the test, do Steps 5a–e with a small group of 2–3 students. You can earn 50 percent of the original credit for each question you missed (that is, you can raise a score of 60 percent to a score of 80 percent).
   a. Write your raw score as a percentage in the upper right corner of your answer sheet.
   b. List under your score the number of the questions that you missed.
   c. Represent the original question in a different way than it was presented on the test. For example, if the question was mostly words, represent it now with a labeled sketch. Or try representing a sketch with words or phrases. Do not copy questions word for word.
   d. Work with a small group (no more than 3 students) to identify and explain the mistakes that you each made on

the test. Be sure to explain conceptual misunderstandings that you might have had. A correct answer with no clear explanation does not receive additional credit.

Explanations like "I read the problem wrong" or "I pushed the wrong button on the calculator" will receive no credit.

e. Show the correct answer or solution. As you can, provide any governing equations with symbolic form, followed by numeric values. Correct answers must include labels on sketches and units for values.

6. Listen to instructions from your teacher about when your corrected explanations are due. This may be at the end of the class period or at the beginning of the next class. For credit, you must include your original answer sheet with your explanations and sketches.

CHAPTER 12

Evidence for the Ice Ages

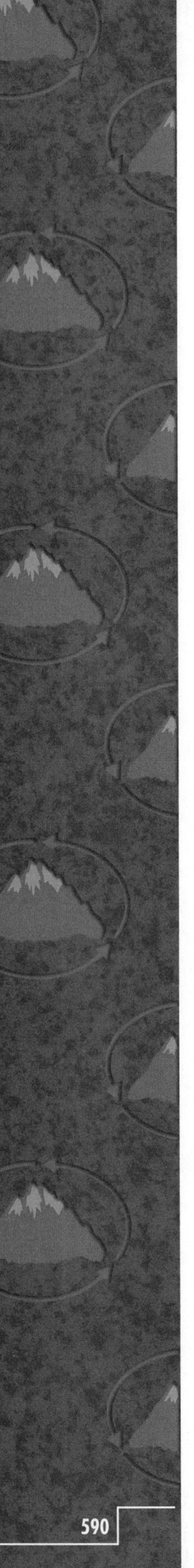

Evidence for the Ice Ages

Take a look out a window, or think about coming to school this morning. What is the weather like today in your town? Is it sunny or cloudy? Warm or cold? Your answer about the weather might be different than if a friend asked you to describe the climate in your town. What would you say? In describing climate, you might describe patterns you notice for seasons, such as fall, winter, spring, and summer.

But what if the friend asked you about the climate of your town in the past—the geologic past? What was the climate like 500,000 years ago? Was it generally warm? Cold? Could you tell by looking at the kinds of animals and plants living then? What might daily weather have looked like back then?

In unit 3, *Moving Matter*, you have been learning about Earth as one big geologic system. When you considered a single chemical moving between reservoirs such as the ocean or continents, you used the term geochemical cycles. Familiar examples are water and various forms of carbon. Perhaps you have heard of other geochemical cycles linked to nitrogen (N), calcium (Ca), or phosphorus (P). Looking at how chemicals are stored and moved among reservoirs helps you better understand earth systems.

As you have seen, many factors affect how rapidly chemicals move around Earth. With H_2O, for example, a key variable is temperature and movement of heat from the equator to the poles. Scientists study recent changes in climate by measuring patterns of temperature, humidity, and rainfall. They also look at the distribution and depth of snow and ice and changes in winds and currents. But these records only extend back to the late 1800s. How do scientists know about past climate changes on Earth—changes that occurred hundreds, thousands, or even millions of years ago? To learn about ancient climates, scientists need to gather other types of evidence. This research is a field called **paleoclimatology,** the study of ancient climates.

Goals for the Chapter

In chapter 12, *Evidence for the Ice Ages*, you will investigate evidence of past climates on Earth. You will revisit the water cycle and see how ancient patterns in the water cycle relate to past climates. One focus will be on Earth climates during the ice ages. You will also consider how this evidence relates to ancient ecosystems. When you finish this chapter, you should be able to answer questions like these:

- What is the evidence that Earth's climate has changed between periods of overall cold climate (glacials) and overall warm climate (interglacials)?
- What causes patterns of ice ages on Earth?
- What kind of geologic evidence is used to learn about ancient ecosystems?
- How are water and carbon part of the record of Earth's past climate patterns?
- Is there any evidence for ice ages in tropical, equatorial oceans?

You will be better able to answer these questions by participating in the following activities:

ENGAGE	How Did They Get There?
EXPLORE	Ice Blocks: Growing, Shrinking
EXPLORE / EXPLAIN	The Core of the Matter
ELABORATE	The Astronomical Theory
EVALUATE	More Than Forams

A chapter organizer will help you with your learning. Check the organizer at the start of class each day. It will help you see where you are in the flow of the chapter. The chapter organizer will also help you see where you are headed in your study of earth systems.

Evidence for the Ice Ages

Linking Question

Does an Ice Age affect the water cycle or sea level?

Engage

How Did They Get There?

Key Idea:

Discoveries in geology lead to new explanations about Earth's climate.

Explore

Ice Blocks: Growing, Shrinking Part I — Miniglaciers

Key Idea:

Ice melts at a rate that depends on the amount of heat.

Ice Blocks: Growing, Shrinking Part II — Glaciers Melting

Key Idea:

Changes in solar radiation play a key role in Earth's climate patterns.

Ice Blocks: Growing, Shrinking Part III — Glacier Melting Rates

Key Idea:

Sea level changes as glaciers and ice sheets grow during glacials, and melt during interglacials.

Linking Question

Do ocean sediments record evidence of Ice Ages?

Explore Explain

The Core of the Matter Part I — Heavy Water, Light Water

Key Idea:

Water molecules with the heavy isotope of oxygen ($H_2{}^{18}O$) behave slightly differently than "lighter" water ($H_2{}^{16}O$) in the water cycle.

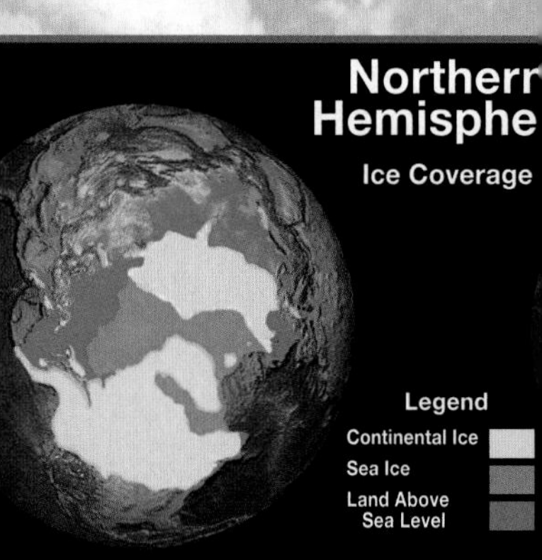

EVALUATE

More Than Forams

Key Idea:
Geologic evidence from pollen and dust is another way to test models for the cause of the Ice Ages.

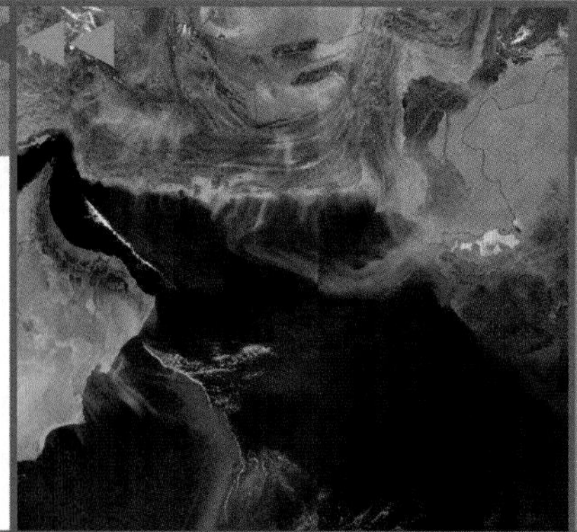

Linking Question

What other kinds of geologic data are used to understand climate cycles on Earth?

ELABORATE

The Astronomical Theory

Key Idea:
The solar radiation reaching Earth varies in a regular way due to changes in the shape of Earth's orbital path around the Sun.

Linking Question

What caused the Ice Ages?

CHAPTER 12 Major Concepts

- **Earth's climate changes between overall cold (glacials) and warm (interglacials) cycles; patterns of oxygen isotopes in foram shells ($CaCO_3$) from the seafloor are one way to study these climate cycles.**
- **Climate is the average weather pattern over many years. Weather is the atmospheric condition at a given time.**
- **Many technologies are used to measure cycles of climate change on Earth.**
- **Geologic evidence (forams, dust, pollen, CO_2), are used to test models for the cause of the Ice Ages.**

EXPLORE EXPLAIN

The Core of the Matter
Part II — The Oxygen Connection

Key Idea:
Foram shells in ocean sediments record a "fingerprint" of oxygen isotopes in seawater.

EXPLORE EXPLAIN

The Core of the Matter
Part III — Analyzing Foram Data

Key Idea:
Oxygen isotope records from foram shells reveal past cycles of glacial and interglacial periods.

ENGAGE

How Did They Get There?

A key part of science is observing. Simple observations often lead to puzzling questions for scientists. In *How Did They Get There?*, you will work in a team of three to read about some strange discoveries. Then your team will propose an explanation for each discovery.

Materials

For each team of 3 students

1 *Mysterious Headlines* handout

Process and Procedure

Sometimes newspaper headlines are difficult to believe. The headlines in this investigation might seem unreal, but they are based on actual discoveries and observations. How can you explain these strange occurrences?

1. Look carefully at figure 12.1. Have you ever seen a creature like this?
   a. Read the newspaper passage in the figure and discuss it with your group.
   b. What might have caused this strange event? Come up with a list of 2–3 possible explanations. Record these in your science notebook.

▼ **Figure 12.1**
Mammoth headlines. This front-page article describes the find of a woolly mammoth.

Mammoth Tooth Discovered by Fisherman

A fossil tooth of a woolly mammoth was recently discovered by a fisherman. He found it while fishing along the Atlantic Coast near New Jersey. Scientists used radiocarbon (C-14) dating to measure its age at about 20,000 years old. Other woolly mammoth fossils have been found in the midwestern United States, Europe, and Siberia. Scientists are now searching the area for *continued on A12*

Artist's rendering of a woolly mammoth.

c. Decide as a team which explanation seems most reasonable and place a check by it.

2. Obtain the *Mysterious Headlines* handout from your teacher with *Headline A*. Repeat Step 1 for this handout.
3. After finishing *Headline A*, repeat Step 1 for the handouts with *Headline B* and then *Headline C*.
4. You might be surprised to learn that the same process caused all of the strange occurrences you read about. What was that process? Discuss your ideas with your team and record them in your science notebook. Be prepared to share your ideas.
5. Participate in a class discussion about the cause of these strange occurrences. Share what you already know about this process and the questions you have about it.

Reflect and Connect

Answer the following questions individually in your science notebook.

1. Identify 2 things you already know about the process that caused the strange occurrences in the headlines. Then identify 2 questions you still have about the process.
2. How do you think it is possible that the same process affected such different regions of Earth (Swiss Alps, New York, Illinois, Wisconsin, and Ireland)?
3. What do scientists do when they find evidence that does not make sense or does not fit their current understanding?
4. You considered elephant evolution in chapter 6, *Exploring Change*. Where were mammoths in the line of descent?

Ice Blocks: Growing, Shrinking

EXPLORE

In the engage activity, *How Did They Get There?*, you investigated strange occurrences linked by a common explanation—an ice age. You might recognize an ice age as a time when large parts of Earth had thick ice and a cold climate. What might cause an ice age? Why is there less ice now? How much ice counts as an ice age?

In *Ice Blocks: Growing, Shrinking*, you will explore questions like these and learn more about Earth's climate. You will also look at how an ice age affects the water cycle. You will work alone and in a team of three students in this investigation.

Part I: Miniglaciers

Materials

For each team of 3 students

1 25-mL graduated cylinder

access to an electronic balance

1 small, resealable bag containing an ice cube

1 calculator (optional)

Process and Procedure

In the engage activity, discoveries in headlines suggested large amounts of ice on Earth. You related these discoveries to evidence for ice ages. At present, those areas do not have a lot of ice. This suggests that we are not experiencing an ice age.

But why does the climate of Earth enter or exit an ice age? To begin to answer this question, we will first explore ice on a small scale.

1. Your team will get an ice cube in a resealable bag. Your challenge will be to melt as much of the ice cube as possible in 2 minutes (min). Decide on a strategy for your team. How can you melt the ice faster than other teams?

   There are some rules you must follow:

   - You cannot win unless you calculate accurately the percentage of change in volume.
   - You may not remove the ice cube from the bag.
   - You may not have access to any materials other than those on the materials list.
2. Obtain the ice cube from your teacher.
   a. Quickly measure the mass of your ice cube.
   b. Decide with your team how to convert the mass of ice (grams, or g) to volume of ice (cubic centimeters, or cm^3).
   c. Carefully show these steps in your science notebook.
3. Begin the melting process when your teacher tells you to start.
4. After your 2 min are up, measure how much of the ice cube you melted by pouring the water into a 25-mL graduated cylinder.
5. In order to win, you must make the calculations in Steps 5a–b.
   a. Calculate the melting rate of your ice cube. What volume melted in 2 min?

Recall that a rate tells how fast something changes per amount of time.

   b. Determine the percentage of change in your ice cube during melting. Write the steps in your science notebook.

6. Which team melted the most of its ice cube? How did the team do it? As a class, discuss the various methods that teams used. What made some methods more successful than others? Did teams document their melting rate and percentage of change properly?
7. Imagine a slightly different melting race with ice cubes. The setup is shown in figure 12.2. Which ice cube do you think will melt faster: the one in front of heat lamp A or the one in front of heat lamp B? Write your reasons in your science notebook.

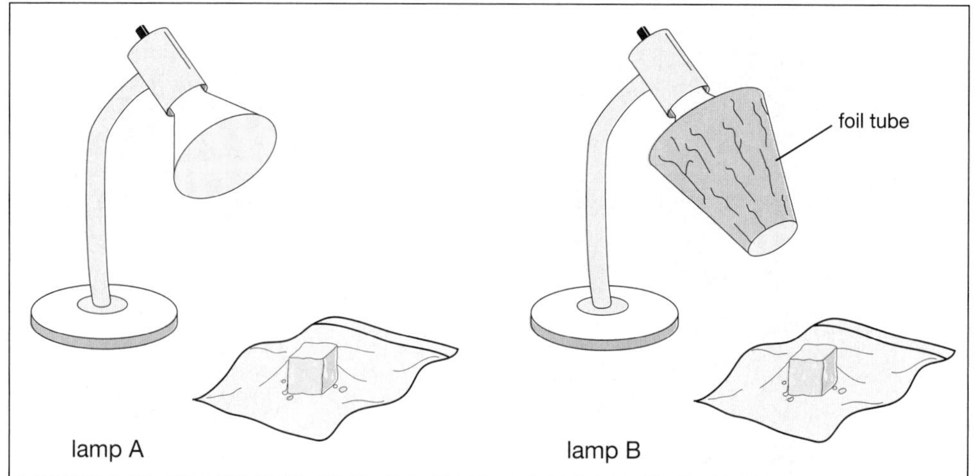

Figure 12.2 Two lamps, one with foil. Which ice cube will melt faster? Both heat lamps are 20 centimeters (cm) from the ice cube. Lamp B has been wrapped in foil to direct the light.

8. Look at figure 12.2 again. Discuss with your team how you would design an experiment to measure the relative difference in heat between lamps A and B.
9. A team of students used the setup in figure 12.2 to heat 2 ice cubes for 5 min. The data from their science notebooks are in figure 12.3. Copy their data into your science notebook and complete the cells that are empty.

	Heat Lamp A	Heat Lamp B
Initial volume of ice cube	28 cm^3	30 cm^3
Volume of water melted	4 cm^3	6 cm^3
Melting rate (cm^3/min)		
Percent of cube melted		

Figure 12.3 Ice melting table. Copy this table of experiment results into your science notebook. Fill in the cells without answers.

Stop & THINK

PART I

Discuss the following questions with your team. Record your answers in your science notebook.

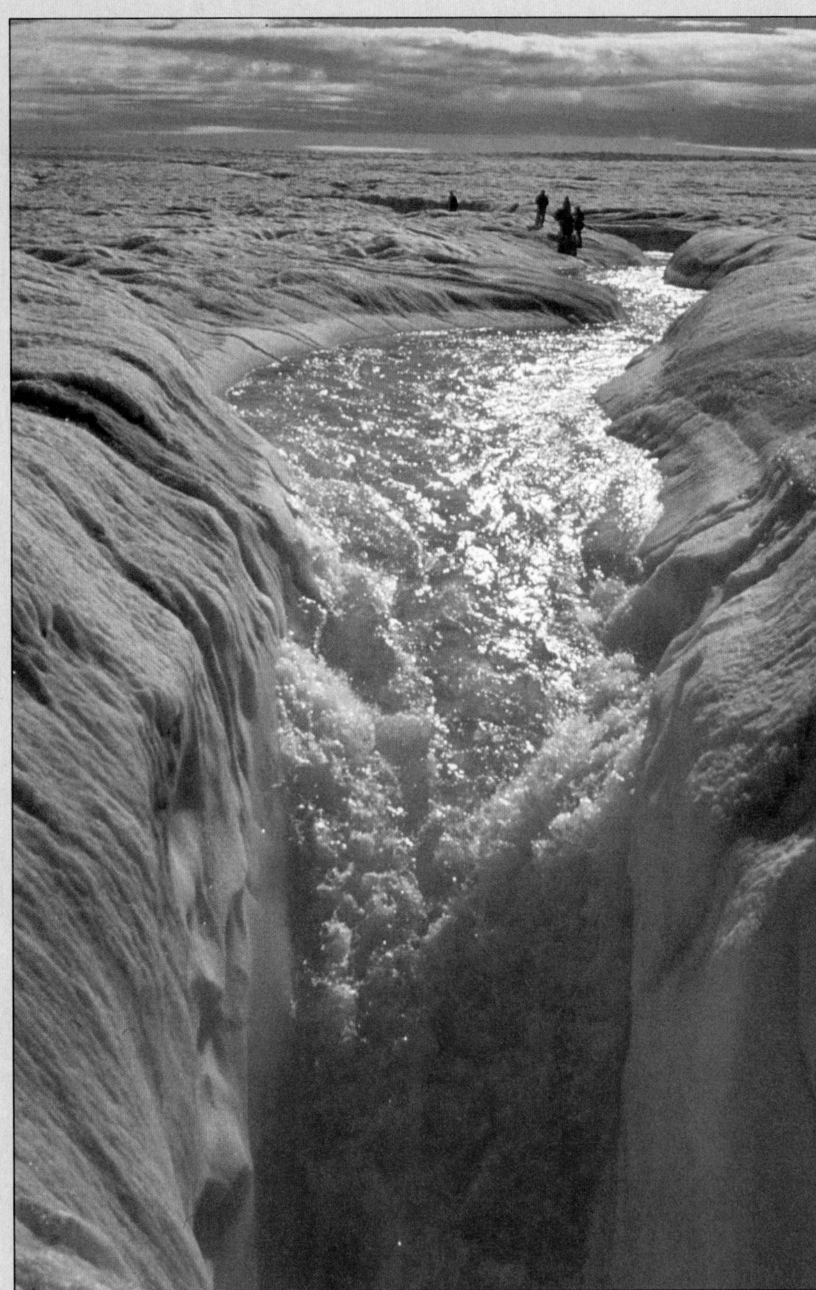

Figure 12.4 Streaming meltwater. This photo shows meltwater streaming off the top of the Greenland ice sheet. (The humans show scale.) What part of the water cycle does this represent?

1 Recall the strategy you used to melt the ice in Step 3. What other strategies might you have used if you had access to other materials or equipment?

2 Predict how long it would take to melt an entire ice cube using the same strategy your team used in Step 3. Use examples of data in your answer.

3 How does the small-scale melting of an ice cube relate to the larger-scale melting of glaciers on Earth? What is similar and what is different?

4 Examine figure 12.4. It shows meltwater flowing off the top of the Greenland continental ice sheet. Think back to your work with the water cycle. Where do you think this water is going? What part of the water cycle is this? Draw a diagram or sketch to show your ideas.

Part II: Glaciers Melting

Materials

none

Process and Procedure

In Part I, you explored how fast an ice cube melts. You also noted that it takes energy to melt an ice cube. In the *Stop and Think* questions, you began to examine how your experience with ice cubes relates to glaciers. But what does it really take for a glacier to melt? Work with your team to think more about that question in Part II.

1. Why do most glaciers tend to be located near the poles? Record the best thinking of your team for this question in your science notebook.

It is useful for you and your team to diagram ideas about glaciers in your science notebooks. If you draw a map, ask yourselves, "Where do glaciers occur on Earth?"

2. You know it takes energy to melt an ice cube. It also takes energy to melt the ice of glaciers. Where does the energy come from? Read the following paragraphs to learn more about that energy.

   The source of energy coming to Earth's surface is the Sun. That energy arrives here as **solar radiation.** Most of the solar radiation coming to Earth is in the form of visible light. You studied this in Level 1 of *BSCS Science: An Inquiry Approach.* Overall, the solar radiation that Earth receives is relatively constant. However, different parts of Earth have different

intensities of solar radiation. It all depends on which parts of Earth are most directly "facing" the Sun.

In Part I of this activity, you noticed a difference in how the ice cubes melted between the more and less concentrated outputs from two lamps. Solar radiation coming to Earth varies in a similar way. At low latitudes near the equator, solar radiation affects Earth most directly. At higher latitudes, the intensity of radiation decreases due to the curvature of Earth. This is because the same amount of radiation must be spread over a larger surface area. At the North and South poles, solar radiation has the lowest intensities because the Sun's rays are at such a low angle to Earth's surface. This is shown in figure 12.5.

Still, the poles get solar radiation during their "summers" due to the tilt of Earth's axis of rotation. **Tilt** is the angle between the Earth's rotation axis and incoming solar radiation. The tilt of Earth's rotation axis is toward the Sun (with north facing up) in figure 12.5. Central and North America receive direct radiation from the Sun. Solar radiation falls upon the North Pole, but not the South Pole. This is when it is summer for continents in the Northern Hemisphere (North America, Europe, Asia). The Southern Hemisphere receives less solar radiation at this time. This is their winter (Australia, South America). You probably know that tilt and radiation tell the seasons. You will learn more about variations in solar radiation in the elaborate activity, *The Astronomical Theory*, later in this chapter.

3. Figure 12.5 shows solar radiation striking Earth during summer for the Northern Hemisphere. Draw in your science notebook a diagram showing solar radiation during winter for the Northern Hemisphere.

Figure 12.5 Solar radiation and Earth. The amount of solar radiation varies with the curvature of Earth and the tilt of the rotation axis. What season is shown for the South Pole?

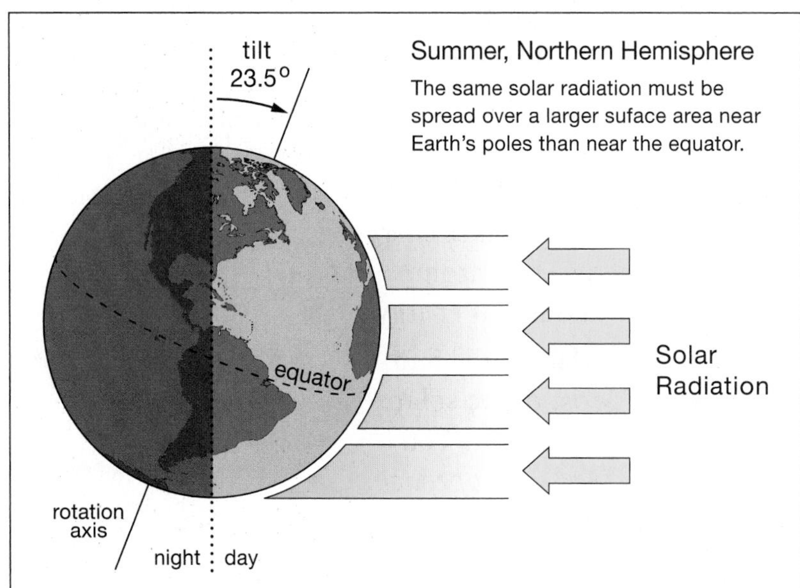
tilt
23.5°
Summer, Northern Hemisphere
The same solar radiation must be spread over a larger suface area near Earth's poles than near the equator.
equator
Solar
Radiation
rotation
axis
night
day

4. Summer and winter are the extremes in climate for North America. Draw in your science notebook a diagram of Earth orbiting the Sun. For a tilt of 23.5 degrees (°), show 4 positions for fall, winter, spring, and summer for the Northern Hemisphere.
5. The seasonal changes in solar radiation described in Step 2 take place in annual cycles. These changes in radiation affect Earth's climate.

Climate versus Weather

"How's the weather?" "What is the weather like where you live?" All you would have to do to answer these questions is to walk outside. Is it hot or cold, wet or dry, sunny or cloudy, windy or calm? **Weather** includes the conditions we experience in relatively short periods of time, like hours or days. Weather can be the passing of an afternoon thunderstorm, a cold front, or a persistent heat wave. Weather is a snapshot of the atmosphere at a particular time and place.

Climate is different from weather. **Climate** is the average weather in a region over longer periods of time—a year, a decade, a century, or even longer. Descriptions of climates often include average weather conditions (usually averaged over 30 years) as well as statistics of weather extremes. The daily weather report often includes average temperature highs and lows and precipitation rates. These data reflect local climate. The term climate can also be used to describe regions. A region that has consistently high temperatures and rainfall can be described as having a hot, wet, or tropical climate.

Climate refers to the general weather conditions over a long period of time. For instance, in Colorado, the summers tend to be warm and the winters tend to be cold. This is very different from areas around the equator, where temperatures are warm all year.

Topic: climate
Go to: www.scilinks.org
Code: 2Inquiry601

a. Read *FYI—Climate versus Weather.*

b. How would you describe the climate where you live?

Do not confuse climate with weather. If you are not sure what the difference is, refer to *FYI—Climate versus Weather.*

c. The strange discoveries you read about in the engage activity are evidence of the most recent ice age. What do you think Earth's climate was like during the last ice age?

6. Read the following paragraphs to learn more about ice ages and their link to climate. Check your understanding with your team.

The overall climate on Earth is cold during an ice age. The climate is so much colder that glaciers can cover much of the continents. These massive continental glaciers are called **ice sheets**. These blankets of ice can be several kilometers (km) thick. Ice ages have occurred many times in the past. In fact, in recent geologic history, Earth has switched back and forth between warm and cold periods. The cold periods are referred to as ice ages, or **glacials**. Periods of warm overall climate, such as now, are called **interglacials**.

The most recent glacial period is called the **Last Glacial Maximum** (LGM). This peak was at 21,000 years ago (21 kya).

To save time and space, you can abbreviate thousands of years ago as "kya."

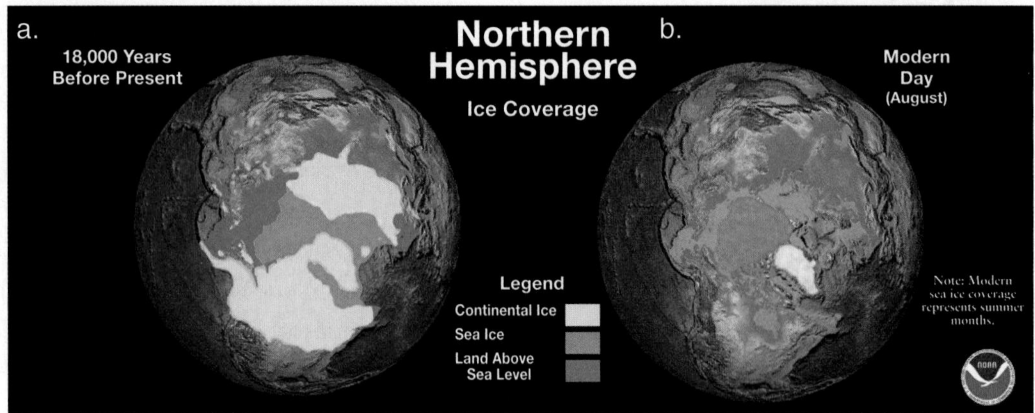

Figure 12.6 Earth today versus Earth during the Last Glacial Maximum (LGM). (a) During the LGM, about 6 percent of the world's water was stored in the global ice reservoir. Glaciers covered as much as 30 percent of Earth's land area. (b) Today, only about 3 percent of Earth's water is trapped in the form of ice, covering about 10 percent of Earth's land area.

As shown in figure 12.6a, glaciers covered a large portion of Europe and the North American continent during this period. We are currently experiencing an interglacial period on Earth. This is shown in figure 12.6b. During an interglacial, the climate is warmer overall and ice sheets are restricted to polar regions.

7. Use your understanding of the global water system to discuss Questions 7a–c with your team. Write your answers in your science notebook.
   a. How does the volume of water in different global reservoirs change from glacial periods to interglacial periods? Explain your reasoning.
   b. How do you think sea level has varied from the LGM (21 kya) to today?
   c. Copy the graph in figure 12.7 into your science notebook. Draw a line in your sketch to show the relationship you would predict.

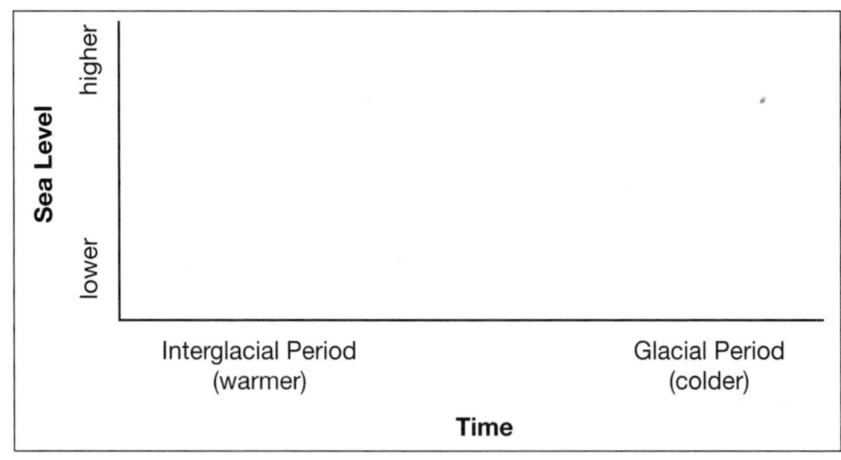

Figure 12.7 Sea level graph. These axes show sea level as a function of whether Earth was in a glacial or interglacial period. What will your line look like on this graph?

Stop & THINK

PART II

Answer the following questions individually in your science notebook.

1. Do you understand the difference between the terms *climate* and *weather*? Show this by filling in each blank in the following sentences.
   a. Some meteorologists say that "__________ is what you expect but __________ is what you get."
   b. According to one student, "__________ tells you what clothes to buy, but __________ tells you what clothes to wear."
   c. Have you heard of tree rings? Do you think that a series of tree rings tells you about weather or climate? Use a sketch with labels to explain your answer.
2. Describe the conditions that would be necessary for glaciers to melt or to advance.
3. Which do you think would be more likely to cause a glacial period—colder winters or colder summers? Why?
4. Imagine that the rotation axis for Earth had zero tilt. What would this imply for the climate during the year in your community?

   It is best to use sketches to help understand the question and to show your answer.

Part III: Glacier Melting Rates

Materials

For each team of 3 students

1 calculator (optional)

Process and Procedure

In Part I, you melted an ice cube and calculated its melting rate. In Part II, you began to think about how really large chunks of ice—glaciers and ice sheets—can melt. You also looked at some of the factors that increased melting and the advance of glaciers.

In this part, you will investigate the melting rate for glaciers and ice sheets since the most recent ice age. This is the LGM. Work in your team to complete this part of the investigation.

1. The LGM ended around 21 kya. Since then, large amounts of ice have melted, reducing the size of glaciers on Earth. Discuss the following questions with your team and record ideas in your science notebook.
   a. How fast do you think the ice melted?
   b. How do you think scientists figure out how fast the ice melted?
2. Geologists cannot measure directly how much ice was on Earth during the LGM. Instead, they rely on the water cycle to relate changes in sea level to the melting of ice. Read the following paragraphs to learn more about how sea level links to the amount of ice on Earth.

   Water from the sea travels through the atmosphere and falls as precipitation on the continents. Some of the precipitation is winter snow. If all of that winter snow does not melt in the next summer, the snow will accumulate. Year after year of compacted, piled snow develops into glaciers and ice sheets. This frozen water remains on continents; it cannot return to the ocean. Thus, sea level goes down. A lot of ice must accumulate for a small drop in sea level. Scientists estimate that it takes about 350,000–400,000 cubic kilometers (km^3) of ice for a 1-meter (m) drop in sea level. Of course, there are a number of variables for this estimate. But a value in this range is a good starting point.

   How do scientists measure past changes in sea level? One method is to study coral reefs. The flat tops for some coral species correspond to sea level at low tide when the coral was living. Some types of coral grow at very specific depths in the ocean (figure 12.8). Scientists search for dead corals and measure their height above or below the current sea level. Then they date the corals using radiometric age dating. You learned about age dating in chapter 6. These data tell how long it has been since the sea level was at a given height. Figure 12.9 shows the changes in sea level in meters since the last ice age at about 21 kya.

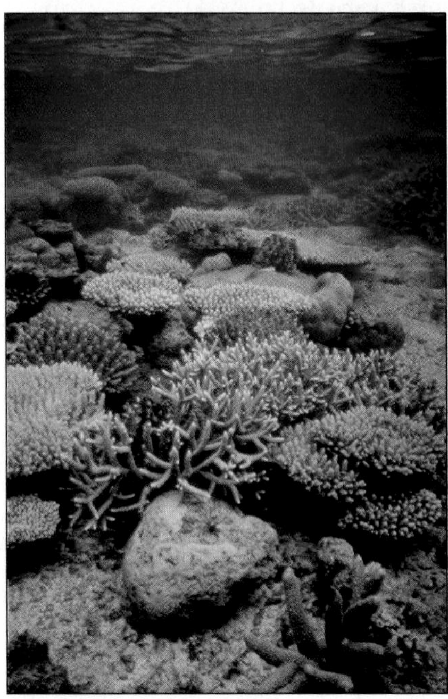

▲ **Figure 12.8 Reef ecosystem near sea level.** Some species of coral in reefs grow at specific depths. These coral are about 1–2 m beneath the surface of the ocean.

3. Use Step 2 and figure 12.9 to answer Questions 3a–d about sea level change.
   a. When was the rate of melting the fastest?
   b. When did the glaciers effectively stop melting?
   c. Write a single statement that summarizes the main point of figure 12.9.
   d. Figure 12.10 shows a map of Earth at the LGM. How does this map differ from a current map of Earth?

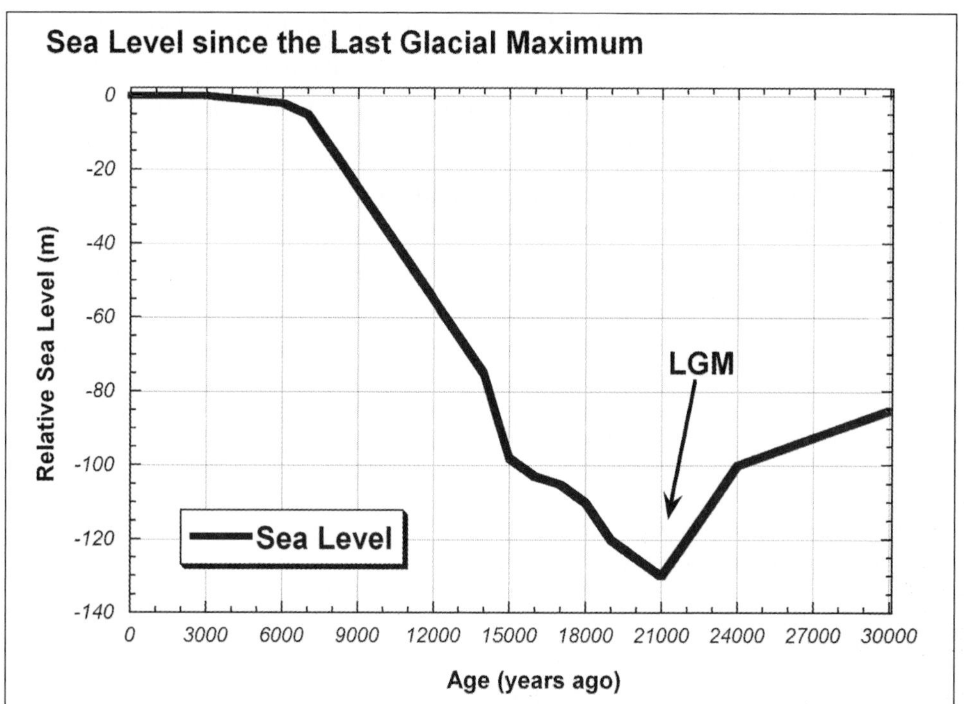

Source: Quinn, T. M. (2000). Shallow water science and ocean drilling face challenges. *Eos, Transactions of the American Geophysical Union, 81*, 397-404. and Cutler, et al. (2003). Rapid sea-level fall and deep-ocean temperature change since the last interglacial period. Earth and Planetary Science Letters, 206, 253–271.

▲ **Figure 12.9 Sea level from the LGM to today.** Negative numbers indicate lower sea levels in the past relative to today. Today, sea level is at 0 m.

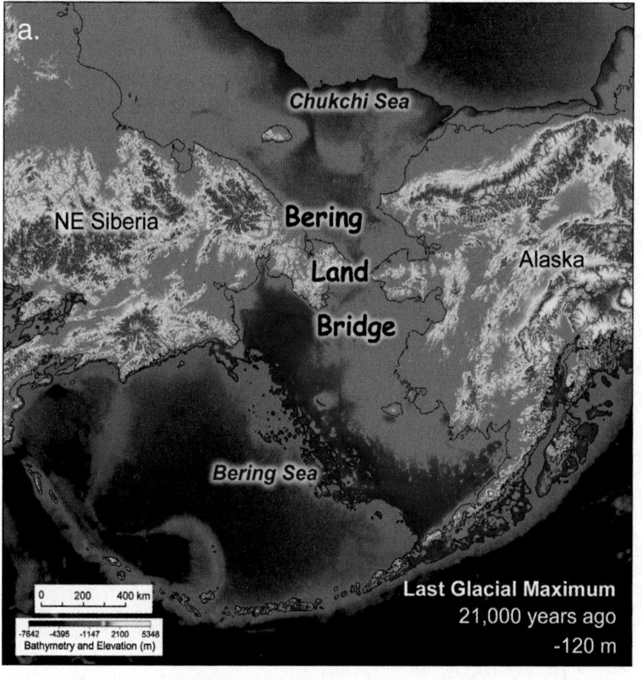

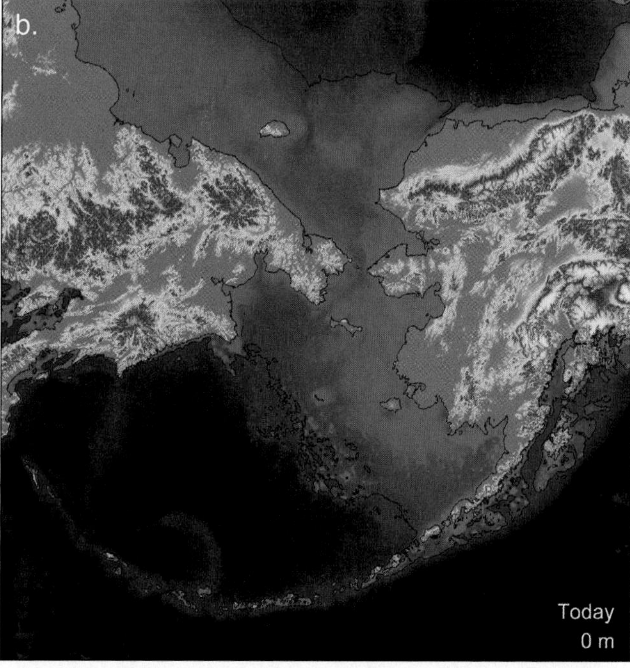

▲ **Figure 12.10 Two maps: Bering Land Bridge at the LGM, and today.** The first map shows the Bering Land Bridge during the LGM about 21 kya. Sea level is about 120 m lower than the current sea level, shown in the second map (today). The map in figure 12.6 shows the locations of continental ice sheets in northeast Siberia and Alaska during the LGM.

4. Use Step 2 and figure 12.9 to estimate the melting rate of glaciers and ice sheets since the LGM. Follow the method in Steps 4a–c to estimate the volume melted per time, just as you did with the ice cube.
   a. Select 2 points on the curve in figure 12.9 between 6 kya and the LGM.
   b. Write in your science notebook the change in sea level for those 2 points.
   c. Use this change in height of sea level to estimate the volume of water added to the ocean by melting glaciers. Show your answer (and all your work) in units of km^3.

$$\text{Volume} = \text{area} \times \text{height}$$

The surface area of the ocean is about 362 million square kilometers (km^2). Can you show this numerically?

   d. Return to the 2 points in Step 4a with figure 12.9. Write the amount of time between the points.
   e. Calculate the melting rate for the 2 points on figure 12.9. Check that you have units of cubic kilometers per year (km^3/yr).

Recall that a rate tells a change in something, such as sea level, per unit time. The melting rate is the slope ($\Delta y/\Delta x$, or rise over run) of the sea level curve.

5. How does the melting rate for glaciers in Step 4 compare with the melting rate for ice cubes? Read the following information and do the steps to make the comparison.

   In Part I, you measured the melting rate of an ice cube in cubic centimeters per minute (cm^3/min). Then you estimated the melting rate of glaciers in units of km^3/yr. To compare these two rates, you will need to use the same units. Which unit should you use? Because an ice cube melts in a few minutes, it would not make sense to use years as the time factor. So it is easiest to convert the melting rates of glaciers to cm^3/min.

   a. Take your answer from Step 4a in units of km^3/yr and first convert it to cubic kilometers per minute (km^3/min). You need to fill in the "?" in the following conversion for this first step.

$$\left(\frac{?\ \text{km}^3}{1\ \text{yr}}\right) \times \left(\frac{1\ \text{yr}}{?\ \text{days}}\right) \times \left(\frac{1\ \text{day}}{?\ \text{hr}}\right) \times \left(\frac{1\ \text{hr}}{?\ \text{min}}\right) = ?\ \frac{\text{km}^3}{\text{min}}$$

Be sure to draw a slash through units that cancel.

b. Convert your answer from Step 5a from units of km^3/min to cm^3/min. Use the conversion that 1 km^3 equals 10^{15} cm^3.

If you cannot cleanly cancel units on the top and bottom here, then the conversion may not be set up properly.

c. Now you should have 2 melting rates, both in units of cm^3/min. One melting rate is for your ice cube, and the other is for glaciers and ice sheets after the LGM. How do the rates compare? Are they what you expected? What might explain the difference in melting rates? Explain with complete sentences in your science notebook.

6. Read the following paragraphs to learn about **proxy data**.

Paleoclimatology is the study of past climates. Records of past climates from satellites and other human measurements (thermometers, rain gauges) only go back about 100–150 years. This range of time is too small to record the full variation in climates. For example, you have been considering glacial and climate change occurring over thousands of years.

To learn about ancient climates, paleoclimatologists cannot rely on direct measurements. Instead, they rely on indirect measurements, or proxy data, to infer the history of past climates. A **proxy** is something that stands in for something else. It is an indirect measure.

You are probably familiar with one type of proxy data: tree rings. Look at the section of a tree trunk in figure 12.11. The cross section shows the number of rings and their thickness.

Figure 12.11 Tree rings. Tree rings give proxy data on the growth history of a tree. Those data often include information about patterns of climate.

The total number of rings tells the age of the tree. The thickness of the rings gives information about moisture and temperature conditions during a given year. Thicker rings often mean high rainfall. Thinner rings also can tell of past drought. Scientists do not have to cut a tree down to study its rings. They can simply remove a horizontal core from the tree. They can then analyze the cores for the number and thickness of rings. This gives proxy data about past climates. Some of these climate records extend up to 8,000 years.

7. Answer Questions 7a–c to show your understanding of proxy data.
   a. Explain why sea level data are considered proxy data.
   b. Describe another type of proxy data used to gather information about past climates.
   c. Why do scientists need different kinds of data to test the idea that Earth has had ice ages in the past?

Reflect and Connect

Work in your team to answer the following questions. Record your answers in your science notebook.

1. What are some characteristics of glacial and of interglacial periods on Earth? Think in terms of sea level, climate, or animals.
2. Compare the water cycle during glacial periods with the water cycle during interglacial periods. Address both the storage of water in global reservoirs and the movement of water between global reservoirs.

It may be most useful to use a diagram or sketch here with a written explanation.

3. What factors influence the advance and retreat of glaciers?
4. What do you think would happen to the climate of the Northern Hemisphere if Earth tilted 50° instead of the current 23.5°? Illustrate your answer with a simple sketch. Explain the effect on seasons and climates in your community.
5. How does your past experience with ice and ice cubes help you understand glaciers and ice ages?

The Core of the Matter

EXPLORE
EXPLAIN

In the engage activity, you analyzed evidence for past ice ages. In the explore activity, *Ice Blocks: Growing, Shrinking*, you learned about ice in the form of glaciers. You explored why and how fast these huge reservoirs of ice melt. You also learned about the link between these global ice reservoirs and sea level.

But how exactly would the ocean tell you about an ice age? How do oceans at the equator reflect the formation of ice sheets at the North and South poles? In *The Core of the Matter*, you will work alone and in teams to make the connection between the ocean and another key piece of evidence of past ice ages.

Part I: Heavy Water, Light Water

Materials

For each team of 6 students

1 shallow plastic box

10 light objects (white Styrofoam balls)

10 heavy objects (black Styrofoam balls)

1 large sheet (plastic drop cloth, bedsheet, or blanket)

1 stopwatch

1 calculator

Process and Procedure

In the explore activity, you looked at some characteristics of ice ages. You explored the melting of ice to form water and related this to changes in sea level. In particular, you used the water cycle to explore how water moved from one reservoir to another during glacial and interglacial periods. As you saw in chapter 10, *The Water System*, the water cycle is one example of a geochemical cycle. (Remember, a geochemical cycle describes the storage and movement of a particular element in the earth system.) In Part I of this investigation, you will take a closer look at the water cycle.

1. Ice melting and changing the sea level is one way water moves from reservoir to reservoir in the earth system. How does water move out of the ocean reservoir? Observe your teacher's demonstration of the most common process. Write the name of this process in your science notebook.
2. What would happen in a model if some balls that represent water molecules were heavier than other balls that represent water molecules? Work in a team of 6 students to explore this model.

a. Read the steps described in figure 12.12 for the What's Shaking? model. Ask for clarification if you do not understand what you will be doing.
b. Based on what you think might happen, develop a table with your team to record your data. Your table needs to include a column expressing the number of heavy objects to light objects as a ratio.
c. Have 1 person from the team pick up the materials from your teacher. Work together to follow the protocol.
d. Analyze your data by calculating the initial and final ratios of heavy to light objects in the box. Be prepared to share these data with your class.

3. Share your results with your class.
4. This model represents water evaporation from the ocean. As a class, discuss what conclusions you could draw about water evaporation based on this model. Record your answers to Questions 4a–e in your science notebook.

▲ **Figure 12.12 What's Shaking? model.** Use these steps to model water evaporation. What is the difference between the heavy and light water?

(1) Place 10 heavy and 10 light objects in a shallow plastic box. These objects should be the same shape and size.
(2) Open a sheet and place it below the plastic box. Have 4 students hold 1 corner of the sheet.
(3) Have 1 student firmly rap the side of the plastic box with his hand for 15 seconds (sec). Some objects should come out of the box and fall onto the large sheet.
(4) Count and record the number of heavy and light objects remaining in the box.
(5) Return all of the objects to the box. Mix up the objects so that the different types are spread evenly throughout.
(6) Repeat Steps 3–5 twice.

a. In this water evaporation model, what does the plastic box represent?
b. What do you think the heavy objects represent? The light objects?
c. What does the tapping represent?
d. In this model, which water molecules (heavy or light) are more likely to evaporate? Why?
e. What happens to the water that evaporates? Where does it end up?

5. What will happen to the ratio of heavy to light water molecules in the ocean during a glacial period? How would you modify the model from Step 2 and gather additional data? Be prepared to share your answer to this question with your class.

Recall that a major difference between glacial and interglacial periods is where water is stored. During a glacial period, more water is stored in ice sheets on continents. This reduces the runoff to the ocean significantly. How could you alter your model to reflect this change?

6. By now you might be wondering what all this talk is about heavy and light water. Isn't all water the same? Read with your team *Water: Is It All the Same?*
7. To get an idea of the relative amounts of oxygen's isotopes, imagine that you have 10,000 oxygen atoms in a container. Work with your team to answer Questions 7a–e.
   a. From the reading, make a T-table showing the 3 oxygen isotopes and their abundance.
   b. How many of these atoms would be ^{16}O atoms? How many would be ^{17}O atoms? How many would be ^{18}O atoms? Show your work.
   c. Which of the 3 oxygen isotopes is the heaviest? The lightest?
   d. Which of the 2 water molecules in figure 12.13 is the heaviest? The lightest? Give the masses.
   e. Given this information, how does the ratio of heavy to light objects in the model from Step 2 compare with the actual ratio of isotopes of heavy to light oxygen atoms found in nature? Explain your answer and clearly use measurements as evidence.
8. Participate in a class discussion of how the model you used relates to what happens with water during glacial and interglacial periods.

Stop & THINK

PART I

Complete the following task individually in your science notebook.

1 Write a short summary of what you learned from your experiences with the What's Shaking? model. Your summary should
- explain how the model relates to water evaporating from the ocean during glacial and interglacial periods,
- explain what happens to the ratio of heavy to light water in the ocean during glacial and interglacial periods,
- include a diagram or sketch showing the relationship to the water cycle, and
- use evidence from your investigation to support points in your summary.

READING

Water: Is It All the Same?

A water molecule consists of two hydrogen atoms and one oxygen atom. It does not matter where the water comes from; if it has two hydrogen atoms and one oxygen atom, it is H_2O. In this sense, all water molecules are the same. However, there are natural variations within each of the atoms that make up water. Look closely at the two water molecules in figure 12.13. What makes each molecule different?

Look more closely at the molecules in figure 12.13. Note that each contains two hydrogen atoms and one oxygen atom. Each hydrogen atom has one proton and one electron. Both oxygen atoms also have the same number of protons and electrons, but they each have a different number of neutrons. One oxygen atom has eight neutrons and the other has 10 neutrons. The two atoms are **isotopes** of oxygen. You might recall that isotopes are atoms of the same element that have different numbers of neutrons.

Both hydrogen and oxygen have naturally occurring isotopes. For the purpose of this investigation, we will look just at isotopes of oxygen. Oxygen has three naturally occurring isotopes that are found in different proportions, or percentages, in nature. These are oxygen-16 (^{16}O, 99.76 percent), oxygen-17 (^{17}O, 0.04 percent), and oxygen-18 (^{18}O, 0.20 percent). These isotopes of oxygen are stable. This means they do not degrade or change mass by radioactive decay or any other process in the nucleus.

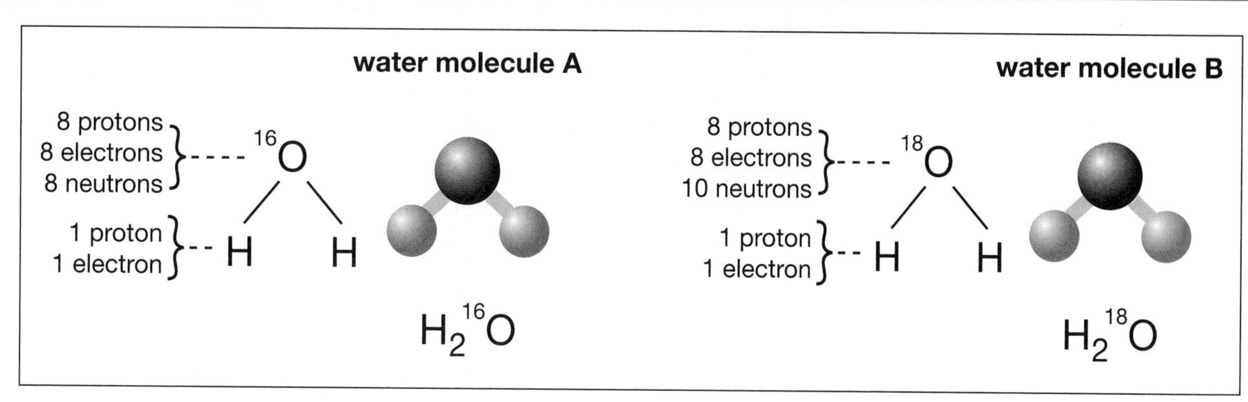

▲ **Figure 12.13 Two water molecules.** This diagram shows two different water molecules, A and B. How are these two water molecules alike or different?

Part II: The Oxygen Connection

Materials

For each team of 3 students

foram sample, if available

access to seafloor model

1 clear plastic straw

1 sheet of white paper

Process and Procedure

In Part I, you learned that not all water is the same. You investigated a simple model that showed how heavy and light water molecules are separated during evaporation. When light water ($H_2{}^{16}O$) evaporates and is stored in ice sheets on continents, the ocean is left enriched in heavy water ($H_2{}^{18}O$). If scientists could measure how the ratio of heavy to light water in the ocean has varied in the past, they would have additional evidence of glacial periods. But how can this be done? You will work in teams to answer this question.

1. Where would a scientist go to find a sample of ancient ocean water? Discuss this question with your class.
2. Scientists needed a way to measure the amount of heavy and light water that was present in the ocean at different times in Earth's history. To address this need, they turned to their understanding of geochemical cycles. Because oxygen isotopes are what cause water molecules to be heavy or light, scientists suspected that the element oxygen held the key to their search. Discuss Questions 2a–c with your team.

a. Take a few minutes to review what you already know about oxygen in the earth system.

b. Where on Earth is the element oxygen found? What forms does it take? What properties does it have?

Think about the different reservoirs in the earth system that you learned about in chapters 10 and 11. Where is oxygen in each of these subsystems? Is it found as an atom, an elemental molecule, or in compounds?

c. Does the amount of oxygen on Earth change across time?

3. Scientists realized that what they needed was to find a reservoir that stored the oxygen from ocean water for long periods of time. Read *Foram Forum* to learn about the reservoir they discovered. Check your understanding with your team by describing to one another how the oxygen atom from a molecule of ocean water becomes part of the shells of foraminifera.

"Foram" is short for "foraminifera." If available, look at the foram shells your teacher has on display.

READING

Foram Forum

Foraminifera are tiny, single-celled organisms that live in the ocean (figure 12.14). Often, these are called **forams**, for short. These organisms are abundant and widespread.

a.

b.

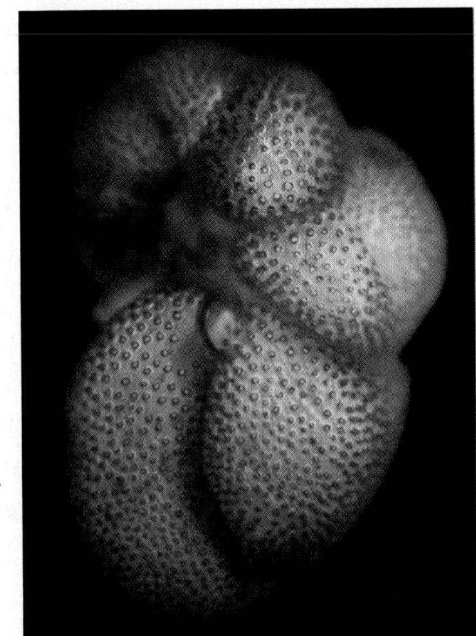

▲ **Figure 12.14 Foraminifera.** Forams are single-celled organisms in the ocean. They consist of an inner shell with many strands of tissue that protrude from the animal into the water (a). When they die, their shells sink to the seafloor (b). The tiny holes show where the strands exited the shell into the water.

A cubic centimeter of ocean sediment contains many living individuals, and even more empty fossil shells. Forams are found in all marine environments, from salt marshes to the deep ocean. They are found from the equator to the poles. Different species are found in different environments, reflecting their preferences for different temperature and nutrient conditions. Of the more than 4,000 species alive today, most live near the ocean bottom. Less than 1 percent of forams, about 40 species, live in the upper regions of the ocean.

As they live, forams build internal shells. These shells are tiny, typically ranging from 0.1 millimeters (mm) to 1 mm. Most are about the size of a pinhead. A foram's shell contains at least one, and often many, openings. The name, foraminifera, is actually a composite of Latin words that mean "bearing pores or openings." The single-celled foram itself is similar to an amoeba. The cell forms long, threadlike strands that stream through the openings in the shell. The strands move out in all directions (figure 12.14). Forams use these strands to catch other organisms they feed on. They can ensnare organisms both smaller and much larger than they are. Some forams also use the strands for locomotion. When forams die, their shells retain the holes (figure 12.14).

Most forams make their shells of calcium carbonate ($CaCO_3$), the same compound that forms larger seashells. Forams build their calcium carbonate shells from calcium ions $(Ca)^{2+}$ and bicarbonate ions $(HCO_3)^{1-}$ in ocean water. In chapter 11, *Carbon on the Move*, you studied how the bicarbonate and calcium ions enter the sea from rivers. These ions come from the chemical weathering of rocks and minerals on continents. These and other ions are carried by rivers to the ocean. The red oxygen in the following reaction indicates the transfer of oxygen from reactant to product:

$$Ca^{2+}_{(aq)} + 2HCO_3{}^{1-}_{(aq)} \longrightarrow CaCO_3 + H_2O + CO_2$$

Note that the oxygen atoms in the bicarbonate ions are some of the same oxygen atoms used in the foram shells. The bicarbonate first comes to the ocean from rivers. But then how does the bicarbonate reflect the oxygen isotopes of the ocean? That is, how can a foram shell preserve information about oxygen isotopes in the ocean water? It can because the bicarbonate is in a chemical equilibrium with the ocean's H_2O. The reaction is continuous, so the bicarbonate always has oxygen isotopes related to the ocean water. You also studied this reaction in chapter 11:

$$\underset{\text{carbon dioxide}}{CO_{2(aq)}} + \underset{\text{ocean water}}{H_2O_{(aq)}} \rightleftharpoons \underset{\text{carbonic acid}}{H_2CO_{3(aq)}}$$

$$\underset{\text{carbonic acid}}{H_2CO_{3(aq)}} \rightleftharpoons \underset{\text{bicarbonate}}{HCO_3{}^{1-}_{(aq)}} + \underset{\text{hydrogen ion}}{H^{1+}_{(aq)}}$$

When forams die, they fall to the ocean floor. The soft tissue of their cells decomposes, leaving the hard shell behind. These shells join other sediments on the seafloor. In time, the sediments build up, layer after layer. The layers of sediment with foram shells capture a record of past oxygen in ocean waters.

With this discovery, scientists found one piece of evidence of past climate changes in the shells of forams scattered in seafloor sediments. The oxygen atoms in the calcium carbonate of foram shells hold a record of the ratio of heavy to light oxygen in ocean water at the time the shell was formed. This record is a vital fingerprint for distinguishing between glacial and interglacial periods.

Topic: foraminifera
Go to: www.scilinks.org
Code: 2Inquiry615

4. In *Foram Forum*, you learned that forams fall to the bottom of the ocean when they die. They mix with other sediments, forming layer upon layer, year after year. How do geologists actually get the samples of forams? They remove samples from the ocean floor. Your teacher has prepared a model that represents a section of sediments on the ocean floor for you to sample.
   a. Use a clear plastic straw to obtain a core sample. Orient the straw vertically and gently push it into the sediment. Twist the straw and then seal it by placing your thumb over the top of the straw. Pull the straw out of the sediment.
   b. Lay the core down on a sheet of white paper. Do not try to remove the sample from the straw. You can view the contents through the clear plastic.
   c. Make a sketch of the sample in your science notebook.
   d. What do you notice about the layers in the sample? What can you infer about this sample?
5. To obtain your core sample, all you needed was a plastic straw, your hand, and access to a sediment sample. Read the information in the sidebar *The Integrated Ocean Drilling Program* to see how scientists in the field gather deep-sea core samples. Write answers to Questions 5a–b in your science notebook.
   a. How was the process of obtaining a model deep-sea core (in the classroom) similar to, and different from, the procedure that actually takes place on an IODP expedition?
   b. How was the model core you obtained similar to, and different from, the actual cores that come from the ocean floor?
6. Once scientists have the core sample, they need to analyze it. Read the information in δ^{18}O—*a Measure of Heavy and Light Oxygen* to find out how scientists analyze the foram samples. Check your understanding with your team. Then answer Questions 6a–b in your science notebook.

The symbol is pronounced "delta oxygen 18" or "dell-oh-18." It is just a chemical indicator. For example, another chemical indicator might be salinity, which indicates concentrations of dissolved salts. Or pH is a chemical indicator that tells the concentration of the H^+ ion in a solution.

   a. How does the information in δ^{18}O—*a Measure of Heavy and Light Oxygen* compare with your experiences with the evaporation model in Part I?

Think about the calculations you did in Part I. How are they like the calculations scientists use to analyze the oxygen in foram shells?

   b. Summarize the relationship between δ^{18}O values in the ocean and glacial and interglacial periods.

SIDEBAR

The Integrated Ocean Drilling Program

How do you get a sea core from the bottom of the ocean? For the answer, look at the Integrated Ocean Drilling Program (IODP). This program has recovered over 160,000 m (almost 100 miles) of deep-sea cores since 1985. IODP uses an oil-drilling ship equipped with state-of-the-art laboratories. For years, the IODP drilling ship, *JOIDES Resolution*, has made about six expeditions per year to recover deep-sea cores for climate researchers. Each expedition lasts about 2 months. During these expeditions, the ship is home to over 100 people, including 50 scientists, engineers, and technicians from around the world. These are examples of professions needed to obtain and study sea cores.

▲ ***JOIDES Resolution.*** This specialized scientific ship, the *JOIDES Resolution*, has been used by climate scientists and oceanographers since about 1985 to recover cores from sediments on the seafloor.

How are the deep-sea cores collected? A hydraulic core sampler is lowered through the drill pipe and driven into sediments on the seafloor. The core is hoisted from the water and taken to shipboard laboratories, where it is carefully opened and studied. An individual core might be up to 9.5 m long and about 10 cm in diameter. Each core is sliced lengthwise. One-half is left intact to provide a permanent record, while scientists sample the other half.

Each core is only one of many from the same hole. As the first core is raised to the surface, the drill penetrates the length of the core just taken. The coring process is repeated many times, thus recovering continuous sections of seafloor sediment. Samples range from hundreds of meters to several kilometers into the seafloor. Scientists study these cores in sequence to construct very long histories of changes in Earth's environment over time.

▲ **Core samples.** Scientists slice in half core samples of sediments from the seafloor. The different sections of a core might add up to thousands of meters in total length.

READING

$\delta^{18}O$—a Measure of Heavy and Light Oxygen

A key piece of evidence of Earth's past climate is recorded in the shells of forams. How do scientists determine and report the ratio of oxygen isotopes in foram shells?

Scientists obtain a sample from deep-sea sediment. They wash the sample in a sieve to remove the finer mud and silt. Then forams are handpicked from the sieve using a small paintbrush with a moistened tip. Only a few shells are needed for the oxygen analysis. These calcium carbonate shells are dissolved in phosphoric acid in a small chamber. One of the reaction products is CO_2 gas. You studied this reaction in chapter 11. The CO_2 gas contains the oxygen atoms that were in the foram shell. Remember, these oxygen atoms initially came from ocean water.

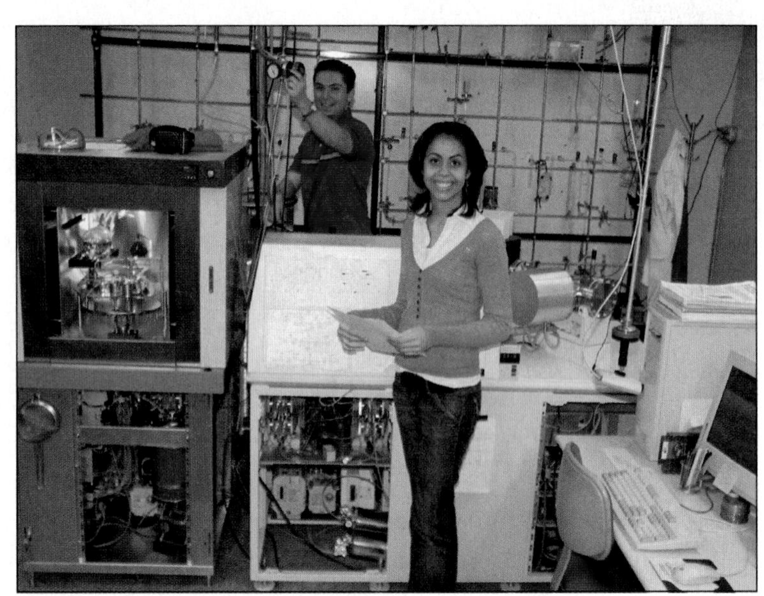

▲ **Figure 12.15 Analyzing CO_2.** Geologists analyze CO_2 from forams in a mass spectrometer. This instrument measures the isotopes of oxygen, ^{18}O and ^{16}O, in CO_2 from the forams.

$$3CaCO_3 + \underset{\text{phosphoric acid}}{2H_3PO_4} \longrightarrow 3Ca^{2+}_{(aq)} + 2PO_4^{3-} + 3H_2O + 3CO_2$$

The scientists put the carbon dioxide into a mass spectrometer. This instrument can detect and measure small differences in atomic mass between the ^{16}O and ^{18}O isotopes in the CO_2 (figure 12.15). This gives a ratio of ^{18}O to ^{16}O in the sample.

Between measuring samples, the geologists make measurements of a carbonate standard. The standard is the same in all laboratories so that data can be compared. The measured value is multiplied by 1,000. This magnifies the small variations in an already small ratio, making the numbers more workable. The calculated values are called "delta oxygen 18" values (or "dell-oh-18," for short). Their symbol is $\delta^{18}O$ and they are reported in parts per thousand (‰). This is also called per mil (as in per thousand).

$$\delta^{18}O_{\text{foram}} = \left(\frac{\left(\frac{^{18}O}{^{16}O}\right)_{\text{foram}} - \left(\frac{^{18}O}{^{16}O}\right)_{\text{standard}}}{\left(\frac{^{18}O}{^{16}O}\right)_{\text{standard}}} \right) \times 1{,}000$$

If a sample has a $\delta^{18}O$ greater than 0, it means that there is more ^{18}O relative to ^{16}O in the sample than there is in the standard. Samples with a lot of ^{18}O are even more positive. They are said to be ^{18}O enriched.

How does the variation in $\delta^{18}O$ values relate to glacial and interglacial periods? Recall the What's Shaking? model from Part I. You learned that $H_2{}^{16}O$ is more likely to evaporate than $H_2{}^{18}O$. During a glacial period, evaporated water enriched in $H_2{}^{16}O$ is stored in glaciers. This is represented in figure 12.16. This increases the relative amount of $H_2{}^{18}O$ remaining in the ocean. There is still $H_2{}^{16}O$ in the ocean during glacials, but the proportion of $H_2{}^{18}O$ has increased, as do values for $\delta^{18}O$.

During an interglacial period (figure 12.16), evaporation over the ocean still occurs. However, during interglacials, rain returns to the ocean by rivers. Moreover, melting ice sheets return the $H_2{}^{16}O$ to the ocean that was stored on continents during the glacial. This decreases the $\delta^{18}O$ values of the ocean during interglacials. The absolute values of $\delta^{18}O$ are an important detail for geologists. Remember, though, that the best way to tell glacials from interglacials is to analyze the pattern of $\delta^{18}O$ in a sediment core.

Forams incorporate the oxygen from ocean water into the calcium carbonate of their shells. If the surrounding ocean water contains a higher ratio of ^{18}O, the foram shells contain a higher ratio of ^{18}O. This means that $\delta^{18}O$ values for forams become larger (more positive) during glacial periods and smaller (less positive) during interglacial periods.

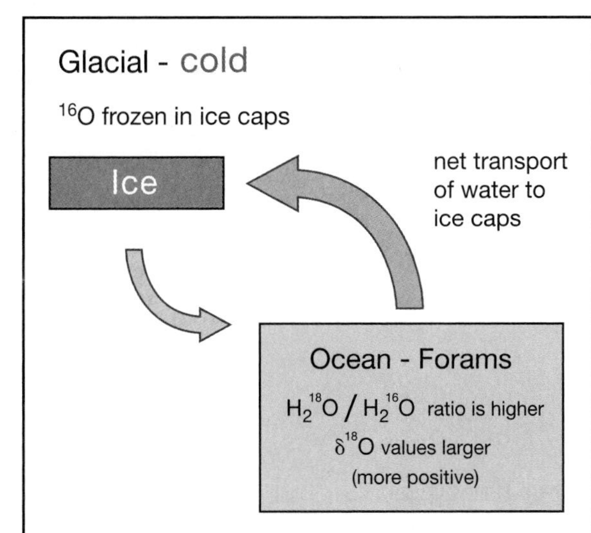

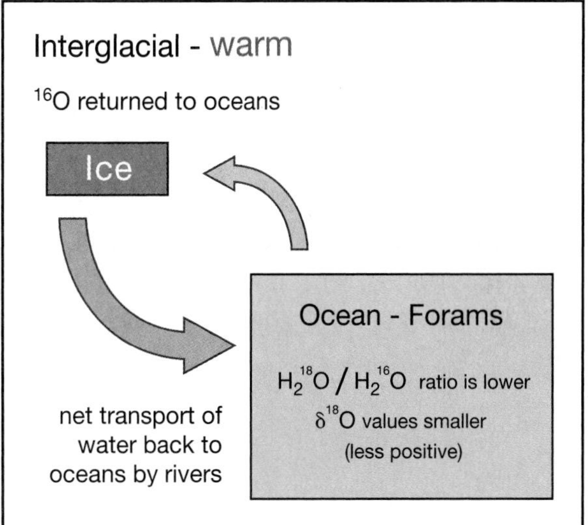

Figure 12.16 Model for glacials, interglacials. This simple model shows the net movement of water to continental ice sheets during glacial periods, and to the ocean during interglacial periods. Note the effect on changing sea level shown in each blue box. The blue boxes represent the ocean and show that $\delta^{18}O$ values for the ocean and forams increase during glacials as light water ($H_2{}^{16}O$) is frozen in continental ice sheets. The $\delta^{18}O$ values of foram shells decrease during interglacials as $H_2{}^{16}O$ is returned to the ocean.

Stop & THINK

PART II

Complete the following tasks individually. Write your responses in your science notebook.

1. Draw a simple diagram that shows examples of reservoirs where oxygen is stored in the earth system. Include examples of reservoirs in each of the earth subsystems (biosphere, atmosphere, geosphere, hydrosphere, cryosphere). Describe a form of oxygen present in each particular reservoir.
2. Describe how the cycling of oxygen connects ancient ocean water to the $\delta^{18}O$ values scientists obtain from the readings of a mass spectrometer. Highlight the journey of oxygen from ancient ocean water to the carbon dioxide (CO_2) analyzed by a modern mass spectrometer.

   Use whatever format you please to complete this task. You may draw a diagram, write a story, or produce a series of journal entries. If you are unsure if your selected format is acceptable, check with your teacher.

Part III: Analyzing Foram Data

Materials

For each team of 3 students

3 *Sea Core Foram Data 677* handouts

3 *Sea Core Foram Data 659* handouts

1 *Bands for Analysis* handout

Process and Procedure

In Part II, you learned that the oxygen isotopes in forams tell glacial periods from interglacial periods. These periods also link with water being transferred back and forth between the ocean and ice sheets. Studying these patterns enables geologists to determine the history of climate on Earth.

But what is the actual evidence from forams? What do the data look like? In this part of the investigation, you will analyze oxygen data that scientists collect from foram shells. Work in teams of three for this part of the investigation. Feel free to mark on your handouts. (Use pencil to mark on your graph, just in case you change your mind about something.)

1. Look at the graph in figure 12.17. This is also the handout *Sea Core Foram Data 677*. The core was obtained near the Galápagos Islands in the equatorial Pacific Ocean (see location in figure 12.24). This graph shows data obtained by geologists. Your team should consider questions like these when analyzing a graph:
   - What are the *x*- and *y*-axes?
   - What are the maximum and minimum values shown for the *x*- and *y*-axes of the graph?
   - How is the grid organized, and how is it set up?
   - What other information is provided?

Look at the title of the graph and the titles of the *x*- and *y*-axes. Read the axis labels below the graph. Notice the range of values for each of the axes. For the *x*-axis, determine where the present and past are located.

2. Now focus on the actual data, the wiggly line. What patterns do you notice in the data? Discuss and record general patterns, but also notice specific details about the patterns. Include numbers in your descriptions of the patterns. Try the following tasks to help you focus on the patterns.
   a. Use your finger to trace over the data. Is there a pattern to the movement of your finger?
   b. Look at the highs and lows on the graph. How much time passes from one major peak to another, or from one major valley to another? Is the time between peaks (or valleys) consistent? How many peaks (or valleys) appear in the 650,000-year time span?

One way to organize your observations is to make a T-table in your science notebook with headings of "peaks" and "valleys" and list the ages down the columns. Feel free to mark in pencil on your handout of figure 12.17 your ideas for any of these questions.

   c. Try tracing the graph with your finger again, but this time begin at the far right side of the graph. Imagine that you are there, 650 kya. Trace the graph as you move toward the left side of it. Is the movement of your finger consistent or does it change?
   d. You have probably been looking at your graph in a landscape orientation. Turn it to a portrait orientation with the *y*-axis on top and the *x*-axis on the left side. How is this

orientation like a sea core? Imagine that the graph represents different layers of sediments. Where are the older, deeper layers? Where are the younger layers?

3. Label glacial and interglacial periods on your handout of figure 12.17. Questions 3a–f will help your team do this.
   a. Where are we now on the graph? What do you predict for current $\delta^{18}O$ values in forams?
   b. What is the age from the graph of the LGM?
   c. What are the $\delta^{18}O$ values for forams at the LGM?
   d. How many glacials do you see in the section? What are typical $\delta^{18}O$ values for glacials? Explain your answer by referring to specific points on the graph.
   e. How many interglacials do you see? What are typical $\delta^{18}O$ values for interglacials? Explain your answer by referring to specific points in figure 12.17.
   f. Label on your graph those areas that represent sea level (high or low), relative size of ice sheets (large or small), $\delta^{18}O$ value (high or low), and global climate cycle (glacial or interglacial).

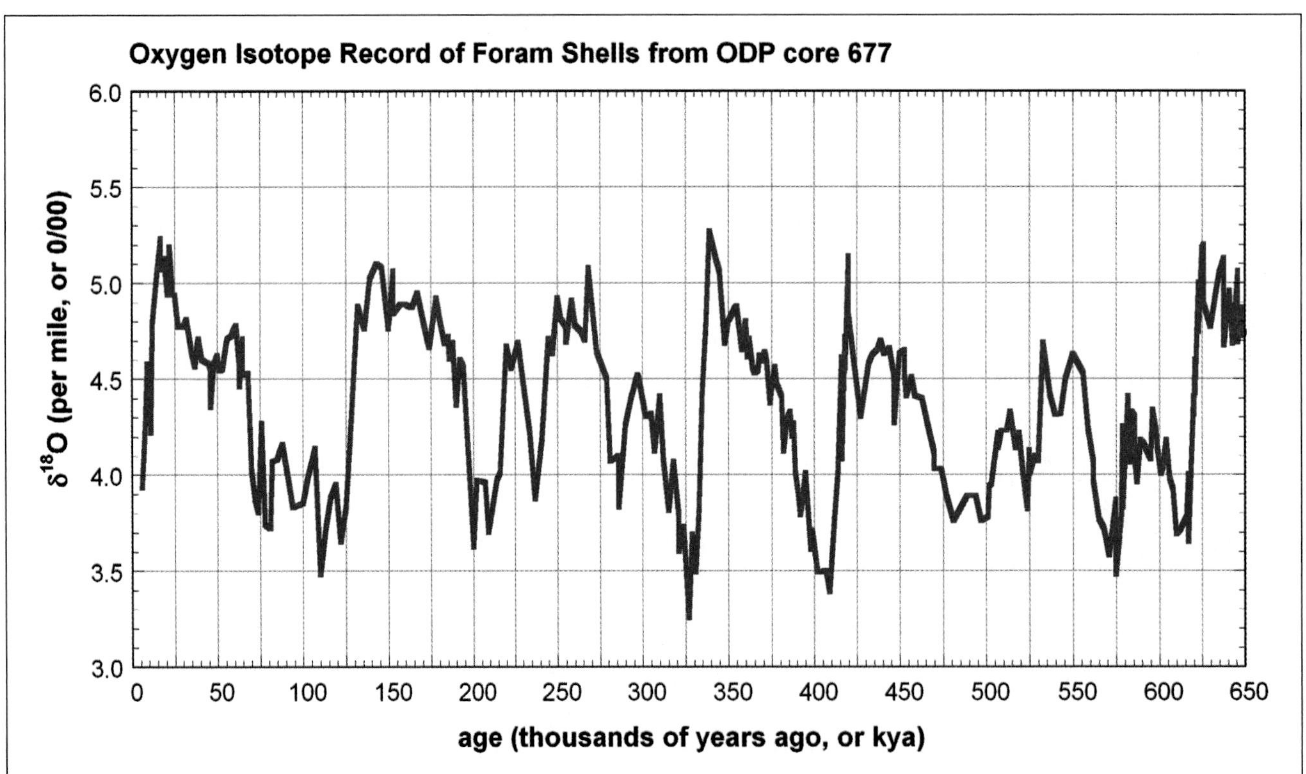

Source: Shackleton, et. al., (1990). An alternative astronomical calibration of the lower Pleistocene timescale based on ODP site 677. Transactions of the Royal Society of Edinburgh: *Earth Sciences*, *81*, 251-261.

▲ **Figure 12.17 ODP site 677.** These data are from site 677 near the Galápagos Islands, Ecuador (see location in figure 12.24). Follow the text to learn what these data tell you about the record of ancient climates on Earth. How do the peaks and valleys relate to glacial periods on Earth?

4. Geologists have analyzed data from many other deep-sea cores to identify interglacials and glacials. Get from your teacher a copy of the handout *Bands for Analysis*. Place this sheet behind the graph on the handout *Sea Core Foram Data 677*. Hold the 2 papers up to a light source.
   a. Identify which bands (white or light gray) are glacials and interglacials. Explain your reasoning.
   b. In your team, discuss how interglacial periods compare with glacial periods on the graph.
   c. How does the banding pattern on the *Bands for Analysis* handout compare with the patterns you noticed in Steps 2 and 3?
5. A key question for geologists studying past climates is, "Do sea cores with $\delta^{18}O$ values for forams tell of global patterns in the ocean?" That is, are glacial periods recorded by forams in other oceans in the world? Use figure 12.18 to answer this question.
   a. Look at the graph in figure 12.18. This is also the handout *Sea Core Foram Data 659*.

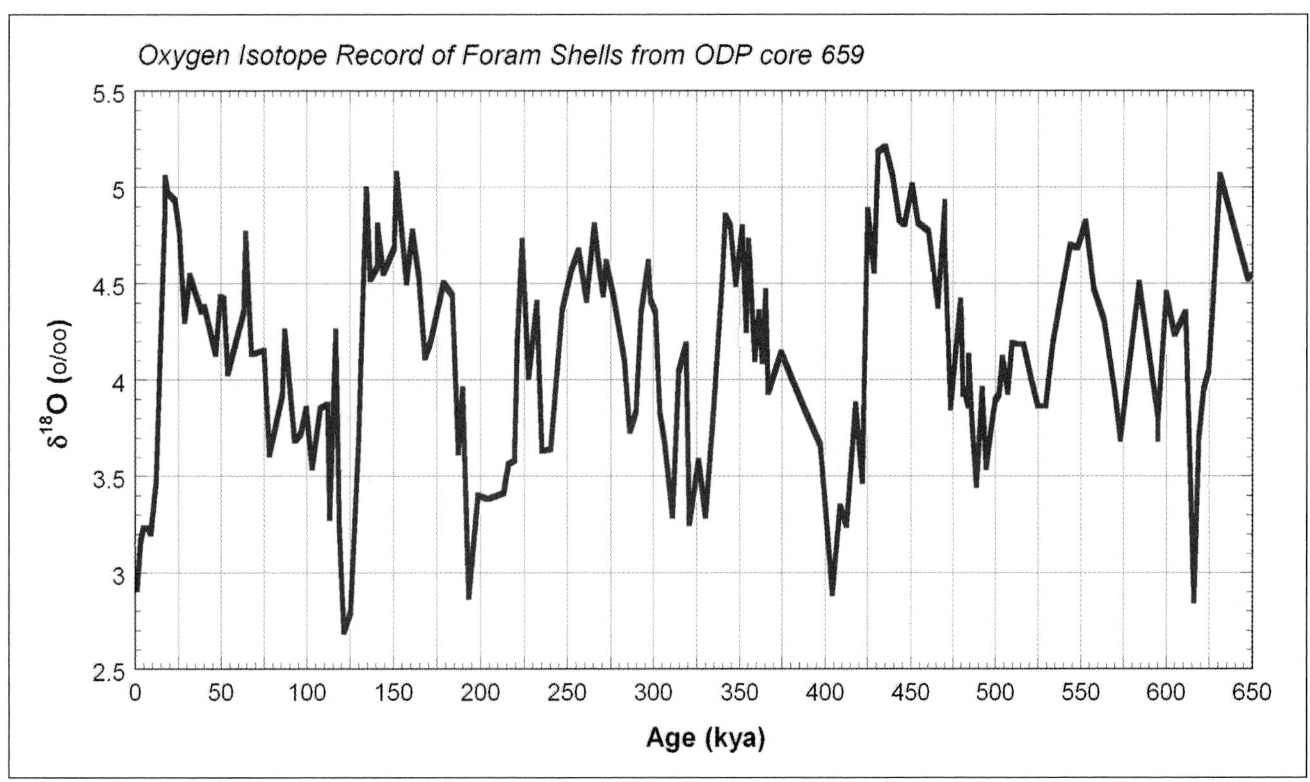

Source: Tiedemann, et. al. (1994). Astronomical timescale for the Pliocene Atlantic delta18-O and dust flux records of Ocean Drilling Program site 659. *Paleoceanography*, 9, 619-638.

▲ **Figure 12.18 ODP site 659.** These data are from ODP site 659 from the ocean offshore of northwestern Africa (see location in figure 12.24). Do you think that this sea core tells the same history of past climates as site 677?

b. The location of sea core 659 is shown in figure 12.24. Where is the location? Describe whether it is near the poles or near the equator.
c. Are glacial and interglacial periods recorded in figure 12.18? What is your evidence? For example, how many glacials are recorded? When were they?
d. How does figure 12.18 compare with figure 12.17? Do these look similar or different? Do they appear to record a global or a local pattern? List your evidence.

Reflect and Connect

Discuss the following questions with your team. Record your best thinking about these questions in your science notebook.

1. In the explore activity, you learned about proxy data. Explain why data from deep-sea cores are proxy data. Use evidence from your exercises.
2. Describe what you have learned so far about how oxygen cycles in the earth system. How has an understanding of the oxygen cycle helped scientists learn about Earth's past climates?
3. How does technology help scientists understand past climates? In your response, use specific examples of technology you have encountered in this activity.
4. Do you need to look at sea core samples from the poles to understand the history of the ice ages? Explain with evidence from this activity.
5. In chapter 11, you investigated records of CO_2 in the atmosphere in the carbon cycle. Those records went back about 1,000 years. Figure 12.19 shows a record of CO_2 concentrations in the atmosphere that goes back much further. This record was obtained from bubbles in the Antarctic ice sheet (see location in figure 12.24).
   a. Analyze patterns on the graph. Where do peaks and valleys occur on this graph? How often do they occur? How many years back does the record extend?
   b. Carbon dioxide contents correlate with warm periods, or interglacials. How many interglacials do you see? How often do they occur?

c. What are the ages of glacials? How often do they occur?
d. How does this record of CO_2 in the atmosphere correlate with foram records in sea cores?
e. Compare periods of CO_2 highs in figure 12.19 over the last 650,000 years with the last 1,000 years in figure 11.12. Explain any similarities and differences in the patterns.
f. Are current CO_2 concentrations (figure 11.12) higher or lower than variations between recent glacials and interglacials (figure 12.19)?

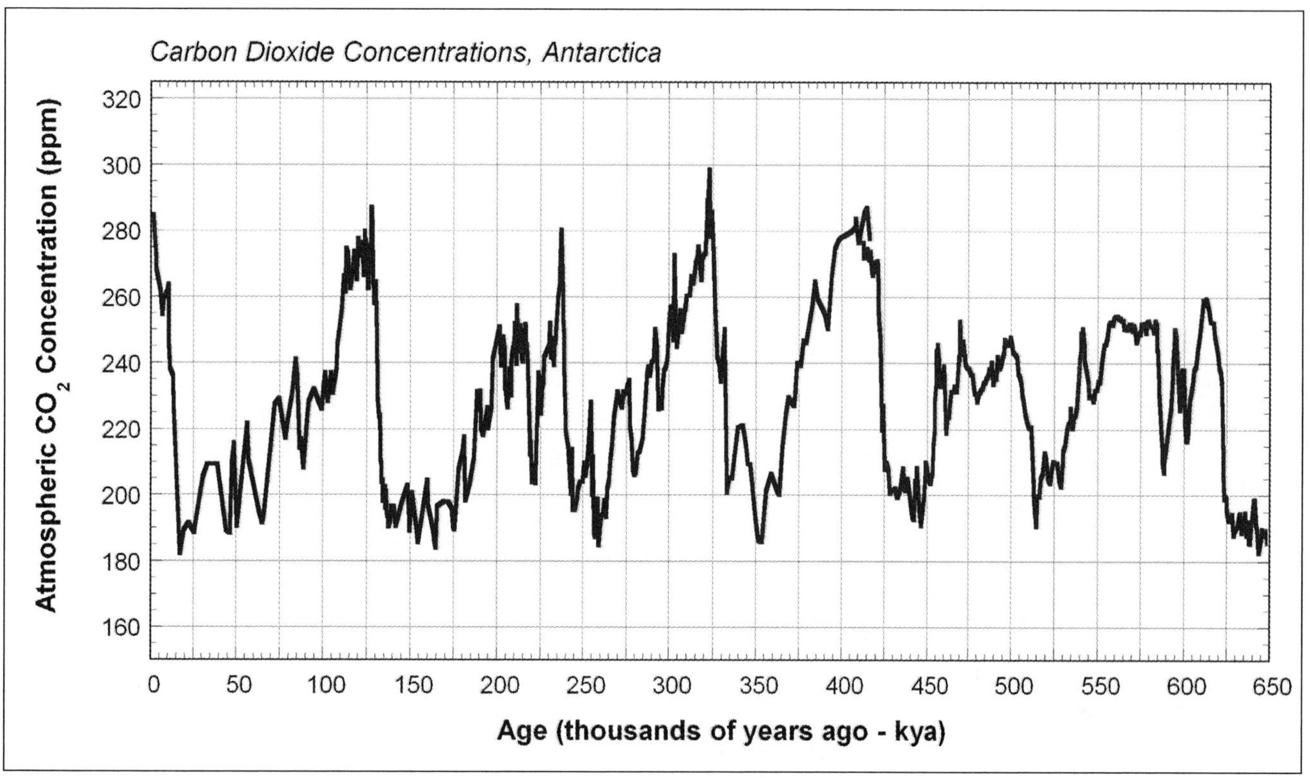

Source: Jouzel, et al. (1993). Extending the Vostok ice-core record of paleoclimate to the penultimate glacial period. *Nature*, *364*, 407–412. and Siegenthaler, et. al. (2005, November 25). Stable carbon cycle-climate relationship during the late Pleistocene. *Science*, *310*, 1313–1317.

▲ **Figure 12.19 Carbon dioxide concentrations, Antarctica.** These data show CO_2 concentrations in the atmosphere from air bubbles in the Antarctic ice sheet. How does the pattern of CO_2 concentrations compare with $\delta^{18}O$ values of forams?

ELABORATE

The Astronomical Theory

Up to this point, you have focused on analyzing patterns in data. This evidence helps you see a history of climate change on Earth between glacial and interglacial periods. You began the chapter by discussing early evidence of ice ages: huge boulders, scratched rocks, and fossils in unusual locations. Next, you analyzed changes in sea level over thousands of years. This is evidence for a large shift in the water cycle from one reservoir to another. You examined the example of moving water from ice sheets to oceans, and back.

In the explore-explain activity, *The Core of the Matter*, you looked to data from deep-sea cores for evidence of past climate changes. You learned that the oxygen locked in the shells of forams provides a proxy record of glacial and interglacial climates from the past. You noted regular patterns in the oxygen isotopes of foram shells. These patterns suggest cycles of climate change in Earth's past. The patterns are global in scale.

Topic: astronomical theory
Go to: www.scilinks.org
Code: 2Inquiry626

But what is the reason for the cycles of climate change? Do the patterns continue back in time before 650 kya? Scientists who study paleoclimatology have wondered that same thing. In *The Astronomical Theory*, you will learn about one theory that scientists have been testing as the cause of the cycling of glacial and interglacial periods.

Materials

For each team of 3 students

1 set of *Graphs A, B, C, D* handout

For each expert group: tilt

1 large Styrofoam ball with a wooden skewer through the center

1 protractor

1 straw cut in half

For each expert group: orbit

1 piece of cardboard

2 pushpins

1 piece of string tied into a circle

oversized paper

1 sharp pencil

1 ruler

For each expert group: wobble

1 spinning top

Process and Procedure

Why does Earth have glacial and interglacial periods? This is a simple question, but the answer has several parts. One way to look at this question is to break it into smaller pieces.

1. Discuss these questions with your team and write your ideas in your notebook.
   a. What conditions favor the growth of glaciers?
   b. What conditions favor the melting of glaciers?
2. Read the following paragraph and discuss your understanding with your team.

   What causes the climate to cycle between glacial and interglacial periods? Scientists have been trying to answer this for over 150 years. In the mid-1800s, scientists first proposed an astronomical theory of climate change. This theory proposes that the orbit of Earth around the Sun causes ice ages. Milutin Milankovitch, a Serbian mathematician, did a lot of work in the 1920s that supported this idea. He calculated how changes in Earth's orbit caused changes in the intensity of solar radiation across time. Milankovitch proposed that variations in solar radiation caused glacial and interglacial patterns. Because of his contributions, scientists sometimes call the astronomical theory of climate change the Milankovitch theory.
3. Make a drawing that reflects what you already know about Earth's orbit around the Sun. Discuss with your team how to include these things with your diagram.
   a. Label the Sun and Earth.
   b. Show the orientation and path of Earth through space.
   c. Include information you know about distance and time.
4. The astronomical theory focuses on 3 factors in the orbital motion of Earth: the tilt of Earth's axis, the changing shape of Earth's orbit around the Sun, and the wobble of the rotation axis. Your team will study these factors, looking at 1 factor at a time.
   a. This activity has 3 reading passages, 1 for each factor. Each team member will focus on 1 of the key factors. For example, one person will become the team expert on tilt, one on wobble, and so on.
   b. Gather with students from other groups who are experts on the same factor. Read the appropriate handout and discuss the information and the diagrams. Complete the *Try This* section of your reading. Be prepared to explain the information to the other students in your team.

READING

Reading 1: Tilt

Earth's axis is tilted about 23.5° from its plane of travel around the Sun. You saw this in figure 12.5. You probably know that this tilt causes the seasons. During summer, the Northern Hemisphere is pointed toward the Sun. In this position, the Northern Hemisphere receives the maximum amount of solar radiation. During winter, the Northern Hemisphere is pointed away from the Sun, and thus receives a minimum amount of solar radiation. If Earth's axis were not tilted, there would be no seasons. This is because every point on Earth would receive the same amount of solar radiation each day of the year.

But did you know that the tilt of the rotation axis changes in time? The tilt varies between 21.5° and 24.5°. The variation occurs on a cycle of about 41 kyr (figure 12.20). If Earth's axis is tilted more, the seasons become more severe. Summers are warmer and winters are colder. If the amount of tilt is less, the seasons become milder. Summers are cooler and winters are warmer.

The cool summers are thought to contribute to glacial advances. During a cool summer, the snow that accumulated during the previous winter cannot quite melt away. Thus, snow and ice can continue to pile up in the far north, eventually building massive ice sheets. As the snow and ice accumulate, they also initiate a positive feedback mechanism. Regions covered with more snow reflect more of the Sun's energy, causing even more cooling.

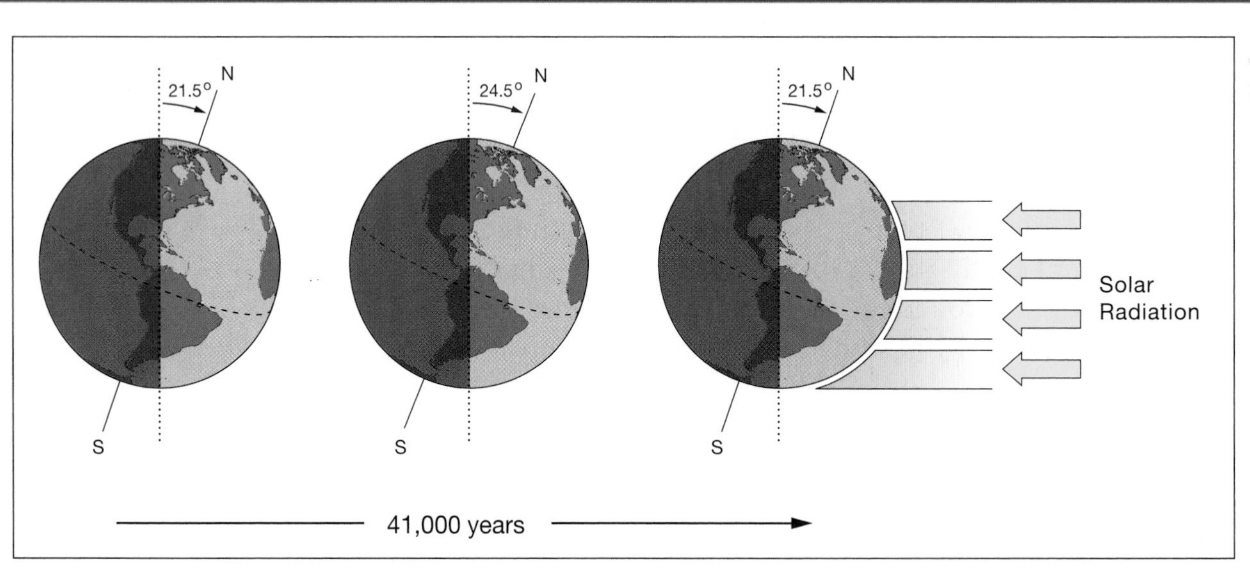

▲ **Figure 12.20 Variation in Earth's tilt.** The tilt of Earth s rotation axis varies from 21.5° to 24.5° and back to 21.5° every 41 kyr. Currently, the tilt is about 23.5°.

Try This

1. Look at the Styrofoam ball or a globe of Earth. The wooden skewer represents the rotational axis of Earth. The straw represents a line that is perpendicular to the plane of Earth's orbit around the Sun. Orient the ball so that it looks like Earth in the diagram in figure 12.20. Notice that the Northern Hemisphere is tilted toward the Sun. Is the Northern Hemisphere receiving more or less incoming solar radiation in this position than the Southern Hemisphere?
2. Change the tilt of Earth by removing the straw and repositioning it so that the angle between the skewer and the straw is larger. (Although the actual variation is only a degree or two in either direction, it might help you see the difference if you exaggerate the change in angle.) Does the Northern Hemisphere receive more or less incoming solar radiation than it did before?
3. Repeat Step 2, but this time make the angle between the skewer and the straw smaller than before. Does the Northern Hemisphere receive more or less incoming solar radiation than it did before?

READING

Reading 2: Eccentricity of Orbit

Earth revolves around the Sun in an elliptical path. The shape of this path changes with time. Sometimes it is nearly circular, other times it is slightly more elliptical. This is shown in figure 12.21. The cycle of this change is about 100 kyr. Currently, Earth's orbit is slightly elliptical.

The change in elliptical shape of Earth's orbit means that Earth's distance to the Sun changes only a very small amount. As Earth's orbit changes shape, the amount of solar radiation Earth receives also varies only a small amount. When the orbit is nearly circular, the distance between Earth and the Sun is nearly equal throughout the year. The total solar radiation received by Earth is nearly equal throughout the year. However, when the orbit is slightly elliptical, the distance between Earth and the Sun varies. But these changes in solar radiation due to distance are very, very small. They would have almost no direct effect on patterns of climate change.

These observations relate to current scientific questions in understanding past climates on Earth. From the discussion above, you would predict that the eccentricity of orbit would have little effect on past climate. You would not expect climate change to relate to 100-kyr cycles. However, data that you investigated also show a strong variation between glacials and interglacials about every 100 kyr. While scientists now understand many parts of past climate cycles, they are still working to solve important details.

Try This

1. Place a blank sheet of paper on top of a piece of cardboard. Place 2 pushpins about 5 cm apart near the center of the paper. Tie the ends of a 30-cm-long piece of string together. Place the string around the pushpins. Place a sharp pencil

Reading 2: Eccentricity of Orbit, continued

inside the string and pull the string tight. Keeping the string tight at all times, draw an ellipse by moving the pencil around the pushpins.

The pushpins represent the foci of the ellipse of Earth's orbit. In a real orbit, the Sun would lie at one of these foci. In reality, however, Earth's orbit is nearly a circle.

2. Repeat Step 1, but this time place the pushpins 10 cm apart.
3. Predict what would happen if you removed 1 of the pushpins. Try it.
4. Which ellipse was more elliptical, the one with pushpins 5 cm apart, 10 cm apart, or with only 1 pushpin?
5. In this model, where is the Sun? Earth? Earth's orbit?

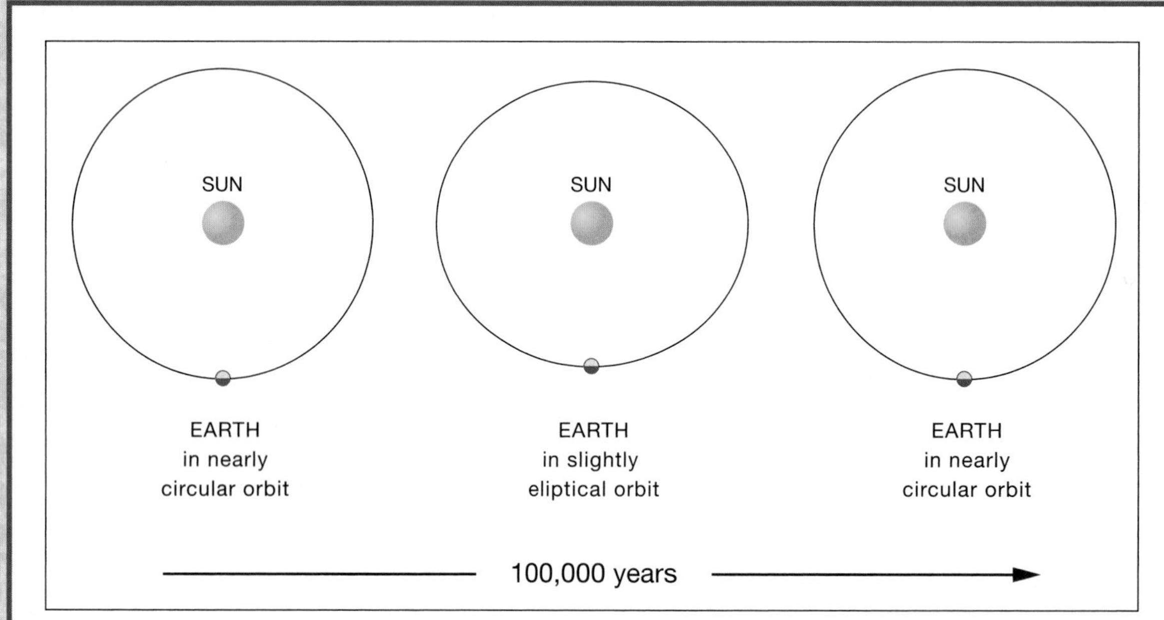

▲ **Figure 12.21 Variation in orbit eccentricity.** The shape of Earth's orbit changes from nearly circular, to slightly elliptical, and back to almost circular. This cycle occurs over about 100 kyr.

READING

Reading 3: Wobble (Precession)

Earth's axis of rotation wobbles like a spinning top (figure 12.22). Of course, Earth spins around the axis with one revolution per day. But then the orientation of the axis itself wobbles in space, making a near circle. A top might complete one cycle of wobble every second or so. In contrast, the Earth takes about 21 kyr to complete a full "wobble." This wobble is known as the precession cycle because of how Earth's axis moves, or precesses, through space.

How does the wobble affect climate on Earth? The wobble affects the axis and the orbit of Earth. Because of the wobble, Earth's axis points in different directions through time. Right

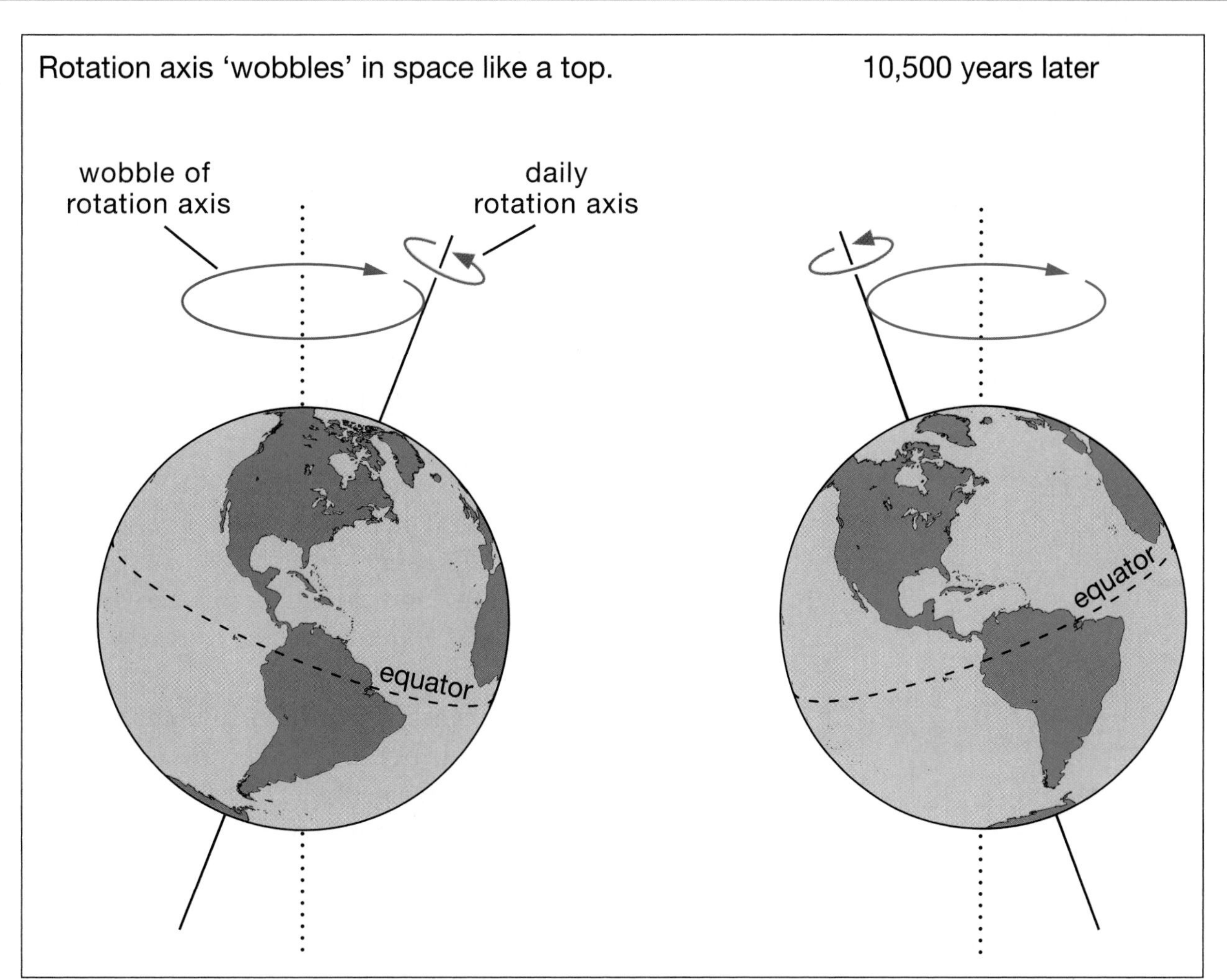

Figure 12.22 Wobble of rotation axis. The rotation axis of Earth wobbles much like the motion of a spinning top. The axis moves through space and describes a circle each 21 kyr.

Reading 3: Wobble (Precession), continued

now, Earth's axis is pointed toward the North Star, Polaris. At other times, the axis has pointed elsewhere in the sky.

What does this mean in the long term? Currently, Earth is closest to the Sun during winter in the Northern Hemisphere. Because Earth is closest to the Sun at this point in its orbit, it receives slightly more solar radiation than it would if it were farther away. But because the axis is pointing away, the Northern Hemisphere still experiences winter.

Summers currently occur in the Northern Hemisphere when Earth is at its maximum distance from the Sun. In about 10,500 years, Earth will experience winters when it is farthest from the Sun and summers when it is closest.

Another way to think of this is that the shortest day of the year will keep moving. In 10,500 years, the shortest day will be June 21. At that time, the middle of summer and the longest day of the year will be December 21. In another 10,500 years, radiation conditions will have precessed back to where we are today.

Try This

1. Observe a spinning top. Look carefully at the motion of the top around its central axis. Notice how the top spins around this central axis, but also notice how the axis itself seems to wobble, forming a circle in space. Each time the wobble completes a circuit, it equals a precession cycle.

5. Return to your original team to share what you have learned in your expert group.
6. After you have discussed all 3 key factors, answer Questions 6a–b with your team.
   a. Which factor do you think would have the greatest impact on past climate changes? Which one would have the least impact? Explain your reasoning.
   b. How does what you now know about Earth's movements in space compare with what you included in your response to Step 3?
7. The astronomical theory regards the history of climate change as being due to interactions between the 3 key cycles. No single cycle can completely explain the geologic evidence, such as forams or records of CO_2 concentrations in the atmosphere. Complete Steps 7a–d to see the patterns that emerge when different factors are combined.
   a. Get from your teacher a set of 4 handouts. Three of the handouts contain a completed graph. Each team member needs to take responsibility for 1 of these graphs (A, B, or C). The fourth handout contains a table and a grid for graphing.
   b. What do you think the first 3 graphs represent?

c. Your task, as a team, is to combine the 3 graphs together to produce a fourth graph (D). The following sequence provides one strategy for doing this:

- Decide on the spacing that your team will use between *x* values. Think about a trade-off so that you do not have too many, or too few, *x* values.
- Use the curve in the graph to determine the *y* value for each *x* value.
- Record all *xy* pairs neatly in a T-table or similar format. Note that your team could also record all the data in a single table with several columns.
- Add together the *y* value for individual *x* values in the 3 graphs.
- Make a new table (or set of columns) for the *x* value and the sum of the 3 *y* values.
- Take turns plotting the *x* and *y* values for graph D.

d. Compare graph D with graphs A, B, and C from the *Graphs A, B, C, D* handout. What similarities and differences do you notice?

8. The data you used in Step 7 simulate the solar radiation that reaches Earth. Although they are not actual data, they are based on the physics of Earth's orbit around the Sun. They can be compared with other evidence.

a. Imagine that the *x*-axis on each of graphs A, B, and C represents age in thousands of years. How long is 1 cycle on each of these graphs? Which of the astronomical cycles could each graph represent?

To save time and space, you can abbreviate thousands of years as "kyr." However, be careful not to confuse kyr (thousands of years) with kya (thousands of years ago).

b. Compare graph D with one or all of the graphs you worked with in the explore-explain activity (figures 12.17, 12.18, 12.19). What similarities and differences do you notice?

As you compare graph D with ice or sea core data, note the different *x*-axis scales. You can still compare them by just looking from 0 to 150 kya. Another option is to obtain graph E from your teacher. This graph is an extension of graph D out to 650 kya. (Remember, kya stands for thousands of years ago.)

9. The graphs you worked with in Step 7 actually simulate the work done by Milankovitch and other scientists. Learn more about their thoughts on these cycles and how they interact by completing the following tasks.

a. Read the following paragraphs to see what Milankovitch and other scientists thought about the role of the 3 factors in modifying Earth's climate. Milankovitch proposed that changes in global climate are due to changes in 3 key factors:

i. The tilt of Earth's axis (41-kyr)
ii. The wobble of the spinning Earth (21-kyr cycle)
iii. The changing shape of Earth's orbit around the Sun (100-kyr cycle)

Milankovitch proposed that climate change was greatest when all three cycles reinforced one another. At times, all the cycles work either to minimize or to maximize the solar radiation on Earth. Milankovitch believed that the tilt and wobble cycles would dominate over the orbit cycle. According to his theory, the combination of cycles affects the relative intensity of solar radiation in summer. This, in turn, controls the growth and retreat of glaciers. Cool summers in the Northern Hemisphere, where most of Earth's landmass is located, would allow snow and ice to persist to the next winter. This allows large glaciers to develop over tens of thousands of years. This links with the movement of water from oceans to continents. In contrast, warmer summers melt all snow from the previous winter, plus a little more. This reduces the mass of glaciers and ice sheets.

Computer models and historical evidence suggest that the Milankovitch cycles exert their greatest cooling and warming influences when the peaks and troughs of all three cycles coincide with one another. This probably accounts for the previous major interglacial at 125 kya.

b. Return to figures 12.17, 12.18, and 12.19. Which of the 3 cycles appears to dominate in those data?

c. From the passage in Step 9a, what cycles did Milankovitch predict would dominate? Is this consistent with your answer in Step 9b? Write an explanation in your science notebook.

10. In this investigation, you have learned about the astronomical theory, which is important to studying past climates. As a class, discuss Questions 10a–c.

a. What makes the astronomical theory a theory and not just a hypothesis?

b. What features of the astronomical theory might we still be trying to understand?

c. Are there any other ideas or theories that attempt to explain the cycles of glacials and interglacials in Earth's past? How would you test those ideas?

11. Read *Coral Dating* to find out how corals are used to anchor the astronomical theory in real geologic time.

READING

Coral Dating

The idea that the shape of Earth's orbit around the Sun changed in a regular and predictable manner has been around for a while. In the 1860s, James Croll first argued for a link between Earth's orbit and changes between glacial and interglacial cycles. His work was the first version of an astronomical theory for the history of climate change. The problem was that in the past there was no good way to determine the age when the glacials and interglacials actually occurred. Some other data were needed that would anchor the theory in real time. This was also true of early work with the fossil record. The ability to anchor these geologic records in time did not emerge for another 100 years.

In the late 1950s, scientists turned to coral reefs to measure ages for periods of high sea levels. They expected that high sea levels and coral ages would correspond with interglacial periods. Elkhorn coral (*Acropora palmata*) provided that key piece of information. These coral tend to grow near the surface of the water. They grow upward, then stop growing right at the level of low tide. This gives them a flat-topped appearance (figure 12.23). If the sea level rises,

▲ **Figure 12.23 Elkhorn coral.** Elkhorn coral (*Acropora palmata*) grows upward in shallow seas. It stops growing at the level of low tide. This gives a flat-topped appearance from the side. When geologists measure ages for fossil elkhorn coral, they can determine the sea level at a time in the geologic past.

Coral Dating, continued

elkhorn coral are "drowned" in water too deep for them. If the sea level falls, or the land is pushed upward, they are stranded in air.

To see changes in sea level in the geologic past, a geologist first must find a dead elkhorn coral still attached at its base. This is where detailed fieldwork is vital. The base of that elkhorn coral was probably about 2 m below sea level at low tide when it was alive. Next, the geologist measures a radiometric age for when the coral was alive. This tells the position of sea level at the time of the coral age.

Spectacular examples of fossil elkhorn reefs have been dated in locations such as Florida, the Bahamas, the Hawaiian Islands, Australia, Barbados, and New Guinea. Such research is used for constructing the sea level curve, such as the one you used in the explore activity. This research has also been used to date high sea levels during the last two interglacial periods. For example, much of the perimeter of Florida is composed of a giant reef that grew approximately 125 kya. At that time, there was even less ice on Earth than today and the sea level was several meters higher. This high sea level at 125 kya is clear in figures 12.17 and 12.18.

Once scientists realized the link between the coral reefs, ancient climate, and sea level, they used radiometric dating for other coral reefs. Work with coral age dating in the 1960s indicated that sea levels were high at time periods such as 82 kya, 105 kya, 125 kya, and 200 kya. Improved laboratory methods in the mid-1980s confirmed these results.

The ages of the coral terraces indicate periods of high sea level and correspond closely to the interglacials predicted by the astronomical theory. You can see these interglacial periods as individual peaks on the deep-sea cores you studied in the explore-explain activity. Take another look at the handout *Sea Core Foram Data* 677. Can you pick out these peaks? This correlation provides compelling evidence for a link between the astronomical theory and the history of glacial and interglacial cycles on Earth.

Dating coral reefs was an important way to test a scientific idea. These data also show that a detailed record of glaciations and climate history is found at the equator in coral reefs.

SCILINKS® NSTA
Topic: coral dating
Go to: www.scilinks.org
Code: 2Inquiry636

Reflect and Connect

Work individually to complete the following tasks.

1. Make a chart that summarizes what you understand about each of the 3 key astronomical factors that influence Earth's climate.
2. Describe how the combination of the 3 key factors can lead to more extreme seasons (colder winters, hotter summers). Then describe how the severity of seasons can lead to glacial or interglacial periods.
3. Use what you understand about the astronomical theory to explain the patterns in the sea core data you analyzed in the explore-explain activity.

4. Describe how corals can provide both direct and indirect data that relate to the study of past climates.
5. What makes the astronomical theory widely accepted by scientists today? What types of observations might be required for scientists to reject this theory?

More Than Forams

EVALUATE

In the explore-explain activity, you used data from cores from the seafloor. You also examined a core of ice from Antarctica. These data told about patterns of climate change on Earth. In *More Than Forams*, you will look again at core data from seafloors. But this time, you will have to use what you know to interpret some new kinds of data from new locations.

Part of the data you will study is forams, but another part of the data set is quite different. You and a partner will act as two scientists interpreting data. You will share your findings with another pair of scientists. The final part of the activity consists of using that evidence to write answers to three questions. Look at the questions ahead of time with your partner. Keep them in mind as you analyze the new data. You should even practice writing answers to these questions ahead of time with your partner. This will show how well you understand the ideas in the chapter.

Part I: Probing for Patterns

Materials

For each team of 2 students

1 *Arabian Sea Data* (*ODP 722*) handout or 1 *Pacific Ocean Data* (*ODP 1020*) handout

pencils

1 colored pencil

2 *More Than Forams Scoring Rubric* handouts

Process and Procedure

You and your partner are geologists who study the history of climates on Earth. You will receive some sea core data from one of two locations. Use the expertise you have acquired to interpret these data.

The two deep-sea cores are from different parts of the globe (figure 12.24). One site is from the Arabian Sea (ODP site 722; 16.4° north, 59.5° east). The second site is from the Pacific Ocean about 170 km west of Northern California (ODP site 1020; 41° north, 126° west). As you look at the data for evidence of past climate changes, also consider the data and handouts from your work with prior cores from seafloors. Do you see any similarities and differences? Can you identify patterns?

The Pacific Ocean teams will look at pollen records. The Arabian Sea teams will look at dust records. You will discuss how these data relate to the foram data you receive from the same location. Later, you will share your findings with another pair of student scientists.

1. You have learned a lot about past climates and the ice ages. You will write about what you have learned by answering the 3 questions in Part II of this activity. Review these questions with your partner before beginning the activity. Also review again the *More Than Forams Scoring Rubric* for this final chapter activity.
2. Obtain data for the dust or pollen sample from your teacher. Examine the deep-sea core data from that location. Read the 1-page description in your handout to learn how scientists get dust and pollen records from sea sediments. Feel free to

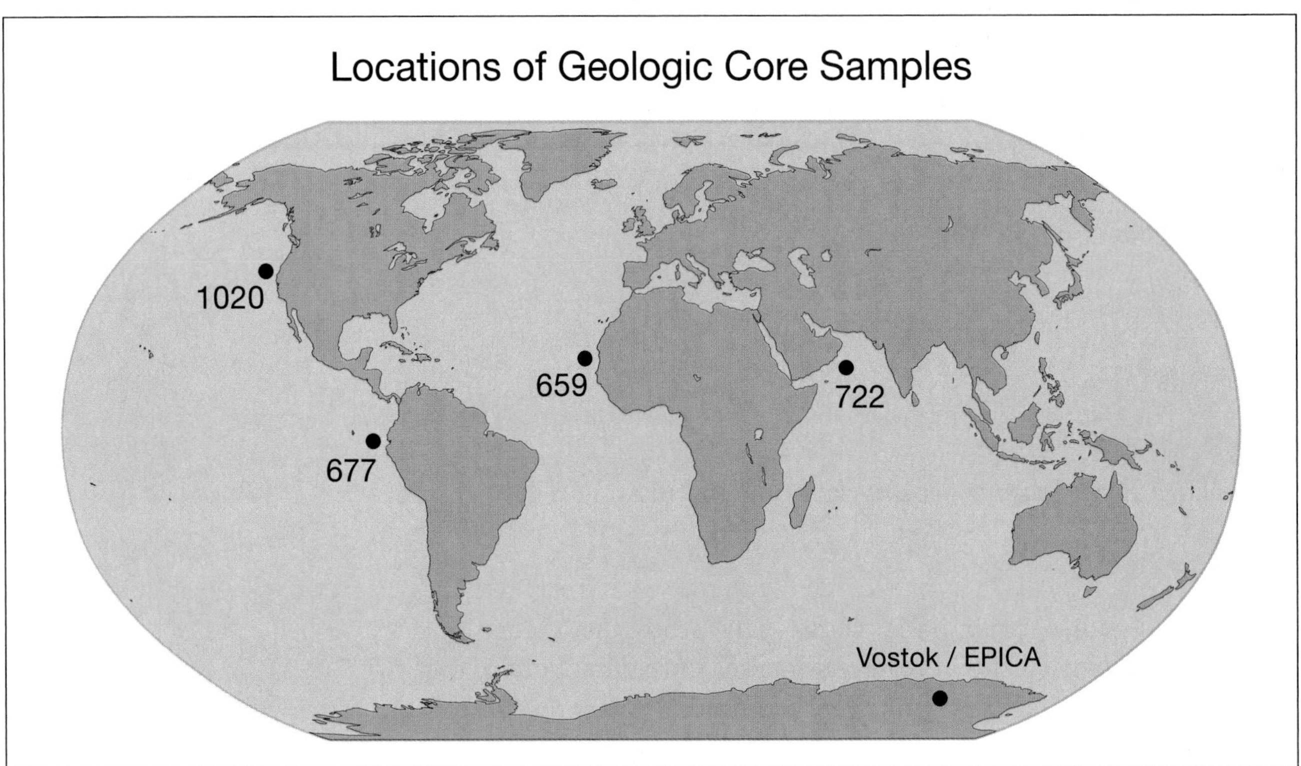

Figure 12.24 Locations of sea and ice cores. This map shows the locations of cores discussed in the text. Marine cores are ODP 677, 659, 722, and 1020. The locations of the Vostok and EPICA ice cores are represented on the Antarctic ice sheet. Do the data suggest that paleoclimate patterns are global in nature?

review any other materials from this chapter. Check your understanding with your partner.

3. Your handout also includes 3 graphs for you to analyze. As you work through Steps 3a–c, record your ideas in your science notebook. Take good notes because you will need them later as you share your findings with another team.
   a. What patterns do you notice in the graphs of dust or pollen data? Label your graphs with the major patterns you see. You might want to use a pencil in case you need to make changes.

Begin by identifying the present time period on the graph and thinking about the climate associated with it.

   b. Explain the patterns you see in the dust or pollen data. Why do you think the amount of dust or pollen moving into the seas has changed during Earth's history?
   c. Now look at the foram graphs. Are the patterns in the dust or pollen graphs similar to or different from the patterns you see in the foram data? Note any patterns you see.

Select 1 foram graph and 1 dust or pollen graph. Trace over the lines on the graphs for both cores beginning at the "bottom" of the core (the oldest data). Do the lines move up and down at the same places on the timescale? You might want to review your notes from earlier investigations in this chapter.

4. Consider the patterns you noted in the foram and dust or pollen data. Explain how these data seem to support or refute the astronomical theory. Discuss your thoughts with your partner and record your ideas in your science notebook.
5. Consider the following bullets, depending on your data set:
   - For the dust record for the Arabian Sea, what sort of conditions on the land do you think relate to more or less dust? What does this tell you about changes in the ecosystems of land near the Arabian Sea (figure 12.25)?
   - For the sequoia and alder record, what sort of conditions on the land favor more of these types of plants to grow? Warm interglacials or cold glacials? Use data from the cores to support your answer (figure 12.26).
6. Get together with another team of scientists that has a different core from you. Each team should take about 5–10 minutes sharing information about its core.
   a. What cores did you examine? Where are they from?
   b. What patterns do you see in the data? Do different data sets from the same core show the similar types of patterns?
   c. How do you interpret the patterns? What do the patterns mean in terms of past climates on Earth?

d. Do the pollen and dust records tell an overall similar or different story?

e. How do these data relate to other data in the chapter? List specific evidence.

7. Review as a group how these data relate to the sea core data you studied (677 and 659) or even the ice core data.
8. Review as a group any new ideas for answering the 3 questions in Part II.

Part II: Climate Questions

Materials

For each student

1 *More Than Forams Scoring Rubric* handout

access to all graphs in chapter

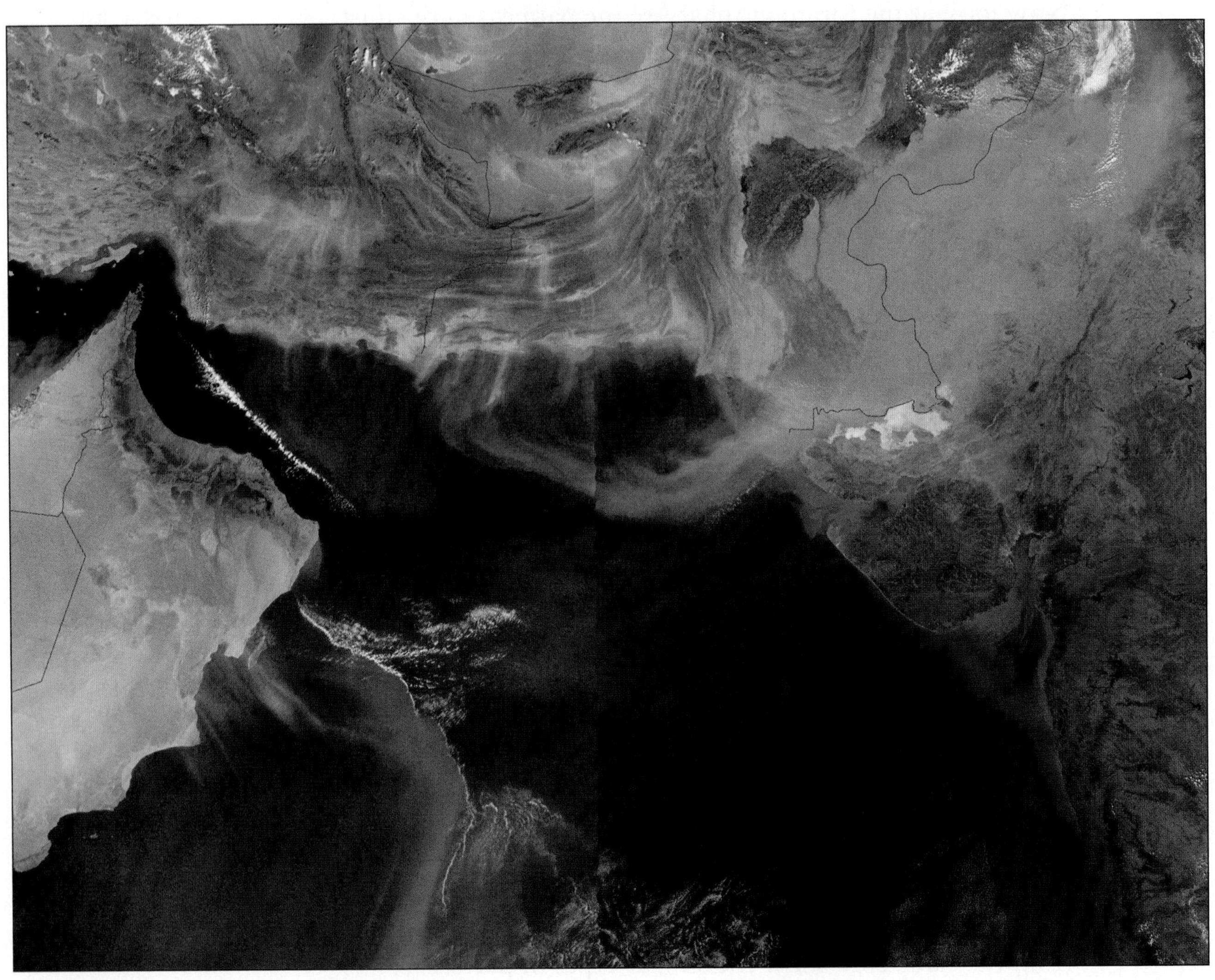

▲ **Figure 12.25 Dust storm over the Arabian Sea.** This satellite photograph shows dust being blown into the Arabian Sea. Do you think that more dust enters the Arabian Sea during glacial or interglacial periods? How would you test your answer?

Process and Procedure

Listen to directions from your teacher to answer the questions in Steps 1–3 on your own. You will have about 15–20 min to write your answers on a sheet of paper. You must use clear sentences and references to data to answer these questions.

1. Are the cores that you have studied part of a global system? Are they part of a global cycle? Revisit the locations in figure 12.24. Use at least 2 pieces of evidence or examples from these sites to explain, in writing, why or why not. Feel free to use what you have learned in chapters 10 and 11.
2. Are the data from sites 1020 (pollen) and 722 (dust) consistent with astronomical theory? You have studied the astronomical theory of climate history using data from forams in sea cores. Now use data from sites 1020 and 722 to explain why, or why not.
3. How was the process that you and your partner used to analyze new data from sea cores similar to the work that a scientist does?

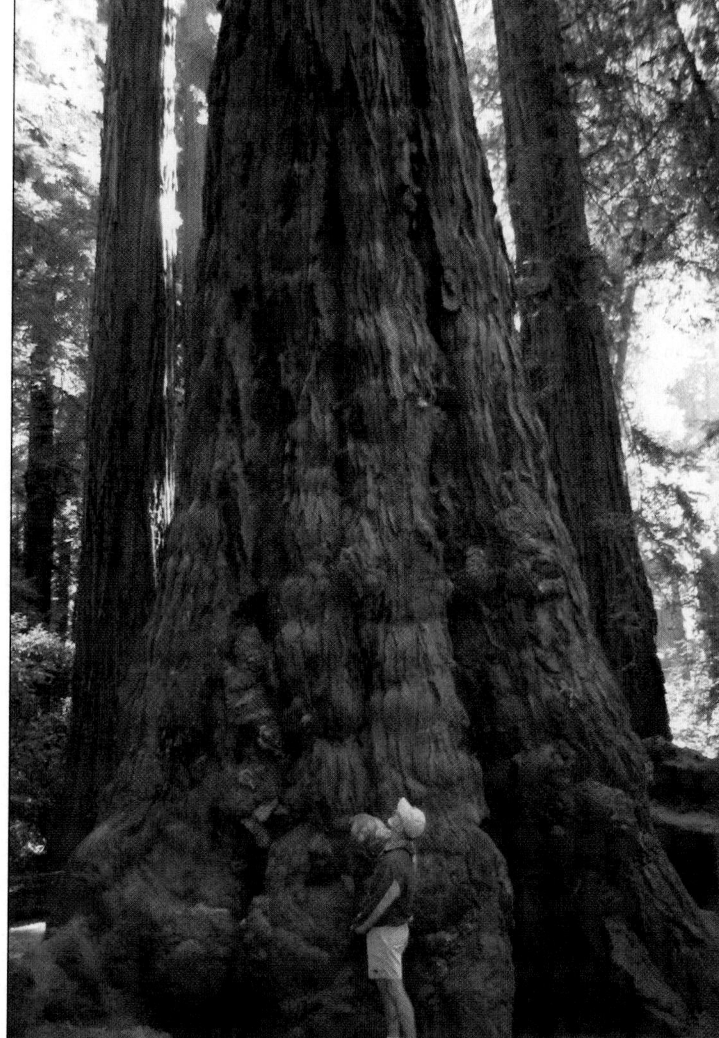

▲ **Figure 12.26 Redwood forest.** Massive redwood trees (*Sequoia*) like this live in Northern California. This tree is about 7.6 m in diameter at the base. Redwoods form a moist, coastal rain forest with about 50–80 inches (about 130–200 cm) of rain per year. How much pollen do you think a redwood forest produces?

CHAPTER 13

Time for Change

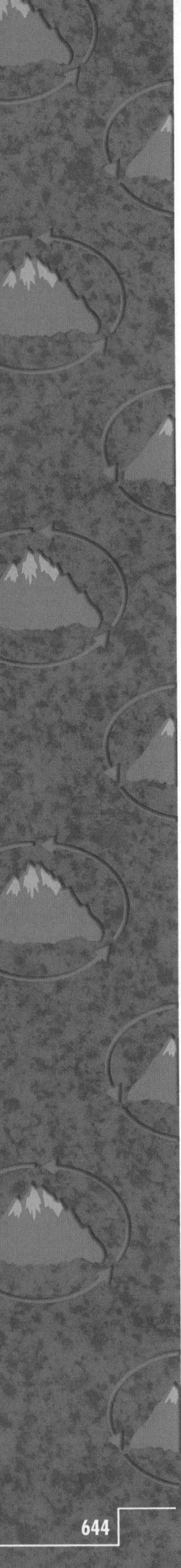

Time for Change

Change. You see it all around you. You see change occurring in your school, in your family, and in your community. An obvious change might be construction in your community. You probably also notice changes that occur naturally in your body. Change is part of our lives.

But what exactly is a change? How much time needs to pass before you can see a change? Beyond your community, can you see changes that occur in ecosystems or the earth around you? Is there a part of Earth that you heard about recently that had a change such as an earthquake or a volcanic eruption? What was it like in the age of the dinosaurs? There has been a big change in Earth from then to now.

Depending on your perspective, change may be fairly easy to define. For example, you learned in earlier chapters that a change in distance for a given time defines velocity. You measured velocities in several settings. And you saw how reactants changed to make new products in a chemical reaction. If you can identify a change, can you also tell when something else doesn't change and is constant? For example, is there something in your classroom that is constant?

Goals for the Chapter

Let's think more about earth systems. Is it easy to identify when things are constant and when they change? You'll explore such questions in chapter 13, *Time for Change*. This will also help you better understand the interactions that occur between the geologic and biological parts of earth systems. In fact, by the end of this chapter, you will learn about

- the rates that tectonic plates move across Earth and the ways that plates interact,
- the driving forces for plate tectonics,
- the patterns and cycles of life on Earth related to plate tectonics,
- the differences between continental drift and plate tectonics, and
- how plate tectonics links with the record of life on Earth (the fossil record).

In chapter 13, you will complete these activities:

ENGAGE	Mile High Time Machine
EXPLORE	Scaling Up to Mountainous Change
EXPLAIN	Rates of Plates
EXPLORE	Sinking Slabs and Convection Connections
ELABORATE	Building Bridges
EVALUATE	Falling into the Ocean

Chapter organizers can help you remember what you have learned and where you are headed. They also help you recognize the most important ideas to learn in a chapter. Look at the chapter organizer every day. Think about where you are in its organization. Compare what you know now with what you knew a week ago. Let the chapter organizer help you map your learning and monitor your progress. That way, you can look back and see what you have accomplished.

Time for Change

Linking Question

How do many small changes add up to one large, geologic change?

Engage

Mile High Time Machine

Key Idea:

You can find evidence of change between an ecosystem today and the same location during the age of the dinosaurs. You do this by comparing plants, animals, and features of the land.

Explore

Scaling Up to Mountainous Change Part I — Paper Plates

Key Ideas:

- Given enough time, small movements add up to large, geologic changes.
- Models help show the velocity that tectonic plates move on Earth.

Scaling Up to Mountainous Change Part II — Ups and Downs of Mountains

Key Idea:

Tectonic uplift builds mountains, and other forces tear down mountains.

a. Geologic diagram of Papua New Guinea

239 ka
198 ka
125 ka
100 ka
81 ka

Linking Question

How do tectonic plates interact and change the surface of Earth?

Explain

Rates of Plates

Key Idea:

Tectonic plates interact by crashing together, splitting apart, or grinding past one another.

Linking Question

Why do tectonic plates move?

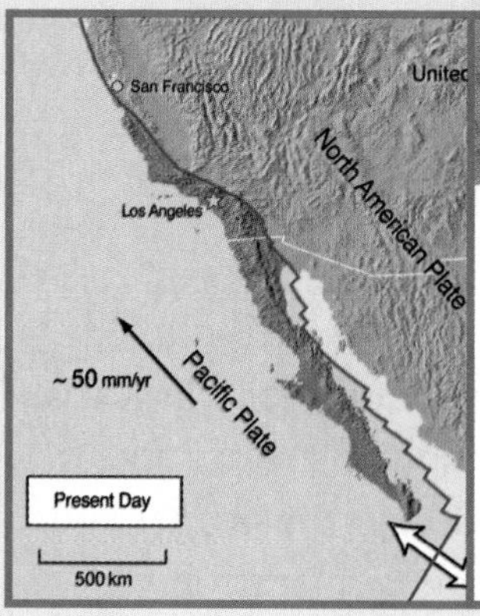

EVALUATE

Falling into the Ocean

Key Idea:

Vectors of plate velocities give evidence about where a plate has been and are used to predict where a plate is going.

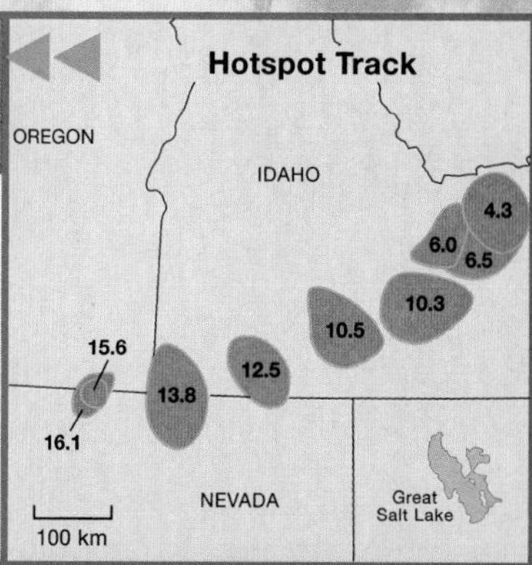

Linking Question

Can geologists predict changes in Earth that occur due to plate tectonics?

CHAPTER 13 Major Concepts

- Different parts of earth systems change at different rates.
- Plate tectonics, mountain building, and erosion have shaped the surface of Earth.
- Tectonic plates interact by crashing together, pulling apart, or grinding past one another.
- Some tectonic events are rapid. It takes many such events over long periods of time to build mountains.
- Many patterns of life on Earth are linked to patterns of plate tectonics.

ELABORATE

Building Bridges

Key Idea:

Connections between continents let animals migrate between them. This alters the animal families preserved in the fossil record.

EXPLORE

Sinking Slabs and Convection Connections

Key Idea:

Mantle convection moves heat out of Earth's interior. Yet a key force in plate tectonics is the downward "pull" on sinking plates at subduction zones.

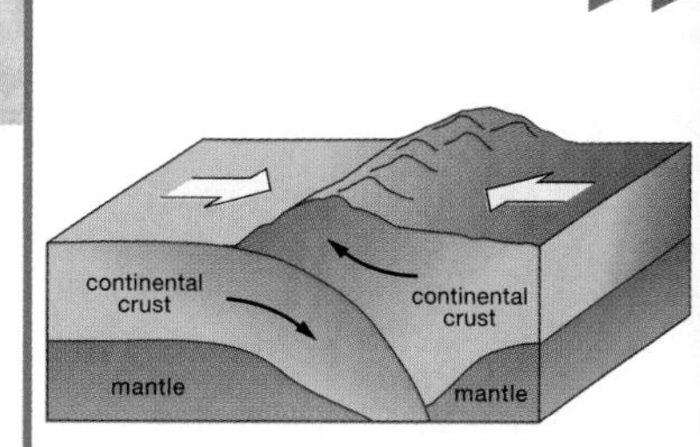

Linking Question

Does plate tectonics affect things like the fossil record of animals on continents?

ENGAGE

Mile High Time Machine

Time machines. They are a favorite of science fiction thrillers. They can propel you into the future with space travel through wormholes, as you eat nourishing meals of orange-flavored capsules. Time machines in science fiction can also send you back in time. They can propel you back to the American Revolution, the signing of the Declaration of Independence, or the building of the pyramids in Egypt. But imagine that you can dial your time machine back still further in time.

Let's take a part of North America today—the state of Colorado—in the center of the continent. Denver is a large city near the center of Colorado, with the Rocky Mountains lying directly to the west (figure 13.1). Because its official elevation is 5,280 feet (ft), Denver is called the "Mile High City." But has Denver always been like that? What would it be like to travel in a time machine to Denver 70 million years ago (Mya)? How has Denver changed since then?

In real life, there is something that acts just like a time machine. It is the geologic record. You've studied the geologic record in other parts of this program. In *Mile High Time Machine*, you will work with a partner to compare scenes around Denver, Colorado, at two very different time periods. What did Denver look like many millions of years of ago? What can you infer from the scenes? Examining scenes around Denver will help you think about other changes on Earth that take a long time.

Materials

For each team of 3 students

3 *Falling into the Ocean Scoring Rubric* handouts

Process and Procedure

1. By yourself, examine and think about the scene from Colorado in figure 13.1. Answer the following questions about the scene and list your ideas in your science notebook.
   a. What kinds of animals do you think are living there?
   b. What types of plants do you think are living there?
   c. What evidence do you see for what the climate is like?
   d. What evidence do you see for what the elevation is like?
2. Get with a partner. Share your ideas about the questions in Step 1. What inferences can you and your teammate make about the types of animals and plants and the ecosystem?

▲ **Figure 13.1 Rocky Mountain ecosystem today.** This scene is just west of Denver, Colorado. How does it compare with scenes of the same area from the geologic past?

3. Look at the chapter opener image. It is another scene from central Colorado during the age of the dinosaurs. Pteranodons soar above the shoreline of a continental sea, while dinosaurs like iguanodon amble along warm, palm- and mangrove-lined beaches. With your partner, answer the questions in Step 1 for the scene in the chapter opener.
4. Work as a team to compare the 2 scenes from Colorado, figure 13.1 and the chapter opener.
   a. What things are similar between the 2 scenes?
   b. What things have changed between the 2 scenes?

It will help you to organize your observations in columns of similarities and differences.

5. One of the Colorado images shows mountains. Write in your science notebook all the ideas that you and your partner have for how mountains form.

Reflect and Connect

Discuss the following questions with your partner and write answers in your science notebook.

1. With your partner, estimate how many years ago the scene in the chapter opener occurred. Perhaps you have studied the age of the dinosaurs in other science classes.

Be as specific as you can. It may help you to refer back to chapter 6, *Exploring Change*. You can modify your answer as you learn more.

2. One image you studied had mammals, and the other had reptiles. What are your current ideas about the differences between mammals and reptiles, such as dinosaurs? Write your ideas in your science notebook. You might consider differences and similarities such as food, habitat, or body features.
3. Discuss with your partner questions you may have about the topography, elevation, or climate for the 2 scenes from the Denver area.
   a. Decide on the most interesting question you and your partner have and write it in your science notebook.
   b. Can you answer part of the question at this time? Write a possible answer to that question.

Feel free to draw a labeled sketch as well. This is a good way to represent ideas that you are developing in science.

4. Review the 2 scenes of the Denver area. When do you think the Rocky Mountains formed? Use the words *before* and *after* to explain your evidence.

You can also draw a sequence of 2 to 3 sketches or diagrams showing this change from coastal plain to sharp-peaked mountains.

EXPLORE

Scaling Up to Mountainous Change

Denver, Colorado, sure has changed a lot. If you went to Denver in the geologic past, it might have had dinosaurs and sandy beaches at the edge of a continental sea. Plants would have included palms, cypresses, and mangroves—plants typical of warm, tropical climates. Today, the Rocky Mountains at Denver are not at all like this. There are rivers, cold-water fish such as trout in rushing mountain streams, lizards and snakes, and many types of large mammals. The plants and animals—the flora and fauna—have changed rather dramatically.

But how can you explain the changes that occur over long periods of time? For example, how does land change in elevation from sea level to towering, snowcapped peaks? How long does this take? What sorts of movements affect Earth's surface and how the surface looks?

In *Scaling Up to Mountainous Change*, you and two teammates will learn how to scale up from small movements to really large ones. The large movements are truly geologic in scale. You will use simple paper plates to simulate Earth movements.

Part I: Paper Plates

Materials

For each team of 3 students

1 timer or stopwatch

1 paper plate

1 small plastic animal

1 pair of scissors

1 length of masking tape (15 cm)

1 meterstick

1 calculator

1 red pen

1 *Lower 48 States Map* handout

Process and Procedure

1. Obtain 1 paper plate for your team. Cut the plate in the shape of your favorite continent and attach a plastic animal to the plate. Cut or tear the masking tape into 10–15 small pieces.
2. Clear a path across the surface of your team's work surface (your desk, a large table, or a lab counter). Place a piece of tape as a marker every 10 centimeters (cm). Do this across the length of the table.
3. Move your paper plate with your hand from one end of the work surface to the other at a constant rate of 10 centimeters per 5 seconds (10 cm/5 sec).

It may help to designate one teammate as timer and one as recorder.

4. How long does it take for your paper plate to move from one end of your work surface to the other end? Show your answer in seconds and in minutes. Explain in your science notebook 2 different ways that you could determine the time.
5. Return the plate to its initial spot. You and your teammates will scale up the movement of the paper plate. You will calculate how long it would take for the paper plate to move to 2 other locations in your school at 2 cm/sec.

Your teacher may write an estimate of distance on the board. Or your class might use other locations if you know their distances.

Figure 13.2 will help you organize your calculations. Record all your work in your science notebook.

a. Rewrite your plate's velocity from Step 3 as seconds per centimeter (sec/cm).
b. Convert this rate to units of seconds per meter (sec/m).
c. What is this rate in units of minutes per meter (min/m)?

Location	Distance (meter, or m)	Time (minute, or min)	Time (hour, or hr)
Cafeteria			
Principal's office			
Gymnasium			

▲ **Figure 13.2 Timetable for recording the distances of the paper plate.** Use a table like this to help organize the distances and times for a paper plate to move to areas like these at a rate of 2 cm/sec. Under the table, show all work and the units canceled.

6. For a paper plate with a velocity of 10 cm/5 sec (or 2 cm/sec), use Steps 6a–f to show how far the plate moves in 1 year. Show all work in your science notebook.
   a. Write the velocity in units of centimeters per 1 second (cm/sec).
   b. Convert the velocity to units of centimeters per minute (cm/min).
   c. Convert the velocity to units of centimeters per year (cm/yr).
   d. Scale up by converting the velocity to units of meters per year (m/yr).
   e. Scale up again to units of kilometers per year (km/yr).
   f. Check your conversion for Step 6e again with your team. When your team thinks you have it, run it by your teacher.

A vital skill that will help you is canceling the units in the numerator and the denominator. Check that you and your teammates understand how to do this.

7. How many years would it take to move your plate to a farther location using the same velocity (km/yr) from Step 6e? Follow Steps 7a–d to find out.
   a. Obtain for your team 1 copy of the handout *Lower 48 States Map*. Place a red star at the location of your school.

Figure 13.3 is a map of the Lower 48 states with a line from San Francisco, California, to Chicago, Illinois. Be sure that you and your teammates can use the scale on the map to show that the line is about 2,900 kilometers (km) long.

b. Select any 4 states from the map and note the location of their capitals. Draw a line from each capital to your school.
c. Use the scale on the map to determine the distance in kilometers from your school to each capital.

Each teammate should make a table like figure 13.2 in his or her science notebook to organize these data. What table headings will you use? Use Steps 7a–d to decide.

d. Calculate how many years it would take to slide your paper plate to another capital. Use your distances and plate velocity to determine this for each capital.

You may slide your plate to other parts of the globe, such as a vacation destination. But you also need to obtain a map showing the United States and that location, along with the distance in kilometers.

8. Return to the question in Step 4. How long would it take for your paper plate to move from one end of your work surface to the other end at a rate of 3 cm/yr? This is a typical rate for tectonic plates, which you will learn about in this chapter.

There are several ways to determine the answer. Show clearly in your science notebook how your team got the answer.

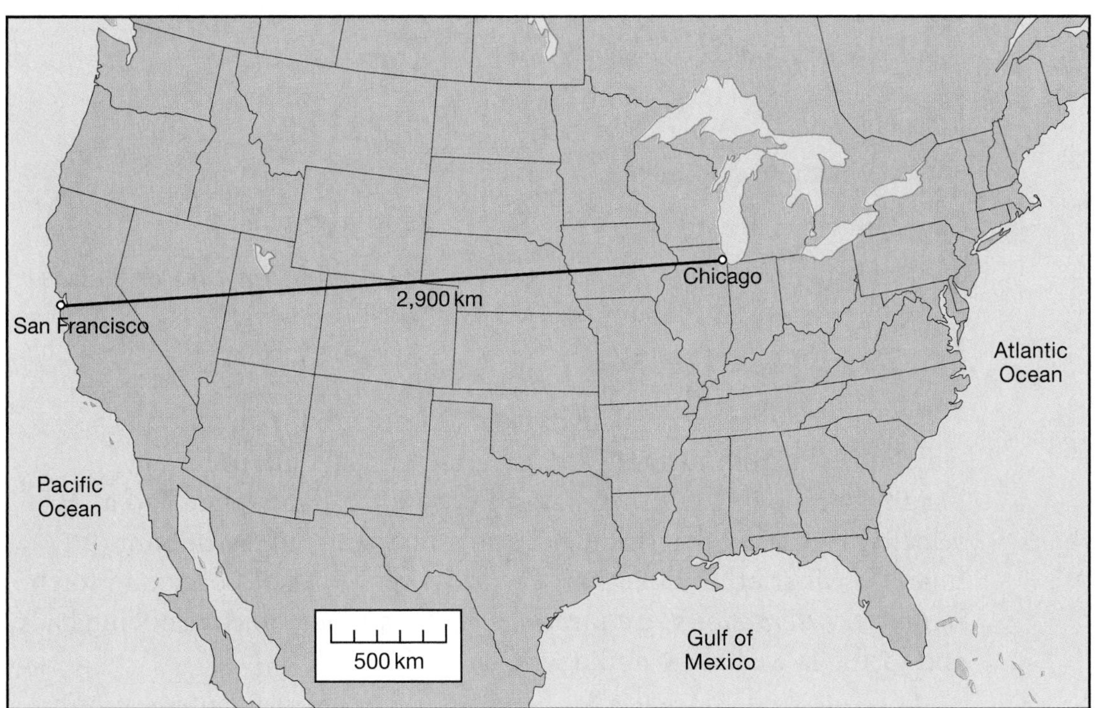

Figure 13.3 Map of the Lower 48 states. The line on this map connects San Francisco and Chicago. Be sure that you can use the scale bar (500 km) to show that the length of the San Francisco–Chicago line is about 2,900 km.

Stop & THINK

PART I

Answer the following question about paper plates with your team.

1. Compare the velocity of your paper plate in Step 6 with the movements of continents over the surface of Earth. Except for Australia, continents move about 3 cm/yr.
   - **a.** What step from Step 6 has units that are easiest to compare with a velocity of 3 cm/yr? Explain why.
   - **b.** Is the paper plate's or a continent's velocity faster? How different are the 2 velocities?

Recall that this type of question is best answered with a ratio. A ratio tells you how many times bigger or faster one number is than the other.

Part II: Ups and Downs of Mountains

Materials

For each team of 3 students

- 1 ruler
- 1 calculator
- colored pencils
- 3 *Mountain Profiles* handouts

Process and Procedure

In Part I, your paper plate moved in a horizontal direction. The plate moved across surfaces and around your school. You even imagined it moving to other states. Because the paper plate had a velocity, you could determine how far it would go in an amount of time. But what other directions do things move besides back and forth? In unit 1, *Interactions Are Interesting*, you studied objects moving back and forth, as well as up and down.

How about mountains? You saw that tectonic plates move across Earth at rates of roughly 3 cm/yr. How does this compare with how fast mountains can be pushed up? Work with your team to do the following activity. It will help you understand how fast mountains grow and how fast they can change Earth's surface.

1. With your team, view the flat-topped coral terrace in figure 13.4. Then read the following paragraph.

   You learned in the last chapter that the sea level has changed between glacial and interglacial periods. When the sea level drops, a reef ecosystem will be stranded above sea level and will die. The stranded, flat-topped part of the coral reef is called a **terrace.** You learned that radiometric dating of corals can measure when the sea level last covered the terrace with 1–2 meters (m) of water. The terrace in figure 13.4a formed during a sea level high about 125,000 years ago (125 kya). (Remember, kya means thousands of years ago.) The sea level then was about 5 m above the current sea level.

2. Imagine you've just returned from exciting geological fieldwork in Papua New Guinea. Papua New Guinea is an area of active mountain formation located just north of Australia. Your work and diagrams show coral terraces on a hillside (figure 13.5.) Complete Steps 2a–f to determine the geologic history of the coral deposits.

   a. Write down the relationship you observe between the age of the corals and the elevation on the hillside.

Note that all these terraces formed during sea level highs, or interglacials. How do the ages of the terraces compare with the climate patterns in chapter 12, *Evidence for the Ice Ages*?

▲ **Figure 13.4 Exposed coral reef, Bahamas.** (a) This flat-topped, exposed coral terrace is at San Salvador, Bahamas. The top of this coral terrace is about 5 m above the current sea level. The close-ups (b and c) show fossil corals in the terrace.

b. Explain the relationship you identified in Step 2a. That is, what does this relationship tell you about the geologic history of this hillside over the past 350,000 years (350 kyr)? (Remember, kyr means thousands of years.)

Make a quick sketch of figure 13.5 in your science notebook and complete the phrases "What I see" and "What it means."

c. Use a strategy to organize your observations of elevation (in meters) as a function of coral age (in thousands of years). Do this in your science notebook.

d. Make a graph to determine a rate of change shown by these data.

Recall that rates show a change in something per amount of time. Extend time on your graph out to 400 kya.

e. Draw a best-fit line through these data with a pencil and determine the value of the slope. Be sure to check the units for your slope. This is the uplift rate.

It may help your team to review the *How To* section on determining slopes: *How to Use Graphs, Measure Slopes, and Estimate Uncertainty* located in the back of your book.

f. Use highlight comments on your graph ("What I see," "What it means") to explain what the slope on the graph indicates about this region of Papua New Guinea.

3. Complete Steps 2a–f for figure 13.5b for a colleague's diagram. She has just returned from mapping coral terraces on the island of Barbados, an area of active mountain formation in the Caribbean Sea. Add these data for Barbados to the graph you did in Step 2 for Papua New Guinea.

You can use a different symbol or color for these data.

4. Develop a sentence with your team comparing the Papua New Guinea and the Barbados data in your graph.
5. How does the upward movement of coral terraces relate to the making of mountains? Read the following paragraph to learn more about the rates at which mountains are made.

World maps show continents, oceans, or countries. But it can be hard to tell from maps where mountains are growing. In active mountains, such changes are happening all the time. Maybe the evidence is an occasional earthquake or a volcanic eruption. Pushing the land up to form mountains is called **uplift**. Examples of active uplift include the Andes mountains, the islands of New Zealand, the Himalaya mountains, and

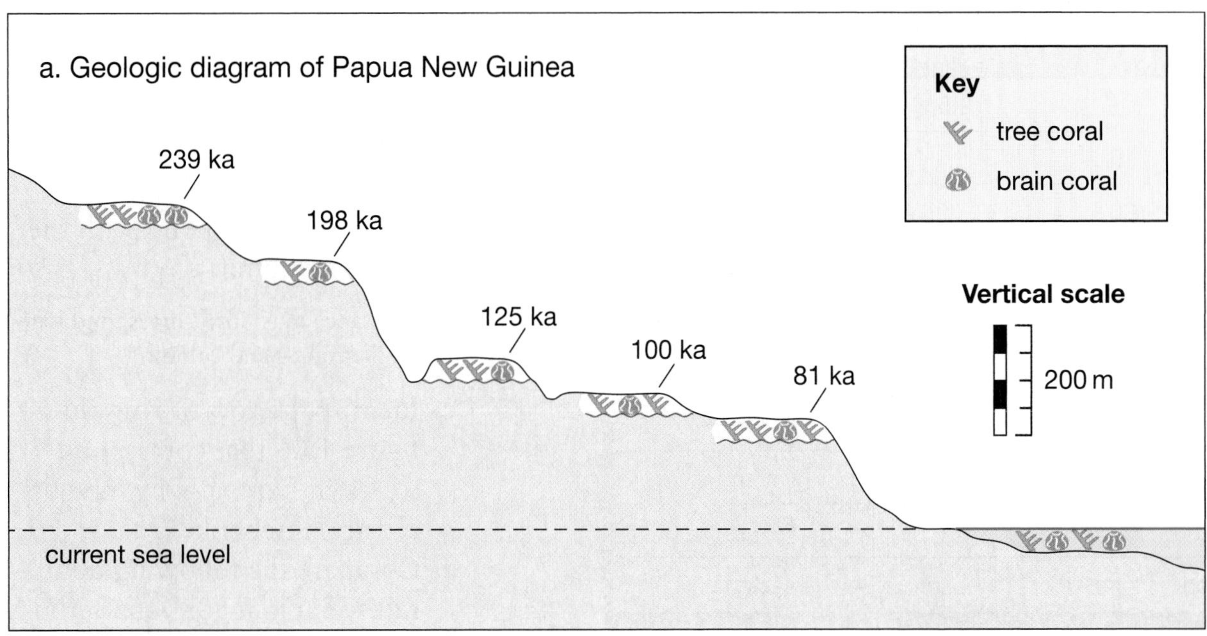

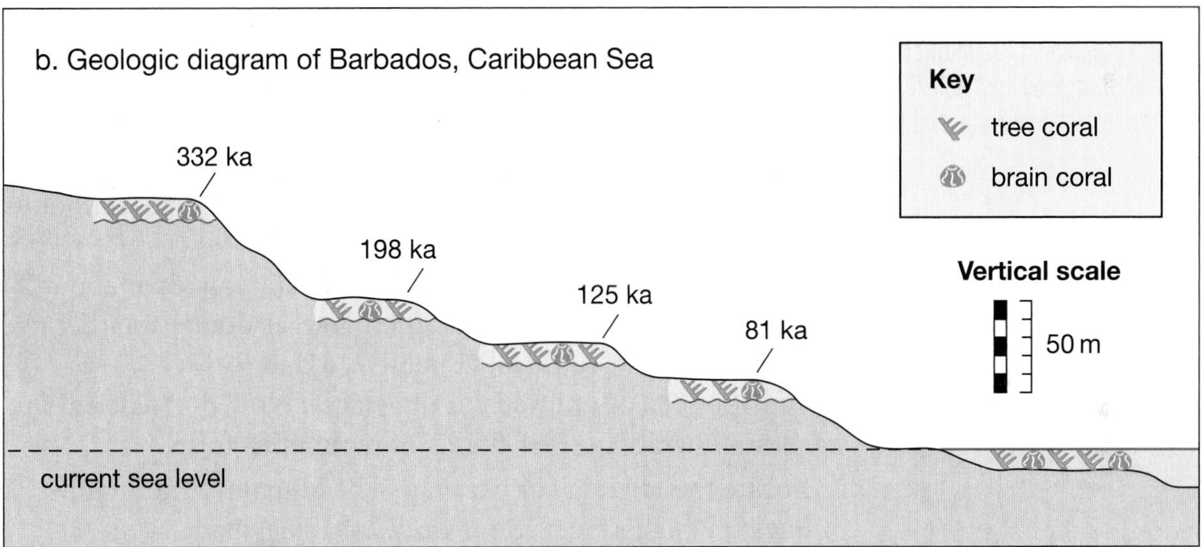

▲ **Figure 13.5 Coral terraces in (a) Papua New Guinea and (b) Barbados.** The geologic diagrams show coral terraces cut into hillsides on Papua New Guinea and Barbados. Radiometric dating tells the age when the corals were living at sea level (as thousands of years ago, or kya). Examples of fossilized tree and brain coral appear in figure 13.4. Living examples are in chapter 12.

parts of the Middle East and western North America. In these areas, uplift rates can be as high as +10 millimeters per year (mm/yr). That may not sound like a lot, but with a lot of time, this uplift can make massive mountains.

6. Uplift over geologic lengths of time is harder to envision than small uplifts each year. Work through Steps 6a–d to estimate how many kilometers can be uplifted in 1 million years (Myr).

Time (yr)	Distance	Units for distance
1	2.5	mm
10		mm
100		mm
1,000		mm
1,000		m
10,000		m
100,000		m
1,000,000		m
1,000,000		km
1 million = 1×10^6		km

▲ **Figure 13.6 Rates for scaling up tectonic uplift.** Tectonic uplift in mountains is a slow process. Uplift occurs over millions of years. Complete this table for an uplift rate of 2.5 mm/yr. This will help you estimate how much uplift can occur in 1 Myr.

a. Study figure 13.6 with your partner. Copy it into your science notebook.
b. Fill in all the blank cells in the "distance" column so that they correspond with the "time" column.

Note that distance must also correspond with the units in the right-hand column.

c. Identify the row or rows in figure 13.6 that correspond to 1 kyr. Explain why in your science notebook.
d. Compare the following uplift rates. Explain your answer in your science notebook.
    i. 2.5 millimeters per year (mm/yr)
    ii. 2.5 meters per thousand years (m/kyr)
    iii. 2.5 kilometers per million years (km/Myr)

7. Read *FYI—Weather to Erode*. This will help you learn about 2 processes that describe how mountains wear down: weathering and erosion. Refer to this FYI in Steps 8 and 9.
8. You just looked at uplifted coral terraces. Now do Steps 8a–f to start thinking about how chains of mountains form.
    a. Locate the Himalaya on a map. The Himalaya mountains have the highest elevations on Earth. They have been forming for 30–40 Myr. The limestone at Mount Everest (the highest peak on Earth) shows that those rocks were near sea level in the past (figure 13.7).
    b. Determine how much uplift occurs in 1 Myr when there is an uplift rate of 2.5 mm/yr.

Use your work in Step 6 and figure 13.6 to help with this conversion.

c. Determine how high a mountain such as Mount Everest would grow in 10 Myr with an uplift rate of 2.5 mm/yr.
d. Geologic evidence shows that Mount Everest has grown to about 8,850 m (29,035 ft) in about 30 Myr. Compare this with your result in Step 8b.

A good way to make comparisons is to use words like "greater than" and "less than" or to estimate how many times slower or faster something is.

Weather to Erode

You certainly have experienced things wearing out. Perhaps it's your shoes, your car's tires, a soccer ball, or a pencil eraser. An object loses mass as small bits or fragments of material are taken away.

But by "wear out," you also could mean a chemical change. Maybe wear out refers to the chemical reaction in batteries as they lose their "juice." Or perhaps the change is the deterioration of lawn furniture exposed to rain and solar radiation. What about a hammer left out in the rain? It gets a rust coating that can be wiped off with your finger.

Mountains wear out, too. And just like car tires and outdoor lawn furniture, they do it by chemical and physical processes. Think about a rock outside, on a mountain, or even on a building's facade. As the rock is exposed to the weather, minerals in the rock begin subtle chemical changes. A good analogy is the hammer—iron metal turns to iron oxide, or rust. The process of the natural chemical alteration of minerals is called **weathering**. Water is often part of a weathering change.

Chemical changes by themselves, however, do not decrease the mass of the rock. Another process must move matter away. This is how mountains can wear down. **Erosion** is the process where weathered rock fragments and soils are transported and moved downward due to gravity. Erosion of mountains occurs along steep slopes and river valleys. Erosion by flowing rivers moves sand and silt away from mountains and closer to oceans. Some parts of rocks, such as carbonate or salt deposits, will even dissolve right into rivers and be carried away to the ocean.

How long does it take for mountains to weather and erode? How would you tell this? Effects that you might notice are a decrease in elevation or a gentle rounding of mountain peaks. An easy way to estimate the decrease in elevation is with the concept of half-lives. You already used half-lives in chapter 6 with radioactive elements. For mountains, the **erosion half-life** is the time needed for the elevations of a profile to decrease by about half.

Consider mountains made of hard granite that have an average elevation of 12,000 ft and an erosion half-life of 10 Myr (see the graph). After about 10 Myr (one half-life), the elevation would have been reduced by about 6,000 ft to an elevation of about 6,000 ft. After a total of 20 Myr (two half-lives), the elevation would have decreased by about 9,000 ft, to an elevation of about 3,000 ft.

This is a simple way to quantify how Earth's surface wears out. Of course, Earth is much more complex than radioactive isotopes in decay. Still, it's nice to have a good rule of thumb to help learn about rates of erosion and weathering.

Go to: www.scilinks.org
Topic: weathering
Code: 2Inquiry659a
Topic: erosion
Code: 2Inquiry659b

Graph showing erosional half-lives of mountains. This graph shows the average elevation of mountains with time due to erosion. The average elevation decreases by half every 10 Myr. How tall will the mountains be in about 40 Myr?

e. Discuss with your teammates the factors or processes on Earth that can help explain the comparison in Step 8d.

What factors or processes can you think of that make mountains appear to be growing more slowly than the actual uplift rate? What would you expect in the areas between mountain peaks in the Himalaya?

f. Examine figure 13.7 with your teammates. What evidence in the figures supports the idea that the peaks may not grow at 2.5 mm/yr, even when they are being pushed up that fast?

9. Obtain 3 copies of the *Mountain Profiles* handout. Then follow Steps 9a–e to see how a mountain chain such as the Appalachians changes when it is not being uplifted.
   a. With your teammates, trace your fingers over the profile of elevation in the handout. Label the elevations of the peaks and valleys on your handout.
   b. The profile mimics a mountain chain like the Appalachians, which has an erosion half-life of about 5 Myr. On your diagram, draw a prediction for the elevations of the peaks and valleys in about 5 Myr.

Connect points with lines to make a full profile. Use colored lines or labels to help indicate the future profile of elevation.

c. Use the concept of erosion half-life again to predict the elevations of the peaks and valleys after another 5 Myr (10 Myr total). Draw your prediction on your diagram.

What color will you use for this line? How will you organize your different profiles in a legend?

d. Explain how you can predict the elevation profile 5 Myr before the initial profile on the handout.
e. The erosion half-life model is a good tool for making predictions. List in your science notebook possible limitations to this tool.

10. In Step 2, you investigated a region of current tectonic uplift in Papua New Guinea.
    a. Look up the tectonic uplift rate you determined in Step 2.
    b. With your team, list how erosion and uplift affect mountains. Write in your science notebook what you think would happen if these processes were occurring at the same time.
    c. Predict how the erosion half-lives for mountains like the Appalachians in Step 9 might compare with the erosion half-lives in other areas. Geologists have shown that conditions at Papua New Guinea give an erosion half-life of about 1 Myr. Rocks there are loose volcanic rocks on steep slopes that get heavy tropical rains.

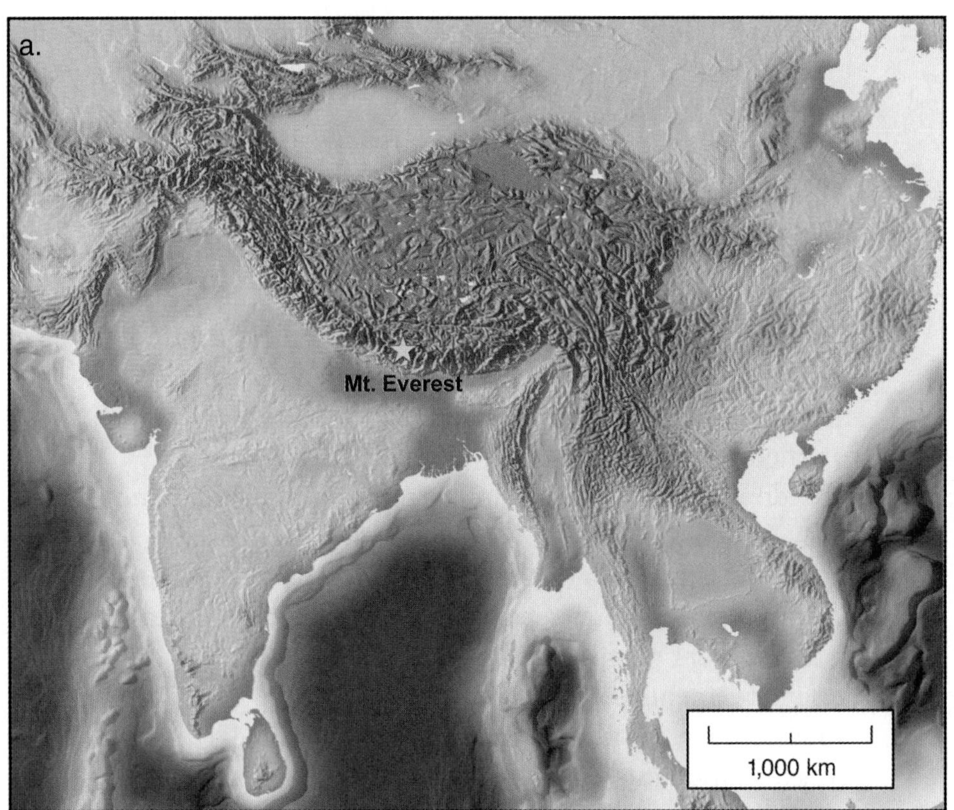

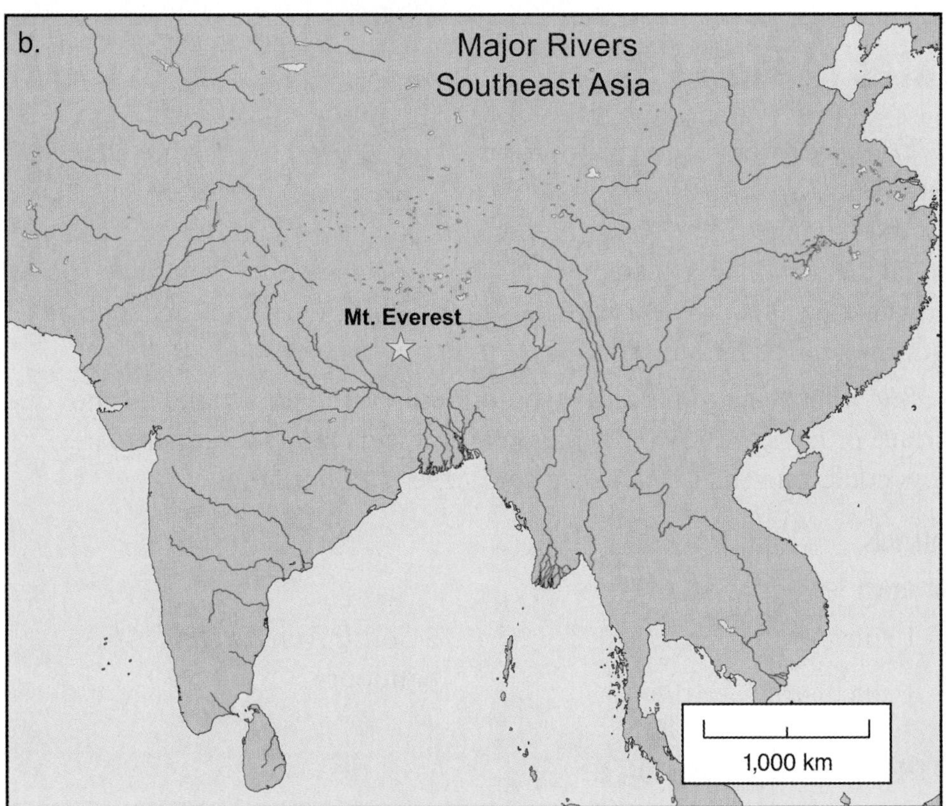

Figure 13.7 Two views of the high Himalaya. (a) The map extends from Iran to China and is centered on the high Himalaya. The star marks Mount Everest. (b) The diagram shows the same region with the land tan, the ocean blue, and major rivers superposed.

d. What is the change in elevation for mountains when the rate of erosion equals the rate of uplift? Write your ideas in your science notebook.

Reflect and Connect

Discuss the following questions with your teammates. Write your answers in your science notebook.

1. View the 5 overhead transparencies of patterns around Earth that your teacher will show you. Share with the class the patterns you see about where earthquakes, volcanoes, continents, and several other geologic features occur.
2. How do you think animals might respond to tectonic movements of several centimeters per year? Consider a tectonically active region like California or the Pacific Northwest. Do you think an earthquake could change ecosystems? Explain your reasoning.
3. Consider rates of plate movement of 15 mm/yr. Sometimes these movements don't occur at a steady pace of 15 mm/yr, but rather happen in sudden lurches. Consider an earthquake that gives a sudden movement of 2 m. How often would events with 2 m of displacement occur to give a net rate of 15 mm/yr?

EXPLAIN

Rates of Plates

You have probably heard that rates can be used to indicate change. Rates tell how fast something happens. For example, velocity tells how distance changes in a given time, as you saw in earlier chapters. Maybe the rate is for a paper plate moving in your classroom. Or maybe you're investigating slow, steady velocities in the up-down direction, such as with the uplift of mountains.

But what sorts of patterns would these movements make on the surface of Earth? How do geologic movements relate to paper plates? How could movements across a surface lead to uplift?

Materials

For each team of 3 students

1 ruler

1 calculator

3 *South America and Africa* handouts

Process and Procedure

Complete the following reading with two teammates to learn more about tectonic plates on Earth. Follow your teacher's instructions about using a strategy to better understand and share ideas from the reading.

READING

Crash, Stretch, and Grind

It's a major scientific discovery of the past 50 years. It's a unifying theory for understanding the surface of Earth. It helps explain the continents, the location of mountains and oceans, natural resources, climate patterns, biological evolution, and many other phenomena. Have you heard of it? It's the **theory of plate tectonics**. You likely studied plate tectonics in middle school. This theory explains the formation of some of the largest features and structures on Earth.

The plate tectonics theory holds that 12 or so rigid **plates** move slowly over Earth. They travel atop the Earth's **mantle**. These plates interact in a number of ways and affect virtually everything in the earth system. Continents ride above sea level and are important parts of several tectonic plates. These parts of plates consist of **continental crust**, the basic rock material of the continents. But there is more to tectonic plates than continents. The other main part is denser than continents and lies beneath the ocean. Rocks in this part of the plate make up what is called **oceanic crust** (figure 13.8).

In many cases, the same plate includes both continental and ocean crust. An example is the eastern margin of the North American Plate. There, continental crust meets oceanic crust at the Atlantic shore (figure 13.9). The South American and African plates are also much larger than their continents alone. In contrast, one of Earth's largest plates, the Pacific Plate, is made up almost entirely of oceanic crust. The Pacific Plate does not have any continents, but only fragments of continental crust in some areas. You'll learn more about this later in the chapter.

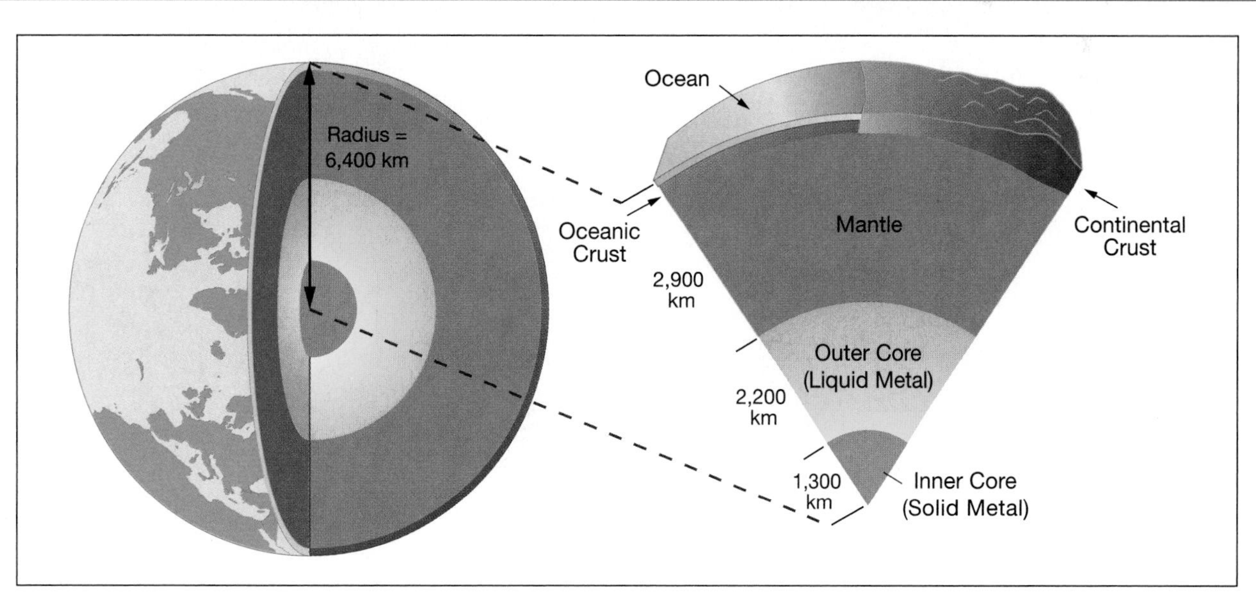

▲ **Figure 13.8 Internal structure of Earth.** Earth consists of several layers arranged like the layers of an onion. Tectonic plates of oceanic crust or continental crust move slowly atop the mantle of Earth.

Crash, Stretch, and Grind, continued

Another important idea led to the theory of plate tectonics. This was **continental drift**, the idea that continents drift slowly across Earth's surface. This idea has proven correct. But, you can also now see that tectonic plates consist of much more than drifting continents. All ocean floors are also part of moving plates.

To better understand tectonic plates, you must look at their interactions. What happens where plates come together? What about where they split apart? Do these interactions affect humans? Where plates meet, they can interact in three general ways. They can either crash, stretch and split apart, or grind past each other. A way to describe these interactions is as three main tectonic settings. To help you answer those earlier questions, read on to learn more about these interactions.

Tectonic Setting 1: Crash—Colossal Collisions

Collisions are dangerous, especially when you are in a car. In a car collision, a car and an object come together too fast. The area where they meet has several characteristic shapes. Some of those shapes are shown in figure 13.10. What evidence do you see to indicate a collision?

Tectonic collisions are similar to car collisions. Of course, a tectonic collision is much slower. But still, zones of collision can be thousands of kilometers long. These collision zones form long chains of mountains. They are distinct areas of uplift, just like the area on the car hood in figure 13.10.

Sometimes the collision zones occur when regions of continental crust crash together

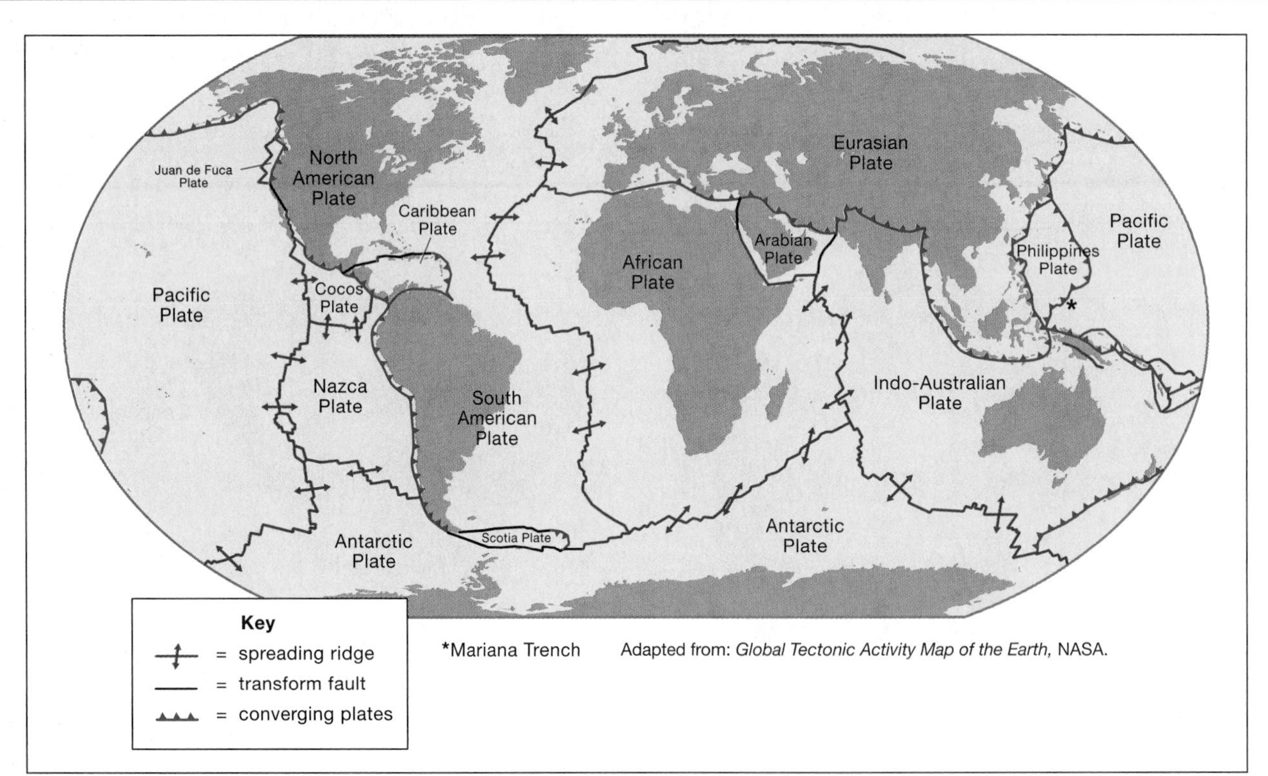

▲ **Figure 13.9 Tectonic plates of Earth.** This map shows the 12 main tectonic plates on Earth. Note that plates can consist of continents as well as large areas of ocean and oceanic crust. Tectonic plates are more than just continents.

▲ **Figure 13.10 Car collision.** This car has collided with a pole. What evidence do you see to indicate the collision?

(figure 13.11). Because the crust comes together, or converges, at the edges of plates, such areas are called **convergent zones**. Examples include the Himalaya, the Alps, and the Appalachian mountains.

At other times, the parts of tectonic plates made of oceanic crust collide with continents. These are also convergent zones since plates are crashing together. Because the oceanic crust is more dense than continental crust, it is thrust downward, or **subducted**, beneath the continent (figure 13.11). This dense oceanic crust then sinks into the mantle.

Several large tectonic features form where oceanic crust sinks into the mantle. The down-going crust forms **subduction zones**. Deep **trenches** on the ocean floor indicate where ocean crust is being subducted. The subducted oceanic crust is sometimes called a slab. Lines of volcanoes above subduction zones are called **volcanic arcs**. For example, a deep trench and line of volcanoes are found as the Juan de Fuca Plate is subducted beneath North America in the Pacific Northwest (figure 13.11). They are called volcanic arcs because of their broad, curved shape. Examples are the Indonesian and Caribbean volcanic arcs in figure 13.9 and the spectacular Aleutian and Japan arcs.

SCiLINKS
NSTA
Go to: www.scilinks.org
Topic: theory of plate tectonics
Code: 2Inquiry665a
Topic: subduction zones
Code: 2Inquiry665b
Topic: volcanic arcs
Code: 2Inquiry665c

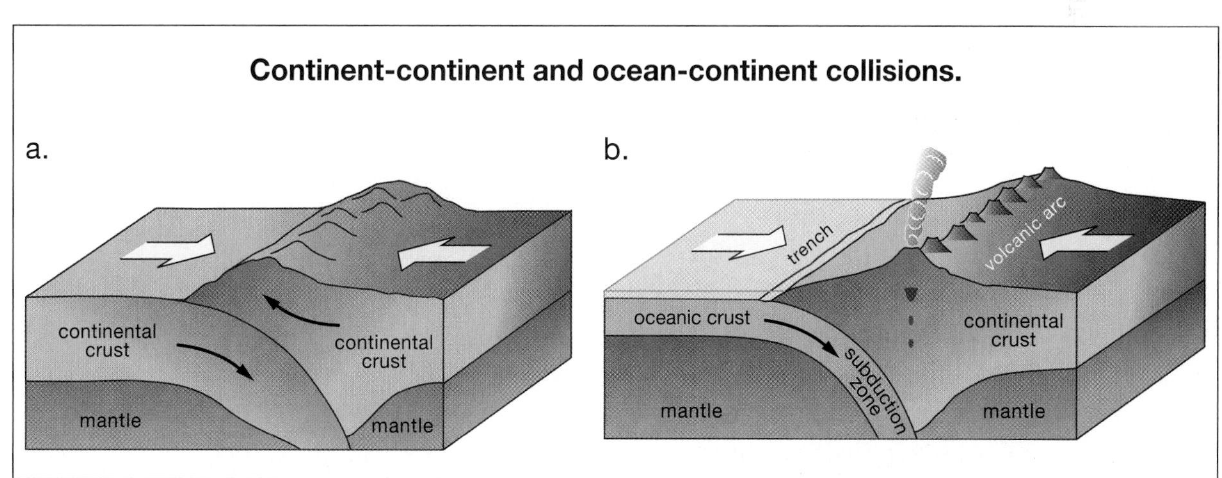

▲ **Figure 13.11 Two tectonic collisions.** Collisions between (a) continents and (b) oceanic crust and continental crust result in chains of mountains. Regions where oceanic crust is pushed beneath continental crust are called subduction zones.

Stop & THINK

Work with your teammates to complete the following tasks about tectonics.

1. Use a T-table to group the tectonic plates in figure 13.9.
   a. In the left-hand column, list plates consisting of both continental and oceanic crust.
   b. In the right-hand column, list plates made up of oceanic crust.

2. The ocean is deepest at the Mariana Trench, at about 11 km deep (figure 13.9). What kind of plate boundary do you think this is, and what is your evidence? What tectonic features are found there?

3. Figure 13.12 shows 5 positions of India in the past 71 Myr. The collision between India and Eurasia made the Himalaya. What was the tectonic velocity for India on its journey to this colossal collision?
   a. For each of the 5 positions shown, draw a small, dark circle on the southern tip of India.
   b. Compare the distance of each position with the same point on India today. Measure the distance from tip to tip in centimeters. Enter

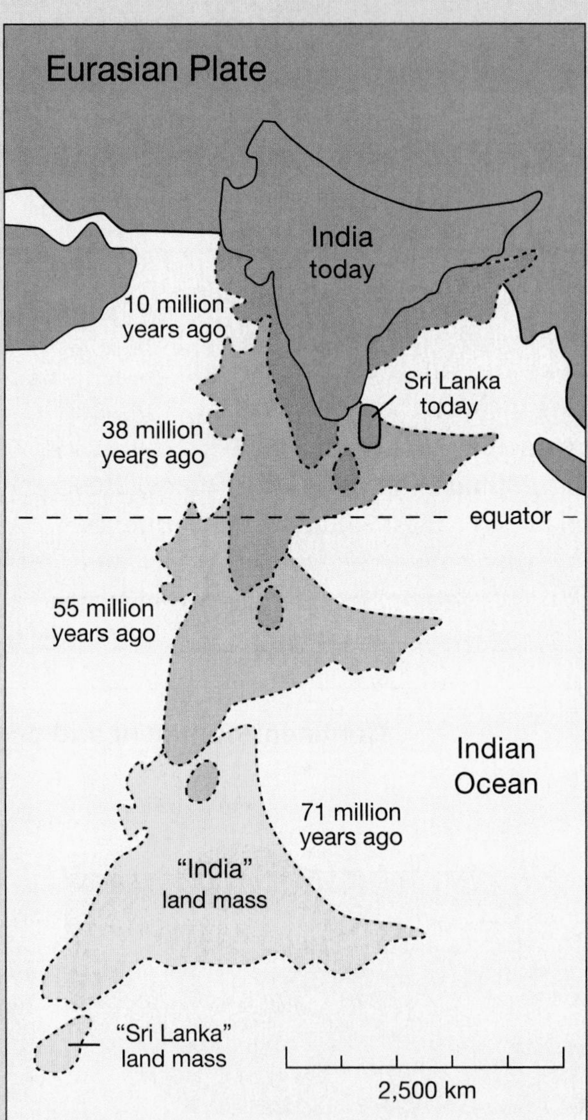

Figure 13.12 Northward tectonic movement of India. India has moved northward over the past 71 Myr. Determine the velocity of India by examining this record of distance and time.

these measurements in your science notebook in a table like figure 13.13.

c. Use the map scale to convert the centimeters that you measured to kilometers.

d. Plot 5 points on a graph of distance (in kilometers on the *y*-axis) as a function of time (in millions of years on the *x*-axis).

e. Use a pencil and ruler to draw a best-fit line through the points. What are the units for the slope of the line on your graph? What does the slope of the line tell you? Explain your answer.

Time (Myr)	Distance (cm)	Distance (km)
0	0	
10		
38		
55		
71		

Figure 13.13 Table for recording India's tectonics. Use a table like this to record distances for India at the times given in figure 13.12. Use the scale at the bottom of the map to convert centimeters on the map to kilometers on the ground.

Check that the line goes through zero. It's OK if the line does not connect all points. This is how you get a quick estimate.

4 Consider again your measurements for India. What if you connect data on your graph from point to point? What inferences can you make about the velocity of India? How might you explain the "low" point on your graph at about 40 Myr?

Crash, Stretch, and Grind, continued

Tectonic Setting 2: Stretch—Breaking Up Is Hard to Do

It's not too hard to imagine tectonic plates crashing together. They've been doing that for millions of years! One possible result is that plates collide to form mountains chains. Another result is one plate can be pushed into a subduction zone beneath the other. But what about the opposite? What happens when plates move in opposite directions? What happens when plates are stretched to the limit?

Just as with stretching chewing gum or rubber bands, plates will eventually break and begin to rip apart. Geologists can observe this process happening at many places today on Earth. The point where plates have broken is called a **rift**. Rifts often form long valleys, or **rift valleys**. These can be many thousands of feet deep. Examples of rifts on continents are the Rio Grande Rift, extending from northern Mexico to Colorado in the United States. A famous rift is the East African Rift. There, a large fragment of continental Africa is being torn away to the east. The floor of the rift valley provides a rich, unique ecosystem for many species. This rift valley also records the history of hominids (the family and ancestors of humans) in many famous fossil finds.

Continental rifts can grow wider and wider with more stretching. They also can get deeper, leaving the land surface below sea level. When these rift valleys meet the ocean, marine waters can move in to submerge the floor of the rift valley. Modern examples of this are the Red Sea and the Gulf of California.

Rifts are not only found on continents. In fact, the largest system of rifts on Earth is found beneath the ocean where tectonic plates are moving apart, or diverging. Rift zones are sometimes called **divergent zones**. These rifts form wide ridges of high topography, even though they are underwater. The areas of rifting are sometimes called **mid-oceanic ridges** due to their historic link with the ridge down the center of the Atlantic Ocean. This long oceanic ridge is also a divergent boundary (figure 13.9) between spreading plates. Figure 13.9 also shows that not all oceanic ridges are in the centers of oceans.

Tectonic Setting 3: Grind—Living on the Edge

How do tectonic plates interact when they are not crashing together or pulling apart? Parking lots offer a clue. Have you ever seen a car try to squeeze through a space that is too small? The result could be a dramatic screeching and grinding as one car scrapes past the other.

Tectonic plates do the same thing. The surface where the two plates grind past each other is called a **transform fault**. Perhaps the best-known transform fault between two plates is on the southwest part of North America.

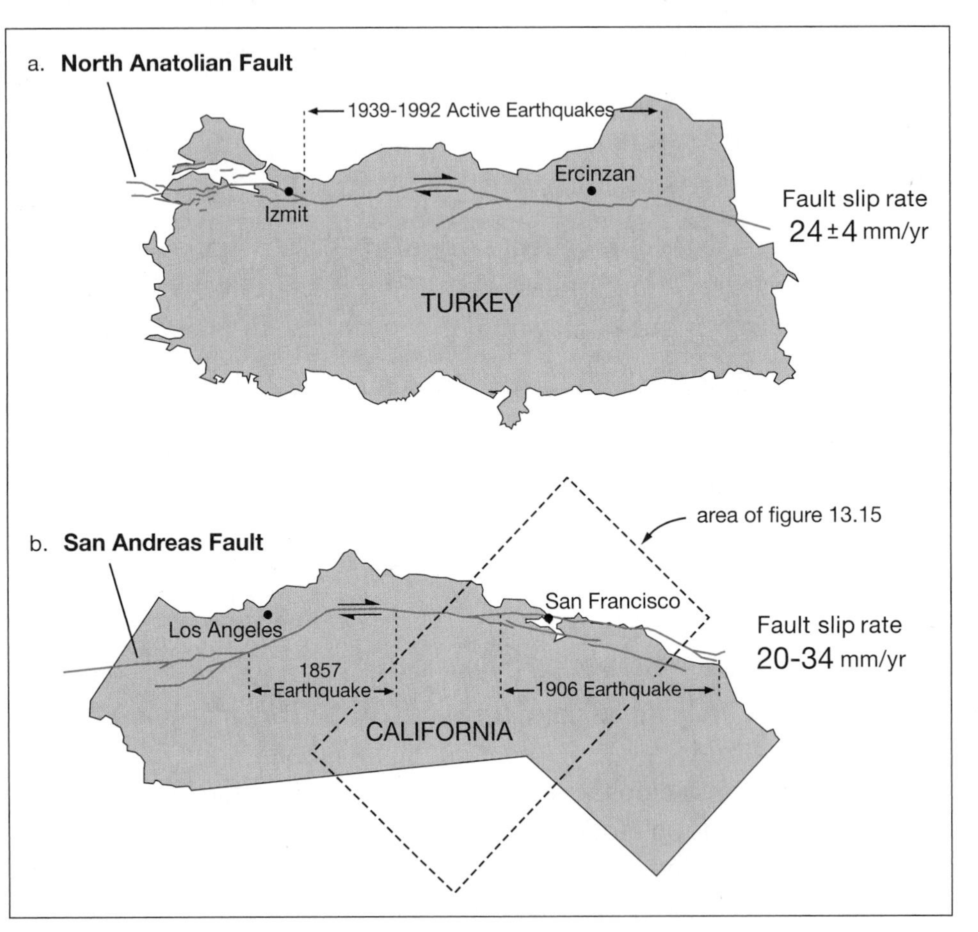

Figure 13.14 North Anatolian and San Andreas faults. These maps show two transform faults: (a) the North Anatolian Fault and (b) the San Andreas Fault. Each fault has ruptured in massive earthquakes during the past 100–200 years. The net movement along each fault is several centimeters per year, about the growth rate of your fingernails.

There, the San Andreas Fault marks where the Pacific Plate is grinding its way northwest along the edge of the North American Plate. A massive lurch along the San Andreas Fault was the cause of the massive 1906 earthquake in San Francisco. This earthquake and the fires that resulted destroyed three-quarters of San Francisco and killed more than 3,000 people. Other devastating earthquakes have struck along the San Andreas Fault since 1906. A massive earthquake in October 1989 hit the San Francisco Bay area in the middle of the World Series between the San Francisco Giants and the Oakland Athletics. The death toll was 65, with thousands injured and an estimated $8 billion of damage.

Another example of a transform fault on a continent is the North Anatolian Fault in Turkey (figure 13.14). It also has a dangerous history of sudden movements, violent earthquakes, and significant damage and deaths.

Geologists used to think that transform faults were sharp zones of slip between rigid blocks. But modern technology shows that this is only part of the story. For example, geology clearly shows a history of movement exactly on the San Andreas Fault. At the same time, sensors show that the total slip at the boundary is spread over a zone about 200 km wide. The increasing total slip is shown by longer and longer velocity vectors as one moves from Nevada to the ocean near San Francisco (figure 13.15). The same is true in Southern California, where the fault slip is spread across a wide region.

So boundaries between tectonic plates may be shown on maps as distinct faults. In reality, transform faults can be broad zones of broken rock that are tens to hundreds of kilometers wide. Large earthquakes will likely occur within these zones. Similarly, wide zones of mountains show that collisions between plates do not form only a single fault. The boundaries are broad and dynamic.

SCILINKS® NSTA
Topic: rift valleys
Go to: www.scilinks.org
Code: 2Inquiry669

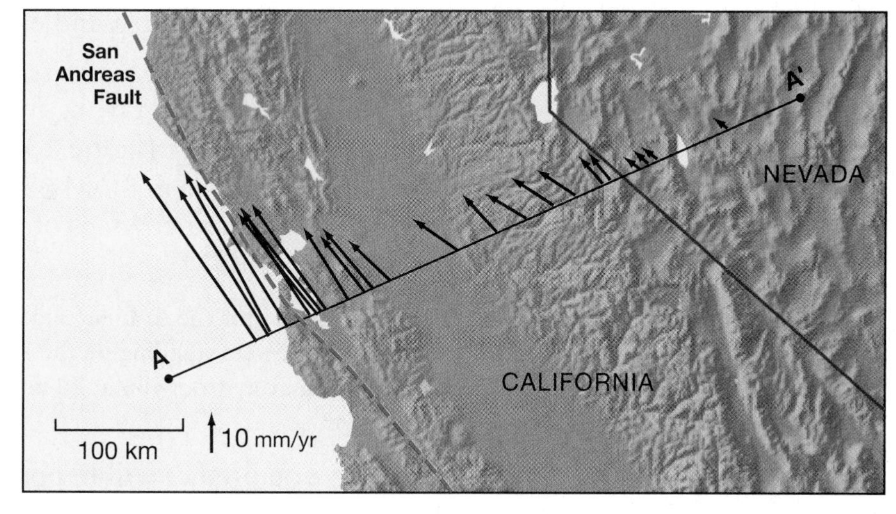

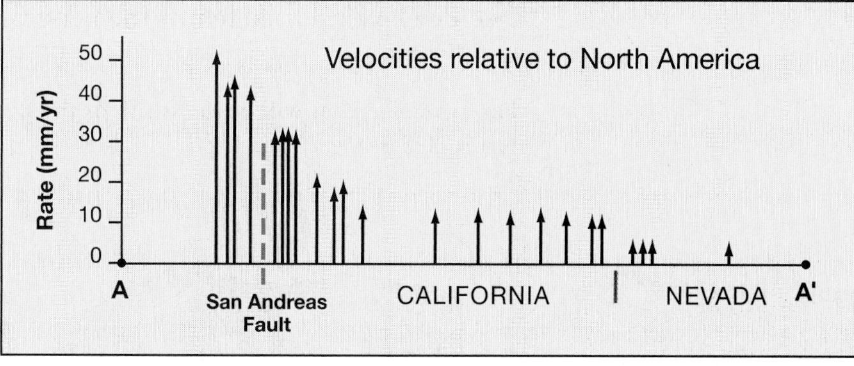

▲ **Figure 13.15 San Andreas Fault slip.** Vectors indicate the slip in an east-west cross section of California. The slip relates to deformation centered on the San Andreas Fault. Arrows show velocity of points relative to stable parts of North America (for example, Missouri).

Reflect and Connect

1. Basins in rifts on continents, like the Rio Grande Rift, can be over 10 km deep. Why do you think they appear as broad valleys instead of deep troughs that are 10 km deep? What processes can you infer are occurring in the land or mountains on the flanks of the rifts?

Think back to the last activity. What factor makes mountain peaks never really grow at the rate of tectonic uplift?

2. Models are a key part of science. In geology, simple block models can show how tectonic plates move past each other. Compare the blocks in figure 13.16 with the velocity vectors in figure 13.15. Which block model do you think most accurately shows slip between the Pacific and North American plates? Use sketches of block models in your answer to explain.
3. What does the future hold for the geology of the Middle East? Predict the tectonic changes and evolution of the Middle East in the next 10 Myr.
   a. The Arabian Plate is moving away from Africa with a velocity of 20 mm/yr (figure 13.17). How far will the Arabian Plate move in 10 Myr?
   b. Where do you predict zones of rifting? Where do you predict zones of collision?

Remember that velocities for the Arabian and Eurasian plates are relative to Africa. This is as if you were standing on the African Plate and noting the Arabian Plate moving away from you at 20 mm/yr, while the Eurasian Plate got closer by 10 mm/yr.

   c. What do you predict will happen to the Red Sea? To the Persian Gulf?
   d. Develop a sketch of the geography of the Middle East in 10 Myr.

For example, what will be the width of the Red Sea? Use the scale to diagram the future Red Sea.

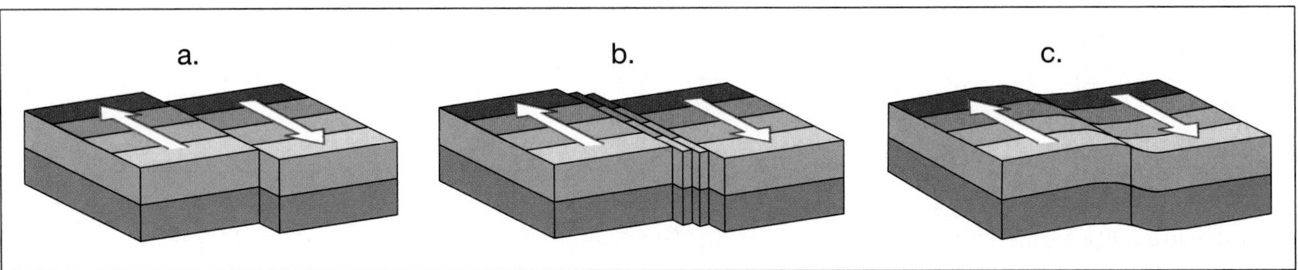

Figure 13.16 Block models of slip at faults. The 3 models illustrate how plates deform as they slide past each other. Which model do you think most closely relates to the data—the current velocity vectors—along the San Andreas Fault (figure 13.15)? Note the style of faulting, not the direction of the arrows.

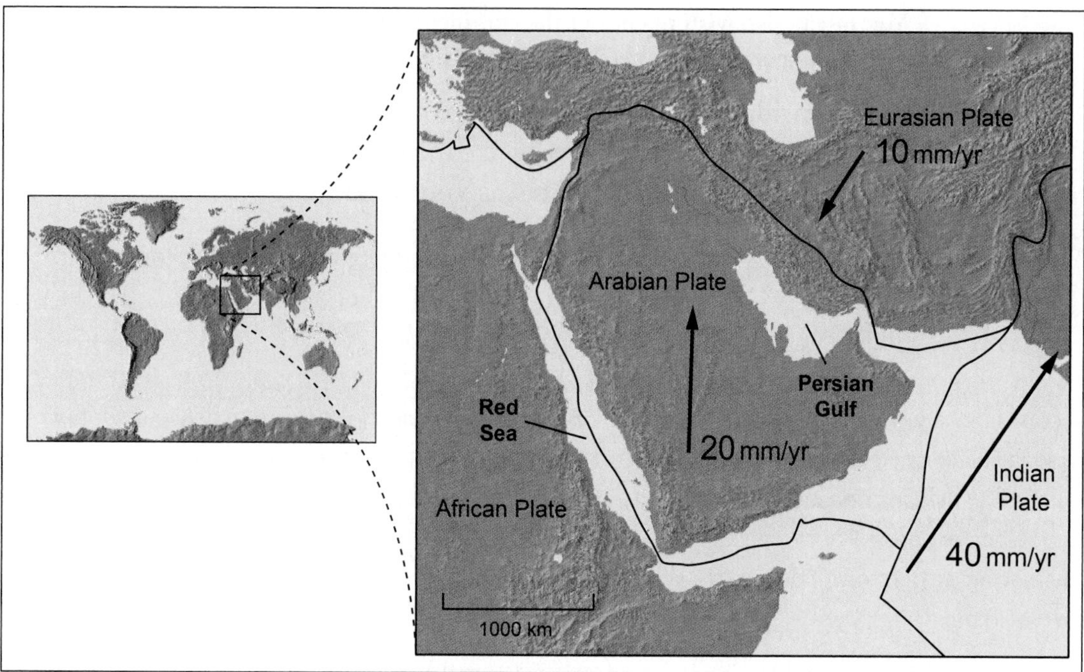

▲ **Figure 13.17 The Arabian Plate's velocity.** The map shows the Arabian Plate and its boundaries. The plate's velocity vector shows its projected movement relative to Africa. What might the Red Sea and the Persian Gulf look like in 5 Myr?

e. Consider an African elephant that wishes to visit its cousin, an Asian elephant, in India. What migration routes could the African elephant take to get to India? Show this with a colored pen or pencil. Describe the migration options.

Challenge Opportunity

4. Early evidence for plate tectonics was the jigsaw fit of South America and Africa. Use the handout *South America and Africa* from your teacher to reconstruct the Atlantic Ocean between these 2 continents. Show your work in your science notebook.
   a. Measure the distance in kilometers (in the east-west direction) between the coasts of South America and Africa. How similar or different are the measurements at different latitudes?
   b. Calculate the average of your distances in Question 4a.
   c. Assume that South America and Africa started rifting apart at 120 Mya. Estimate the velocity of South America relative to Africa.
   d. Consider your calculations for the Atlantic Ocean. What can you infer about changes in the size of the Pacific Ocean over that same time period?
   e. Draw a sketch of what Africa and South America might have looked like with no Atlantic Ocean between them. Draw this in your science notebook or on a sheet of paper.

You might also wish to cut out the continents and glue them together on another piece of paper. Refer as needed to *FYI—Going to Great Lengths.*

5. Consider what you noted for South America and Africa in Question 4. What inference can you make about the history of the North Atlantic? What is your evidence?

Going to Great Lengths

Some simple conversions will make it easy for you to do quick calculations. These are called back-of-the-envelope calculations because you can do them on a small piece of paper. For example, if something is only moving at 12 mm/yr, how could you tell how far it would travel in 2 Myr?

This is easier than it sounds. In fact, you already did this when you completed figure 13.6 by scaling up with factors of 10. You showed that 2.5 mm/yr equals 2.5 km/Myr. You also need to be able to show this by canceling units.

For example, how would you convert 12 cm/yr to kilometers per million years? First, change the 12 cm to millimeters (mm). Then include two factors: one factor of 10^6 from millimeters to kilometers, and then another factor of 10^6 from years to millions of years. These steps are easier to see:

$$\left(\frac{12\ \cancel{\text{cm}}}{1\ \text{yr}}\right) \times \left(\frac{10\ \text{mm}}{1\ \cancel{\text{cm}}}\right) = \left(\frac{120\ \text{mm}}{1\ \text{yr}}\right) = 120\,\frac{\text{mm}}{\text{yr}}$$

Second, complete the conversion to kilometer per million years either in separate steps or all together. They are the same thing. The separate steps are

$$\left(\frac{120\ \text{mm}}{1\ \cancel{\text{yr}}}\right) \times \left(\frac{10^6\ \cancel{\text{yr}}}{1\ \text{Myr}}\right) = \frac{120 \times 10^6\ \text{mm}}{\text{Myr}}, \text{ and then}$$

$$\left(\frac{120 \times 10^6\ \cancel{\text{mm}}}{\text{Myr}}\right) \times \left(\frac{1\ \text{km}}{10^6\ \cancel{\text{mm}}}\right) = 120\,\frac{\text{km}}{\text{Myr}}.$$

You should also be able to show a single step with all units canceling:

$$\left(\frac{120\ \cancel{\text{mm}}}{1\ \cancel{\text{yr}}}\right) \times \left(\frac{10^6\ \cancel{\text{yr}}}{1\ \text{Myr}}\right) \times \left(\frac{1\ \text{km}}{10^6\ \cancel{\text{mm}}}\right) = \frac{120\ \text{km}}{\text{Myr}}$$

So the rule of thumb is that units of millimeters per year transfer directly to kilometers per million years. A plate moving 12 cm/yr moves 120 km in a million years. You can also show that it would move 240 km in 2 Myr, or 1,200 km in 10 Myr. This is handy to remember for quick calculations. Now you should be able to prove it, too!

EXPLORE

Sinking Slabs and Convection Connections

Tectonic plates are always changing, but why do they move? What causes large pieces of crust to move about the surface of Earth? How do plate interactions relate to the oceans, continents, mountain chains, or natural resources? Is there a simple way to explain these changes on Earth's surface?

Indeed, this has been one of the more vexing questions in science: What makes tectonic plates move? Because of several modern technologies, geologists are better able to answer this question now than when plate tectonics was first proposed in the early 1960s. *Sinking Slabs and Convection Connections* will help you better understand why tectonic plates change position on Earth. You will gather as a class to observe and diagram two demonstrations that your teacher will show you.

Materials

For each student

1 blank sheet of paper

1 pencil

1 ruler

Process and Procedure

1. As a class, discuss the first setup. Do Steps 1a–d during the demonstration.
   a. Draw a clear sketch of the setup.

Remember that when you do scientific sketches, it is helpful to include a title, data, appropriate labels, a scale, and the orientation.

   b. Identify the source of energy for the system. Clearly label it on your diagram.
   c. How does the system respond to that source of energy? Use arrows in your diagram to show any movement in the system.
   d. Explain how you think the system relates to plate tectonics.

Be prepared to share your ideas and questions in a class discussion.

2. Read the following paragraph. Record in your science notebook any words that you are not familiar with.

   Many people have learned that the mantle is a key layer in the structure of Earth. But did you know that about 80 percent of the volume of Earth consists of mantle (figure 13.8)? Most of the rest of Earth is a metal core consisting mostly of iron and nickel. Some heat escaping Earth's core travels up through the mantle in plumes. These plumes of upwelling through the mantle create hot spots when they reach Earth's surface. Hot spots are characterized by outpourings of molten rock (lava) at volcanoes. Examples of hot spots are the Hawaiian volcanoes, the island of Iceland, the Galápagos Islands, and the Yellowstone hot spot. Do you know of others? After upwelling toward the crust, other parts of the mantle must also go back down into the earth. The slow movement of the mantle due to upwelling and sinking is called mantle convection.

3. As a class, develop a list of words from the paragraph in Step 2 that you do not know. Discuss these words and link them to features in the setup from Step 1. Record your best thinking in your science notebook.
   a. What might have represented mantle in the demonstration?
   b. Did you observe upwelling, downwelling, or a hot spot?
   c. Did convection move the piece of wood? What might the wood represent?
4. Your teacher will show a second setup to your class. Listen carefully for instructions on observing that system.
   a. Sketch the setup. What do you predict will happen when your teacher lets go of the weight?
   b. What forces act on the system and move the block? Use arrows to show these forces in your diagram.
   c. Does the velocity of the weight or block change? Explain whether there is a net force on the system.
   d. If there are no net forces, what force is resisting the motion on the block? Identify what is keeping the weight from accelerating.

Recall from chapter 2, *Collision Course*, where you dropped the coffee filter in the elaborate activity, *With and Without a Net*.

   e. Write in your science notebook how this setup may relate to plate tectonics. What plate tectonic setting might this represent?
5. You have seen 2 setups: a sliding block and a falling weight. Combine these into a single, simple diagram to represent elements of plate tectonics. Steps 5a–c may help.
   a. Obtain a blank sheet of paper from your teacher.
   b. Sketch the setup from Step 1 near the middle of the paper.
   c. Use arrows to show the direction of motion in the system.
   d. Add a sketch of the setup from Step 4.

Your diagram should include the container, convection, the string, the weight, the block, and arrows for the direction of motion.

   e. How many areas of convection do you have? If helpful, add 1 block-and-weight combination per convection cell.
6. Complete the following sentences to help you better understand why plates move.
   a. "If plate motion is only driven by mantle convection and upwelling, then plates should be moving __________ hot spots."

b. "If plate motion is only driven by plates being pulled, then plates should be moving __________ subduction zones."

7. Get with a partner at your work area. Use evidence and examples from figures 13.9 and 13.18 to complete Steps 7a–c.
   a. Review your answers for Step 6. Then read the caption for figure 13.18 together.
   b. Write in your science notebook how many hot spots you see.
   c. Describe the directions that plates move, in general, relative to the positions of hot spots. Use specific examples to explain.

In other words, do plates move away from the upwelling at hot spots?

   d. Describe the directions that plates move, in general, relative to subduction zones. Use specific examples to explain.
   e. Discuss with your partner what these movements tell you about the forces that drive plate tectonic motions across Earth's surface.

It may help to relate this question to the demonstrations that you saw.

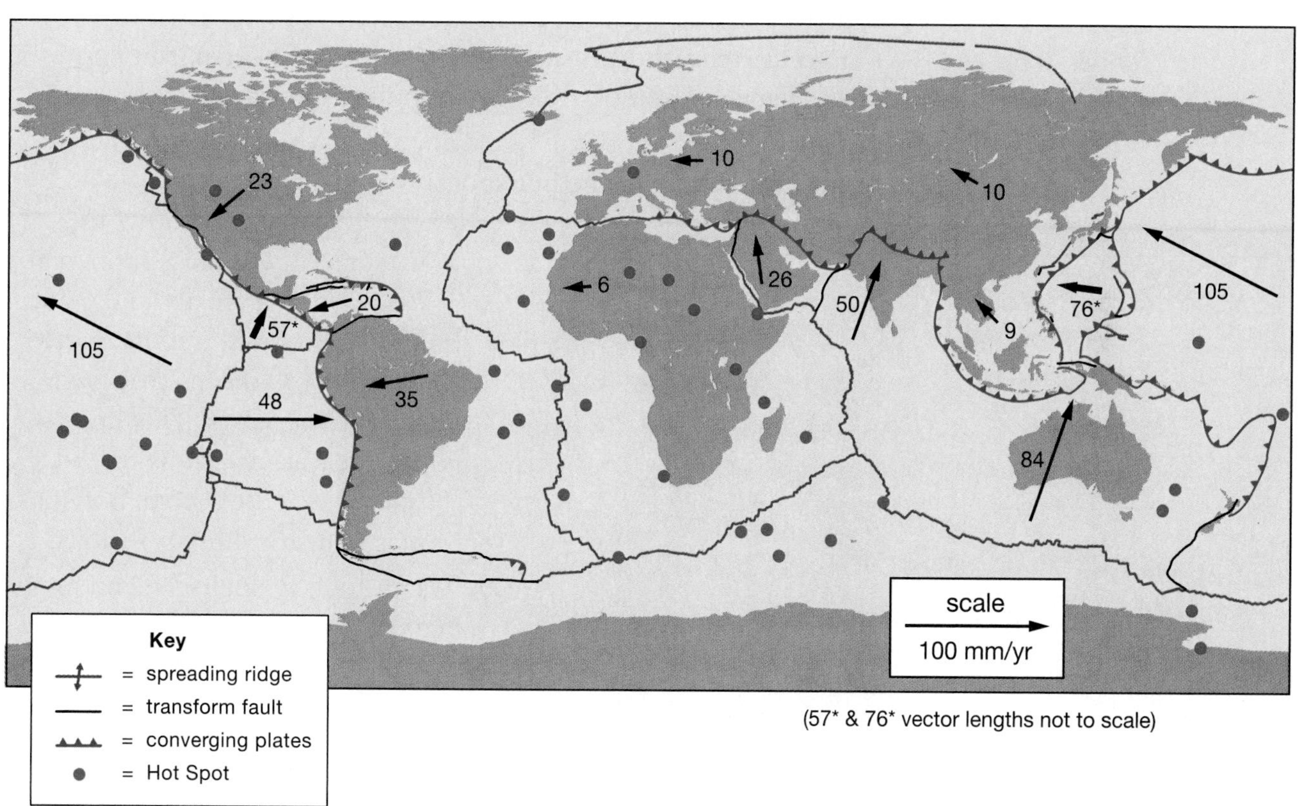

Figure 13.18 Tectonic boundaries, hot spots, and plate velocities. This map shows the 12 main tectonic plates on Earth, locations of ridges and trenches, and hot spots. Estimates for velocity vectors are also shown. Use this map to evaluate whether plates move away from hot spots, toward trenches, or some combination.

Reflect and Connect

Complete the following steps.

1. Your teacher will show you an overhead transparency. Each circle represents an earthquake, and the color indicates how deep underground (in kilometers) the earthquake occurred.
   a. What part of the world is shown? How can you figure this out?
   b. What tectonic plates are included in the figure?
   c. Look at the pattern of earthquakes. Write in your science notebook the relationship between earthquakes and depth.
   d. What kind of tectonic setting do you think is shown by the pattern of earthquakes?
   e. A line is labeled "A–A′." Sketch in your science notebook where earthquakes occur along this line. What does the depth of the earthquakes indicate?
2. Figure 13.19 shows the history of volcanic eruptions (in millions of years ago) for the Yellowstone hot spot beneath North America.
   a. Determine a vector for the velocity of North America relative to the Yellowstone hot spot and sketch it in your science notebook. Keep these points in mind:
      - View this hot spot as stationary, with North America moving over the hot spot.
      - The "0.6" symbol shows the most recent volcanic eruption at Yellowstone Park about 0.6 Mya.
      - The shapes with numbers give the ages of volcanic rocks in millions of years. This line of volcanic eruptions records when the Yellowstone hot spot was beneath those positions.
   b. What does "velocity" mean in regard to a tectonic plate?
   c. How would you represent the velocity of North America in a graph from these data?

Watch the demonstration your teacher does with aluminum foil, a candle, wax, and a syringe.

Remember how you determined the velocity of India in figure 13.12 in the explain activity, *Rates of Plates*.

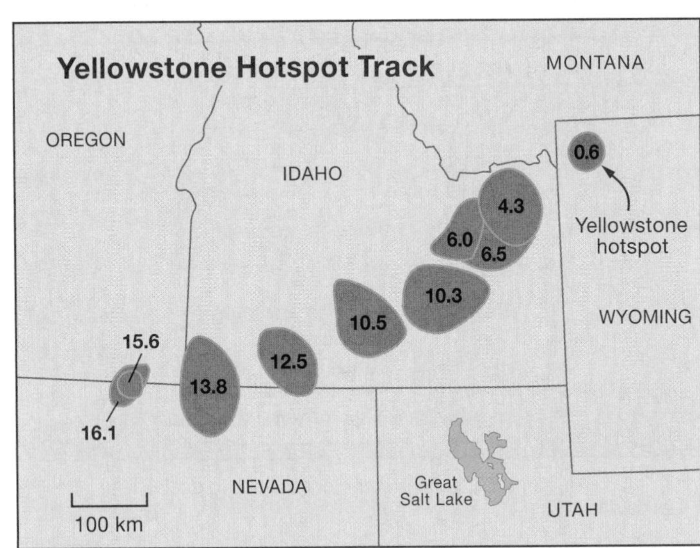

Data source: Smith, R.B., and Siegel, L. (2000). *Windows into the Earth: The geologic story of Yellowstone and Grand Teton National Parks.* New York: Oxford Univeristy Press.

▲ **Figure 13.19 Yellowstone hot spot track.** The Yellowstone hot spot has a history of volcanic eruptions that crosses several states. The age of eruptions are shown as millions of years ago. How fast is North America moving over the Yellowstone hot spot?

SIDEBAR

Shakin' Like Jell-O

Have you ever eaten molded gelatin for dessert or a snack? It's funny how it shakes and quivers. But during a massive earthquake, wiggling back and forth isn't merely funny—it is a good thing for a building with people in it to do. Being rigid and stiff can lead to the collapse of buildings or bridges, especially for those constructed of brick, stone, or cinder blocks. Collapsed buildings have killed tens of thousands of people. It is the job of seismic and civil engineers to ensure that buildings can move during earthquakes.
This saves human lives.

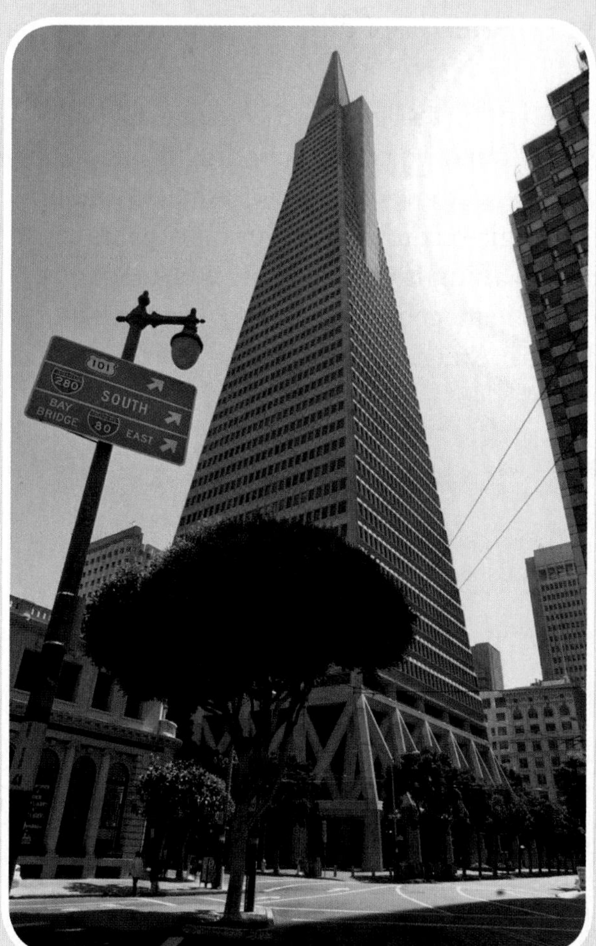

▲ **Transamerica Pyramid Building.**

So what do seismic or civil engineers do? In areas prone to earthquakes, they have several vital tasks. One is to design buildings that shake like Jell-O! Take the Loma Prieta earthquake in the San Francisco Bay area in 1989. The Transamerica Pyramid Building swayed back and forth several feet. This is exactly what earthquake engineers had hoped it would do.

Another vital task is analyzing existing buildings. Engineers decide how to strengthen them to withstand earthquakes. This is called seismic retrofitting. It is a very important job in cities prone to large earthquakes, such as San Francisco, California; Seattle, Washington; Tokyo, Japan; and Istanbul, Turkey. Seismic retrofitting can save thousands of lives when the next big earthquake hits. Sadly, it's hard to know when that will be.

SRCD

Seismic and civil engineers are also very involved in planning. Their roles include planning for structures such as bridges, stadiums, subways, roadways, and public utilities. These are areas where humans would be at risk during a large earthquake.

So, remember next time you eat gelatin: shakin' like Jell-O during an earthquake is a good thing. Professions of seismic and civil engineers ensure that things keep shakin'.

3. Yellowstone National Park is famous for many things. One is large mammals. At Yellowstone, visitors can see bison grazing in the park. But during the last volcanic eruption of the Yellowstone hot spot about 0.6 Mya, a much larger bison was present on the Great Plains—*Bison latifrons*. Evidence shows that this species is ancestral to the modern bison, *Bison bison*. What does it mean for *B. latifrons* to be **ancestral** to the current bison, *B. bison*, in Yellowstone?

ELABORATE

Building Bridges

Have you ever seen an armadillo or an opossum? They may seem like typical North American mammals. But what does the geologic record say about animals like armadillos and opossums in North America? Can we trace records of other animal families in the geologic record? What might the geologic record say about animals on other continents, such as zebras in Africa or kangaroos in Australia? Can plate tectonics explain the occurrences of different families of animals on different continents?

In *Building Bridges*, you will investigate real evidence for why certain mammal families are found on certain continents. You and your partner will analyze how plate tectonics affects ecosystems and how it plays a key role in the geologic record and evolution of mammals. This might even include some animals that are now common pets. Work with a partner to investigate geologic evidence for the history of mammals on North and South America.

Materials

For each team of 2 students

colored highlighters

access to reference materials such as atlases and maps

2 *Six Strata from North and South America* handouts

Process and Procedure

1. Study the 2 maps in figure 13.20. Use a T-table to list how they are similar and different. You may wish to use an atlas to identify geographic features that you do not know.
2. Review your T-table and the major differences between the maps. Explain the differences.

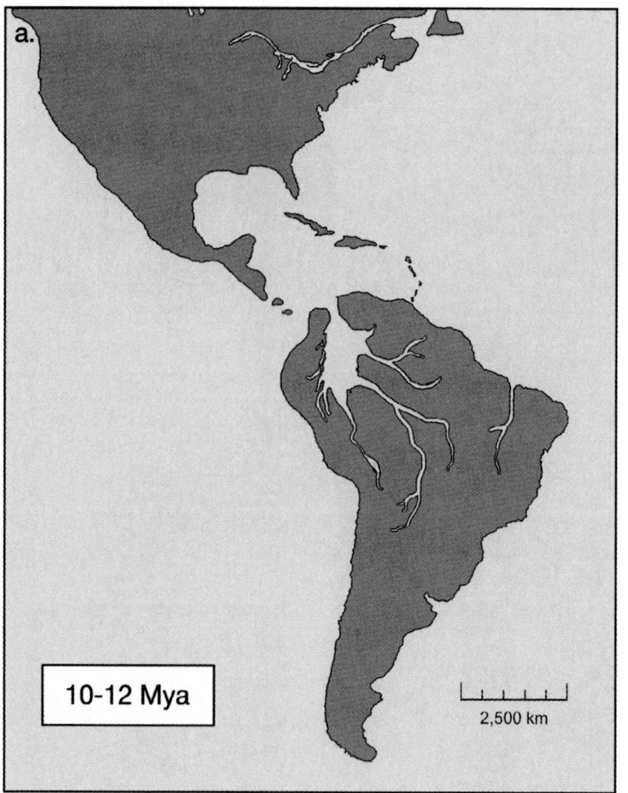

Figure 13.20 North and South America at 2 geologic times. The maps show the outlines of North America and South America at (a) 12–10 Mya and (b) today. What changes do you see in the landforms over approximately 10 Myr?

3. The Caribbean region has hosted a coral reef ecosystem for at least 20–30 Myr. Use the maps in figure 13.20 to explain where else you think the reef ecosystem might be found during that time.

Would the organisms in that reef ecosystem have been isolated in the Caribbean during that time period?

4. Figure 13.21 shows geologic sections (rock layers, or strata) with fossil finds at 6 sites in North and South America. Obtain a copy of this figure from your teacher. The strata span from today back to 10 Mya. At a given site, are older rocks found at a deeper or shallower position? Explain how you know.

The singular form of strata is stratum.

5. Pick a site in figure 13.21 and make a list of all the mammals recorded at that site. Which sites have the most mammals? Which have the fewest?

Making a table that shows mammals per site may help you here. Also check that you can locate the states and countries where each stratum is found on figure 13.20.

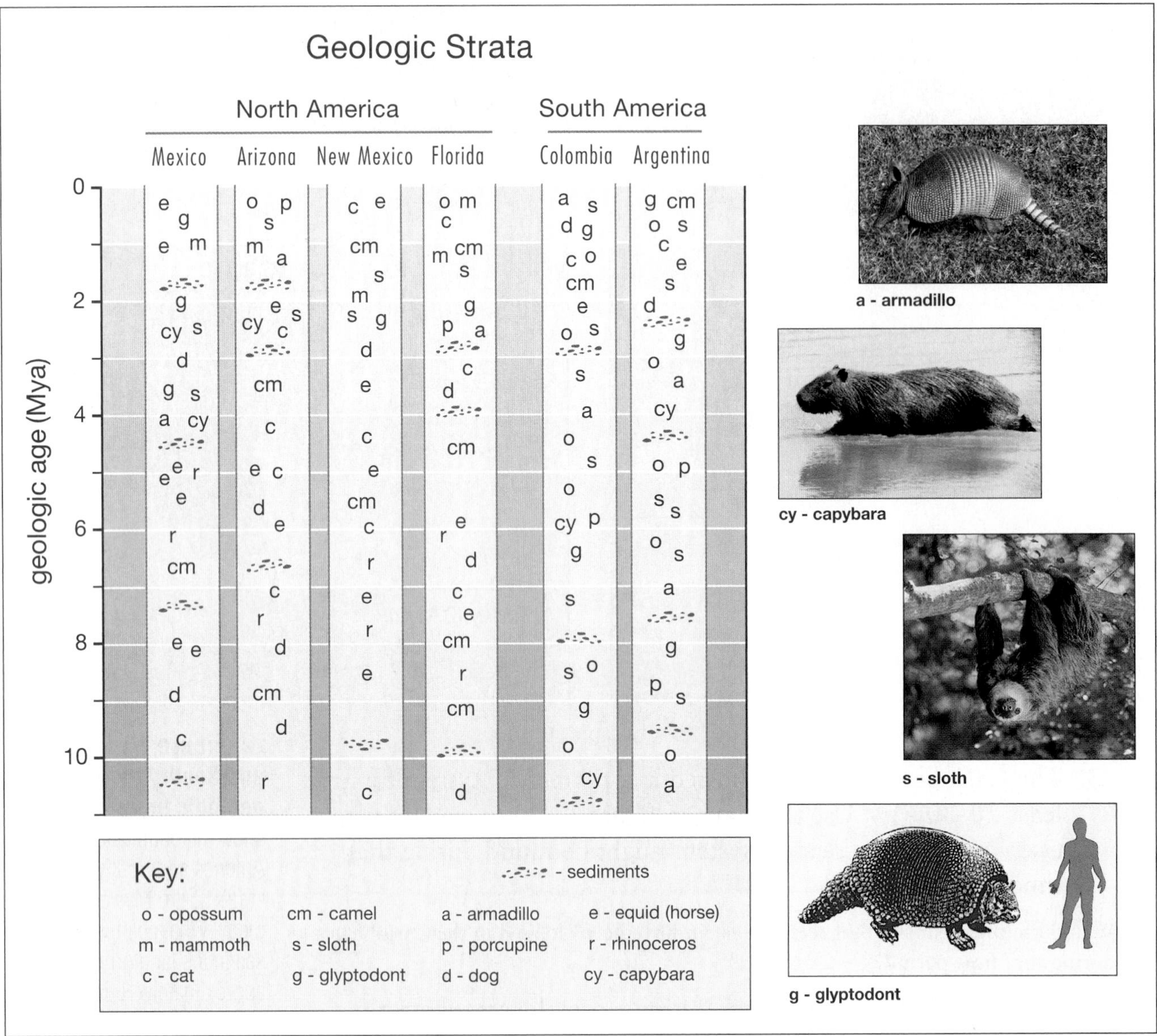

▲ **Figure 13.21 Six geologic strata from North and South America.** The fossil finds from 6 locations (across top) are a function of geologic age (left). The key lists 12 representatives of animal families from North and South America. Current examples (right) are the sloth, the capybara (a large rodent), and the armadillo. Glyptodonts are extinct.

6. Animals or plants that are restricted to a specific region are called **endemic.** Follow Steps 6a–d to evaluate what animals were endemic to South America 12–10 Mya.
   a. Determine with your partner how to tell whether an animal is endemic to a continent based on the geologic record. Explain this strategy in your science notebook from the geologic strata.
   b. Explain which sites you would study in order to list the mammals that were endemic to South America. Would you search the tops or bottoms of those strata? Write your best response in your science notebook.

c. Make a T-table showing animals that were endemic to South America and animals that might be endemic to North America.
d. Explain why you think Step 6c said animals that "might" be endemic to North America.

7. Answer Questions 7a–d for the animal groups endemic to South America 12–10 Mya.
   a. When do South American animals arrive in North America? List specific evidence from fossils in the strata in figure 13.21.
   b. How can you explain the arrival of South American endemics in North America?
   c. When do North American animals arrive in South America?
   d. How can you explain the arrival of North American animals in South America?
8. Examine the geologic record of the rhinoceros family in figure 13.21. What is the time period of when they are found? What inferences can you make about the history of the rhinoceros family?

It is helpful to highlight all fossil finds of rhinos. A relative of the rhinoceros family is the horse.

9. Based on figure 13.21, make some inferences about the mammoth family. What is the earliest evidence of its appearance in the fossil record?

It is helpful to highlight mammoths in another color.

10. Discuss with your partner the concept of a **land bridge**. Consider Questions 10a–f related to land bridges and write specific examples from figures in the activity.
    a. What do you think is the land bridge between North America and South America?
    b. When do you think the land bridge formed? What is your evidence?
    c. Which animals did or did not use a land bridge?
    d. Which tectonic plates were involved in the land bridge? Use a map to describe the tectonic setting of the land bridge between North and South America.

Consult figure 13.9 and draw a simple sketch of the plates involved.

   e. Which of the 3 main types of tectonic settings best applies to the Central American land bridge?
   f. What process resulted in the Central American land bridge? Is this consistent with the tectonic setting? Base your answers on your responses to Questions 10a–e.

Reflect and Connect

Work individually on the following tasks. Write ideas and evidence in your science notebook. Be prepared to contribute your ideas to a class discussion.

1. In the engage activity, *Mile High Time Machine*, you developed a question about climate, elevation, or topography related to figures 13.1 and the chapter opener. These show the Denver area at different geologic times. Write in your science notebook how you would answer that question now.

Some questions aren't always easy to answer, or they take a while to figure out. Even a little progress, though, moves you toward a better understanding.

2. Consider figure 13.21 again. Do you think each site indicates all the animals that were living at that site at a geologic time? Explain why or why not.
3. Recall the geologic strata in figure 13.21. Would you expect the sites to be near the tops of mountains? Write why or why not in your science notebook.
4. Refer to the image of the Bering land bridge in chapter 12 (figure 12.10). Compare the causes of that land bridge with the development of the Central America land bridge discussed in this activity.
5. Make a list of all the geographic areas that you have studied in this chapter. Decide whether to list them by city, country, continent, or tectonic plate.

EVALUATE

Falling into the Ocean

"This just in from our affiliate station in Los Angeles. A massive earthquake has just struck Southern California. Initial geologic reports are a magnitude of 8.6 and an epicenter in the rugged mountains 15 miles east of San Diego. Reports of damage are coming in from Los Angeles, San Diego, and south to Ensenada, Mexico. It's too early to tell about human casualties. This earthquake is sure to rekindle fears, once again, that California is going to fall into the ocean."

You've probably heard that California is going to "fall into the ocean." Could this really happen with a massive earthquake, even if it was "the Big One"? What sort of changes might there be? Could earthquakes affect the many types of habitats and ecosystems in coastal California? While the short-term effects could be catastrophic, what does the future—the geologic future—hold for the Golden State?

In *Falling into the Ocean*, you will work with your teammates to address questions like those. You will become a geology team making real predictions about tectonic and ecological changes in California and northwestern Mexico. You'll have the data and evidence to argue whether or not California is really poised to fall into the ocean.

Materials

For each team of 3 students

3 pairs of scissors

colored pencils

clear tape

several sheets of blank white paper

1 calculator

1 ruler

6 *Tectonic Map of PAC and NAM* handouts

3 *Falling into the Ocean Scoring Rubric* handouts

Process and Procedure

1. Review the *Falling into the Ocean Scoring Rubric* before you begin the activity. This will help you understand your teacher's expectations for your work. You will do this as a class.
2. Work with your teammates to critically evaluate this question: "In a massive earthquake, could the state of California break off and fall into the ocean?"
   a. Discuss each teammate's answer to the question.
   b. Write on a blank sheet of paper whether you think that California could fall into the ocean. If you think it could, record the reasons why and describe what California would look like afterward. If you think it couldn't, make a list of reasons why not.

Another strategy is to make a T-table on the blank sheet of paper outlining "reasons for" and "reasons against."

   c. Turn in this paper to your teacher.
3. Work with your teammates to complete the following reading. It gives some information to help you analyze whether California might fall into the ocean.
4. Work with your teammates to determine how the Mexican Peninsular Ranges and the Gulf of California formed. Follow Steps 4a–d in your reconstruction.
   a. Consider the movements of the Pacific and North American plates. Use a vector to demonstrate how the movements could form the Gulf of California.

READING

Tectonic Changes in the Southwest

It is a striking feature of our North American continent. It's shaped like Florida, yet nearly twice as long. And it's part of Mexico. Do you know what it is? It's a long spit of land surrounded by water—a **peninsula**—called the Mexican Peninsular Ranges (figure 13.22). Some maps show this peninsula as Baja California.

But the Peninsular Ranges are more than just a long spit of land. They host a unique desert ecosystem that extends from sea level to jagged peaks. The peninsula is bound by the warm waters of the Pacific Ocean to the west and the Gulf of California to the east. The Gulf of California harbors a rich reef ecosystem. The gulf is also a valuable breeding and wintering ground for many larger fish, sharks, seabirds, and mammals.

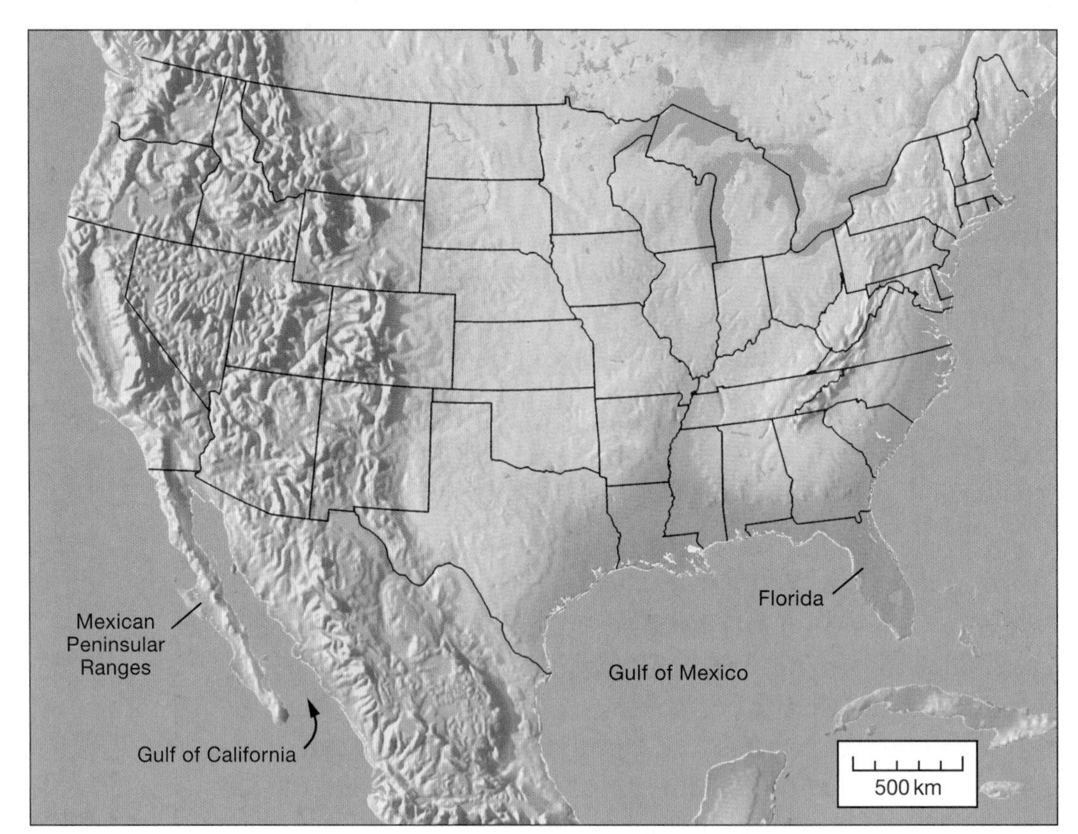

▲ **Figure 13.22 North America with Mexico's Peninsular Ranges.** This map of the southern part of North America shows the location and scale of the Mexican Peninsular Ranges and the Gulf of California. This peninsula is nearly twice the size of Florida, one of the United States's largest states.

The rugged desert mountains of the Peninsular Ranges go farther north than the Gulf of California. They form a long chain of mountains that connects with the Coast Ranges east of San Diego and Los Angeles, California. In fact, rugged, tectonically active mountains extend along the entire West Coast to Canada.

Moving north from the tip of the peninsula, the mountains pass through a sequence of ecosystems (figure 13.23). This is due to increasing precipitation (rainfall) as one moves north (see the key in figure 13.23). For example, upon going from Mexico to Southern California, the desert ecosystem gives way to chaparral at low elevations and mixed chaparral and coniferous forests at higher elevations.

Farther north, the Coast Ranges undergo another ecosystem change. Central California is largely mixed chaparral, oaks, and grasslands. Then from central California north, chaparral and mixed coniferous forests give way to a much more humid, coniferous rain forest. This transition occurs in central California (figure 13.23). This rain forest is dense, hosting plants such as ferns, Douglas fir, and coast redwood (*Sequoia sempervirens*). You learned about pollen from redwoods in the last chapter.

This region hosts an active tectonic boundary. Figure 13.24 shows that the boundary lies between the Pacific Plate and the North American Plate. It is localized in the center of the Gulf of California as a rifting or opening gulf. Farther north, the rift zone changes to the renowned San Andreas Fault. This fault trends northward to the east of San Diego and Los Angeles, extending through the San Francisco Bay area. The San Andreas Fault then enters the Pacific Ocean in northern California. It also passes through a region where tens of millions of people live.

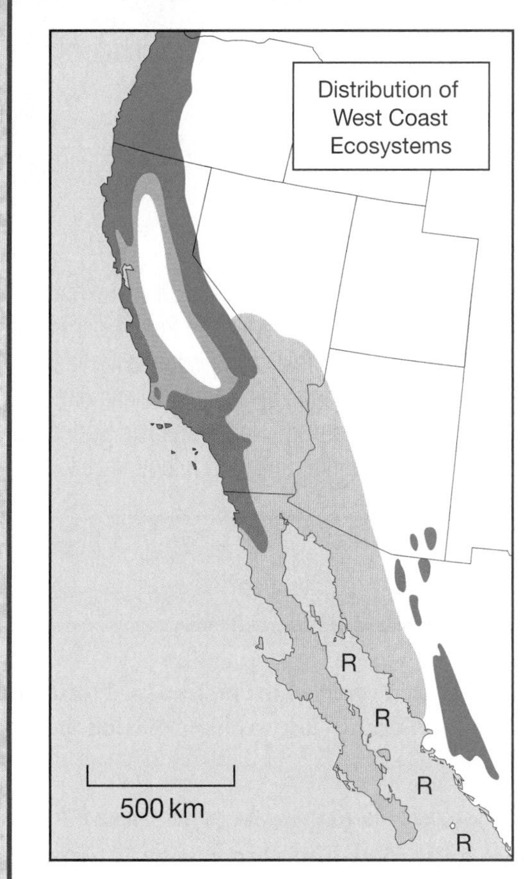

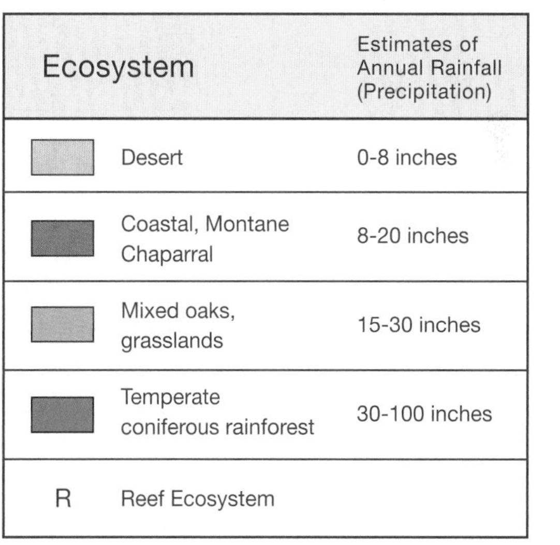

	Ecosystem	Estimates of Annual Rainfall (Precipitation)
	Desert	0-8 inches
	Coastal, Montane Chaparral	8-20 inches
	Mixed oaks, grasslands	15-30 inches
	Temperate coniferous rainforest	30-100 inches
R	Reef Ecosystem	

▲ **Figure 13.23 Ecosystems of southwestern North America.** This map shows the major ecosystems of southwestern North America from the Mexican Peninsular Ranges to northern California. The key matches ecosystems with estimates for annual rainfall.

Tectonic Changes in the Southwest, continued

Due to a history of big earthquakes, the San Andreas Fault is watched closely. Current work shows that the Pacific Plate is sliding to the northwest at about 50 mm/yr. This is not fast if the sliding is steady. The risk for massive earthquakes arises when the fault locks up. The result can be sudden, massive lurches along the fault every 100–200 years. Events like this probably caused the great 1906 San Francisco earthquake and even many other large earthquakes along the fault in the past 20–25 Myr.

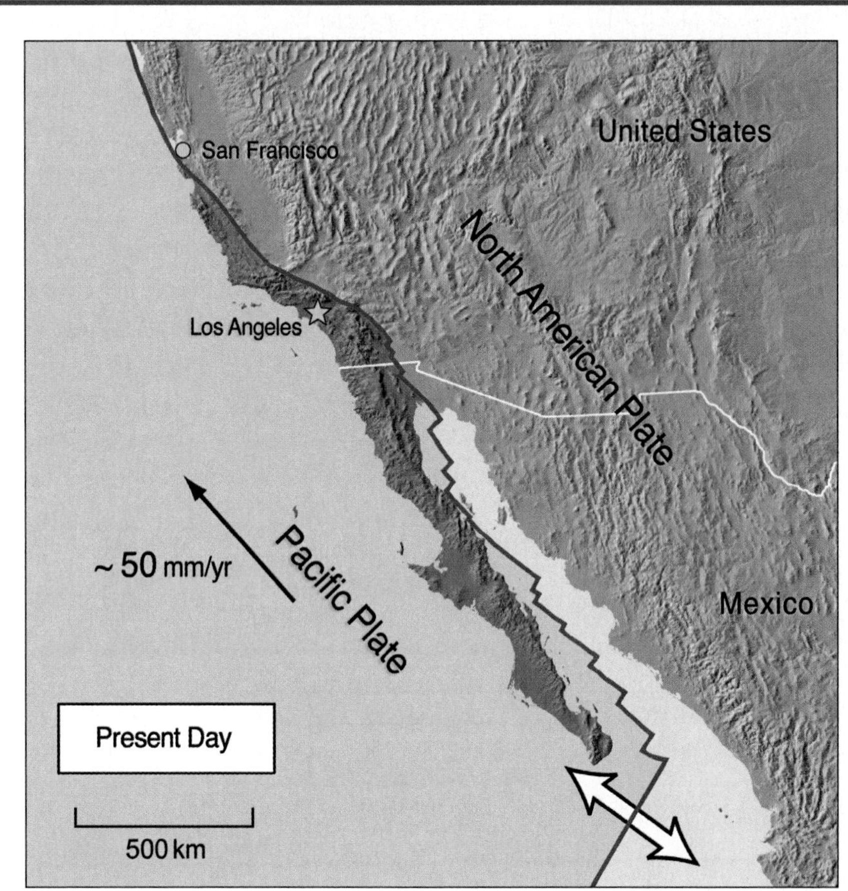

▲ **Figure 13.24 Tectonic map of the Pacific and North American plates.** The region shown extends from the tip of the Mexican Peninsular Ranges to northern California. Rifting in the Gulf of California changes to the north and slips along the San Andreas Fault. The vector shows the magnitude and direction of the Pacific Plate (in millimeters per year) relative to North America. Northward movement of the Pacific Plate causes a spreading ridge (red) in bottom left.

Recall the steps in the explain activity that reversed the motion for North and South America and closed the Atlantic Ocean. This was like "playing the movie backward" with the Atlantic Ocean.

b. Use your handout *Tectonic Map of PAC and NAM* to sketch the coastline of the Mexican Peninsular Ranges at intervals of about 5 and 10 Mya.

It may help to indicate the coastline with colored pencils. For example, use orange for 5 Mya and red for 10 Mya.

c. Organize your data in a T-table that lists millions of years ago and distance (in kilometers).

d. Imagine you are a geologist. Would there have been a rich reef ecosystem extending up into the Gulf of California 10 Mya? Explain your answer.

5. Predict the geologic future for the Mexican Peninsular Ranges, the Gulf of California, and the state of California in 20 Myr. What might the geography of the shoreline look like?

   a. Use the *magnitude* of the Pacific Plate vector to determine how far it will travel relative to North America in 20 Myr (20×10^6 years).

For full credit, you must show all your work. You might also add this row to your T-table from Step 4c.

   b. Use the *direction* of the Pacific Plate vector to show how far it will go along the San Andreas Fault in 20 Myr.

Before you do this step, try sketching the progress of the Mexican Peninsular Ranges 10 Myr into the future.

   c. Identify the part of the Pacific Plate that moves north. Use a pair of scissors to cut it out of your *Tectonic Map of PAC and NAM* handout. Place small pieces of tape to show the parts of the Pacific Plate in their future positions. Use the scale on the map to determine the size of each piece of tape.

   d. Predict what will happen to the size of the Gulf of California. List evidence to support your ideas.

   e. Draw a star on your diagram to show the position of Los Angeles in 20 Myr.

If you wish, draw stars in increments of 5 Myr.

6. Predict the types of ecosystem in different sections of the Mexican Peninsular Ranges in about 20 Myr. Refer to the succession of ecosystems up the Pacific coast in figure 13.23.

It is OK to predict, but only use data from the activity as evidence to support your speculation.

   a. Add neat labels to your diagram from Step 5c to indicate the type of ecosystems.

Colored pencils and a key will best illustrate your predicted distribution of ecosystems along the west coast in 20 Myr.

b. Go to the farthest, northwestern edge of the Pacific Plate in figure 13.9. This is in Siberia and Japan. What geologic process is occurring there to allow 20 Myr of slip along the San Andreas Fault?

7. Obtain from your teacher your team's response to Step 2 about whether California will sink into the ocean during the Big One. With your teammates, critically evaluate the answers that you gave for Step 2.

Critically evaluating an issue means to give real evidence and documentation for your position. If your position is the same, you review this position, giving any new supporting evidence. If your position has changed, you outline the new position, giving evidence for your revisions.

8. Turn in all of the following to your teacher:
   - Initial ideas and evidence (Step 2b)
   - The sketch and answers for Steps 4b–d
   - The sketch and notes from Steps 5 and 6
   - The critical evaluation from Step 7

Conducting Your Own Inquiry

As you have been learning, science is a way of knowing the world around you, whether it becomes your career or you use it to make informed decisions. In *Conducting Your Own Inquiry*, you will use your understanding and skills of inquiry to conduct an interdisciplinary investigation that interests you. By now, you should have enough experience to realize that thinking scientifically is a valuable way of answering many questions.

In this special section, you will investigate a scientific question of your own. You need to decide what you want to explore, where you will find background information, and how you will conduct your investigation. You may work alone or in a team of two or three.

The goal is for you to conceive, design, and conduct a scientific investigation of your choice about the natural or human-made world—one that integrates concepts from more than one discipline of science. If you used Level 1 of this program, you may have conducted an inquiry that left you with additional questions to explore. Consider following up on one of those questions.

One reason to study science is to learn how to use the methods of science as you study the natural world around you. Another reason is to understand the events that influence your life. As you design and conduct your own inquiry, remember that each of the *thinking* steps, such as asking a good question, deciding how to test it, and analyzing the meaning of the data, is just as important as the hands-on steps of *doing* an investigation. Your performance in this activity will demonstrate your understanding of the following:

- science concepts that you investigate,
- your understanding of the nature of science,
- your ability to think scientifically, and
- your ability to use scientific processes.

Materials

For each student

Materials will depend on the investigation you design. You will need your teacher's approval before you assemble materials.

1 *Conducting Your Own Investigation Scoring Rubric* handout

Cautions

Depending on what you choose to investigate, you may be working with harmful chemicals.

Process and Procedure

Part I: Preparation

1. Study figure 1.10 in chapter 1, *Investigations by Design*, as you discuss the following questions with a partner. Record your best ideas in your science notebook.
    a. How has your understanding of the ideas represented in figure 1.10 changed since the beginning of the year?
    b. Identify 4–5 specific times during this program when you have used these processes.

Looking through your science notebook may help you answer this question.

2. Obtain a copy of the *Conducting Your Own Investigation Scoring Rubric* handout from your teacher. Examine the tasks and the criteria your teacher will use to score your investigation.

Part II: Asking the Question

You will begin your inquiry with a question. As you proceed, you will record all your work in your science notebook.

1. Choose a problem or topic in the natural or human-made world that interests you. Think of problems or topics that involve an integrated science perspective. In other words, the problem you select should include more than 1 discipline of science, such as life science and physical science or physical science and earth and space science.

If you are having difficulty thinking of an area or a problem, consider looking through your science notebook. Review the investigations, readings, and activities that most interested you. You also might want to do some Web or library research about a topic that interests you. This new information will provide useful background and may give you an idea for a testable question.

2. Consider some focused and testable questions that you might want to investigate related to this area or problem. Record 2 or 3 good questions in your science notebook and discuss them with a partner.
   a. Select 1 question to investigate.

Consider which question interests you the most and which one best meets the criteria of a testable question.

   b. Explain why your question is significant and how it is testable.

Write several sentences describing what is already known about the topic that you wish to investigate. Be sure to explain why your question meets the criteria of a testable question.

   c. Restate your question as a hypothesis that can be tested.
   d. Record the major concepts in the sciences that relate to your question and hypothesis. Then explain how those concepts represent an integrated science perspective.
3. Show your question to your teacher for approval before you proceed.

Part III: Gathering Information and Conducting Your Investigation

1. Use the Web, the library, local scientists, or other available resources to gather information related to your question.

Scientists use data that others collect as well as data that they collect directly through experimental investigations. You should use a similar process.

2. Design an investigation to test or answer your question by doing Steps 2a–b.
   a. Describe your experimental design in your science notebook and include the following:
      - rationale, that is, how this investigation will test your question (include a description of your controls and the role that they will play);
      - hypothesis (explain what you think the answer to your question may be and why you think so);
      - procedure (include a step-by-step procedure along with a list of the materials you will need); and
      - data analysis (explain how you will analyze the data).

Remember, you learned many important ideas about designing a scientific investigation in chapter 1. You may want to refer to that chapter in your book and to your science notebook as you design this investigation. Also, your teacher may have specific suggestions about the length of time you will have to conduct your investigation and the equipment that will be available.

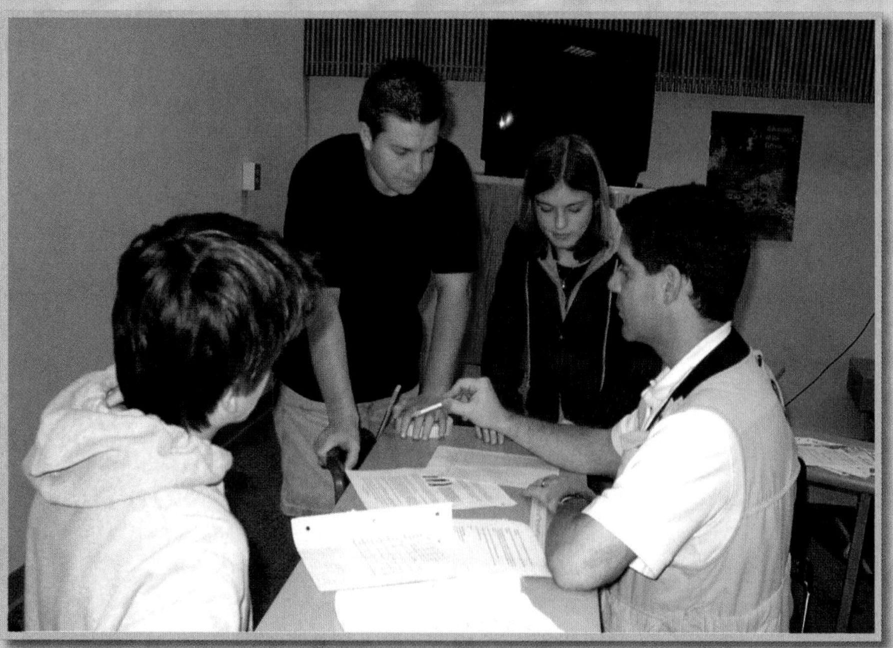

b. Write in your science notebook a safety plan for your investigation. In your procedure, record the precautions that you will follow when you
   - use chemicals,
   - handle equipment, and
   - handle biological hazards such as bacteria or yeast.

Ask your teacher to explain any hazards that you do not understand and to help you identify the precautions necessary to prevent harm from an accident.

Cautions

Review *Laboratory Safety* in the back of your student book and be sure that you understand all the safety considerations involved in your experimental design. Make sure that you have read and understood the hazards and precautions described on the labels and Material Safety Data Sheets for all the chemicals you plan to use in your experiment. Report all accidents, no matter how small, to your teacher.

3. Discuss your library research and experimental design with your teacher and have your teacher approve your safety plan before you continue. If your plans are reasonable and safe, your teacher will approve further work.
4. When you have your teacher's approval, carry out the investigation you have designed to test your hypothesis.

Remember, use the proper controls to make it a valid test and record data in your science notebook in a way that will be most useful.

Part IV: Analyzing Your Data

1. Reorganize your data in a way that makes it easier to see patterns or understand what the data show you.

Consider the many ways you have represented data in other investigations in this program: graphs, tables, diagrams, formulas, and words, for example. Which ways will best show the important information about your results? Also, remember to keep your original data.

2. Decide what your data tell you and record these ideas in your science notebook.
   a. How confident are you that your results will help you answer your question?

b. Do you think your experimental design could be improved to help you get results that would better answer your question?
c. Did you have any unexpected results? Explain your answer.

The strategies "What I see" and "What it means" might be useful as you complete this step.

Part V: Drawing Conclusions

1. Use the evidence that you have collected to develop an explanation and preliminary conclusions for your investigation.

What can you say based on the evidence you have?

2. Explain what your conclusions mean at this point. Do your conclusions help you answer your question? Why or why not?
3. Describe how your results
   a. connect to the major concepts in the sciences that you selected,
   b. deepen your understanding of these concepts, and
   c. represent an integrated science perspective.

Part VI: Communicating Your Results

1. Develop a presentation of your inquiry that makes it possible for someone else to understand what you did, why you did it, and what you found out.

Your teacher will provide you with guidelines for your presentation. You might also want to refer to *How to Write a Lab Report* in the back of your book for some additional guidance. Also, consider the many different ways you have presented and communicated information to your classmates and your teacher during the year.

2. Identify the connections between your investigation and any of the following that are relevant:
   - How the investigation represents an integrated science perspective
   - How the investigation deepened your understanding of specific concepts in the sciences that you have been studying this year
   - The processes of inquiry that are featured in figure 1.10 in chapter 1

- Your understanding about inquiry and the nature of science
- Additional questions that your findings generate
- Society and technology
- The history of science

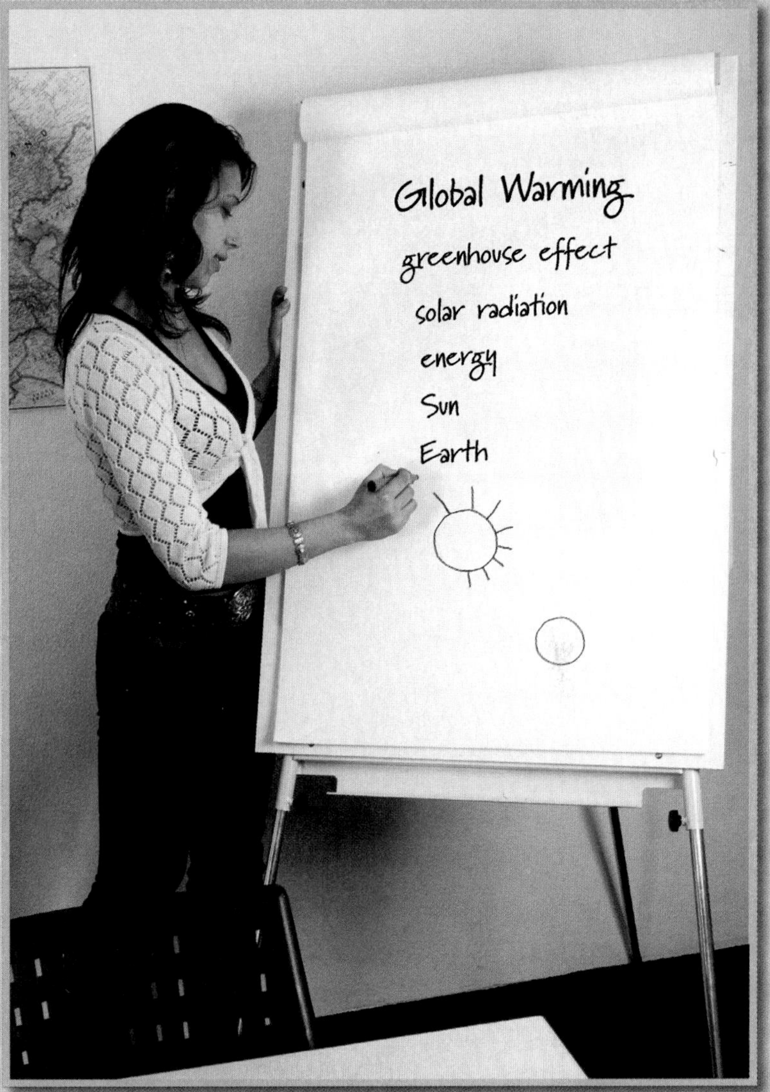

3. Present your work as your teacher directs.
4. Your teacher may assign you several of your classmates' presentations to pay particular attention to. Record your ideas about these presentations using the scoring rubric or other device your teacher provides. Justify the ideas you record using examples from the presentations.
   a. What evidence or examples illustrate that they used a scientific approach to answer their question?
   b. Can you suggest other ways to improve their designs?
   c. Did the presenters use evidence and logic to communicate their findings?
   d. Was their means of presenting their findings effective?
   e. How do their findings lead to other questions?
5. According to your teacher's instructions, share your ideas about the presentations with the teams that gave them.
6. Participate in a class discussion of important ideas that arise during this special investigation.

UNIT 4

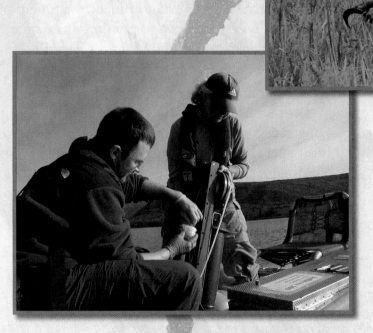

Sustaining Earth Systems

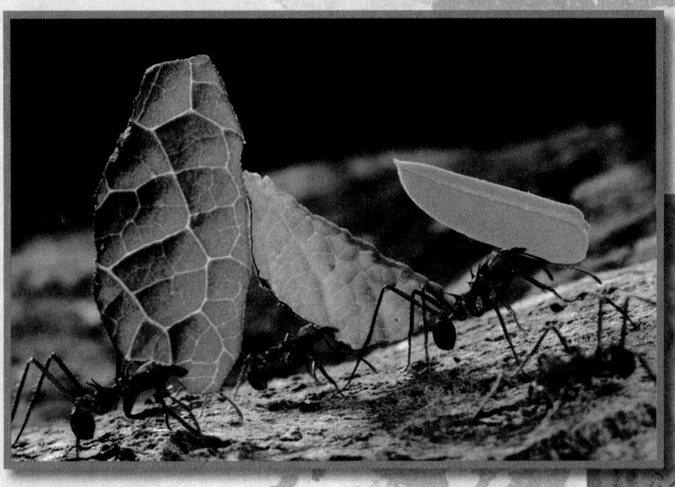

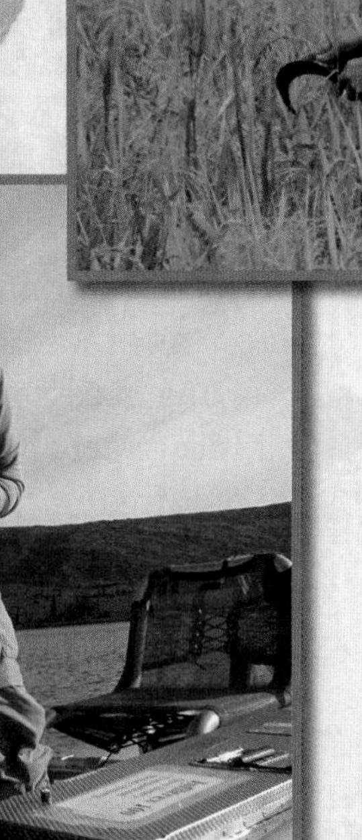

Sustaining Earth Systems

How are you connected to the natural world? Are you affected by changes in earth systems? All organisms, including humans, depend on Earth's physical and biological resources. In turn, all organisms influence earth systems. Living things and the environment are interdependent. Humans need to understand this relationship. A sustainable society needs to balance development and growth with the protection of functional earth systems. That way, future generations can continue to thrive on Earth.

Notice the satellite photo of Egypt. The Nile River valley, shown in green, is a stark contrast to the surrounding desert of northeastern Africa. The city of Cairo appears as a gray smudge where the river widens. Smaller cities give the Nile River valley its speckled appearance. What resources do the people living in these cities rely on? And how does the presence of these people affect the Nile River valley?

In unit 4, *Sustaining Earth Systems*, you will continue investigating systems on Earth. You learned a lot about cycles on Earth in unit 3, *Moving Matter.* Now you will learn about the living environment on Earth and how it relates to the nonliving environment. You will begin by investigating what influences population size. Then you will learn how populations cooperate, compete, and depend on resources in ecosystems. How are the ants interacting in the opening photograph?

Human populations are influenced by the same factors as other organisms. We face the same challenge of having access to the resources we need for our current and future generations to survive. The person harvesting rice pictured in the opening art depends on this resource for food. What resources do you depend on? How do humans influence ecosystems as our population grows and we consume those resources?

You will learn that many of our actions affect environmental quality. The scientists pictured are monitoring water quality. What could you do to protect environmental quality? Understanding interactions in earth systems requires knowledge from all fields of science. At the end of unit 4, you will use what you have learned this year to investigate an environmental quality issue. You will then propose ways to improve environmental quality.

Goals for the Unit

In unit 4, you will learn how populations of organisms and the nonliving environment interact and are interdependent. You will discover the importance of these interactions. At the same time, you will see how humans depend on natural processes in ecosystems. By the end of this unit, you should understand the following:

- Populations grow or decline through the combined effects of births, deaths, immigration, and emigration.
- There are limits to population growth and a maximum number of individuals an environment can support.
- Ecosystems are made up of the biotic and abiotic environments.
- Organisms both cooperate and compete in an ecosystem.
- Technology influences human population growth and Earth's capacity to support human populations.
- Humans depend on natural processes that occur in ecosystems.
- Human activities modify natural processes and alter the distribution of species and resources in ecosystems.
- Environmental quality is influenced by human population growth, resource use, and technology.

As you learn about living systems, you also will refine your ability to do science. You will develop a better understanding of scientific inquiry as well. You will

- design investigations to answer questions about populations and ecosystems,
- create and analyze tables and graphs to formulate explanations, and
- understand that scientists are influenced by current and historical scientific knowledge as they investigate how systems function.

CHAPTER 14

Population Interactions

Population Interactions

Why does a particular species live in one place and not another? All life on Earth is interconnected. Populations of organisms constantly interact. Individuals within populations interact among themselves and with other populations. They also interact with the nonliving environment. What interactions do you see in the opening art? The actions of these organisms affect their environment. And the environment influences these organisms. These interactions help determine the distribution of organisms on Earth.

The study of the living and nonliving parts of the environment and how they affect organisms is called **ecology**. Ecology is the branch of science that focuses on natural systems. In fact, the natural systems you will study are called *eco*systems. You studied physical and chemical systems in unit 1, *Interactions Are Interesting*, and living systems in unit 2, *Inside Life*. In unit 3, you studied systems on a global scale. You learned how matter, such as water and carbon, moves between different reservoirs. This matter is important for both the nonliving, or physical, environment and the biological environment on Earth.

In chapter 14, *Population Interactions*, you will focus on populations and ecosystems on a regional scale. You will analyze changes in growth for different populations and learn what influences population growth. Then you will look at examples of how populations interact in ecosystems. You will find that there is both the cycling of matter and the transfer of much energy in ecosystems.

Goals for the Chapter

By the end of chapter 14, you will be able to answer the following questions:

- What makes population size change?
- Is there a limit to population size? If so, what limits population size?
- What is the relationship between populations and ecosystems?
- What components make up an ecosystem?
- What kinds of interactions do organisms have in ecosystems?
- How are ecosystems related to geochemical cycles?
- How are the interactions among organisms and the environment related to the diversity of life on Earth?

The following activities will help you learn how populations interact with one another and with the environment.

ENGAGE	What Do You Know about Populations?
EXPLORE	Changing Populations
EXPLAIN	Systems in Balance
ELABORATE	Finding Your Niche
EVALUATE	Interpret the Interactions

This chapter organizer is your guide for learning about populations and ecosystems. Use it to review what you have learned and to see what new things you will be learning.

Linking Question

How can I build on what I know about populations to determine what factors affect population size?

ENGAGE

What Do You Know about Populations?

Key Ideas:

- Population size can change.
- Different kinds of interactions occur in ecosystems.

EXPLORE

Changing Populations

Key Idea:

The size of a population is affected by environmental factors and interactions with other organisms.

Population Interactions

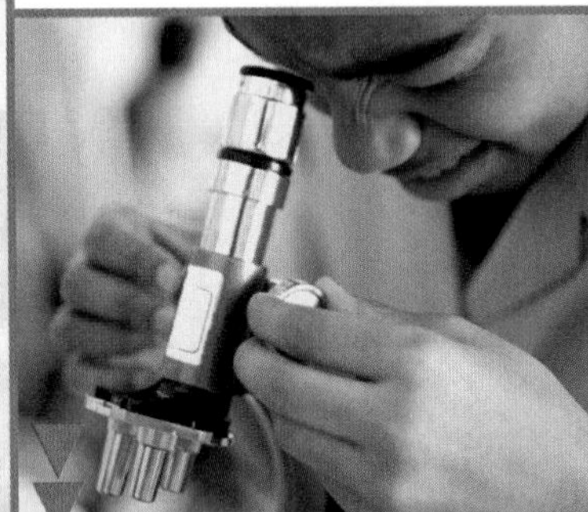

Linking Question

How are populations and ecosystems related?

EVALUATE

Interpret the Interactions

Key Ideas:
- Population growth is affected by many factors.
- The interactions between the biotic and abiotic parts of an ecosystem result in the transfer of energy and the cycling of matter.
- Interactions can lead to natural selection.

Linking Question

How can I use what I have learned to demonstrate my understanding of populations and ecosystems?

CHAPTER 14 Major Concepts

- **Populations grow and decline.**
- **There are limits to population growth.**
- **Ecosystems are made up of the biotic and abiotic environments.**
- **Organisms both cooperate and compete in an ecosystem.**
- **Interactions among populations can lead to natural selection and contribute to the diversity of organisms on Earth.**

ELABORATE

Finding Your Niche

Key Idea:

Interactions among organisms are part of the process of natural selection and can lead to diverse species on Earth.

EXPLAIN

Systems in Balance

Key Ideas:
- Population growth is limited by limiting factors that can be abiotic or biotic.
- Interactions occur between organisms and between organisms and the abiotic environment.
- Ecosystems are important for the flow of energy and the cycling of matter.

Linking Question

How are competitive interactions related to natural selection?

ENGAGE

What Do You Know about Populations?

▲ **Figure 14.1 Student population.** Does your school population change? What might limit the size of the population at your school?

Every day populations of organisms surround you. For example, all the students in your school system make up a population (figure 14.1). Many things influence the size of the student population and how the students in the school system interact. Your school population shares some characteristics with biological populations.Do you ever think about the interactions between organisms in other systems? In *What Do You Know about Populations?*, you will share your current ideas about populations and natural systems.

Materials

none

Process and Procedure

1. Record in your science notebook whether you think each of the following statements is true or false. Provide a 1 or 2 sentence explanation for each of your answers.
   a. Populations can grow indefinitely. (T or F)
   b. You have a population of fruit flies in a large building. If you gave the population all the food and water it needs, the population would continue to increase in size. (T or F)
   c. All of the species in an environment have the same maximum population size. (T or F)
   d. A species of fish can cooperate with one organism and can compete with another. (T or F)
   e. Light, water, and nutrients are abiotic parts of an ecosystem. (T or F)
   f. Temperature can influence the size of a population. (T or F)
   g. A forest contains as many woodpeckers that eat insects as there are insects. (T or F)
   h. When one organism eats another, all the energy stored as food is passed to the consumer. (T or F)
2. Add a specific example to support each of your explanations in Step 1.
3. Compare your examples and explanations from Steps 1 and 2 to those of a classmate.
4. Record in your science notebook why each explanation is or is not valid for each statement.

You will revisit your explanations in the evaluate activity, *Interpret the Interactions*.

Reflect and Connect

Record your ideas to the following questions in your science notebook.

1. List 2 factors that you think might increase a population of plants. Then list 2 factors that might decrease the same population. For each factor, explain why it would cause an increase or a decrease.
2. Recall what you learned about cycles in chapter 11, *Carbon on the Move*. Use what you learned in unit 3 to describe how you think organisms contribute to the cycling of carbon. For example, how would a pine tree contribute to the cycling of carbon?

Changing Populations

EXPLORE

A group of individuals of the same species that lives in a particular area and interbreeds is called a **population.** Each population has certain characteristics, such as size, density, and distribution. In *Changing Populations*, you will investigate how the size of populations changes across time. In Part I, you will discover how different environments result in yeast populations of different sizes. In Part II, you will review almost 50 years of data to learn how populations of wolves, moose, and balsam fir interact on an island.

Part I: Yeast Population Explosion

Changes in the population size of organisms are difficult to investigate in the classroom. The changes occur over long periods of time. For example, scientists monitor changes in animal populations across years. Even changes in the size of insect and plant populations take weeks to occur. Can you think of any populations that change size in a shorter time frame? Scientists use different techniques to estimate population size, depending on the organism they are investigating (see figure 14.2).

Microorganisms are small, reproduce rapidly, and have short life spans, so they are good to study in the classroom. Bacteria and yeast are examples of microorganisms. If you have had food poisoning, you have experienced a bacterium population rapidly growing and causing illness.

In this investigation, you will use common baker's yeast (*Saccharomyces cerevisiae*) to observe a population of yeast cells. The cells are growing in a test tube in a liquid called a broth medium. This population is a closed population. A closed population lets you estimate the rate of population growth more easily than an open system. In nature, open populations increase or decrease in size as organisms enter or leave them. Matter can cycle through the open population.

▲ **Figure 14.2 Determining population size.** Scientists estimate population size in different ways, depending on the organism they are studying. (a) In the laboratory, scientists can use microscopes to estimate the population size of microorganisms such as bacteria or yeast. (b) In nature, scientists use techniques such as aerial surveys to sample populations of larger organisms. During aerial surveys, scientists count animals such as birds, elk, or whales from a plane or helicopter. Why might it be valuable to know the population size of different organisms?

Materials

For each team of 3 students

- 3 pairs of safety goggles
- 2 16×150-mm test tubes with screw caps, each with 10 mL yeast suspension
- 2 18×150-mm test tubes
- 1 dropping pipet
- microscope slides
- coverslips
- 1 compound microscope
- 1 test-tube rack
- methylene blue (optional)
- 1-mL graduated pipet (optional)
- water (optional)
- paper towel
- 1 glass-marking pencil
- 1 transparent metric ruler
- 4 sheets of graph paper
- 1 tally counter

Cautions

Wear safety goggles when working with any liquid. Culture test tubes should be inverted gently to avoid foaming, which would result in inaccurate counts. Caps on culture tubes should be loosened slightly before storage to prevent gas buildup. Avoid contact with methylene blue because it will dye your skin and clothes. Methylene blue is harmful if ingested. Wash your hands thoroughly before leaving the classroom.

Process and Procedure

1. Read the following 2 paragraphs about yeast. Use this question to focus your reading: "What do yeast need to survive?"

   Yeast are fungi that grow as single cells. They can reproduce asexually by budding, or they can reproduce sexually. They reproduce rapidly in moist environments that have a supply of nutrients such as sugars and amino acids.

   Like all organisms, yeast undergo cellular respiration. Cellular respiration produces the energy needed for growth and reproduction. Recall that you investigated cellular respiration in decaying vegetation in chapter 11. Yeast undergo cellular respiration with oxygen present (aerobic respiration) and without oxygen (anaerobic respiration). Anaerobic respiration is also called fermentation. When yeast respire anaerobically, they break down sugars into carbon dioxide and ethanol. These two reaction products alter the environment and affect the yeast's growth and reproduction.

2. Participate in a class discussion about different conditions you could create for a yeast population. Use Questions 2a–c to guide your discussion.
   a. What conditions do you think affect a yeast population?
   b. What conditions might increase reproduction?
   c. What conditions might decrease reproduction?

3. As a team, develop 2 or 3 hypotheses that might explain how different conditions will affect the size of a yeast population. Record these in your science notebook.

A hypothesis is a statement that suggests an explanation of an observation or an answer to a scientific problem.

4. Discuss with your team how you could design an investigation to study yeast population growth under different conditions. Be prepared to share your ideas with the class.

Focus on how to create different environments. In Step 7, you will read a protocol describing how to measure yeast population growth. Remember that a control may help you understand variables, which in this case are the different environments.

5. Participate in a class discussion to decide how to design investigations to study yeast population growth in different environments. Consider how each team could test different conditions.

6. Decide on 1 design for your team and record it in your science notebook. Have your teacher approve your design.

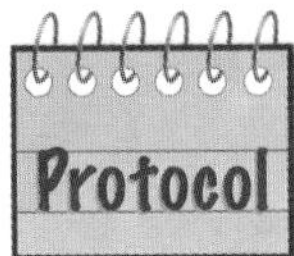

7. Read *Measuring Population Growth in Yeast Protocol.* Then decide how to create a data table for your investigation. Use an entire sheet of paper for the data table.

Make sure you include space in your table to record the yeast population for different environmental conditions.

8. Collect the materials you need and begin your investigation.

This investigation will continue for 7 class periods. Make population counts each day, then continue with other activities as your teacher directs.

9. Once you have finished collecting data, graph the change in the yeast population size. Include a caption and highlight comments on the graph.

Stop & THINK

PART I

Participate in a class discussion of the following questions. Record your answers in your science notebook.

1. Is there a general trend in how the population size changed? Is the trend the same for all teams? Describe the trend in your own words.
2. Review the hypotheses you developed in Step 3. Are any of them supported by the data the class gathered? Are any of them not supported by these data? Explain.

   A hypothesis is supported when it is consistent with the data collected. For example, consider this hypothesis: "A yeast population will grow faster in an environment where 5 grams (g) of sugar is added than in an environment where no sugar is added." Next, study your graphed data. Does the yeast with the sugar have a steeper slope than the yeast without sugar? If so, the data are consistent with the hypothesis, and thus support it.

3. What factors contributed to population growth? What factors contributed to a decline in population growth? What evidence do you have?

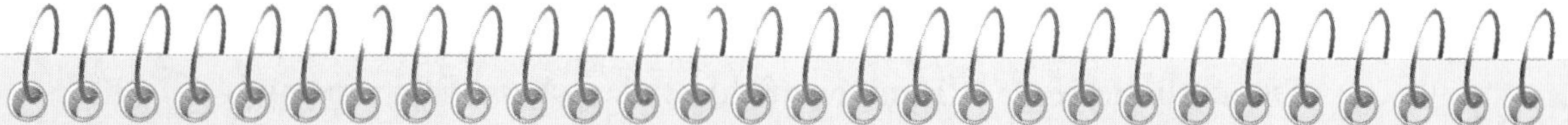

Protocol

Measuring Population Growth in Yeast Protocol

To determine how fast the yeast population grows, make population counts during the course of the investigation.

1. Yeast cells settle to the bottom of test tubes. Before counting the yeast population, gently invert the test tube several times to distribute the yeast.
2. Use a dropping pipet to transfer a drop from the test tube to a slide. Carefully place a clean coverslip over the drop. Try not to trap any air bubbles.
3. Examine the slide with the high-power lens of a microscope, such as the 400× lens. Adjust the focus and the amount of light until you can easily see yeast cells.

If the light is too bright, yeast cells are difficult to see. Adding a stain such as methylene blue to the slide will make it easier to see yeast cells. Add the stain to the drop of water when first preparing the slide, or later, after viewing the cells. Add stain to a prepared slide by carefully holding a small piece of paper towel on one side of a coverslip while you drop stain on the other side (see illustration).

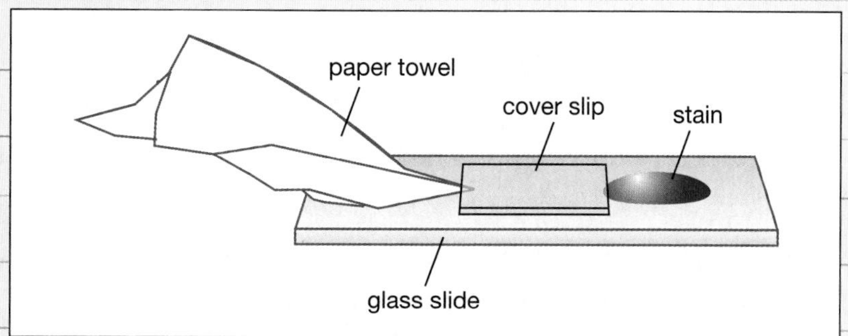

Adding stain to a slide. Carefully hold a small piece of paper towel on one side while you drop stain on the other side.

Cautions

Avoid contact with methylene blue because it will dye your skin and clothes. Methylene blue is harmful if ingested.

4. Count all the yeast cells in your field of view. Your field of view is the circular area you see when you look through the microscope. If your count is more than 300 or too many to count, make a dilution by following Steps 4a–c.

Make certain you are counting yeast cells and not other material. Buds also count as individual yeast cells. The yeast cells often stick together. Don't count clumps of 3 or more cells as one cell. Refer to the following figure to see the appearance of yeast cells.

a. Use the 1-milliliter (mL) graduated pipet to transfer 0.9 mL water to a clean test tube. Then add 0.1 mL culture to the test tube. Label this test tube "D1" for first dilution.

b. Invert test tube D1 several times to mix, and then use the dropping pipet to transfer 1 drop to the grid of the slide. Add a coverslip as in Step 2.

c. Count the yeast cells.

If there are still too many yeast cells to count, make another dilution by transferring 0.1 mL of D1 to a clean test tube with 0.9 mL water. Label this test tube "D2" for second dilution.

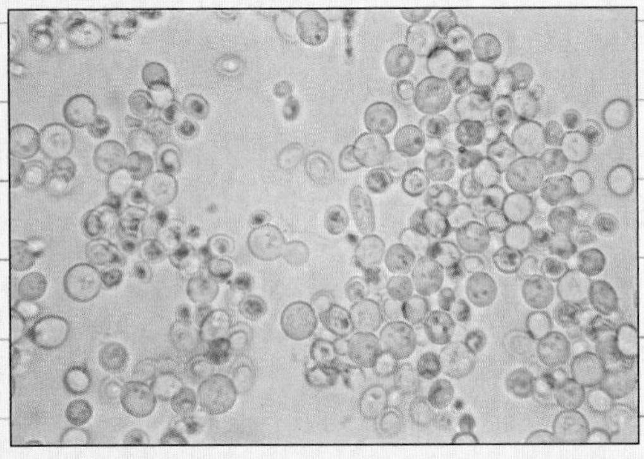

▲ **Yeast cells you might see in your light microscope.** Note the buds that are still attached to the yeast cells. These buds will become new individuals.

d. Record the count, the dilution you made, if any, and the magnification of the lens you are using in your science notebook.

5. Record the count as the number of yeast cells per milliliter in the data table. Assume that the drop you placed on the slide is 0.1 mL.

What additional calculations must you make if you made the first dilution? The second dilution?

6. Make multiple counts. Do this by moving the slide to different positions without changing the magnification of the microscope. Record each count in your data table.
7. Calculate the average number of yeast cells per field of view. Do this by dividing the number of yeast cells by the number of fields of view counted. Record the average count as yeast cells per milliliter.
8. Continue to make counts of the number of yeast cells in culture each day for 7 days (except for weekends). Repeat the counting procedure from Steps 4–7.
9. Wash your hands thoroughly before leaving the classroom.

Part II: Interacting Populations

There is another way to investigate populations from your classroom. You can look at data that scientists have already gathered about populations in nature. How does population growth in a natural environment compare with yeast growing in a lab? The conditions you grew the yeast in varied, just as conditions in nature vary. But populations in nature interact with one another. A yeast population in nature would interact with other populations, such as bacteria.

In Part II, you and a partner will analyze scientists' data from Isle Royale National Park. You will learn how the interactions of three populations affect their size. Isle Royale is the largest island in Lake Superior (see figure 14.3). Its isolation gives scientists a unique opportunity to study the interactions of mammal populations. It is a closed system because mammals cannot regularly enter or leave the island. Scientists have learned valuable information about population interactions from this system.

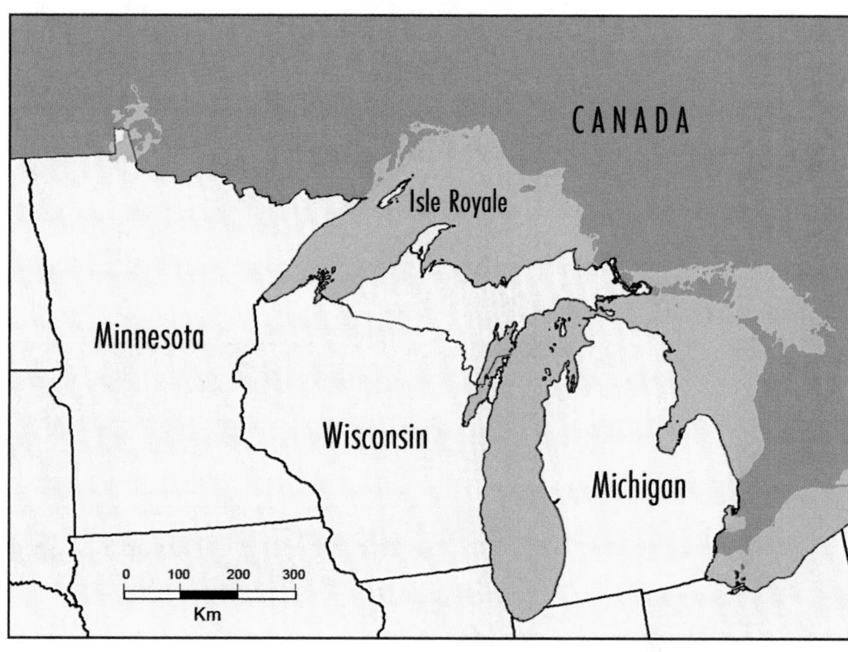

Figure 14.3 Map of Lake Superior and surrounding region. Isle Royale is located off the northern coast of Lake Superior. The island is about 72 kilometers (km) long and 14 km wide at its widest point. It was designated as a national park in 1931.

Materials

none

Process and Procedure

1. Study the graphs in figure 14.4.
   a. Sketch the essential features of the graphs in your science notebook.
   b. Write highlight comments and a caption for each figure.

   Focus on any changes you observe.

   c. Look at the change in the moose population between 1995 and 1998. Then look at the wolf population between 1995 and 1998. What do you notice? Describe the changes in the moose and wolf populations. How do you think the moose and wolf populations might be related?

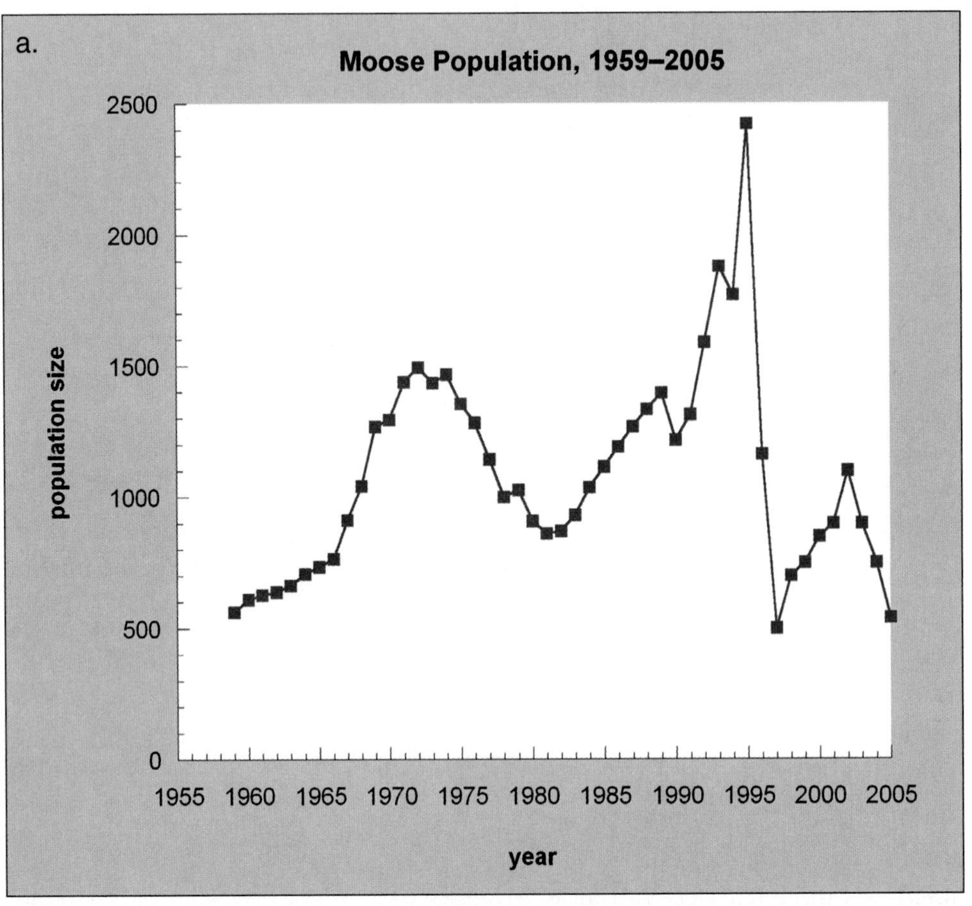

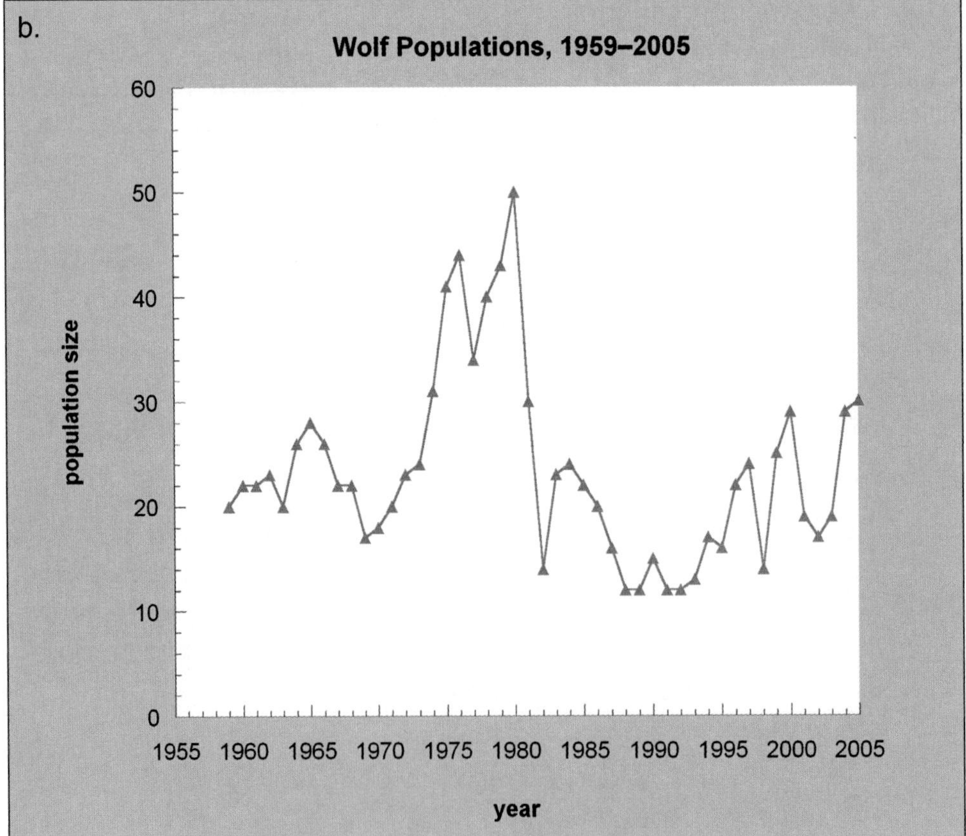

▶ **Figure 14.4 Moose and wolf populations on Isle Royale.** Biologists estimated the (a) moose and (b) wolf populations on Isle Royale from 1959 to 2005. What changes do you notice in the moose and wolf populations?

d. Read to a partner your highlight comments, captions, and description of how the moose and wolf populations are related. Modify what you have written if necessary.

2. Read *Moose and Wolves on Isle Royale* to learn what scientists know about these populations.
   a. As you read, draw a food web in your science notebook that shows the relationship between the organisms described. Include a caption with your drawing.
   b. Read your caption aloud to a partner. Then adjust your caption based on feedback from your partner.

READING

Moose and Wolves on Isle Royale

The research on Isle Royale constitutes one of the world's longest, continuous studies of either wolves or moose. Moose arrived on the island around 1900. They either swam or crossed an ice bridge, which rarely forms, from the mainland (see figure 14.5). Wolves crossed an ice bridge around 1950. The monitoring of the moose and wolf populations began in 1959 and has continued since. Isle Royale is essentially a single prey–single predator system. The simplicity of this system is not typical but makes it well suited for research. Scientists hope that studying this simple system will help them better understand more complex systems.

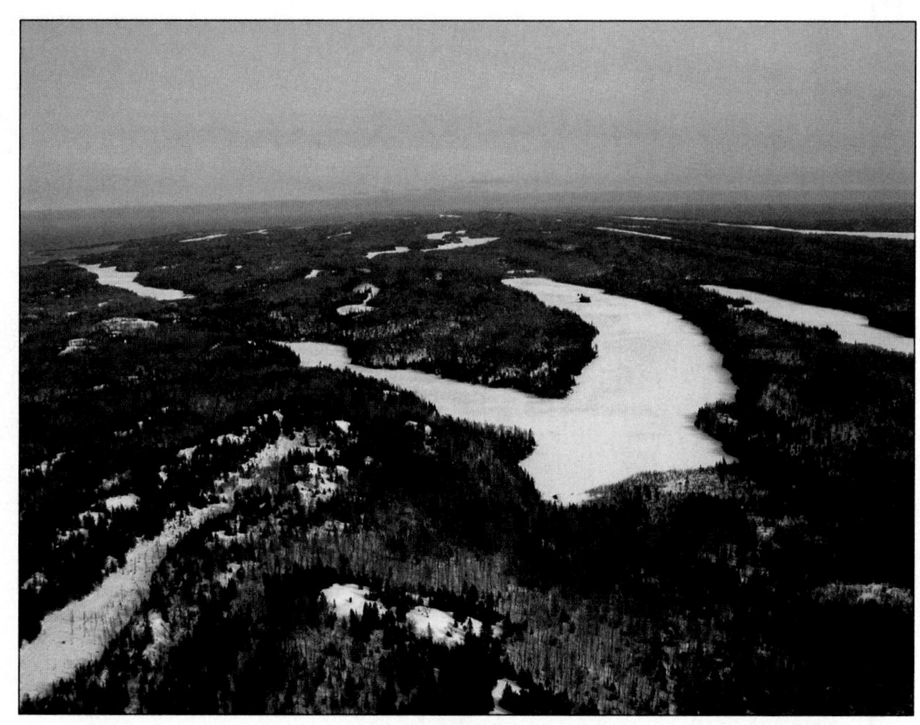

▲ **Figure 14.5 Isle Royale in the winter.** Isle Royale is separated from the mainland by more than 24 km of water. Very few species have colonized the island. What might bring more organisms to the island?

Moose and Wolves on Isle Royale, continued

Moose (*Alces alces*) are the only large herbivores on Isle Royale (figure 14.6). Moose feed on aquatic vegetation in the summer and woody vegetation in the winter. They prefer to feed on balsam fir (*Abies balsamea*) seedlings over other tree species. In 2005, the moose population consisted predominantly of old moose, those that were more than 10 years old. These moose survived a large die-off in their population in 1996, which was caused by a severe winter and delayed spring. Mild winters can also be difficult for moose because of the increased number of winter ticks. A high number of ticks in moose can lead to anemia and reduced feeding. Older moose and moose weakened by winter ticks are more vulnerable to wolf attacks.

▲ **Figure 14.6 Moose in the winter.** Moose have difficulty moving and finding food in deep snow.

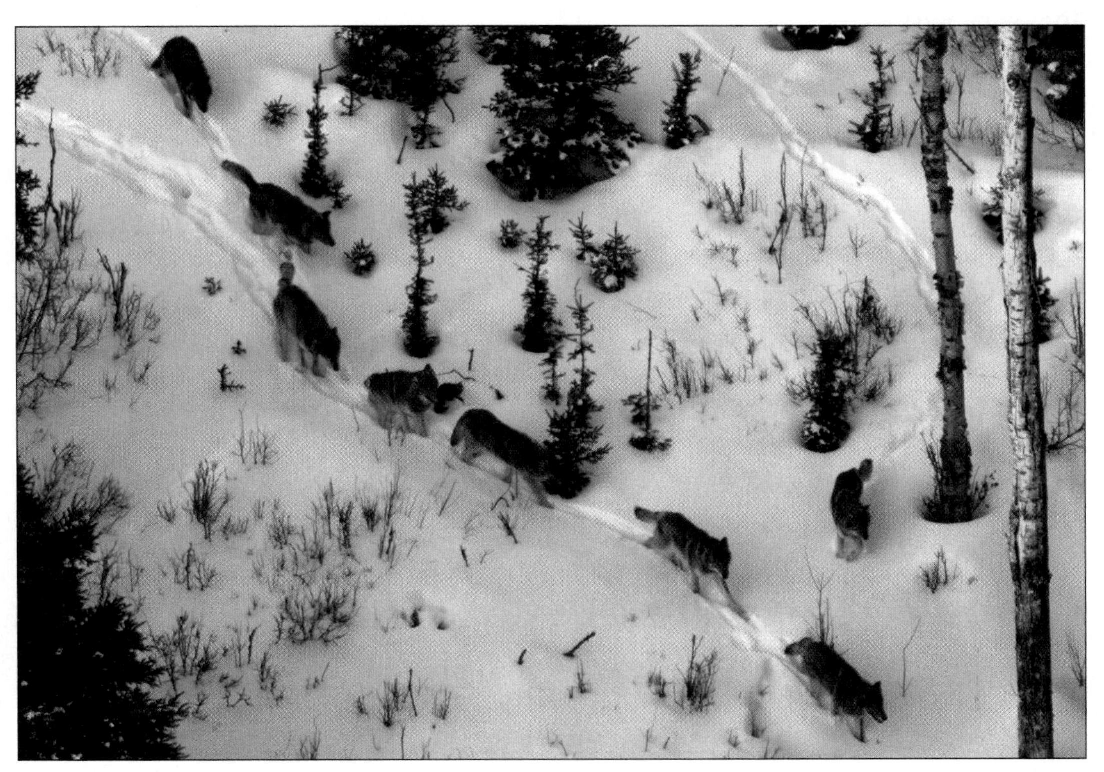

▲ **Figure 14.7 Wolf pack.** Wolves work together in packs to catch their prey. How do you think deep snow affects the likelihood of a wolf pack attacking a moose?

Hunting of moose and wolves on the island is prohibited. Gray wolves (*Canis lupus*) are the only predators of the moose on the island (figure 14.7). Moose make up 90 percent of the wolves' diet. The other 10 percent of the diet consists of beavers (*Castor canadensis*) and snowshoe hares (*Lepus americanus*). Beavers eat balsam fir, and hares eat grass. The wolf population responds to fluctuations in its prey population (moose), but it is also influenced by other factors. In the early 1980s, many wolves died from canine parvovirus accidentally introduced by humans or their pet dogs. A decline in genetic diversity might also have the potential to affect the wolf population. Some species inbreeding makes populations more vulnerable to fitness loss. (Inbreeding is breeding between closely related individuals. Fitness is the ability of an organism to survive and reproduce in its environment.) For example, inbreeding might increase the likelihood that individuals in the wolf population will have a genetic disorder. Scientists have gathered evidence of vertebrae abnormalities in the Isle Royale wolf population. But so far, there is no evidence that the survival rate of wolves with the abnormality has changed.

3. Now that you know a little more about moose and wolves on Isle Royale, complete the tasks in Steps 3a–b.
   a. List at least 2 factors that you think might cause the moose population to *increase.* Then list at least 2 factors that might cause the moose population to *decrease.* Explain why for each factor.
   b. Repeat Step 3a for the wolf population.
4. Study the graph in figure 14.8. Then answer Questions 4a–b about the balsam fir population.

Look for and try to explain any changes you see. This is one of many effective ways to study graphs and charts.

   a. Describe the trend for tagged balsam fir trees.

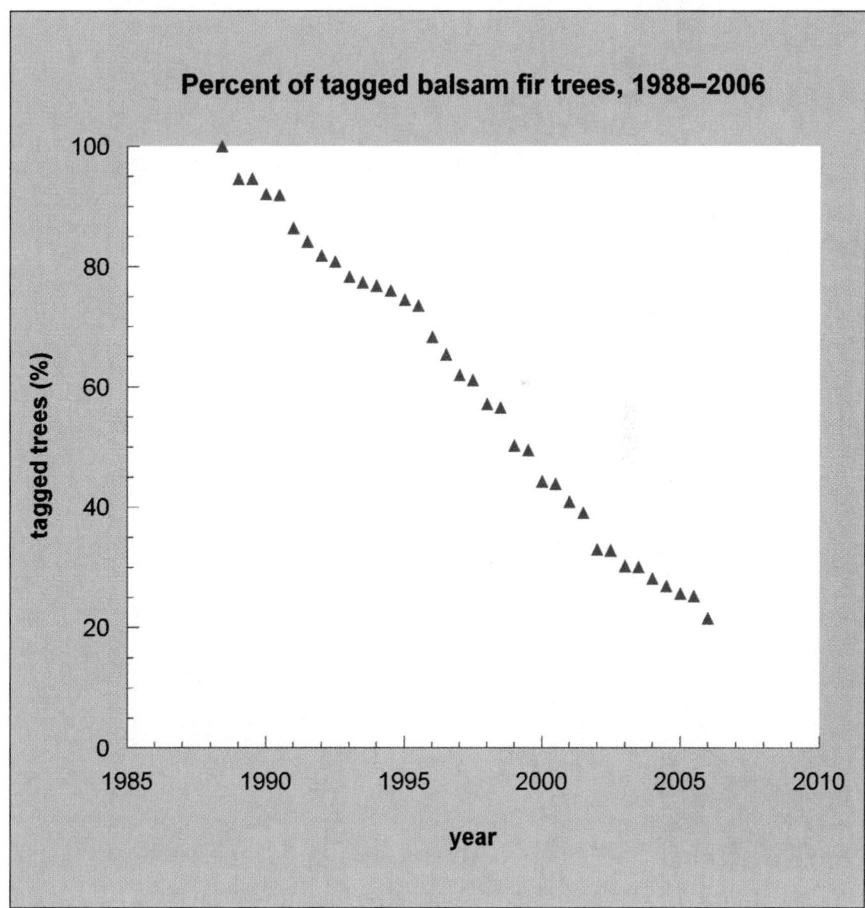

Figure 14.8 Percentage of tagged balsam fir trees. Scientists tagged a portion of the balsam fir trees on Isle Royale in 1988. All of the trees were mature, meaning they were able to produce seeds. Since 1988, the number of tagged trees has declined. What has happened to the number of mature fir trees since 1988? What might have caused this change?

b. The data in figure 14.8 show the percentage of tagged mature fir trees that remain each year since 1988. Mature trees produce seeds. These trees are necessary for saplings (young trees) to become established and contribute new growth in the forest. How do you think the change in the abundance of mature balsam fir trees will affect the overall abundance of balsam fir trees?

Think about a factor that should increase the population.

5. Read the following paragraph about the forest vegetation on Isle Royale. Use the following questions to focus your reading:
   - "How does the age and number of trees on the east end of the island compare with the trees on the west end of the island?"
   - "What factors contribute to the differences?"

   Forests on the east end of the island have more young balsam fir trees than forests on the west end of the island. After a wildfire burned many trees on the east end, the number of new balsam fir trees there has been gradually increasing. On the west end of the island, the growth of new balsam firs is very low. As moose feed on balsam fir saplings, they prevent the saplings from growing (see figure 14.9). Most of the trees on the west end are old and produce fewer seeds. Many of the older trees are expected to die in the next 10 years.

6. Complete Steps 6a–d to show what you have learned about the abundance of balsam fir trees and how the abundance might change in the future.

▲ **Figure 14.9 The effect of moose on balsam fir.** (a) Balsam fir growth is hindered where moose feed intensely. Moose can feed in this forest, where there is an open canopy and very few mature balsam fir. (b) An exclosure is an area fenced off to keep organisms out. This 50-year-old exclosure shows that where moose are excluded, balsam fir are abundant and healthy. This forest is protected from moose and contains mature balsam firs and a dense canopy.

a. Represent in a sketch what you read about the current abundance of firs. Consider making a map of the island that uses simple drawings to represent the abundance of balsam firs. (A map of Isle Royale is shown in figure 14.10.) Include highlight comments and a caption with your sketch.
b. Create another labeled sketch that represents the abundance of firs on Isle Royale in 10 years.
c. Use an effective strategy to get feedback on your sketch.
d. Record the results of your feedback in your science notebook.

SCILINKS NSTA
Go to: www.scilinks.org
Topic: moose population
Code: 2Inquiry719a
Topic: wolf population
Code: 2Inquiry719b

Reflect and Connect

Work alone to answer the following questions in your science notebook.

1. Study figure 14.10. Explain why moose are distributed unevenly across Isle Royale during the winter of 2002.

Review the paragraph from Step 5 to help you answer the question.

2. Copy figure 14.8 into your science notebook and extend the x-axis to 2055.
   a. Predict how the balsam fir population will change over the next 50 years.

Extending the line will help you make your prediction.

   b. Add highlight comments to the graph to explain why you think those changes will occur.
3. Copy figure 14.4 into your science notebook. Extend the x-axis to 2055.
   a. Predict how the moose and wolf populations will change over the next 50 years.

Extending the line for both populations will help you make your predictions.

Figure 14.10 Moose distribution on Isle Royale during winter 2002. Moose are more common on one end of the island. What might cause this distribution?

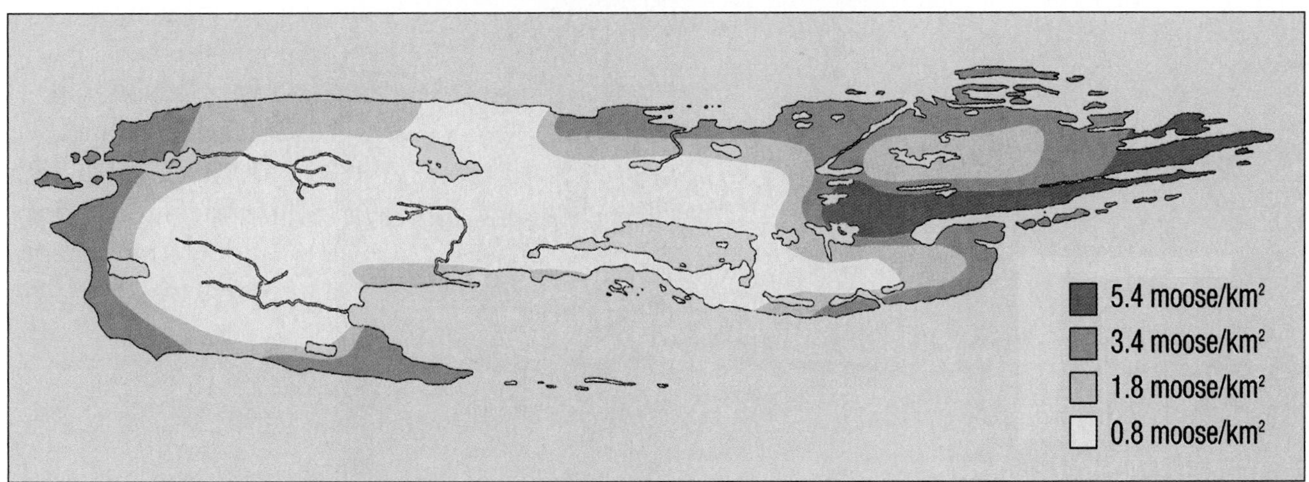

b. Add highlight comments to the graph to explain why you think those changes will occur.

4. In Part I, you investigated different environmental conditions for a population of yeast. What environmental conditions do you think might affect the populations on Isle Royale? List at least 2 conditions.
5. Suppose you could add an organism that feeds on yeast to the yeast culture. Explain how you think the yeast population would be affected. Give your answer as a graph that shows the resulting yeast population and the population of another organism across time. Include a caption with your graph.

EXPLAIN

Systems in Balance

Natural processes are important to the maintenance of systems. Chemical reactions are one type of natural process. You learned in unit 1 that many chemical reactions are reversible under the right conditions. A chemical system is at equilibrium when the rate of the forward reaction equals the rate of the reverse reaction. These reactions are an important part of processes in living systems. In unit 3, you learned that fluxes into and out of a system maintain the system. In the global carbon cycle, many of the carbon fluxes depend on processes that involve chemical reactions. (Remember, a carbon flux is the movement of carbon between reservoirs.)

In *Systems in Balance*, you will learn how natural processes maintain ecosystems from year to year (figure 14.11). Changes in populations are part of these natural processes. For example, fluxes into and out of a population eventually cause a population to reach equilibrium. Interactions between populations, just like interactions between molecules, influence a system. In this case, the system is an ecosystem. In Part I, you will learn what influences populations. Then in Part II, you will learn what shapes ecosystems, including how the interactions of populations shape ecosystems.

Figure 14.11 Oak-grassland ecosystem. Oak-grassland ecosystems consist of a mixture of oak forest, meadows, and grasslands. What natural process might help maintain this ecosystem?

Part I: Population Dynamics

Materials

For each student

1 calculator

graph paper

graphs of the yeast population from the activity *Changing Populations*

Process and Procedure

You have investigated several populations. Did these populations stay the same or change across time? What makes a population change? Given enough space and **resources**, a population can potentially continue to grow indefinitely. In Part I, you will work alone or with a partner to learn what characterizes populations and what limits population growth.

1. Imagine a single bacterium cell in a large container of nutrient medium. If the cell and its descendants divide every 30 minutes (min), how many cells would you expect to find in the container in 24 hours (hr)? Model the population growth of bacteria through calculations and graphing. Steps 1a–e will help you.
   a. Copy the table in figure 14.12 into your science notebook. Add enough rows so that you can calculate for 24 hr in Step 1d. You will calculate the increase in the number of bacterium cells in 3 hr. Perform the calculations and complete the column titled "number of bacterium cells."
   b. Identify the mathematical relationship in the right-hand column. First, read down the middle columns. How much does the number of bacterium cells increase by? Now read down the right-hand column. Calculate what n is by using the amount of increase.

For example, if $2 = 2^n$, then n must be 1 for the second row.

Time (hours)	Number of cell divisions	Number of bacterium cells	Mathematical representation
0.0	0	1	$= 2^n$
0.5	1	2	$= 2^n$
1.0	2	4	$= 2^n$
1.5	3	8	$= 2^n$
2.0	4		$= 2^n$
2.5	5		$= 2^n$
3.0	6		$= 2^n$

Figure 14.12 Modeling bacterium population growth. How does the number of bacterium cells change every 30 min?

c. Notice how the population doubles every 30 min. What does the 2 in the right-hand column represent? What does *n* represent?

d. Now calculate the bacterium population after 24 hr. Show your work. Consider rounding the number and giving your answer in scientific notation.

For example, the scientific notation for 5,869,481 is 5.9×10^6.

e. Draw a graph of this bacterium population for a 12-hr period. Include highlight comments on your graph. Your graph represents 1 type of population growth curve.

2. Read the following 2 paragraphs to learn about exponential growth. Then write an answer in your science notebook for the question in the second paragraph.

   The graph of the bacterium population is an example of **exponential growth**. Exponential growth happens when an increase occurs at a constant *rate* per unit of *time*. At first, the population grows slowly, then it increases progressively faster and faster. The number of individuals added to the population gets larger and larger across time. This occurs because the constant rate of growth applies to a larger and larger population. Eventually, the population reaches a very large size. Exponential growth occurs in other situations as well. For example, compound interest makes the money in your savings account grow quickly. The amount your money grows depends on your interest rate.

   Think about this. Would you rather start with \$1 in your savings account and have it double every month for 1 year, or get \$100 each month for a year? Calculate the total for your savings account for both situations after 1 year. Then explain why you would choose \$1 that doubles every month or \$100 a month. Show your calculations.

3. Complete the tasks in Steps 3a–c to learn how exponential growth affects populations.

   a. Read the information in the following paragraph. You will use it to create a graph showing the relationship between population growth and population density.

      Why hasn't exponential growth resulted in enormous numbers of organisms that completely overwhelm Earth's resources? In reality, populations rarely grow exponentially. As a population grows, its **population density** increases as well. Population density is the number of individuals per unit of land area or water volume.

b. Look at the data in figure 14.13. Decide how you will label the axes of your graph. Then graph the data to see how the growth of a paramecium population changes as the population density increases. Include highlight comments on your graph.

c. How is the paramecium graph similar to the bacterium graph? How is it different?

4. Add a horizontal line to your graph indicating the *carrying capacity* of the paramecium population. Read the following 2 paragraphs to learn what carrying capacity is.

The pattern of a population's size growing slowly, then rapidly, and finally leveling off is called **logistic growth.** You are familiar with logistic growth in other situations. For example, wages increase steadily when you begin working. Then they level off as you approach retirement.

Let's look at what happens in natural systems. As a population's density increases in an environment, the amount of space and resources decreases. Competition within the population increases as nutrients and other resources are used up. Toxic bodily wastes may build up in the environment. Predators and parasites may become common. All these factors reduce reproduction and increase the number of deaths in the population. This slows population growth. A population that develops in a new environment may begin to grow exponentially. But it soon slows and eventually approaches a maximum size. This maximum is called the **carrying capacity.** Carrying capacity is the largest population of a species that the environment can support in a given period of time. Carrying capacities are not fixed.

Time (days)	Number of organisms
1	25
2	120
3	310
4	375
5	375
6	375

Source: G. F. Gause. (1934). *The struggle for existence.* Baltimore: Williams and Wilkins.

▲ **Figure 14.13 Paramecium population data.** Paramecia are single-celled organisms. How will a graph of these data compare with the graph of the bacterium population in Step 1?

5. Read *Population Growth* to learn what causes populations to change size.

a. Use this question to focus your reading: "How is population size related to births, deaths, immigration, and emigration?"

b. Fill in the T-table in figure 14.14 as you read.

Term	How it is related to the focus question
birthrate	
mortality rate	
immigration	
emigration	
limiting factor	

▲ **Figure 14.14 Relationship to population size.** Describe how each term on the left is related to the focus question. Add any terms to the T-table that you think are important.

READING

Population Growth

Imagine a park with 125 oak trees. Thirty years later, the park has only 115 oak trees. What does the decrease of 10 oak trees represent? Because trees cannot wander away, they must have died or been cut down. In this situation, the decrease represents the death rate, or **mortality rate**, of the oak tree population. The number of deaths in the oak tree population per unit of time is the mortality rate. Mortality is not the only change that can affect a population, however. While some of the trees may have died, some young oak trees may have started to grow from seed. Death decreases a population; reproduction increases it. The rate at which reproduction increases the population is called the **birthrate**.

Immigration and emigration are two other ways that change population size in organisms that can move. Imagine you studied the pigeon population in your city. You discovered that in 1 year a certain number of pigeons flew into the city and a certain number flew out. **Immigration** occurs when one or more individuals move into an area where others of their type can be found. Immigration increases the population. **Emigration** occurs when individuals leave the area. Emigration decreases the population. A simple way to remember the difference is that during *immigration* organisms move *into* an area. During *emigration*, organisms *exit* an area.

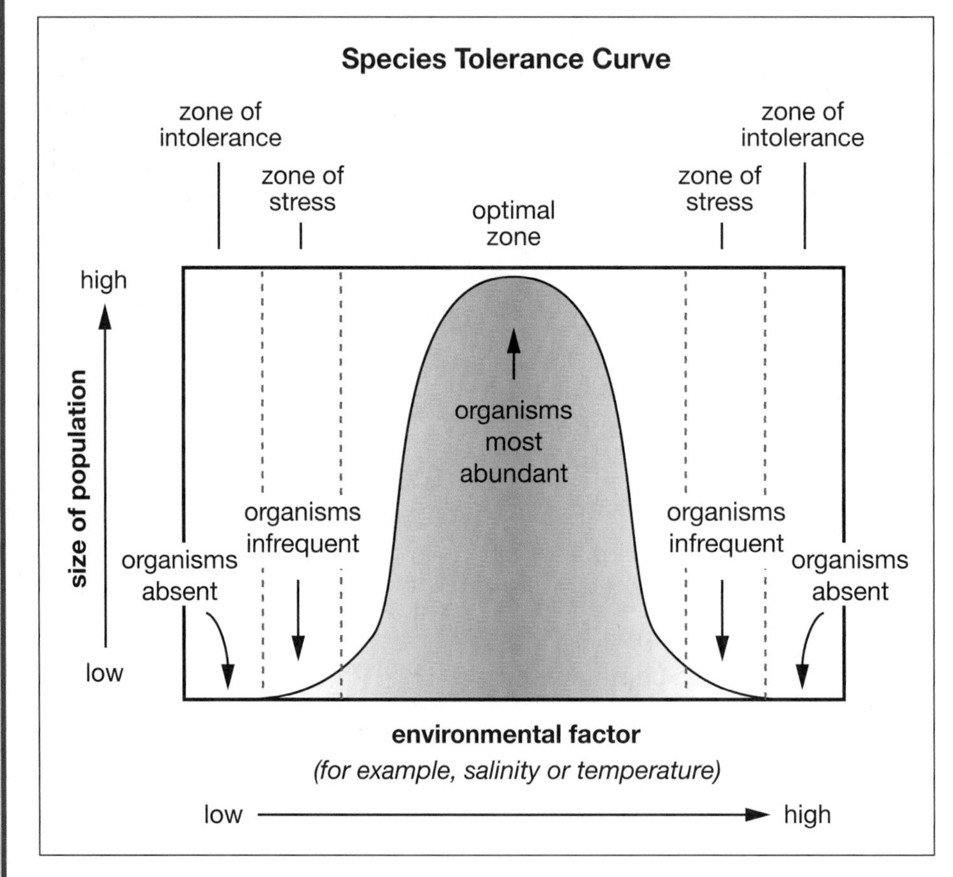

▲ **Figure 14.15 Species tolerance curve.** There are maximum and minimum levels of environmental factors that affect where an organism can survive. These levels might be determined by abiotic factors such as salinity or temperature. Can you think of other environmental factors that will affect where an organism lives?

In any population that can move, birthrate and immigration increase the population. And mortality and emigration decrease the population. Thus, a population's size is the result of the relationships among these rates.

What are some things that might decrease population growth? That is, what could reduce the birthrate or increase the mortality rate? Are there factors that could increase emigration? How does the environment influence population growth?

The **environment** is everything that surrounds and affects an organism. The environment has two parts. The living part is called the **biotic** environment. The biotic environment for a wolf on Isle Royale includes all the plants, animals, and microorganisms that live or once lived on the island. The nonliving part is called the **abiotic** environment. The abiotic environment includes such things as sunlight, water, nutrients, and physical structure.

The environment affects individuals. The environment may slow the individual's growth, kill it, or stimulate its growth and reproduction. Any biotic or abiotic factor that can *limit* the growth of a population is a **limiting factor**. For example, predators like coyotes are biotic limiting factors for a population of rabbits. Temperature is an example of an abiotic limiting factor. Many plants and animals only survive in a specific range of temperatures. Figure 14.15 shows a species tolerance curve. This graph illustrates how environmental factors affect the abundance of organisms.

6. Complete the following 2 tasks to show your understanding of population growth.
   a. Finish the following equation to show how population size is related to births, deaths, immigration, and emigration.

      population size = ______________

   b. Calculate the size of a population of least bitterns (see figure 14.16) over a period of 4 years using data in figure 14.17.

▲ **Figure 14.16 Least bittern and chicks (*Ixobrychus exilis*).** Least bitterns are secretive marsh birds that live in wetlands with tall vegetation.

Time	Starting population	Birthrate (chicks/ year)	Mortality rate (birds/ year)	Immigration (birds/year)	Emigration (birds/ year)
Begin	30	4	6	10	2
year 1	?	3	3	2	5
year 2	?	3	3	2	5
year 3	?	3	4	3	6
year 4	?				

◀ **Figure 14.17 Information about a least bittern population.** How does the population change from one year to the next?

Stop & THINK

PART I

Work alone or with a partner to answer the following questions in your science notebook.

1. What are the 4 factors that determine population size?
2. How is a limiting reagent in a chemical reaction similar to a limiting factor for a population? How is it different? Use a Venn diagram to show the similarities and differences.
3. You have learned about exponential and logistic growth. Apply this new knowledge to the yeast investigation from the explore activity, *Changing Populations*, and answer Questions 3a–c. Refer to your graph of the yeast population and the graphs from other teams.
   - **a.** What growth pattern (exponential or logistic) did the yeast population have? Explain your answer.
   - **b.** What was the carrying capacity of your team's yeast population? Provide evidence for your answer. If your yeast population did not reach carrying capacity, then estimate what the carrying capacity might have been if you had continued to monitor the yeast population. Provide an explanation for your estimate.
   - **c.** Was the carrying capacity for your team's yeast population different from the carrying capacity for other teams? Explain why or why not, and discuss possible limiting factors in your response.
4. Answer Questions 4a–d about the moose and wolf populations on Isle Royale. Review the text and graphs from the explore activity as necessary.
   - **a.** Which of these factors affect the moose and wolf populations: birthrate, mortality rate, immigration, and emigration?
   - **b.** Predict the carrying capacity for moose and wolves on Isle Royale.
   - **c.** List 4 limiting factors for the population of moose. At least 1 of the factors must be abiotic.
   - **d.** How do you think the change in the balsam fir population will affect the carrying capacity for moose on Isle Royale? Explain your answer.

Part II: Ecosystems

Materials

none

Process and Procedure

The world around you consists of more than populations of living organisms. How do the conditions in an environment influence populations? In Part II, you will work with a partner to learn about the systems that affect and are affected by living organisms. You also will relate what you learn about these systems to the cycling of matter and the flow of energy.

1. Think about what kind of relationships you have with the people you encounter. You also have relationships with organisms other than people. In fact, organisms are constantly interacting with other organisms. Work with your partner to consider these relationships.
   a. Read *Relationships among Populations* to learn about some of these interactions.
   b. Look ahead to Steps 2 and 3 to guide your reading. Take turns talking about your ideas. Revise your responses if you get new information after talking with your partner. Remember, this is the think-share-advise-revise (TSAR) strategy.

READING

Relationships among Populations

All populations of organisms, including human populations, interact with one another. The interactions form a complex web of relationships. These interactions can be beneficial or harmful. But all involve the cycling of matter and the flow of energy.

All the populations of different species in a designated area make up a **community**. Each environment has a community of different organisms. Many types of relationships help form a community's web of life. Each relationship involves at least two different organisms. The most obvious relationship between organisms is who eats whom. This is called a feeding relationship. Most organisms get their food from many sources.

We can use a food web to illustrate the feeding relationships in a community of

Relationships among Populations, continued

organisms. Figure 14.18 shows one example of a food web. Notice how many of the relationships are between predators and prey. Also notice the decomposers that break down the dead bodies of plants and animals. There are other common relationships between organisms besides predator-prey relationships. These include competition and mutualism (see figure 14.19).

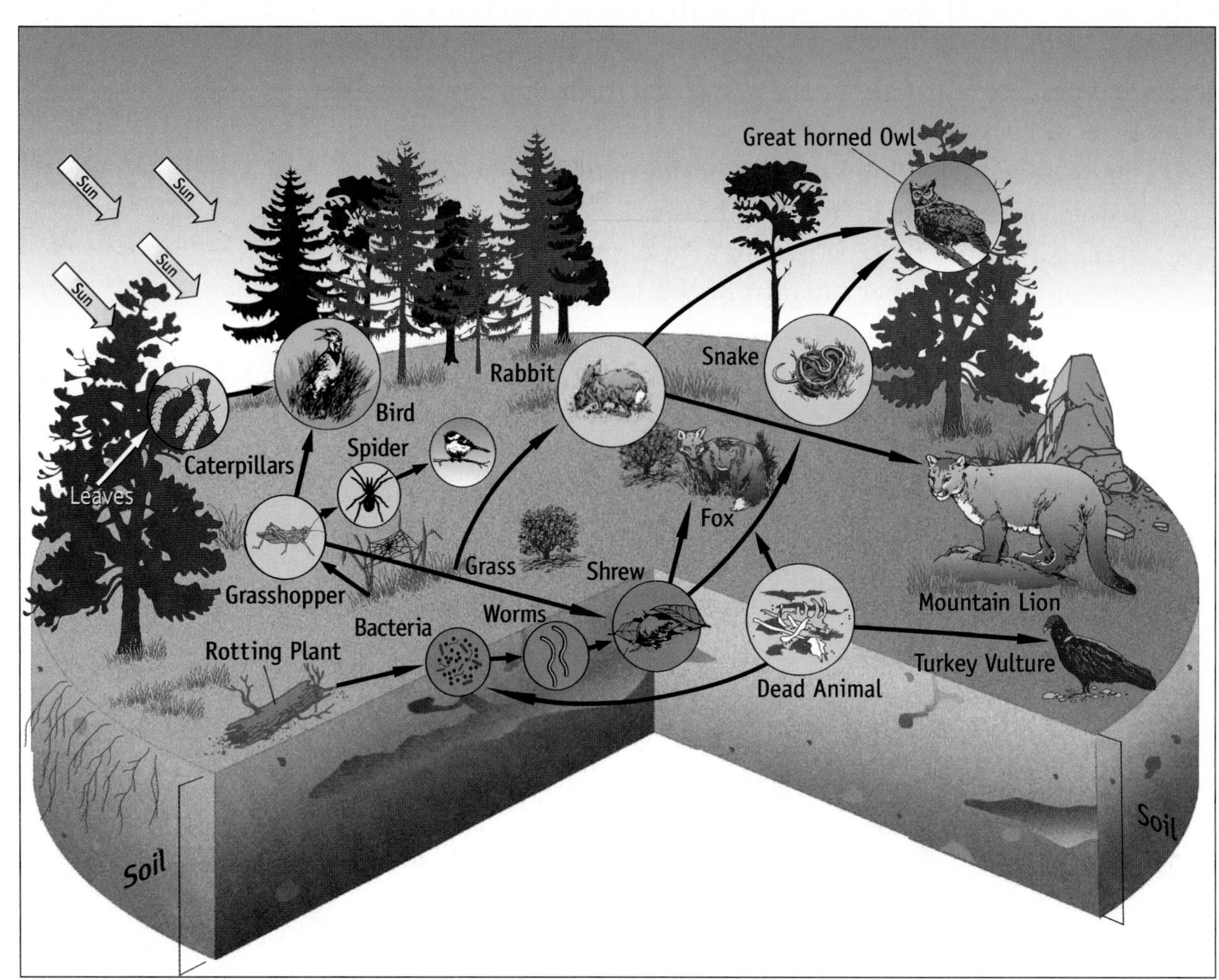

▲ **Figure 14.18 Food web.** Food webs show the feeding relationships among different species within a community. Arrows in the diagram show the direction of energy flow. The arrow points from the organisms getting consumed to the consumer. For example, worms get eaten by shrews, which in turn get eaten by foxes. Recall that producers are organisms that make their own food and consumers obtain their food by eating or breaking down other organisms. Can you think of other arrows that you would include for the organisms shown in this community?

Relationship	Effect of the relationship	Description
Mutualism	+ / +	A relationship among organisms in which both organisms benefit. For example, lichens often consist of an alga and a fungus that live in close association. The alga produces food through photosynthesis and the fungus provides moisture and nutrients. Another example is the relationships between some plant species and insects. Insects eat pollen or nectar provided by the plant and the insect helps the plants reproduce through pollination.
Predator-prey	+ / −	One organism (predator) eats another (prey). This relationship is lethal to the prey but is not an intimate association.
Parasitism	+ / −	One organism (parasite) lives on or in another organism (the host), using it as a food source. The relationship between the two species is more intimate, but not usually as lethal as predator-prey.
Herbivory	+ / −	The consumption of living plant material by a consumer (grazers). The relationship is usually not as lethal as predator-prey and is not intimate.
Competition	− / −	Organisms may compete for such things as food, space, sunlight, nutrients, or water. The competition is often for a resource that limits the growth of a population. In competition, both organisms are harmed.

▲ **Figure 14.19 Relationships in ecosystems classified by effects of the relationship.** In figure 14.18, organisms were classified by feeding relationships. It is sometimes useful to classify species in a community by the effect they have on each other. The survival or reproduction of a species may benefit from the presence of another species (+) or be harmed by it (−). In the table, + / + indicates that both species benefit from a relationship, + / − indicates that one species is harmed and the other benefits, and − / − indicates that both species are harmed.

Topic: food webs
Go to: www.scilinks.org
Code: 2Inquiry729

2. After completing the reading, identify the following relationships as predator-prey, parasitism, herbivory, competition, or mutualism. Justify your response and record it in your science notebook. You will use your responses in a class discussion.
   a. A hummingbird getting nectar from a flower and getting pollen on its back
   b. Prairie dogs and bison feeding on grass
   c. Wolves and moose on Isle Royale
   d. Leeches on a fish
   e. A bird removing seeds from a pinecone

3. Answer Questions 3a–b about how relationships can affect population size. Provide a brief explanation for each answer.
   a. How does a predator-prey relationship affect the population size of the 2 organisms involved?
   b. How do you think competition between 2 organisms affects their population sizes?
4. Read *Structure of an Ecosystem* to learn what characteristics ecosystems have and how energy and matter move into and out of ecosystems. Look ahead to Step 5 to guide your reading.

READING

Structure of an Ecosystem

A community (the biotic environment) and the abiotic environment make up an ecological system, or **ecosystem**. You learned that the biotic and abiotic environments influence populations. Scientists look at the abiotic and biotic environments to understand how natural systems work. Suppose a trout population in one river ecosystem is wiped out. Yet a trout population in a different river ecosystem flourishes. You may wonder why. So you would compare the abiotic environments in the two ecosystems. From that, you would learn that the first ecosystem had water temperatures above the trout's tolerance limit. As a result, the temperatures wiped out the trout in that ecosystem. Read FYI—*Climatic and Topographic Effects* to learn how climate and topography affect the biotic and abiotic environments in ecosystems.

Ecosystems are open systems. Things constantly enter and leave them. Energy is one of the largest inputs into ecosystems. The Sun is the ultimate source of energy for most ecosystems. Other sources include wind, rain, water flow, or fuel (for ecosystems with humans). Energy outputs can be in the form of heat and organic matter (food and waste products). Other fluxes for ecosystems include water, air, nutrients, and organisms. If you find learning about ecosystems interesting, you might enjoy a career in ecology. You can learn more about careers in ecology in the sidebar *Working for the Environment*.

All organisms require energy. Thus, the amount of energy and material entering and leaving an ecosystem determines the size and diversity of the biotic community. The flow of energy and the cycling of matter from one organism to another tie organisms together. The flow of energy begins with producers. Producers convert light energy from the Sun into food (chemical energy). The conversion occurs through photosynthesis, which involves a series of chemical reactions.

How does energy flow through an ecosystem? The answer is in the ecosystem's trophic structure. The trophic structure is made up of the feeding relationships among the producers and consumers. Each step in a food web is a trophic level. The relationships between trophic levels determine the flow of energy and the cycling of matter in the ecosystem.

Producers make up the trophic level that supports an ecosystem. Consumers are another trophic level. Consumers can depend directly or indirectly on producers for energy and matter.

Herbivores (organisms that consume plants or algae) are the primary consumers. Deer, grasshoppers, and garden snails are primary consumers. Carnivores that eat herbivores are secondary consumers. Carnivores that eat other carnivores are tertiary (third-level) consumers. Finally, decomposers consume organic material and dead organisms from all trophic levels. Can you identify the trophic levels of the organisms in figure 14.18?

You can use trophic levels to illustrate the amount of energy entering and leaving an ecosystem. Study figure 14.20 to see how energy is distributed from one trophic level to another. Notice that primary producers are the foundation. Each trophic level above them receives less energy. In many ecosystems, each trophic level receives about one-tenth the energy of the level below it. Where does the energy go? Most of the energy is lost to the environment as heat and also to activities needed to keep an organism alive.

You know that the available energy declines at higher trophic levels. So does **biomass**. Biomass is the total amount of living organic matter for a given area of the environment. Living organic matter includes all the living organisms in an area such as plants and animals. Recall that all organisms are composed of organic molecules.

The rate at which new biomass forms, or the **productivity**, is highest among producers. Consumers at higher tropic levels generate less biomass and so are less productive. Therefore, an ecosystem can sustain far fewer top-level carnivores than low-level consumers and producers. For example, the total mass of the coyotes in a grassland is much less than the total mass of rabbits and other prey. The total mass of the coyotes also is less than all the mass of the grass.

In the next chapter, you will learn how the productivity of different ecosystems and agricultural systems has implications for humans.

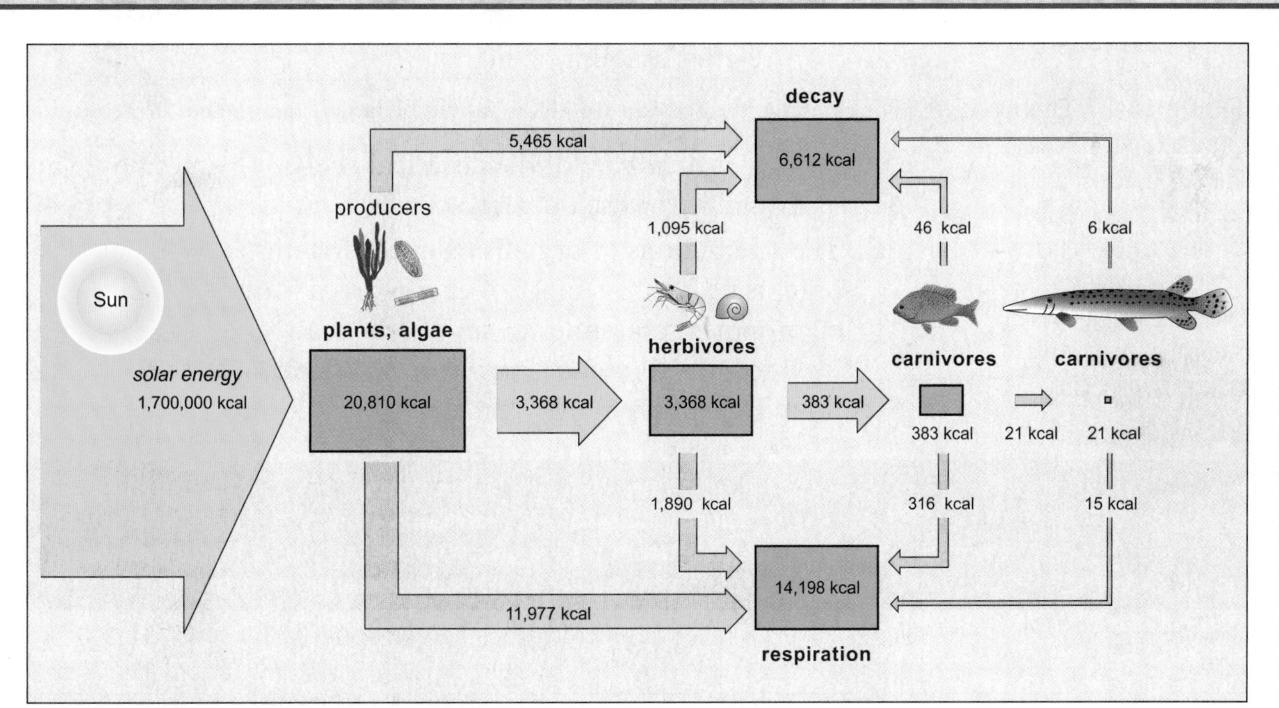

▲ **Figure 14.20 Energy flow diagram for Silver Springs, Florida.** How does the amount of energy (in kilocalories, or kcal) differ from one trophic level to the next? Can you calculate what percentage of energy is transferred from producers to herbivores (primary consumers)?

5. After completing the reading, answer Questions 5a–d about ecosystems.
   a. Would you expect most ecosystems to contain more primary consumers or more secondary consumers? Explain your answer.
   b. Imagine a grassland ecosystem with mice, other herbivores, and predators, such as weasels, which eat mice. Use a sketch or diagram to represent the relative biomass of different trophic levels in this ecosystem. For example, trophic levels often are shown as horizontal, stacked bars inside a pyramid. The lowest trophic level is on the bottom.
   c. Figure 14.21 shows how energy might be distributed in the different trophic levels for the grassland ecosystem described in Step 5b. Create a diagram like the one in figure 14.20 to show the flow of energy for the grassland. Your diagram should include the following:
      - Inputs and outputs of energy
      - Three trophic levels that are labeled
      - The total energy lost through cellular respiration and the energy stored in the remains of organisms

Calculate the total energy lost based on the information in figure 14.21.

      - Sizes of boxes and arrows that are scaled to represent the relative amount of energy

For example, the box for producers should be larger than the box for consumers.

   d. Why is only *part* of the chemical energy produced by plants available for use by herbivores?
6. The interactions of organisms in ecosystems ensure that all organisms have a supply of energy from food. The abiotic environment continues to supply the matter that organisms need to survive. Read *Cycling of Matter in Ecosystems* to learn how. Take notes as you read.

Figure 14.21 Energy for a grassland. Calculate the total energy lost through cellular respiration and the energy stored in the remains of organisms. The units for the values are kcal/m²/year. The amount of energy available as sunlight is 4,700,000 kcal.

Trophic Level	Energy available as biomass	Energy loss to space from cell respiration	Energy as remains that are available to decomposers	Energy in next trophic level
Plants (primarily grass)	52,800	11,550	26,950	14,300
Herbivores 1° consumers	14,300	4,094	10,200	6
Carnivores 2° consumers	6	5	1	0

READING

Cycling of Matter in Ecosystems

How are conditions in ecosystems maintained for hundreds or thousands of years? A constant recycling of materials between the biotic and abiotic environments is required. Recall that the amount of chemical elements on Earth is fixed. Essentially, the same atoms and molecules are used over and over. Many of the processes that allow atoms and molecules to be used again occur in ecosystems. In chapter 3, *Collisions—Atomic Style*, you learned about the law of conservation of matter. This law states that matter is conserved in ordinary chemical and physical changes. In other words, matter is transformed, but it doesn't disappear. It cycles endlessly.

You learned about the cycling of water and carbon in unit 3. You know that water cycles between global reservoirs. But it also cycles through ecosystems. Plants absorb water from the soil. Land animals, other consumers, and decomposers absorb water from food or drink it directly. Aquatic organisms are constantly bathed in water. Water returns to the atmosphere through cellular respiration, transpiration (water loss by plants), and evaporation, mostly from the oceans.

Carbon is important for ecosystems. It must cycle through ecosystems to provide the raw materials living organisms need. Living organisms are made up of organic molecules that are based on a skeleton of carbon atoms. Recall from chapter 11 and Level 1 of this program that plants take in carbon dioxide during photosynthesis. Then a series of chemical reactions makes organic molecules. Some of the carbon remains in the bodies of producers and consumers. The carbon leaves them when their bodies decay on a forest or ocean floor. The remaining carbon returns to the air as carbon dioxide through cellular respiration in producers, consumers, and decomposers.

Reflect and Connect

Complete the following tasks individually in your science notebook.

1. Explain how an abiotic factor can affect biotic factors in an ecosystem.
2. Why is energy said to *flow through* an ecosystem in one direction, whereas matter such as carbon *cycles* through an ecosystem? Think about what the source of energy and matter is for ecosystems.
3. Explain why ecosystems typically have so few top-level consumers such as tigers, eagles, and sharks. Think about what you learned about the amount of energy that flows through the different trophic levels in ecosystems.

Climatic and Topographic Effects

Climate

Climate is an important abiotic factor that shapes ecosystems. Climate is the weather conditions in an area over long periods of time. Climate depends on factors such as temperature, precipitation, humidity, and wind. For example, the climate of a tropical rain forest ecosystem is hot and humid year-round. This ecosystem also receives a lot of precipitation. In contrast, a desert ecosystem can have hot or cool temperatures depending on the time of year. This ecosystem gets very little precipitation.

Topography

Topography, the elevation and shape of Earth's surface, contributes to climate. For example, mountains cause rain shadows. Rain shadows are dry areas on the leeward (downwind) slopes of mountain ranges (see the illustration). Topography also affects temperature. Have you ever driven up a mountain? You probably noticed that the air gets colder as you go up in elevation. Similarly, temperatures are cooler at higher latitudes. Solar radiation is less at the poles than at the equator because of the angle of incoming radiation.

Topography affects the location of water reservoirs. Remember that water is an important abiotic factor in ecosystems. Contours of the land, such as ridges and valleys, determine where water accumulates in ponds or lakes and runs in rivers. Different species of plants grow depending on the availability of water. For example, you will never find lily pads growing in a desert. Changes in elevation also determine how fast water flows in rivers. Have you ever noticed that water seems to run faster in mountain streams? There is more dissolved oxygen in fast-flowing rivers than in slower rivers. Water temperatures are also colder in mountain streams, allowing more oxygen to dissolve. As a result, trout only survive in cold, fast-flowing rivers because they need higher levels of oxygen to survive. Oxygen is an important abiotic factor for many organisms.

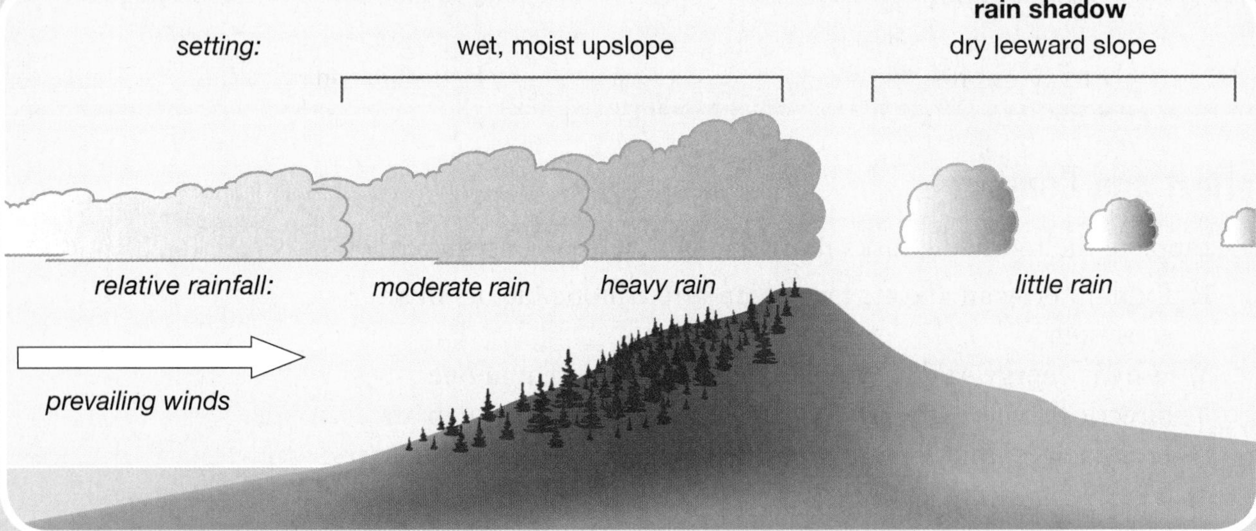

Rain shadow effect. Rain shadows are areas of low rainfall on the leeward (downwind) slope of a mountain range. They form as warm, moist air rises to higher elevations where temperatures are cooler. Cool air holds less moisture than warm air, causing precipitation to fall on the windward side. The air has lost most of its moisture by the time it reaches the leeward slope.

Earth is a patchwork of distinctive ecosystems called **biomes**. Biomes are large habitats created by major types of climates. They feature a characteristic type of vegetation. For example, warm, arid climates are associated with desert vegetation. Semiarid climates usually are covered with grassland. Moist climates support forests. Each type of plant life, in turn, supports a characteristic variety of animal life. The resulting community of plants and animals forms the biome.

Scientists benefit from studying the physical surroundings that organisms live in. They can better understand the ways that matter and energy are stored or move between parts of an ecosystem. They also learn how an ecosystem works by studying its organization and function.

SIDEBAR

Working for the Environment

Careers in ecology are diverse and often fun and rewarding. The type and location of the work depend on the job. Ecology jobs can take place indoors in the lab or outdoors in a unique ecosystem. The work can be solitary or with a team of people. Recall that ecology is the study of how living things interact with one another and their environment. People who work in the ecology field are curious about the natural world, enjoy investigating problems, and often want to contribute to society. Their work adds to our understanding and preservation of the natural world.

People with ecology careers need a background in science and certain skills. Ecology involves biotic and abiotic systems. Thus, ecologists need to understand all fields of science. These sciences help them study the links between living things and their environment. Mathematics is also important for making measurements and predictions about the natural world. Sometimes researchers use mathematical models to study processes in ecosystems. Computer skills are important for using tools to analyze data. Communicating ideas in written and oral form is another needed skill. Finally, some ecological issues involve more than the natural world. They may require an understanding of economics or engineering.

Careers in ecology exist for different interests and levels of education. If you like being outdoors, you can find a job that involves fieldwork. Fieldwork can be sampling plants or taking soil samples in a local ecosystem. It can take place far away in a rain forest or on an ice field. Fieldwork involves research. However, research can also take place in the laboratory. With a two-year associate's degree, you can be a field technician, lab assistant, or teaching assistant. With more training, you could become a

Working for the Environment, continued

wildlife biologist or an ecologist. Maybe you are more interested in managing or restoring populations and ecosystems. Then you could become a manager for a state park or a wildlife refuge. If you enjoy teaching as well as ecology, you could work at a high school, museum, or college or university. Some people bring their teaching interest outdoors by working as an educator at a nature center or as a naturalist at a park. To help solve environmental problems or influence policy makers, you could become an environmental consultant, environmental planner, or even an environmental lawyer.

Careers in ecology. Do any of these careers interest you?

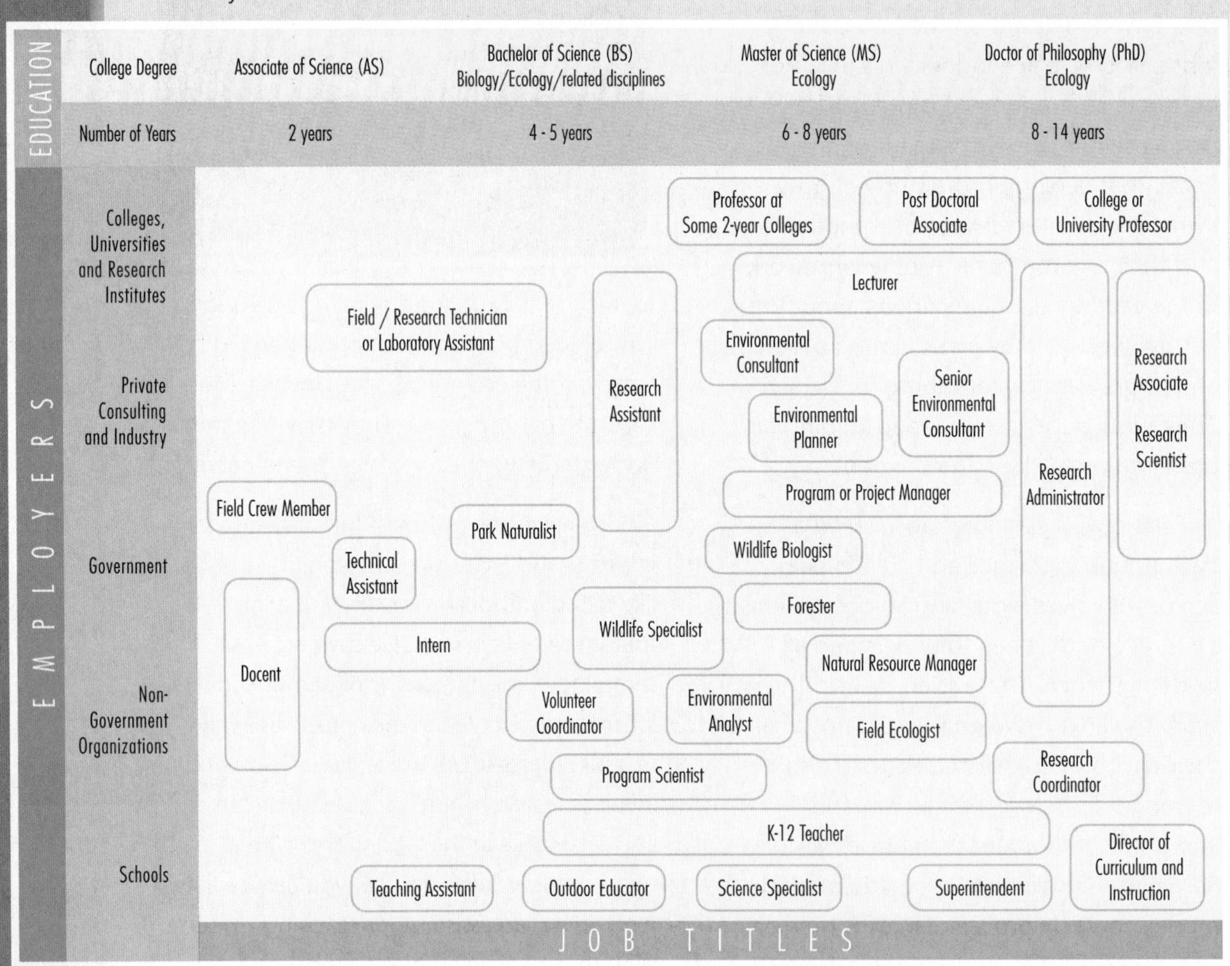

Ecological and environmental jobs will always be available because we depend on ecosystems. Disturbances to ecosystems are likely to increase because humans will continue to interact with ecosystems. Thus, more people with ecological backgrounds will be needed to better understand how ecosystems work. They will also need to educate the public and develop management plans to sustain and restore ecosystems. Job opportunities are expected to grow in private companies, nongovernment organizations, and precollege schools. The number of jobs with universities and the federal government is expected to stay the same.

Finding Your Niche

ELABORATE

How do you think species' interactions influence the traits of species? Could interactions be important for evolution? Competition for limited resources is a common interaction among species in ecosystems. For example, foxes and coyotes compete for some of the same food resources, such as rabbits. Because they compete, foxes are less abundant in areas where coyotes also live. Foxes and coyotes are species in the same trophic level that coexist because they do not use the same resources entirely. Scientists have evidence that the great diversity of organisms on Earth is a result of interactions.

In *Finding Your Niche*, you will think about how six species of shorebird use the same habitat in a way that minimizes competition. Shorebirds are a group of birds that are adapted to live near water. You will work alone and with your classmates to discover how interactions may have led to diverse species of shorebirds.

Materials

For each student

colored pencils   1 *Shorebird Habitat* handout

Process and Procedure

1. Read about the shorebirds shown in figure 14.22. Are these shorebirds competing for the same resources? Why or why not?
2. Shorebirds live in a variety of habitats. A **habitat** is the specific environment where an organism lives. Shorebirds live in habitats such as seashores, coastal wetlands, inland wetlands, and grasslands. Wetlands are just as they sound—areas that are saturated with water for at least part of the year. Obtain the *Shorebird Habitat* handout from your teacher to see how a wetland habitat for shorebirds might look in South Dakota.
3. Use the *Shorebird Habitat* handout and Steps 3a–d to create a guide that shows where each shorebird in figure 14.22 feeds.
   a. Use a different-colored pencil to shade in areas for each shorebird.
   b. The shaded areas should indicate if shorebirds find food in different depths of soil or different parts of the water. Some of the shaded areas may overlap.
   c. Create a key for your guide.
   d. Use the TSAR strategy to compare your guide with the guides of 2 other classmates. Revise your guide if you learn something new after talking with a classmate. Continue using this strategy throughout the activity.

Semipalmated plovers (*Charadrius semipalmatus*) are small shorebirds. They are about 18 centimeters (cm) long, with short legs and a very short bill. They feed by picking invertebrates off the soil's surface or off plants.

Wilson's phalaropes (*Phalaropus tricolor*) are small shorebirds. They are about 22 cm long, with short legs and a medium-length bill. They feed by wading in shallow water or swimming in deeper water and picking invertebrates off the water's surface. In deep water, they use their legs to churn up the water and bring invertebrates closer to the surface.

Greater yellowlegs (*Tringa melanoleuca*) are medium-sized shorebirds. They are about 30 cm long, with long legs and a long, thin bill. They feed by wading in water and picking invertebrates off the water's surface or plants.

Baird's sandpipers (*Calidris bairdii*) are small shorebirds. They are about 15 cm long, with medium-length legs and a short bill. They feed by probing their bills into soil to find invertebrates. They search for food on wet mud and in shallow water.

Dowitchers (*Limnodromus sp.*) are medium-sized birds. They are about 30 cm long, with medium-length legs and a long, straight bill. They feed by probing their bills into soil to find invertebrates. They search for food on wet mud and in shallow water.

Pectoral sandpipers (*Calidris melanotos*) are medium-sized shorebirds. They are about 20 cm long, with medium-length legs and a medium-length bill. They feed by probing their bills into soil to find invertebrates or by picking invertebrates off wet mud or water. They search for food on wet mud and in shallow water.

▲ **Figure 14.22 Shorebirds found in shallow wetlands.** How do you think natural selection might have led to so many species of shorebirds?

4. Are the shorebirds using different parts of the same habitat? Based on your guide, describe how these 6 shorebird species interact in a wetland habitat.
5. Read *An Ecological Niche* to learn how scientists describe the different roles of species in habitats. Answer Questions 5a–c in your science notebook as you read. Then use the TSAR strategy to refine your answers.
   a. Are shorebirds generalists or specialists? Explain your answer.
   b. How are shorebirds minimizing competition in the same habitat? Include in your answer how the traits of the species differ.
   c. Suppose 2 populations of the same species are competing for the same resource. Both populations have variations in their traits that make them use resources slightly differently, as shown in figure 14.24. Describe how natural selection could result in a new species.

Remember that natural selection occurs when members of a population with the most successful adaptations to their environment are more likely to survive and reproduce than members of the same population with less successful adaptations.

READING

An Ecological Niche

The role that each species plays in the community is its **ecological niche**. A habitat is an organism's address, and a niche is its profession. A niche includes where an organism lives, what it eats, how it obtains its food, and how it interacts with other species. Some species are specialists and occupy a narrow niche. For example, black-footed ferrets (*Mustela nigripes*, see figure 14.23a)

Figure 14.23 Specialist (black-footed ferret) and generalist (long-tailed weasel). (a) Black-footed ferrets have a narrow niche that is limited to habitats containing prairie dogs. (b) Long-tailed weasels have a broad niche that includes different habitats and foods.

An Ecological Niche, continued

rely exclusively on prairie dog towns for food and shelter. Long-tailed weasels (*Mustela frenata*, see figure 14.23b) are related to black-footed ferrets. But they are generalists, eat a wide variety of foods, and occur in a wide variety of habitats.

No two species occupy the same, exact niche in a community for very long. Eventually, one species gains a larger share of the resources. The other migrates to a new area, becomes extinct, or adapts to reduce competition. Recall that adaptations are traits that help an organism survive and reproduce in a particular environment. Adaptations can be physical or behavioral traits. Adaptations allow species to use resources differently and occupy different niches. To understand how humans can affect the balance of species in an ecosystem read the sidebar *Invasive Populations*.

You can show graphically how differences in niches can reduce competition. You did this when you shaded different areas of a wetland used by shorebirds. You can also show differences in niches with a graph like the one in figure 14.24. The x-axis shows the use of resources such as food or habitat. The y-axis shows the abundance of organisms. Competition occurs where the niches of two species overlap (figure 14.24a). Across time, individuals occupying the part of the niche where competition occurs are less successful. Fewer of these individuals survive and reproduce. Eventually, the two species might have fewer variations in their traits and they become more specialized. This means their niches become narrower (figure 14.24b). Specialization allows different species to use resources differently and coexist in the same habitat.

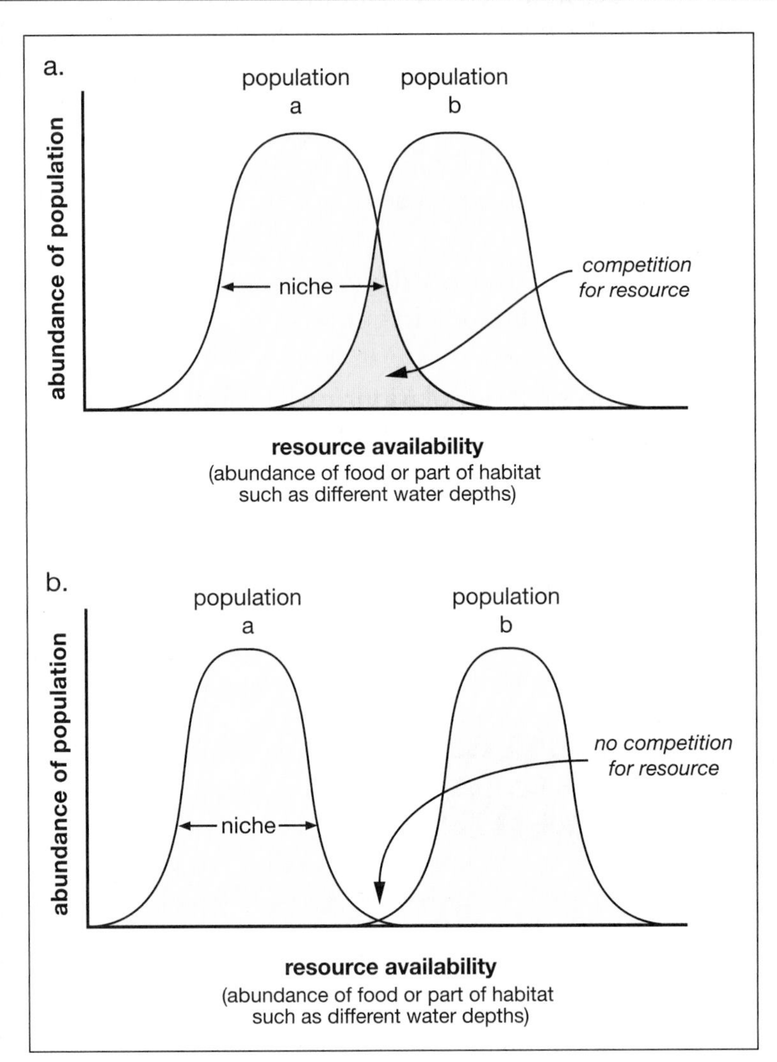

▲ **Figure 14.24 Niches of two species.** (a) The niches of two species using the same habitat may overlap because some individuals from each population use the same resources. The shaded area shows the part of the two populations competing for resources. (b) Competition is reduced when niches do not overlap.

SCILINKS® NSTA
Topic: ecological niche
Go to: www.scilinks.org
Code: 2Inquiry740

Invasive Populations

SIDEBAR

You have been learning about how plant and animal populations interact in ecosystems. Humans also interact with these populations. In fact, human populations can unintentionally disrupt the balance of species in an ecosystem. Humans can affect the balance by introducing a new species or changing the conditions in an ecosystem in a way that favors some species over others.

Humans transport plants and animals to new locations for food or enjoyment, and sometimes by accident. Arriving with the plants and animals are the bacteria, fungi, and diseases associated with those species. In most cases, when organisms are moved away from their native habitat, they die out once humans no longer use them. Sometimes, however, the limiting factors that were present in a species' natural habitat are not present at a new location. Or a species might invade a new niche that didn't exist in its natural habitat. If non-native species thrive, they can potentially cause harm. These introduced species are called invasive species. Some well-known examples of invasive species are purple loosestrife, zebra mussels, fire ants, and whirling disease.

Purple loosestrife (*Lythrum salicaria*) is a plant brought to the wetlands in northeastern North America from Europe in the 1800s. Immigrants may have brought the seeds because of their value as an herb and ornamental plant. Although purple loosestrife is attractive, it outcompetes and replaces native wetland plants (see the photographs). It produces abundant nectar, but it is a poorer source of nutrition for wildlife than native plants.

Zebra mussels (*Dreissena polymorpha*) are small, fingernail-sized mussels native to the Caspian and Black Seas between Europe and Asia. They are now found in the United Kingdom, western Europe, Canada, and the United States. In 1988, they arrived in the Great Lakes in the ballast water of a transoceanic ship. Ballast water is water held in a ship's ballast tanks and cargo holds to provide stability. This water is taken from a coastal port area and transported to the next port, where it may be discharged. Zebra mussels breed prolifically and live and feed in many aquatic habitats. They filter large amounts of food from the water. This action reduces

Before and after purple loosestrife establishment. (a) The photograph shows a wildlife refuge in New York in 1968. (b) Ten years later, the native vegetation has been replaced by purple loosestrife.

Invasive Populations, continued

the food supply for other organisms and causes some animal populations to decline.

Black and red fire ants (*Solenopsis sp.*) were accidentally brought to the United States from South America in the early 1900s. As of 2006, they have spread to 14 states. Fire ants sting their victims repeatedly. The sting injects venom that causes a burning sensation. Fire ants sometimes attack and kill newborn domestic animals as well as pets and wildlife. They can also damage some crops.

Whirling disease was brought to North America from Europe in the 1950s. Whirling disease is caused by a parasite (*Myxobolus cerebralis*) that penetrates the head and spinal cartilage of trout and salmon. It does not infect humans. Fish infected with the parasite swim erratically (whirl) and have difficulty feeding and avoiding predators. Water sources with severe infections result in high mortality rates of young fish. This disease is one of the biggest threats to native trout populations.

Some problem populations are viruses that need a host organism such as a bird or human to reproduce and spread. For example, West Nile virus and the avian flu are viruses that mainly infect birds but can spread to humans. West Nile was found in North America in 1999. It is common in Africa, Europe, the Middle East, and west and central Asia. The virus might have arrived in the United States through illegally imported birds, a person who was infected with the virus, or mosquitoes trapped on a plane or boat. Mosquitoes spread West Nile between birds and to humans. When a mosquito feeds on the blood of an infected individual, it can transmit the virus to an uninfected individual during its next feeding. Most cases of West Nile virus in humans occur in people who are immune compromised—their immune systems are not strong.

The avian flu is an infection caused by avian flu viruses. There are many subtypes of avian flu viruses. These viruses occur naturally in birds worldwide. Wild birds usually do not get sick from the viruses, but the viruses are very contagious and spread quickly. The avian flu virus can cause domesticated birds such as chickens, ducks, and turkeys to become very sick and die. Avian flu viruses occur mainly in birds, but occasionally they infect humans. Most human infections result from direct contact with infected domesticated birds. These infections usually do not pass from person to person. However, because flu viruses are constantly changing, they might adapt over time to infect and spread among humans.

New species from other countries are introduced in the United States every year. They may be introduced intentionally or accidentally, but their introduction can potentially create problems for native populations and human health.

6. Create a graph like figure 14.24. Show the niches of 2 shorebirds that you choose. Your graph should have the following:
   - An x-axis labeled "habitat type"

Choose the appropriate habitat type depending on which shorebirds you graph.

- A y-axis labeled "abundance"
- Each curve labeled with the names of the shorebirds
- A caption and highlight comments

Reflect and Connect

Work alone to answer the following questions in your science notebook.

1. Describe how a niche is different from a habitat. Use an example in your answer.
2. Describe in a short paragraph how interactions between populations of shorebirds in the past might have led to diverse species of shorebirds.

Interpret the Interactions

EVALUATE

One of the important parts of doing science is reviewing data that other scientists have collected. In *Interpret the Interactions*, you will use what you have learned about populations and ecosystems to *interpret* the results from different real scientific studies. For example, you will look at data from a study of populations in a kelp forest ecosystem (see figure 14.25). As you analyze and interpret the results of these studies, you will be acting like real scientists.

▲ **Figure 14.25 Sea otter.** This sea otter is eating a sea urchin. Sea urchins are marine invertebrates that feed on kelp, a type of alga. Sea otters and sea urchins live in kelp forest ecosystems in coastal waters.

In Part I, you will work alone and with your classmates to revisit the true-false statements from the engage activity, *What Do You Know about Populations?* You will decide whether your responses have changed now that you have completed the activities in this chapter. Then in Part II, you will take a test that asks you to analyze data from current and past research and answer a series of questions about how the populations change and what interactions are taking place in the ecosystems.

Part I: What Have You Learned about Populations?

Materials

For each student

1 *Interpret the Interactions Scoring Rubric* handout

answers from the engage activity

Process and Procedure

1. Get a copy of the *Interpret the Interactions Scoring Rubric* handout from your teacher. Review it with your class.
2. Review your true or false answers to the statements from the engage activity.
3. Use the TSAR strategy to decide whether to change any of your answers based on what you and your classmates have learned in the chapter. Consult with at least 2 other students. Record any evidence you have for keeping or changing each answer.

Even though your answers may not have changed, your reasoning may have. You should have more knowledge now and be able to write better explanations than you did in the engage activity.

Part II: Analyzing Research

Materials

For each student

1 *Analyzing Research* handout

Process and Procedure

1. Get the *Analyzing Research* handout from your teacher and see what you have learned. Steps 1a–c will help you.
   a. Review the graphs carefully before answering each question. Focus on any changes you see.
   b. Write and mark on the graphs as necessary to show what you understand about the data.
   c. You must complete the test in the time allotted by your teacher.

CHAPTER 15

Earth's Capacity

Earth's Capacity

In chapter 14, *Population Interactions*, you learned how organisms interact with their environment. You learned that population growth depends on factors that affect birth- and death rates. You also learned that there are limits to how much populations can grow. Do you think there are limits to human population growth?

Currently, Earth has about 6.6 billion humans. How many people do you think Earth can support? In chapter 15, *Earth's Capacity*, you will begin to form answers to these questions. You will learn about the factors affecting the growth of human populations. One of these factors is the availability of natural resources. Natural resources are materials that come from Earth, such as water, soil, wood, minerals, or oil. What natural resources are shown in the opening images? You will learn how much we rely on natural systems to provide the resources we need. As you complete the activities, you will consider how the size of human populations and human consumption of resources affect the carrying capacity of Earth.

Goals for the Chapter

By the end of chapter 15, you will be able to answer the following questions:

- What factors influence birthrates, fertility rates, and mortality rates in human populations?
- What kinds of resources do natural systems provide for human populations?
- Are there limited amounts of resources on Earth?
- How does consumption affect the availability of resources?
- What effect does technology have on the capacity of earth systems to provide resources?

To help you answer these questions and others, you will be involved in the following activities:

ENGAGE	Your Ecological Footprint
EXPLORE	Eat, Drink, and Be Merry
EXPLAIN	Too Much Is Never Enough: Consumption and Human Population
EXPLAIN	Limits to Growth
ELABORATE	Managing an Ecosystem
EVALUATE	Sustaining Human Populations

Use your chapter organizer as a road map for your learning journey through this chapter. Look at it daily to review what you have studied and to see what you will study today and in the days to come. It will help map your learning about human populations and the availability of resources in ecosystems.

Earth's Capacity

ENGAGE

Your Ecological Footprint

Key Idea:
Humans rely on resources to support their daily lives.

Linking Question

How are the resources we use distributed across the world?

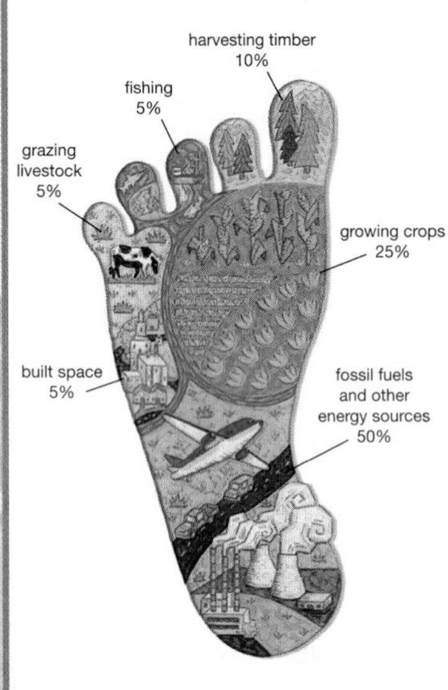

EXPLORE

Eat, Drink, and Be Merry

Key Idea:
Humans and resources are unevenly distributed across the world. People in different parts of the world consume resources at different rates.

Linking Question

How are human populations changing across time and how will this affect ecosystems?

EXPLAIN

Too Much Is Never Enough: Consumption and Human Population

Key Idea:
Human population growth is influenced by a variety of factors such as birthrate, mortality rate, fertility rate, and life expectancy.

Linking Question

Where do the resources come from that support human populations?

EVALUATE

Sustaining Human Populations

Key Ideas:

- Human population growth is affected by many factors.
- Humans rely on ecosystems for resources and natural processes.
- Consumption affects the number of people Earth can support.

Linking Question

How can I use what I have learned to demonstrate my understanding of human populations and natural resources?

CHAPTER 15 Major Concepts

- Various factors affect human birthrates, fertility rates, and mortality rates.
- Human populations rely on natural systems for resources.
- Earth does not have infinite resources.
- Human consumption places pressure on natural processes; it renews some resources and depletes resources that cannot be renewed.
- Technology can cause either positive or negative changes in the capacity of earth systems to provide resources for human populations.

ELABORATE

Managing an Ecosystem

Key Idea:

Limits are often placed on consumption to make ecosystems sustainable.

EXPLAIN

Limits to Growth

Key Ideas:

- Ecosystems provide resources and services for humans.
- Consumption affects the capacity of ecosystems to provide resources and services.

Linking Question

How are resources managed for sustainability?

ENGAGE Your Ecological Footprint

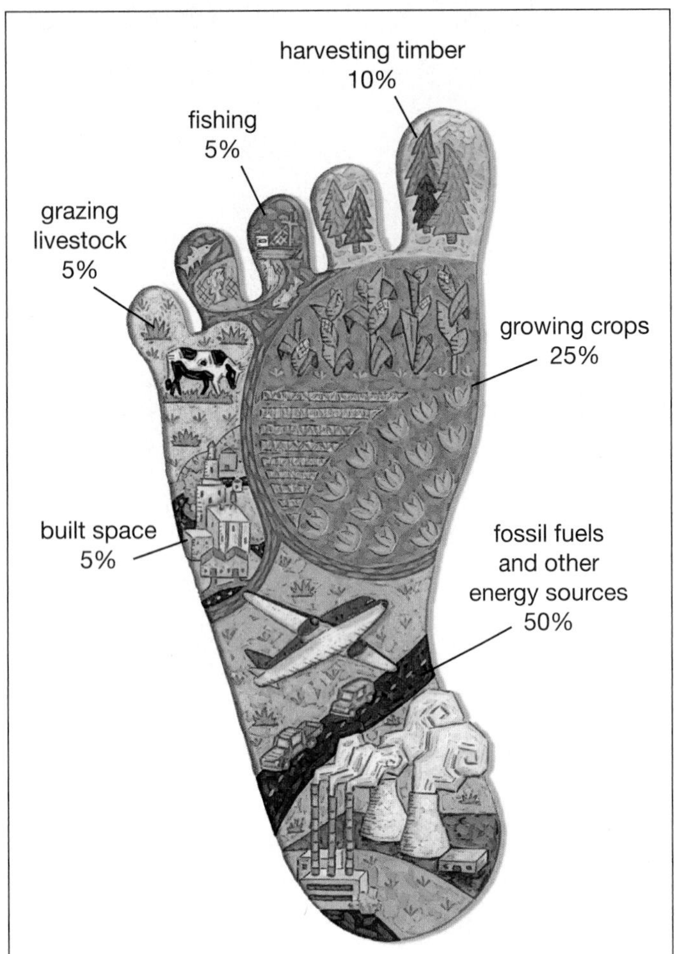

▲ **Figure 15.1 An ecological footprint.** In this activity, you will estimate how much land you need in order to provide all the resources you use.

What do you need to live? For animals like humans, perhaps you think of their needs for food and shelter. How much space do you need to live comfortably? You might be thinking about the amount of space in your dream apartment once you are on your own. Would you include the acres of land needed to provide the food you eat or the materials in your bedroom or home? What about your trash and sewage? Would you set aside space for that? In *Your Ecological Footprint*, you will work with your classmates to think about all the resources you use every day. Then you will work alone to estimate your ecological footprint (see figure 15.1). An ecological footprint is a measure of how much land you need to support what you use (inputs) and what you discard (outputs).

Materials

For each team of 3 students

3 *Ecological Footprint* handouts

Process and Procedure

1. Write down things that you use every day. In your science notebook, record at least 3 things in each of the following categories.
   a. Food
   b. Shelter
   c. Clothing
   d. Transportation
   e. Communication and entertainment
2. Work in a team of 3 and identify what resources are necessary to make or supply the things on your lists from Step 1. Record all the resources you identified.

Make sure you include energy in your list of resources. Write down the different sources of energy that might be necessary for the things on your list. For example, coal might be used to generate the electricity that heats or cools your home.

3. Make a T-table with the headings "resource" and "natural system." Match the resources from Step 2 with the natural system that provides the resource by aligning them in the T-table. For example, water is a resource that everyone uses daily, and it might come from a natural system such as a river, lake, or groundwater reservoir.
4. Predict how much land area is necessary for the natural systems to supply the resources you use. Give your answer as the number of bedrooms it would take.

An average bedroom is around 11 × 10 feet (ft), or 110 square feet (ft^2). To give you some perspective, you could fit about 524 bedrooms of this size in a soccer field or 396 bedrooms of this size in an acre.

5. Fill in the *Ecological Footprint* handout on your own and complete the calculations.
6. Compare the size of your ecological footprint with those of your teammates. Then follow Steps 6a–b to compare each teammate's footprint with America's average footprint of 9.7 hectares.

1 hectare (ha) = 10,000 meters squared (m^2)

A hectare is an area 100 × 100 meters (m), which is about the size of a soccer field.

   a. Use a ratio to compare your footprint with America's footprint. Then write a sentence that explains what the ratio means.
   b. Discuss what factors make your team's footprints similar to or different from the average American's footprint. Write at least 2 factors in your science notebook.
7. How does your prediction from Step 4 compare with the ecological footprint you calculated in Step 5?
   a. Make the comparison by converting your footprint in hectares to the number of bedrooms: 1 ha = 10,000 m^2, 1 m^2 = 10.76 ft^2.
   b. Does the size of your ecological footprint surprise you? Why or why not?
8. List 3 ways you could make your ecological footprint smaller. Provide an explanation for each way.

Reflect and Connect

Answer the following questions by yourself. Record your answers in your science notebook.

1. Why does footprint size matter? Why might a smaller footprint be advantageous?

2. How do personal and cultural differences affect ecological footprint size?
   a. Why would a vegetarian's footprint be smaller than a meat eater's footprint? (Assume that they have the same lifestyle except for their differences in diet.)

Use what you know about the amount of energy transfer between trophic levels. Think about how much energy it takes to produce vegetables compared with the amount of energy to raise a chicken or a cow.

   b. Predict the ecological footprint size for an Aborigine from Australia. Provide your reasoning for your answer.
3. Study figure 15.2 and compare the ecological footprints of different countries with the amount of biologically productive space.

Biologically productive space is the amount of land and water area that has a large amount of photosynthetic activity. As a result of this activity, it has a lot of plant and animal matter.

   a. Some countries have an ecological footprint that is greater than their biologically productive space. How do they get the resources to sustain the footprint?
   b. How do you think someone from India or Kenya might feel about the impact Americans are having on the global environment?
4. If a country wanted to make its ecological footprint smaller, how could it do that? List at least 3 things a country could do. Then explain how you think each would make the footprint smaller.
5. What are some limitations to the "footprint model"?

Country	Ecological footprint per person (ha)	Biologically productive space per person (ha)
Australia	7.6	14.6
Germany	4.7	1.7
India	0.8	0.7
Kenya	1.1	1.1
Mexico	2.5	1.7
United States	9.7	5.3

Source: © 2002 Redefining Progress. All rights reserved. Permission to reprint granted by Redefining Progress, www.rprogress.org/education

▲ **Figure 15.2 Ecological footprints and biologically productive space for 6 countries.** The values in this table are based on data from 2002.

Eat, Drink, and Be Merry

EXPLORE

Have you ever thought about where the resources you use come from? The resources that plants and wild animals use must be in their immediate area (see figure 15.3). They get their resources from the surrounding environment. Some animals such as birds migrate to get their resources. Other animals such as mountain lions have home ranges that extend up to 260 kilometers squared (km^2), which is 26,000 ha or about 100 square miles (mi^2). Even so, these animals must come into direct contact with the resources they use.

How do humans in modern urban, suburban, and rural societies get their resources? For example, do you gather the food you eat or the water you drink? Humans in many societies transport resources to where they need them. In *Eat, Drink, and Be Merry*, you will work with a partner to map where some of the resources originate. Then you will compare the locations of those resources with population size and the consumption of those resources.

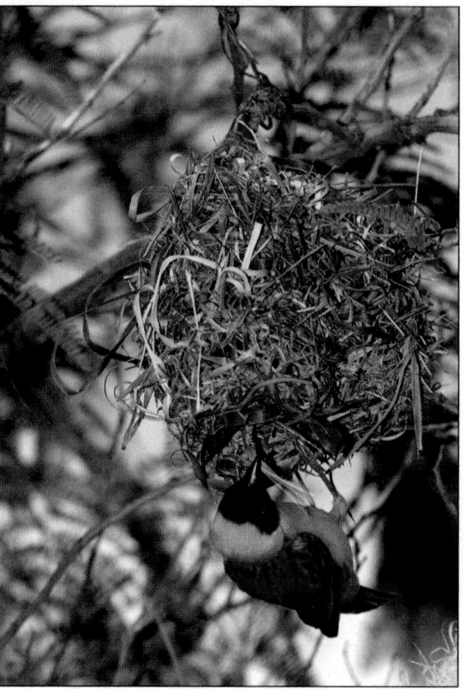

▲ **Figure 15.3**
Resources. The resources birds need to survive, such as nest-building material and food, are in their immediate environment. Where do the resources that you use come from?

Materials

For each team of 2 students

3 *World Region Map* handouts

colored pencils

transparent tape

Process and Procedure

1. Divide into teams of 2 and get 3 copies of the *World Region Map* handout.
2. Study figures 15.4–15.7. Discuss as a team how you could represent the amount of each resource on a world map.

For example, sometimes maps use color or patterns to represent different values. Other maps use icons such as water drops or trees to represent a specific unit of material.

3. Create world maps showing the available resources and resource consumption. Steps 3a–c will help you.
   a. Meet with another team and divide the work so that each team generates 2 different maps from the data shown in the 4 tables in figures 15.4–15.7. For example, one team could create maps of figures 15.4 and 15.6 and the other team could create maps of 15.5 and 15.7.

Region	Total freshwater resources (km^3/yr)	Total forest area (km^2)	Total agricultural area (km^2)
North America	6,709	5,257,690	5,869,030
Central America and Caribbean	787	232,650	344,960
South America	12,380	8,856,180	6,424,820
Western and central Europe	2,181	1,617,430	2,108,110
Eastern Europe	4,693	8,776,800	2,761,640
Africa	3,950	6,498,660	11,109,740
Near East	491	257,520	3,220,080
Central Asia	289	206,260	3,195,150
Southern and eastern Asia	11,720	5,320,160	10,432,910
Oceania and Pacific	911	1,670,220	4,656,180

Source: Food and Agriculture Organization of the United Nations, "Review of World Water Resources by Country, 2003", "State of the World's Forests, 2005", http://faostat.fao.org

▲ **Figure 15.4 World resources by region.** Total freshwater resources are calculated as the average flow of rivers and groundwater from precipitation. They also include the amount of water flowing into the region from other regions. Total forest area is the land area covered by natural or planted stands of trees. Agricultural area is the land area covered by crops or pasture.

Region	Oil reserves (billion tons)	Coal reserves (million tons)	Natural gas reserves (trillion m^3)
North America	8.0	254,432	7.3
Central America and Caribbean	0.3	2,690	0.7
South America	14.1	17,203	6.4
Western and central Europe	3.6	60,467	7.2
Eastern Europe	9.9	191,163	49.1
Africa	14.9	50,336	14.1
Near East	100.0	4,605	78.2
Central Asia	5.5	31,279	7.8
Southern and eastern Asia	4.9	217,506	11.4
Oceania and Pacific	0.6	79,383	2.84

Source: Putting Energy in the Spotlight: BP Statistical Review of World Energy June 2005

▲ **Figure 15.5 World energy resources by region.** Geologists and engineers estimate the amount of reserves there are. They estimate how much oil, coal, and natural gas can be recovered based on the use of current technology and the cost of extraction. Their estimates may change if new technologies are developed.

Region	Total water withdrawal (km³/yr)	Total wood products (1,000 m³)	Average food calorie supply (kcal)	Food calories from animal products (%)
North America	603	719,615	3,432	23
Central America and Caribbean	22	109,018	2,489	15
South America	165	186,112	2,845	21
Western and central Europe	289	502,018	3,368	27
Eastern Europe	120	137,549	2,943	23
Africa	161	73,761	3,034	9
Near East	210	27,903	2,840	14
Central Asia	163	3,012	2,386	18
Southern and eastern Asia	2,004	374,074	2,477	12
Oceania and Pacific	26	48,037	2,865	24

Source: water data and wood product data: Food and Agriculture Organization of the United Nations, AQUASTAT database, "State of the World's Forests, 2005". World Resources Institute. 2006. food calorie data: EarthTrends: The Environmental Information Portal. Available at http://earthtrends.wri.org. Washington, DC: World Resources Institute.

▲ **Figure 15.6 World water, wood, and food consumption.** Water withdrawal includes any water use, such as industrial, agricultural, and residential uses. Total wood products include wood used for building materials, but does not include paper products. The average food calorie supply is the average amount of food available (in kcal) per person per day.

Region	Oil (thousand million tons)	Coal (million tons)	Natural gas (trillion m³)	Wood fuel (million m³)
North America	1,122.4	603.8	784.3	114
Central America and Caribbean	58.3	1.0	17.6	45
South America	163.4	17.7	100.3	190
Western and central Europe	756.4	340.0	560.5	55
Eastern Europe	148.4	145.5	475.9	57
Africa	124.3	0	68.6	546
Near East	282.9	32.1	264.3	8
Central Asia	20.5	28.7	50.0	1
Southern and eastern Asia	1,025.2	1,425.3	331.8	778
Oceania and Pacific	65.3	81.0	35.9	7

Source: Putting Energy in the Spotlight: BP Statistical Review of World Energy June 2005

▲ **Figure 15.7 Annual world energy consumption for 2004.** The oil, coal, and natural gas totals include energy used for all purposes, such as electricity and gasoline. Wood fuel includes charcoal and wood cut directly from forests and used for heating or cooking. Why do you think some regions use more wood fuel than others?

b. Use the strategy you developed in Step 2 to generate the maps.

For the data in figure 15.6, you might use a different color to show the percentage of food calories (kcal) from animal products.

c. Include a title and legend on each map.

4. Examine the maps your team of 4 created. What patterns do you see? Why might these patterns be important? Discuss the patterns and other important things you notice and record what you learn in your science notebook.

Consider using highlight comments to describe the patterns and to explain what the patterns mean.

5. Study the world precipitation map that your teacher displays. Compare the amount of precipitation with the availability of resources for each region.
   a. Describe the relationship between precipitation and where water, forest, and agricultural land resources are located.
   b. Identify any factors that might influence the availability of water, forest, and agricultural land resources.
6. Consider how human populations in different parts of the world can affect Earth's resources.
   a. Which 2 regions have the greatest water withdrawal and consumption of wood products? Why do these regions consume more water and wood products? See figure 15.6.
   b. Why might it be important to look at the percentage of food calories (kcal) from animal products in addition to the total kcal? See figure 15.6.
   c. The United States and Europe have a higher percentage of food calories from animals than Africa and southern and eastern Asia have. What factors might explain this observation? See figure 15.6.

The average daily food supply for Americans is 3,754 kcal, of which 28 percent is composed of animal products.

   d. Each region uses different amounts of oil, coal, and natural gas. Is the usage affected more by the size of the population or by the kind of lifestyle people have? Figure 15.7 should help you answer this question. Be sure to explain your answer.
   e. Why do you think Africa and southern and eastern Asia use more wood fuel than other regions in the world? See figure 15.7.
7. Compare the maps showing the available resources with the maps showing resource consumption. Steps 7a–c will help you do this. See also figures 15.4–15.7.

a. Discuss with your partner the similarities and differences in where the resources are located and where they are used. Record at least 1 similarity and 1 difference.
b. Identify which regions seem to consume more resources than are available. How might you explain this?
c. Identify which regions seem to have more resources than they consume. How might you explain this?

8. Use Steps 8a–b to help you determine how resources are distributed for the total land area of each region. Use the total land area given in figure 15.8 to make your calculations.
   a. Create a data table to record the following in your science notebook:
      - Amount of freshwater resources (cubic meters, m^3) per km^2 for each region
      - Percentage of area covered by forest per total km^2 for each region
      - Percentage of area covered by agricultural land per total km^2 for each region
      - Amount of oil reserves (tons) per km^2 for each region
   b. Describe the patterns you see.
9. Complete Steps 9a–e to help you think about how human populations are distributed across the world.
   a. Predict which 3 regions have the largest population densities. Provide your reasoning in your answer.
   b. Calculate the population density for each region using the data in figure 15.8. Give the population density in people per kilometers squared (people/km^2).

Region	Total area ($\times 10^6$ km^2)	Total population (millions)
North America	22.0	429
Central America and Caribbean	0.8	78
South America	17.8	362
Western and central Europe	4.9	513
Eastern Europe	18.1	213
Africa	30.3	851
Near East	6.3	250
Central Asia	4.7	82
Southern and eastern Asia	21.4	3,497
Oceania and Pacific	8.1	27

◄ **Figure 15.8 Total land area and population for each region.** The total land area includes the area under inland water bodies. How does the population size compare with the total area of each region?

Source: Food and Agriculture Organization of the United Nations, http://faostat.fao.org, AQUASTAT database

c. Create a human population map that shows the relative population densities of each region. Include a title and a legend with your map.
d. Compare the human population map with the maps of resources. Are the densest populations located where the resources are most plentiful? What does the pattern of human populations and resources mean?
e. Compare the human population map with the maps of resource and energy consumption. Does the greatest consumption occur where the largest populations are? Why or why not?

10. Determine which regions consume the most water and oil resources per person.
    a. Create a data table to record the following in your science notebook:
       - Amount of water withdrawal per person in cubic meters per year (m^3/yr) for each region
       - Amount of oil consumed per person in tons per year (tons/yr) for each region
    b. Describe which regions are the biggest consumers and which are the smallest consumers.

Reflect and Connect

Answer the following questions by yourself and write your answers in your science notebook. Check your answers with those of another student and revise them if necessary.

1. How might the differences in ecosystems explain the differences in resource availability? Provide an explanation for both energy and nonenergy resources.

Remember that ecosystems include both the biotic and abiotic environments and that ecosystems change across time.

2. Describe at least 2 ways that ecosystems provide resources that support human populations.

Use what you know about populations and some of the processes that occur in ecosystems.

3. Review your answer to Step 6d. Has your position changed? Is consumption of energy related more to the size of the population or the lifestyle people have? Use evidence to explain why or why not.
4. Consider what would happen if other regions consumed oil at the same rate per person that North America does.

a. Calculate the amount of oil (thousand million tons) that southern and eastern Asia would use annually if it consumed the same amount per person as North America.
b. Describe how the world's oil resources would be affected if regions such as southern and eastern Asia started using more oil.

EXPLAIN

Too Much Is Never Enough: Consumption and Human Population

Population size is one factor that affects the quantity of resources a country uses. What do you know about human populations? You learned in the explore activity, *Eat, Drink, and Be Merry*, how human populations are distributed across Earth. In *Too Much Is Never Enough*, you will look at world population data and learn the factors that affect human population growth. Then you will learn about the different goods and services ecosystems provide. You will use what you know about human populations and resources to propose a carrying capacity for Earth.

Materials

For each student

1 *Age Structure* handout

access to a computer and the Web

Process and Procedure

1. Read the following paragraph to learn about a prediction made in 1798 about the future of human populations.

   In 1798, Thomas Malthus published *An Essay on the Principle of Population as It Affects the Future Improvement of Society*. He said that human populations tend to grow at an exponential rate. But food is produced at a stable or slowly increasing rate. He predicted that, as a result, the world would face famine and misery. He argued that the only way to stabilize human populations was for wars or disease to increase mortality rates or for birthrates to decrease.

2. Explain why you think Malthus's prediction about human populations was right or wrong. Steps 2a–e will help you form your explanation.
   a. Read *History of Human Population Growth* to learn how human populations have changed across time. Use this

question to focus your reading: "What factors have affected human population growth?"

b. What aspects of Malthus's argument have merit or value?
c. What things have happened across time that he didn't predict?
d. Describe in your science notebook at least 3 reasons why human populations have not collapsed as Malthus predicted. Include justifications from the reading in your answer.
e. Predict what you think the graph in figure 15.9 will look like in another 200 years. Make your prediction by drawing a new graph in your science notebook. Include a caption describing what changes, if any, have occurred that account for the population size.

Consider using the think-share-advise-revise (TSAR) strategy to compare your graph with another student's.

READING

History of Human Population Growth

More than 6.5 billion people live on Earth today. The human population wasn't always this large. It became large only recently. Scientists estimate that the world's population around 8000 BC was near 10 million. The current population size of Los Angeles County, California, is about the same.

Around 8000 BC, many human cultures changed from hunting and gathering societies to farming communities (see figure 15.9). This agricultural revolution provided a more dependable food supply. The food supply allowed human populations to grow and groups of people to live in one place. By 200 BC, the human population had increased to as many as 200 million people. The human population didn't reach 1 billion until the 1800s. Since then, it has increased rapidly.

Many technological changes took place in the 1700s. These changes were the start of the industrial revolution. The technology developed at this time brought about many of the conveniences we enjoy today. Machines and factories became widespread. Many people left agricultural lifestyles and moved to cities. Railroads improved transportation. The telegraph improved communication. Scientific discoveries and technological advances improved medical care and sanitation. People began living longer and healthier lives.

As the human population grew, some countries began having food shortages. In the 1940s, scientists began to research ways to improve crop yields. They used selective breeding to develop grains that were resistant to pests and diseases. The new plants yielded two to three times more grain. New agricultural techniques also were developed. Some of the techniques used fertilizers, pesticides, and herbicides. Irrigation methods improved. Machines replaced human labor in almost every agricultural process (see figure 15.10).

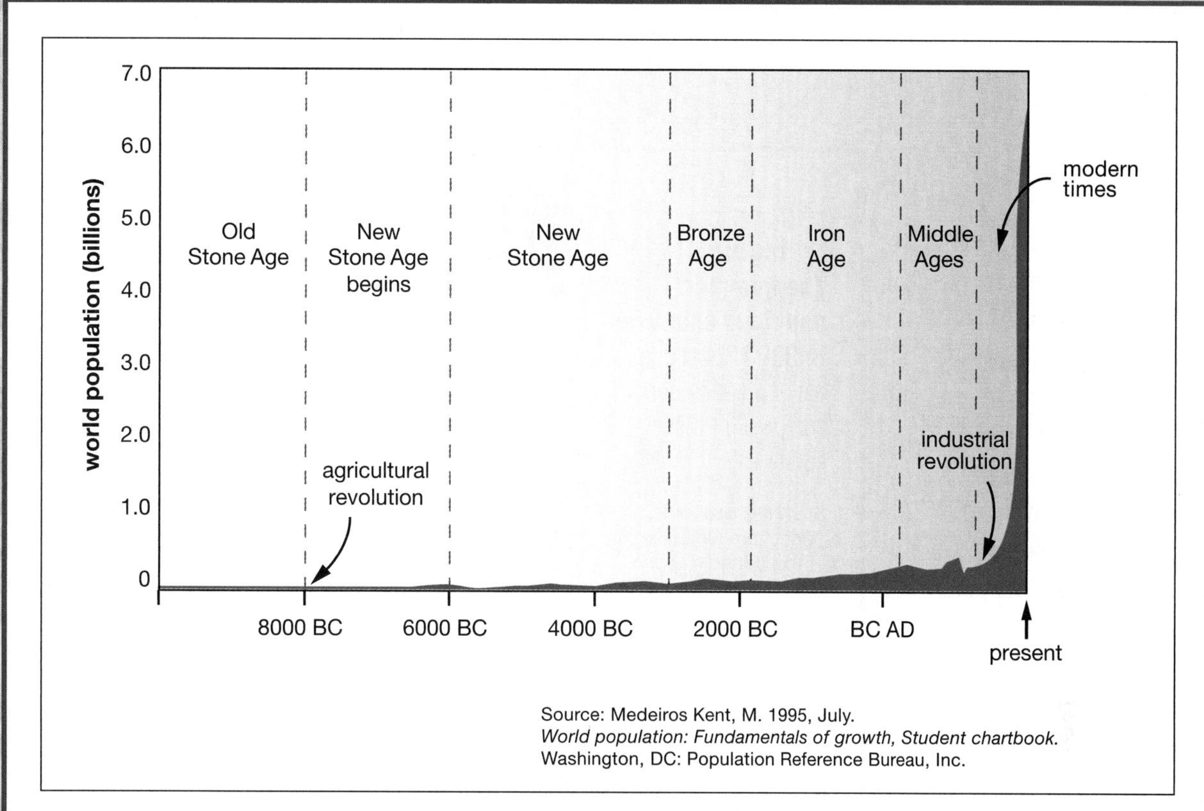

▲ **Figure 15.9 Human population size across history.** What do you notice about the shape of the graph?

▲ **Figure 15.10 Resource extraction.** How does technology influence the extraction of resources? Consider whether different techniques yield the same amount of resources. How do the techniques affect the surrounding environment?

History of Human Population Growth, continued

All these changes increased efficiency. This period of technological advances is referred to as the green revolution.

Today, more than 6.5 billion people live on Earth. The most populous countries are shown in figure 15.11. The world continues to become more urbanized. In 1950, most people lived in rural areas. Now the number of people living in rural and urban areas is nearly equal (figure 15.12).

Although the rural and urban populations are about the same size, more of the world's population lives in developing regions than in developed regions (figure 15.13). Developing regions have a low standard of living and are not very industrialized. Standard of living is a measure of income per person. It includes the availability of health care, education, and goods such as appliances.

Figure 15.11 The five most populous countries in 2003. How does the population density compare for these countries?

Source: Food and Agriculture Organization of the United Nations, http://faostat.fao.org

Country	Population size in billions ($\times 10^9$)	Density (people/km²)
China	1.31	137
India	1.07	324
United States	2.94	31
Indonesia	2.20	115
Brazil	1.78	21

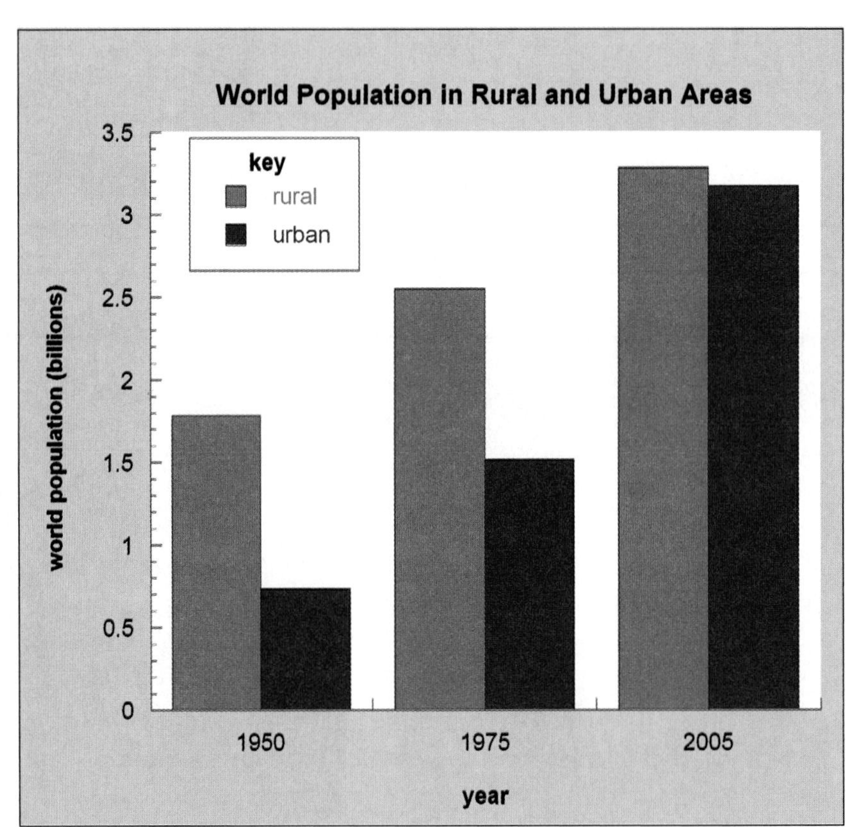

Source: Food and Agriculture Organization of the United Nations, http://faostat.fao.org

Figure 15.12 Total world population in rural and urban areas. What effect on the environment do you think the shift of the population to urban areas has had?

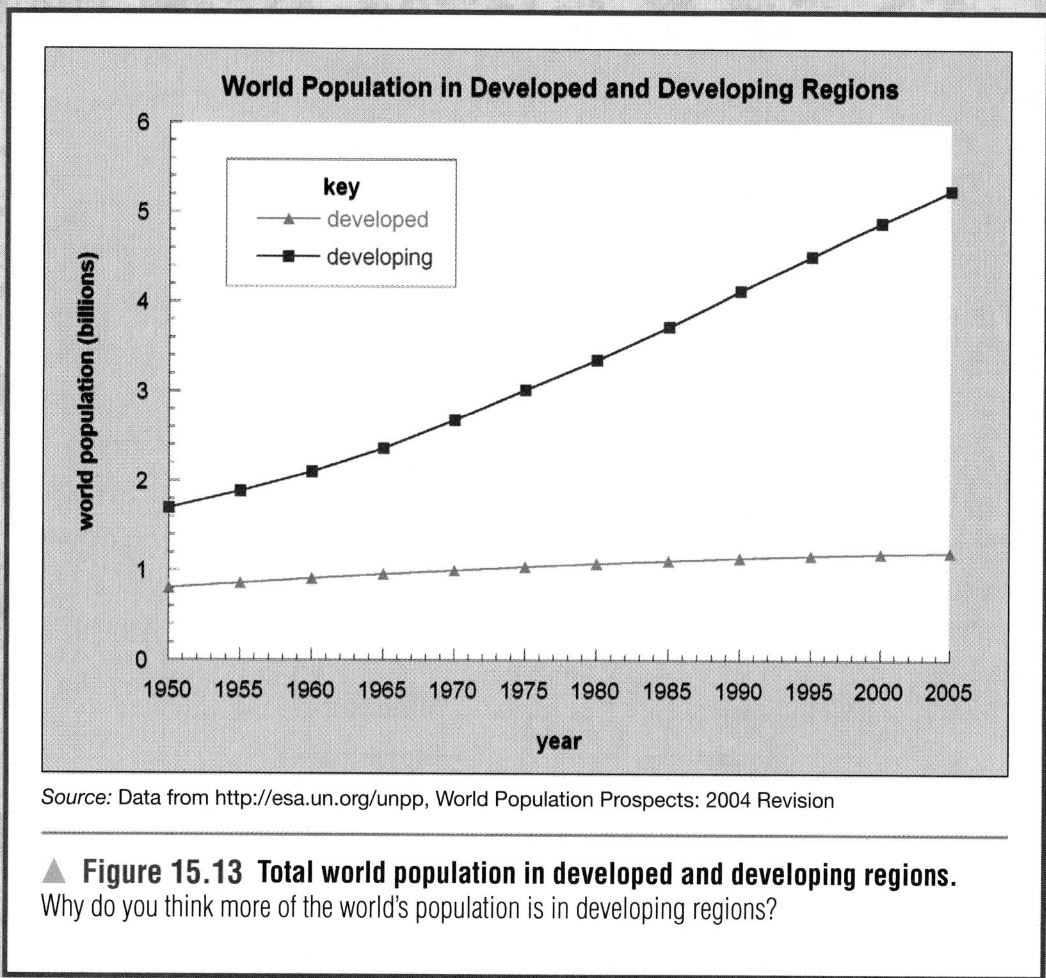

Source: Data from http://esa.un.org/unpp, World Population Prospects: 2004 Revision

Figure 15.13 Total world population in developed and developing regions. Why do you think more of the world's population is in developing regions?

Developed regions have a high standard of living (see figure 15.10). The economies of these regions are based on industry and technology. Developed regions include Europe, North America, Australia, New Zealand, and Japan. The remaining regions are considered developing.

Developing regions include Africa, Asia, South America, Central America, the Caribbean, and the Pacific islands. These regions tend to rely on agriculture and natural resource extraction to support their economies. Many countries in developing regions are on the fast track for development. They are becoming more industrialized and their education systems are improving. These changes gradually increase the standard of living.

SCILINKS® NSTA
Topic: world population
Go to: www.scilinks.org
Code: 2Inquiry763

3. Read *Birth and Death*. Then complete Steps 3a–b to learn how birthrates and mortality rates affect human population growth. Record your ideas in your science notebook.
   a. Study figure 15.14 and compare the *birthrates* and *mortality rates* for developed and developing regions.
   b. What patterns do you see and why do you think these patterns exist?

READING

Birth and Death

Recall that mortality rate is one important factor used to determine the growth rate of a population. Mortality rate is the number of deaths in a year per 1,000 people. From the 1700s to 1900, the mortality rate for the world's population was 35–40 deaths per 1,000. Since then, the mortality rate has declined dramatically. It is now around 10 deaths per 1,000.

Another factor in population growth is birthrate. Birthrate for humans is the average number of births in a year per 1,000 people. From the 1700s to 1900, the birthrate for the world's population was 35–45 births per 1,000. Like the mortality rate, the birthrate began declining dramatically after 1900. Now the birthrate varies around the world. It ranges from 10 to 22 births per 1,000. Figure 15.14 (a) and (b) show how birth- and mortality rates in developed and developing countries have changed during the last 55 years.

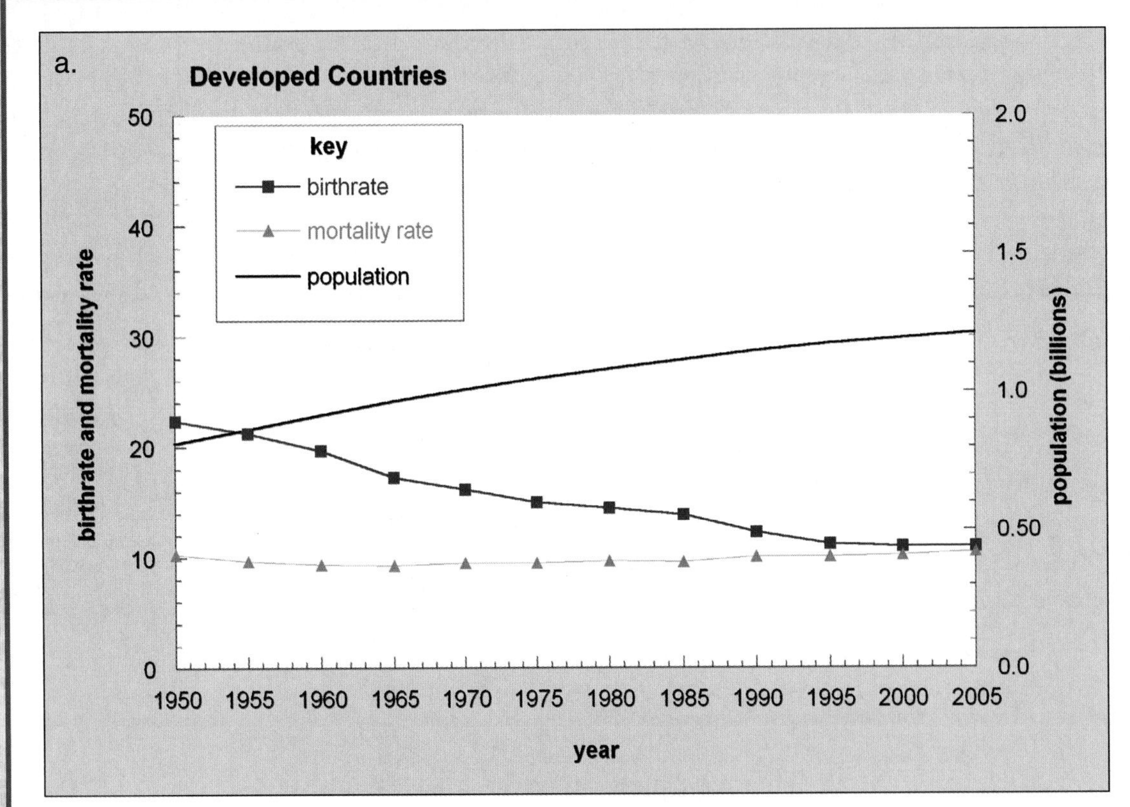

Source: Data from http://esa.un.org/unpp, World Population Prospects: 2004 Revision

▲ **Figure 15.14 Birthrates, mortality rates, and population for developed and developing countries.** Birthrates and mortality rates are on the left axis. Population is on the right axis. How does the slope for the population compare with the change in birthrates and mortality rates?

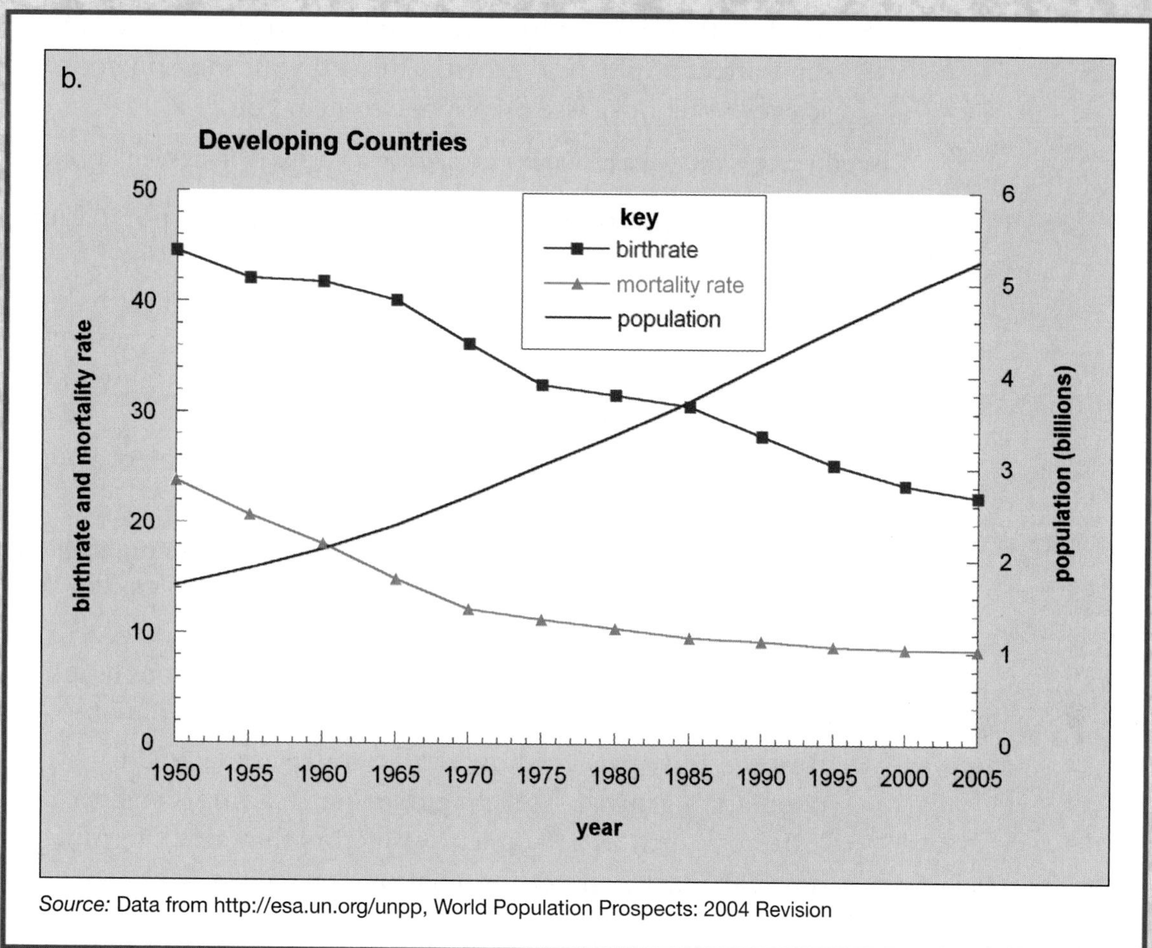

Source: Data from http://esa.un.org/unpp, World Population Prospects: 2004 Revision

4. Answer the questions in Step 4a–c in your science notebook to show your understanding of how birthrates and mortality rates affect human population growth.
   a. Why might there be a difference between birthrates and mortality rates for developed and developing countries?
   b. How does the change in population size compare for developed and developing countries? Discuss the rate of increase (slope) in your answer.
   c. How can you explain the difference in the rate of increase for developed and developing countries? Use what you know about birthrate and mortality rate to explain the rate of population increase.

Recall this equation: ***population size = population size + births – deaths + immigration – emigration.***

5. Work with a partner to discuss and investigate how fertility rates affect population growth. Record your ideas in your science notebook. Use Steps 5a–e to help you.

Fertility rate is the average number of children a woman will have in her lifetime.

   a. How do you think fertility rates are related to population growth?
   b. What questions do you have about fertility rates?
   c. What information do you need to answer your questions? Discuss which of your questions can be answered with information you might find on the Web.
   d. Look for information on the Web to answer one of your questions. Document what you find.

Remember to document your references. For information on citing other people's work, see *How to Cite References and Avoid Plagiarism* in the *How To* section in the back of the book.

   e. Describe how what you learned is related to population growth.

6. Read *Fertility* to learn how fertility rates are related to population growth. To help guide your reading, consider using a strategy such as a T-table. List factors that affect fertility and how each factor affects population growth.

READING

Fertility

To predict how populations will change, you need to know the number of children born and the number of women who are of reproductive age. The fertility rate provides this measure. Total fertility rate is the average number of children born to a woman during her entire reproductive life. The total fertility rate has remained fairly constant for developed regions since 1975. During this same time period, the fertility rate in developing regions has decreased by half (see figure 15.15).

Many factors affect how many children a woman has. In the past, families may have had many children because infant mortality rates were high. Children often have been, and in some countries still are, important for providing income and helping with chores. For example, they might work in factories, take care of animals and siblings, help grow crops, and gather water and firewood. Some couples have more children in an attempt to have a son because boys may be given special social status. Religious or cultural beliefs may dictate that families should not control fertility and that they should have as many children as possible. In some societies, women's status is tied to children. In these societies, a woman without children has no financial support.

Other factors tend to reduce fertility. Women with higher educations often choose to have fewer children (see figure 15.16). Similarly, women who enter the workforce are less likely to stay home and have many children. Women have more freedom to make their own choices when they have their own source of income. The choice of how many children to have also is different for developed and developing countries. In developing countries, adding a child doesn't cost a lot more for the family and may provide additional income or labor that will help the family. However, the cost of raising a child in a developed country such as the United States is high. In 2004, the U.S. Department of Agriculture estimated the cost of raising a child to age 17 averaged about $10,000 a year. With a high cost of raising children, many families in developed countries choose to have only one or two children.

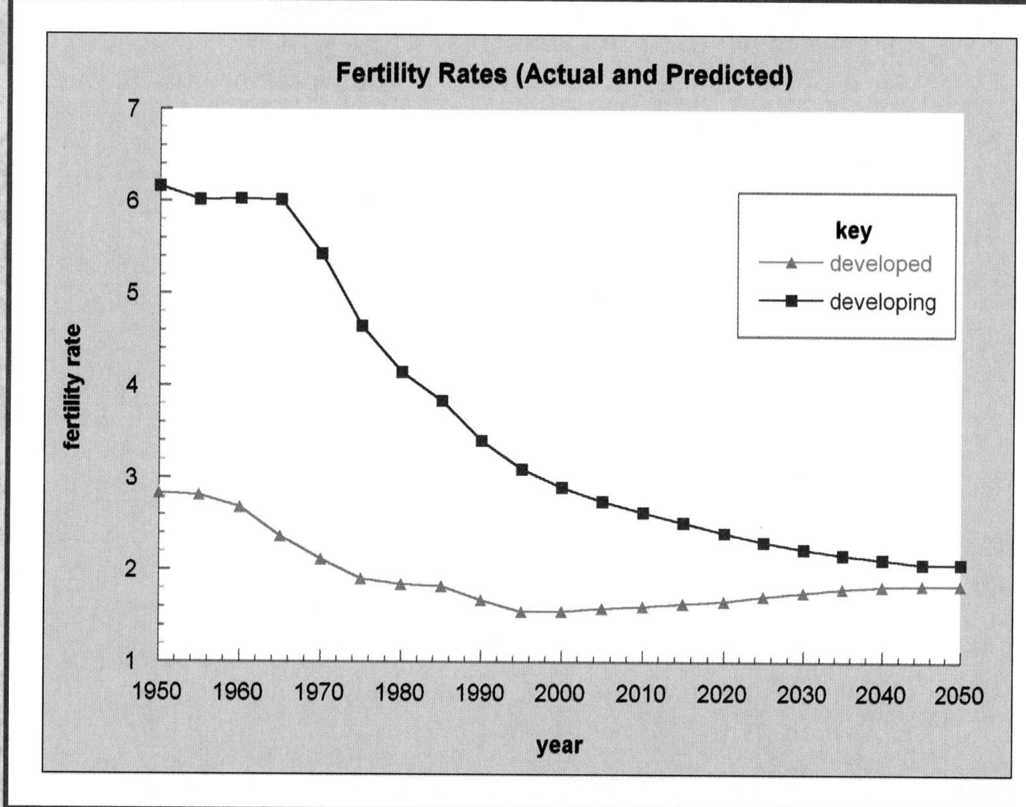

Figure 15.15 Actual and predicted fertility rates for developed and developing regions. The United Nations uses current data to project future fertility rates. What do you notice about the fertility rates predicted for 2050?

Source: Data from http://esa.un.org/unpp, World Population Prospects: 2004 Revision

Fertility rate and education statistics	Developed regions	Developing regions
Total fertility rate	1.6 births per woman	3.0 births per woman
Literacy rate for women aged 15–24	100%	81%
Secondary school enrollment of women	100%	55%

Source: Data from http://esa.un.org/unpp, World Population Prospects: 2004 Revision

Figure 15.16 Fertility and education statistics for women in developed and developing regions. For a woman to be literate, she must be able to write, read, and understand a short, simple statement about her everyday life. Why do you think literacy rates and secondary school enrollment are different for developed and developing countries?

7. Complete Steps 7a–e to show your understanding of what influences fertility rates and how fertility affects human population growth.
   a. Study figure 15.15 and describe the change in the fertility rate during the past 50 years.
   b. Compare the fertility rate with the birthrate shown in figure 15.14. Do both rates show the same trend? Justify your answer using evidence.
   c. Describe at least 3 things that influence fertility rate.
   d. Look at the fertility levels predicted for 2005 to 2050 in figure 15.15. What is the trend? Use evidence from the reading to explain your answer.
   e. What do you think the fertility rate would be if there were zero population growth? Explain your answer.

Zero population growth is the number of births that keep the population size the same. At zero population growth, the birthrate equals the mortality rate.

8. Work with a partner to discuss and investigate how age structure affects population growth. Record your ideas for Steps 8a–b in your science notebook.

Age structure is the distribution of individuals in a population according to age. Age structure varies among populations.

   a. How do you think the age of people is related to population size?
   b. Repeat Steps 5b–e. Make sure you describe how the age structure of a population helps explain population growth.
9. To learn more about how life expectancy affects population size, read *Aging Populations* and study figure 15.17.

READING

Aging Populations

Life expectancy has been increasing in many countries in the past 50 years (see figure 15.17). Life expectancy is the average number of years a person in a given society can expect to live. For much of human history, life expectancy was from 35 to 40 years. Now the average life expectancy for the world as a whole is 65 years. The increase in life expectancy can be attributed to improved health conditions. In the past, most people died from infectious diseases and parasites. Now many people die from chronic conditions and diseases that cannot be passed from one individual to another. These conditions tend to show up later in life. This health transition has occurred as countries become more modernized and the standard of living increases.

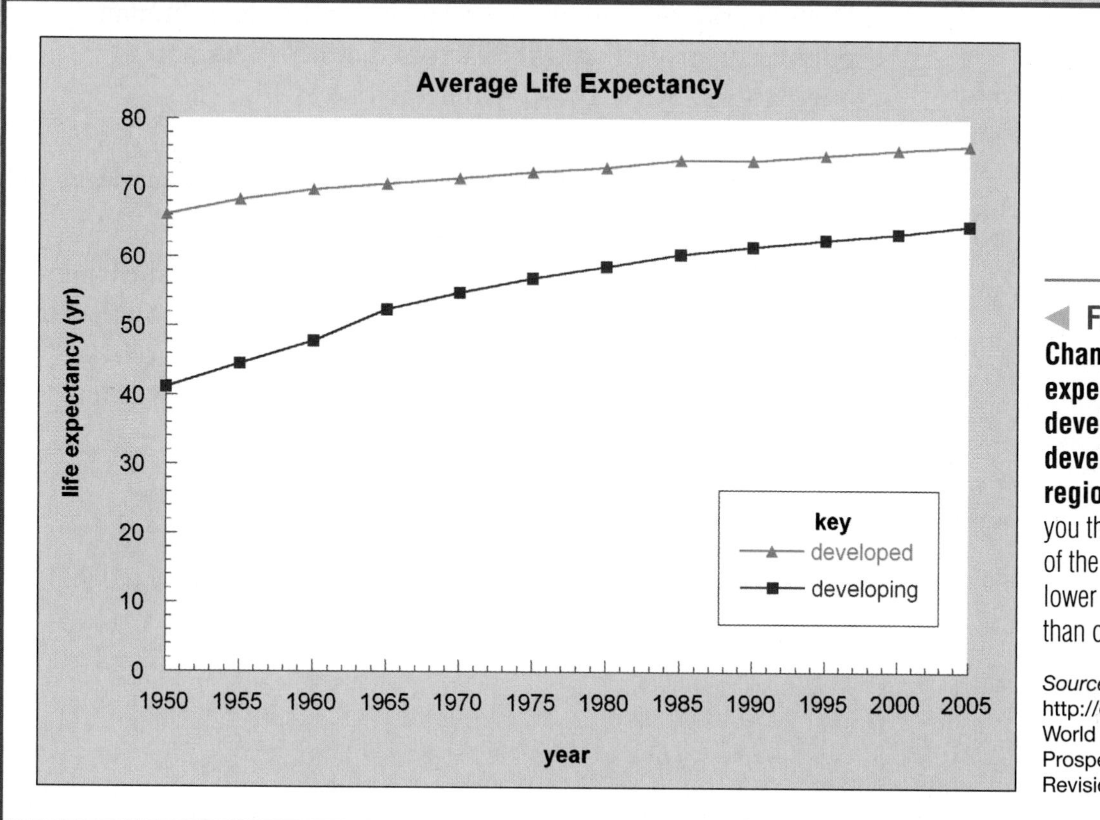

◀ **Figure 15.17 Change in life expectancy for developed and developing regions.** Why do you think some parts of the world have a lower life expectancy than others?

Source: Data from http://esa.un.org/unpp, World Population Prospects: 2004 Revision

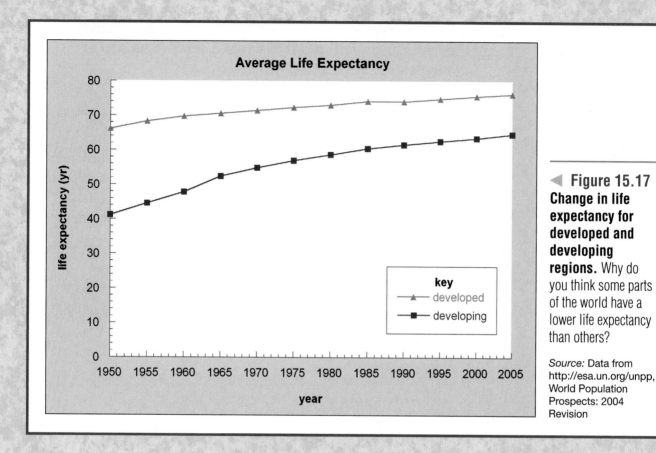

10. Consider how the age structure of a population is related to population growth.
    a. Study figure 15.17 and describe how life expectancy is changing across time.
    b. List 2 reasons why life expectancy is increasing.
    c. Get the *Age Structure* handout from your teacher.
    d. Which population (Kenya or Italy) has more young people? Which has more old people?
    e. Use the diagram on the *Age Structure* handout to help explain why Kenya's population size is increasing and Italy's population size stays the same.
    f. Suppose the average life expectancy for Kenya increased to 65 years. Draw how you think its age structure diagram would look.

The current average life expectancy is 50 years in Kenya and 80 years in Italy.

    g. Use age structure to explain why Kenya's birthrate is higher (40 births per 1,000) than Italy's (9 births per 1,000).

11. Draw 3 graphs showing the relationship between human population growth and the factors that affect human populations. Steps 11a–c will help you.

Population growth rate is the percentage change in a population in 1 year. It reflects the number of births and deaths and the number of people moving to and from a region.

a. Use figure 15.18 as a template to create a graph showing the relationship between birthrate and population growth rate.
b. Add highlight comments and a caption to the graph.
c. Repeat Steps 11a–b for mortality rate and fertility rate.

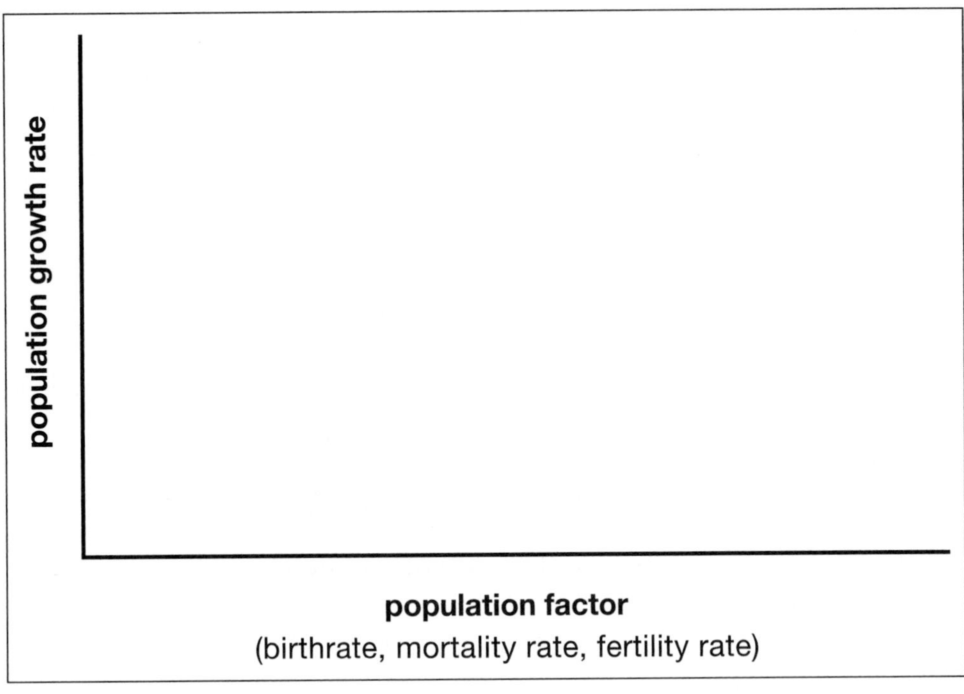

Figure 15.18 Graph template for showing the relationship between population factors and population growth. Is the relationship between birthrate and population growth rate direct or inverse? What about mortality rate or fertility rate?

12. Calculate growth rate and doubling time for the world's populations at different times in history. Show your work.
a. Calculate the growth rate from 1700 to 1800, 1800 to 1900, and 1900 to 2000 using the data in figure 15.19. Average growth rate is calculated as

$$\textit{growth rate (percent)} = \frac{\textit{population at time 2} - \textit{population at time 1}}{\textit{population at time 1} \times \textit{number of years}} \times 100.$$

b. Calculate the doubling time for each growth rate in Step 12a. Doubling time is the amount of time required for a population to double in size.

$$\textit{doubling time} = \frac{0.7}{\textit{growth rate}}$$

Year	Population ($\times 10^9$)
1700	0.6
1800	0.8
1900	1.6
2000	6.1

Figure 15.19 World population. How has the growth rate changed each century since 1700?

If the annual growth rate is 7 percent, the doubling time is 10 years $\left(\frac{0.7}{0.07/\text{yr}} = 10 \text{ yr}\right)$.

13. Study figure 15.20 to learn how the world population growth rate has changed and is expected to change in the future.
    a. Describe the trend in the world's population growth rate from 1950 to 2005.
    b. In what year will the 2005 world population double? What will the population size be in that year? In 2005, the population was 6.45 billion and the growth rate was 1.15 percent.
    c. Give 3 reasons why you think the growth rate has decreased even though the total population has increased since 1950. Include quantitative evidence in your answer.
    d. Explain why you think the world's population growth rate will continue to decline in the future.

Remember, population growth rate and population size are not the same. Even with a low population growth rate, the population will continue to grow.

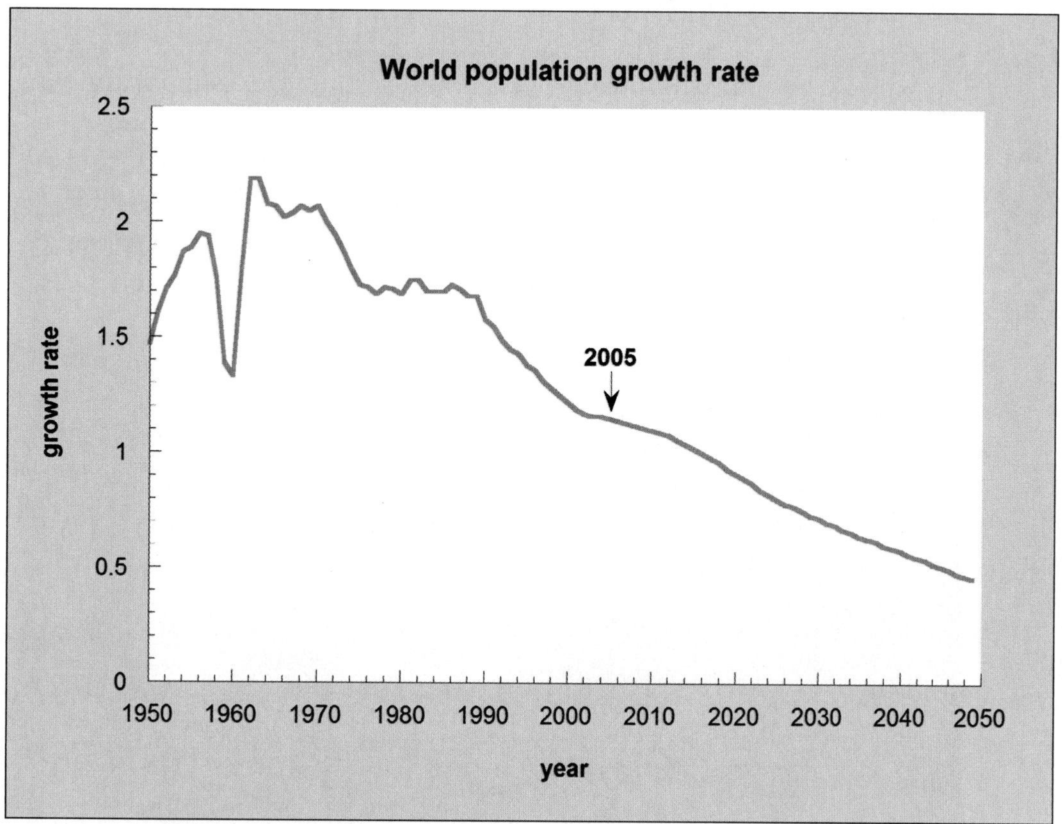

Source: Data from http://esa.un.org/unpp, World Population Prospects: 2004 Revision

▲ **Figure 15.20 World population growth in the past and future.** This graph shows actual population growth measured from 1950 to 2005. Population growth declined from 1965 to 2005. Scientists predict that population growth will continue to decline in the future.

Reflect and Connect

Answer the following questions by yourself in your science notebook.

1. List at least 3 limiting factors for human populations and describe why each is a limiting factor.

Recall from chapter 14 that limiting factors such as availability of resources and space, predators, and environmental conditions keep plant and animal populations in check.

2. Look back at the last 1,000 years shown in figure 15.9.
   a. Does the graph show exponential growth? Why or why not?
   b. Explain why you think limiting factors have not stopped human populations from getting larger. Include the role of technology in your answer.
   c. Do you think there is a carrying capacity for humans on Earth? Why or why not?

Recall that carrying capacity is the maximum number of a species that an environment can support.

EXPLAIN

Limits to Growth

We rely on many natural processes and resources to support human life. Ecosystems provide important services such as air and water purification (see figure 15.21), nutrient cycling, climate control, and soil production. You might be more familiar with the resources that ecosystems provide, such as food and water. Recall the list of resources you developed in the engage activity, *Your Ecological Footprint.*

Figure 15.21
Wetland. Wetlands play an important role in purifying water. Plants and soils in wetlands effectively remove nutrients such as phosphorus and nitrogen. These nutrients are commonly found in agricultural runoff and when in large amounts can pollute streams. Many wetland plants can also remove toxic substances from industrial waste and mining activities.

You thought about the resources needed to provide everyday things such as food, shelter, clothing, and transportation. Now you will consider where those resources come from. In *Limits to Growth*, you will examine how four types of ecosystems support human life.

Materials

none

Process and Procedure

1. Identify 1 question you have about the resources and services that ecosystems provide. Record your question in your science notebook.
2. Read *Our Dependency on Ecosystems*. Then complete Steps 2a–e to show your understanding of how ecosystems sustain human populations.
   a. Work in a team of 4 and divide the reading into 4 sections. Each teammate should read about 1 type of ecosystem, as directed by your teacher.
   b. Draw a table in your science notebook with these 4 headings: "ecosystem," "resources," "natural processes and services," and "threats to the system."
   c. Fill in the table with examples as you read about your ecosystem.
   d. Meet with the other classmates who read about the same ecosystem. Discuss your findings and add new information to your table or revise your examples based on what you learn.
   e. Meet again with your team of 4 and read the information from your table. Then add information about the other ecosystems to your table.

READING

Our Dependency on Ecosystems

Ecosystems provide direct and indirect benefits. Direct benefits include things that can be harvested, such as crops, fish, livestock, and wood. Indirect benefits come from interactions and feedback. The interactions and feedback occur among organisms. They also occur between organisms and the abiotic environment. Some familiar examples are water purification, pollination, erosion control, and seed dispersal. There are four types of ecosystem—marine, freshwater, forest, and grassland. Each type provides a unique set of benefits through its resources and natural processes.

Our Dependency on Ecosystems, continued

Marine Ecosystems

Marine ecosystems include the open ocean and coastal areas. The ocean is important for climate. The heat stored in the ocean drives air circulation and ocean currents. Circulating air carries water vapor from the ocean over land surfaces, where it falls as rain or snow. Ocean currents also affect climate because they redistribute heat. For example, the Gulf Stream makes western Europe much warmer than Canada, which is at similar latitude. In unit 3, *Moving Matter*, you learned that the ocean is important for the global water cycle and the global carbon cycle.

One group of organisms, called phytoplankton, is very important to the carbon cycle. Phytoplankton are microscopic algae that live suspended in the water column, which extends from the ocean's surface to the bottom. Phytoplankton take in the carbon dioxide dissolved in the ocean during photosynthesis. They give off oxygen. As primary producers, they are the basis for the ocean's food chains. Although phytoplankton are an important food source for many organisms, most phytoplankton die before being consumed and sink to the bottom of the ocean. The calcium carbonate in their shells accumulates on the ocean floor. The accumulation of organic matter from phytoplankton makes the ocean a carbon sink. Remember that a carbon sink is a reservoir of carbon that has inputs of carbon greater than the outputs.

Most organisms in the ocean live in coastal areas. More organisms can survive in shallower water where light can penetrate and nutrients are more plentiful. As a result, as much as 95 percent of the world's fish and shellfish supply comes from coastal areas. Almost 40 percent of the world's population lives along the coast. Fish and shellfish account for one-sixth of the animal protein consumed by the world's population. Many small countries, such as Iceland, Bangladesh, Ghana, Indonesia, and Japan, depend on fish as their main source of protein.

Coastal areas are areas up to 200 m deep, tidal areas, and the nearby land areas. Habitats such as mangroves, estuaries, coral reefs, and tidal wetlands are found in coastal areas. Tidal wetlands are wetlands that are flooded with tidal waters. Mangroves are coastal, forested wetlands. Estuaries are wetlands where freshwater and ocean water meet. Some well-known estuaries are located in Puget Sound in Washington state and Chesapeake Bay in Maryland and Virginia. Mangroves and estuaries provide spawning areas for fish. Mangroves also provide wood for building materials and fuel. In the United States, mangroves are found mainly along the Atlantic and Gulf coasts of Florida (see figure 15.22). In December 2004, large mangrove forests in Malaysia and India protected some people from the tsunami that hit southeast Asia. Coral reefs provide areas for small-scale fishing.

Coastal areas also help maintain water quality. These ecosystems filter toxic pollutants and absorb large amounts of nutrients that run off agricultural and urban areas. All the habitats in coastal areas help protect coastlines from storm damage. For example, plants help decrease erosion. Unfortunately, the loss of estuaries along the coast leaves cities more exposed to hurricanes. This happened when New Orleans, Louisiana, was hit by Hurricane Katrina in 2005.

Some of the biggest threats to marine ecosystems are population growth, pollution, and overharvesting. As human populations grow, rivers deliver more pollutants to coastal waters. Increased use of fertilizers on crops has brought more nutrients to coastal areas. The extra nutrients cause harmful algal blooms. Overharvesting has become more of a problem as the fishing industry has grown. New equipment allows one fishing vessel to capture many more fish than in the past. Coastal areas are producing less fish because of overfishing, damaging fishing techniques, and the destruction of nursery habitats.

Freshwater Ecosystems

Freshwater ecosystems contain a fraction of Earth's water. But most ecosystem services depend on a consistent supply of freshwater. Freshwater is essential for people to consume as well as for agriculture and industry. Freshwater ecosystems maintain water quality by breaking down contaminants and organic waste. Many species live only in freshwater ecosystems or depend on freshwater ecosystems for a part of their life cycle. Inland fish are an important source of protein for much of the world's population, especially the poor.

Wetlands are an especially important part of freshwater ecosystems. Wetlands are habitats that are flooded for a given period of time and contain water-loving plant species. Wetlands include flooded forests, river floodplains, shallow lakes, and marshes. Wetlands provide flood control; water filtration; carbon storage; and goods such as fish, shellfish, and timber. At least half the wetlands in the world have been drained for settlement or agriculture. Wetlands once covered much of Iowa, for example, but they were drained and filled in. Now most of the area is cultivated for crops.

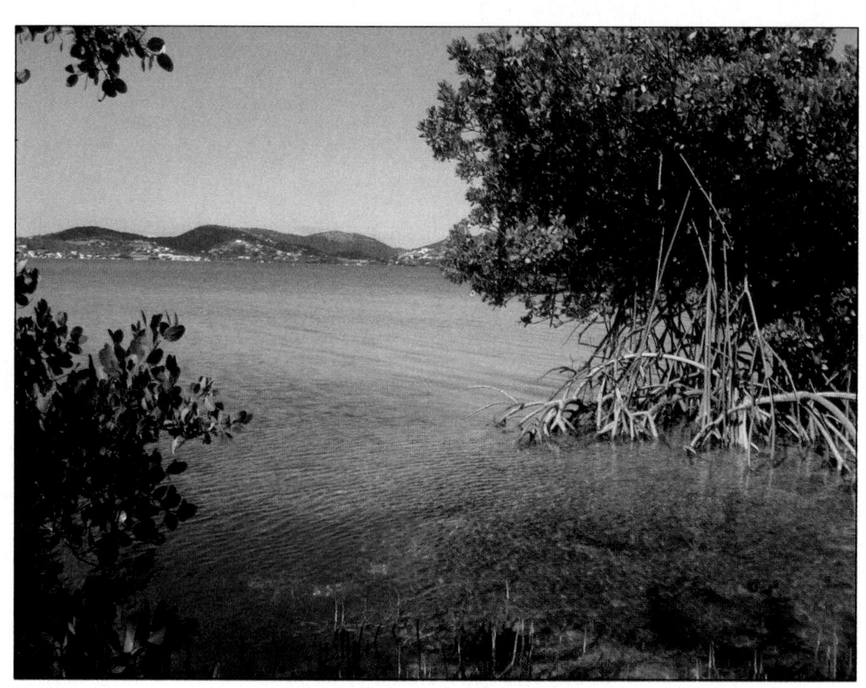

▲ **Figure 15.22 Mangrove swamps.** Mangroves are coastal, forested wetlands. The roots of mangrove plants stabilize surrounding mud and sand.

Freshwater ecosystems are threatened when humans alter them and pollution enters them. Rivers have been disconnected from their floodplains to control the flow of water for human uses. Dams capture 14 percent of the world's runoff. Altered freshwater ecosystems have increased agricultural output, made water transport easier, and provided hydropower. But the alteration has dramatically changed where and how much water flows. As population increases, reduced water flows and increased inputs of nutrients and pollutants affect water quality. Changes in water flow have made it easier for non-native species such as zebra mussels and exotic fish to invade freshwater ecosystems. Non-native species compete with native species, and thus threaten or endanger many native species.

Forest Ecosystems

Forests have provided humans with food, shelter, fuel, and building materials throughout history. Today, millions of people still rely on forests for all their needs. Commercial timber production is a major global industry. North America and Europe produce more timber than less developed countries. However, many less developed countries depend on timber to support their economies. For example, wood fuels account for at least half the energy consumed in less developed countries.

Forests are also important for reasons other than for food and shelter. Forests help maintain water quality by filtering water and reducing erosion and sedimentation. Forests are a much smaller reservoir for carbon than the ocean. However, forests are an important part of the global carbon cycle tied to land. They store 39 percent of the carbon in terrestrial ecosystems. Carbon is stored in the living plant matter and the organic matter in forest soils. Forest ecosystems have the highest biodiversity of any ecosystem. The diverse species found in forests are sources of new drugs and nontimber products such as resins, fruits, and mushrooms.

Less than 40 percent of Earth's forests are undisturbed by humans. Forest cover has been reduced 20–50 percent since pre-agricultural times (figure 15.23). Since 1980, forest cover has increased slightly in more developed countries. But it has decreased by 10 percent in less developed countries. The biggest threats to forests are converting the forest land for agriculture and building roads. In Africa, only 49 percent of the forest area consists of large forest blocks (10,000 km^2 or larger). If there were no roads there, large forest blocks would make up 83 percent of the area.

Grassland Ecosystems

Grassland ecosystems cover 40 percent of the land on Earth's surface and are crucial for the world's food supply. These ecosystems include grasslands, savanna, shrublands, and tundra. More grasslands have been converted for agricultural use than any other ecosystem. All of the grains, such as wheat, rice, rye, and corn, were selectively bred from wild grasses. Grasslands will continue to be a source for genetic material to improve crops in the future. Grasslands support grazing livestock such as cattle, sheep, and goats. They also are a source of animals for hunting and for medicinal plants. Grasslands store 33 percent of the carbon in terrestrial ecosystems. Like forests, carbon is stored in the living plant matter as well as in the organic matter in grassland soils. The amount of carbon stored in grasslands is

▲ **Figure 15.23 Cleared trees.** Using forest resources for timber and other purposes affects natural processes in forests. For example, how does clearing trees affect a forest's ability to filter water?

about half that of forests because grasslands cover twice the area of forests.

Humans have also modified grasslands. Agriculture, urbanization, and road building fragment grasslands into smaller, disconnected areas. Agriculture is important for providing food for human populations, but some farming practices can deplete soils and negatively affect the environment. To learn about farming techniques that have less impact, read the sidebar *Sustainable Agriculture*. Grazing techniques can help maintain grassland ecosystems or degrade them. Grazing cuts back vegetation and prevents bushes and trees from replacing grasses. However, when many animals graze in an area, they destroy vegetation, compact the soil, and increase soil erosion. For example, some grasslands in northern China are becoming deserts (figure 15.24). Growing populations that farm and graze intensively are overusing the land. In addition, they are misusing water resources.

▲ **Figure 15.24 Desertification.** Desertification is the spread of desert conditions in once fertile land. A well-known example of desertification occurred in the 1930s. Drought and poor farming practices turned the grasslands (the Great Plains) in the United States into a dust bowl until rain brought back vegetation. Improvements in land and water management have prevented this from occurring again in the United States.

3. Did the information in the reading answer your question from Step 1 about the resources and services that ecosystems provide? If so, document your answer here. Otherwise, describe what information you need to answer your question.

You can also look for information on the Web to answer your question.

4. Provide a 1- or 2-sentence definition of renewable resources. The resources described in *Our Dependency on Ecosystems* are considered renewable resources.
5. Read *Energy Resources* to learn how ecosystems have provided energy in the form of fossil fuels.

Topic: limits to growth
Go to: www.scilinks.org
Code: 2Inquiry777

READING

Energy Resources

The industrialization of the world created a need for energy to power machinery. Historically, people used wood for fuel. During the industrial revolution, people began using fossil fuels such as coal. By the early 1900s, oil and natural gas were used as well.

Coal, oil, and natural gas form where organic matter was abundant millions of years ago. Coal formed where plant matter accumulated in large amounts, such as in wetlands. Waterlogged soils in some wetlands create anaerobic conditions (conditions without oxygen). Most decomposers require aerobic conditions to break down organic matter. As plants died, they accumulated and gradually turned into peat. Across time, peat was buried under more and more plant matter or sediment. Burial compressed and heated the peat. After millions of years, chemical changes in the peat, which was already high in carbon, transformed it into coal. Coal is 70–90 percent carbon, depending on the conditions in which it was formed.

The formation of oil and natural gas is similar to the formation of coal. Oil and natural gas form in coastal areas where marine organisms were abundant in the past. Many of the marine organisms were buried under sediment before they decomposed. After millions of years, higher temperatures and chemical reactions transformed some of the organic matter into oil and natural gas.

Many countries depend on sources other than fossil fuels for their energy. Nuclear energy provides 7 percent of the world's energy. Nuclear energy requires uranium, which is present in very small amounts on Earth. One problem with nuclear energy is that scientists are still working on the best way to dispose of nuclear waste. Some renewable sources of energy are hydroelectric, solar, geothermal, wind, and tidal energy. These account for less than 1 percent of the world's energy use.

6. Describe the connection between fossil fuels and ecosystems.
7. Provide a 1- or 2-sentence definition for nonrenewable resources. Fossil fuels are considered nonrenewable resources.
8. Think about the relationship between consumption and the resources and services ecosystems provide.
   a. How does consumption of resources affect the natural processes that occur in ecosystems? Look at the table you created in Step 2 to help you.
   b. How does consumption affect the supply of renewable resources differently from nonrenewable resources?
   c. Why are renewable resources finite (limited) even though they can be replenished?

d. Why are fossil fuels considered nonrenewable even though they were made from plant material?

e. Predictions of how long nonrenewable resources will last keep changing. For example, in 1989, reserves of oil and natural gas were estimated to last for 41 years of production. By 1998, the estimate had increased to 57 years. Why do you think the predictions change?

9. Read *Earth's Carrying Capacity* to learn what limits the population size that Earth can support.

READING

Earth's Carrying Capacity

Scientists estimate Earth's carrying capacity to be from 7.7 to 12 billion people. Estimates of Earth's carrying capacity have increased across time. Scientists use factors such as water, energy, food, and the things needed to produce food to make their estimates. Their estimates are often based on the minimal needs of humans. For example, one estimate is based on the fact that the world currently produces enough grains to feed 10 billion people. This estimate assumes that all people on Earth live on a vegetarian diet.

Calculating the carrying capacity of Earth is difficult. The factors affecting carrying capacity depend on one another. For example, crop productivity may decrease if agricultural land is converted to urban areas or if fertilizers become scarce. If water is scarce and energy is abundant, then it may be possible to transport water or remove salt from salt water. If energy is scarce or too expensive, then it may be impractical to make water available in these ways. People might face water shortages. Carrying capacity for humans depends less on the number of people and more on the choices societies make. Although many parts of the world have unused land, this land may not provide the resources that humans use. Recall what you learned in the engage activity. We need land not only to provide space to live, but also to provide the resources we use.

10. Consider how land area and consumption are related to Earth's carrying capacity. Use Steps 10a–b to help you.

a. Explain why the amount of space (land) doesn't determine how many people Earth can support.

b. Based on what you have learned about population and resource consumption, describe 2 ways you think the carrying capacity of Earth could be increased. Explain why these changes would make a difference.

Reflect and Connect

Work individually to answer the following questions in your science notebook. Then check your answers with another student and revise them based on anything new you learn.

1. Why are fossil fuels considered nonrenewable resources?
2. Study figure 15.25 and predict how human populations and ecosystems will be affected if the world population reaches 7.7, 9, and 10.6 billion, respectively, in 2050. For each answer, use evidence from the chapter to justify your answer.

Notice that this graph of world population size looks different from earlier graphs. This graph only shows population size since the year 2000.

   a. Which 3 resources do you think will be in shortest supply? Explain.
   b. Which natural process in ecosystems do you think will be affected the most?
   c. Where will the human populations that are affected the most by the changes be located?

3. How does technology affect the carrying capacity of Earth? Technology includes new equipment and techniques used in medicine, agriculture, and industry.
   a. List 2 ways technology has increased the carrying capacity for the number of people on Earth. Explain why.
   b. List 2 ways that technology negatively affects the capacity of Earth to support human populations. Explain why the technology has this effect.
4. Has this activity changed your opinion about human population issues? If so, how? If not, why not?

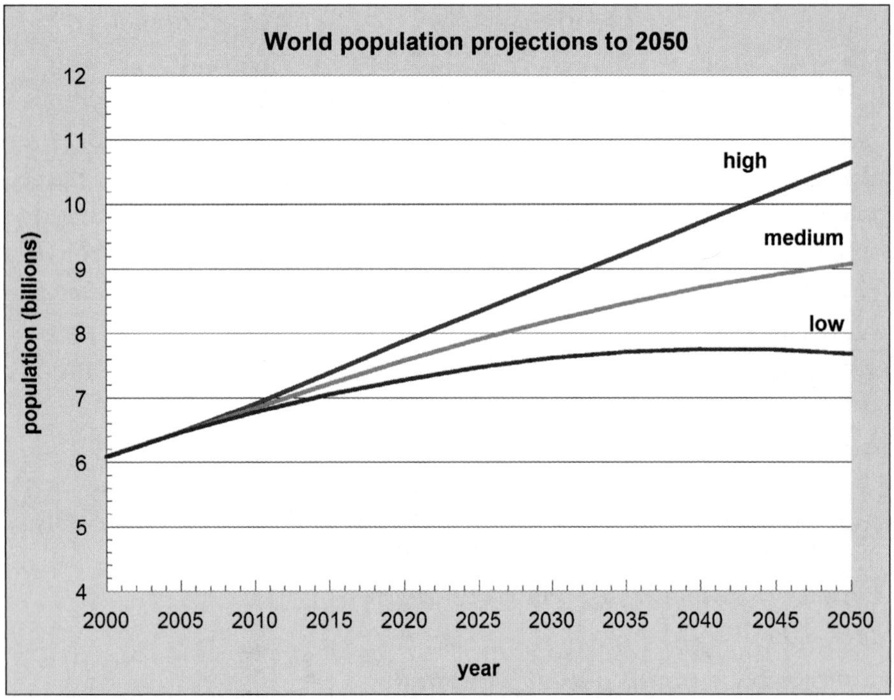

Source: Data from http://esa.un.org/unpp, World Population Prospects: 2004 Revision

▲ **Figure 15.25 World population projections to 2050.** The United Nations has 3 different predictions for the future of the world's population. Each prediction makes different assumptions about how mortality rates and fertility rates will change in the future. Which prediction do you think will be more accurate: a conservative (low) estimate, a high estimate, or an estimate somewhere in between?

Sustainable Agriculture

SIDEBAR

Sustainable agriculture produces an abundance of food, while it conserves resources and minimizes pollution. It combines some aspects of existing agricultural systems with new agricultural techniques. It is based on systems for raising crops that are self-sustaining, just as natural systems are. For example, sustainable agriculture takes advantage of local climates, soils, and resources. Sustainable farms use smaller amounts of fossil fuels than farms that use most of the existing agricultural techniques. Sustainable farms conserve topsoil and water. And they control pests with little, if any, use of pesticides. A common practice is low-till or no-till farming, where crop residue is left as cover for new crops being planted.

Most agriculture practices in developed countries focus on the short-term productivity of one crop. That is, they focus on how much crop is produced in a growing season. Sustainable agricultural systems focus on the long-term condition of the soil. Instead of producing a single type of crop, sustainable systems produce a diverse mix of fruit and vegetable crops. These systems also use organic fertilizers made from animal and crop wastes. Special fast-growing trees are planted along with the food crops. The trees supply fuelwood and add nitrogen to the soil. Whenever it is affordable, sustainable farmers use locally available alternatives to fossil fuels. Such alternatives include wind energy and solar power.

A central part of sustainable agricultural systems is crop rotation. Crop rotation is the planned planting of various crops, one after the other, on one field. Rotation provides better weed and insect control. It also improves nutrient cycling, which improves crop yields. Rotating crops reduces disease and insect pests. Since both tend to be linked to specific plants, planting different crops disturbs the life cycles of many insects and diseases. Rotating nitrogen-fixing crops such as legumes (beans and peas) with other crops helps increase the amount of nitrogen available in the soil. This supports soil fertility and helps provide nutrients needed by the next crop.

▲ **No-till farming.** No-till farming prevents erosion and helps soil retain moisture. This photo shows young soybean plants growing in the residue of a wheat crop.

A second component of sustainable agricultural systems is the addition of organic matter, such as crop waste and manure, to the soil. Organic matter improves the soil in many ways. It builds topsoil, increases the ability of soil to store water, and enhances soil fertility. Soil in good condition is easier to till, and it allows seedlings to emerge and root more easily. Water readily seeps into rich soil, thus reducing surface runoff and erosion. Organic materials also provide food for earthworms and other soil organisms. These organisms in turn improve the condition of the soil.

Sustainable Agriculture, continued

A shift to more sustainable agriculture is difficult to accomplish. Some experts believe that the government's support of research, subsidies and tax breaks, and training programs may encourage some farmers to adopt these practices. However, no agricultural practice is sustainable unless it is also profitable. Sustainable agriculture may be best for smaller family farms that serve local markets. Creating new markets for sustainable agriculture will be one of the challenges for increasing its use.

ELABORATE

Managing an Ecosystem

You learned in the explore activity *Limits to Growth* that human populations depend on and affect ecosystems. In some cases, humans have a direct effect on populations of organisms. For example, overfishing threatens the future supply of fish. U.S. fishermen know that the Pacific halibut is one of the most profitable fish species to harvest. Pacific halibut are large flatfish that weigh up to 200 to 300 kilograms (kg) and grow up to 2.7 m long (figure 15.26). They are found along the continental shelf from California to the Bering Sea in Alaska. Larval halibut feed on plankton. Adults are carnivorous. They feed on octopuses, crabs, clams, and fishes such as cod, pollock, rockfish, and sablefish. Halibut are occasionally eaten by marine mammals, but are rarely eaten by other fish.

▲ **Figure 15.26 Halibut.** Halibut have flattened bodies that make them well suited to live on the ocean floor. They typically have both eyes on the right side or "top" of the body.

Commercial fishing began in the early 1900s. Today, fishermen catch halibut by long-lining. Long-lining uses hundreds of baited hooks on a line that can be many miles long. Fishing for Pacific halibut is concentrated off Alaska and the west coast of Canada (figure 15.27).

Like most countries, the United States limits the number of halibut and other fish species that can be caught each year. In *Managing an Ecosystem*, you will experience this firsthand.

You will play the role of a Pacific halibut fisherman in Alaska. First, you will model how fishing affects the halibut population. Then you will propose different ways to manage your fishery to keep your income while sustaining that halibut population.

Materials

For each team of 4 students

1 bag of "halibut" (20 small paper clips, 30 large paper clips)

1 stopwatch

1 calculator

Process and Procedure

▲ **Figure 15.27 Sampling the commercial catch.** A portion of the halibut caught by commercial fisherman is sampled by the International Pacific Halibut Commission. This group gathers information about age and size to set limits on halibut fishing. This photo shows a large halibut caught by a sport fisherman being weighed.

1. Get into teams of 4.
2. Read the following information to become familiar with the halibut you will harvest. Each teammate will act as a Pacific halibut fisherman in this activity.
   - Each paper clip represents 1,000 halibut.
   - Large paper clips represent mature fish that can reproduce.
   - Small paper clips represent immature fish.
   - Fish mature at 10 years.
   - Each mature female can produce 50 eggs.
3. Get the bag of fish from your teacher and scatter all but 1 of the large paper clips across the table or floor. This 1 paper clip represents the mature fish that are hidden; you will not be able to catch these 1,000 halibut.
4. Harvest as many fish as you can by grabbing with both hands for 20 seconds. Remember that as a fisherman, catching fish is your livelihood. This round of "fishing" represents an annual harvest.
5. Record the catch for each fishing vessel in your science notebook. Each hand represents a separate fishing vessel.

Remember to keep the paper clips in each hand separate.

6. Calculate your gross income for each fishing vessel, counting each hand as a fishing vessel. Show your calculations in your science notebook.
   - An average harvested fish weighs 10 kg.
   - The standard price a fisherman in Alaska received in 2004 was about $2.40 per kilogram.

Gross income is the amount of money earned before operating costs and taxes are subtracted. Your calculations do not represent profits because they do not include your business costs, such as the cost of the equipment, fuel, and paying people to fish and run the vessel.

7. Describe the effect of your harvest on the halibut population by completing Steps 7a–c. Record your answers in your science notebook and show your calculations.
   a. Use the information in Step 2 to calculate the size of the halibut population for the next 15 years. Give your answer in the numbers of mature and immature fish. Assume that each year
      - you set aside 1 large paper clip from the population, which represents those fish you could not catch;
      - half the fish are male and half are female;
      - all mature females reproduce (50 eggs per female); and
      - you caught the same number of fish each year.
   b. Calculate the size of the fish population after your first harvest. List the number of mature and immature fish in your answer.
   c. Explain what effect this harvest rate has on the fish population and on the fishermen. Discuss whether each fishing vessel would make as much money after the first harvest.
8. Discuss as a team how you could adjust your harvest to continue to make income and to have a population survive and sustain itself. Use this goal as a guide:

   Goal: Allow halibut fishing to continue while ensuring the survival of the halibut population.

Think about whether the length of your harvest, the number of fishing vessels, or other variables should be adjusted.

9. Write a management plan in your science notebook. Then record your team's ideas for adjusting your harvest based on your management plan.
10. Carry out and adjust your management plan by using Steps 10a–f as a guide.
    a. Repeat the harvest you did in Step 4, but this time restrict your harvest according to your management plan.
    b. Calculate the income for each fishing vessel.
    c. Calculate the size of the halibut population for the next 15 years based on your management plan.

d. Decide as a team whether your management plan meets the goal in Step 8.
e. Use evidence to explain why your management plan is effective if you decide not to revise it.
f. Repeat Steps 10a–e if you revise your management plan. Document all revisions of your plan, especially *why* you made a change.

11. Make a list of at least 4 factors, other than removing fish, that might affect the halibut population. Your list should include the influence of other aspects of fishing as well as nonfishing activities.
12. Participate in a class discussion about managing a fishery. Be prepared to do the following.
    a. Describe how harvests affect fish populations.
    b. Describe your team's final management plan.
    c. Compare the advantages and disadvantages of your management plan with other teams' plans.

Reflect and Connect

Answer the following questions on your own in your science notebook.

1. What criteria did you use to decide on a final management plan?
2. Do you think open access to resources will always lead to overexploitation? Explain why or why not.

You modeled an open-access fishery during the first round of fishing in Step 4. An open-access fishery has no limit on the number of fishermen or the number of fish caught. Overexploitation is using a resource beyond its capacity to regenerate. In this case, overexploitation means that reproduction cannot replace the number of fish caught.

3. Think of another example where resources are managed. For example, consider the resources you mapped in the explore activity such as water and forests. Explain why you think the resource is managed, how the resource is managed, and the effectiveness of the management.

In the United States, management of resources may occur at the level of the city, county, state, or federal government.

Your values and attitudes toward nature probably influence how you would choose to manage a resource. Read the sidebar Environmental Ethics and You to learn about different views of humanity's relationship to the natural world.

Topic: managing ecosystems
Go to: www.scilinks.org
Code: 2Inquiry785

SIDEBAR

Environmental Ethics and You

Environmental ethics is a branch of ethics that considers the relationship between humans and the natural world. People have different perspectives about humanity's relationship to nature. Their perspectives are based on different values, beliefs, and attitudes. People's values, beliefs, and attitudes about nature are formed by a variety of influences, including the values and attitudes of their culture. People's attitudes about nature also are influenced by their personal experiences, the people they talk to, and the books they read. Together, these values influence how people behave toward the environment. Our behavior has a major impact on the state of the natural world around us.

Brief descriptions of two distinctive ethics follow that show how different people's perspectives can be. How similar or different is your personal environmental ethic from the two views described here? What factors have influenced your environmental ethic? What other environmental ethical views are you aware of?

- *The human-centered environmental ethic.* People who support a human-centered environmental ethic take the position that humans dominate the natural world. People with this view see humans as different from all other life-forms and separate from nature. The value of nonhuman organisms is tied to their usefulness to humans. People with this ethic tend to view Earth as a collection of natural resources that can be used to promote economic growth. People who support this position also think that Earth is vast and has many resources in abundant supply. They point out that human history has been characterized by continual progress. Through technology, people find solutions to all problems (including those of resource depletion and pollution), and progress continues.
- *The deep ecology environmental ethic.* The deep ecology ethic is a life-centered ethic. People who support this view think that all life-forms on Earth have inborn value regardless of their usefulness to humans. From this view, humans have no right to reduce Earth's resources except to satisfy essential needs. People who support this position think that Earth's resources are in limited supply. They think that resources are for all life-forms, not just for humans. This view takes the position that human population growth must be reduced for both human and nonhuman life to flourish. People with this view think that the human impact on Earth's environment must be minimized. People must make economic and technological changes and changes in the way they think in order to promote a sustainable lifestyle. A sustainable lifestyle protects the function of earth systems.

Most people's views are somewhere in between the two ethics described here. Where you fall depends on how you answer questions such as, "What value does the natural world have?" This question has become increasingly important because we have more decisions to make about the fate of the natural environment. For example, should we consider drilling for natural gas on public lands? Where will we dispose of hazardous waste? Technological advancements that increase our capacity to take advantage of Earth's resources force us to make choices about our responsibility to nature.

Protecting ecosystems. The National Wildlife Refuge System was established in 1903 by Theodore Roosevelt. The system protects wildlife through habitat preservation. There are over 500 refuges distributed across all 50 states. This is a photo of the Edwin B. Forsythe Wildlife Refuge in New Jersey.

Sustaining Human Populations

EVALUATE

You have investigated human populations in a large open system called Earth. The resources we need are provided by the natural processes occurring on Earth. What if humans were to live in space or on the Moon? One such project is going on right now. The International Space Station is a joint project of six space agencies from different countries. The space station can support two to four people and has 425 m^3 of living space. For comparison, an average bedroom has around 31 m^3 of living space and an average house (2,000 ft^2) has around 1,900 m^3 of living space. Even with its small size, assembly of the station is still in progress, and it requires many inputs from outside sources.

Science fiction stories often describe humans colonizing the Moon or living in space. The people live in space stations that provide everything they need. Based on what you know about how Earth sustains human populations, do you think it might be possible for space stations to be self-sustaining in the future? What decisions would people living in a space station face?

In *Sustaining Human Populations*, you will begin by reading about an attempt to create a self-sustaining ecosystem called Biosphere 2. You will discover the challenges its designers faced to keep the system functioning without outside inputs. Then you will apply what you learned about human populations on Earth to decide how well three different populations will fare in a space station. Finally, you will work in a team to propose how a human population could sustain itself and its resources in a space station.

Part I: Analyzing and Evaluating Biosphere 2

Materials

For each student

1 *Sustaining Human Populations Scoring Rubric* handout

1 *Population Description* handout

Process and Procedure

1. Review the *Sustaining Human Populations Scoring Rubric* handout to understand all the evaluation expectations *before* you begin the activity.
2. Complete Steps 2a–b to show your understanding of how natural systems on Earth provide the resources and conditions we need to survive. Remember that natural systems are self-sustaining.
   a. Read *An Experimental Earth System* to learn what happened when scientists tried to create a self-sustaining system.
   b. As you read, compare how natural processes occur in a natural system with how the same processes occurred in Biosphere 2. Show your ideas by filling in a T-table with the 3 headings "natural process," "how it works in a natural system," and "what happened in Biosphere 2."

READING

An Experimental Earth System

In the late 1980s, Biosphere 2 was built in the southern Arizona desert. (Biosphere 1 is Earth itself.) Biosphere 2 is a glass enclosure containing living ecosystems (figure 15.28). Biosphere 2 was designed to grow food and recirculate air and water without exchanging materials with the outside world. The only inputs into the system were energy for external supporting systems (air pressure, cooling, and other utilities) and information (radio, television, and telephone). The intent was to see if humans could live self-sufficiently in a closed environment. It was designed with connected buildings containing different environments including rain forest, ocean, desert, agriculture, and human habitat.

In 1991, eight people entered Biosphere 2 to live for 2 years without outside intervention. After 1 year, the oxygen level in the closed atmosphere fell from 21 percent to 14 percent. This oxygen level was barely enough to support the residents. Oxygen was added to the closed atmosphere from outside to fix the problem. At the same time that oxygen levels were decreasing, carbon dioxide levels were increasing. Scientists later discovered that

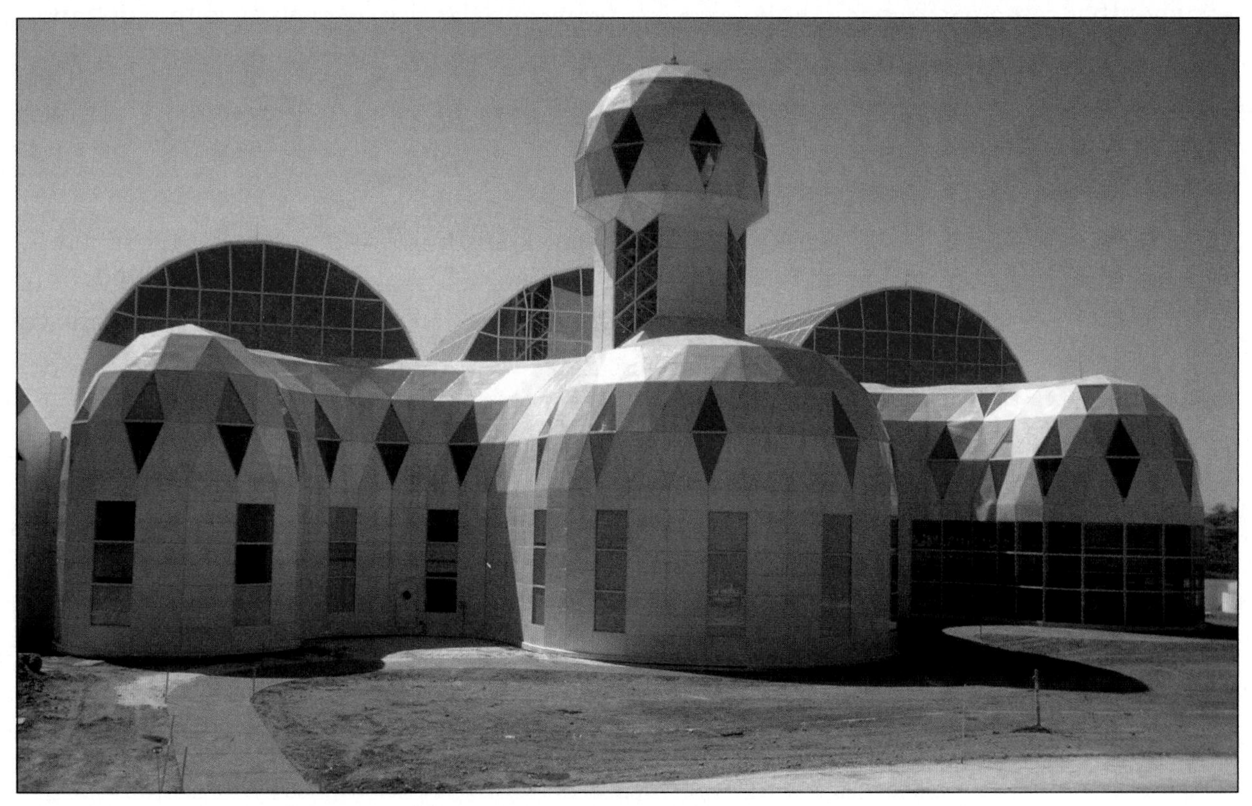

▲ **Figure 15.28 Biosphere 2.** Biosphere 2 is located on about 100 ha in Arizona, 56 km northeast of Tucson.

An Experimental Earth System, continued

respiration from microbes living in the fertile soils was responsible for the changes. The microbes were consuming large amounts of oxygen and releasing large amounts of carbon dioxide. The concrete used in the structure was releasing carbon dioxide as well.

There were other unexpected problems in Biosphere 2. All the insect pollinators died off, which caused food supplies to decline. Without pollination, flowering plants cannot produce seeds. Vines introduced to absorb carbon dioxide grew aggressively. Residents had to spend a lot of time weeding to keep the vines from overrunning food plants. Water pollution also became a problem as water systems became loaded with nutrients. Excessive nutrients cause blooms of harmful algae. Air temperatures in the upper parts of the facility were higher than anticipated, but light levels were lower because glass cut the sunlight by nearly half. Areas designed to be deserts became grasslands or chaparral filled with shrubby plants. The humidity inside was much higher than outside in the Sonoran Desert.

Biosphere 2 cost nearly $200 million to build. Energy costs were about $1 million per year to keep pumps, fans, and other systems running. In 1996, Columbia University began managing Biosphere 2 for scientific research and educational programs. From 1996 to 2003, scientists studied how high carbon dioxide levels affected forest ecosystems and coral reef communities in the artificial environment. In 2003, Columbia ended its contract and research stopped. In 2006, Biosphere 2 was for sale while tourists continued to visit the unusual facility. A developer made an offer to purchase the facility. The developer is likely to build a community of homes on the site. We will have to wait and see what happens to the Biosphere 2 facility.

3. Think carefully about Questions 3a–d regarding Biosphere 2. Record your best ideas in your science notebook, and then use the TSAR strategy with another classmate to compare answers.
   a. Did Biosphere 2 accomplish its purpose of acting as a self-sustaining environment? Use evidence to explain why or why not.
   b. How is Biosphere 2 different from Biosphere 1 (Earth)?
   c. What do you think scientists learned from Biosphere 2? Use evidence from the reading to describe your thoughts.
   d. If you tried to create your own biosphere, what would you do differently? Document *why* you would make the changes you mention.
4. Read the following paragraph to apply your understanding to a space station.

   Only eight people lived in Biosphere 2. Now imagine you are in the future and scientists have designed a space station that 1,000 people will live in. Your job is to compare three populations and their resource use on different space stations. You will decide what the biggest challenge facing each population would be. The following list explains the same conditions for all three populations.

- A starting population of 1,000 people
- Identical resources including water, soils, plants, animals, microorganisms, and energy sources used for fuel
- Identical environmental conditions such as physical space, available area for growing crops, temperature, and sunlight

Keep in mind that these things may change after people colonize the space station.

5. Get the *Population Description* handout from your teacher and begin reviewing the characteristics of the 3 populations.
6. In your science notebook, document your ideas about the populations by thinking carefully about Questions 6a–i. Then record your answers. After answering each question on your own, use the TSAR strategy to review your responses with another student.
   a. Technology can affect populations in different ways. How are differences in mortality rates and agricultural production related to the availability of technology?
   b. How do you think religious or cultural ideas affect the birthrate?
   c. Consider the difference in the education of the women in each population. How would the fertility rate of each population compare?

Remember that fertility rate is the average number of children born to each woman, and birthrate is the number of births in a year per 1,000 people.

   d. What does the age structure of each colonizing population tell you about how the populations might change across time?
   e. How would each population change across time? Draw graphs to show your prediction. Include highlight comments and a caption with each graph.
   f. Which population do you think will run out of resources first? Explain why.
   g. Which population do you think will be the largest while resources are still plentiful?
   h. Each population will face its own struggle to live comfortably while growing. What do you think will be the biggest challenge for each population? Describe the challenge in your science notebook.

i. How might the space stations manage their resources to support their populations?

Part II: A Space Station Challenge

Now that you have thought about the difficulties that populations might face on a space station, it's time to confront those challenges with your team.

Materials

For each team of 2 students

materials for creating a poster

Process and Procedure

1. Read and discuss the following team goal:

   Goal: Propose the maximum number of people (carrying capacity) who could live comfortably on a space station the size of Earth.
2. Review the scoring rubric and the following considerations as you develop your proposal:
   - Your team must agree upon an operational definition for "living comfortably." Remember that how a population lives determines its influence on ecosystems.
   - The conditions you describe must apply to everyone in the human population. Everyone must be able to use resources at the same rate.
   - Ecosystems on the space station must operate in the same way as ecosystems on Earth. In other words, you can't create ecosystems that function differently from ecosystems on Earth.
3. Discuss as a team the resources and ecosystem services your space station needs. Use the questions listed here as a guide for your discussion. Record ideas from the discussion.
   - What ecosystems are present?
   - What resources are supplied by each ecosystem?
   - What natural processes are supplied by each ecosystem?
4. Discuss as a team what characteristics you think the population should have. Use the questions listed here as a guide for your discussion. Record ideas from the discussion.
   - What is the growth rate of the population?
   - What are some of the resources the population uses?
   - How will the population get the energy it needs?

- Will the population be made up of individuals who consume a lot or those who consume less? Why?
- How does the population affect the ecosystems?

5. Prepare a poster to share your proposal with the class. Your poster should include the following:
   - **a.** Labeled sketches showing the ecosystems on the station and the resources and services that the ecosystems provide
   - **b.** A description of how the population manages its resources and maintains the function of ecosystems
   - **c.** The growth rate of the population and an explanation of why your population has this growth rate
   - **d.** A graph showing how the population will change across time and the carrying capacity for the space station; include highlight comments and a caption
   - **e.** A logical flow from one idea to the next made clear with graphic features
6. Work with a partner to critically review your posters.
   - **a.** Read your poster and provide explanations for your sketches and graphs.
   - **b.** Listen as your partner describes his or her poster. Note any parts that are confusing or could be improved.
   - **c.** Revise your poster based on your partner's comments.
7. Describe how your proposed space station is similar to or different from Earth today.

CHAPTER 16

Sustaining Earth's Environmental Quality

Sustaining Earth's Environmental Quality

Our Earth is changing. It began as a hot, lifeless chunk of rock and gas swirling around a young sun. Now we live on a planet that is full of life and dominated by humans in many respects. Today, we continue to wonder if our world is changing for the better, or for the worse. How could you tell?

Planet Earth is a complex system of cycles. You have learned a lot about cycles in previous chapters. Other cycles that you already know about may include life cycles, weather cycles, rock cycles, and chemical cycles like the carbon cycle. These cycles interact to make our earth system one that can sustain life.

At the same time, we can't become a part of these cycles without affecting earth systems in some way. These disruptions could change our environmental quality. What factors have the potential to change our environmental quality? Do our lifestyles benefit or harm our environment? Should we make changes to ensure that our planet will continue to host life, including human life?

Developing sources of energy is a good example. Look at the chapter opening photo. Wind energy is generated at wind farms, and hydroelectric energy is produced at dams. These sources of energy are independent of fossil fuels. But what other sorts of environmental issues do you think are involved in producing these kinds of energy?

▼ **Cars on a busy highway.** Is your lifestyle changing our environment? Are there changes in your lifestyle that you can make that will help to preserve or improve the quality of our environment?

The way in which we live on Earth contributes to the quality of our atmosphere, our water, and our soil. These in turn affect the overall health of our biosphere. What questions can you formulate about our effect on Earth's environmental quality? What recommendations can you make to the citizens of our planet to promote changes that will benefit both humans and the environment? In this last chapter of your year in science, you have the opportunity to use your learning from this unit and others to answer these questions and participate with your class in a world conference on environmental quality.

Goals for the Chapter

By the end of this chapter, you will be able to answer the following questions:

- How do human activities affect ecosystems?
- How do population growth, resource use, and overconsumption influence environmental quality?
- What is the role of science in improving global environmental quality?

To help you answer these questions and others, you will be involved in the following activities:

ENGAGE	Think Globally
EXPLORE	Pay Me Now, or Pay Me Later
EXPLAIN	The Times, They Are a Changing
ELABORATE	Be Prepared
EVALUATE	A Meeting of the Minds

Use your chapter organizer as a road map for your learning journey through this chapter. Look at it daily to review what you have studied and to see what you will study today and in the days to come.

Linking Question

How are populations, resources, and lifestyles related to environmental issues?

ENGAGE

Think Globally

Key Idea:
A variety of environmental issues affect Earth.

Sustaining Earth's Environmental Quality

EXPLORE

Pay Me Now, or Pay Me Later

Key Ideas:
- Humans affect ecosystems.
- Many factors influence environmental quality.

Linking Question

How can evidence be used to improve environmental quality?

EXPLAIN

The Times, They Are a Changing

Key Ideas:
- Science and technology help us understand how humans affect environmental quality.
- Policy decisions should be based on scientific knowledge, but are influenced by societal issues and funding as well.

EVALUATE

A Meeting of the Minds

Key Ideas:

- Humans affect ecosystems.
- Many factors influence environmental quality.
- Science and technology can only indicate what can happen, not what should happen.
- Policy decisions should be based on scientific knowledge; however science alone cannot resolve global challenges.

Linking Question

How can I use what I have learned to demonstrate my understanding of environmental quality?

CHAPTER 16 Major Concepts

- **Humans affect basic processes in ecosystems.**
- **Many factors such as population growth, resource use, and overconsumption influence environmental quality.**
- **Science and technology can only indicate what can happen, not what should happen.**
- **Policy decisions should be based on scientific knowledge; however science alone cannot resolve global challenges.**

ELABORATE

Be Prepared

Key Idea:

Communicating scientific knowledge involves organizing information, developing explanations, and making revisions based on comments.

Linking Question

How can recommendations be effectively communicated?

ENGAGE

Think Globally

You and your classmates are invited to attend the upcoming Global Conference on Environmental Quality. This conference will be held in the evaluate activity, *A Meeting of the Minds*. The conference will address environmental issues related to sustaining environmental quality on Earth. Before you can participate in the conference, however, you have some work to do. Work individually or in teams, as instructed by your teacher, as you prepare for this conference.

Materials

For each student

access to the Web

scientific or environmental articles in journals or newspapers

1 *A Meeting of the Minds Scoring Rubric* handout

Process and Procedure

1. Become familiar with conferences that address our environment. Use the Web to search for environmental conferences. Then complete Steps 1a–d.
   a. Find a conference that you think addresses global environmental issues and access the conference program.
   b. Record in your notebook the sponsor of the conference. Consider if there are any biases that would be apparent in the conference with this particular sponsor. Record your ideas in your notebook.

Bias is an unfair preference for or dislike of something. Depending on the sponsor of the conference, the invited speakers could show bias toward the environmental issue.

   c. Make a list of the types of presenters who are participating in the conference. Examples include college professors, scientists, business leaders, and government officials.
   d. Consider whether or not there are any special requirements for the presentations. If so, what are they? You might find this type of information in a "call for papers" or with other preliminary arrangements for the conference.

If you do not find this information for the conference you selected, choose a conference that is scheduled for some time in the future.

2. Think about the conference that your class will hold in a few days as you complete Steps 2a–c.

a. In what ways might you model the environmental conferences that you read about on the Web?
b. Think about the logistics of the conference as well as the presentations. Which conferences appeal to you and why?
c. Write down at least 3 ideas you have for your class conference. Be prepared to share them in a class discussion.

3. Share your ideas about the conference in a class discussion led by your teacher.
4. Gather information related to environmental issues in Steps 4a–b. These should be issues that affect environmental quality on a local, regional, national, or even global level.
   a. Use the Web and your library to find articles about environmental issues. Your teacher will assign a time frame for you to complete this step.
   b. Collect 3–5 articles about different environmental issues. Be sure to collect articles about local, regional, national, and global issues.

You should be able to describe how each issue you choose affects some natural system. For example, say you choose the overuse of pesticides or pesticide runoff. These issues would affect the water system.

5. Display the articles collected in Step 4b around the room. Arrange the articles in groups according to topic, region, or another factor that your class identifies. Review the articles in their groups.
6. If you have been working individually, choose a team of 2 or 3 other classmates and complete Steps 6a–c.
   a. Choose 1 of the groups of articles that the class collected. Review the articles in that group.
   b. Generate at least 3 questions related to environmental issues that can be answered by science. These questions may relate to population growth, resources, lifestyles, or another issue linked to how humans affect the environment. Record these questions in your science notebook.

You may want to visit other teams and review their articles.

   c. Be prepared to share your questions in a class discussion.

7. Participate in a class discussion and complete Steps 7a–c.
   a. Record the categories your teacher has written on the board.
   b. Share your questions with the class and listen as other teams report their questions.
   c. Decide as a class how to group the questions in 1 of the categories on the board.

8. Review the handout *A Meeting of the Minds Scoring Rubric.* This is the rubric that your teacher will use to evaluate your performance throughout this chapter. Think about what is expected of you to receive the highest credit for your work.

If you have questions about the scoring rubric and how your teacher will use the rubric to evaluate your work at the conference, be sure to ask them now.

9. Listen as your teacher discusses the timeline you will follow as you work toward the goals in the rubric. Record important due dates in your science notebook.

Reflect and Connect

Work with your team to answer the following questions. Record your best ideas in your science notebook.

1. Look at the group of articles that your team selected in Step 6 and answer Questions 1a–b.
   a. What patterns do you see in your group of articles?

   Examples of patterns you should look for include the types of issues; issues that relate to the same natural system, for example, all the articles concerning water quality; patterns that indicate that environmental quality is improving or declining; and patterns of issues that all target the same industry.

   b. Are the issues the same or different for articles at a local level compared with those at a regional, national, or global level? Justify and explain your answer.
2. Use the scoring rubric to answer Questions 2a–d in your science notebook.
   a. What constitutes "sound evidence," which is referred to in the first task on the rubric? Where will you find this evidence?
   b. What questions do you have about the science principles listed in the second task on the rubric?
   c. What are your initial ideas about how you will present your recommendations?
   d. Consider the strengths of each member of your team. What types of presentation aids can you use that will draw on these strengths? For example, you may have a team member who is an artist or is very good at designing computer presentations. Use these strengths to select the type of aids you will use in your presentation.

Pay Me Now, or Pay Me Later

EXPLORE

You have discovered that many environmental issues affect Earth. Each of these issues is tied to a human activity (figure 16.1). For example, exhaust from cars contributes to air pollution, and some farming practices cause loss of topsoil. These actions result in reduced air and soil quality. As you prepare for the Global Conference on Environmental Quality, you will focus on this relationship between human activity and environmental quality. In *Pay Me Now, or Pay Me Later*, your team continues its preparation by deciding what environmental quality issue it will address. Then you will generate questions about that issue and collect evidence to answer your questions. Throughout your preparations, focus your work to answer the question, "How is this environmental issue related to global environmental quality?"

▲ **Figure 16.1 Center-pivot irrigation.** Agriculture has become a vital way for humans to produce the food that we need. In what ways do you think agriculture and food production relates to ecosystems?

Materials

For each team of 3 students

access to the Web

3 *A Meeting of the Minds Scoring Rubric* handouts

Process and Procedure

1. Get into your team and read over the articles and questions collected by the class in Steps 4 and 6 of the engage activity, *Think Globally*. Discuss what environmental issues interest you the most and briefly describe them in your science notebook.
2. Choose 1 environmental issue related to environmental quality to present at the conference. Remember, you are participating in a global conference, so the issue must be common to people in all parts of the world or be a local issue of global concern.

Examples of issues include managing waste, contaminants from industry, road or agricultural runoff, and clearing forests or grasslands for other uses.

3. Generate at least 3 questions about the environmental issue that can be answered by science.

You might be able to adjust or improve upon one of the questions from the engage activity. Be sure that your questions are related.

4. Have your teacher approve your questions.
5. Discuss as a team what information you need to answer your questions. Record your ideas in your science notebook.
6. Develop a plan for gathering evidence for the global conference by completing Steps 6a–e.
   a. Review the *A Meeting of the Minds Scoring Rubric* handout.
   b. Discuss what evidence you need to gather about populations, resources, and lifestyles.
   c. Discuss what you need to know about how the issue you chose affects air, water, and soil quality.
   d. Decide as a team which member will gather what evidence from Steps 6b–c.
   e. Record your plan in your science notebook.

Recall that an important part of this conference is justifying your recommendations with evidence.

7. Carry out your plan and collect evidence about the environmental issue you chose by completing Steps 7a–c.
   a. Use the Web and your library to find evidence about the environmental issue. Your teacher will assign a time frame for you to complete this step.
   b. Keep a list of references including the Web sites and other sources you use.
   c. Record in your notebook a summary of each article that you will use for your presentation. Include the reference for the article.

▲ **Figure 16.2 Group of students working.** Work with your team as the students in this investigation are doing.

Reflect and Connect

Answer the following questions individually in your science notebook.

1. Describe what you have learned about the environmental issue you chose by completing Steps 1a–c.
   a. Give 1 example of the relationship between human activity and environmental quality. Use something you learned while researching information about your environmental issue.
   b. Explain how humans affected environmental quality.

c. Propose what humans could do differently to improve environmental quality.

2. List 1 or 2 new questions you have about the environmental issue after having gathered your evidence.

You do not need to search for evidence to answer these questions. Simply reflect on what you have learned and what you are curious about.

The Times, They Are a Changing

EXPLAIN

Soon you will be making decisions about your life after high school. Will you go to college? If so, what information do you need to make the best decision? You would probably investigate the colleges and universities that interest you. You may base your decision on location, academic programs, or cost. Even if you know everything there is to know about the university, the decision is yours. You likely will make that decision based on information you have gathered.

Policy makers go through a similar process when addressing global challenges such as sustaining environmental quality (figures 16.3 and 16.4). Science provides society with information about what *can* happen, not about what *should* happen. In *The Times, They Are a Changing*, you will go through this process as you continue to prepare for the conference. You will work in your team to develop a set of recommendations based on the evidence you gathered in the explore activity, *Pay Me Now, or Pay Me Later.*

▲ **Figure 16.3 Oil rig.** An oil rig is a structure used to drill for and extract oil. How do you think this process of oil extraction affects environmental quality?

◄ **Figure 16.4 Growing populations.** As populations in cities increase, how will they affect consumption rates and pollution?

Materials

For each team of 3 students

access to the Web

3 *A Meeting of the Minds Scoring Rubric* handouts

Process and Procedure

1. Review the evidence you collected in Steps 7a–c in the explore activity and cross-check it with the plan you developed.
   a. Do you have evidence showing how populations, resources, and lifestyles are related to the environmental issue?
   b. Do you have evidence showing how the environmental issue affects environmental quality?

You might have found that the issue affects air, water, and soil quality, or only 1 of these. Perhaps the issue affects environmental quality in another way such as reducing biodiversity—the diversity of organisms in an area.

   c. Decide whether you have enough evidence to meet the needs of your plan. If you do, continue with Step 2. If not, spend some more time gathering information.

Consult with your teacher before going on to Step 2.

2. Organize the evidence you have gathered about the environmental issue by following these guidelines.
   a. Use tables, graphs, or other visual strategies to arrange any data you have collected.
   b. Decide as a team how you can sort the evidence into types or categories of evidence.

Be sure to document your decisions in your notebook, as well as any discussions you have as a team.

3. Revisit the questions you developed in Step 3 of the explore activity. Use the evidence you gathered to answer your questions. Record your answers in your science notebook.

Consider collecting more information if you were unable to answer one of your questions.

4. Review the scoring rubric handout, specifically the task of making a set of evidence-based recommendations.
5. Read *Making London a More Sustainable City* to learn about the strategies of the mayor of London for sustaining environmental quality. This short reading might give you some ideas to develop in more detail when making your recommendations.

READING

Making London a More Sustainable City

In October 2005, representatives from 20 world cities met at the World Cities Leadership Climate Change Summit. The summit brought together city leaders to discuss climate change and how to reduce greenhouse emissions. Some of the mayor of London's strategies are outlined here.

Air quality

- Reduce traffic by charging a fee for traveling roads in central London during business hours and by improving public transportation and conditions for walking and cycling.
- Reduce emissions by targeting reductions in the most polluting vehicles and by increasing the use of cleaner fuels and vehicles.

Biodiversity

- Increase open space in new housing developments and along transport routes.
- Improve water quality and maintain wildlife habitat.

Energy

- Use less energy.
- Use renewable energy sources.
- Investigate more efficient energy production.

Water

- Install water meters in households that currently don't have them.
- Provide the public with tips on water conservation.

Waste

- Strategically build new waste management facilities and provide equal access to reuse and recycling centers (figure 16.5).

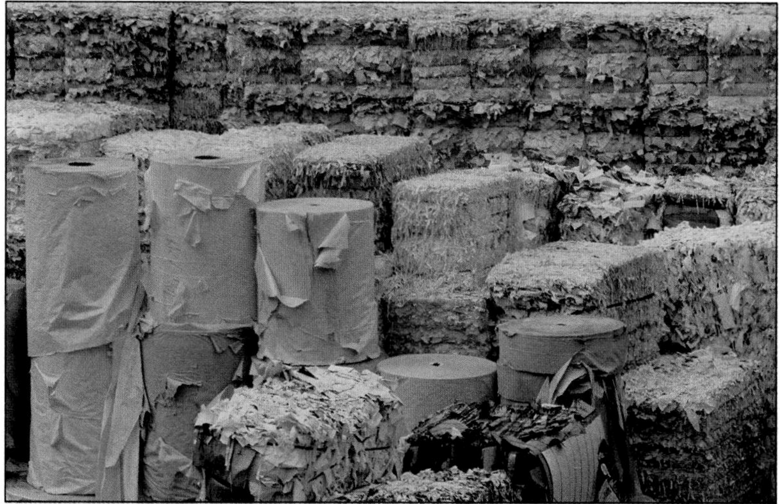

▲ **Figure 16.5 Recycling.** This photograph shows paper and cardboard packed at a recycling center. Recycling paper and cardboard reduces waste in landfills. What other measures could be taken to reduce waste?

6. Discuss with your team what recommendations you might want to consider after completing your research. Recommendations you plan to present at the conference should describe what steps could be taken to sustain Earth's environmental quality. Record your team's ideas for recommendations in your science notebook.
7. Agree as a team on a set of 3 or 4 recommendations for the Global Conference on Environmental Quality. Your recommendations
   - must be based on the evidence you gathered about environmental issues,
   - should be challenging but feasible, and
   - should reflect the relationship between human activity and environmental quality.

Reflect and Connect

Answer the following questions individually in your science notebook.

1. Describe how 1 of your recommendations would change human activities and improve environmental quality.

Each team member should choose a different recommendation.

2. Answer Questions 2a–b about making and justifying recommendations to sustain environmental quality.
   a. How did gathering scientific evidence help you develop your set of recommendations?
   b. Can scientific evidence and technology alone solve environmental quality issues? Why or why not?

To learn more about science and technology, read the sidebar *Science and Technology*.

3. Recall the reading about making London a more sustainable city. Write in your science notebook a profession or occupation for each of the five categories of recommendations that would help London be more sustainable (air quality, biodiversity, energy, water, and waste).

Be prepared to share your list of professions with the class.

Science and Technology

SIDEBAR

Certainly you've heard the phrase "science and technology." You see it in the news and hear it at school. And you've heard a lot about science and technology in this program. These two words often appear together. But what do we really mean by science and technology, and how does this relate to you? Are there important distinctions? You bet.

Both science and technology are vital to understanding our physical world and to solving human problems. Science begins in questions about the natural world. This is shown in the figure below. Those who use science get information by inquiring and by proposing and testing explanations about the natural world. Examples of broad fields in science include the life, physical, earth, and space sciences.

In contrast, technology stems from problems and challenges that humans face in their environment. Technology is more than shiny equipment or computers. Technology is a process of using problem-solving strategies to propose and develop solutions (see figure). Examples of technology fields include areas

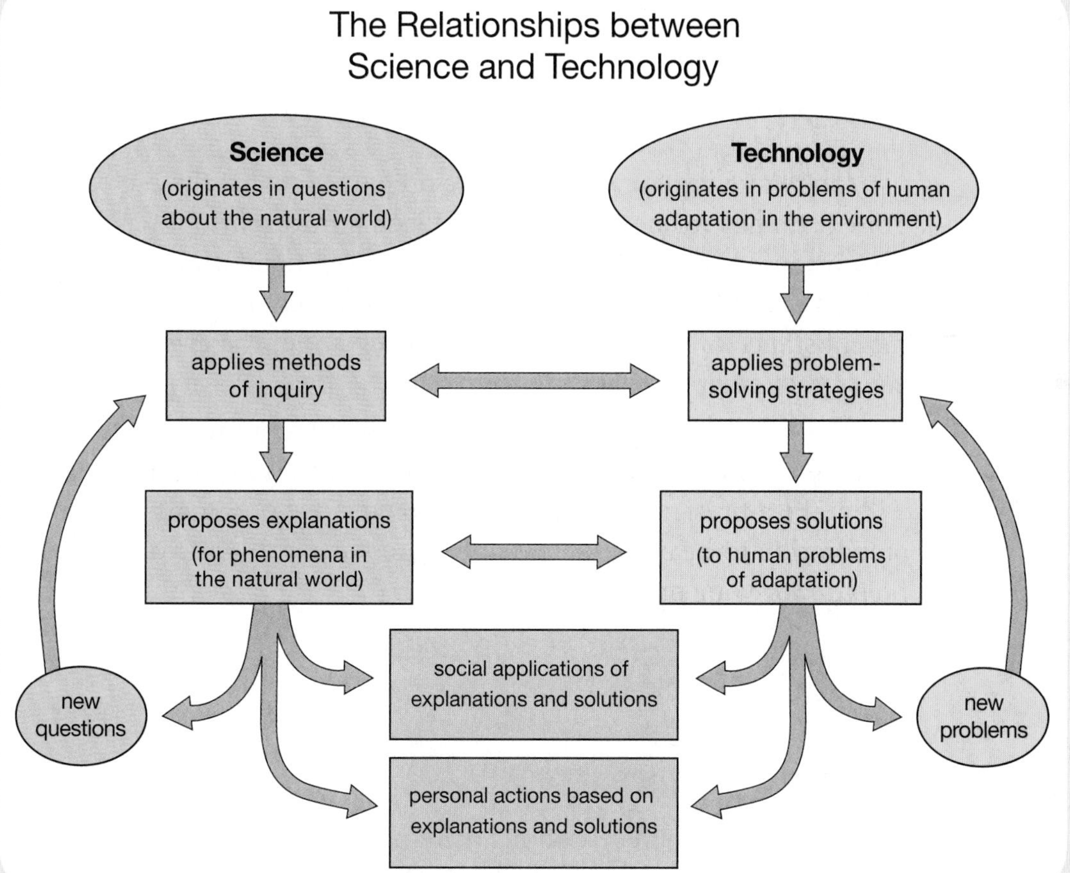

▲ **Relationship between science and technology.** This diagram shows that science focuses on explaining the natural world, whereas technology centers on solutions to human problems. Both science and technology join to solve problems of society.

Science and Technology, continued

of computer science, information technology, and engineering. Thus, technology complements science. Using science and technology together helps you solve different kinds of problems for society. And each can also generate engaging new questions.

The Apollo missions to the Moon are a great example of science and technology. The missions were undertaken to answer very fundamental scientific questions. These included questions about lunar geology, the origin of the Moon, moon-planet systems, and the evolution of our solar system.

Answering these questions required that we obtain rocks from the Moon. To do that, many technological challenges would have to be solved to get astronaut-geologists to the Moon, collect the lunar rocks, and return the samples and astronaut-geologists safely to Earth. Virtually all obstacles were cleared for a series of successful missions. Technologies developed and tested in the 1960s formed a foundation for the many exciting NASA missions occurring today.

ELABORATE

Be Prepared

You're moving forward on your preparations for the big conference. Your team has formed questions, collected information, reached conclusions, and is ready to present its recommendations. Each of these tasks is crucial to effective scientific communication. They represent the substance of what you want to convey about the effect of human activity on environmental quality.

Now it's time to share your findings and recommendations with a larger community of concerned scientists. To do this, your team will make a presentation at the conference. But presentations require preparation to be effective. So in this activity, you and your team will prepare for your presentation.

Materials

none

Process and Procedure

Effective team presentations demand strong team communications. This involves ensuring that each member understands his or her responsibilities, performs those responsibilities, and gets feedback from team members. You will begin by working individually and in a team to assemble a first draft of your presentation. Then you will use team feedback to improve the presentation.

1. Review the handout *A Meeting of the Minds Scoring Rubric* again to be clear about the goals and requirements of your presentation. To help you focus your presentation even more, consider the criteria in Steps 1a–c.
   a. The presentation will demonstrate the connection between findings and recommendations.
   b. The presentation will include 3 forms of communication:
      - Language (written reports and oral presentation)
      - Spatial representation (graphs, charts, models, demonstrations, and posters)
      - Mathematical representation (formulas, data, spreadsheets, and proofs)

There can be some overlap of forms. For example, graphs should have labels and captions, which involve language.

   c. The presentation will last no more than 10 minutes or a time specified by your teacher.
2. Decide as a team which member will be responsible for each segment of the presentation.
3. Develop each segment of the presentation according to an agreed-upon time schedule.
4. Present your individual segment to your team, using the following team roles:
   - Listeners: Nonpresenting team members listen to the presentation and generate questions they think audience members might ask. Listeners also use the scoring rubric to evaluate this segment of the presentation.
   - Presenter: Answers questions posed by the listeners in his or her science notebook and adjusts the segment of the presentation appropriately.

Remember that responses should be based on what you know about populations, resources, and environmental quality.

5. Meet as a team and reach consensus on what changes to make based on feedback from Step 4.
6. Record how and why you made changes to your original presentation.

Remember, it is a good practice to record any changes to your original ideas in a different-colored pen or pencil.

Reflect and Connect

1. Answer the focus question from the introduction to the explore activity: "How is this environmental issue related

to global environmental quality?" Base your answer on the environmental issue that you have chosen for your presentation.

2. If you had more time to spend researching an environmental issue, what other information would you want to gather?

EVALUATE

A Meeting of the Minds

The opening day of the conference has arrived! During the next few days, think about the significance of your findings and recommendations. You interact with the environment every day of your life and make important decisions about sustaining Earth. Keep this in mind as you participate in the conference and learn from your classmates.

Materials

For the entire class

assorted presentation aids

A Meeting of the Minds Scoring Rubric handout

Process and Procedure

Scientists frequently present their ideas and recommendations to their peers (figure 16.6). You and your classmates are ready to participate in the conference for which you have been preparing during the last 2 weeks. Make the most of your experience as a conference participant.

1. Meet with your team to go over the last-minute details of your presentation. Be sure you are ready when it is your team's turn to present.
2. Listen to the introductory comments that launch the conference. Record the big ideas that you hear.
3. As each team presents, listen carefully to its recommendations. Record the important ideas along with the justification from science and technology for each idea the team presents.

▼ **Figure 16.6 Scientist making a presentation.** What are some important things to consider when making a presentation?

4. When each team finishes, think about 1 or 2 questions you might have about something you heard. Participate in a brief class discussion of the group's presentation.
5. Using the scoring rubric, assign each team a score, based on what you heard.
6. When all teams have presented, participate in a class discussion of the best ideas that you heard. Use the following criteria as a guide:
   - The recommendations are based on principles of science and technology.
   - There is evidence that these recommendations have a good chance of working.
   - The recommendations are feasible.
7. At the end of the class discussion, revisit the questions that each of you asked in the engage and explore activities. Discuss as a class whether you are better able to answer these questions now than you were before you began this chapter.
8. As a class, agree on the top 3–5 recommendations from across the teams and a convincing set of justifications (figure 16.7).

Reflect and Connect

Answer the following questions individually in your science notebook.

1. If you could add 1 more recommendation to the set of recommendations that the class agreed on, what would it be and why?
2. Think about the set of class recommendations, including the one you added from the last step. What might the world look like 50 years from now if people began implementing the recommendations next year?
3. What might the situation be 50 years from now if none of these recommendations is implemented? Cite evidence to support your prediction.

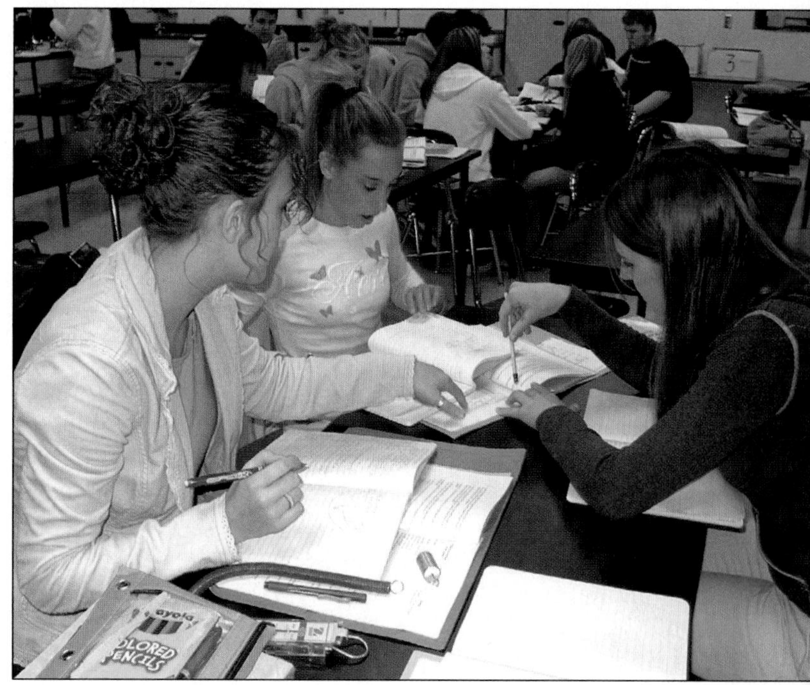

▲ **Figure 16.7**
Working together. How does communicating with your teammates and class help you decide on the best recommendations?

1 HOW TO Use Chapter Organizers

Some of the skills you will improve this year will be your skills of organization. You know that an organized room or file system is easier to work with than one that is disorganized. Knowledge can be organized as well. You will work this year at organizing your thoughts and knowledge in a science notebook. In addition, you will learn to use the organizational tools that the student book provides. You will notice one of these tools as you look through your student book. You will see that we have included a chapter organizer at the beginning of each chapter. This organizer will help you see the big picture. Your understanding will deepen and strengthen as you see that what you have learned today connects to what you will learn tomorrow.

Work with a partner to complete the following tasks. Record your answers and thoughts in your science notebook. Organize your science notebook by including the title "using the chapter organizers."

1. Look through the table of contents of your student book and find a chapter title that most interests you. Do not turn to your chapter yet; just look at the title. Make sure that you and your partner choose *different* chapters. If you both like the same one, work out a plan to have 2 different chapters. Learning to compromise in a group is another skill you will develop this year. Complete the following tasks based on the chapter you select.
   - **a.** Explain to your partner why you think this chapter will be interesting to you. Listen as your partner explains his or her thinking to you. Record the title of your chapter and at least 1 statement explaining why you think this chapter will be interesting.
   - **b.** Think of as many concepts and ideas as you can that might be included in your chapter. List these concepts in your science notebook.
   - **c.** Share your list with your partner and listen as your partner shares with you. Think about your partner's chapter selection. Can you add to his or her list of topics? Add new topics to your list that emerge during this discussion.

2. Turn to your chapter and find the chapter organizer. It is found at the beginning of the chapter. Look at it carefully. All the chapters in this book follow the BSCS 5E instructional model. The 5Es provide a structure for active learning that will have you *doing* and *understanding* science, not just reading about it. Taken together, the

5Es will help you build a strong understanding of science. Can you find each of the 5Es included in your chapter organizer? List them in your science notebook.

3. What do you think each *E* represents in the learning sequence? Record your ideas in your science notebook.

Include in your answer what you think you should be doing in each activity. For example, what will you be doing in the explore activity? How will you be interacting with your teacher and with your teammates?

4. Every *E* is an activity that builds on the previous one and helps prepare you for the next one—the next *E*. Do you notice that between each activity there is a linking question? Discuss with your partner what you think the purpose of the linking question might be. Record your best ideas in your science notebook.

5. Look back at your original ideas from Steps 1b–c about the concepts you thought would be included in your chapter.
   a. Circle the ones that appear to be covered in this chapter.
   b. Look at the other chapters in this same unit. Highlight topics that will be covered in those other chapters.
   c. What feature of the chapter organizer helped you determine the topics covered in your chapter?

6. Look at another chapter organizer from your book. Discuss with your partner how this organizer can help you with your learning. Record at least 3 ways that you can use the chapter organizers to enhance your learning.

7. Look at your list. Are there things that you will do at the beginning of the chapter, during the middle of the chapter, and at the end of the chapter? Add them to your list so that you have at least 1 from each place.

8. From the chapter organizer that you chose in Step 1, record what you think is the main idea of that chapter. Try to sum it up in 1 sentence.

9. What part or parts of the chapter organizer did you use in Step 8 to write your main idea sentence? What part of the organizer helped you the most?

2 HOW TO Use the Science Notebook

In *BSCS Science: An Inquiry Approach*, you will use a science notebook on a regular basis. Science notebooks serve many purposes. They provide a place to record data, take notes, reflect on your progress, or respond to questions. This science notebook will become your permanent record of your work, and you will refer to it often during discussions and assessments. The more complete your science notebook is, the more valuable it will be for you.

Your science notebook should be a spiral notebook or a hardcover book that is permanently bound. (Do not use a loose-leaf notebook or a spiral notebook with perforated pages that tear out.) A notebook with square-grid (graph paper) pages will make any graphing that you do much easier.

The following sections describe the major ways in which you will use your science notebook in this program.

Recording Data

Science depends on accurate data. No one—not even the original observer—can trust the accuracy of confusing, vague, or incomplete data. Scientific record keeping is the process by which you maintain neat, organized, and accurate records of your observations and data. Use a pen to record data. Although your interpretation of the data may change, *the original data are a permanent record.* If you learn new or additional things and your thinking changes, make changes in your science notebook in a different-colored pen or pencil. That way, both you and your teacher have a record of your ongoing learning.

Keep records in a diary form, and record your name and the date at the beginning of each entry. Keep the records of each activity separate. Be brief but to the point when recording data in words. It may not be necessary to use complete sentences, but single words seldom are descriptive enough to represent accurately what you have observed or done.

Sometimes the easiest way to record data is in the form of a drawing or sketch. Such drawings need not be works of art, but they should be accurate representations of what you have observed. Place your sketches or drawings in the middle of the page, leaving room for captions, revisions, and highlights. Keep the drawings simple, use a hard pencil, and include clearly written labels. Often, the easiest way to record numerical data is in the form of a table. When you record data for counts or measurements with numbers, include the units of the measurements you used, for example, degrees Celsius or centimeters.

Do not record your data on other papers and then copy them into your science notebook. Doing so may increase neatness, but it will decrease accuracy. Your science notebook is your book, and blots and stains are a normal circumstance of field and laboratory work.

You will do much of your laboratory work as a member of a team. Your science notebook, therefore, will contain data that other team members have contributed. Keep track of the source of those observations by circling (or recording in a different color) the data that others reported.

Responding to Questions

When you answer discussion or activity questions in your science notebook, record the date and the activity title. Then number each response. You also may find it useful to record the questions. Sometimes you will respond to questions individually and sometimes with your team; indicate whether your responses are your own or those of your team. As you are writing your responses, practice writing in complete sentences; this will help you when you synthesize and present ideas. After each answer that you write, leave a blank space where you can add questions or comments that arise as your understanding grows.

Taking Notes

Always begin with the date. Then record the source of information. Often, this is a person or a book, but it could be a video, a Web site, or a computer program. When recording notes, start each new idea on a new line. Try to group related ideas under broad headings that will help you remember the important ideas and how they are connected. Write down more than you think you will need; it is hard to make sense of a few words when you look back at them later. Include diagrams and charts to clarify ideas.

It is often valuable to take notes during team and class discussions as well as when your teacher is presenting ideas or instructions. In addition, taking notes in your science notebook as you read helps you better absorb the written information.

You can use the information in your science notebook to prepare for discussions or to review what you have learned. At times, you also will use the information that you have recorded in your science notebook to complete assessment activities.

Keeping Track of Your Questions

Often, as you read or work through an activity, a question will come to mind or you will find that you are confused about something. If you cannot talk with your teammates or your teacher right away, jot down your question or confusion in your science notebook so that you will remember to ask about it when you have the opportunity. You also may use this technique to record questions that you want to answer yourself.

Keeping Track of Your Responsibilities

Because you will use your science notebook every day in science class, this notebook is a good place to record your class assignments and responsibilities. Each day, you may want to record these in red in the upper corner of your science notebook page.

Using Your Science Notebook during Assessment

At times throughout this program, you will use your science notebook during assessments—both ongoing assessments, such as class discussions and team presentations, and more formal, end-of-unit assessments. Your teacher will collect your science notebook periodically to assess your progress. Using a science notebook for assessment will be a rewarding experience if your entries are complete, detailed, and well organized. Remember to make it easy for someone else reading your science notebook to understand what you have recorded. Use blank space to separate activities, notes, and data. This will make your science notebook easier to assess, and it will provide space for you to add new information if needed. Keep this in mind as you make entries in your science notebook.

Learning Strategies

Use Multiple Forms of Representation

Sometimes what you're asked to do in school seems like a waste of your time. How do you evaluate whether it's worthwhile? One way is to examine the evidence. Does what you're being asked to do benefit you now and in the future?

Using multiple forms of representation for the same information is an example. That is, your teacher asks you to make a sketch of what you read, convert a line graph into an equation, or write a paragraph about lab observations. Why represent what you know in more than one way?

Generating different ways to represent knowledge helps you solve problems, enhances your memory, and improves your ability to communicate. Just think how these outcomes affect your performance in school and ultimately in your chosen profession. You can start learning now how to represent knowledge in a variety of ways. First, become aware of the common forms of representation. Second, know which situations use what forms of representation. Third, practice translating among the forms.

1. Read the table in figure H3A.1 and study the example it contains.
2. Practice generating your own tables, similar to this one, for the following scenarios.
   - **a.** A comparison of the number of males to females in your classroom
   - **b.** The force of wind needed to move a sailboat
   - **c.** How fast trees grow

Forms of representation	Source	Example
Language	Textbooks, science notebook, the Web, magazines, text messages, conversations, lectures, music lyrics	Ants are ten percent of the animal biomass on Earth.
Mathematics/Logic	Equations, science notebook, proportions, comparisons, percents, differences, summation	$\frac{M_{ants}}{M_{all\ animals\ in\ biomass}} \times 100 = 10$ Key: M = mass
Spatial/Dimensional	Sketches, charts, real objects, maps, demonstrations, science notebook, lab equipment	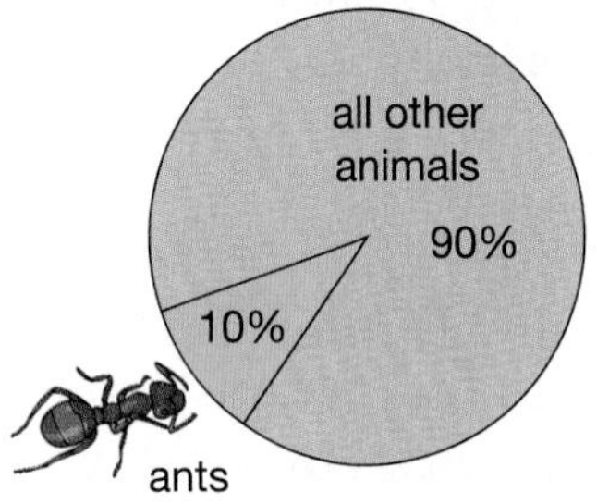 all other animals 90%; 10% ants

▲ **Figure H3A.1 Forms of representation.**

Learning Strategies

Use the Think-Share-Advise-Revise (TSAR) Strategy

Does learning stop when your paper comes back with a grade on it? It shouldn't. The same is true for experiences *during* class. That is, you get the most out of school when you get ongoing feedback on your thinking, then revise your original ideas to reflect what you've learned. This cycle of thinking on your own, sharing your ideas, getting advice from others, and revising what you think is essential in the workplace as well as in school. Work with a partner to learn about the think-share-advise-revise (TSAR) strategy.

1. Chapter 2, *Collision Course*, has an example of using the TSAR strategy for answering a science question. Find it in the engage activity, *Forces Make a Lovely Pair* (p. 52), and read through the process.

2. Match each step from chapter 2 to the descriptions listed in the table in figure H3B.1. You'll see generalized tasks in the table and specific examples in chapter 2. The combination of the tasks and the examples provides you with why, what, and how to use the TSAR process. Use this strategy for any problem, especially in team situations.

Step	What you do	What others do
Think	• access what you already know and understand and the skills you already have • work individually • pinpoint what you do and don't know • generate questions • document your thoughts in your science notebook	• respect your private thinking time
Share	• read aloud your thinking to a teammate • explain any diagrams, charts, or sketches • respond to requests for clarification	• listen attentively • ask questions respectfully
Advise	• offer suggestions, elaborations, or alternative explanations to what your teammate read • respond to questions about your advice	• listen to your advice without interruption • ask for clarification if needed
Revise	• record what you changed in your original answer in response to advice • record why you changed your original answer in response to advice (remember, not all advice leads to changes)	• respect your private time to revise your first thoughts

▲ **Figure H3B.1 TSAR table.**

Learning Strategies

Use and Create Organizing Tables

Organizing information helps you see patterns and better understand text materials. There are many different kinds of organizing tables. For example, you can use tables to organize data in an investigation, to make comparisons and analogies, and to show relationships between information in reading passages. Here are 3 common organizing tables you might use.

1. *T-tables* show relationships between information listed in the horizontal rows. T-tables can have 2, 3, or even 4 columns. You can use T-tables to show similarities or differences or to organize what you know before or after you read.

Reading about genetics

Fact or idea I read	Questions I have about the fact or idea

▲ **Figure H3C.1 T-table example.** This is an example of a T-table you could use as you read about genetics. As you read a passage, record your ideas in a table to help you organize your thoughts.

2 *Analogy maps* are a special type of table that allows you to connect new ideas with ideas you are familiar with.

Feature of a road trip	is like . . .	aspect of scientific inquiry . . .	because . . .
A detour on the road	is like . . .	getting unexpected results from an investigation	when you encounter something you do not expect, you change the way you approach your investigation.
Circling back on a portion of the road to look for a turn	is like . . .	adjusting the design of an investigation	you return to your design and adjust it to get the results you need to answer your question.
Trying different routes on a road trip	is like . . .		
Encountering car trouble and returning home	is like . . .		
Abandoning your car on the road	is like . . .		
Starting your trip and changing the destination	is like . . .		

▲ **Figure H3C.2 Analogy map example.** This analogy map is one you could use to compare a road trip you might take with the process of scientific inquiry.

3 *Data tables* provide a place to record observations or data from an investigation. You can create graphs from the information in these tables or interpret your data directly from the tables themselves.

Material	Volume of liquid sample (mL)	Mass of cylinder with liquid sample (g)	Mass of cylinder alone (g)
Sample A	100	142.54	2.54
Sample B	100	93.21	2.54
Sample C	100	83.44	2.54

▲ **Figure H3C.3 Data table example.** Data tables are a place to record both qualitative and quantitative observations or data from an investigation. This data table shows data recorded as students conduct an investigation about density. The data can be used to make a graph or do calculations.

Learning Strategies

3D HOW TO Use and Create Venn Diagrams

Venn diagrams are a powerful strategy for comparing topics or concepts. You can use them to visually show similarities and differences. A Venn diagram is made up of two or three overlapping circles. Each circle represents one topic or concept. The region inside each circle lists characteristics of the topic or concept. The part of the circle that overlaps contains characteristics common to both concepts. See the example in figure H3D.1. Then try creating your own Venn diagrams using Steps 1–5 to help you.

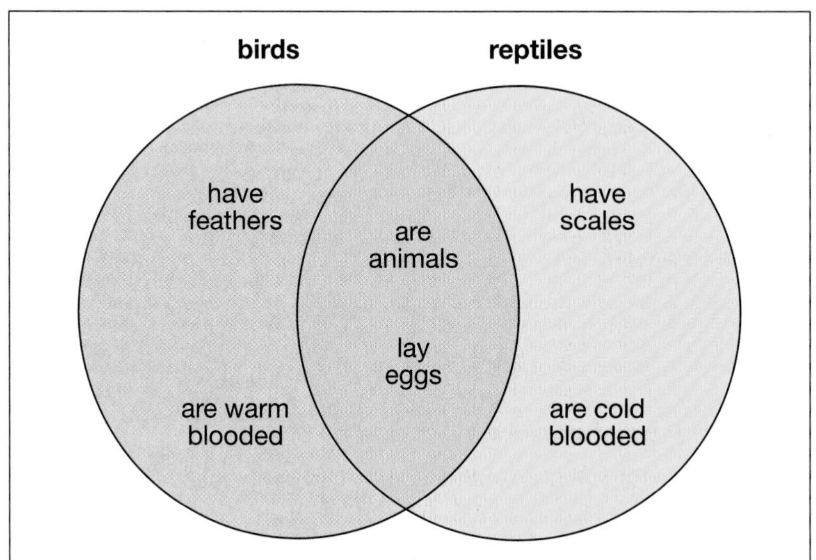

▲ **Figure H3D.1 Venn diagram comparing birds and reptiles.**

Venn Diagram Guidelines

1. Draw 2 overlapping circles like the ones shown in figure H3D.1. Use at least a half sheet of paper for the circles to give you enough room to write inside the circles.
2. Label each circle with the topics or concepts you are comparing.
3. Identify the important characteristics of the topics or concepts.
4. Write the characteristics that are specific to only 1 of the 2 topics or concepts in the circle, outside the overlapping area.
5. Write the characteristics that are common to the topics or concepts in the area where the circles overlap.

Learning Strategies

Make Better Observations

You were not born knowing how to make good-quality scientific observations. But you can learn. Effective scientists have made good-quality observations for centuries. The following questions related to making observations are not a step-by-step procedure. Rather, they are guidelines (in the form of questions) to help you *think* your way through observations. When done well, observations help you link what you see to what it means—the very heart of science.

Observation Guidelines

- How is each procedural step related to the focus question or problem you are investigating?
- What is the best way to represent the initial conditions (with tables, sketches, graphs, equations, or sentences)?
- What is the best way to record the final conditions?
- What is the best way to record what happens *during* the investigation?

You need to focus on what is happening during the investigation, but sometimes changes occur very quickly. In these cases, you must plan carefully so that you are not distracted by writing down your data.

- How do you know that the changes you see are the result of the variable that you are manipulating and not other variables?
- Will multiple trials increase your confidence in what you see?
- What is the best way to keep a record of your initial ideas and how those ideas change during the course of the investigation?

Learning Strategies

Write Highlight Comments and Captions

How do you make sense of charts, diagrams, graphs, and sketches? You do what scientists have been doing for centuries. You note what you see, then you try to say what it means. This process helps you connect evidence to interpretations—a hallmark of scientific inquiry.

Highlight comments help you link observations from graphs, charts, and other spatial forms of representation to possible interpretations. Captions assemble highlight comments into sentences that form a coherent paragraph. This paragraph tells the story of the graph, chart, or sketch and communicates the "executive summary" of the essential understandings displayed. The combination of highlight comments and captions helps you communicate scientific information with increasing effectiveness, improving your performance and deepening your understanding of the natural world.

Suppose you investigated the uptake of a nutrient by a tree over 24 hours. How would you make sense of the data? Follow the steps in figure H3F.1 and use them as a general guide for any graph, chart, diagram, or sketch you make.

Commenting step	Example and comments
1. Look for changes, trends, or differences. Draw an arrow to each of these you notice in the graph.	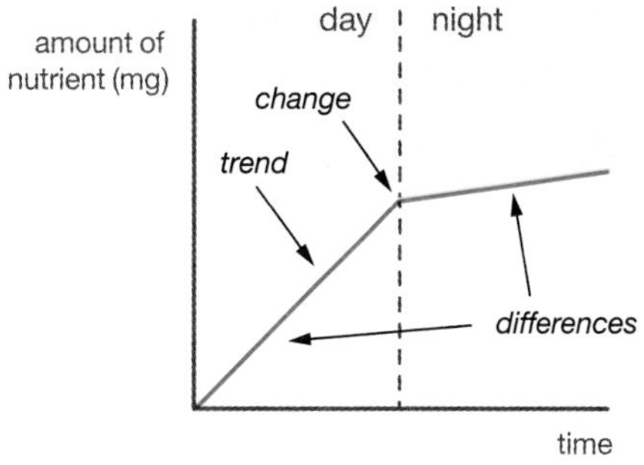 amount of nutrient (mg) day / night *change* *trend* *differences* time
2. Write what you see. Each arrow has a different description. Be concise. Write only the essence, or *highlights*, of what you see.	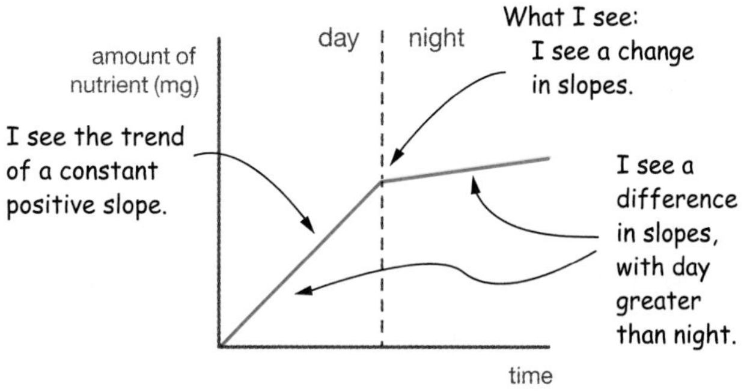 amount of nutrient (mg) day / night What I see: I see a change in slopes. I see the trend of a constant positive slope. I see a difference in slopes, with day greater than night. time
3. Interpret what you see. Write what each observation means. Don't interpret the entire figure at once, just one observation at a time.	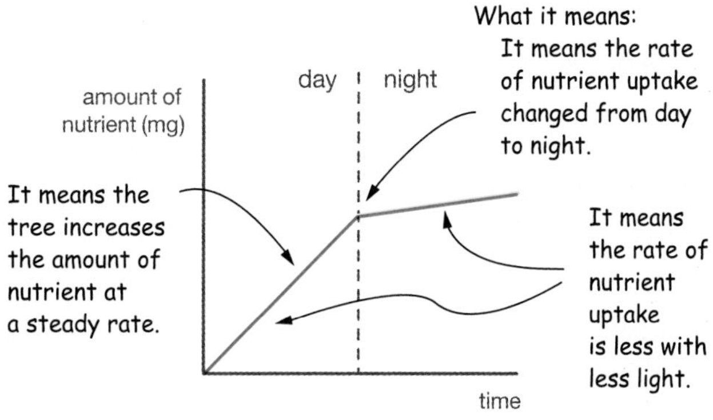 amount of nutrient (mg) day / night What it means: It means the rate of nutrient uptake changed from day to night. It means the tree increases the amount of nutrient at a steady rate. It means the rate of nutrient uptake is less with less light. time
4. Write a caption. Think of the caption as an executive summary. Start by joining each "What I see" to its "What it means" to form a sentence. Then build a coherent paragraph out of the sentences. Begin your caption with a topic sentence describing the overview of the figure.	Caption: This graph shows the uptake of nutrients in a tree over a 24-hour period. During the day, the graph shows a constant, positive slope, meaning there is a steady rate of uptake. At night, the rate changes as shown by change in slopes. This suggests that light changes the rate of uptake. Finally, the night slope is less than the day slope, meaning the uptake of nutrients slows at night.

▲ **Figure H3F.1 Steps for writing highlight comments and captions.**

Learning Strategies

Use the *Learn from Mistakes (LFM) Protocol*

School isn't just a place to deposit right answers. Sometimes we make mistakes. In fact, most humans make mistakes when they try to learn something, especially when the subject is difficult or new. When you learn to identify and explain what's incorrect about a wrong answer, you have a better chance of avoiding that mistake next time.

The *Learn from Mistakes* (*LFM*) *Protocol* was designed to help you learn from wrong answers. You will use it after you take certain tests. For each of the questions you missed on the test, perform the following steps. If you do, you can earn up to 50 percent of the difference between your raw percentage score and 100 percent. Be sure to write your raw percentage score at the top of the test along with a list of the numbers of the questions you missed.

Learn from Mistakes Protocol

1. Represent the original question in a different way than it was represented on the test. For example, if the question was mostly words, represent it as a sketch. If it was mostly a sketch, represent it in words. When you use words, paraphrase the question in your own words. Do not copy the question word for word. Label any sketch with all the variables, especially the unknown. If the problem mentions any change in condition, then show a before-and-after sketch.

2. Identify and explain the mistake you made in the answer you selected. Focus on explaining any conceptual misunderstanding. When you explain what is incorrect, show how the misconception would lead to a contradiction with what you see in nature. Explanations like, "I read the problem wrong" and "I pushed the wrong button on the calculator" will receive no credit.

3. Show the correct solution or answer. When necessary, show all governing equations, first in symbol form, then followed by substitution with number values. Always place proper units and labels on answers. Include why the answer is reasonable.

Learning Strategies

Solve Problems

Humans aren't born knowing how to build dams, determine why a baby is crying, or understand when *i* comes before *e*. We have to learn how to solve these problems. That's one of the primary benefits of school. You learn how to solve problems.

Every problem seems different. But successful problem solvers use a general approach that works for a large variety of everyday and school problems. Read the following problem, then learn how expert problem solvers find a solution. Try to use this approach with the next problem you're asked to solve. An example follows.

Problem-Solving Guidelines

1. *Read the problem.* Often, reading the problem aloud helps you to understand what the problem is asking you to do.

    Example problem: You push a 20-kilogram (kg) box across the floor at 3.0 meters per second (m/sec) with a constant force of 10 newtons (N). What force does the box exert on you?

2. *Adjust your mind-set.* Your attitude toward problem solving matters. The brain that thinks, also feels. Get rid of fears of failure or incompetence. Don't allow resentment or anger to cloud your thinking.

    Example mind-set statements to avoid: "I can't do science, so I'm not going to try." "I never get these right. I give up." "I'll never use this. Why should I do the problem?" "I hate not knowing what to do, so I'm not going to do it."

3. *Sort the problem.* Read the problem and use your prior experiences to determine what you know and don't know in the problem. This step clears your mind so that it can focus on the important features of the problem. It starts you thinking about the real question, not the things that distract you from the solution. The following table is an example of a way to organize your thoughts.

What I know, understand, or assume	What I don't know or understand
I pushed with 10 N force.	How does the box exert a force?
The box has a mass of 20 kg.	How do I find out the amount of box force?
The velocity is 3.0 m/sec.	Why is the box force "pushing back" on me?
The box moves in the same direction as the push and doesn't leave the floor (my assumption).	

▲ **Figure H3H.1 Problem-solving table.**

4 *Represent the problem.* Translate what you know and don't know into some form other than writing. Sketches, graphs, charts, and lists are examples. Be sure to transfer the items from your problem-solving table to the representation.

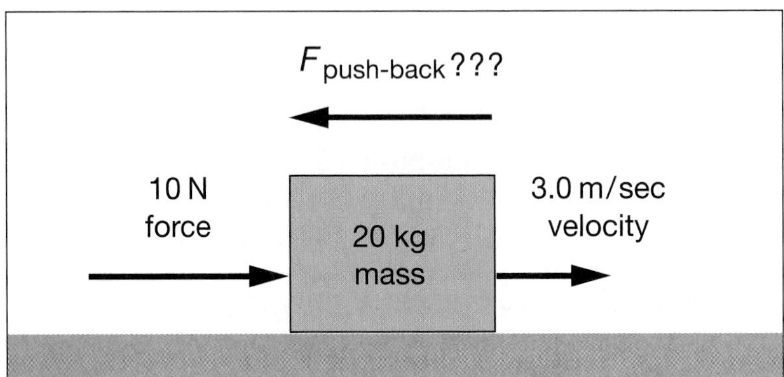

▲ **Figure H3H.2 Example representation of forces on mass.**

5 *Apply a strategy.* Expert problem solvers use a variety of methods, not just one. Successful methods include applying key concepts, using logic, trying to guess and then check, finding a pattern, working backward, and acting it out. Don't let yourself get stuck! If one method isn't working, try another.

Example application of the key concepts to the strategy: "I remember learning that all objects push back if you push on them. That makes me think of Newton's third law—forces come in pairs that are equal in size and opposite in direction. So if I push with 10 N, that means the box pushes back with 10 N. The velocity isn't important in the problem."

6 *Check for reasonableness.* Build confidence in your answer. Check it against your everyday experience or scientific theory. If there's a contradiction, then repeat the problem-solving steps as needed.

Example: "I feel something when I push on a box or a wall. That must mean the object pushes back. I remember that a net force causes acceleration. Since the box has a constant velocity, the net force must be zero. That means the push-back force has to be equal to my force. If I thought my force was greater, then the box would accelerate, which contradicts the problem statement."

4 HOW TO Construct a Concept Map

Concept maps are tools that help you organize ideas in a way that shows the relationships among them. There is no one right concept map for a body of information. But together, the concept words, connecting lines, and linking words should be an accurate representation of the content. To create a concept map, follow these steps.

Concept Map Guidelines

1. Identify the major concept that you will map. Then list several words or phrases that are important to understanding this concept. These should be words or phrases that identify parts of your major concept, such as parts of a system, a key idea, or an important process.
2. On a new page in your science notebook, write the major concept that you will map at the top of the page and draw a box around it. Arrange the related words or phases below this box. Arrange these words so that the bigger ideas are near the top and the more specific ideas are near the bottom. Draw boxes around these words as well.
3. Draw lines between the boxes to show relationships between the concept words. Lines can crisscross to show complex relationships.
4. Label the lines with linking words that describe the relationships.

   Study the sample concept map in figure H4.1 of AIDS concept words, connecting lines, and linking words on the map.

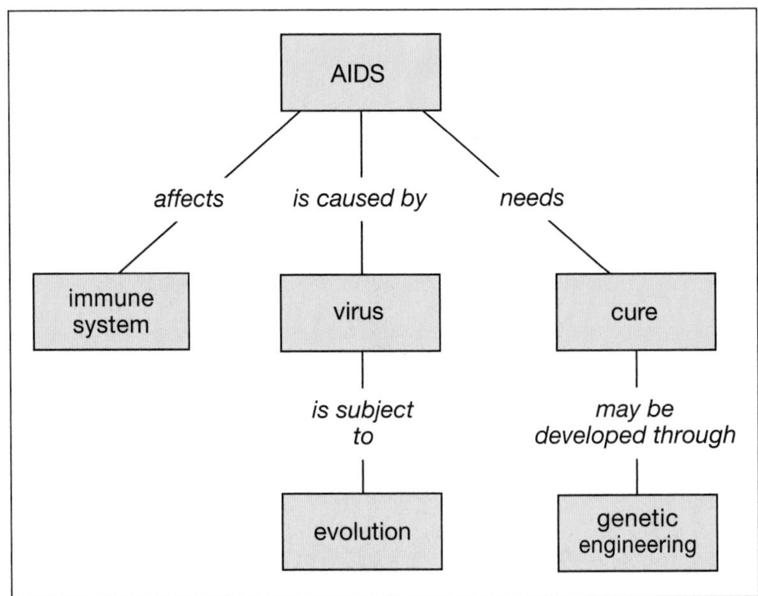

▲ **Figure H4.1 AIDS concept map.**

Improving Math Skills

Use Graphs, Measure Slopes, and Estimate Uncertainty

Do you like sports? Do you follow how certain teams or players do in football, baseball, or basketball? Or do you note how the price of music CDs or snack foods changes? Perhaps you need to show results from an investigation in a business, science, or math class.

For these and other cases, it is important to be able to show observations or data in graphs and plots. This skill helps you show a bigger picture of trends in data. Similarly, you also need to be able to read and interpret a few basic types of charts and graphs. This is true for many professions and for fields besides science.

The Basics: Labels and Limits

For most graphs, you typically show a variable across the bottom of the graph. This direction of the graph is called the *x-axis*, or *horizontal axis*. The amount that this variable changes is shown in a horizontal direction. The amount that a variable changes in the vertical direction is shown on the *vertical axis*, or *y-axis*. The axes have these names because you often plot data points with x and y values. The data points are also called the *xy coordinates*, written as (x,y). Examples of this follow.

An important next step in plotting a group of data is deciding the limits for the x-axis and the y-axis. To do this, examine your data and write down the high values and the low values for the x and y variables. Your axes must extend a little bit beyond the highest number, typically about 10–20 percent further. For a variable you measured, the difference between the high value and the low value is called the *spread*, or w. Starting the x- and y-axes at the value of zero is useful, depending on the data you are plotting.

You will see examples where the x-axis represents a category of a thing. The section titled *The Bar Graph* shows this. The type of thing is on the x-axis, while the amount of each thing is shown on the y-axis.

Let's look at examples of types of graphs that you will use in science and other fields.

The *xy* Plot

The *xy* plot is a simple plot where pairs of *xy* data are plotted as data points in a graph. Sometimes people call an *xy* plot a scatter plot. As you will see, this name really isn't appropriate because the data can define very straight lines (correlations) rather than scattered points.

For example, the table in figure H5A.1 shows the population densities of two kinds of squirrels that live in the ponderosa pine forests in northern Arizona. The population density is the number of squirrels counted for an area 100 × 100 meters, about the area of two soccer fields. By examining the table, you can quickly see that red squirrels are more common overall than Kaibab squirrels in these forests. Note the shading on the high and low values in the table. You can see that the spread, *w*, for the red squirrel is about 1.1 (= 1.38−0.31) and the spread for the Kaibab squirrel is about 0.23 (= 0.26−0.038).

Red squirrel	Kaibab squirrel
0.3685	0.0844
0.4955	0.1931
0.5317	0.1083
0.4739	0.0993
0.9713	0.1671
1.0529	0.1263
1.3779	0.2607
0.3126	0.0657
0.3770	0.0377

▲ **Figure H5A.1 Data on red and Kaibab squirrels.**

The values in the table help you decide the limits for the graph. You have some options, but the values of $x = 1.6$ and $y = 0.4$ work well for plot limits in this example.

The *xy* plot in figure H5A.2 helps you see relationships much better than the data table. The *xy* plot shows clearly that as the number of red squirrels

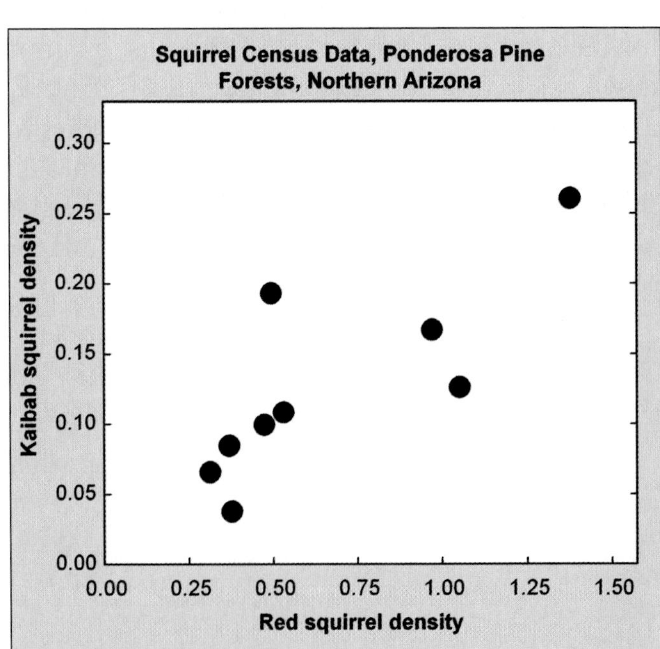

▶ **Figure H5A.2 Plot for red and Kaibab squirrels.** *xy* plot showing the relationship between the density of red and Kaibab squirrels in northern Arizona ponderosa forests.

increases, the number of Kaibab squirrels also increases. We say that such data show a *correlation* between red and Kaibab squirrel populations. But why would that be? After viewing these data, a biologist might be interested in further exploring the factors that might cause the number of red and Kaibab squirrels to change together. In Level 1 of *BSCS Science: An Inquiry Approach*, you actually learn about the culprit behind why the numbers of red and Kaibab squirrels are correlated in these ponderosa forests.

Determining the Slope

An important feature of xy plots is that they show relationships between pairs of x and y values. When xy pairs define a line, you can calculate the slope to find out how much the y value changes for each change in the x value. You are probably familiar with this as rise over run, or $\frac{\Delta y}{\Delta x}$. When the variable on the x-axis is time, slope is very important because it gives you a rate of change. You have seen that this is part of calculating velocities.

Take an example of a car. You have a record of the total distance that the car has traveled at certain points in time. The data are shown in the graph in figure H5A.3. For example, after about 3 hours (hr), the car has traveled about 190 miles (mi). On average, what is the velocity of the car?

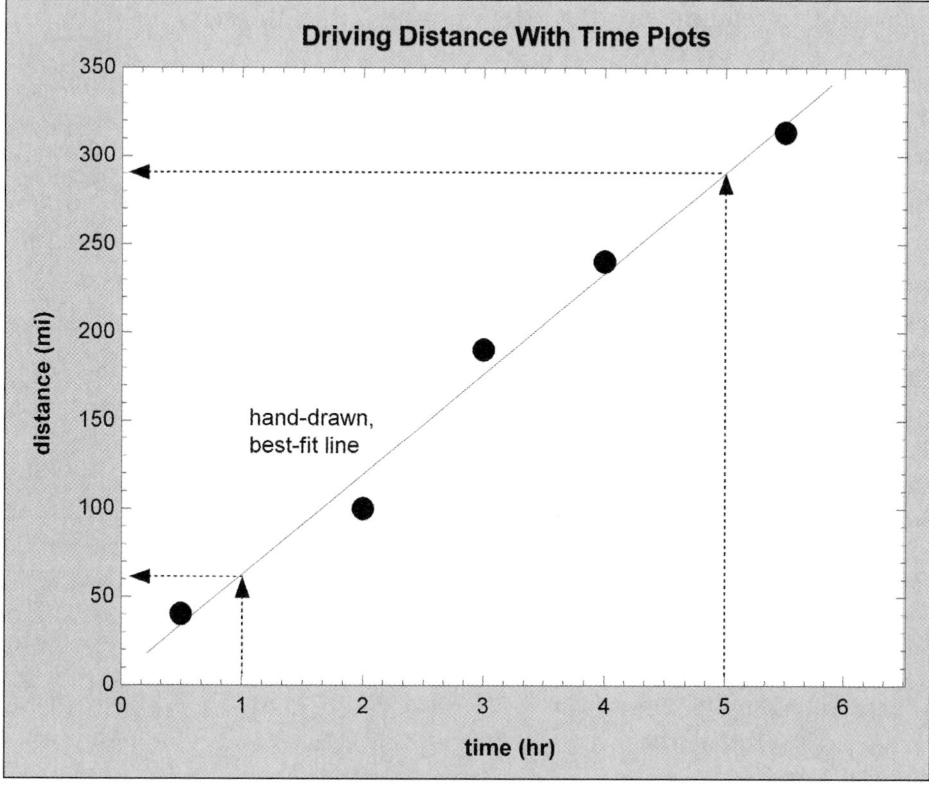

Figure H5A.3 Driving distance with time plots.

You can determine the average velocity by finding the slope using Steps 1–5.

1. Draw a line that goes as closely as possible through the points.
2. Pick any 2 values on the x-axis, even if they do not have actual data points. You can select values of 1 and 5 hr from the graph in figure H5A.3.
3. Project these points up to where they intersect the best-fit line that you have drawn.
4. Read the y-axis value where the x-axis intersects the slope. By doing this, you obtain the xy coordinates of 2 locations on the line. You can show these locations in a T-table or designate them as x_1,y_1 and x_2,y_2.
5. You calculate the slope with a series of points on the line. By being careful to keep units for the x- and y-axes, this example shows that slope also tells you velocity when time is on the x-axis.

$$slope = \frac{\Delta y}{\Delta x} = \frac{(y_2 - y_1)}{(x_2 - x_1)}$$

$$= \frac{(290 - 61)\text{ mi}}{(5 - 1)\text{ hr}} = \frac{229\text{ mi}}{4\text{ hr}} = 57.3\,\frac{\text{mi}}{\text{hr}}$$

You'll want to remember a few extra points. First, the slope, $\frac{\Delta y}{\Delta x}$, is a rate when the change in the denominator of the slope, Δx, is time. For example, the car's velocity was a rate with units of miles per hour. Second, at times you can draw a best-fit line, but keep in mind that not all physical relationships are linear. You'll see a nonlinear example using radioactivity in the next section, *The Time-Trend Plot*. Other examples in this program use acceleration, population growth, erosion of mountains, and cyclical changes. Thus, slope is only valid for lines, or nearly linear relationships.

The Time-Trend Plot

The *time-trend plot* is a kind of xy plot where the x-axis has the units of time. These types of plots are used for testing whether a variable changes in a predictable way as a function of time. The measured variable is shown on the y-axis, with time on the x-axis.

Take records of monthly temperatures in Denver, Colorado, for example. Figure H5A.4 shows temperature data for 5 years from 2000–2004. Temperature is on the *y*-axis, with year and month on the *x*-axis. The bold line shows the average monthly temperature. This line is bound by the average high temperature (the average of daily high temperatures for the month) and the average low temperature (usually the average of daily low temperatures for the month). The plot shows annual temperature cycles. Moreover, the graph shows differences among the years.

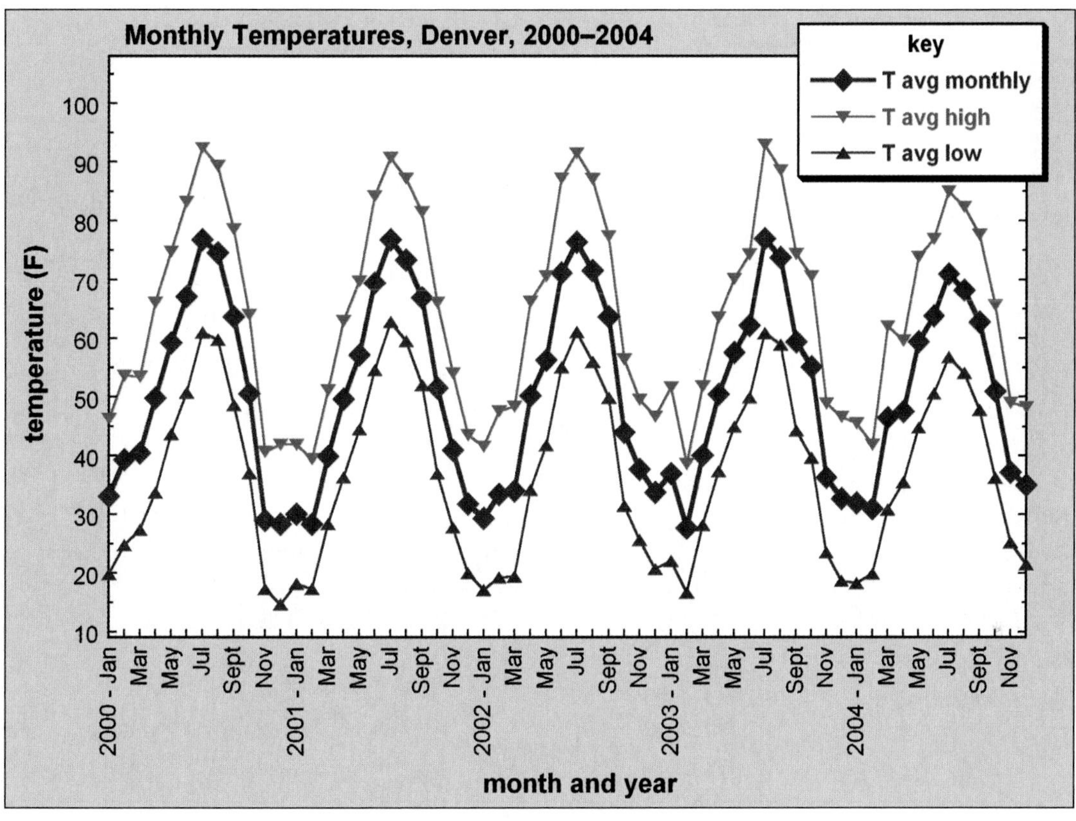

Figure H5A.4 Temperature plot for Denver, Colorado.

Another useful type of xy plot is called a "double y" plot. This plot uses both the left and the right y-axes to show the values for two variables against a common variable on the x-axis. Double y plots are useful for time trends, as shown in figure H5A.5 for temperature and rainfall over 5 years in Denver. (Note that low rainfall in winter correlates with snow.)

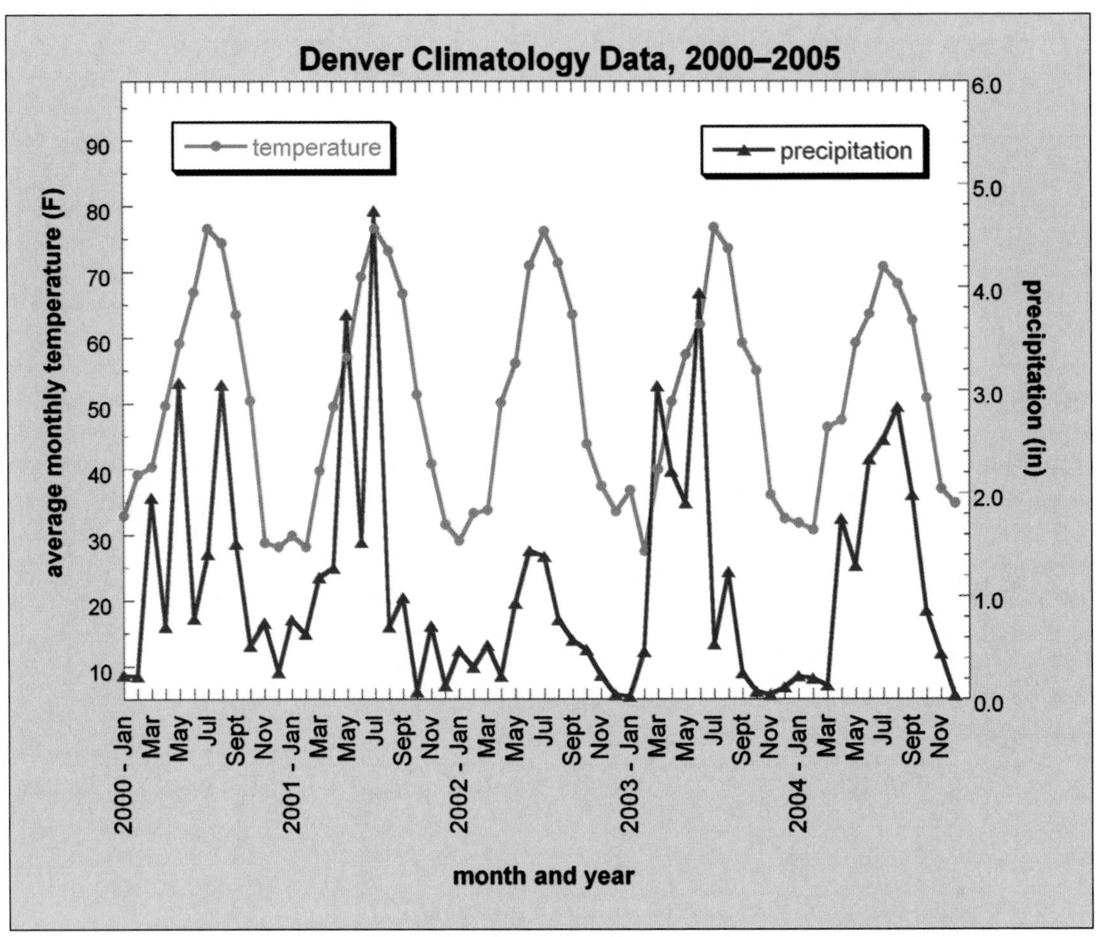

▲ **Figure H5A.5 Denver temperature and precipitation using a double *y* plot.**

The xy graph can also be used to show another technique for graphing. Often, we use a regular scale for tick marks on the axes. These plots are *linear.* At other times, the major tick marks on the axes are compressed and show factors of 10. Usually, these axes denote a logarithmic pattern. We call these *log* axes.

Consider a nuclear disaster. A product of nuclear reactions with the element uranium (U-235) is radioactive atoms of strontium-90 (Sr-90). Authorities have been concerned about radioactive Sr-90 because it is similar to calcium and it lodges rapidly in the bones of humans. Human bodies use calcium for bones. Radioactive atoms of Sr-90 in your bones are not good.

The mass of radioactive Sr-90 in a sample decreases by one-half (50 percent) in about 30 years (28.8 years, to be exact). This is the *half-life* of Sr-90. The table in figure H5A.6 shows that starting with an initial mass of 100 grams (g) of Sr-90, the mass of Sr-90 decreases by half, or 50 percent, every 30 years.

The data from the table are much easier to see and examine in a graph. For every 30 years that pass, the mass of Sr-90 decreases by about half. For example, after 60 years (two half-lives), only about 25 percent of the initial Sr-90 atoms remain. It appears from the plot in figure H5A.7 that the Sr-90 is gone after about 240 years. But on this linear scale, how would you tell if amounts still existed that were too small to show up on this graph? Even a gram or less of Sr-90 can be a health hazard.

Years	Mass of Sr-90 (g)
0	100.0000
30	50.0000
60	25.0000
90	12.5000
120	6.2500
150	3.1250
180	1.5625
210	0.7813
240	0.3906
270	0.1953
300	0.0977
330	0.0488
360	0.0244
390	0.0122
420	0.0061
450	0.0031
480	0.0015
510	0.0008
540	0.0004
570	0.0002
600	0.0001

▲ **Figure H5A.6 Sr-90 decay table.**

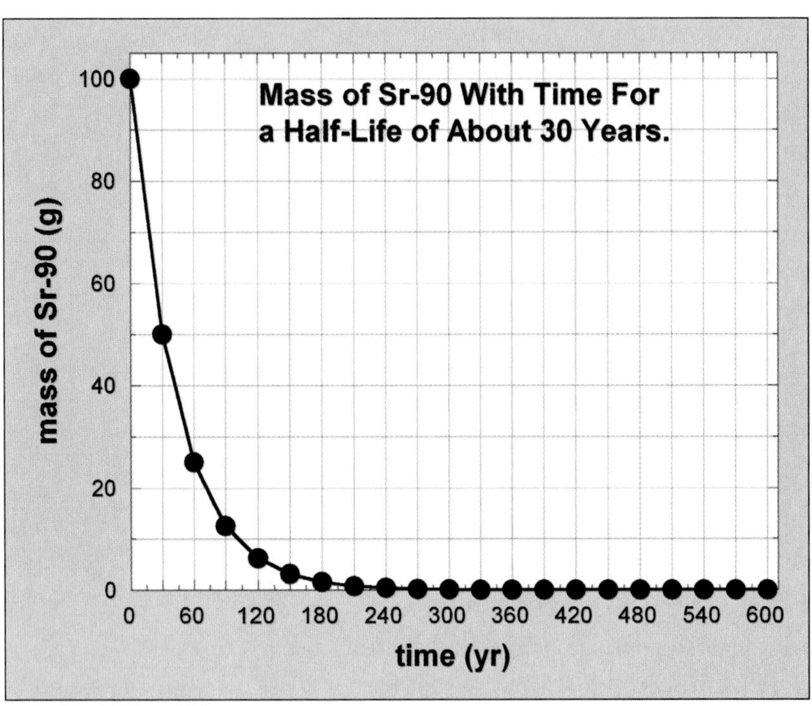

▲ **Figure H5A.7 Linear plot of Sr-90.**

You would use a log scale on an axis in what's called a *log plot*. In a log plot, the scale of the *y*-axis is modified so that increments are divided for each factor of 10. In general, values increase from 0.01, 0.1, 1.0, 10, 100, 1,000, and so on.

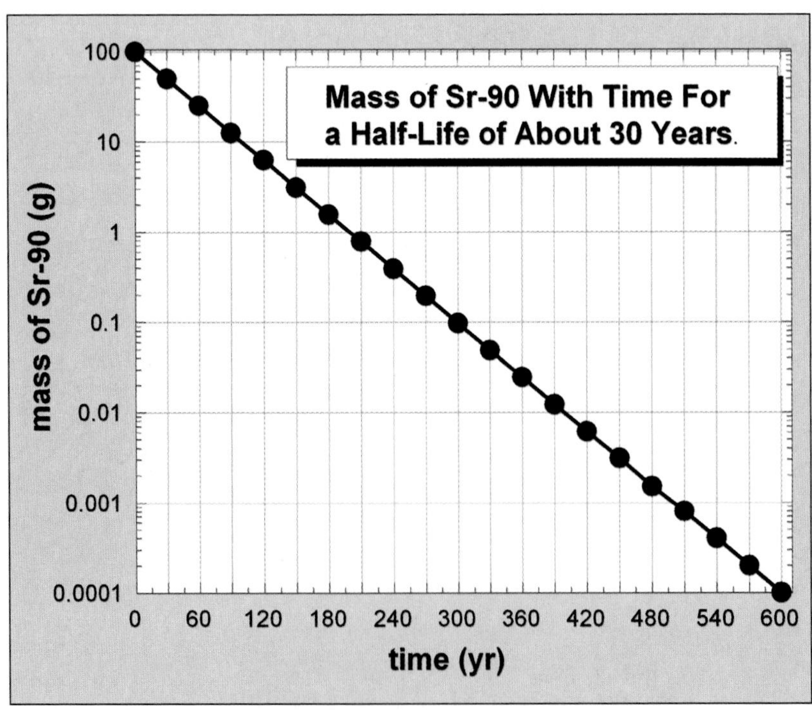

▲ **Figure H5A.8 Log plot of Sr-90.**

A key feature of the log plot is that the *y*-axis never goes to zero. Also, a value halfway between factors of 10 is roughly three, compared with five (between 0 and 10) on a linear scale. The graph in figure H5A.8 shows the same Sr-90 data in a log plot.

The Bar Graph

Bar graphs show the values or frequencies (on the *y*-axis) as a function of categories of things (on the *x*-axis). The *x*-axis does not have a numeric scale, either linear or log.

How could we show the frequency by month of tropical storms or hurricanes for the Atlantic Ocean in 1998? Bar graphs are perfect for this. Figure H5A.9 shows that for 1998, tropical storms occurred from July to September, with hurricanes occurring from August to November. Hurricanes also had a pronounced peak in September. Given such data, a scientist could then examine other years to test whether the pattern applies to those years.

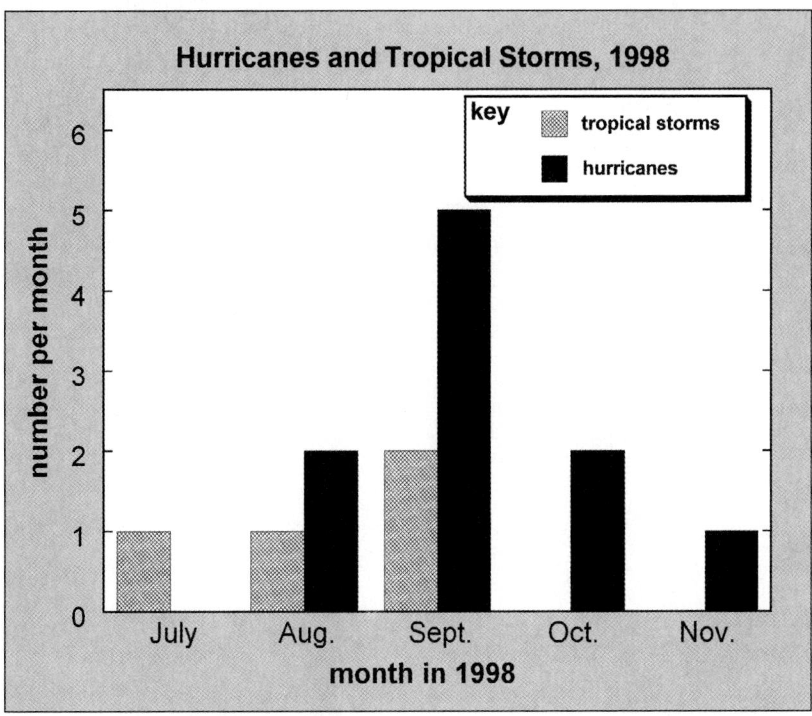

▲ **Figure H5A.9 Hurricanes and storms bar graph.** This bar graph shows the frequency in 1998 of tropical storms and hurricanes in the Atlantic Ocean.

The Histogram

Histograms are another type of graph. They show how often a result occurs. Let's take an example showing scores in geology class. The following histograms show the scores for 27 students on a final mapping project for a geology class. The first histogram (figure H5A.10) shows compartments, or *bins*, where the scores are tallied. Bin sizes of two and five are shown for the same set of scores. The average score is 88.1, which falls in the bar with the highest value in figure H5A.10. The histograms show the *variability* of data about the mean.

▶ Figure H5A.10 Geology scores histogram where bin = 5. This histogram shows scores for 27 geology projects with a bin size of five.

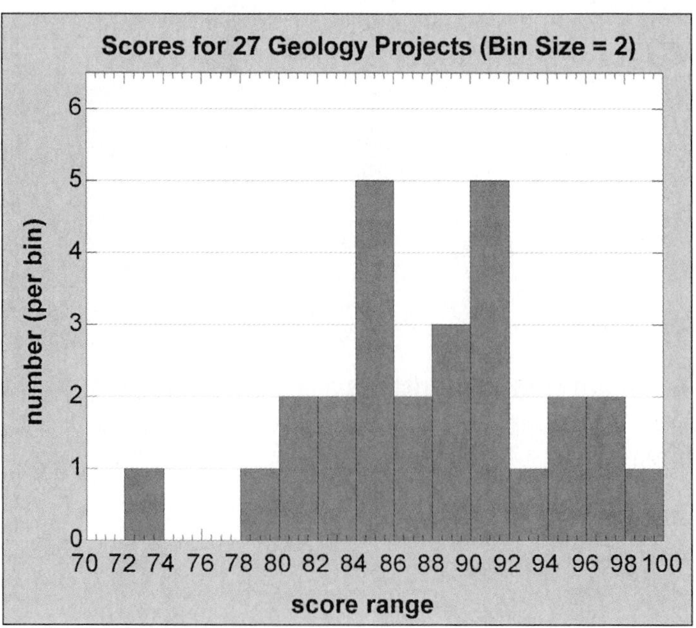

▶ Figure H5A.11 Geology scores histogram where bin = 2. Histogram of scores for 27 geology projects with a bin size of two.

For comparison, the second histogram (figure H5A.11) shows the same scores ($n = 27$) using a finer bin size of two. The result is similar, but shows two distinct peaks on each side of the mean of 88.1. You may wish to test different bin sizes to show important points in a histogram that you wish to make.

Note several things about histograms. In the histogram where the bin size equals five, values are distributed about a peak in the center. Sometimes this is called a *bell-shaped curve.* This happens when the number and positions of observations to the right and to the left of the peak are approximately equal. You might see a pattern like this by plotting a histogram of the heights of all students in your class. Your graph might have a peak value around 5.5 feet (ft), with a smattering of values in bins above and below 5 ft, 6 inches.

The key to making histograms is to first record your data or observations in a long column. Then decide the size of your bins. Finally, tabulate how many values in your column fall in each bin. Following these suggestions will help you successfully plot your histogram.

The Pie Chart

Another way to represent measurements or data is with a *pie chart.* This type of graph is called a pie chart because categories are spread around a circle, rather than along an x-axis, and look like slices of pie. The amount per category is given as a percentage of a total. Your teacher can show you how to take percentages for categories and divide them proportionately into a circle of 360 degrees.

Consider the human body. You may have heard statements such as, "Most of the human body is water." But what elements are in the human body? The pie chart in figure H5A.12 shows clearly that we are about 92 percent oxygen, carbon, and hydrogen.

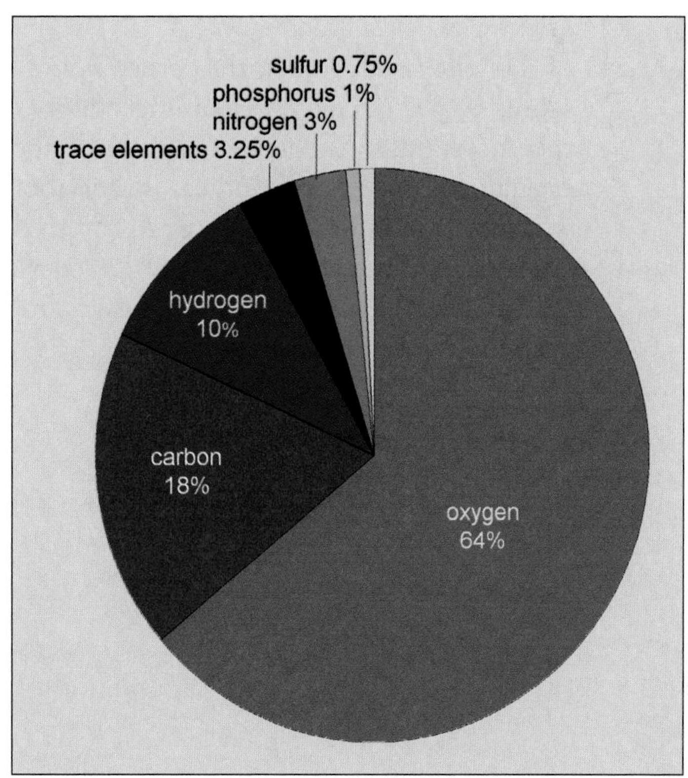

Figure H5A.12 A pie chart showing the body's elements.

Showing Uncertainty (or Error) in Measurements

A good experimental design often requires that you repeat a measurement several times. Because experiments are not perfect, it is unlikely that you will get the same exact measurement in each trial. An average, $\bar{x}$ or "mean," is one way to estimate the actual value from your measurements. You are used to calculating averages. But how would you show the variability of your measurements around that mean? There are several ways to do this.

One way is to show all measured values around the average. Consider the scores on the final project in the geology class from the section *The Histogram*. The plot in figure H5A.13 shows all 27 student scores, along with a large symbol for the mean. For comparison, individual scores with means are plotted for two prior assignments (a quiz and a midterm) in that geology class.

A second way to represent all measured values is to calculate an indicator of uncertainty around the average. This is a quick way to estimate the standard deviation, another term that you might have heard. First, calculate the spread, w, between the high and low values. Next, to estimate the uncertainty (or error), e, divide the spread by the square root of the number of measurements, n.

$$e = \frac{w}{\sqrt{n}}$$

For the final project, the spread is $w = (98.3 - 73.1) = 25.2$. For 27 scores ($n = 27$), this gives an uncertainty of ± 4.8. The $\pm$ sign shows that the uncertainty in scores extends both above and below the mean. This estimate of uncertainty indicates that about 60–70 percent of the scores will have values bracketed by $\bar{x} \pm e$. With the geology final projects, this is 88.1 $\pm$4.8. (That is, about 60–70 percent of the scores fall in a range from 83.3 to 92.9.) This can also be shown graphically by error bars on the graph in figure H5A.14.

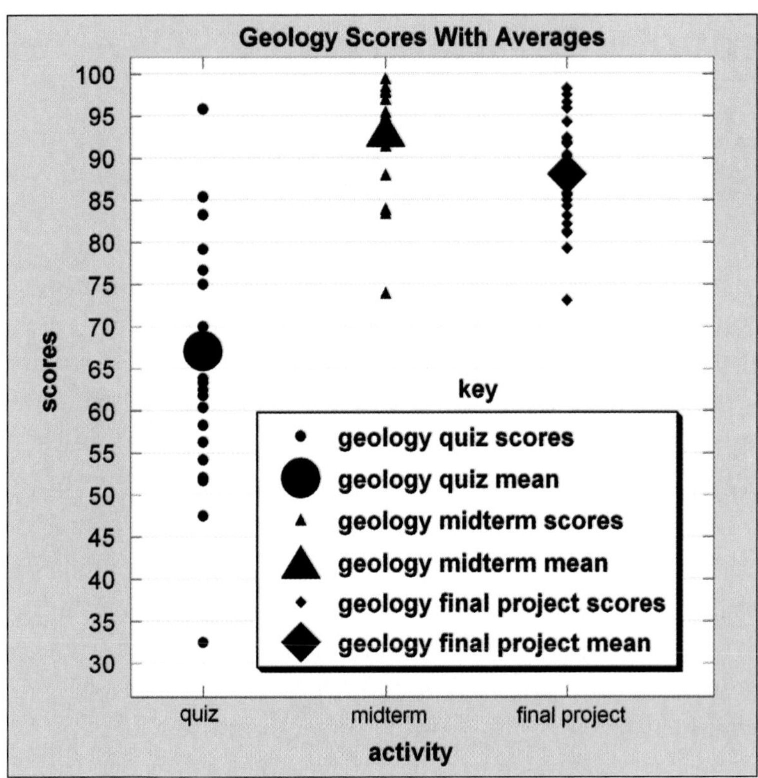

Figure H5A.13 Geology scores with averages.

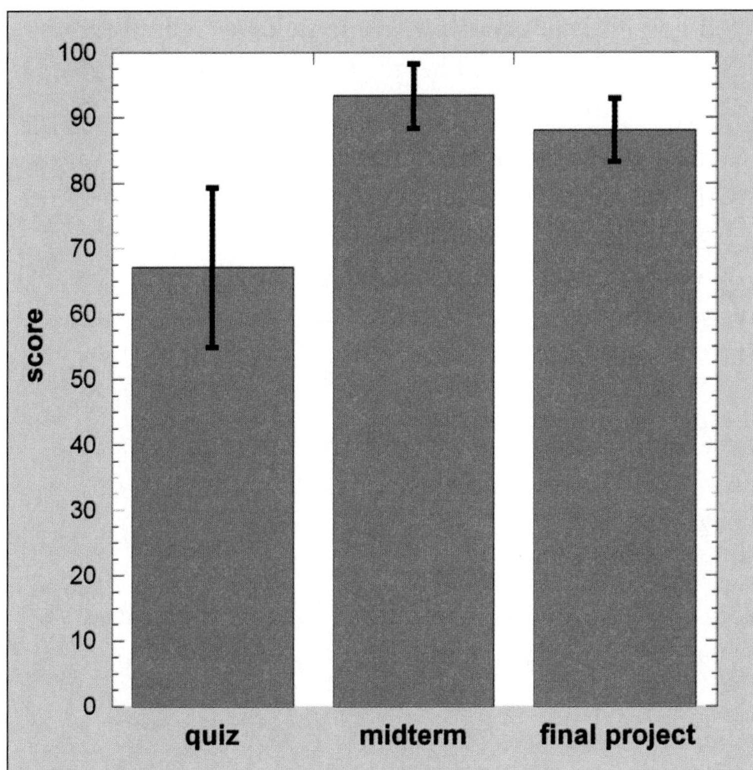

Figure H5A.14 Geology scores with errors.

Improving Math Skills

Do Unit Conversions

When you measure something, you always need to indicate what units you are using. For example, suppose someone told you that her cat had a weight of "20." That doesn't mean much without units. Does the cat weigh 20 pounds, 20 newtons, 20 ounces, or 20 tons? Distance measurements (length) also need units such as feet, inches, meters, kilometers, and miles. If you are measuring time, you use units such as seconds, minutes, hours, and years.

Converting between units is also very important. For example, what if a friend told you that he would phone you in 86,400 seconds (sec)? When would that be? After this activity, you will be able to show that this is the same as 1 day. Unit conversions are also important for comparing two measurements made with different units. For example, suppose a person who is 5 feet (ft) 8 inches (in) tall has a hat on that is 0.30 meters (m) tall. What is the total height of the person, including the hat? Unfortunately, you cannot simply add the lengths. You must convert all of them to the same unit, and then you can add the lengths. You may have to convert again to a more reasonable unit. The total height of the person would be 79.8 in, 6 ft 7.8 in, or 2.03 m tall.

How do you make these conversions? The method is called unit analysis (or dimensional analysis). These terms may sound complicated, but the method is pretty simple. The method uses conversion factors to convert units step-by-step, canceling units at each step. Using these guidelines, unit analysis is simple.

Unit Analysis Guidelines

1. Conversion factors relate different units and are different ways of expressing the number 1. For example, there are 12 in in 1 ft, or
$12 \text{ in} = 1 \text{ ft, or} \left(\frac{12 \text{ in}}{1 \text{ ft}}\right) = 1.$
2. Conversion factors can be flipped (inverted) as long as the units stay with the number. For example, you can write
$\left(\frac{12 \text{ in}}{1 \text{ ft}}\right) = 1, \text{ or} \left(\frac{1 \text{ ft}}{12 \text{ in}}\right) = 1.$
This is the same thing.

3. Units behave as numbers do when you multiply fractions. The units in the numerator of fractions will cancel the same units in the denominator of fractions. For example, $\left(\frac{12\ \cancel{in}}{3\ \cancel{in}}\right) = 4$.

4. In unit analysis, your goal is to cancel the same units in the numerators and denominators until you end up with the units you want.

5. When you convert between units, follow these steps.
   a. Identify the units that you have.
   b. See which units you want.
   c. Note the conversion factors that get you from Steps 5a and 5b.

6. Work through the following example to practice using the guidelines for unit analysis from Steps 1–5.

   How many inches are there in 1 mile (mi)?

Conversion steps (from Step 5)	Answers
What unit do you have now?	1 mi
What unit do you want?	"How many inches"
What are the conversion factors?	$1\ \text{mi} = 5{,}280\ \text{ft}$ or $\left(\frac{5{,}280\ \text{ft}}{1\ \text{mi}}\right) = 1$ $1\ \text{ft} = 12\ \text{in}$ or $\left(\frac{12\ \text{in}}{1\ \text{ft}}\right) = 1$

Figure H5B.1 Conversion table for miles to inches.

To convert miles to inches, start with what you know (1 mi). Then use conversion factors (figure H5B.1) to cancel units as you go until you get to the units that you want (inches). When the same units are on both the bottom and the top, they cancel. Work with your teacher to see how to cancel these units on the top and bottom.

$$(1\ \cancel{mi}) \times \left(\frac{5{,}280\ \cancel{ft}}{1\ \cancel{mi}}\right) \times \left(\frac{12\ \text{in}}{1\ \cancel{ft}}\right)$$

The units cancel, so you are left with units of inches. You can then multiply the numerator numbers together for the answer in inches.

$$(1\ \cancel{mi}) \times \left(\frac{5{,}280\ \cancel{ft}}{1\ \cancel{mi}}\right) \times \left(\frac{12\ \text{in}}{1\ \cancel{ft}}\right) = \left(\frac{1 \times 5{,}280 \times 12\ \text{in}}{1 \times 1}\right) = 63{,}360\ \text{in}$$

7 Work through a more complicated example using dimensional analysis. Suppose that you want to convert 75 miles per hour (mph) into feet per second (ft/sec).

Conversion steps (from Step 5)	Answers
What unit do you have now?	$75 \frac{\text{mi}}{\text{hr}}$ (mph)
What unit do you want?	$\frac{\text{ft}}{\text{sec}}$ (ft /sec)
What are the conversion factors?	1 hour (hr) = 60 minutes (min) 1 minute (min) = 60 seconds (sec) 1 mi = 5,280 ft

▲ **Figure H5B.2 Conversion table for miles per hour to feet per second.**

Now what? Take your conversions (figure H5B.2) one step at a time, canceling units as you go until you arrive at the units you want.

$$\left(\frac{75\ \cancel{\text{mi}}}{1\ \cancel{\text{hr}}}\right) \times \left(\frac{5{,}280\ \text{ft}}{1\ \cancel{\text{mi}}}\right) \times \left(\frac{1\ \cancel{\text{hr}}}{60\ \cancel{\text{min}}}\right) \times \left(\frac{1\ \cancel{\text{min}}}{60\ \text{sec}}\right) =$$

$$\left(\frac{75 \times 5{,}280\ \text{ft} \times 1 \times 1}{1 \times 1 \times 60 \times 60\ \text{sec}}\right) = \left(\frac{396{,}000\ \text{ft}}{3{,}600\ \text{sec}}\right) = \left(\frac{110\ \text{ft}}{1\ \text{sec}}\right) = 110\ \frac{\text{ft}}{\text{sec}}$$

8 Try the conversions in Steps 8a–c on your own. Use the following conversion factors, and show your calculations for each conversion.

1 slink = 7 zips　　1 sliff = 5 zips

4 voles = 3 sliffs　　8 lampos = 7 flies

12 voles = 1 lampo

a. How many sliffs are in 1 lampo?
b. One vole is how many zips?
c. How many flies are in 1 slink?

Improving Math Skills

Understand Very Large and Very Small Numbers

When it comes to studying the universe, scientists must work with very large and very small numbers. Scientists use numbers in the millions and billions because quantities, distances, timescales, and temperatures in the universe are so vast. Consider this:

- Our galaxy has billions of stars, and the universe has hundreds of billions of galaxies.
- Distances between objects in the universe can be greater than billions of miles; it would take light over 10 billion years to travel across the universe.
- Astronomers measure time spans of the universe in billions of years.
- Temperatures in the universe once were hotter than billions of degrees Celsius.

You know that 1 million is a lot—but how much is it? For instance, if someone offered you a million dollars in a pile, you'd sure take it. But how could you test that the pile actually had 1 million dollar bills in it? Would you count dollar bills one by one? How long would this take? Now suppose that someone gave you a billion dollars in $1 bills. How much more is this, really?

In *How to Understand Very Large and Very Small Numbers*, you'll explore how big the numbers million and billion really are. Get ready to share your ideas with your classmates.

Part I: How Many Is 1 Million?

Materials

none

1. With your teammate, find or think of a million of 1 type of item. You do not need to actually collect the items, but decide how you will convince the rest of the class that you could gather 1 million of the item. Think through this step carefully. You can change items to arrive at the best example.

2. Work with your partner on a method to prove that you have 1 million of the objects. You will share your ideas and prove your work to your classmates.

3. Discuss these questions in your class and write your answers in your science notebook.
   a. What were some of the difficulties you had finding a million of something?
   b. What were some different methods that groups used to prove their findings?

Part II: Millions or Billions: What's the Difference?

Materials

stopwatch or clock with second hand

calculators

In Part I, you had to prove that you have 1 million of an item. This might have seemed difficult at first, but you probably quickly figured out how to meet the challenge. As you worked, you should have seen how big 1 million of something really is. You also probably saw that counting every single item would not work too well.

Astronomers work with numbers even larger than 1 million. In fact, numbers in the billions and larger are quite common in astronomy. You will work again with your partner to better understand the real size of 1 billion (1,000,000,000).

1. Individually, predict how long you think it would take you to count to 1 million saying each number aloud without stopping. Write this prediction in your science notebook and title it "prediction." What did your partner predict?

2. With your partner, calculate how long it takes to count to 1 million (1,000,000).
   a. Have one person say the number 383,262 ("three hundred eighty-three thousand two hundred sixty-two") while the other person times how long it takes to say the number. Record the time in your science notebook.

You said this number because most numbers between 1 and 1 million are in the hundred thousands.

b. It took you a certain number of seconds to say that single number. How many numbers are there between 1 and 1 million? Using multiplication, calculate how many seconds it would take you to say all these numbers and, thus, count to 1 million. Record your calculations and this number in your science notebook.

3. You probably calculated many millions of seconds, which probably doesn't make a lot of sense. Convert your answer from seconds to a more appropriate unit. Show your calculations in your science notebook. What did others in your class find?

4. You now know that it takes a significant amount of time to count to 1 million. But many measurements in the universe need billions or even hundreds of billions. Let's see how 1 billion compares with 1 million. Predict how long it would take you to count to 1 billion by ones. Record your prediction in your science notebook.

5. Calculate how long it would take you to count to 1 billion (1,000,000,000) by ones. Use the same method you used in Step 2 and record your answer in the units that make the most sense. Review the unit conversions as necessary.

A good number to say is 504,394,568 (pronounced "five hundred four million three hundred ninety-four thousand five hundred sixty-eight") because most numbers from 1 to 1 billion are in the hundreds of millions.

6. Share your calculation from Step 5 with the class. What did you find?

7. Discuss Questions 7a–c with your class and write your answers in your science notebook.
   a. Were you surprised at how long it would take you to count to a billion versus counting to a million? Explain your thoughts.
   b. How did measuring 1 million of an object help you to understand the enormity of 1 million?
   c. What was the range of values your class had for counting to 1 billion? What might account for this range of results?

Improving Math Skills

Use Very Large and Very Small Numbers

By now, you understand numbers like million and billion better. Astronomers have to work with numbers in the billions—and bigger—all the time. For example, how many stars are in the sky? Are there more stars that you cannot see? All stars that you see are part of the galaxy in which we live, the Milky Way Galaxy. A galaxy is an enormous group of stars in a massive cluster. The Milky Way has more than 100 billion stars. The universe contains hundreds of billions of different galaxies, many of which are made up of hundreds of billions of stars. How do astronomers know this?

Astronomers are scientists who study the matter in outer space, particularly the many types of stars. When they cannot count stars or galaxies, they need to calculate estimates based on what they can clearly see and count. For example, astronomers cannot see each star in our galaxy because some stars are behind other stars or clouds of gas and dust. So astronomers base their estimates on mass. The laws of physics also allow astronomers to estimate the mass of the Milky Way Galaxy. Dividing this by the mass of an average star like the Sun gives estimates of up to several hundred billion stars in the Milky Way Galaxy.

Part I: Big Numbers

Materials

calculators

You have seen how large numbers can be difficult to manage. It would be awkward for astronomers to use terms such as a million billion billion or to write out numbers like 1,000,000,000,000,000,000,000,000. Rather, astronomers (and other scientists) use a special way of expressing numbers called scientific notation.

Scientific notation is a way to abbreviate numbers to make them easier to work with. To show numbers with scientific notation, you must first be comfortable with exponents. Exponents are shorthand for the number of times a number, called the base, is multiplied by itself. A base with an exponent is said to be "raised to the power" of that exponent. For example, the number 2^4 means $2 \times 2 \times 2 \times 2$, or 16. Here, 2 is the base and 4 is the exponent. In scientific notation, the base number is always 10. Having

10 as the base works well because the exponent shows how many zeros you would need to write out in the long form of the number. So 10,000 is expressed as 10^4, because $10 \times 10 \times 10 \times 10 = 10{,}000$.

Numbers in astronomy work best with powers of 10. With scientific notation, you simply move the decimal point of a number to obtain a more manageable number. Then you write the number of places you moved the decimal as an exponent of 10. For example, you would write the number 4,600,000,000 as 4.6×10^9 with scientific notation. The second number is a lot simpler, and it says the same thing as the first. You write it like this because you moved the decimal nine places to the left to get to the numeral 4.6. This is shown in figure H5D.1.

Other large numbers are also easy to write using scientific notation. You would write the number 34,000 as 3.4×10^4. You would write the number 286,000,000 as 2.86×10^8. You might remember that the metric system is based on multiples of 10. The table in figure H5D.2 shows how large numbers convert to powers of 10. It also shows prefixes for these numbers in the metric system. Using the example above, 286,000,000 is also the same as 286×10^6, or just 286 million.

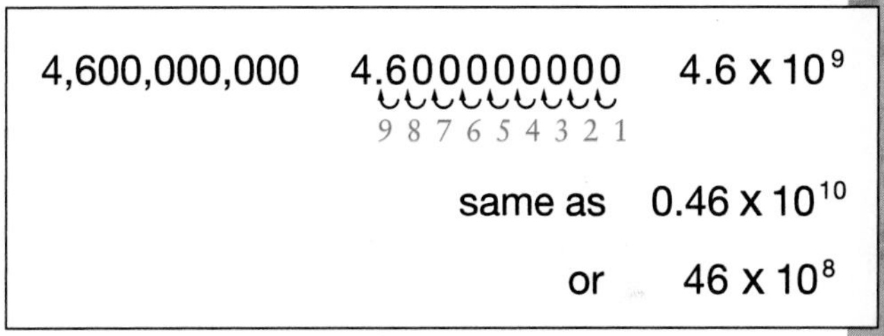

4,600,000,000 4.600000000 4.6×10^9
9 8 7 6 5 4 3 2 1
same as 0.46×10^{10}
or 46×10^8

Figure H5D.1 Example of moving decimals for positive exponents. This diagram shows the conversion of the number 4,600,000,000 to scientific notation, 4.6×10^9. The illustration in the center shows the decimal place moving left nine times. The table in figure H5D.2 explains why 4.6×10^9 is the same as 4.6 billion.

Pronounced	Number	Powers of ten (scientific notation)	Unit prefix in the metric system (SI)
Trillion	1,000,000,000,000	10^{12} or 1×10^{12}	tera-
Billion	1,000,000,000	10^9 or 1×10^9	giga-
Million	1,000,000	10^6 or 1×10^6	mega-
Thousand	1,000	10^3 or 1×10^3	kilo-
Hundred	100	10^2 or 1×10^2	hecto-
Ten	10	10^1 or 1×10^1	deka-
One	1	10^0 or 1×10^0	
Three hundred twenty-seven thousand	327,000	3.27×10^5	

Figure H5D.2 Table for large numbers.

Work through these problems individually and write your answers in your science notebook. When you finish, join with another student and compare your answers. Discuss and resolve any differences you have in your answers.

1. One kilometer (km) is the same as 1,000 meters (m). How would you write 1,000 m using scientific notation?
2. A googol is one of the biggest named numbers. It is written as the number 1 followed by 100 zeros. Write this number using scientific notation.
3. The speed of light is 3.0×10^8 meters per second (m/sec). What is this value written without using scientific notation?
4. Use scientific notation to write $87 billion and 248 million stars.

Part II: Small Numbers

Materials

calculators

Astronomers often work with countless billions of stars and galaxies, but they also work with extremely small numbers. For example, you will see that a key property of light is wavelength. Wavelengths of light are commonly about 1 billion times shorter than a meter.

You write numbers less than 1.0 in scientific notation in the same general way that you write large numbers. The key difference is that the power of 10 is a negative exponent. The exponent still tells you how many places the decimal is from the number 1.0, but the decimal is moved in the other direction (to the right). When writing small numbers using powers of 10, you imagine moving the decimal to the right. The number of places you moved the decimal is the power of 10 expressed as a negative number. We would write the number 0.0000001 in scientific notation as 1×10^{-7} because the decimal moves seven places to the right to get to the number 1.0. Another example is shown in figure H5D.3 for 0.00000035, which is the same as 3.5×10^{-7}.

0.00000035	00000003.5 1 2 3 4 5 6 7	3.5×10^{-7}
	same as	0.35×10^{-6}
	or	350×10^{-9}

Figure H5D.3 Example of moving decimals for negative exponents. This diagram shows the conversion of the number 0.00000035 to scientific notation, 3.5×10^{-7}. The illustration in the top center shows the decimal place moving to the right seven times.

Pronounced	Number	Powers of ten (scientific notation)	Unit prefix in the metric system (SI)
Tenth	0.1	1×10^{-1} or 10^{-1}	deci-
Hundredth	0.01	1×10^{-2} or 10^{-2}	centi-
Thousandth	0.001	1×10^{-3} or 10^{-3}	milli-
Millionth	0.000001	1×10^{-6} or 10^{-6}	micro-
Billionth	0.000000001	1×10^{-9} or 10^{-9}	nano-

▲ **Figure H5D.4 Prefixes for small numbers.**

Work through these problems individually and write your answers in your science notebook. When you finish, join with another student and compare your answers. Discuss and resolve any differences you have in your answers.

1. A micron is an abbreviation for the term micrometer (μm). How would you express 1 μm using scientific notation? Look at the prefixes in the table in figure H5D.4.
2. How many meters are in 1 millimeter (mm)?
3. Scientists often measure wavelengths of light in units called nanometers (nm). A nanometer is 0.000000001 m. Write this number using scientific notation.

Conduct an Effective Web Search

Searching for information on the Web can be rewarding as well as frustrating. It may take hours to sift through the thousands of sites that pop up from a poorly designed search. *How to Conduct an Effective Web Search* gives you a few pointers for using any search engine to look for information on the Web. There are times when you want to broaden the search to include more documents, and there are times when you will want to narrow the search to return fewer documents. The following 7 steps will give you a balanced search that is broad enough to find documents that pertain to your topic, but narrow enough to be useful.

Web Searching Guidelines

1. **Choose your keywords carefully.** You will type keywords that relate to your topic into a search engine. Choose nouns and objects as your keywords. For example, if you were searching for information about new planets discovered outside our solar system, using the keyword *planet* or *planets* would be a good start. Verbs, adjectives, adverbs, and similar terms will either be thrown out by the search engine or will be too variable to be useful.
2. **Use several keywords in your search.** Using six to eight appropriate keywords can greatly reduce the number of documents that are returned with your search. Using the example in Step 1, the keywords *new*, *planet*, *solar*, *system*, and *discovery* would return useful documents.
3. **Use appropriate variations in your words connected by OR.** For example, use *planet OR planets* to make sure the search engine picks up both variations of the word "planet."
4. **Use synonyms connected by OR where possible.** *Discovery OR find* is an example of using 2 synonyms connected by *OR* that will cover the different ways a concept can be described.
5. **Combine words into phrases where possible and place phrases in quotation marks (" ").** For example, *"solar system"* is a phrase in our example that should be combined and put in quotation marks. This will restrict the search to exact matches of the phrase.

6. **Combining 2 or 3 concepts in 1 search, distinguished by parentheses, will narrow your results and possibly give you just what you want.** For our current example, using *("solar system")("new planet")(discover OR find)* would be the best selection.

7. **Order your concepts with the main subject first.** Search engines tend to rank documents that match the first keywords in the search higher than those that match the later keywords. For our example search, you would order the concepts as *("new planet")(discover OR find)("solar system").*

7 HOW TO Write a Lab Report

Adapted from BSCS. (2006). *Biological perspectives laboratory manual: Thinking biologically* (3rd ed.). Dubuque, IA: Kendall/Hunt.

When scientists have enough information, data, and evidence about a particular scientific matter, they summarize their results in a formal, scientific paper and submit it for publication in a professional journal. These papers are organized in specific sections as required by the particular journal. You, too, will be writing lab reports this year, and your report should have sections similar to a scientific paper. Those 5 sections are listed here with a brief description of what you should include in each section.

Lab Report Guidelines

1. **Introduction.** The introduction includes background information from scientific papers, textbooks, newspapers, or magazine articles. Be sure to cite your references at the end of your paper. (See *How to Cite References and Avoid Plagiarism*.) The introduction should also include the purpose of your investigation or the question you are trying to answer.
2. **Materials and methods.** List the materials that you used in the investigation. Also include your step-by-step procedure.
3. **Results.** Describe your results in written form in this section. You should also include appropriate tables, graphs, and diagrams with captions.
4. **Discussion.** This section is where you discuss the results of this particular investigation. How do the results relate to what you already know?
5. **Conclusion.** Summarize the findings of your investigation in the conclusion. Try to answer questions such as, "What trends do I see in the data?" "What general statement can I make about the results?" "What do the data mean?" "What do they tell me about what is happening with the object, organism, or phenomenon?"

8 HOW TO

Cite References and Avoid Plagiarism

When doing research in your classes, you'll quickly find that you will need to rely on the results and work of others. These are usually professionals who have had the chance to consider a topic in much more detail than you. You will gain insight from their work, and their work will even make yours much stronger. The important thing is to review with your teacher how to reference that work in your write-up or presentation.

Sometimes students may forget to list sources, or they may even use other people's work without a clear reference. Claiming someone else's work as your own is cheating.

Using the creative work, scientific results, or ideas of other people without a specific reference is a form of stealing. This form of stealing is called *plagiarism*. It's easy to be sure not to plagiarize—*just cite in all your work any sources of information, data, creative work, or ideas that you are borrowing from someone else*. It's fine to borrow, but you have to be clear about when you are doing so.

Referencing any materials or facts that you use in your work is a key part of writing a good paper. Accurate references will actually make your work a lot better. If you have questions, be sure to check with your teacher on his or her methods for documenting references. Your teacher should also be able to tell you the policies at your school for plagiarism.

It is common practice to use the Web to do research on school projects. The Web sites that you use in your report must be cited just as you cite a book or an article from a journal. Your teacher can provide you with the format for citing Web resources.

When doing research or projects in any of your classes, it is vital to keep a list of all references that you use. This convention is part of doing research. It is the official way to recognize the results and prior hard work of others, and it is the proper way to confirm your research and interpretations. Two steps are needed to have accurate references.

1. *Clearly indicate, or cite, the prior research or findings directly within your text or write-up*. This is called a *citation*, and it includes the last names of the authors plus the year the work was published (see the following example). Some results in your work may be widely known facts in science (for example, the speed of light and the atomic masses for elements of the periodic table). These facts don't need text citations.

But suppose that you are researching changes in the rates of cigarette smoking among adults over the past 20 years. Here's an example of citing resources directly in your text:

> Recent data show that smoking rates are decreasing somewhat, and that about one-fourth (22.5 percent) of all Americans still smoke (Centers for Disease Control and Prevention [CDC], 2004). Factors related to smoking rates include the socioeconomic status of the person (Adler, Boyce, Chesney, Folkman, & Syme, 1993; Sorenson, Barbeau, Hunt, & Emmons, 2004), or where the person works (Nelson, Emont, Brackbill, Cameron, Peddicord, & Fiore, 1994). Another factor is where the person learns about quitting smoking, such as at work or by television or radio (CDC, 1999; Haviland et al., 2004).

2 *Each of the resources you cite must be listed in a reference section at the end of your report.* Your teacher may have a preferred format. The following example cites the resources for the short reading on smoking in adults.

Reference List

Adler, N. E., Boyce, W. T., Chesney, M. A., Folkman, S., & Syme, L. S. (1993). Socioeconomic inequalities in health: No easy solution. *Journal of the American Medical Association*, *269*, 3140–3145.

Centers for Disease Control and Prevention. (1999). *Best practices for comprehensive tobacco control programs*. Atlanta, GA: U.S. Department of Health and Human Services, Centers for Disease Control and Prevention.

Centers for Disease Control and Prevention. (2004). Cigarette smoking among adults—United States, 2004. *Morbidity and Mortality Weekly Report*, *53*, 427–431.

Haviland, L., Thornton, A. H., Carothers, S., Hund, L., Allen, J. A., Kastens, B., et al. (2004). Giving infants a great start: Launching a national smoking cessation program for pregnant women. *Nicotine and Tobacco Research*, 6, S181–188.

Nelson, D. E., Emont, S. L., Brackbill, R. M., Cameron, L. L., Peddicord, J., & Fiore, M. C. (1994). Cigarette smoking prevalence by occupation in the United States: A comparison between 1978 to 1980 and 1987 to 1990. *Journal of Occupational Medicine*, *36*, 516–525.

Sorensen, G., Barbeau, E., Hunt, M. K., & Emmons, K. (2004). Reducing social disparities in tobacco use: A social-contextual model for reducing tobacco use among blue-collar workers. *American Journal of Public Health*, *94*, 230–239.

9 HOW TO Use a Compound Microscope

The human eye cannot distinguish objects much smaller than 0.1 millimeter in diameter. The compound microscope is a technology often used in biology to extend vision. It allows observation of much smaller objects. The most commonly used compound microscope is monocular (that is, it has one eyepiece). Figure H9.1 shows a binocular microscope. Light reaches the eye after it has passed through the objects being examined. In *How to Use a Compound Microscope*, you will learn how to use and care for a microscope.

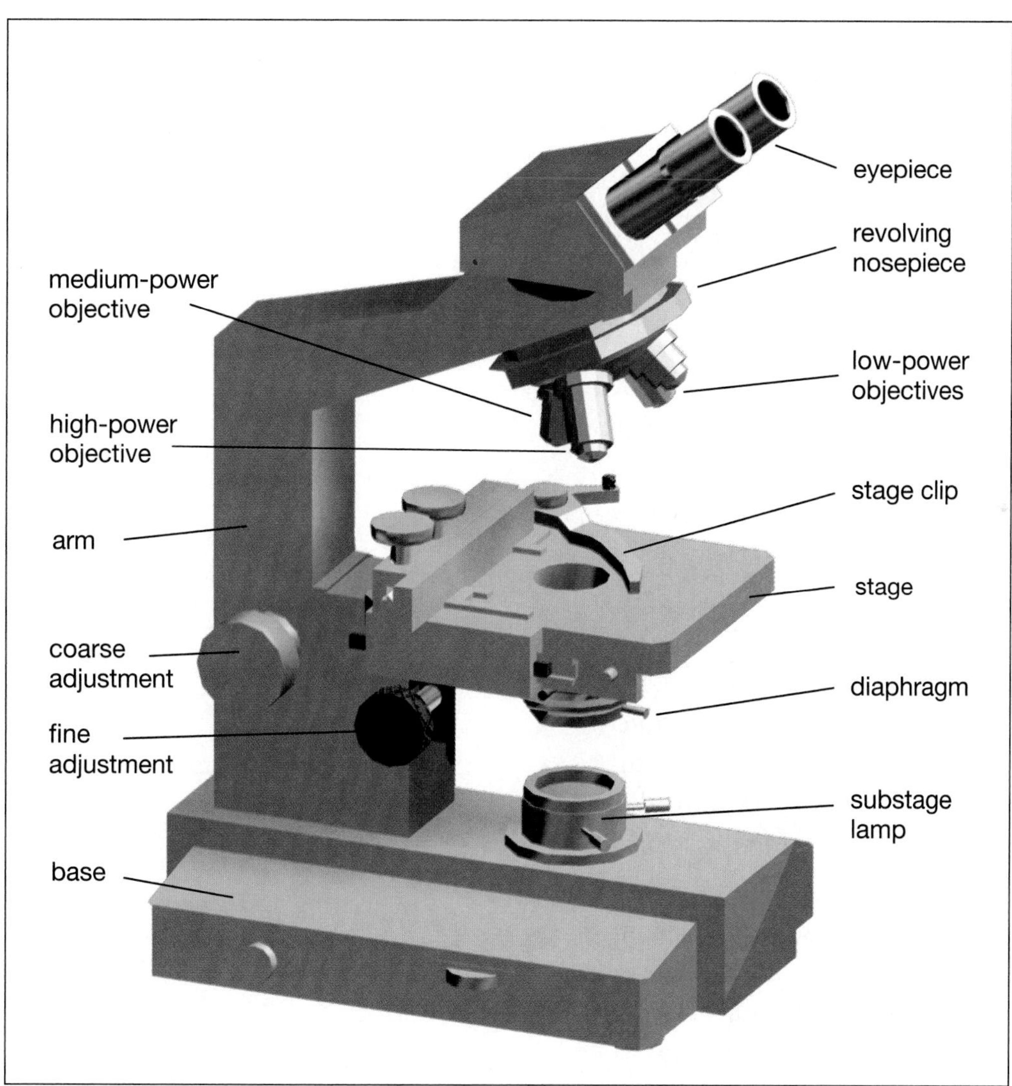

▲ **Figure H9.1 Compound microscope.** Use this figure to help locate the parts of a compound microscope.

Part I: Setting Up the Microscope

Materials

For each team of 2 students

- 3 coverslips
- 3 microscope slides
- 1 100-mL beaker or small jar
- 1 dropping pipet
- 1 compound microscope
- 1 pair of scissors
- 1 transparent metric ruler
- lens paper
- newspaper
- water

1. Read *Care of the Microscope* to learn how to properly care for a microscope.

Care of the Microscope

- The microscope is a precision instrument that requires proper care. Always carry the microscope with both hands. Put one hand under its base, the other on its arm (see figure H9.2).
- Keep the microscope away from the edge of the table. If a lamp is attached to the microscope, keep its cord out of the way. Move everything not needed for microscope studies off your lab table.
- Avoid tilting the microscope when using temporary slides made with water.
- The lenses of the microscope cost almost as much as all the other parts put together. Never clean lenses with anything other than the lens paper designed for this task.
- Always return the microscope to the low-power setting before putting it away. The high-power objective extends too close to the stage to be left in place safely.

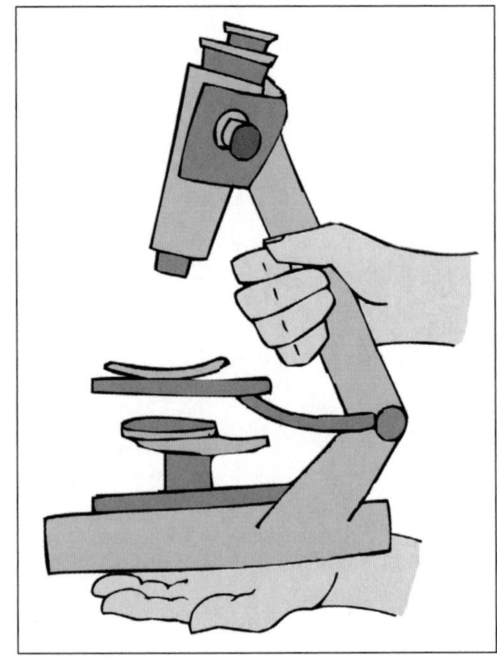

▲ **Figure H9.2 How to carry a microscope.** Always place one hand under the base and the other hand on the arm.

2. Rotate the low-power objective into place if it is not already there. When you change from one objective to another, you will hear the objective click into position.

3. Move the mirror so that you obtain even illumination through the opening in the stage. Or turn on the substage lamp. Most microscopes are equipped with a diaphragm for regulating light intensity. Some materials are best viewed in dim light, others in bright light.

Cautions

Never use a microscope mirror to capture direct sunlight when illuminating objects under a microscope. The mirror concentrates light rays, which can permanently damage the retina of the eye. Always use indirect light.

4. Make sure the lenses are dry and free of fingerprints and debris. Wipe lenses with lens paper only.

Part II: Using the Microscope

Materials

For each team of 2 students

supplies from Part I

1. In your science notebook, prepare a data table similar to the one in figure H9.3.

Object being viewed	Observations and comments
Letter *o*	
Letter *c*	
Letter *e* or *r*	

Figure H9.3 Microscope observations.

2. Cut a lowercase letter *o* from a piece of newspaper. Place it right side up on a clean slide. With a dropping pipet, place 1 drop of water on the letter. This type of slide is called a wet mount.

3. Wait until the paper is soaked before adding a coverslip. Hold the coverslip at about a 45-degree angle, with the bottom edge of the coverslip touching both the slide and the drop of water. Then slowly lower the coverslip. Figure H9.4 shows these first steps.

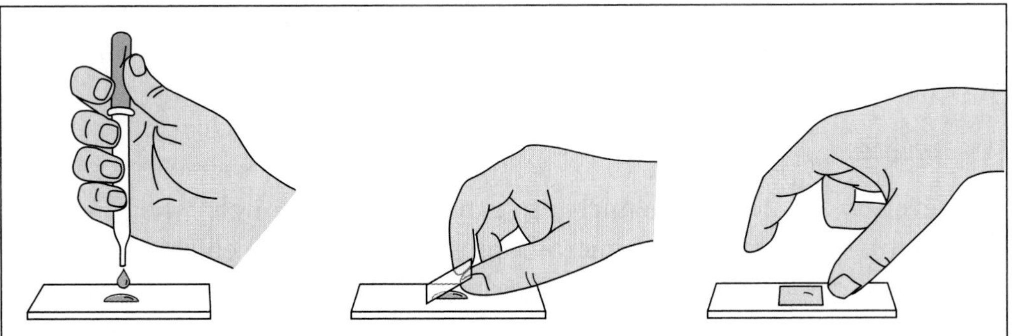

▲ **Figure H9.4 Preparing a wet mount.** This figure shows the steps to prepare a wet mount with a microscope slide and coverslip.

4. Place the slide on the microscope stage. Clamp it down with the stage clips. Move the slide so that the letter is in the middle of the hole in the stage. Use the coarse-adjustment knob to lower the low-power objective to the lowest position.
5. Look through the eyepiece. Use the coarse-adjustment knob to *raise* the objective slowly, until the letter *o* is in view.
6. If you cannot find the *o* on the first try, start the process again by repeating Steps 4 and 5.
7. Once you have the *o* in view, use the fine-adjustment knob to sharpen the focus. Position the diaphragm for the best light. Compare the way the letter looks through the microscope with the way it looks to the naked eye. Record your observations in your data table.
8. To determine how magnified the view is, multiply the number inscribed on the eyepiece by the number of the objective lens being used. For example:

   eyepiece (10×) × objective lens (10×) = total (100×)

9. Follow the same procedure with a lowercase *c*. Describe in your data table how the letter appears when viewed through a microscope.
10. Make a wet mount of the letter *e* or the letter *r*. Describe how the letter appears when viewed through the microscope. What new information (not revealed by the letter *c*) is revealed by the *e* or *r*?

11 Look through the eyepiece at the letter as you use your thumbs and forefingers to move the slide slowly *away* from you. Which way does your view of the letter move? Move the slide to the right. Which way does the image move?

12 Make a sketch of the letter as you see it under the microscope. Label the changes in image and in movement that take place under the microscope.

Part III: Using High Power

Materials

For each team of 2 students

supplies from Part I

1 light-colored hair

1 dark-colored hair

1 Make a wet mount of 2 different-colored hairs, 1 light and 1 dark. Cross 1 hair over the other. Sketch the hairs as they appear under low power.

2 With the crossed hairs centered under low power, adjust the diaphragm for the best light.

3 Turn the high-power objective into viewing position. Do *not* change the focus.

4 Sharpen the focus with the *fine-adjustment knob only. Do not focus under high power with the coarse-adjustment knob.* The high-power objective will touch the slide if it is in its lowest position. So you must not make large adjustments toward the slide. *Doing so can damage the objective and the slide by driving the objective into the slide.*

5 Readjust the diaphragm to get the best light. If you are not successful in finding the object under high power the first time, return to Step 2. Repeat the entire procedure carefully.

6 Using the fine-adjustment knob, focus on the hairs at the point where they cross. Can you see both hairs sharply at the same focus level? How can you use the fine-adjustment knob to determine which hair is crossed over the other? Sketch the hairs as they appear under high power.

Reflect and Connect

Work with your partner to answer the following questions in your science notebook.

1. Summarize the differences between an image viewed through a microscope and the same image viewed with the unaided eye.
2. When you view an object through the high-power objective, not all of the object may be in focus. Explain why.

Laboratory Safety

The science laboratory has the potential to be either a safe place or a dangerous place. The difference depends on how well you know and follow safe laboratory practices. It is important that you read the information here and learn how to recognize and avoid potentially hazardous situations. Follow your teacher's instructions about specific safety concerns related to your science classroom. Basic rules for working safely in the laboratory include the following.

Basic Safety

1. Be prepared. Study the assigned activity before you come to class. Resolve any questions about the procedures before you begin to work.
2. Be organized. Arrange the materials you need for the activity in an orderly way.
3. Maintain a clean, open work area, free of anything except those materials you need for the assigned activity. Store books, backpacks, and purses out of the way. Keep laboratory materials away from the edge of the work surface.
4. Tie back long hair and remove dangling jewelry. Roll up long sleeves and tuck in long clothing. Do not wear loose-fitting sleeves or open-toed shoes in the laboratory.
5. Wear safety goggles and a lab apron whenever you work with chemicals, hot liquids, lab burners, hot plates, or apparatuses that could break or shatter. Wear protective gloves when working with preserved specimens, toxic and corrosive chemicals, or when otherwise directed to do so.
6. Never wear contact lenses while conducting any experiment involving chemicals. If you must wear them (by a physician's order), inform your teacher before conducting any experiment involving chemicals.
7. Never use direct or reflected sunlight to illuminate your microscope or any other optical device. Direct or reflected sunlight can cause serious damage to your retinas.
8. Keep your hands away from the sharp or pointed ends of equipment, such as scalpels, dissecting needles, or scissors.
9. Observe all cautions in the procedural steps of the activities. **Caution** is a signal word used in the text and on labeled chemicals or reagents that tells you about the potential for harm and injury. It reminds you to observe specific safety practices. **Always read and follow this statement.** It is meant to help keep you and your fellow students safe.

Caution statements advise you that the material or procedure has some potential risk of harm or injury if directions are not followed.

10. Become familiar with the caution symbols identified in the following table.

Cautions

The caution symbol alerts you to procedures or materials that may be harmful if directions are not followed properly. You may encounter the common hazards listed in this table during this course.

Caution items	Precautions
Sharp object	Sharp objects can cause injury, either a cut or puncture. Handle all sharp objects with caution and use them only as your teacher instructs you. Do not use them for any purpose other than the intended one. If you do get a cut or puncture wound, call your teacher and get first aid.
Irritant	An irritant is any substance that, on contact, can cause reddening of living tissue. Wear safety goggles, a lab apron, and protective gloves when handling any irritating chemical. In case of contact, flush the affected area with soap and water for at least 15 minutes and call your teacher. Remove contaminated clothing.
Reactive	These chemicals are capable of reacting with any other substance, including water, and can cause a violent reaction. ***Do not*** mix a reactive chemical with any other substance, including water, unless directed to do so by your teacher. Wear your safety goggles, a lab apron, and protective gloves.
Corrosive	A corrosive substance injures or destroys body tissue on contact by direct chemical action. When handling any corrosive substance, wear safety goggles, a lab apron, and protective gloves. In case of contact with a corrosive material, immediately flush the affected area with water and call your teacher.
Biohazard	Any biological substance that can cause infection through exposure is a biohazard. Before handling any material so labeled, review your teacher's specific instructions. ***Do not*** handle in any manner other than as instructed. Wear safety goggles, a lab apron, and protective gloves. Any contact with a biohazard should be reported to your teacher immediately.
Safety goggles	Safety goggles are for eye protection. Wear goggles whenever you see this symbol. If you wear glasses, be sure the goggles fit comfortably over them. In case of splashes in your eyes, flush your eyes (including under the lid) at an eyewash station for 15–20 minutes. If you wear contact lenses, remove them ***immediately*** and flush your eyes as directed. Call your teacher.
Lab apron	A lab apron is intended to protect your clothing. Whenever you see this symbol, put on your apron and tie it securely behind you. If you spill any substance on your clothing, call your teacher.
Gloves	Wear gloves when you see this symbol or whenever your teacher directs you to do so. Wear them when using ***any*** chemical or reagent solution. Do not wear your gloves for an extended period of time.
Flammable	A flammable substance is any material capable of igniting under certain conditions. ***Do not*** bring flammable materials into contact with open flames or near heat sources unless instructed to do so by your teacher. Remember that flammable liquids give off vapors that can be ignited by a nearby heat source. Should a fire occur, ***do not*** attempt to extinguish it yourself. Call your teacher. Wear safety goggles, a lab apron, and protective gloves whenever you handle a flammable substance.
Poison	Poisons can cause injury by direct action within a body system through direct contact with skin, inhalation, ingestion, or penetration. Always wear safety goggles, a lab apron, and protective gloves when handling any material with this label. If you have any preexisting injuries to your skin, inform your teacher before you handle any poison. In case of contact, call your teacher immediately.

Caution symbol. Refer to this table when you see a caution icon in your text for precautions to take in the activity.

1. Never put anything in your mouth and never touch or taste substances in the laboratory unless you teacher specifically instructs you to do so.
2. Never smell substances in the laboratory without specific instructions from your teacher. Even then, do not inhale fumes directly; wave the air above the substance toward your nose and sniff carefully.
3. Never eat, drink, chew gum, or apply cosmetics in the laboratory. Do not store food or beverages in the lab area.
4. Know the location of all safety equipment and learn how to use each piece of equipment.
5. If you witness an unsafe incident, an accident, or a chemical spill, report it to your teacher immediately.
6. Use materials only from containers labeled with the name of the chemical and the precautions to be used. Become familiar with the safety precautions for each chemical by reading the label before use.
7. To dilute acid with water, **always add the acid to the water.**
8. Never return unused chemicals to the stock bottles. Do not put any object into a chemical bottle, except the dropper with which it may be equipped.
9. Clean up thoroughly. Dispose of chemicals and wash used glassware and instruments according to your teacher's instructions. Clean tables and sinks. Put away all equipment and supplies. Make sure all water, gas jets, burners, and electrical appliances are turned off. Return all laboratory materials and equipment to their proper places.
10. Wash your hands thoroughly after handling any living organisms or hazardous materials and before leaving the laboratory.
11. Never perform unauthorized experiments. Do only those experiments your teacher approves.
12. Never work alone in the laboratory and never work without your teacher's supervision.
13. Approach laboratory work with maturity. Never run, push, or engage in horseplay or practical jokes of any type in the laboratory. Use laboratory materials and equipment only as directed.
14. Use the smallest amount of material necessary to conduct an experiment successfully.

In addition to observing these general safety precautions, you need to know about some specific categories of safety. Before you do any laboratory work, familiarize yourself with the following precautions.

Heat

1. Use only the heat source specified in the activity.
2. Never allow flammable materials such as alcohol near a flame or any other source of ignition.
3. When heating a substance in a test tube, point the mouth of the tube away from other students and you.

4. Never leave a lighted lab burner, hot plate, or any other hot objects unattended.
5. Never reach over an exposed flame or other heat source.
6. Use tongs, test-tube clamps, insulated gloves, or pot holders to handle hot equipment.
7. Shut off all sources of natural gas after use.
8. Never touch equipment such as glassware or iron rings that have been heated. They can be very hot, even though they may not look hot.

Glassware

1. Never use cracked or chipped glassware.
2. Use caution and proper equipment when handling hot glassware; remember that hot glass looks the same as cool glass.
3. Make sure glassware is clean before you use it and when you store it.
4. To put glass tubing into a rubber stopper, moisten the tubing and the stopper. Protect your hands with a heavy cloth when you insert or remove glass tubing from a rubber stopper. Never force or twist the tubing.
5. Immediately sweep up broken glassware and discard it in a special, labeled container for broken glass. **Never pick up broken glass with your fingers.**

Electrical Equipment and Other Apparatuses

1. Before you begin any work, learn how to use each piece of apparatus safely and correctly in order to obtain accurate scientific information.
2. Never use equipment with frayed insulation or loose or broken wires.
3. Make sure the area in and around the electrical equipment is dry and free of flammable materials. Never touch electrical equipment with wet hands.
4. Turn off all power switches before plugging an appliance into an outlet. Never jerk wires from outlets or pull appliance plugs out by the wire.
5. Assemble lab apparatuses so that the setup does not tip easily.

Living and Preserved Specimens

1. Be sure that specimens for dissection are properly mounted and supported. Do not cut a specimen while holding it in your hand.
2. Wash your work surface with a disinfectant solution both before and after using live microorganisms.
3. Always wash your hands with soap and water after working with live or preserved specimens.
4. Care for animals humanely. General rules for their care are listed below.
   a. Always follow carefully your teacher's instructions about the care of laboratory animals.

b. Keep the animals in a suitable, escape-proof container in a location where they will not be disturbed constantly.
c. Keep the containers clean. Clean cages of small birds and mammals daily. Provide proper ventilation, light, and temperature.
d. Provide water at all times.
e. Feed regularly, depending on the animals' needs.
f. Treat laboratory animals gently and with kindness in all situations.
g. If you are responsible for the regular care of any animals, be sure to make arrangements for their care during weekends, holidays, and vacations.
h. Your teacher will provide a suitable method to dispose of or release animals, if it becomes necessary.

5. Many plants or plant parts are poisonous. Work only with the plants your teacher specifies. Never put any plant or plant parts in your mouth.
6. Handle plants carefully and gently. Most plants must have light, soil, and water, although the specific requirements differ.
7. Wear the following personal protective equipment when handling or dissecting preserved specimens: safety goggles, a lab apron, and protective gloves.

Accident Procedures

1. Report **all** accidents, incidents, and injuries, and all breakage and spills, no matter how minor, to your teacher.
2. If a chemical spills on your skin or clothing, wash it off immediately with plenty of water and have a classmate notify your teacher immediately.
3. If a chemical gets in your eyes or on your face, wash immediately at the eyewash fountain with plenty of water. Flush your eyes for at least 15 minutes, including under each eyelid. Have a classmate notify your teacher immediately.
4. If a chemical spills on the floor or work surface, do not clean it up yourself. Notify your teacher immediately.
5. If a thermometer breaks, do not touch the broken pieces with your bare hands. Notify your teacher immediately.
6. In case of a lab table fire, notify your teacher immediately. In case of a clothing fire, drop to the floor and roll. Use a fire blanket if one is available. Have a classmate notify your teacher immediately.
7. Report to your teacher all cuts and abrasions received in the laboratory, no matter how small.

Chemical Safety

All chemicals are hazardous in some way. A hazardous chemical is defined as a substance that is likely to cause injury. Chemicals can be placed in four hazard categories: flammable, toxic, corrosive, and reactive.

In the laboratory investigations for this course, every effort is made to minimize the use of dangerous materials. However, many "less hazardous" chemicals can cause injury if not handled properly. The following information will help you become aware of the types of chemical hazards that exist and of how you can reduce the risk of injury when using chemicals. Before you work with any chemical, be sure to review safety rules 1 through 10 described at the beginning of this safety appendix.

Flammable Substances

Flammable substances are solids, liquids, or gases that will burn. The process of burning involves three interrelated components—fuel (any substance capable of burning), oxidizer (often air or a specific chemical), and ignition source (a spark, flame, or heat). To control fire hazard, one must remove, or otherwise make inaccessible, at least one side of this fire triangle.

Flammable chemicals should not be used in the presence of ignition sources, such as lab burners, hot plates, and sparks from electrical equipment or static electricity. Containers of flammables should be closed when not in use. Sufficient ventilation in the laboratory will help to keep the concentration of flammable vapors to a minimum.

Toxic Substances

Most of the chemicals you encounter in a laboratory are toxic, or poisonous to life. The degree of toxicity depends on the properties of the specific substance, its concentration, the type of exposure, and other variables. The effects of exposure to a toxic substance can range from minor discomfort to serious illness or death. Exposure to toxic substances can occur through ingestion, skin contact, or inhalation of toxic vapors. Wearing a lab apron, safety goggles, and protective gloves is an important precautionary measure when using toxic chemicals. A clean work area, prompt spill cleanup, and good ventilation also are important.

Corrosive Substances

Corrosive chemicals are solids, liquids, or gases that by direct chemical action either destroy living tissue or cause permanent changes in the tissue. Corrosive substances can destroy eye and respiratory tract tissues. The consequences of mishandling a corrosive substance can be impaired sight or permanent blindness, severe disfigurement, permanent severe breathing difficulties, and even death. As with toxic substances, wear a lab apron, safety goggles, and protective gloves when handling corrosive chemicals to help prevent contact with your skin or eyes. Immediately wash off splashes on your skin or eyes with water, while a classmate notifies the teacher.

Reactive Substances

Under certain conditions, reactive chemicals promote violent reactions. A chemical may explode spontaneously or when it is mechanically disturbed. Reactive chemicals also include those that react rapidly when mixed with another chemical, releasing a large amount of energy. Keep chemicals separate from one another unless they are being combined according to specific instructions in an activity. Heed any other cautions your teacher may give you.

Glossary

A

abiotic [abiótico]: The physical and chemical (nonliving) components of an environment, such as light or water.

acceleration (*a*) [aceleración (*a*)]: The time rate of change in velocity; it is represented by the symbol *a*. The mathematical relationship describing acceleration is $a = \frac{\Delta v}{\Delta t}$.

acid [ácido]: A chemical compound that increases the concentration of hydrogen ions (H^+) in solution. This definition represents one of several views of acids.

acre-feet (af) [acre-pie (ap)]: The volume of water that covers 1 acre of land with water that is 1 foot deep.

activation energy (E_a) [energía de activación (E_a)]: The energy associated with the particles formed with the highest potential energy during a chemical process.

adaptations [adaptaciones]: Characteristics that help an organism survive and reproduce within a particular environment.

aerobic respiration [respiración aerobia]: A type of cellular respiration that requires the presence of oxygen.

agarose gel electrophoresis [electroforesis de gel de agarosa]: A process in which scientists separate DNA fragments by size. An electric current is used to propel the DNA through a porous gel matrix.

allele [alelo]: One of two or more possible forms of a gene. Each allele affects the hereditary trait a little differently.

amino acid [aminoácido]: The building blocks of polypeptides and proteins. Amino acids are organic compounds. They are composed of a central carbon atom to which are bonded a hydrogen atom, an amino group ($—NH_2$), an acid group (—COOH), and one of a variety of other atoms or groups of atoms.

anaerobe [anaerobio]: An organism that lives in the absence of oxygen.

anaerobic respiration [respiración anaeróbica]: A type of cellular respiration that does not require oxygen.

ancestral [ancestral]: Something from which a later generation or form is derived.

anion [anión]: A negatively charged particle typically associated with redox reactions.

anode [ánodo]: The electrode of an electrochemical cell, where oxidation takes place.

anticodon [anticodón]: A three-nucleotide sequence in a transfer RNA molecule. It is complementary to, and base-pairs with, a specific codon in mitochondrial RNA.

asexual reproduction [reproducción asexuada]: Any method of reproduction that requires only one parent or one parent cell.

atmospheric mixing [mezcla atmosférica]: The process of transporting and mixing components of the atmosphere on a regional or global scale.

autosome [autosoma]: A chromosome that is not directly involved in determining sex.

B

base [base]: A chemical compound that increases the concentration of hydroxide ions (OH^-) in solution. This definition represents one of several views of bases.

bioethics [bioética]: The study of ethical issues that are raised by developments in life science technologies, such as new medical technologies.

biologic carbon cycle [ciclo biológico del carbono]: A carbon cycle that consists of *active* or *mobile* carbon that moves between reservoirs on timescales of days to hundreds of years. This part of the carbon cycle operates largely at the surface of Earth and involves organisms.

biomass [biomasa]: The dry weight of organic matter that makes up a group of organisms in a particular habitat.

biome [bioma]: The distinctive plant cover and the rest of the community of organisms associated with a particular physical environment; often the biome is named for its plant cover. Some examples of biomes include tundra, tropical rain forest, desert, and temperate grassland.

bioremediation [biorremediación]: The use of microorganisms to degrade waste.

biotechnology [biotecnología]: A solution to a problem that involves technology *and* living organisms. Recombinant DNA technology has created many new forms of biotechnology.

biotic [bióticos]: The living or recently living components of an ecosystem.

birthrate [índice de natalidad]: The rate at which reproduction increases the population; often expressed as new individuals per 1,000 or 10,000 in the population.

boundaries [límites]: The limits of a system within which interactions occur.

C

carrying capacity [capacidad máxima]: The maximum population size that can be supported by the available resources of a given area.

catalyst [catalizador]: A chemical species that increases the rate of a chemical reaction without being changed permanently by the reaction.

cathode [cátodo]: The electrode of an electrochemical cell, where reduction takes place.

cation [catión]: A positively charged particle typically associated with redox reactions.

chromosome [cromosoma]: A long, threadlike group of genes found in the nucleus of all eukaryotic cells. Chromosomes are most visible during mitosis and meiosis. Chromosomes consist of DNA and protein.

climate [clima]: The general atmospheric conditions that repeat over long periods of time.

codon [codón]: The basic unit of the genetic code; a sequence of three adjacent nucleotides in DNA or messenger RNA.

community [comunidad]: All the organisms that inhabit a particular area.

complementary base pairing [formación de pares de bases complementarias]: The predictable interaction between nitrogen bases on opposite strands of DNA and between DNA and RNA. Adenine pairs with thymine and guanine pairs with cytosine in DNA; in RNA, adenine pairs with uracil.

concentration [concentración]: A means of expressing the number of particles per unit of space. A common unit of concentration in chemistry is molarity. It has the units of moles per liter (mol/L).

conservation of mass [conservación de la masa]: The concept that the mass of the reactants in a reaction must equal the mass of the products.

constant [constante]: A factor or attribute that remains unchanged during the course of an investigation. A constant can also be a quantity or value that is assumed not to vary for the purposes of a theory or experiment, for example, the speed of light.

continental crust [corteza continental]: The varied, basic rock material that is 40–70 kilometers thick and makes up continents.

continental drift [deriva continental]: The hypothesis proposed in 1912 by Alfred Wegener that, at one time, Earth's landmasses were joined in a supercontinent that broke up to form the present continents. Continental drift is now considered part of the broader theory of plate tectonics.

control [control]: In an investigation, the control is the individual thing, or group designated to receive no treatment (the unchanged group). All other groups are compared against the control.

convergent zones [zonas convergentes]: Regions where tectonic plates crash together.

cubic feet per second (cfs) [pies cúbicos por segundo (pcs)]: Units of water flow that measure 1 cubic foot of water moving past a point in 1 second.

D

daughter element [elemento derivado]: The chemical substance on the product side of a radioactive decay equation. The nuclei of daughter elements are produced from parent elements.

deoxyribonucleic acid (DNA) [ácido desoxirribonucleico (ADN)]: The hereditary material of most organisms. DNA makes up genes and contains deoxyribose, a phosphate group, and one of four DNA bases.

diploid [diploide]: Refers to a cell that contains both members of every chromosome pair that is characteristic of a species.

dissolved inorganic carbon (DIC) [carbono inorgánico disuelto (CID)]: The component of carbon derived from inorganic sources, such as bicarbonate and carbonate ions, that is dissolved in natural waters.

dissolved load [carga disuelta]: The elements and molecules in an ionic form that are dissolved in natural waters.

dissolved organic carbon (DOC) [carbono orgánico disuelto (COD)]: The component of carbon derived from organic matter, such as plant leaves, that is dissolved in natural waters.

divergent zones [zonas divergentes]: Zones where tectonic plates move apart, forming rifts on continents or on the ocean floor.

DNA polymerase [polimerasa de ADN]: An enzyme that catalyzes the synthesis of a new DNA strand by using one of the original strands as a template.

DNA replication [replicación del ADN]: The process of making a copy of a chromosome in a cell nucleus as well as other genes in certain organelles outside the nucleus, particularly chloroplasts and mitochrondria.
The process is different from duplication because each gene and each chromosome in the double set contains new parts and parts of the old gene or chromosome.

dominant [dominante]: Refers to alleles or traits that mask the presence of another allele of the same gene in a heterozygous organism.

E

eccentricity [excentricidad]: Refers to the shape of Earth's orbit around the Sun. Eccentricity varies on timescales of about 100,000 years.

ecological niche [nicho ecológico]: All the adaptations an organism uses to survive in its environment. These include what its role in the community is, what it eats, and what interactions it has with other organisms and with its environment.

ecology [ecología]: A field in biology that studies organisms and their relationship to their environment.

ecosystem [ecosistema]: The biological community and its abiotic environment.

elastic collision [choque elástico]: A collision that occurs when the energy and momenta of objects in a system remain the same before and after collisions. Elastic collisions can occur when colliding objects rebound or bounce off each other.

electric current [corriente eléctrica]: The flow of charge in a particular direction.

electrolytic cell [célula electrolítica]: An electrochemical reaction such as electrolysis. This reaction is characterized by using electrical energy to reverse a spontaneous redox reaction.

embryo [embrión]: An organism in its earliest stages of development.

emigration [emigración]: The departure of individuals from a population; emigration decreases the size of the population.

endemic [endémico]: Animals or plants that are restricted to a specific region.

endothermic [endotérmico]: Processes that absorb heat from the surroundings, resulting in a temperature decrease. Endothermic reactions have a positive net enthalpy ($+\Delta H$).

enthalpy [entalpía]: The net energy ($E_{final} - E_{initial}$ = net energy) associated with a chemical reaction. Its symbol is ΔH.

environment [medio ambiente]: Everything living and nonliving in an organism's surroundings, including light, temperature, air, soil, water, and other organisms.

enzymes [enzimas]: Any chemical species, usually proteins or molecules that include proteins, that catalyze, or speed up, biological reactions. Enzymes are made by an organism.

equilibrium [equilibrio]: A description of the state of any reversible chemical reaction in which the rate of its forward reaction equals the rate of its reverse reaction.

equilibrium position [punto de equilibrio]: An indication of the relative amounts of reactants and products present for a chemical system at equilibrium. When more products are present, the equilibrium position favors the products. The equilibrium position is to the right. When more reactants are present, the equilibrium position favors the reactants. The equilibrium position is to the left.

erosion [erosión]: The process where weathered rock fragments and soils are transported and moved downward due to gravity. Erosion of mountains occurs along steep slopes and river valleys.

erosion half-life [período de semidesintegración por erosión]: The time for the elevations of a topographic profile to decrease by about half.

ethics [ética]: Refers to the morals of individuals and society. Morals are values and beliefs about what is acceptable behavior.

evaporation [evaporación]: The change when molecules of a liquid absorb heat and change into the vapor phase.

evapotranspiration [evapotranspiración]: The total loss of water from land settings due to evaporation and to transpiration from plants.

evolution [evolución]: A cumulative change in the characteristics of organisms or populations from generation to generation.

exothermic [exotérmico]: Processes that release heat to the surroundings, resulting in a temperature increase. Exothermic reactions have a negative net enthalpy ($-\Delta H$).

exponential [exponencial]: A way to describe a line on a graph that is curved. The equations that generate these lines have exponents in them and represent the changing rates of some phenomenon.

exponential growth [crecimiento exponencial]: Growth that occurs at a rate proportional to its size.

F

flux [flujo]: The rate at which matter enters or exits a reservoir or system. Fluxes are typically given as rates relative to a duration of time, such as days or years.

foraminifera (forams) [foraminífera (forams)]: Single-celled, photosynthesizing organisms that live in the ocean. Forams form the base of the marine food web.

fossil fuels [combustibles fósiles]: Fuels that consist of hydrogen and carbon compounds from geologic deposits of organic carbon. They are a primary energy source for humans.

G

gamete [gameto]: A sex cell, either an egg or a sperm, formed by meiosis. Gametes have half the number of chromosomes that body cells have.

gene [gen]: The fundamental unit of heredity, which transmits a set of specifications from one generation to the next; a segment of DNA that codes for a specific product.

gene therapy [terapia de genes]: The insertion of normal or genetically altered genes into cells as part of the treatment of genetic disorders.

genetic engineering [ingeniería genética]: The experimental technology developed to alter the genome of a living cell for medical or industrial use. Genetic engineering introduces new traits to organisms.

genome [genoma]: All the genetic material in any given species or complement of a haploid cell from any given species.

genotype [genotipo]: The genetic makeup of an organism.

geochemical cycle [ciclo geoquímico]: A term that describes the storage and movement of a chemical, element, or nutrient such as carbon, water, phosphorus, or calcium through the earth systems.

geologic carbon cycle [ciclo geológico del carbono]: A carbon cycle that consists largely of *inactive* or *immobile* carbon that moves between reservoirs on timescales of hundreds to millions of years. Carbon in geologic reservoirs is stored mainly inside Earth.

glacials [glaciaciones]: Also known as **ice ages.** Periods where the overall global climate is cold. Glacials are characterized by low sea level and the widespread extent of ice sheets.

H

habitat [hábitat]: The place where an organism lives. Even in the same ecosystem, different organisms differ in their habitats.

half-life [período de semidesintegración]: The length of time it takes for exactly one-half of the parent atoms to decay to daughter atoms. Half-life reflects the time rate of decay.

half reactions [semi-reacciones]: Either the oxidation or reduction portion of a redox chemical reaction.

haploid [haploide]: Refers to a cell that contains only one member (n) of each chromosome pair characteristic of a species.

heterozygous [heterocigoto]: Refers to having two different alleles for a given trait.

homozygous [homocigoto]: Refers to having two identical alleles for a given trait.

humus [humus]: Decayed litter on forest floors and within soils.

hydrocarbon [hidrocarburo]: An organic substance made of hydrogen and carbon.

hypothesis [hipótesis]: A statement that is based on current knowledge and suggests an explanation for an observation or an answer to a scientific problem. A hypothesis suggests that there is a cause-and-effect or an if-then relationship for the observation or problem.

I

ice sheet [capa de hielo]: Thick, glacial ice that accumulates on continents and can be up to several kilometers thick.

immigration [inmigración]: The arrival of new individuals into a population; immigration increases the size of a population.

impulse [impulso]: The product of force and change in time ($F\Delta t$).

independent assortment [muestreo independiente]: The inheritance of the alleles for a trait.

indicator [indicador]: A chemical substance that undergoes a measurable change. A color change during a chemical reaction is an example. The change signals a point of interest during a particular reaction.

inelastic collision [colisión inelástica]: An inelastic collision occurs when the energy of the objects in a system is less after the collision than before the collision. A common example occurs when objects hit and stick together after the collision.

input [entrada]: The amount or mass of material entering a reservoir or system.

interglacials [períodos interglaciares]: Periods where the overall global climate is warm. Interglacials are characterized by high sea level and a limited extent of ice sheets.

isotopes [isótopos]: Atoms of the same element that have different numbers of neutrons.

L

land bridge [puente terrestre]: A bridge of land above sea level that links two continents.

Last Glacial Maximum (LGM) [Máximo de la Última Glaciación (LGM por sus siglas en inglés)]: The most recent of many glacials. The LGM has a strong influence on geology and occurred about 21,000 years ago.

law of conservation of matter [ley de conservación de la materia]: A principle of nature that states that matter is neither created nor destroyed during ordinary chemical and physical changes.

law of conservation of momentum [ley de conservación de la energía]: A principle of nature that states that, in any interaction, the momentum of the system before the interaction will be the same as the momentum of the system after the interaction.

Le Châtelier's principle [principio de Le Châtelier]: A way to predict shifts in equilibrium position. The method depends on changes imposed on a system at equilibrium. Imposed changes such as temperature, concentration, pressure, and volume cause shifts in the equilibrium position. The shift always moves in a direction that lessens the imposed change and restores equilibrium.

ligase [ligasa]: An enzyme that assists in the formation of bonds between adjacent, complementary DNA segments.

limiting factor [factor limitante]: An environmental condition such as food, temperature, water, or sunlight that restricts the types of organisms and the population numbers that an environment can support.

litter [materia]: Litter is the buildup of leaves and plant limbs beneath trees on forest floors. Forming litter moves carbon from trees to the forest floor. When litter starts to decay, it is sometimes called humus.

logistic growth [crecimiento logístico]: Growth that starts as exponential growth then slows and eventually stops. In logistic growth, a population levels off at the carrying capacity of the environment.

M

mantle [manto]: The layer of Earth that lies beneath Earth's crust. The mantle consists mostly of the minerals olivine and pyroxene, and the elements magnesium, iron, silicon, and oxygen.

meiosis [meiosis]: Meiosis is the process in which two cell divisions, including division of the nucleus, produces gametes (in animals) or sexual spores (in plants). The gametes or sexual spores have one-half of the genetic material of the original cell.

messenger RNA (mRNA) [ARN mensajero (ARNm)]: A class of RNA molecule that is complementary to one strand of DNA; mRNA is transcribed from genes and translated by ribosomes into protein (see transcription and translation).

microbe [microbio]: A general term for microorganism.

mid-oceanic ridges [dorsales oceánicas]: Areas of high topography on the ocean floor that form due to the rifting of tectonic plates. They were originally linked with the mid-Atlantic ridge.

millions of gallons (Mgal) [millones de galones (Mgal)]: A standard unit for the volume of water in systems.

millions of gallons per day (Mgal/d) [millones de galones por día (Mgal/d)]: A standard flux for water in systems.

mitosis [mitosis]: The replication of the chromosomes and the production of two nuclei in one cell; mitosis is usually followed by the division of the cytoplasm in the cell; it forms new cells.

molar mass [masa molar]: The average atomic mass of any element (found on the periodic table) in grams. Molar mass is equal to the amount of mass in grams in 1 mole (mol) of that element.

molarity [molaridad]: One of several ways to communicate the concentration of a substance. Molarity has the units of moles per liter (mol/L) and is abbreviated M.

mole (mol) [mol (mol)]: A unit that refers to an amount of a substance associated with 6.02×10^{23} particles of that substance.

momentum (p) [cantidad de movimiento (p)]: The product of mass and velocity (mv); it is represented by the symbol p. Momentum can be thought of as mass in motion.

monohybrid cross [cruce monohíbrido]: A mating between individuals that differ in one allele.

mortality rate [índice de mortalidad]: Death rate, measured as the proportion of deaths to total population over a given period; often expressed as the number of deaths per 1,000 or 10,000 individuals.

mutation [mutación]: A chemical change in a gene that results in a new allele or a change in the portion of a chromosome that regulates the gene. In either case, the change is hereditary.

N

natural selection [selección natural]: A mechanism for biological evolution. In natural selection, members of a population with the most successful adaptations to their environment are more likely to survive and reproduce than members with less successful adaptations.

net force [fuerza neta]: The force resulting from the vector addition of all forces acting on an object.

Newton's laws [leyes de Newton]: History reports three governing principles of nature called Newton's laws. (1) The law of inertia is often used to describe Newton's first law. It states that there will be no change in an object's motion unless acted upon by an outside force. (2) Newton's second law states that the net force on an object is equal to the product of the object's mass and acceleration. It is represented by the equation $F_{net} = ma$. (3) Newton's third law is the principle of nature that states that forces come in pairs, equal in magnitude and opposite in direction. These forces always act on two different objects.

nucleotide [nucleótido]: A subunit or building block of DNA or RNA. It consists of a 5-carbon sugar, a nitrogen base, and a phosphate group.

O

oceanic crust [corteza oceánica]: The outer part of Earth that resides beneath oceans. Oceanic crust is attached to several continents to form tectonic plates.

output [salida]: The amount or mass of material leaving a reservoir or system.

oxidation [oxidación]: A reaction in which electrons appear on the product side of the reaction or half reaction. That is, electrons are lost by the half reaction.

oxidation-reduction reactions (redox reactions) [reacciones de oxidación-reducción (reacciones redox)]: A chemical process involving the transfer of electrons to produce new chemical substances.

oxidized [oxidado]: A description of atoms or ions that have lost electrons.

oxidizing agent [agente oxidante]: A particle involved in a redox reaction that gains an electron or electrons. Oxidizing agents are reduced in redox reactions.

P

paleoclimatology [paleoclimatología]: The study of past climates.

parent element [elemento precursor]: The original chemical substance on the reactant side of a radioactive decay equation. The nuclei of parent elements decay radioactively into daughter elements and other particles.

pathogenic [patógeno]: Microorganisms that cause disease.

pedigree [pedigrí]: A diagram showing the occurrence of heritable traits across many generations.

peninsula [península]: A long spit of land surrounded by water.

phenotype [fenotipo]: The expression of a genotype in the appearance or function of an organism; the observed trait.

pheromone [feromona]: A chemical signal that functions in communication between animals. Pheromones act much like hormones to influence physiology and behavior.

phytoplankton [fitoplancton]: Very small aquatic organisms, many microscopic, that carry on photosynthesis. Phytoplankton form the basis of aquatic food webs.

plasmid [plásmido]: A small ring of DNA in bacteria. Plasmids carry genes separate from those of the chromosome.

plate tectonics, theory of [tectónica de placas, teoría de]: Plate tectonics is the theory that 12 or so rigid *plates* move slowly over Earth atop the mantle. Plates interact in many ways and affect all systems on Earth.

population [población]: A group of organisms of the same species that lives in the same place at the same time.

population density [densidad de población]: The number of organisms per unit of habitat area.

precession [precesión]: *See* wobble (precession).

principle of independent assortment [principio del muestreo independiente]: A principle that states that the inheritance of alleles for one trait does not affect the inheritance of alleles for another trait.

principle of segregation [principio de segregación]: A principle that states that during meiosis, chromosome pairs separate so that each of the two alleles for any given trait appears in a different gamete.

probability [probabilidad]: The chance that any given event will occur.

producer [productor]: Any organism that produces its own food using matter and energy from the nonliving world.

productivity [productividad]: The amount of available solar energy that is converted to chemical energy by producers during any given period.

products [productos]: The new substances that form as a result of a chemical reaction.

projectile motion [movimiento de proyectil]: A motion in the horizontal plane (often parallel to the ground) and in the vertical plane (perpendicular to the ground). In projectile motion, the horizontal motion and the vertical motion are independent of each other, that is, neither motion affects the other.

proxy [representante]: Something that stands in for, or represents something else.

proxy data [datos de representación]: Data as records that represent and stand in for other patterns of change. For example, the thickness of tree rings is an important proxy for annual climate.

Q

qualitative [cualitativo]: Something is qualitative if it describes features, characteristics, observations, or relative comparisons.

quantitative [cuantitativo]: Something is quantitative if it represents measurements or specific numbers, amounts (quantities), or ratios.

R

radioactive decay [desintegración radiactiva]: The spontaneous breakdown of one kind of nuclei into nuclei of different elements.

reactants [reactivos]: The starting ingredients for a chemical reaction.

recessive [recesivo]: Refers to alleles or traits that are masked by a dominant allele or trait.

recombinant DNA technology [tecnología de recombinación del ADN]: A technique used to cut apart segments of DNA and then put different segments of DNA together. Usually DNA segments from one organism are introduced into a different organism for genetic research, genetic engineering, or medical treatment.

reduced [reducidos]: A description of atoms or ions that have gained electrons.

reducing agent [agente reductor]: A particle involved in a redox reaction that loses an electron or electrons. Reducing agents are oxidized in redox reactions.

reduction [reducción]: A reaction in which electrons appear on the reactant side of the reaction of half reaction. That is, electrons are gained by the half reaction.

reservoir [depósito]: A volume or container that holds a given mass of matter.

residence time [tiempo de residencia]: The average length of time that matter in a system is in a reservoir. This value is estimated when there is no long-term change in the system. Residence time is the mass of material in the reservoir divided by either the flux in or the flux out ($residence\ time = mass / flux_{in}$ or $residence\ time = mass / flux_{out}$).

resource [recurso]: In ecology, a supply of one or more of an organism's requirements from the environment (light, food energy, water, oxygen or carbon dioxide, living space, protective cover, and so on). In human society, a resource may be anything useful.

restriction enzyme [enzima de restricción]: An enzyme that recognizes specific nucleotide sequences in DNA and breaks the DNA chain at those points.

restriction site [punto de restricción]: Restriction enzymes that cut at a unique DNA sequence.

ribonucleic acid (RNA) [ácido ribonucleico (ARN)]: RNA is the material coded by the DNA of cells to carry out specific genetic functions; for example, messenger RNA and transfer RNA carry out different functions. It is also the hereditary material of certain viruses.

ribosomal RNA (rRNA) [ARN ribosómico (ARNr)]: A class of RNA molecule found, together with characteristic proteins, in ribosomes; it is involved in the process of translation.

rift valley (rift) [valle tectónico (grieta)]: Zones where plates separate or move apart to form a deep valley. Examples are the East African Rift and the Rio Grande Rift.

S

salinity [salinidad]: A measure of the mass of dissolved ions in natural waters.

salt [sal]: The ionic compound formed when acids and bases react to neutralize each other.

satellite [satélite]: Any object that orbits another object.

scientific inquiry [enfoque científico]: The approach to learning used in this program, in which learners ask questions about the natural world and seek answers based on evidence, logic, and interaction with others. In scientific inquiry, students learn science in the way that science is practiced.

selective pressure [presión selectiva]: A biotic or abiotic factor that drives natural selection. Selective pressures influence an organism's ability to survive and reproduce.

sex chromosome [cromosoma del sexo]: One of a pair of chromosomes that differentiates between and is partially responsible for determining the sexes.

simulation [simulación]: A small-scale model or test of a much larger physical process.

sink [vertedero]: A reservoir that accumulates and gains matter with time.

soil [suelo]: The organic and bacteria-rich layer between the geosphere and the biosphere and atmosphere.

solar radiation [radiación solar]: The external source of energy coming to Earth's surface from the Sun. This energy fuels photosynthesis and food cycles.

solubility [solubilidad]: An indicator of the mass of a substance that will dissolve into a liquid.

source [fuente]: A reservoir that loses matter with time.

species [especies]: A group of organisms that successfully reproduce with individuals of the same type.

spectator ions [iones espectadores]: Charged particles that are not changed during a chemical reaction.

strong acid [ácido fuerte]: An acid that dissociates completely or nearly completely.

subducted [subducido]: Pushed down.

subduction zones [zonas de subducción]: Regions where slabs of oceanic crust sink into the mantle.

subsystems [subsistemas]: Smaller systems within a larger system that have distinct boundaries, inputs, and outputs.

suspended load [arrastre en suspensión]: The fine particles of silt, clay, organic matter, and microorganisms carried by rivers or streams.

system [sistema]: A collection of things that interact within given limits or boundaries. *Open systems* exchange both energy and matter with their surroundings; *closed systems* exchange only energy with their surroundings.

T

tectonic plate [placa tectónica]: The outer, rigid layers of oceanic and continental crust. Tectonic plates move on the order of several centimeters per year over Earth's surface.

terminal velocity [velocidad terminal]: The maximum constant velocity of an object that is moving through a fluid. Terminal velocity occurs when the forces of motion in one direction balance each other after some initial acceleration.

terrace [terraza]: A flat surface formed by ocean waves eroding a surface or plane. When geologists date terraces, the dates can be used to determine the rates of tectonic uplift.

terrestrial [terrestre]: Found on land.

tilt [inclinación]: Refers to the angle of Earth's rotation axis relative to incoming solar radiation. Tilt changes by several degrees every 41,000 years.

trait [rasgo]: An inherited characteristic; a trait is determined by genes.

transcription [transcripción]: The assembly of an RNA molecule that is complementary to a strand of DNA. The product may be messenger RNA, transfer RNA, or ribosomal RNA. Transcription is part of protein synthesis, the process of making proteins.

transfer RNA (tRNA) [ARN de transferencia (ARNt)]: A class of RNA molecule with two functional sites. One site is for the attachment of a specific amino acid. The other site is for carrying the three-nucleotide sequence (anticodon) for that amino acid. Each type of tRNA transfers a specific amino acid to a growing polypeptide chain.

transform fault [falla de transformación]: A zone where two tectonic plates move past each other. Examples are the San Andreas Fault in California and the North Anatolian Fault in Turkey.

transgenic [transgénico]: Refers to when one or more genes, usually from another species, are added to an organism; the organism being changed is called a transgenic organism.

translation [traducción]: The assembly of proteins on ribosomes, using messenger RNA to direct the order of amino acids. Translation is part of protein synthesis, the process of making proteins.

transpiration [transpiración]: The loss of water to the atmosphere by plants through the stomates in their leaves.

trenches [fosas submarinas]: Linear regions of deep water where oceanic crust sinks into the mantle. *See* subduction zones.

U

uplift [alzamiento]: The process of land moving vertically relative to sea level.

V

variable [variable]: A factor or attribute that can be measured or described. Scientific investigations look for changes in variables.

variation [variación]: Small differences among individuals within a population or species that provide the raw material for evolution.

vectors [vectores]: In physical science, vectors are variables that have both magnitude (size) and direction. Force, velocity, and acceleration are vectors as well as any change in these quantities. In biology, researchers use vectors to carry a gene to an organism. A plasmid can be used as a vector.

volcanic arcs [arcos volcánicos]: Curved chains of volcanoes residing above subduction zones.

volcanic degassing [desgasificación volcánica]: The movement of gases, such as carbon dioxide and water, from Earth's interior to the atmosphere.

voltaic cell [pila voltaica]: A spontaneous chemical reaction that generates an electric current by the physical separation of redox half reactions.

W

watershed [cuenca hidrográfica]: The area of land that drains into a body of water.

weak acid [ácido débil]: An acid that does not dissociate readily.

weather [tiempo]: Environmental conditions experienced over periods of time from hours to days, such as an afternoon thunderstorm, a cold front, or a persistent heat wave.

weathering [meteorización]: The process of natural, chemical alteration of minerals in rocks.

wobble (precession) [giro excéntrico (precesión)]: The cyclic motion of Earth's rotation axis in a circular motion, like a spinning top. The period of precession is about 21,000 years.

Z

zygote [cigoto]: The diploid product of the union of haploid gametes during conception; a fertilized egg.

Glosario

A

abiótico [abiotic]: Componentes físicos y químicos (no vivientes) de un medio ambiente, como la luz o el agua.

aceleración (*a*) [acceleration (*a*)]: Rapidez con que cambia la velocidad vectorial; se representa con el símbolo *a*. La relación matemática que describe la aceleración es $a = \frac{\Delta v}{\Delta t}$.

ácido [acid]: Compuesto químico que aumenta la concentración de los iones de hidrógeno (H^+) en una solución. Esta definición es una de las diversas formas de concebir los ácidos.

ácido débil [weak acid]: Ácido que no se disocia fácilmente.

ácido desoxirribonucleico (ADN) [deoxyribonucleic acid (DNA)]: Material hereditario de la mayoría de los organismos. El ADN forma los genes y contiene desoxirribosa, un grupo de fosfatos, y una de las cuatro bases de ADN.

ácido fuerte [strong acid]: Ácido que se disocia totalmente o casi totalmente.

ácido ribonucleico (ARN) [ribonucleic acid (RNA)]: El ARN es el material codificado por el ADN de las células para llevar a cabo las funciones genéticas específicas; por ejemplo, el ARN mensajero y el ARN de transferencia llevan a cabo diferentes funciones. También es el material hereditario de ciertos virus.

acre-pie (ap) [acre-feet (af)]: Volumen de agua que cubre 1 acre de tierra con agua y posee 1 pie de profundidad.

adaptaciones [adaptations]: Características que ayudan a que un organismo sobreviva y se reproduzca dentro de un medio ambiente determinado.

agente oxidante [oxidizing agent]: Partícula que participa en una reacción redox que gana un electrón o electrones. Los agentes oxidantes se reducen en las reacciones redox.

agente reductor [reducing agent]: Partícula que participa en la reacción redox que pierde un electrón o electrones. Los agentes reductores se oxidan en las reacciones redox.

alelo [allele]: Una de las dos o más formas posibles de un gen. Cada alelo afecta al rasgo hereditario de forma levemente diferente.

alzamiento [uplift]: El proceso de movimiento de la tierra en sentido vertical con respecto al nivel del mar.

aminoácido [amino acid]: Los componentes básicos de los polipéptidos y proteínas. Los aminoácidos son compuestos orgánicos. Están compuestos por un átomo central de carbono unido a un átomo de hidrógeno, un grupo de aminos (—NH_2), un grupo de ácidos (—COOH), y un átomo de una variedad de otros átomos o grupos de átomos.

anaerobio [anaerobe]: Organismo que vive en ausencia de oxígeno.

ancestral [ancestral]: Algo de lo cual proviene una generación o forma posterior.

anión [anion]: Partícula cargada negativamente, típicamente asociada a las reacciones redox.

ánodo [anode]: Electrodo de una célula electroquímica donde tiene lugar la oxidación.

anticodón [anticodon]: Secuencia de tres nucleótidos en una molécula de transferencia de ARN. Se complementa y forma pares de bases con un codón específico en el ARN mitocondrial.

arcos volcánicos [volcanic arcs]: Cadenas curvas de volcanes que residen por encima de las zonas de subducción.

ARN de transferencia (ARNt) [transfer RNA (tRNA)]: Clase de molécula de ARN con dos lugares funcionales. Un lugar es donde se anexan los aminoácidos específicos. El otro lugar es donde se halla la secuencia de trinucleótidos (anticodones) para ese aminoácido. Cada tipo de ARNt transfiere un aminoácido específico a una cadena de polipéptidos en crecimiento.

ARN mensajero (ARNm) [messenger RNA (mRNA)]: Tipo de molécula de ARN complementaria de una cadena de ADN; el ARNm se transcribe desde los genes y los ribosomas lo traducen a proteínas (ver transcripción y traducción).

ARN ribosómico (ARNr) [ribosomal RNA (rRNA)]: Clase de molécula de ARN que se encuentra en los ribosomas, junto con las proteínas características de éstos; participa en el proceso de traducción.

arrastre en suspensión [suspended load]: Partículas finas de limo, arcilla, materia orgánica y microorganismos que son transportadas por los ríos o arroyos.

autosoma [autosome]: Cromosoma que no está directamente involucrado en la determinación del sexo.

B

base [base]: Compuesto químico que aumenta la concentración de los iones de hidróxido (OH^-) en una solución. Esta definición es una de las diversas formas de concebir las bases.

bioética [bioethics]: Estudio de los temas éticos que se plantean a raíz de los acontecimientos que se desarrollan en las tecnologías de las ciencias biológicas, como las nuevas tecnologías médicas.

bioma [biome]: Conjunto formado por la cubierta vegetal característica y el resto de la comunidad de organismos asociados a un medio ambiente físico en particular; a menudo el bioma recibe el nombre de la cubierta vegetal que lo recubre. Algunos ejemplos de biomas incluyen la tundra, el bosque tropical, el desierto y la pradera de clima templado.

biomasa [biomass]: Peso seco de toda la materia orgánica de un grupo de organismos dentro de un hábitat en particular.

biorremediación [bioremediation]: El uso de microorganismos para degradar los desechos.

biotecnología [biotechnology]: La solución a un problema que involucra a la tecnología *y* a los seres vivos. La tecnología de recombinación de ADN creó varias formas nuevas de biotecnología.

bióticos [biotic]: Los componentes vivos o recién nacidos de un ecosistema.

C

cantidad de movimiento (*p*) [momentum (*p*)]: El producto de la masa por la velocidad (*mv*); se representa con el símbolo *p*. La cantidad de movimiento puede concebirse como la masa en movimiento.

capa de hielo [ice sheet]: Hielo glaciar grueso que se acumula sobre los continentes y puede tener un espesor de incluso varios kilómetros.

capacidad máxima [carrying capacity]: El mayor tamaño de una población capaz de abastecerse con los recursos disponibles de una cierta zona.

carbono inorgánico disuelto (CID) [dissolved inorganic carbon (DIC)]: Componente del carbono que deriva de fuentes inorgánicas, como los iones de bicarbonato y carbonato, que se disuelve en el agua natural.

carbono orgánico disuelto (COD) [dissolved organic carbon (DOC)]: Componente del carbono que deriva de la materia orgánica, como las hojas de plantas, que se disuelve en el agua natural.

carga disuelta [dissolved load]: Elementos y moléculas en forma iónica que se disuelven en agua natural.

catalizador [catalyst]: Especie química que aumenta la velocidad de una reacción química sin que la reacción lo altere en forma permanente.

catión [cation]: Partícula cargada positivamente, típicamente asociada a las reacciones redox.

cátodo [cathode]: Electrodo de una célula electroquímica donde tiene lugar la reducción.

célula electrolítica [electrolytic cell]: Reacción electroquímica, como la electrólisis. Esta reacción se caracteriza por usar la energía eléctrica para revertir una reacción redox espontánea.

choque elástico [elastic collision]: Choque que se produce cuando la energía y el impulso de los objetos de un sistema se mantienen inalterados antes y después de los choques. Los choques elásticos pueden producirse cuando los objetos que chocan rebotan o colisionan repetidamente entre sí.

ciclo biológico del carbono [biologic carbon cycle]: Ciclo del carbono que consiste en carbono *activo* o *móvil* que se mueve entre los depósitos en lapsos que abarcan desde días a cientos de años. Esta parte del ciclo del carbono opera fundamentalmente sobre la superficie de la tierra e involucra a los organismos.

ciclo geológico del carbono [geologic carbon cycle]: Ciclo del carbono que consiste principalmente en el carbono *inactivo* o *inmóvil* que se desplaza entre los depósitos en escalas temporales de cientos a millones de años. El carbono en los depósitos geológicos se almacena principalmente dentro de la Tierra.

ciclo geoquímico [geochemical cycle]: Expresión que describe el almacenamiento y movimiento de una sustancia química, elemento o nutriente como el carbón, el agua, el fósforo o el calcio a través de los sistemas terrestres.

cigoto [zygote]: El producto diploide de la unión de los gametos haploides durante la concepción; el óvulo fertilizado.

clima [climate]: Condiciones atmosféricas generales que se repiten a lo largo de lapsos prolongados.

codón [codon]: Unidad básica del código genético; secuencia de tres nucleótidos adyacentes de ADN o ARN mensajero.

colisión inelástica [inelastic collision]: Se produce una colisión inelástica cuando la energía de los objetos de un sistema es menor después de la colisión que antes de ella. Un ejemplo común se da cuando los objetos se golpean y se quedan adheridos después de la colisión.

combustibles fósiles [fossil fuels]: Combustibles que constan de compuestos de hidrógeno y carbono de los depósitos geológicos del carbono orgánico. Son una fuente de energía primaria para los seres humanos.

comunidad [community]: Todos los organismos que habitan en una zona en particular.

concentración [concentration]: Medida para expresar la cantidad de partículas por unidad de espacio. Una unidad de concentración muy frecuente en química es la molaridad: indica las unidades de moles por litro (mol/L).

conservación de la masa [conservation of mass]: Concepto por el cual la masa de reactivos de una reacción debe ser igual a la masa de los productos.

constante [constant]: Factor o atributo que permanece inalterado durante el curso de una investigación. Una constante también puede ser una cantidad o valor que se asume no variará a los efectos de una teoría o experimento, por ejemplo, la velocidad de la luz.

control [control]: En una investigación el control es el individuo o el grupo designado para no recibir tratamiento (el grupo que no cambia). Todos los demás grupos se comparan con el grupo de control.

corriente eléctrica [electric current]: El flujo de la carga en una dirección en particular.

corteza continental [continental crust]: Material variado, de roca básica, que posee un espesor de 40–70 kilómetros que forma los continentes.

corteza oceánica [oceanic crust]: La parte externa de la Tierra que yace bajo los océanos. La corteza oceánica está unida a varios continentes y forma las placas tectónicas.

crecimiento exponencial [exponential growth]: Crecimiento que ocurre a una velocidad que es proporcional a su tamaño.

crecimiento logístico [logistic growth]: Crecimiento que comienza como un crecimiento exponencial y luego se hace más lento hasta finalmente detenerse. En el crecimiento logístico la población alcanza su nivel ideal en la capacidad máxima del medio ambiente.

cromosoma del sexo [sex chromosome]: Uno de un par de cromosomas que se diferencia y es parcialmente responsable de la determinación del sexo.

cromosoma [chromosome]: Grupo de genes largos y en forma de hebra que se encuentra en el núcleo de todas las células eucariotas. Los cromosomas son más visibles durante la mitosis y la meiosis. Los cromosomas están formados por ADN y proteínas.

cruce monohíbrido [monohybrid cross]: Apareamiento entre individuos que difieren en un alelo.

cualitativo [qualitative]: Algo es cualitativo si describe los rasgos, características, observaciones o comparaciones relativas.

cuantitativo [quantitative]: Algo es cuantitativo si representa las mediciones o números, montos (cantidades) o índices específicos.

cuenca hidrográfica [watershed]: El área de tierra con drenaje hacia una masa de agua.

D

datos de representación [proxy data]: Datos de registros que representan y están en lugar de otros patrones de cambio. Por ejemplo, el grosor de los anillos de un árbol es un dato de representación importante para el clima anual.

densidad de población [population density]: La cantidad de organismos por unidad o superficie de hábitat.

depósito [reservoir]: Volumen o recipiente que contiene una determinada masa de materia.

deriva continental [continental drift]: Hipótesis propuesta en 1912 por Alfred Wegener según la cual, en un momento determinado, las masas terrestres de la Tierra estaban unidas, formando un supercontinente que luego se separó para dar lugar a los continentes actuales. Ahora se considera que la deriva continental es parte de la teoría mayor de la tectónica de placas.

desgasificación volcánica [volcanic degassing]: El movimiento de los gases, como el dióxido de carbono y el agua, desde el interior de la Tierra a la atmósfera.

desintegración radiactiva [radioactive decay]: La descomposición espontánea de un tipo de núcleos en núcleos con diferentes elementos.

diploide [diploid]: Se refiere a una célula que contiene miembros de cada par de cromosomas que le es característico a una especie.

dominante [dominant]: Se refiere a los alelos o rasgos que enmascaran la presencia de otro alelo del mismo gen en un organismo heterocigoto.

dorsales oceánicas [mid-oceanic ridges]: Zonas de topografía elevada en el suelo oceánico que se forman debido a las grietas de las placas tectónicas. Estaban originalmente unidas a la dorsal meso-Atlántica.

E

ecología [ecology]: Campo de la biología que estudia los organismos y su relación con el medio ambiente.

ecosistema [ecosystem]: La comunidad biológica y su entorno abiótico.

electroforesis de gel de agarosa [agarose gel electrophoresis]: Proceso en el cual los científicos separan los fragmentos de ADN por su tamaño. Se utiliza una corriente eléctrica para impulsar el ADN a través de una matriz de gel poroso.

elemento derivado [daughter element]: Sustancia química del lado de los productos de una ecuación de desintegración radiactiva. Los núcleos de los elementos derivados se producen de los elementos madre.

elemento precursor [parent element]: Sustancia química original del lado de los reactivos en una ecuación de descomposición radiactiva. Los núcleos de los elementos precursores se desintegran radiactivamente para formar elementos derivados y otras partículas.

embrión [embryo]: Organismo en las etapas iniciales de desarrollo.

emigración [emigration]: Partida de los individuos de una población; la emigración disminuye el tamaño de una población.

endémico [endemic]: Animales o plantas cuya presencia se restringe a una región específica.

endotérmico [endothermic]: Procesos que absorben el calor del entorno, provocando una disminución de la temperatura. Las reacciones endotérmicas tienen una entalpía neta positiva ($+\Delta H$).

energía de activación (E_a) [activation energy (E_a)]: Energía vinculada a las partículas que se forman con la energía de mayor potencial durante un proceso químico.

enfoque científico [scientific inquiry]: El abordaje del aprendizaje que se usa en este programa, en el cual los estudiantes formulan preguntas acerca del mundo natural y buscan las respuestas basándose en la evidencia, la lógica y la interacción con los demás. En el enfoque científico, los estudiantes aprenden ciencia en la forma en que se ejerce la ciencia.

entalpía [enthalpy]: Energía neta ($E_{final} - E_{inicial}$ = energía neta) asociada a las reacciones químicas. Se representa con el símbolo ΔH.

entrada [input]: La cantidad de masa o material que ingresa en un depósito o sistema.

enzima de restricción [restriction enzyme]: Enzima que reconoce las secuencias de nucleótidos específicas en el ADN y descompone la cadena de ADN en esos puntos.

enzimas [enzymes]: Cualquier especie química, generalmente proteínas o moléculas que incluyen proteínas que catalizan o aceleran las reacciones biológicas. Las enzimas son producidas por un organismo.

equilibrio [equilibrium]: Descripción del estado de cualquier reacción química reversible en la cual la velocidad de su reacción directa equivale a la velocidad de su reacción inversa.

erosión [erosion]: Proceso por el cual se transporta tierra y fragmentos de roca sometidos a la meteorización y se desplazan hacia abajo debido a la acción de la gravedad. La erosión de las montañas se produce a lo largo de laderas pronunciadas y de valles de los ríos.

especies [species]: Grupo de organismos que se reproducen satisfactoriamente con los seres de su mismo tipo.

ética [ethics]: Se refiere a la moral de las personas y la sociedad. La moral son los valores y creencias sobre lo que se considera un comportamiento aceptable.

evaporación [evaporation]: El cambio producido cuando las moléculas de un líquido absorben calor y cambian a la fase de vapor.

evapotranspiración [evapotranspiration]: La pérdida total de agua del entorno terrestre debido a la evaporación y a la transpiración de las plantas.

evolución [evolution]: Cambio acumulativo en las características de los organismos o poblaciones de generación a generación.

excentricidad [eccentricity]: Se refiere a la forma de la órbita de la Tierra alrededor del Sol. La excentricidad varía en escalas temporales de alrededor de 100,000 años.

exotérmico [exothermic]: Procesos que liberan calor al entorno, provocando un aumento de la temperatura. Las reacciones exotérmicas poseen una entalpía neta negativa ($-\Delta H$).

exponencial [exponential]: Forma de describir una línea en una gráfica curva. Las ecuaciones que generan estas líneas contienen exponentes y representan los cambios de velocidad de algunos fenómenos.

F

factor limitante [limiting factor]: Condición ambiental como alimento, temperatura, agua o luz natural que restringe el tipo de organismos y la cantidad de habitantes que un medio ambiente puede sustentar.

falla de transformación [transform fault]: Zona donde se superponen dos placas tectónicas. Ejemplos de ello son la Falla de San Andrés en California y la Falla de Anatolia del Norte en Turquía.

fenotipo [phenotype]: Expresión del genotipo en el aspecto o función de un organismo; el rasgo que se observa.

feromona [pheromone]: Señal química que funciona en las comunicaciones entre los animales. Las feromonas actúan en forma similar a las hormonas para influir en la fisiología y el comportamiento.

fitoplancton [phytoplankton]: Organismos acuáticos muy pequeños, muchos de ellos microscópicos, que llevan a cabo la fotosíntesis. El fitoplancton forma la base de las redes alimentarias acuáticas.

flujo [flux]: La velocidad a la cual la materia ingresa o egresa de un depósito o sistema. Los flujos generalmente se expresan como velocidades relativas al transcurso del tiempo, como pueden ser días o años.

foraminífera (forams) [foraminifera (forams)]: Organismos unicelulares con capacidad fotosintética que viven en el océano. Las forams forman la base de la red alimentaria marina.

formación de pares de bases complementarias [complementary base pairing]: Interacción predecible entre las bases de nitrógeno de las cadenas opuestas de ADN, y entre el ADN y el ARN. Los pares de adenina con timina, y los pares de guanina con citosina en el ADN; en el ARN, los pares de adenina con uracil.

fosas submarinas [trenches]: Regiones lineales de agua profunda donde la corteza oceánica se hunde en el manto. *Ver* zonas de subducción.

fuente [source]: Depósito que pierde materia con el paso del tiempo.

fuerza neta [net force]: La fuerza que resulta de la suma de los vectores de todas las fuerzas que actúan sobre un objeto.

G

gameto [gamete]: Célula sexual, ya sea un óvulo o esperma, formada por la meiosis. Los gametos poseen la mitad de la cantidad de cromosomas que poseen las células del cuerpo.

gen [gene]: Unidad fundamental de la herencia genética, que transmite un conjunto de especificaciones de una generación a la siguiente; segmento de ADN que codifica un producto específico.

genoma [genome]: Todo el material genético de una especie determinada o el complemento de una célula haploide de cualquier especie.

genotipo [genotype]: Composición genética de un organismo.

giro excéntrico (precesión) [wobble (precession)]: El movimiento cíclico del eje de rotación de la Tierra en sentido circular, como el de un trompo. El lapso de precesión es de alrededor de 21,000 años.

glaciaciones [glacials]: También conocidas como **edades del hielo** o **períodos glaciales.** Son épocas en que el clima global general es frío. Las glaciaciones se caracterizan por el bajo nivel del mar y la presencia de capas de hielo sobre grandes extensiones de la superficie terrestre.

H

hábitat [habitat]: Lugar donde vive un organismo. Incluso en el mismo ecosistema los diferentes organismos difieren de hábitat.

haploide [haploid]: Se refiere a una célula que contiene solamente un miembro (n) de cada par cromosómico característico de una especie.

heterocigoto [heterozygous]: Se refiere a poseer dos alelos diferentes para un rasgo dado.

hidrocarburo [hydrocarbon]: Sustancia orgánica compuesta por hidrógeno y carbono.

hipótesis [hypothesis]: Enunciado que se basa en el conocimiento actual y sugiere una explicación para una observación o una respuesta a un problema científico. Una hipótesis sugiere que hay una causa y un efecto o una relación del tipo "si...entonces" para la observación o problema.

homocigoto [homozygous]: Se refiere a poseer dos alelos idénticos para un rasgo dado.

humus [humus]: Materia descompuesta en el piso de los bosques y dentro del suelo.

I

impulso [impulse]: El producto de la fuerza y el cambio en el tiempo ($F\Delta t$).

inclinación [tilt]: Se refiere al ángulo del eje de rotación de la Tierra relativo a la entrada de la radiación solar. La inclinación cambia en varios grados cada 41,000 años.

indicador [indicator]: Sustancia química que sufre un cambio medible. Un cambio de color durante una reacción química es un ejemplo. El cambio señala un punto de interés durante una reacción en particular.

índice de mortalidad [mortality rate]: Índice de muerte, medido como la proporción de muertes con respecto a la población total a lo largo de un lapso dado; a menudo se expresa como la cantidad de muertes por cada 1,000 ó 10,000 personas.

índice de natalidad [birthrate]: La velocidad con que crece la población a través de la reproducción; a menudo se expresa en función de los individuos nacidos por cada 1,000 ó 10,000 en la población.

ingeniería genética [genetic engineering]: Tecnología experimental desarrollada para alterar el genoma de una célula viva para uso médico o industrial. La ingeniería genética introduce nuevos rasgos en los organismos.

inmigración [immigration]: Llegada de nuevas personas a una población; la inmigración aumenta el tamaño de una población.

iones espectadores [spectator ions]: Partículas cargadas que no cambian durante una reacción química.

isótopos [isotopes]: Átomos del mismo elemento que poseen diferentes cantidades de neutrones.

L

ley de conservación de la energía [law of conservation of momentum]: Principio de la naturaleza que indica que, en toda interacción la energía del sistema antes de la interacción será la misma que la energía del sistema después de la interacción.

ley de conservación de la materia [law of conservation of matter]: Principio de la naturaleza que indica que la materia no se crea ni se destruye durante los cambios físicos y químicos comunes.

leyes de Newton [Newton's laws]: La historia da cuenta de tres principios que rigen la naturaleza, llamados leyes de Newton. (1) La ley de la inercia se utiliza a menudo para describir la primera ley de Newton. Enuncia que no habrá cambios en el movimiento de un objeto a menos una fuerza externa actúe sobre él. (2) La segunda ley de Newton enuncia que la fuerza neta de un objeto es igual al producto de la masa por la aceleración del objeto. Se representa con la ecuación $F_{neta} = ma$. (3) La tercera ley de Newton es el principio de la naturaleza que describe que las fuerzas se presentan en pares, iguales en magnitud y opuestas en dirección. Estas fuerzas siempre actúan sobre dos objetos diferentes.

ligasa [ligase]: Enzima que contribuye a la formación de enlaces entre los segmentos adyacentes y complementarios de ADN.

límites [boundaries]: Fronteras que delimitan un sistema dentro del cual se producen interacciones.

M

manto [mantle]: La capa de la Tierra que se encuentra debajo de la corteza terrestre. El manto consiste principalmente en los minerales olivino y piroxeno, y los elementos, magnesio, hierro, sílice y oxígeno.

masa molar [molar mass]: El promedio de masa atómica de cualquier elemento (de la tabla periódica) en gramos. La masa molar equivale a la cantidad de masa en gramos en 1 mol de ese elemento.

materia [litter]: Materia es la acumulación de hojas y ramas vegetales debajo de los árboles en el suelo de los bosques. La materia en formación moviliza el carbón de los árboles hacia el suelo del bosque. Cuando la materia comienza a descomponerse, a veces recibe el nombre de humus.

Máximo de la Última Glaciación (LGM por sus siglas en inglés) [Last Glacial Maximum (LGM)]: La más reciente de muchas glaciaciones. El LGM tuvo una fuerte influencia en la geología y se produjo hace alrededor de 21,000 años.

medio ambiente [environment]: Todos los seres vivos y no vivos del entorno de un organismo, incluyendo la luz, temperatura, aire, suelo, agua y demás organismos.

meiosis [meiosis]: La meiosis es el proceso en el cual las divisiones de dos células, incluyendo la división del núcleo, producen gametos (en los animales) o esporas sexuales (en las plantas). Los gametos o esporas sexuales poseen la mitad del material genético de la célula de origen.

meteorización [weathering]: El proceso de la alteración química natural de los minerales en las rocas.

mezcla atmosférica [atmospheric mixing]: Proceso de transportar y mezclar componentes de la atmósfera en una escala global o regional.

microbio [microbe]: Término general para microorganismo.

millones de galones (Mgal) [millions of gallons (Mgal)]: Unidad estándar del volumen de agua en los sistemas.

millones de galones por día (Mgal/d) [millions of gallons per day (Mgal/d)]: Unidad estándar del flujo de agua en los sistemas.

mitosis [mitosis]: Replicación de los cromosomas y producción de dos núcleos en una célula; la mitosis está generalmente seguida de la división del citoplasma en la célula; se forman nuevas células.

mol (mol) [mole (mol)]: Unidad que se refiere a una cantidad de una sustancia asociada con 6.02×10^{23} partículas de esa sustancia.

molaridad [molarity]: Una de las diversas formas de expresar la concentración de una sustancia. La molaridad posee las unidades de moles por litro (mol/L) y se abrevia M.

movimiento de proyectil [projectile motion]: Movimiento en el plano horizontal (a menudo paralelo al suelo) y en el plano vertical (perpendicular al suelo). En el movimiento de proyectil el movimiento horizontal y el movimiento vertical son independientes entre sí, es decir que ninguno afecta al otro.

muestreo independiente [independent assortment]: La transmisión hereditaria de los alelos para un rasgo.

mutación [mutation]: Cambio químico en un gen que da como resultado un nuevo alelo o un cambio en la porción de un cromosoma que regula a ese gen. En cualquiera de los casos el cambio es hereditario.

N

nicho ecológico [ecological niche]: Todas las adaptaciones que un organismo utiliza para sobrevivir en su medio ambiente. Éstas incluyen su función dentro de la comunidad, lo que come y las interacciones que posee con los demás organismos y su medio ambiente.

nucleótido [nucleotide]: Subunidad o componente de ADN o ARN. Consta de un glúcido de 5 carbonos, una base de nitrógeno, y un grupo de fosfatos.

O

oxidación [oxidation]: Reacción en la cual los electrones aparecen del lado del producto de la reacción o semi-reacción. Es decir, los electrones se pierden en la semi-reacción.

oxidado [oxidized]: Descripción de los átomos o iones que perdieron electrones.

P

paleoclimatología [paleoclimatology]: El estudio de los climas del pasado.

patógeno [pathogenic]: Microorganismos que provocan enfermedades.

pedigrí [pedigree]: Diagrama que muestra la aparición de rasgos hereditarios a lo largo de varias generaciones.

península [peninsula]: Punta larga de tierra rodeada de agua.

período de semidesintegración [half-life]: También conocido como vida media. El tiempo necesario para que la mitad exacta de los átomos originales se degraden hasta convertirse en átomos derivados. La vida media refleja la constante de degradación.

período de semidesintegración por erosión [erosion half-life]: El tiempo que debe transcurrir para que se reduzcan a la mitad las elevaciones de un perfil topográfico.

períodos interglaciares [interglacials]: Lapsos en los cuales hay un clima global general cálido. Los períodos interglaciares se caracterizan por el elevado nivel del mar y la presencia limitada de capas de hielo.

pies cúbicos por segundo (pcs) [cubic feet per second (cfs)]: Unidades de flujo de agua que miden 1 pie cúbico de agua y se desplazan en 1 segundo con respecto a un punto.

pila voltaica [voltaic cell]: Reacción química espontánea que genera una corriente eléctrica mediante la separación física de las semi-reacciones redox.

placa tectónica [tectonic plate]: Las capas externas rígidas de la corteza oceánica y continental. Las placas tectónicas se mueven en el orden de varios centímetros por año sobre la superficie terrestre.

plásmido [plasmid]: Pequeño anillo de ADN en las bacterias. Los plásmidos transportan los genes separados de los genes de los cromosomas.

población [population]: Grupo de organismos de la misma especie que habitan en el mismo lugar al mismo tiempo.

polimerasa de ADN [DNA polymerase]: Enzima que cataliza la síntesis de una nueva cadena de ADN utilizando una de las cadenas originales como plantilla modelo.

precesión [precession]: *Ver* giro excéntrico (precesión).

presión selectiva [selective pressure]: Factor biótico o abiótico que fomenta la selección natural. Las presiones selectivas influyen en la capacidad de un organismo para sobrevivir y reproducirse.

principio de Le Châtelier [Le Châtelier's principle]: Forma de predecir los cambios en el punto de equilibrio. El método depende de los cambios que se le impongan a un sistema en equilibrio. Los cambios impuestos como temperatura, concentración, presión y volumen provocan cambios en el punto de equilibrio. El cambio siempre se desplaza en la dirección que disminuya el cambio impuesto y restablezca el equilibrio.

principio de segregación [principle of segregation]: Principio que enuncia que durante la meiosis los pares de cromosomas se separan de forma tal que cada uno de los dos alelos que determinan cualquier rasgo aparece en un gameto diferente.

principio del muestreo independiente [principle of independent assortment]: Principio que enuncia que la herencia de los alelos para un rasgo no afecta la herencia de los alelos para otro rasgo.

probabilidad [probability]: La posibilidad de que tenga lugar un acontecimiento dado.

productividad [productivity]: La cantidad de energía solar que los productores convierten en energía química durante cualquier período dado.

productor [producer]: Todo organismo que produce su propio alimento utilizando materia y energía del mundo no vivo.

productos [products]: Las nuevas sustancias que se forman como consecuencia de una reacción química.

puente terrestre [land bridge]: Puente de tierra por encima del nivel del mar que une a dos continentes.

punto de equilibrio [equilibrium position]: Medida de las cantidades relativas de reactivos y productos que deberán estar presentes para que un sistema químico se encuentre en equilibrio. Cuando hay más productos presentes, la posición de equilibrio favorece a los productos. El punto de equilibrio está a la derecha. Cuando hay más reactivos presentes, la posición de equilibrio favorece a los reactivos. El punto de equilibrio está a la izquierda.

punto de restricción [restriction site]: Enzimas de restricción que efectúan un corte en una secuencia única de ADN.

R

radiación solar [solar radiation]: Fuente externa de energía que llega a la superficie de la Tierra y proviene del Sol. Esta energía alimenta a la fotosíntesis y los ciclos alimentarios.

rasgo [trait]: Una característica que se hereda; los rasgos son determinados por los genes.

reacciones de oxidación-reducción (reacciones redox) [oxidation-reduction reactions (redox reactions)]: Proceso químico que involucra la transferencia de electrones para producir nuevas sustancias químicas.

reactivos [reactants]: Ingredientes iniciales de una reacción química.

recesivo [recessive]: Se refiere a los alelos o rasgos que quedan enmascarados por un alelo o rasgo dominante.

recurso [resource]: En ecología, el abastecimiento por parte del medio ambiente de uno o más de los requisitos de un organismo (luz, energía de los alimentos, agua, oxígeno o dióxido de carbono, espacio vital, cubierta protectora, y demás). En la sociedad humana, un recurso puede ser cualquier cosa que resulte útil.

reducción [reduction]: Reacción en la cual los electrones aparecen del lado de los reactivos de la reacción o semi-reacción. Es decir, se ganan electrones en la semi-reacción.

reducidos [reduced]: Descripción de los átomos o iones que ganaron electrones.

replicación del ADN [DNA replication]: Proceso para fabricar una copia de un cromosoma en el núcleo de una célula, así como en otros genes de ciertos organelos fuera del núcleo, particularmente los cloroplastos y las mitocondrias. El proceso es diferente de la duplicación porque cada gen y cada cromosoma en el doble par contiene partes nuevas y partes del antiguo gen o cromosoma.

representante [proxy]: Algo que representa o está en lugar de otra cosa.

reproducción asexuada [asexual reproduction]: Cualquier método de reproducción que requiera únicamente de un progenitor o una célula madre.

respiración aerobia [aerobic respiration]: Tipo de respiración celular que requiere de la presencia de oxígeno.

respiración anaeróbica [anaerobic respiration]: Tipo de respiración celular que no requiere de oxígeno.

S

sal [salt]: Compuesto iónico que se forma cuando los ácidos y las bases reaccionan para neutralizarse entre sí.

salida [output]: La cantidad de masa o material que sale de un depósito o sistema.

salinidad [salinity]: Medida de la masa de iones disueltos en aguas naturales.

satélite [satellite]: Todo objeto que orbita en torno a otro objeto.

selección natural [natural selection]: Mecanismo de la evolución biológica. En la selección natural los integrantes de la población que posea el mejor poder de adaptación al medio ambiente tendrán mayores probabilidades de sobrevivir y reproducirse que los integrantes con menor capacidad de adaptación.

semi-reacciones [half reactions]: La porción de oxidación o reducción de una reacción química redox.

simulación [simulation]: Modelo o prueba a pequeña escala de un proceso físico mucho mayor.

sistema [system]: Conjunto de cosas que interaccionan dentro de ciertos límites o fronteras. Los *sistemas abiertos* intercambian energía y materia con su entorno; los *sistemas cerrados* intercambian solamente energía con su entorno.

solubilidad [solubility]: Indicador de la masa de una sustancia que se disuelve en un líquido.

subducido [subducted]: Algo sometido a una fuerza que lo empujó hacia abajo.

subsistemas [subsystems]: Sistemas más pequeños dentro de un sistema mayor que poseen límites bien delineados, elementos de entrada y de salida.

suelo [soil]: Capa orgánica rica en bacterias entre la geoesfera, la biosfera y la atmósfera.

T

tecnología de recombinación del ADN [recombinant DNA technology]: Técnica utilizada para recortar segmentos de ADN y luego unir diferentes segmentos de ADN. Generalmente se introducen los segmentos de ADN de un organismo en diferentes organismos a los efectos de realizar investigación genética, ingeniería genética o tratamientos médicos.

tectónica de placas, teoría de [plate tectonics, theory of]: La tectónica de placas es la teoría que expresa que hay alrededor de 12 *placas* rígidas que se mueven lentamente sobre la Tierra por encima del manto. Las placas interactúan de muchas formas y afectan a todos los sistemas de la Tierra.

terapia de genes [gene therapy]: Inserción de genes normales o genéticamente alterados en las células como parte de un tratamiento de los trastornos genéticos.

terraza [terrace]: Superficie plana formada por las olas oceánicas que erosionan una superficie o plano. Cuando los geólogos determinan la antigüedad de las terrazas, las fechas pueden utilizarse para determinar la frecuencia del alzamiento tectónico.

terrestre [terrestrial]: Que se encuentra sobre la tierra.

tiempo de residencia [residence time]: El lapso promedio en el cual la materia de un sistema permanece en el depósito. Este valor se estima cuando no hay cambios a largo plazo en el sistema. El tiempo de residencia es la masa de material en el depósito dividida por el flujo entrante o el flujo saliente ($tiempo\ de\ residencia = masa / flujo_{en}$ o $tiempo\ de\ residencia = masa / flux_{sal}$).

tiempo [weather]: Condiciones ambientales que se experimentan a lo largo de lapsos que abarcan desde horas a días, como una tormenta eléctrica vespertina, un frente frío o una ola de calor persistente.

traducción [translation]: La formación de proteínas sobre los ribosomas, utilizando el ARN mensajero para dirigir el orden de los aminoácidos. La traducción es parte de la síntesis proteica, el proceso para la fabricación de las proteínas.

transcripción [transcription]: La formación de una molécula de ARN que complementa a una cadena de ADN. El producto puede ser el ARN mensajero, el ARN de transferencia o el ARN de los ribosomas. La transcripción es parte de una síntesis de proteínas, el proceso para fabricar las proteínas.

transgénico [transgenic]: Se refiere a cuando uno o más genes, generalmente de otras especies, se agregan a un organismo; el organismo que se altera recibe el nombre de organismo transgénico.

transpiración [transpiration]: Pérdida de agua de las plantas hacia la atmósfera a través de los estomas que poseen en las hojas.

V

valle tectónico (grieta) [rift valley (rift)]: Zonas donde se separan o se desplazan las placas para formar un valle profundo. Los ejemplos son la grieta del Este de África y la grieta del Río Grande.

variable [variable]: Factor o atributo que puede medirse o describirse. Las investigaciones científicas buscan cambios en las variables.

variación [variation]: Pequeñas diferencias entre los individuos dentro de una población o especie que proporcionan la materia prima para la evolución.

vectores [vectors]: En la ciencia física los vectores son variables que poseen magnitud (tamaño) y dirección. La fuerza, la velocidad vectorial y la aceleración son vectores, al igual que cualquier cambio en esas cantidades. En biología los investigadores utilizan vectores para transportar un gen a un organismo. Un plásmido puede utilizarse como vector.

velocidad terminal [terminal velocity]: La máxima velocidad constante de un objeto que se desplaza a través de un fluido. La velocidad terminal ocurre cuando las fuerzas del movimiento en una dirección se contrarrestan entre sí después de cierta aceleración inicial.

vertedero [sink]: Depósito que acumula y gana materia con el paso del tiempo.

Z

zonas convergentes [convergent zones]: Regiones donde chocan las placas tectónicas.

zonas de subducción [subduction zones]: Regiones donde las placas de la corteza oceánica se hunden en el manto.

zonas divergentes [divergent zones]: Zonas donde las placas tectónicas se separan, formando grietas en los continentes o en el suelo oceánico.

Credits

CHAPTER 1: **Opener** (operating room) Corbis, (pendulum clock, insect colony) iStockphoto, (workers in food prep area) U.S. Department of Agriculture, (space view of Earth) NASA Goddard Space Flight Center Image by Reto Stöckli [land surface, shallow water, clouds]. Enhancements by Robert Simmon [ocean color, compositing, 3D globes, animation]. Data and technical support: MODIS Land Group; MODIS Science Data Support Team; MODIS Atmosphere Group; MODIS Ocean Group Additional data: USGS EROS Data Center [topography]; USGS Terrestrial Remote Sensing Flagstaff Field Center [Antarctica]; Defense Meteorological Satellite Program [city lights]; **Two Students Talking** Comstock **1.3** Dr. Tony Brain & David Parker/Photo Researchers, Inc.; **1.4** Comstock; **1.12** HIP/Oxford Science Archive/Art Resource, NY; **1.13** Used with permission from Pfizer Inc. All rights reserved.; **City Skyline** Corel; **Getting Glass of Water from Faucet** iStockphoto; **Getting Fast Food at Drive-up Window** iStockphoto; **George Strait** Peg Skorpinski; **Cocci (sphere) Bacteria** © Dr. David Phillips/Visuals Unlimited; **Bacilli (rods) Bacteria** © Dr. David Phillips/Visuals Unlimited; **Spirochetes (corkscrew) Bacteria** © George Wilder/Visuals Unlimited; **Virus Micrograph** M. Wurtz/ Biozentrum, University of Basel/Photo Researchers, Inc.

Unit 1

Unit Opener (amusement park ride) Dreamstime, (karate kick) iStockphoto, (pouring chemicals) iStockphoto, (painting of Volta) HIP/Ann Ronan Picture Library/Art Resource, NY; **Boy Giving Girl Balloons** iStockphoto; **Rapeller** Dreamstime/Joe Gough.

CHAPTER 2: **Opener** (friendly game of football) PhotoDisc, (parachute jumper) iStockphoto, (football tackle) iStockphoto; **Chapter Organizer** (vehicle crash scene) iStockphoto; **2.2** EyeWire; **2.9** Dreamstime; **2.13** (solar flare) SOHO, NASA/ESA; **Soccer Head Shot** iStockphoto; **Comparison of Impact Gs Chart** Data from Maunhelin, R. S., Standeven, J., Richter, C., & Lewis, L. M. (2000). Comparison of Impact Data in Hockey, Football, and Soccer. *The Journal of Trauma: Injury, Infection, and Critical Care, 48*(5). p. 940, figure 3. Used by permission of Dr. Rosanne Naunheim and John Standeven.; **2.20** iStockphoto; **Sir Isaac Newton** National Portrait Gallery, London; **2.21** iStockphoto; **2.22** iStockphoto; **Billiards Player** iStockphoto; **2.23** (satellite view of hurricane) NASA Goddard Space Flight Center [NASA-GSFC], (Space Shuttle Atlantis landing) NASA; **2.31** (building demolition, roller coaster) iStockphoto, (car crash) Dreamstime.

CHAPTER 3: **Opener** (metallic balls in wood bowl) iStockphoto, (tennis balls) Dreamstime/Stasys Eidiejus, (eyedropper and bottle) Dreamstime/Scott Rothstein; **3.2a** Dreamstime/Tyler Olson; **3.2b** Dreamstime; **3.5** NASA; **Chemist at Work** iStockphoto; **Fe-TAML and Hydrogen Peroxide Molecule** Terry Collins; **3.12** iStockphoto.

CHAPTER 4: **Opener** (amusement park swings, bungee jump, Ferris wheel, amusement park rocker) iStockphoto, (roller coaster) Dreamstime; **4.1** (astronauts) NASA, (cheerleader) Digital Stock; **4.9** iStockphoto; **4.16** iStockphoto; **Roller Coaster** Dreamstime; **4.19** iStockphoto; **4.31** iStockphoto.

CHAPTER 5: **Opener** (photos) iStockphoto; **Painting of Volta** HIP/Ann Ronan Picture Library/Art Resource, NY; **Cross Section of Carbon-Zinc Battery** © C. R. Nave, 2006. Adapted by permission.

Unit 2

Unit Opener (elephants) PhotoDisc, (ducks) Corel, (scientists) PhotoDisc, (humans) Brand X Pictures, (2 dinosaur illustrations) Douglas Henderson, (marten) Friends of the Loomis Forest, (platypus) Tom McHugh/Photo Researchers, Inc.

CHAPTER 6: **Opener** (bird photos) Gerald and Buff Corsi © California Academy of Sciences; **6.1** USGS "This Dynamic Earth"; **6.3** Helen Richardson/The Denver Post; **6.8** Chip Clark, Museum of Natural History, Smithsonian Institution; **6.13** (crater) Corel, (meteorite) Courtesy Rhian Jones, University of New Mexico; **6.15** Corel; **6.17a, b, c** Corel; **6.18** Corbis; **6.19** Darwin Museum Down House, Courtesy of the Royal College of Surgeons of England; **6.20** (penguin, rhea) Corel, (steamer duck) Gerald and Buff Corsi © California Academy of Sciences; **6.22** Adapted from page 142 of *Morphological Differentiation and Adaptation in the Galapagos Finches* by Robert I. Bowman, University of California Publication in Zoology, volume 58 (1961).

CHAPTER 7: **Opener** (ducks, elephants) Corel, (iguanas) iStockphoto, (humans) BrandX Pictures; **7.1** iStockphoto; **7.3a** Biophoto Associates/Photo Researchers, Inc.; **7.3b** © Dr. Robert Calentine/Visuals Unlimited; **7.3c** PhotoDisc; **7.3d** EyeWire; **7.5a** Corel; **7.5b** iStockphoto; **7.6** Courtesy of Dr. Vítézslav Orel, Mendelianum, Moravian Museum, Brno, Czech Republic; **7.7** Photograph by Marie Schmerkova. Courtesy of Marie Schmerkova and the City of Brno.; **7.11** Based on data from I. I. Gottesman and L. L. Heston in Genetic, Environment, and Behavior, © 1972 by Academic Press; **Budding Potatoes** iStockphoto; **Normal Female Karyotype** PhotoDisc; **Down Syndrome and Turner's Syndrome Karyotypes** Science VU/Visuals Unlimited; **Genetics Counselor** Reprinted with permission of the University of Maryland Medical Center (www.umm.edu).

CHAPTER 8: **Opener** (SEM: chromosome, TEM: transcription) © Dr. K. G. Murti/Visuals Unlimited, (STM: DNA molecule double helix) Driscoll, Youngquist & Baldeschwieler, CalTech/Photo Researchers, Inc., (translation) © Kiseleva and Donald Fawcett/Visuals Unlimited, (protein molecule illustration) Houdusse, A., Cohen, C. Structure of the regulatory domain of scallop myosin at 2 A resolution: implications for regulation. *Structure, v4*, pp. 21–32, 1996.; **8.1** iStockphoto; **8.5, 8.12a** Adapted from art courtesy of National Human Genome Research Institute; **Franklin's DNA X-ray** Courtesy James D. Watson Collection, Cold Spring Harbor Laboratory Archives; **DNA Timeline** (Avery, Wilkins, Franklin) James L. Koevenig, (McClintock) Courtesy Barbara McClintock Collection, Cold Spring Harbor Laboratory Archives, (Miescher) Courtesy of the Friedrich Miescher Institute, (Watson and Crick) Courtesy James D. Watson Collection, Cold Spring Harbor Laboratory Archives, (electrophoresis result) Panackal, A. A., Imhof, A., Hanley, E. W., Marr, K. A. (2006). *Aspergillus ustus* infections among transplant recipients. *Emerg Infect Dis.* 12:406, (chromosomes) U.S. Department of Energy Human Genome Program http://www.ornl.gov/hgmis, (scientists with gel results) PhotoDisc, (*Haemophilis influenzae* TEM) Wadsworth Center, New York State Department of Health, (cover of Nature) Reprinted by permission from Macmillan Publishers Ltd: *Nature, 409* (15 Feb. 2001), (boxer) Corel; **8.17** Adapted from art courtesy of National Human Genome Research Institute; **Automated DNA Sequencing Machines** U.S. Department of Energy Joint Genome Institute, http://www.jgi.doe.gov; ***Clostridium difficile* Bacteria** © Dr. David Phillips/Visuals Unlimited.

CHAPTER 9: **Opener** (plant growing room) Institute for Plant Genomics and Biotechnology, Texas Agricultural Experiment Station, Texas A&M University, (pills, mortar, pestle) Province of Manitoba, Canada, (tomato plant) iStockphoto, (scientist with petri dish) Scott Bauer, U.S. Department of Agriculture; **9.1** Courtesy of Pacific Northwest National Laboratory; **9.3** Adapted with compliments of Eden Foods, www.edenfoods.com; **9.2** © Nick Cobbing/Peter Arnold, Inc.; **9.4** (plasmid TEM) © Dr. Gopal Murti/Visuals Unlimited; **Students Loading an Electrophoresis Gel** Karen Spuck; **Electrophoresis Result** Panackal, A. A., Imhof, A., Hanley, E. W., Marr, K. A. (2006). Aspergillus ustus infections among transplant recipients. *Emerg Infect Dis.* 12:406; **9.9** (tomato plant, produce in grocery store) iStockphoto, (sheep) Corel; **Biomedical Engineering Careers** (background– healthcare professional in lab) Corbis; **9.11** Houdusse, A., & Cohen, C. (1996). Structure of the regulatory domain of scallop myosin at 2 A resolution: implications for regulation. *Structure, v4*, pp. 21-32.; **9.13** © Science VU/Visuals Unlimited; **9.14** iStockphoto; **9.15** Codelco (Corporación Nacional del Cobre de Chile) ; **Bollworm on Cotton Boll** Clemson University - USDA Cooperative Extension Slide Series, www.ipmimages.org; **Genetic Engineering of Cotton** (cotton photo) iStockphoto; **9.17** iStockphoto; **9.19** Human Growth Foundation; **9.20** U.S. Department of Agriculture.

Unit 3

Unit Opener (Mt. Rainier) Shutterstock, (forest fire) Dreamstime/Aleksandr Klimashin, (Earth) PhotoDisc, (reef) Jerry Wellington, Department of Biology, University of Houston, (exposed coral terrace) Ron Capen.

CHAPTER 10: **Opener** (Earth) PhotoDisc, (ocean, river, irrigation) Comstock; **10.1** (satellite image) U.S. Department of Interior, U.S. Geological Survey, Reston, VA, USA, (Great Salt Lake causeway) Corbis; **10.2** Comstock; **10.11** These data are distributed by the EROS Data Center Distributed Active Archive Center (EDC DAAC), located at the U.S. Geological Survey's EROS Data Center in Sioux Falls, South Dakota.; **10.12** George H. Taylor; **10.17** Lonnie G. Thompson; **10.19** U.S. Geological Survey; **10.20** © David Wrobel/Visuals Unlimited; **Salts along Shore of Great Salt Lake** iStockphoto.

CHAPTER 11: **Opener** (satellite image) Jacques Descloitres, MODIS Land Rapid Response Team, NASA/GSFC, (corals) Ron Capen; **11.6** iStockphoto; **11.8** Dreamstime/Carolina K. Smith; **11.9** iStockphoto; **11.11** Dreamstime/Tyler Olson; **11.12** (graph) Keeling, C.D. and T.P. Whorf. 2005. Atmospheric CO_2 records from sites in the SIO air sampling network. In Trends: A Compendium of Data on Global Change. Carbon Dioxide Information Analysis Center, Oak Ridge National Laboratory, U.S. Department of Energy, Oak Ridge, Tenn., U.S.A., (photo) Courtesy USGS—Hawaiian Volcano Observatory; **11.14** Oceanic and Atmospheric Administration Paleoclimatology Program/Department of Commerce, Mark Twickler, University of New Hampshire; **Pumping Gas** iStockphoto; **Three Views of Hydrocarbons on Titan** (a. Titan's atmosphere) NASA/JPL/Space Science Institute, (b. river channels and c. blocks of "dirty ice" and CH4) NASA/JPL/ESA/University of Arizona; **11.18** www.Mountain.RU collection.

CHAPTER 12: **Opener** © Wim van Egmond/Visuals Unlimited; **12.1** (mammoth) Corel; **12.4** © Roger Braithwaite/Peter Arnold, Inc.; **12.6** Paleoclimatology Branch, NOAA/NCDC; **12.8** Jerry Wellington, Department of Biology, University of Houston; **12.10** Manley, W.F., 2002, Postglacial Flooding of the Bering Land Bridge: A Geospatial Animation: INSTAAR, University of Colorado, v1, http://instaar.colorado.edu/QGISL/bering_land_bridge; **12.11** Copyright © 2006 Henri D. Grissino-Mayer, University of Tennessee; **12.14a** Dr. Howard Spero, Department of Geology, University of California Davis; **12.14b** © Wim van Egmond/Visuals Unlimited; **Drilling Ship *JOIDES Resolution*, Scientists Examining Core Samples** IODP/TAMU; **12.15** Steven C. Clemens; **12.23** Andrew Bruckner; **12.25** Jacques Descloitres, MODIS Rapid Response Team, NASA/GSFC.

CHAPTER 13: **Opener** (inland sea) Douglas Henderson, (close-up image) All rights reserved, Image Archives, Denver Museum of Nature & Science; **13.1** (mountain stream painting) Dreamstime/Larry Jacobsen, (beaver, moose) Shutterstock, (elk) iStockphoto, (mountain lion) EyeWire; **13.4** Ron Capen; **13.7a** Image courtesy of PLATES, University of Texas Institute for Geophysics. PLATES retains all copyrights to this image; **13.7b** Map image from ARC Science Simulations Inc.'s "Face of the Earth" produced on UNAVCO's map server http://jules.unavco.org; **13.8** Adapted from *This Dynamic Earth*, USGS; **13.9** Adapted from *Global Tectonic Activity Map of the Earth*, NASA; **13.10** iStockphoto, **13.12** Adapted from *This Dynamic Earth*, USGS; **13.14** Adapted from USGS; **13.15, 13.17, 13.18, 13.20, 13.24** Map image from ARC Science Simulations Inc.'s "Face of the Earth" produced on UNAVCO's map server http://jules.unavco.org; **13.19** Adapted from "Windows into the Earth," Robert B. Smith, University of Utah; **TransAmerica Building** AP Photo/Paul Sakuma; **13.21** (armadillo) iStockphoto, (capybara, sloth) Corel.

Conducting Your Own Inquiry: **Student Writing on Easel Pad** Dreamstime/Simone Vandenberg.

Unit 4

Unit Opener (satellite image of Nile River) http://visibleearth.nasa.gov, Jacques Descloitres, MODIS Rapid Response Team, NASA/GSFC, (leaf cutter ants) © Mark Moffett/Minden Pictures, (worker in paddy field) iStockphoto, (scientists sampling water quality) National Park Service.

CHAPTER 14: **Opener** (butterflies and flowers) EyeWire, (fish and shark) iStockphoto, (hippos in mud) Comstock; **14.1** BSCS/Carlye Calvin; **14.2a** Corbis; **14.2b** Used by permission of Provincetown Center for Coastal Studies; **Yeast Cells** BSCS by Doug Sokell; **14.3** National Atlas of the United States, http://nationalatlas.gov; **14.4, 14.10** John Vucetich and Rolf Peterson, Michigan Technological University; **14.5, 14.7, 14.9** John Vucetich, Michigan Technological University; **14.6, 14.8** Rolf Peterson, Michigan Technological University; **14.11** iStockphoto; **14.16** Corel; **14.20** Based on data gathered by H. T. Odum from a river ecosystem in Silver Springs, Florida; **Ecologists** Photo by Mike Haramis, USGS; **Careers Chart** *Careers in Ecology* [brochure]. Used by permission of The Ecological Society of America.; **14.22** (semipalmated plover, Wilson's phalarope) Tim Avery, www.timaverybirding.com, (greater yellowlegs, Baird's sandpiper) Jack Binch, (dowitcher) U.S. Fish and Wildlife Service, (pectoral sandpiper) Brian L. Currie; **14.23a** U.S. Fish and Wildlife Service; **14.23b** Robert Barber/Painet Inc.; **Wetland Before and After Purple Loosestrife Growth** D. Q. Thompson, U. S. Fish & Wildlife Service; **14.25** NOAA National Estuarine Research Reserve Collection.

CHAPTER 15: **Opener** (tractor farming) Dreamstime/Stuart Blyth, (irrigated crops) Dreamstime/Jim Parkin, (coal mine conveyors) Dreamstime/Dan Bannister, (fishing trawlers) Dreamstime/Don Mace, (crowd of people) Dreamstime/Norman Chan; **15.2** © 2002 Redefining Progress. All rights reserved. Permission to reprint granted by Redefining Progress, www.rprogress.org/education; **15.3** Dreamstime/Francois Etienne du Plessis; **15.4** Food and Agriculture Organization of the United Nations, "Review of World Water Resources by Country, 2003", "State of the World's Forests, 2005", http://faostat.fao.org; **15.5, 15.7** BP Statistical Review of World Energy 2005; **15.6** (water data and wood product data) Food and Agriculture Organization of the United Nations, AQUASTAT database, "State of the World's Forests, 2005" World Resources Institute 2006, (food calorie data) *EarthTrends: The Environmental Information Portal*. Available at http://earthtrends.wri.org. Washington, DC: World Resources Institute. **15.8** Food and Agriculture Organization of the United Nations, http://faostat.fao.org, AQUASTAT database; **15.10** (manually harvesting rice) Dreamstime/Jan Dejong, (mechanically harvesting rice) Photo by Gary Kramer, USDA Natural Resources Conservation Service; **15.11, 15.12** Food and Agriculture Organization of the United Nations, http://faostat.fao.org; **15.13, 15.14, 15.15, 15.16, 15.17, 15.19, 15.20, 15.25** The United Nations is the author of the original material. Data from http://esa.un.org/unpp, *World Population Prospects: 2004 Revision*; **15.21** Dreamstime/Robert Simon; **15.22** Dreamstime/Alex Fairest; **15.23** PhotoDisc; **15.24** Corel; **No-till Farming** Courtesy of USDA NRCS; **15.26, 15.27** International Pacific Halibut Commission; **Wildlife Refuge** iStockphoto; **15.28** Corel.

CHAPTER 16: **Opener** (wind farm) Dreamstime, (hydroelectric dam) digitalvision; **Cars on Busy Highway** Comstock; **16.1** U.S. Environmental Protection Agency; **16.3, 16.4** Corel; **16.5** Comstock; **16.6** Mark Lohaus, Center for Science and Technology Policy Research.

Index

A

B

C

F

G

H

I

J

K

L

M

R

X

Y

Z